PHILIP'S

C000112732

STREET ATLAS
Hertfordshire

First published in 1986 by

Philip's, a division of
Octopus Publishing Group Ltd
2-4 Heron Quays, London E14 4JP

Third colour edition 2004
First impression 2004

ISBN-10   0-540-08495-6 (hardback)
ISBN-13   978-0-540-08495-1 (hardback)

ISBN-10   0-540-08496-4 (spiral)
ISBN-13   978-0-540-08496-8 (spiral)

© Philip's 2004

Ordnance Survey®

This product includes mapping data licensed
from Ordnance Survey® with the permission of
the Controller of Her Majesty's Stationery Office.
© Crown copyright 2004. All rights reserved.
Licence number 100011710.

Printed and bound in Spain
by Cayfosa-Quebecor

Contents

III	**Key to map symbols**
IV	**Key to map pages**
VI	**Route planning**
VIII	**Administrative and Postcode boundaries**
1	**Street maps** at 3½ inches to 1 mile
177	**Index** of towns and villages
179	**Index** of streets, hospitals, industrial estates, railway stations, schools, shopping centres, universities and places of interest

Digital Data

The exceptionally high-quality mapping found in this atlas is available as digital data in TIFF format, which is easily convertible to other bitmapped (raster) image formats.

The index is also available in digital form as a standard database table. It contains all the details found in the printed index together with the National Grid reference for the map square in which each entry is named.

For further information and to discuss your requirements, please contact Philip's on 020 7644 6932 or james.mann@philips-maps.co.uk

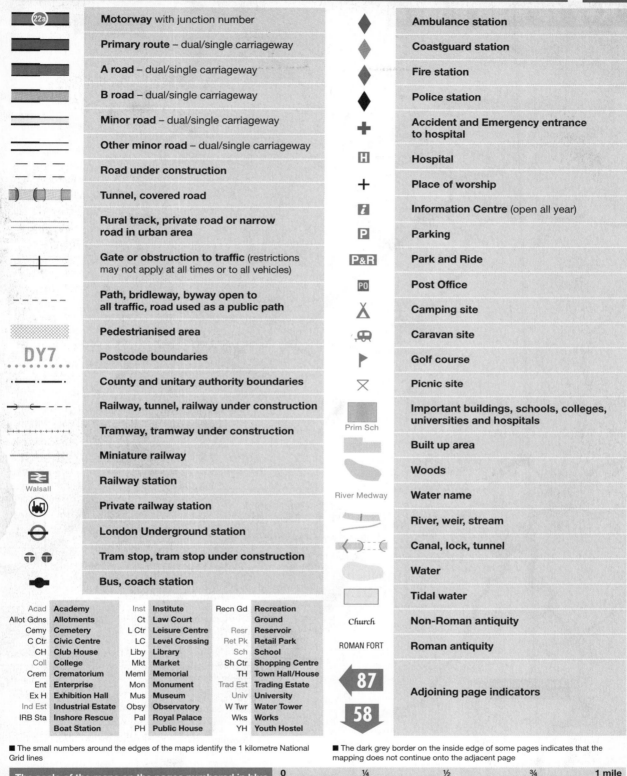

Motorway with junction number	◆ **Ambulance station**
Primary route – dual/single carriageway	◆ **Coastguard station**
A road – dual/single carriageway	◆ **Fire station**
B road – dual/single carriageway	◆ **Police station**
Minor road – dual/single carriageway	✚ **Accident and Emergency entrance to hospital**
Other minor road – dual/single carriageway	
Road under construction	**H** **Hospital**
Tunnel, covered road	✛ **Place of worship**
Rural track, private road or narrow road in urban area	**i** **Information Centre** (open all year)
Gate or obstruction to traffic (restrictions may not apply at all times or to all vehicles)	**P** **Parking**
	P&R **Park and Ride**
Path, bridleway, byway open to all traffic, road used as a public path	**PO** **Post Office**
	Å **Camping site**
Pedestrianised area	**Caravan site**
DY7 **Postcode boundaries**	▶ **Golf course**
County and unitary authority boundaries	⊠ **Picnic site**
Railway, tunnel, railway under construction	**Prim Sch** **Important buildings, schools, colleges, universities and hospitals**
Tramway, tramway under construction	**Built up area**
Miniature railway	**Woods**
Railway station Walsall	**River Medway** **Water name**
Private railway station	**River, weir, stream**
London Underground station	**Canal, lock, tunnel**
Tram stop, tram stop under construction	**Water**
Bus, coach station	**Tidal water**
	Church **Non-Roman antiquity**
	ROMAN FORT **Roman antiquity**

Acad	**Academy**	Inst	**Institute**	Recn Gd	**Recreation Ground**
Allot Gdns	**Allotments**	Ct	**Law Court**		
Cemy	**Cemetery**	L Ctr	**Leisure Centre**	Resr	**Reservoir**
C Ctr	**Civic Centre**	LC	**Level Crossing**	Ret Pk	**Retail Park**
CH	**Club House**	Liby	**Library**	Sch	**School**
Coll	**College**	Mkt	**Market**	Sh Ctr	**Shopping Centre**
Crem	**Crematorium**	Meml	**Memorial**	TH	**Town Hall/House**
Ent	**Enterprise**	Mon	**Monument**	Trad Est	**Trading Estate**
Ex H	**Exhibition Hall**	Mus	**Museum**	Univ	**University**
Ind Est	**Industrial Estate**	Obsy	**Observatory**	W Twr	**Water Tower**
IRB Sta	**Inshore Rescue Boat Station**	Pal	**Royal Palace**	Wks	**Works**
		PH	**Public House**	YH	**Youth Hostel**

87 / **58** **Adjoining page indicators**

■ The small numbers around the edges of the maps identify the 1 kilometre National Grid lines

■ The dark grey border on the inside edge of some pages indicates that the mapping does not continue onto the adjacent page

The scale of the maps on the pages numbered in blue is 5.52 cm to 1 km • 3½ inches to 1 mile • 1: 18103

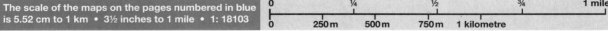

0	¼	½	¾	1 mile
0	250 m	500 m	750 m	1 kilometre

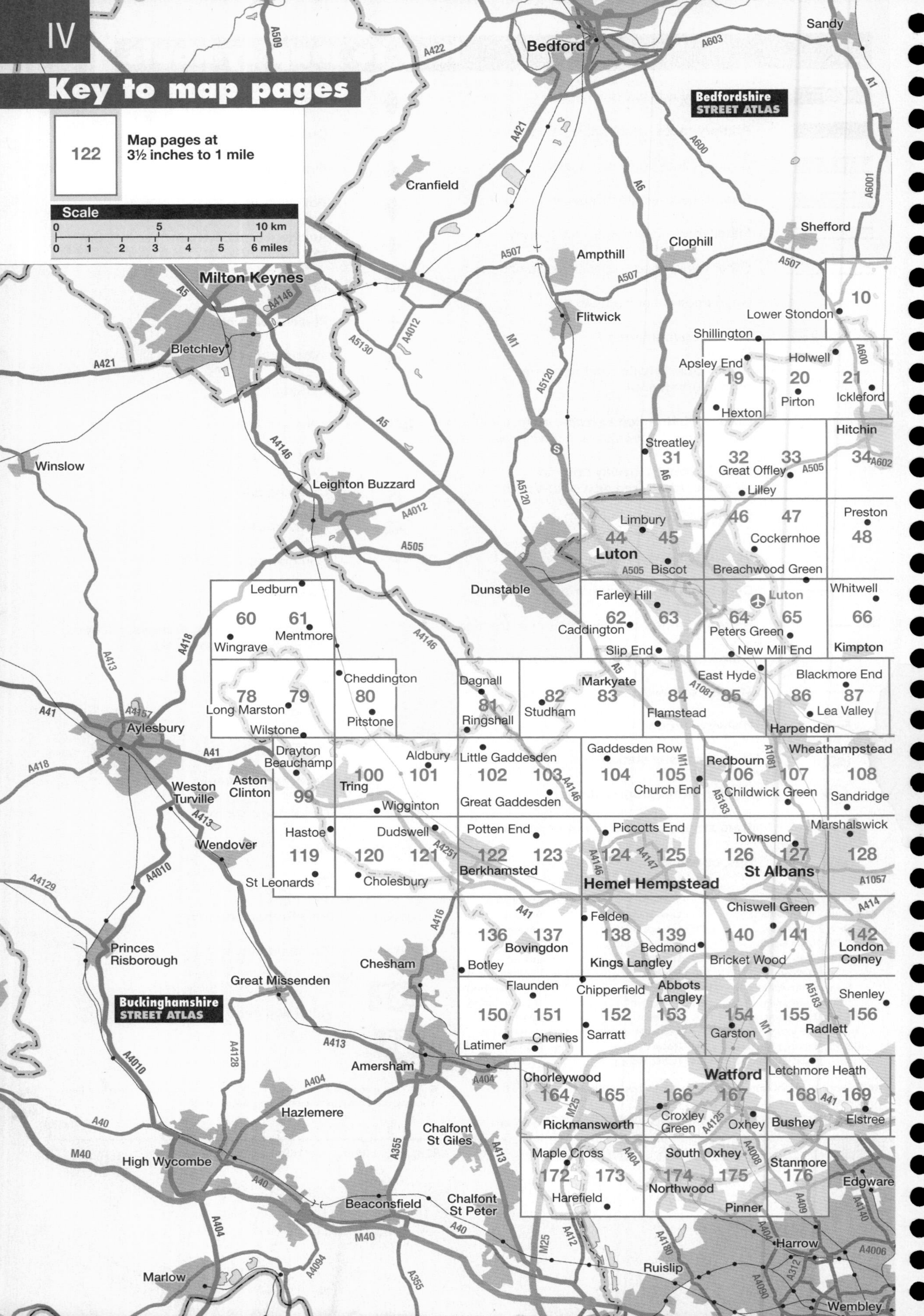

IV

Key to map pages

122 — Map pages at 3½ inches to 1 mile

Scale

0 ——— 5 ——— 10 km
0 — 1 — 2 — 3 — 4 — 5 — 6 miles

Bedfordshire STREET ATLAS

Buckinghamshire STREET ATLAS

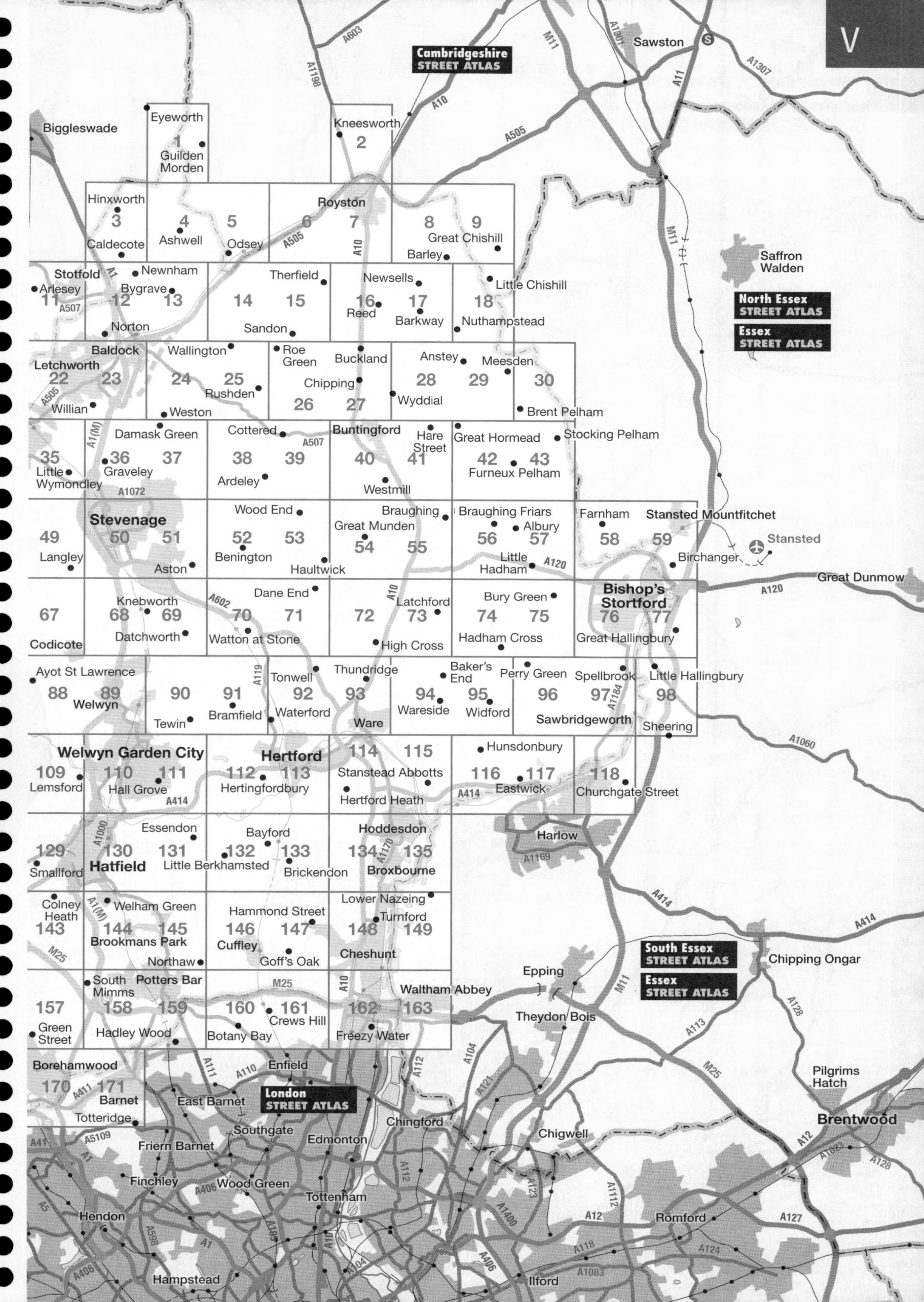

Biggleswade

Eyeworth
1
Guilden Morden

Kneesworth
2

Cambridgeshire
STREET ATLAS

Sawston

Hinxworth
3
Caldecote

Ashwell
4

5
Odsey

Royston
6
A505

7
A10

8

9
Great Chishill
Barley

Saffron Walden

North Essex
STREET ATLAS

Essex
STREET ATLAS

Stotfold
Arlesey
11
A507

Newnham
Bygrave
12

13
Norton

Therfield
14

15
Sandon

Newsells
16
Reed

17
Barkway

18
Nuthampstead

Little Chishill

Baldock
Letchworth
22

23
Willian
A505

Wallington
24
Weston

Roe Green
25
Rushden

Buckland
26
Chipping

27
Wyddial

Anstey
28

29
Meesden

30
Brent Pelham

Damask Green
Little Wymondley
35

36
Graveley

37
A1072

Cottered
38
Ardeley

A507
39

Buntingford
40
Westmill

Hare Street
41

Great Hormead
42
Furneux Pelham

43

Stocking Pelham

Stevenage
49
Langley

50

51
Aston

Wood End
52
Benington

53
Haultwick

Great Munden
54

55

Braughing Friars
56
Little Hadham

Albury
57
A120

Farnham
58

59
Birchanger

Stansted Mountfitchet

Stansted

Great Dunmow

A602
Knebworth
67
Codicote

68
Datchworth

69

Dane End
70
Watton at Stone

71

72

Latchford
73
High Cross

Bury Green
74

75
Hadham Cross

Bishop's Stortford
76

77
Great Hallingbury

A120

Ayot St Lawrence
88
Welwyn

89

90
Tewin

A419
Tonwell
Bramfield
91

92
Waterford

Thundridge
93
Ware

94
Wareside

Baker's End
Widford
95

Perry Green
96

Spellbrook
97
A1184

Little Hallingbury
98
Sheering

Sawbridgeworth

Welwyn Garden City
109
Lemsford

Hall Grove
110

111
A414

Hertford
112
Hertingfordbury

113

114

115
Stanstead Abbotts
Hertford Heath

Hunsdonbury

116

117
Eastwick
A414

118
Churchgate Street

A1060

Essendon
129
Smallford

A1000
130
Hatfield

Little Berkhamsted
131

Bayford
132
Brickendon

133

Hoddesdon
134
A1170

135
Broxbourne

Harlow
A1169

Colney Heath
143
M25

Welham Green
144
Brookmans Park

145
Northaw

Hammond Street
146
Cuffley

147
Goff's Oak

Lower Nazeing
148
Cheshunt

Turnford
149

Epping

A414

South Essex
STREET ATLAS

Essex
STREET ATLAS

Chipping Ongar

Green Street
157

South Mimms
158
Hadley Wood

Potters Bar
159

160
Botany Bay

Crews Hill
161

162

Freezy Water

163

Waltham Abbey

M11

Theydon Bois

A113

Pilgrims Hatch

Brentwood

Borehamwood
170
A411

171
Barnet
Totteridge

London
STREET ATLAS

A111
A110
East Barnet

Enfield

Chingford

Chigwell

M25

A41
A5109
A1

Friern Barnet
Southgate

Edmonton

Finchley
A406 Wood Green

Hendon

Tottenham

Romford

Hampstead

Ilford

Route Planning

Scale
0 5 10 km
0 1 2 3 4 5 6 miles
Milton Keynes
Bedford
Herts
Ravenstone
Stoke Goldington
Emberton
Newton Blossomville
Clifton Reynes
Weston Underwood
Filgrave
Hardmead
Astwood
Stagsden
Box End
Kempston
Biddenham
Queen's Park
Goldington
Willington
Moggerhanger
Fenlake
Cople
Sandy
Girtford
Beeston
Hatch
Thorncote Green
Northill
Upper Caldecote
Ickwell Green
Cardington
Harrowden
Shortstown
Elstow
Cotton End
Keeley Green
Kempston Hardwick
Littleworth
Wilstead
North Crawley
Bourne End
Wootton
Upper Shelton
Lower Shelton
Broad Green
Cranfield
Moulsoe
Marston Moretaine
Stewartby
How End
Houghton Conquest
Haynes
Haynes Church End
Old Warden
Southill
Broom
Stanford
Shefford
Clifton
Henlow
Beadlow
Clophill
Maulden
Ampthill
Millbrook
Lidlington
Brogborough
Salford
Cosgrove
Stony Stratford
Wolverton
New Bradwell
Linford
Willen
Milton Keynes
Passenham
Bradwell
Broughton
Calverton
Woolstone
Milton Keynes Village
Upper Weald
Beachampton
Loughton
Woughton on the Green
Shenley Church End
Shenley Brook End
Simpson
Walton
Wavendon
Aspley Guise
Woburn Sands
Bow Brickhill
Aspley Heath
Husborne Crawley
Ridgmont
Steppingley
Flitwick
Flitton
Silsoe
Upper Gravenhurst
Campton
Meppershall
Upper Stondon
Arlesey
Greenfield
Pulloxhill
Higham Gobion
Shillington
Holwell
Whaddon
Bletchley
Fenny Stratford
Far Bletchley
Nash
Newton Longville
Little Brickhill
Woburn
Eversholt
Church End
Tingrith
Westoning
Harlington
Apsley End
Pirton
LETCHWORTH
Barton-le-Clay
Hexton
Pegsdon
Sharpenhoe
Little Horwood
Great Horwood
Great Brickhill
Potsgrove
Milton Bryan
Battlesden
Toddington
TODDINGTON SERVICES
HITCHIN
Drayton Parslow
Stoke Hammond
Mursley
Swanbourne
North End
Soulbury
Heath and Reach
Hockliffe
Tebworth
Streatley
Upper Sundon
Lower Sundon
Charlton
Great Offley
Lilley
Gosmore
Winslow
Stewkley
South End
Leighton Buzzard
Eggington
Wingfield
Chalton
Sundon Park
Limbury
GALLEY HILL
Granborough
Hoggeston
Dunton
Linslade
Burcott
Tilsworth
Stanbridge
Houghton Regis
Leagrave
Luton
Stopsley
Cockernhoe Green
King's Walden
St Paul's Walden
North Marston
Creslow
Wing
Cublington
Billington
Lower End
Totternhoe
Dunstable
Biscot
Hart Hill
Breachwood Green
Oving
Whitchurch
Pitchcott
Aston Abbotts
Ledburn
Slapton
Eaton Green
Eaton Bray
Church End
Farley Hill
LONDON LUTON
Whitwell
Hardwick
Mentmore
Wingrave
Horton
Edlesborough
Kensworth
Caddington
Peter's Green
Weedon
Rowsham
Hulcott
Ivinghoe Aston
Cheddington
Ivinghoe
Whipsnade
Kensworth Common
Slip End
East Hyde
Kinsbourne Green
Blackmore End
Long Marston
Marsworth
Pitstone Green
Pitstone
Dagnall
Studham
Markyate
Batford
Bierton
Aylesbury
Puttenham
Wilstone
Ringshall
Jockey End
Flamstead
Trowley Bottom
HARPENDEN
Marshall's Heath
Wheathampstead
Waddesdon
Upper Winchendon
Stone
Southcourt
Buckland
Drayton Beauchamp
Tring Wharf
New Mill
Tring
Aldbury
Little Gaddesden
Great Gaddesden
Hatching Green
Redbourn
Dinton
Westlington
Stoke Mandeville
Weston Turville
Aston Clinton
Bishopstone
Halton
TOLL
Nettleden
Water End
Childwick Green
Sandridge
Jersey Farm
Ford
Kimble Wick
North Lee
Terrick
Nash Lee
Wendover
Wigginton
Hastoe
Northchurch
Potten End
Piccotts End
Townsend
Marshalswick
Aston Sandford
Little Kimble
Butler's Cross
Berkhamsted
Gadebridge
St Albans
Fleetville
Owlswick
Meadle
Ellesborough
St Leonard's
Buckland Common
Cholesbury
Bourne End
Boxmoor
Hemel Hempstead
St Stephens
The Camp
Colney Heath
Ilmer
Longwick
Great Kimble
Dunsmore
The Lee
Bellingdon
Ashley Green
Felden
Chiswell Green
London Colney
Monks Risborough
Lee Clump
Chartridge
Lye Green
Whelpley Hill
Bovingdon
Bedmond
Pitch Green
Princes Risborough
Bledlow
Little Hampden
Ballinger Common
South Heath
Botley
Ley Hill
Bovingdon Green
Primrose Hill
Kings Langley
Abbots Langley
Colney Street
Bricket Wood
Shenley
Saunderton
Chinnor
Great Hampden
Loosley Row
Great Missenden
Chesham
Chipperfield
Flaunden
Radlett
Prestwood
Hyde Heath
Lacey Green
Speen
Little Kingshill
Great Kingshill
Chesham Bois
Latimer
Sarratt
Aldenham
Letchmore Heath
Radnage
Bledlow Ridge
Walters Ash
Upper North Dean
Cryers Hill
Widmer End
Holmer Green
Little Missenden
Amersham
Chenies
BOREHAMWOOD
The City
Stokenchurch
Bradenham
Naphill
Hughenden Valley
Little Chalfont
Chorleywood
Croxley Green
Watford
Beacon's Bottom
West Wycombe
Downley
Hazlemere
Penn Street
Coleshill
Winchmore Hill
Chalfont St Giles
RICKMANSWORTH
Oxhey
Bushey
Bushey Heath
Ibstone
High Wycombe
Tylers Green
Penn
Knotty Green
Seer Green
Jordans
Chalfont Common
Maple Cross
South Oxhey
Eastbury
Batchworth Heath
Stanmore
Edgware
Cadmore End
Bolter End
Fingest
Lane End
Booker
Wycombe Marsh
Forty Green
Loudwater
Beaconsfield
Chalfont St Peter
Harefield
Northwood
Hatch End
Harrow Weald
Turville
Skirmett
Frieth
WYCOMBE AIR PARK
Marlow Bottom
Little Marlow
Flackwell Heath
Wooburn Green
Gerrards Cross
DENHAM
Denham Green
Ruislip Common
Pinner
HARROW
Wealdstone
Greenhill
Rockwell End
Lower Woodend
Well End
Wooburn
Hedgerley
Ruislip
Eastcote
Rayners Lane
Harrow on the Hill
Fawley
Hambleden
Bovingdon Green
Bourne End
Cores End
Hedsor
Tatling End
Denham
Ickenham
Greenlands
Marlow
Mill End
Cookham Dean
Cookham
Fulmer
NORTHOLT
Wembley
M1
M10
M25
M40
A5
A6
A41
A413
A421
A505
A4010
A4146
A418
A355
A404
A509
A1
A600
A4012
A507

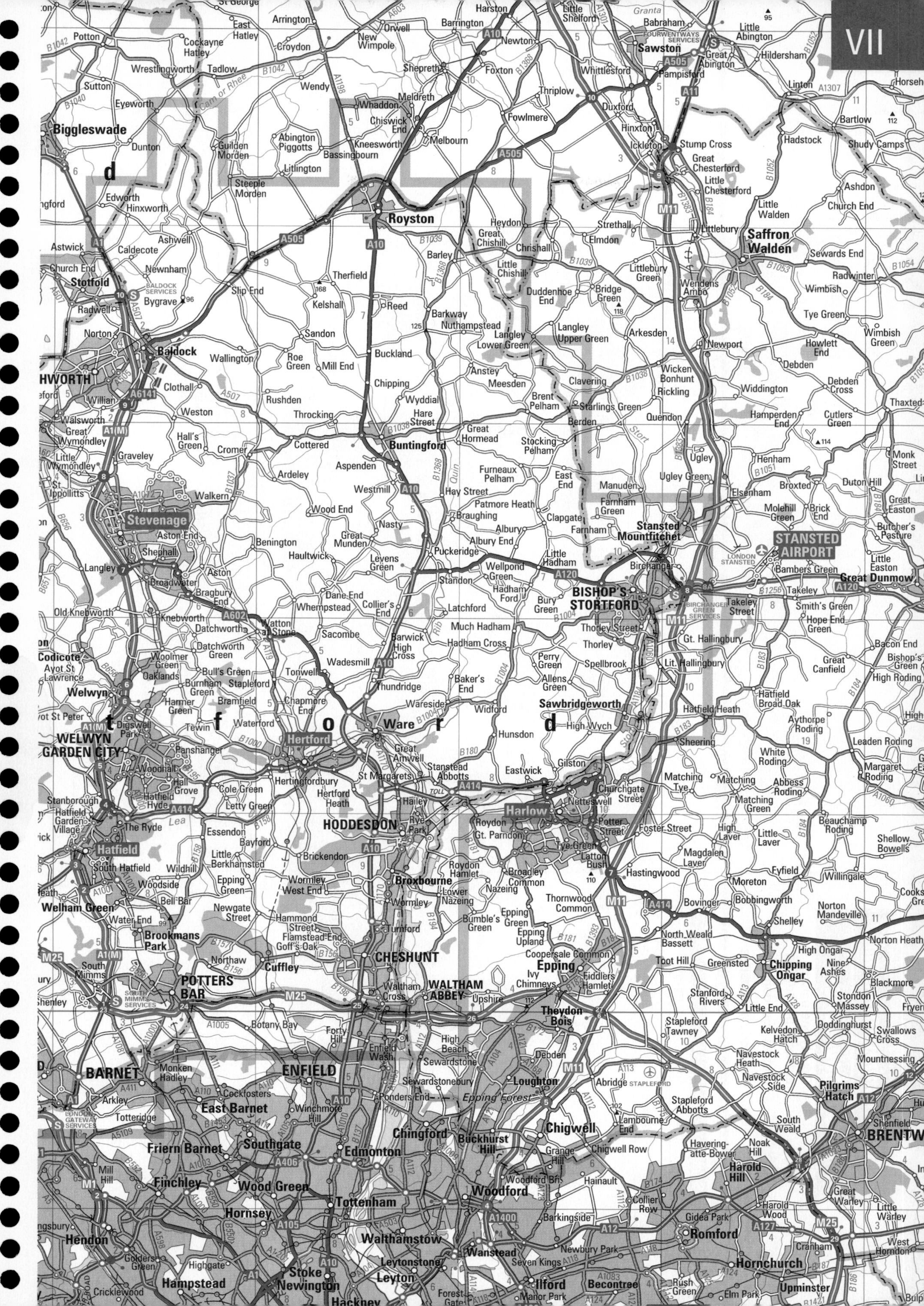

Potton
Cockayne Hatley
East Hatley
Arrington
Croydon
Orwell
New Wimpole
Barrington
Harston
Newton
Little Shelford
Granta
Babraham
Sawston
Great Abington
Little Abington
Hildersham
Pampisford
Whittlesford
Wrestlingworth
Tadlow
Sutton
Wendy
Shepreth
Foxton
Thriplow
Duxford
Linton
Horseheath
Eyeworth
Whaddon
Meldreth
Fowlmere
Bartlow
Biggleswade
Dunton
Guilden Morden
Abington Piggotts
Chiswick End
Kneesworth
Bassingbourn
Melbourn
Hinxton
Ickleton
Stump Cross
Great Chesterford
Little Chesterford
Hadstock
Shudy Camps
Ashdon
Litlington
Steeple Morden
Edworth
Hinxworth
Royston
Heydon
Great Chishill
Chrishall
Strethall
Elmdon
Littlebury
Saffron Walden
Little Walden
Church End
Sewards End
Radwinter
Astwick
Caldecote
Ashwell
Church End
Stotfold
Newnham
Barley
Little Chishill
Littlebury Green
Wendens Ambo
Wimbish
Baldock Services
Bygrave
Therfield
Kelshall
Reed
Duddenhoe End
Bridge Green
Radwell
Norton
Baldock
Sandon
Barkway
Nuthampstead
Langley Upper Green
Langley Lower Green
Arkesden
Newport
Tye Green
Howlett End
Wimbish Green
Wallington
Roe Green
Mill End
Buckland
Anstey
Meesden
Clavering
Wicken Bonhunt
Debden
Debden Cross
Letchworth
Willian
Clothall
Rushden
Chipping
Wyddial
Brent Pelham
Rickling
Widdington
Thaxted
Walsworth
Great Wymondley
Little Wymondley
Weston
Throcking
Hare Street
Starlings Green
Berden
Quendon
Hamperden End
Cutlers Green
Hall's Green
Cromer
Cottered
Great Hormead
Buntingford
Stocking Pelham
Graveley
Aspenden
Ardeley
Furneaux Pelham
East End
Manuden
Ugley
Ugley Green
Henham
Monk Street
St Ippolitts
Walkern
Westmill
Hay Street
Patmore Heath
Farnham Green
Elsenham
Broxted
Duton Hill
Stevenage
Wood End
Nasty
Braughing
Clapgate
Farnham
Stansted Mountfitchet
Molehill Green
Brick End
Great Easton
Aston End
Benington
Great Munden
Albury
Albury End
Stansted Airport
Butcher's Pasture
Shephall
Langley
Aston
Haultwick
Levens Green
Puckeridge
Little Hadham
Birchanger
Little Easton
Bambers Green
Great Dunmow
Bragbury End
Broadwater
Dane End
Standon
Wellpond Green
Hadham Ford
Bishop's Stortford
Takeley
Takeley Street
Smith's Green
Old Knebworth
Whempstead
Collier's End
Latchford
Bury Green
Birchanger Green Services
Hope End Green
Knebworth
Datchworth
Watton at Stone
Much Hadham
Thorley Street
Thorley
Gt. Hallingbury
Bacon End
Codicote
Datchworth Green
Sacombe
Barwick
High Cross
Hadham Cross
Woolmer Green
Wadesmill
Perry Green
Spellbrook
Lit. Hallingbury
Great Canfield
Bishop's Green
Ayot St Lawrence
Oaklands
Bull's Green
Tonwell
Baker's End
Allens Green
High Roding
Welwyn
Burnham Green
Stapleford
Thundridge
Sawbridgeworth
Hatfield Broad Oak
Harmer Green
Bramfield
Chapmore End
Wareside
Widford
Hatfield Heath
Ayot St Peter
Digswell Park
Tewin
Waterford
Ware
High Wych
Aythorpe Roding
Welwyn Garden City
Hertford
Hunsdon
Sheering
Leaden Roding
Panshanger
Great Amwell
White Roding
Woodhall
Hertingfordbury
Stanstead Abbotts
St Margarets
Eastwick
Gilston
Matching Tye
Matching
Abbess Roding
Margaret Roding
Hall Grove
Cole Green
Hertford Heath
Churchgate Street
Stanborough
Hatfield Hyde
Letty Green
Hailey
Netteswell
Matching Green
Hatfield Garden Village
The Ryde
Lea
Hoddesdon
Rye Park
Roydon
Harlow
Potter Street
Foster Street
High Laver
Little Laver
Beauchamp Roding
Essendon
Bayford
Gt. Parndon
Tye Green
Magdalen Laver
Shellow Bowells
Hatfield
Little Berkhamsted
Brickendon
Latton Bush
Hastingwood
Fyfield
Willingale
South Hatfield
Wildhill
Roydon Hamlet
Broadley Common
Woodside
Epping Green
Wormley West End
Broxbourne
Nazeing
Lower Nazeing
Moreton
Cooksmill Green
Welham Green
Bell Bar
Wormley
Thornwood Common
Bovinger
Bobbingworth
Newgate Street
Hammond Street
Bumble's Green
Epping Green
Norton Mandeville
Water End
Brookmans Park
Flamstead End
Turnford
Epping Upland
North Weald Bassett
Shelley
Goff's Oak
Coopersale Common
Norton Heath
South Mimms
Northaw
Cuffley
Cheshunt
Epping
High Ongar
Toot Hill
Greensted
Chipping Ongar
Nine Ashes
South Mimms Services
Potters Bar
Waltham Cross
Waltham Abbey
Ivy Chimneys
Fiddlers Hamlet
Stanford Rivers
Blackmore
Shenley
Upshire
Theydon Bois
Stondon Massey
Little End
Fryerning
Botany Bay
Forty Hill
Stapleford Tawney
Doddinghurst
Kelvedon Hatch
Swallows Cross
High Beach
Enfield Wash
Debden
Sewardstone
Monken Hadley
Barnet
Enfield
Sewardstonebury
Loughton
Abridge
Stapleford
Navestock Heath
Navestock Side
Mountnessing
Pilgrims Hatch
Arkley
Cockfosters
Ponders End
Epping Forest
East Barnet
Winchmore Hill
Lambourne End
Stapleford Abbotts
London Gateway Services
Totteridge
Chingford
Buckhurst Hill
Chigwell
South Weald
Shenfield
Brentwood
Friern Barnet
Southgate
Edmonton
Grange Hill
Chigwell Row
Havering-atte-Bower
Noak Hill
Mill Hill
Woodford Bridge
Hainault
Harold Hill
Finchley
Wood Green
Woodford
Tottenham
Collier Row
Great Warley
Hornsey
Harold Wood
Little Warley
Hendon
Walthamstow
Barkingside
Gidea Park
Romford
Wanstead
Newbury Park
Cranham
West Horndon
Golders Green
Highgate
Leytonstone
Seven Kings
Hornchurch
Hampstead
Stoke Newington
Leyton
Ilford
Becontree
Rush Green
Upminster
Cricklewood
Hackney
Forest Gate
Manor Park
Elm Park
M11
M25
A1(M)
A10
A505
A120
A414
A602
A11
A12
A406

Major administrative and Postcode boundaries

County and unitary authority boundaries
District boundaries
Postcode boundaries
Area covered by this atlas

Scale

0   5   10 miles
0   5   10   15 km

Cambridgeshire

Essex

Bedfordshire

Buckinghamshire

London

East Hertfordshire

North Hertfordshire

Hertfordshire

Welwyn Hatfield

St Albans

Dacorum

Three Rivers

Watford

Hertsmere

Broxbourne

Stevenage

Luton

TL
TQ

SP
TL

SU
TQ

SP
SU

Stansted Mountfitchet
CM24
CB11
Furneux Pelham
Bishop's Stortford
CM23
CM22
SG10
Much Hadham
CM21
Sawbridgeworth
CM20
CM17
Harlow
Braughing
SG11
SG9
Buntingford
SG12
Ware
Stansted Abbotts
CM19
Hoddesdon
EN11
EN9
Anstey
Barkway
Barley
SG8
Royston
Kelshall
Sandon
Thundridge
Hertford Heath
EN10
Broxbourne
EN7
Cheshunt
Cuffley
EN8
Goff's Oak
EN3
Enfield
E4
Crews Hill
EN2
EN1
Dane End
Bayford
SG13
Cromer
Benington
SG2
Watton at Stone
Hertford
SG14
Ashwell
SG19
SG7
Baldock
SG3
Welwyn
AL9
Welham Green
EN6
Potters Bar
EN4
Barnet
N20
Letchworth
SG1
Stevenage
Knebworth
SG6
AL6
AL7
Welwyn Garden City
AL8
Welwyn
AL10
Hatfield
EN5
Borehamwood
WD6
HA8
NW7
SG18
SG15
Stotfold
SG5
Hitchin
Graveley
SG4
Whitwell
Kimpton
London Colney
AL2
Radlett
WD7
Bushey
WD23
HA7
HA6
SG17
SG16
Pirton
Great Offley
Preston
AL5
Harpenden
Wheathampstead
Sandridge
AL4
St Albans
AL1
Bedmond
WD24
Watford
WD25
WD19
HA5
HA3
Lilley
Peters Green
AL3
Redbourn
WD17
Sarratt
Three Rivers
WD18
WD3
Northwood
HA4
MK45
LU2
Markyate
Jockey End
HP2
Kings Langley
WD4
WD5
Watford
Chorleywood
Rickmansworth
UB9
Harefield
SL9
LU3
LU4
LU1
Caddington
Luton
Hemel Hempstead
HP1
HP3
Bovingdon
LU6
Dagnall
Aldbury
HP4
Berkhamsted
Bourne End
HP5
Mentmore
LU7
Long Marston
Marsworth
HP23
Tring
Cholesbury
HP22
Wingrave

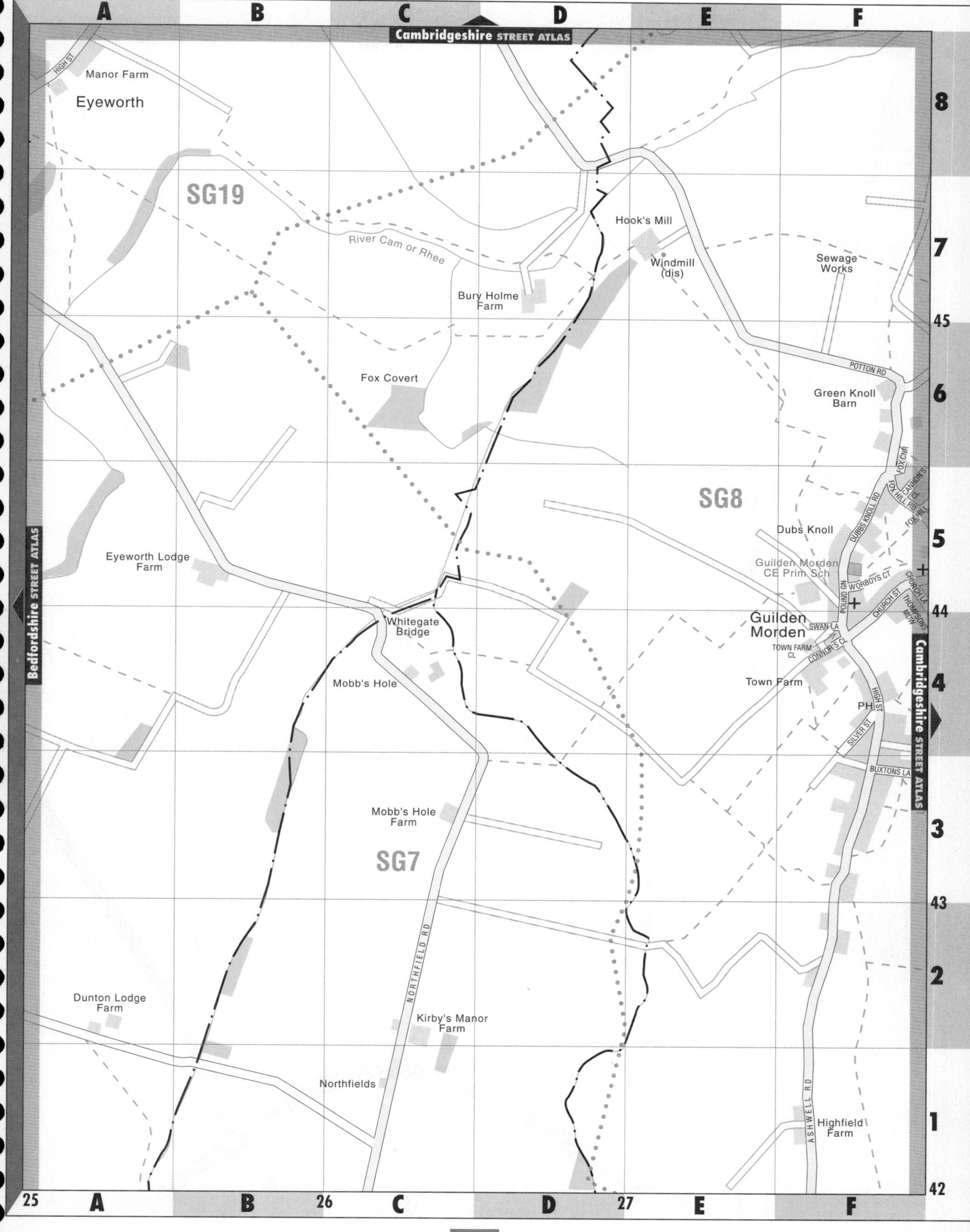

A B C D E F

8
7
45
6
5
44
4
43
3
2
43
1
42

Manor Farm
Eyeworth
High St

SG19

River Cam or Rhee

Hook's Mill
Windmill (dis)
Bury Holme Farm

Sewage Works

Fox Covert

Green Knoll Barn

Potton Rd

SG8

Dubs Knoll
Guilden Morden CE Prim Sch

Fox Hall
Caxmon's
Dubs Knoll Rd
Fox Hall Rd
Churcella

Eyeworth Lodge Farm

Guilden Morden
Pound Gn Worboys Ct
Swan La
Thompsons Mdw
Church St

Bedfordshire STREET ATLAS

Whitegate Bridge

Town Farm Cl
Connor's Cl
Town Farm

Mobb's Hole

PH
High St

Silver St
Buxtons La

Mobb's Hole Farm

SG7

Northfield Rd

Dunton Lodge Farm

Kirby's Manor Farm

Northfields

Ashwell Rd
Highfield Farm

Cambridgeshire STREET ATLAS

25 A B 26 C D 27 E F

A1198 Huntingdon (A14)
Cambridgeshire STREET ATLAS
Mettle Hill Farm
NEW FARM TRAVELLER'S SITE
Mettle Hill
Meldreth
Dyer's Green
Ermine Farm
Bassingbourn Barracks
Frog Hall
DANGER AREA
OXFORD CL
Harcamlow Way
EDINBURGH SQ
DANGER AREA
Resr
CHESTNUT LA
WELLINGTON PL
NIGHTINGALE AVE
THE CAUSEWAY
PH
PH
SWINNELL CL
Kneesworth
Kneesworth House
SG8
OLD NORTH RD
Beauval Farm
TUDOR CT
Icknield Way Path
Harcamlow Way
A10 Cambridge
Bury Farm
ASHWELL ST
Nurseries
Holland Hall
Sewage Works
Highfield Farm
1 SWINBURNE CL
2 SCOTT CL
3 ST PANCRAS HO
New Farm
Royston
A505
Schs

7

4

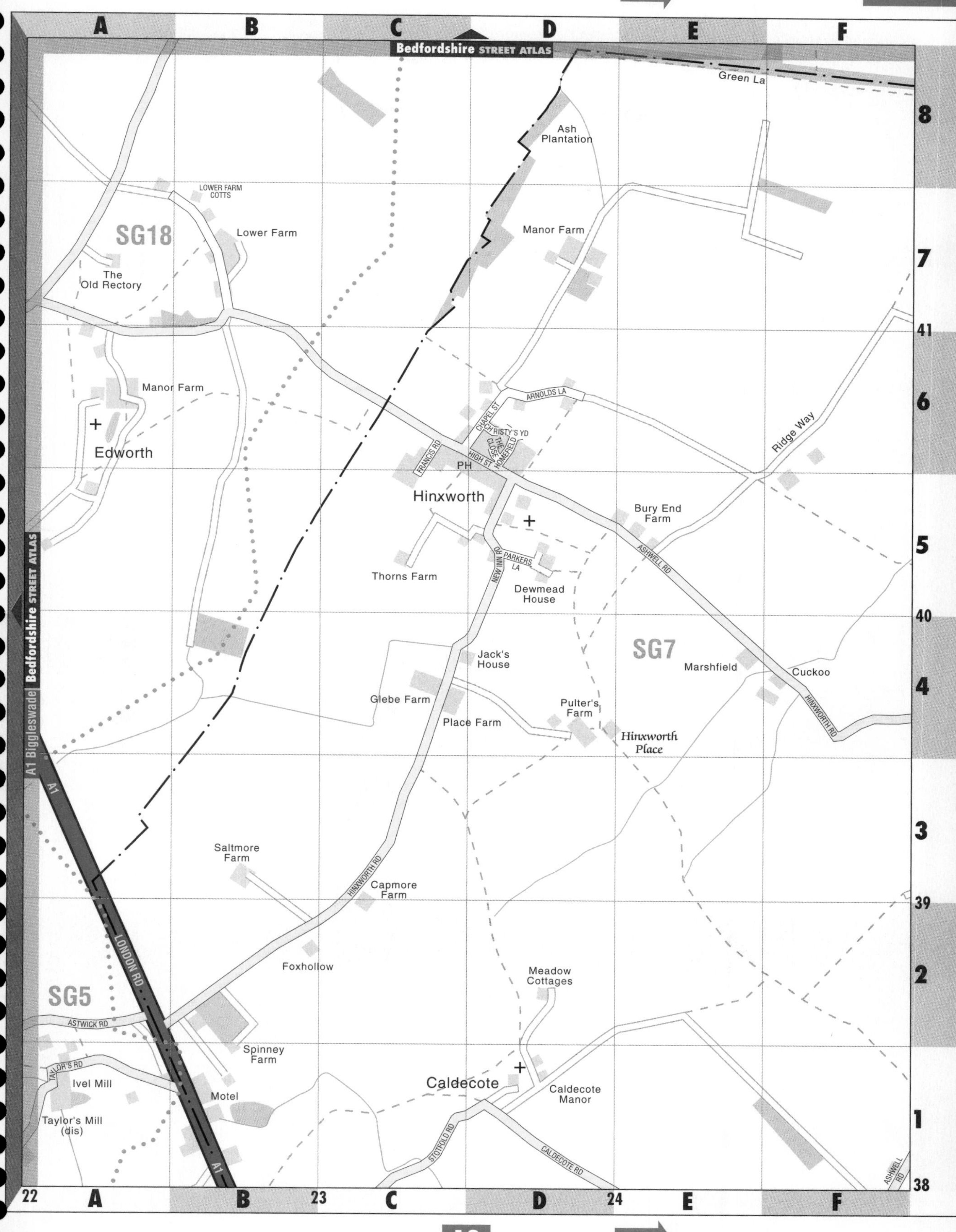
Bedfordshire STREET ATLAS
A1 Biggleswade Bedfordshire STREET ATLAS
A
B
C
D
E
F
8
7
41
6
5
40
4
3
39
2
1
38
22
23
24
Green La
Ash Plantation
LOWER FARM COTTS
Lower Farm
SG18
The Old Rectory
Manor Farm
Manor Farm
Edworth
ARNOLDS LA
CHAPEL ST
CHRISTY'S YD
THE CLOSE
HOMEFIELD
FRANCIS RD
HIGH ST
PH
Hinxworth
Ridge Way
Bury End Farm
ASHWELL RD
PARKERS LA
NEW INN RD
Thorns Farm
Dewmead House
SG7
Jack's House
Marshfield
Cuckoo
Glebe Farm
Place Farm
Pulter's Farm
Hinxworth Place
HINXWORTH RD
A1
Saltmore Farm
Capmore Farm
HINXWORTH RD
LONDON RD
Foxhollow
Meadow Cottages
SG5
ASTWICK RD
Spinney Farm
TAYLOR'S RD
Ivel Mill
Motel
Caldecote
Caldecote Manor
Taylor's Mill (dis)
STOTFOLD RD
CALDECOTE RD
ASHWELL RD

12
4

A B C D E F

8 Green La
Barrowsford Bridge
Ridge Way

SG8
Ashwell Rd

Cold Harbour

7

Northfield Rd

41

Sewage Works
Common La

6

Bluegates Farm
River Rhee

Ashwell End

Bluegates Dairy
Elbrook House

5
SG7
Baldwin's Corner

Ashwell Bury
Cemy

40
Love's Farm
Love La
Fordham Cl
Springhead
Lucas La
Icknield Way Path
Ashridge Farm

Rollys La
Alms La
Hotel
Gardners La
Church La
Mill St
High St
Hodwell

4
Quarry Hills Farm
Whittington Farm
Ashwell Village Mus
WOLVERLEY HO 1
THE OLD GRANARY 2
THE DOVECOTE 3
Bacons La
Swan St
PO
Station Rd
Hinxworth Rd
PH
Silver St Cl
Silver St
Angell's Mdw
Kingsland Way
Woodforde Cl
West St
Back St
Wilsons La
Bear La
Ashwell
Coombes Cl
Dixies Cl
Claybush Rd
Ashwell Prim Sch

3
Partridge Hill
Ashwell

39
Newnham Hill

2
Newnham Way
Arbury Banks
Claybush Hill
Icknield Way Path

1
Ashwell Rd
Ash Hill

38
25 A B 26 C D 27 E F

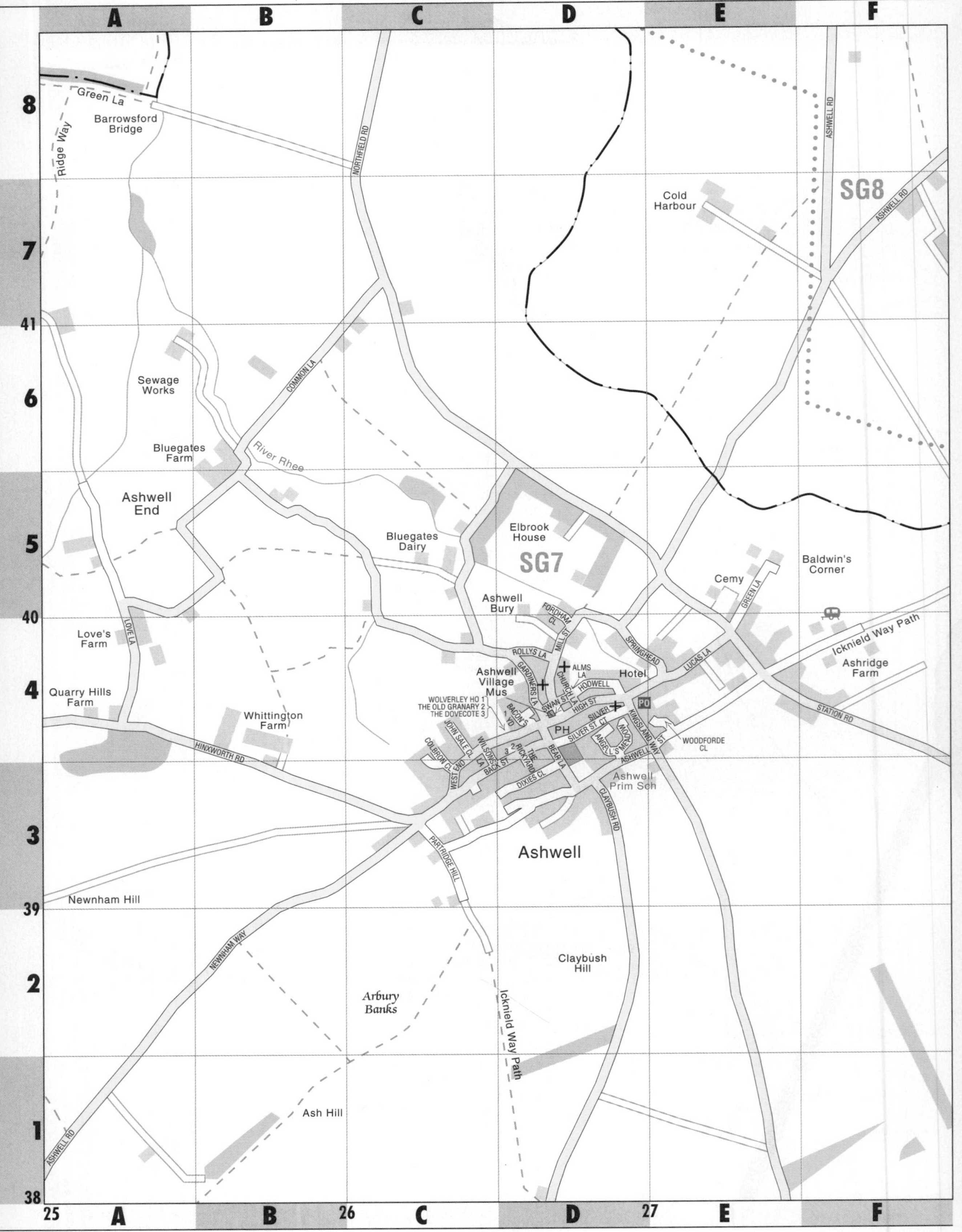

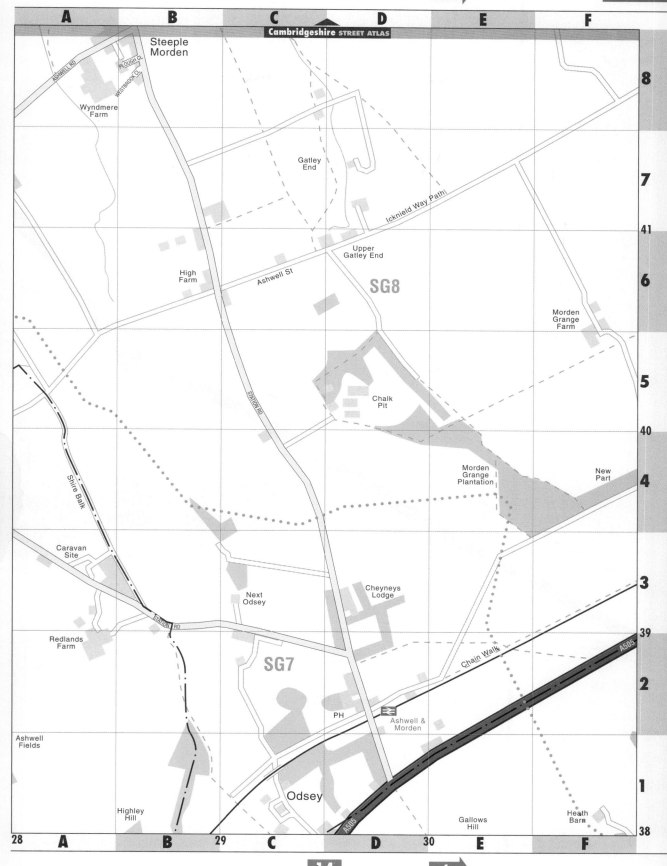

Cambridgeshire STREET ATLAS

A B C D E F

8
7
41
6
SG8
5
40
4
3
39
2
1
38

Steeple
Morden

ASHWELL RD
PLOUGH CL
WESTBROOK CL

Wyndmere
Farm

Gatley
End

Icknield Way Path

Upper
Gatley End

High
Farm

Ashwell St

STATION RD

Morden
Grange
Farm

Chalk
Pit

Morden
Grange
Plantation

New
Part

Shire Balk

Caravan
Site

Next
Odsey

Cheyneys
Lodge

Chain Walk

A505

Redlands
Farm

STATION RD

SG7

Ashwell
Fields

PH

Ashwell &
Morden

Highley
Hill

Odsey

A505

Gallows
Hill

Heath
Barn

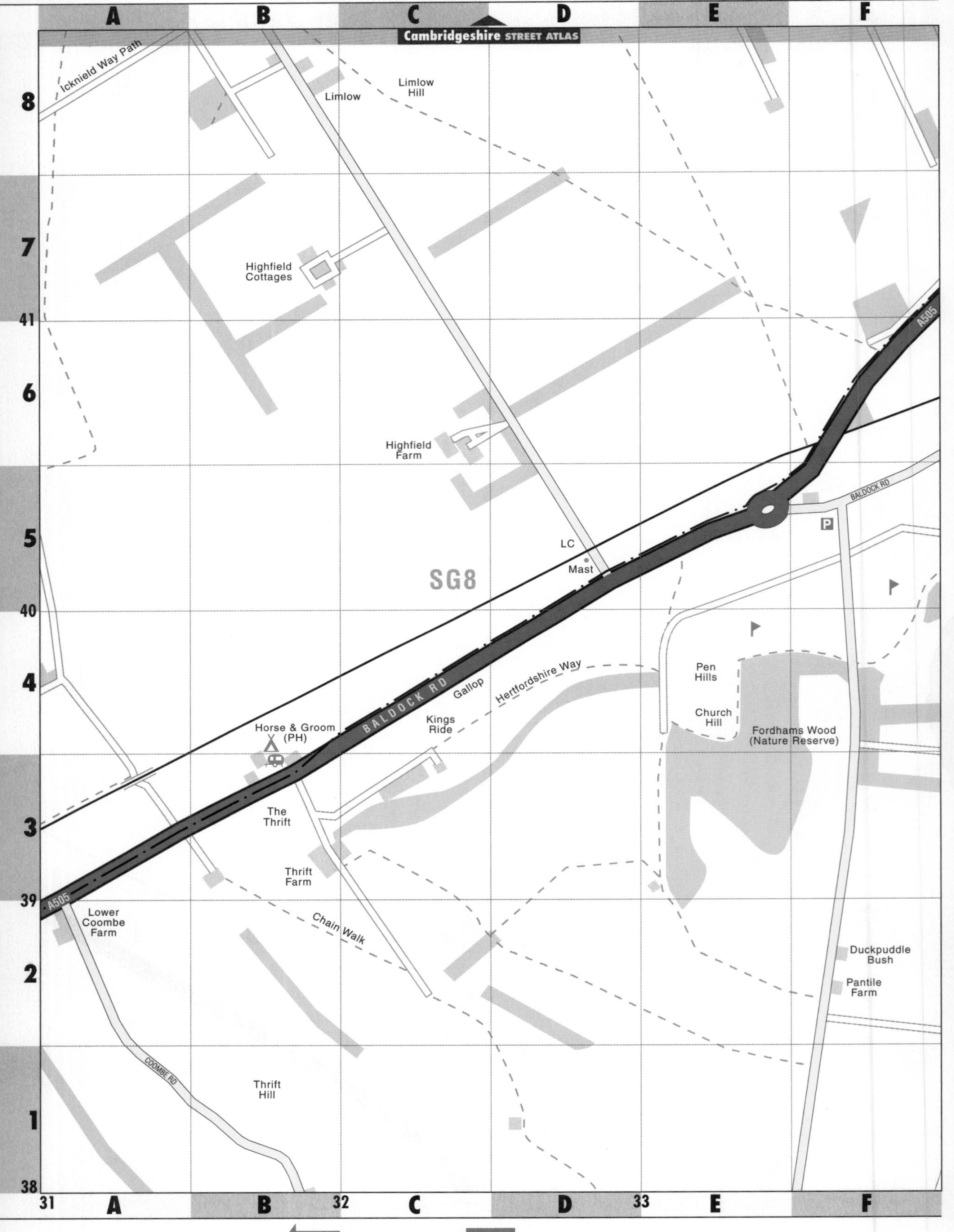

Cambridgeshire STREET ATLAS

Icknield Way Path

Limlow Hill

Limlow

Highfield Cottages

Highfield Farm

LC

Mast

SG8

A505

BALDOCK RD

Baldock Rd

Gallop

Hertfordshire Way

Kings Ride

Horse & Groom (PH)

The Thrift

Thrift Farm

Chain Walk

Lower Coombe Farm

A505

COOMBE RD

Thrift Hill

Pen Hills

Church Hill

Fordhams Wood (Nature Reserve)

Duckpuddle Bush

Pantile Farm

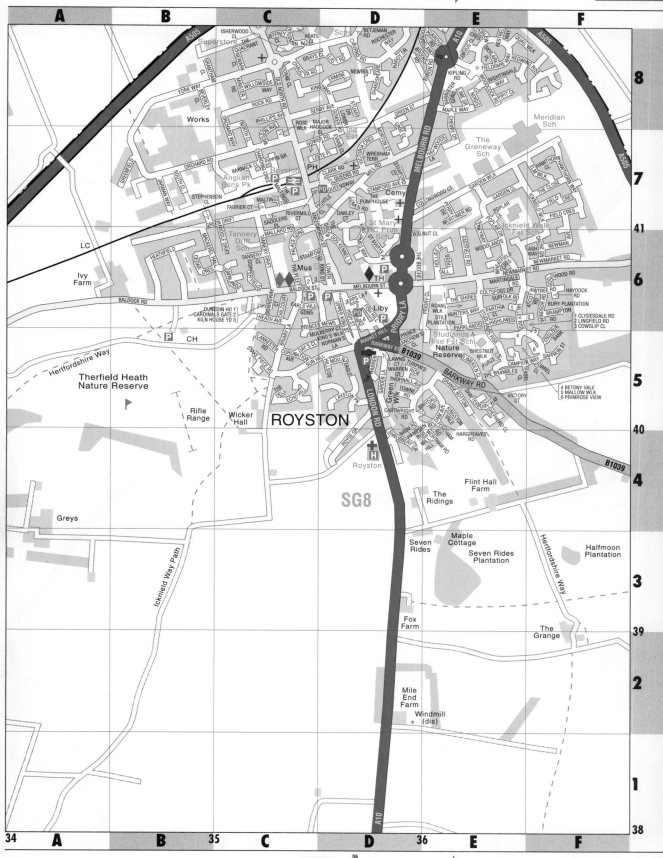

2
8

ROYSTON

SG8

16
8

D6
1 ABBOTTS YD
2 KING ST
3 JOHN ST
4 CHURCH LA
5 GEORGE LA
6 MARKET HILL
7 ANGEL PAVEMENT

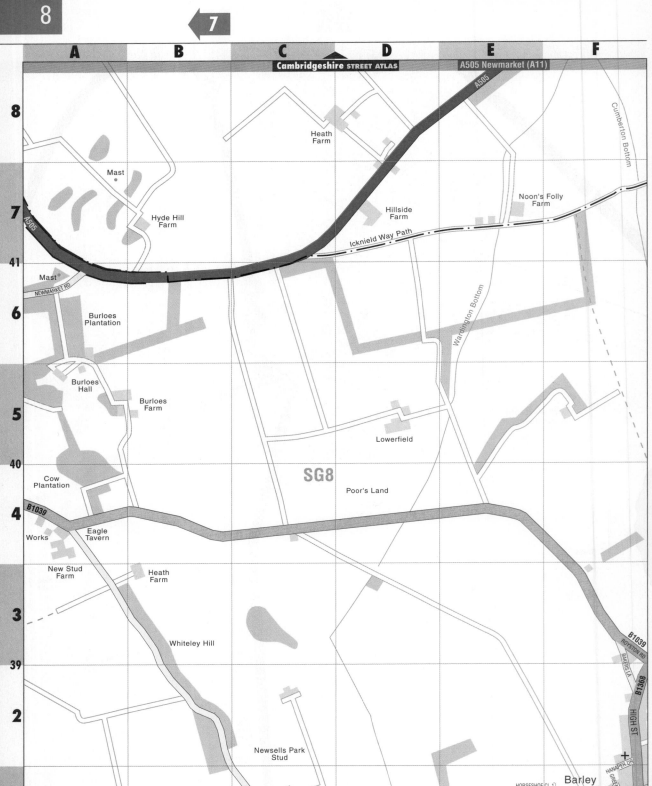

Cambridgeshire STREET ATLAS

A505 Newmarket (A11)

A505

Heath
Farm

Mast

Hyde Hill
Farm

Hillside
Farm

Noon's Folly
Farm

Cumberton Bottom

Icknield Way Path

A505

Mast

NEWMARKET RD

Burloes
Plantation

Wardington Bottom

Burloes
Hall

Burloes
Farm

Lowerfield

Cow
Plantation

SG8

Poor's Land

B1039

Works

Eagle
Tavern

New Stud
Farm

Heath
Farm

Whiteley Hill

B1039

ROYSTON RD

BAKERS LA

B1368

HIGH ST

Newsells Park
Stud

HANAPER DR

GREENBURY CL

Barley

HORSESHOE CL 1
TOMLINS CL 2

CHURCH
END

Newsells Barn
Farm

THE MOUNT

LONDON RD

CROSSWAYS

SMITH'S END LA

Horeshoe
Farm

Smith
End
Farm

Duck's
Nest

CAMBRIDGE
RD

B1368

STOCK BANK

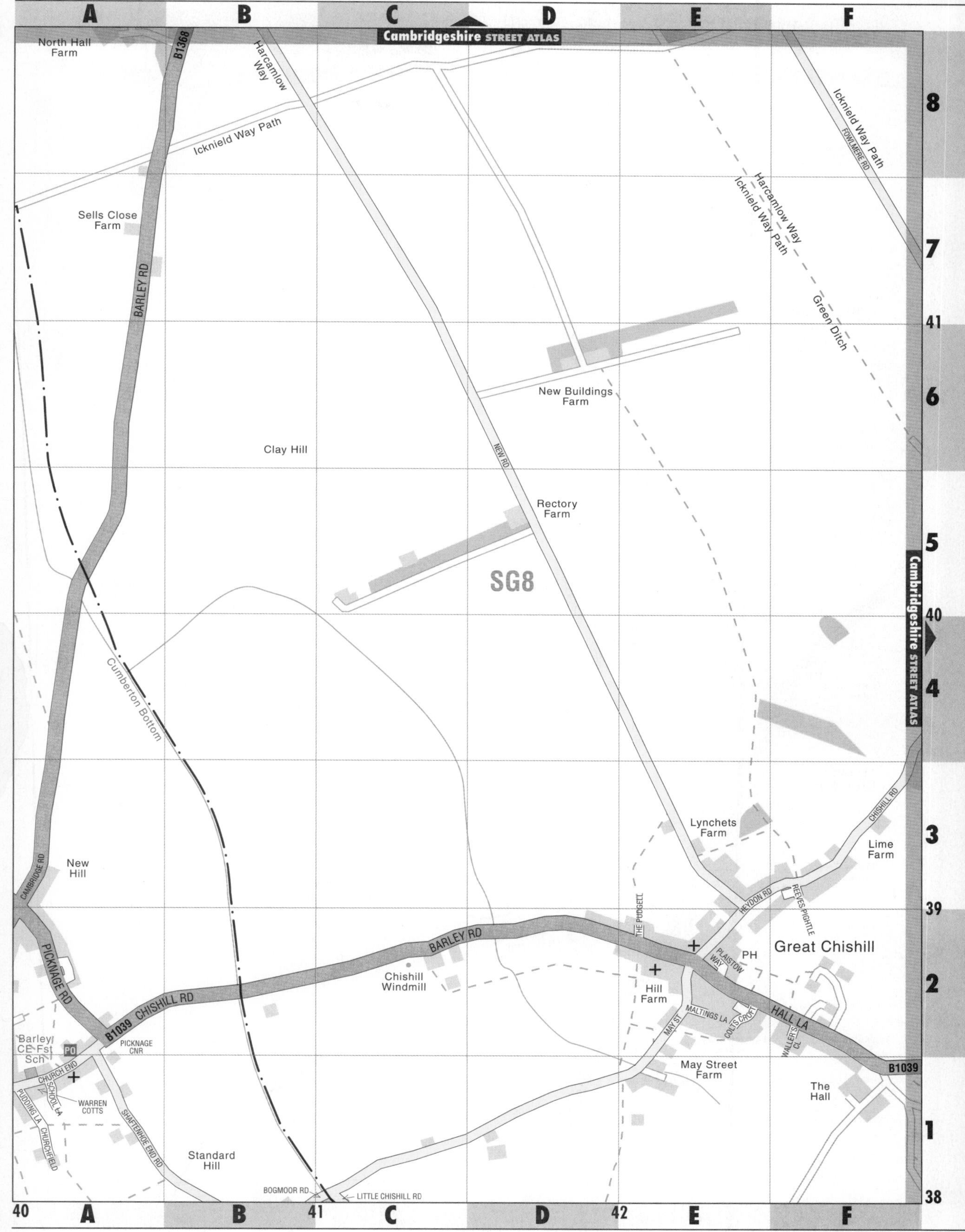

North Hall Farm

Sells Close Farm

Icknield Way Path

Harcamlow Way

B1368

BARLEY RD

Clay Hill

New Buildings Farm

NEW RD

Rectory Farm

SG8

Cumberton Bottom

Icknield Way Path

FOWLMERE RD

Harcamlow Way
Icknield Way Path

Green Ditch

Cambridgeshire STREET ATLAS

CHISHILL RD

Lynchets Farm

Lime Farm

Great Chishill

HEYDON RD

REEVES PIGHTLE

New Hill

CAMBRIDGE RD

BARLEY RD

THE PIGHTLE

PLAISTOW WAY

PH

Hill Farm

Chishill Windmill

PICKNAGE RD

CHISHILL RD

B1039

PICKNAGE CNR

Barley CE Fst Sch

PO

CHURCH END

SCHOOL LA

WARREN COTTS

PUDDING LA

CHURCHFIELD

SHAFTENHOE END RD

MAY ST

MALTINGS LA

COL'S CROFT

WALLER'S CL

HALL LA

B1039

May Street Farm

The Hall

Standard Hill

BOGMOOR RD

LITTLE CHISHILL RD

40   41   42

8   7   41   6   5   40   4   3   39   2   1   38

A   B   C   D   E   F

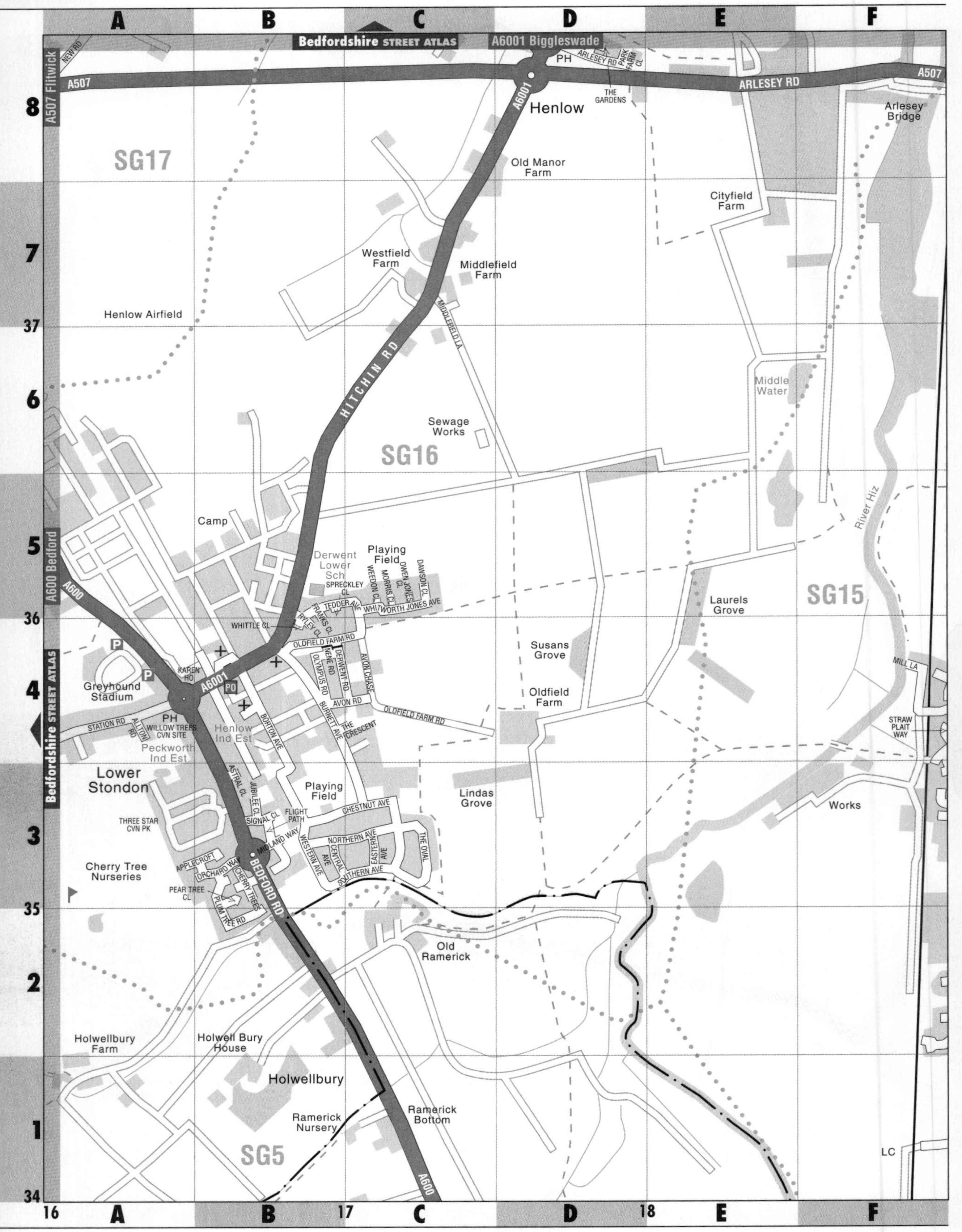

Bedfordshire STREET ATLAS

A6001 Biggleswade

Henlow

SG17

SG16

SG15

SG5

Henlow Airfield

Old Manor Farm

Westfield Farm

Middlefield Farm

Cityfield Farm

Arlesey Bridge

ARLESEY RD

HITCHIN RD

MIDDLEFIELD LA

Sewage Works

Middle Water

River Hiz

Camp

Derwent Lower Sch

Playing Field

Laurels Grove

Greyhound Stadium

Susans Grove

Oldfield Farm

OLDFIELD FARM RD

Henlow Ind Est

Lower Stondon

Peckworth Ind Est

THREE STAR CVN PK

Cherry Tree Nurseries

Playing Field

Lindas Grove

Works

STRAW PLAIT WAY

MILL LA

Old Ramerick

BEDFORD RD

Holwellbury Farm

Holwell Bury House

Holwellbury

Ramerick Nursery

Ramerick Bottom

A600

LC

12

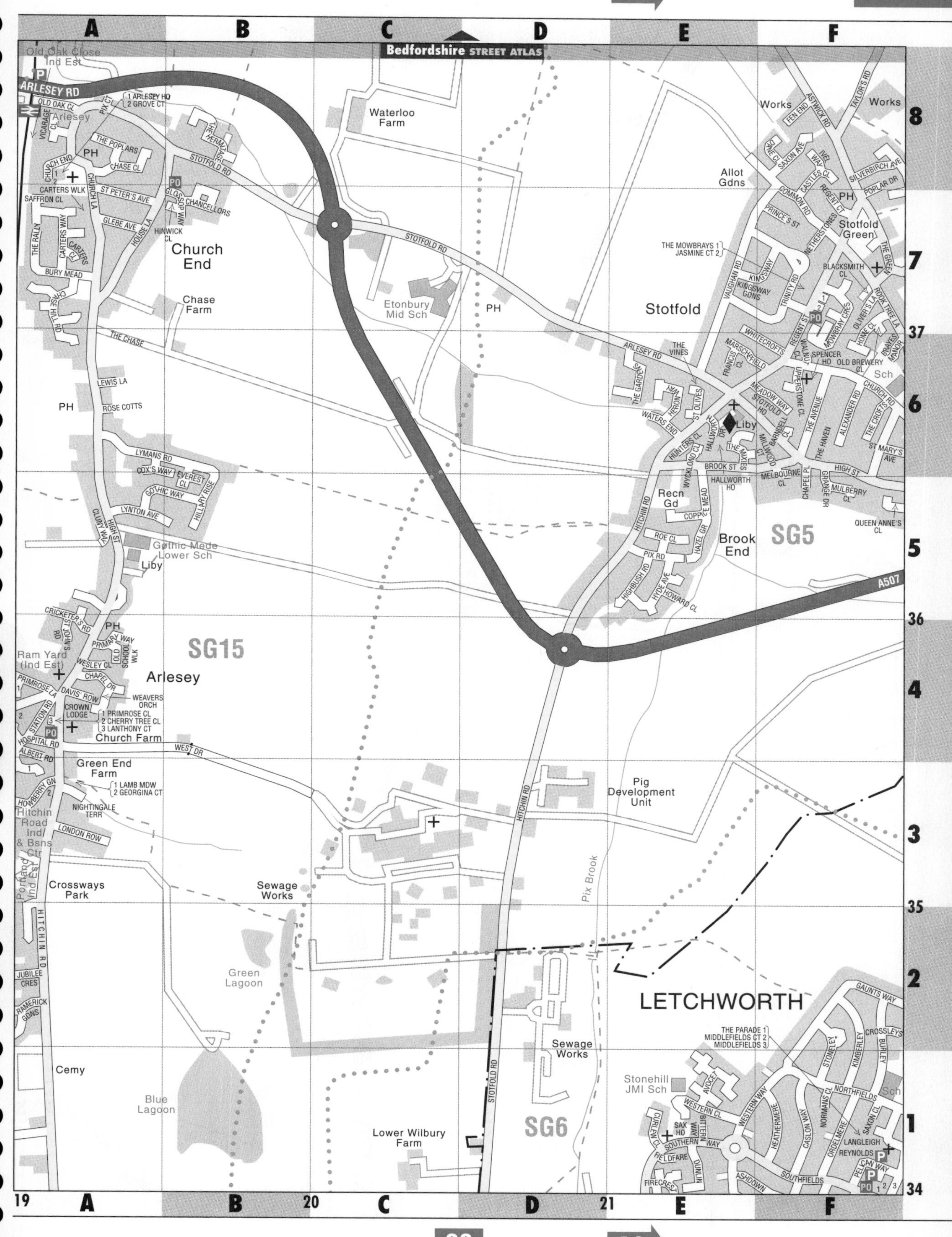

A
B
C
D
E
F
Bedfordshire STREET ATLAS
Old Oak Close Ind Est
ARLESEY RD
OLD OAK CL
1 ARLESEY HO
2 GROVE CT
PIN CL
Arlesey
VICARAGE CL
THE POPLARS
PH
CHASE CL
THE HERMITAGE
STOTFOLD RD
PO
CHURCH END
CARTERS WLK
SAFFRON CL
CHURCH LA
ST PETER'S AVE
GLOSSOP WAY
CHANCELLORS
GLEBE AVE
HOUSE LA
HINWICK CL
THE RALLY
CARTERS WAY
CARTERS CL
Church End
BURY MEAD
CHASE HILL RD
Chase Farm
Waterloo Farm
Etonbury Mid Sch
PH
THE CHASE
LEWIS LA
ROSE COTTS
PH
LYMANS RD
COX'S WAY
EVEREST CL
GOTHIC WAY
HILLARY RISE
LYNTON AVE
CLUNY WAY
HIGH ST
Gothic Mede Lower Sch
Liby
CRICKETERS RD
ST JOHN'S RD
PH
PRIMARY WAY
OLD SCHOOL WLK
SG15
Arlesey
Ram Yard (Ind Est)
WESLEY CL
CHAPEL DR
PRIMROSE LA
DAVIS' ROW
WEAVERS ORCH
CROWN LODGE
1 PRIMROSE CL
2 CHERRY TREE CL
3 LANTHONY CT
STATION RD
PO
HOSPITAL RD
Church Farm
WEST DR
ALBERT RD
Green End Farm
1 LAMB MDW
2 GEORGINA CT
HOWBERRY GN
NIGHTINGALE TERR
Hitchin Road Ind/ & Bsns Ctr
LONDON ROW
Portland Ind Est
Crossways Park
Sewage Works
HITCHIN RD
JUBILEE CRES
RAMERICK GDNS
Green Lagoon
Cemy
Blue Lagoon
Lower Wilbury Farm
STOTFOLD RD
HITCHIN RD
Pig Development Unit
Pix Brook
Sewage Works
SG6
LETCHWORTH
Works
FEN END
ASTWICK RD
TAYLOR'S RD
Works
Allot Gdns
SAXON AVE
IVEL WAY
SILVERBIRCH AVE
POPLAR DR
COMMON RD
CASTLES CL
REGENT CT
PH
PRINCE'S ST
NETHERSTONES
Stotfold Green
THE MOWBRAYS 1
JASMINE CT 2
KINGSWAY
KINGSWAY GDNS
VAUGHAN RD
TRINITY RD
BLACKSMITH CL
THE GREEN
Stotfold
REGENT ST
PO
MOWBRAY CRES
OLIVER'S LA
ROOK TREE LA
HOME CL
BRAYES MANOR
WHITECROFTS
ARLESEY RD
THE VINES
MARSCHEFIELD
FRANCIS CL
WALNUT CL
SPENCER HO
OLD BREWERY CL
Sch
THE GARDENS
HERON WAY
UPPERSTONE CL
CHURCH RD
MEADOW WAY
STOTFOLD HO
THE AVENUE
ALEXANDER RD
THE CROFTS RD
WATERS END
ST OLIVES
HALLWORTH DR
Liby
BARNDELL CL
MILLWOOD CT
THE HAVEN
ST MARY'S AVE
HUNTERS CL
WYCKLOND CL
THE MALTINGS
BROOK ST
HIGH ST
HALLWORTH HO
MELBOURNE CL
CHAPEL PL
GRANGE DR
MULBERRY CL
HITCHIN RD
Recn Gd
COPPICE MEAD
QUEEN ANNE'S CL
Brook End
SG5
ROE CL
HAZEL GR
PIX RD
HIGHBUSH RD
HYDE AVE
HOWARD CL
A507
GAUNTS WAY
THE PARADE 1
MIDDLEFIELDS CT 2
MIDDLEFIELDS 3
CROSSLEYS
BURLEY
STONELEY
KIMBERLEY
Stonehill JMI Sch
AVOCET
NORTHFIELDS
Sch
WESTERN CL
WESTERN WAY
HEATHERMERE
CASLON WAY
NORMANS CL
ORDELMERE
SAXON CL
CURLEW CL
SAX HO
BITTERN WAY
SOUTHERN WAY
LANGLEIGH
REYNOLDS
FIELDFARE
DUNLIN
ASHDOWN
SOUTHFIELDS
PELICAN WAY
FIRECREST
PO
8
7
37
6
5
36
4
3
35
2
1
34
19
20
21

22

12

3

A B C D E F

8
7
37
6
5
36
4
3
35
2
1
34

Nursery
SILVERBIRCH AVE
SPOTFOLD RD
WRAYFIELDS
A1
Cat Ditch
CALDECOTE RD
Newnham Hall
White House
ASHWELL RD
Newnham
Radwell Grange Spinney
Manor Farm
THE GREEN
PO
MALTHOUSE LA
Ford Bridge
SG5
Radwell Grange
Cemy
St Mary's Lower Sch
MILL LA
ROOK TREE CL
ROOK TREE LA
MILL CL
Grange Cottages
A1(M)
Hullockpit Hill
NEWNHAM RD
Hullockpit Plantation
Baldock Services
PH
CHEQUERS CL
ST MARY'S AVE
QUEEN ST
VICTORIA DR
SG7
Works
New Bridge
MURRELL LA
BALDOCK RD
A507
10
QUEEN ANNE'S CL
THE COPPENS
GROVELAND WAY
LITTLEBURY CL
Boundary Farm
Mill House
Radwell
COUNCIL COTTS
RADWELL LA
THE PEBBLES
Bury Farm
Radwell House
Capra
Garden Cottages
Landing Strip
Poultry Farm
Icknield Way Path
River Ivel
GREAT NORTH RD
The Nook
Countryside Walk
NORTON MILL LA
Norton Mill (disused)
NORTON RD
NORTON BURY LA
P
Norton Bury
Blackhorse Farm
Grange Playing Field
SG6
NORTH RD
BALDOCK
1 BRAMLEY CL
2 LAUREL MEWS
3 RABAN CT
4 PRYORS CT
5 GROSVENOR RD W
6 MAGDALENE CT
7 PEARL CT
Nursery
Laymore Farm
Equitation Ctr
Grange Jun Sch
GAUNTS WAY
SPARHAWKE
WHITEHICKS
MAYCROFT
SALISBURY RD
FARRIERS CL 1
FOOTBALL CL 2
MEETING HOUSE LA 3
EAGLE CT 4
LAVENDER CT 5
ALDRIDGE CT 6
BUTLERS YD 7
BREWERY COTTS 8
BREWERY LA 9
BYGRAVE RD
Works
CHURCH LA
St Nicholas CE Prim Sch
LARKINS CL
Baldock
Payne's Farm
NORTHFIELDS
EASTERN WAY
THE MEWS
THE RICKYARD
THE MALTINGS
ICKNIELD WAY E
ROYSTON RD
A505
SALE DR
GRANGE CT
DANESCROFT
THE LINK
LINDENCROFT
CROFT LA
PAYNES CL
FARM CL
CASHIO LA
Playing Field
Allot Gdns
Norton
GREEN LA
TALBOT WAY
CADE CL
SYCAMORES
ICKNIELD WAY
JACKSON ST
CHURCH ST
ORCHARD RD
STATION RD
WHITEHORSE ST
CALIFORNIA
GROSVENOR RD
CLOTHALL RD
Hartsfield JMI Sch

22 A B 23 C D 24 E F

11

23

4
14

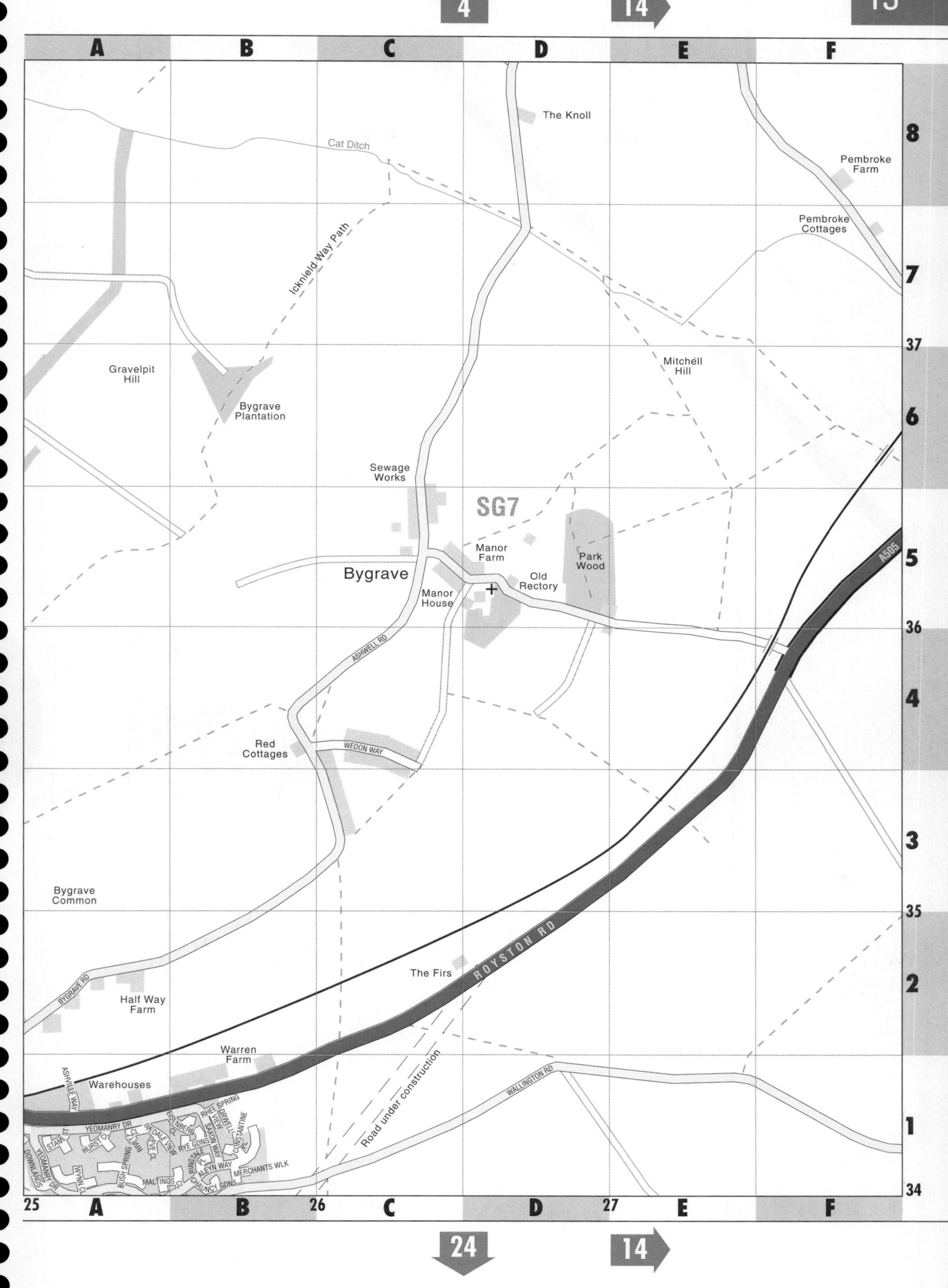
A
B
C
D
E
F
The Knoll
Cat Ditch
Pembroke Farm
Pembroke Cottages
Icknield Way Path
Gravelpit Hill
Bygrave Plantation
Mitchell Hill
Sewage Works
SG7
Manor Farm
Bygrave
Park Wood
Old Rectory
Manor House
ASHWELL RD
A505
Red Cottages
WEDON WAY
Bygrave Common
ROYSTON RD
The Firs
BYGRAVE RD
Half Way Farm
Warren Farm
Warehouses
ASHVILLE WAY
Road under construction
WALLINGTON RD
RHEE SPRING
YEOMANRY DR
MERCHANTS WLK
ALEYN WAY
MALTINGS
CHAUNCY GDNS
DOWNLANDS
BUSH SPRING
RYE GDNS
SAXON WAY
CONSTANTINE PL
8
7
37
6
5
36
4
3
35
2
1
34
25
26
27

24
14

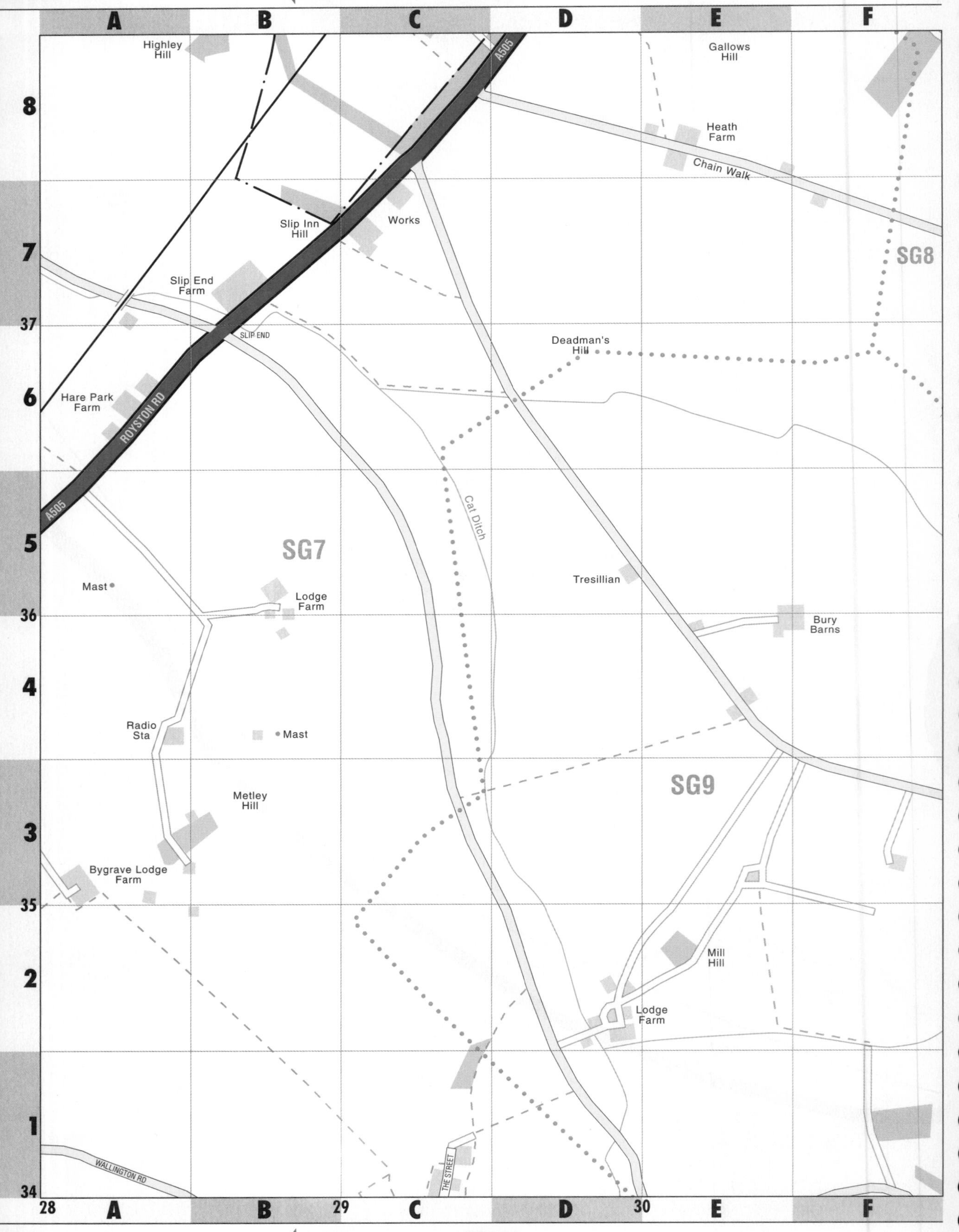

A B C D E F

8

7

37

6

5

36

4

3

35

2

1

34

SG8

SG7

SG9

Highley Hill

Slip Inn Hill

Slip End Farm

SLIP END

Works

Hare Park Farm

ROYSTON RD

A505

A505

Gallows Hill

Heath Farm

Chain Walk

Deadman's Hill

Cat Ditch

Tresillian

Bury Barns

Mast

Lodge Farm

Radio Sta

Mast

Metley Hill

Bygrave Lodge Farm

Mill Hill

Lodge Farm

WALLINGTON RD

THE STREET

28 A B 29 C D 30 E F

6
16

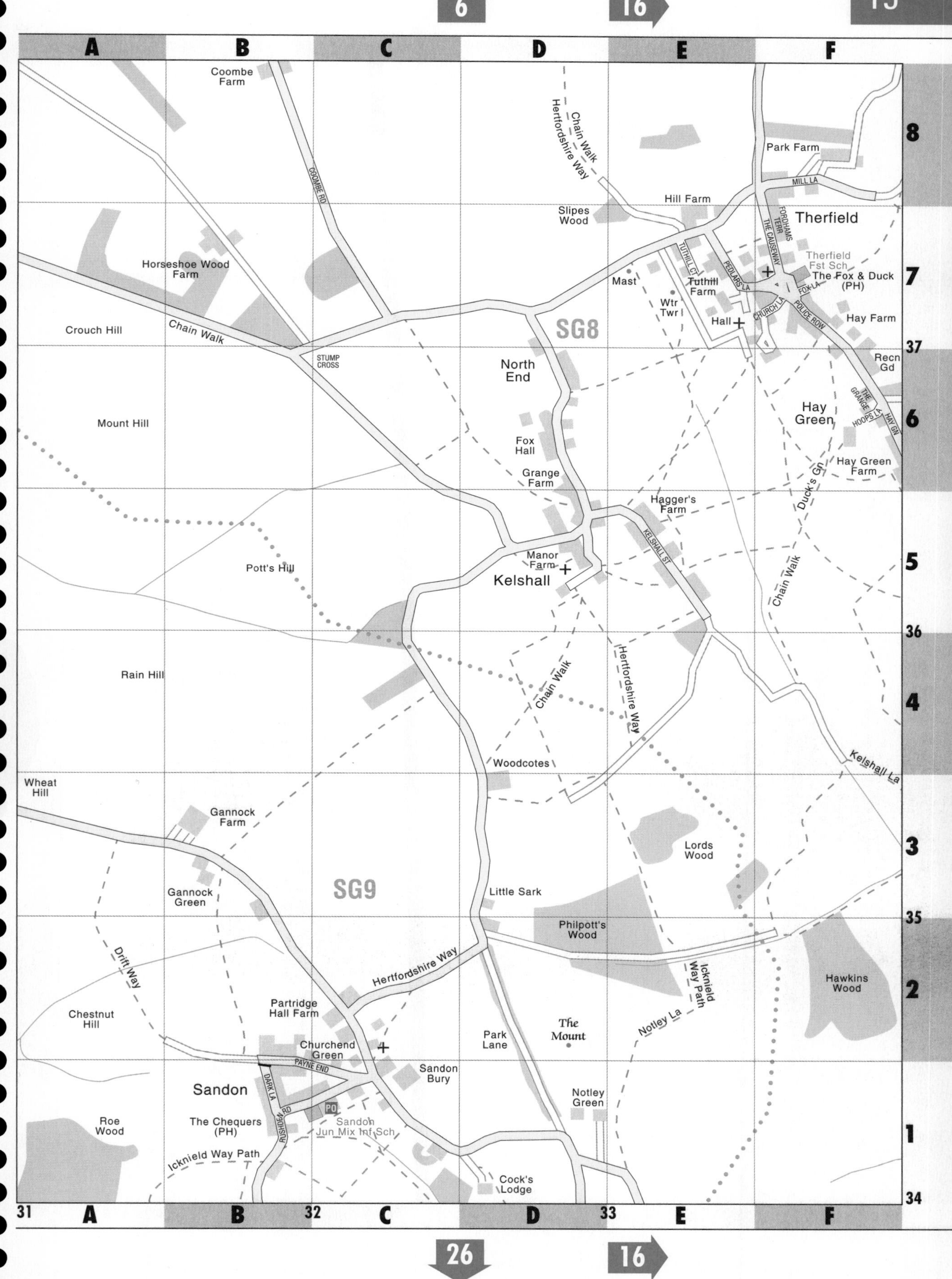
A
B
C
D
E
F
8
7
37
6
5
36
4
3
35
2
1
34
31
32
33
Coombe Farm
COOMBE RD
Chain Walk
Hertfordshire Way
Park Farm
MILL LA
Hill Farm
Slipes Wood
Therfield
FORDHAMS TERR
THE CAUSEWAY
TUTHILL CT
PEDLARS LA
Therfield Fst Sch
The Fox & Duck (PH)
FOX LA
CHURCH LA
POLICE ROW
Horseshoe Wood Farm
Mast
Tuthill Farm
Wtr Twr
Hall
Hay Farm
Crouch Hill
Chain Walk
STUMP CROSS
SG8
North End
Recn Gd
Mount Hill
Hay Green
THE GRANGE
HOOPS LA
HAY GN
Fox Hall
Grange Farm
Hay Green Farm
Duck's Gn
Hagger's Farm
Manor Farm
Kelshall
KELSHALL ST
Pott's Hill
Chain Walk
Rain Hill
Chain Walk
Hertfordshire Way
Woodcotes
Kelshall La
Wheat Hill
Gannock Farm
Lords Wood
SG9
Gannock Green
Little Sark
Philpott's Wood
Drift Way
Hertfordshire Way
Icknield Way Path
Hawkins Wood
Chestnut Hill
Partridge Hall Farm
Park Lane
The Mount
Notley La
Churchend Green
PAYNE END
Sandon Bury
Sandon
DARK LA
RUSHDEN RD
PO
The Chequers (PH)
Sandon Jun Mix Inf Sch
Notley Green
Roe Wood
Icknield Way Path
Cock's Lodge

26
16

15 7

A B C D E F
8
7
37
6
5
36
4
3
35
2
1
34
Icknield Way Path
A10
Hatchpen
Hertfordshire Way
MEADOW WAY
Washingditch Green
HAYWOOD LA
River Rib
Mardlebury
THE JOINT
BRICKYARD LA
Mast
Reed End
SG8
JACKSON'S LA
WILLOW CL
BLACKSMITH'S LA
HOBBS HAYES
CROW LA
Reed Fst Sch
Wisbridge Farm
Holborn Farm
Mast
ROOKS NEST LA
HIGH ST
Reed
CHURCH LA
The Cabinet (PH)
Southview
DRIFTWAY
Dane End
Queenbury
Mast
CHURCH CL
Rooksnest Farm
Reed Hall
DANE END
Gannock Grove
Kelshall La
Icknield Way Path
Gannock Green
Chapel Green
Reed Wood
River Rib
Sewage Works
Hilly Wood
Southfield Grove
Brandish Wood
SG9
Slate Hall Farm
34 A B 35 C D 36 E F

15 27

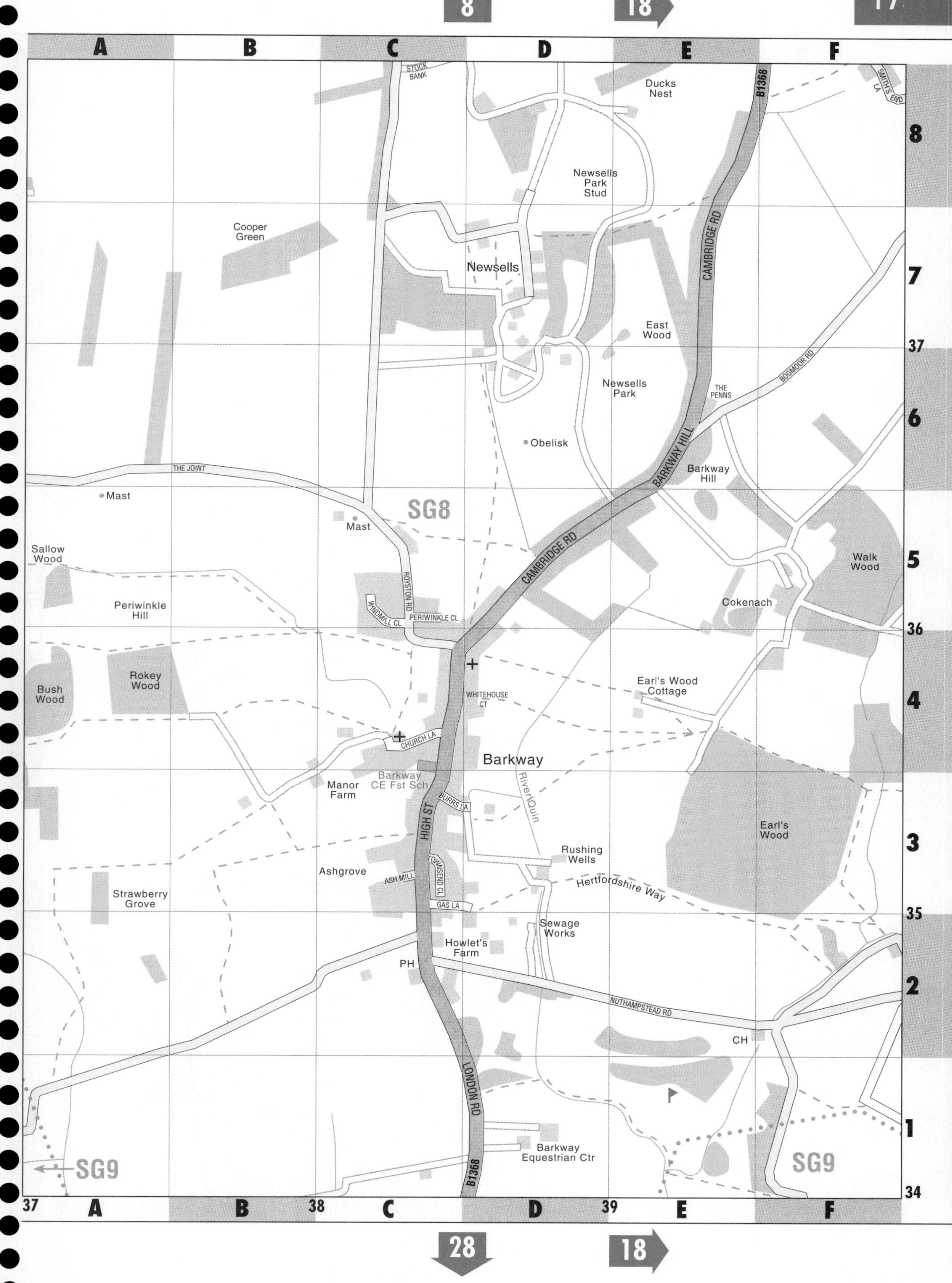
8
18
A
B
C
D
E
F
STOCK BANK
Ducks Nest
B1368
SMITH'S END LA
Newsells Park Stud
Cooper Green
CAMBRIDGE RD
Newsells
East Wood
Newsells Park
THE PENNS
BOGMOOR RD
Obelisk
BARKWAY HILL
Barkway Hill
THE JOINT
Mast
SG8
Mast
Sallow Wood
CAMBRIDGE RD
Walk Wood
ROYSTON RD
Periwinkle Hill
WINDMILL CL
PERIWINKLE CL
Cokenach
Rokey Wood
Bush Wood
WHITEHOUSE CT
Earl's Wood Cottage
CHURCH LA
Barkway
Manor Farm
Barkway CE Fst Sch
River Quin
BURRS LA
HIGH ST
Earl's Wood
Rushing Wells
Ashgrove
TOWNSEND CL
ASH MILL
Strawberry Grove
Hertfordshire Way
GAS LA
Sewage Works
Howlet's Farm
PH
NUTHAMPSTEAD RD
CH
LONDON RD
Barkway Equestrian Ctr
B1368
SG9
SG9
8
7
37
6
5
36
4
3
35
2
1
34
37
38
39
28
18

17
9

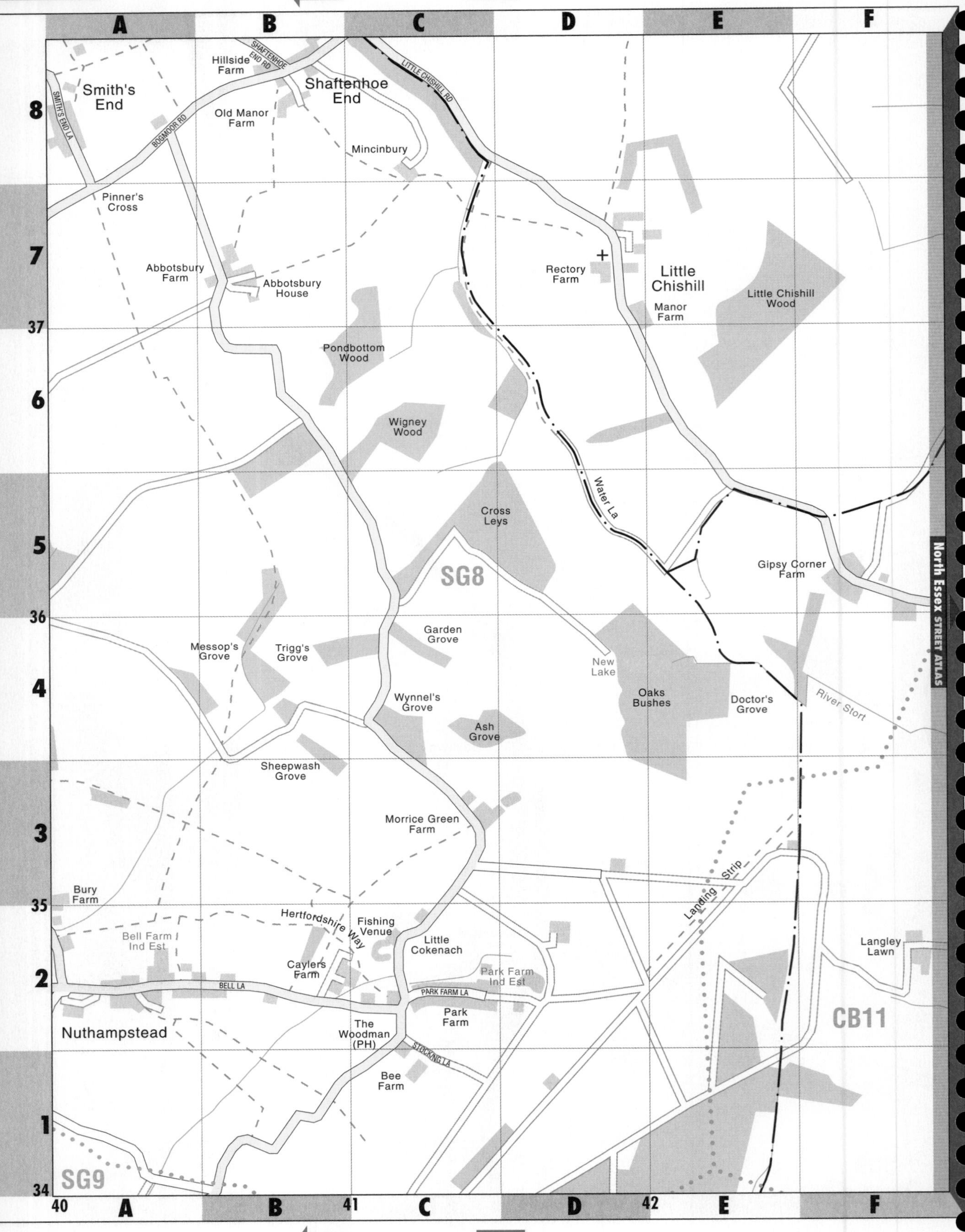

A B C D E F

8

Smith's End

Hillside Farm

SHAFTENHOE END RD

Shaftenhoe End

LITTLE CHISHILL RD

Old Manor Farm

BOGMOOR RD

Mincinbury

Pinner's Cross

7

Rectory Farm

Little Chishill

Abbotsbury Farm

Abbotsbury House

Manor Farm

Little Chishill Wood

37

Pondbottom Wood

6

Wigney Wood

Water La

5

Cross Leys

SG8

Gipsy Corner Farm

36

Garden Grove

Messop's Grove

Trigg's Grove

New Lake

4

Wynnel's Grove

Oaks Bushes

Doctor's Grove

River Stort

Ash Grove

Sheepwash Grove

3

Morrice Green Farm

Landing Strip

Bury Farm

35

Hertfordshire Way

Fishing Venue

Little Cokenach

Langley Lawn

Bell Farm Ind Est

Caylers Farm

Park Farm Ind Est

2

BELL LA

PARK FARM LA

CB11

Nuthampstead

The Woodman (PH)

Park Farm

STOCKING LA

Bee Farm

1

SG9

34

40 A B 41 C D 42 E F

North Essex STREET ATLAS

17
29

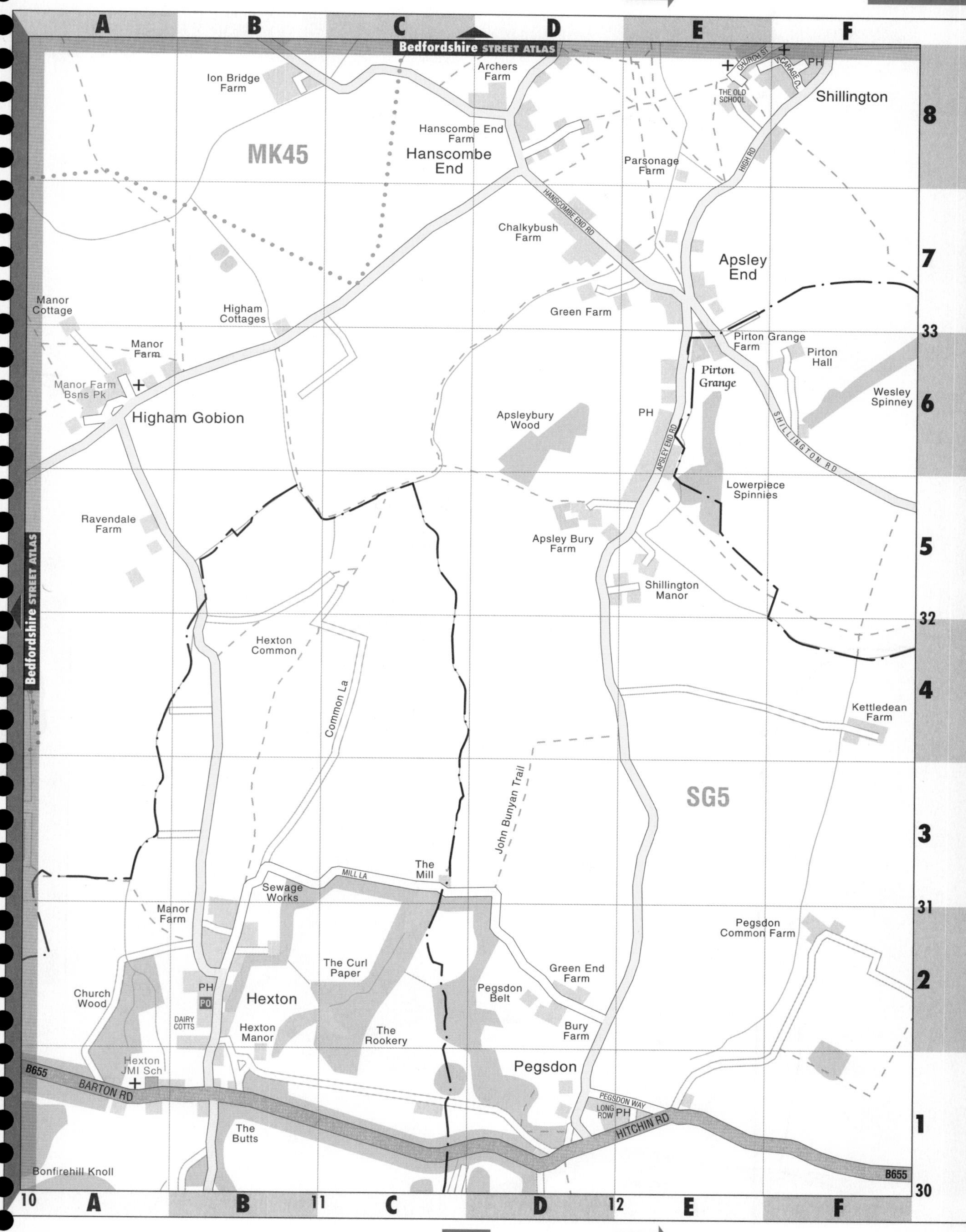

Bedfordshire STREET ATLAS

A **B** **C** **D** **E** **F**

Ion Bridge Farm

Archers Farm

MK45

Hanscombe End Farm

Hanscombe End

8

Parsonage Farm

THE OLD SCHOOL

CHURCH ST

VICARAGE CL

PH

Shillington

HIGH RD

Chalkybush Farm

HANSCOMBE END RD

Apsley End

7

Manor Cottage

Higham Cottages

Green Farm

33

Manor Farm

Pirton Grange Farm

Pirton Hall

Manor Farm Bsns Pk

Pirton Grange

Wesley Spinney

6

Higham Gobion

Apsleybury Wood

PH

APSLEY END RD

SHILLINGTON RD

Lowerpiece Spinnies

Ravendale Farm

Apsley Bury Farm

5

Shillington Manor

32

Hexton Common

Kettledean Farm

4

Common La

John Bunyan Trail

SG5

3

The Mill

MILL LA

31

Sewage Works

Manor Farm

Pegsdon Common Farm

The Curl Paper

Green End Farm

2

Church Wood

PH

PO

Hexton

Pegsdon Belt

DAIRY COTTS

Hexton Manor

The Rookery

Bury Farm

B655

BARTON RD

Hexton JMI Sch

Pegsdon

PEGSDON WAY

LONG ROW

PH

The Butts

HITCHIN RD

1

Bonfirehill Knoll

B655

30

10 **A** **B** **11** **C** **D** **12** **E** **F**

19

Bedfordshire STREET ATLAS

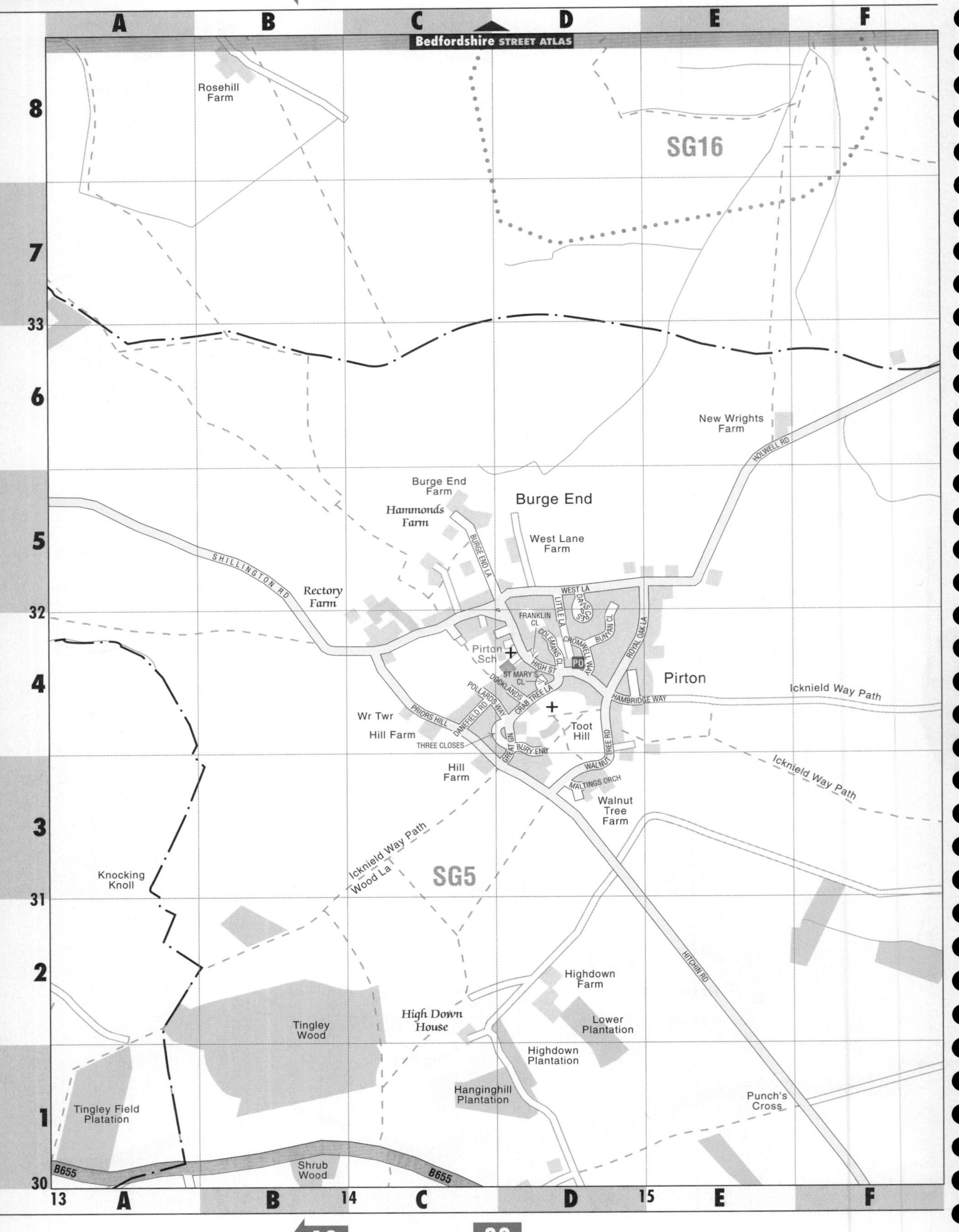

A
B
C
D
E
F
8
7
33
6
5
32
4
3
31
2
1
30
13
14
15
Rosehill Farm
SG16
New Wrights Farm
HOLWELL RD
Burge End Farm
Burge End
Hammonds Farm
West Lane Farm
SHILLINGTON RD
BURGE END LA
Rectory Farm
WEST LA
LITTLE LA
DAYS CL
FRANKLIN CL
COLEMANS CL
CROMWELL WAY
BUNYAN CL
ROYAL OAK LA
Pirton Sch
HIGH ST
PO
ST MARY'S CL
DOCKLANDS
CRAB TREE LA
POLLARDS WAY
HAMBRIDGE WAY
Pirton
Icknield Way Path
Wr Twr
PRIORS HILL
DANEFIELD RD
Toot Hill
Hill Farm
THREE CLOSES
GREAT GN
BURY END
WALNUT TREE RD
Hill Farm
WALNUT
MALTINGS ORCH
Walnut Tree Farm
Icknield Way Path
Icknield Way Path
Wood La
SG5
Knocking Knoll
HITCHIN RD
Highdown Farm
Tingley Wood
High Down House
Lower Plantation
Highdown Plantation
Hanginghill Plantation
Punch's Cross
Tingley Field Platation
Shrub Wood
B655
B655

19

33

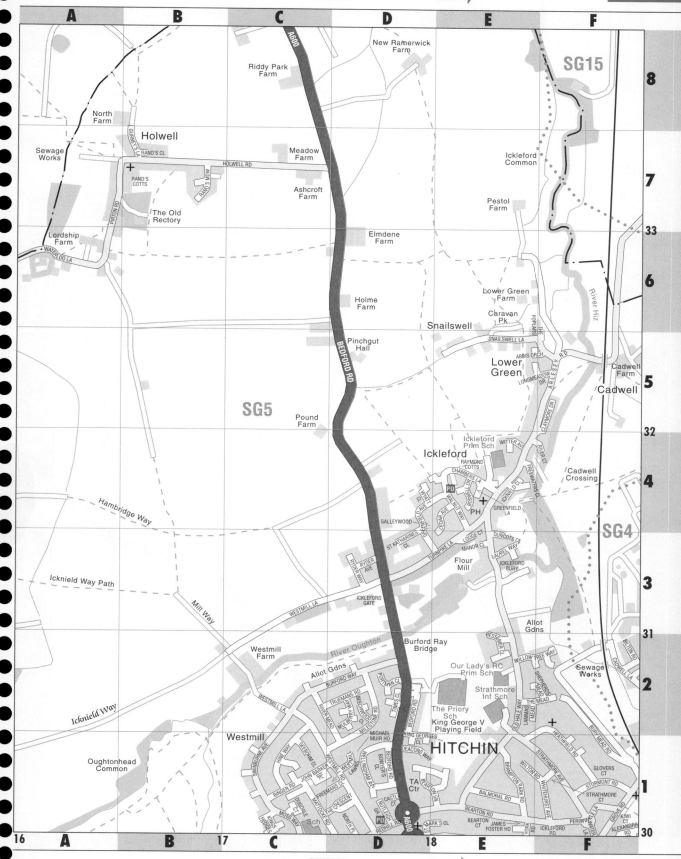

A   B   C   D   E   F

8

SG15

New Ramerwick Farm

Riddy Park Farm

Ickleford Common

North Farm

Holwell

7

Meadow Farm

Sewage Works

RAND'S CL

HOLWELL RD

Pestol Farm

33

The Old Rectory

Ashcroft Farm

RAND'S MDW

RAND'S COTTS

PIRTON RD

GURNEY'S LA

Elmdene Farm

6

Lordship Farm

WATERLOO LA

Lower Green Farm

Holme Farm

Caravan Pk

River Hiz

THE POPLARS

Snailswell

Cadwell Farm

SG5

Pinchgut Hall

SNAILSWELL LA

Lower Green

ABBIS ORCH

LONGMEADOW DR

ARLESEY RD

Cadwell

5

CLAYMORE DR

Pound Farm

32

Ickleford Prim Sch

WITTER AVE

RIVER CT

FREEMATERS CL

Ickleford

Cadwell Crossing

RAYMOND COTTS

CHAMBERS LA

WYATT CL

4

Hambridge Way

PO

WALNUT WAY

PH

GREENFIELD LA

ICKNIELD CL

GREENFIELD AVE

GALLEYWOOD

CEDAR AVE

SG4

Icknield Way Path

ST KATHARINES CL

TURNPIKE LA

LODGE CT

MANOR CL

DUNCOTS CL

LAUREL WAY

Flour Mill

Ickleford Bury

Mill Way

RYDER AVE

ICKLEFORD GATE

3

WESTMILL LA

BESSEMER CL

Allot Gdns

31

Westmill Farm

River Oughton

Burford Ray Bridge

WILLOW TREE WAY

Our Lady's RC Prim Sch

SHEPHERDS MEAD

Sewage Works

BURY MEAD RD

CALDWELL LA

BILTON RD

Allot Gdns

BURFORD WAY

PORTMAN RD

BEECHWOOD AVE

TIMES CL

BEDFORD RD

Strathmore Inf Sch

THE MEAD

LAMMAS MEAD

OLD HALE WAY

2

Westmill

WESTMILL LA

TRUEMANS RD

MULBERRY WAY

RIVER MEAD

MILLSTONE CL

MICHAEL MUIR HO

The Priory Sch

King George V Playing Field

HITCHIN

STRATHMORE AVE

WILTON RD

BRAMPTON PARK RD

HEATHFIELD RD

WHITEHURST AVE

Oughtonhead Common

SWINBURNE AVE

HINE WAY

SEEOHM CL

JOHN BARKER PL

WESTMILL WEST RD

TIMES CL

THE LAWNS

WELLINGHAM AVE

KING GEORGES CL

DEACONS WAY

BEARTON GRN

BALMORAL RD

GLOVERS CT

STORMONT CT

STRATHMORE CT

1

Icknield Way

BINGEN RD

BEDFORD RD

MATTOCKE RD

THE CRESCENT

NORTH PL

CASTLE CL

PO

BOWER'S CT

Sch

TA Ctr

ST MARK'S CL

BEARTON RD

BEARTON CT

JAMES FOSTER HO

ICKLEFORD RD

PERIWINKLE

GROVE RD

K/WI CT

ALEXANDRA RD

30

A   B   C   D   E   F

16   17   18

A B C D E F

8
SG15

White Hill
Fairfield Kennels

Hitchin Rd

Standalone Farm

PH

SG6

Southern Way
Hawkfield
Western Way
Midhurst
Sherwood
Orchard Cl
Orchard Way
Woodhurst
Lammas Way
Stonnells Cl
Westholm
Grange Rd

The Riches
Kite Way
Linnet Cl
Wilbury Rd
Wheat Hill
Hawthorn Hill

7
Wilbury Farm

Arlesey New Rd

COOPERS FIELD 1
HAMMERDELL 2
WYSELLS CT 3

David Evans Ct
Beech Hill
Furlay Cl
Haymoor
Longmead

Longfield Ct
Chasten Hill
Valley Rd
Warren Cl
Rivers Ct

Pix Brook
Norton Common

Arlesey Rd

33
Fox Covert

Wilburyhill Farm

Wilbury Hills Rd
Wilbury Cl
Romany Cl

Hibberts Ct
Runalow
Bedford Rd

STATION PAR 1
THE GALLERY 2
THE ARCADE 3
THE WYND 4
CENTRAL APP 5
COMMERCE WAY 6

Redhoods Way E
Rowan Cres
Cowslip Hill

Cross St
Nevells Rd

6
PH
Cemy

Cvn Pk

Wilbury Hill

Mull Way
Hall Mead
Monklands
Monks Cl
Abbots Rd
Burslam

Icknield Inf Sch

Wilbury Jun Sch

Corner Cl

Haslefoot
Saffron Hill
Redhoods Way W
Icknield Way

Chasny Cl
Martins Way

Station Way
The Meads
The Dale

TA Ctr Letchworth

Bridge Rd

Station Rd
Bennett Ct
Leys Ave

Superstore

Rowland Way
Eastcheap
Arena Par

Gernon Rd
Pixmore Way
Broadway

5

Cadwell Farm

SG5

Icknield Way Path

Allot Gdns

Fearnhill Sch

Ampfield Way
Highover Rd

Burnell Rise
Campers Rd
Springshott

Broadwater Ave
Broadwater Dale

Gost Dl

Liby
TH

Letchworth Mus & Art Gall

West View
Meadow Way
Lytton Ave
Paddock Cl

LETCHWORTH

Campers Ave
West View

Broadway
Spring Rd

St Francis' Coll

Souberie Ave
South View

32

Chiltern View
Hillbrow
High Ave

Sch

Robert Saunders Ct
Parker Cl
Unwin Cl

Field La
Sollersmotte

South View
A505

Sollershott

4

St Thomas More RC Prim Sch

The Highfield Sch

Highfield

Sollershott W

Sollershott Hall

PO

Barrington Rd

Baldock Rd
Cloisters Rd
Cloister Lawns

3

The Hitchin Bsns Ctr
Hillgate
Theobald Bsns Ctr
KNOWL PIECE
Hunting Gate

Wilbury Way

North Area Pupil Referral Unit
Briar Patch

Briar Patch La

Playing Field

Hitchin Rd

Broadway Ct

Pasture Rd
The Glade

Manor Rd

Letchworth Ga

St Christopher Sch

Earlsmead
Dagnall La
Aubreys

2
SG4

Cam Sch
Cam Ctr

HITCHIN
Highover Farm

Wallace Way
Hillside Ave
Girdle Rd
Cadwell
Cadwell La

Collison Cl
Roundwood Rd

Nursery

Garden Ctr

Lodge

Keysheath

Garth Rd

CH

Hotel

Manor Way
Manor Rd
St Michaels
Broadcroft
Aubreys

Fiveways House

31

High Dane
Sturgeon's Way
Armour Rise
Grove Lands Ave
Gainsford Cres
Frensham Dr

Grove Rd

Tristram Rd
West Cl
Highover Way
Chennells Way
Harkness Way
Millard Way

Highover JMI Sch

River Purwell

Walsworth Common
Walsworth

Redoubt Cl
Grove Rd
Woolgrove Rd
East Cl
Woolgrove Ct
Orchard Cl
Green La
St Hays Cl
St Franklin Cl
Harness Ct

Hampden Rd
Granville Rd

Queenswood Dr

CAMBRIDGE RD

Willian Rd

The Orchard

Longwood

Kingswood Dr
Wilshere Cres

1

SG5
MIDLAND COTTS

Cadwell La
Grove Rd
Mill Stream Way

Sharps Way
Comton Rise
Cooks Way
Meadowbank
Meadow Way

A505
Bradleys Cnr
Mount Joy

30
19 A 20 B C 21 D E F

12
24

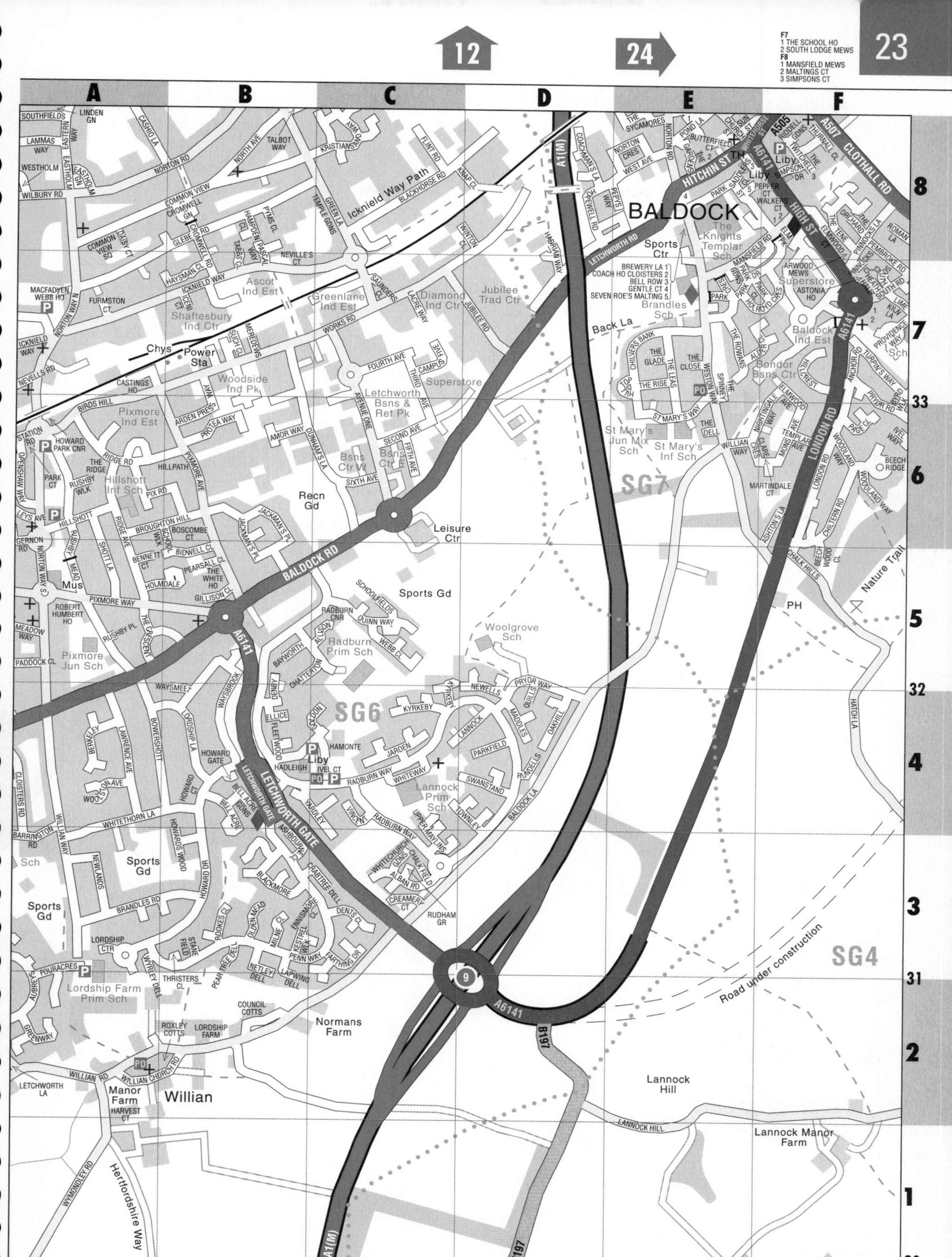
BALDOCK
Willian
SG6
SG7
SG4
Letchworth Bsns & Ret Pk
Sports Gd
Recn Gd
Leisure Ctr
Woolgrove Sch
Radburn Prim Sch
Lannock Prim Sch
Lannock Hill
Lannock Manor Farm
Normans Farm
Manor Farm
Pixmore Jun Sch
Lordship Farm Prim Sch
St Mary's Jun Mix Sch
St Mary's Inf Sch
The Knights Templar Sch
Brandles Sch
Baldock Ind Est
Bondor Bsns Ctr
Woodside Ind Pk
Pixmore Ind Est
Shaftesbury Ind Ctr
Ascot Ind Est
Greenlane Ind Est
Diamond Ind Ctr
Jubilee Trad Ctr
Power Sta
Icknield Way Path
Hertfordshire Way
Nature Trail
Road under construction
BALDOCK RD
LETCHWORTH GATE
LETCHWORTH RD
HITCHIN ST
HIGH ST
LONDON RD
CLOTHALL RD
LANNOCK HILL
A1(M)
A6141
A505
A507
B197
A B C D E F
8 7 6 5 4 3 2 1
33 32 31 30
22 23 24

36
24

23 13

A B C D E F

8

WEAVERS WAY
MERCIA RD
WESTELL RD
YEOMANRY RD
BARLEY RISE
YEOMANRY DR

Nursery
Home Land

SOUTH RD
WALINS
WALINS AVE
LAXTON GDNS

Clothall Common

A507

LIMEKILN
Sch
BYRD WLK
PENFOLD
PRYOR RD

Cambrai Farm

7

33

The Homestead

TIVEL WAY

Nature Trail

Baldock By-Pass under construction

Icknield Way Path

CLOTHALL RD

WARREN LA

Icknield Way Path

Cockpit

Quickswood

6

Welbury Farm

Windmill Hill

Bird Hill

SG7

Weston Hills

Newfield Hill

5

32

Ashanger Hill

Clothall

Clothall Bury

4

Hertfordshire Way

Green Grove

HICKMAN'S HILL

ASHANGER LA

A507

Bush Wood

The Barley Mow (PH)

3

31

HATCH LA

SG4

Green End

2

Mill Farm

Weston Windmill (dis)

Darnall's Hall Farm

PH

Old Farm

Weston

Weston Bury

1

THE SNIPE

FRIARS RD

HITCHIN RD

POST OFFICE ROW

FORE ST

MILL LA

MILL GROUND COTTS

MAIDEN ST

HUNTS MEADOW

SCHOOL LA

Weston Prim Sch

Oakley's Farm

PO

DAMASK GREEN

Works

Manor House

Recn Gd

Church End

CHURCH LA

30

Town Farm

25 A B 26 C D 27 E F

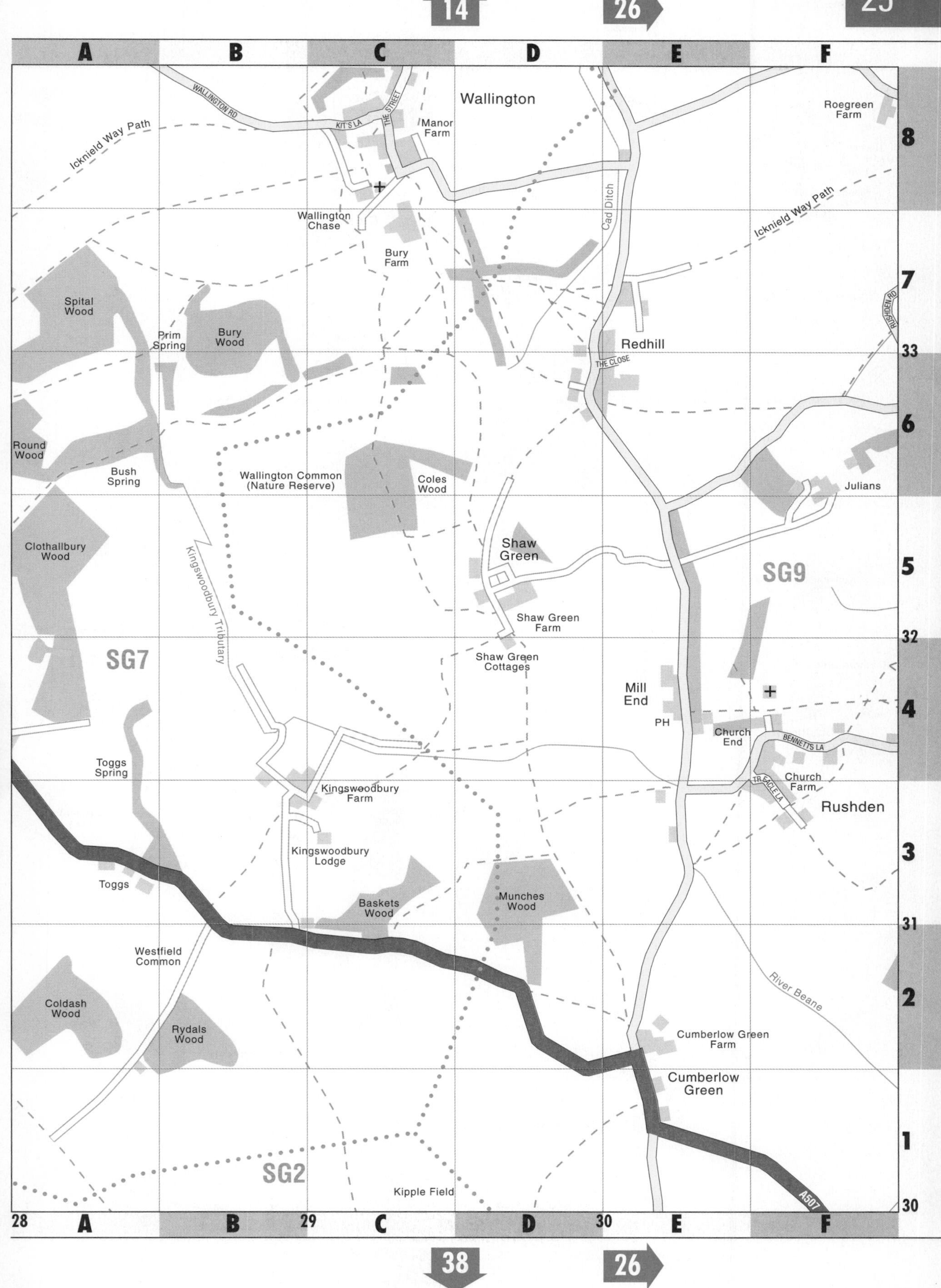

A **B** **C** **D** **E** **F**

WALLINGTON RD

Icknield Way Path

KIT'S LA

THE STREET

Wallington

Manor Farm

Roegreen Farm

8

Wallington Chase

Bury Farm

Cad Ditch

Icknield Way Path

7

Spital Wood

Prim Spring

Bury Wood

Redhill

THE CLOSE

REDHOEN RD

33

6

Round Wood

Bush Spring

Wallington Common (Nature Reserve)

Coles Wood

Julians

Clothallbury Wood

Kingswoodbury Tributary

Shaw Green

SG9

5

SG7

Shaw Green Farm

Shaw Green Cottages

32

Mill End

PH

Church End

BENNETTS LA

4

Toggs Spring

Kingswoodbury Farm

Church Farm

TREACLE LA

Rushden

Toggs

Kingswoodbury Lodge

Baskets Wood

Munches Wood

3

Westfield Common

River Beane

31

Coldash Wood

Rydals Wood

Cumberlow Green Farm

2

Cumberlow Green

SG2

Kipple Field

A507

1

30

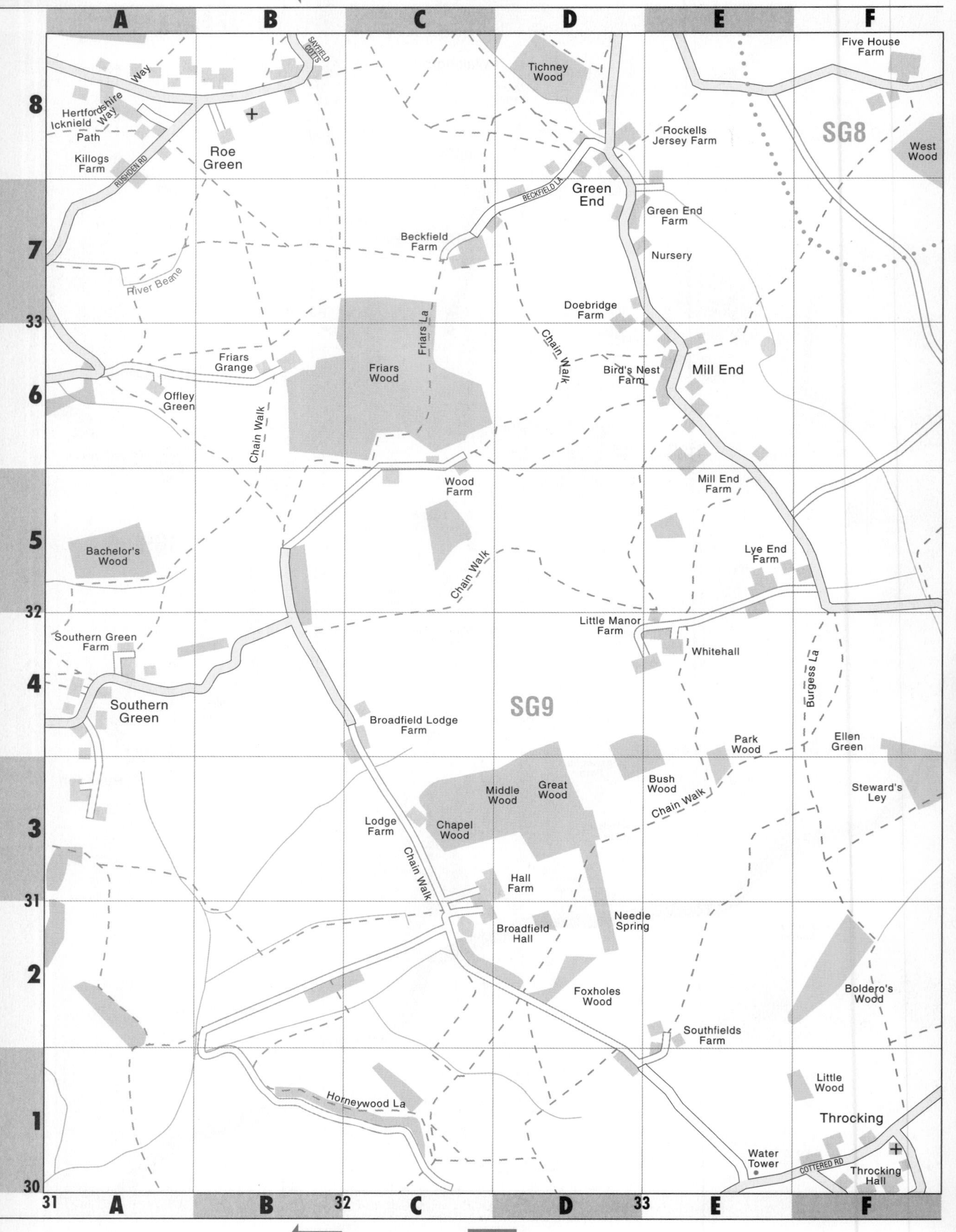

A B C D E F

8

7

33

6

5

32

4

31

3

2

1

30

Five House Farm

SG8

West Wood

Tichney Wood

Rockells Jersey Farm

Green End

Green End Farm

Nursery

Beckfield Farm

Beckfield La

Doebridge Farm

Chain Walk

Bird's Nest Farm

Mill End

Friars La

Friars Grange

Friars Wood

Offley Green

Chain Walk

Hertfordshire Way

Icknield Path

Killogs Farm

Roe Green

RUSHDEN RD

SAYFIELD CROFTS

River Beane

Way

Bachelor's Wood

Wood Farm

Chain Walk

Mill End Farm

Lye End Farm

Little Manor Farm

Whitehall

Southern Green Farm

Southern Green

Broadfield Lodge Farm

SG9

Park Wood

Burgess La

Ellen Green

Steward's Ley

Lodge Farm

Chapel Wood

Middle Wood

Great Wood

Bush Wood

Chain Walk

Chain Walk

Hall Farm

Broadfield Hall

Needle Spring

Boldero's Wood

Horneywood La

Foxholes Wood

Southfields Farm

Little Wood

Throcking

Water Tower

COTTERED RD

Throcking Hall

31 A B 32 C D 33 E F

16
28

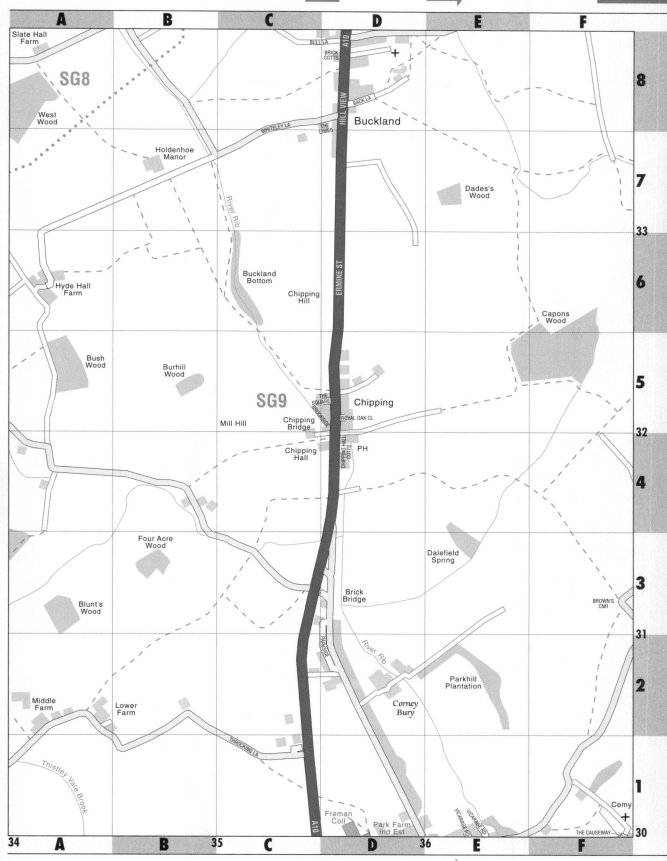
A
B
C
D
E
F
Slate Hall Farm
SG8
West Wood
BULL LA
A10
BRICK COTTS
HILL VIEW
BACK LA
Buckland
WHITELEY LA
THE LIMES
Holdenhoe Manor
Dades's Wood
River Rib
Buckland Bottom
Chipping Hill
ERMINE ST
Hyde Hall Farm
Capons Wood
Bush Wood
Burhill Wood
SG9
THE SQUARE
BROOKSIDE
Chipping
ROYAL OAK CL
Mill Hill
Chipping Bridge
Chipping Hall
CHIPPING HALL COTTS
PH
Four Acre Wood
Dalefield Spring
Brick Bridge
BROWN'S CNR
Blunt's Wood
PARKSIDE
River Rib
Parkhill Plantation
Middle Farm
Lower Farm
Corney Bury
THROCKING LA
Thistley Vale Brook
Freman Coll
Park Farm Ind Est
VICARAGE RD
VICARAGE RD
Cemy
THE CAUSEWAY
A10
8
7
33
6
5
32
4
3
31
2
1
30
34
35
36

40
28

27
17

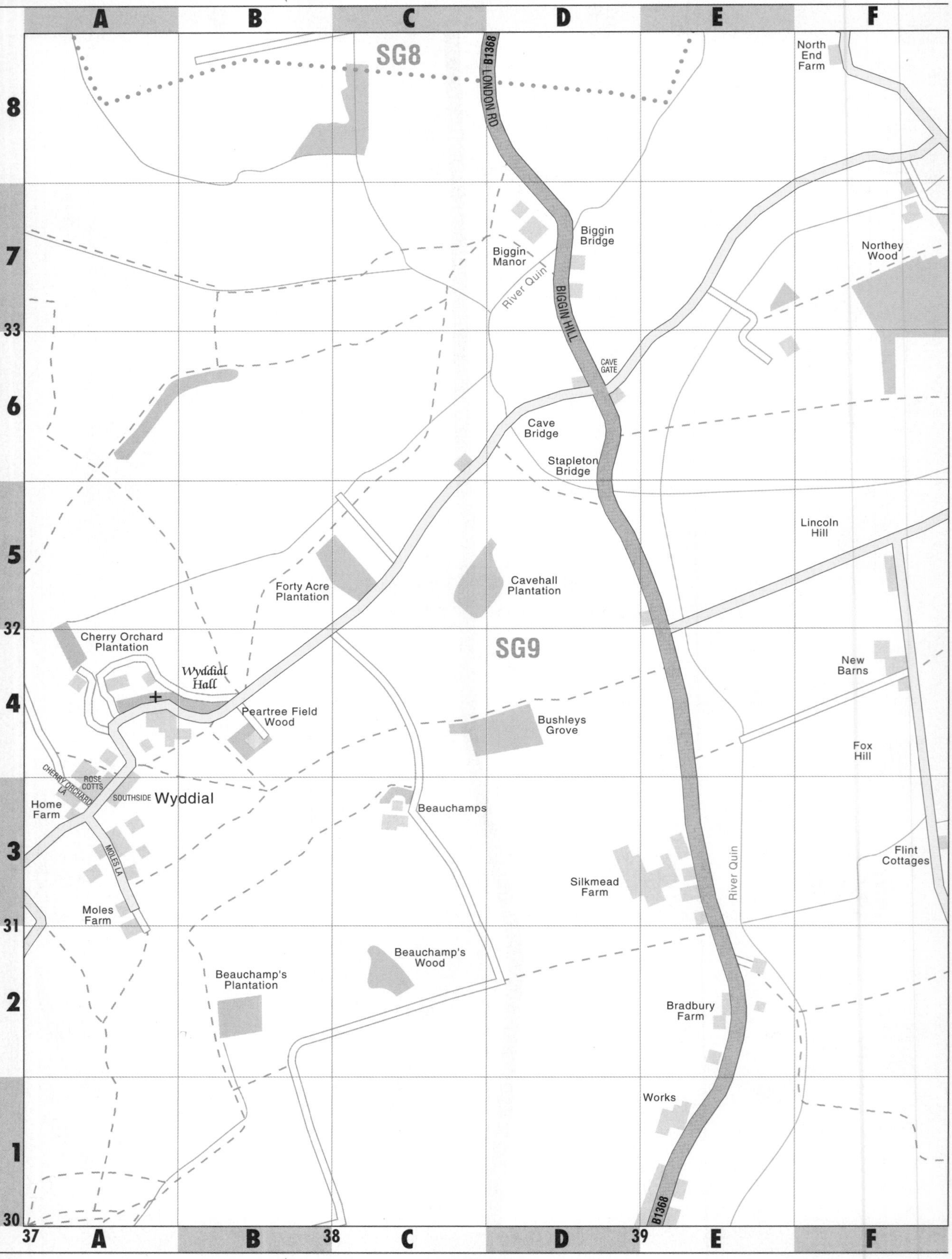

A   B   C   D   E   F

8

SG8

B1368 LONDON RD

North
End
Farm

7

Biggin
Manor

Biggin
Bridge

River Quin

BIGGIN HILL

Northey
Wood

33

CAVE
GATE

6

Cave
Bridge

Stapleton
Bridge

Lincoln
Hill

5

Forty Acre
Plantation

Cavehall
Plantation

32

Cherry Orchard
Plantation

SG9

New
Barns

Wyddial
Hall

4

Peartree Field
Wood

Bushleys
Grove

Fox
Hill

CHERRY ORCHARD LA

ROSE
COTTS

SOUTHSIDE Wyddial

Home
Farm

Beauchamps

Flint
Cottages

MOLES LA

River Quin

3

Silkmead
Farm

Moles
Farm

31

Beauchamp's
Plantation

Beauchamp's
Wood

2

Bradbury
Farm

Works

1

B1368

30

27
41

18
30

A
B
C
D
E
F
SG8
CB11
Scales Park
8
Bandons
Pain's End
DIMSDALE COTTS
Two Acres Farm
Northey Wood
Cheapside
CASTLE COTTS
White Hill
7
Anstey Castle
MOATSIDE
BURY FIELD
The Chequers (PH)
33
ST GEORGES END
The Hale
Lower Green
Anstey
Anstey Fst Sch
6
ELM COTTS
Meesden
Snow End
The Fox (PH)
LINCOLN HILL
ROGER'S LA
Daw's End
Coltsfoot Farm
Manor Farm
5
SILVER ST
32
Anstey Bury
River Ash
Hertfordshire Way
4
Puttock's End
SG9
Cole Green
3
Mill Mound
Brick House Farm
31
2
B1038
Borley Green Cottage
ANDERSON'S LA
Hormead Hall
Three Acre Wood
1
HALL LA
Black Ditch
HALL COTTS
CONDUIT LA
B1038
Dane End House
30
40
41
42

42
30

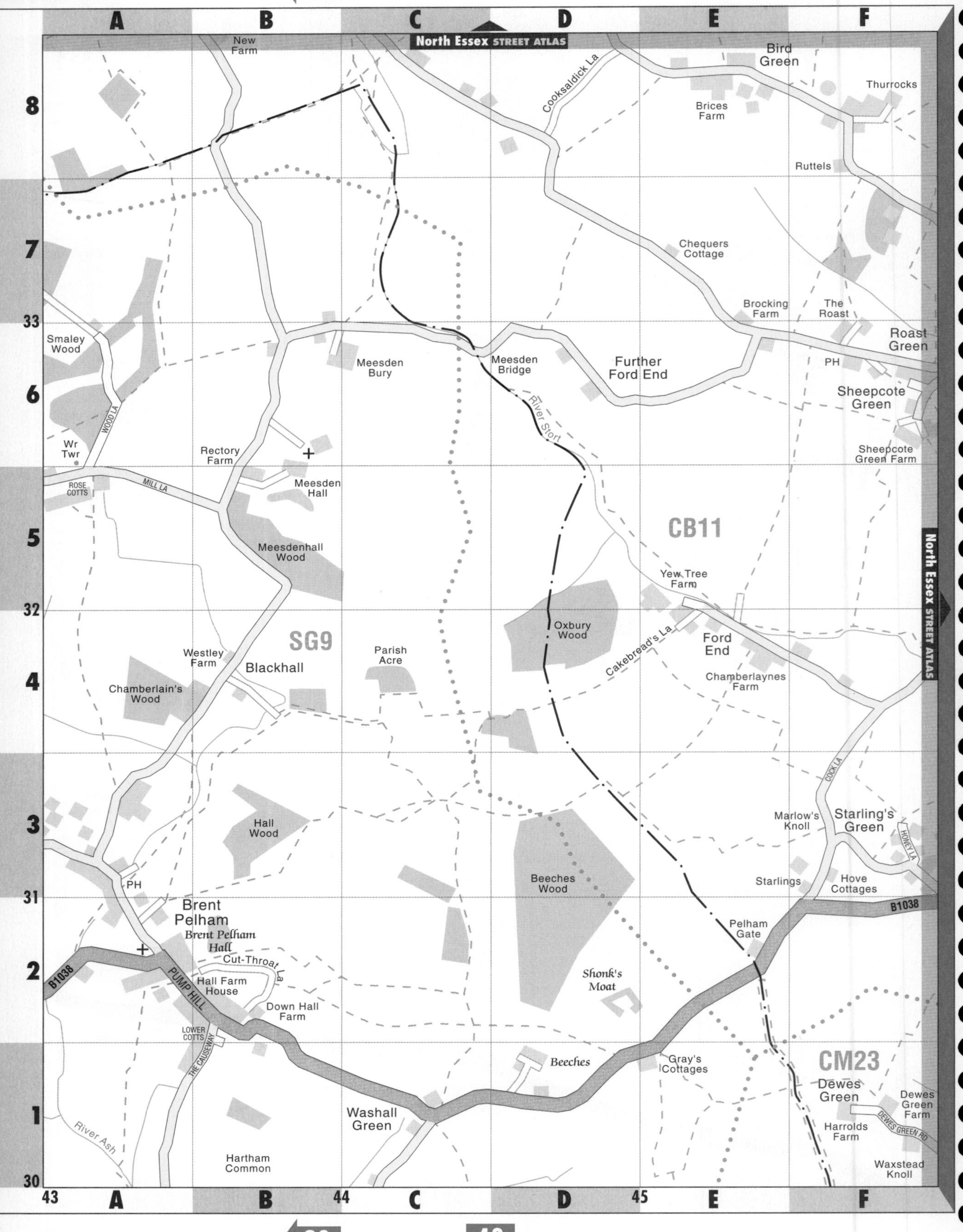

A   B   C   D   E   F

8

7

33

6

32

5

4

3

31

2

1

30

New Farm

Cooksaidick La

Bird Green

Brices Farm

Thurrocks

Ruttels

Chequers Cottage

Brocking Farm

The Roast

Roast Green

PH

Smaley Wood

Sheepcote Green

WOOD LA

Wr Twr

ROSE COTTS

MILL LA

Rectory Farm

Meesden Bury

Meesden Bridge

Meesden Hall

Further Ford End

River Stort

Sheepcote Green Farm

CB11

Meesdenhall Wood

Yew Tree Farm

SG9

Westley Farm

Blackhall

Parish Acre

Oxbury Wood

Cakebread's La

Ford End

Chamberlaynes Farm

Chamberlain's Wood

Hall Wood

Beeches Wood

Marlow's Knoll

Starling's Green

COCK LA

Starlings

Hove Cottages

HOVE LA

PH

Brent Pelham

Brent Pelham Hall

Cut-Throat La

Pelham Gate

B1038

B1038

PUMP HILL

Hall Farm House

Down Hall Farm

Shonk's Moat

CM23

Dewes Green

LOWER COTTS

THE CAUSEWAY

Beeches

Gray's Cottages

Dewes Green Farm

DEWES GREEN RD

River Ash

Washall Green

Harrolds Farm

Waxstead Knoll

Hartham Common

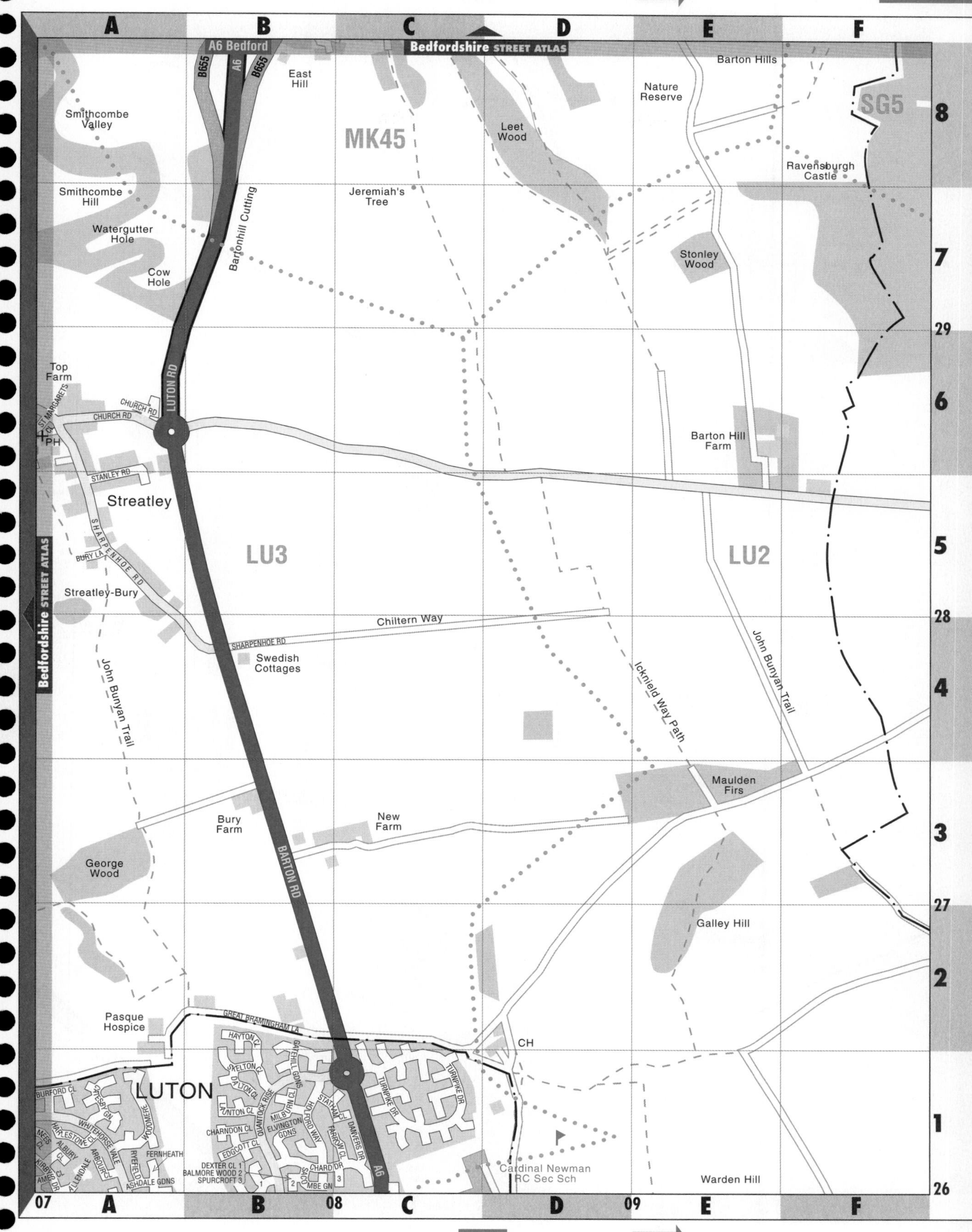

Bedfordshire STREET ATLAS

A6 Bedford
A6

East Hill

Smithcombe Valley

MK45

Leet Wood

Nature Reserve

Barton Hills

SG5

Smithcombe Hill

Jeremiah's Tree

Ravensburgh Castle

Watergutter Hole

Bartonhill Cutting

Cow Hole

Stonley Wood

LUTON RD

Top Farm

CHURCH RD
ST MARGARETS CL
CHURCH RD
PH

Barton Hill Farm

STANLEY RD

Streatley

SHARPENHOE RD

LU3

LU2

Bury La

Streatley-Bury

John Bunyan Trail

Chiltern Way

SHARPENHOE RD

John Bunyan Trail

Swedish Cottages

Icknield Way Path

Bury Farm

New Farm

Maulden Firs

George Wood

BARTON RD

Galley Hill

Pasque Hospice

GREAT BRAMINGHAM LA

CH

HAYTON CL
SKELTON CL
CAYFELL GDNS
HAYFORD WAY
STAMP CL
DANVERS DR
TURNPIKE DR
TURNPIKE DR

LUTON

BURFORD CL
GREET CL
HARTOPP CL
CHARNDON CL
LINTON CL
MILO DR
EDGCOTT CL
ELVINGTON GDNS
PARROY CL
CHARD DR
SLOW CL
BAMBE GN

HAR ESTONE
WHITERRS VALE
AL BURY
ARBOUR
RYEFIELD
FERNHEATH
DEXTER CL 1
BALMORE WOOD 2
SPURCROFT 3

ANES CL
KIRBY CL
AMES CL
ALLENDALE GDNS
ASHDALE GDNS

A6

Cardinal Newman RC Sec Sch

Warden Hill

07   A   B   08   C   D   09   E   F

8   29   7   6   5   28   4   3   27   2   1   26

31
19

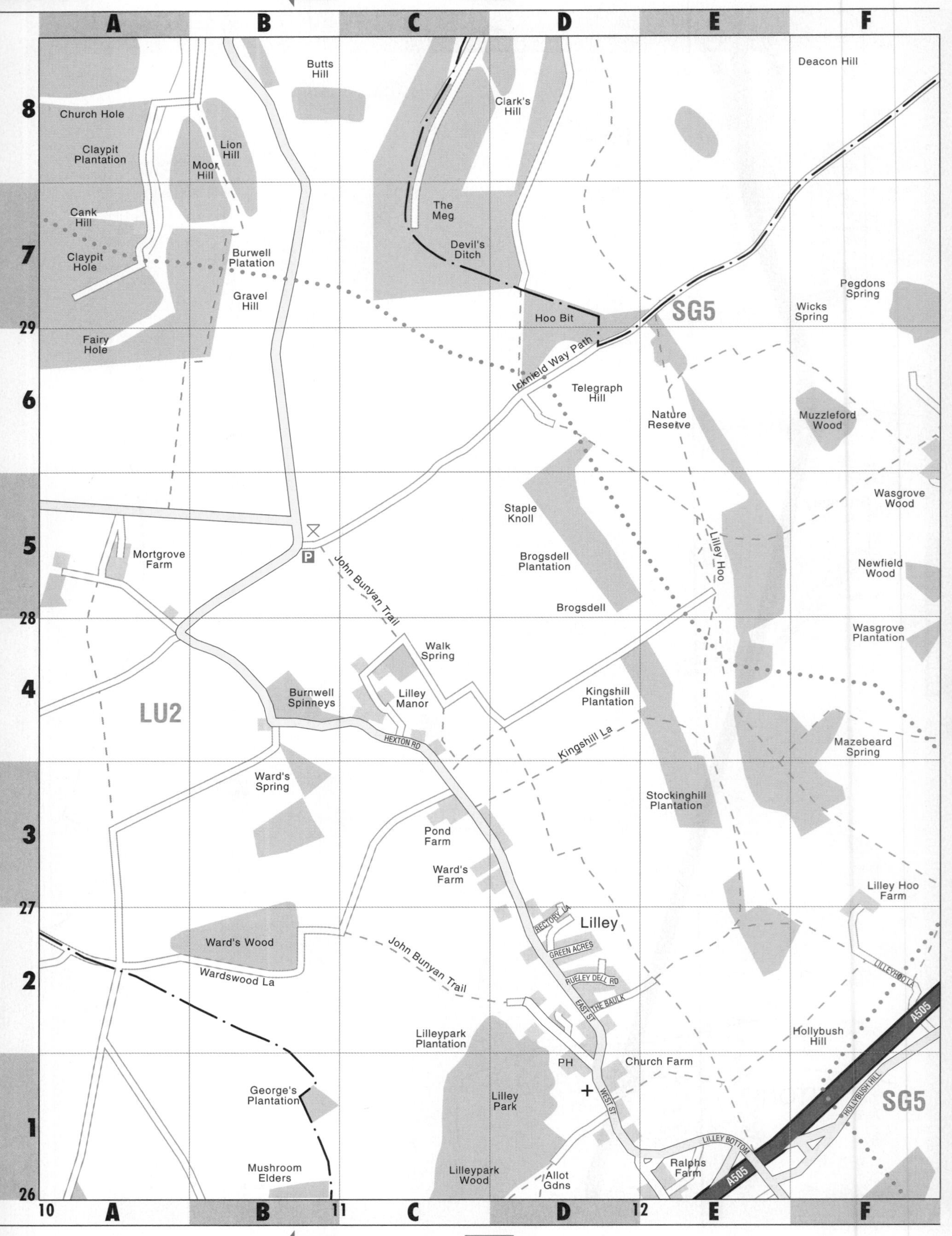
A
B
C
D
E
F
8
7
29
6
5
28
4
3
27
2
1
26
10
11
12
Deacon Hill
Butts Hill
Church Hole
Clark's Hill
Claypit Plantation
Lion Hill
Moor Hill
Cank Hill
The Meg
Devil's Ditch
Claypit Hole
Burwell Platation
Gravel Hill
Pegdons Spring
Wicks Spring
SG5
Hoo Bit
Fairy Hole
Icknield Way Path
Telegraph Hill
Nature Reserve
Muzzleford Wood
Wasgrove Wood
Staple Knoll
Mortgrove Farm
John Bunyan Trail
Brogsdell Plantation
Lilley Hoo
Newfield Wood
Brogsdell
Wasgrove Plantation
Walk Spring
Burnwell Spinneys
Lilley Manor
Kingshill Plantation
LU2
HEXTON RD
Kingshill La
Mazebeard Spring
Ward's Spring
Stockinghill Plantation
Pond Farm
Ward's Farm
Lilley Hoo Farm
RECTORY LA
Lilley
Ward's Wood
GREEN ACRES
John Bunyan Trail
Wardswood La
LILLEYHOO LA
RUELEY DELL RD
EAST ST
THE BAULK
A505
Lilleypark Plantation
Hollybush Hill
PH
Church Farm
George's Plantation
Lilley Park
WEST ST
HOLLYBUSH HILL
SG5
LILLEY BOTTOM
Ralphs Farm
Mushroom Elders
Lilleypark Wood
Allot Gdns
A505

31
46

20
34

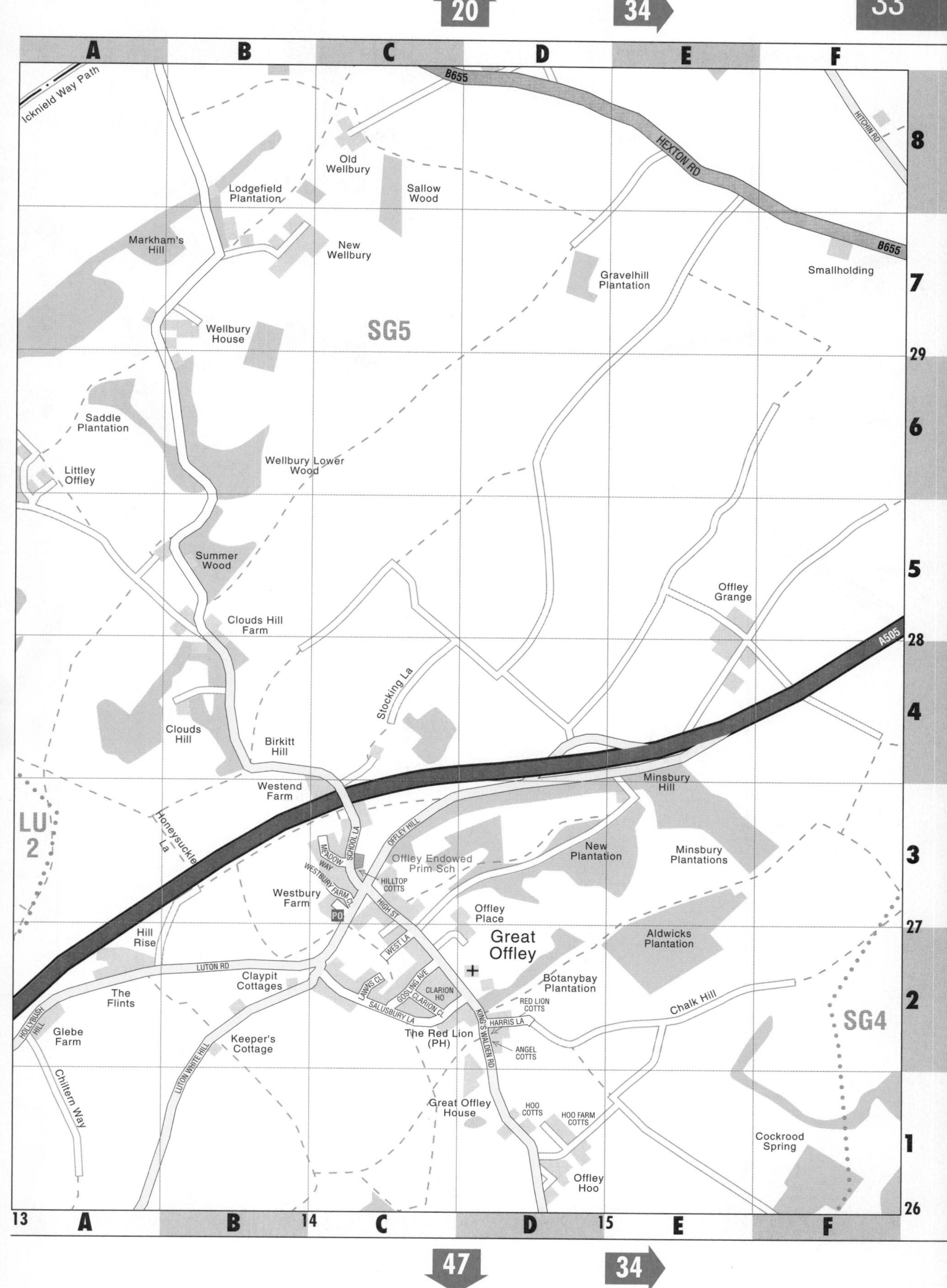
A
B
C
D
E
F
8
7
29
6
5
28
4
3
27
2
1
26
13
14
15
Icknield Way Path
B655
HEXTON RD
HITCHIN RD
Old Wellbury
Sallow Wood
Lodgefield Plantation
Markham's Hill
New Wellbury
Gravelhill Plantation
Smallholding
Wellbury House
SG5
Saddle Plantation
Littley Offley
Wellbury Lower Wood
Summer Wood
Offley Grange
Clouds Hill Farm
A505
Stocking La
Clouds Hill
Birkitt Hill
Westend Farm
Minsbury Hill
LU 2
Honeysuckle La
SCHOOL LA
MEADOW WAY
OFFLEY HILL
Offley Endowed Prim Sch
New Plantation
Minsbury Plantations
WESTBURY FARM CL
HILLTOP COTTS
Westbury Farm
HIGH ST
PO
Offley Place
Hill Rise
WEST LA
Great Offley
Aldwicks Plantation
LUTON RD
Claypit Cottages
LAWNS CL
GOSLING AVE
CLARION HO
CLARION CL
Botanybay Plantation
The Flints
SALUSBURY LA
RED LION COTTS
Chalk Hill
HOLLYBUSH HILL
Glebe Farm
Keeper's Cottage
The Red Lion (PH)
HARRIS LA
KING'S WALDEN RD
ANGEL COTTS
SG4
LUTON WHITE HILL
Chiltern Way
Great Offley House
HOO COTTS
HOO FARM COTTS
Cockrood Spring
Offley Hoo

47
34

33
21

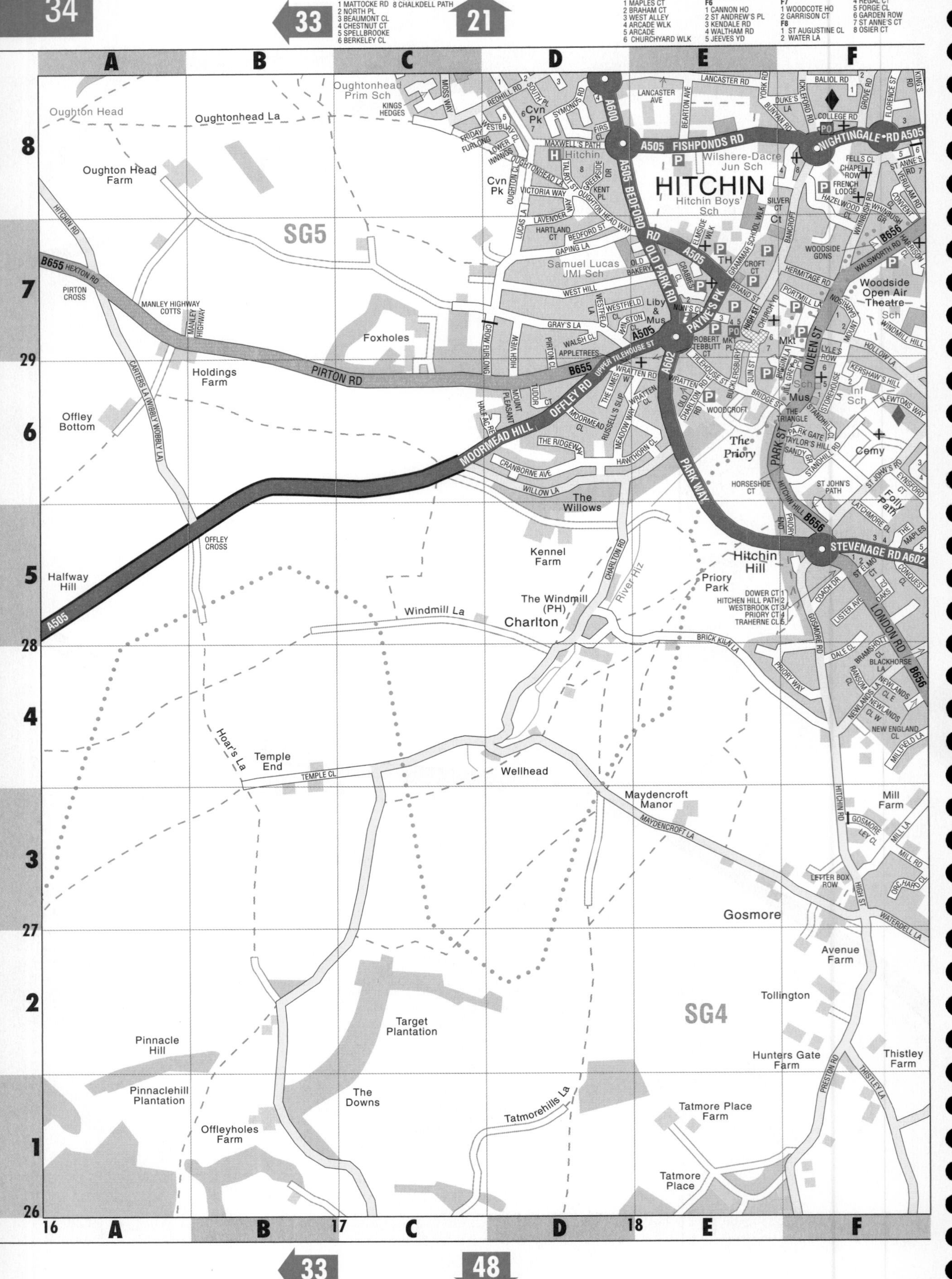
D8
1 MATTOCKE RD
2 NORTH PL
3 BEAUMONT CL
4 CHESTNUT CT
5 SPELLBROOKE
6 BERKELEY CL
7 FOSMAN CL
8 CHALKDELL PATH
E7
1 MAPLES CT
2 BRAHAM CT
3 WEST ALLEY
4 ARCADE WLK
5 ARCADE
6 CHURCHYARD WLK
7 CHURCHGATE
F6
1 CANNON HO
2 ST ANDREW'S PL
3 KENDALE RD
4 WALTHAM RD
5 JEEVES YD
6 SAXON CT
F7
1 WOODCOTE HO
2 GARRISON CT
F8
1 ST AUGUSTINE CL
2 WATER LA
3 ANDERSON'S HO
4 REGAL CT
5 FORGE CL
6 GARDEN ROW
7 ST ANNE'S CT
8 OSIER CT
A
B
C
D
E
F
8
7
29
6
5
28
4
3
27
2
1
26
16
17
18
HITCHIN
SG5
SG4
Oughton Head
Oughtonhead La
Oughtonhead Prim Sch
Oughton Head Farm
Hitchin Boys' Sch
Wilshere-Dacre Jun Sch
Samuel Lucas JMI Sch
A505 FISHPONDS RD
NIGHTINGALE RD A505
A505 BEDFORD RD
OLD PARK RD
PAYNE'S PK
B655 HEXTON RD
PIRTON CROSS
MANLEY HIGHWAY COTTS
PIRTON RD
Foxholes
Holdings Farm
Offley Bottom
MOORMEAD HILL
OFFLEY RD
UPPER TILEHOUSE ST
A602
PARK WAY
The Priory
The Willows
Kennel Farm
OFFLEY CROSS
Halfway Hill
A505
Windmill La
The Windmill (PH)
Charlton
River Hiz
Hitchin Hill
Priory Park
STEVENAGE RD A602
LONDON RD
B656
QUEEN ST
PARK ST
Woodside Open Air Theatre
Cemy
Folly Path
BRICK KILN LA
Hoar's La
Temple End
TEMPLE CL
Wellhead
Maydencroft Manor
MAYDENCROFT LA
Mill Farm
Gosmore
Avenue Farm
Tollington
Target Plantation
Pinnacle Hill
Pinnaclehill Plantation
The Downs
Offleyholes Farm
Tatmorehills La
Tatmore Place Farm
Tatmore Place
Hunters Gate Farm
Thistley Farm
PRESTON RD
THISTLEY LA
HITCHIN RD
HIGH ST
WATERDELL LA

33
48

22
36

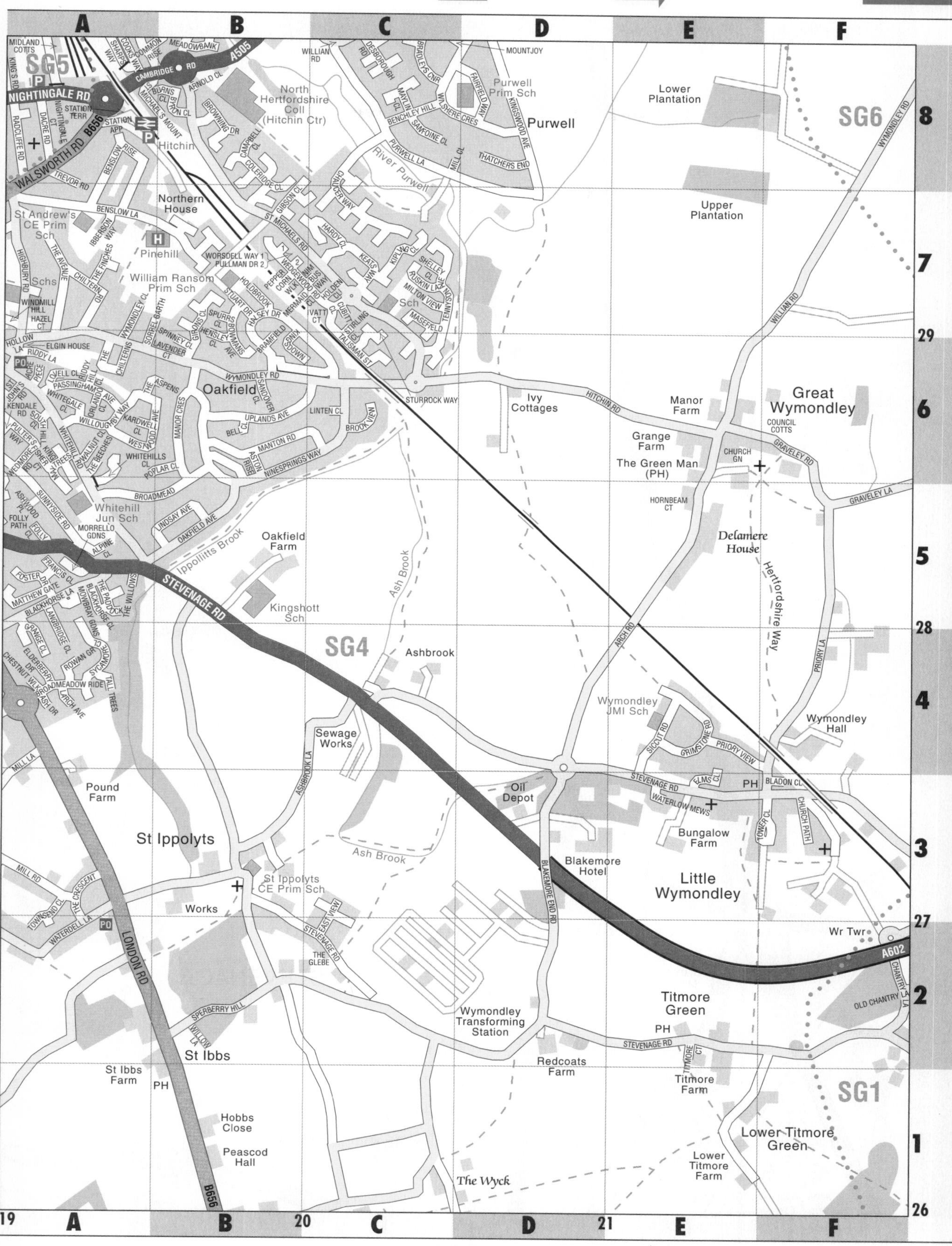
A
B
C
D
E
F
SG5
SG6
SG4
SG1
8
7
29
6
5
28
4
3
27
2
1
26
19
20
21
MIDLAND COTTS
KING'S RD
MEADOWBANK
A505
CAMBRIDGE RD
NIGHTINGALE RD
STATION TERR
STATION APP
RADCLIFFE RD
DACRE RD
NIGHTINGALE CT
WALSWORTH RD B656
TREVOR RD
ARNOLD CL
BURNS CL
BYRON CL
MICHAEL'S MOUNT
Hitchin
BENSLOW RISE
BROWNING DR
CAMPBELL CL
COLERIDGE CL
North Hertfordshire Coll (Hitchin Ctr)
WILLIAN RD
DESBOROUGH RD
BRADLEYS CNR
MAYLIN CL
BENCHLEY HILL
SAINFOINE CL
WILSHERE CRES
FAIRFIELD WAY
KINGSWOOD AVE
MOUNTJOY
Purwell Prim Sch
Purwell
MILL CL
THATCHERS END
PURWELL LA
River Purwell
CHAUCER WAY
GIBSON CL
Lower Plantation
Upper Plantation
WYMONDLEY RD
Northern House
St Andrew's CE Prim Sch
BENSLOW LA
IBBERSON WAY
ST MICHAELS RD
HARDY CL
KEATS WAY
KIPLING CL
SHELLEY CL
RUSKIN LA
TENNYSON AVE
MILTON VIEW
MASEFIELD
Pinehill
WORSDELL WAY 1
PULLMAN DR 2
THE AVENUE
HIGHBURY RD
THE FINCHES
CHILTERN RD
William Ransom Prim Sch
Schs
WINDMILL HILL
HAZEL CT
WYMONDLEY CL
SORREL GARTH
SPINNEY CL
LAVENDER CT
GIRONS CL
SPURRS CL
HENSLEY CL
BOWMANS AVE
HOLDBROOK
STUART DR
HALSEY DR
BRAMFIELD
ONYX
SODWON
PEPPER CT
CORN
MERMAID CL
HOLDEN CL
CUBITT CL
STIRLING
VATT CT
TALISMAN ST
Sch
HOLLOW LA
ELGIN HOUSE
RIDDY LA
PO
ACRE PIECE
LOVELL CL
PASSINGHAM AVE
WHITEGALE CL
ORLANDO CL
THE CHILTERNS
THE ASPENS
Oakfield
SANDOVER CL
UPLANDS AVE
LINTEN CL
BROOK VIEW
BELL CL
MANTON RD
MANOR CRES
KARDWELL CL
WESTWOOD AVE
WILLOUGHBY WAY
KENDALE RD
ST JOHN'S RD
SOUTH HILL CL
WHITEHILL RD
WALNUT CL
THE BEECHES
WHITEHILLS CL
POPLAR CL
ASTON RISE
NINESPRINGS WAY
BROADMEAD
LINDSAY AVE
OAKFIELD AVE
Whitehill Jun Sch
SUNNYSIDE RD
ASHWOOD PL
FOLLY PATH
FOLLY CL
MORRELLO GDNS
ALPINE CL
Ippollitts Brook
Oakfield Farm
STURROCK WAY
Ivy Cottages
HITCHIN RD
Manor Farm
Great Wymondley
COUNCIL COTTS
Grange Farm
CHURCH GN
GRAVELEY RD
The Green Man (PH)
HORNBEAM CT
GRAVELEY LA
Delamere House
Hertfordshire Way
WYMONDLEY RD
WILLIAN RD
FRANCIS CL
FOSTER DR
MATTHEW GATE
BLACKHORSE LA
MOWBRAY GDNS
THE PADDOCK
THE WILLOWS
STEVENAGE RD
Kingshott Sch
Ash Brook
Ashbrook
ARCH RD
PRIORY LA
GRANGE CL
LANGBRIDGE CL
ELDERBERRY DR
CHESTNUT WLK
ROWAN GR
SYCAMORE AVE
BROADMEADOW RIDE
LARCH AVE
TALL TREES
ASH DR
Wymondley JMI Sch
Wymondley Hall
SICCUT RD
GRIMSTONE RD
PRIORY VIEW
Sewage Works
ASHBROOK LA
MILL LA
Pound Farm
Oil Depot
ELMS CL
PH
BLADON CL
WATERLOW MEWS
CHURCH PATH
TOWER CL
Bungalow Farm
St Ippolyts
Ash Brook
Blakemore Hotel
BLAKEMORE END RD
Little Wymondley
MILL RD
THE CRESCENT
TOWNSEND CL
WATERDELL LA
PO
St Ippolyts CE Prim Sch
Works
EAST VIEW
THE GLEBE
LONDON RD
Wr Twr
A602
CHANTRY LA
OLD CHANTRY
Titmore Green
SPERBERRY HILL
WILLOW LA
Wymondley Transforming Station
Redcoats Farm
TITMORE CT
St Ibbs
St Ibbs Farm
Titmore Farm
Hobbs Close
Peascod Hall
Lower Titmore Green
Lower Titmore Farm
The Wyck
B656

49
36

35 23

A B C D E F
8 7 29 6 5 28 4 3 27 2 1 26
22 23 24
WYMONDLEY RD
A1(M)
B197
Jack's Hill Farm
The Lodge
ROXLEY MANOR
The Old Stables
SG6
CH
Jack's Hill
Hertfordshire Way
How Wood
Caravan Site
Stonesley Wood
GRAVELEY LA
The Ranch
Mast
Landing Strip (Private)
SG4
The Beeches
Riding Sch
Ledge Side Plantation
Manor Farm
MILKSEY LA
Graveley Hall Farm
CHURCH LA
Lodge
TURE LA
OAK LA
HIGH ST
Graveley Bury
ASHWELL COMM
ASHWELL CL
PONDSIDE
Graveley
George & Dragon (PH)
Hertfordshire Way
GRINDERS END
Graveley Prim Sch
Chesfield Park
HUMBER CT
Ten Acre Plantation
KENMARE CL
Park Plantation
RICCAT LA 1
WENSUM RD 2
KENNETT WAY 3
ORWELL AVE
DOVE RD
RYE CL
TEES CL
SEVERN WAY
GRAVELEY RD
CHANTRY LA
STEVENAGE RD
MIDDLESBOROUGH CL
MANCHESTER CL
NEWCASTLE CL
GREAT ASHBY WAY
B197
8
A602
LISTER CL 1
ASTON CL 2
GRAVELEY CL 3
HOLWELL 4
ASHWELL 5
BYGRAVE 6
GODSMORE 7
FROGMORE HO 8
EASTHALL HO 9
DANE END HO 10
CODICOTE HO 11
ST ANDREWS DR
ISLINGTON WAY
WESTON RD
RIPON RD
Corey's Mill
STEVENAGE
NORTH RD
UNDERWOOD RD
GRANBY RD
FOWLER GDNS
Recn Gd
Todd's Green
SG1
LANCASTER CL 1
GLOUCESTER CL 2
ROOKS NEST COTTS 3
TATES WAY
Lister
DALTRY RD
DALTRY CL
TURNER CL
BRAMBLES
THURLOW CL
ARNOLD CL
NEWBURY CL
ROOKS NEST FARM
IONA CL
GUILDFORD CL
CANTERBURY WAY
Superstore
HITCHIN RD
ST ALBANS LINK
CHANCELLORS RD
MORGAN CL
STEVENAGE RD
BARON CT
COREYS MILL LA
NORMAN CT
CAISTER CL
INGLESIDE DR
1 CRANBOURNE
2 CAVALIER
WOODFIELD RD
FOSTER CL
BOSWELL GDNS
WILSON CL
MATHEWS CL
HERNE RD
ANSELL CT
THE OLD WALLED GDN
WESTON RD
ST ALBANS DR
YORK RD
KESSINGLAND
GORLESTON
CHAPMAN RD
KNOWLE
HIGGINS WLK
WHITNEY DR
RECTORY LA
The Bury
Cemy
FOVANT
TARRANT
ALDEBURGH CL
FISHERS GN
SHERINGHAM AVE
TUDOR CL
NICHOLAS PL
CHESTNUT WLK
A1072
JESSOP RD
WISDEN RD
MUNDESLEY CL
The John Henry Newman RC Sch
BURYMEAD
MARTINS WAY
GRACE WAY
BADER CL
CONSTANTINE CL
JESSOP RD
Fishers Green
BAWDSEY CL
A602
A1072
TRAFFORD CL
TRENT CL
TRUMPER RD
Trotts Hill Prim Sch

35 50

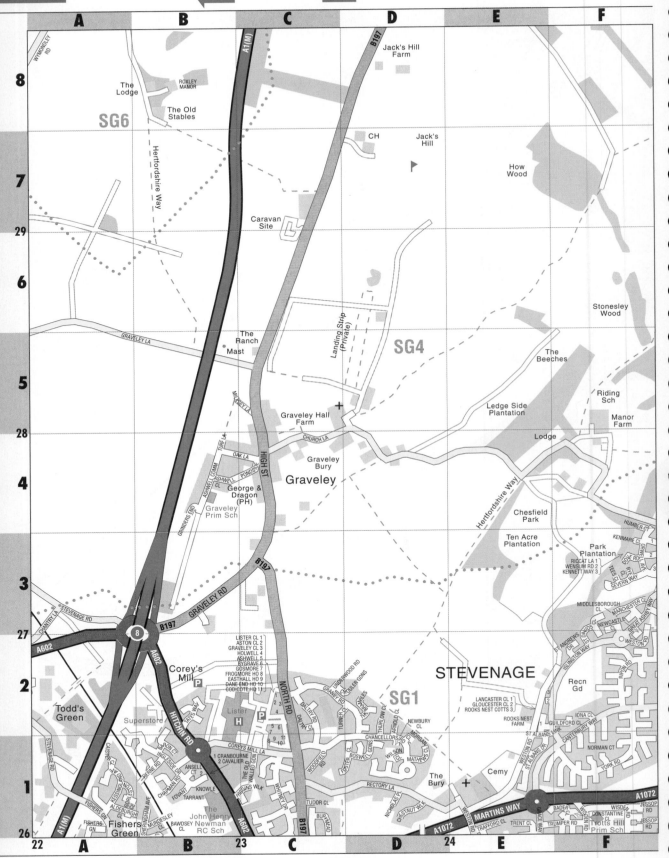

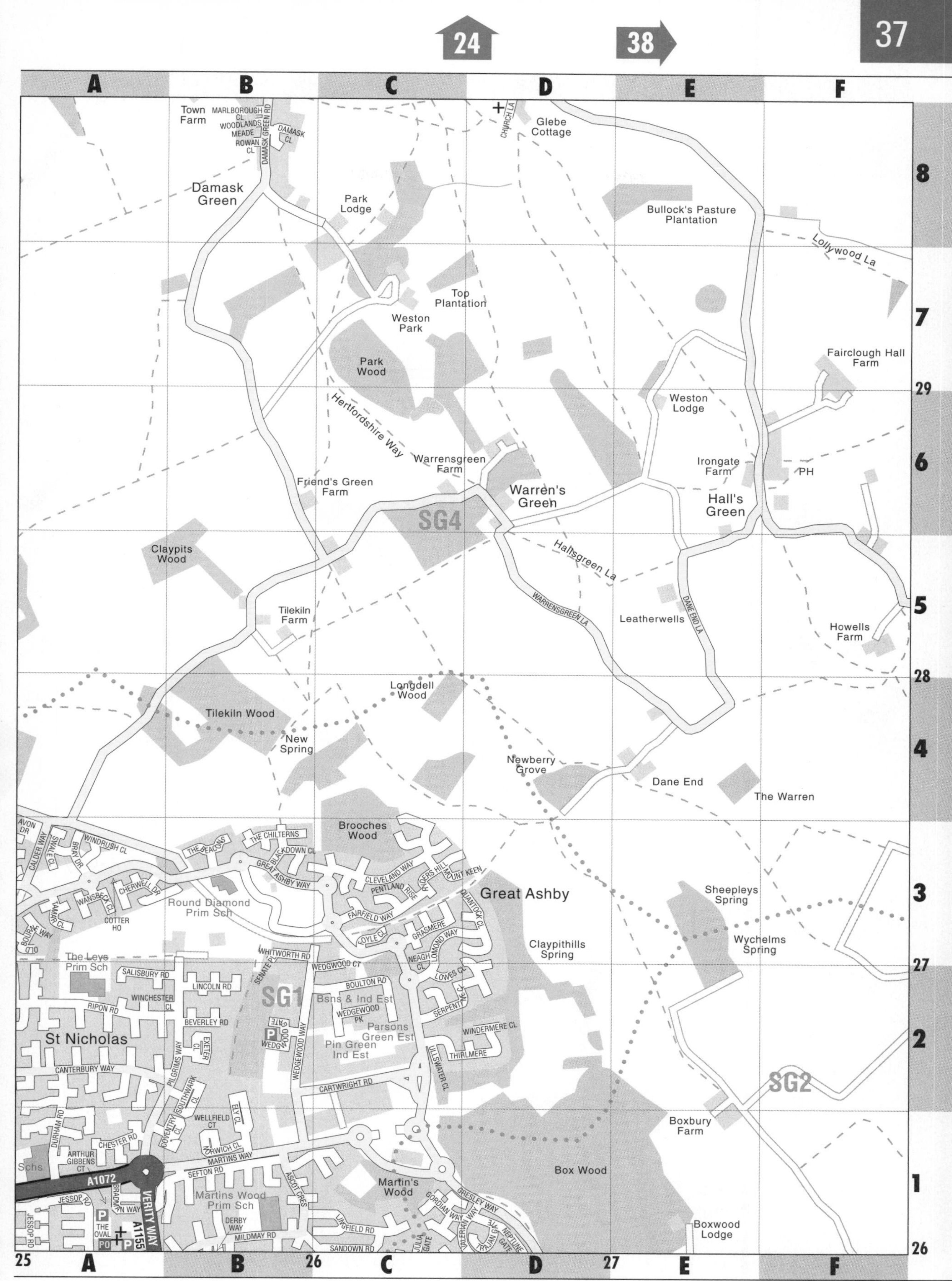
24
38
A
B
C
D
E
F
Town Farm
MARLBOROUGH CL
WOODLANDS
MEADE
ROWAN CL
DAMASK GREEN RD
DAMASK CL
CHURCH LA
Glebe Cottage
Damask Green
Park Lodge
Bullock's Pasture Plantation
Lollywood La
Top Plantation
Weston Park
Park Wood
Fairclough Hall Farm
Weston Lodge
Hertfordshire Way
Warrensgreen Farm
Irongate Farm
PH
Friend's Green Farm
Warren's Green
Hall's Green
SG4
Claypits Wood
Hallsgreen La
WARRENSGREEN LA
DANE END LA
Tilekiln Farm
Leatherwells
Howells Farm
Longdell Wood
Tilekiln Wood
New Spring
Newberry Grove
Dane End
The Warren
Brooches Wood
THE CHILTERNS
THE BEACONS
WINDRUSH CL
BLACKDOWN CL
GREAT ASHBY WAY
CLEVELAND WAY
PENTLAND RISE
RYDERS HILL
MOUNT KEEN
QUANTOCK CL
Great Ashby
Sheepleys Spring
Round Diamond Prim Sch
CHERWELL DR
WANSBECK CL
TAMAR CL
CALDER WAY
SWALE CL
BRAY DR
AVON DR
COTTER HO
BOURNE WAY
FAIRFIELD WAY
COYLE CL
GRASMERE
LOMOND WAY
NEAGH CL
Claypithills Spring
Wychelms Spring
The Leys Prim Sch
WHITWORTH RD
WEDGWOOD CT
SALISBURY RD
LINCOLN RD
BOULTON RD
LOWES CL
WINCHESTER CL
SG1
Bsns & Ind Est
SERPENTINE CL
RIPON RD
WEDGEWOOD PK
BEVERLEY RD
Parsons Green Est
WINDERMERE CL
St Nicholas
Pin Green Ind Est
PILGRIMS WAY
EXETER CL
WEDGWOOD WAY
THIRLMERE
ULLSWATER CL
CANTERBURY WAY
CARTWRIGHT RD
SOUTHWARK CL
COVENTRY CL
WELLFIELD CT
ELY CL
SG2
DURHAM RD
CHESTER RD
NORWICH CL
Boxbury Farm
ARTHUR GIBBENS CT
Schs
MARTINS WAY
SEFTON RD
A1072
ASCOT CRES
Box Wood
Martin's Wood
JESSOP RD
BRADMAN WAY
VERITY WAY
A1155
Martins Wood Prim Sch
GRESLEY WAY
GORDIAN WAY
NEPTUNE GATE
TRAJAN GATE
VALERIAN WAY
JULIA GATE
THE OVAL
PO
P
DERBY WAY
MILDMAY RD
LINGFIELD RD
SANDOWN RD
Boxwood Lodge
JESSOP RD
8
7
29
6
5
28
4
3
27
2
1
26
25
26
27
51
38

37
25

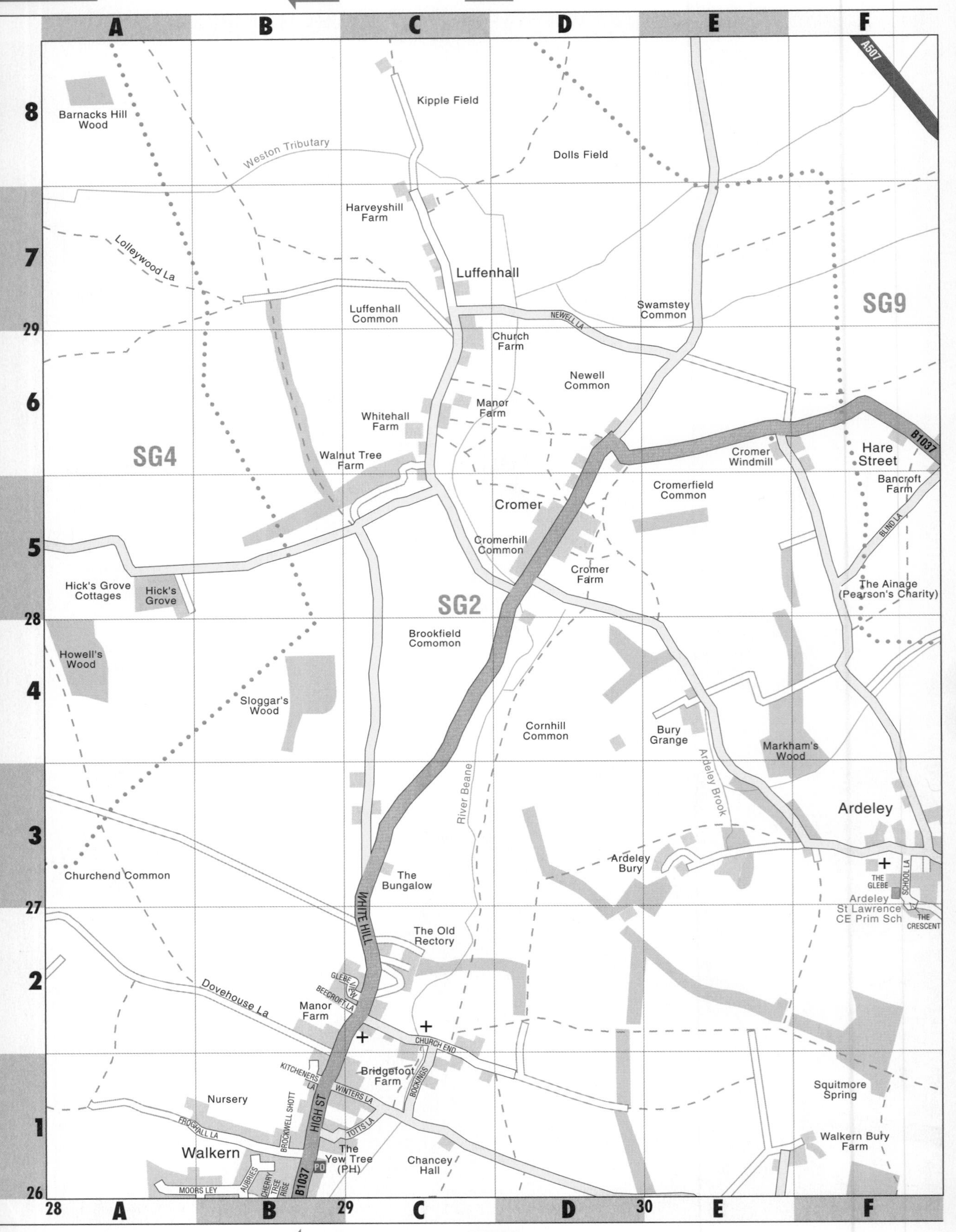

A B C D E F

8

Barnacks Hill Wood

Kipple Field

Weston Tributary

Dolls Field

7

Lolleywood La

Harveyshill Farm

Luffenhall

29

Luffenhall Common

Swamstey Common

SG9

NEWELL LA

Church Farm

6

Whitehall Farm

Manor Farm

Newell Common

SG4

Walnut Tree Farm

Cromer Windmill

Hare Street

B1037

Bancroft Farm

Cromerfield Common

5

Hick's Grove Cottages

Hick's Grove

Cromer

SG2

Cromerhill Common

Cromer Farm

BLIND LA

The Ainage (Pearson's Charity)

28

Howell's Wood

Brookfield Comomon

4

Sloggar's Wood

Cornhill Common

Bury Grange

Markham's Wood

Ardeley

River Beane

Ardeley Brook

3

Churchend Common

Ardeley Bury

Ardeley St Lawrence CE Prim Sch

THE GLEBE

SCHOOL LA

27

WHITE HILL

The Bungalow

THE CRESCENT

2

Dovehouse La

The Old Rectory

GLEBE RD

BEECROFT LA

Manor Farm

CHURCH END

Squitmore Spring

KITCHENERS LA

Bridgefoot Farm

WINTERS LA

BROCKINGS

1

Nursery

BROCKWELL SHOTT

HIGH ST

TUTTS LA

Walkern Bury Farm

FROGHALL LA

Walkern

The Yew Tree (PH)

PO

Chancey Hall

26

MOORS LEY

AUBRIES

CHERRY TREE RISE

B1037

28 A B 29 C D 30 E F

A507

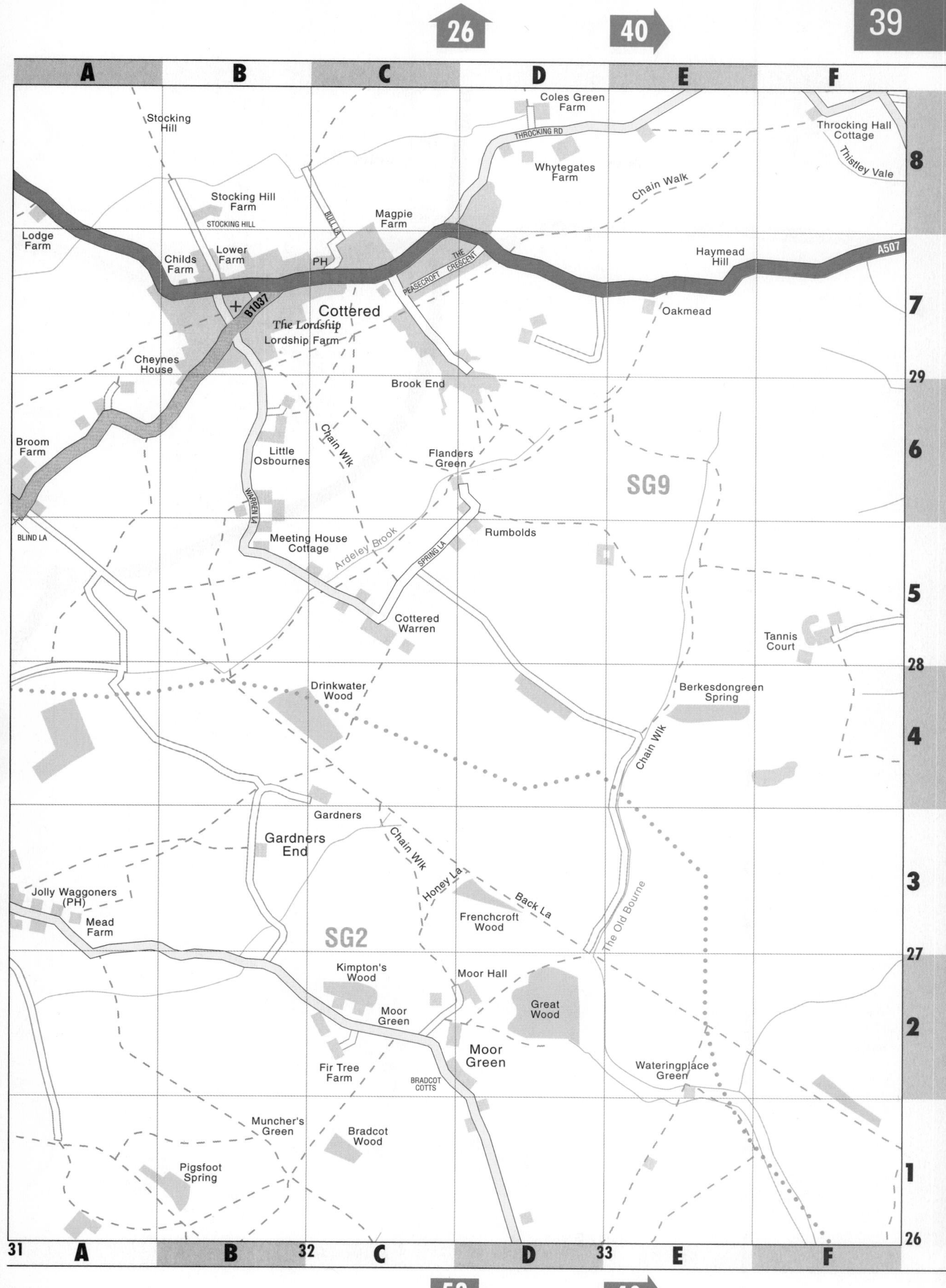
26
40
A
B
C
D
E
F
Coles Green Farm
Stocking Hill
Throcking Hall Cottage
THROCKING RD
Thistley Vale
Whytegates Farm
Chain Walk
Stocking Hill Farm
STOCKING HILL
BULL LA
Magpie Farm
Lodge Farm
Lower Farm
Childs Farm
PH
THE CRESCENT
PEASECROFT
Haymead Hill
A507
B1037
Cottered
The Lordship
Lordship Farm
Oakmead
Cheynes House
Brook End
Broom Farm
Little Osbournes
Chain Wlk
Flanders Green
SG9
WARREN LA
BLIND LA
Meeting House Cottage
Ardeley Brook
SPRING LA
Rumbolds
Cottered Warren
Tannis Court
Drinkwater Wood
Berkesdongreen Spring
Chain Wlk
Gardners
Gardners End
Chain Wlk
Honey La
Back La
Jolly Waggoners (PH)
Mead Farm
Frenchcroft Wood
The Old Bourne
SG2
Kimpton's Wood
Moor Hall
Great Wood
Moor Green
Moor Green
Wateringplace Green
Fir Tree Farm
BRADCOT COTTS
Muncher's Green
Bradcot Wood
Pigsfoot Spring
8
7
29
6
5
28
4
3
27
2
1
26
31
32
33
A
B
C
D
E
F
53
40

A B C D E F

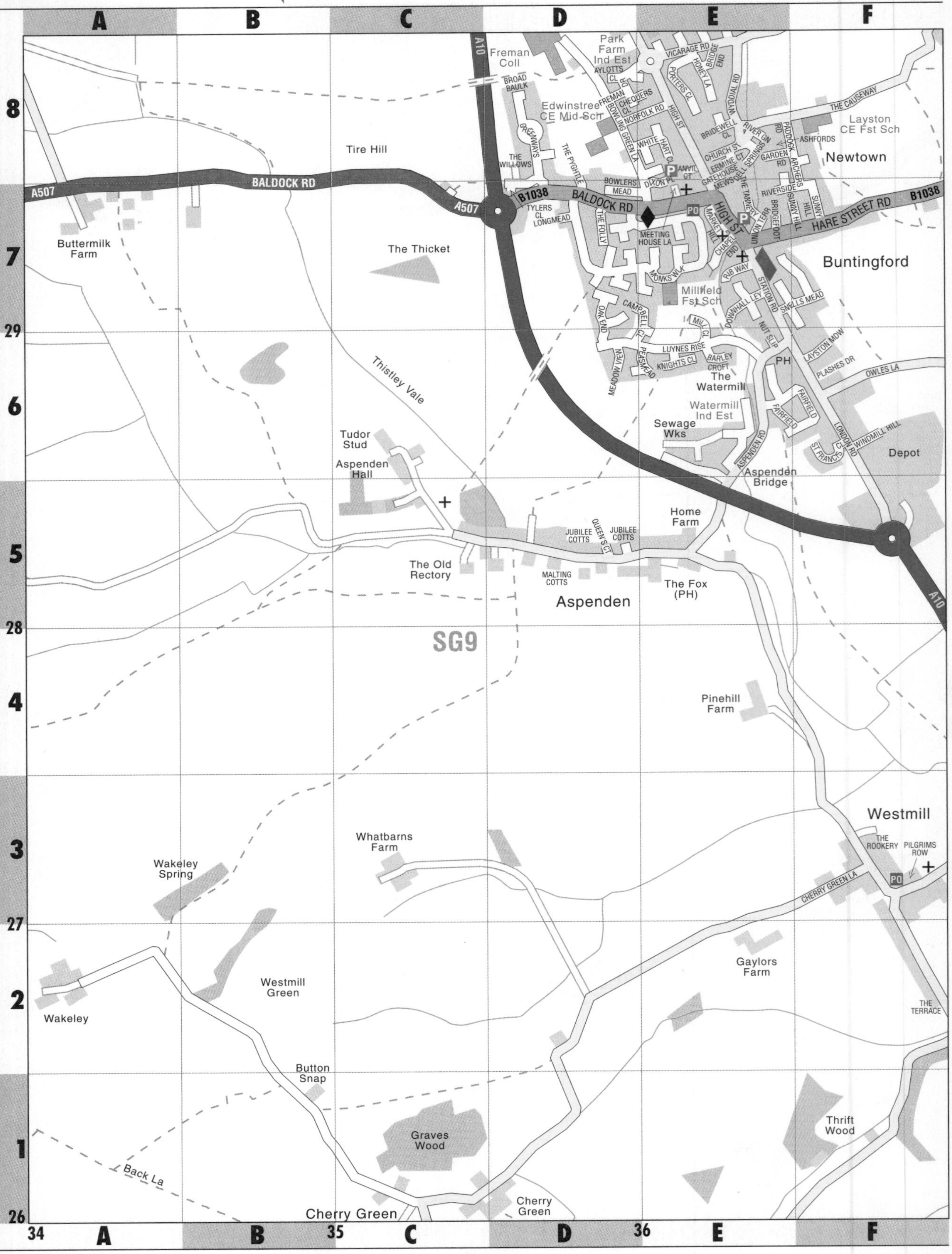

8

Tire Hill

Freman Coll

Park Farm Ind Est
AYLOTTS
VICARAGE RD
HONEY LA
PORTERS CL
THE CAUSEWAY

Edwinstree CE Mid Sch
FREMAN

Layston CE Fst Sch
ASHFORDS

BROAD BAULK

WHITE HART CL
WYDDIAL RD

Newtown

BALDOCK RD

A507

THE WILLOWS
GREENWAYS
DIXON PL

BRIDEWELL

CHURCH ST
GATEHOUSE RD
THE TANNERY

GARDEN RD
PADDOCK
ARCHERS

B1038

BALDOCK RD

TYLERS CL
LONGMEAD
THE FOLLY

BOWLERS MEAD

HIGH ST

RIVERSIDE
SUNNY HILL
BRIDGEFOOT

HARE STREET RD

B1038

7

The Thicket

MEETING HOUSE LA

MONKS WLK

CHART

PO

P

Buttermilk Farm

Buntingford

29

Thistley Vale

CAMPBELL

MEADOW VIEW

PEARMEAD

LUYNES RISE
KNIGHTS CL
NUT SLIP

Millfield Fst Sch
I A MULT CL

DOWNHALL LEY

BARLEY CROFT

STATION RD
SNELLS MEAD

LAYSTON MDW
PLASHES DR

OWLES LA

6

Tudor Stud

The Watermill

PH

Aspenden Hall

Sewage Wks

Watermill Ind Est

FAIRFIELD

LONDON RD
WINDMILL HILL

ST FRANCIS

Depot

5

The Old Rectory

JUBILEE COTTS
QUEEN'S ST
JUBILEE COTTS

MALTING COTTS

Home Farm

Aspenden Bridge

ASPENDEN RD

A10

Aspenden

The Fox (PH)

28

SG9

4

Pinehill Farm

3

Whatbarns Farm

Westmill

Wakeley Spring

THE ROOKERY
PILGRIMS ROW

PO

27

Wakeley

Westmill Green

Gaylors Farm

CHERRY GREEN LA

THE TERRACE

2

Button Snap

Graves Wood

Thrift Wood

1

Back La

26

Cherry Green

Cherry Green

34 A B 35 C D 36 E F

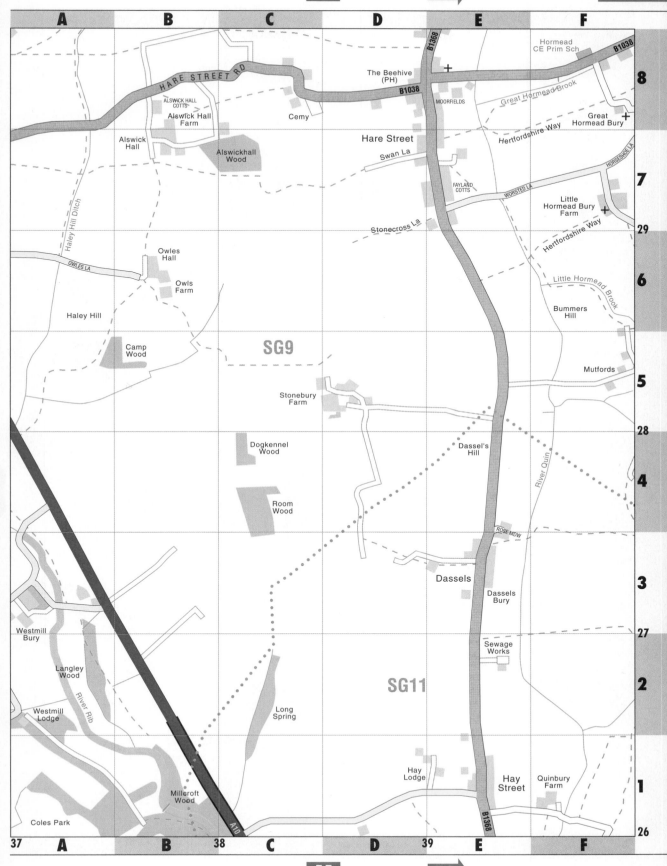

A B C D E F

Hare Street Rd

ALSWICK HALL COTTS
Alswick Hall Farm
Cemy
Alswick Hall
Alswickhall Wood

B1368
Hormead CE Prim Sch
B1038
The Beehive (PH)
B1038
MOORFIELDS
Great Hormead Bury
Hertfordshire Way

Hare Street
Swan La
FAYLAND COTTS
WORSTED LA
HORSESHOE LA
Little Hormead Bury Farm
Hertfordshire Way

Haley Hill Ditch
OWLES LA
Owles Hall
Owls Farm
Haley Hill

Stonecross La

8
7
29
6
5
28
4
27
2
3
1
26

Little Hormead Brook
Bummers Hill
Mutfords

SG9

Camp Wood
Stonebury Farm

Dogkennel Wood

Dassel's Hill
River Quin

Room Wood
ROSE MDW

Dassels
Dassels Bury

Westmill Bury
Langley Wood
River Rib
Westmill Lodge

Long Spring

SG11

Sewage Works

Hay Lodge
Hay Street
Quinbury Farm

Millcroft Wood
A10
B1368

Coles Park

37 A 38 B C 39 D E F
26

41
29

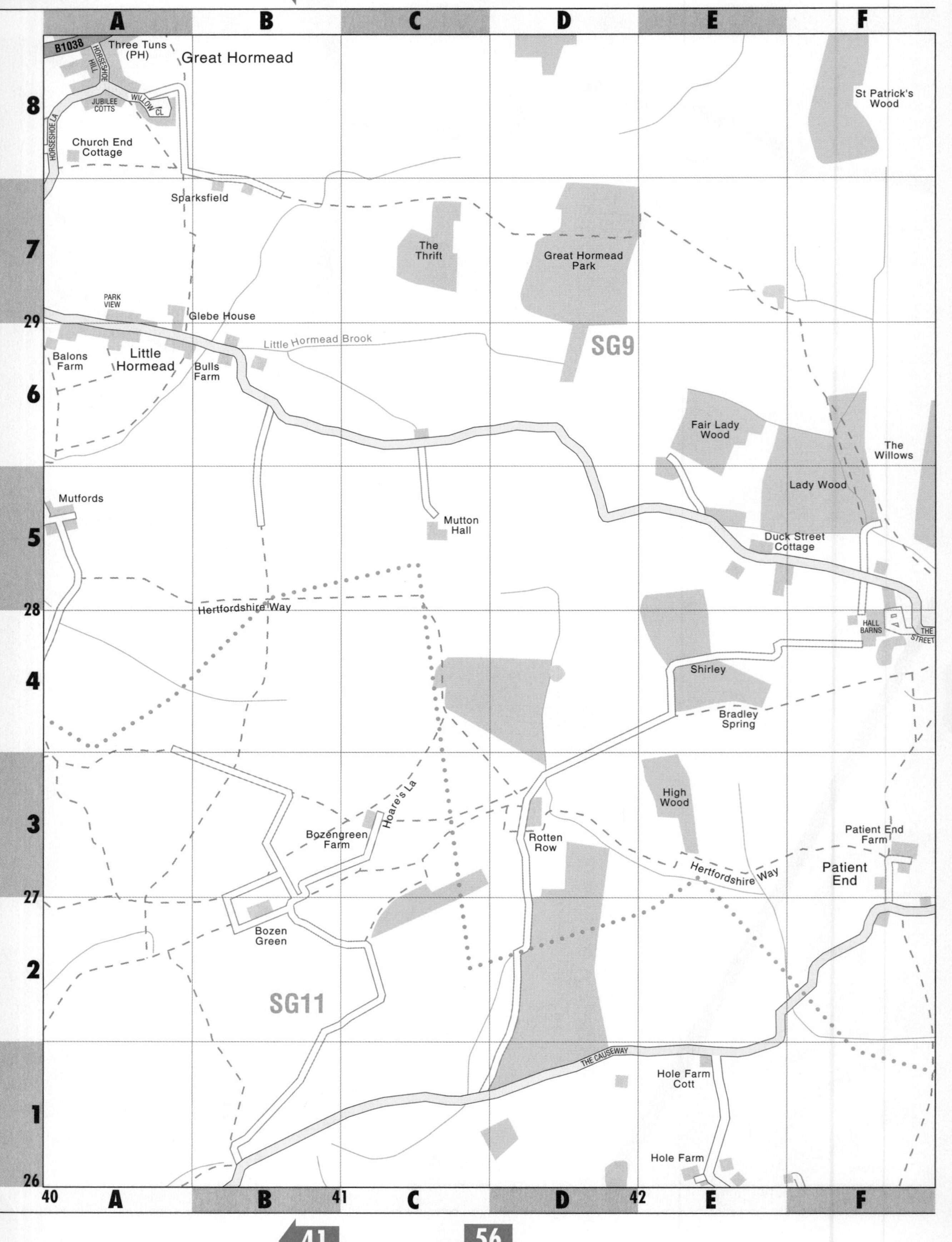
A
B
C
D
E
F
8
7
29
6
5
28
4
3
27
2
1
26
40
41
42
B1038
HORSESHOE HILL
Three Tuns (PH)
Great Hormead
JUBILEE COTTS
WILLOW CL
HORSESHOE LA
Church End Cottage
Sparksfield
The Thrift
Great Hormead Park
St Patrick's Wood
PARK VIEW
Glebe House
Little Hormead Brook
SG9
Balons Farm
Little Hormead
Bulls Farm
Fair Lady Wood
The Willows
Lady Wood
Mutfords
Mutton Hall
Duck Street Cottage
Hertfordshire Way
HALL BARNS
THE STREET
Shirley
Bradley Spring
High Wood
Hoare's La
Bozengreen Farm
Rotten Row
Patient End Farm
Patient End
Hertfordshire Way
Bozen Green
SG11
THE CAUSEWAY
Hole Farm Cott
Hole Farm

41
56

CM23

8

Hall Wood

Stocking Farm

Stocking Pelham Hall

The Cock (PH)

Violets Spring

7

Stocking Pelham

White Hart

Whitebarns

MEAD VIEW

29

WHITEBARNS LA

Sports Ground

Crabb's Green

6

Silla Farm

Whitebarns Cottages

GINNS RD

CRABB'S LA

Crabb's Green Farm

The Willows

El Sub Sta

River Ash

VIOLETS LA

Willows Farm

SG9

5

28

North Essex Street Atlas

WHITEBARNS

Furneux Pelham

THE WASH

GINNS RD

Brewery

Lower Farm

East End

Green's Farm

+ PO

THE STREET

The Star (PH)

Furneux Pelham CE Sch

+

The Brewery Tap (PH)

LAKE VILLAS

Old Mill House

Eastend Farm

4

THE OLD COMMON

Barleycroft End

BROOKSIDE

Recn Gd

Clay Chimneys

The Brook

3

THE CAUSEWAY

Pheasant Hall

Sewage Works

27

Hixham Cottages

Hixham Hall

2

Kings Cottage

SG11

Kings

CM23

1

Oaken Spring

Heath Farm

26

Bedfordshire STREET ATLAS

C5
1 CHAWORTH GN
2 ACWORTH CT
3 MOSSDALE CT
4 WOLFSBURG CT
5 THORNTONDALE
6 GREEN CT

7 WHARFDALE

LU3

LU4

LU5

LU1

DUNSTABLE

M1 Milton Keynes, Northampton

A505 Dunstable

Sundon Park

Marsh Farm

Leagrave

Limbury

Luton & Dunstable (Faringdon Wing)

Luton Maternity

Luton & Dunstable

Icknield Way Path

Great Bramingham
Lea Manor Wood

Waulud's Bank

Source of the River Lea or Lee

Leagrave Common

HATTERS WAY

TODDINGTON ROAD

LUTON RD

MARSH RD

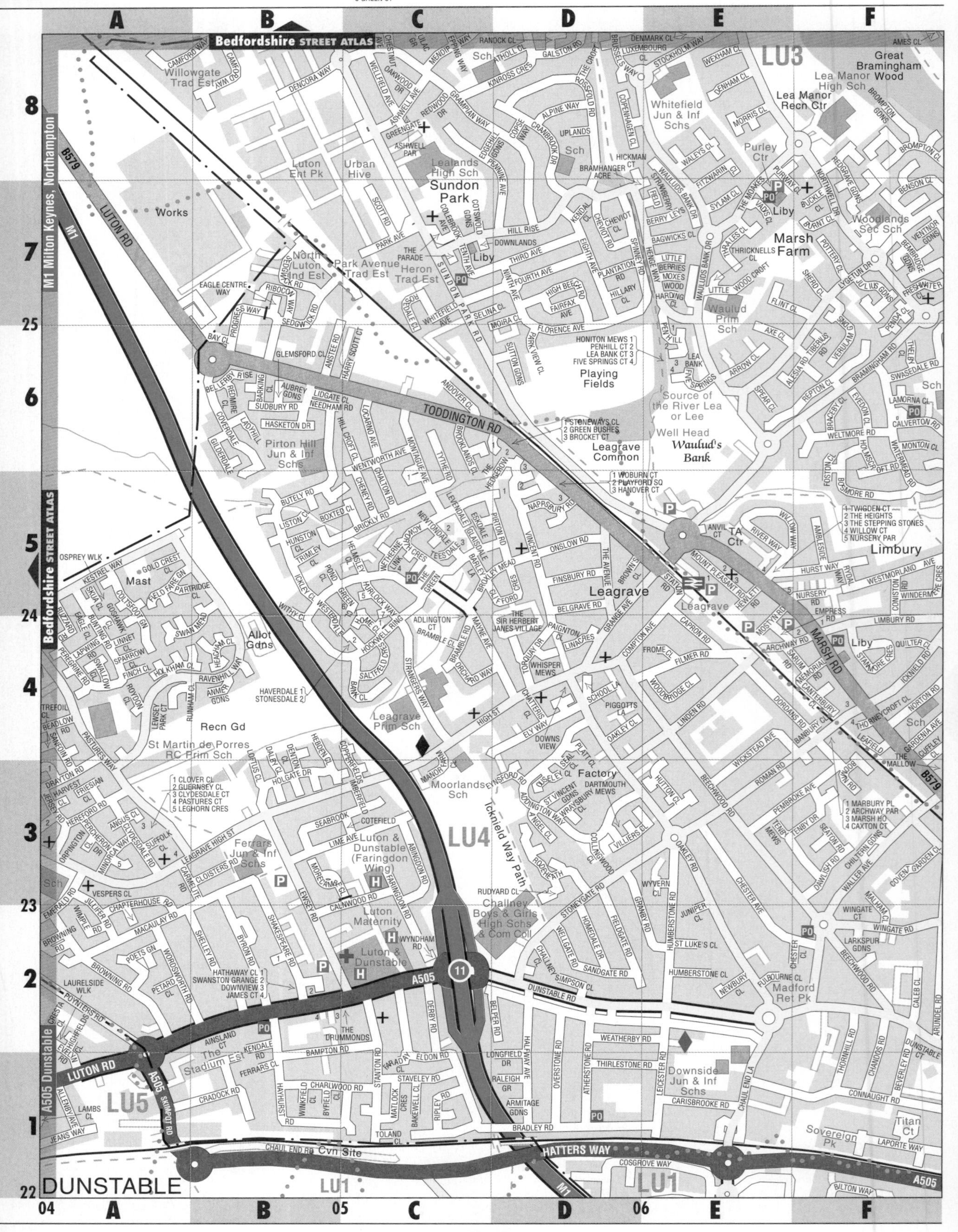

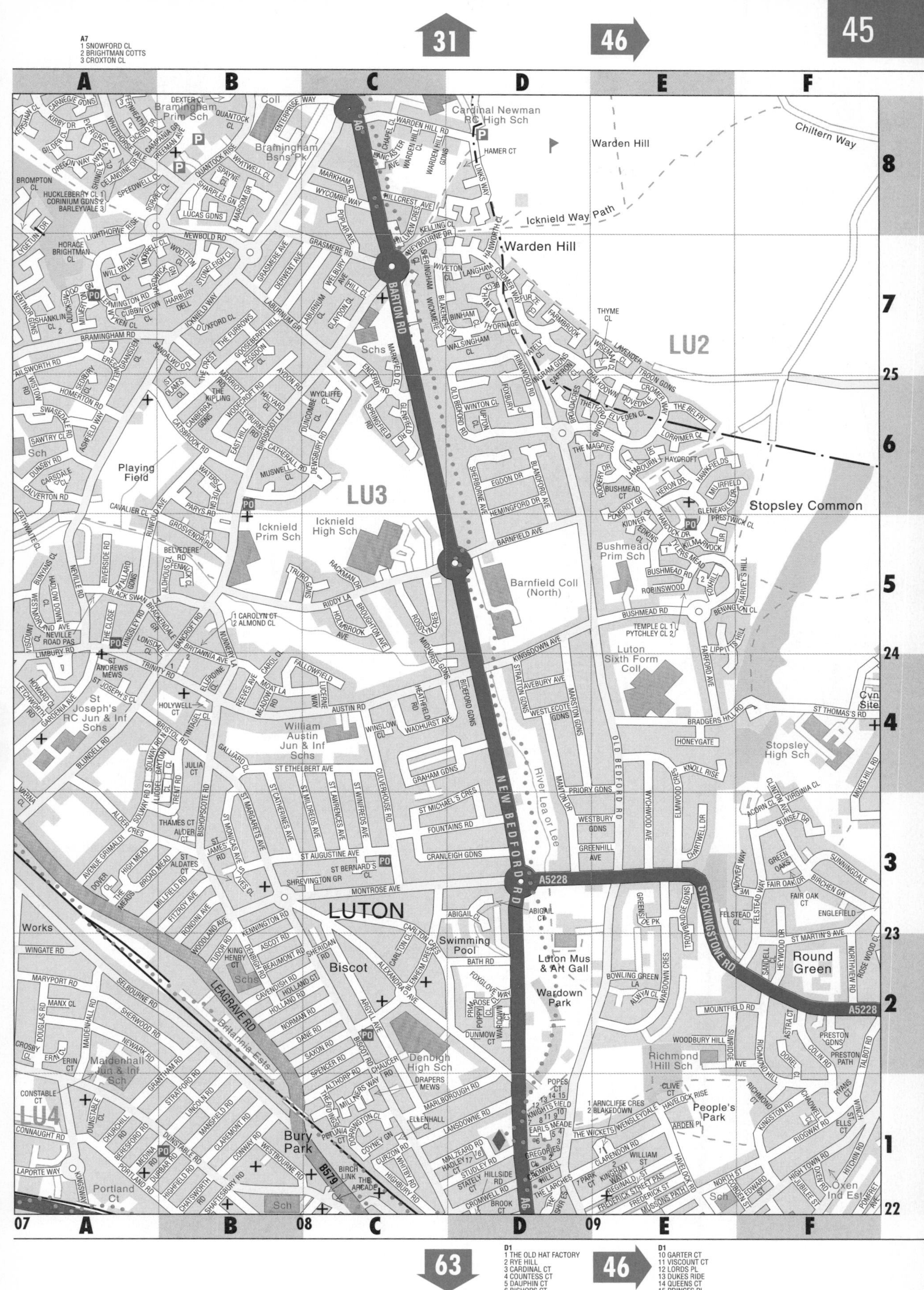
A7
1 SNOWFORD CL
2 BRIGHTMAN COTTS
3 CROXTON CL
31
46
A
B
C
D
E
F
8
7
25
6
5
24
4
3
23
2
1
22
07
08
09
Bramingham Prim Sch
Bramingham Bsns Pk
Coll
Cardinal Newman RC High Sch
Warden Hill
Chiltern Way
Icknield Way Path
Warden Hill
BARTON RD
LU2
LU3
Playing Field
Icknield Prim Sch
Icknield High Sch
Schs
Barnfield Coll (North)
Bushmead Prim Sch
Stopsley Common
Luton Sixth Form Coll
Cvn Site
St Joseph's RC Jun & Inf Schs
William Austin Jun & Inf Schs
Stopsley High Sch
NEW BEDFORD RD
River Lea or Lee
A5228
STOCKINGSTONE RD
LUTON
Swimming Pool
Luton Mus & Art Gall
Wardown Park
Round Green
Biscot
Works
Maidenhall Jun & Inf Sch
Denbigh High Sch
Richmond Hill Sch
People's Park
LEAGRAVE RD
Britannia Ests
LU4
Bury Park
B579
Portland Ct
Oxen Ind Est
A6
1 CAROLYN CT
2 ALMOND CL
TEMPLE CL 1
PYTCHLEY CL 2
1 ARNCLIFFE CRES
2 BLAKEDOWN
63
46
D1
1 THE OLD HAT FACTORY
2 RYE HILL
3 CARDINAL CT
4 COUNTESS CT
5 DAUPHIN CT
6 BISHOPS CT
7 BARONS CT
8 ERMINE PL
9 MARQUIS CT
D1
10 GARTER CT
11 VISCOUNT CT
12 LORDS PL
13 DUKES RIDE
14 QUEENS CT
15 PRINCES PL
16 BRAITHWAITE CT
17 MALZEARD CT

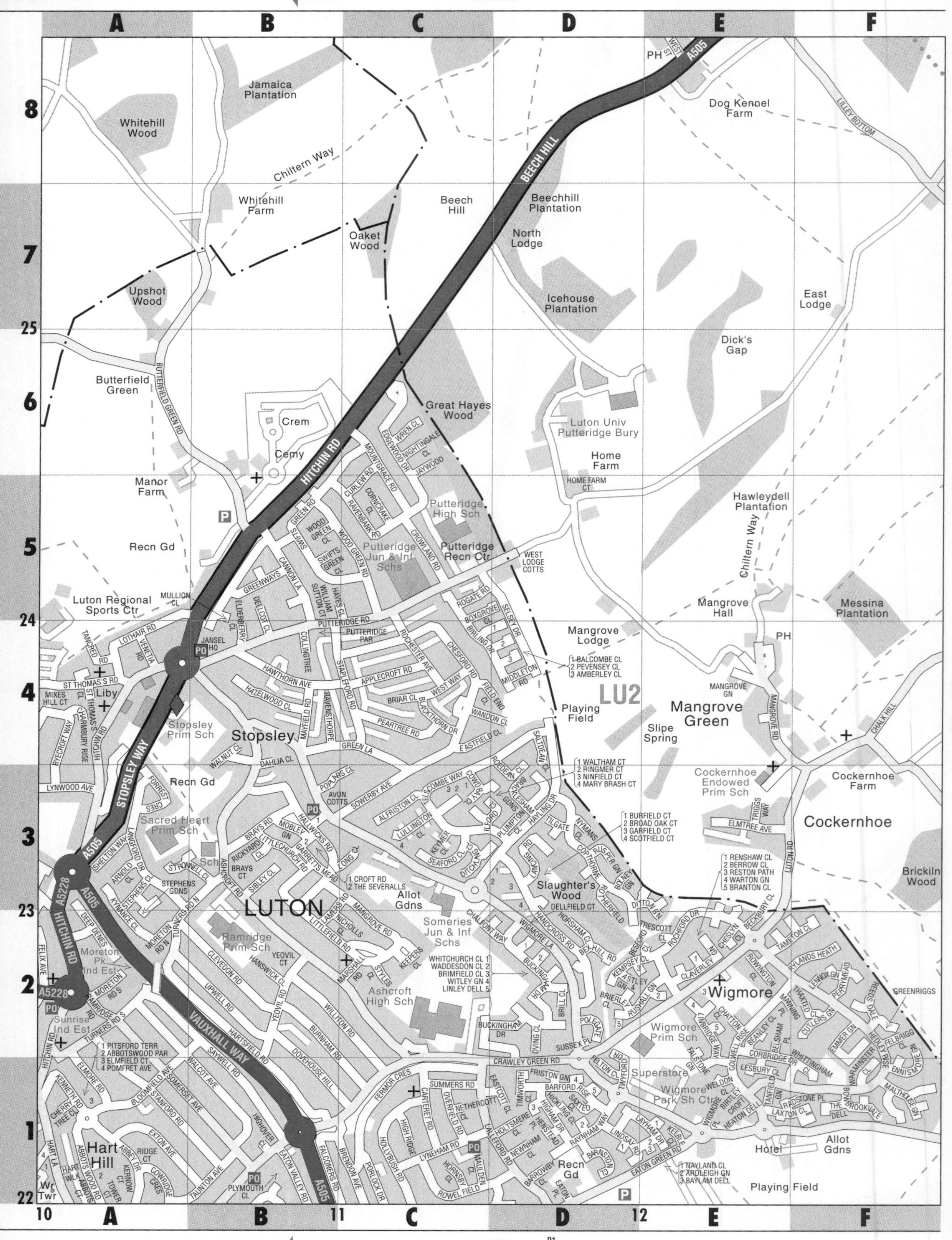

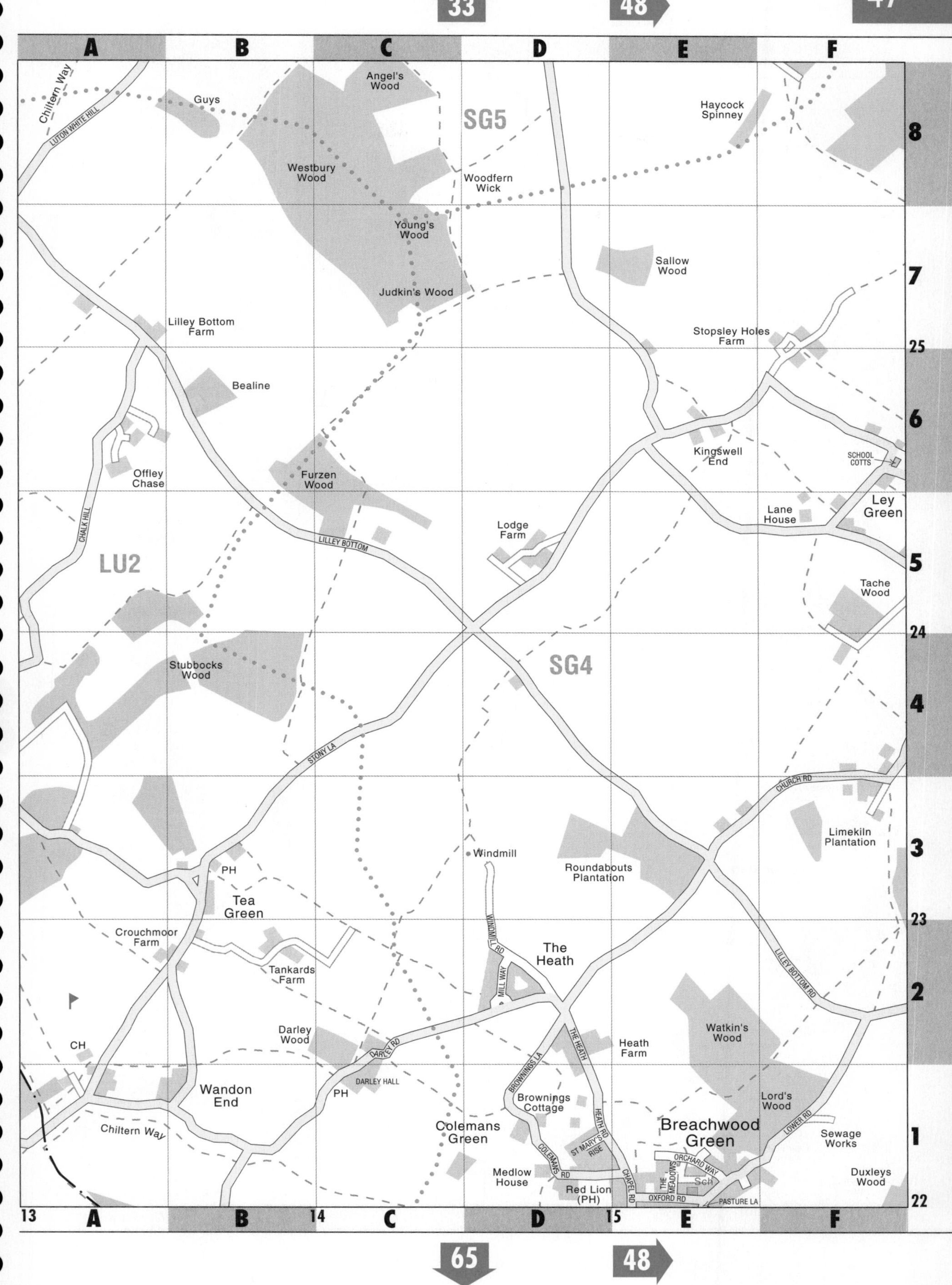

Chiltern Way
LUTON WHITE HILL

Guys

Angel's
Wood

SG5

Haycock
Spinney

Westbury
Wood

Woodfern
Wick

Young's
Wood

Sallow
Wood

Judkin's Wood

Lilley Bottom
Farm

Stopsley Holes
Farm

25

Bealine

CHALK HILL

Offley
Chase

Furzen
Wood

LILLEY BOTTOM

Kingswell
End

SCHOOL
COTTS

Lane
House

Ley
Green

Lodge
Farm

LU2

Tache
Wood

5

24

Stubbocks
Wood

SG4

4

STONY LA

CHURCH RD

Limekiln
Plantation

Windmill

Roundabouts
Plantation

3

LILLEY BOTTOM RD

23

PH

Tea
Green

The
Heath

2

Crouchmoor
Farm

WINDMILL RD

MILL WAY

Tankards
Farm

Watkin's
Wood

CH

Darley
Wood

THE HEATH

Heath
Farm

DARL'S RD

Wandon
End

DARLEY HALL

PH

BROWNINGS LA

Brownings
Cottage

Lord's
Wood

LOWER RD

Breachwood
Green

Sewage
Works

Chiltern Way

Colemans
Green

HEATH RD

ST MARY'S RISE

ORCHARD WAY

Medlow
House

COLEMANS RD

Red Lion
(PH)

CHAPEL RD

THE MEADOWS

OXFORD RD

ScH

PASTURE LA

Duxleys
Wood

22

13   A   14   B   C   D   15   E   F

47
34

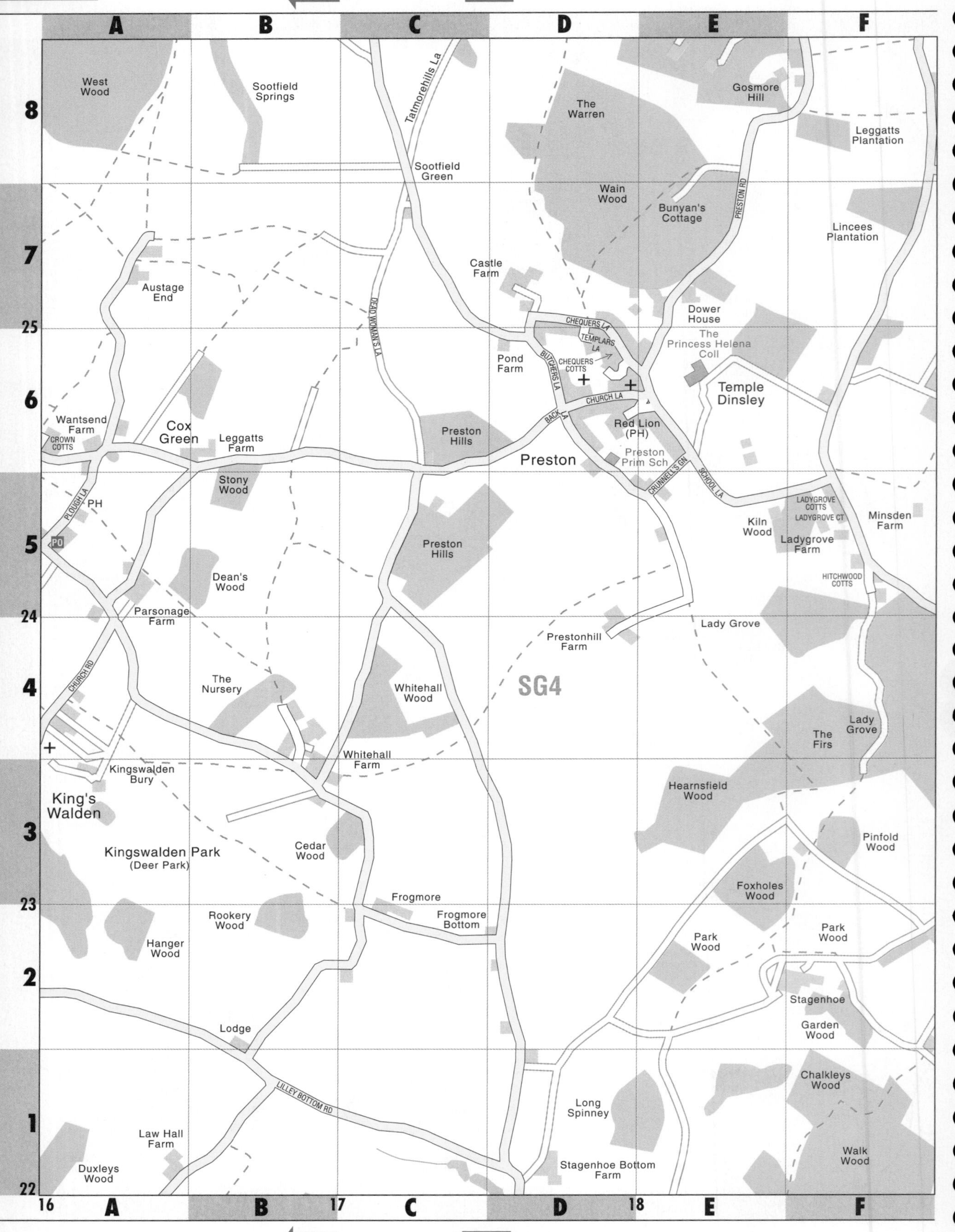
A
B
C
D
E
F
West Wood
Sootfield Springs
Tatmorehills La
The Warren
Gosmore Hill
Leggatts Plantation
Sootfield Green
Wain Wood
Bunyan's Cottage
PRESTON RD
Lincees Plantation
Castle Farm
Austage End
DEAD WOMAN'S LA
Dower House
CHEQUERS LA
TEMPLARS LA
The Princess Helena Coll
Pond Farm
BUTCHERS LA
CHEQUERS COTTS
Temple Dinsley
CHURCH LA
Wantsend Farm
CROWN COTTS
Cox Green
Leggatts Farm
Preston Hills
BACK LA
Red Lion (PH)
Preston
Preston Prim Sch
CRUNNELL'S GN
SCHOOL LA
Stony Wood
PLOUGH LA
PH
PO
LADYGROVE COTTS
LADYGROVE CT
Kiln Wood
Ladygrove Farm
Minsden Farm
Preston Hills
Dean's Wood
HITCHWOOD COTTS
Parsonage Farm
Lady Grove
Prestonhill Farm
CHURCH RD
The Nursery
Whitehall Wood
SG4
Lady Grove
The Firs
Whitehall Farm
Kingswalden Bury
King's Walden
Hearnsfield Wood
Kingswalden Park (Deer Park)
Cedar Wood
Pinfold Wood
Foxholes Wood
Frogmore
Rookery Wood
Frogmore Bottom
Park Wood
Park Wood
Hanger Wood
Stagenhoe
Garden Wood
Lodge
LILLEY BOTTOM RD
Chalkleys Wood
Long Spinney
Law Hall Farm
Duxleys Wood
Stagenhoe Bottom Farm
Walk Wood
8
7
25
6
5
24
4
3
23
2
1
22
16
17
18

47
66

35
50

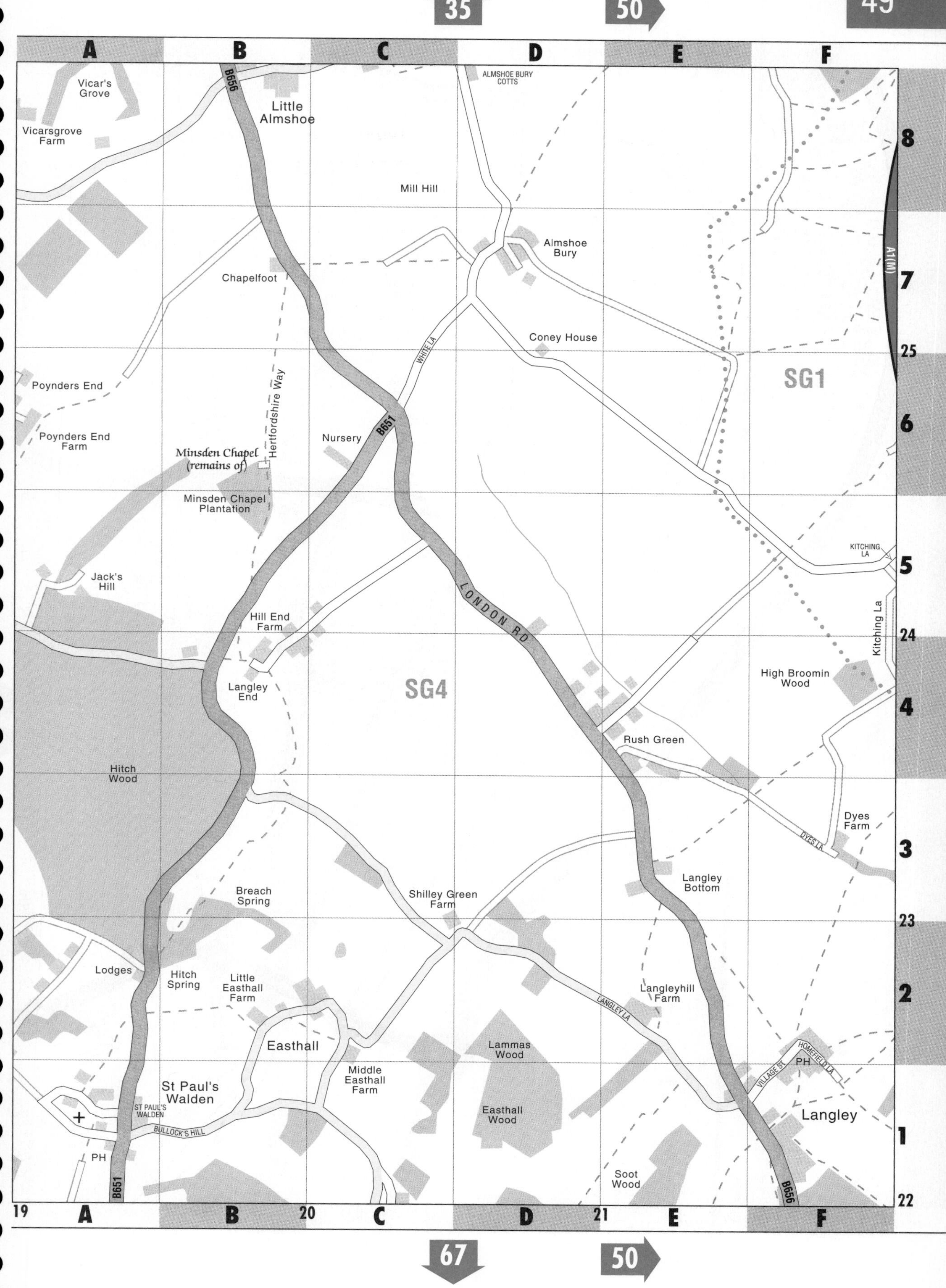
Vicar's Grove
Vicarsgrove Farm
Little Almshoe
B656
ALMSHOE BURY COTTS
Mill Hill
Almshoe Bury
Chapelfoot
Coney House
WHITE LA
SG1
A1(M)
Poynders End
Poynders End Farm
Hertfordshire Way
Nursery
B651
Minsden Chapel (remains of)
Minsden Chapel Plantation
Jack's Hill
KITCHING LA
Kitching La
LONDON RD
Hill End Farm
SG4
Langley End
High Broomin Wood
Rush Green
Hitch Wood
Dyes Farm
DYES LA
Breach Spring
Shilley Green Farm
Langley Bottom
Lodges
Hitch Spring
Little Easthall Farm
Langleyhill Farm
LANGLEY LA
Easthall
Lammas Wood
Middle Easthall Farm
HOMEFIELD LA
VILLAGE ST
PH
St Paul's Walden
ST PAUL'S WALDEN
BULLOCK'S HILL
Easthall Wood
Langley
PH
Soot Wood
A B C D E F
8 7 25 6 5 24 4 3 23 2 1 22
19 20 21

67
50

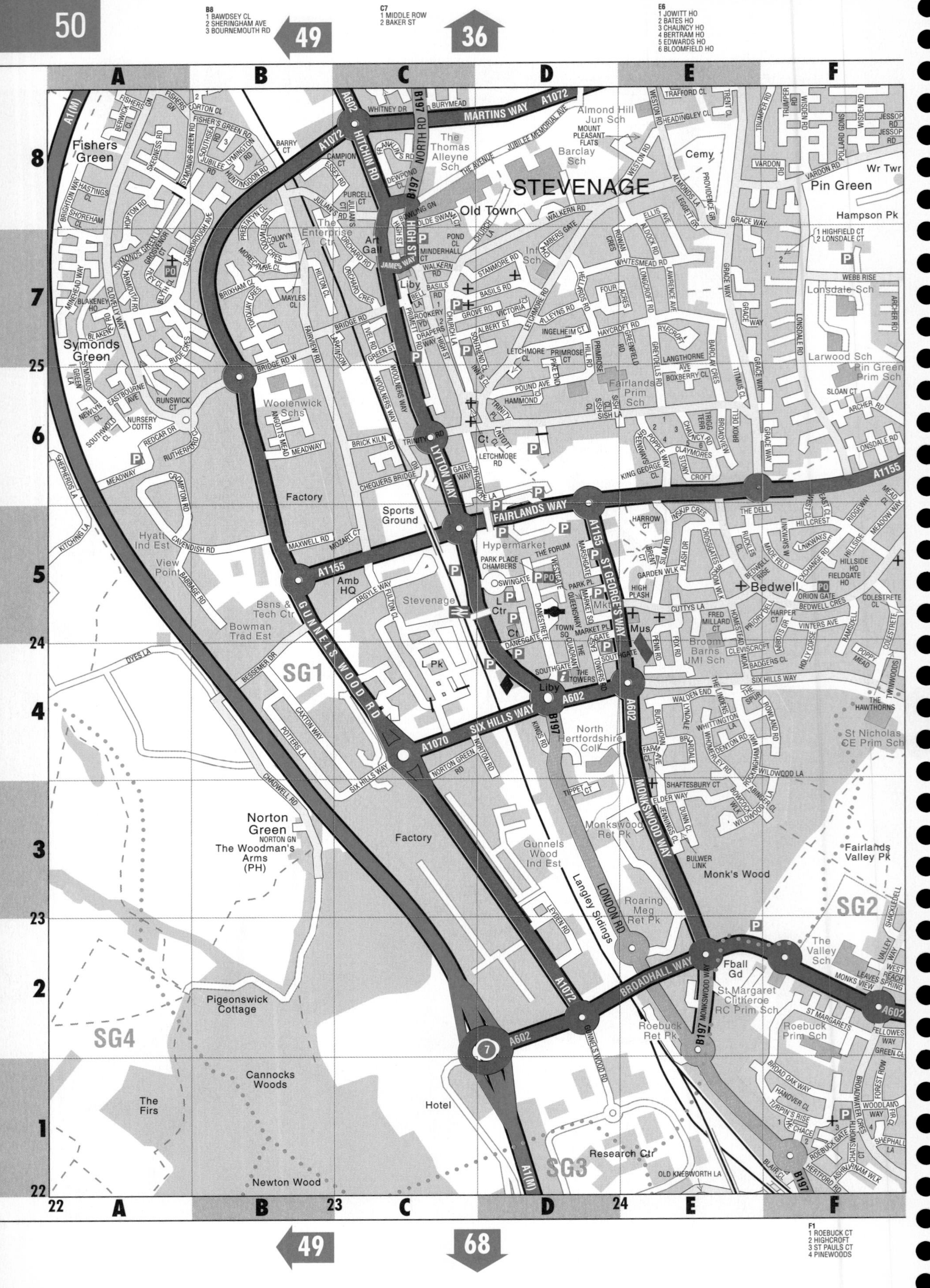
B8
1 BAWDSEY CL
2 SHERINGHAM AVE
3 BOURNEMOUTH RD
49
C7
1 MIDDLE ROW
2 BAKER ST
36
E6
1 JOWITT HO
2 BATES HO
3 CHAUNCY HO
4 BERTRAM HO
5 EDWARDS HO
6 BLOOMFIELD HO
A
B
C
D
E
F
8
7
25
6
5
24
4
3
23
2
1
22
STEVENAGE
Old Town
Fishers Green
Symonds Green
Pin Green
Bedwell
Norton Green
The Woodman's Arms (PH)
Pigeonswick Cottage
Cannocks Woods
The Firs
Newton Wood
Research Ctr
Hotel
Factory
Sports Ground
Hypermarket
Stevenage
Hyatt Ind Est
View Point
Bsns & Tech Ctr
Bowman Trad Est
Amb HQ
Woolenwick Schs
The Thomas Alleyne Sch
Almond Hill Jun Sch
Barclay Sch
Cemy
Lonsdale Sch
Larwood Sch
Pin Green Prim Sch
Fairlands Prim Sch
Broom Barns JMI Sch
North Hertfordshire Coll
Monkswood Ret Pk
Gunnels Wood Ind Est
Langley Sidings
Roaring Meg Ret Pk
Monk's Wood
Fairlands Valley Pk
St Nicholas CE Prim Sch
The Valley Sch
Fball Gd
St Margaret Clitheroe RC Prim Sch
Roebuck Ret Pk
Roebuck Prim Sch
Hampson Pk
Wr Twr
SG1
SG2
SG3
SG4
A1(M)
A602
A1072
A1155
A1070
B197
MARTINS WAY
HITCHIN RD
NORTH RD
HIGH ST
LYTTON WAY
FAIRLANDS WAY
GUNNELS WOOD RD
SIX HILLS WAY
ST GEORGE'S WAY
MONKSWOOD WAY
BROADHALL WAY
LONDON RD
GRACE WAY
OLD KNEBWORTH LA
68
F1
1 ROEBUCK CT
2 HIGHCROFT
3 ST PAULS CT
4 PINEWOODS

A8
1 JARDINE CT
2 HENDREN CT

C8
1 MARCUS CL
2 TACITUS CL
3 MINERVA CL

37
52

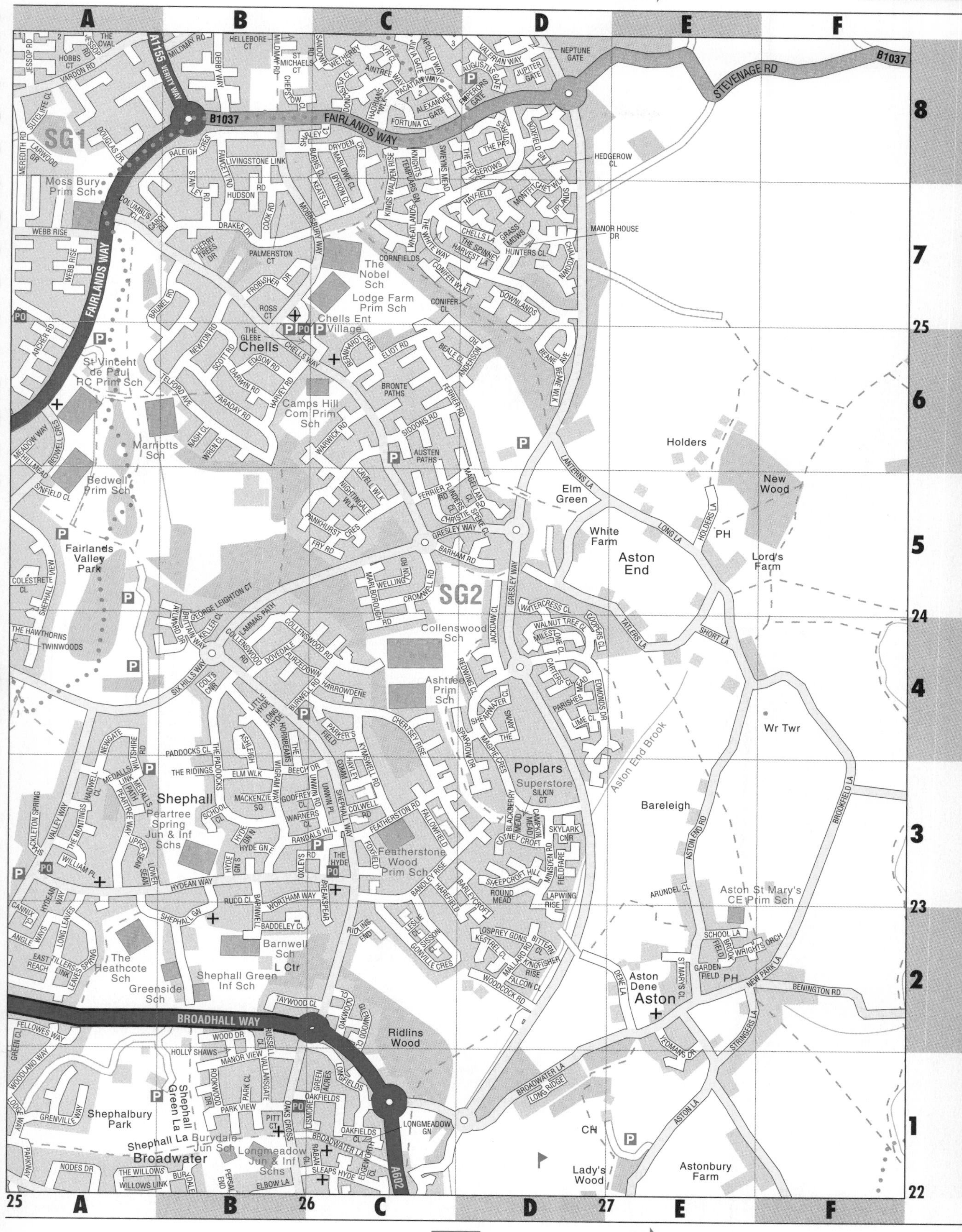

69
52

51
38

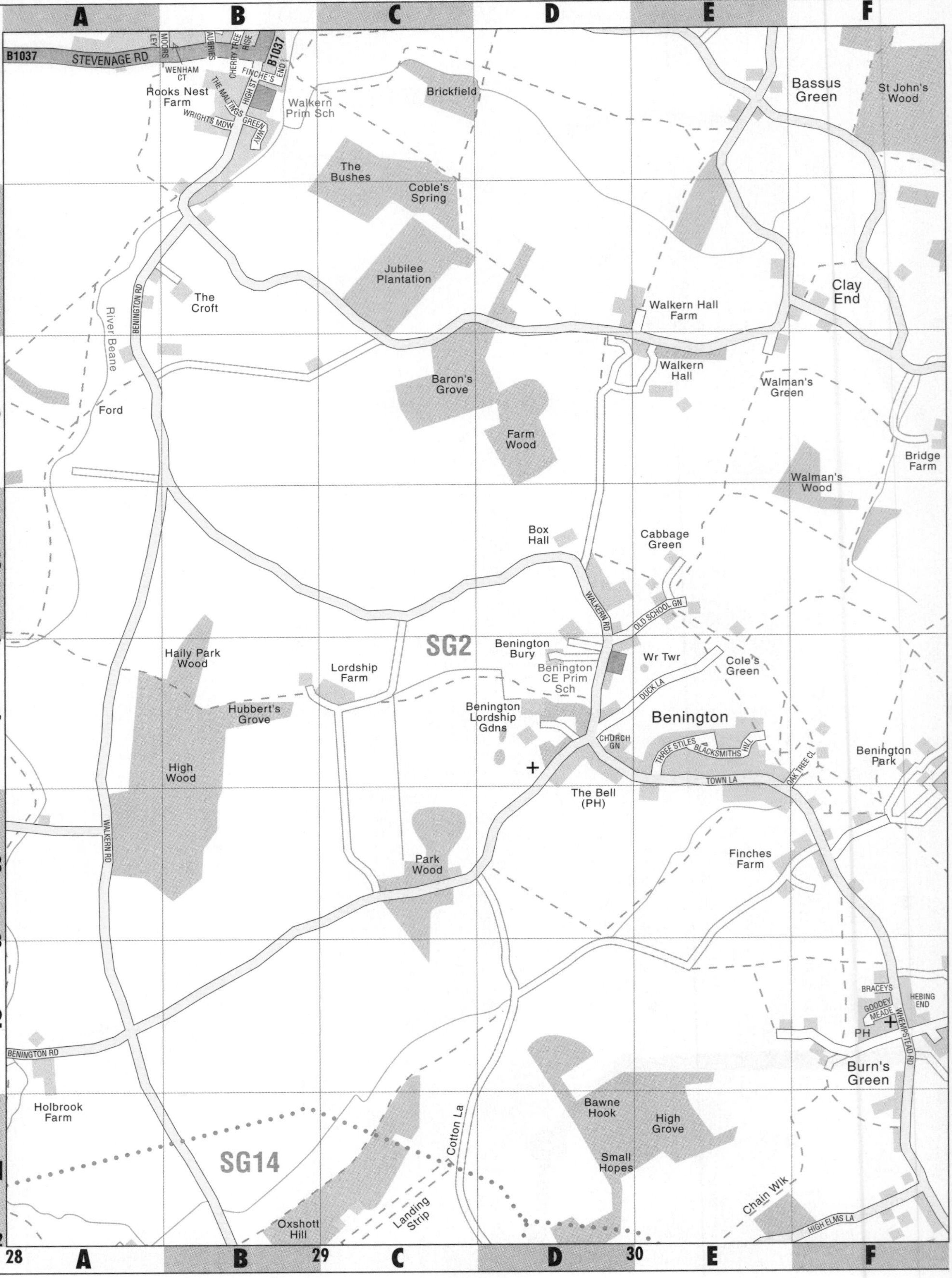

A B C D E F

8

B1037 STEVENAGE RD

Rooks Nest Farm
WENHAM CT
THE MALTINGS
WRIGHTS MDW
CHERRY TREE RISE
HIGH ST
FINCHE'S
B1037 END
AUBRIES
MOORS
LEY
GREEN
AWAY

Walkern Prim Sch

Brickfield

Bassus Green

St John's Wood

The Bushes

Coble's Spring

7

Benington Rd
The Croft

Jubilee Plantation

Walkern Hall Farm

Clay End

25

River Beane

Ford

Baron's Grove

Walkern Hall

Walman's Green

6

Farm Wood

Walman's Wood

Bridge Farm

5

Box Hall

Cabbage Green

24

Haily Park Wood

Lordship Farm

SG2

Benington Bury

Walkern Rd
Old School Gn

Wr Twr

Cole's Green

Benington CE Prim Sch

4

Hubbert's Grove

Benington Lordship Gdns

Duck La

Benington

High Wood

Walkern Rd

Church Gn

Three Stiles
Blacksmiths Hill

Oak Tree Cl

Benington Park

The Bell (PH)

Town La

3

Park Wood

Finches Farm

23

Benington Rd

2

Benington Rd

Braceys
Goodey Meade
Hebing End
Whempstead Rd
PH

Burn's Green

Holbrook Farm

1

SG14

Bawne Hook

High Grove

Cotton La

Small Hopes

Chain Wlk

Oxshott Hill

Landing Strip

High Elms La

22

28 A B 29 C D 30 E F

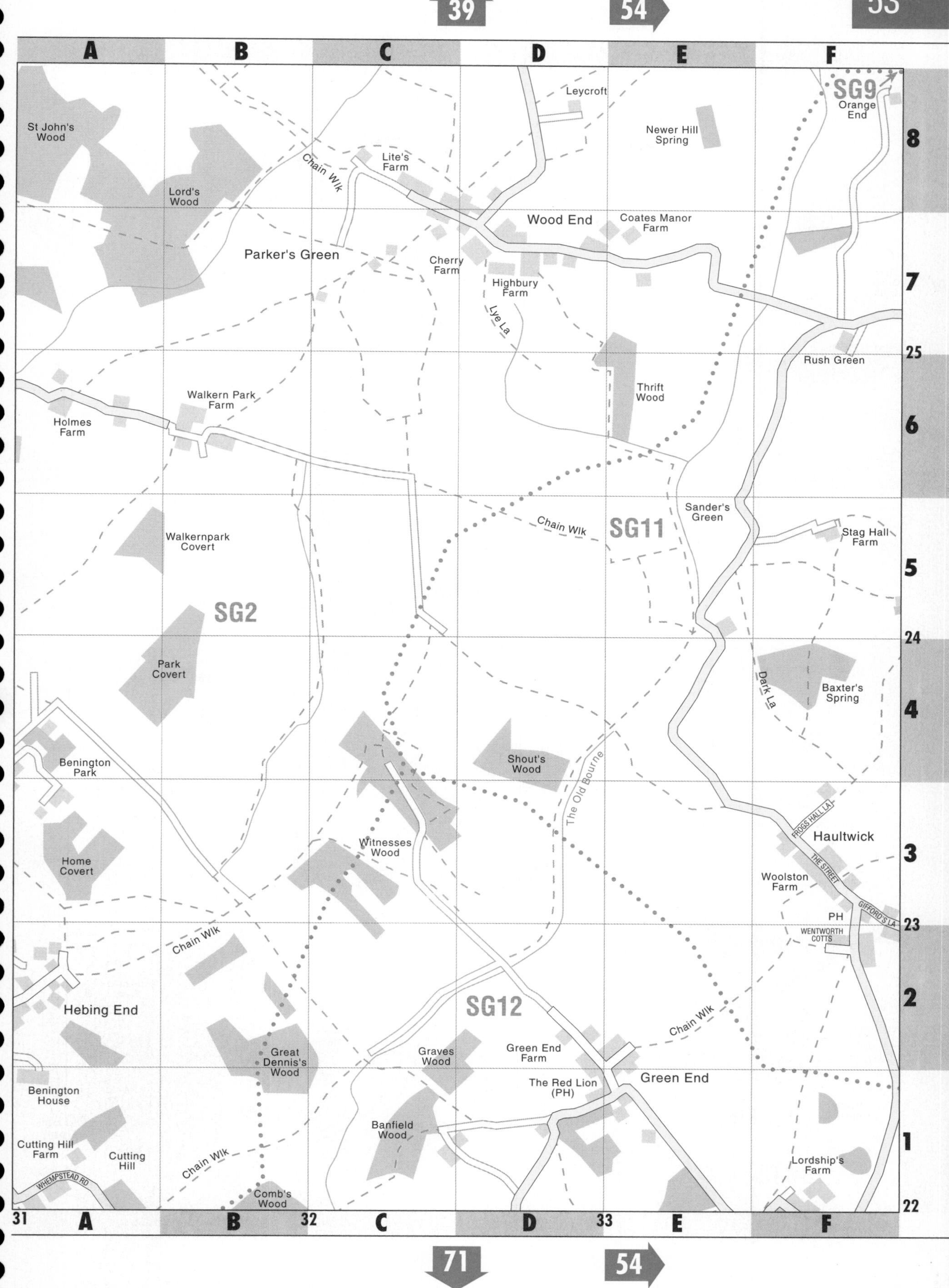

A B C D E F

8

Leycroft

St John's
Wood

Newer Hill
Spring

SG9
Orange
End

Lord's
Wood

Chain Wlk

Lite's
Farm

Wood End

Coates Manor
Farm

7

Parker's Green

Cherry
Farm

Highbury
Farm

Lye La

25

Rush Green

Walkern Park
Farm

Thrift
Wood

6

Holmes
Farm

Chain Wlk

SG11

Sander's
Green

Stag Hall
Farm

5

Walkernpark
Covert

SG2

24

Park
Covert

Dark La

Baxter's
Spring

4

Benington
Park

Shout's
Wood

The Old Bourne

FROGS HALL LA

Haultwick

3

Home
Covert

Witnesses
Wood

Woolston
Farm

THE STREET

Chain Wlk

PH

GIFFORD'S LA

23

WENTWORTH
COTTS

2

Hebing End

SG12

Chain Wlk

Great
Dennis's
Wood

Graves
Wood

Green End
Farm

Green End

Benington
House

The Red Lion
(PH)

1

Cutting Hill
Farm

Cutting
Hill

Chain Wlk

Banfield
Wood

Lordship's
Farm

WHEMPSTEAD RD

Comb's
Wood

22

31 A B 32 C D 33 E F

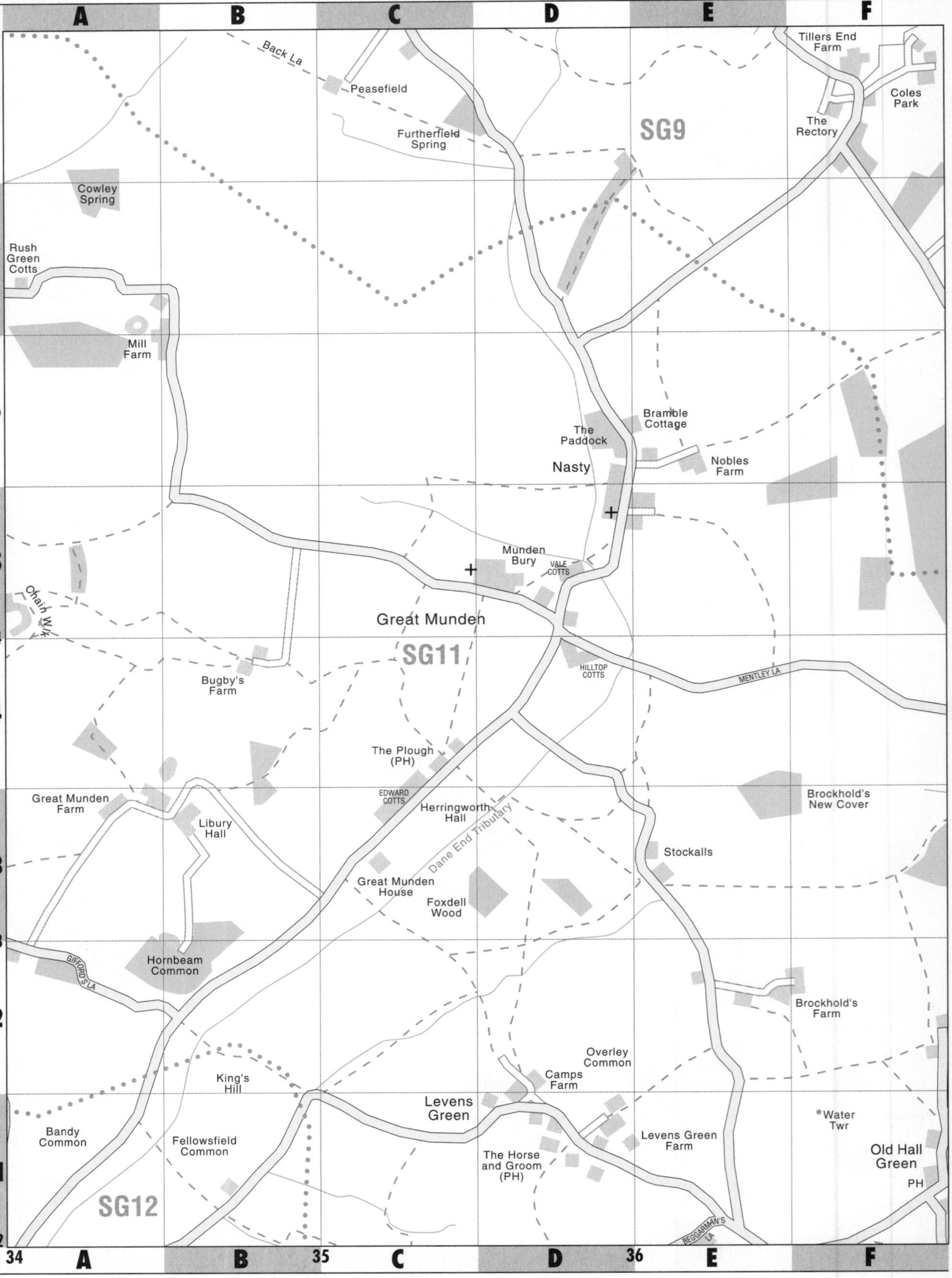

A B C D E F

8

Back La

Peasefield

Furtherfield
Spring

SG9

Tillers End
Farm

Coles
Park

The
Rectory

Cowley
Spring

7

Rush
Green
Cotts

Mill
Farm

25

6

Bramble
Cottage

The
Paddock

Nobles
Farm

Nasty

Chain Wk

5

Munden
Bury

VALE
COTTS

Great Munden

SG11

24

HILLTOP
COTTS

MENTLEY LA

Bugby's
Farm

4

The Plough
(PH)

EDWARD
COTTS

Herringworth
Hall

Brockhold's
New Cover

Great Munden
Farm

Libury
Hall

Dane End Tributary

Great Munden
House

Foxdell
Wood

Stockalls

3

GIFFORD'S LA

Hornbeam
Common

23

Brockhold's
Farm

2

Overley
Common

King's
Hill

Camps
Farm

Levens
Green

Levens Green
Farm

Water
Twr

Bandy
Common

Fellowsfield
Common

The Horse
and Groom
(PH)

Old Hall
Green

PH

1

SG12

BEGGARMAN'S LA

22

34 A B 35 C D 36 E F

41
56

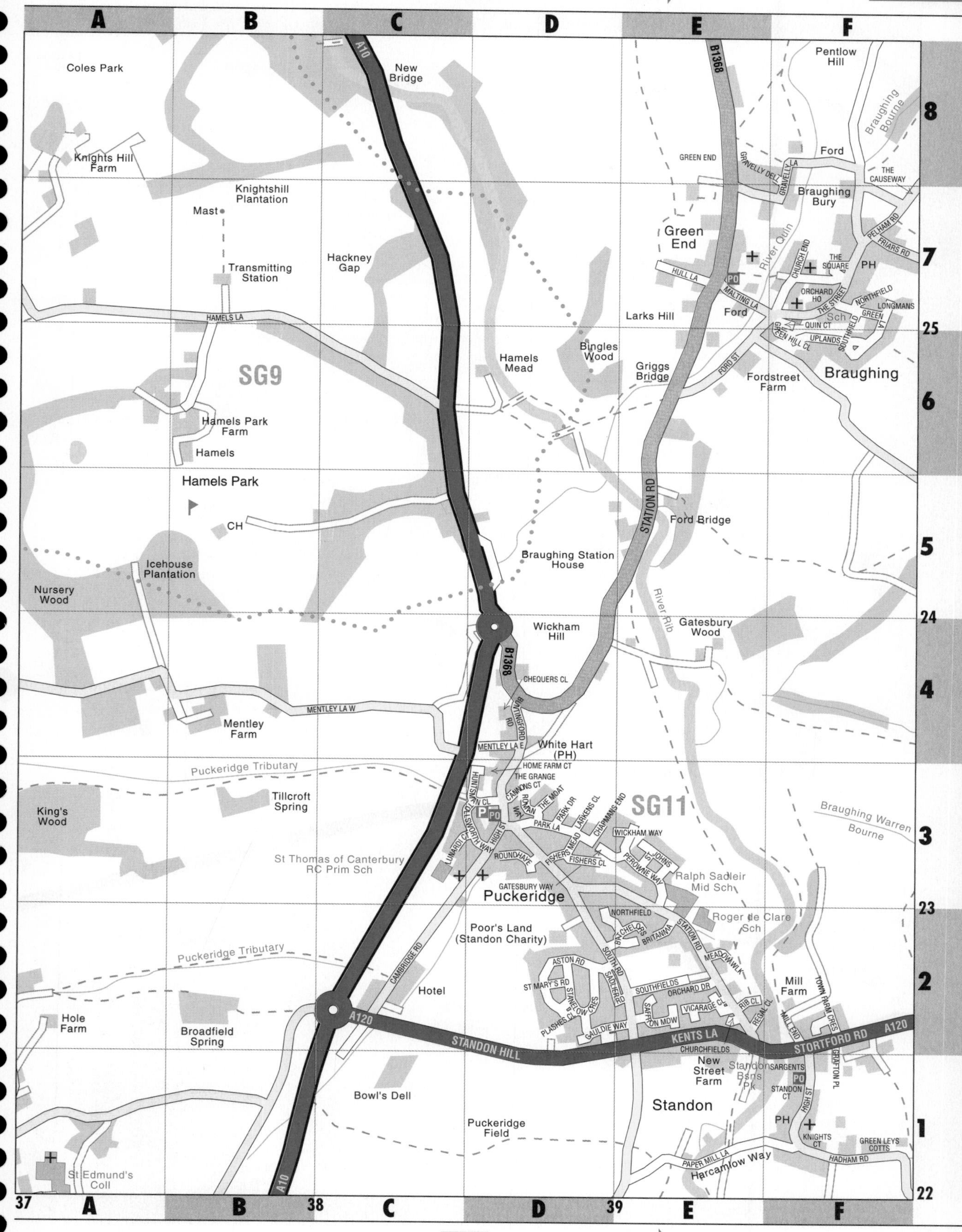

A
B
C
D
E
F
Coles Park
New Bridge
Pentlow Hill
Braughing Bourne
8
Knights Hill Farm
Knightshill Plantation
Mast
GREEN END
GRAVELLY DELL
GRAVELLY LA
Ford
THE CAUSEWAY
Braughing Bury
PELHAM RD
FRIARS RD
Green End
River Quin
CHURCH END
THE SQUARE
PH
7
Transmitting Station
Hackney Gap
HULL LA
PO
MALTING LA
ORCHARD HO
THE STREET
NORTHFIELD
LONGMANS
HAMELS LA
Larks Hill
Ford
QUIN CT
Sch
GREEN LA
GREEN HILL CL
UPLANDS
SOUTHFIELD
25
SG9
Hamels Mead
Bingles Wood
Griggs Bridge
FORD ST
Fordstreet Farm
Braughing
6
Hamels Park Farm
Hamels
Hamels Park
STATION RD
CH
Ford Bridge
5
Icehouse Plantation
Braughing Station House
Nursery Wood
River Rib
24
Wickham Hill
Gatesbury Wood
B1368
CHEQUERS CL
BUNTINGFORD RD
4
MENTLEY LA W
Mentley Farm
MENTLEY LA E
White Hart (PH)
HOME FARM CT
Puckeridge Tributary
THE GRANGE
CANNONS CT
Tillcroft Spring
HUNTSMAN CL
ROMAN WAY
THE MOAT
PARK DR
LARKENS CL
CHAPMANS END
SG11
King's Wood
ELLSWORTH WAY
P
PO
PARK LA
Braughing Warren Bourne
3
HIGH ST
WICKHAM WAY
JOHNS
LUNARDI CT
ROUNDHAYE
FISHERS MEAD
FISHERS CL
PEROWNE WAY
St Thomas of Canterbury RC Prim Sch
Ralph Sadleir Mid Sch
GATESBURY WAY
Puckeridge
23
NORTHFIELD
Roger de Clare Sch
Poor's Land (Standon Charity)
BATCHELORS
BRITANNIA
STATION RD
Puckeridge Tributary
CAMBRIDGE RD
ASTON RD
SOUTH RD
MEADOW WALK
Mill Farm
TOWN FARM CRES
2
ST MARY'S RD
STANELOW CRES
SADLER RD
SOUTHFIELDS
ORCHARD DR
Hotel
VICARAGE CL
RIB CL
REGAL CL
MILL END
Hole Farm
A120
PLASHES CL
GAULDIE WAY
SAFFRON MDW
KENTS LA
STORTFORD RD
A120
Broadfield Spring
STANDON HILL
CHURCHFIELDS
GRAFTON PL
New Street Farm
Standon Bsns Pk
SARGENTS
PO
Bowl's Dell
Standon
STANDON CT
HIGH ST
Puckeridge Field
PH
1
KNIGHTS CT
GREEN LEYS COTTS
PAPER MILL LA
Harcamlow Way
HADHAM RD
St Edmund's Coll
A10
22
37
38
39

73
56

55
42

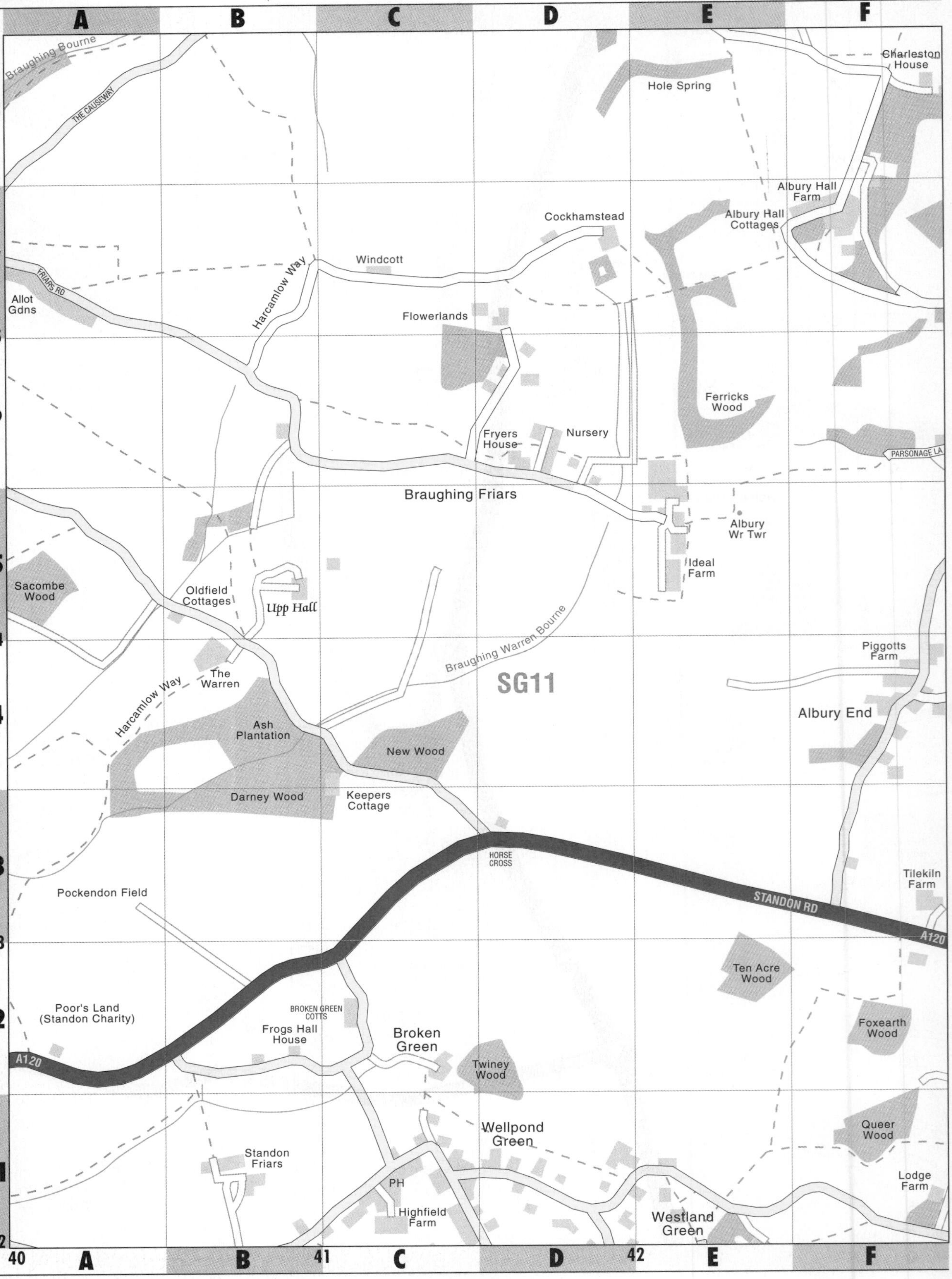

A B C D E F

8

7

25

6

5

24

4

3

23

2

1

22

40 41 42

Braughing Bourne
THE CAUSWAY
FRIARS RD
Allot Gdns
Harcamlow Way
Windcott
Flowerlands
Hole Spring
Cockhamstead
Charleston House
Albury Hall Farm
Albury Hall Cottages
Ferricks Wood
PARSONAGE LA
Fryers House
Nursery
Braughing Friars
Albury Wr Twr
Ideal Farm
Sacombe Wood
Oldfield Cottages
Upp Hall
Braughing Warren Bourne
SG11
Piggotts Farm
Harcamlow Way
The Warren
Ash Plantation
New Wood
Darney Wood
Keepers Cottage
Albury End
HORSE CROSS
STANDON RD
A120
Tilekiln Farm
Pockendon Field
Ten Acre Wood
Poor's Land (Standon Charity)
A120
BROKEN GREEN COTTS
Frogs Hall House
Broken Green
Twiney Wood
Foxearth Wood
Wellpond Green
Queer Wood
Standon Friars
PH
Highfield Farm
Westland Green
Lodge Farm

55
74

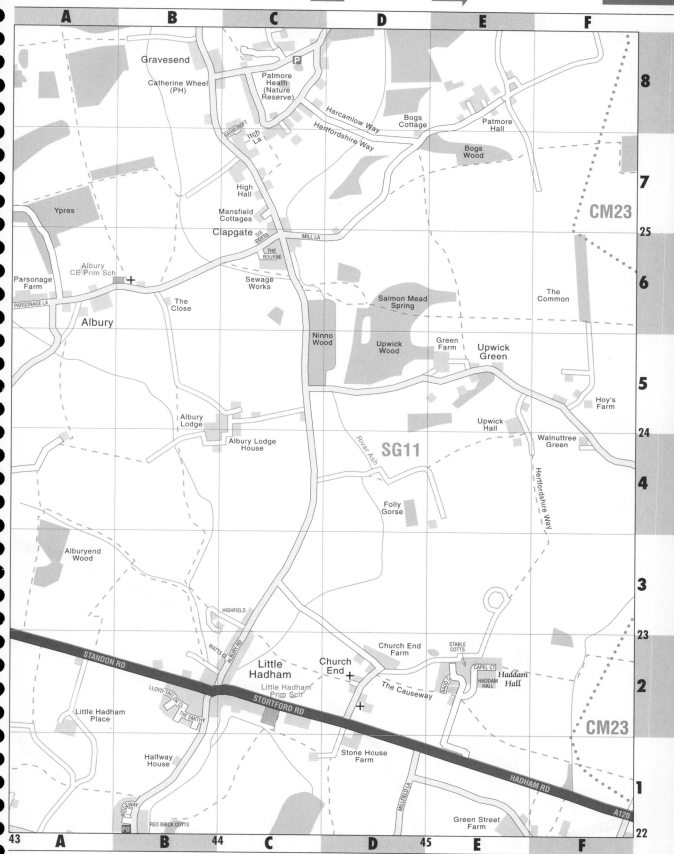

A   B   C   D   E   F

8

Gravesend

Catherine Wheel
(PH)

Patmore
Heath
(Nature
Reserve)

Bogs
Cottage

Patmore
Hall

Harcamlow Way

Hertfordshire Way

BARNCROFT

Itch
La

Bogs
Wood

7

High
Hall

CM23

Ypres

Mansfield
Cottages

SIX
COTTS

MILL LA

25

Clapgate

THE
BOURNE

The Common

6

Parsonage
Farm

Albury
CE Prim Sch

Sewage
Works

Salmon Mead
Spring

PARSONAGE LA

The
Close

Ninno
Wood

Upwick
Wood

Green
Farm

Upwick
Green

Albury

Hoy's
Farm

5

Albury
Lodge

Albury Lodge
House

River Ash

SG11

Upwick
Hall

Walnuttree
Green

24

Hertfordshire Way

4

Alburyend
Wood

Folly
Gorse

3

HIGHFIELD

23

STANDON RD

Church End
Farm

STABLE
COTTS

WATTS CL

ALBURY RD

Little
Hadham

Church
End

The Causeway

CAPEL CT

BAUD CL

HADDAM
HALL

Haddam
Hall

2

Little Hadham
Prim Sch

LLOYD-TAYLOR CL

THE SMITHY

STORTFORD RD

Little Hadham
Place

Halfway
House

Stone House
Farm

MILLFIELD LA

CM23

RIDGEWAY

PO

RED BRICK COTTS

Green Street
Farm

HADHAM RD

A120

1

22

57

A
B
C
D
E
F
North Essex STREET ATLAS
8
7
25
6
5
24
4
3
23
2
1
22
46
47
48
The Folly
Lincolns
Harcamlow Way
Oozes Wood
Home Wood
Shaw Wood
Farnham Green
Savenend Cottage
Savenend Farm
Shawwood Cottage
Farnham Hall
Thrifts
Chatter End
Hassobury
Farnham CE Prim Sch
New Wood
THRIMLEY LA
RECTORY LA
GLOBE CRES
RECTORY DR
Globe Farm
Thrimley La
Thrimley House
Farnham
Long Belt
Walkers
Oak Plantation
Bourne Bridge
Ford
Longdown Plantation
Level's Green
Hill Farm
Earlsbury
MILL HILL
SG11
CM23
Hudshill Plantation
Moorfield Spring
WALNUT TREE LA
Walnut Tree Cottages
Bourne Brook
Bailey Hills
FARNHAM RD
A120
Mast
Wickham Hall
Foxdells Farm
Hoggate's Wood
Bloodhounds' Wood
GRANGESIDE
FOXDELLS LA
BROADFIELD
THE GRANGE
DANE O'COYS RD
Whitehall Coll
WHITEHALL RD
WHITEHALL LA
GRANGE PK
B1004
Blackthorn Spring
Hadham Park
High Wood
FRERE CT
PINELANDS
CEDAR CT
RYE ST
Hertfordshire Way
Wr Twr
Ash Grove
ROBERT WALLACE CL
BARRELLS DOWN RD
LINDSEY RD
GALLOWAY RD
LINDSEY CL
REYNARD COPSE
STANE CL
Savernake
Hadham Lodge
Mast
Dane O'Coys Farm
CRICKETFIELD LA
HADHAM RD A120
A120
P

57
76

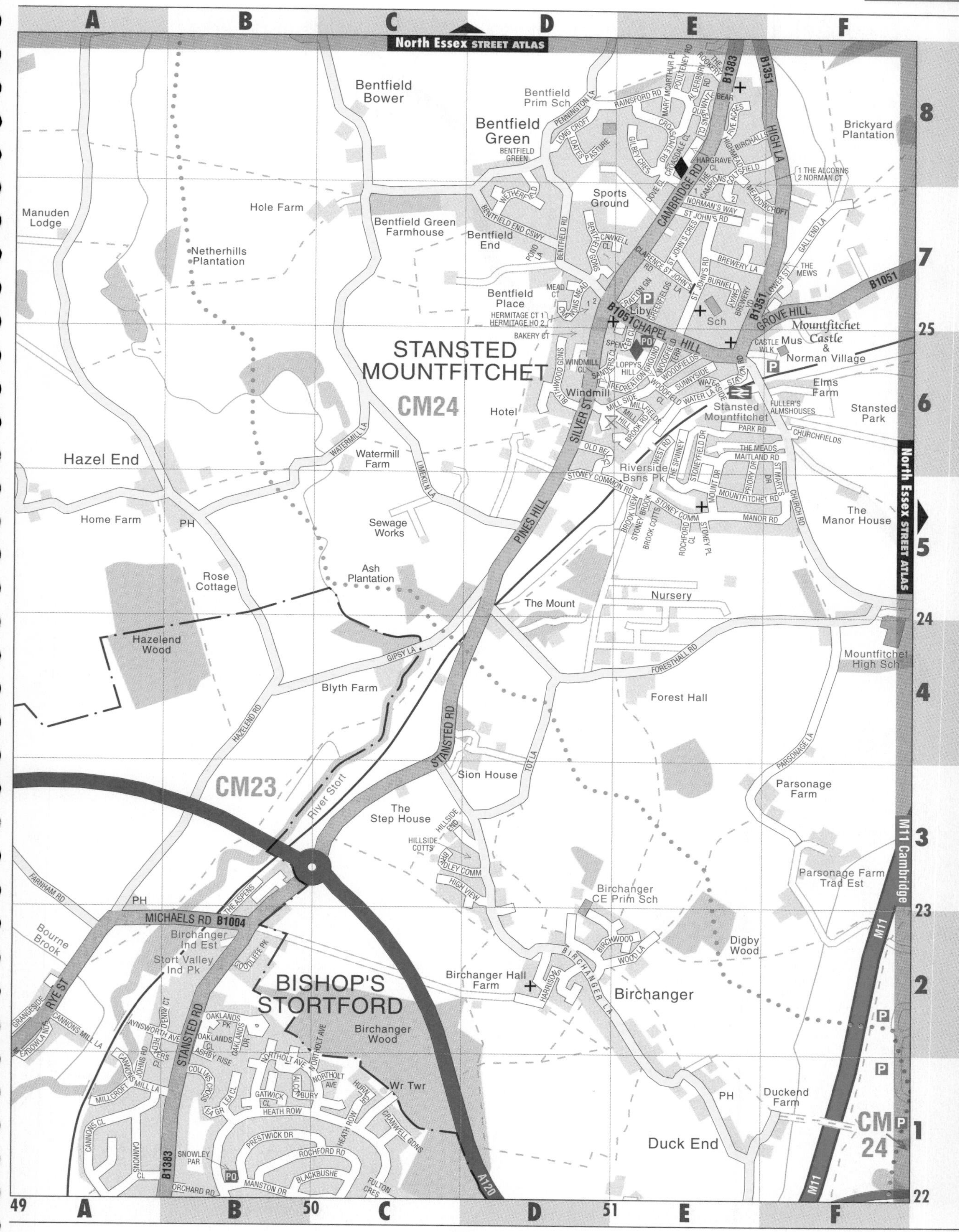

Bentfield
Bower

Bentfield
Prim Sch

Bentfield
Green

Brickyard
Plantation

1 THE ALCORNS
2 NORMAN CT

Manuden
Lodge

Hole Farm

Netherhills
Plantation

Bentfield Green
Farmhouse

Bentfield
End

Sports
Ground

THE
MEWS

Bentfield
Place

HERMITAGE CT 1
HERMITAGE HO 2

Mountfitchet
Castle
& Norman Village

Mus

Elms
Farm

Stansted
Park

STANSTED
MOUNTFITCHET

CM24

Hotel

Windmill

Stansted
Mountfitchet

FULLER'S
ALMSHOUSES

Hazel End

Watermill
Farm

Riverside
Bsns Pk

The
Manor House

Home Farm

PH

Sewage
Works

The Mount

Nursery

Mountfitchet
High Sch

Rose
Cottage

Ash
Plantation

Hazelend
Wood

Blyth Farm

Forest Hall

CM23

Sion House

Parsonage
Farm

River Stort

The
Step House

Hillside
Cotts

Parsonage Farm
Trad Est

HIGH VIEW

Birchanger
CE Prim Sch

Digby
Wood

FARNHAM RD

PH

MICHAELS RD B1004

THE ASPERS

Birchanger
Ind Est

Bourne
Brook

Stort Valley
Ind Pk

BISHOP'S
STORTFORD

Birchanger Hall
Farm

Birchanger

RYE ST

Birchanger
Wood

PH

Duckend
Farm

CM
24

Wr Twr

Duck End

PO

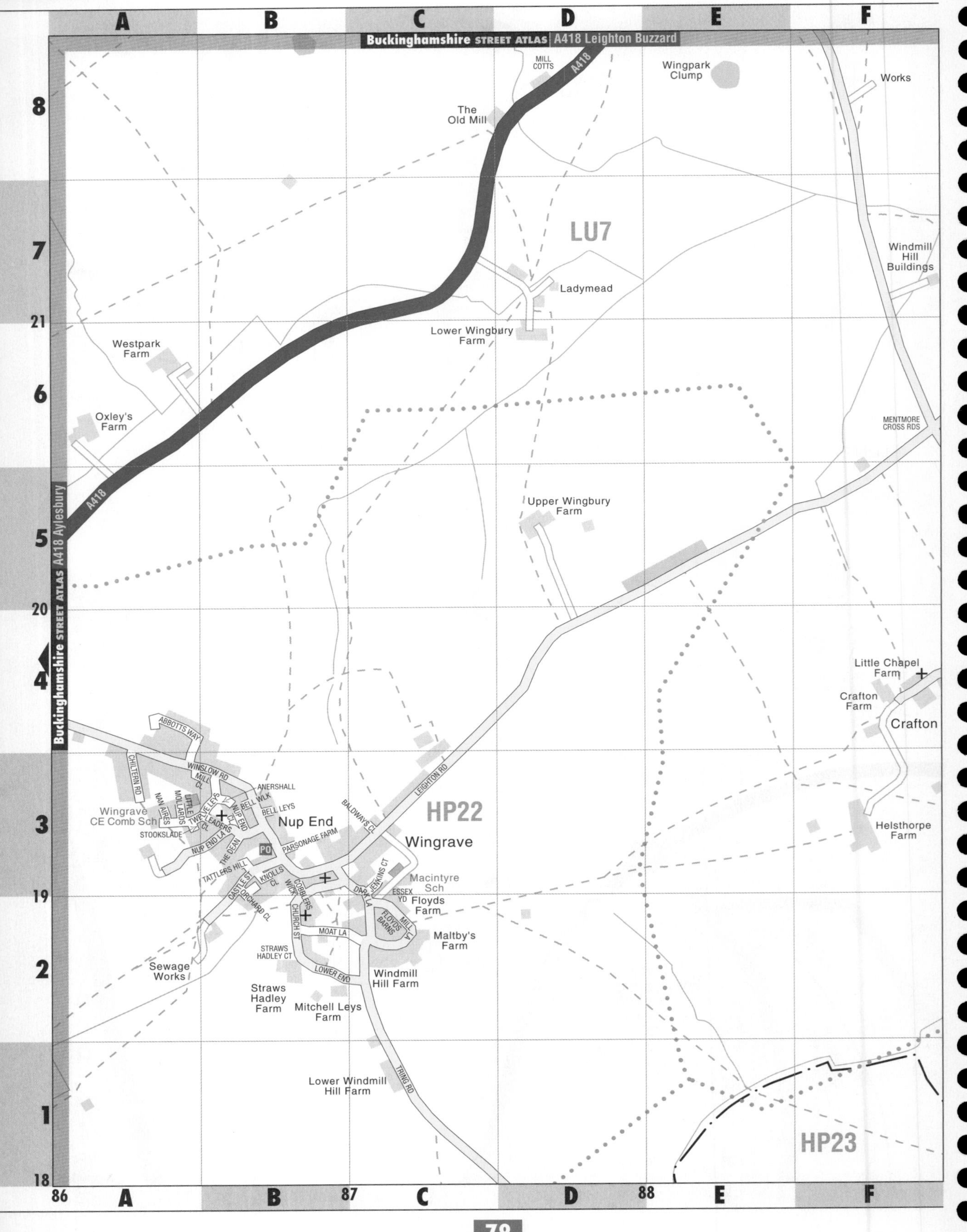

LU7

Mill Cotts

Wingpark Clump

Works

The Old Mill

A418

Windmill Hill Buildings

Ladymead

Lower Wingbury Farm

Westpark Farm

Mentmore Cross Rds

Oxley's Farm

A418 Aylesbury

Upper Wingbury Farm

Little Chapel Farm

Crafton Farm

Crafton

Abbotts Way

Winslow Rd

Mill Cl

Chiltern Rd

Nan Aires

Mollards Cl

Little Leaders Cl

Anershall

Bell Wlk

Bell Leys

Baldways Cl

Leighton Rd

HP22

Helsthorpe Farm

Wingrave CE Comb Sch

Stookslade

The Dean

Nup End La

Nup End

Parsonage Farm

PO

Nup End

Tattlers Hill

Castle St

Orchard Cl

Knolls Cl

Cobblers

Wick

Church Rd

Dmb La

Essex Yd

Gelvins Ct

Mill La

Floyds Barns

Macintyre Sch

Wingrave

Floyds Farm

Maltby's Farm

Sewage Works

Moat La

Straws Hadley Ct

Lower End

Windmill Hill Farm

Straws Hadley Farm

Mitchell Leys Farm

Tring Rd

Lower Windmill Hill Farm

HP23

Ledburn

Buckinghamshire STREET ATLAS

Manor Farm

MANOR FARM LA

LEYBURNE CL

WELL LA

Ledburn Farm

Whaddon Farm Cottages

Windmill Hill

Rowden Farm

B488

B488

LU7

Cricket Ground

Mentmore Stud

HOWELL HILL CL

The Belt

Wing Lodge

Mentmore

THE GREEN

PH

Home Farm

Mansom

Crafton Stud Farm

Mentmore

ROSEBERY MEWS

Big Wood

New Spinney

Mentmore Park

Crafton Stud

Crafton Lodge

Model Farm

CH

Bedfordshire STREET ATLAS

The Belt

HP23

STATION RD

89   90   91

LU5

LU4

LU4

Skimpot
Wood

Stanner's
Wood

Cultivation
Terraces

Mast

Chaul End
Farm

Foxdell
Jun Sch

COULSON CT

Ind
Est

Works

HAREFIELD
CT

BASINGWOLD GDNS
WARREN RD
DALLOW RD
KENT RD
SUMMERFIELD RD
RUNLEY RD
BILTON WAY
BILTON WAY
HAREFIELD RD

Chaul End

Tunnels

Zouches
Farm

Round
Wood

WOOD CL

Mast

Twentynine
Wood

CH

Bush
Wood

Badgerdell
Wood

BLUEBELL
WOOD CL

M1

Thirty
Wood

Blossom
Spring

Bedfordshire STREET ATLAS

Dame Ellen's
Wood

Castlecroft
Wood

Brickkiln
Farm

CHAUL END RD

LU1

Little John's
Wood

Folly
Wood

Cvn
Pk

Manor
Farm

RUSHMEAD CL
WELLER CL
COLLINGS
CADRIA
FOLLY LA
LUTON RD
MANOR CT
MEADOW CROFT

A5 Dunstable, Milton Keynes

Turnpike
Farm

Bury
Farm

Cradle
Spinney

ORCHARD CL
DELFIELD GDNS
MOSSMAN DR
PH
PO
MEADOW WAY
HEATHFIELD CL
HYDE RD
Heathfield
Lower Sch
FIVE OAKS
THE CRESCENT

Willowfield
Lower Sch

A5

Lodge
Farm

Gatehouse

HOLLY FARM CL
HAWTHORN CRES
SUTTON GDNS
OULWORTH CL
THE BELL
ELM AVE
AYSTONE RD
EDGECOTE CL
LEDWELL RD
FAIRGREEN CL
THE GLEN

Five Oaks
Mid Sch

Buncer's
Wood

Garden
Centre

Caddington

MILLFIELD WAY
CROSS PONDS
MARDLE CL
LITTLE GREEN LA
WOODLANDS
ENSLOW CL
MANOR RD

Tipplehill
Farm

Jockey
Farm

LU6

Kensworth
House

PH

Herons
Farm

Piper's
Farm

MANCROFT RD

Cvn
Pk

Aley
Green

Corner
Farm

Lynch
Farm

Nurseries

MILLFIELD LA

Cotswold
Bsns Pk

Millfield
Farm

PIPERS LA

Cemy

Kensworth
Lynch

AL3

Hill Farm

DUNSTABLE RD

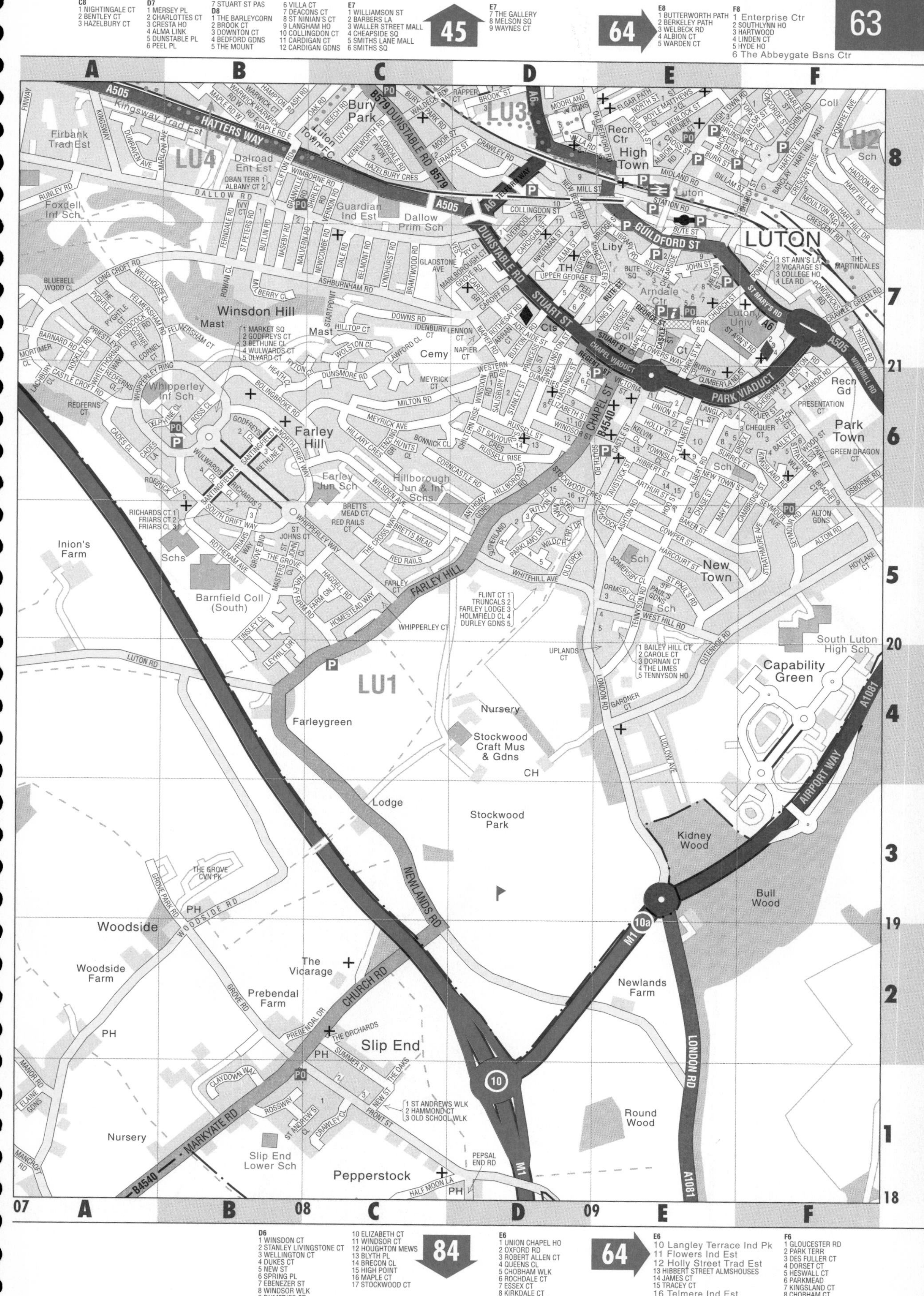
C8
1 NIGHTINGALE CT
2 BENTLEY CT
3 HAZELBURY CT
D7
1 MERSEY PL
2 CHARLOTTES CT
3 CRESTA HO
4 ALMA LINK
5 DUNSTABLE PL
6 PEEL PL
7 STUART ST PAS
D8
1 THE BARLEYCORN
2 BROOK CT
3 DOWNTON CT
4 BEDFORD GDNS
5 THE MOUNT
6 VILLA CT
7 DEACONS CT
8 ST NINIAN'S CT
9 LANGHAM HO
10 COLLINGDON CT
11 CARDIGAN CT
12 CARDIGAN GDNS
E7
1 WILLIAMSON ST
2 BARBERS LA
3 WALLER STREET MALL
4 CHEAPSIDE SQ
5 SMITHS LANE MALL
6 SMITHS SQ
45
E7
7 THE GALLERY
8 MELSON SQ
9 WAYNES CT
64
E8
1 BUTTERWORTH PATH
2 BERKELEY PATH
3 WELBECK RD
4 ALBION CT
5 WARDEN CT
F8
1 Enterprise Ctr
2 SOUTHLYNN HO
3 HARTWOOD
4 LINDEN CT
5 HYDE HO
6 The Abbeygate Bsns Ctr
A
B
C
D
E
F
A505
HATTERS WAY
Kingsway Trad Est
Firbank Trad Est
LU4
Dalroad Ent Est
Bury Park
Luton Town FC
B579
DUNSTABLE RD
LU3
A6
High Town
Recn Ctr
Foxdell Inf Sch
DALLOW RD
Guardian Ind Est
Dallow Prim Sch
Luton
LUTON
GUILDFORD ST
Liby
TH
Arndale Ctr
Luton Univ
ST MARY'S RD
STUART ST
PARK VIADUCT
Winsdon Hill
Mast
Cemy
Cts
Whipperley Inf Sch
Farley Hill
Farley Jun Sch
Hillborough Jun & Inf Schs
Recn Gd
Park Town
Inion's Farm
Schs
Barnfield Coll (South)
FARLEY HILL
CHAPEL ST
B4540
New Town
Sch
South Luton High Sch
Capability Green
LU1
Farleygreen
Nursery
Stockwood Craft Mus & Gdns
CH
Lodge
Stockwood Park
Kidney Wood
AIRPORT WAY
A1081
THE GROVE CVN PK
PH
Woodside
Woodside Farm
NEWLANDS RD
Bull Wood
M1
10a
The Vicarage
Prebendal Farm
CHURCH RD
Newlands Farm
Slip End
THE ORCHARDS
10
LONDON RD
MARKYATE RD
B4540
Nursery
Slip End Lower Sch
Pepperstock
HALF MOON LA
PEPSAL END RD
Round Wood
1 ST ANDREWS WLK
2 HAMMOND CT
3 OLD SCHOOL WLK
8
7
21
6
5
20
4
3
19
2
1
18
07
08
09
D6
1 WINSDON CT
2 STANLEY LIVINGSTONE CT
3 WELLINGTON CT
4 DUKES CT
5 NEW ST
6 SPRING PL
7 EBENEZER ST
8 WINDSOR WLK
9 DUMFRIES CT
10 ELIZABETH CT
11 WINDSOR CT
12 HOUGHTON MEWS
13 BLYTH PL
14 BRECON CL
15 HIGH POINT
16 MAPLE CT
17 STOCKWOOD CT
84
E6
1 UNION CHAPEL HO
2 OXFORD RD
3 ROBERT ALLEN CT
4 QUEENS CL
5 CHOBHAM WLK
6 ROCHDALE CT
7 ESSEX CT
8 KIRKDALE CT
9 NEW TOWN RD
64
E6
10 Langley Terrace Ind Pk
11 Flowers Ind Est
12 Holly Street Trad Est
13 HIBBERT STREET ALMSHOUSES
14 JAMES CT
15 TRACEY CT
16 Telmere Ind Est
F6
1 GLOUCESTER RD
2 PARK TERR
3 DES FULLER CT
4 DORSET CT
5 HESWALL CT
6 PARKMEAD
7 KINGSLAND CT
8 CHOBHAM CT
9 OSBORNE CT

A B C D E F

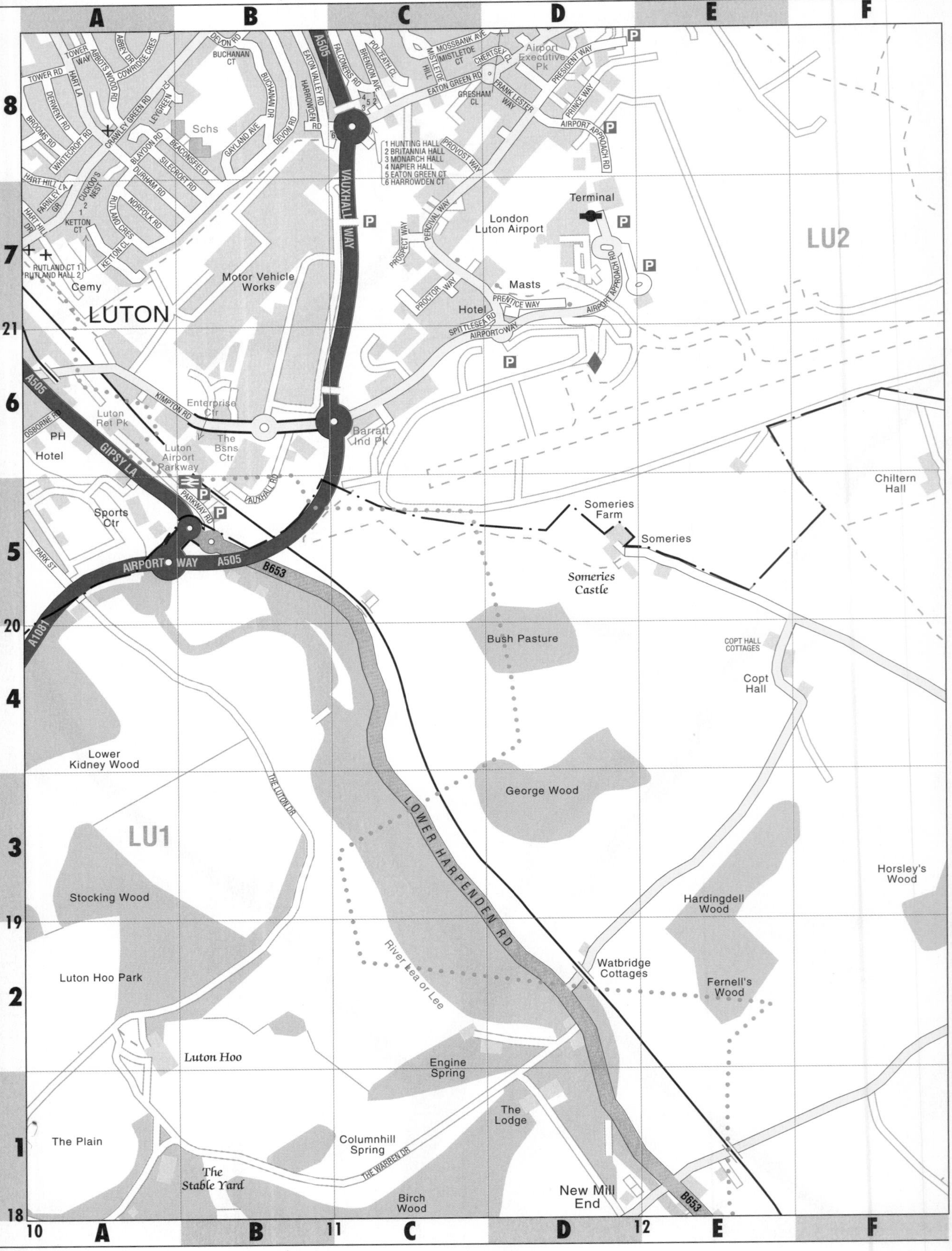

8

1 HUNTING HALL
2 BRITANNIA HALL
3 MONARCH HALL
4 NAPIER HALL
5 EATON GREEN CT
6 HARROWDEN CT

Airport
Executive
Pk

Terminal

LU2

7

Schs

Motor Vehicle
Works

London
Luton Airport

Masts

Cemy

Hotel

LUTON

RUTLAND CT 1
RUTLAND HALL 2

21

Chiltern
Hall

6

Luton Ret Pk

Enterprise
Ctr

The
Bsns
Ctr

Barratt
Ind Pk

PH

Hotel

Luton
Airport
Parkway

Someries
Farm

Someries

Sports
Ctr

5

AIRPORT WAY A505

B653

Someries
Castle

20

COPT HALL
COTTAGES

Bush Pasture

Copt
Hall

4

Lower
Kidney Wood

George Wood

Horsley's
Wood

LU1

3

Stocking Wood

Hardingdell
Wood

19

Luton Hoo Park

Watbridge
Cottages

Fernell's
Wood

2

Luton Hoo

Engine
Spring

The
Lodge

The Plain

Columnhill
Spring

Birch
Wood

New Mill
End

B653

18

1

10 A B 11 C D 12 E F

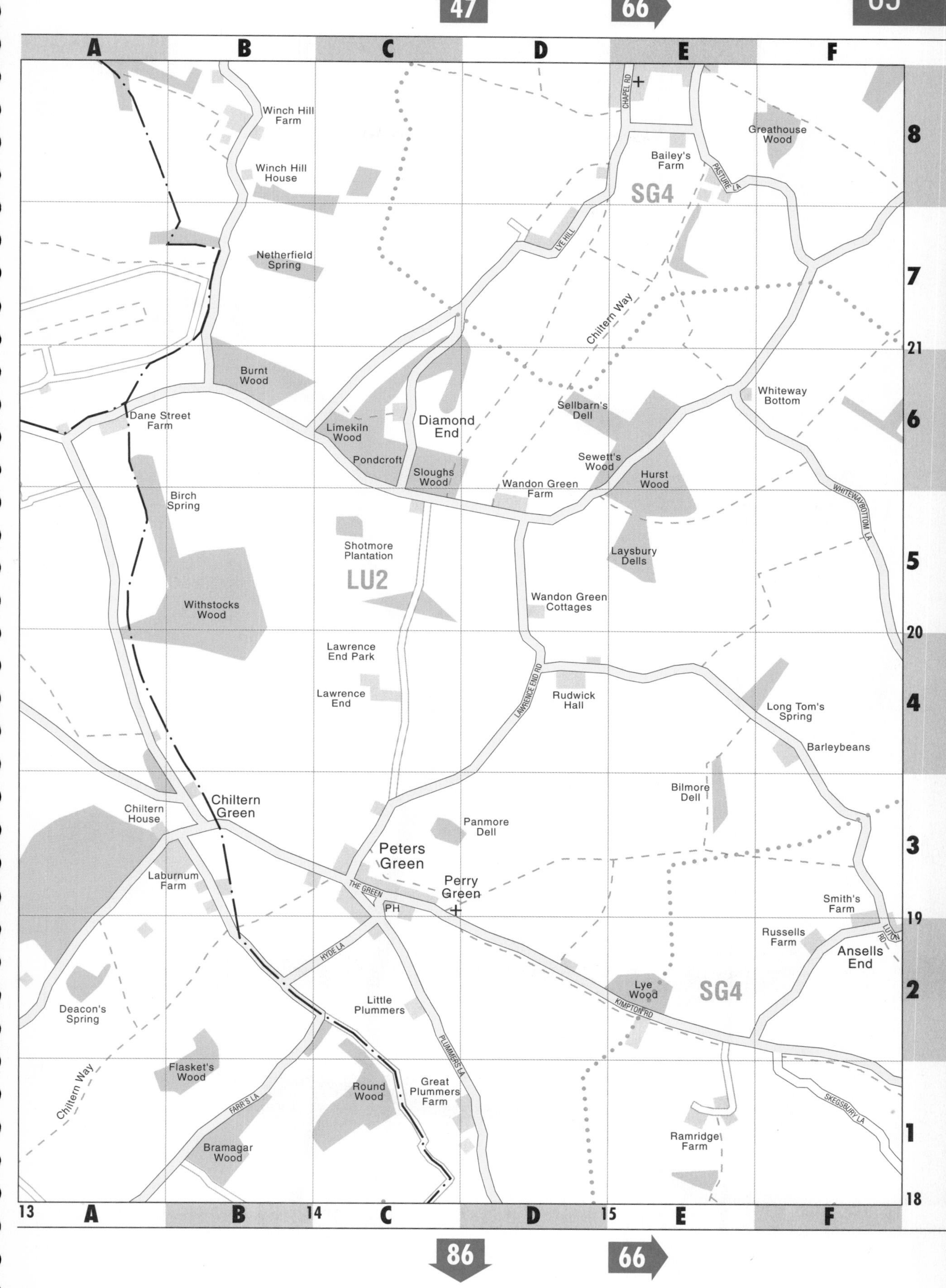

A B C D E F

8
Winch Hill Farm
Winch Hill House
Greathouse Wood
Bailey's Farm
SG4
CHAPEL RD
PASTURE LA

7
Netherfield Spring
Chiltern Way
21
Burnt Wood
Whiteway Bottom

6
Dane Street Farm
Limekiln Wood
Diamond End
Sellbarn's Dell
Pondcroft
Sloughs Wood
Sewett's Wood
Wandon Green Farm
Hurst Wood
WHITEWAYBOTTOM LA

5
Birch Spring
Shotmore Plantation
LU2
Laysbury Dells
Wandon Green Cottages

20
Withstocks Wood

4
Lawrence End Park
Lawrence End
LAWRENCE END RD
Rudwick Hall
Long Tom's Spring
Barleybeans

3
Chiltern House
Chiltern Green
Panmore Dell
Peters Green
Bilmore Dell
Smith's Farm

19
Laburnum Farm
THE GREEN
PH
Perry Green
Russells Farm
Ansells End
LUTON RD

2
HYDE LA
Lye Wood
SG4
KIMPTON RD

Deacon's Spring
Little Plummers
PLUMMERS LA

1
Chiltern Way
Flasket's Wood
FARR'S LA
Round Wood
Great Plummers Farm
Ramridge Farm
SKEGSBURY LA
Bramagar Wood

18

65
48

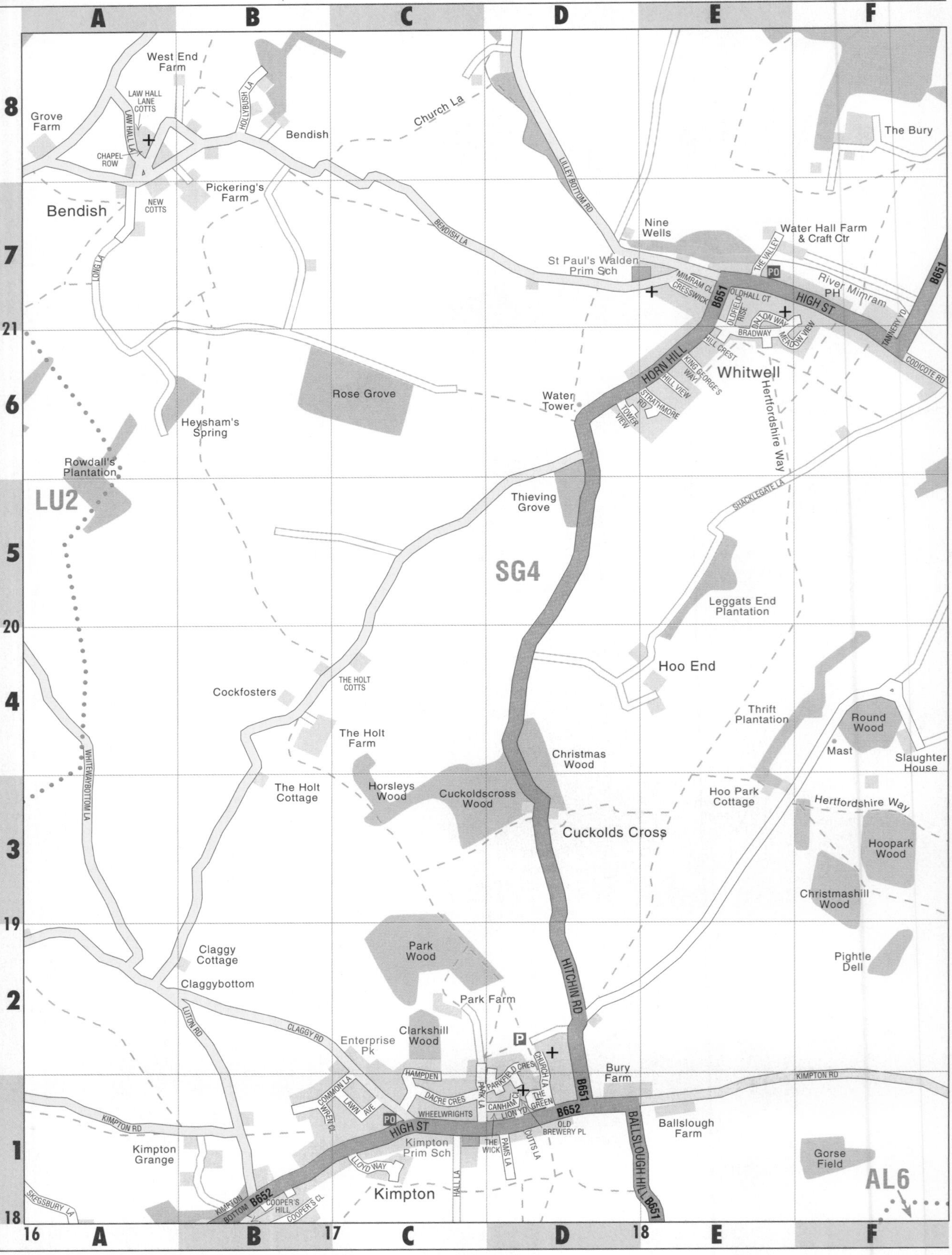

A **B** **C** **D** **E** **F**

8

Grove Farm

West End Farm

LAW HALL LANE COTTS

LAW HALL LA

Bendish

CHAPEL ROW

Church La

The Bury

NEW COTTS

Pickering's Farm

Bendish

HOLLYBUSH LA

BENDISH LA

LILLEY BOTTOM RD

Nine Wells

Water Hall Farm & Craft Ctr

7

St Paul's Walden Prim Sch

MIMRAM CL
CRESSWICK

OLDHALL CT

River Mimram

PH

B651

21

HORN HILL

HILL CREST

KING GEORGE'S WAY

OLDFIELD RISE

HIGH ST

TANNERY LA

6

Rose Grove

Heysham's Spring

Water Tower

STRATHMORE RD

TOWER VIEW

Whitwell

Hertfordshire Way

CODICOTE RD

Rowdall's Plantation

LU2

Thieving Grove

SHACKLEGATE LA

5

SG4

Leggats End Plantation

20

Cockfosters

THE HOLT COTTS

Hoo End

Thrift Plantation

Round Wood

Mast

Slaughter House

4

The Holt Farm

Christmas Wood

Hoo Park Cottage

Hertfordshire Way

The Holt Cottage

Horsleys Wood

Cuckoldscross Wood

Hoopark Wood

3

Cuckolds Cross

Christmashill Wood

WHITEWAYBOTTOM LA

19

Claggy Cottage

Park Wood

Pightle Dell

2

Claggybottom

CLAGGY RD

LUTON RD

Park Farm

HITCHIN RD

Enterprise Pk

Clarkshill Wood

P

Bury Farm

KIMPTON RD

COMMON LA

LARCH PL

HAMPDEN

LAWN AVE

PARKFIELD CRES

PARK LA

CHURCH LA

B651

Ballslough Farm

KIMPTON RD

DACRE CRES

CANHAM

THE WICK

LION YD GREEN

BALLSLOUGH HILL

B651

PO

WHEELWRIGHTS

OLD BREWERY PL

B652

Gorse Field

AL6

KIMPTON RD

HIGH ST

Kimpton Prim Sch

THE WICK

HALL LA

PARKS LA

CUTTS LA

Kimpton Grange

LLOYD WAY

1

KIMPTON BOTTOM

B652

COOPER'S HILL

COOPER'S CL

Kimpton

18

SKEGSBURY LA

16 **A** **B** **17** **C** **D** **18** **E** **F**

65
87

A B C D E F

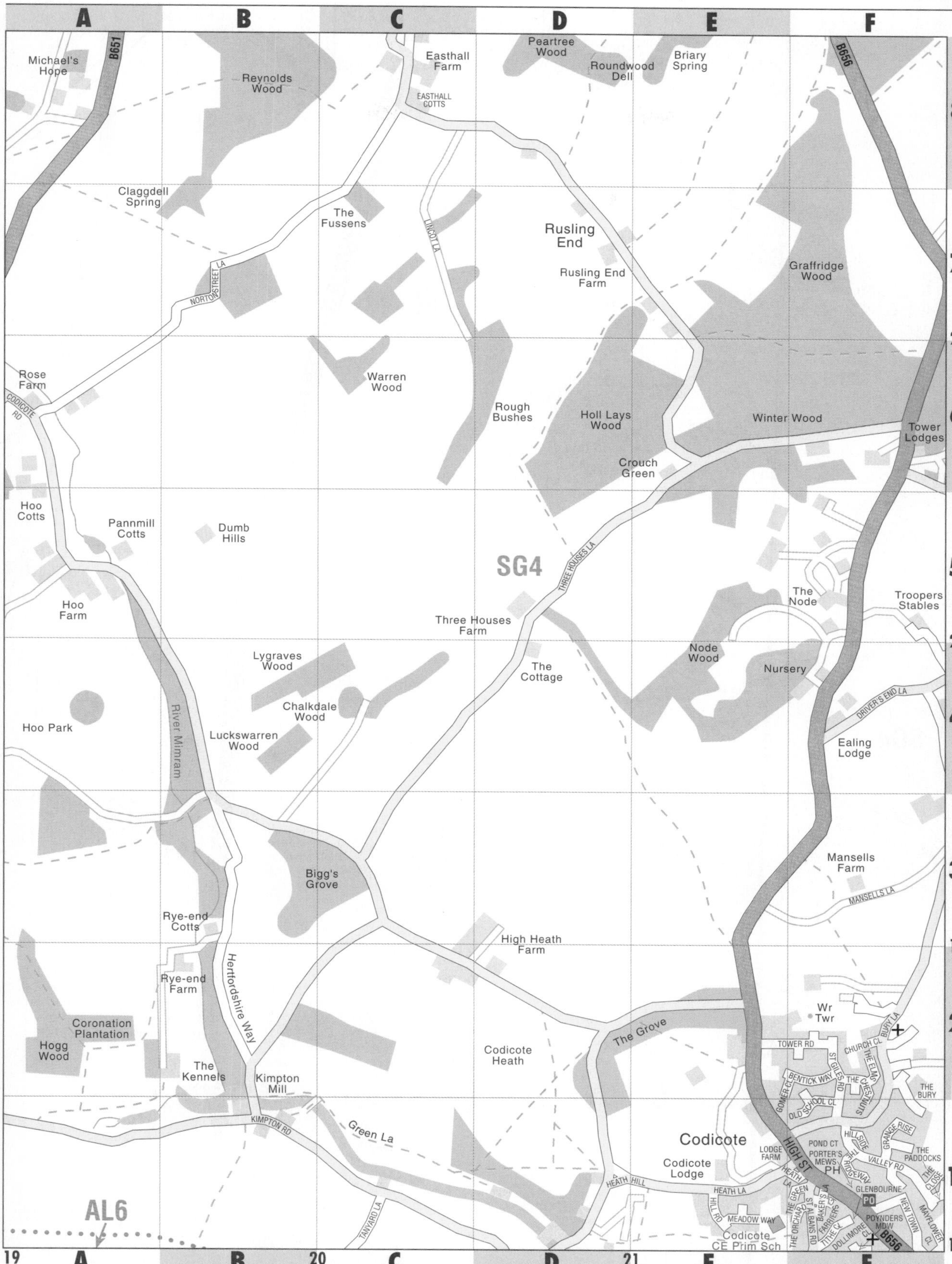

B651

B656

Michael's Hope

Reynolds Wood

Easthall Farm

Peartree Wood

Roundwood Dell

Briary Spring

8

EASTHALL COTTS

Claggdell Spring

The Fussens

LINCOT LA

Rusling End

Graffridge Wood

7

NORTON STREET LA

Rusling End Farm

21

Rose Farm

CODICOTE RD

Warren Wood

Rough Bushes

Holl Lays Wood

Winter Wood

Tower Lodges

6

Crouch Green

Hoo Cotts

Pannmill Cotts

Dumb Hills

THREE HOUSES LA

SG4

The Node

Troopers Stables

5

Hoo Farm

Three Houses Farm

Node Wood

Nursery

20

Lygraves Wood

The Cottage

DRIVER'S END LA

4

River Mimram

Chalkdale Wood

Ealing Lodge

Hoo Park

Luckswarren Wood

Mansells Farm

3

Bigg's Grove

MANSELLS LA

Rye-end Cotts

Hertfordshire Way

High Heath Farm

19

Rye-end Farm

Wr Twr

2

Coronation Plantation

The Grove

TOWER RD

CHURCH CL

THE BURY

Hogg Wood

The Kennels

Kimpton Mill

Codicote Heath

BENTICK WAY

ST GILES RD

OLD SCHOOL CL

THE ELMS

THE PADDOCKS

KIMPTON RD

Green La

Codicote

HIGH ST

Codicote Lodge

Lodge Farm

PORTER'S MEWS

POND CT

PH

HILL SIDE

VALLEY RD

GRANGE RISE

GLENBOURNE

1

AL6

TANYARD LA

Heath Hill

HEATH HILL

HEATH LA

MEADOW WAY

THE GREEN

ST ALBAN RD

BAKER ST

BARBERS

TITHE CL

P.O

B656

POYNDERS MDW

NEWTOWN

MAYFLOWER

18

Codicote CE Prim Sch

DOLLIMORE

67
50

A B C D E F

8
7
21
6

Burleigh Grove
Cowley's Corner Wood
North Lodges
A1(M)
Hotel
LONDON RD
HERTFORD RD
SKIPTON CL
BROOKHILL
KIMBOLTON CRES
B197
SG2
Burleigh Farm
OLD KNEBWORTH LA
Knebworth Country Park
Wintergreen Wood
B656
STEVENAGE RD
Mausoleum
CH
BADGER CL
Knebworth House
Miniature Rly
SG3
Lodge Farm
B197
PETERS WAY
NEW CL
DEARD'S END LA
STOBARTS CL
Manor Farm
Old Knebworth

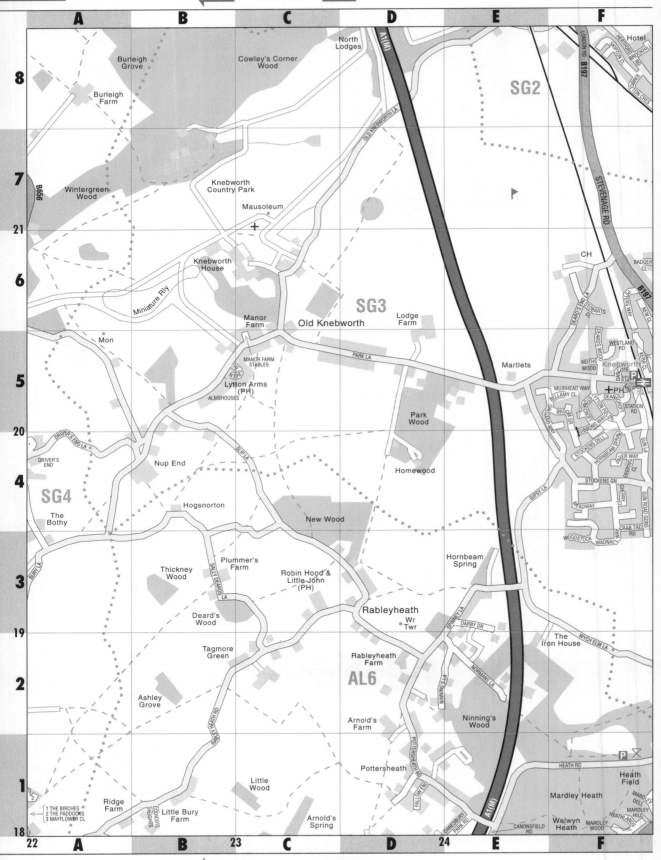

5
20
4
3
19
2
1
18

Hornbeam Spring
BURY LA
Thickney Wood
Plummer's Farm
SALLY DEARDS LA
Robin Hood & Little John (PH)
Rableyheath
Wr Twr
Deard's Wood
SPINNEY LA
DARBY DR
The Iron House
WYCH ELM LA
Tagmore Green
Rableyheath Farm
AL6
NORMANS LA
NINNING'S LA
Ashley Grove
Arnold's Farm
Ninning's Wood
RABLEY HEATH RD
POTTERSHEATH RD
P
HEATH RD
Heath Field
Pottersheath
Little Wood
Mardley Heath
MARDLEY DELL
MARDLEY HILL
HEATHLANDS
Ridge Farm
CODICOTE HEIGHTS
Little Bury Farm
FALLOW END
1 THE BIRCHES
2 THE PADDOCKS
3 MAYFLOWER CL
Arnold's Spring
DANESBURY PARK RD
A1(M)
CANONSFIELD RD
Welwyn Heath
MARDLEY WOOD

22 A B 23 C D 24 E F

51
70

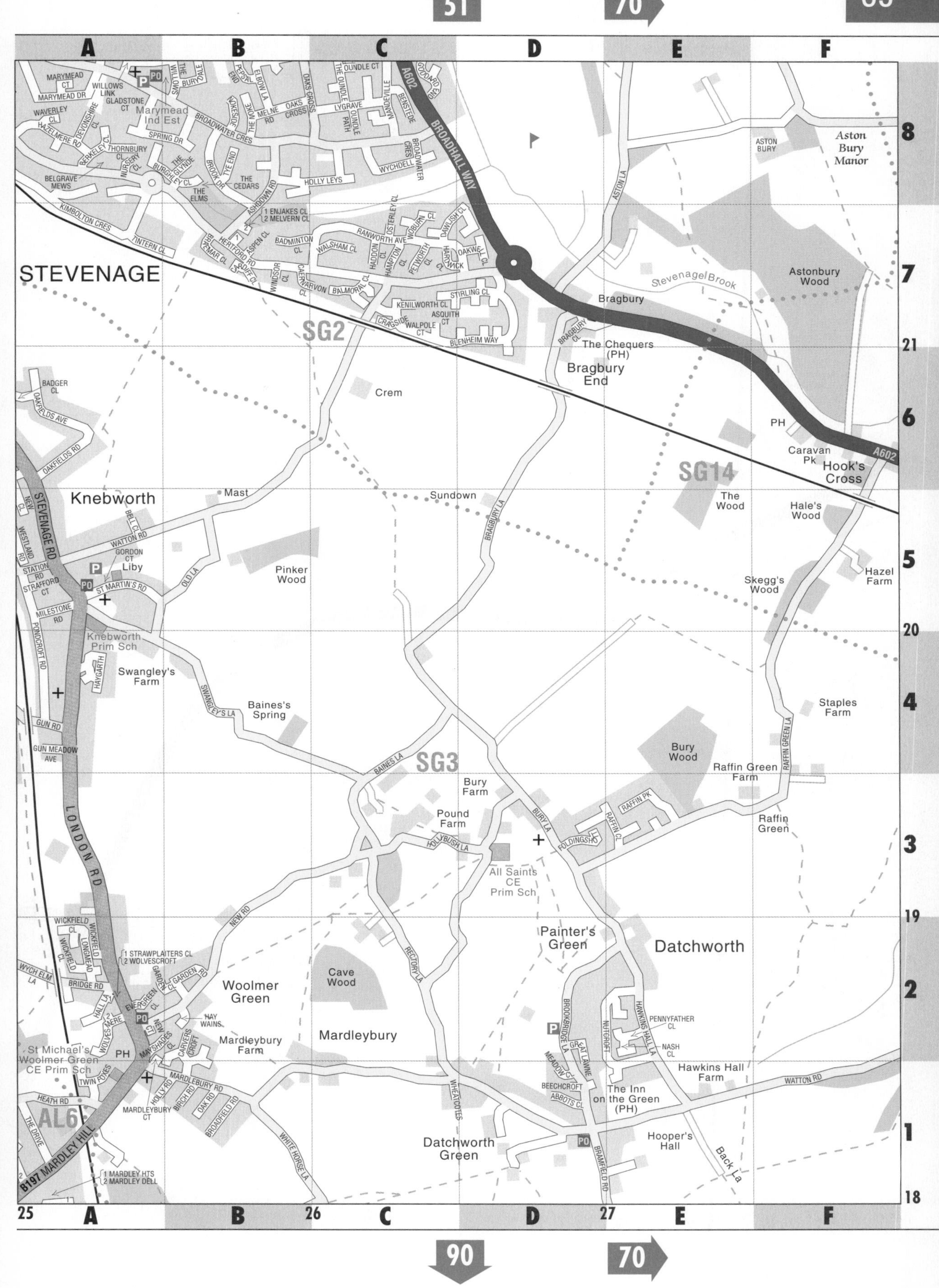
A
B
C
D
E
F
8
7
21
6
5
20
4
3
19
2
1
18
25
26
27
STEVENAGE
SG2
Marymead Ind Est
BROADHALL WAY
A602
Aston Bury Manor
ASTON BURY
ASTON LA
Astonbury Wood
Stevenage Brook
Bragbury
The Chequers (PH)
Bragbury End
Crem
PH
Caravan Pk
Hook's Cross
SG14
The Wood
Hale's Wood
Hazel Farm
Skegg's Wood
Knebworth
Mast
Sundown
BRAGBURY LA
Liby
Pinker Wood
STEVENAGE RD
Knebworth Prim Sch
Swangley's Farm
SWANGLEY'S LA
Baines's Spring
BAINES LA
SG3
Staples Farm
Bury Wood
Raffin Green Farm
RAFFIN GREEN LA
Bury Farm
Pound Farm
BURY LA
Raffin Green
LONDON RD
HOLLYBUSH LA
All Saints CE Prim Sch
NEW RD
Painter's Green
Datchworth
Cave Wood
RECTORY LA
Woolmer Green
Mardleybury
Mardleybury Farm
Hawkins Hall Farm
WATTON RD
St Michael's Woolmer Green CE Prim Sch
PH
The Inn on the Green (PH)
AL6
WHEATCOTES
BRAMFIELD RD
Datchworth Green
Hooper's Hall
Back La
WHITE HORSE LA
B197 MARDLEY HILL

90
70

69
52

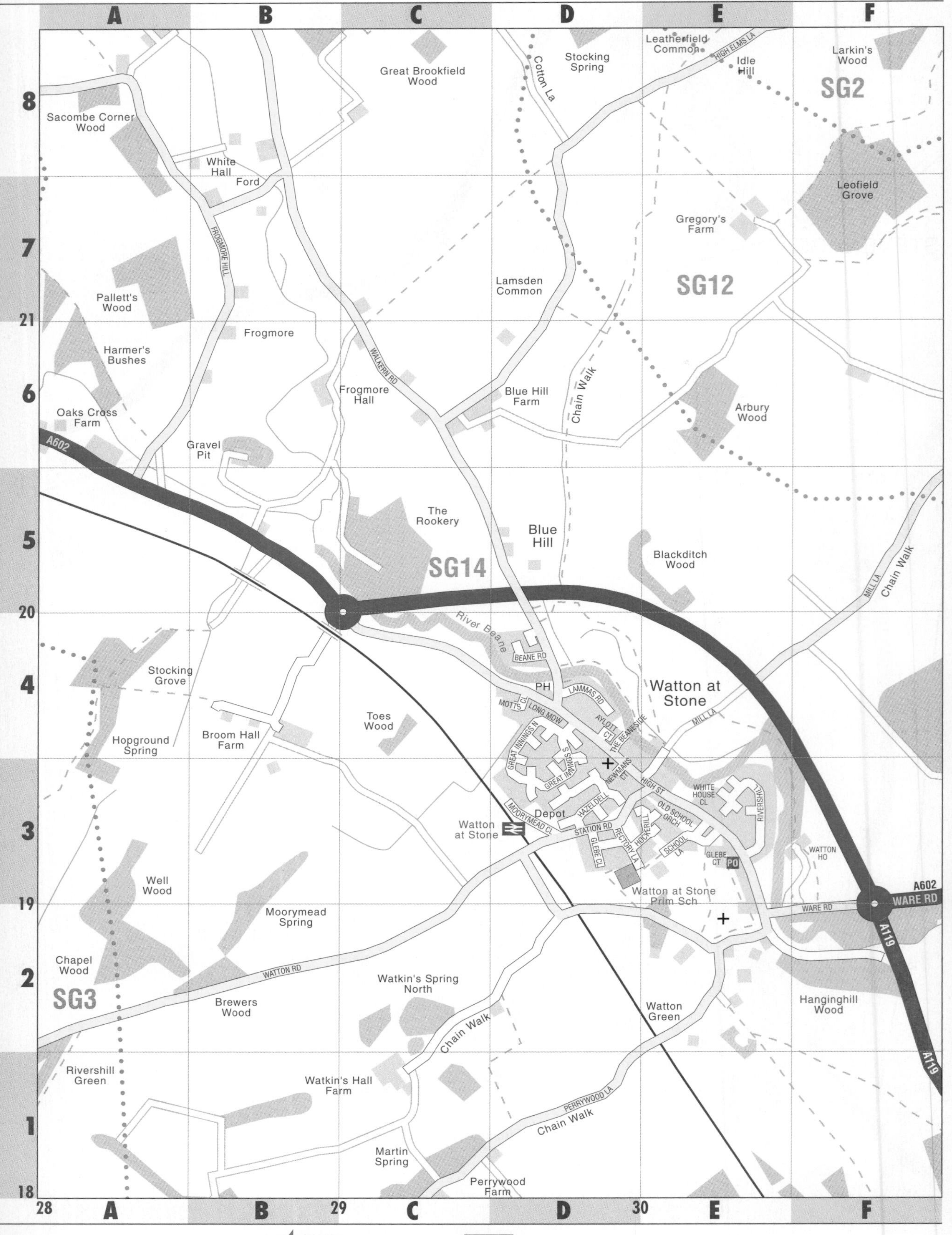
A
B
C
D
E
F
Leatherfield Common
HIGH ELMS LA
Stocking Spring
Great Brookfield Wood
Cotton La
Idle Hill
Larkin's Wood
SG2
Sacombe Corner Wood
White Hall
Ford
Leofield Grove
Gregory's Farm
FROGMORE HILL
Pallett's Wood
Lamsden Common
SG12
Frogmore
Harmer's Bushes
WALKERN RD
Chain Walk
Frogmore Hall
Blue Hill Farm
Arbury Wood
Oaks Cross Farm
A602
Gravel Pit
The Rookery
Blue Hill
Blackditch Wood
SG14
MILL LA
Chain Walk
River Beane
BEANE RD
Stocking Grove
PH
LAMMAS RD
Watton at Stone
MOTTS CL
LONG MDW
AYLOTT CT
THE BEANESIDE
MILL LA
Hopground Spring
Broom Hall Farm
Toes Wood
GREAT INNINGS N
GREAT INNINGS S
NEWMANS CT
HIGH ST
WHITE HOUSE CL
RIVERSHILL
MOORYMEAD CL
HAZELDELL
Depot
OLD SCHOOL ORCH
Watton at Stone
STATION RD
RECTORY LA
HOCKERILL
SCHOOL LA
GLEBE CL
GLEBE CT
PO
WATTON HO
Well Wood
Watton at Stone Prim Sch
A602
WARE RD
WARE RD
Moorymead Spring
A119
Chapel Wood
WATTON RD
Watkin's Spring North
SG3
Brewers Wood
Watton Green
Hanginghill Wood
Chain Walk
A119
Rivershill Green
Watkin's Hall Farm
PERRYWOOD LA
Chain Walk
Martin Spring
Perrywood Farm
8
7
21
6
5
20
4
3
19
2
1
18
28
29
30

69
91

A B C D E F

Chain Walk
SG2
Comb's Wood
Customs Wood
Apsley Common
Little Munden CE Prim Sch
Short Whiteley Common
Easington Common
Dane End
CHURCH LA
GLADSTONE RD
WINDMILLS
FOUNCELEY AVE
KINGSFIELD RD
WHITELEY CL
WINDY RISE
EASINGTON RD
KENNEDY RD
MUNDEN RD
PO
PH
PAGET COTTS
Long Spring
The Old Bourne
Chapel Farm
WHEMPSTEAD RD
Whempstead Green
Dane End House
PEARMAN DR
Home Farm
Whempstead
Cottonborough Common
Claypits Wood
MILL LA
Whempstead Farm
Whempstead Gate Farm
Hog's Wood
WHEMPSTEAD LA
Wicks Wood
Lodge Farm
Brookfield Common
Smart's Hill
Longcroft Wood
Bromley Common
Bushy Leys Spring
SG12
Willeycotes Wood
Dane End Tributary
Sacombe Hill Farm
Sacombe Hill
Bardolphspark Wood
SACOMBE GREEN RD
Bardolphs
Sacombe
SG14
WARE RD
SACOMBE POUND
Heath Mount Sch
Sacombebury Farm
Sacombe House
The Springs
Woodhall Park
Sacombe Park
The Clumps
Sacombe Lake
River Beane
Broad Water
Home Farm
The Cuts
Ware Lodge
King Edward's Gorse
A119
A602

8
7
21
6
5
20
4
3
19
2
1
18

31 A B 32 C D 33 E F

| |  A | B | C | D | E | F |

8 Fullar's Common · Moorfield Common · High Trees Farm · Hatchett Poultry Farm · Beggarman's Wood · Hatchett Farm

Trenchern Hills · Hill Farm

7 Whitehill Farm · Langton's La · Shelly's Wood · Roughground Wood

21 CH · Cock's Wood · Rigery Farm

6 Potter's Green · Potter's Hall Farm

Labdens Farm

5 Rowney La · Rowney Priory · Black Grove · Willowtree Farm

Rowney Wood · Lowgate La · Standon Green End Farm

20 Knoll Farm

4 Lowgate La · SG12 · Standon Green End · SG11

Sacombe Green · Mott's Wood · Barwick Tributary

3 Church Wood · Dilly Wood · Low Wood · Salmonsley Wood · A10

Home Wood

19 Home Farm · Marshall's La · Sutes · Cambridge Cotts

2 Gages Wood · Marshall's Farm PH · Pullar Memorial Prim Sch · High Cross

Furzeground Wood · Marshall's · North Dr · Poplar Cl · Passfield Cotts

1 Rennesley Garden Wood · Hazelwood Farm · Mark's Wood · SG12

18 Highcross Hill · Gravelpit Wood · A10

| 34 | A | B | 35 | C | D | 36 | E | F |

The Bourne · Dane End Rd

55
74

A B C D E F

8
7
21
6
5
20
4
3
19
2
1
18

St Hugh's Sch
FARM LA
GARDEN COTTS
Ryders Grove
A10
Kitchencroft Wood
Sewage Works
New Plantation
Nurseries
WELLINGTON COTTS
The Lordship
RIGERY LA
Dowsett's Farm
Harcamlow Way
Fisher's Farm
WEST VIEW
PH
Colliers End
PARKINS CL
Plashes Wood
Ford
Latchford Farm
Latchford
Plashes Farm
Hangingwood Plantation
SG11
ARCHES HALL COTTS
MORLEY LA
Arches Hall
FB
River Rib
Hanging Wood
Ford
Barwick Tributary
Blackey Mead Wood
Badger's Eye Plantation
Wellington House
ASHLEIGH CVN PK
BARWICK LA
Cook's Wood
Biggin's Wood
Barwick
Sutes Wood
Furzeground Wood
GORE LA
Round Wood
Heathfield Wood
Biggin's Farm
Barwick Ford
Great Barwick
Ash Plantation
Tyler's Hill
Little Barwick Farm
New Plantation
SG10
Gutteridge Lye
Great Southey Wood
Harcamlow Way
Round Wood
Sawtrees Wood
SG12
Rush Green
Aldeck Spring
Steere Wood

37 A B 38 C D 39 E F

94
74

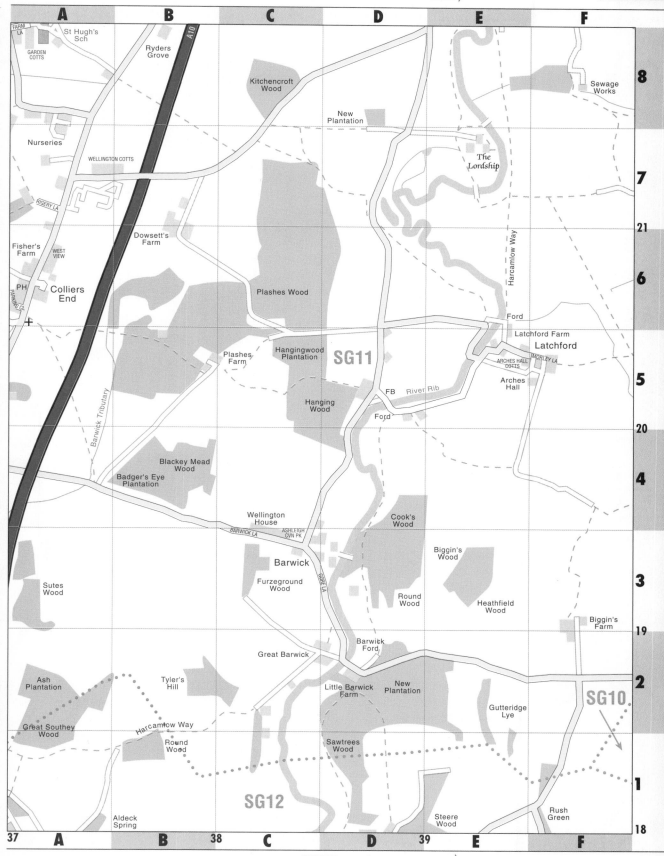

A   B   C   D   E   F

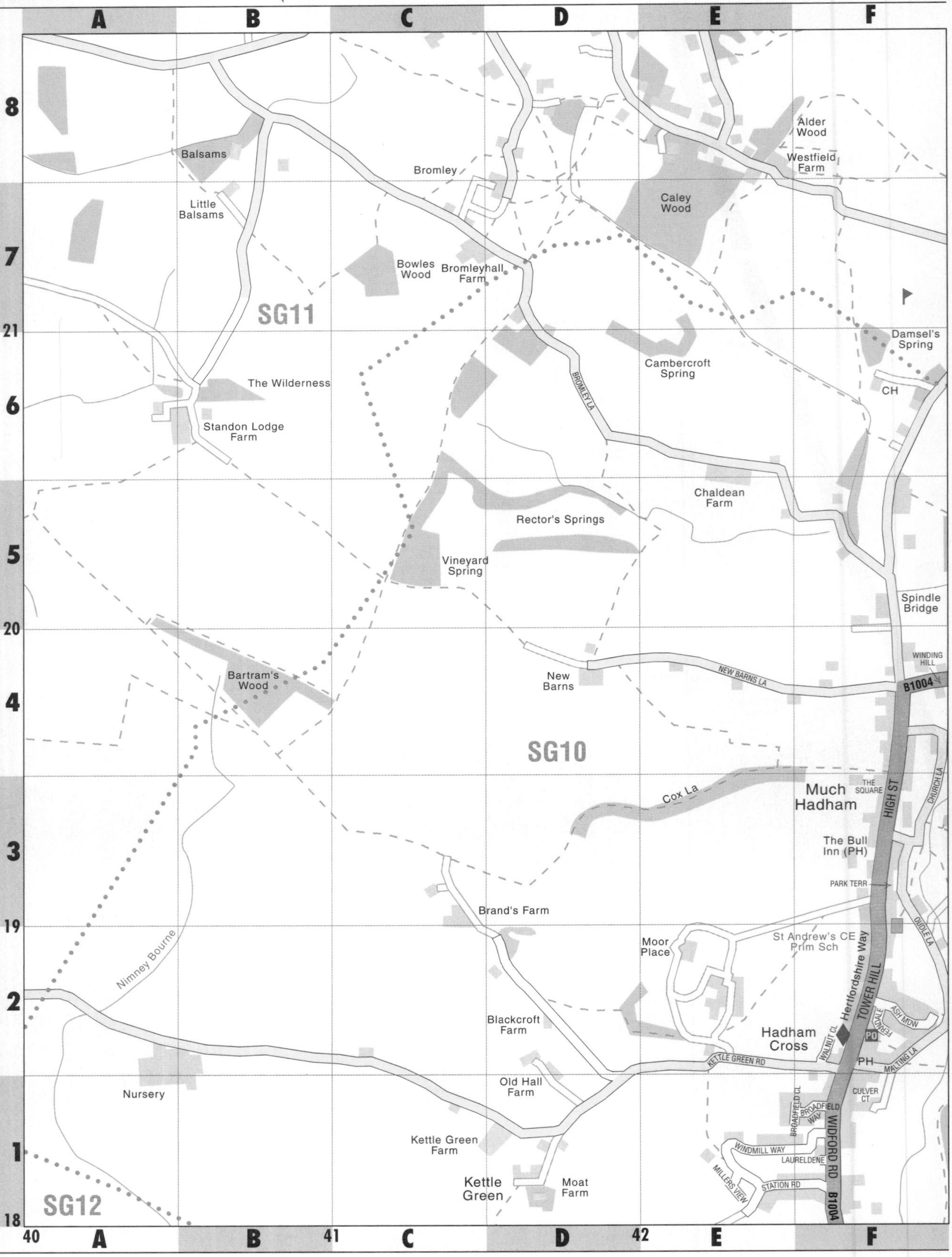

8

Balsams

Bromley

Alder
Wood

Westfield
Farm

Caley
Wood

Little
Balsams

Bowles
Wood

Bromleyhall
Farm

7

SG11

21

Cambercroft
Spring

Damsel's
Spring

The Wilderness

BROMLEY LA

CH

6

Standon Lodge
Farm

Chaldean
Farm

Rector's Springs

5

Vineyard
Spring

Spindle
Bridge

20

WINDING
HILL

Bartram's
Wood

New
Barns

NEW BARNS LA

B1004

4

SG10

Cox La

Much
Hadham

THE
SQUARE

HIGH ST

CHURCH LA

3

The Bull
Inn (PH)

PARK TERR

OLD LA

Brand's Farm

19

Moor
Place

St Andrew's CE
Prim Sch

Hertfordshire Way

TOWER HILL

Nimney Bourne

2

Blackcroft
Farm

KETTLE GREEN RD

Hadham
Cross

WALNUT CL

PENROSE

ASH MDW

MALTING LA

PO

PH

Nursery

Old Hall
Farm

BROADFIELD
WAY

BRAMFIELD CL

CULVER
CT

WIDFORD RD

1

Kettle Green
Farm

WINDMILL WAY

LAURELDENE

MILLERS VIEW

STATION RD

B1004

Kettle
Green

Moat
Farm

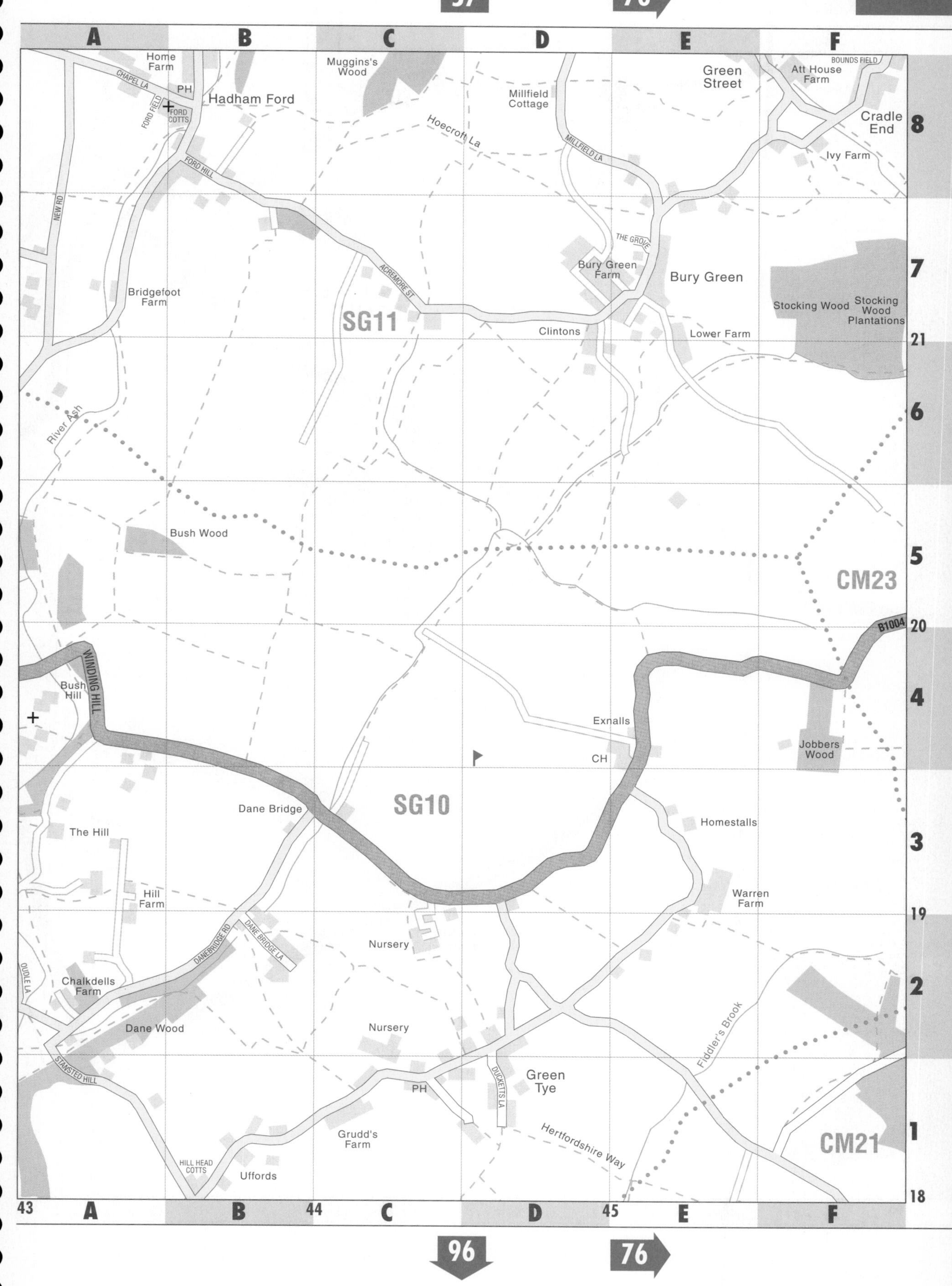
57
76
A
B
C
D
E
F
Home Farm
CHAPEL LA
PH
Hadham Ford
FORD FIELD
FORD COTTS
Muggins's Wood
Millfield Cottage
Hoecroft La
MILLFIELD LA
Green Street
BOUNDS FIELD
Att House Farm
Cradle End
Ivy Farm
8
FORD HILL
NEW RD
THE GROVE
Bury Green Farm
Bury Green
ACREMORE ST
7
Bridgefoot Farm
SG11
Stocking Wood
Stocking Wood Plantations
Clintons
Lower Farm
21
River Ash
6
Bush Wood
5
CM23
B1004
20
WINDING HILL
Bush Hill
Exnalls
4
CH
Jobbers Wood
SG10
Dane Bridge
Homestalls
The Hill
3
Hill Farm
Warren Farm
19
DANEBRIDGE RD
DANE BRIDGE LA
Nursery
OUDLE LA
Chalkdells Farm
2
Dane Wood
Nursery
Fiddler's Brook
STANSTED HILL
DUCKETTS LA
Green Tye
PH
Hertfordshire Way
1
Grudd's Farm
CM21
HILL HEAD COTTS
Uffords
18
43
44
45
96
76

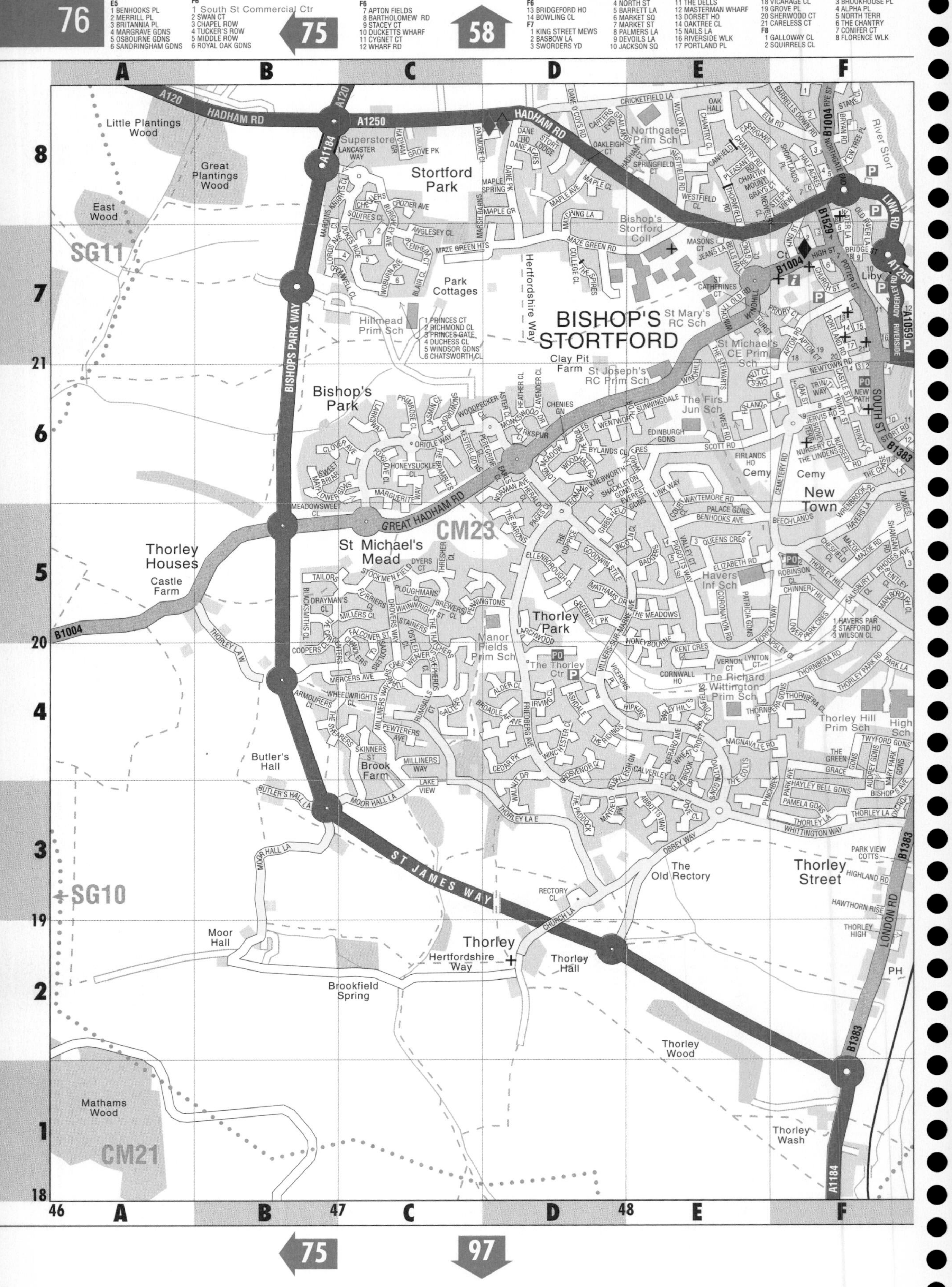
E5
1 BENHOOKS PL
2 MERRILL PL
3 BRITANNIA PL
4 MARGRAVE GDNS
5 OSBOURNE GDNS
6 SANDRINGHAM GDNS
F6
1 South St Commercial Ctr
2 SWAN CT
3 CHAPEL ROW
4 TUCKER'S ROW
5 MIDDLE ROW
6 ROYAL OAK GDNS
75
F6
7 APTON FIELDS
8 BARTHOLOMEW RD
9 STACEY CT
10 DUCKETTS WHARF
11 CYGNET CT
12 WHARF RD
58
F6
13 BRIDGEFORD HO
14 BOWLING CL
F7
1 KING STREET MEWS
2 BASBOW LA
3 SWORDERS YD
4 NORTH ST
5 BARRETT LA
6 MARKET SQ
7 MARKET ST
8 PALMERS LA
9 DEVOILS LA
10 JACKSON SQ
11 THE DELLS
12 MASTERMAN WHARF
13 DORSET HO
14 OAKTREE CL
15 NAILS LA
16 RIVERSIDE WLK
17 PORTLAND PL
18 VICARAGE CL
19 GROVE PL
20 SHERWOOD CT
21 CARELESS CT
F8
1 GALLOWAY CL
2 SQUIRRELS CL
3 BROOKHOUSE PL
4 ALPHA PL
5 NORTH TERR
6 THE CHANTRY
7 CONIFER CT
8 FLORENCE WLK
A
B
C
D
E
F
8
7
21
6
5
20
4
3
19
2
1
18
46
47
48
BISHOP'S STORTFORD
Little Plantings Wood
Great Plantings Wood
East Wood
SG11
A120
HADHAM RD
A1250
A1184
Superstore
Stortford Park
Park Cottages
Hillmead Prim Sch
1 PRINCES CT
2 RICHMOND CL
3 PRINCES GATE
4 DUCHESS CL
5 WINDSOR GDNS
6 CHATSWORTH CL
Hertfordshire Way
Northgate Prim Sch
Bishop's Stortford Coll
St Mary's RC Sch
Clay Pit Farm
St Joseph's RC Prim Sch
St Michael's CE Prim Sch
The Firs Jun Sch
Bishop's Park
BISHOPS PARK WAY
GREAT HADHAM RD
CM23
St Michael's Mead
Thorley Houses
Castle Farm
B1004
B1529
B1383
A1059
LINK RD
River Stort
Cemy
New Town
Havers Inf Sch
Thorley Park
Manor Fields Prim Sch
The Thorley Ctr
The Richard Wittington Prim Sch
Thorley Hill Prim Sch
1 HAVERS PAR
2 STAFFORD HO
3 WILSON CL
Butler's Hall
Brook Farm
ST JAMES WAY
Old Rectory
Thorley Street
SG10
Moor Hall
Thorley
Hertfordshire Way
Thorley Hall
Brookfield Spring
LONDON RD
Thorley Wood
Mathams Wood
CM21
Thorley Wash
A1184
75
97

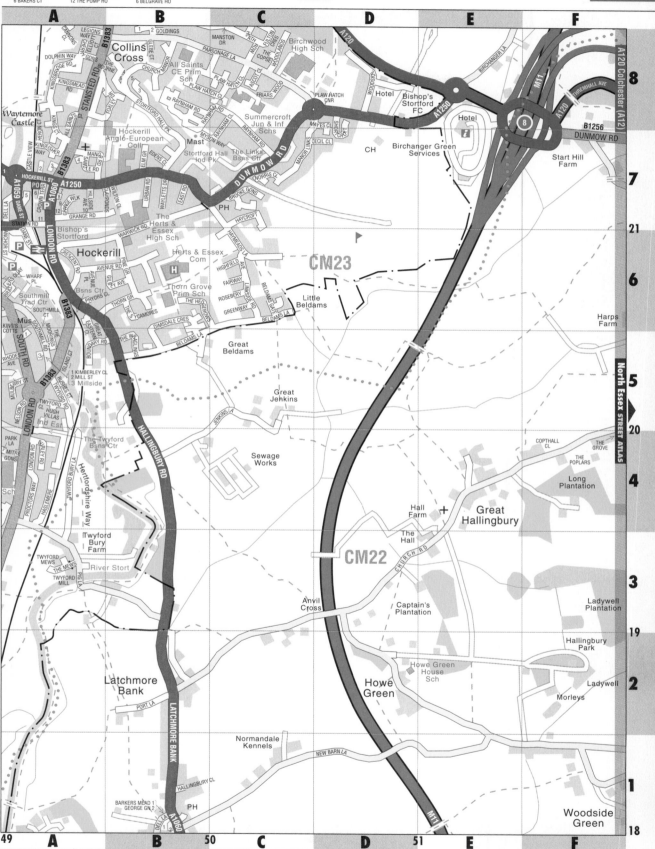

A7
1 THE CAUSEWAY
2 THE OLD MALTINGS
3 FULLER CT
4 LIMES CRES
5 RED LION CT
6 BAKERS CT
7 HOCKERILL CT
8 HARRINGTON CL
9 PRIORS
10 CLIFFORD CT
11 THOMAS HESKIN CT
12 THE PUMP HO

B8
1 BOYD CL
2 HEATH ROW
3 STORTFORD HALL RD
4 GROSVENOR HO
5 EATON HO
6 BELGRAVE HO

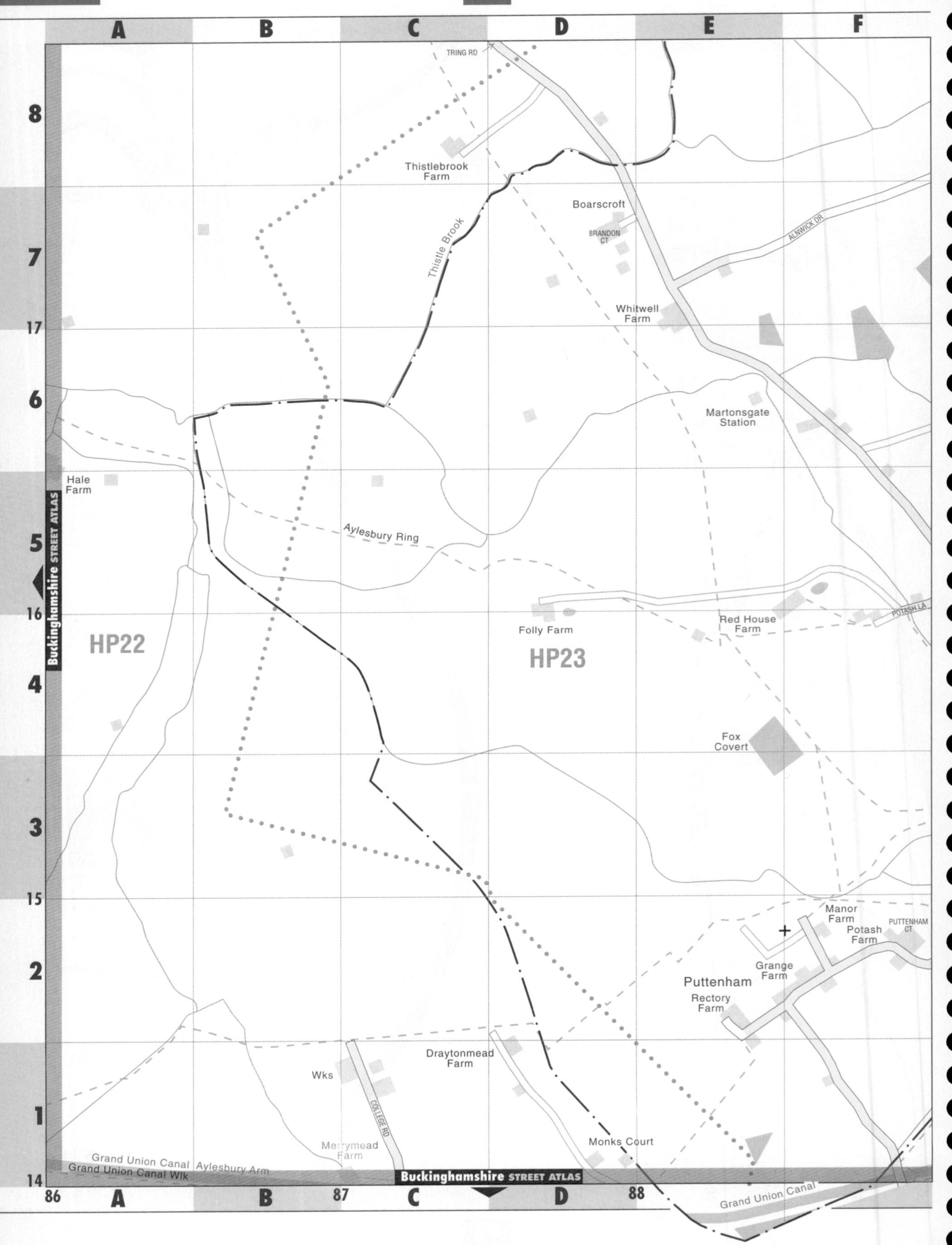

A B C D E F

8

Thistlebrook
Farm

Boarscroft

BRANDON
CT

ALNWICK DR

7

Thistle Brook

17

Whitwell
Farm

6

Martonsgate
Station

Hale
Farm

5

Aylesbury Ring

16

Red House
Farm

POTASH LA

Folly Farm

HP22

HP23

4

Fox
Covert

3

15

Manor
Farm

Potash
Farm

PUTTENHAM
CT

2

Grange
Farm

Puttenham

Rectory
Farm

Draytonmead
Farm

Wks

COLLEGE RD

1

Monks Court

Merrymead
Farm

14

Grand Union Canal Aylesbury Arm
Grand Union Canal Wlk

Grand Union Canal

86 A B 87 C D 88 F

TRING RD

Buckinghamshire STREET ATLAS

61
80

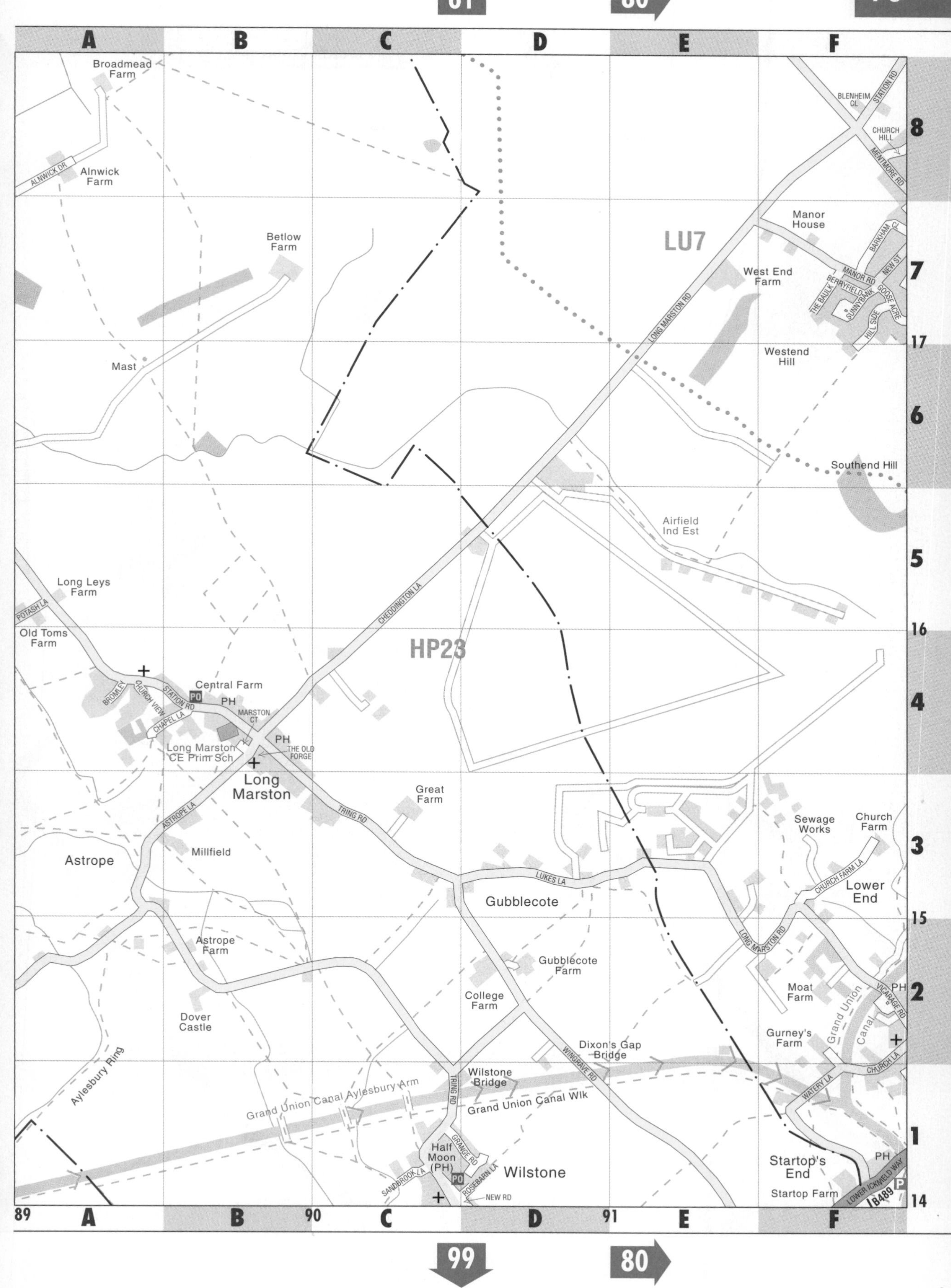
A
B
C
D
E
F
Broadmead Farm
Alnwick Farm
ALNWICK DR
Betlow Farm
Mast
LU7
Manor House
West End Farm
Westend Hill
LONG MARSTON RD
BLENHEIM CL
STATION RD
CHURCH HILL
MENTMORE RD
BARKHAM CL
MANOR RD
NEW ST
BERRYFIELD
THE BAULK
SUNNYBANK
GOOSE ACRE
HILL SIDE
Southend Hill
Airfield Ind Est
Long Leys Farm
POTASH LA
Old Toms Farm
CHEDDINGTON LA
HP23
Central Farm
PH
BROMLEY
CHURCH VIEW
STATION RD
CHAPEL LA
MARSTON CT
PH
THE OLD FORGE
Long Marston CE Prim Sch
Long Marston
Great Farm
ASTROPE LA
TRING RD
Astrope
Millfield
LUKES LA
Gubblecote
Sewage Works
Church Farm
CHURCH FARM LA
Lower End
LONG MARSTON RD
Astrope Farm
Gubblecote Farm
Moat Farm
PH
VICARAGE RD
Dover Castle
College Farm
Gurney's Farm
Grand Union Canal
Aylesbury Ring
Dixon's Gap Bridge
WINGRAVE RD
Wilstone Bridge
TRING RD
Grand Union Canal Aylesbury Arm
Grand Union Canal Wlk
WATERY LA
CHURCH LA
Half Moon (PH)
GRANGE RD
SANDBROOK LA
ROSEBARN LA
Wilstone
NEW RD
Startop's End
Startop Farm
PH
LOWER ICKNIELD WAY
B489
8
7
17
6
5
16
4
3
15
2
1
14
89
90
91

99
80

79

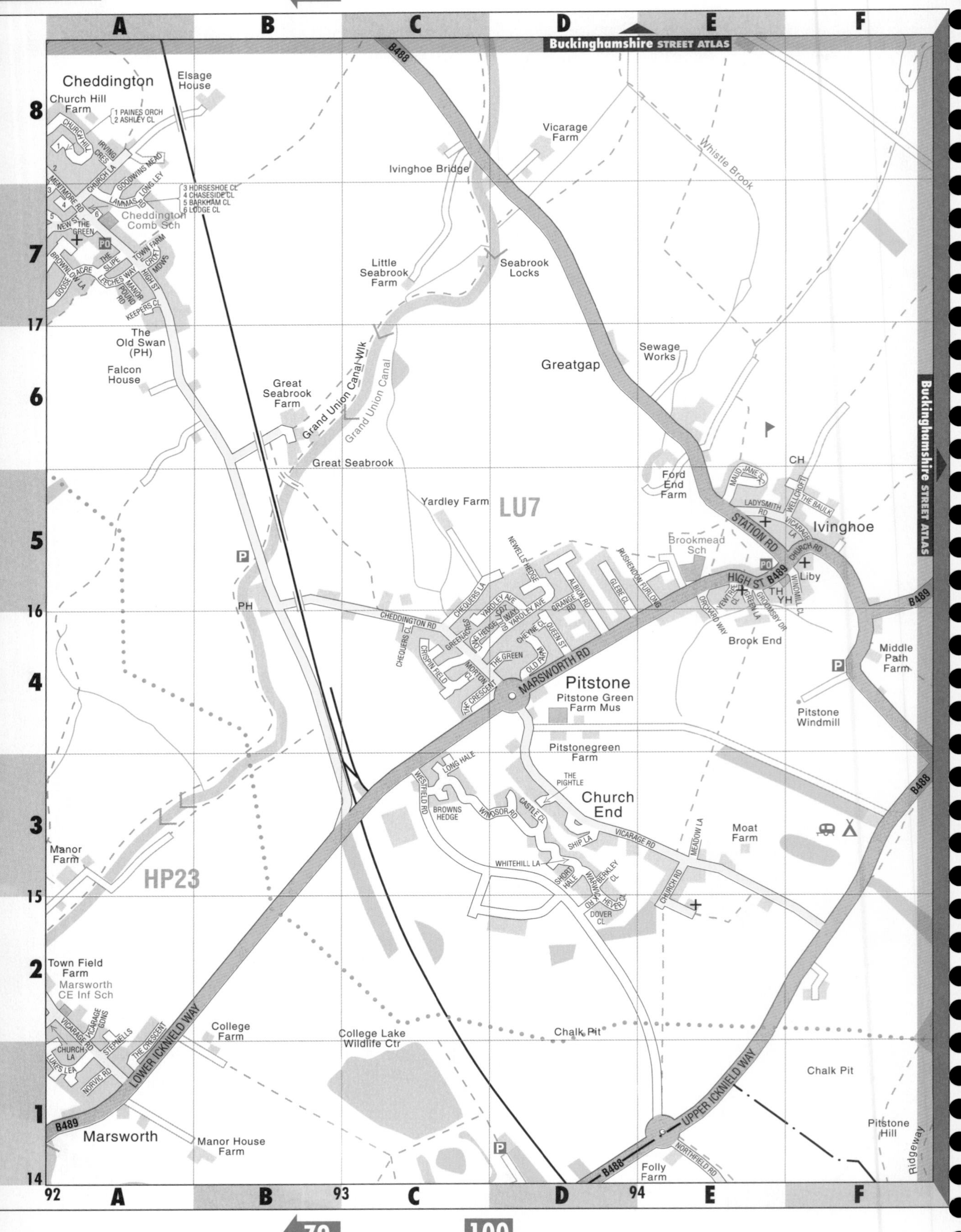

Buckinghamshire STREET ATLAS
Cheddington
Church Hill Farm
Elsage House
Cheddington Comb Sch
The Old Swan (PH)
Falcon House
Great Seabrook Farm
Grand Union Canal Wlk
Grand Union Canal
Great Seabrook
Ivinghoe Bridge
Little Seabrook Farm
Seabrook Locks
Vicarage Farm
Whistle Brook
Greatgap
Sewage Works
Ford End Farm
Yardley Farm
LU7
Brookmead Sch
Ivinghoe
Brook End
Middle Path Farm
Pitstone
Pitstone Green Farm Mus
Pitstone Windmill
Pitstonegreen Farm
Church End
Moat Farm
Manor Farm
HP23
Town Field Farm
Marsworth CE Inf Sch
College Farm
College Lake Wildlife Ctr
Chalk Pit
Marsworth
Manor House Farm
Folly Farm
Pitstone Hill
Ridgeway
MARSWORTH RD
CHEDDINGTON RD
HIGH ST B489
STATION RD
LOWER ICKNIELD WAY
UPPER ICKNIELD WAY
B488
B489

79
100

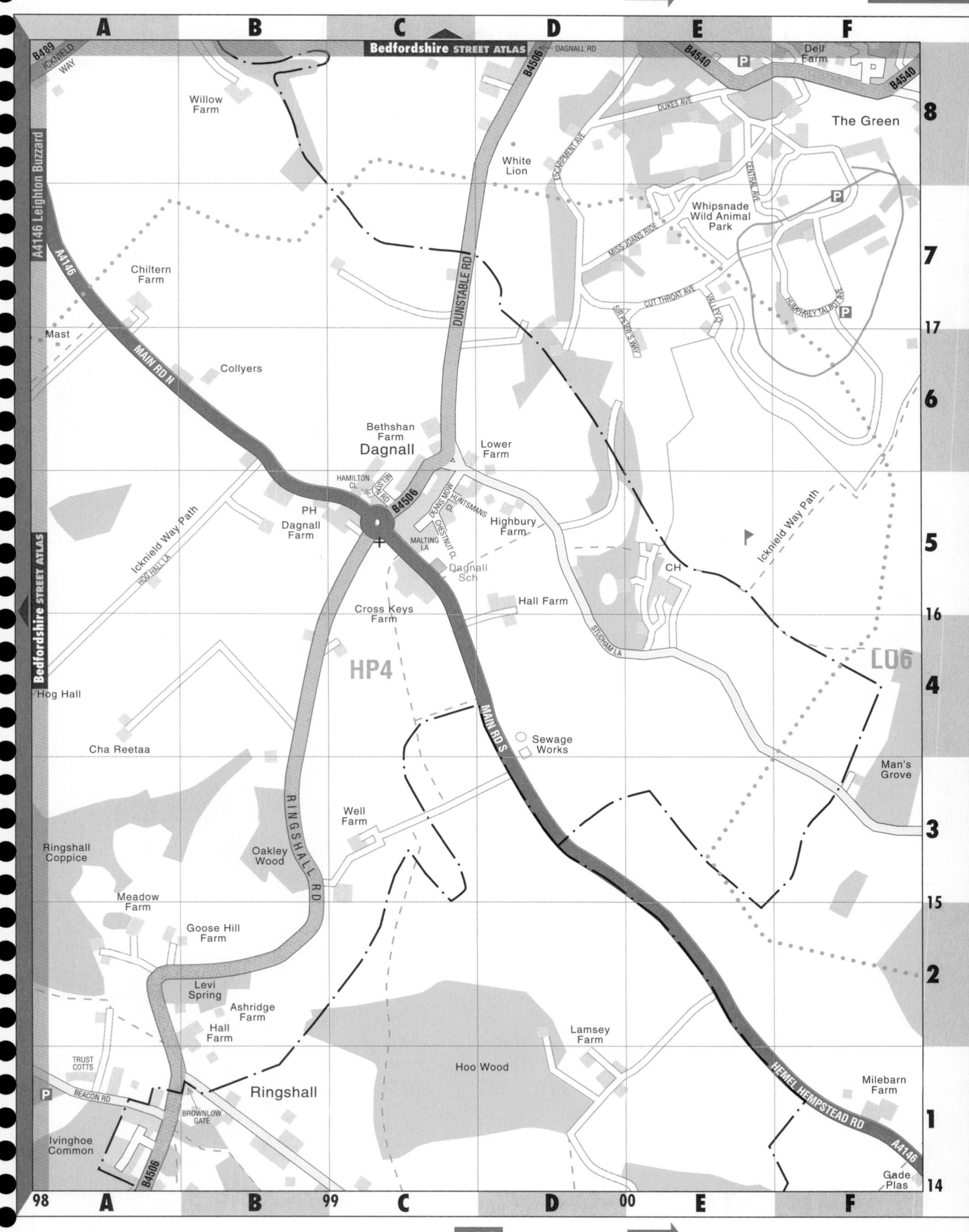

82 ➤

Bedfordshire STREET ATLAS

Bedfordshire STREET ATLAS

A **B** **C** **D** **E** **F**

B489
ICKNIELD WAY
← DAGNALL RD
B4506
DAGNALL RD
B4540
B4540

A4146 Leighton Buzzard

Dell Farm

Willow Farm

White Lion

The Green **8**

DUKES AVE

ESCARPMENT AVE

CENTRAL AVE

Whipsnade Wild Animal Park

A4146

MISS JOANS RIDE

P

7

Chiltern Farm

DUNSTABLE RD

CUT THROAT AVE

VALLEY CT

HUMPHREY TALBOT

P

17

Mast

Collyers

SIR PETER'S WAY

6

MAIN RD N

Bethshan Farm

Dagnall

Lower Farm

Icknield Way Path **5**

HAMILTON CL

NEVS CSS RD

Huntsmans

B4506

CHESTNUT CL

MALTING LA

Highbury Farm

PH
Dagnall Farm

Icknield Way Path

HOG HALL LA

MAIN CHESTNUT CL

Dagnall Sch

CH

L06

Hall Farm

16

Hog Hall

Cross Keys Farm

STUDHAM LA

HP4

4

Cha Reetaa

Man's Grove

MAIN RD S

○ Sewage
□ Works

Ringshall Coppice

RINGSHALL RD

Well Farm

3

Oakley Wood

15

Meadow Farm

Goose Hill Farm

2

Levi Spring

Ashridge Farm

Lamsey Farm

Hall Farm

Hoo Wood

HEMEL HEMPSTEAD RD

Milebarn Farm

TRUST COTTS

P

BEACON RD

Ringshall

BROWNLOW GATE

1

Ivinghoe Common

B4506

A4146

Gade Plas

14

81

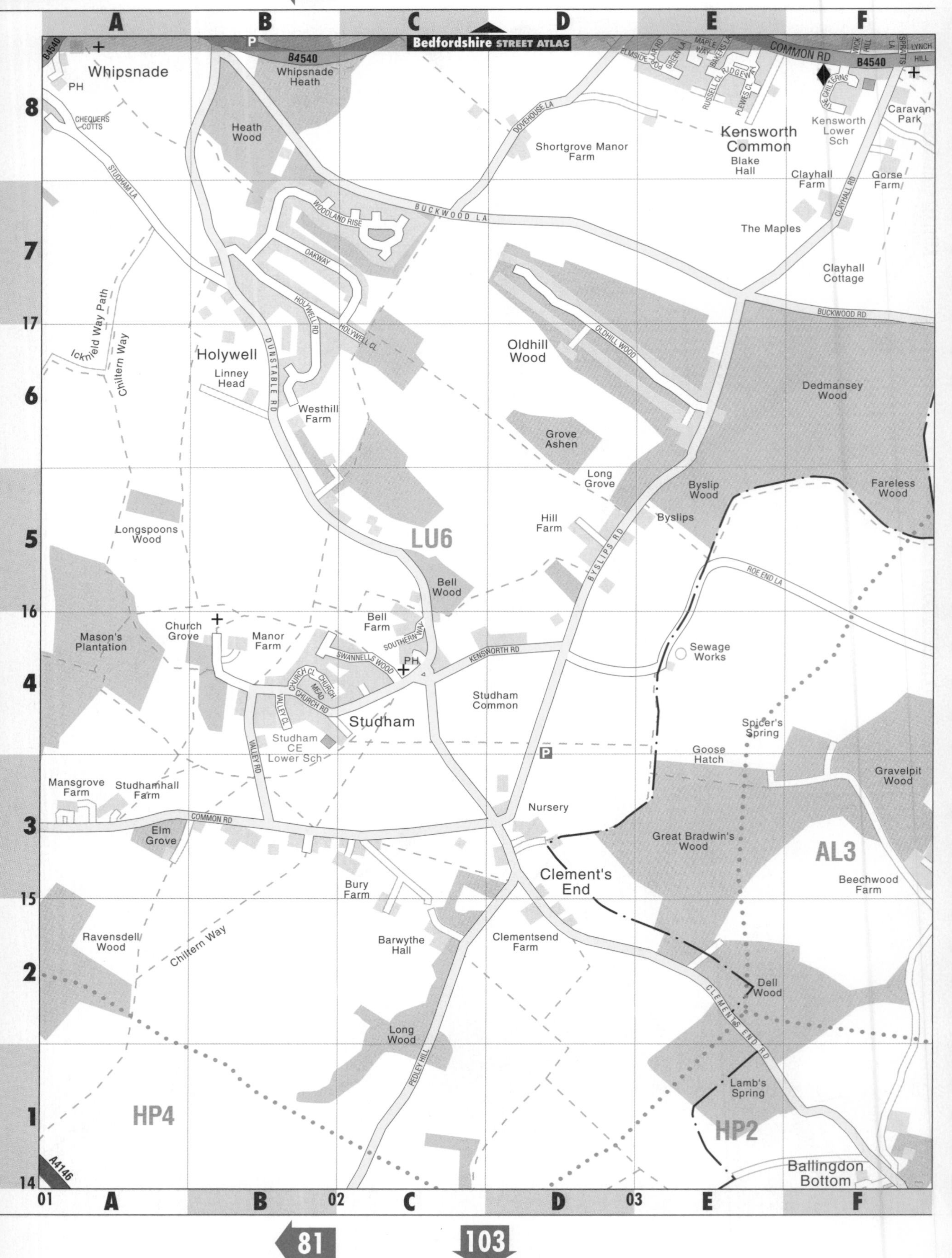

Bedfordshire STREET ATLAS
Whipsnade
Whipsnade Heath
Heath Wood
Kensworth Common
Kensworth Lower Sch
Caravan Park
Shortgrove Manor Farm
Blake Hall
Clayhall Farm
Gorse Farm
The Maples
Clayhall Cottage
BUCKWOOD LA
BUCKWOOD RD
Holywell
Linney Head
Westhill Farm
Oldhill Wood
Dedmansey Wood
Grove Ashen
Long Grove
Byslip Wood
Byslips
Fareless Wood
Hill Farm
Longspoons Wood
LU6
Bell Wood
ROE END LA
Bell Farm
Church Grove
Manor Farm
Mason's Plantation
Sewage Works
Studham Common
Studham
Studham CE Lower Sch
Spicer's Spring
Goose Hatch
Gravelpit Wood
Mansgrove Farm
Studhamhall Farm
Nursery
COMMON RD
Elm Grove
Great Bradwin's Wood
AL3
Clement's End
Beechwood Farm
Bury Farm
Ravensdell Wood
Barwythe Hall
Clementsend Farm
Chiltern Way
Icknield Way Path
Dell Wood
Long Wood
Lamb's Spring
HP4
HP2
Ballingdon Bottom
B4540
A4146

81
103

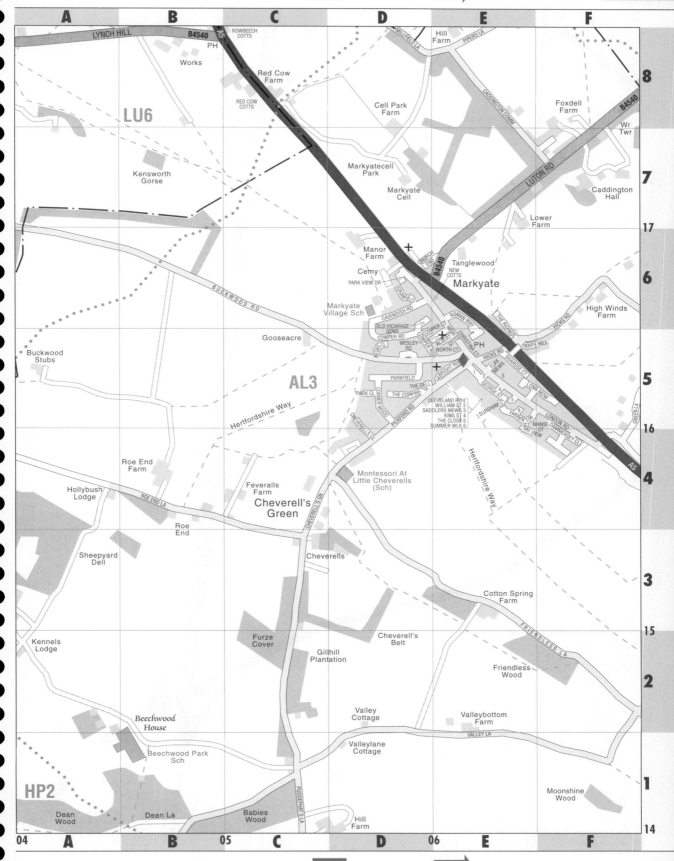

83
63

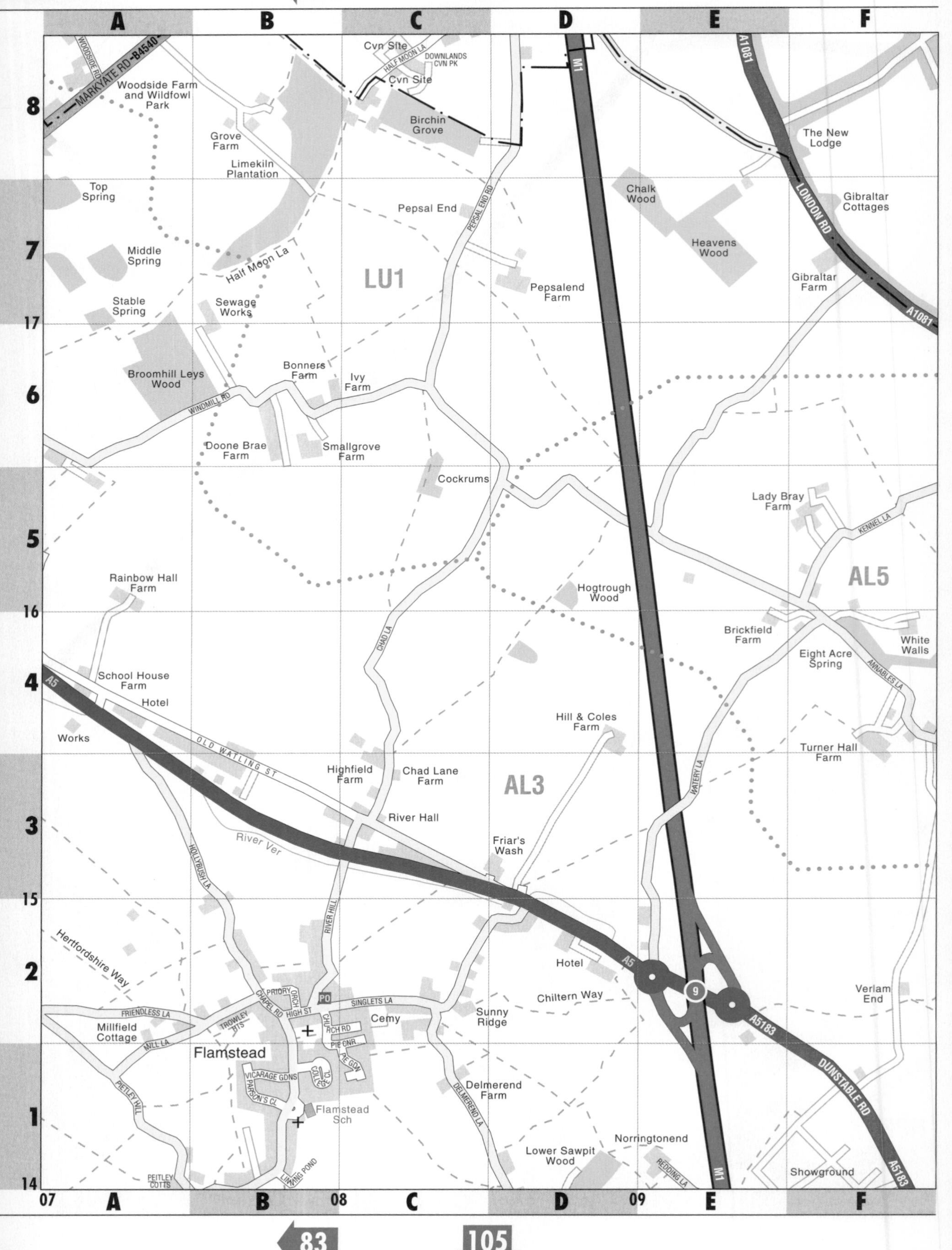
A
B
C
D
E
F
8
7
17
6
5
16
4
3
15
2
1
14
07
08
09
MARKYATE RD B4540
WOODSIDE RD
Woodside Farm and Wildfowl Park
Cvn Site
HALF MOON LA
DOWNLANDS CVN PK
Cvn Site
Birchin Grove
Grove Farm
Limekiln Plantation
Top Spring
Pepsal End
PEPSAL END RD
Middle Spring
Half Moon La
LU1
Stable Spring
Sewage Works
Pepsalend Farm
Broomhill Leys Wood
Bonners Farm
Ivy Farm
WINDMILL RD
Doone Brae Farm
Smallgrove Farm
Cockrums
M1
A1081
The New Lodge
Chalk Wood
LONDON RD
Gibraltar Cottages
Heavens Wood
Gibraltar Farm
Lady Bray Farm
KENNEL LA
AL5
Rainbow Hall Farm
Hogtrough Wood
Brickfield Farm
White Walls
Eight Acre Spring
ANNABLES LA
School House Farm
A5
Hotel
Works
CHAD LA
Hill & Coles Farm
Turner Hall Farm
OLD WATLING ST
Highfield Farm
Chad Lane Farm
AL3
WATERY LA
River Hall
River Ver
Friar's Wash
HOLLYBUSH LA
RIVER HILL
Hertfordshire Way
Hotel
Chiltern Way
9
Verlam End
A5183
PRIORY
ORCH
CHAPEL RD
PO
SINGLETS LA
FRIENDLESS LA
HIGH ST
Sunny Ridge
Millfield Cottage
TROWLEY HTS
CHURCH RD
Cemy
MILL LA
PIE CNR
PIE GDN
Flamstead
VICARAGE GDNS
COLLEGE CL
PARSON'S CL
DUNSTABLE RD
Delmerend Farm
DELMEREND LA
PIETLEY HILL
Flamstead Sch
Norringtonend
Lower Sawpit Wood
REDDING LA
PEITLEY COTTS
LINING POND
Showground
A5183
A
B
C
D
E
F

83
105

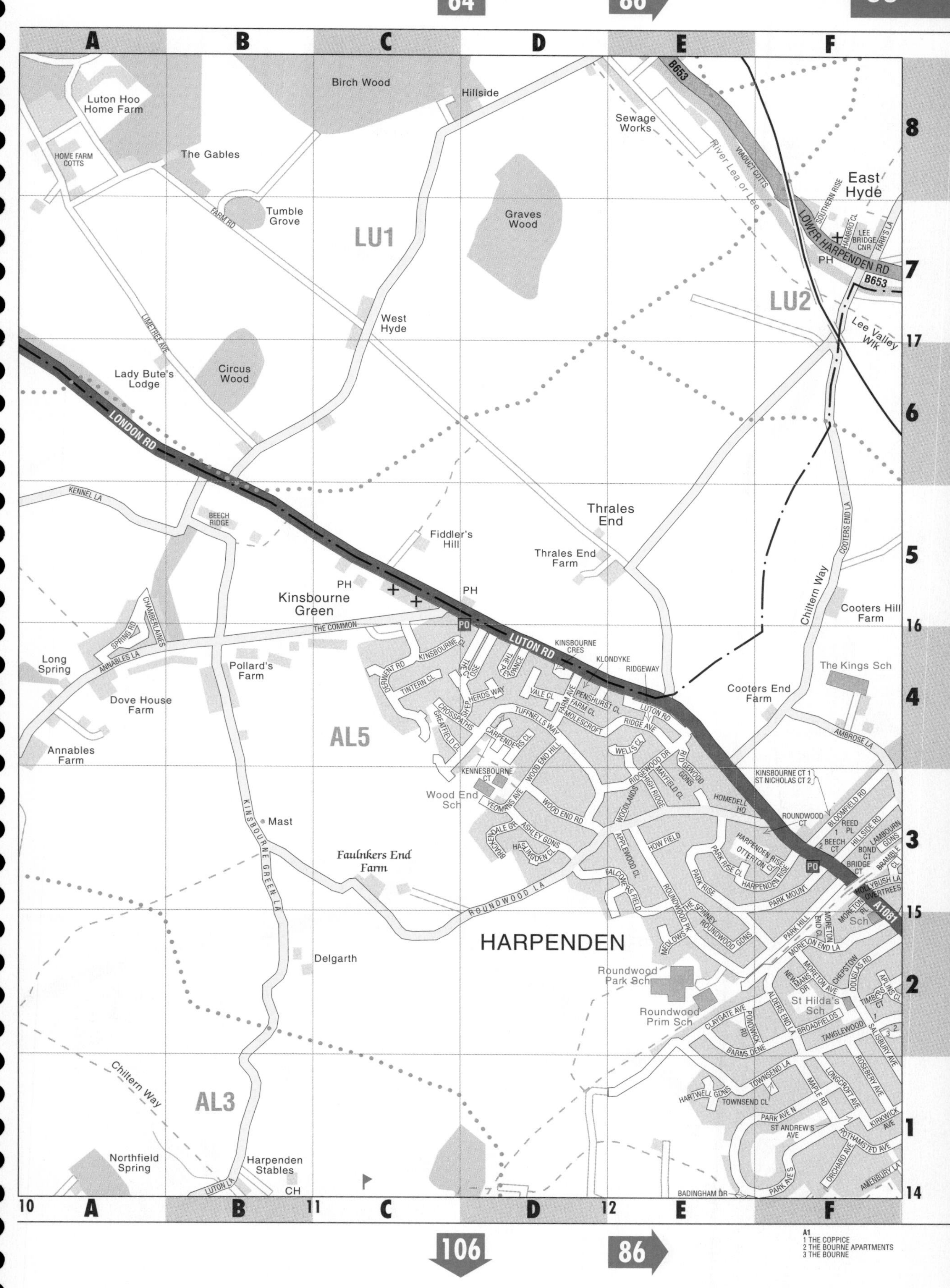

A1
1 THE COPPICE
2 THE BOURNE APARTMENTS
3 THE BOURNE

85 65

A B C D E F

8 7 17 6 5 16 4 3 15 2 1 14

Chiltern Way
Hyde Home Farm
Garden Wood
Home Wood
The Hyde
Little Cutts Farm
Plummers La
Bishey Wood
Tallents Farm
SG4
B652
Hill Farm
East Hyde Park
Dane Farm
LU2
Lower Harpenden Rd
B653
Kimpton Bottom
Animal Welfare Centre
Dane Spring
Ladies Spring
Holly Farm
Holly La
Hyde Mill Farm
Bower Heath Farm
Broadlands
Wall Wood
Old Raisins Farm
Bower Heath La
Bower Heath
Kings Heath Pk
The Slype
Saunceys Wood La
River Lea or Lee
Lea Valley Wlk
Common La
AL5
Turners Hall Farm
Cold Hartbour
1 Riverbanks Cl
2 Barley Rise
3 St Martins Cl
Westfield Wood
Saunceys Wood
Sauncey Wood
The Lea Prim Sch
Cemy
Sauncey Wood Prim Sch
Mackerye End
Mackerye End Farm
Harpenden (private)
Riverside Est
Allied Bsns Ctr
Lower Luton Rd
Manland Prim Sch
Sir John Lawes Sch
Batford
Leacroft
Martham Ct
Lea Valley
Manor Rd
Lower Luton Rd
Marshalls Way
St George's Sch
HARPENDEN
Harpenden Memorial
Ford
The Firs
Ambleside
Marquis La
Station Rd
Luton Rd
A1081
B653
AL4
Sewage Works
Lea Valley Wlk
High St
Crabtree Inf Sch
1 Dalewood
2 Fairfield Cl
3 Englehurst
Piggottshill La
Piggottshill Wood
Liby
Coll
Harpenden
James Marshall Commercial Ctr
St Albans Rd
Southdown Rd
High Beeches Prim Sch
CH
Leasey Bridge La

13 A B 14 C D 15 E F

A2
1 LYDEKKER MEWS
2 GERARD CT
3 CORNELIA CT
4 HARDENWICK CT
5 SOUTHGATE CT
6 BERKELEY CT
7 FERNDALE
8 ANVIL HO

B1
1 CARLTON CT
2 CARLTON BANK
3 THE MEWS
4 CROFT CT
5 DEVONSHIRE RD
6 KINLOCH CT
7 VICTORIA RD
8 HARDING PAR
9 COLERIDGE CT

B1
10 BEAUMONT CT
11 COPPER BEECHES
12 MILTON CT
13 THE CEDARS
14 YARDLEY CT
15 KEATS HO
16 SHELLEY CT
17 AVON CT
18 FURZEDOWN CT
19 CHILTERN CT
20 HADDON CT

85 107

66
88

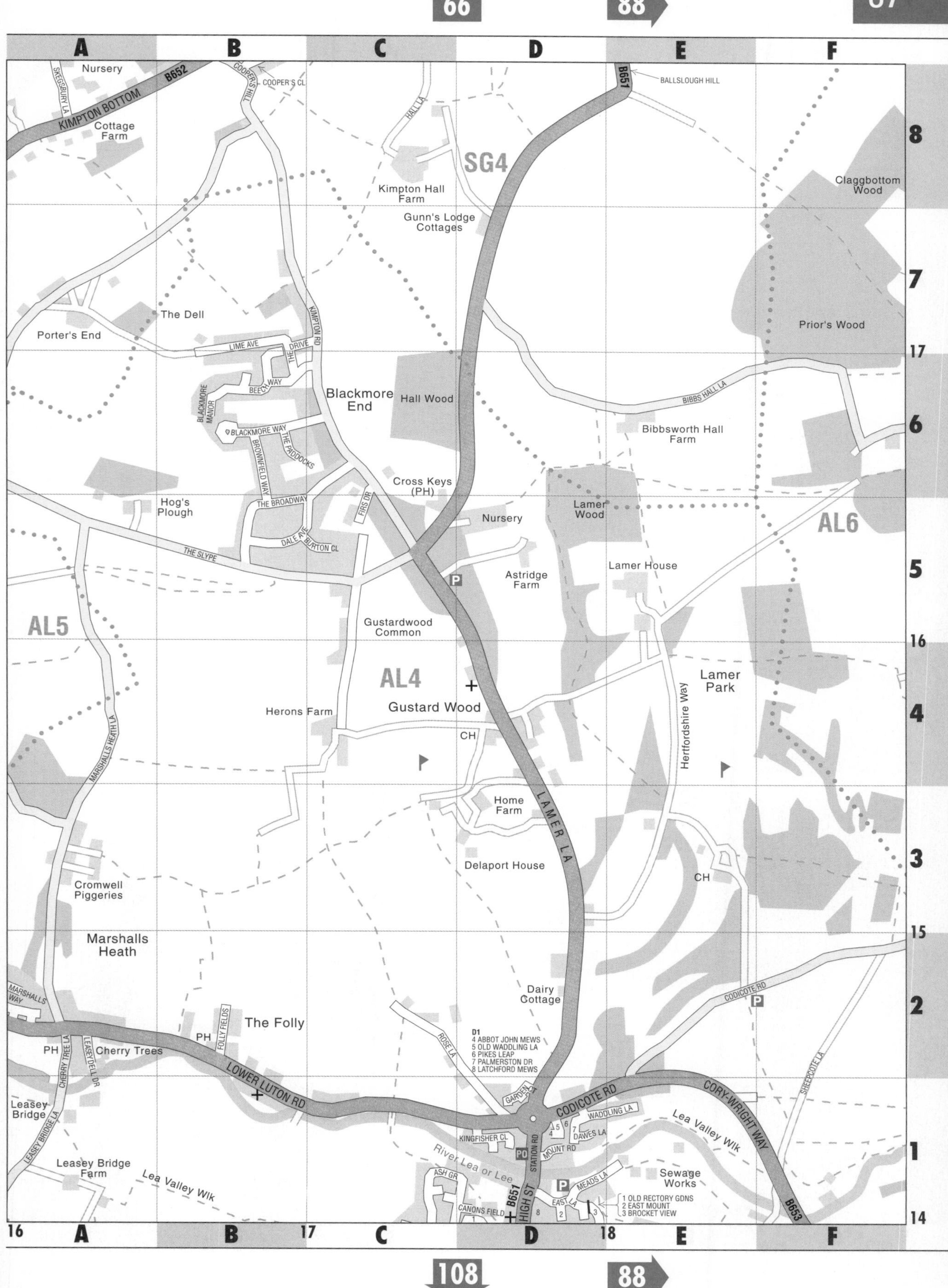
A
B
C
D
E
F
Nursery
SKEGSBURY LA
B652
KIMPTON BOTTOM
COOPER'S HILL
COOPER'S CL
B651
BALLSLOUGH HILL
Cottage Farm
HALL LA
SG4
8
Kimpton Hall Farm
Claggbottom Wood
Gunn's Lodge Cottages
7
The Dell
KIMPTON RD
Prior's Wood
Porter's End
LIME AVE
THE DRIVE
17
BEECH WAY
Blackmore End
Hall Wood
BIBBS HALL LA
BLACKMORE MANOR
BLACKMORE WAY
Bibbsworth Hall Farm
6
THE PADDOCKS
BROWNFIELD WAY
Cross Keys (PH)
Hog's Plough
THE BROADWAY
FIRS DR
Nursery
Lamer Wood
AL6
DALE AVE
BURTON CL
THE SLYPE
Astridge Farm
Lamer House
5
P
AL5
Gustardwood Common
16
AL4
Lamer Park
Herons Farm
Gustard Wood
Hertfordshire Way
4
CH
MARSHALLS HEATH LA
Home Farm
LAMER LA
3
Delaport House
CH
Cromwell Piggeries
15
Marshalls Heath
Dairy Cottage
MARSHALLS WAY
CODICOTE RD
P
2
FOLLY FIELDS
The Folly
PH
D1
4 ABBOT JOHN MEWS
5 OLD WADDLING LA
6 PIKES LEAP
7 PALMERSTON DR
8 LATCHFORD MEWS
PH
CHERRY TREE LA
LEASEY DELL DR
Cherry Trees
ROSE LA
SHEEPCOTE LA
LOWER LUTON RD
GARDEN CT
CODICOTE RD
CORY-WRIGHT WAY
Leasey Bridge
LEASEY BRIDGE LA
WADDLING LA
Lea Valley Wlk
KINGFISHER CL
DAWES LA
1
STATION RD
MOUNT RD
PO
River Lea or Lee
Leasey Bridge Farm
ASH GR
Sewage Works
Lea Valley Wlk
B651
P
MEADS LA
HIGH ST
1 OLD RECTORY GDNS
2 EAST MOUNT
3 BROCKET VIEW
CANONS FIELD
EAST LA
B653
14
16
17
18

108
88

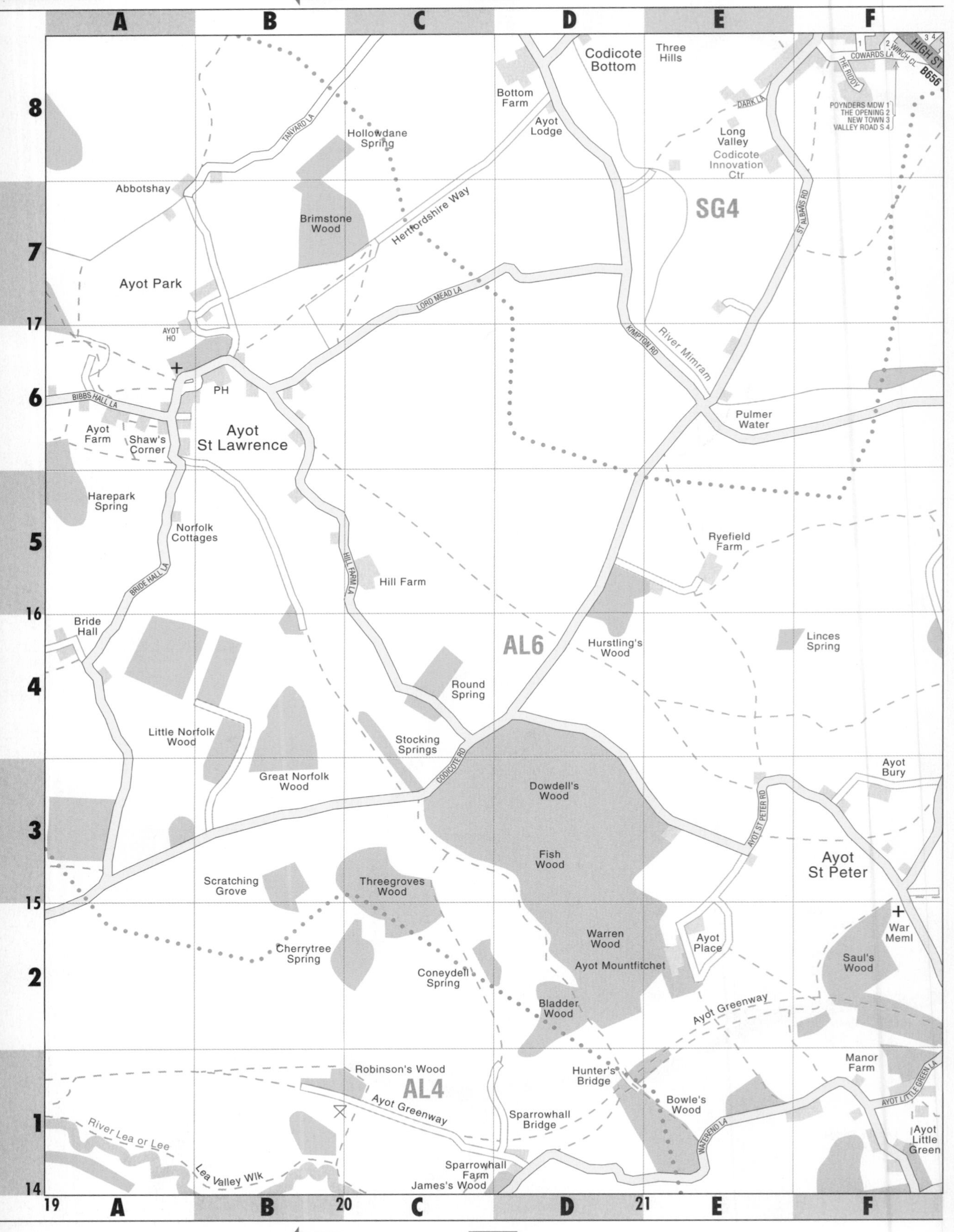

Codicote Bottom

Three Hills

Bottom Farm

Ayot Lodge

Hollowdane Spring

TANYARD LA

Abbotshay

Brimstone Wood

Hertfordshire Way

DARK LA

Long Valley

Codicote Innovation Ctr

SG4

ST ALBANS RD

THE BURY

COWARDS LA

HIGH ST

B656

POYNDERS MDW 1
THE OPENING 2
NEW TOWN 3
VALLEY ROAD S 4

Ayot Park

LORD MEAD LA

KIMPTON RD

River Mimram

AYOT HO

PH

BIBBS HALL LA

Ayot St Lawrence

Ayot Farm

Shaw's Corner

Pulmer Water

Harepark Spring

Norfolk Cottages

BRIDE HALL LA

HILL FARM LA

Hill Farm

Ryefield Farm

Linces Spring

Bride Hall

AL6

Hurstling's Wood

Round Spring

Little Norfolk Wood

Stocking Springs

CODICOTE RD

Dowdell's Wood

AYOT ST PETER RD

Ayot Bury

Great Norfolk Wood

Ayot St Peter

Scratching Grove

Threegroves Wood

Fish Wood

War Meml

Cherrytree Spring

Coneydell Spring

Warren Wood

Ayot Mountfitchet

Ayot Place

Saul's Wood

Bladder Wood

Ayot Greenway

Robinson's Wood

AL4

Ayot Greenway

Hunter's Bridge

Bowle's Wood

Manor Farm

AYOT LITTLE GREEN LA

River Lea or Lee

Sparrowhall Bridge

WATEREND LA

Ayot Little Green

Lea Valley Wlk

Sparrowhall Farm

James's Wood

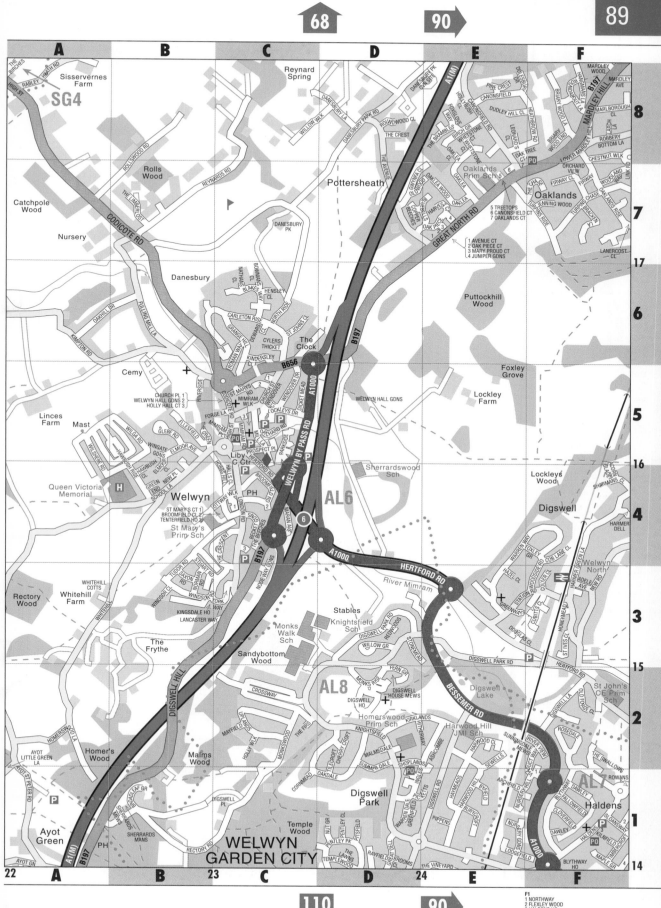

A B C D E F

8
7
17
6
5
16
4
3
15
2
1
14

22 23 24

SG4
Sisservernes Farm
Reynard Spring
Rolls Wood
Catchpole Wood
Nursery
Pottersheath
Oaklands
Oaklands Prim Sch
Danesbury
Puttockhill Wood
The Clock
Cemy
Foxley Grove
Lockley Farm
Linces Farm
Mast
Liby C Ctr
Sherrardswood Sch
Queen Victoria Memorial
Welwyn
AL6
Lockleys Wood
Digswell
St Mary's Prim Sch
Welwyn North
Rectory Wood
Whitehill Farm
River Mimram
Stables
Knightsfield Sch
Monks Walk Sch
The Frythe
Sandybottom Wood
AL8
Digswell Lake
St John's CE Prim Sch
Homerswood Prim Sch
Harwood Hill JMI Sch
Homer's Wood
Malms Wood
Digswell Park
AL7
Haldens
Temple Wood
Ayot Green
WELWYN GARDEN CITY

CODICOTE RD
GREAT NORTH RD
WELWYN BY PASS RD
HERTFORD RD
BESSEMER RD
DIGSWELL HILL
A1(M)
A1000
B197
B656

5 TREETOPS
6 CANONSFIELD CT
7 OAKLANDS CT

1 AVENUE CT
2 OAK PIECE CT
3 MARY PROUD CT
4 JUNIPER GDNS

CHURCH PL 1
WELWYN HALL GDNS 2
HOLLY HALL CT 3

ST MARY'S CT 1
BROOMFIELD CL 2
TENTERFIELD HO 3

110
90

F1
1 NORTHWAY
2 FLEXLEY WOOD
3 HALDENS HO
4 RUNSLEY

89 69

A B C D E F
8 7 17 6 5 16 4 3 15 2 1 14
25 26 27
Gover's Green
Backlane Wood
Sedge Green
Hempstall Spinney
SG3
The Horns (PH)
Coltsfoot Farm
Moathouse Farm
Welches Farm
Bull's Green
Wr Twr
Nurseries
Green's Wood
Harmergreen Wood
Barnes Wood
White Horse (PH)
Burnham Green
Caravan Site
Brickground Wood
Nursery
Harmer Green
Tewin Wood
Nancybury Gorse
Nursery
Little Hillfoot Wood
Queen Hoo Hall
Sidehill Wood
Seven Acre Wood
Cooks Wood
AL6
Tewin Hill Farm
Beal's Wood
Dawley Wood
PH
Upper Green
Dawley Plantation
Digswell Water
Margery Green
Crown Farm
Tewin
Rose & Crown (PH)
Muspatts Farm
River Mimram
Home Wood
Tewin Cowper CE Prim Sch
The Rowans Prim Sch
Holy Family RC JMI Sch
Westley Wood
Rectory Wood
Tewin Bury Farm
Lamb Dell Wood
Home Wood
SG14
Marden Hill
AL7
MARDLEY HTS
MARDLEY AVE
WOODACRE DR
ROSECROFT LA
HILLSIDE WAY
MARLBOROUGH CL
ROBBERY
BOTTOM LA
COPSE HILL
CHESTNUT WLK
BROOM HILL
WOODLAND WAY
TURPINS CHASE
PEACE GR
TANGLEWOOD
SPINDLEBERRY CL
LANERCOST CL
BRAMFIELD RD
Back La
COLTSFOOT LA
WHITE HORSE LA
PURCELL CL
BURNHAM GREEN RD
BISHOPS RD
QUEEN HOO LA
TWO OAKS DR
BURNHAM CL
TYLERS WOOD
COWPERS WAY
FIRS WLK
TEWIN CL
Chain Wlk
DESBOROUGH DR
HARMER GREEN LA
WEST RIDING
EAST RIDING
ORCHARD RD
BADGERS WLK
TEWIN HILL
Park La
PENNYFEATHERS LA
VERA LA
SHARMANS CL
THE DELL
HARMER DELL
NEW RD
MORNINGTON
UPPER GN
UPPER GREEN RD
GODFREYS CL
HARWOOD CL
BACK LA
LOWER GN
HERTFORD RD
THE STABLE BLOCK
THE WALLED GDN
THE HAZELS
CANNONS MDW
SCHOOL LA
MARGERY WOOD
NUTFIELD
HERTFORD RD
FLEXLEY WOOD
SWANHILL
ROBIN MEAD
ROWANS
SALMON CL
CHURCHFIELD RD
GRASS WARREN
POSTFIELD
LUMBARDS
EASTOR
SLOANSWAY
CROOKHAMS
QUICK BEAMS
POND FIELD
RUNSLEY
B1000 WATERSIDE
B1000
ARCHERS GREEN LA
P
PO

89 111

70
92

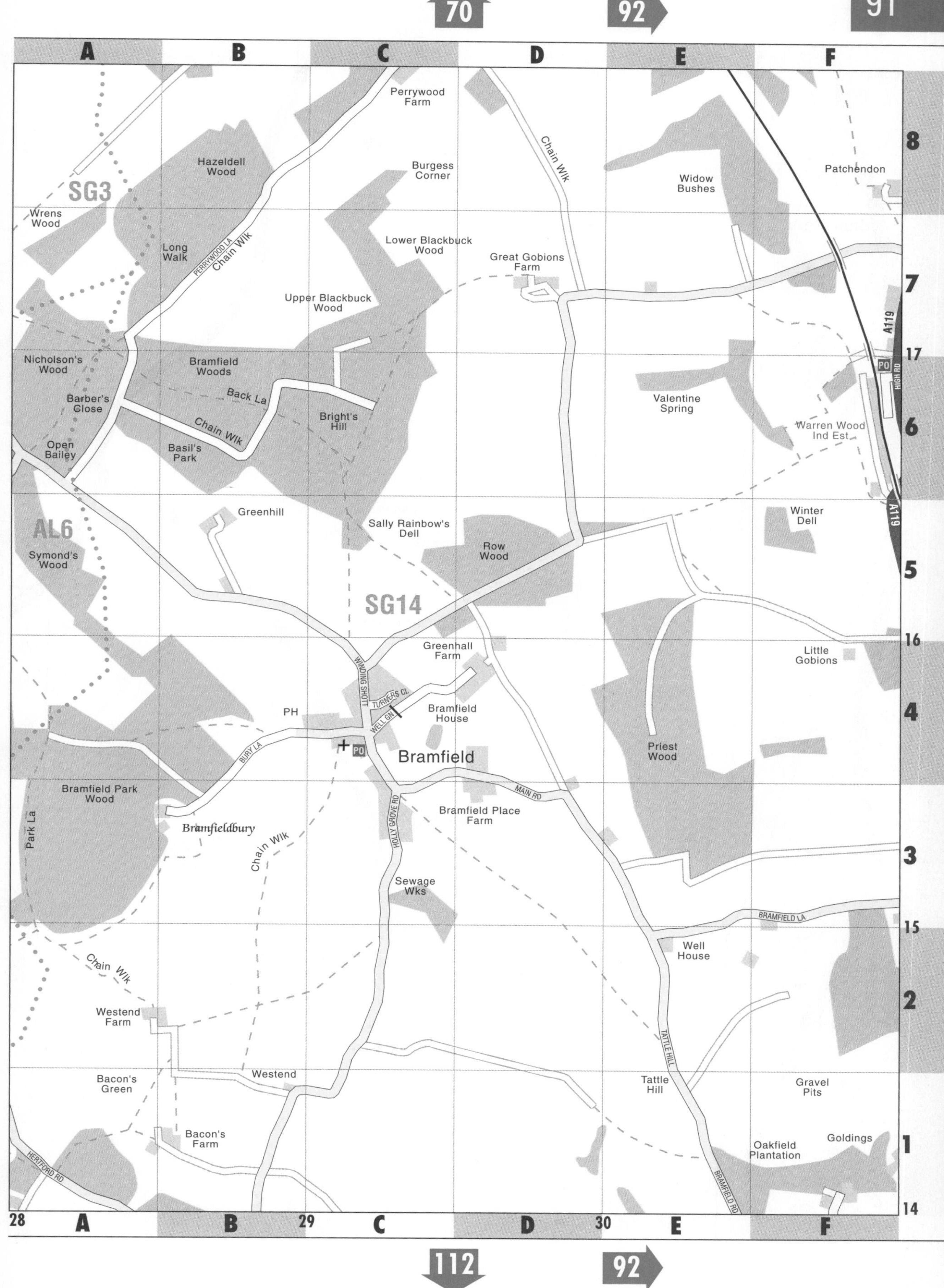
A
B
C
D
E
F
Perrywood Farm
Chain Wlk
8
Hazeldell Wood
Burgess Corner
Widow Bushes
Patchendon
SG3
Wrens Wood
Long Walk
PERRYWOOD LA
Lower Blackbuck Wood
Great Gobions Farm
7
Upper Blackbuck Wood
A119
17
Nicholson's Wood
Bramfield Woods
PO
HIGH RD
Back La
Barber's Close
Valentine Spring
Bright's Hill
Chain Wlk
Warren Wood Ind Est
6
Open Bailey
Basil's Park
Greenhill
Winter Dell
A119
AL6
Sally Rainbow's Dell
Row Wood
Symond's Wood
5
SG14
16
Greenhall Farm
Little Gobions
WINDING SHOTT
TURNERS CL
Bramfield House
4
PH
WELL GN
PO
Bramfield
BURY LA
Priest Wood
Bramfield Park Wood
MAIN RD
Bramfield Place Farm
Park La
Bramfieldbury
HOLLY GROVE RD
Chain Wlk
3
Sewage Wks
BRAMFIELD LA
15
Well House
Chain Wlk
2
Westend Farm
TATTLE HILL
Westend
Bacon's Green
Tattle Hill
Gravel Pits
Goldings
Oakfield Plantation
1
Bacon's Farm
HERTFORD RD
BRAMFIELD RD
14
28
29
30

112
92

91
71

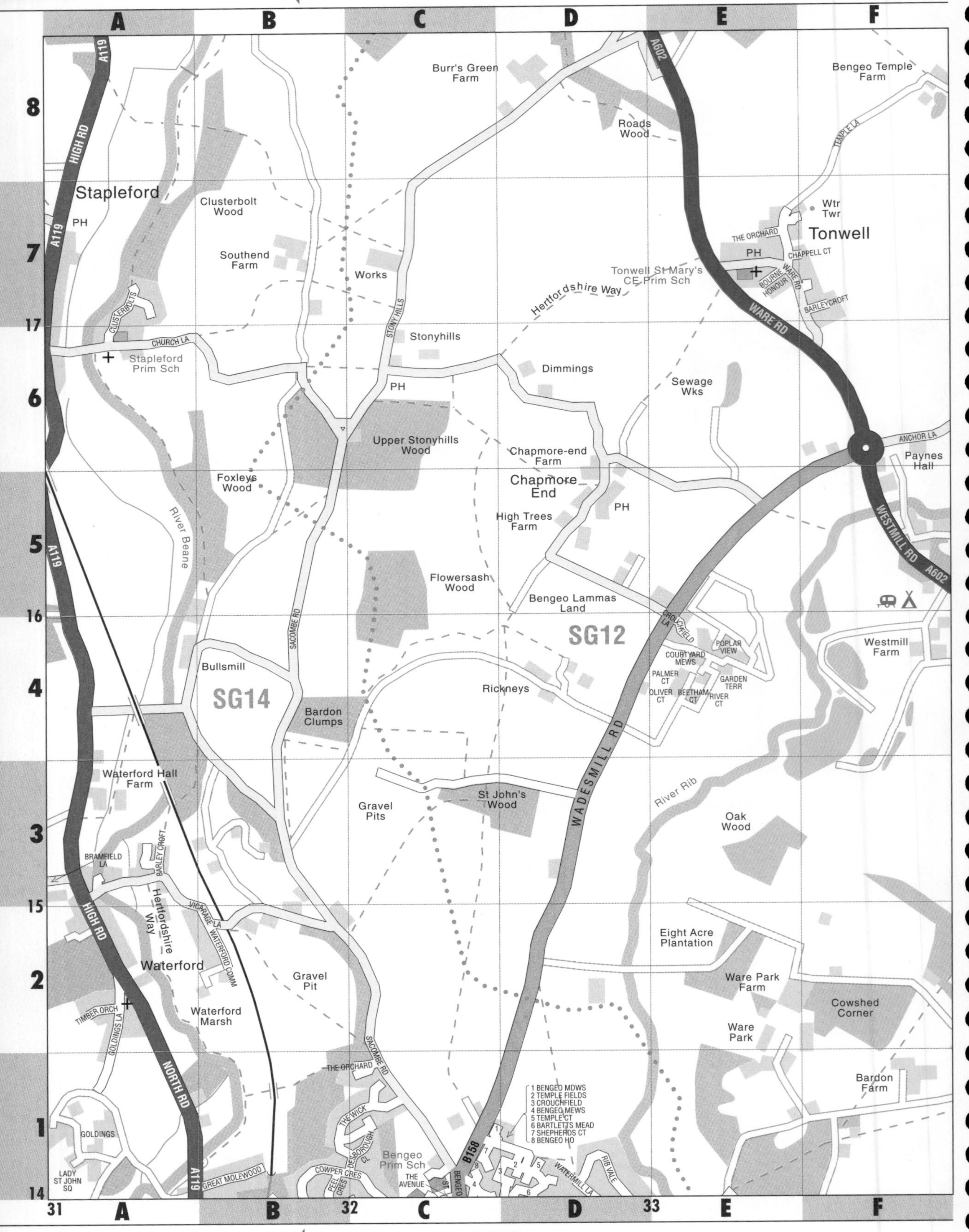
Stapleford
Clusterbolt Wood
Southend Farm
Burr's Green Farm
Roads Wood
Bengeo Temple Farm
Tonwell
Wtr Twr
Works
Stonyhills
Tonwell St Mary's CE Prim Sch
Hertfordshire Way
Stapleford Prim Sch
Dimmings
Sewage Wks
Upper Stonyhills Wood
Chapmore-end Farm
Chapmore End
Paynes Hall
Foxleys Wood
High Trees Farm
River Beane
Flowersash Wood
Bengeo Lammas Land
SG12
Westmill Farm
Bullsmill
SG14
Rickneys
Bardon Clumps
Waterford Hall Farm
Gravel Pits
St John's Wood
River Rib
Oak Wood
Eight Acre Plantation
Waterford
Gravel Pit
Waterford Marsh
Ware Park Farm
Cowshed Corner
Ware Park
Bardon Farm
Bengeo Prim Sch
GOLDINGS
LADY ST JOHN SQ
HIGH RD
NORTH RD
A119
A602
B158
WARE RD
WADESMILL RD
WESTMILL RD
SACOMBE RD
STONY HILLS
CHURCH LA
VICARAGE LA
WATERFORD COMM
GREAT MOLEWOOD
THE ORCHARD
THE WICK
COWPER CRES
PEEL CRES
DESBOROUGH CL
THE AVENUE
BENGEO ST
WATERMILL LA
RIB VALE
TIMBER ORCH
GOLDINGS LA
BRAMFIELD LA
BARLEY CROFT
CLUSTERBOLTS
TEMPLE LA
BARLEYCROFT
CHAPPELL CT
BOURNE HONOUR
ANCHOR LA
CROUCHFIELD LA
POPLAR VIEW
COURTYARD MEWS
PALMER CT
OLIVER CT
BEETHAM CT
GARDEN TERR
RIVER CT
PH
1 BENGEO MDWS
2 TEMPLE FIELDS
3 CROUCHFIELD
4 BENGEO MEWS
5 TEMPLE CT
6 BARTLETTS MEAD
7 SHEPHERDS CT
8 BENGEO HO
A B C D E F
8 7 17 6 5 16 4 3 15 2 1 14
31 32 33

91
113

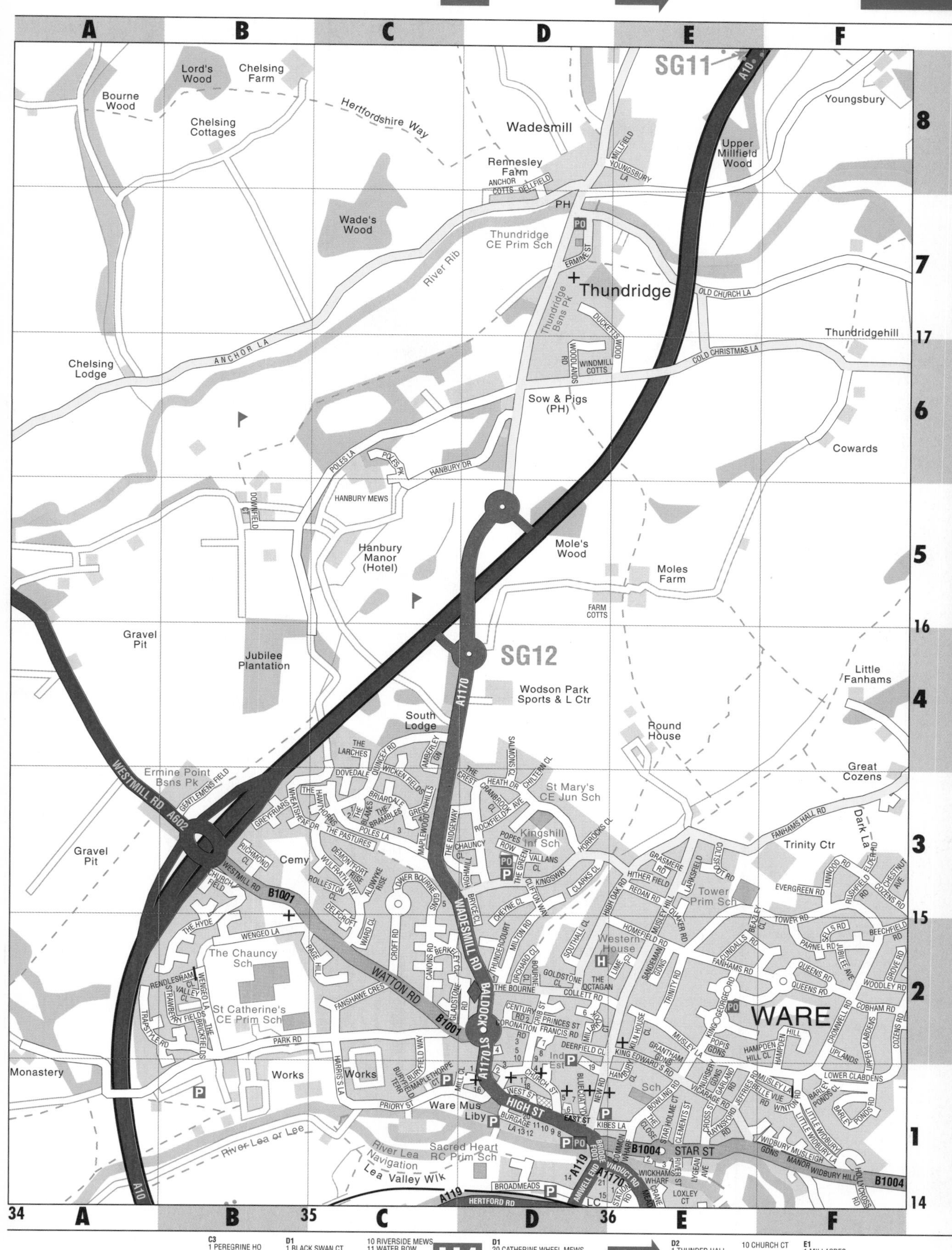

C3
1 PEREGRINE HO
2 FALCON CT
3 OSPREY HO
4 KESTREL CT
5 LOWER BOURNE CL

D1
1 BLACK SWAN CT
2 CHURCH ROW MEWS
3 ST MARY'S CTYD
4 OMEGA CT
5 FRENCH HORN CT
6 LEASIDE WLK
7 DOLPHIN YD
8 WELLS YD
9 GEORGE WLK

10 RIVERSIDE MEWS
11 WATER ROW
12 BURGAGE CT
13 CHRISTOPHER CT
14 BECKETS WLK
15 STATION CT
16 YORKES MEWS
17 TUDOR WLK
18 TUDOR SQ
19 DICKENSON WAY

D1
20 CATHERINE WHEEL MEWS
21 FRENCHES YD

D2
1 THUNDER HALL
2 THE BAKERY
3 ROKEWOOD MEWS
4 WAGGONERS YD
5 ST EVROUL CT
6 HARTFIELD CT
7 MONKS ROW
8 CAMERON CT
9 THE ALBION

10 CHURCH CT

E1
1 MILLACRES
2 OMEGA MALTINGS
3 ALBANY MEWS

93 73

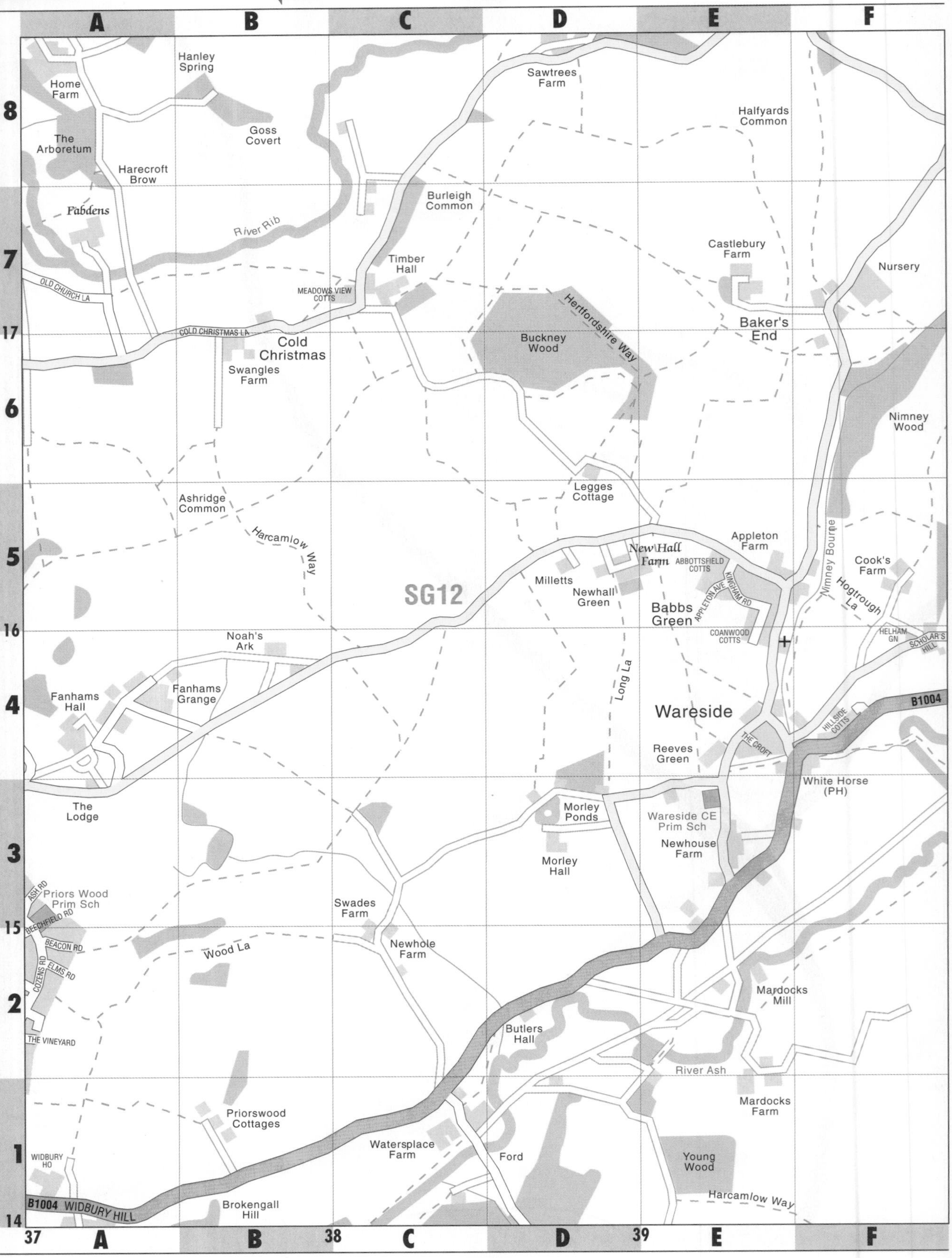

A B C D E F

8

Home Farm

Hanley Spring

Goss Covert

The Arboretum

Harecroft Brow

Fabdens

River Rib

Sawtrees Farm

Halfyards Common

Burleigh Common

7

OLD CHURCH LA

Timber Hall

MEADOWS VIEW COTTS

Castlebury Farm

Nursery

17

COLD CHRISTMAS LA

Cold Christmas

Buckney Wood

Hertfordshire Way

Baker's End

Swangles Farm

6

Nimney Wood

Legges Cottage

Ashridge Common

Harcamlow Way

Appleton Farm

Cook's Farm

5

SG12

Milletts

New Hall Farm

ABBOTTSFIELD COTTS

Hogtrough La

Nimney Bourne

Newhall Green

KINGHAM RD

16

Noah's Ark

Babbs Green

COANWOOD COTTS

HELHAM GN

SCHOLAR'S HILL

APPLETON AVE

4

Fanhams Hall

Fanhams Grange

Wareside

B1004

HILLSIDE COTTS

THE CROFT

Reeves Green

White Horse (PH)

The Lodge

Morley Ponds

Wareside CE Prim Sch

Mardocks Mill

3

Priors Wood Prim Sch

Morley Hall

Newhouse Farm

ASH RD

BEECHFIELD RD

15

Swades Farm

Wood La

Newhole Farm

BEACON RD

COZENS RD

ELMS RD

2

THE VINEYARD

River Ash

Butlers Hall

Mardocks Farm

Priorswood Cottages

1

WIDBURY HO

Watersplace Farm

Ford

Young Wood

Harcamlow Way

14

B1004 WIDBURY HILL

Brokengall Hill

37 A B 38 C D 39 E F

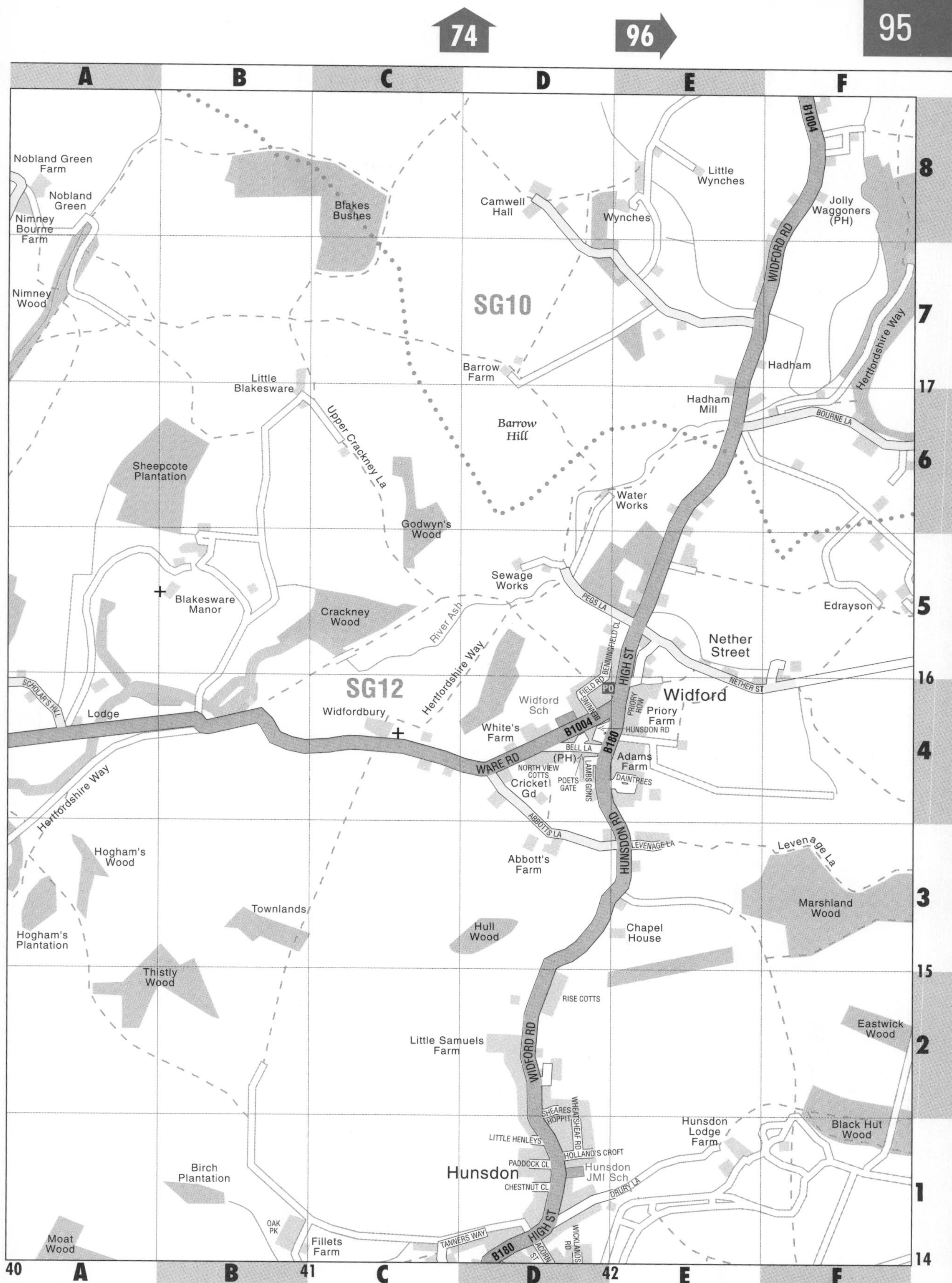

A   B   C   D   E   F

Nobland Green
Farm

Nobland
Green

Nimney
Bourne
Farm

Nimney
Wood

Blakes
Bushes

Camwell
Hall

Little
Wynches

Wynches

B1004

WIDFORD RD

Jolly
Waggoners
(PH)

Hertfordshire Way

SG10

8

7

Little
Blakesware

Barrow
Farm

Hadham

17

Upper Crackney La

*Barrow
Hill*

Hadham
Mill

BOURNE LA

6

Sheepcote
Plantation

Godwyn's
Wood

Water
Works

Edrayson

5

+
Blakesware
Manor

Crackney
Wood

River Ash

Hertfordshire Way

Sewage
Works

PEGS LA

Nether
Street

NETHER ST

SG12

Lodge

Widfordbury

+

White's
Farm

Widford
Sch

FIELD RD

BENINGFIELD CL

PO

HIGH ST

Widford

Priory
Farm

PRIORY
ROW

HUNSDON RD

16

SCHOLAR'S

Hertfordshire Way

WARE RD

NORTH VIEW
COTTS

Cricket
Gd

POETS
GATE

BELL LA
(PH)

LAMBS GDNS

B1004

B180

Adams
Farm

DAINTREES

4

ABBOTT'S LA

HUNSDON RD

LEVENAGE LA

Levenage La

Hogham's
Wood

Abbott's
Farm

Hull
Wood

Chapel
House

Marshland
Wood

3

Hogham's
Plantation

Townlands

15

Thistly
Wood

RISE COTTS

Eastwick
Wood

WIDFORD RD

Little Samuels
Farm

2

Birch
Plantation

SHEARES

WHEATSHEAF RD

CROPPIT

Hunsdon
Lodge
Farm

Black Hut
Wood

LITTLE HENLEYS

HOLLAND'S CROFT

PADDOCK CL

CHESTNUT CL

Hunsdon

HIGH ST

Hunsdon
JMI Sch

DRURY LA

1

Moat
Wood

OAK
PK

Fillets
Farm

TANNERS WAY

B180

ACORN
ST

WICKLANDS
RD

14

40   A   B   41   C   D   42   E   F

95

75

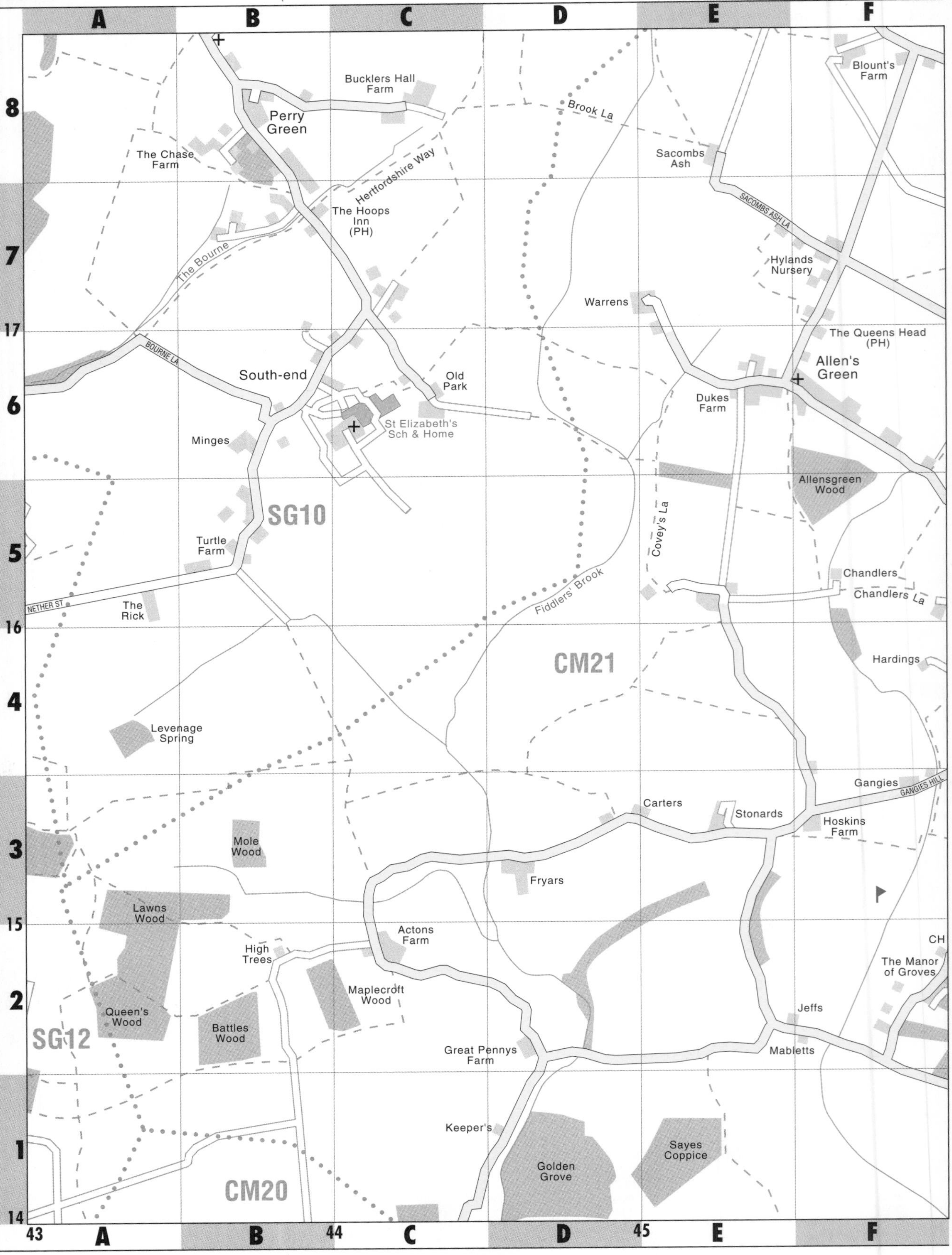

A B C D E F

8

Blount's Farm

Bucklers Hall Farm

Brook La

Perry Green

Sacombs Ash

The Chase Farm

Hertfordshire Way

SACOMBS ASH LA

The Hoops Inn (PH)

7

Hylands Nursery

The Bourne

17

Warrens

The Queens Head (PH)

BOURNE LA

South-end

Old Park

Allen's Green

6

Minges

St Elizabeth's Sch & Home

Dukes Farm

Allensgreen Wood

SG10

Turtle Farm

Covey's La

Chandlers

Chandlers La

5

NETHER ST

The Rick

16

Fiddlers' Brook

CM21

Hardings

4

Levenage Spring

Gangies

GANGIES HILL

Carters

Stonards

Hoskins Farm

3

Mole Wood

Fryars

Lawns Wood

15

Actons Farm

High Trees

The Manor of Groves

CH

Maplecroft Wood

2

Jeffs

Queen's Wood

Battles Wood

Great Pennys Farm

Mabletts

SG12

Keeper's

1

Sayes Coppice

Golden Grove

CM20

14

43 A B 44 C D 45 E F

95

117

76
98

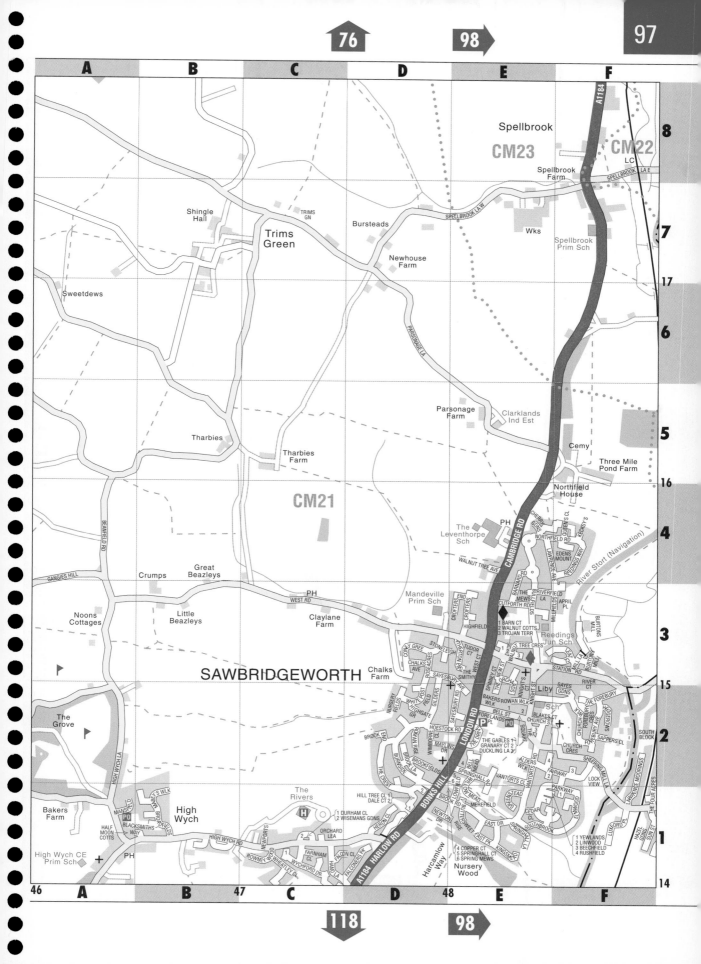
A
B
C
D
E
F
Spellbrook
CM23
CM22
A1184
LC
Spellbrook Farm
SPELLBROOK LA E
Shingle Hall
TRIMS GN
Trims Green
Bursteads
SPELLBROOK LA W
Wks
Spellbrook Prim Sch
Newhouse Farm
Sweetdews
PARSONAGE LA
Parsonage Farm
Clarklands Ind Est
Tharbies
Tharbies Farm
Cemy
Three Mile Pond Farm
Northfield House
CM21
The Leventhorpe Sch
PH
CAMBRIDGE RD
River Stort (Navigation)
BEANFIELD RD
WALNUT TREE AVE
GANGIES HILL
Crumps
Great Beazleys
Mandeville Prim Sch
WEST RD
Noons Cottages
Little Beazleys
Claylane Farm
Reedings Jun Sch
SAWBRIDGEWORTH
Chalks Farm
STATION RD
Liby
Sch
The Grove
LONDON RD
PO
SOUTH BLOCK
HIGH WYCH LA
Bakers Farm
High Wych
The Rivers
HALF MOON COTTS
HIGH WYCH RD
BONKS HILL
HARLOW RD
High Wych CE Prim Sch
Harcamlow Way
Nursery Wood
1 BARN CT
2 WALNUT COTTS
3 TROJAN TERR
THE GABLES 1
GRANARY CT 2
DUCKLING LA 3
HILL TREE CL 1
DALE CT 2
1 DURHAM CL
2 WISEMANS GDNS
4 COPPER CT
5 SPRINGHALL CT
6 SPRING MEWS
1 YEWLANDS
2 LINWOOD
3 BEECHFIELD
4 RUSHFIELD
8
7
17
6
5
16
4
3
15
2
1
14
46
47
48

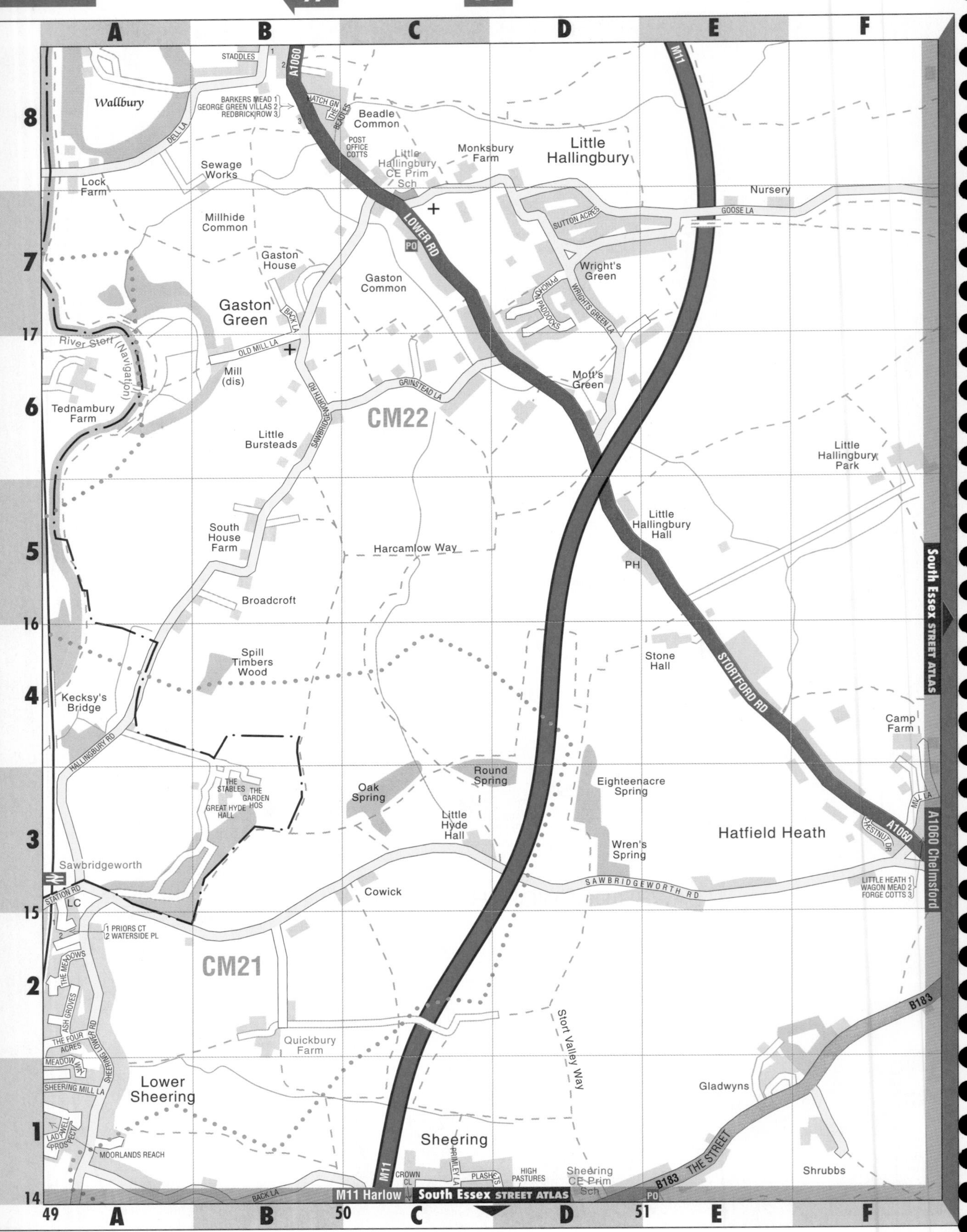

A B C D E F

8
STADDLES
Wallbury
BARKERS MEAD 1
GEORGE GREEN VILLAS 2
REDBRICK ROW 3
HATCH GN
Beadle
Common
Little Hallingbury CE Prim Sch
Monksbury Farm
Little Hallingbury

Sewage Works
POST OFFICE COTTS
Little Hallingbury
Nursery
GOOSE LA

Lock Farm
Millhide Common
LOWER RD
PO
SUTTON ACRES
Wright's Green

7
Gaston House
Gaston Common
PADDOCKS
WRIGHT'S GREEN LA

17
River Stort (Navigation)
Gaston Green
BACK LA
OLD MILL LA
Mott's Green

Tednambury Farm
Mill (dis)
GRINSTEAD LA
CM22
Little Hallingbury Park

6
Little Bursteads
SAWBRIDGEWORTH RD
Little Hallingbury Hall

5
South House Farm
Harcamlow Way
PH
STORTFORD RD

16
Broadcroft
Stone Hall

4
Kecksy's Bridge
Spill Timbers Wood
Camp Farm
MILL LA
CHESTNUT DR
A1060

HALLINGBURY RD
THE STABLES
THE GARDEN
GREAT HYDE HALL
HOS
Oak Spring
Round Spring
Eighteenacre Spring
Hatfield Heath
A1060 Chelmsford

3
Sawbridgeworth
STATION RD
LC
Little Hyde Hall
Wren's Spring
LITTLE HEATH 1
WAGON MEAD 2
FORGE COTTS 3

15
1 PRIORS CT
2 WATERSIDE PL
Cowick
SAWBRIDGEWORTH RD

2
THE MEADOWS
CM21
Quickbury Farm
STORT VALLEY WAY
B183

ASH GROVES
SHEERING RD
THE FOUR ACRES
Gladwyns

MEADOW
Lower Sheering
THE STREET

1
LADY WELL
PROSPECT
Sheering
B183
Shrubbs

MOORLANDS REACH
M11
CROWN CL
PRIMLEY LA
PLASH CS
HIGH PASTURES
Sheering CE Prim Sch
PO

SHEERING MILL LA
BACK LA
14
49 A B 50 C D 51 E F

M11 Harlow
South Essex STREET ATLAS

South Essex STREET ATLAS

97

79
100

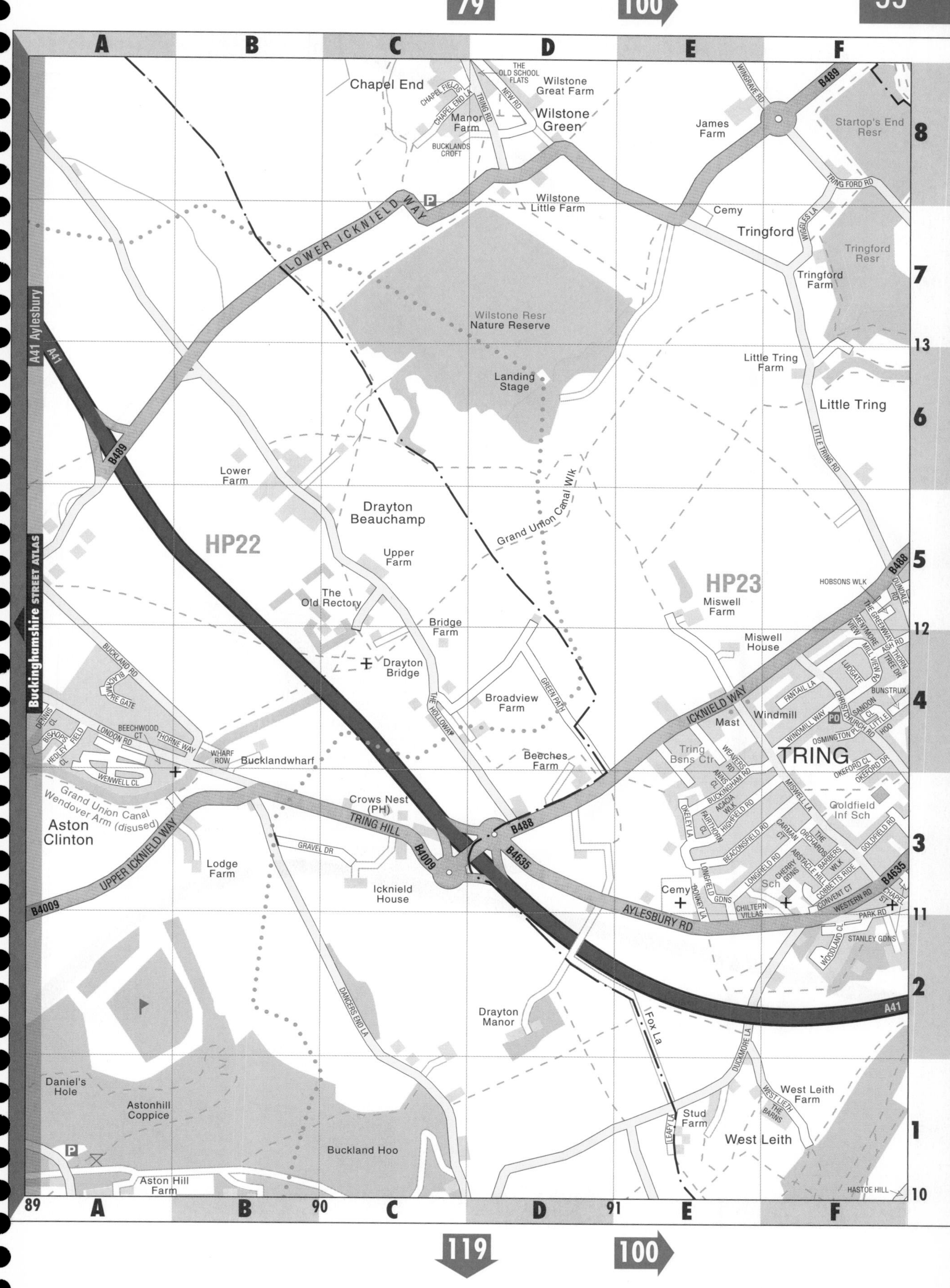
Chapel End
Wilstone Great Farm
Wilstone Green
Manor Farm
James Farm
Startop's End Resr
Wilstone Little Farm
Cemy
Tringford
LOWER ICKNIELD WAY
Tringford Resr
Tringford Farm
Wilstone Resr Nature Reserve
Landing Stage
Little Tring Farm
Little Tring
Lower Farm
Drayton Beauchamp
HP22
Grand Union Canal Wlk
Upper Farm
The Old Rectory
HP23
Miswell Farm
Bridge Farm
Miswell House
Drayton Bridge
Broadview Farm
ICKNIELD WAY
Windmill
Mast
Tring Bsns Ctr
TRING
Beeches Farm
Bucklandwharf
Grand Union Canal Wendover Arm (disused)
Aston Clinton
Crows Nest (PH)
TRING HILL
Goldfield Inf Sch
UPPER ICKNIELD WAY
Lodge Farm
Icknield House
Cemy
Sch
AYLESBURY RD
Drayton Manor
Fox La
Daniel's Hole
West Leith Farm
Astonhill Coppice
Stud Farm
West Leith
Buckland Hoo
Aston Hill Farm
A41 Aylesbury
Buckinghamshire STREET ATLAS
A B C D E F
8 7 13 6 5 12 4 3 11 2 1 10
89 90 91

119
100

99
80

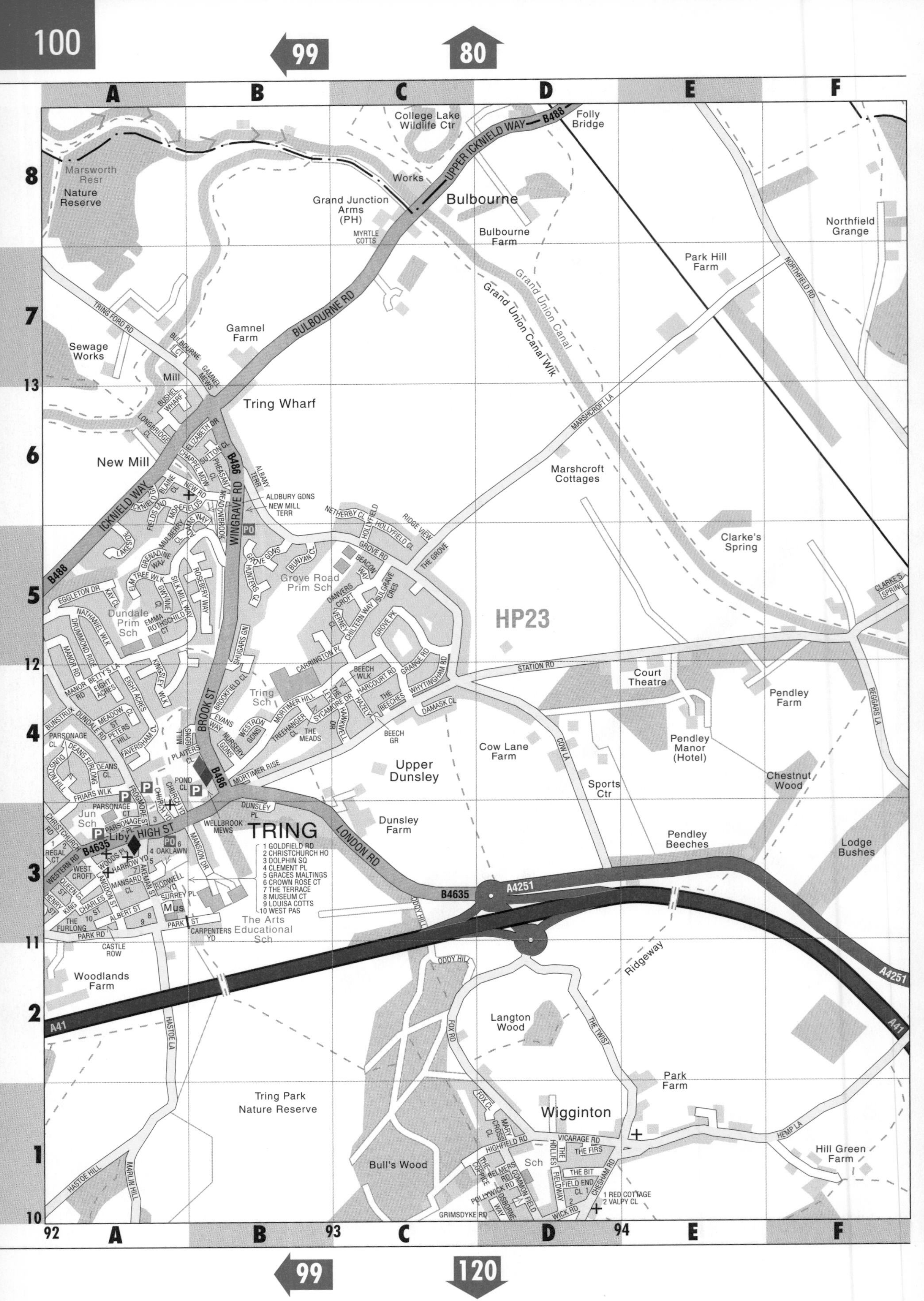
A
B
C
D
E
F
College Lake
Wildlife Ctr
Folly
Bridge
UPPER ICKNIELD WAY
B488
Marsworth
Resr
Nature
Reserve
Works
Grand Junction
Arms
(PH)
Bulbourne
MYRTLE
COTTS
Bulbourne
Farm
Northfield
Grange
Park Hill
Farm
NORTHFIELD RD
Grand Union Canal
Grand Union Canal Wlk
TRING FORD RD
BULBOURNE RD
Gamnel
Farm
Sewage
Works
BULBOURNE
CT
GAMNEL
MEWS
Mill
BUSHEL
WHARF
Tring Wharf
LONGBRIDGE
CL
MARSHCROFT LA
ELIZABETH DR
New Mill
SUTTON CL
CHAPPEL MDW
B486
ALBANY
TERR
Marshcroft
Cottages
ICKNIELD WAY
NEW RD
PHEASANT CL
MEADOWBROOK
ALDBURY GDNS
NEW MILL
TERR
FIELDS END
WINGRAVE RD
NETHERBY CL
HOLLYFIELD
RIDGE VIEW
HOLLYFIELD CL
Clarke's
Spring
PO
LAKESIDE
MULBERRY
GRENADINE
WAY
GROVE GDNS
BUNYAN CL
GROVE RD
BEACON WAY
THE GROVE
B488
ELM TREE WLK
HUNTERS CL
Grove Road
Prim Sch
SULGRAVE CRES
ROSEBERY WAY
SILK MILL WAY
GWYNNE CL
EGGLETON DR
KAY CL
DANVERS CROFT
CHILTERN WAY
CLARKE'S
SPRING
NATHANIEL WLK
Dundale
Prim
Sch
EMMA
ROTHSCHILD
CT
VERNEY CL
GROVE PK
HP23
DRUMMOND RIDE
SHUGARS GN
CARRINGTON PL
GRANGE RD
WHYTINGHAM RD
MANOR RD
BETTY'S LA
BEECH
WLK
HARCOURT RD
STATION RD
Court
Theatre
KINGSLEY WLK
BROOKFIELD CL
Tring
Sch
MANOR
RD
EIGHT
ACRES
EIGHT ACRES
Pendley
Farm
BROOK ST
MORTIMER HILL
THE LIMES
SYCAMORE DR
HAZELY
THE BEECHES
DAMASK CL
BEGGARS LA
BUNSTRUX
DUNDALE RD
MEADOW CL
ST PETERS HILL
EVANS WAY
WESTRON GDNS
TREEHANGER CL
THE MEADS
HAWKWELL DR
BEECH GR
Cow Lane
Farm
COW LA
Pendley
Manor
(Hotel)
PARSONAGE
CL
DEANS FURLONG
FAVERSHAM CL
MILL VIEW
NURSERY GDNS
PLATTERS CL
Upper
Dunsley
MORTIMER RISE
DEANS
CL
B486
POND
CL
Sports
Ctr
Chestnut
Wood
FRIARS WLK
P
P
P
PARSONAGE
CT
CHURCH YD
DUNSLEY
PL
Dunsley
Farm
Jun
Sch
PARSONAGE
PL
HIGH ST
WELLBROOK
MEWS
TRING
LONDON RD
Pendley
Beeches
Lodge
Bushes
CHRISTCHURCH RD
Liby
P
B4635
PO
REGAL
CT
WOODS PL
4 OAKLAWN
MANSION DR
1 GOLDFIELD RD
2 CHRISTCHURCH HO
3 DOLPHIN SQ
4 CLEMENT PL
5 GRACES MALTINGS
6 CROWN ROSE CT
7 THE TERRACE
8 MUSEUM CT
9 LOUISA COTTS
10 WEST PAS
WESTERN RD
WEST
CROFT
HARROW YD
MANSARD
CL
AKEMAN ST
RODWELL
YD
SURREY PL
Mus
B4635
A4251
ODDY HILL
QUEEN ST
LANGDON ST
HENRY ST
KING ST
CHARLES ST
ALBERT ST
THE
FURLONG
PARK RD
PARK ST
CARPENTERS
YD
The Arts
Educational
Sch
CASTLE
ROW
Ridgeway
ODDY HILL
Woodlands
Farm
A4251
Langton
Wood
A41
HASTOE LA
FOX RD
THE TWIST
A41
Park
Farm
Tring Park
Nature Reserve
FOX CL
Wigginton
MARY
CROSS
CL
HIGHFIELD RD
VICARAGE RD
HEMP LA
THE FIRS
THE HOLLIES
Sch
Hill Green
Farm
HASTOE HILL
MARLIN HILL
Bull's Wood
THE COPPICE
BELMERS RD
POLLYWICK RD
COMMON FIELD
FIELDWAY
THE BIT
FIELD END
CL
CHESHAM RD
OSBORNE WAY
1 RED COTTAGE
2 VALPY CL
WICK RD
GRIMSDYKE RD
8
7
13
6
5
12
4
3
11
2
1
10
92
93
94

99
120

102

Buckinghamshire STREET ATLAS

Golding's Spring

Hanging Isley

Moneybury Hill

8

Aldbury Nowers

Icknield Way Path

Sallow Copse

Howlett's Wood

Walk Wood

Tim's Spring

CH

7

Hotel

Stocks

Little Stocks

The Bridgewater Monument

Forest Trails

Pitstone Common

Hertfordshire Way

13

Visitor Centre

6

Ridgeway

Aldbury CE Prim Sch

PH

Thunderdell Cottages

Westland Farm

Church Farm

Old Copse

HP4

5

Tring

STATION RD

PO

Aldbury

Aldbury Common

POSTING HO

ROYAL CT

FOG COTTS

HP23

Chiltern Way

12

MALTING LA

TOMS HILL CL

TOMS HILL RD

Gryme's Dell

Hertfordshire Way

STONEYCROFT

TROOPER RD

BECHWOOD RD

4

Brightwood

Rail Copse

NEWGROUND RD

The Hangings

Tom's Hill

Tom's Hill House

Broomfield Spring

The Scrubs

11

BEGGARS LA

Bottom Spring

3

High Spring

New Ground Farm

Grand Union Canal Wlk

Grand Union Canal

Norcott Hill

Northchurch Common

2

HEMPL LA

New Ground

Marina

Norcott Hall Farm

BOTTOM HOUSE LA

Norcott Court Farm

Hill Farm

Cow Roast

Norcott Court

1

A41

PH

A4251

WHARF LA

B4506

10

95

A

B

96

C

D

97

E

F

121

102

B4506

ALDERTON DR

GATESFERDE CL

RINGSHALL DR

Chiltern Way

Pitstone Park Copse

B4506

Ashridge

CH

Old Park Lodge

Prince's Riding

Ashridge Park

Golden Valley

The Rookery

Hertfordshire Way

Thunderdell Wood

Ashridge College Gdns

Ashridge Management Coll

HP4

Harding's Rookery

Woodyard Cottage

Berkhamstead Common

Toll

Little Coldharbour Farm

Coldharbour Spring

Coldharbour Farm

Furzefield Wood

Hertfordshire Way

Ashridge

Brickkiln Cottage

PO

BRIDGEWATER CT

Bridgewater Arms (PH)

Little Gaddesden CE Prim Sch

CHURCH RD

BEE CT

Church Farm

Little Gaddesden

THE LYE

CHAPEL LA

Robin Hood Farm

Little Brownlow Farm

LITTLE GADDESDEN HO

Home Farm

Cromer Wood

ASHRIDGE COTTS

CROMER CL

CROMER CL

NETTLEDEN RD

Badger Wood

Hudnall Common Plantation

Hudnall Common

HUDNALL LA

POND LA

Hudnall

Hudnall Farm

Lady Grove

Pulridge Wood

Golden Valley Farm

Nettleden Lodge

Webb's Copse

Bluebell Spring

HP1

Frithsden Beeches

Frithsden Gardens

82
104

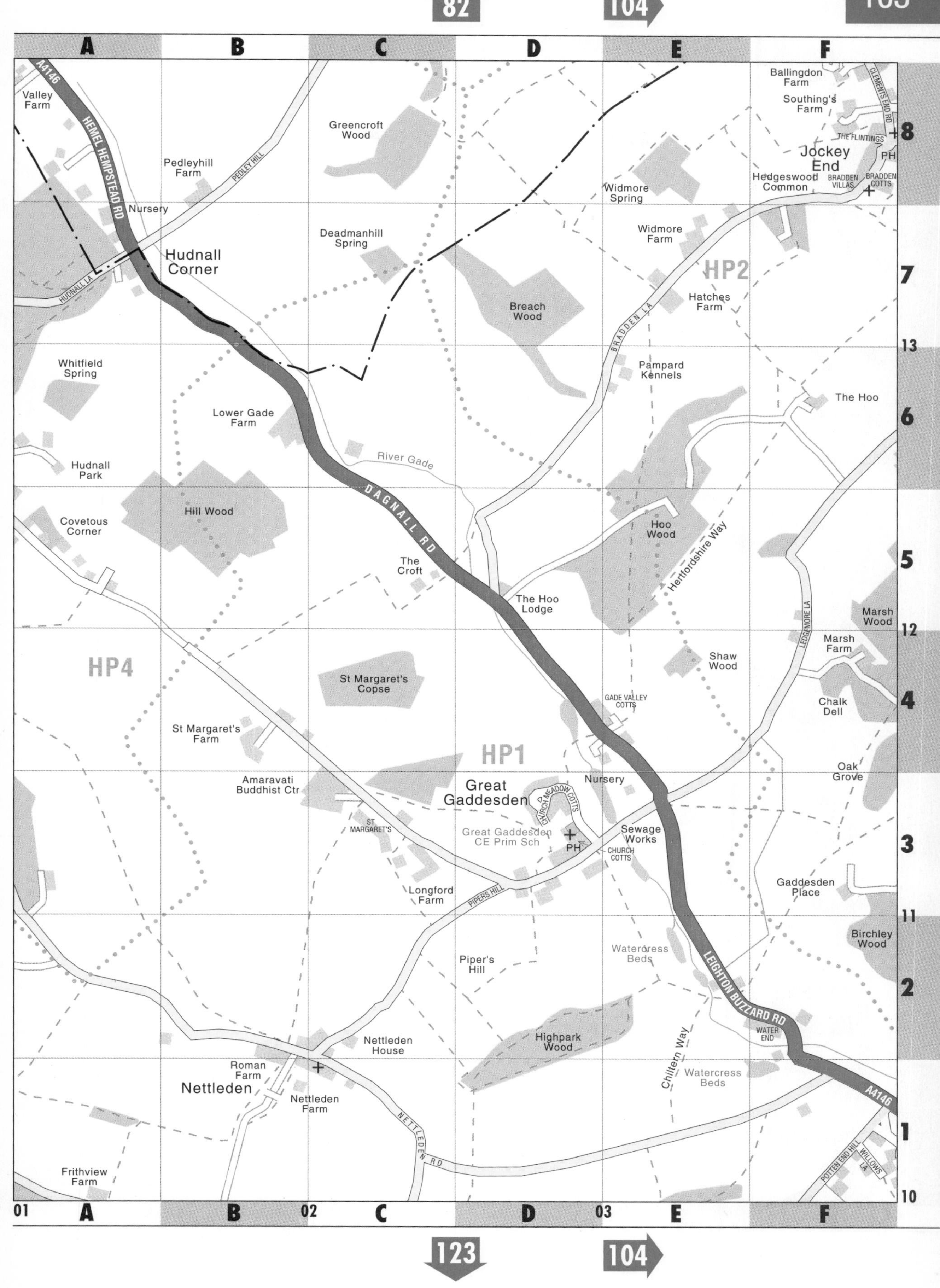
A
B
C
D
E
F
A4146
HEMEL HEMPSTEAD RD
Valley Farm
Greencroft Wood
Pedleyhill Farm
PEDLEY HILL
Nursery
Hudnall Corner
HUDNALL LA
Deadmanhill Spring
Widmore Spring
Widmore Farm
Ballingdon Farm
Southing's Farm
CLEMENTS END RD
THE FLINTINGS
Jockey End
PH
Hedgeswood Common
BRADDEN VILLAS
BRADDEN COTTS
HP2
Hatches Farm
Breach Wood
BRADDEN LA
Pampard Kennels
Whitfield Spring
Lower Gade Farm
The Hoo
River Gade
Hudnall Park
DAGNALL RD
Covetous Corner
Hill Wood
Hoo Wood
Hertfordshire Way
The Croft
The Hoo Lodge
LEDGEMORE LA
Marsh Wood
Marsh Farm
HP4
Shaw Wood
St Margaret's Copse
GADE VALLEY COTTS
Chalk Dell
St Margaret's Farm
HP1
Oak Grove
Amaravati Buddhist Ctr
Great Gaddesden
CHURCH MEADOW COTTS
Nursery
ST MARGARET'S
Great Gaddesden CE Prim Sch
PH
Sewage Works
CHURCH COTTS
Gaddesden Place
Longford Farm
PIPERS HILL
Birchley Wood
Piper's Hill
Watercress Beds
LEIGHTON BUZZARD RD
Highpark Wood
Nettleden House
WATER END
Chiltern Way
Roman Farm
Watercress Beds
Nettleden
Nettleden Farm
A4146
NETTLEDEN RD
Frithview Farm
POTTEN END HILL
WILLOWS LA
8
7
13
6
5
12
4
3
11
2
1
10
01
02
03

123
104

103
83

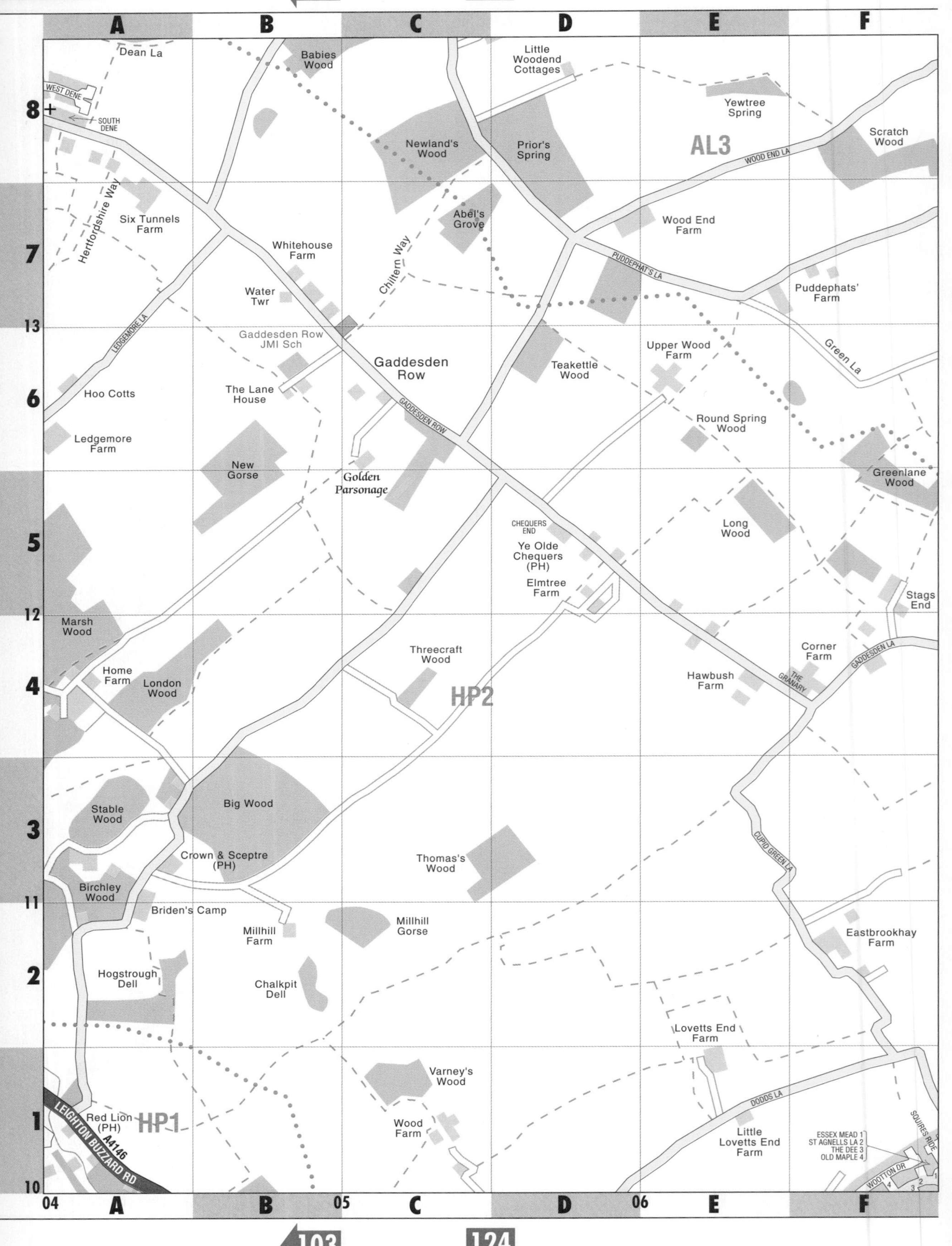
A
B
C
D
E
F
Dean La
Babies Wood
Little Woodend Cottages
Yewtree Spring
Scratch Wood
WEST DENE
SOUTH DENE
Newland's Wood
Prior's Spring
AL3
WOOD END LA
Hertfordshire Way
Six Tunnels Farm
Abel's Grove
Wood End Farm
Whitehouse Farm
Chiltern Way
PUDDEPHAT'S LA
Puddephats' Farm
Water Twr
Gaddesden Row JMI Sch
LEDGEMORE LA
Gaddesden Row
Teakettle Wood
Upper Wood Farm
Green La
Hoo Cotts
The Lane House
GADDESDEN ROW
Round Spring Wood
Ledgemore Farm
New Gorse
Golden Parsonage
Greenlane Wood
CHEQUERS END
Ye Olde Chequers (PH)
Long Wood
Elmtree Farm
Stags End
Marsh Wood
Threecraft Wood
Corner Farm
GADDESDEN LA
Home Farm
London Wood
HP2
Hawbush Farm
THE GRANARY
Big Wood
Stable Wood
CUPID GREEN LA
Crown & Sceptre (PH)
Thomas's Wood
Birchley Wood
Briden's Camp
Millhill Farm
Millhill Gorse
Eastbrookhay Farm
Hogstrough Dell
Chalkpit Dell
Lovetts End Farm
Varney's Wood
DODDS LA
Red Lion (PH)
HP1
LEIGHTON BUZZARD RD
A4146
Wood Farm
Little Lovetts End Farm
ESSEX MEAD 1
ST AGNELLS LA 2
THE DEE 3
OLD MAPLE 4
SQUIRES RIDE
WOOTTON DR
8
7
13
6
5
12
4
3
11
2
1
10
04
05
06

103
124

84
106

A
B
C
D
E
F
PH
WOOD END LA
TROWLEY BOTTOM
WHITE HILL
Trowley Bottom
Trowley Bottom Farm
DELMEREND LA
St Agnells Farm
M1
Wr Twr
Redding Wood
REDDING LA
A5183
DUNSTABLE RD
8
PUDDEPHAT'S LA
Grove Farm
7
LYBURY LA
Nursery
Nicholls Farm
13
Green La
Nicholl's Great Wood
Hertfordshire Way
HILLTOP
TASSELL HALL
6
Nirvana
Rabbitfield Spring
THE SQUARE
ROSE ACRE
NICHOLLS CL
Greenlane Farm
New Wood
DOWN EDGE
5
Flamsteadbury Farm
BURY COTTS
STEPHENS WAY
Bury Wood
12
MANSDALE RD
AL3
Church End
4
GADDESDEN LA
Hay Wood
SABERTON CL
HEMEL HEMPSTEAD RD
B487
3
The Aubreys
Woodside
Holtsmore End Farm
Hotel
Great Revel End Farm
Pantake Wood
Holtsmore End
11
AUBREY LA
Smallholding
HP2
2
The Beeches
Little Revel End
HEMEL HEMPSTEAD RD
Nicky Way
1 ASHBY CT
2 EVERSDEN CT
3 LONGSTANTON CT
4 SEDGEWICK CT
5 HADDENHAM CT
6 MILTON CT
ST AGNELL'S FARM MEWS
HIGH WYCH WAY
ASTON VIEW
BRAEMAR
TATTERSHALL DR
BLAIR CL
VALLEY GN
SHENLEY RD
ELSTREE RD
BRAMFIELD PL
WARESIDE
SANDRIDGE CL
HORTON GDNS
ROYDON CT
DUNSTER RD
KIPLING GR
KEATS CL
BRONTE CRES
BYRON PL
COLERIDGE CRES
CODICOTE ROW
HOLTSMERE END LANE
Brockswood Prim Sch
BERKELEY SQ
NIGHTINGALE WLK
CUPID GREEN LA
YEOMANS RIDE
ESSEX MEAD
B487
1
10
07
08
09

125
106

105
85

A B C D E F

8

CH
New Cottages
Chiltern Way

Harpendenbury Farm

Rothamsted Experimental Farm

Scout Spring

Knott Wood

Nicky Way

7

BYLANDS HO

Rothamsted Experimental Station

Redbourn Recn Ctr

Rothamsted

13

St Luke's Sch

BLACKHORSE LA

DUNSTABLE RD

LINSEY CL

PIPERS CL

PEPPARD CL

LINDEN RD

AYSGARTH RD

CRECY GDNS

CAVAN RD

Redbourn

REDBOURN LA

6

BETTESPOL MDWS

CROUCH HALL LA

CROUCH RD

HOLTS MDW

Scout Farm

HARPENDEN LA

MAPLETREE

VER RD

Nursery

AL5

B487

B487

HILLTOP MDW

LONG CUT

Schs

Liby

PO

CUMBERLAND DR

FLINT COPSE

BASSETT CL

CROWN'S

VER MDW CVN SITE

HAMMOND END LA

CH

OAKHURST AVE

GEDOWN

SNATCHUP

DOWN EDGE

TINGEYS CL

WHEAT CL

MEAD

LORDS MDW

NEW FORGE

SHEPHERD'S ROW

HARDING'S

WATEREND LA

Hammondsend Farm

OAKVIEW CL

OAKWOOD DR

5

RICKYARD MDW

NORTH COMM

WEYBRIDGE CL

TOTTEN MEWS THE RUINS

MONKS CL

HIGH ST

ARCHERS CL

FISH ST

Nursery

WHEATFIELD RD

HAMMONDS HILL

CHARRINGTON WAY

LIBURY WAY

BRACHE CL

ST STEPHEN'S CL

VAUGHAN WAY

Redbourn Common

PONDSMEADE

Redbourn Ind Ctr

THE UPLANDS

PROSPECT LA

12

Mus

SOUTH COMM

MULBERRY PL

FISH STREET FARM

AL3

BEN AUSTINS

ELMS CLEABURY LA

THE TERRACE

BROOK

SILK MILL RD

THE PARK

Hammondsend Wood

4

WOOLLAMS

WEST COMM

EAST COMM

HEMEL HEMPSTEAD RD

NORTH COMMON RD

CHURCH END

CHEQUER LA

B487

CHEQUER LA

PH

Nicky Way

B487

STATHAMS CT

The Elms

ST ALBANS RD

3

River Ver

BEESONEND LA

Flowers Farm

Hertfordshire Way

11

BEAUMONT HALL LA

2

Baeumont Hall

Redbournbury Water Mill

CROWN YD

Redbournbury

REDBOURNBURY LA

Dane-End Farm

REDBOURN RD

1

PH

Works

A5183

HILL FARM LA

PUNCH BOWL LA

10

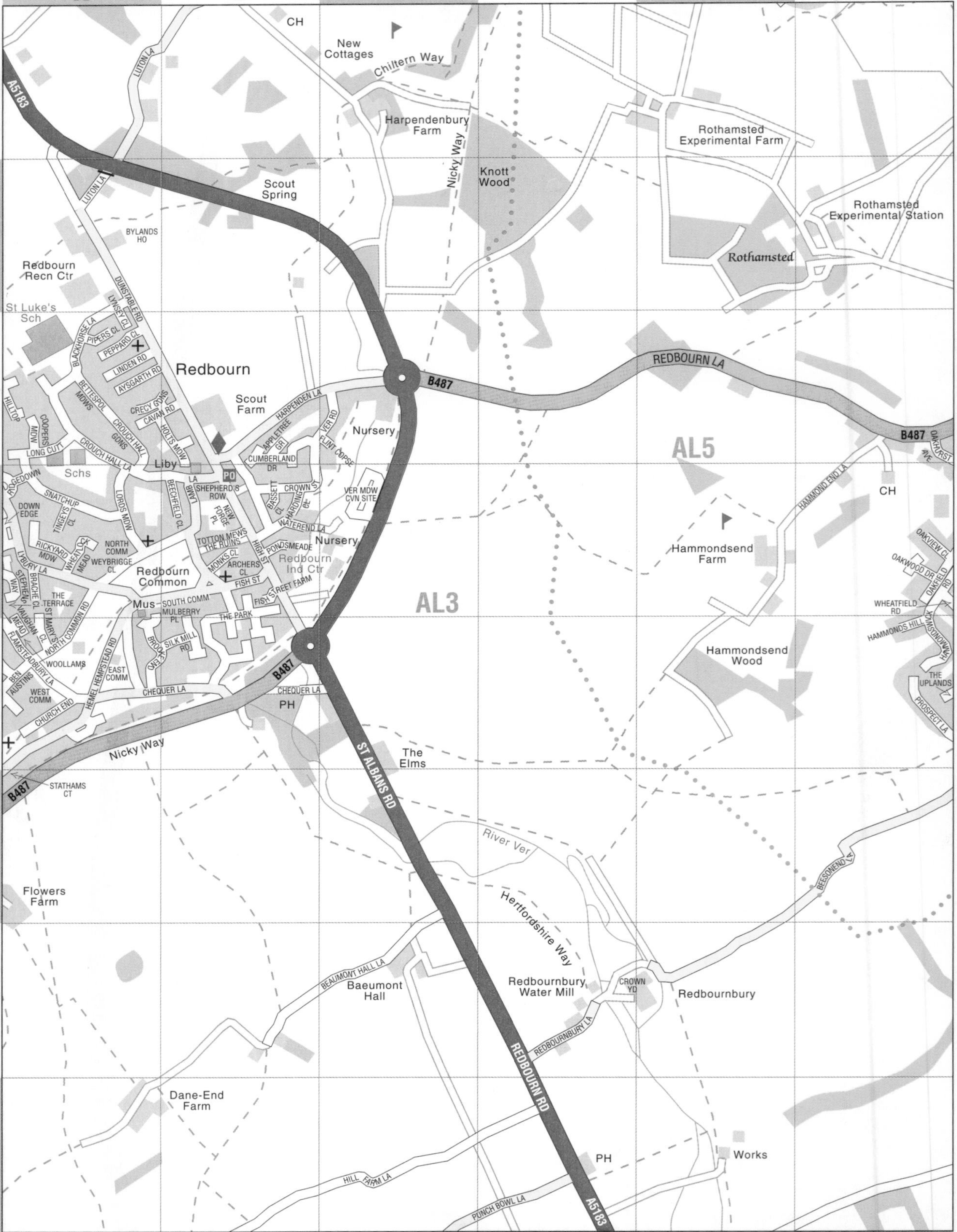

10 A 11 B C D 12 E F

86

108

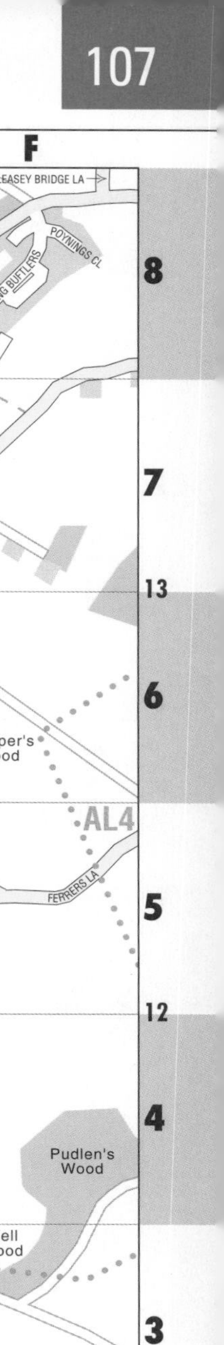

A
B
C
D
E
F
8
7
13
6
5
12
4
3
11
2
1
10
Rothamsted
Experimental Sta
Coach La
Hotel
St Dominic
RC Prim Sch
Southdown
Ind Est
Aldwickbury
Farm
Aldwickbury
Sch
Green La
The Grove
Inf & Jun Schs
Grove
Wood
Grove
Farm
The
Grove
Harpenden
Common
Hatching
Green
Limbrick
Hall
CH
HARPENDEN
Cross
Farm
Secret
Spring
Clapper's
Wood
Thames
Wood
AL4
Mud La
Eight Acre
Wood
AL5
Ayres End
BAMVILLE
WOOD
MAPLE COTTS
Bamville
Farm
Three
Horseshoes
(PH)
White
House
Pudlen's
Wood
Beesonend
Farm
Well
Wood
Childwick
Stud
Childwick
Hall
Pismire
Spring
Hedge's
Farm
Childwick
Green
AL3
Cheapside
Farm
The
White House
Green
Wood
Water
Tower
Bush
Wood
Greens
Cottages
Childwick
Bury Ho
A1081
B487
ST ALBANS RD
HARPENDEN RD
REDBOURN LA
AYRES END LA
BEESONEND LA
SANDRIDGEBURY LA
LEASEY BRIDGE LA
WHEATHAMPSTEAD RD
FERRERS LA
PIPERS LA
1 HADLEIGH CT
2 TIVERTON CT
13
14
15

127

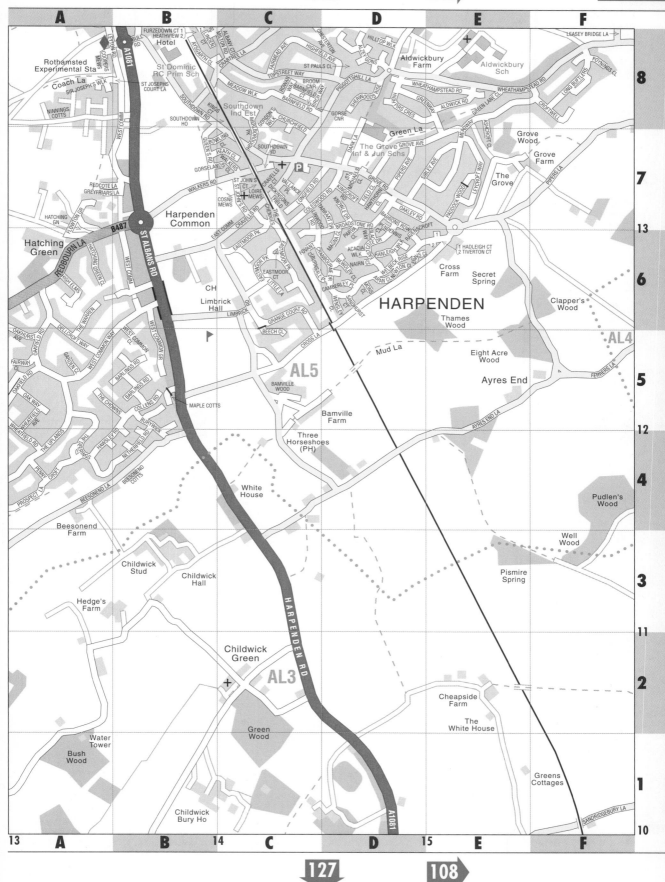

107
87

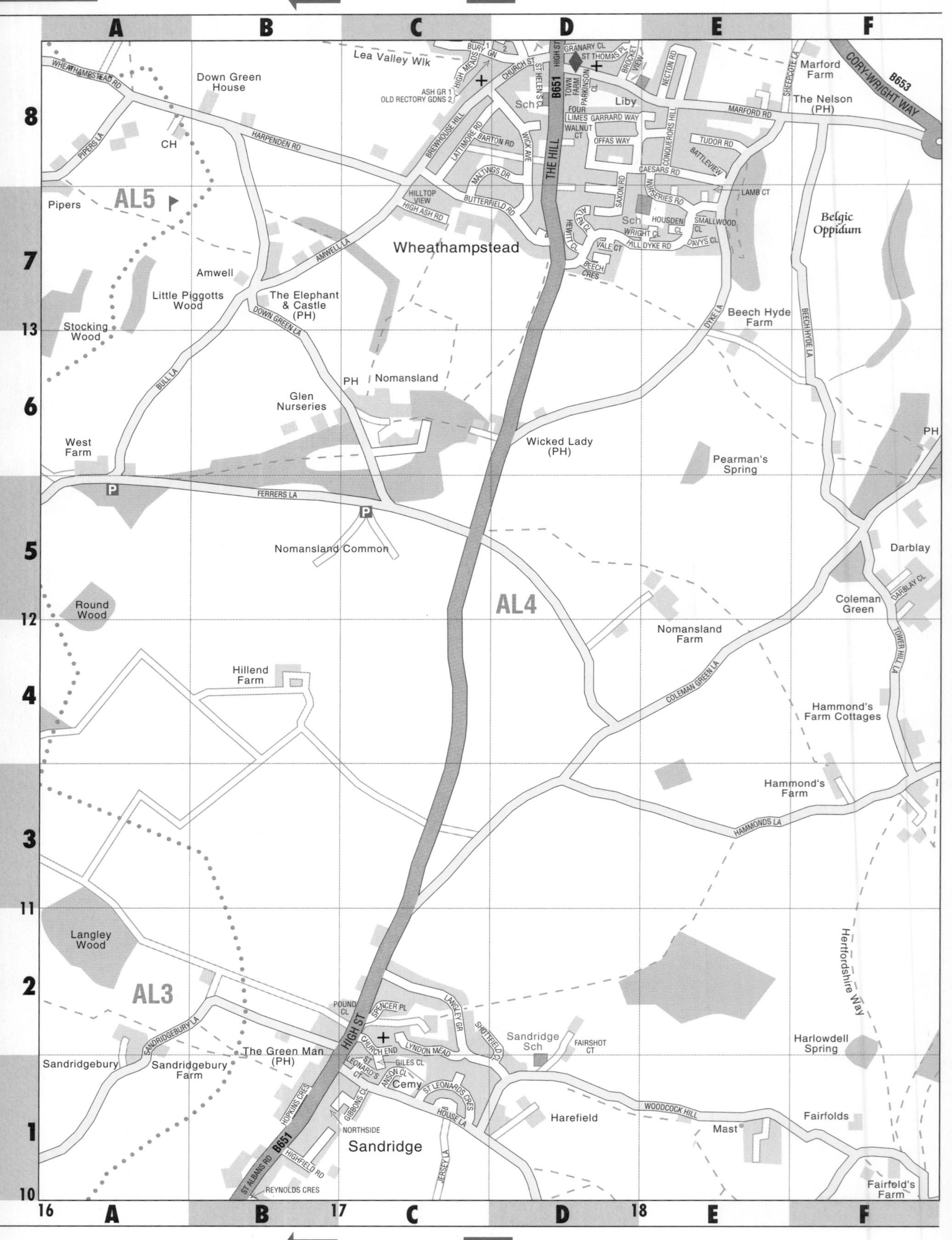
A
B
C
D
E
F
8
7
13
6
5
12
4
3
11
2
1
10
16
17
18
Lea Valley Wlk
Down Green House
CH
Pipers
AL5
Wheathampstead
Amwell
Little Piggotts Wood
Stocking Wood
The Elephant & Castle (PH)
Nomansland
PH
Glen Nurseries
West Farm
Wicked Lady (PH)
Liby
Sch
Marford Farm
The Nelson (PH)
Belgic Oppidum
Beech Hyde Farm
Pearman's Spring
PH
Darblay
Coleman Green
Nomansland Common
Round Wood
AL4
Nomansland Farm
Hillend Farm
Hammond's Farm Cottages
Hammond's Farm
Langley Wood
AL3
Hertfordshire Way
The Green Man (PH)
Sandridgebury
Sandridgebury Farm
Sandridge Sch
Cemy
Harefield
Mast
Fairfolds
Harlowdell Spring
Sandridge
Fairfold's Farm
WHEATHAMPSTEAD RD
PIPERS LA
HARPENDEN RD
AMWELL LA
HILLTOP VIEW
HIGH ASH RD
DOWN GREEN LA
BULL LA
FERRERS LA
THE HILL
B651
HIGH ST
CHURCH ST
BURY GN
HIGH MEADS
ASH GR
OLD RECTORY GDNS
BREWHOUSE HILL
LATTIMORE RD
BARTON RD
MALTINGS DR
BUTTERFIELD RD
WICK AVE
ST HELEN'S CL
GRANARY CL
ST THOMAS PL
TOWN FARM
PARKINSON CL
BROCKET VIEW
NECTON RD
FOUR LIMES
GARRARD WAY
WALNUT CT
OFFAS WAY
CONQUERORS HILL
TUDOR RD
BATTLEVIEW
CAESARS RD
SAXON RD
NURSERIES RD
LAMB CT
ALLEN CL
HEWITT CL
HOUSDEN CL
SMALLWOOD CL
WRIGHT CL
HILL DYKE RD
DAVYS CL
VALE CT
BEECH CRES
MARFORD RD
SHEEPCOTE LA
CORY-WRIGHT WAY
B653
DYKE LA
BEECHHYDE LA
DARBLAY CL
TOWER HILL LA
COLEMAN GREEN LA
HAMMONDS LA
SANDRIDGEBURY LA
POUND CL
SPENCER PL
LANGLEY GR
SHOTTFIELD CL
FAIRSHOT CT
CHURCH END
LYNDON MEAD
ST LEONARD'S CT
GILES CL
ANSON CL
ST LEONARDS CRES
HOPKINS CRES
GIBBONS CL
HOUSE LA
WOODCOCK HILL
NORTHSIDE
JERSEY LA
HIGHFIELD RD
ST ALBANS RD
REYNOLDS CRES

107
128

88
110

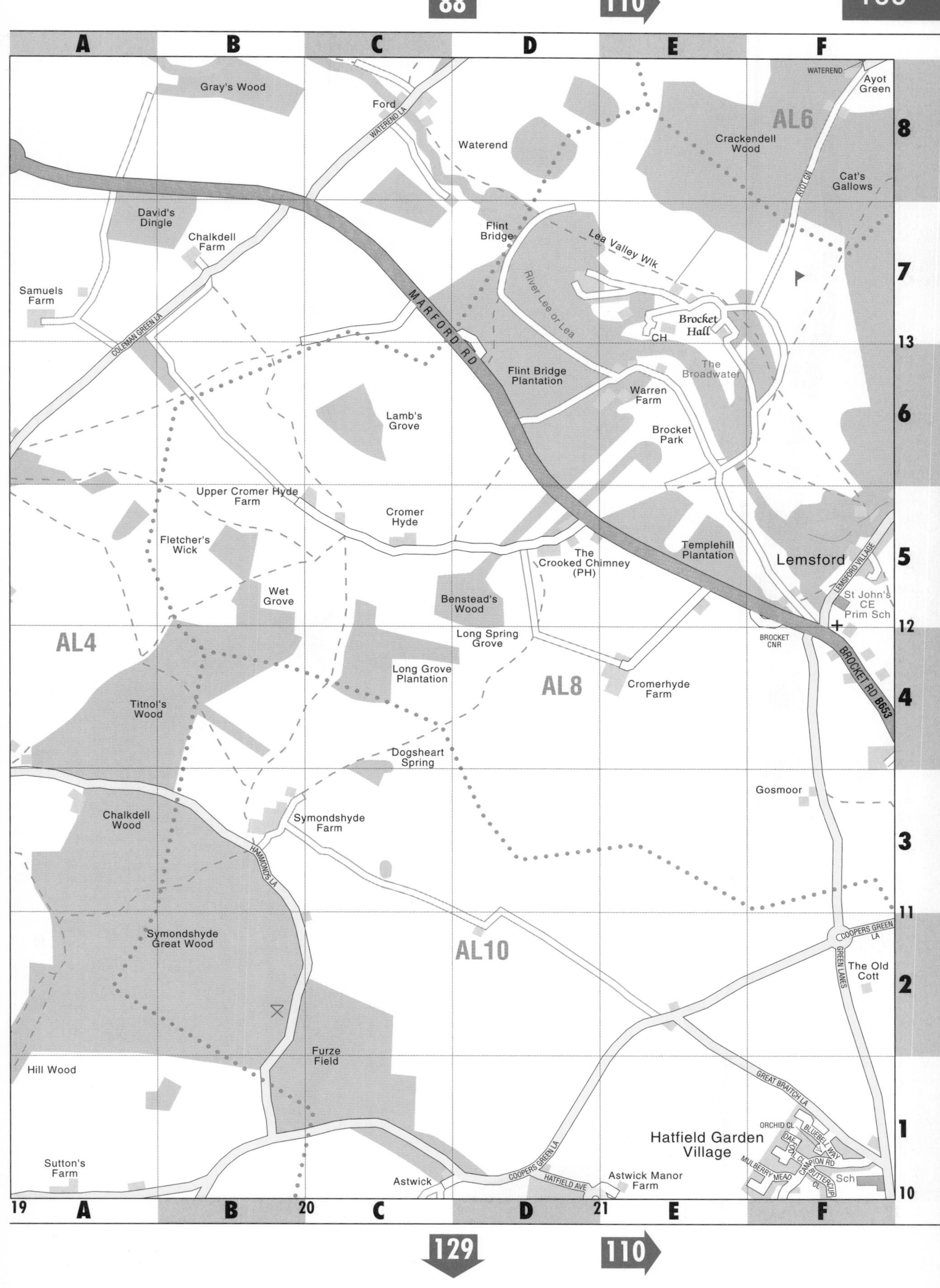
Gray's Wood
Ford
WATEREND LA
Waterend
AL6
Crackendell Wood
WATEREND
Ayot Green
Cat's Gallows
AYOT GN
David's Dingle
Chalkdell Farm
Flint Bridge
Lea Valley Wlk
River Lee or Lea
Samuels Farm
MARFORD RD
Brocket Hall
CH
COLEMAN GREEN LA
The Broadwater
Flint Bridge Plantation
Warren Farm
Lamb's Grove
Brocket Park
Upper Cromer Hyde Farm
Cromer Hyde
Fletcher's Wick
The Crooked Chimney (PH)
Templehill Plantation
Lemsford
LEMSFORD VILLAGE
Wet Grove
Benstead's Wood
St John's CE Prim Sch
AL4
Long Spring Grove
BROCKET CNR
Long Grove Plantation
AL8
Cromerhyde Farm
BROCKET RD B653
Titnol's Wood
Dogsheart Spring
Gosmoor
Chalkdell Wood
Symondshyde Farm
HAMMONDS LA
Symondshyde Great Wood
AL10
COOPERS GREEN LA
GREEN LANES
The Old Cott
Furze Field
Hill Wood
GREAT BRAITCH LA
ORCHID CL
BLUEBELL WAY
Hatfield Garden Village
DAFFODIL CL
CAMPION RD
MULBERRY MEAD
BUTTERCUP CL
Sch
Sutton's Farm
Astwick
COOPERS GREEN LA
HATFIELD AVE
Astwick Manor Farm
A B C D E F
8 7 13 6 5 12 4 3 11 2 1 10
19 20 21

129
110

109
89

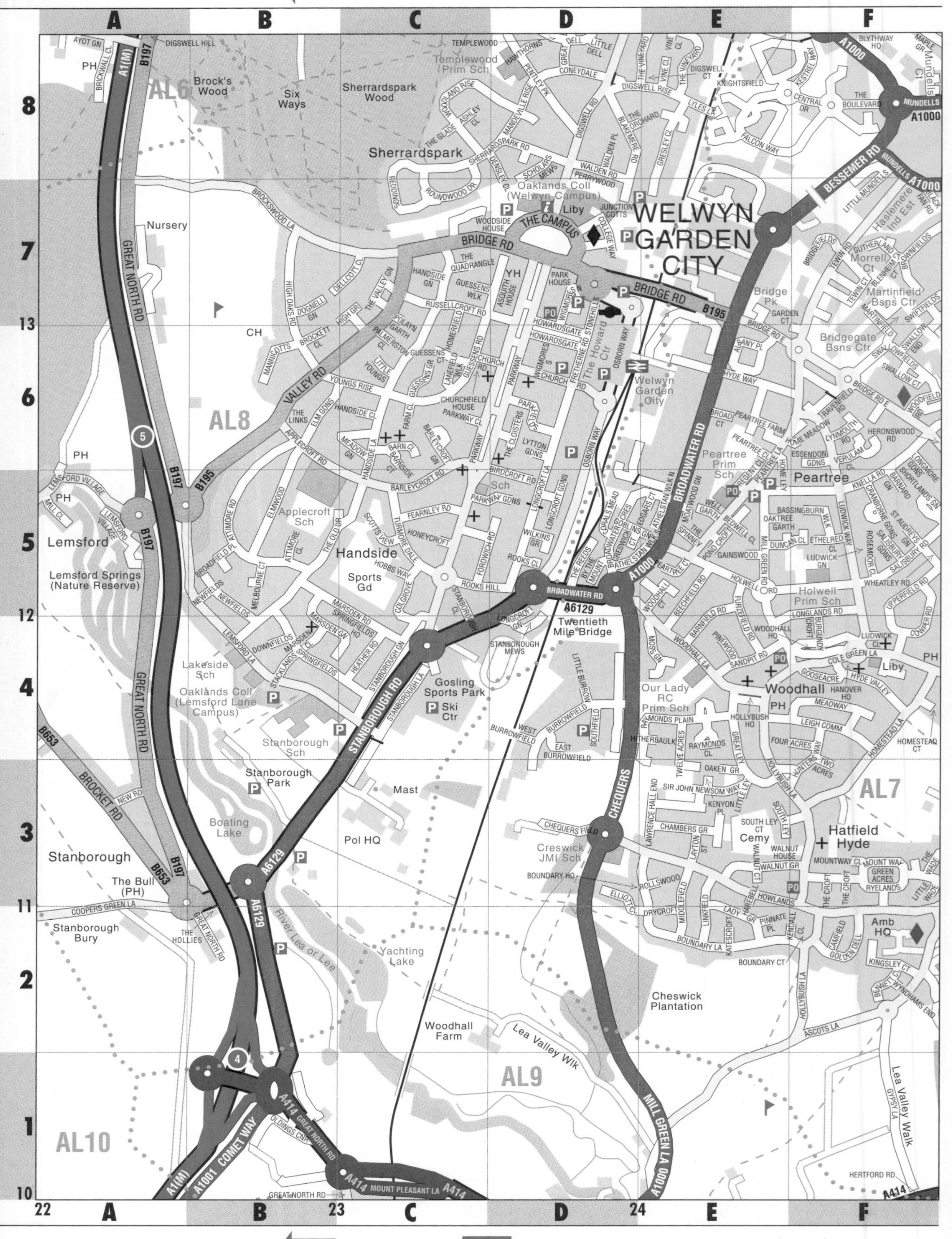
A
B
C
D
E
F
8
7
13
6
5
12
4
3
11
2
1
10
22
23
24
AYOT GN
DIGSWELL HILL
TEMPLEWOOD
Templewood Prim Sch
HAWTHORNS
PENTLEY PK
GREAT DELL
LITTLE DELL
CONEYDALE
THE VINEYARD
VINE CL
THE VINEYARD
DIGSWELL CT
KNIGHTSFIELD
KESTREL WAY
BLYTHWAY HO
MAPLE GR
Mundells Ct
A1000
MUNDELLS
THE BOULEVARD
CENTRAL DR
FALCON WAY
LYLES LA
DIGSWELL RISE
THE ORCHARD
THE BLAKEMERE RD
GRESLEY CL
WALDEN PL
DIGSWELL RD
PH
BRICKWALL CL
A1(M)
B197
AL6
Brock's Wood
Six Ways
Sherrardspark Wood
WOODLAND RISE
THE GLADE
ASHLEY CL
MANDEVILLE RISE
SHERRARDSPARK RD
Sherrardspark
DENSLEY CL
SCHOLARS MEWS
WALDEN RD
PERRYWOOD
REDDINGS
ROUNDWOOD DR
Oaklands Coll (Welwyn Campus)
Liby
JUNCTION COTTS
WELWYN GARDEN CITY
BESSEMER RD
MUNDELLS
LITTLE MUNDELLS
Haslemere Ind Est
BROCKSWOOD LA
Nursery
WOODSIDE HOUSE
THE CAMPUS
COLLEGE WAY
BRIDGE RD
THE QUADRANGLE
HANDSIDE GN
GUESSENS WLK
YH
ASQUITH HOUSE
PARK HOUSE
WIGMORES N
BRIDGE RD
B195
Bridge Pk
GARDEN CT
BRIDGE RD E
TEWIN RD
TEWIN CT
SUTHERLAND CL
Morrell Ct
BLENHEIM CT
BROWNFIELDS
Martinfield Bsns Ctr
MARTINFIELD
SWIFTFIELDS
Bridgegate Bsns Ctr
SWALLOWFIELDS
SWALLOW END
SWALLOW CT
GREAT NORTH RD
HIGH OAKS RD
DELLCOTT CL
THE VALLEY GN
DOGNELL GN
HIGH GR
BROCKETT CL
MANNICOTTS
RUSSELLCROFT RD
POLAYN GARTH
PALMERSTON CL
GUESSENS CT
HOMERFIELD
HOWARDSGATE
STONEHILLS
The Howard Ctr
OSBORN WAY
CH
VALLEY RD
YOUNGS RISE
LITTLE YOUNGS
GUESSENS GR
LANEFIELD WLK
GUESSENS RD
CHURCH RD
PARKWAY
WIGMORES S
FRETHERNE RD
CHURCH RD
Welwyn Garden City
ALBANY PL
HYDE WAY
BRIDGE RD E
RAVENFIELD RD
WOODFIELD
AL8
THE LINKS
ELM GDNS
HANDSIDE CL
FARM CL
CHURCHFIELD HOUSE
PARKWAY CL
PARKFIELDS
THE CLOISTERS
LYTTON GDNS
BROADWATER RD
BROAD CT
PEARTREE FARM
HOME MEADOW
LYNMOUTH RD
HERONSWOOD RD
APPLECROFT RD
MEADOW GN
HANDSIDE LA
BARN CL
BARNSIDE CT
BARLEYCROFT GN
BIRDCROFT RD
Sch
PEARTREE CL
Peartree Prim Sch
ESSENDON GDNS
VERULAM CL
Peartree
KNELLA RD
BARNARD GN
SHORTLANDS GN
LONGMORE GDNS
PH
LEMSFORD VILLAGE
MILL CL
LEMSFORD VILLAGE
B197
B195
ATTIMORE RD
ELMWOOD
Applecroft Sch
BARLEYCROFT RD
PARKWAY GDNS
LONGCROFT LA
LONGCROFT GDNS
OSBORN WAY
MOATWOOD GN
REGENT CL
HOME LETE
WELL GARTH
BEDWELL CL
BASSINGBURN WLK
OAKTREE GARTH
LUDWICK WAY
CRANBORNE GDNS
ST AUDREYS GN
SALISBURY GDNS
SALISBURY RD
Lemsford
ATTIMORE CL
THE OLD DR
SCOTTS VIEW
TURMORE DALE
FEARNLEY RD
HONEYCROFT
Handside
FORDWICH RD
WILKINS GR
OPALS MEAD
THE REEDS
BROADWATER CRES
CRESWICK CT
COLLINS GR
EDGARS CT
ATHELSTAN WLK N
ATHELSTAN WLK S
THE SPINNEY
POND CROFT
GAINSWOOD
MILL GREEN RD
DUNCAN CL
ETHELRED CL
LUDWICK GN
ROSEMOOR CL
Lemsford Springs (Nature Reserve)
BROADFIELD PL
MELBOURNE CT
Sports Gd
HOBBS WAY
ROOKS CL
ROOKS HILL
BROADWATER RD
A1000
EARLS CT
WOODHALL CT
BEECHFIELD RD
HOLWELL RD
Holwell Prim Sch
WHEATLEY RD
UPPERFIELD RD
NEWFIELDS
A6129
Twentieth Mile Bridge
LONGLANDS RD
LEMSFORD LA
DOWNFIELDS
MARSDEN RD
SPRINGFIELDS
MARSDEN GN
HEATHER RD
STANBOROUGH GN
COLGROVE
STANBOROUGH CL
LONGCROFT GN
STANBOROUGH MEWS
MOSS GN
WOODHALL LA
BARNFIELD RD
PINEWOOD
FURZEFIELD RD
SANDPIT RD
WOODHALL HO
CROFT GN
BURGUNDY
LUDWICK CL
COLE GREEN LA
Liby
COWPER RD
PH
STACKLANDS
Lakeside Sch
Oaklands Coll (Lemsford Lane Campus)
STANBOROUGH RD
STANBOROUGH LA
Gosling Sports Park
Ski Ctr
LITTLE BURROW
SOUTHFIELD
WEST BURROWFIELD
EAST BURROWFIELD
Our Lady RC Prim Sch
GOOSEACRE
HYDE VALLEY
Woodhall
HANOVER HO
MEADWAY
HOLLYBUSH HO
LEIGH COMM
HOMESTEAD LA
HOMESTEAD CT
B653
Stanborough Sch
RAYMONDS PLAIN
HITHERBAULK
RAYMONDS CL
TWELVE ACRES
FOUR ACRES
HUNTERS WAY
TWO ACRES
AL7
BROCKET RD
NEW RD
Stanborough Park
Mast
OAKEN GR
SIR JOHN NEWSOM WAY
KENYON PL
LITTLE LEY
HOLLYBUSH LA
GREAT LEY
CHEQUERS
Boating Lake
Pol HQ
CHEQUERS FIELD
LAWRENCE HALL END
CHAMBERS GR
AYTON
ST
SOUTH LEY CT
Cemy
SOUTH LEY
Hatfield Hyde
Stanborough
The Bull (PH)
B653
B197
A6129
Creswick JMI Sch
BOUNDARY HO
WALNUT HOUSE
WALNUT GR
MOUNTWAY CL
MOUNT WAY
GREEN ACRES
RYELANDS
LITTLE WADE
THE WADE
THE CROFT
ROLLSWOOD
MIDDLEFIELD
LINKFIELD
HAREBELL
HOWLANDS
COOPERS GREEN LA
Stanborough Bury
THE HOLLIES
GREAT NORTH RD
River Lea or Lee
Yachting Lake
ELLIOTT CL
DRYCROFT
LADY GR
PINNATE PL
KENDALL CL
CAMFIELD
GOLDEN DELL
Amb HQ
KATESCROFT
BOUNDARY LA
BOUNDARY CT
KINGSLEY CT
BENNETTS CL
WYNDHAMS END
Cheswick Plantation
Woodhall Farm
Lea Valley Wlk
ASCOTS LA
AL9
Lea Valley Walk
GYPSY LA
AL10
A414
GREAT NORTH RD
OLDINGS CNR
A1001 COMET WAY
A1(M)
A414
MOUNT PLEASANT LA
A414
GREAT NORTH RD
MILL GREEN LA
A1000
HERTFORD RD
A414

109
130

90
112

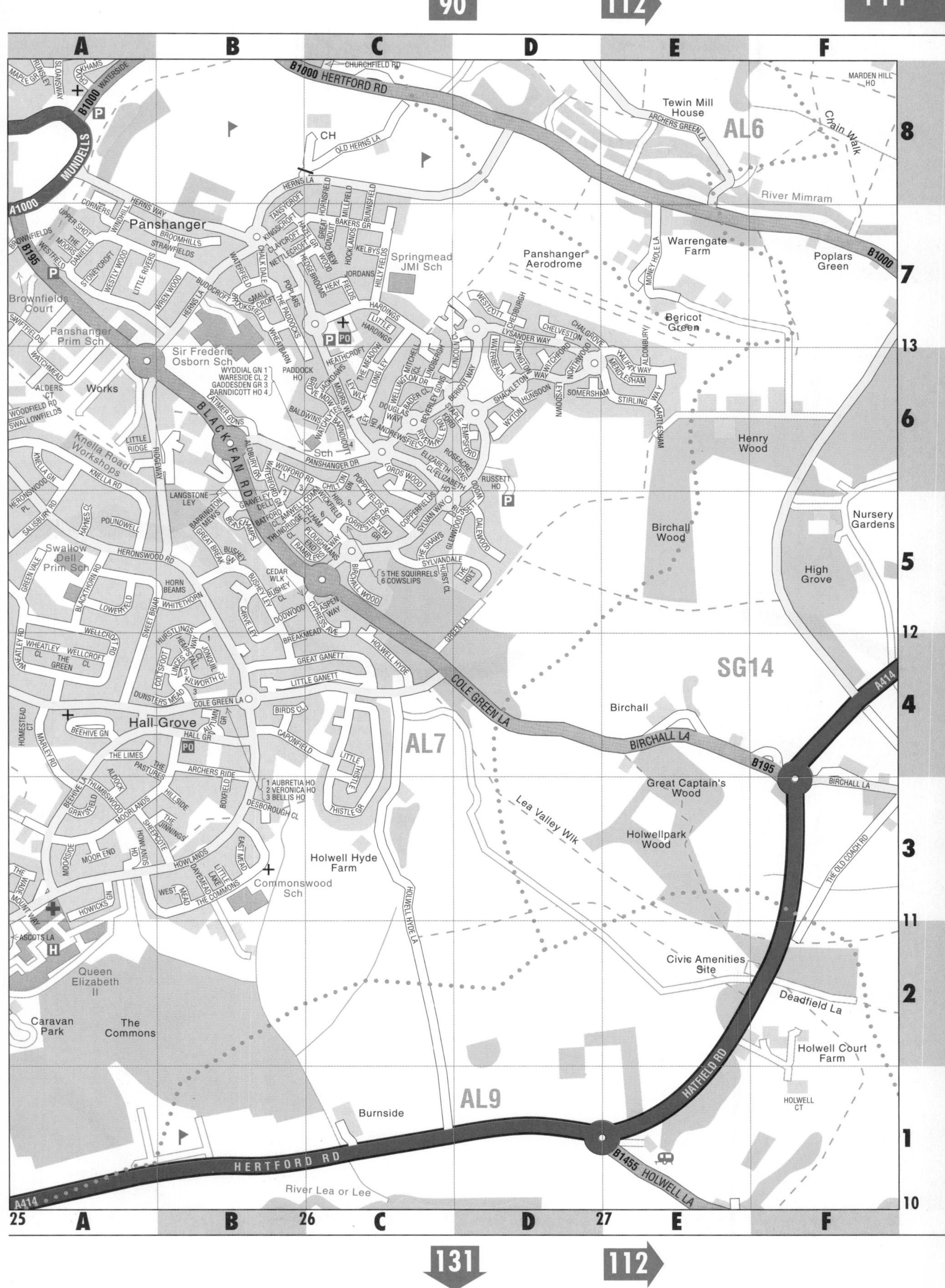
B1000 HERTFORD RD
Tewin Mill House
AL6
Chain Walk
River Mimram
Panshanger
Springmead JMI Sch
Panshanger Aerodrome
Warrengate Farm
Poplars Green
Bericot Green
Brownfields Court
Panshanger Prim Sch
Sir Frederic Osborn Sch
Works
BLACKFAN RD
Knella Road Workshops
Henry Wood
Birchall Wood
Nursery Gardens
Swallow Dell Prim Sch
High Grove
SG14
COLE GREEN LA
Birchall
Hall Grove
AL7
BIRCHALL LA
Great Captain's Wood
Lea Valley Wlk
Holwellpark Wood
Holwell Hyde Farm
Commonswood Sch
Queen Elizabeth II
Civic Amenities Site
Deadfield La
Caravan Park
The Commons
Holwell Court Farm
AL9
HATFIELD RD
Burnside
HERTFORD RD
B1455 HOLWELL LA
River Lea or Lee
A414

131
112

111
91

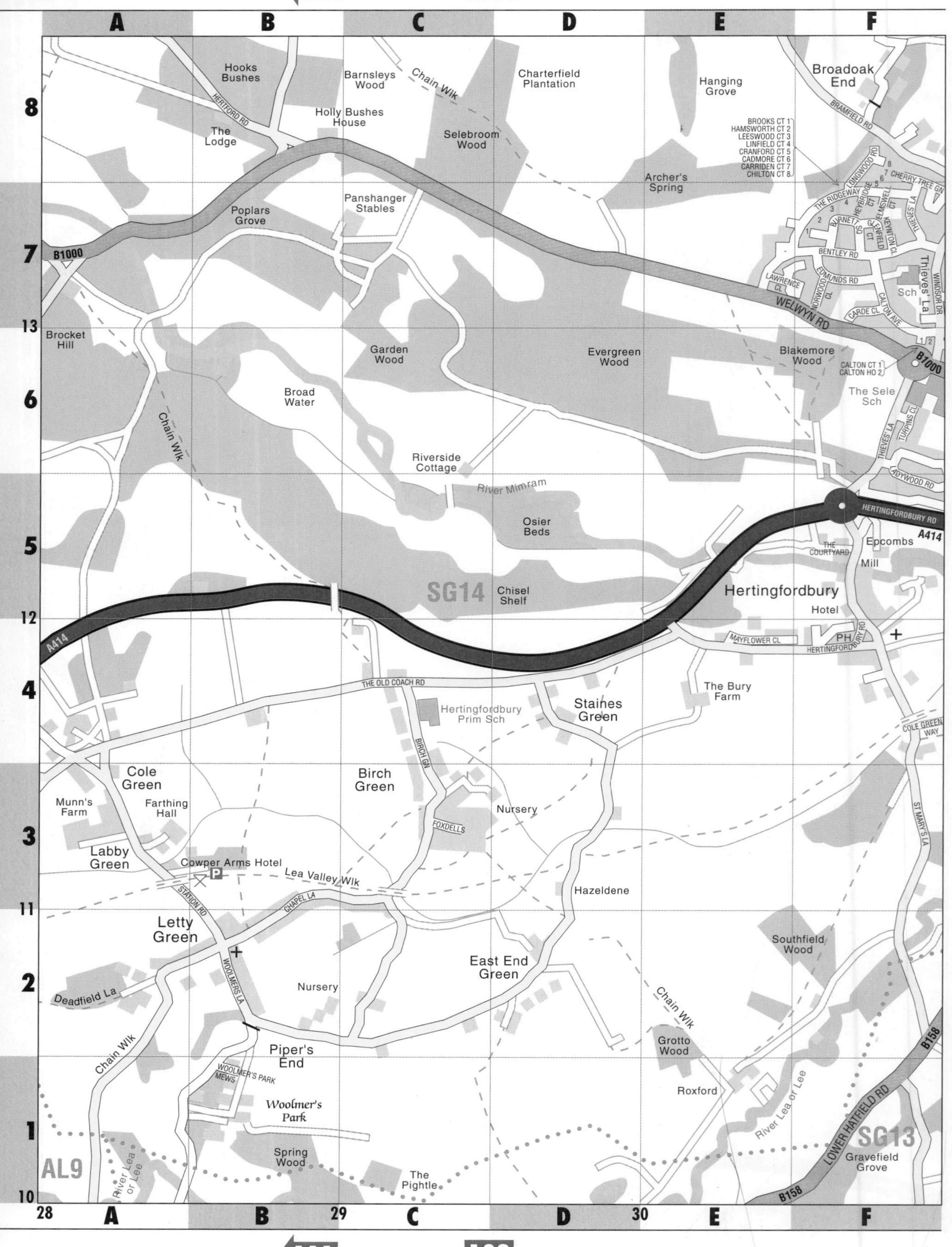
Hooks Bushes
Barnsleys Wood
Chain Wlk
Charterfield Plantation
Hanging Grove
Broadoak End
Hertford Rd
The Lodge
Holly Bushes House
Selebroom Wood
Archer's Spring
Bramfield Rd
Panshanger Stables
Poplars Grove
B1000
Welwyn Rd
Brocket Hill
Garden Wood
Evergreen Wood
Blakemore Wood
The Sele Sch
Broad Water
Riverside Cottage
River Mimram
Osier Beds
Hertingfordbury Rd
A414
Epcombs
Mill
SG14
Chisel Shelf
Hertingfordbury
Hotel
Mayflower Cl
PH
The Old Coach Rd
Hertingfordbury Prim Sch
Staines Green
The Bury Farm
Cole Green Way
Cole Green
Birch Green
Birch Gn
Munn's Farm
Farthing Hall
Nursery
Foxdells
St Mary's La
Labby Green
Cowper Arms Hotel
Lea Valley Wlk
Hazeldene
Station Rd
Chapel La
Letty Green
East End Green
Southfield Wood
Deadfield La
Woolmers La
Piper's End
Grotto Wood
Roxford
Woolmer's Park Mews
Woolmer's Park
River Lea or Lee
B158
Lower Hatfield Rd
SG13
AL9
Spring Wood
The Pightle
Gravefield Grove

111
132

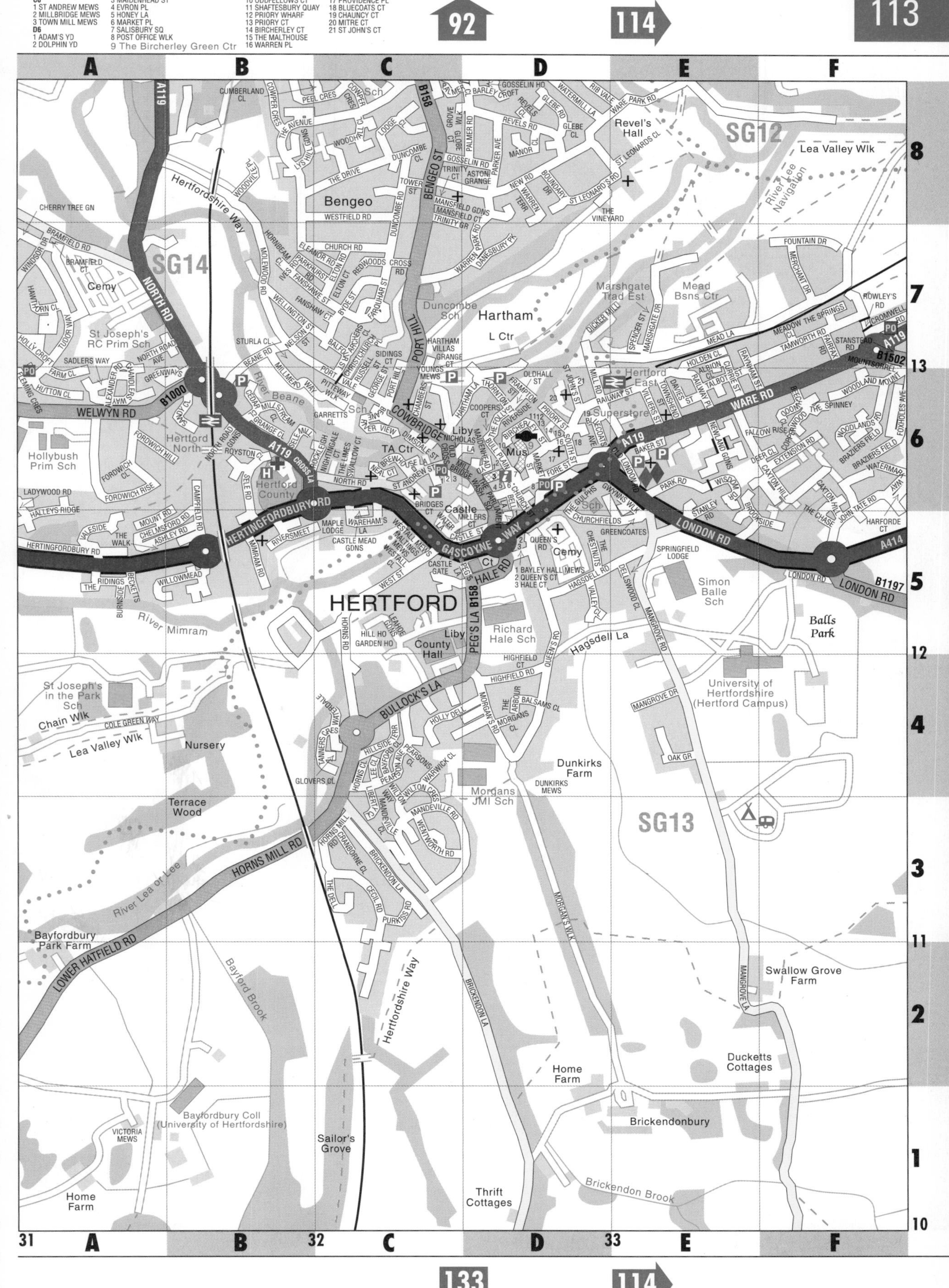

C6
1 ST ANDREW MEWS
2 MILLBRIDGE MEWS
3 TOWN MILL MEWS
D6
1 ADAM'S YD
2 DOLPHIN YD

3 MAIDENHEAD ST
4 EVRON PL
5 HONEY LA
6 MARKET PL
7 SALISBURY SQ
8 POST OFFICE WLK
9 The Bircherley Green Ctr

10 ODDFELLOWS CT
11 SHAFTESBURY QUAY
12 PRIORY WHARF
13 PRIORY CT
14 BIRCHERLEY CT
15 The MALTHOUSE
16 WARREN PL

17 PROVIDENCE PL
18 BLUECOATS CT
19 CHAUNCY CT
20 MITRE CT
21 ST JOHN'S CT

HERTFORD

SG14

SG12

SG13

Bengeo

Hartham

113
93

A
B
C
D
E
F
8
7
13
6
5
12
4
3
11
2
1
10
34
35
36
SG12
Lea Valley Wlk
New River
King's Mead
HERTFORD RD
HILLSIDE
Hertford Regional Coll
Ware
CRANE MEAD
1 DIXON'S CT
2 COOPER'S CT
3 SOMMER'S CT
4 SUTTON CT
5 WILLOW VIEW
Crane Mead Bsns Pk
River Lee or Lea
River Lee Navigation
Lea Valley Wlk
HOLLYCROSS RD
A119 LONDON RD
A1170 VIADUCT RD
Scott's Grotto
WARE
CH
MEADVIEW RD
SPRING VIEW RD
FAIRWAY
LITTLE ACRES
CEDAR CL
WARNER RD
COLLEGE CL
MARSH LA
Peerglow Ctr
PRESDALES CT
PRESDALES DR
GILPIN RD
RED HOUSE CL
POST WOOD RD
LONDON RD
A1170
BEECH MEWS
HOE LA
HERTFORD
WARE RD
NAGS HEAD CL
Taylor Trad Est
RAINSBOROUGH CT 1
WILDMAN CT 2
CROMWELL RD
A119
BURLEIGH RD
Wheatcroft Prim Sch
ALBATROSS CT
PAR CL
RYDER CL
Thieve's La
Presdales Sch
Pinewood Sch
Middleton Middle Sch
Presdales
Post Wood
SG12
LC
YEARLING CL
ASCOT TERR
B1502
STANSTEAD RD
BIRDIE WAY
TEE SIDE
THE FINCHES
MARTINS DR
HAREBELL CL
PRIMROSE DR
THE COPSE
THE BRIARS
VIXEN DR
THE ELMS
THE SQUIRRELS
BADGERS CL
A414
B1502
Amwellbury Farm
WALNUT TREE WLK
LOWER RD
FURLONG WAY
OAKTREE COTTS
AMWELL HILL
CHURCH PATH
Hardforde Ct
Rush Green Farm
Mast
Great Amwell
MADGEWAYS CL
MADGEWAYS LA
A414
Foxholes Farm
STANSTEAD RD
Leafyoak Farm
A1170
PEPPER HILL
CAUTHERLY LA
B1197
Jenningsbury Farm
JENNINGSBURY CT
DOWNFIELD RD
AMWELL PL
WOODSTOCK CL
DOWNFIELD CL
SG13
Leafyoak Wood
GYPSY LA
GYPSY CL
HERTFORD RD
B1502
Much Wood
VICARAGE CSWY
Hertford Heath JMI Sch
CHURCH HILL
MOUNT PLEASANT
THE OLD SCHOOL
RUSHEN DR
TRINITY WLK
BEACON CT
Golding's Wood
Chardingleye Farm
A10
Hertford Heath
LONDON RD
PRIORS CL
WOODLAND RD
TRINITY RD
OAK TREE CL
HARRINGTON CT
Great Stock Wood
Springle House
WOODLAND RD
POSTWOOD GN
PO
OLD FORGE ROW
HEATHGATE
WOODSIDE
HEATH LA
TOWER CL
HARLINGS
COLLEGE RD
Hailey Wood
SPRINGLE LA
Hailey
THE ROUNDINGS
Balls Wood (Nature reserve)
Brides Farm
Haileybury & Imperial Service Coll
THE MEADOW
HAILEY LA
HAILEY CL
Hailey Farm
Hailey Hall Sch
THE ROUNDINGS
High Wood
Roselands Prim Sch
HOWFIELD GN
ELBOW LA
Hobbyhorse Wood
B1197 HERTFORD RD
Dells Wood
EN11
A10
DELLS WOOD CL
HIGH WOOD RD
HOBSONS CL
CHEFFINS RD
WESTBUSH CL
GODDINGTON CL
ROSELANDS AVE
MORICE RD

113
134

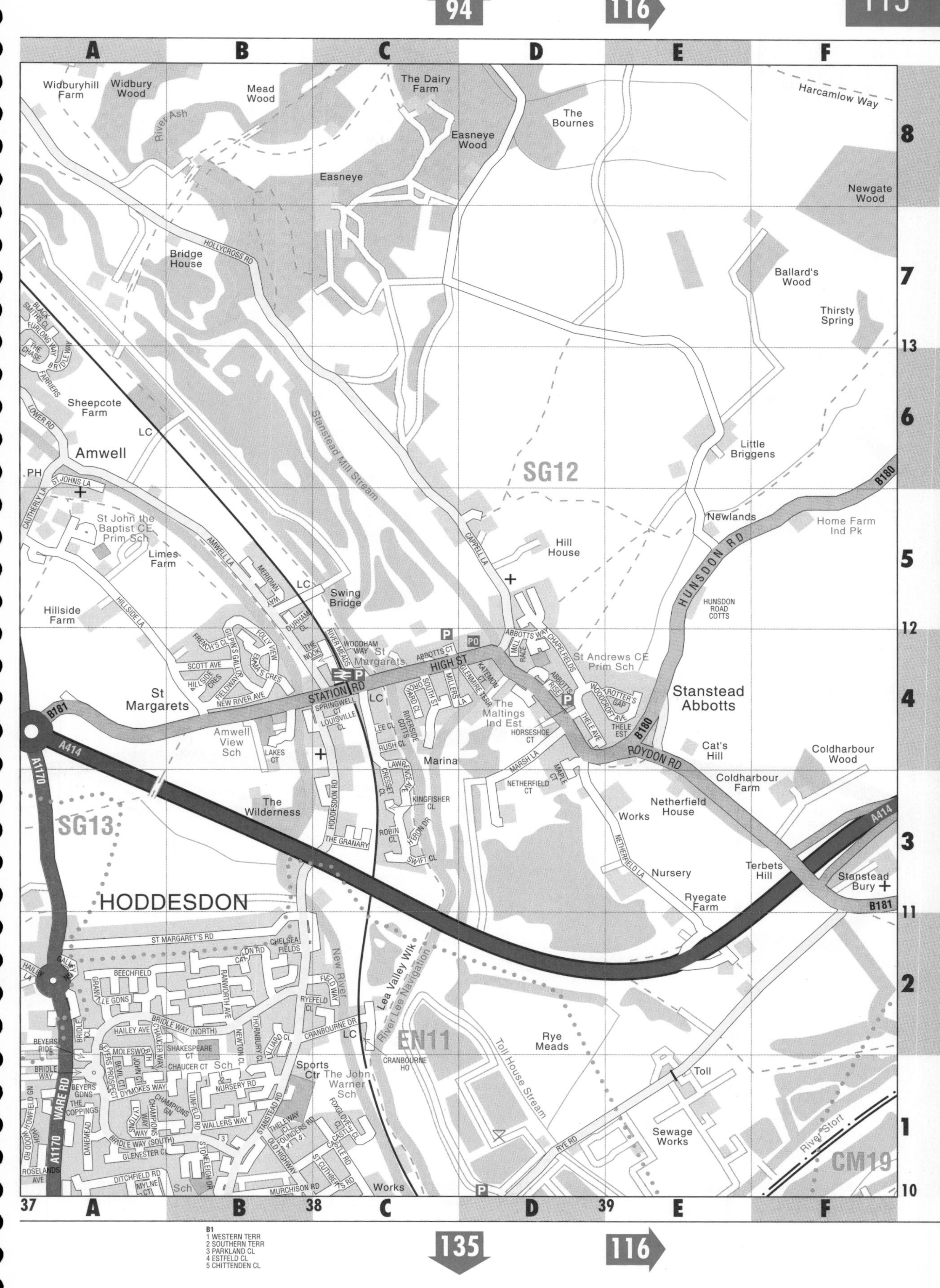

A B C D E F

8

Moat
Wood

Tuck's
Spring

Newfield
Plantation

The
Wilderness

Little
Spellers

Spellers

7

Black
Bushes

Bonningtons

Nine Ashes
Farmhouse

Eastwick Hall
Farm

13

Halfway
House

Hunsdonbury

Copt
Hall

HUNSDON RD

Hunsdon
House

CM20

6

B180

Olives
Farm

Bury
Plantation

Cemy

Square
Spring

Hunsdon Brook

SG12

Lord's
Wood

5

Long
Spring

12

Brickhouse
Farm

Stone Basin
Spring

4

Harcamlow Way

Pogden's
Wood

Briggens Home
Farm

Hunsdon Mill
House

A414

A414

The
Grove

Briggens
Park

Mead
Lodge

Eastwick
Mead

3

Stanstead
Lodge

Briggens
(Hotel)

Hunsdon
Mead

Stanstead
Bury Farm

B181

Three Forests Way

Stort Valley Way

Oak
Pollard

11

Roydon
Mead

2

Roydon
Lea

Roydon

LC

River Stort (Navigation)

CM19

Roydon
Mead

Roydon
Lea

River Stort

LC

ROYDON LODGE
CHALET EST

Harlow
Stadium
(Greyhounds)

CYGNET WAY

ROYDON MILL
LEISURE PK

THE GRANARY

DUCKETTS MEAD

Eastend

MALLARD WAY

ROYDON
MILL

1 KINGFISHER WAY
2 MOORHEN WAY
3 HOLY ACRE

HIGH ST

Roydon

Barrows
Farm

ELIZABETH
WAY

1

Temple
Farm

FARM CL

CHURCH MEAD

East End
Farm

EASTEND
COTTS

STADIUM WAY

Mast

A1169

TEMPLE MEAD

PO

B181

PH

Mount
Pleasant

ROYDON RD

40 A B 41 C D 42 E F

A B C D E F

SG12
Sayes Park Farm
CM21
8
Overhall Farm
Golden Hill
COCKROBIN LA
Gibson's Shaw
CHURCH COTTS
CHANNOCK'S FARM COTTS
Channocks Farm
Fox Earths
HIGH WYCH RD
7
Rectory Plantation
13
Gilston Park
GILSTON PK
GILSTON MEWS
Gilston Rectory
Home Wood
REDRICKS LA
6
Pole Hole Farm
EASTWICK RD
Pole Hill
VINE GR
Fiddlers' Brook
EASTWICK HALL LA
PH
PYE CNR
Hollingson Meads
5
Gilston
Latton Island
CM20
Fiddler's Bridge
12
Stort Valley Way
Three Forests Way
Mead Park Ind Est
Eastwick
Eastwick Lodge Farm
ROSELEY COTTS
BURNTMILL CNR
PH
EASTWICK RD
4
Eastwick Manor
GREEN MAN CT
EASTWICK RD
River Stort (Navigation)
Queensgate Ctr
A414
Astra Ctr
FIFTH AVENUE / ALLENDE AVE
Burnt Mill Lock
BURNTMILL LA
Harlow Town
P
EDINBURGH WAY
Princes Gate
Oaks Ret Pk
Parndon Mead
Harcamlow Way
BURNTMILL CL
3
Burnt Mill
MARSHGATE
NETTESWELL RD
GLEBELANDS
Mill (dis)
Francis Ct
PARNDON MILL LA
A414
RUSHMEAD VILLAS
ALTHAM GR
TARLINGS
BURNT MILL
A1169
A1019
HARLOW
11
Ram Gorse
CROUCH CT
CONYERS
RIVERMILL
NETTESWELL CROSS
Burnt Mill Comp Sch
St Alban's RC Prim Sch
GREAT PLATTS
ELIZABETH WAY
THE HORNBEAMS
FIFTH AVENUE / ALLENDE AVE
Town Park
UMTREE
HERONS WOOD
WINTONS
Harlow Sports Ctr
SCHOOL LA
FIRST AVENUE / MANDELA AVE
Service Ind Bays
2
ASH TREE FIELD
RAM GORSE
HERONS WOOD
HODINGS RD
HESTER HO
PARK LA
Peace Wood
DESORMEAUX
JIM BOLWS
OLDHOUSE CROFT
HALLING HILL
MALLORIES
HOWARD WAY
THE STOW
CANONS GATE
SPRING HILLS
HAMMARSKJOLD RD
MORLEY GR
ST ANDREW'S HO
SEWELL HARRIS CL
HOBTOE RD
SPRING HILLS
PARK MEAD
Supermkt
NETTESWELL ORCH
AMBERRY CT
PARK CT
ADINGTONS
COLT HATCH
Little Parndon Sch
Rectory Wood
THE DASHES
COMMONFIELDS
PITTMANS FIELD
CH
SPRING HILLS TWR
KERRIL CROFT
Oak Wood
HAMSTEL RD
RECTORY WOOD
BRAMBLE RISE
A1019
THE GLEBE
THE DRIVE
Canons Brook
FOLD CROFT
Little Parndon
WYCH ELM
NETTESWELL TWR
VELIZY AVE
THE DASHES
FRESHWATERS
VICTORIA CT
LAVENDER CL
Sch
MONKSWICK RD
VICARAGE WOOD
1
THE HIDES
POST OFFICE RD
FOURTH AVE
Princess Alexandra
UPPER PK
WEST SQ 1
MITRE BLDGS 2
ADAMS HO
EAST GATE
3 THE ROWS
4 MARKET HO
5 STONE CROSS
Harlow Coll
MADDOX RD
ST MICHAELS CT
ARKWRIGHTS
WELL LA
CORAL HO
STANTONS
STANFIELDS CT
FISHERS HATCH
BROADFIELD
Netteswell
LONG LEY
10

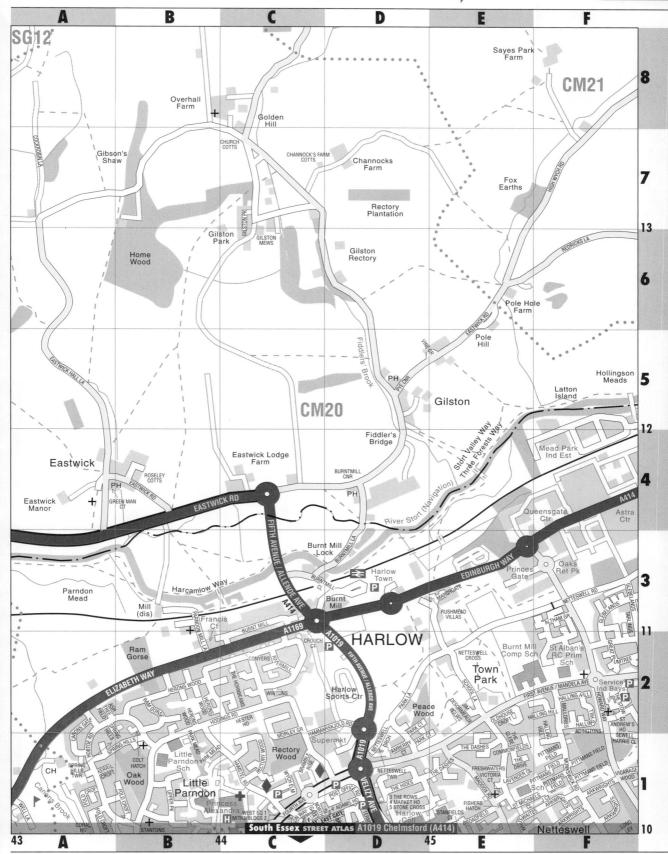

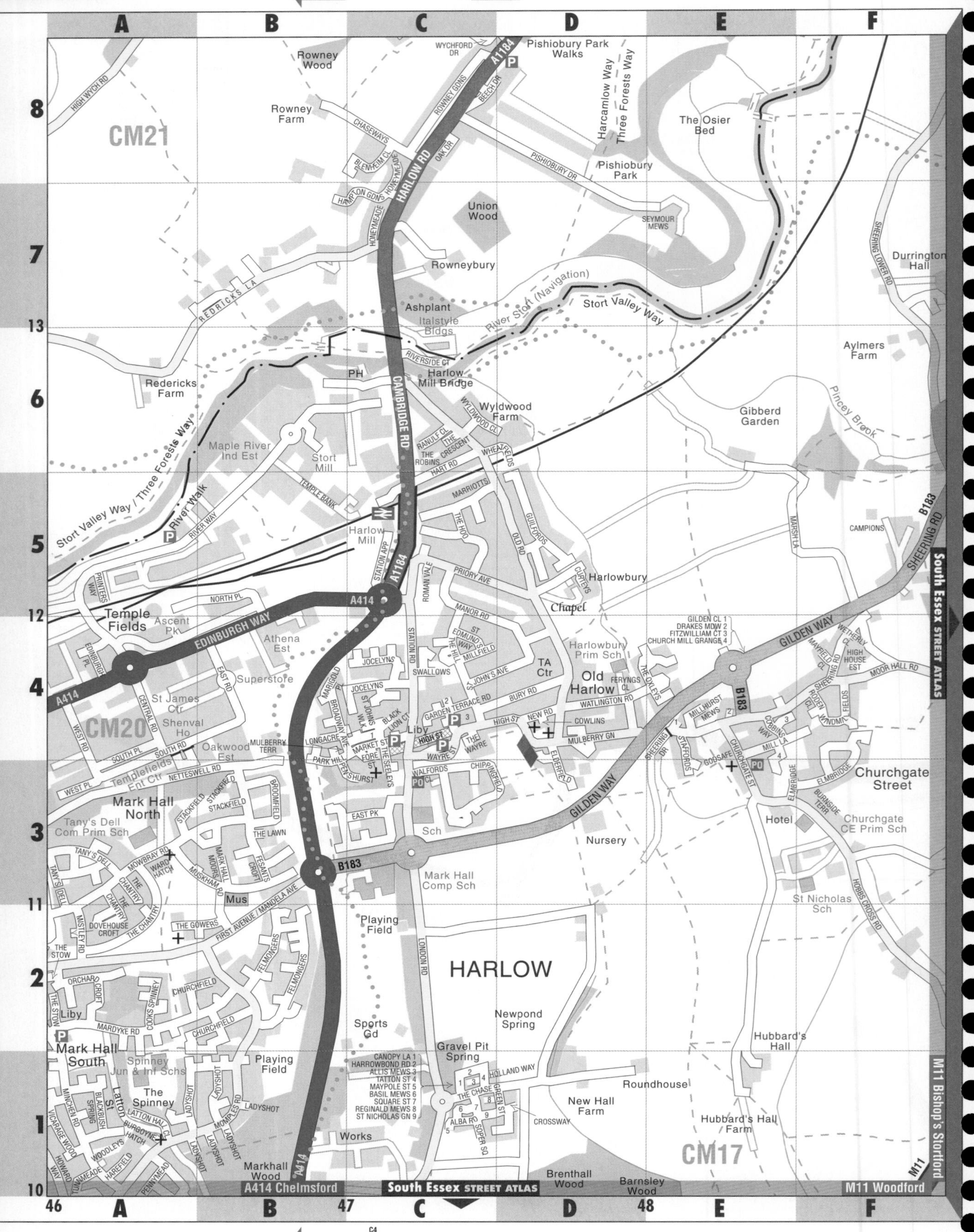

C4
1 DELLFIELD CT
2 CHERRY BLOSSOM CL
3 ROSEMARY CL

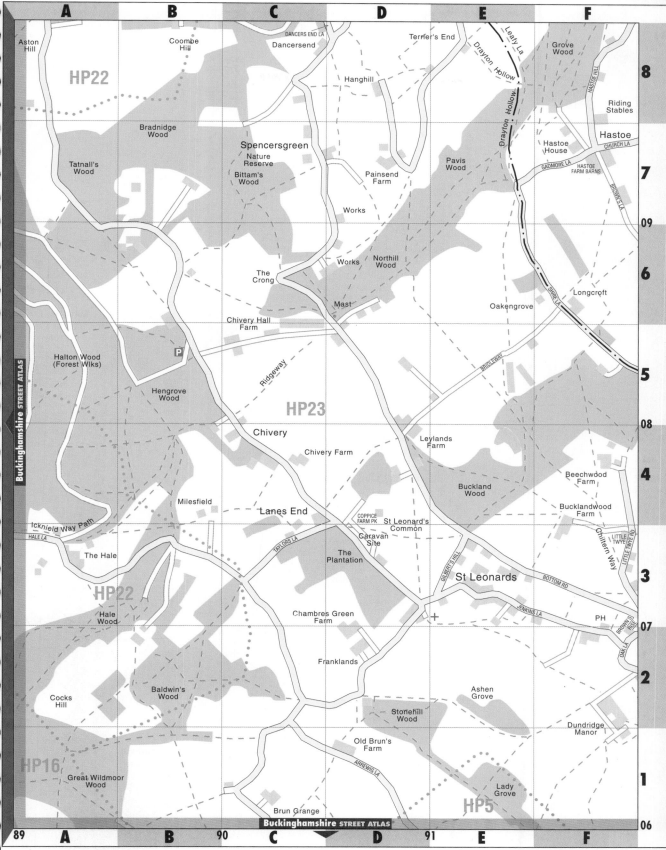

A   B   C   D   E   F

Aston Hill

HP22

Coombe Hill

DANCERS END LA
Dancersend

Terrier's End

Leafy La

Drayton Hollow

Grove Wood

HASTOE HILL

8

Hanghill

Drayton Hollow

Riding Stables

Bradnidge Wood

Spencersgreen

Pavis Wood

Hastoe House

Hastoe

CHURCH LA

Tatnall's Wood

Nature Reserve

Painsend Farm

GADMORE LA

HASTOE FARM BARNS

7

Bittam's Wood

Works

BROWN'S LA

09

Works

Northill Wood

The Crong

Mast

Oakengrove

Longcroft

6

Chivery Hall Farm

SHIRE LA

Halton Wood (Forest Wlks)

P

Ridgeway

BRIDLEWAY

5

Hengrove Wood

HP23

Leylands Farm

08

Chivery

Chivery Farm

Beechwood Farm

4

Milesfield

Buckland Wood

Bucklandwood Farm

Lanes End

COPPICE FARM PK

St Leonard's Common

CHILTERN WAY

LITTLE TWYE RD

Icknield Way Path

HALE LA

TAYLORS LA

Caravan Site

GILBERT'S HILL

St Leonards

BOTTOM RD

LITTLE TWYE

PH

3

The Hale

The Plantation

JENKINS LA

BROWN'S RISE

HP22

Hale Wood

Chambres Green Farm

OAK LA

07

Franklands

Ashen Grove

2

Cocks Hill

Baldwin's Wood

Stonehill Wood

Dundridge Manor

HP16

Great Wildmoor Wood

Old Brun's Farm

ARREWIG LA

Lady Grove

HP5

1

Brun Grange

06

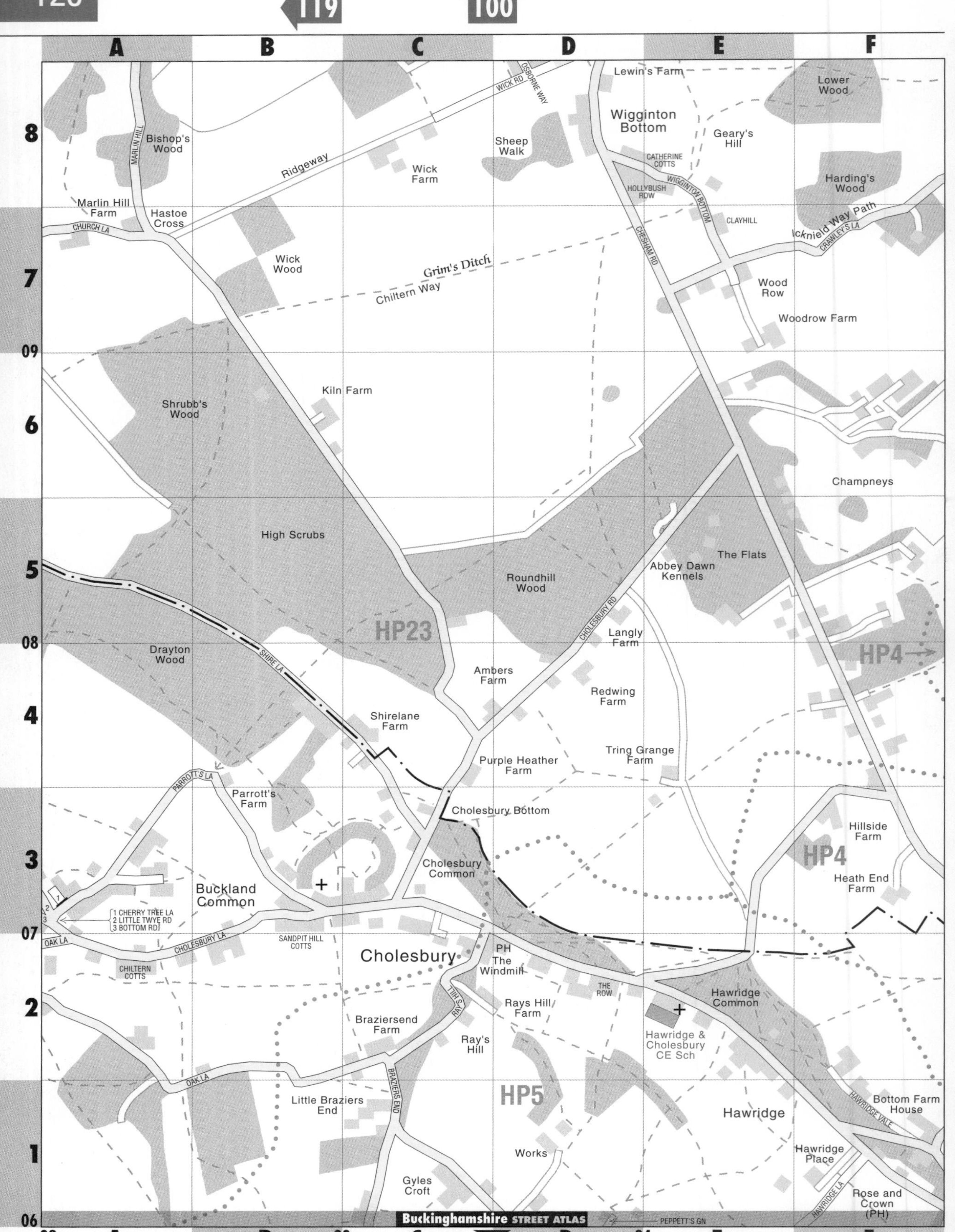

A   B   C   D   E   F

8

7

09

6

5

08

4

3

07

2

1

06

Marlin Hill Farm
Bishop's Wood
Hastoe Cross
CHURCH LA
MARLIN HILL

Ridgeway
Wick Farm
Sheep Walk
WICK RD
OSBORNE WAY

Lewin's Farm
Wigginton Bottom
Geary's Hill
CATHERINE COTTS
HOLLYBUSH ROW
WIGGINTON BOTTOM
CHESHAM RD
CLAYHILL
Lower Wood
Harding's Wood
Icknield Way Path
CRANLEY'S LA

Wick Wood
Grim's Ditch
Chiltern Way

Wood Row
Woodrow Farm

Kiln Farm

Shrubb's Wood

Champneys

High Scrubs

Roundhill Wood
Abbey Dawn Kennels
The Flats

HP23

Drayton Wood
SHIRE LA

Ambers Farm
CHOLESBURY RD
Langly Farm

HP4 →

HP4

Shirelane Farm
Redwing Farm

Purple Heather Farm
Tring Grange Farm

Hillside Farm

Parrott's Farm
PARROTT'S LA

Cholesbury Bottom
Cholesbury Common

Heath End Farm

Buckland Common
1 CHERRY TREE LA
2 LITTLE TWYE RD
3 BOTTOM RD
OAK LA
CHOLESBURY LA
SANDPIT HILL COTTS
CHILTERN COTTS

Cholesbury
PH The Windmill
THE ROW

Hawridge Common

Braziersend Farm
Rays Hill Farm
Ray's Hill
BRAZIERS END
THE SCRUBS

Hawridge & Cholesbury CE Sch

Bottom Farm House
RAWRIDGE VALE

OAK LA
Little Braziers End

HP5

Hawridge

Hawridge Place
HAWRIDGE LA

Works

Gyles Croft

Rose and Crown (PH)

PEPPETT'S GN

92   A   B   93   C   D   94   E   F

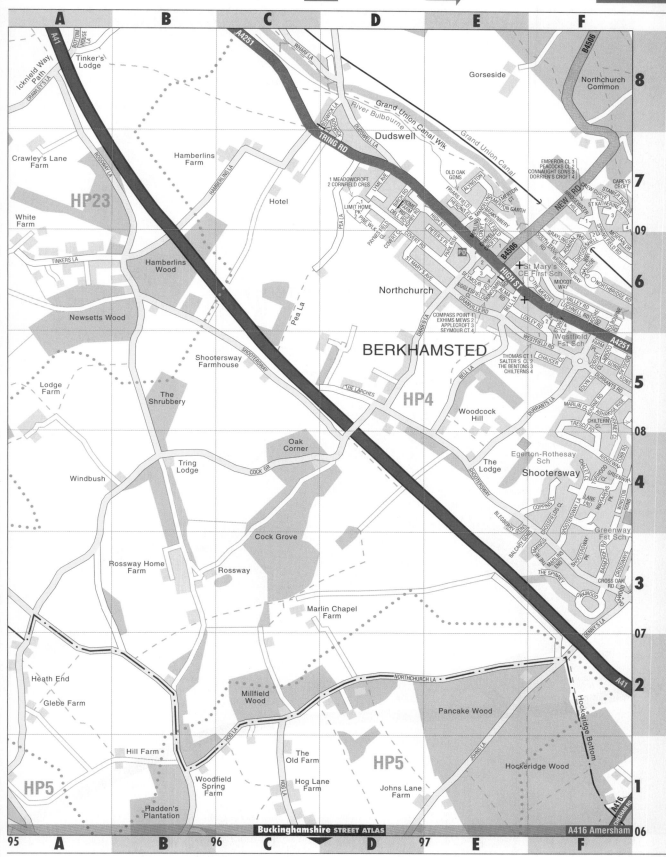

Icknield Way Path
Crawley's La
A41
BOTTOM HOUSE LA
Tinker's Lodge

Gorseside

Northchurch Common

B4506

8

Crawley's Lane Farm

HP23

ROSSWAY LA

Hamberlins Farm

HAMBERLINS LA

Hotel

Wharf La

Grand Union Canal Wlk
River Bulbourne

Dudswell

BESWICK LA
BESWICK LA
DUDSWELL LA
Tring Rd
TRING RD

Grand Union Canal

EMPEROR CL 1
PEACOCKS CL 2
CONNAUGHT GDNS 3
DORRIEN'S CROFT 4

NEW RD

CAREYS CROFT
STANIER RD
CREW CURVE
St KATHERINE'S WAY

7

09

White Farm

TINKERS LA

Hamberlins Wood

Newsetts Wood

PEA LA

1 MEADOWCROFT
2 CORNFIELD CRES

LIMIT HOME
PK
1 PINE WLK
2

BIRCH RD
HOME FARM CL
DEL RD
COVERT CL
COVERT RD
ST MARY'S AVE
PAVINGS CL
LIME AVE
FRIARS FIELD
HEADONS LA
HIGH ST
PETER'S PL
PARK RISE
B4506
HIGH ST

OLD OAK GDNS
ALYNGTON
EMERTON CT
EMERTON GARTH
NANBERRY
KITE FIELD
PROPERTY

Northchurch

PO
SEYMOUR CL
EGGLESFIELD
GRANVILLE RD
DARR-B LA
ALMA RD
BELL LA
BUCKINGHAM
DUNGROVE
MIDCOT WAY

St Mary's CE First Sch

GRAYLING CT
SOUTH BANK
BRIDGESTONE
DUCHESS CL
MORTAIN DR
SPRINGFIELD RD
ON ORTHBRIDGE RD
VALLEY RD
LOCHNELL RD

6

BERKHAMSTED

Pea La

Shootersway Farmhouse
SHOOTERSWAY

THE LARCHES

HP4

BELL LA

Woodcock Hill

COMPASS POINT 1
EXHIMS MEWS 2
APPLECROFT 3
SEYMOUR CT 4

WESTFIELD RD
LOXLEY RD

THOMAS CT 1
SALTER'S CL 2
THE BENTONS 3
CHILTERNS 4

Westfield Fst Sch

CHAUCER

A4251

DURRANTS LA
MARLIN CL
ASHRIDGE RISE
VERNEY CL
CHILTERN RD
TRESCO RD
RIDGEWAY

5

08

Lodge Farm

The Shrubbery

Windbush

Tring Lodge

COCK GR

Oak Corner

Egerton-Rothesay Sch

The Lodge
SHOOTERSWAY

Shootersway

COPPINS CL
CROSSFIELDS CL
SHOOTERSWAY LA
CHALET CL
TORSWOOD
GREENWAY
LANE END
WATMERS
WINSTON CL

Greenway Fst Sch

4

Cock Grove

BLEGBERRY GDNS
BALCARY GDNS
SIMMONS
THE MARLINS
BARNCROFT RD
SHOOTERSWAY
THE SPINNEY
OAKWOOD
CROSS OAK RD

CROSS OAK RD

3

07

Rossway Home Farm

Rossway

Marlin Chapel Farm

NORTHCHURCH LA

DENNY'S LA

A41

Hockeridge Bottom

2

Heath End

Glebe Farm

Millfield Wood

HOG LA

JOHNS LA

Pancake Wood

Hockeridge Wood

A416 CHESHAM RD

Hill Farm

HP5

Woodfield Spring Farm

Hadden's Plantation

HOG LA

The Old Farm

Hog Lane Farm

HP5

Johns Lane Farm

1

A416

06

121 102

A B C D E F

8 Northchurch Farm

Berkhamsted Common

Hertfordshire Way

7 Well Farm

FRITHSDEN COPSE

09
CAREYS CROFT
1 ST KATHERINE'S WAY
2 MORTAIN DR
3 MONTGOMERIE CL
4 BECKETS SQ

HILL VIEW
HAYNES MEAD
BRIDLE WAY
LONG VIEW

Bridgewater Mid Sch

WHYBROW GDNS
CH
FARMERY CT
PRIESTLAND GDNS
BRITWELL DR
BENNINGFIELD GDNS
THE MANSION
LADY COOPER CT
RAVENS CT

SPRING FIELD RD
ALTERN PARK AVE

6
EGERTON RD
MEADOW RD

Castle Hill Farm
CASTLE HILL CT
CASTLE GATE WAY

BERKHAMSTED

HP4

THE COMMON
GUTTERIDGE FARM
NETTLEDEN RD

NORTHBRIDGE RD

River Park Ind Est
BELTON RD
RIVERSIDE GDNS

GOSSOM'S END
A4251

HIGH ST

Berkhamsted Castle

GRAVEL PATH
GILPIN'S RIDE
HEADLANDS DR
BRACKENHILL
BYWNS
HUMPERS PK
BRACKENHILL

5
Sp Ctr
VICTORY RD
DOUGLAS GONS
GOSSOMS RD
CHILTERN CNR
DURRANT'S CT

Berkhamsted Station
WHITEHILL CT
WHITEHILL
BEECHILL
MALLFIELD
MEADOW
IVY HOUSE LA

08
LARCH
WHITEWOOD
ROTHESAY CT

Nightingale Lodge
Berkhamsted Schs
CHAPEL ST
STATION RD
CANTHAM MEWS
ELLESMERE RD

4
St Thomas More RC Prim Sch
Liby
TH
C Ctr
MANOR
WATERSIDE
GEORGE ST
THE CEDARS
BANK MILL

Victoria CE Fst Sch
FROST HO

Grand Union Canal Wlk
OLD MILL GDNS
GEORGE ST
BANK MILL LA

3
Greenway Fst Sch
GRAEMESDYKE RD
MARLBOROUGH HO
KINGSDALE RD
KINGS RD

Berkhamsted Collegiate Sch
ASHLYNS RD
ALDERLEY CT

Swing Gate Fst Sch
CURTIS WAY
HOLLY DR
GREENE WLK CAPTAINS WLK
LOMBARDY DR
CEDAR
HALL PK
River Bulbourne
Bankmill Bridge

LONDON RD
A4251

07
SHOOTERSWAY
POWER CL
OXFIELD CT
OLD MEADOW
BALLINGER CT

CORAM CL
HILLTOP RD
BRIAR WAY
CHESTNUT DR
WOODLANDS AVE
OAK DR
HAZEL RD
ST MARGARET'S CL
HILLSIDE GDNS
UPPER HALL PK
HALL PARK HILL
HALL PARK GATE
FIELDWAY

2
A416
National Film Archive
Cemy
KINGSHILL WAY
A416

Ashlyn's Hall

Ashlyns Sch

The Thomas Coram CE Mid Sch
SWING GATE LA
Long Green

A41

1
A416 CHESHAM RD

Sandpit Green

Bottom Farm

HP1

A41

06
98 A B 99 C D 00 E F

Haresfoot Sch
Haresfoot Farm
Kingshill
Cemy

103
124

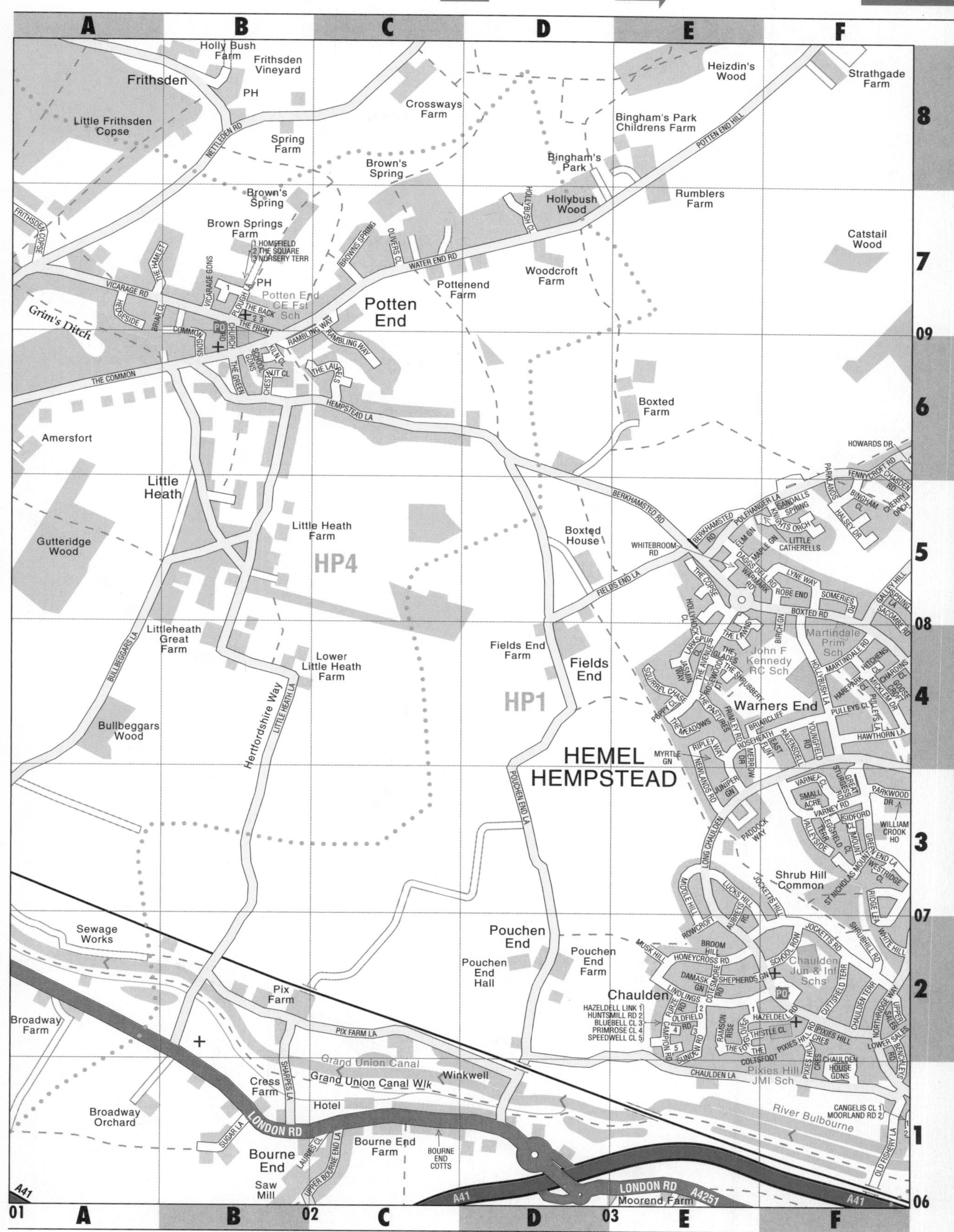
Frithsden
Potten End
Little Heath
HP4
HP1
HEMEL HEMPSTEAD
Warners End
Fields End
Pouchen End
Chaulden
Bourne End
Winkwell
Grand Union Canal
River Bulbourne
LONDON RD
A41
A4251

137
124

123
104

HEMEL HEMPSTEAD

Grovehill

Highfield

Gadebridge

Hammerfield

Counter's End

Green End

Boxmoor

Paradise

HP1

HP2

HP3

Piccotts End

Grist House Farm

Thrift Wood

Noake Mill

Gaddesden Hall

Dell Wood

Warnersend Wood

Boar's Head (PH)

Marchmont Arms (PH)

Marchmont Farm

Howe Grove

Barncroft Prim Sch

Aycliffe Drive Prim Sch

The Hammond Prim Sch

Bellgate Prim Sch

Rossgate Prim Sch

Gadebridge Park

St Cuthbert Mayne RC Jun Sch

Gade Valley Jun Mix Inf Sch

The Cavendish Sch

The Collett Sch

Lockers Park Sch

Lockers Park

South Hill Prim Sch

The Hemel Hempstead Sch

St Rose's RC Infants Sch

Hemel Hempstead General

Hemel Hempstead Sports Ctr

Broadfield Jun & Inf Schs

Tudor JMI Sch

Athletics Gd

Ski Ctr

Lime Walk Prim Sch

Superstore

Grand Union Canal

Grand Union Canal Wlk

A4146 LONDON RD A4251

A4146

A4147 LINK RD

LEIGHTON BUZZARD RD

B487

QUEENSWAY

ST ALBANS RD

A414

A4147

B487

TWO WATERS RD

STATION RD

123
138

105
126

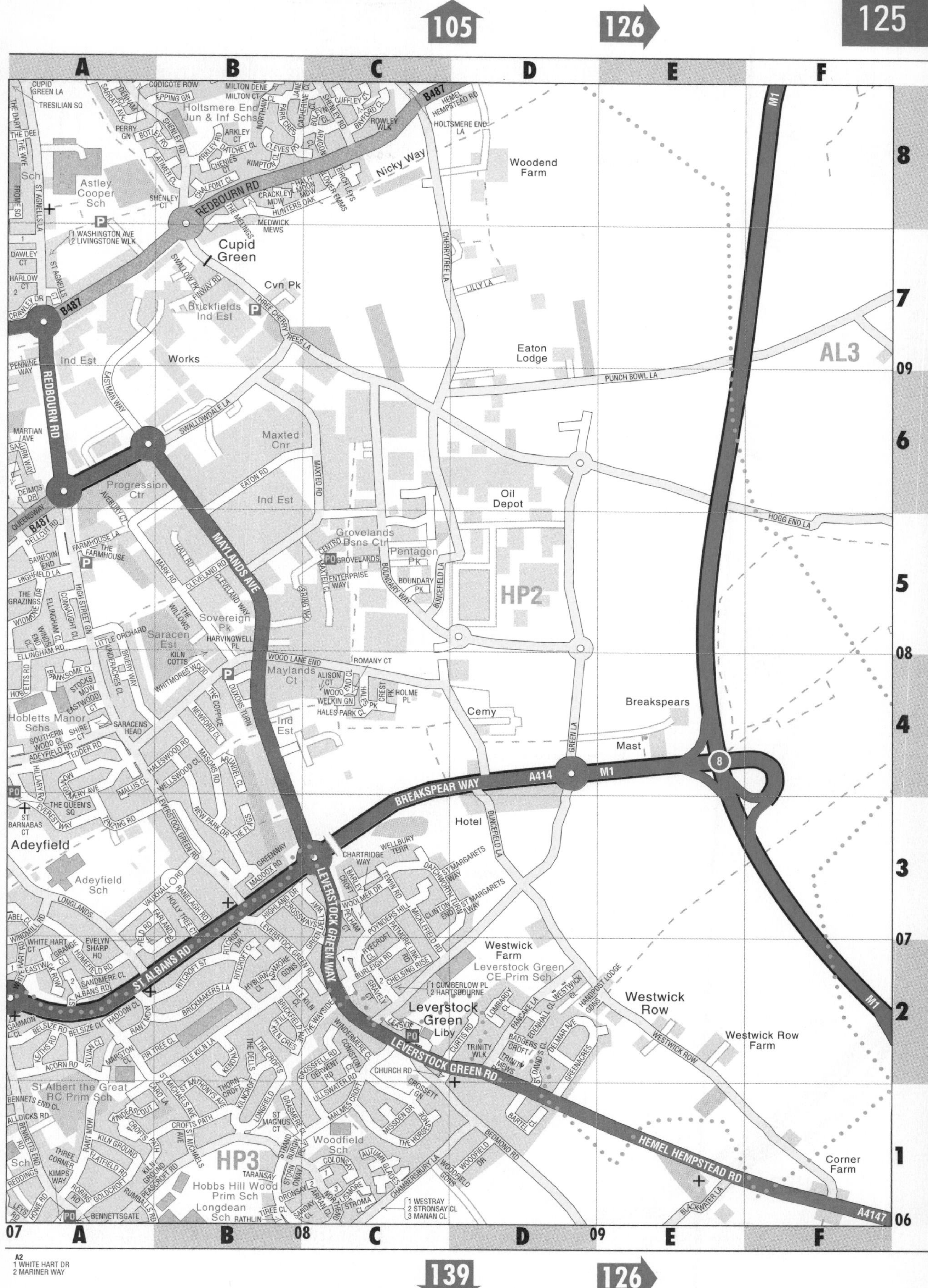
A
B
C
D
E
F
8
7
09
6
5
08
4
3
07
2
1
06
07
08
09
Holtsmere End Jun & Inf Schs
Astley Cooper Sch
Sch
Cupid Green
REDBOURN RD
B487
Nicky Way
Woodend Farm
HEMEL HEMPSTEAD RD
HOLTSMERE END LA
M1
Cvn Pk
Brickfields Ind Est
THREE CHERRY TREES LA
CHERRYTREE LA
LILLY LA
Eaton Lodge
AL3
PUNCH BOWL LA
Ind Est
Works
SWALLOWDALE LA
EASTMAN WAY
Maxted Cnr
MAXTED RD
Progression Ctr
EATON RD
Ind Est
Oil Depot
HOGG END LA
QUEENSWAY
Grovelands Bsns Ctr
GROVELANDS
Pentagon Pk
ENTERPRISE WAY
BOUNDARY PK
BOUNDARY WAY
BUNCEFIELD LA
HP2
MAYLANDS AVE
Sovereign Pk
Saracen Est
HARVINGWELL PL
WOOD LANE END
ROMANY CT
Maylands Ct
HOLME PL
HALES PARK CL
Cemy
Breakspears
Hobletts Manor Schs
Ind Est
Mast
GREEN LA
BREAKSPEAR WAY
A414
8
Hotel
Adeyfield
Adeyfield Sch
LEVERSTOCK GREEN WAY
ST ALBANS RD
LONGLANDS
Westwick Farm
Leverstock Green CE Prim Sch
Westwick Row
WESTWICK ROW
Westwick Row Farm
Leverstock Green
Liby
LEVERSTOCK GREEN RD
CHURCH RD
St Albert the Great RC Prim Sch
HEMEL HEMPSTEAD RD
Woodfield Sch
HP3
Hobbs Hill Wood Prim Sch
Longdean Sch
BENNETTSGATE
BLACKWATER LA
Corner Farm
A4147
1 WESTRAY
2 STRONSAY CL
3 MANAN CL
1 CUMBERLOW PL
2 HARTSBOURNE
1 WASHINGTON AVE
2 LIVINGSTONE WLK

A2
1 WHITE HART DR
2 MARINER WAY

139
126

125
106

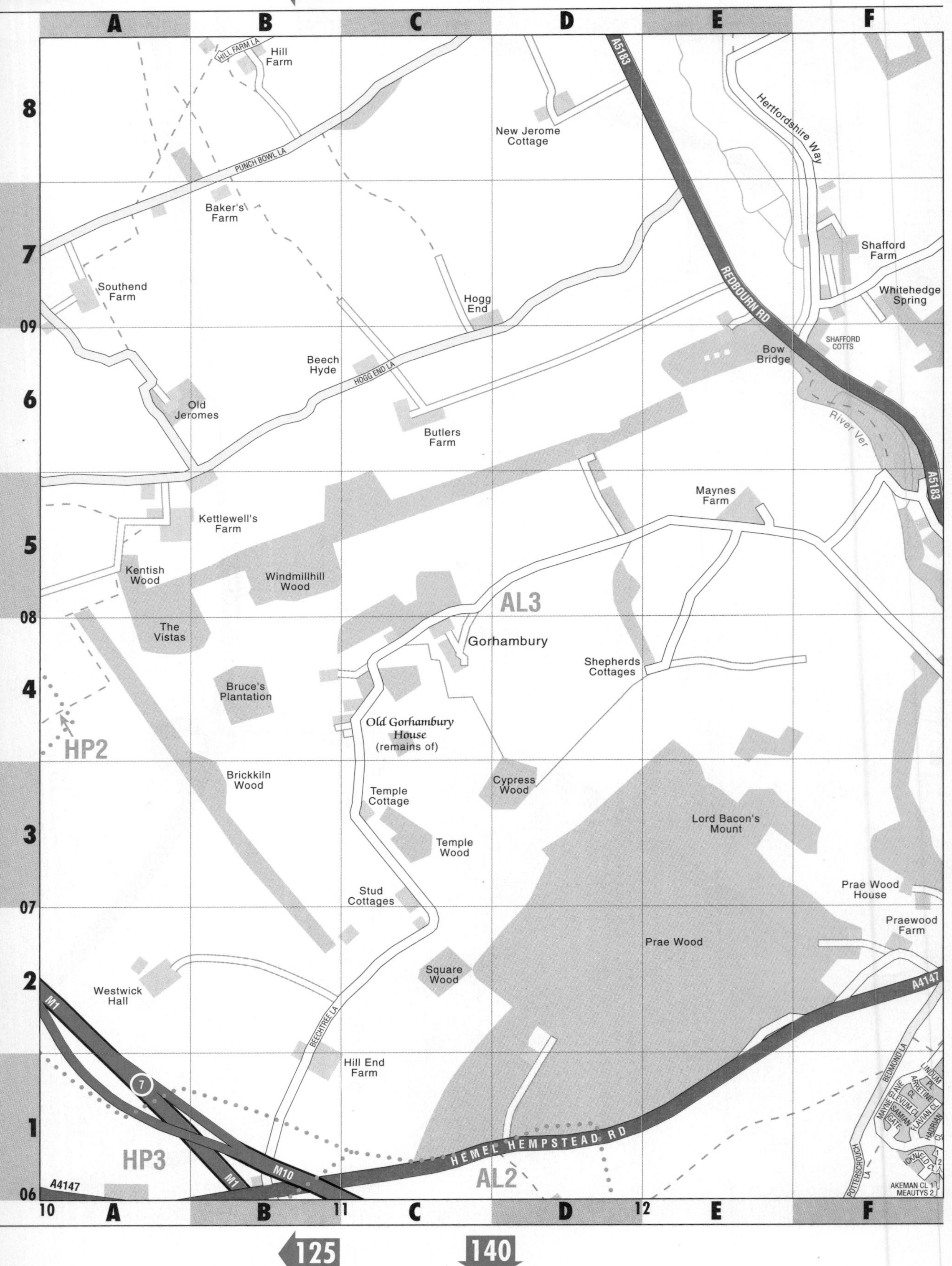
A
B
C
D
E
F
8
7
09
6
5
08
4
3
07
2
1
06
10
11
12
HILL FARM LA
Hill Farm
A5183
New Jerome Cottage
Hertfordshire Way
PUNCH BOWL LA
Baker's Farm
Shafford Farm
Southend Farm
Hogg End
Whitehedge Spring
REDBOURN RD
SHAFFORD COTTS
Beech Hyde
HOGG END LA
Bow Bridge
Old Jeromes
Butlers Farm
River Ver
Maynes Farm
Kettlewell's Farm
Kentish Wood
Windmillhill Wood
AL3
The Vistas
Gorhambury
Shepherds Cottages
Bruce's Plantation
Old Gorhambury House
(remains of)
HP2
Brickkiln Wood
Cypress Wood
Temple Cottage
Lord Bacon's Mount
Temple Wood
Stud Cottages
Prae Wood House
Praewood Farm
Prae Wood
Square Wood
A4147
Westwick Hall
M1
BEECHTREE LA
Hill End Farm
BEDMOND LA
7
HEMEL HEMPSTEAD RD
HP3
M10
AL2
A4147
POTTERSCROUCH LA
AKEMAN CL 1
MEAUTYS 2

125
140

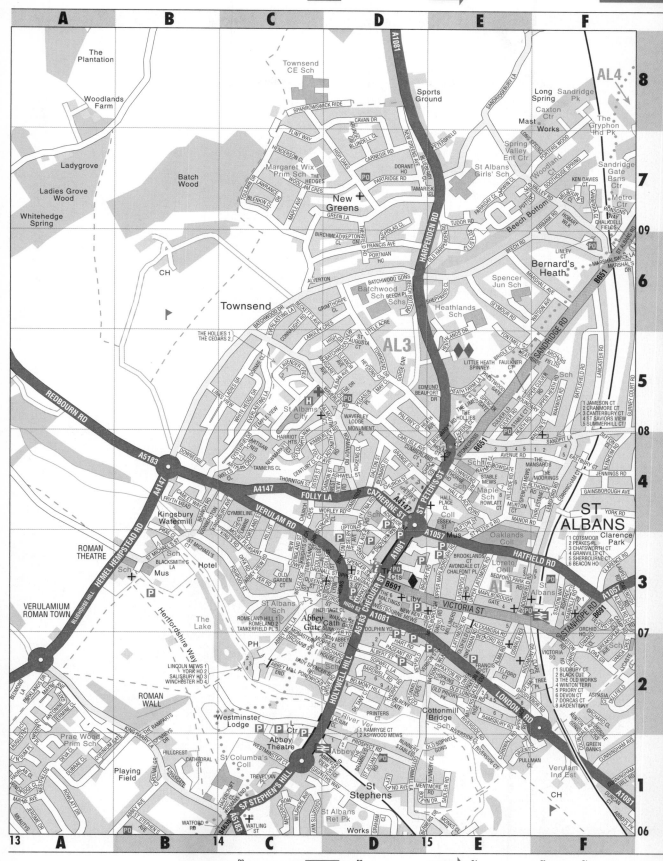

141   128 →

D2
1 SARACENS HEAD YD
2 SAMUEL SQ
3 RYDER SEED MEWS
4 PEARCES WLK
5 MALTHOUSE CT
6 BARDWELL CT
7 BELMONT CT
8 THE SYCAMORES
9 PAT LARNER HO

D3
1 WADDINGTON RD
2 CROSS ST
3 CHRISTOPHER PL
4 FRENCH ROW
5 HALF MOON MEWS
6 ART SCHOOL YD
7 WESLEY HO

D4
1 DENNIS CT
2 GRAHAM CT
3 GRANGE CT
4 PEMBERTON ALMSHOUSES

E3
1 DITCHLING CT
2 LAGUNA CT
3 YARRA HO
4 GARLAND CT
5 MIDLAND HO

E4
1 RAYMER CT
2 HEATHFIELD CT
3 WEYVER CT
4 HIGHCLERE CT
5 ST RAPHAELS CT
6 HILLSIDE GATE
7 RAMSEY LODGE LA
8 HILLSIDE CT

127 108

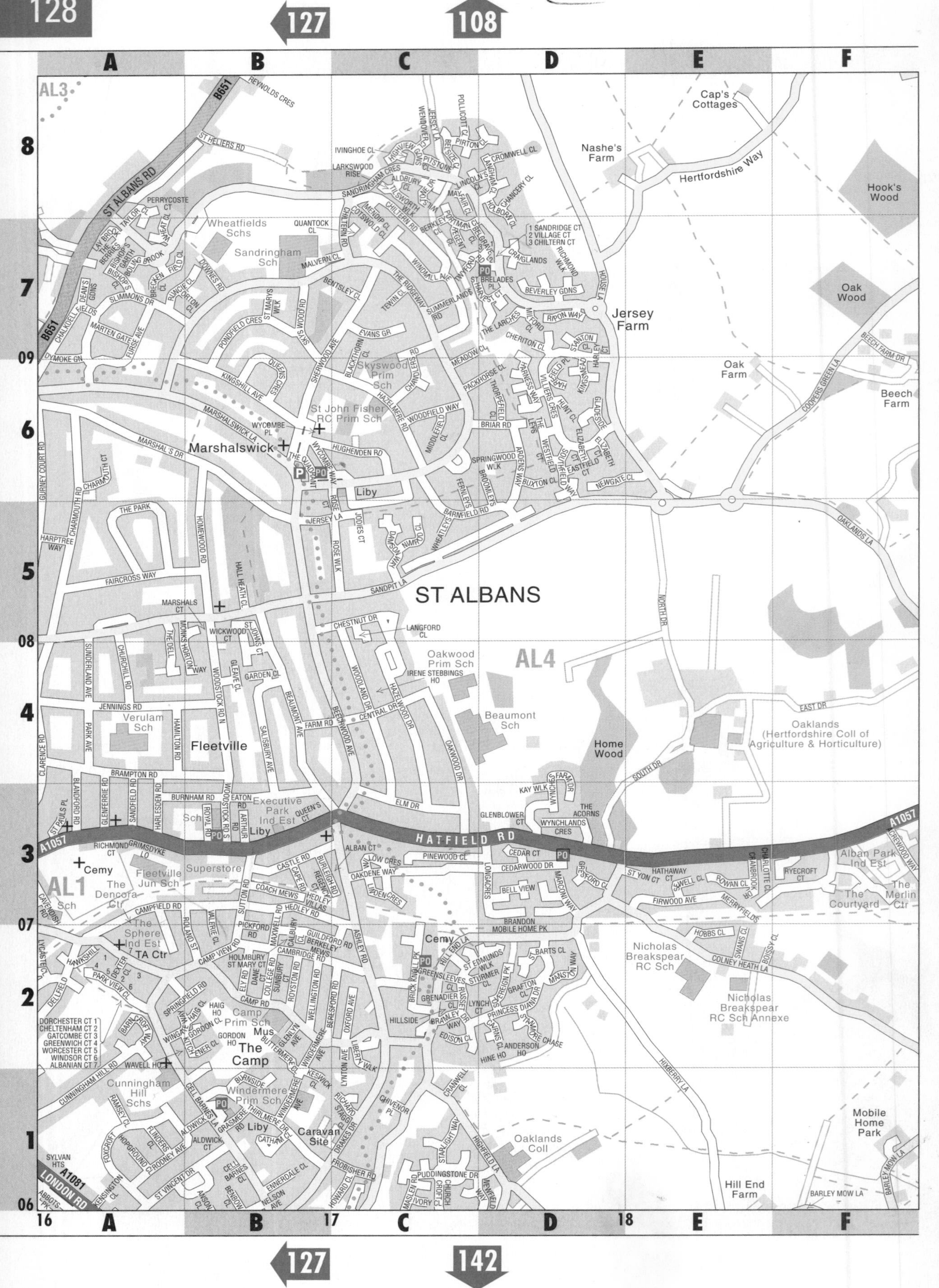
ST ALBANS
Marshalswick
Fleetville
The Camp
Jersey Farm
AL1
AL3
AL4
HATFIELD RD
A1057
B651
A1081

127 142

109
130

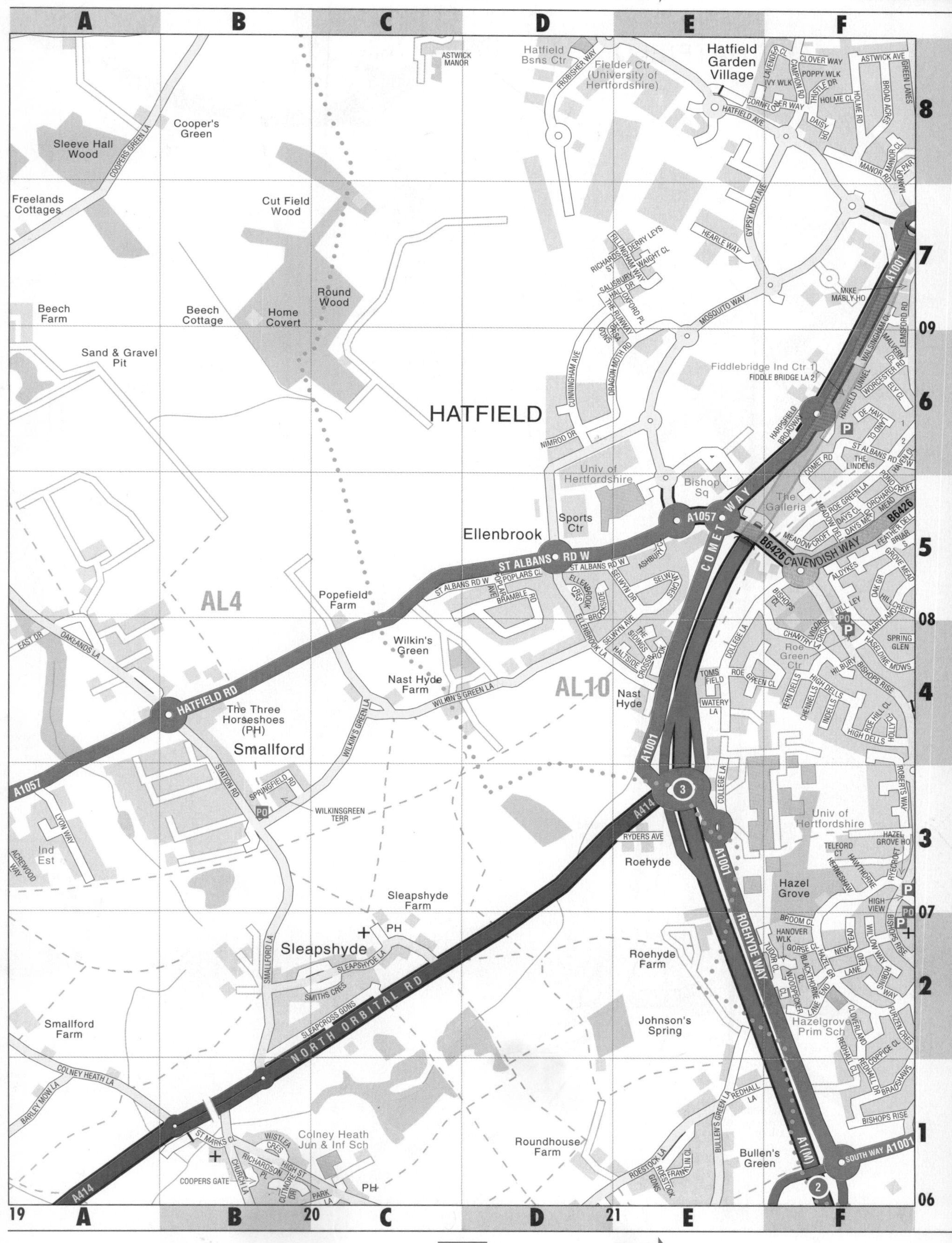
A
B
C
D
E
F
ASTWICK MANOR
Hatfield Bsns Ctr
FROBISHER WAY
Fielder Ctr (University of Hertfordshire)
Hatfield Garden Village
LAVENDER CL
CAMPION RD
CLOVER WAY
POPPY WLK
IVY WLK
THISTLE DR
ASTWICK AVE
GREEN LANES
BROAD ACRES
HOLME CL
HOLME RD
CORNFLOWER WAY
DAISY DR
HATFIELD AVE
MANOR RD
MANOR CL
MANOR PAR
8
Cooper's Green
COOPERS GREEN LA
Sleeve Hall Wood
Freelands Cottages
Cut Field Wood
GYPSY MOTH AVE
HEARLE WAY
FILLINGHAM WAY
DERRY LEYS
RICHARDS ST
WAIGHT CL
SALISBURY HALL DR
OXFORD PL
THE RUNWAY
TRISA GDNS
7
A1001
MIKE MABLY HO
Beech Farm
Beech Cottage
Home Covert
Round Wood
MOSQUITO WAY
09
Sand & Gravel Pit
CUNNINGHAM AVE
DRAGON MOTH RD
Fiddlebridge Ind Ctr
FIDDLE BRIDGE LA
WALSINGHAM CL
LEMSFORD RD
MALVERN CL
WORCESTER RD
ELY CL
HATFIELD TUNNEL
HARPSFIELD BROADWAY
HATFIELD
6
NIMROD DR
Univ of Hertfordshire
Bishop Sq
COMET RD
ST ALBANS RD W
THE LINDENS
HAVEN CL
POND CROFT
The Galleria
ROE GREEN LA
MEADOW DR
DAYS CL
DAYS MEAD
ORCHARD MEAD
Sports Ctr
A1057
COMET WAY
B6426
Ellenbrook
MEADOWCROFT
CAVENDISH WAY
FEATHERBED
BRIAR
5
ST ALBANS RD W
ASHBURY CL
ALDYKES
GROVE MEAD
SELWYN CRES
SELWYN DR
POPLARS CL
ST ALBANS RD W
POPLAR AVE
BRAMBLE RD
ELLENBROOK CRES
BROOKSIDE
ELLENBROOK LA
AL4
Popefield Farm
BISHOPS CL
HILL LEY
OAK GR
HILLCREST
MARYLANDS
08
EAST DR
OAKLANDS LA
Wilkin's Green
SELWYN AVE
THE SIDINGS
HALTSIDE
CROSSBROOK
CHANTRY LA
VICORS CROFT
COLLEGE LA
Roe Green Ctr
SPRING GLEN
HASELDINE MDWS
HILBURY
BISHOPS RISE
Nast Hyde Farm
WILKIN'S GREEN LA
AL10
Nast Hyde
TOMS FIELD
ROE GREEN CL
FERN DELLS
CHENNELLS
HIGH DELLS
INDELLS
ROE HILL CL
4
HATFIELD RD
The Three Horseshoes (PH)
Smallford
WILKIN'S GREEN LA
WATERY LA
HIGH DELLS
A1001
ROBERTS WAY
A1057
STATION RD
SPRINGFIELD RD
WILKINSGREEN TERR
3
COLLEGE LA
LYON WAY
A414
Univ of Hertfordshire
HAZEL GROVE HO
Ind Est
ACREWOOD WAY
RYDERS AVE
Roehyde
A1001
TELFORD CT
HAWTHORNE
RYECROFT
3
Hazel Grove
Sleapshyde Farm
PH
HIGH VIEW
07
BROOM CL
HANOVER WLK
Sleapshyde
SLEAPSHYDE LA
ROEHYDE WAY
GORSE CL
NEWSTEAD
WILLOW WAY
BISHOPS RISE
Roehyde Farm
TUDOR CL
HAZEL GR
BLACKTHORNE LA
LANE END
ROBINS WAY
SMALLFORD LA
SMITHS CRES
NORTH ORBITAL RD
WOODPECKER CL
2
Smallford Farm
SLEAPCROSS GDNS
Johnson's Spring
Hazelgrove Prim Sch
CLOVERLAND
FURZEN CRES
REDHALL CL
COPPICE CL
BRADSHAWS
COLNEY HEATH LA
BARLEY MOW LA
REDHALL LA
REDHALL DR
BISHOPS RISE
1
ST MARKS CL
WISTLEA CRES
Colney Heath Jun & Inf Sch
Roundhouse Farm
BULLEN'S GREEN LA
Bullen's Green
SOUTH WAY
A1001
RICHARDSON PL
HIGH ST
CHURCH LA
CUTMORE DR
COOPERS GATE
PARK LA
PH
A414
ROESTOCK LA
FRANKLIN CL
ROESTOCK GDNS
A1(M)
2
06
19
20
21

143
130

130

A6
1 Queensway Ho
2 Broomfield Ct
3 Lothair Ct
4 Galleycroft Ct

129   110

A   B   C   D   E   F

HATFIELD

Bush Hall

LEA GREEN
Mill Green

Lea Valley Wlk

A414

The Ryde

HERTFORD RD

The Warren

COMET WAY   A1(M)   A1001

Mus   PH

The Broadwater

The Vineyard

Birchwood

The Lodge House

Home Park

The Ryde Sch

Wellfield

St Albans Rd E   B6426

Old Hatfield

1 NORTHCOTTS
2 ARCHWAY HO
3 SALISBURY SQ
4 ENDYMION CT

Roe Green

Queensway

B6426

French Horn La   B197

Bishop's Palace (rem of)

Hatfield House & Gdns

AL9

Conduit Wood

Hatfield Park

Oxlease

GREAT NORTH RD

Onslow St Audrey's Sch

Playing Field

Howe Dell Prim Sch

Cemy

Home Farm

Coombe Wood

Park Dairy

AL10

Playing Field

Jun & Inf Sch

Oxleys

Buttfield Cottage

Millward's Park

South Hatfield

SOUTH WAY   A1001

1 BRICKFIELD CT
2 FIVE OAKS

Southfield Sch

New Barnfield (Central Resources Liby)

Cemy

Apex Point

Marshmoor Nurseries

Lodge

GREAT NORTH RD   A1000

Marshmoor

WOODSIDE LA

Longmeadow

Lower Woodside

22   A   B   23   C   D   24   E   F

A2
1 ALMOND WLK
2 ROWAN WLK
3 GEAN WLK
4 SCHOLARS WLK
5 HAZEL GR
6 SHALLCROSS CRES
7 FURZEN CRES
8 STRAWBERRY FIELD

A3
1 LINNET WLK
2 MAGPIE WLK
B3
1 KINGSMILL CT
2 ALLEN CT
3 HAMILTON CT
4 RICHMOND CT

129   144

111
132
A
B
C
D
E
F
B1455
HOLWELL LA
Holwell Manor
Holwell Bridge
B158
LOW RD
Essendonbury Farm
MILLGREEN COTTS
Lodge
Hillend Farm
Ox Wood
ESSENDON HILL
THE BUNGALOWS
Larkinshill Grove
Parsonage
Hillend Cottages
Essendon
THE TERRACE
CHURCH COTTS
HANBURY COTTS
CHURCH ST
GLEBE CL
GLEBE COTTS
EAST VIEW
GLEBE HO
RECTORY CL
FORGE COTTS
SCHOOL LA
SCHOOL CL
Essendon CE Prim Sch
The Furze Field
Lower Westend Farm
Pollard Wood
West End
ROSE LA
Rose & Crown (PH)
The Candlestick (PH)
Brickkiln Wood
WEST END LA
Edwards Wood
HIGH RD
AL9
Hertfordshire Way
Wellington Wood
Essendon Place
Essendon Place Farm
The Roughs
Pope's Pondholes
Harefield Wood
Bedwell Park
Pope's Farm
CH
Bath Wood
Belvedere Farm
Home Wood
BERKHAMSTED LA
Green St
Duncan's Wood
Panther's Wood
Bedwell Lodge Farm
Woodside
CUCUMBER LA
Woodside Place Farm
Brewhouse Farm
Camfield Place
CUMCUM HILL
Hoppett's Wood
WILDHILL RD
The Woodman (PH)
Wildhill
Woodside Green
HORNBEAM LA
Whitbury Wood
Warrenwood Park
KENTISH LA
Nine Acre Wood
WOODSIDE LA
GRUBBS LA
WESTFIELD
B158
8
7
09
6
5
08
4
3
07
2
1
06
25
26
27
145
132

131
112

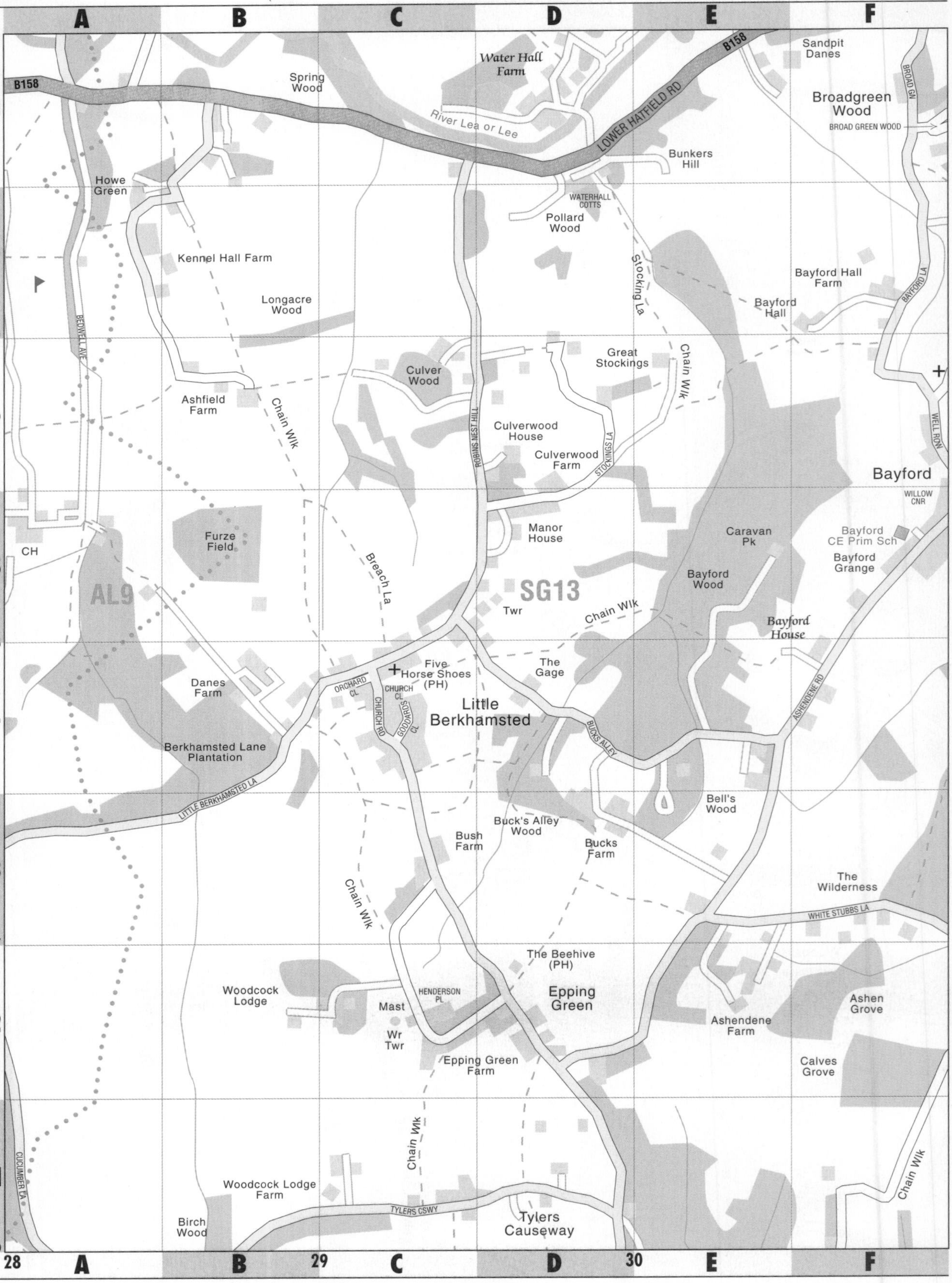

A B C D E F

8

B158

Water Hall Farm

Spring Wood

River Lea or Lee

Sandpit Danes

B158

Broadgreen Wood

BROAD GREEN WOOD

Howe Green

Bunkers Hill

WATERHALL COTTS

Pollard Wood

LOWER HATFIELD RD

BROAD GM

7

Kennel Hall Farm

Bayford Hall Farm

Stocking La

Bayford Hall

BAYFORD LA

09

Longacre Wood

Great Stockings

6

Ashfield Farm

Chain Wlk

Culver Wood

Culverwood House

Chain Wlk

Bayford

WILLOW CNR

WELL RON

ROBINS NEST HILL

Culverwood Farm

STOCKINGS LA

Bayford CE Prim Sch

CH

Furze Field

Breach La

Manor House

SG13

Caravan Pk

Bayford Wood

Bayford Grange

5

AL9

Twr

Chain Wlk

Bayford House

08

Danes Farm

ORCHARD CL

Five Horse Shoes (PH)

CHURCH CL

The Gage

ASHENDENE RD

4

Berkhamsted Lane Plantation

CHURCH RD

ORCHARD CL

Little Berkhamsted

BUCKS ALLEY

Bell's Wood

LITTLE BERKHAMSTED LA

Bush Farm

Buck's Alley Wood

Bucks Farm

The Wilderness

3

Chain Wlk

WHITE STUBBS LA

07

The Beehive (PH)

Ashen Grove

Woodcock Lodge

HENDERSON PL

Epping Green

Ashendene Farm

2

Mast

Wr Twr

Epping Green Farm

Calves Grove

CUCUMBER LA

Chain Wlk

1

Woodcock Lodge Farm

Birch Wood

TYLERS CSWY

Tylers Causeway

Chain Wlk

06

28 A B 29 C D 30 E F

113
134

A
B
C
D
E
F
Hook's Grove
Clements Farm
Blackfields Farm
CLEMENTSBURY
The Grove
BROAD GREEN WOOD
Broadgreen Wood
Weepings Wood
Hertfordshire Way
Owls Hatch Cottages
MANGROVE LA
Edwards Green Farm
Back La
Monk's Wood
Harmond's Wood
Bayford Brook
Warren House
BRICKENDON LA
Sewards Farm
BAYFORD GN
WELL ROW
Monks Green
Jepp's Wood
Manor House
SG13
Great Groves
FOURWAYS
PH
Mast
Sewage Wks
Bayford
ASHENDENE RD
Bourne Orchard
Bramble's Wood
Fanshaws
FANSHAWS LA
Stocking La
Chain Wlk
Bourne Wood
Fanshaws Farm
The Farmer's Boy (PH)
Brickendon
Brickendon Grange
Cowheath Wood
Morley Grove
CH
Broad Riding Wood
Nature Trails
Blackfan Wood
Claypits Wood
Broxbourne Wood
Hedgerows Wood
Hedgegrove Farm
Devil's La
P
Nature Reserve
PEMBRIDGE LA
Old Claypits Farm
WOOD HOUSE LA
Calais Wood
Pembridge Lane Farm
Paradise Wildlife Park
Ettridge Farm
Stocking Wood
Ponsbourne Tunnel
EN10
WHITE STUBBS LA
Mortals Wood
Old Grove
Emanuel Pollards
Bencroft Wood
Chain Wlk
Nature Trail
Manor Farm
WEST END RD
Wormley Wood
Westlea
8
7
09
6
5
08
4
3
07
2
1
06
31
32
33

147
134

133
114

SG13
EN11
EN10
Broxbourne
Goose Green
Carneles Green
Elbowlane Farm
Dalmonds
Dalmond's Wood
Highfield Farm
Highfield Wood
Hoddesdonpark Wood
Hoddesdon Lodge
Box Wood
Lanthorn's Wood
The Huntsman (PH)
The Woodman (PH)
Woollensbrook
High Leigh Farm
High Leigh
Danemead Wood
Nursery Grove
Chestnut Grove
Great Grove
Icehouse Grove
Broxbournebury Mansion
Edgewood Farm
Lower White Stubbs
White Stubbs Farm
Cold Hall
Baas Hill
Baas Manor Farm
Tudor Farm
Manor House
Bury Farm
Cozens Grove
The Broxbourne Sch
Sheredes Sch
Sheredes Prim Sch
Westfield Com Prim Sch
Broxbourne CE Prim Sch
Ley Park Prim Sch
Recn Gd
Sports Gd
Beech Wlk
Spital Brook
Woollens Brook
New River
MANGROVE LA
LORD ST
COCK LA
PEMBRIDGE LA
WHITE STUBBS LA
CHURCH LA
BAAS HILL
HERTFORD RD
HIGH ROAD
A10
A1170
B1197
B194

133
148

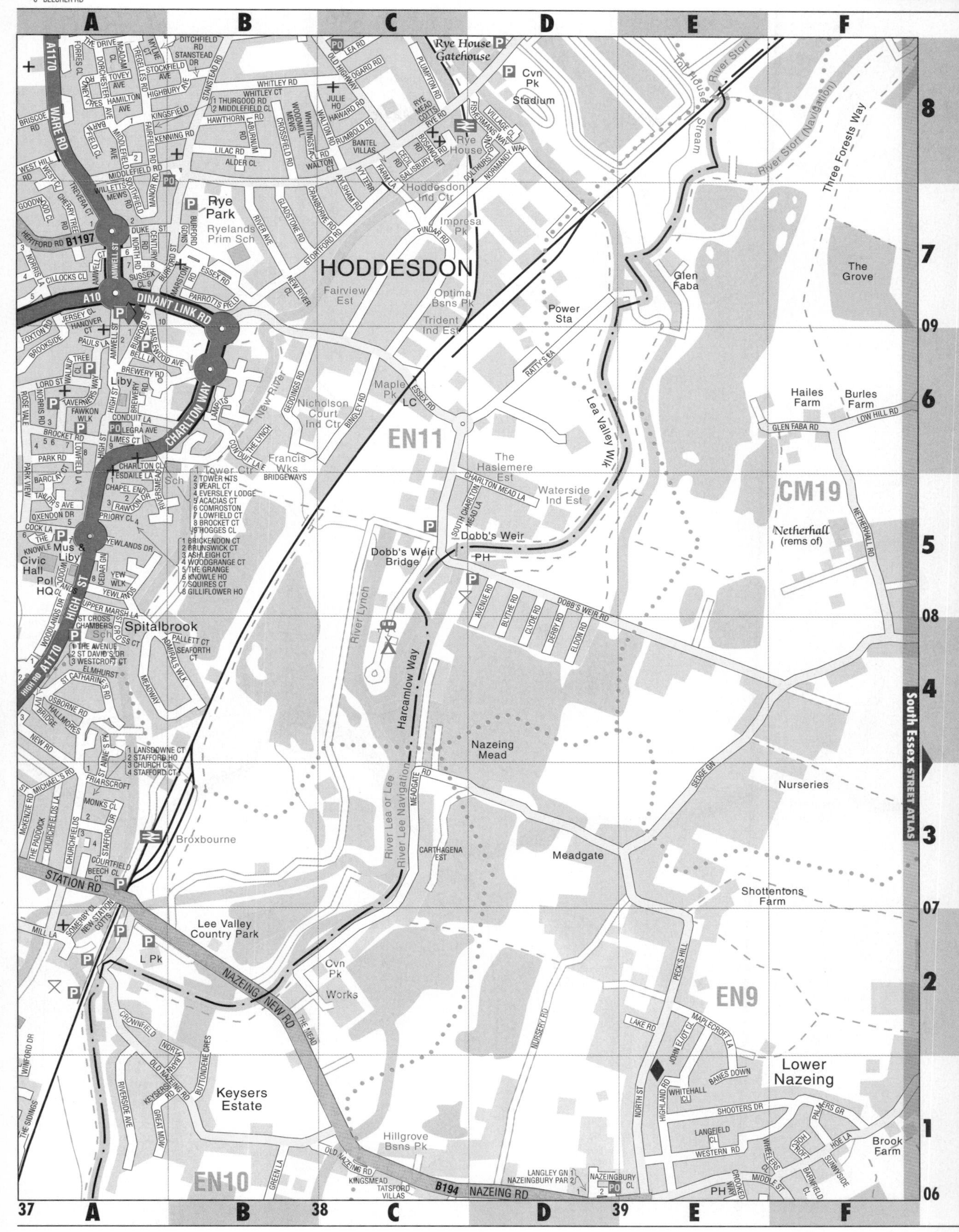

A7
1 FOURWAYS CT
2 CUMBERLAND CT
3 WESTFIELD RD
4 NORRIS RISE
5 WINTERSCROFT RD
6 BELCHER RD

7 ROMAN MEWS
8 ROMAN ST
9 BURFORD MEWS
10 BURFORD PL

HODDESDON

EN11

CM19

EN9

EN10

Lower Nazeing

Keysers Estate

Lee Valley Country Park

Spitalbrook

Broxbourne

Rye Park

South Essex STREET ATLAS

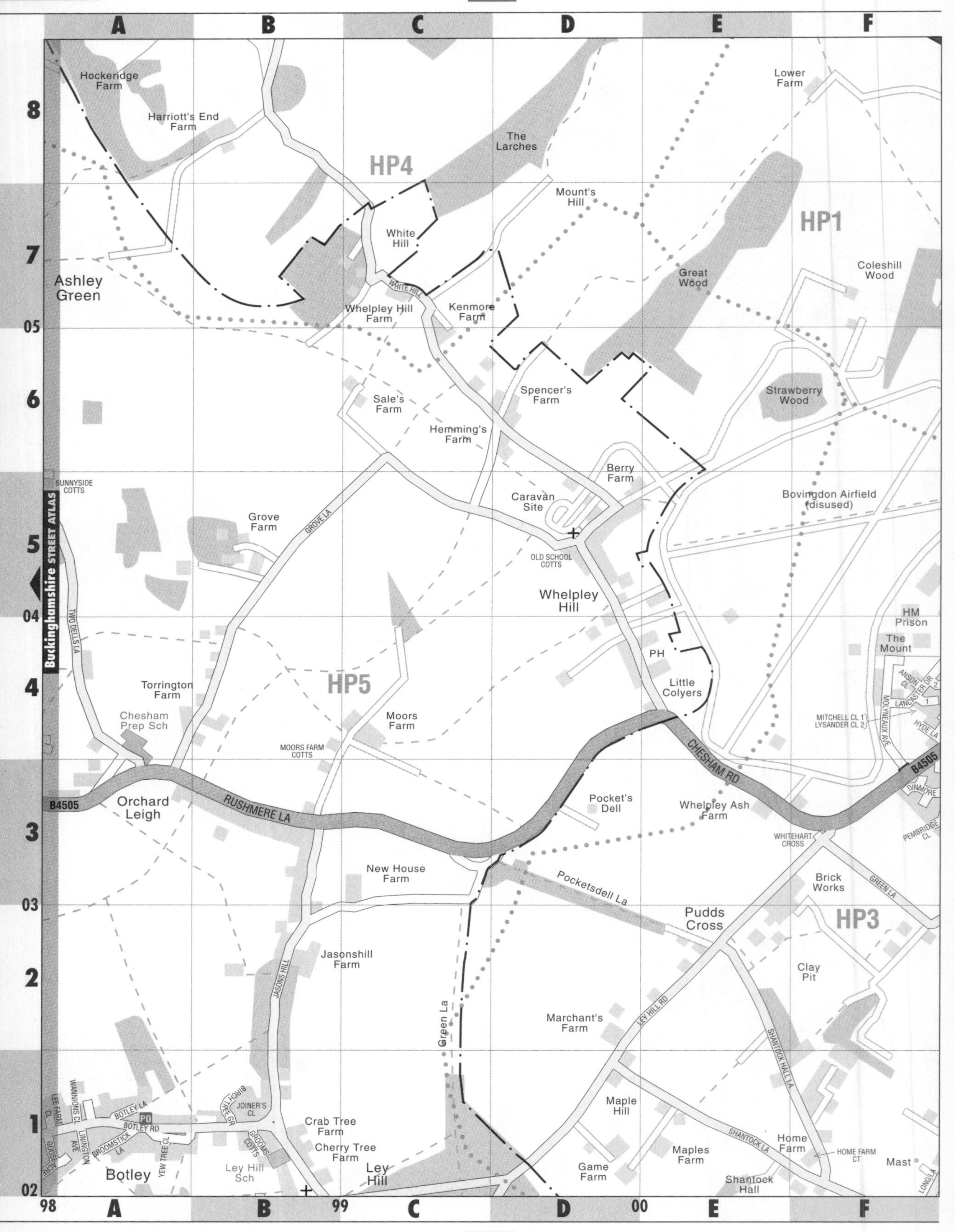

A **B** **C** **D** **E** **F**

Hockeridge Farm

Harriott's End Farm

HP4

The Larches

Lower Farm

8

Mount's Hill

HP1

7

White Hill

Coleshill Wood

WHITE HILL

Ashley Green

Whelpley Hill Farm

Kenmore Farm

Great Wood

05

Sale's Farm

Hemming's Farm

Spencer's Farm

Strawberry Wood

6

SUNNYSIDE COTTS

Berry Farm

Bovingdon Airfield (disused)

Grove Farm

GROVE LA

Caravan Site

OLD SCHOOL COTTS

5

Buckinghamshire STREET ATLAS

TWO DELLS LA

Whelpley Hill

HM Prison

The Mount

04

HP5

PH

ANSON CL

LANCASTER DR

MOLINEAUX AVE

Torrington Farm

Little Colyers

MITCHELL CL 1 LYSANDER CL 2

HYDE LA

4

Chesham Prep Sch

Moors Farm

MOORS FARM COTTS

CHESHAM RD

B4505

DINMORE

B4505

Orchard Leigh

RUSHMERE LA

Pocket's Dell

Whelpley Ash Farm

WHITEHART CROSS

PEMBRIDGE CL

GREEN LA

3

New House Farm

Pocketsdell La

Brick Works

03

JASONS HILL

Jasonshill Farm

Pudds Cross

HP3

Clay Pit

2

Green La

Marchant's Farm

LEY HILL RD

SHANTOCK HALL LA

LEE FARM CL

WANNIONS CL

LININGTON AVE

BROOMSTICK LA

GOODYERS

Botley La

JOINER'S CL

GROOMS CL

GROOMS COTTS

Crab Tree Farm

Cherry Tree Farm

Maple Hill

SHANTOCK LA

Home Farm

HOME FARM CT

Mast

1

PO

Botley Rd

YEW TREE CL

Ley Hill Sch

Ley Hill

Game Farm

Maples Farm

Shantock Hall

LONGLA

Botley

98 **A** **B** 99 **C** **D** 00 **E** **F**

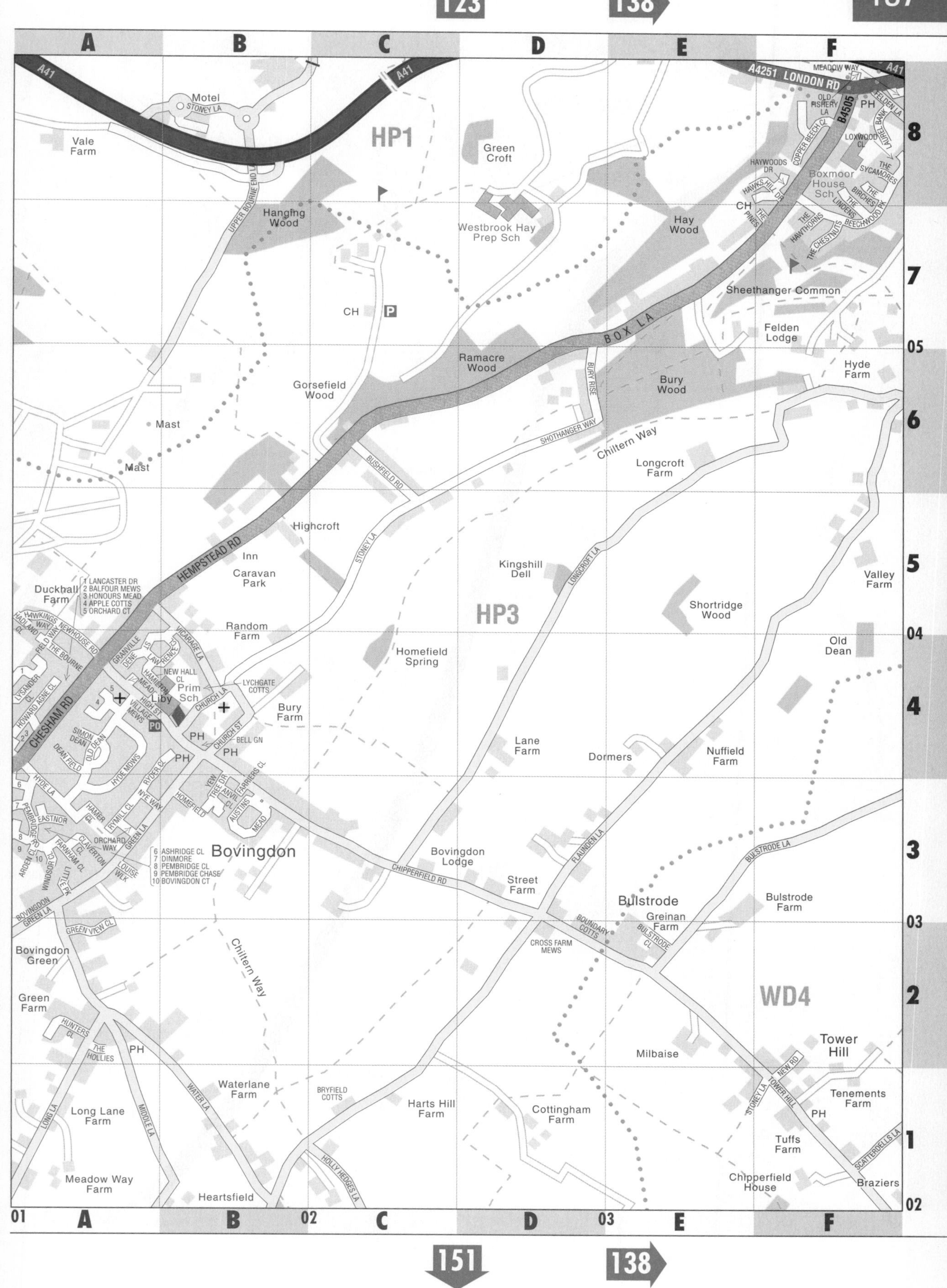
123
138
A
B
C
D
E
F
A41
A4251 LONDON RD
B4505
Motel
STONEY LA
Vale Farm
HP1
Green Croft
Hanging Wood
UPPER BOURNE END LA
Westbrook Hay Prep Sch
Hay Wood
Boxmoor House Sch
Sheethanger Common
Felden Lodge
CH
BOX LA
Ramacre Wood
Bury Wood
BURY RISE
Gorsefield Wood
Hyde Farm
Mast
SHOTHANGER WAY
Chiltern Way
Longcroft Farm
BUSHFIELD RD
Highcroft
STONEY LA
HEMPSTEAD RD
Inn
Caravan Park
Kingshill Dell
LONGCROFT LA
Valley Farm
HP3
Shortridge Wood
Duckhall Farm
1 LANCASTER DR
2 BALFOUR MEWS
3 HONOURS MEAD
4 APPLE COTTS
5 ORCHARD CT
Random Farm
Homefield Spring
Old Dean
CHESHAM RD
Liby
Prim Sch
PO
PH
LYCHGATE COTTS
BELL GN
Bury Farm
Lane Farm
Dormers
Nuffield Farm
Bovingdon
6 ASHRIDGE CL
7 DINMORE
8 PEMBRIDGE CL
9 PEMBRIDGE CHASE
10 BOVINGDON CT
Bovingdon Lodge
CHIPPERFIELD RD
Street Farm
FLAUNDEN LA
BULSTRODE LA
Bulstrode
Greinan Farm
Bulstrode Farm
CROSS FARM MEWS
Bovingdon Green
Green Farm
WD4
Tower Hill
Milbaise
Waterlane Farm
Harts Hill Farm
Cottingham Farm
Tenements Farm
Long Lane Farm
Tuffs Farm
Meadow Way Farm
Heartsfield
Chipperfield House
Braziers
8
7
05
6
5
04
4
3
03
2
1
02
01
02
03
151
138

137
124

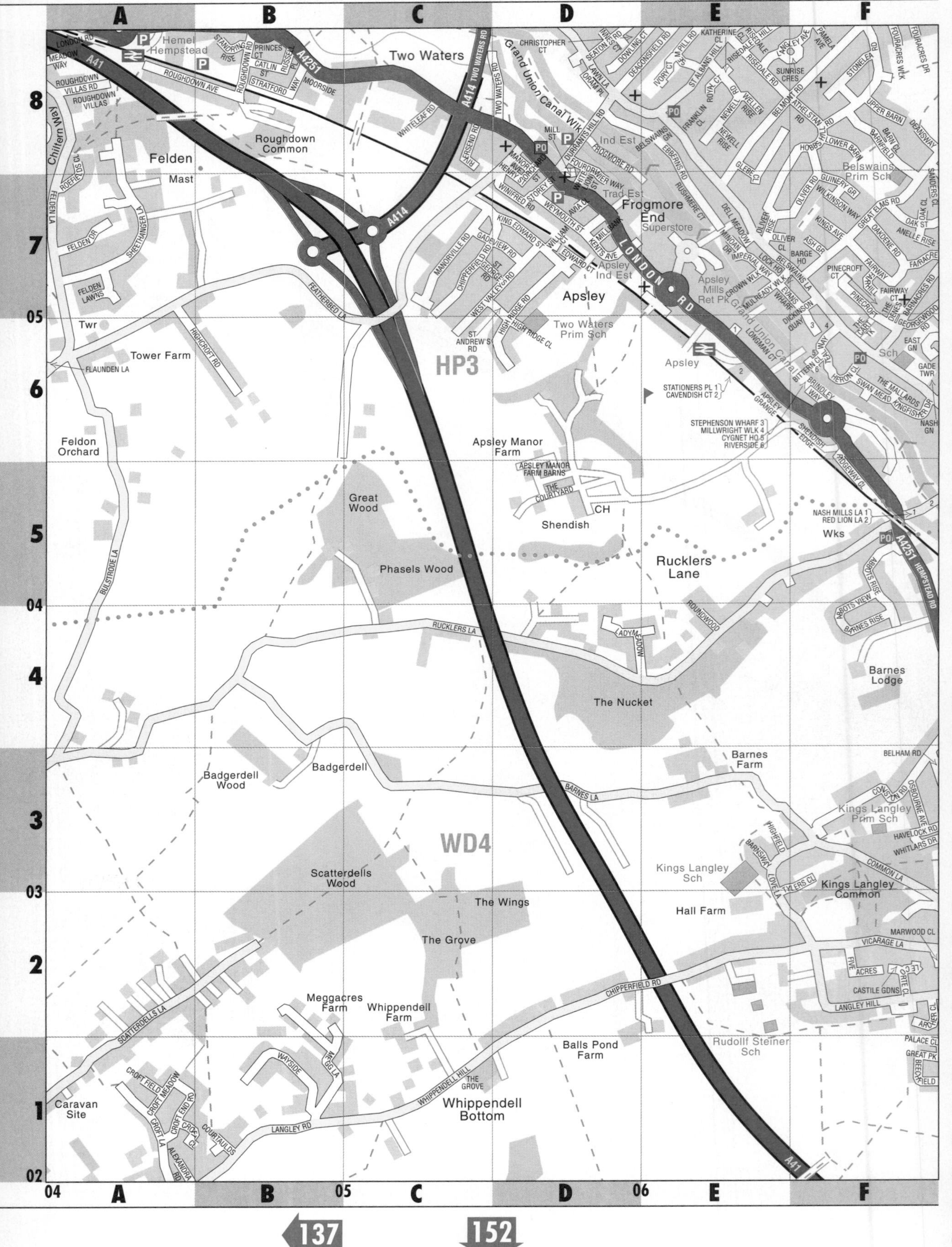
Hemel Hempstead
Two Waters
Roughdown Common
Felden
Mast
Chiltern Way
Twr
Tower Farm
Feldon Orchard
Great Wood
Phasels Wood
Apsley Manor Farm
Shendish
CH
Rucklers Lane
Apsley
Frogmore End
Superstore
Ind Est
Trad Est
Apsley Ind Est
Apsley Mills Ret Pk
Two Waters Prim Sch
Belswains Prim Sch
Grand Union Canal
Grand Union Canal Wlk
LONDON RD
HP3
WD4
A41
A414
A4251
The Nucket
Barnes Lodge
Barnes Farm
Badgerdell
Badgerdell Wood
Scatterdells Wood
The Wings
The Grove
Kings Langley Sch
Kings Langley Prim Sch
Kings Langley Common
Hall Farm
Meggacres Farm
Whippendell Farm
Balls Pond Farm
Rudolf Steiner Sch
Whippendell Bottom
Caravan Site
Wks
Sch
STATIONERS PL 1
CAVENDISH CT 2
STEPHENSON WHARF 3
MILLWRIGHT WLK 4
CYGNET HO 5
RIVERSIDE 6
NASH MILLS LA 1
RED LION LA 2
RUCKLERS LA
BARNES LA
CHIPPERFIELD RD
LANGLEY RD
WHIPPENDELL HILL
SCATTERDELLS LA
FEATHERBED LA
BULSTRODE LA
FLAUNDEN LA
HIGHCROFT RD
ROUGHDOWN AVE
VICARAGE LA
COMMON LA
LANGLEY HILL
A B C D E F
8 7 6 5 4 3 2 1
04 05 06
05 04 03 02

137
152

125
140

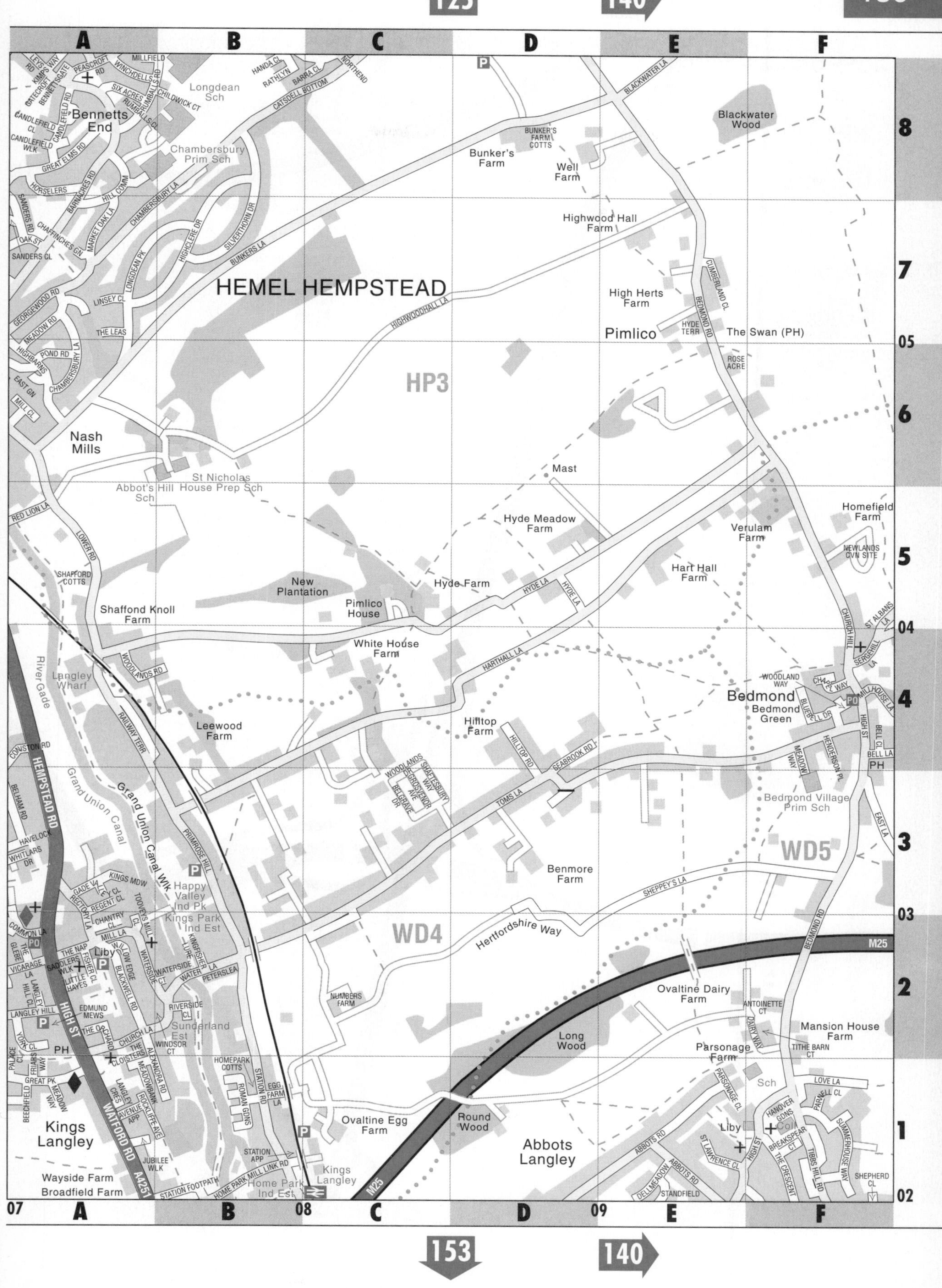
A
B
C
D
E
F
HEMEL HEMPSTEAD
Bennetts End
Longdean Sch
Chambersbury Prim Sch
Blackwater Wood
Bunker's Farm
BUNKER'S FARM COTTS
Well Farm
Highwood Hall Farm
High Herts Farm
Pimlico
The Swan (PH)
HP3
Nash Mills
St Nicholas House Prep Sch
Abbot's Hill Sch
Mast
Hyde Meadow Farm
Homefield Farm
Verulam Farm
NEWLANDS CVN SITE
Hart Hall Farm
New Plantation
Hyde Farm
Pimlico House
Shaffond Knoll Farm
SHAFFORD COTTS
White House Farm
River Gade
Langley Wharf
Bedmond
Bedmond Green
Leewood Farm
Hilltop Farm
Grand Union Canal
Grand Union Canal Wlk
Bedmond Village Prim Sch
WD5
Benmore Farm
Happy Valley Ind Pk
Kings Park Ind Est
WD4
Hertfordshire Way
M25
Ovaltine Dairy Farm
NUMBERS FARM
Sunderland Est
Long Wood
Mansion House Farm
Parsonage Farm
Sch
Coll
Liby
Kings Langley
Ovaltine Egg Farm
Round Wood
Abbots Langley
Wayside Farm
Broadfield Farm
Home Park Ind Est
Kings Langley
HEMPSTEAD RD
HIGH ST
WATFORD RD A4251
BUNKERS LA
HIGHWOODHALL LA
BEDMOND RD
HYDE LA
HARTHALL LA
TOMS LA
SHEPPEY'S LA
BLACKWATER LA
LOWER RD
PRIMROSE HILL
STATION RD
ABBOTS RD
CHURCH HILL
ST ALBANS LA
SERGEHILL LA
MILLHOUSE LA
LOVE LA
07
08
09
02
03
04
05
1
2
3
4
5
6
7
8

153
140

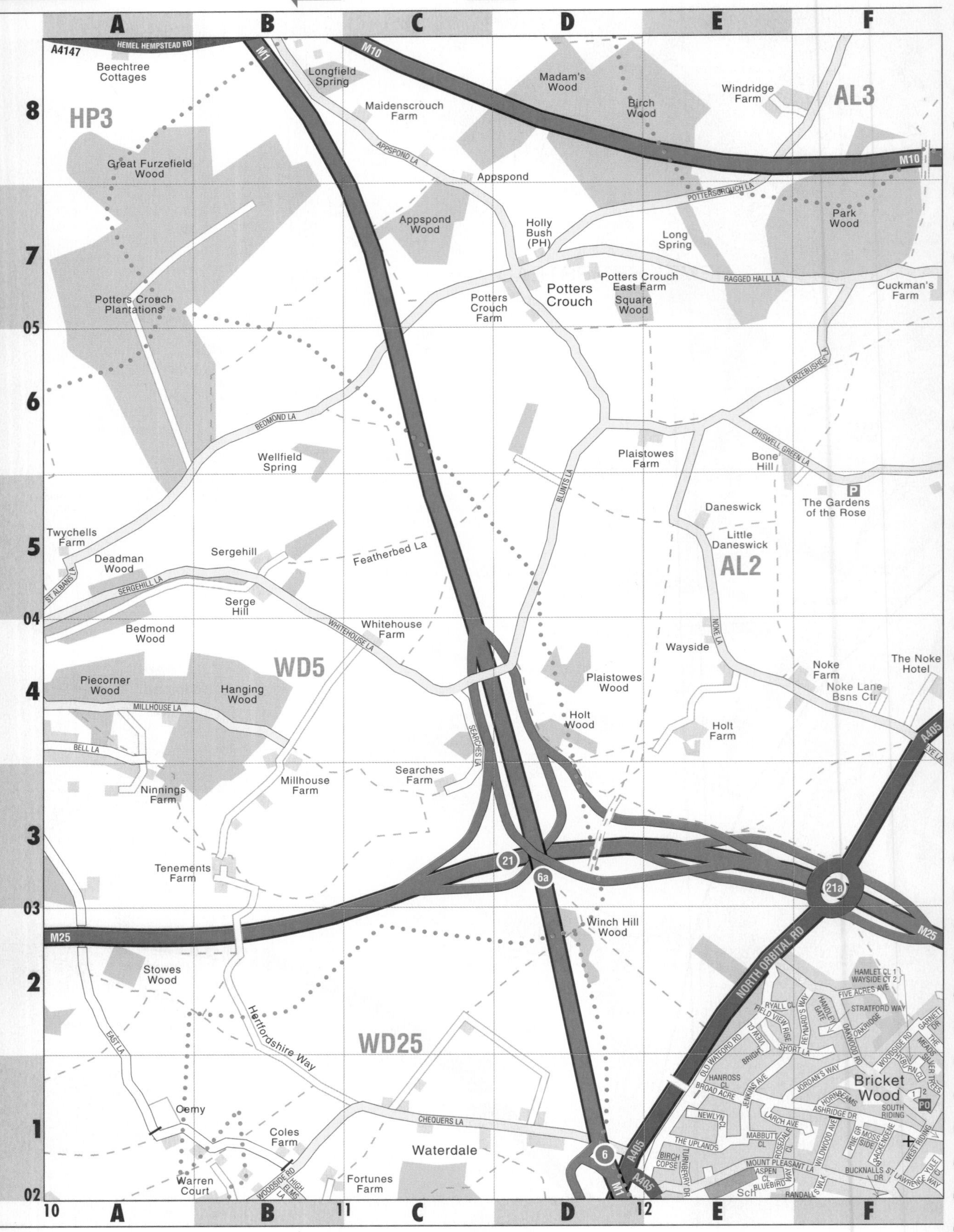
139
126
154
A4147
HEMEL HEMPSTEAD RD
M1
M10
M25
A405
Beechtree Cottages
HP3
AL3
AL2
WD5
WD25
Longfield Spring
Maidenscrouch Farm
Madam's Wood
Birch Wood
Windridge Farm
Great Furzefield Wood
APPSPOND LA
Appspond
POTTERSCROUCH LA
Park Wood
Appspond Wood
Holly Bush (PH)
Long Spring
Potters Crouch East Farm
RAGGED HALL LA
Cuckman's Farm
Potters Crouch Plantations
Potters Crouch Farm
Potters Crouch
Square Wood
FURZEBUSHES LA
BEDMOND LA
CHISWELL GREEN LA
Wellfield Spring
Plaistowes Farm
Bone Hill
BLUNTS LA
The Gardens of the Rose
Daneswick
Twychells Farm
Little Daneswick
Deadman Wood
Sergehill
Featherbed La
ST ALBANS LA
SERGEHILL LA
Serge Hill
Bedmond Wood
WHITEHOUSE LA
Whitehouse Farm
NOKE LA
Wayside
Noke Farm
The Noke Hotel
Piecorner Wood
Hanging Wood
Plaistowes Wood
Noke Lane Bsns Ctr
MILLHOUSE LA
Holt Wood
Holt Farm
BELL LA
SEARCHES LA
LYE LA
Ninnings Farm
Millhouse Farm
Searches Farm
21
6a
21a
Tenements Farm
Winch Hill Wood
Stowes Wood
NORTH ORBITAL RD
HAMLET CL
WAYSIDE CT
FIVE ACRES AVE
RYALL CL
FIELD VIEW RISE
REYNARD'S WAY
HANDLEY GATE
STRATFORD WAY
GARNETT DR
Hertfordshire Way
EAST LA
OLD WATFORD RD
SHORT LA
OAKWOOD RD
OAKRIDGE
WOODSIDE RD
THE MEADS
SILVER TREES
HANROSS CL
BROAD ACRE
JENKINS AVE
JORDAN'S WAY
Bricket Wood
HORNBEAMS
ASHRIDGE DR
SOUTH RIDING
PO
Oemy
NEWLYN CL
LARCH AVE
Coles Farm
CHEQUERS LA
THE UPLANDS
MABBUTT CL
ROSEDALE CL
WILDWOOD AVE
PINE GR
MOSS SIDE
BACKENDENE
WEST RIDING
Waterdale
6
BIRCH COPSE
TURNBERRY DR
MOUNT PLEASANT LA
BUCKNALLS DR
ST LAWRENCE WAY
YULE CL
Warren Court
WOODSIDE RD
HIGH ELMS LA
Fortunes Farm
ASPEN CL
BLUEBIRD WAY
Sch
RANDALLS WLK
A B C D E F
8 7 05 6 5 04 4 3 03 2 1 02
10 11 12

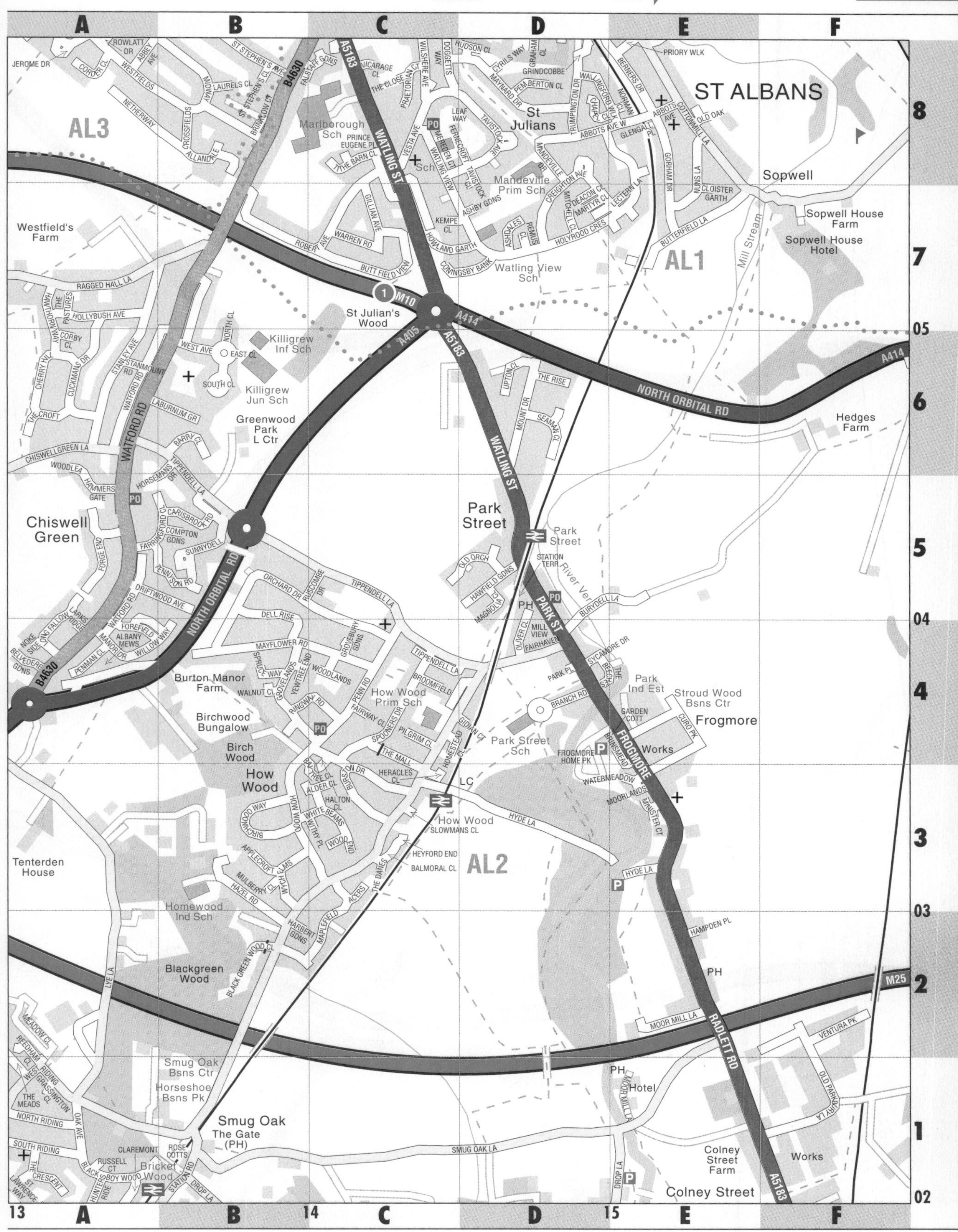
A
B
C
D
E
F
ST ALBANS
AL3
AL1
AL2
St Julians
Marlborough Sch
Mandeville Prim Sch
Sopwell
Sopwell House Farm
Sopwell House Hotel
Westfield's Farm
Watling View Sch
St Julian's Wood
Killigrew Inf Sch
Killigrew Jun Sch
Greenwood Park L Ctr
NORTH ORBITAL RD
WATLING ST
WATFORD RD
Hedges Farm
Chiswell Green
Park Street
Burton Manor Farm
How Wood Prim Sch
Stroud Wood Bsns Ctr
Frogmore
Park Ind Est
Birchwood Bungalow
Birch Wood
How Wood
Park Street Sch
Works
Tenterden House
Homewood Ind Sch
Blackgreen Wood
Smug Oak Bsns Ctr
Horseshoe Bsns Pk
Smug Oak
The Gate (PH)
Bricket Wood
Hotel
Colney Street Farm
Colney Street
RADLETT RD
FROGMORE
M25
M10
A414
A405
A5183
B4630
8
7
6
5
4
3
2
1
05
04
03
02
13
14
15

A B C D E F

8
7
05
6
5
04
4
3
03
2
1
02

ST ALBANS

AL1

AL4

AL2

London
Colney

WD7

A1081
A414
B5378
M25
NORTH ORBITAL RD
LONDON RD
SHENLEY LA
BELL LA
HARPER LA
SHENLEYBURY
A1081
A414

Tyttenhanger
Barley Mow (PH)
Knights Wood
Blout Spring
Highfield Farm
Highfield Hall
Highfield Clinic
Coppice Wood
Bowmansgreen Farm

Francis Bacon Sch
L Ctr
1 MASLEN RD
2 HOUSEFIELD WAY
3 CHUCH CROFT
4 HONEYCROFT DR

North Orbital Commercial Pk
Nursery
Cemy
North Cotts
Caravan Site
Napsbury
Liby
Sch
AL2
South Farm Cotts
Fir Tree Farm
Barley-Mo-Farm
Broad Colney Bridge
River Colne
Broad Colney
All Saints Pastoral Ctr
Colney Park
Springfield Farm
Harperbury
Clore Shalom Sch

St Bernadette RC Prim Sch
ROMAN HO 1
THE GREEN 2
HEATHER CT 3
COULSON CT 4

Armstrong Cl

WATERSPLASH CT 1
SEVERNVALE 2
TYNEDALE 3

Bsns Ctr
P O
Sch
Five Acres
Blst Ctr

THE BELL RDBT
22 M25
B556

THE DRIVE
GREEN LA
NAPSBURY LA
MILE HOUSE LA
NEW BARNES AVE
ABBOTS

141 156

16 A 17 B C 18 D E F

A **B** **C** **D** **E** **F**

NORTH ORBITAL RD
A414

River Colne

P Water Works

HEATH PARK LA
CHURCH LA
PARK CNR
SCHOLARS CT
HIGH ST

Colney Heath
PH
Roestock
ROESTOCK LA
HALL GDNS
MEADWAY
ADMIRALS CL
FELLOWES LA
BENNETTS CL
Colney Heath Farm
BULLEN'S GREEN LA
DELLSOME LA
A1 (M)
2
A1 (M)

Windmill

Warren Farm

Tyttenhanger Farm

Tollgate Farm
Tollgate Wood
TOLLGATE RD

Frederick's Wood

Park Cottage

The Osierbeds

AL4

Garden Wood

The New Plantation

COURSERS FARM COTTS

North Mymms Park

Tyttenhanger Park

COURSERS RD

Coursers Farm

Red Lodge

North Mymms Park

AL9

Lodge Plantation

Walsingham Wood

Cangsley Grove

Cobs Ash

AL2
A1081
22

Round Wood

Potwells

EN6

Salisbury Hall

The de Havilland Aircraft Heritage Mus

Salisbury Hall Farm

Redwell Wood Farm

Oak Lodge

Hawkshead Wood

Redwell Wood

Ridgehill Stud
Shenley Lodge Cottage

Manor Lodge Sch

RECTORY LA

Ridgehill

PACKHORSE LA

WD7

Shenley Lodge Farm

B556
BLACKHORSE LA
ST ALBANS RD
M25
Woodhill Farm

8
7
05
6
5
04
4
3
03
2
1
02

143 130

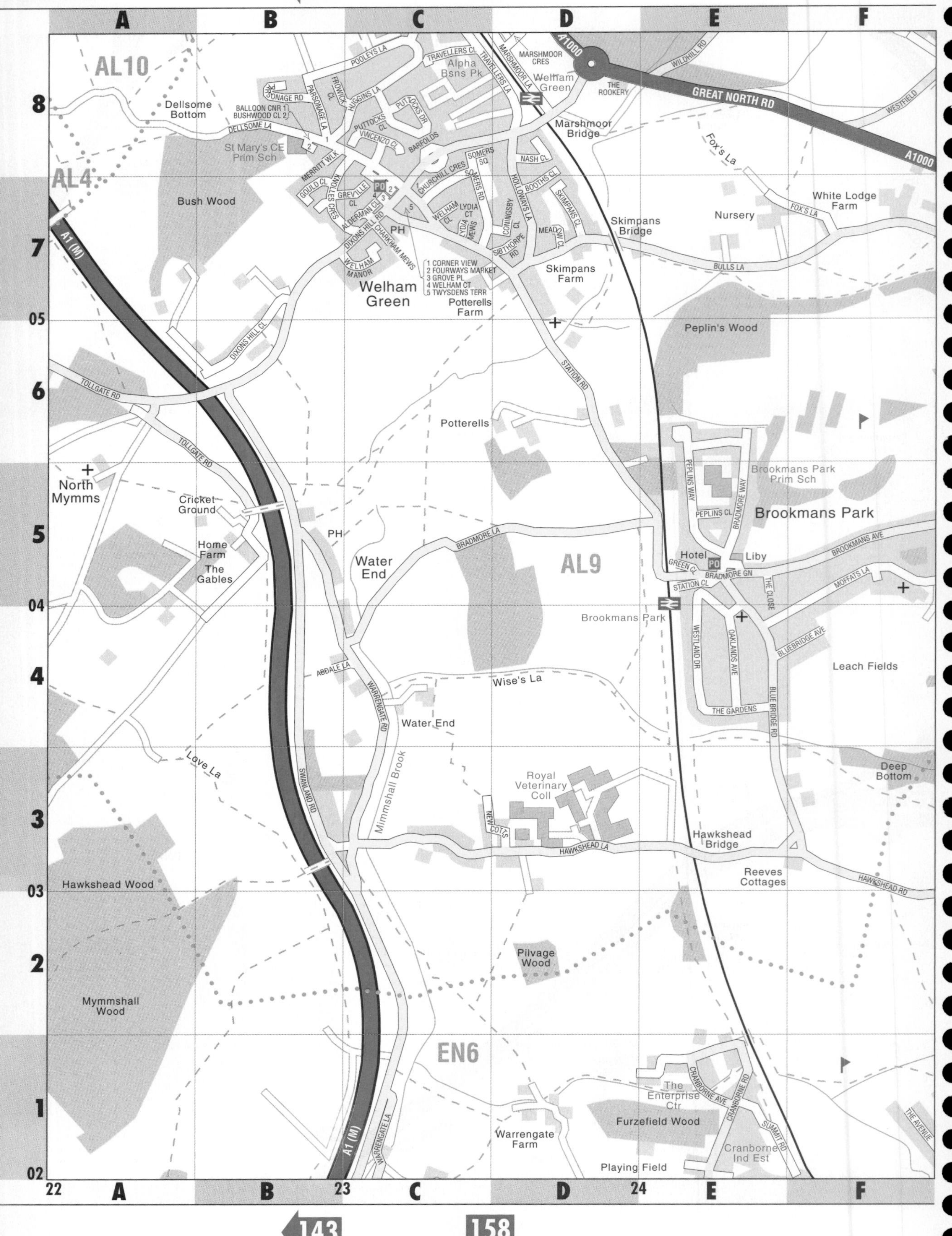
AL10
AL4
AL9
EN6
Dellsome Bottom
St Mary's CE Prim Sch
Bush Wood
Welham Green
Alpha Bsns Pk
Marshmoor Bridge
Skimpans Bridge
Skimpans Farm
Potterells Farm
Nursery
White Lodge Farm
Peplin's Wood
Potterells
Brookmans Park Prim Sch
Brookmans Park
North Mymms
Cricket Ground
Home Farm
The Gables
Water End
Hotel
Liby
Leach Fields
Royal Veterinary Coll
Hawkshead Bridge
Reeves Cottages
Deep Bottom
Hawkshead Wood
Pilvage Wood
Mymmshall Wood
Mimmshall Brook
The Enterprise Ctr
Furzefield Wood
Warrengate Farm
Cranborne Ind Est
Playing Field
GREAT NORTH RD
A1000
A1 (M)
1 CORNER VIEW
2 FOURWAYS MARKET
3 GROVE PL
4 WELHAM CT
5 TWYSDENS TERR
Fox's La
Wise's La
Love La
Station Rd
Bradmore La
Hawkshead La
Tollgate Rd
Swanland Rd
Warrengate Rd
A B C D E F
22 23 24

143 158

131
146

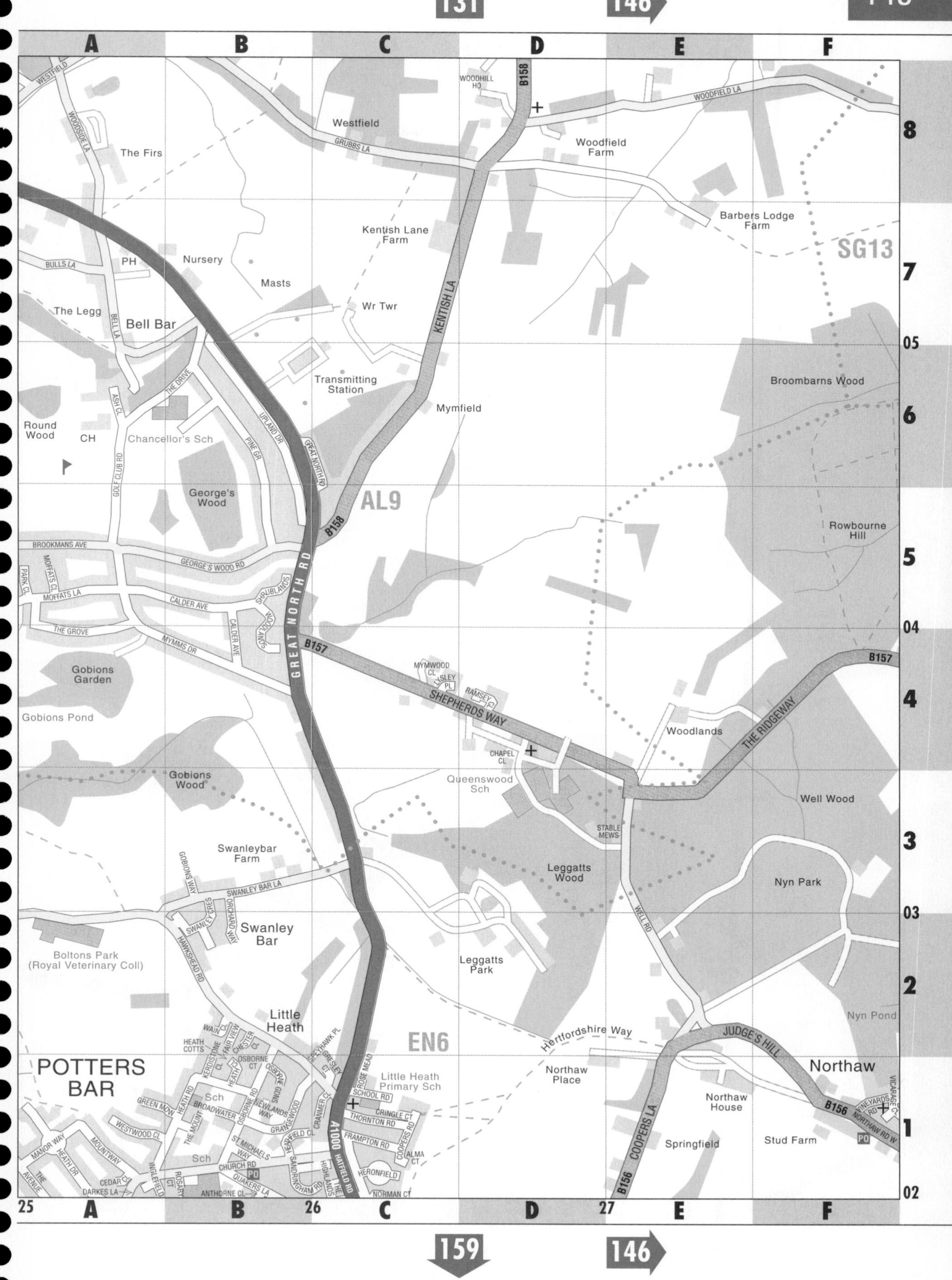
Westfield
The Firs
Woodfield Farm
Barbers Lodge Farm
Kentish Lane Farm
SG13
PH
Nursery
Masts
Wr Twr
The Legg
Bell Bar
Transmitting Station
Broombarns Wood
Round Wood
CH
Chancellor's Sch
Mymfield
George's Wood
AL9
Rowbourne Hill
Gobions Garden
Gobions Pond
Woodlands
Queenswood Sch
Gobions Wood
Well Wood
Swanleybar Farm
Leggatts Wood
Nyn Park
Swanley Bar
Boltons Park (Royal Veterinary Coll)
Leggatts Park
Little Heath
EN6
Hertfordshire Way
Nyn Pond
POTTERS BAR
Northaw Place
Northaw
Little Heath Primary Sch
Northaw House
Springfield
Stud Farm
GREAT NORTH RD
KENTISH LA
SHEPHERDS WAY
THE RIDGEWAY
JUDGE'S HILL
COOPERS LA
WELL RD
B157
B158
B156
A1000 HATFIELD RD

159
146

145 132

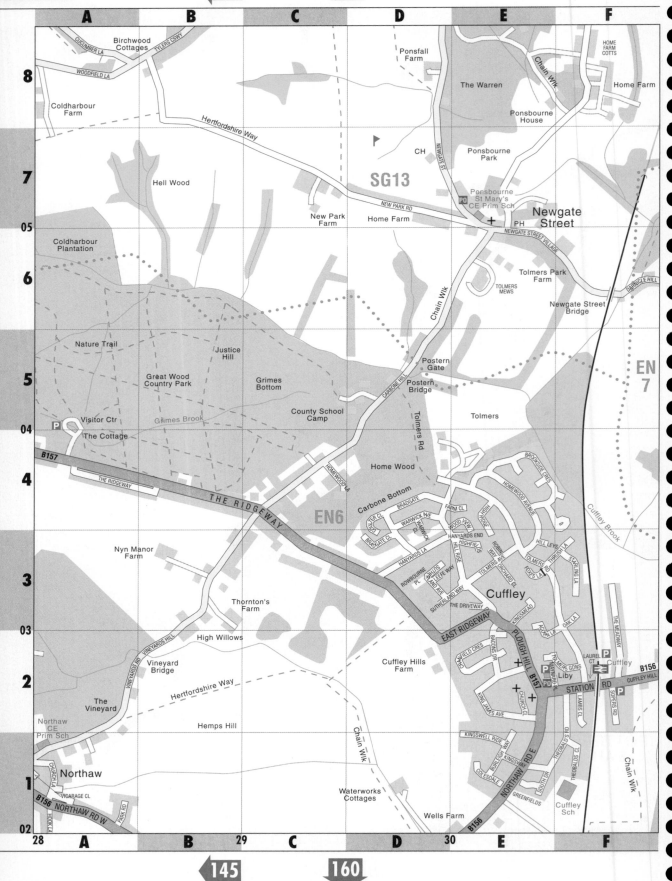

145 160

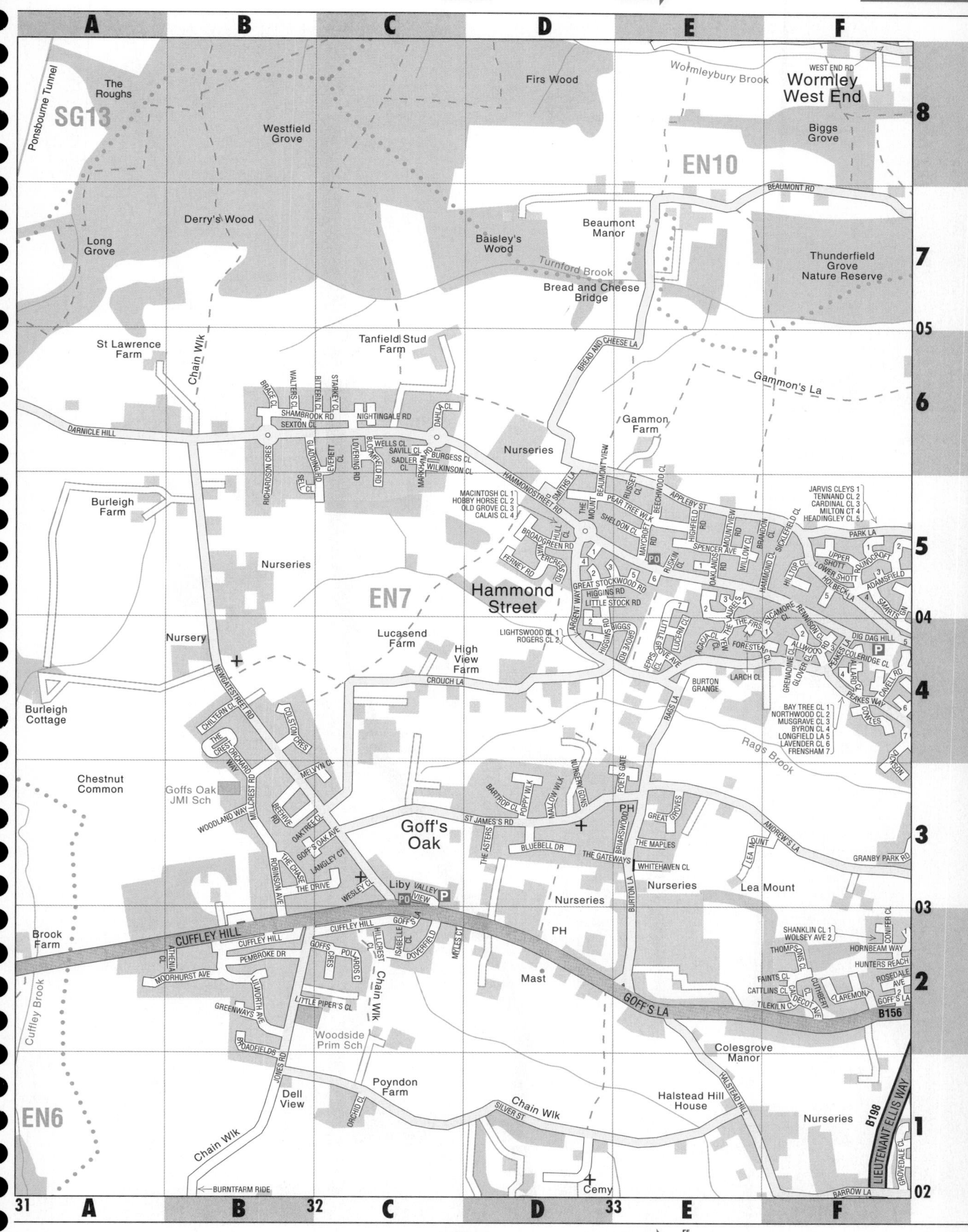

E5
1 SOUTHVIEW CL
2 THE POPLARS
3 HAZEL CL
4 WHITEBEAM CL
5 NUTWOOD GDNS
6 FRIERN CL
7 CONY CL

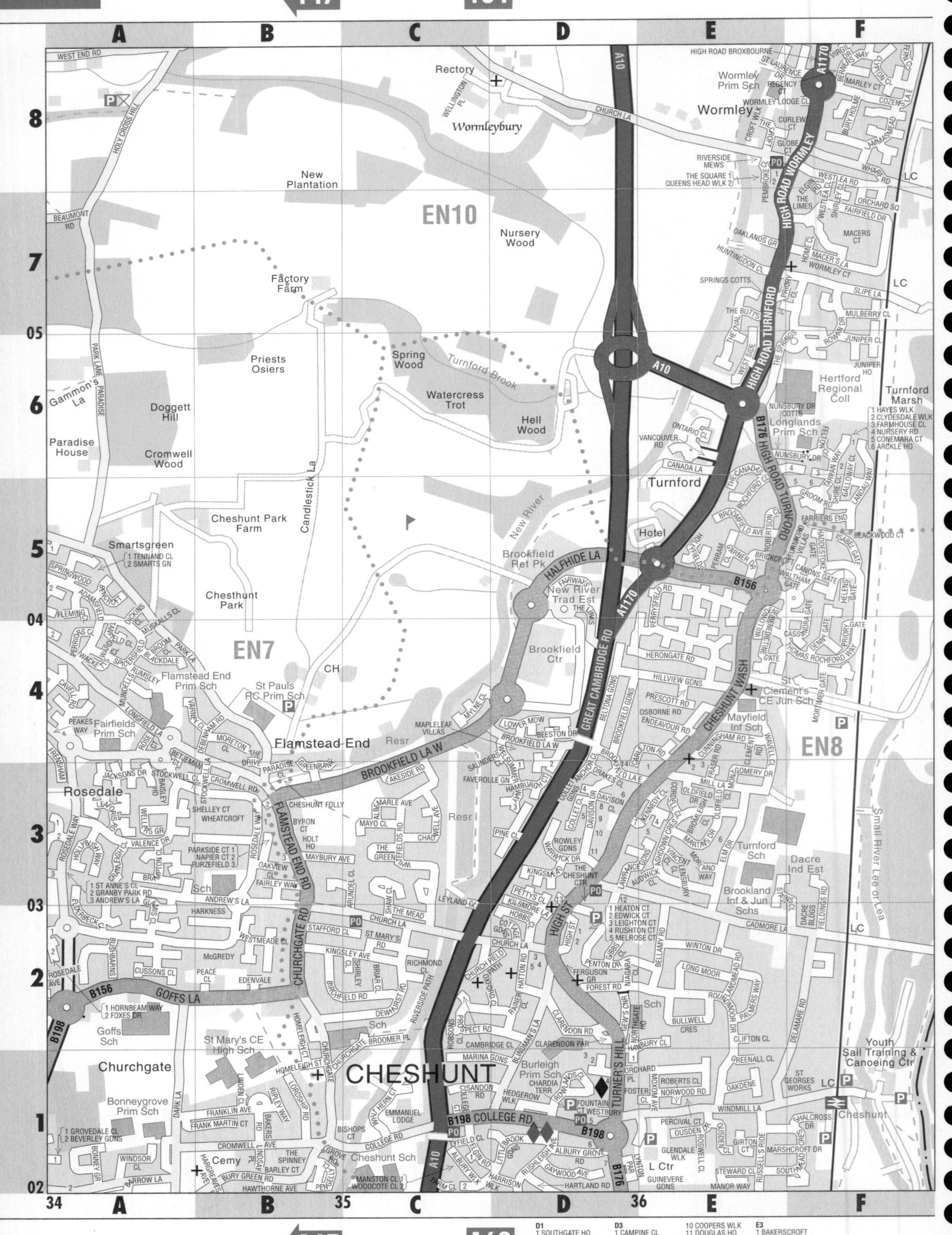

D1
1 SOUTHGATE HO
2 ALEXANDER CT
3 ROWLANDS CT
4 ANCIENT ALMHOS
5 NEWNHAM PAR
6 MANORCROFT PAR
7 CLAYTON PAR

D3
1 CAMPINE CL
2 SOUTHBROOK DR
3 THE SPUR
4 CRAIGS WLK
5 BREEZE TERR
6 THE WHITE HO
7 THE COLONNADE
8 CEDAR LODGE
9 BLAXLAND TERR

10 COOPERS WLK
11 DOUGLAS HO
12 CADMORE CT
13 SYMONDS CT
14 BROOKFIELD CT

E3
1 BAKERSCROFT
2 BRAY LODGE
3 CUNNINGHAM CT
4 GOODWIN CT
5 BEECHOLM MEWS
6 FAIRFIELD WLK

135

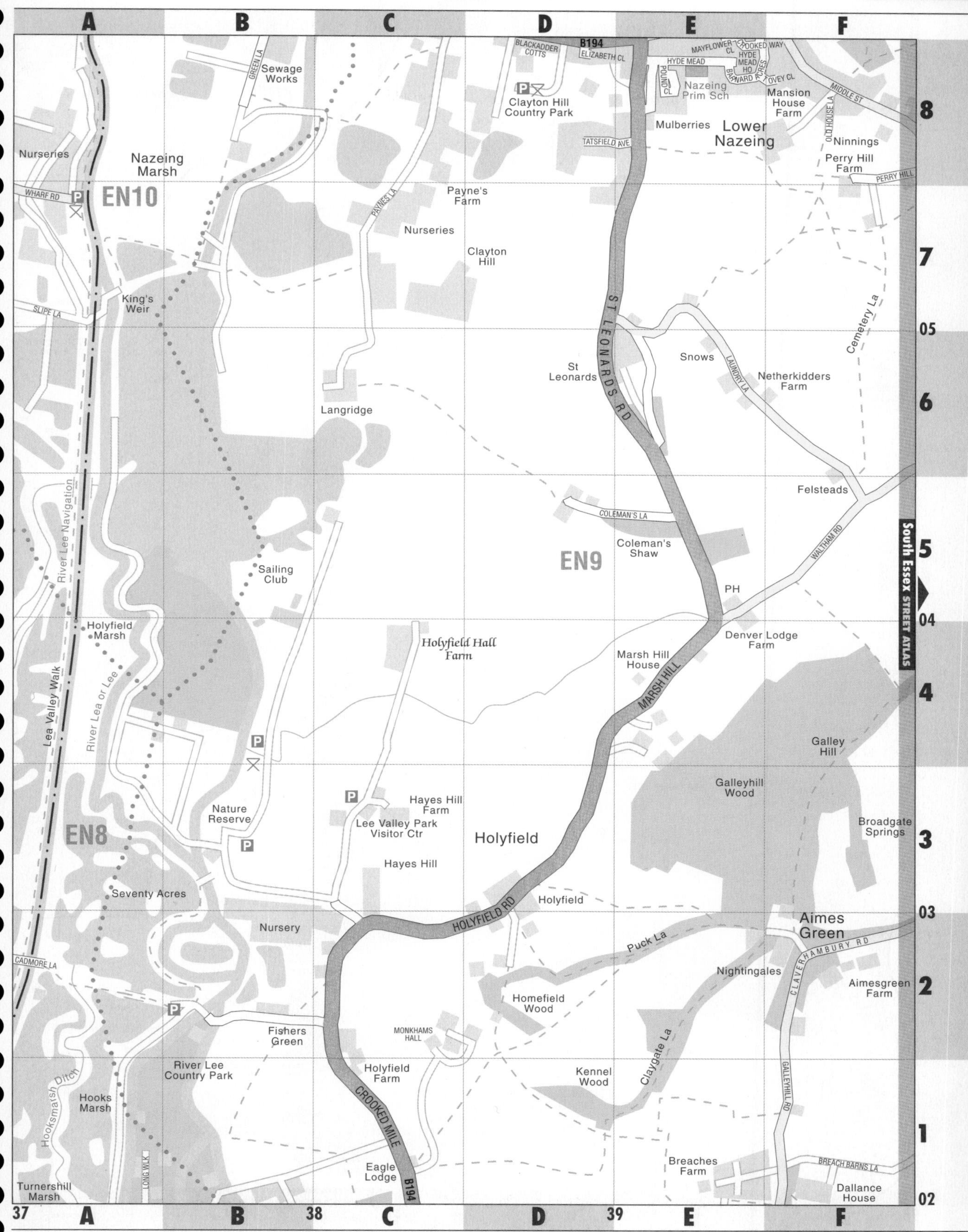
A
B
C
D
E
F
Sewage Works
GREEN LA
BLACKADDER COTTS
B194
ELIZABETH CL
Clayton Hill Country Park
MAYFLOWER CL
CROOKED WAY
HYDE MEAD
HYDE MEAD HO
BARNARD ACRES
POUND CL
OVEY CL
Nazeing Prim Sch
Mansion House Farm
MIDDLE ST
OLD HOUSE LA
Mulberries
Lower Nazeing
Ninnings
Nurseries
Nazeing Marsh
TATSFIELD AVE
Perry Hill Farm
PERRY HILL
WHARF RD
EN10
Payne's Farm
PAYNES LA
Nurseries
Clayton Hill
King's Weir
SLIPE LA
ST LEONARDS RD
Cemetery La
Snows
St Leonards
LAUNDRY LA
Netherkidders Farm
Langridge
Felsteads
COLEMAN'S LA
River Lee Navigation
Coleman's Shaw
WALTHAM RD
EN9
Sailing Club
PH
Holyfield Marsh
Holyfield Hall Farm
Denver Lodge Farm
Marsh Hill House
MARSH HILL
Lea Valley Walk
River Lea or Lee
Galley Hill
Galleyhill Wood
Nature Reserve
Hayes Hill Farm
Lee Valley Park Visitor Ctr
Broadgate Springs
EN8
Holyfield
Hayes Hill
Seventy Acres
Holyfield
HOLYFIELD RD
Aimes Green
Nursery
Puck La
HAMBURY RD
CLAVERHAMBURY RD
CADMORE LA
Nightingales
Homefield Wood
Aimesgreen Farm
Fishers Green
MONKHAMS HALL
Claygate La
River Lee Country Park
Holyfield Farm
Kennel Wood
Hooksmarsh Ditch
Hooks Marsh
GALLEYHILL RD
CROOKED MILE
Breaches Farm
BREACH BARNS LA
LONG WLK
Eagle Lodge
B194
Turnershill Marsh
Dallance House
South Essex STREET ATLAS
8
7
05
6
5
04
4
3
03
2
1
02
37
38
39

163

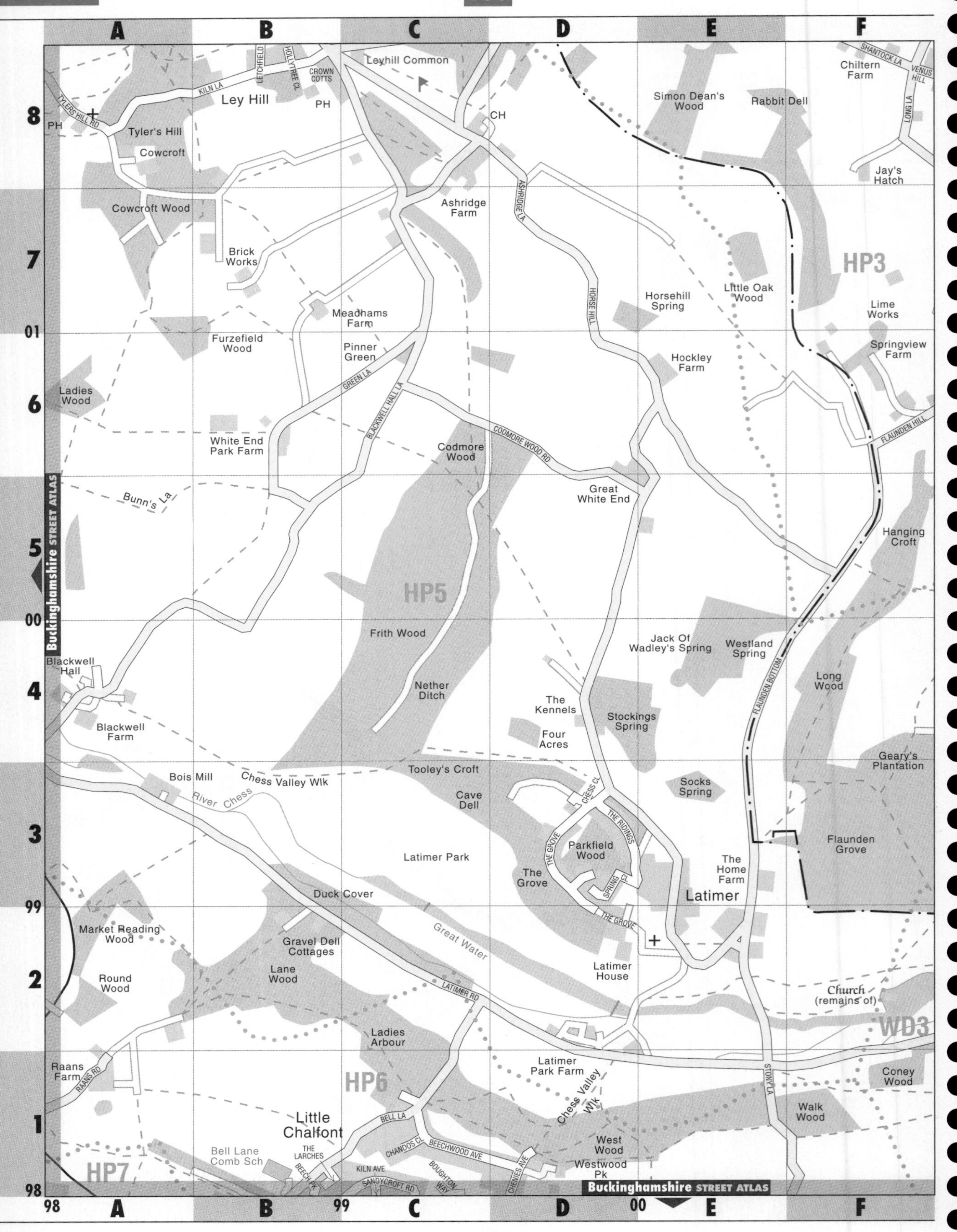

A B C D E F

8

Tyler's Hill Rd
PH
KILN LA
Ley Hill
LETCHFIELD
HOLLYTREE CL
CROWN COTTS
Leyhill Common
CH
ASHRIDGE LA
Simon Dean's Wood
Rabbit Dell
SHANTOCK LA
VENUS HILL
Chiltern Farm
LONG LA
Jay's Hatch
PH
Tyler's Hill
Cowcroft
PH

7

Cowcroft Wood
Brick Works
Ashridge Farm
HORSE HILL
Horsehill Spring
Little Oak Wood
HP3
Lime Works

01

Meadhams Farm
Furzefield Wood
Pinner Green
GREEN LA
BLACKWELL HILL LA
Hockley Farm
Springview Farm

6

Ladies Wood
White End Park Farm
Codmore Wood
CODMORE WOOD RD
Great White End
FLAUNDEN HILL
Hanging Croft

5

Bunn's La
HP5
Jack Of Wadley's Spring
Westland Spring
FLAUNDEN BOTTOM
Long Wood

00

Blackwell Hall
Frith Wood
The Kennels
Stockings Spring
Geary's Plantation

4

Blackwell Farm
Nether Ditch
Four Acres
Bois Mill
Chess Valley Wlk
Tooley's Croft
Cave Dell
CHESS CL
Socks Spring
Long Wood

3

River Chess
Latimer Park
THE GROVE
Parkfield Wood
THE RIDINGS
SPRING CL
The Home Farm
Flaunden Grove
Duck Cover
The Grove
Latimer

99

Market Reading Wood
Gravel Dell Cottages
Great Water
THE GROVE
Church (remains of)
Round Wood
Lane Wood
LATIMER RD
Latimer House

2

Ladies Arbour
Latimer Park Farm
WD3
Raans Farm
RAANS RD
HP6
BELL LA
Chess Valley Wlk
STONY LA
Coney Wood

1

Little Chalfont
CHANDOS CT
BEECHWOOD AVE
West Wood
Walk Wood
Bell Lane Comb Sch
THE LARCHES
BEECH PK
KILN AVE
CHENIES AVE
BOUGHTON WAY
Westwood Pk
HP7
SANDYCROFT RD

98

A B C D E F
98 99 00

137
152

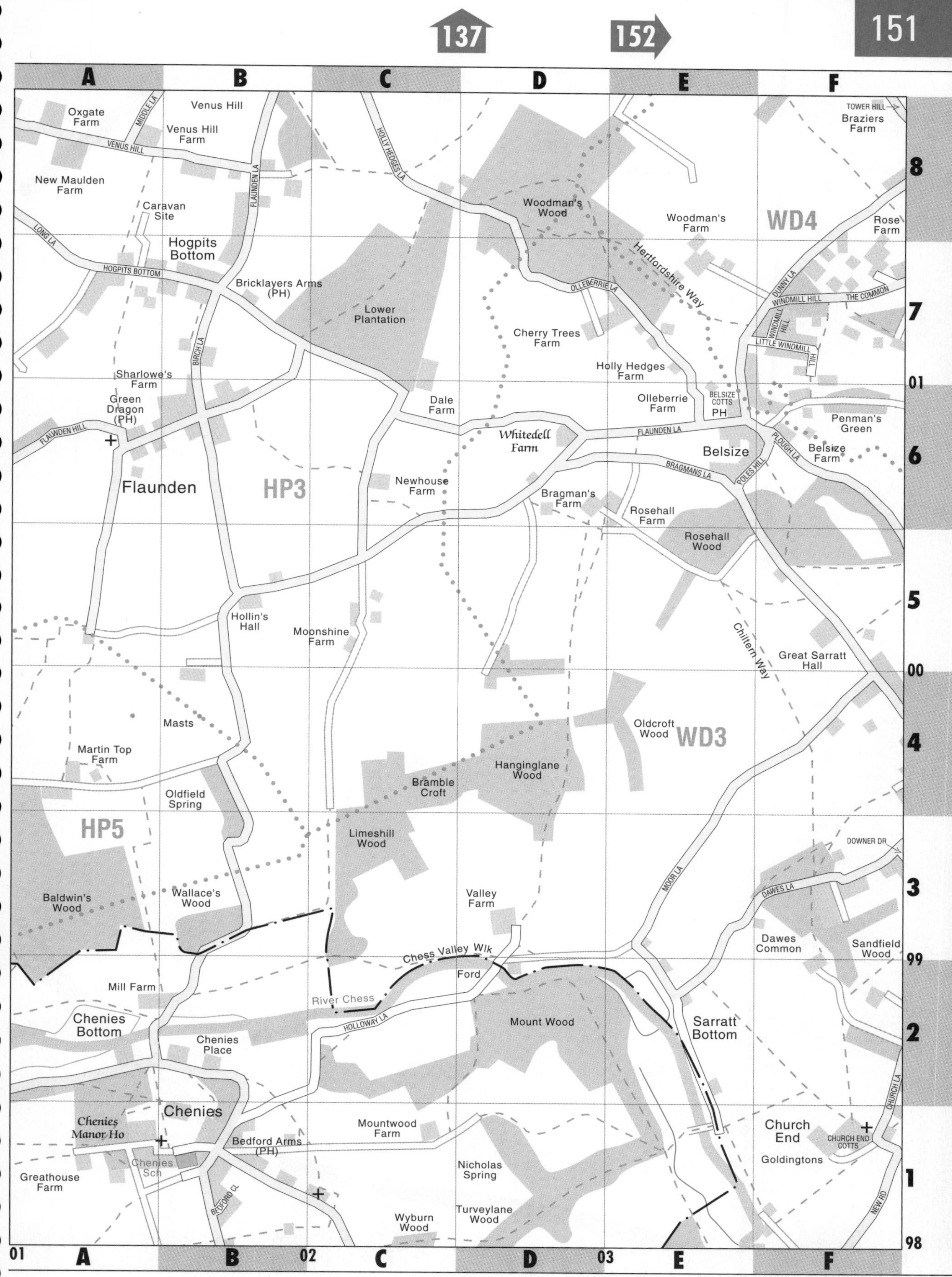

152

151
138

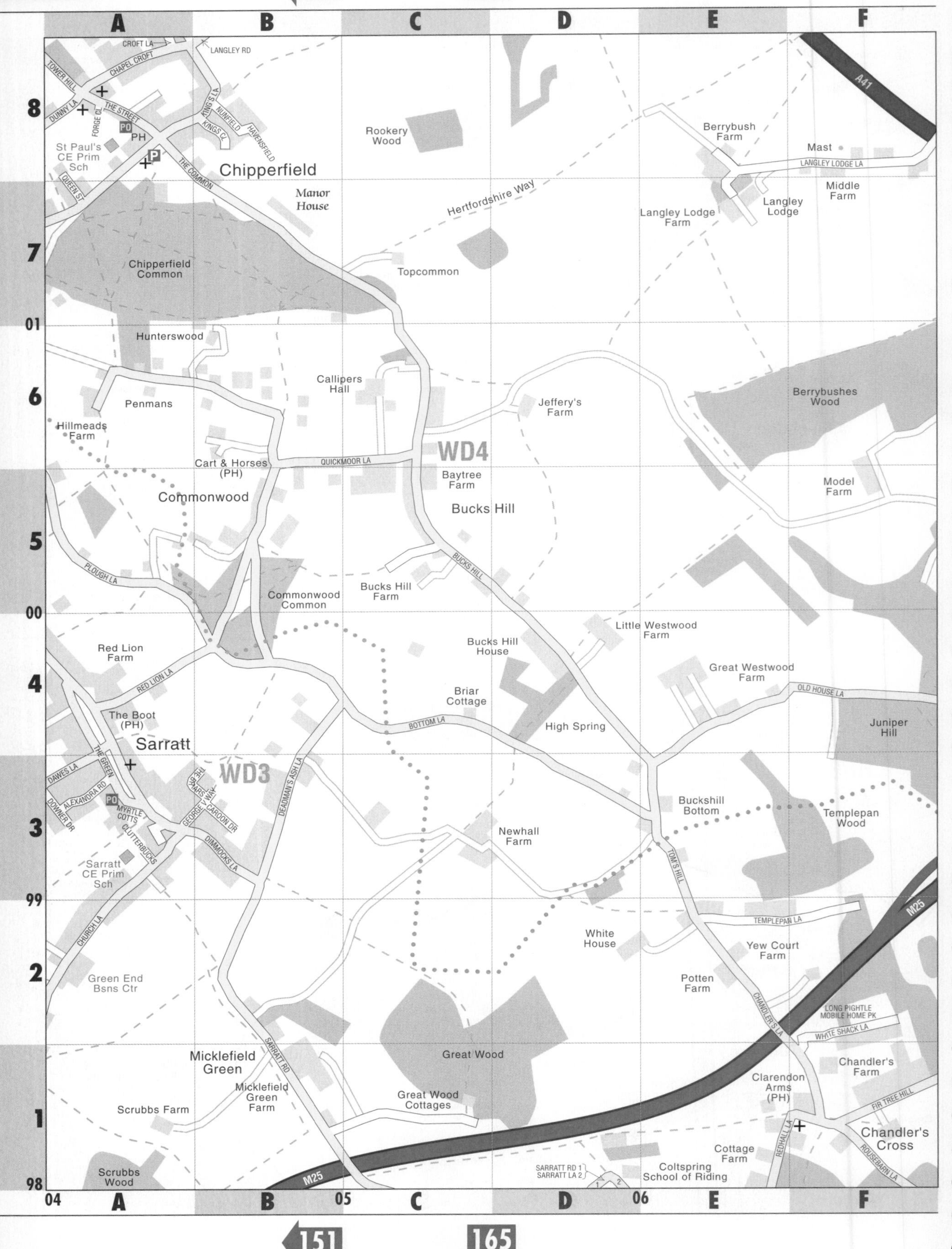
Chipperfield
Manor House
Rookery Wood
Hertfordshire Way
Berrybush Farm
Mast
LANGLEY LODGE LA
Langley Lodge Farm
Langley Lodge
Middle Farm
A41
St Paul's CE Prim Sch
PH
Chipperfield Common
Topcommon
Hunterswood
Callipers Hall
Penmans
Hillmeads Farm
Jeffery's Farm
Berrybushes Wood
QUICKMOOR LA
Cart & Horses (PH)
WD4
Baytree Farm
Model Farm
Commonwood
Bucks Hill
PLOUGH LA
BUCKS HILL
Bucks Hill Farm
Commonwood Common
Little Westwood Farm
Red Lion Farm
Bucks Hill House
Great Westwood Farm
RED LION LA
OLD HOUSE LA
Briar Cottage
The Boot (PH)
BOTTOM LA
High Spring
Juniper Hill
Sarratt
WD3
DEADMAN'S ASH LA
Buckshill Bottom
Templepan Wood
Newhall Farm
DAWES LA
ALEXANDRA RD
DOWNER DR
MYRTLE COTTS
CLUTTERBUCKS
GEORGE V WAY
CAROON DR
DIMMOCKS LA
TOM'S HILL
Sarratt CE Prim Sch
TEMPLEPAN LA
M25
CHURCH LA
White House
Yew Court Farm
Green End Bsns Ctr
Potten Farm
CHANDLER'S LA
LONG PIGHTLE MOBILE HOME PK
WHITE SHACK LA
Great Wood
Micklefield Green
SARRATT RD
Chandler's Farm
Clarendon Arms (PH)
Micklefield Green Farm
Great Wood Cottages
FIR TREE HILL
Scrubbs Farm
REDHALL LA
Chandler's Cross
Cottage Farm
ROUSEBARN LA
SARRATT RD 1
SARRATT LA 2
Coltspring School of Riding
Scrubbs Wood
M25
CROFT LA
LANGLEY RD
CHAPEL CROFT
TOWER HILL
THE STREET
FORGE CL
DUNNY LA
KING'S LA
NUNFIELD
HAVENSFIELD
KINGS CL
THE COMMON
QUEEN ST
THE GREEN
A B C D E F
8 7 01 6 5 00 4 3 99 2 1 98
04 05 06

151
165

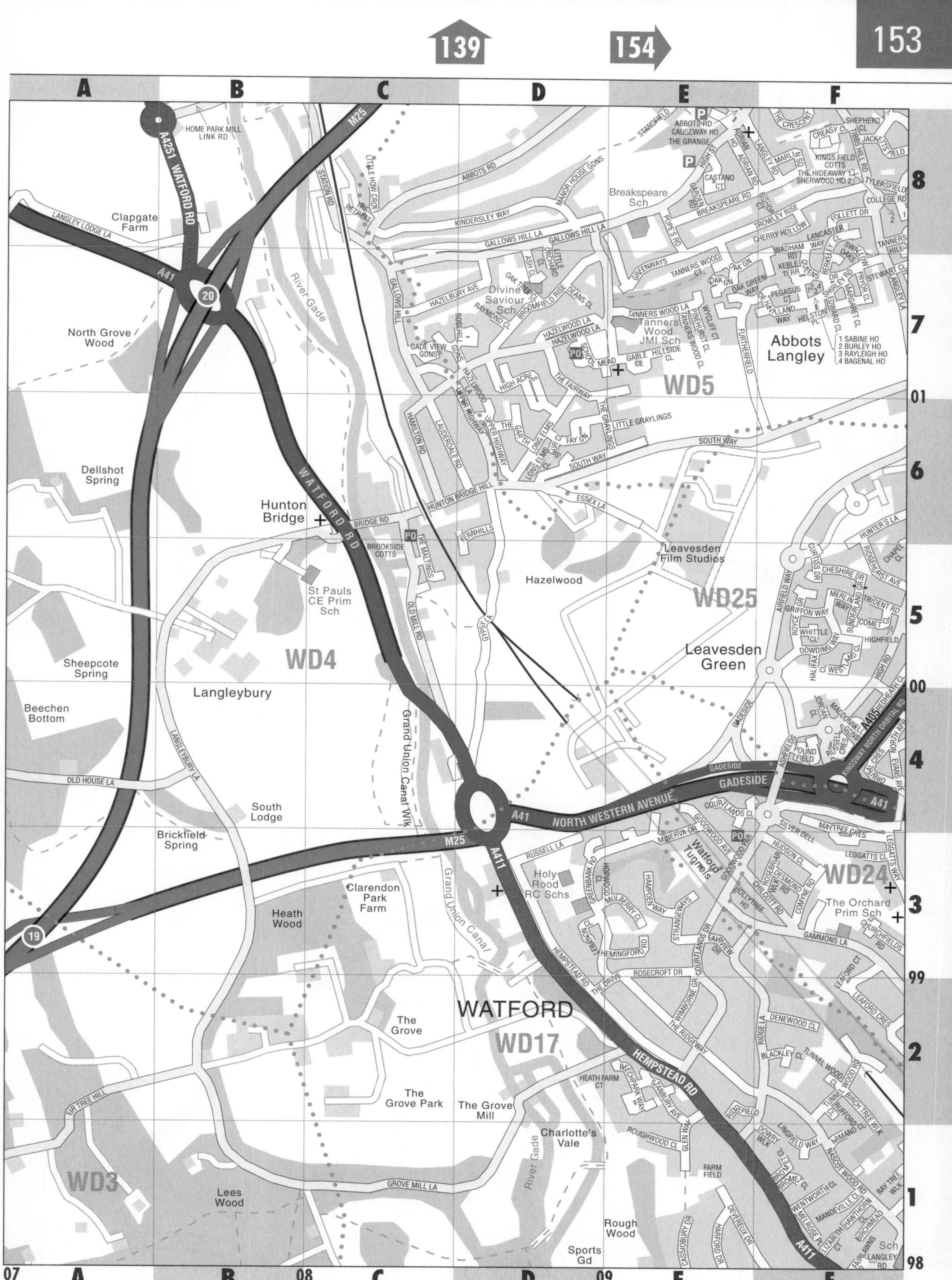

139
154

A B C D E F

166
154

A251 WATFORD RD
HOME PARK MILL LINK RD
STATION RD
LITTLE HOW CROFT
M25
ABBOTS RD
MAYOR HOUSE GDNS
STANDFIELD
ABBOTS RD CAUSEWAY HO
THE GRANGE
THE CRESCENT
SHEPHERD CL
CREASY CL
JACKETTS FIELD
TIBBS HILL RD
KINGS FIELD COTTS
THE HIDEAWAY 1
SHERWOOD HO 2
TYLERSFIELD
COLLEGE RD

Clapgate Farm
Langley Lodge La
A41
KINDERSLEY WAY
GALLOWS HILL LA
Breakspeare Sch
CASTANO CT
ADRIAN RD
MARL
MARLIN CL
BREAKSPEARE RD
CROWLEY RISE
CHERRY HOLLOW
WADHAM RD
KEBLE TERR
FOLLETT DR
LANCASTER WAY
SWAN CL
PRIOR CL
TANNERS HILL

North Grove Wood
20
GALLOWS HILL
GADE VIEW GDNS
ROSEHILL
HAZELBURY AVE
HAZELWOOD LA
OAK TREE
ASH CL
LITTLE ORCHARD
BROOMFIELD RISE DEANS CL
GREENWAYS
TANNERS WOOD
OAK GN
OAK GREEN
PEGASUS CT
SHIRLEY RD
EDWARD CT
HELSTON CL
STEWART LANGLEY LA
BERKELEY RD
MARGARET CL

Abbots Langley
1 SABINE HO
2 BURLEY HO
3 RAYLEIGH HO
4 BAGENAL HO

Dellshot Spring
River Gade
RAYMOND CL
HAZELWOOD LA
SCHOOL MEAD
PO
HIGH ACRE
THE FAIRWAY
GABLE CL
HILLSIDE CL
Tanners Wood JMI Sch
Divine Saviour Sch
PINEHURST CT
TANNERS WOOD CT
TANNERS WOOD CL
FURTHERFIELD

WATFORD RD
WD4
Hunton Bridge
BRIDGE RD
BROOKSIDE COTTS
PO
THE MALTINGS
FERNHILLS
HUNTON BRIDGE HILL
HAMILTON RD
LAUDERDALE RD
UPPER HIGHWAY
THE GATE
LONG ELMS
LONG ELMS CL
FAY GD
SOUTH WAY
LITTLE GRAYLINGS
THE GRAYLINGS
SOUTH WAY
ESSEX LA

WD5
01

St Pauls CE Prim Sch
GYPSY LA
OLD MILL RD
Hazelwood
Leavesden Film Studios
WD25
AIRFIELD WAY
CURTISS DR
CHESHIRE DR
MERLIN CT
TRIDENT RD
COMET
HIGHFIELD
HUNTER'S LA
RIDGEHURST AVE
CHAPEL LA

Langleybury
Leavesden Green
GRIFFON WAY
WAYFARER
WHITTLE CL
DOWDING WAY
HALIFAX
HIGH RD
JORDAN'S WAY

Sheepcote Spring
LANGLEYBURY LA
Grand Union Canal Wlk
00

Beechen Bottom
OLD HOUSE LA
South Lodge
GADESIDE
GADESIDE
POUND FIELD
A405 NORTH ORBITAL RD
KINGSWAY
RUSSELL CT
MACDONALD RD
EVANS AVE
A41
ORB
MAYTREE CRES
4

Brickfield Spring
Clarendon Park Farm
M25
A411
A41 NORTH WESTERN AVENUE
GADESIDE
RUSSELL LA
MINERVA DR
COURTLANDS CL
GOODWOOD AVE
SILVER DELL
LEGGATTS CLOSE
WD24
The Orchard Prim Sch
CHURCHFIELDS RD
LEGGATTS WAY

19
Heath Wood
Holy Rood RC Schs
GREENBANK RD
HAMPER MEWS
Watford Tunnels
HUDSON CL
ROSEGARTH
ROSECROFT RD
COMBE RD
HEMINGFORD RD
GAMMONS LA
STRANGEWAYS

WATFORD
WD17
The Grove
HEMPSTEAD RD
MULBERRY CL
HAMPER MEWS
POLLYTREE
FAIRVIEW DR
ROSECROFT DR
THE DRIVE
DENEWOOD CL
RIDGE LA
BLACKLEY CL
TUNNEL WOOD
99

The Grove Park
The Grove Mill
HEATH FARM CT
THE RIDGEWAY
WINBOURNE GREEN
STANBURY AVE
BEECHPARK WAY
GEFIELD
LINGFIELD WAY
LINGFIELD WAY
BUFFORD RD
TINNE BIRCH TREE WLK
TINNE WOOD CL
2

WD3
Lees Wood
Charlotte's Vale
River Gade
GROVE MILL LA
ROUGHWOOD CL
GLEN VIEW
FARM FIELD
ROUGHWOOD CL
DONRY WLK
NASCOT WOOD RD
BROME CL
WENTWORTH CL
1

FAR TREE HILL
Rough Wood
Sports Gd
CASSIOBURY DR
HARFORD DR
ELIZABETH DR
DEXTREUX DR
MANDEVILLE CL
MELROSE CL
ELIZABETH HAWTHORN
BEECHMEAD
FAIRLAWNS
A411
DOWRY WLK
BAY TREE WLK
LANGLEY RD
Sch
98

07 08 09

153

140

A B C D E F

8
7
01
6
5
00
4
3
99
2
1
98

WD5
AL2
WD25
AL2
WD24
WD23
WD17

WATFORD
Woodside
Kingswood
Garston
North Watford
Meriden
Otterspool

M1
6
5
A405
A412
A41
A4008 STEPHENSON WAY
KINGSWAY NORTH ORBITAL RD
NORTH ORBITAL RD
ST ALBANS RD
NORTH WESTERN AVE
COLNE WAY
OTTERSPOOL WAY

Parmiter's Sch
St Andrews Montessori Prep Sch
Crem
Brookdell Farm
Building Research Sta
Francis Combe Sch & Com Coll
St Michael's RC High Sch
Garston Manor Sch
Alban Wood Inf Sch
Alban Wood Jun Sch
L Ctr
Woodside Playing Fields
Sch
Coates Way JMI Sch
Mutchetts Wood
Coldharbour Plantation
The Old Fox (PH)
Munden Spring
Leavesden Green Sch
Kingsway Schs
Stanborough Prim Sch
Stanborough Sec Sch
North Watford Cemy
Schs
Superstore
Works
West Herts Coll Leggatts Campus
Cherry Tree Prim Sch
Liby
Meriden Sch
Parkgate Inf Sch
Oldhams Trad Est
The Orient Ctr
Wenta Bsns Ctr
Ind Est
LC
Watford North
Paramount Ind Est
Mowat Ind Est
Beechfield Sch
Recn Gnd
Knutsford Sch
Shakespeare Ind Est
Coll
River Colne
Garston

HIGH ELMS
HIGH ELMS LA
MEADOWSIDE
COLLEGE RD
NIGHTINGALE CL
REDWING GR
LINNET RD
PEACOCK WLK
LEAVESDEN CT
LAPWING WAY
GLENMORE GDNS
KATHERINE PL
STEWART CL
MAGNOLIA AVE
HAWTHORN CL
SHACKLETON WAY
CARDIFF WAY
STIRLING CL
LYSANDER WAY
HURRICANE WAY
BLENHEIM RD
OLD FORGE CL
AIRFIELD WAY
HILL FARM CL
HILL FARM AVE
HUNTER'S GATE
HAMMER PAR
CHAPEL CL
SHERWOOD CT
LEVERET CL
LYMINGTON CT
BADGERS CL
FOXLANDS CL
REDHEATH CL
ARUNDEL RD
BALMORAL RD
LONG BARN CL
LODGE CT
HARE CRES
HIGH RD
HORE GN
ABBOTSBURY CT
THE BROW
GANDERS ASH
VALLEY RISE
ST ALBANS VIEW
KENFORD CL
RYDAL CL
GRASMERE CL
BLACKTHORN CL
WEALL GN
LOUDWATER CT
POPLARS CL
FARRIERS CT
BOUNDARY WAY
HORSESHOE LA
COBB GN
NEWHOUSE CRES
COMBEWOOD
HOP GARDEN WAY
COOPERS MEWS
BARLEY BROW
THE SHIRES
ORCHARD AVE
ASHLEY CL
CAMPION CL
QUEENSWOOD CRES
SHEEPCOT LA
MARIAN GDNS
FOREST RD
SPRINGFIELD RD
WOODGATE
SHERIFF WAY
NOTTINGHAM CL
LINDEN LEA
HAINES WAY
ST MICHAELS DR
NORTH APP
MEADOW RD
HILLINGDON RD
KINGSWOOD RD
GREENWOOD DR
MOSS RD
PERIVALE GDNS
BRAMBLE CL
BRIAR RD
FLORENCE CL
FERN WAY
ROSS CRES
HARRIS RD
SUMMERFIELD RD
GOODRICH CL
HEMMING WAY
GREEN EDGE
RUSHTON AVE
GULLET WOOD RD
CLARKE WAY
LEGGATTS RISE
ELDERBERRY WAY
SYCAMORE CL
HAZEL GR
ASH CL
ALDER WLK
ASPEN PARK DR
APPLETREE WLK
CEDAR WOOD DR
CYPRESS WLK
SHEEPCOT VILLAS
ELLWOOD GDNS
THE CONIFERS
LAMB CL
HOLME LEA
SHEEPCOT DR
WESTLOCK CL
MEDWAY
GARSTON CRES
GARSTON DR
SEVERN WAY
AVON CL
ROTHER CL
ROCHESTER DR
THE PIPPINS
LINGMOOR DR
HAWKSHEAD RD
DERWENT CL
LOWESWATER CL
NEWLANDS WLK
HARDING CL
CART PATH
ALL SAINTS CRES
THE GLEBE
LYCH GATE
CROWN RISE
JEWELL CT
LAVINIA AVE
PARK LODGE
WILCON WAY
GARDENER CT
BIDDENHAM TURN
KILBY CL
SIXTH AVE
SECOND AVE
FIRST AVE
THIRD AVE
FIFTH AVE
FOURTH AVE
BEKEN CT
HOLTSMERE CL
HOLLAND GDNS
SPRING GDNS
PURBROCK AVE
EAST DR
WEST DR
COW LA
HERONSLEA
BERRY AVE
POMEROY CRES
LEGGATTS WOOD AVE
OAKDENE RD
BRUSHRISE
CHERRY TREE RD
FOXHILL
YEATMAN HO
BEECHWOOD RISE
CHURCHFIELDS RD
LEGGATTS WAY
WOODSIDE
ACORN PL
CHESTNUT WLK
BEECH RD
FULLER GDNS
FULLER RD
HAZEL TREE RD
GLADESMERE CT
ODEON PAR
BUSHEY MILL CRES
SWANLEY CT
NORTHFIELD GDNS
NESTON RD
LEAFORD CRES
ELM GR
DELL RD
GAMMONS LA
HOWARD CL
DISBURNE WAY
BRANSCOMBE HO
BRETT PL
COWPER CT
THRUMS
MIDDLE WAY
THE HAREBREAKS
LONGSPRING
NICHOLAS CL
ASHBY RD
MERRYFIELD
SUSSEX RD
BRIGHTON RD
BREAKSPEARE CL
POPES LA
JUBILEE RD
DIAMOND RD
GAMMONS LA
COLLEGE YD
ACME RD
CALLOWLAND
LEAVESDEN RD
JUDGE ST
CECIL ST
REGENT ST
HALSEY PL
ST GEORGES DR
MAUDE CRES
LEA RD
RIDGE ST
CROMER RD
YARMOUTH RD
BRUCE GR
SALISBURY
VICTORIA RD
GARFIELD ST
SHAKESPEARE ST
MILTON ST
GRANGE CL
CHATSWORTH MEWS
JUNIPER GR
BAY TREE WLK
BROOM GR
BUCKINGHAM RD
SANDRINGHAM RD
PARKGATE RD
SOUTHWOLD RD
WINDSOR RD
OSBORNE RD
SANDOWN RD
CHISWELL CT
SOUTHFIELD AVE
NORFOLK AVE
MUNDEN GR
KNUTSFORD AVE
HERBERT AVE
WESTFIELD AVE
BALMORAL RD
IMPERIAL WAY
REGAL WAY
FEDERAL WAY
DEVON RD
RADLETT RD
BUSHEY MILL LA
TUDOR WLK
TUDOR AVE
TUDOR DR
HILLRISE AVE
WOODMERE AVE
HORWOOD CT
DOUGLAS AVE
GREYCAINE RD
GARNETT CL
BROOKSIDE CL
COLNE WAY CT
FOXTREE HO
COLDHARBOUR HO
BEARTREE CT
HARVEST END
AUDBURY CL
ABBEY VIEW
MAPLE CT
MUNDEN VIEW
GARSMOUTH WAY
GADSWELL CL
YORK WAY
THE TURNSTONES
PINETREE HO
TEAL HO
MALLARD WAY
WIDGEON WAY
MERIDEN WAY
KELSHALL
WESTLEA AVE
EASTLEA AVE
LEANDER GDNS
BUTTERWICK
THE GOSSAMERS
FAIRFOLDS
BOW MANS GN
LEA BUSHES
PHILLIPERS
IVINGHOE CL
THE PELHAMS
WHITWELL RD
TIBBLES CL
MAXWELL RD
GARSTON LA
TELFORD CL
LANSDOWNE CL
WOODHURST AVE
KIMPTON PL
CUFFLEY AVE
CODICOTE DR
BOVINGDON CRES
GADDESDEN CRES
FELDEN CL
GARSTON PARK PAR
BRAMFIELD
FALCON WAY
RAVENSCROFT
KESTREL CL
PEREGRINE CL
OSPREY CL
KYTES DR
PILGRIM CL
COATES WAY
COATES DELL
MUTCHETTS CL
CHICHESTER WAY
VERDURE CL
BUCKNALLS CL
BUCKNALLS LA
BUCKNALLS DR
TUDOR MANOR GDNS
AVALON CL
BRIDGER CL
LYMONFIELD DR
CRANEFIELD DR
1 GLEBE CT
2 CEDAR CT
3 DEAN CT
4 THE GABLES
HALIFAX CL
FERNDENE
ASH COPSE
ENID CL
MOUNT PLEASANT LA
ST LAWRENCE WAY
THE KESTRELS
MORAN CL
SCHOOL LA
BERRY GROVE LA
OTTERSPOOL LA

10 A B 11 C D 12 E F

153
167

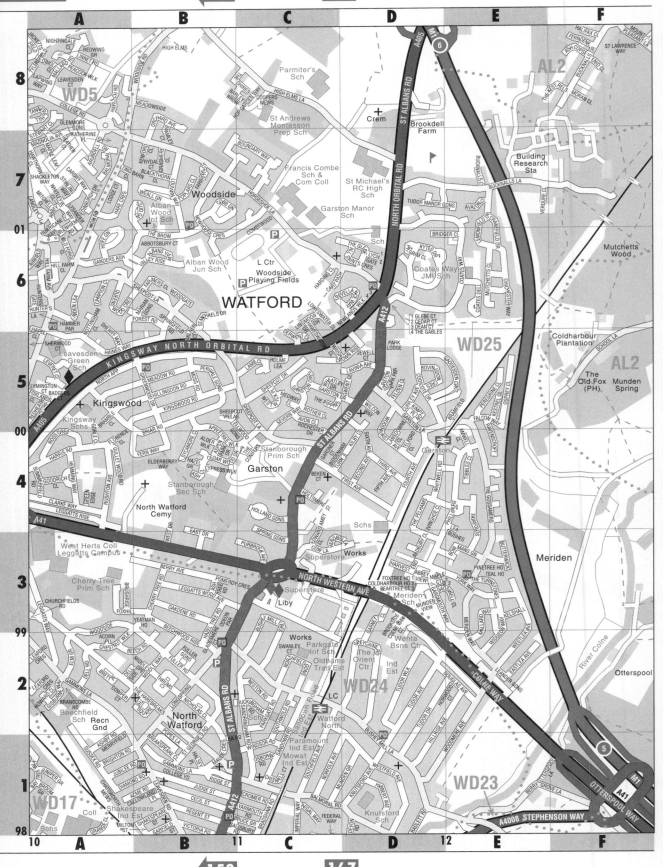

141
156

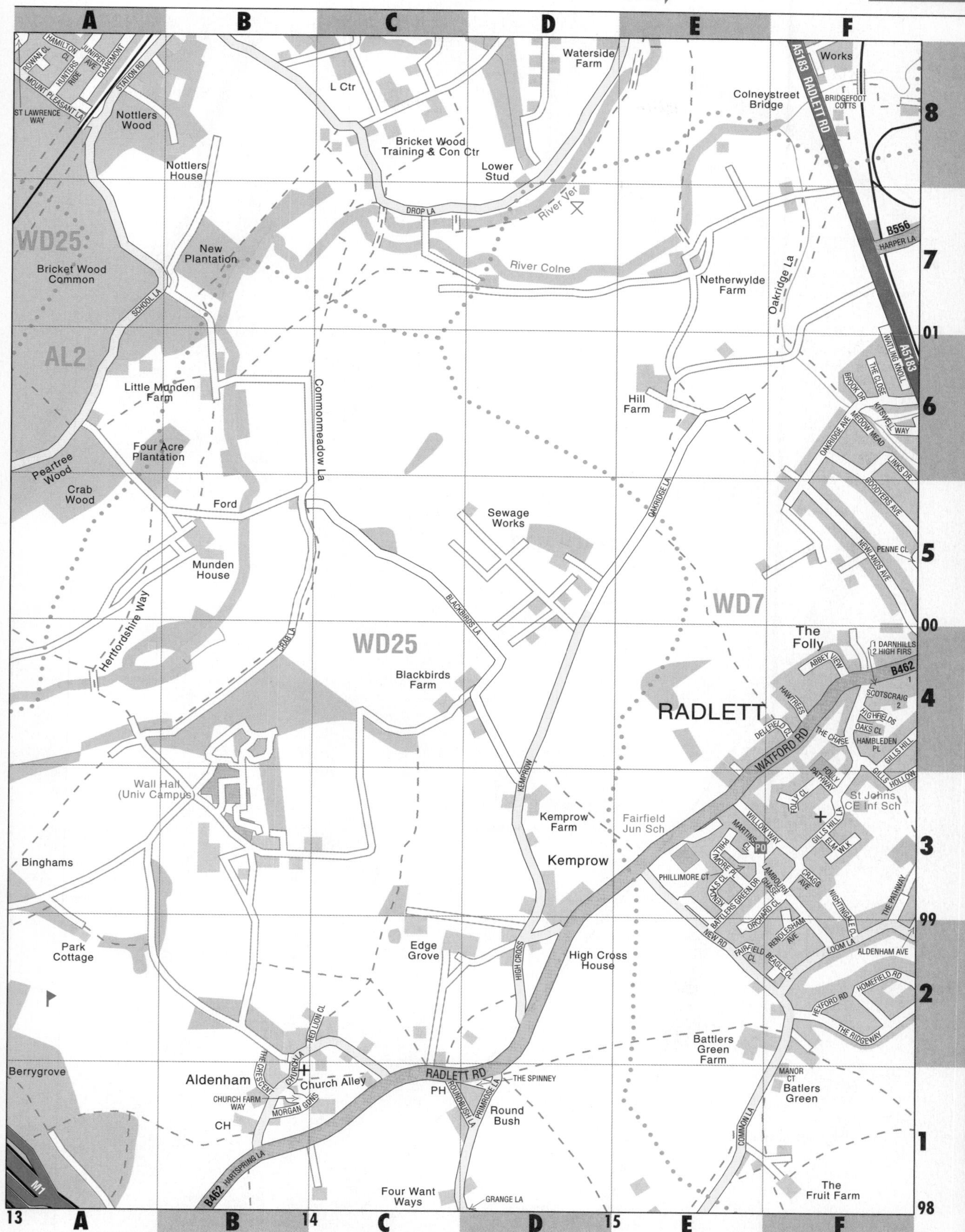
A
B
C
D
E
F
Waterside Farm
Works
L Ctr
Colneystreet Bridge
A5183 RADLETT RD
BRIDGEFOOT COTTS
8
Nottlers Wood
ST LAWRENCE WAY
STATION RD
Bricket Wood Training & Con Ctr
Nottlers House
Lower Stud
DROP LA
River Ver
WD25
Bricket Wood Common
New Plantation
River Colne
B556
HARPER LA
7
Netherwylde Farm
Oakridge La
SCHOOL LA
AL2
01
Little Munden Farm
Commonmeadow La
Hill Farm
6
Four Acre Plantation
Peartree Wood
Crab Wood
Ford
Sewage Works
OAKRIDGE LA
5
Munden House
WD7
Hertfordshire Way
BLACKBIRDS LA
00
CRAB LA
WD25
The Folly
Blackbirds Farm
B462
4
RADLETT
WATFORD RD
Wall Hall (Univ Campus)
KEMPROW
St Johns CE Inf Sch
Kemprow Farm
Fairfield Jun Sch
3
Binghams
Kemprow
PHILLIMORE CT
99
Park Cottage
Edge Grove
HIGH CROSS
High Cross House
2
Battlers Green Farm
Berrygrove
Aldenham
Church Alley
RADLETT RD
PH
THE SPINNEY
CHURCH FARM WAY
MORGAN GDNS
CH
Round Bush
Batlers Green
MANOR CT
COMMON LA
1
M1
B462 HARTSPRING LA
Four Want Ways
GRANGE LA
The Fruit Farm
98
13
14
15

168
156

155 142

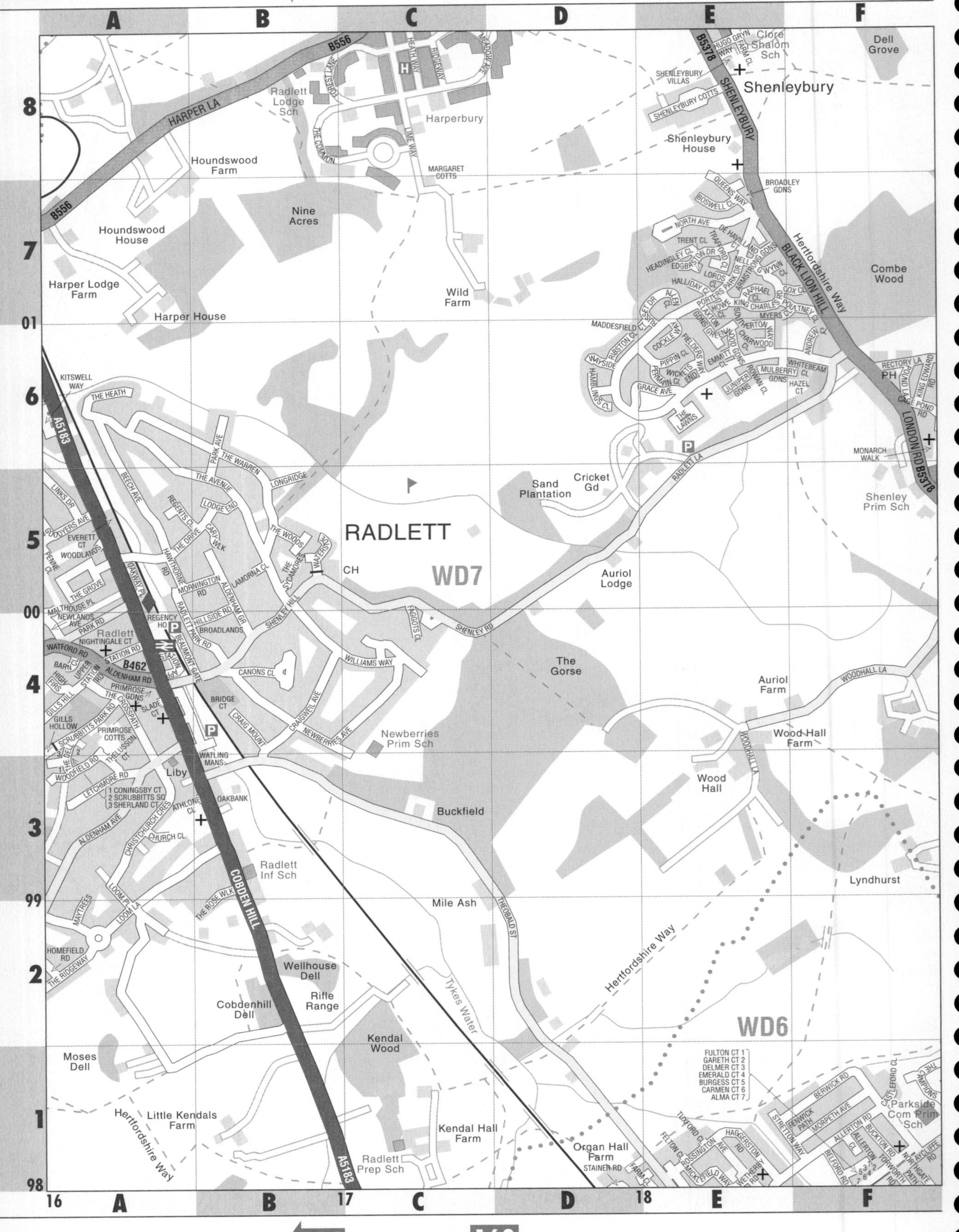
RADLETT
WD7
WD6
Shenleybury
Harperbury
Radlett Lodge Sch
Houndswood Farm
Houndswood House
Nine Acres
Harper Lodge Farm
Harper House
Wild Farm
Shenleybury House
Clore Shalom Sch
Dell Grove
Combe Wood
Hertfordshire Way
Sand Plantation
Cricket Gd
Shenley Prim Sch
Auriol Lodge
The Gorse
Auriol Farm
Wood Hall Farm
Wood Hall
Newberries Prim Sch
Buckfield
Radlett Inf Sch
Mile Ash
Lyndhurst
Wellhouse Dell
Rifle Range
Cobdenhill Dell
Kendal Wood
Moses Dell
Little Kendals Farm
Kendal Hall Farm
Radlett Prep Sch
Organ Hall Farm
Parkside Com Prim Sch
Tykes Water
COBDEN HILL
HARPER LA
SHENLEY RD
RADLETT LA
WOODHALL LA
THEOBALD ST
BLACK LION HILL
LONDON RD
WATLING MANS
Liby
CH
PH

143
158

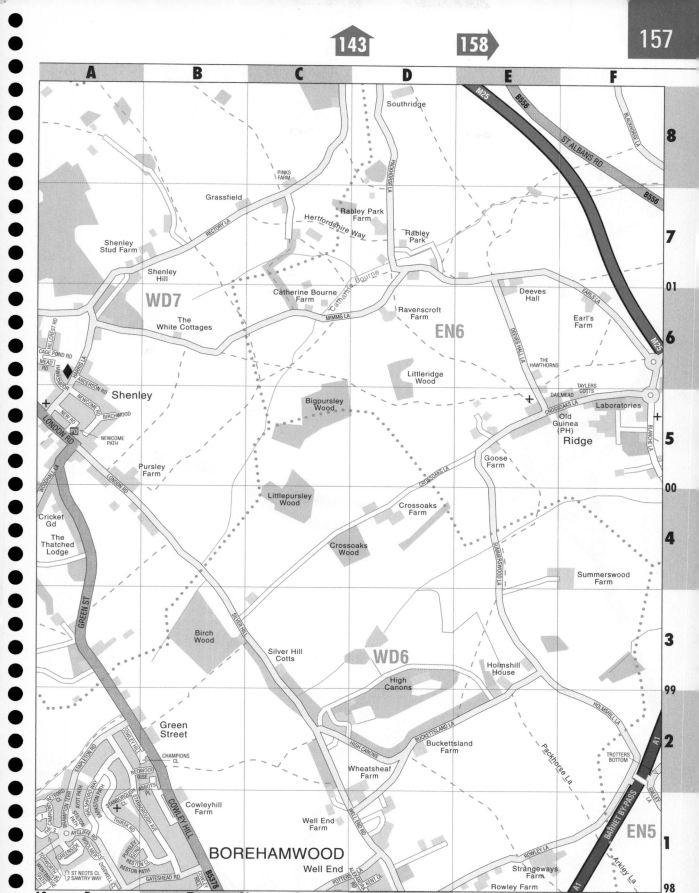
A
B
C
D
E
F
8
7
01
6
5
00
4
3
99
2
1
98
19
20
21
Southridge
M25
B556
ST ALBANS RD
BLACKHORSE LA
PINKS FARM
Grassfield
PACKHORSE LA
Rabley Park Farm
Hertfordshire Way
Rabley Park
RECTORY LA
Shenley Stud Farm
Shenley Hill
Catherine Bourne
Catherine Bourne Farm
WD7
The White Cottages
MIMMS LA
Ravenscroft Farm
EN6
Deeves Hall
EARLS LA
Earl's Farm
DEEVES HALL LA
THE HAWTHORNS
HILLCREST RD
CAGE POND RD
MEAD RD
HAWKSMOOR
HARRIS LA
ANDERSON RD
Shenley
NEWCOME RD
BIRCHWOOD
NEW RD
LONDON RD
PO
NEWCOME PATH
Littleridge Wood
Bigpursley Wood
TAYLERS COTTS
DAILMEAD
CROSSOAKS LA
Laboratories
Old Guinea (PH)
Ridge
BLANCHE LA
Goose Farm
WOODHALL LA
Pursley Farm
Littlepursley Wood
Crossoaks Farm
Cricket Gd
The Thatched Lodge
Crossoaks Wood
SUMMERSWOOD LA
Summerswood Farm
GREEN ST
Birch Wood
SILVER HILL
Silver Hill Cotts
WD6
Holmshill House
High Canons
HOLMSHILL LA
Green Street
COWLEY HILL
CHAMPIONS CL
BUCKETTSLAND LA
Buckettsland Farm
HIGH CANONS
A1
TROTTERS BOTTOM
Packhorse La
STAPLETON RD
REDWOOD RISE
Wheatsheaf Farm
ABBOTS PL
GALLEY LA
RETFORD CL
BRAMPTON TERR
AYOT PATH
WALSHFORD WAY
BANKSTON PATH
STANBOROUGH CL
STANBOROUGH AVE
Cowleyhill Farm
BARNET BY-PASS
THE CAMPIONS
STILTON PATH
THIRSK RD
WELL END RD
Well End Farm
EN5
AYCLIFFE RD
WOOLMER CL
GREENSIDE
PURSLEY GDNS
BOREHAMWOOD
Arkley La
TORWORTH RD
1 ST NEOTS CL
2 SAWTRY WAY
DIGSWELL CL
RESTON CL
RESTON PATH
Well End
ROWLEY LA
Strangeways Farm
WENTBRIDGE PATH
GATESHEAD RD
B5378
POTTERS RD
ALEXANDRA RD
KENT CL
Rowley Farm

157
144

A B C D E F

8
7
01
6
5
00
4
3
99
2
1
98

South Mimms
Hertfordshire Way
BLACKHORSE LA
ARLINGHAM COTTS
HEPBURN CT
BROOKSIDE
GOWAR FIELD
GASCOYNE CL
B556 ST ALBANS RD
CECIL RD
A1 (M)
WARRENGATE LA
Mimms Hall
Warrengate Cottages
The Furzefield Ctr
Playing Field
P
PO
CRANBORNE PARK
WINDMORE HALL
WINDMORE AVE
DEEPDENE
LEXINGTON CT
MUTTON LA
CRANBORNE RD
CRANBORNE CL
CRANBORNE CRES
BORNEHENE
Cranborne Prim Sch
Liby
OAKFIELD CL
PINEWOOD DR
MANOR RD
STATION CL
TEMPLE CT
WROXHAM GDNS
The Wroxham Sch
RANWORTH GDNS
CAMBRIDGE DR
FURZEFIELD CT
LAUREL FIELDS
NEVILLE CL
CLIVE CL
LAUREL AVE
P
Potters Bar
WYLLYOTTS CL
WYLLYOTTS PL
Mus
MANOR CT
DARKES LA
B556
ORMESBY DR
MIMMS HALL RD
SUFFOLK RD
BOROUGH WAY
OULTON CRES
AUCKLAND RD
ALLANDALE CRES
THE APPROACH
BROOKLANDS GDNS
BERKELEY CL
ELMSCROFT GDNS
SHERWOOD AVE
DRAYTON AVE
ABERDALE GDNS
SNOWS
WESTON CL
HEATHER WAY
THE DRIVE
DALESIDE DR
FAIRACRES CL
ELMROYD AVE
ELMROYD CL
Mimmshall Brook
SWANLAND RD
EN6
KIMPTONS MEAD
KIMPTONS CL
SHILLITOE AVE
UPDALE CL
RUSHFIELD
STEVENS CL
DUGDALE HILL LA
ROBERT CL
WELLESLEY CRES
ELMFIELD CL
ELMFIELD RD
THE SHRUBLANDS
SANTERS LA
FROWYKE CRES
ST GILES' AVE
St Giles' CE Prim Sch
BLANCHE LA
HAMILTON CL
NEW RD
GREYHOUND LA
ST ALBANS RD
Bridgefoot
BRIDGEFOOT LA
Dugdale Hill
Grasmere
Dame Alice Owen's Sch
RYDAL MOUNT
GREAT SLADES
OAKROYD AVE
OAKROYD CL
Pope Paul RC Prim Sch
M25
Motel
WASH LA
South Mimms Motorway Service Area
SAWYERS LA
Playing Field
BAKER ST
BIGNELLS CNR
Motel
Blanche Farm
1
23
FB
M25
Elm Farm
BENTLEY HEATH LA
A1081
BLANCHE LA
A1 (M)
DANCERS LA
Dancershill Farm
Norfolk Lodge Farm
Bentley Heath
The Cottage
Dancers Hill
Dancershill House
DANCERS HILL RD
Norfolk Lodge
Dyrham Park Farm
WASH LA
Laurel Lodge La
ST ALBANS RD
Wrotham Park
Wrotham Park
BARNET BY-PASS
DYRHAM LA
EN5
TROTTERS BOTTOM
A1
Home Farm
The Green Dragon (PH)
KITT'S END RD
Lower Kitt's End Farm
Dyrham Park
CH
Knightsland Farm
Kitt's End
Kitt's End Farm
Valentine's Farm
BARNET RD A1000
GALLEY LA
A1081
GREENACRE CL
A1000
BEAUMONT PL

22 A B 23 C D 24 E F

145
160

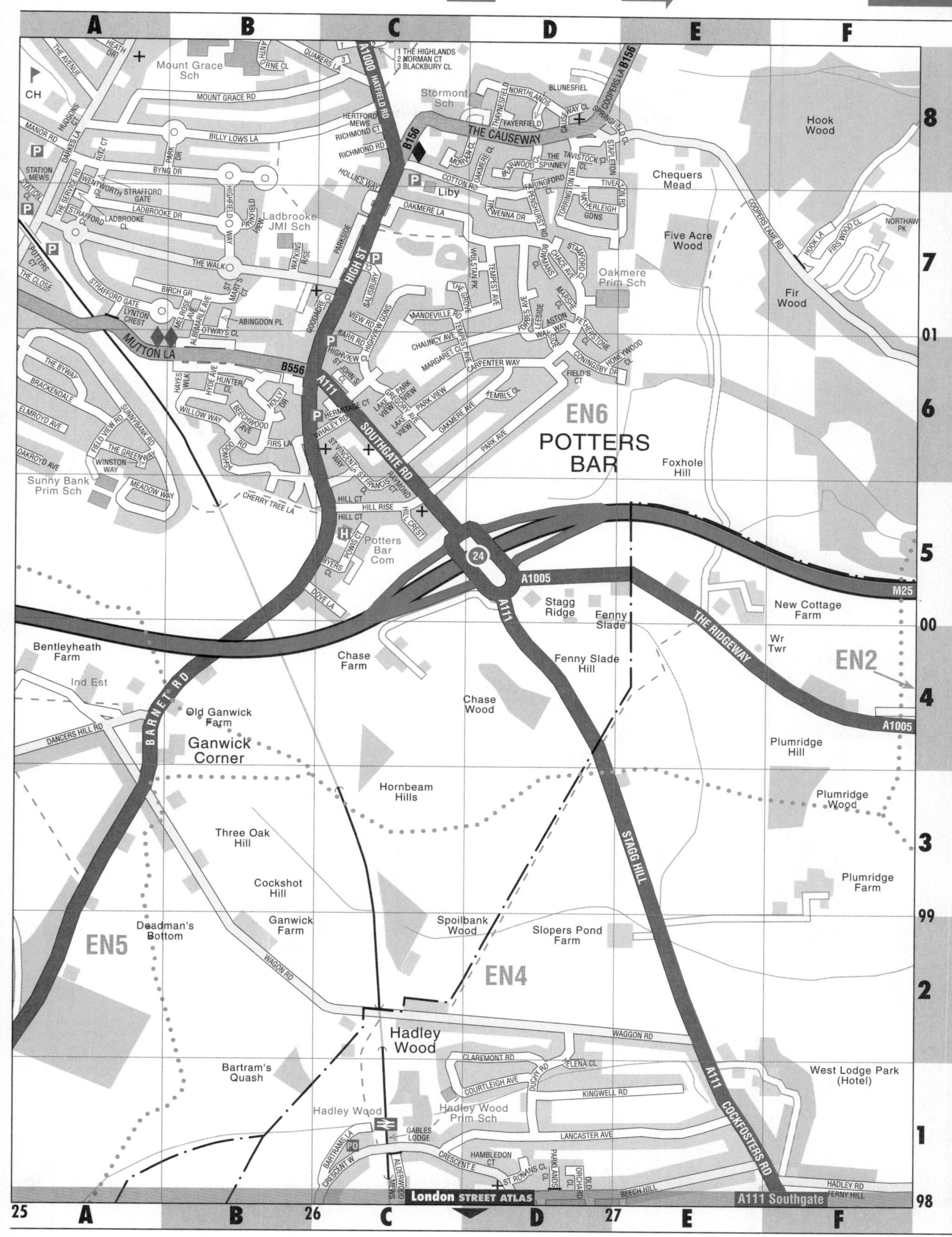
POTTERS BAR
EN6
EN5
EN4
EN2
Mount Grace Sch
Stormont Sch
Ladbrooke JMI Sch
Oakmere Prim Sch
Sunny Bank Prim Sch
Potters Bar Com
Hook Wood
Chequers Mead
Five Acre Wood
Fir Wood
Foxhole Hill
Bentleyheath Farm
Ind Est
Old Ganwick Farm
Ganwick Corner
Chase Farm
Chase Wood
Stagg Ridge
Fenny Slade
Fenny Slade Hill
New Cottage Farm
Wr Twr
Plumridge Hill
Plumridge Wood
Plumridge Farm
Hornbeam Hills
Three Oak Hill
Cockshot Hill
Ganwick Farm
Deadman's Bottom
Spoilbank Wood
Slopers Pond Farm
Hadley Wood
Bartram's Quash
Hadley Wood Prim Sch
West Lodge Park (Hotel)
THE CAUSEWAY
HIGH ST
SOUTHGATE RD
HATFIELD RD
MUTTON LA
BARNET RD
THE RIDGEWAY
STAGG HILL
COCKFOSTERS RD
WAGON RD
WAGGON RD
DANCERS HILL RD
CHERRY TREE LA
COOPERS LANE RD
A1000
A111
A1005
B156
B556
M25
A111 Southgate
London STREET ATLAS

160

159
146

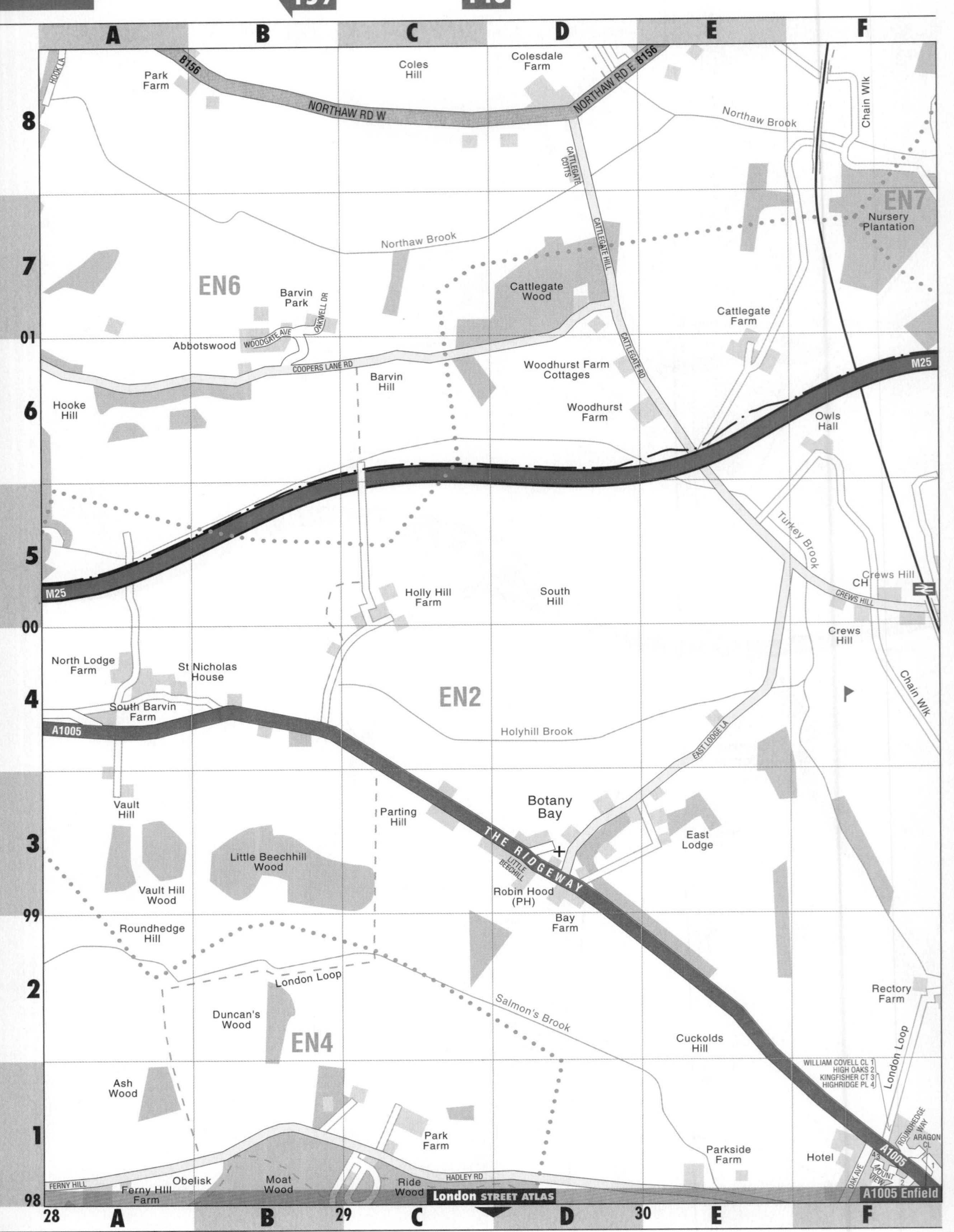
A
B
C
D
E
F
8
7
01
6
5
00
4
3
99
2
1
98
28
29
30
Park Farm
B156
NORTHAW RD W
Coles Hill
Colesdale Farm
NORTHAW RD E
Northaw Brook
Chain Wlk
CATTLEGATE COTTS
EN7
Nursery Plantation
Northaw Brook
CATTLEGATE HILL
EN6
Barvin Park
OAKWELL DR
Cattlegate Wood
Cattlegate Farm
Abbotswood
WOODGATE AVE
COOPERS LANE RD
Barvin Hill
Woodhurst Farm Cottages
CATTLEGATE RD
M25
Hooke Hill
Woodhurst Farm
Owls Hall
Turkey Brook
Crews Hill
CH
CREWS HILL
Holly Hill Farm
South Hill
Crews Hill
North Lodge Farm
St Nicholas House
EN2
Chain Wlk
South Barvin Farm
A1005
Holyhill Brook
EAST LODGE LA
Vault Hill
Parting Hill
Botany Bay
East Lodge
THE RIDGEWAY
Little Beechhill Wood
LITTLE BEECHHILL
Vault Hill Wood
Robin Hood (PH)
Bay Farm
Roundhedge Hill
London Loop
Rectory Farm
Salmon's Brook
Duncan's Wood
EN4
Cuckolds Hill
WILLIAM COVELL CL 1
HIGH OAKS 2
KINGFISHER CT 3
HIGHRIDGE PL 4
London Loop
Ash Wood
ROUNDHEDGE WAY
ARAGON CL
Park Farm
Parkside Farm
Hotel
OAK AVE
MOUNT VIEW
FERNY HILL
Obelisk
Moat Wood
HADLEY RD
Ferny Hill Farm
Ride Wood
London STREET ATLAS
A1005 Enfield

159

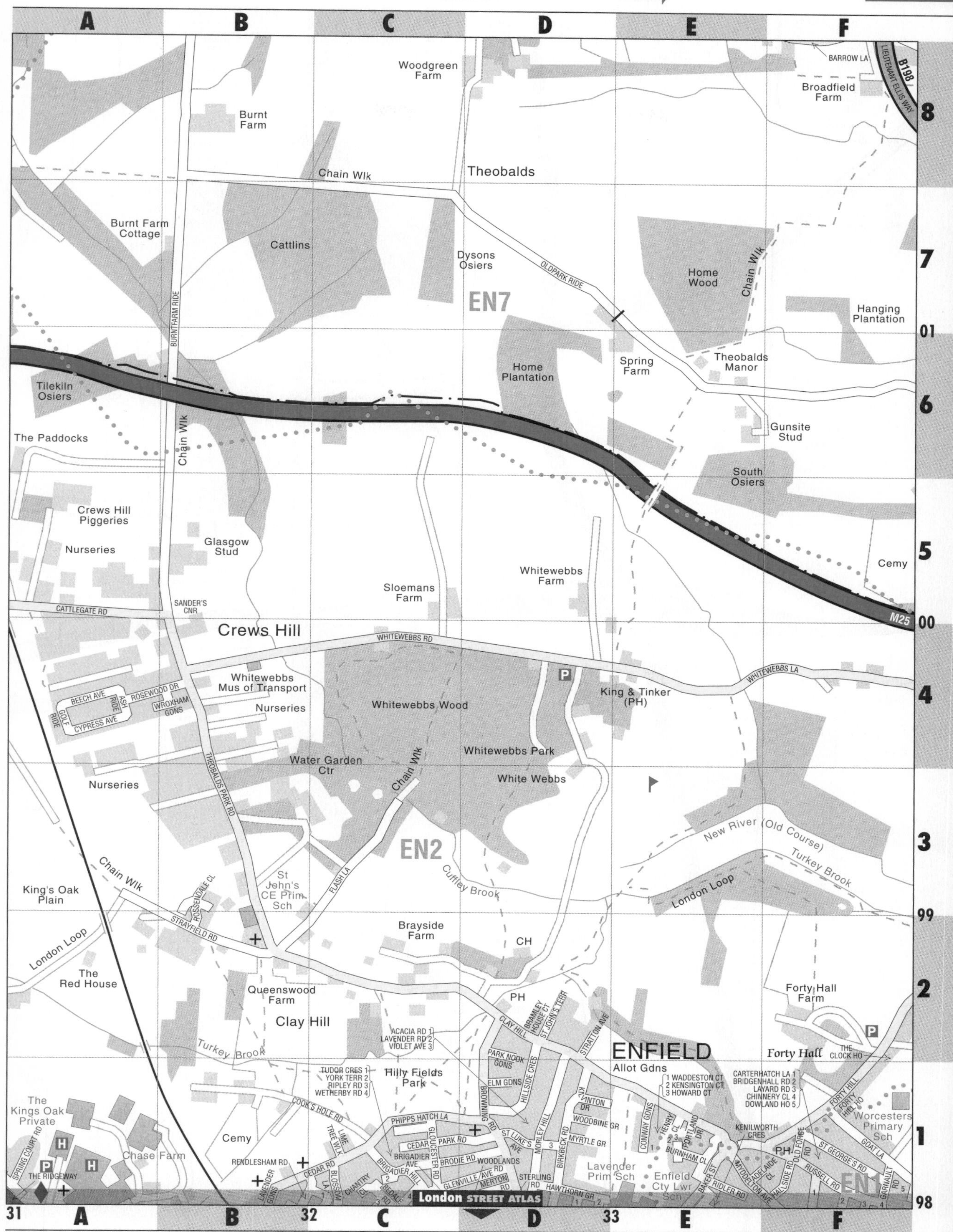
A
B
C
D
E
F
Woodgreen Farm
Burnt Farm
Broadfield Farm
BARROW LA
B198
LIEUTENANT ELLIS WAY
8
Chain Wlk
Theobalds
Burnt Farm Cottage
Cattlins
Dysons Osiers
OLDPARK RIDE
Home Wood
Chain Wlk
7
EN7
Hanging Plantation
BURNTFARM RIDE
01
Home Plantation
Spring Farm
Theobalds Manor
Tilekiln Osiers
6
The Paddocks
Chain Wlk
Gunsite Stud
South Osiers
Crews Hill Piggeries
Nurseries
Glasgow Stud
5
Cemy
Whitewebbs Farm
Sloemans Farm
SANDER'S CNR
CATTLEGATE RD
M25
00
Crews Hill
WHITEWEBBS RD
Whitewebbs Mus of Transport
WHITEWEBBS LA
King & Tinker (PH)
4
BEECH AVE
ROSEWOOD DR
ASH RIDE
WROXHAM GDNS
GOLF RIDE
CYPRESS AVE
Nurseries
Whitewebbs Wood
Whitewebbs Park
Water Garden Ctr
Chain Wlk
White Webbs
Nurseries
THEOBALDS PARK RD
New River (Old Course)
3
EN2
Turkey Brook
Chain Wlk
ROSSENDALE CL
St John's CE Prim Sch
FLASH LA
Cuffley Brook
London Loop
King's Oak Plain
99
STRAYFIELD RD
London Loop
Brayside Farm
CH
The Red House
2
Queenswood Farm
PH
Forty Hall Farm
Clay Hill
CLAY HILL
BRAMLEY HOUSE CT
ST JOHN'S TERR
STRATTON AVE
ACACIA RD 1
LAVENDER RD 2
VIOLET AVE 3
Turkey Brook
ENFIELD
Forty Hall
THE CLOCK HO
PARK NOOK GDNS
Allot Gdns
TUDOR CRES 1
YORK TERR 2
RIPLEY RD 3
WETHERBY RD 4
Hilly Fields Park
1 WADDESTON CT
2 KENSINGTON CT
3 HOWARD CT
CARTERHATCH LA 1
BRIDGENHALL RD 2
LAYARD RD 3
CHINNERY CL 4
DOWLAND HO 5
ELM GDNS
HILLSIDE CRES
BROWNING RD
The Kings Oak Private
COOK'S HOLE RD
KIVINTON DR
CONWAY GDNS
HENRY CL
PORTLAND DR
FORTY HILL HO
Worcesters Primary Sch
PHIPPS HATCH LA
WOODBINE GR
MORLEY HILL
BIRKBECK RD
MYRTLE GR
KENILWORTH CRES
1
SPRING COURT RD
Cemy
TREE WLK
LIME
CEDAR
PARK RD
ST LUKE'S AVE
BURNHAM CL
PH
OLD FORGE RD
ST GEORGE'S RD
GOAT LA
Chase Farm
BRIGADIER AVE
GLOUCESTER RD
BRIGADIER HILL
BRODIE RD
WOODLANDS RD
Lavender Prim Sch
Enfield Cty Lwr Sch
BAKER ST
MYDDELTON AVE
ADELAIDE CL
HALSIDE RD
RUSSELL RD
GARNAULT RD
RENDLESHAM RD
CEDAR RD
BLOSSOM LA
CHANTRY CL
BEDALE RD
GLENVILLE AVE
MERTON RD
STERLING RD
HAWTHORN GR
RIDLER RD
EN1
THE RIDGEWAY
LAVENDER GDNS
98
31
32
33

161
148

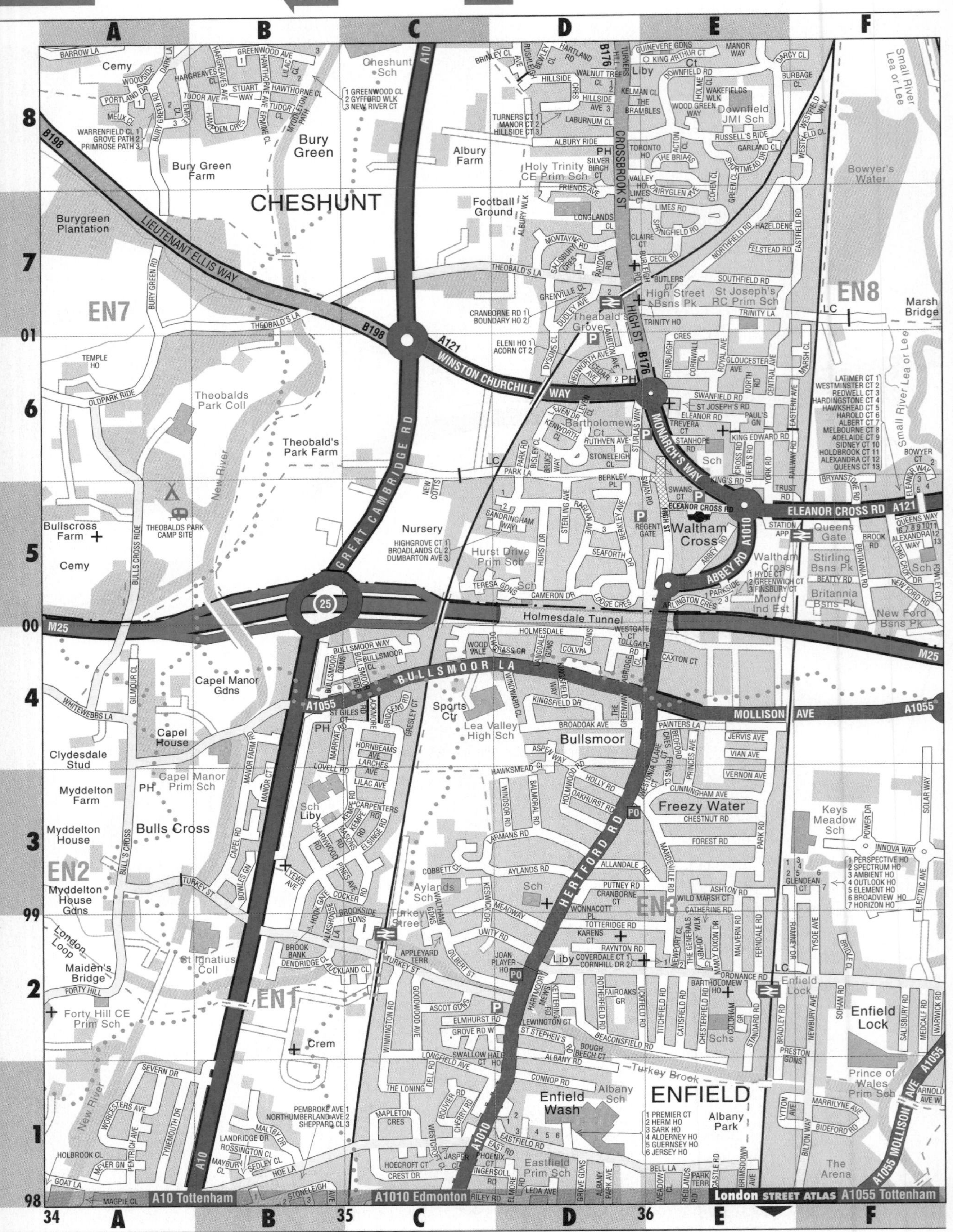
CHESHUNT
Bury Green
Cheshunt Sch
Albury Farm
Bury Green Farm
Burygreen Plantation
LIEUTENANT ELLIS WAY
EN7
EN8
Theobalds Park Coll
Theobald's Park Farm
Bullscross Farm
Cemy
Nursery
Hurst Drive Prim Sch
Waltham Cross
Theobald's Grove
High Street Bsns Pk
St Joseph's RC Prim Sch
Downfield JMI Sch
Holy Trinity CE Prim Sch
Football Ground
Bowyer's Water
Small River Lea or Lee
Marsh Bridge
WINSTON CHURCHILL WAY
GREAT CAMBRIDGE RD
ELEANOR CROSS RD
MONARCH'S WAY
Queens Gate
Stirling Bsns Pk
Britannia Bsns Pk
Monro Ind Est
New Ford Bsns Pk
Holmesdale Tunnel
M25
BULLSMOOR LA
MOLLISON AVE
Capel Manor Gdns
Capel House
Clydesdale Stud
Capel Manor Prim Sch
Myddelton Farm
Myddelton House
Bulls Cross
EN2
Myddelton House Gdns
Sports Ctr
Lea Valley High Sch
Bullsmoor
Freezy Water
HERTFORD RD
Keys Meadow Sch
EN3
Aylands Sch
Turkey Street
St Ignatius Coll
Maiden's Bridge
London Loop
EN1
Forty Hill CE Prim Sch
Crem
Enfield Lock
Turkey Brook
Albany Sch
Enfield Wash
ENFIELD
Albany Park
Prince of Wales Prim Sch
Eastfield Prim Sch
The Arena
New River
A10 Tottenham
A1010 Edmonton
London STREET ATLAS
A1055 Tottenham

161

149

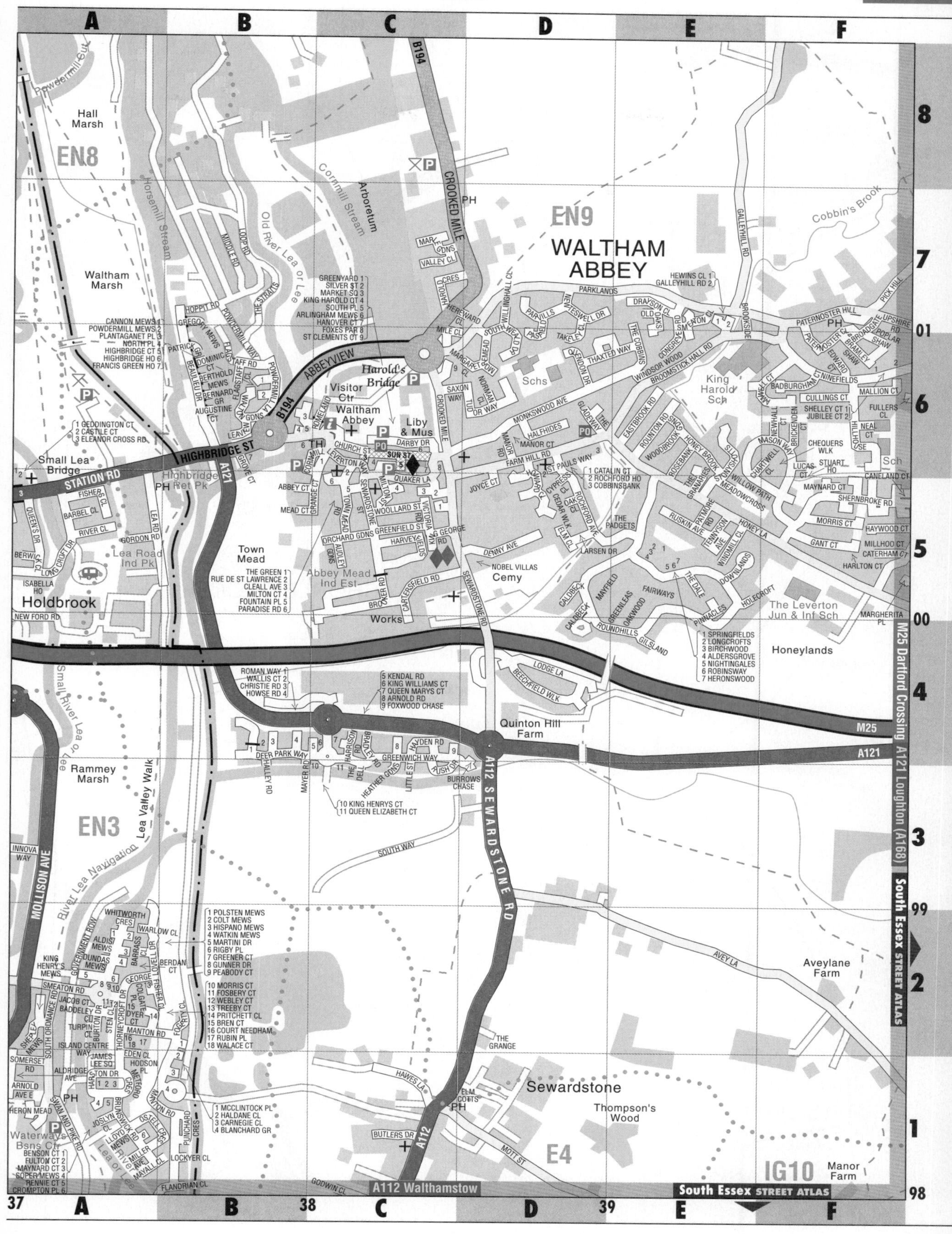
WALTHAM ABBEY
EN9
EN8
EN3
E4
IG10
Hall Marsh
Waltham Marsh
Small Lea Bridge
Holdbrook
Town Mead
Rammey Marsh
Visitor Ctr
Waltham Abbey
Liby & Mus
Harold's Bridge
Arboretum
Schs
King Harold Sch
Cemy
Works
Quinton Hill Farm
Honeylands
The Leverton Jun & Inf Sch
Aveylane Farm
Sewardstone
Thompson's Wood
Manor Farm
Highbridge Ret Pk
Lea Road Ind Pk
Abbey Mead Ind Est
HIGHBRIDGE ST
STATION RD
ABBEYVIEW
CROOKED MILE
SEWARDSTONE RD
A112 SEWARDSTONE RD
M25
A121
MOLLISON AVE
Lea Valley Walk
River Lea Navigation
Cobbin's Brook
AVEY LA
SOUTH WAY
M25 Dartford Crossing A121 Loughton (A168)
A112 Walthamstow

South Essex STREET ATLAS

151

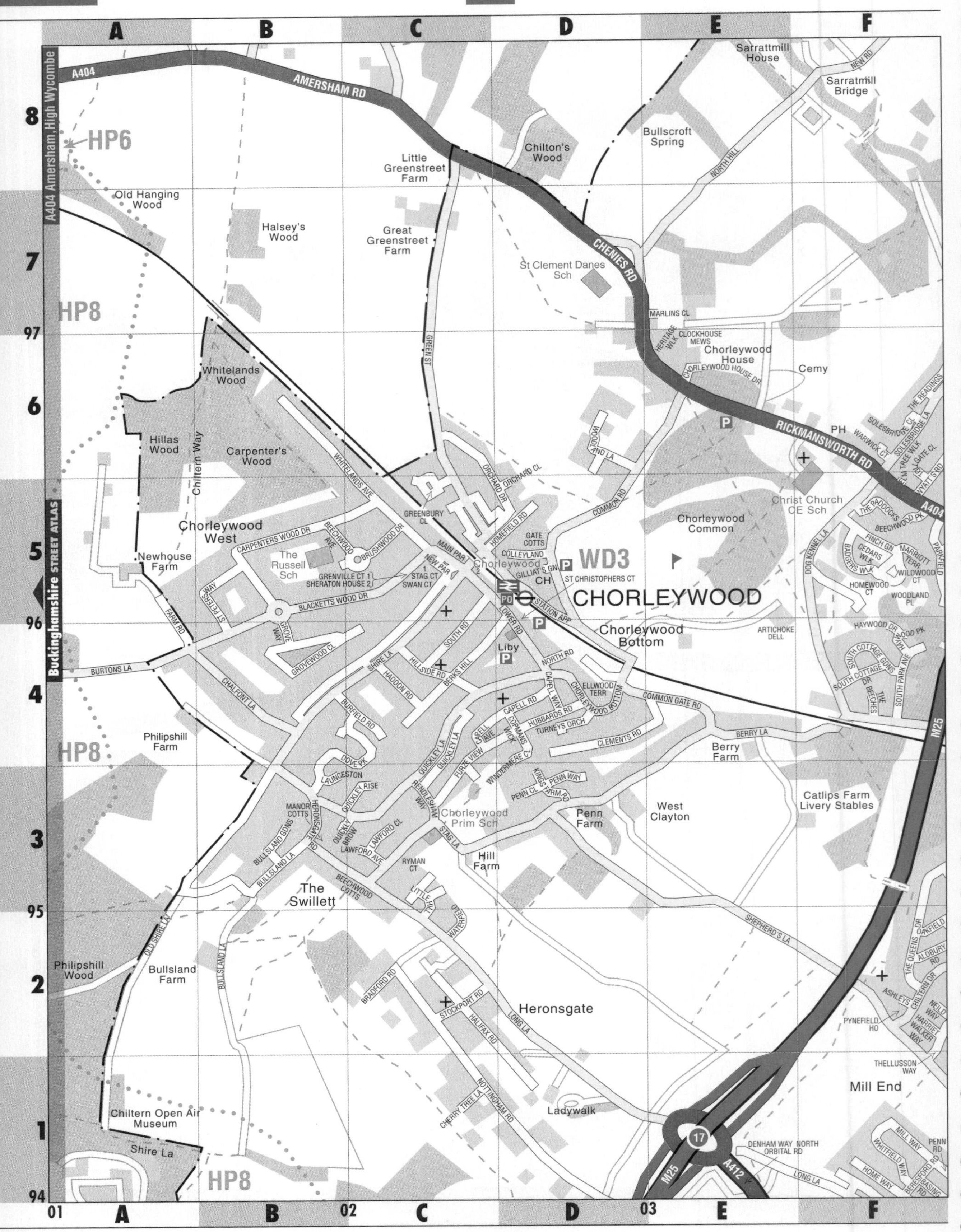
A404 Amersham, High Wycombe
Buckinghamshire STREET ATLAS
A404
AMERSHAM RD
HP6
Old Hanging Wood
Halsey's Wood
Little Greenstreet Farm
Great Greenstreet Farm
Chilton's Wood
Bullscroft Spring
Sarrattmill House
Sarratmill Bridge
NEW RD
NORTH HILL
CHENIES RD
St Clement Danes Sch
HP8
MARLINS CL
HERITAGE WLK
CLOCKHOUSE MEWS
Chorleywood House
CHORLEYWOOD HOUSE DR
Cemy
GREEN ST
Whitelands Wood
Hillas Wood
Chiltern Way
Carpenter's Wood
RICKMANSWORTH RD
PH
Christ Church CE Sch
Chorleywood Common
WHITELANDS AVE
ORCHARD DR
ORCHARD CL
GREENBURY CL
HOMEFIELD RD
GATE COTTS
COMMON RD
Chorleywood West
Newhouse Farm
CARPENTERS WOOD DR
BEECHWOOD AVE
BRUSHWOOD DR
The Russell Sch
GRENVILLE CT
SHERATON HOUSE
STAG CT
SWAN CT
MAIN PAR
NEW PAR
Chorleywood
COLLEYLAND
GILLIAT'S GN
CH
WD3
ST CHRISTOPHERS CT
CHORLEYWOOD
STATION APP
BLACKETTS WOOD DR
ST PETERS WAY
FARM RD
GROVE WAY
GROVEWOOD CL
LOWER RD
Chorleywood Bottom
ARTICHOKE DELL
Liby
SOUTH RD
BURTONS LA
CHALFONT LA
SHIRE LA
HILLSIDE RD
BERKS HILL
HADDON RD
NORTH RD
CAPELL WAY
CHORLEYWOOD BOTTOM
ELLWOOD TERR
COMMON GATE RD
CAPELL RD
HUBBARDS RD
TURNEYS ORCH
CLEMENTS RD
BERRY LA
Berry Farm
Philipshill Farm
BURFIELD RD
DOVE PK
LAUNCESTON
QUICKLEY RISE
QUICKLEY LA
FURZE VIEW
WINDERMERE CL
KINGS FARM RD
PENN WAY
PENN CL
Catlips Farm Livery Stables
West Clayton
Penn Farm
Chorleywood Prim Sch
RENDLESHAM WAY
MANOR COTTS
HERONSGATE RD
QUICKLEY BROW
LAWFORD CL
LAWFORD AVE
STAG LA
BULLSLAND GDNS
BULLSLAND LA
RYMAN CT
Hill Farm
BEECHWOOD COTTS
The Swillett
LITTLE HILL
WATERFIELD
SHEPHERD'S LA
OLD SHIRE LA
Philipshill Wood
Bullsland Farm
BRADFORD RD
STOCKPORT RD
HALIFAX RD
LONG LA
Heronsgate
NOTTINGHAM RD
CHERRY TREE LA
Ladywalk
Chiltern Open Air Museum
Shire La
M25
A412
17
DENHAM WAY NORTH ORBITAL RD
Mill End
THELLUSSON WAY
PYNEFIELD HO
ASHLEYS
CHILTERN DR
THE QUEENS DR
OAKFIELD
ALDBURY RD
HOME WAY
WHITFIELD WAY
BERESFORD RD
BASING RD
PENN RD
MILL WAY
SOLESBRIDGE CL
SOLESBRIDGE LA
WARWICK CL
THE READINGS
WYATT'S RD
THE PADDOCKS
BEECHWOOD PK
FINCH GN
CEDARS WLK
BADGERS WLK
MARRIOTT TERR
WILDWOOD CT
HOMEWOOD CT
WOODLAND PL
PARKFIELD
DOG KENNEL LA
HAYWOOD DR
HAYWOOD PK
SOUTH COTTAGE GDNS
SOUTH COTTAGE DR
THE BEECHES
SOUTH PARK AVE
A B C D E F
8 7 97 6 5 96 4 3 95 2 1 94
01 02 03

172

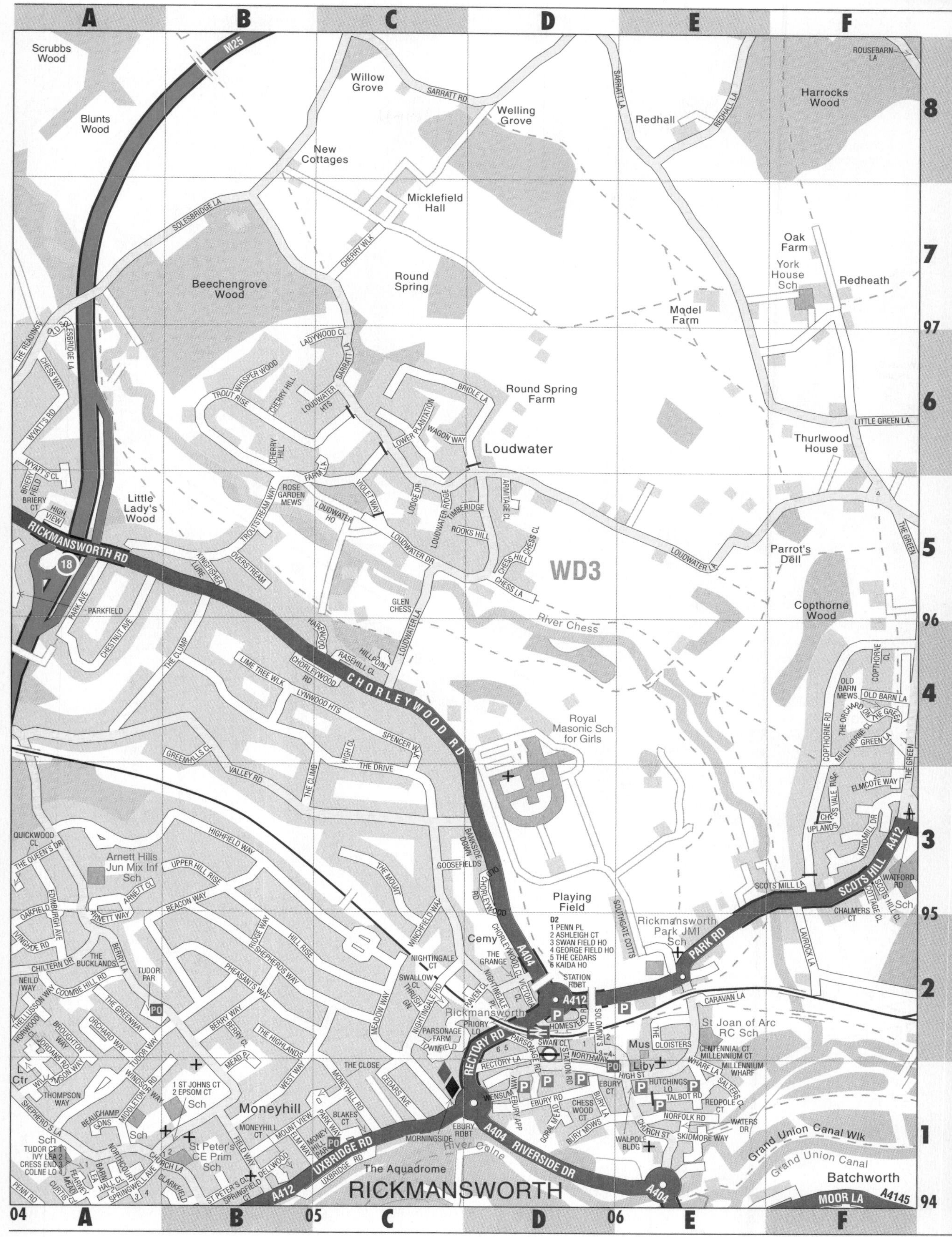
A
B
C
D
E
F
Scrubbs Wood
M25
Blunts Wood
Willow Grove
SARRATT RD
Welling Grove
SARRATT LA
Redhall
REDHALL LA
ROUSEBARN LA
Harrocks Wood
8
New Cottages
Micklefield Hall
SOLESBRIDGE LA
CHERRY WLK
Beechengrove Wood
Round Spring
Oak Farm
York House Sch
Redheath
7
Model Farm
97
THE READINGS
CHESS WAY
LADYWOOD CL
SARRATT LA
WHISPER WOOD
TROUT RISE
CHERRY HILL
LOUDWATER HTS
BRIDLE LA
Round Spring Farm
6
LOWER PLANTATION
WAGON WAY
LITTLE GREEN LA
WYATT'S RD
Loudwater
Thurlwood House
WYATT'S CL
BRIERY FIELD
BRIERY CT
HIGH VIEW
FARM LA
ROSE GARDEN MEWS
VIOLET WAY
LODGE DR
LOUDWATER RIDGE
TIMBERIDGE
ARMITAGE CL
Little Lady's Wood
TROUTSTREAM WAY
LOUDWATER HO
ROOKS HILL
CHESS HILL
CHESS CL
RICKMANSWORTH RD
18
KINGFISHER LURE
OVERSTREAM
LOUDWATER DR
WD3
LOUDWATER LA
Parrot's Dell
THE GREEN
5
CHESS LA
PARKFIELD
PARK AVE
CHESTNUT AVE
GLEN CHESS
Copthorne Wood
River Chess
96
THE CLIMB
HAREWOOD
RASEHILL CL
HILLPOINT
LOUDWATER LA
CHORLEYWOOD RD
COPTHORNE CL
LIME TREE WLK
CHORLEYWOOD RD
LYNWOOD HTS
OLD BARN MEWS
OLD BARN LA
THE ORCHARD
THE GREEN
4
Royal Masonic Sch for Girls
SPENCER WLK
MILLTHORNE CL
GREEN LA
COPTHORNE RD
GREENHILLS CL
HIGH CL
THE DRIVE
VALLEY RD
THE CLIMB
ELMCOTE WAY
VALE RISE
UPLANDS
WINDMILL DR
3
QUICKWOOD CL
THE QUEEN'S DR
HIGHFIELD WAY
BANKSIDE DOWN
THE MOUNT
Arnett Hills Jun Mix Inf Sch
UPPER HILL RISE
GOOSEFIELDS
A412
SCOTS HILL
WATFORD RD
SCOTS MILL LA
ARNETT CL
CHORLEYWOOD RD
Playing Field
OAKFIELD
ARNETT WAY
BEACON WAY
SCOTS HILL CL
COTTAGE CL
Sch
95
EDINBURGH AVE
RIDGE WAY
HILL RISE
WINCHFIELD WAY
D2
1 PENN PL
2 ASHLEIGH CT
3 SWAN FIELD HO
4 GEORGE FIELD HO
5 THE CEDARS
6 KAIDA HO
SOUTHGATE COTTS
Rickmansworth Park JMI Sch
CHALMERS CT
LAURISTON RD
LAVROCK LA
Cemy
IVINGHOE RD
THE BUCKLANDS
SHEPHERDS WAY
NIGHTINGALE CT
THE GRANGE
CHORLEYWOOD CL
A404
PARK RD
CHILTERN DR
BERRY LA
PHEASANTS WAY
SWALLOW CL
STATION RDBT
NEILD WAY
COOMBE HILL RD
TUDOR PAR
THRUSH GN
NIGHTINGALE RD
RAVEN CL
NIGHTINGALE PL
VICTORIA CL
A412
CARAVAN LA
2
PO
P
Rickmansworth
HOMESTEAD RD
SOLOMON'S HILL
THE GREENWAY
BERRY WAY
MEADOW WAY
PRIORY LO
St Joan of Arc RC Sch
HELLUSSON WAY
HORWOOD CL
BROUGHTON WAY
ORCHARD WAY
BERRY CL
THE HIGHLANDS
PARSONAGE FARM
TOWNFIELD
RECTORY RD
PARSONAGE RD
SWAN CL
STATION RD
NORTHWAY
THE CLOISTERS
Mus
CENTENNIAL CT
MILLENNIUM CT
JORDANS RD
MASON WAY
TUDOR WAY
MEAD PL
RECTORY LA
Liby
HIGH ST
WHARF LA
MILLENNIUM WHARF
Ctr
WINDSOR RD
THE CLOSE
HUTCHINGS LO
SALTERS CL
THOMPSON WAY
1 ST JOHNS CT
2 EPSOM CT
WEST WAY
MONEYHILL RD
CEDARS AVE
WENSUM
EBURY APP
EBURY RD
EBURY CT
TALBOT RD
REDPOLE CT
Sch
Moneyhill
BLAKES CT
CHESS WOOD CT
NORFOLK RD
SHEPHERD'S LA
MIDDLETON RD
MONEYHILL CT
MOUNT VIEW
PARK WAY
GORAL MEAD
BURY LA
BEAUCHAMP GDNS
EBURY RDBT
BURY MDWS
CHURCH ST
SKIDMORE WAY
WATERS DR
Sch
A404
RIVERSIDE DR
Grand Union Canal Wlk
1
St Peter's CE Prim Sch
ELM WAY
MONEYHILL PAR
MORNINGSIDE
River Colne
WALPOLE BLDG
Sch
TUDOR CT
IVY LEA
CRESS END
COLNE LO
NORTHCOURT
CHURCH LA
FIELD WAY
DELLWOOD
UXBRIDGE RD
Grand Union Canal
FEARNEY MEAD
BARN LEA
HALL CL
SPRINGWELL AVE
CLARKEFIELD
The Aquadrome
Batchworth
CURTIS CL
PENN RD
ST PETER'S CT
SPRINGFIELD CT
A412
UXBRIDGE RD
RICKMANSWORTH
A404
MOOR LA
A4145
94
04
05
06

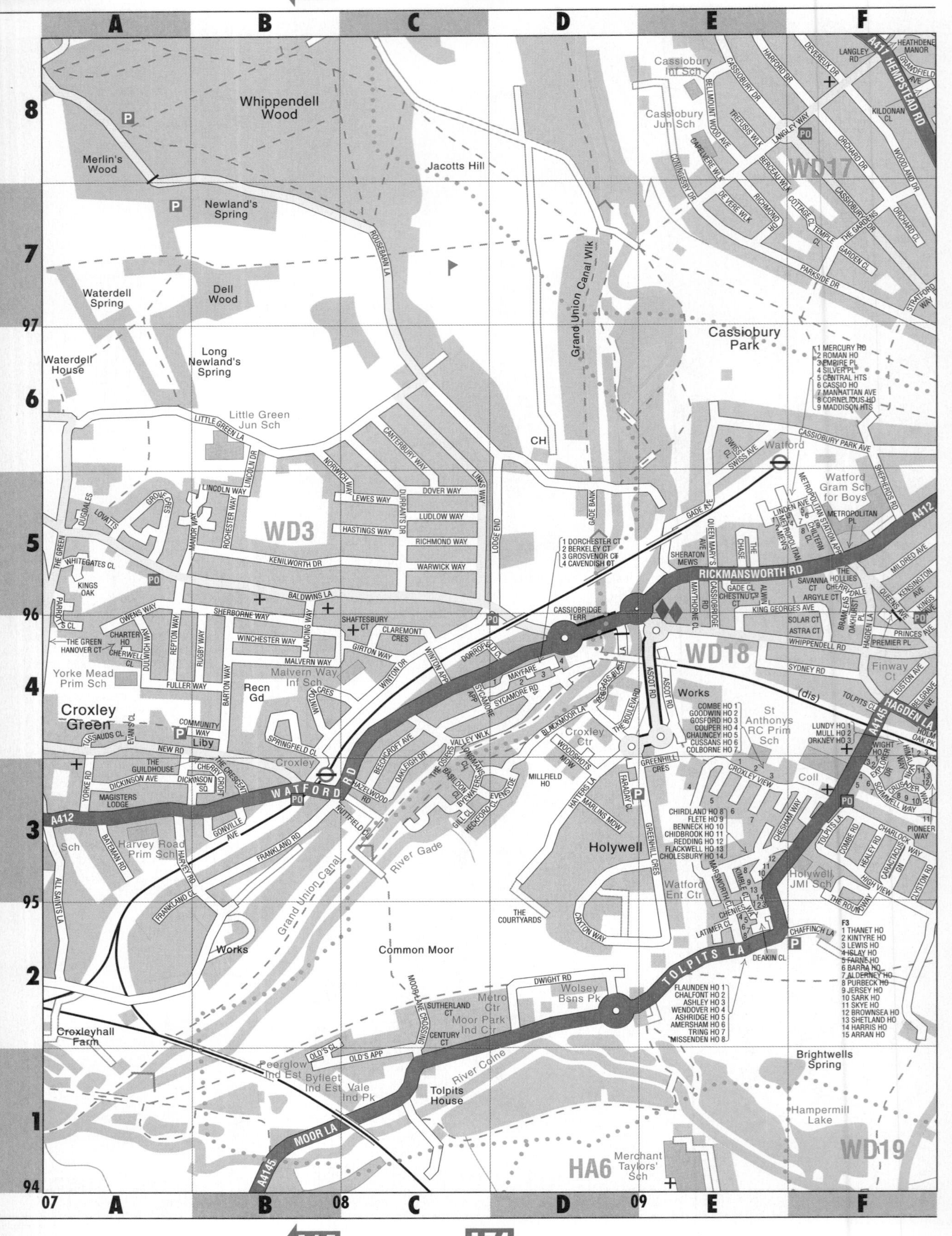

165
153

A B C D E F

8

Whippendell
Wood

Merlin's
Wood

Jacotts Hill

Cassiobury
Inf Sch

Cassiobury
Jun Sch

WD17

HEATHDENE
MANOR

7

Newland's
Spring

ROUSEBARN LA

Cassiobury
Park

97

Waterdell
Spring

Dell
Wood

Long
Newland's
Spring

6

Waterdell
House

Little Green
Jun Sch

LITTLE GREEN LA

CANTERBURY WAY

CH

Watford

Watford
Gram Sch
for Boys

1 MERCURY HO
2 ROMAN HO
3 EMPIRE PL
4 SILVER PL
5 CENTRAL HTS
6 CASSIO HO
7 MANHATTAN AVE
8 CORNELIOUS HO
9 MADDISON HTS

5

WD3

NORWICH WAY

LEWES WAY
HASTINGS WAY

DOVER WAY

LUDLOW WAY
RICHMOND WAY

WARWICK WAY

LODGE END

1 DORCHESTER CT
2 BERKELEY CT
3 GROSVENOR CT
4 CAVENDISH CT

RICKMANSWORTH RD

Metropolitan
PL

A412

96

KENILWORTH DR

BALDWINS LA

SHAFTESBURY
CT

CLAREMONT
CRES

GIRTON WAY

CASSIOBRIDGE
TERR

WD18

SYDNEY RD

WHIPPENDELL RD

Finway
Ct

4

Yorke Mead
Prim Sch

Croxley
Green

Malvern Way
Inf Sch

Recn
Gd

MALVERN WAY

WINTON DR

SYCAMORE RD

MAYFARE

THE BOULEVARD

ASCOT RD

Works

St
Anthonys
RC Prim
Sch

COMBE HO 1
GOODWIN HO 2
GOSFORD HO 3
COUPER HO 4
CHAUNCEY HO 5
CUSSANS HO 6
COLBORNE HO 7

HAGDEN LA

A4145

LUNDY HO 1
MULL HO 2
ORKNEY HO 3

3

Croxley

WATFORD RD

Croxley
Ctr

Millfield
HO

Holywell

GREENHILL
CRES

CROXLEY VIEW

Coll

CHESHAM WAY

CHIRDLAND HO 8
FLETE HO 9
BENNECK HO 10
CHIDBROOK HO 11
REDDING HO 12
FLACKWELL HO 13
CHOLESBURY HO 14

Holywell
JMI Sch

TOLPITS LA

HIGH VIEW

PIONEER
WAY

95

Harvey Road
Prim Sch

FRANKLAND RD

River Gade

Grand Union Canal

THE
COURTYARDS

CAXTON WAY

Watford
Ent Ctr

CHENIES

LATIMER CL

CHAFFINCH LA

F3
1 THANET HO
2 KINTYRE HO
3 LEWIS HO
4 ISLAY HO
5 FARM HO
6 BARRA HO
7 ALDERNEY HO
8 PURBECK HO
9 JERSEY HO
10 SARK HO
11 SKYE HO
12 BROWNSEA HO
13 SHETLAND HO
14 HARRIS HO
15 ARRAN HO

2

Works

Common Moor

MOORHALL CROSSING

DWIGHT RD

Wolsey
Bsns Pk

TOLPITS LA

DEAKIN CL

FLAUNDEN HO 1
CHALFONT HO 2
ASHLEY HO 3
WENDOVER HO 4
ASHRIDGE HO 5
AMERSHAM HO 6
TRING HO 7
MISSENDEN HO 8

Brightwells
Spring

1

Croxleyhall
Farm

Peerglow
Ind Est Byfleet
Ind Est Vale
Ind Pk

OLD'S SE
OLD'S APP

River Colne

Tolpits
House

Hampermill
Lake

WD19

MOOR LA

A4145

HA6

Merchant
Taylors'
Sch

94

07 A B 08 C D 09 E F

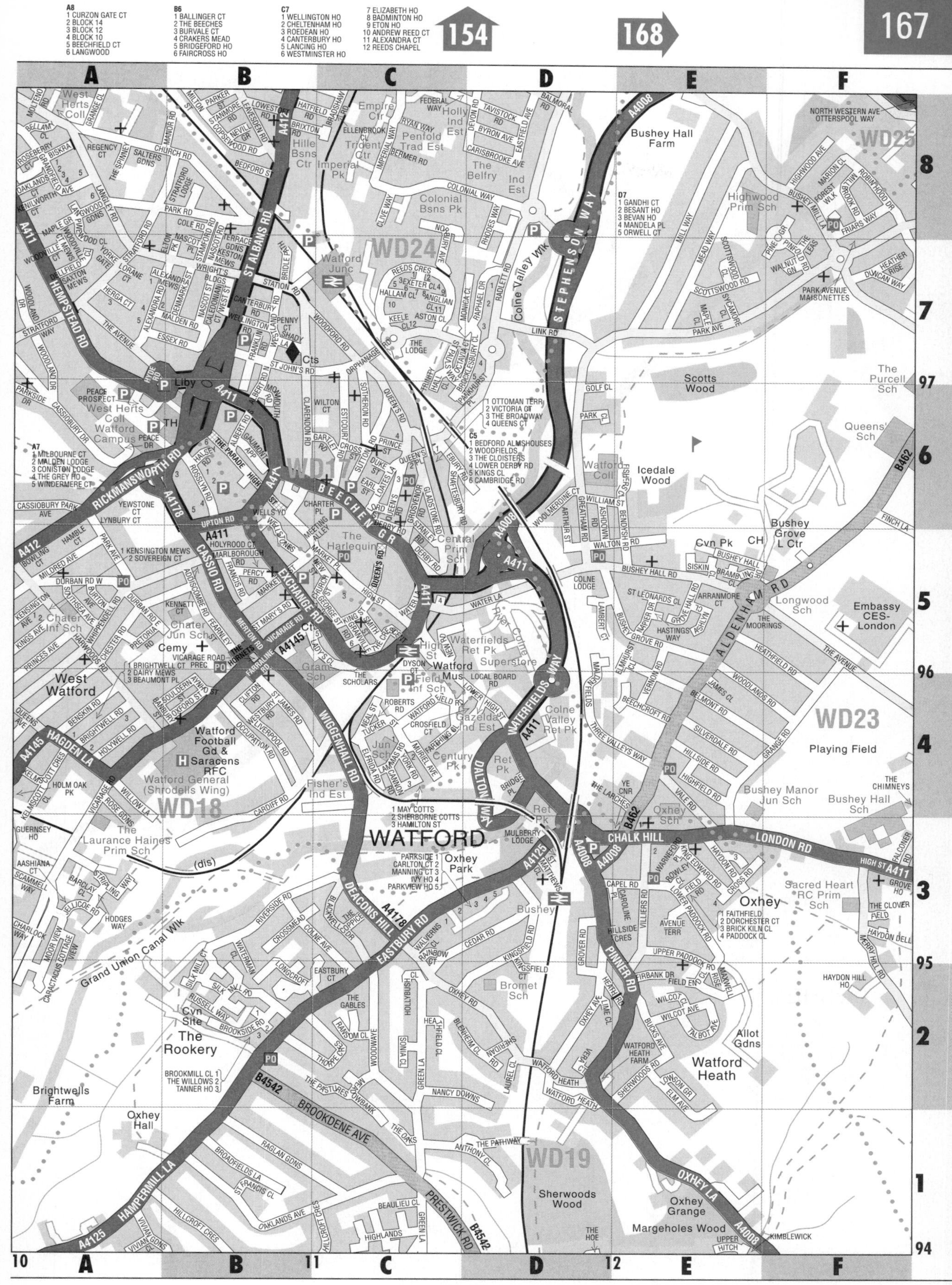

154 ▲
168 ►
168 ►

A8
1 CURZON GATE CT
2 BLOCK 14
3 BLOCK 12
4 BLOCK 10
5 BEECHFIELD CT
6 LANGWOOD

B6
1 BALLINGER CT
2 THE BEECHES
3 BURVALE CT
4 CRAKERS MEAD
5 BRIDGEFORD HO
6 FAIRCROSS HO

C7
1 WELLINGTON HO
2 CHELTENHAM HO
3 ROEDEAN HO
4 CANTERBURY HO
5 LANCING HO
6 WESTMINSTER HO

7 ELIZABETH HO
8 BADMINTON HO
9 ETON HO
10 ANDREW REED CT
11 ALEXANDRA CT
12 REEDS CHAPEL

D7
1 GANDHI CT
2 BESANT HO
3 BEVAN HO
4 MANDELA PL
5 ORWELL CT

A7
1 MELBOURNE CT
2 MALDEN CT
3 CONISTON LODGE
4 THE GREY HO
5 WINDERMERE CT

C5
1 BEDFORD ALMSHOUSES
2 WOODFIELDS
3 THE CLOISTERS
4 LOWER DERBY RD
5 KINGS CL
6 CAMBRIDGE RD

C6
1 OTTOMAN TERR
2 VICTORIA QT
3 THE BROADWAY
4 QUEENS ST

WATFORD

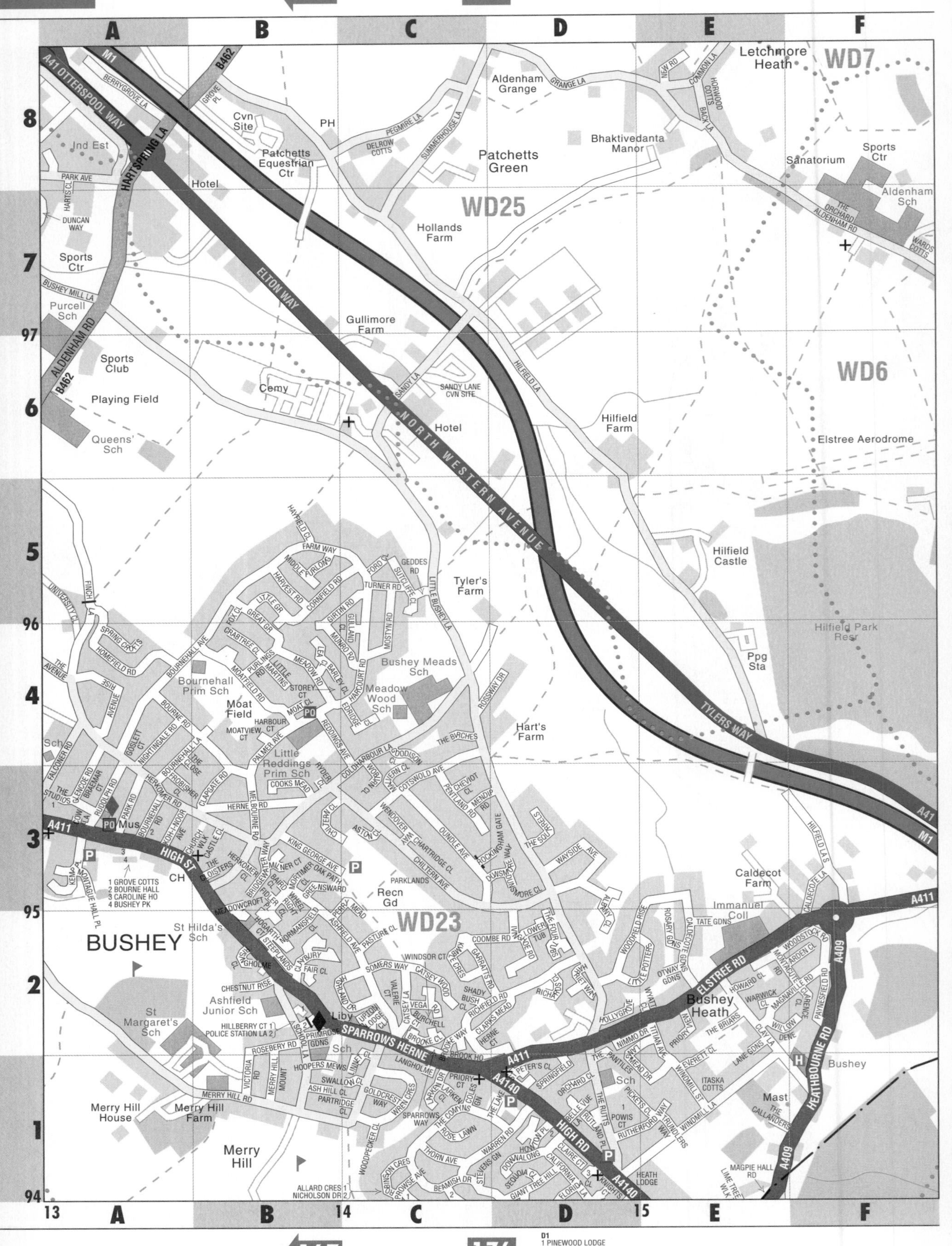

A   B   C   D   E   F

8

7

97

6

5

96

4

3

95

2

1

94

13   A   B   14   C   D   15   E   F

A411 OTTERSPOOL WAY
M1
B462
HART SPRING LA
ELTON WAY
NORTH WESTERN AVENUE
A411
M1
A41
TYLERS WAY
BUSHEY MILL LA
ALDENHAM RD
B462

WD7
WD25
WD6
WD23

Letchmore Heath
Aldenham Grange
Patchetts Green
Bhaktivedanta Manor
Sanatorium
Sports Ctr
Aldenham Sch
Wards Cotts
THE ORCHARD
ALDENHAM RD

Cvn Site
Patchetts Equestrian Ctr
Hotel
PH
DELROW COTTS
PEGMIRE LA
SIMMERHOUSE LA
GRANGE LA
NEW RD
HORWOOD COTTS
COMMON LA
BACK LA

Ind Est
PARK AVE
HARTS CL
DUNCAN WAY
Sports Ctr
Purcell Sch
Sports Club
Playing Field
Queens' Sch

Hollands Farm
Gullimore Farm
Cemy
Hotel
Sandy Lane Cvn Site
SANDY LA
HILFIELD LA
Hilfield Farm
Hilfield Castle
Elstree Aerodrome
Hilfield Park Resr
Ppg Sta

FINCH LA
UNIVERSITY CL
FARM WAY
HAYFIELD RD
MIDDLE CL
AIRLIE
LITTLE GR
HARVEST RD
GREAT GR
CORNFIELD RD
FORD CL
GEDDES RD
SUTCLIFFE RD
LITTLE BUSHEY LA
Tyler's Farm
TURNER RD
BATTLER RD
GILLAND
MONGO RD
Bushey Meads Sch
Meadow Wood Sch
Hart's Farm
THE BIRCHES
ROSEMARY DR
WOODDISON
TYLERS WAY

SPRING CROSS
HOMEFIELD RD
THE AVENUE
Bournehall Prim Sch
Moat Field
MOATVIEW CT
Little Reddings Prim Sch
COOKS MEAD
COLDHARBOUR LA
COTSWOLD AVE
CHEVIOT
PENTLAND
MENDIP
THE SUMMIT

Sch
FALKENER RD
GOSSELT RD
NIGHTINGALE RD
THE STUDIOS
PO Mus
A411
HIGH ST
CH
1 GROVE COTTS
2 BOURNE HALL
3 CAROLINE HO
4 BUSHEY PK
BUSHEY
St Hilda's Sch
St Margaret's Sch
Ashfield Junior Sch
CHESTNUT RISE
HILLBERRY CT 1
Police Station LA 2
Liby
SPARROWS HERNE
Sch
PRIMROSE GDNS
LANGHOLME
King George Ave
OAK PATH
Recn Gd
PARKLANDS
CHILTERN AVE
OUNDLE AVE
ROCKINGHAM GATE
WAYSIDE AVE
Caldecot Farm
Immanuel Coll
TATE GDNS
CALDECOTE RD
HILFIELD LA
A411

ROSEBERY RD
Merry Hill House
Merry Hill Farm
Merry Hill
ALLARD CRES 1
NICHOLSON DR 2
Victoria
MERRY HILL RD
ASH HILL CL
PARTRIDGE CL
WOODPECKER CL
GOLDCREST WAY
WREN CRES
SPARROWS WAY
THE COMYNS
ROSE LAWN
THORN AVE
BEAMISH DR
STEVENS GN
WARREN RD
GIANT TREE HILL
DON A LONG RD
CALIFORNIA CL
HIGH RD
A4140
ELSTREE RD
Bushey Heath
HEATHBOURNE RD
A409
A411
Mast
THE CALLANDERS
Bushey
Magpie Hall Rd
LINE TREE WLK

156
170

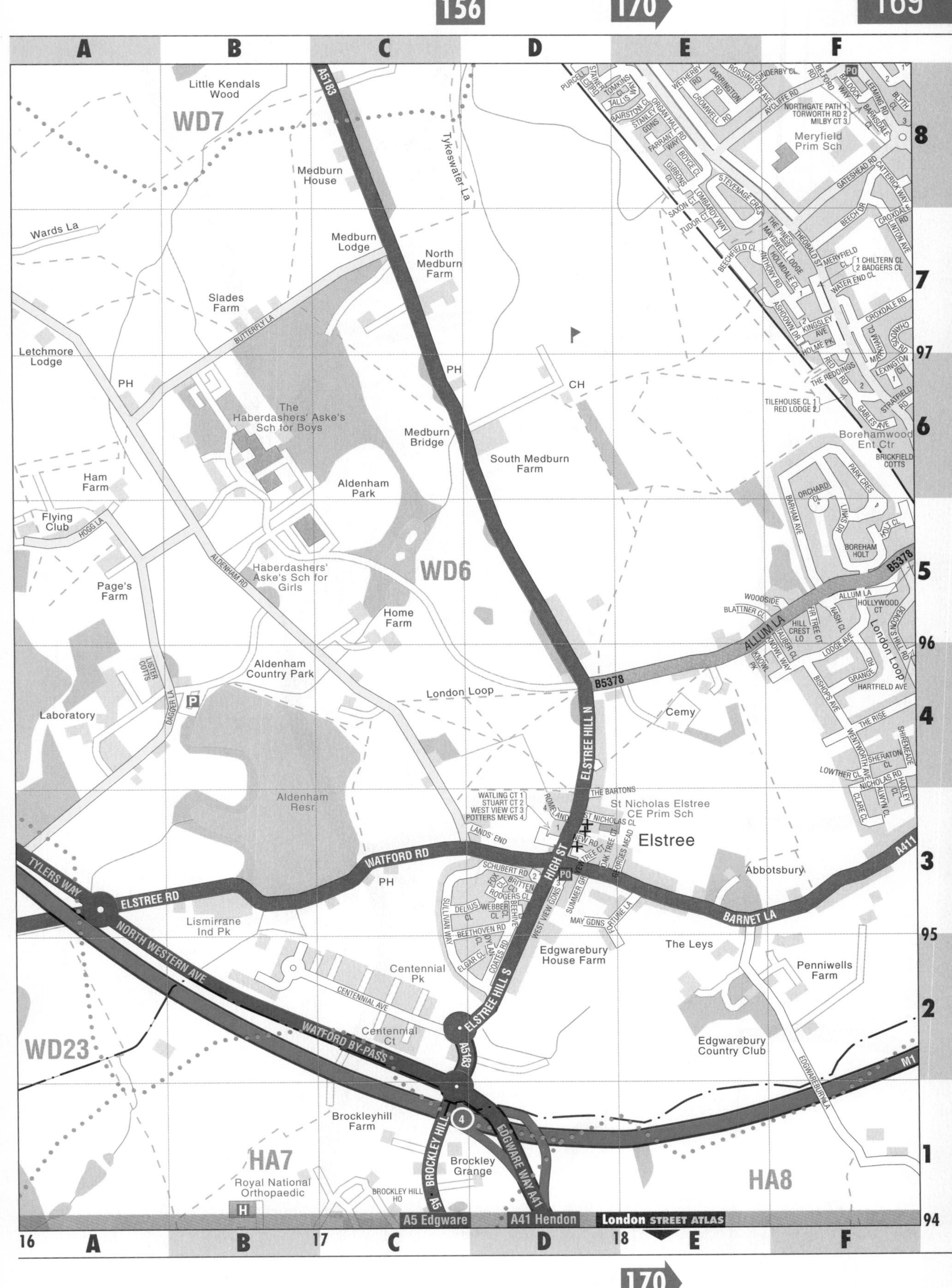
A
B
C
D
E
F
8
7
97
6
5
96
4
3
95
2
1
94
16
17
18
Little Kendals Wood
WD7
A5183
Medburn House
Tykeswater La
Wards La
Medburn Lodge
North Medburn Farm
Slades Farm
BUTTERFLY LA
Letchmore Lodge
PH
CH
The Haberdashers' Aske's Sch for Boys
Medburn Bridge
South Medburn Farm
Ham Farm
Aldenham Park
Flying Club
HOGG LA
ALDENHAM RD
Haberdashers' Aske's Sch for Girls
WD6
Page's Farm
Home Farm
LISTER COTTS
Aldenham Country Park
DAGGER LA
London Loop
Laboratory
B5378
ELSTREE HILL N
Cemy
Aldenham Resr
THE BARTONS
WATLING CT 1
STUART CT 2
WEST VIEW CT 3
POTTERS MEWS 4
St Nicholas Elstree CE Prim Sch
ST NICHOLAS CL
LANDS' END
Elstree
WATFORD RD
HIGH ST
PO
TYLERS WAY
ELSTREE RD
Abbotsbury
A411
SCHUBERT RD
BRITTEN CL
RODGERS CL
DELIUS CL
WEBBER CL
BEETHOVEN RD
ELGAR CL
SULLIVAN WAY
COATES RD
WEST VIEW GDNS
SUMMER GROVE
OAK TREE CT
GEORGES MEAD
MAY GDNS
BARNET LA
Lismirrane Ind Pk
NORTH WESTERN AVE
Edgwarebury House Farm
The Leys
Centennial Pk
CENTENNIAL AVE
Penniwells Farm
ELSTREE HILL S
WATFORD BY-PASS
Centennial Ct
WD23
Edgwarebury Country Club
EDGWAREBURY LA
M1
Brockleyhill Farm
4
BROCKLEY HILL
EDGWARE WAY A41
Brockley Grange
HA7
Royal National Orthopaedic
H
BROCKLEY HILL HO
HA8
A5
Meryfield Prim Sch
NORTHGATE PATH 1
TORWORTH RD 2
MILBY CT 3
WETHERBY RD
DARRINGTON RD
ROSSINGTON AVE
SINDERBY CL
BELFORD RD
BALDOCK WAY
LEEMING RD
BLYTH CL
BARNSDALE CL
AYCLIFFE RD
CROMWELL RD
TALLIS WAY
TOMKINS CL
STAINER CL
PURCELL CL
BAIRSTOW CL
STANLEY GDNS
FARRANT WAY
ORGAN HALL RD
BOYCE CL
GIBBONS CL
SAXON CT
LOMBARDY WAY
TUDOR CT
STEVENAGE CRES
GATESHEAD RD
CATTERICK WAY
BEECH DR
CROXDALE RD
LINTON AVE
THEOBALD ST
THE PINES
MAYOWELL LODGE
HOLMDALE CL
ANTHONY RD
BEECHFIELD CL
MERYFIELD CL
1 CHILTERN CL
2 BADGERS CL
WATER END CL
ASHDOWN DR
KINGSLEY AVE
HOLME PK
THE REDDINGS
RED RD
CHAMPION CL
LEXINGTON CT
STRATFIELD RD
GABLES AVE
TILEHOUSE CL 1
RED LODGE 2
Borehamwood Ent Ctr
BRICKFIELD COTTS
ORCHARD CL
PARK CRES
BARHAM AVE
LINKS DR
HOLT CL
BOREHAM HOLT
WOODSIDE
BLATTNER CL
ALLUM LA
HILL CREST LO
FIR TREE CT
NASH CL
HOLLYWOOD CT
DEACONS HILL RD
London Loop
TAUBER CL
ARNOWL WAY
LODGE AVE
GRANGE RD
HARTFIELD AVE
BISHOPS AVE
THE RISE
WENTWORTH AVE
SHIREHEADE
SHERATON CL
LOWTHER CL
NICHOLAS RD
HADLEY CL
CLARE CL
ALLWYN CL
A5 Edgware
A41 Hendon
London STREET ATLAS

170

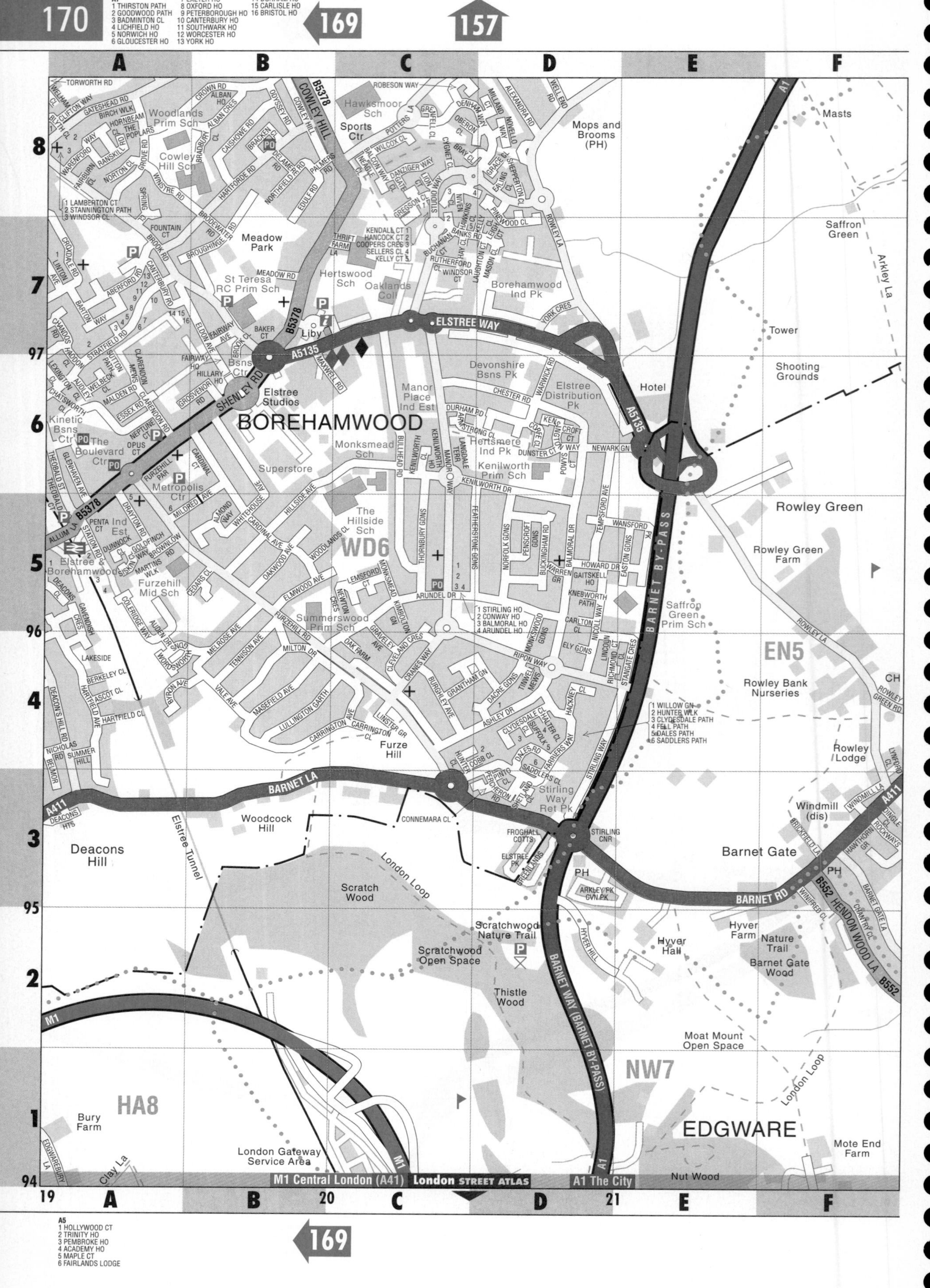

E5
1 HERTSWOOD CT
2 SUNBURY CT
3 MERIDEN HO
4 NORFOLK CT
5 MORRISON CT
6 KINGSHILL CT

7 BARONSMERE CT
8 CHARTWELL CT

E6
1 RICHARD CT
2 ALSTON CT
3 RIDGELEIGH CT
4 BARLETTS COTTS
5 NURSERY ROW
6 HADLEY PAR

7 EXCHANGE BLDGS
8 CHIPPING CL
9 BRUCE RD
10 HART LODGE
11 HOLKHAM HO
12 LEATHERSELLERS CL
13 BRADDON CT

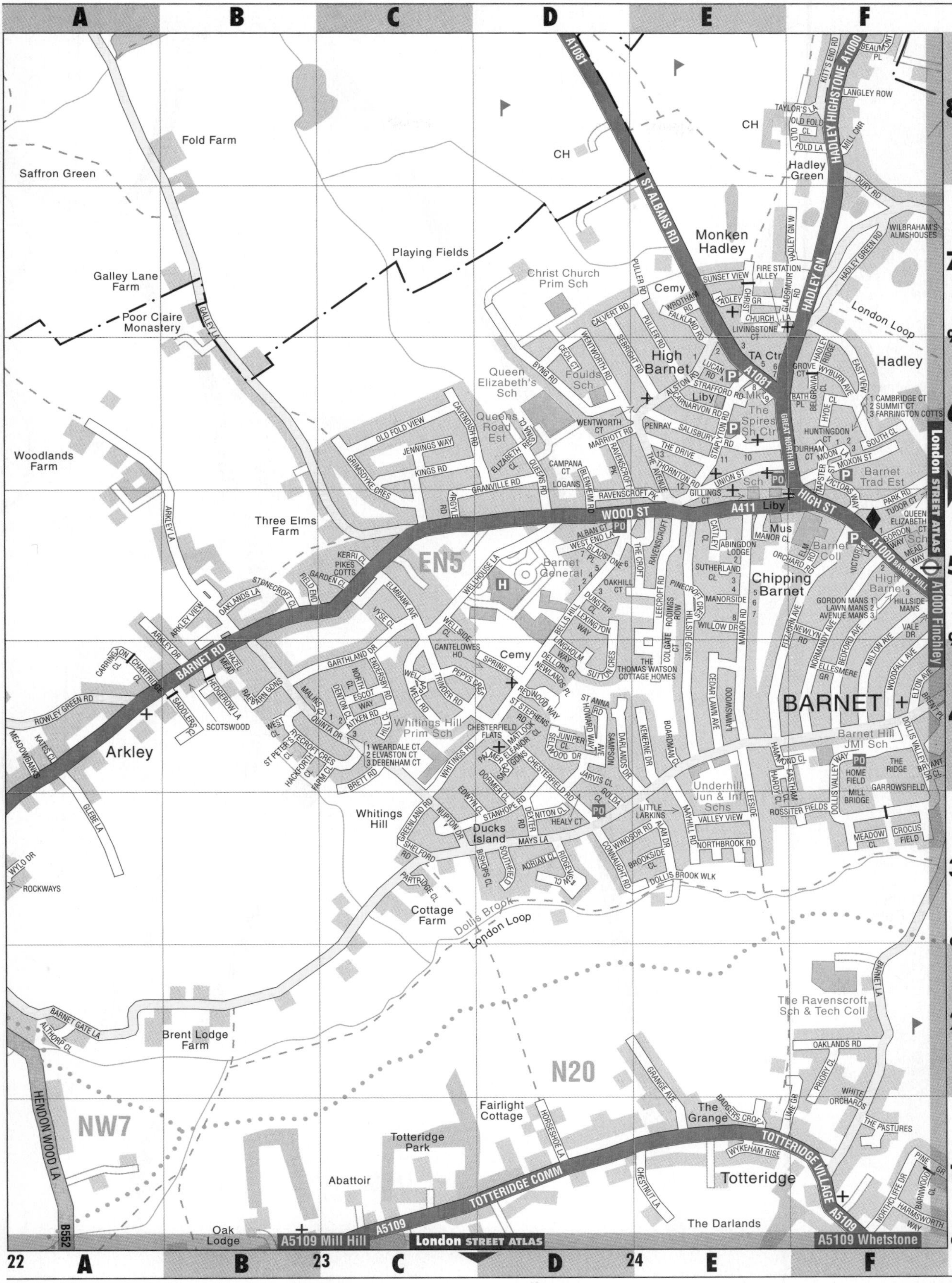

E6
1 CAMBRIDGE CT
2 SUMMIT CT
3 FARRINGTON COTTS

D5
1 BIRNBECK CT
2 WILBURY LODGE
3 CHAUCER HO
4 PINERIDGE CT
5 BYFORD HO
6 OAKMEDE
7 WESSEX CT

London STREET ATLAS

London Street Atlas

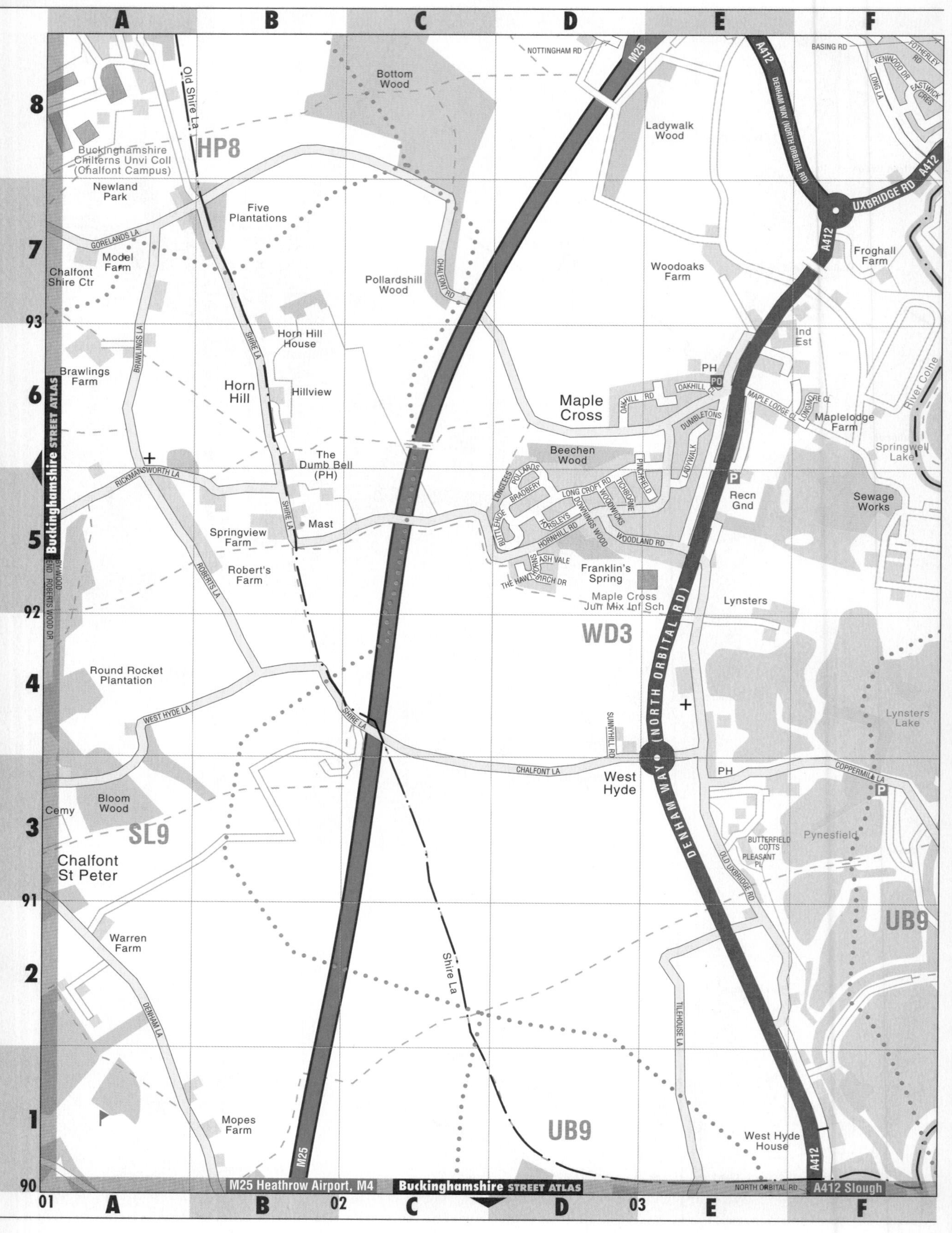

165

174

A B C D E F

8 7 93 6 5 92 4 3 91 2 1 90

Batchworth Lake
The Aquadrome
Bury Lake
Superstore
CH
The Grove
River Colne
Stocker's Lake
Stocker's Farm
St Mary's CE Prim Sch
Juniper Hill
Greenbroom Spring
Andrews Ley Farm
Springwell Farm
Cemy
WD3
Quarry Farm
Springwell Lake
Sixteen Acre Spring
Pipers Farm
Harefield Road Ind Est
Woodcock Hill
Cooks Wood
London Loop
PH
Park Wood
Long Spring
Sewage Wks
Grand Union Canal
Grand Union Canal Wlk
Cripps House Farm
Bishop's Wood Country Park
Weybeards Farm
Pearsons Wood
Hill End
White Heath Farm
Mast
Whiteacres
Harefield Grove
Battlers Wells Farm
Park Wood
UB9
Shepherds Hill Farm
John Penrose Sch
Shepherds Hill House
Harefield
Mount Pleasant
Furzefield
Colney Farm Barns
Schs
Liby
PO
Ashain Spring
Scarlet Spring
HA6
Harefield
Knightscote Farm
Dell

A412 UXBRIDGE RD
A404 CHURCH ST
A4145
MOOR LA
A404
BATCHWORTH HILL LONDON RD
HOME FARM RD
BASING RD
PENN RD
SPRINGWELL AVE
GROVE RD
COLNE AVE
MAXWELL CL
CLARKFIELD
VINE TREE CT
WATERDELL PL
CHURCH LA
MILL STREAM LODGE
COLNE MEAD
THE WILLOWS
1 CURTIS CL
2 DELL CT
3 ARDEN CT
4 SPRINGWELL CT
5 FOTHERLEY RD
6 EASTWICK CRES
FROGMOOR LA
FROGMOOR CT
MOSS CL
HERON CL
RUSHMOOR CL
LANDFORD CL
THE BYEWAY
SHERFIELD AVE
PLAITFORD CL
MALM CL
STOCKERS FARM RD
JUNIPER GATE
JUNIPER CL
HAREFIELD RD
SPRINGWELL LA
HAREFIELD RD
WOODCOCK HILL
SHRUBS RD
SHRUBS
WHITE HILL
JACKETS LA
WATERSIDE MEWS
BANKSIDE CL
LINDEN SQ
CANAL WAY
HERON PL
PLOUGH LA
BELLEVUE TERR
SUMMERHOUSE LA
LONG ROOM
BARRINGTON DR
HILL END RD
RICKMANSWORTH RD
NORTHWOOD RD
COPPER MILL LA
SHELLEY LA
BELFRY AVE
BELFRY VILLAS
ANDERSON CL
MOULT PL
ROMAN CL
PLEASANT
MILNE
SANCTUARY CL
THE LODGE
BARDEN HALL DR
CHAPEL ROW
NEWDIGATE RD
NEWDIGATE GN
NEWDIGATE RD E
SPRINGWOOD CL
NORTHWOOD WAY
NEW PARK RD
ADRIAN CL
VERNON DR
JACKS LA
PARK LA
STAFF COTTS
FALLOWFIELD CL
ASH GR
ASH CL
SPRING CL
MOSSEND CL
LEYS CL
WICKHAM CL
PENZANCE RD
OLIVIA GDNS
SAVOY CL
GILBERT RD
SULLIVAN CRES
KNIGHTSCOTE CL
BREAKSPEAR RD N
DUNSTER CL
HARLAND CT
TAYLOR CT
THE POPLARS
POND CL
MERLE AVE
HIGH ST
LEWIS CL
DEXTER RD
CHILDS AVE
DOVEDALE CL
MORSE CL
WOODFIELD TERR
CHURCH HILL
NEWSTEAD HO
COUNTESS CL
HILL HO

04 A B 05 C D 06 E F

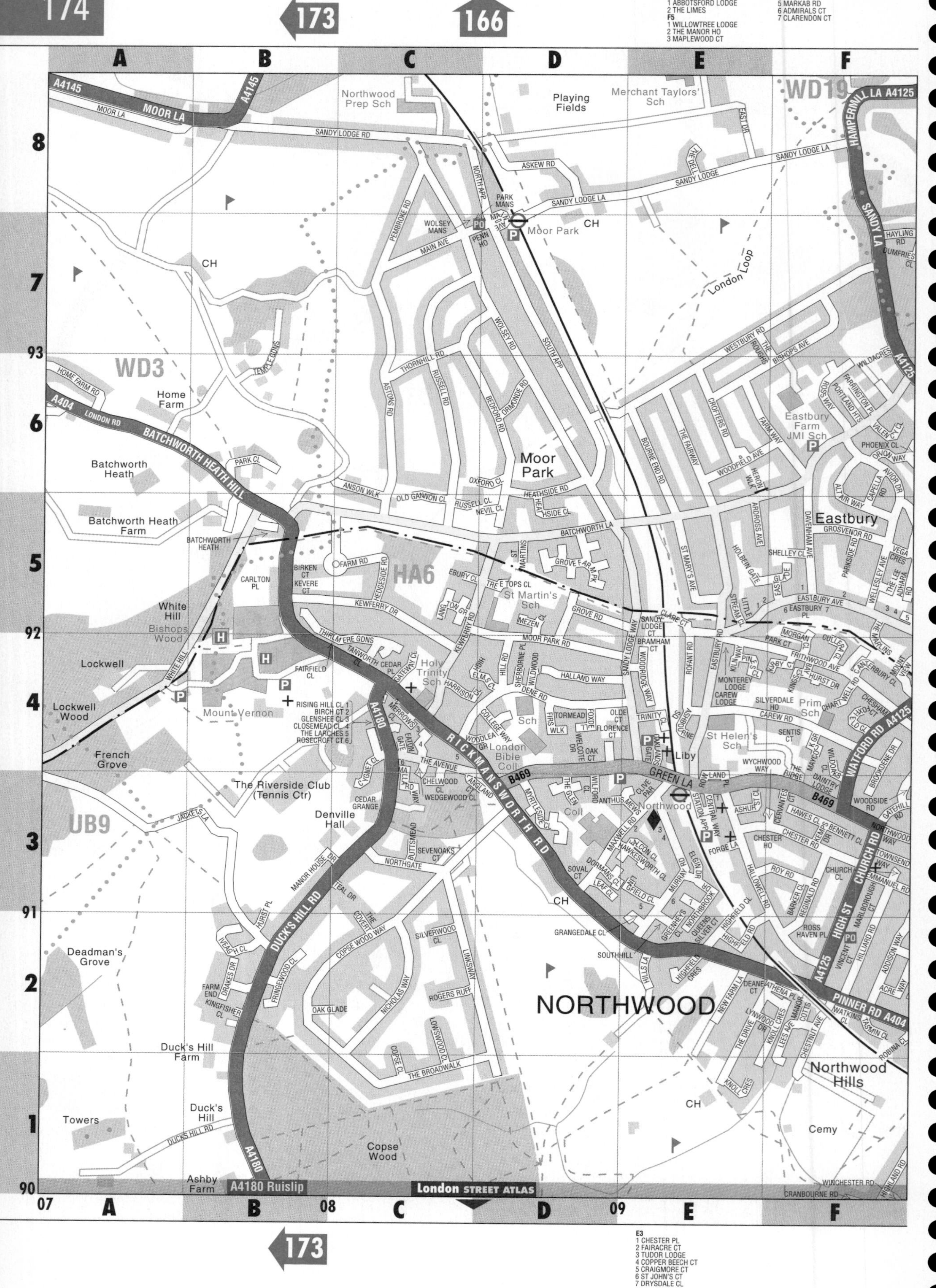

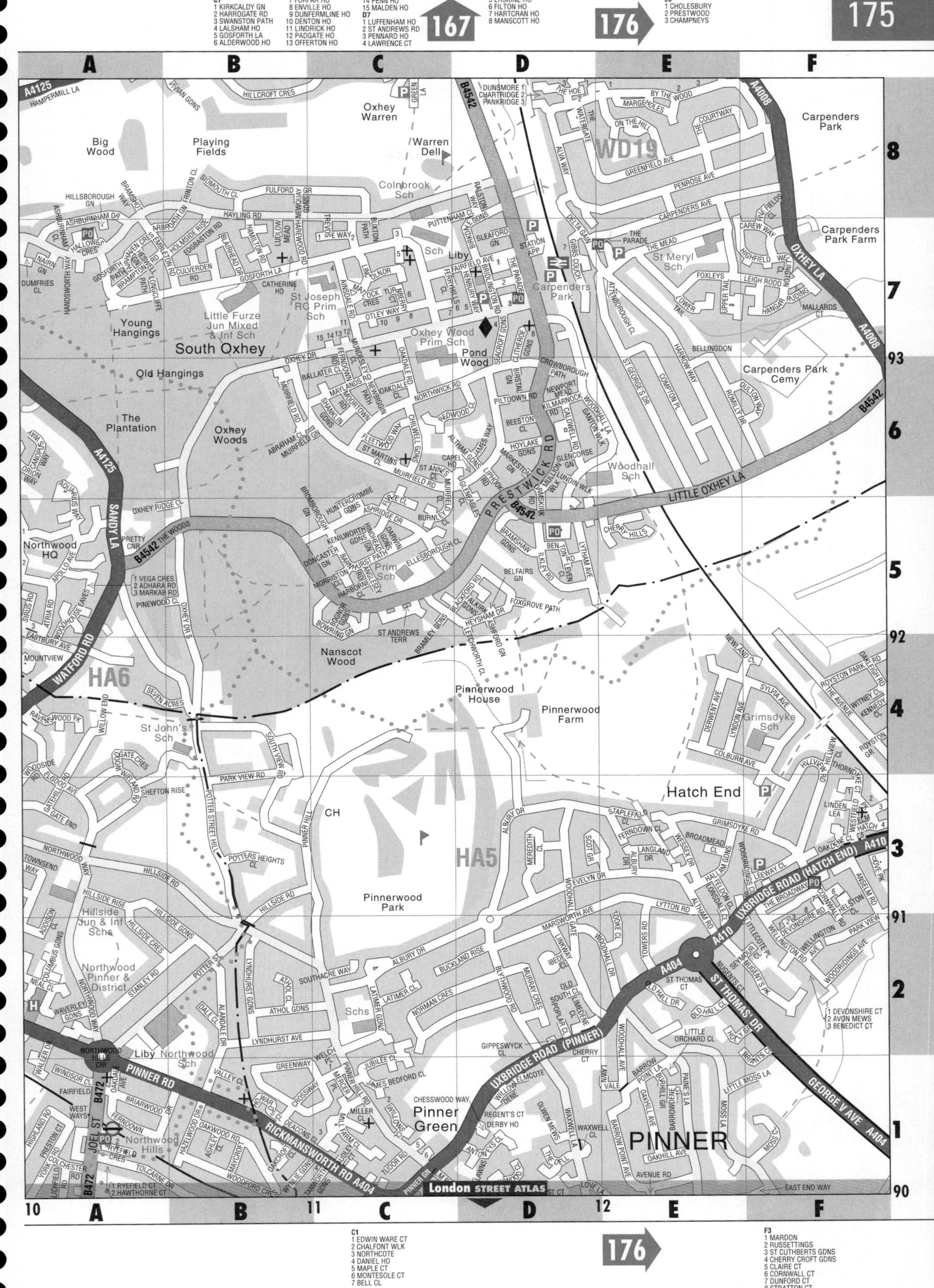

C7
1 KIRKCALDY GN
2 HARROGATE RD
3 SWANSTON PATH
4 LALSHAM HO
5 GOSFORTH LA
6 ALDERWOOD HO
7 FORFAR HO
8 ENVILLE HO
9 DUNFERMLINE HO
10 DENTON HO
11 LINDRICK HO
12 PADGATE HO
13 OFFERTON HO
14 PENN HO
15 MALDEN HO
D7
1 LUFFENHAM HO
2 ST ANDREWS RD
3 PENNARD HO
4 LAWRENCE CT
167
5 ERSKINE HO
6 FILTON HO
7 HARTCRAN HO
8 MANSCOTT HO
176
E8
1 CHOLESBURY
2 PRESTWOOD
3 CHAMPNEYS
A
B
C
D
E
F
Big Wood
Playing Fields
Oxhey Warren
Warren Dell
Colnbrook Sch
WD19
Carpenders Park
Carpenders Park Farm
St Meryl Sch
Carpenders Park
Young Hangings
Little Furze Jun Mixed & Inf Sch
St Joseph RC Prim Sch
Oxhey Wood Prim Sch
Pond Wood
South Oxhey
Old Hangings
Carpenders Park Cemy
The Plantation
Oxhey Woods
Woodhall Sch
Northwood HQ
Prim Sch
Nanscot Wood
HA6
Pinnerwood House
Pinnerwood Farm
St John's Sch
Grimsdyke Sch
Hatch End
CH
HA5
Pinnerwood Park
Hillside Jun & Inf Schs
Northwood Pinner & District
Schs
Liby
Northwood Sch
Northwood Hills
Pinner Green
PINNER
A4125
A4008
B4542
A410
A404
B472
SANDY LA
WATFORD RD
PRESTWICK RD
LITTLE OXHEY LA
OXHEY LA
UXBRIDGE ROAD (HATCH END)
UXBRIDGE ROAD (PINNER)
PINNER RD
RICKMANSWORTH RD
GEORGE V AVE
ST THOMAS' DR
OXHEY DR
HAYLING RD
GOSFORTH LA
CARPENDERS AVE
GREENFIELD AVE
PENROSE AVE
HARROW WAY
ST GEORGE'S DR
COMPTON PL
HILLSIDE RD
MARSWORTH AVE
ALBURY DR
PINNER HILL
POTTER STREET HILL
LYNDHURST AVE
1 VEGA CRES
2 ADHARA RD
3 MARKAB RD
1 DEVONSHIRE CT
2 AVON MEWS
3 BENEDICT CT
1 RYEFIELD CT
2 HAWTHORNE CT
8
7
93
6
5
92
4
3
91
2
1
90
10
11
12
London STREET ATLAS

176

C1
1 EDWIN WARE CT
2 CHALFONT WLK
3 NORTHCOTE
4 DANIEL HO
5 MAPLE CT
6 MONTESOLE CT
7 BELL CL
F3
1 MARDON
2 RUSSETTINGS
3 ST CUTHBERTS GDNS
4 CHERRY CROFT GDNS
5 CLAIRE CT
6 CORNWALL CT
7 DUNFORD CT
8 STRATTON CT
9 HANOVER CT

A B C D E F

8

BUSHEY

WD23

WD19

Nicolson Dr
Hartsbourne Cty Club
Hartsbourne Prim Sch
Hartsbourne Rd

7

Harrow Weald Common

Mutton Wood

Stanmore Common

THE COMMON A4140

Priory Dr
Priory Cl
WARREN LA

A4140 Stanmore

93

Levels Wood

Bentley Priory

COMMON RD

HA7

Deer Park

6

A4008

Valley View Farm

Grimsdyke Hotel

Weald Wood

The Kiln

The Kiln

Heriot's Wood

Priory House

Burnt Oak Farm

CH

Stony Wood

PH

PH

Lower Priory Farm

STANMORE

OXHEY LA

Oxheylane Farm

Copse Farm

Brookshill Dr

Hillside

Bentley Wood High Sch

KEMBLE HO
FLECKER CL

London STREET ATLAS

A4140 Stanmore

5

White Craig Cl
Sadlers Cl

Royston Park Rd
Highlands Ave

BROOKSHILL

Brookshill Ave

Clamp Hill

Harrow Coll Harrow Weald Campus

Harrow Weald Cemy

Bentley Wood High Sch

Kipling Pl

92

HA5

The Bannister Sports Ctr

HA3

Warburton Cl

Lakeland Dr
West Dr
Templars Dr

Harrow Weald Pk

UXBRIDGE RD

Fortnums Acre

4

Meadway
Woodwood Gdns
Sequoia Pk
Pinewoods Ave
Oxhey La

A4008

Birch Pk
Ross Cl

Carrington Sq

Bellfield Ave

West Drive Gdns

Park Dr

Lavender Gdns

Fontwell Cl

3

A410

UXBRIDGE RD (HATCH END)

Hatch End

Superstore

Boniface Wlk
Boniface Gdns
Ufford Cl
Tillotson Rd

Chichester Gdns
Langton Rd

A410

UXBRIDGE RD (HARROW WEALD)

Hutton Wlk
Mepham Cres
Chicheley Rd
Hutton La

Boxtree Rd

Belsize Rd

Recn Gd

Parkview Gdns

High View
Leonard
Superstore

Weald Fst & Mid Schs

91

Hatch End High Sch

Winston Ct

Whittlesea Cl
Whittlesea Path

Stafford Rd

Boxtree La
Colmer Rd
Silver La

Black Well Ct

Harrow Weald

Azure Appartments
Barnview

High Rd

Park Cres

2

Playing Field

Mullion Cl

Shaftesbury High Sch

St Teresa's RC Fst & Mid Sch

St Barnabas Ct

Cedars Fst & Mid Schs

Long Elmes

Weighton Rd

College Ave

Juniper Ct
Willow Ct

College Hill Rd

1

Pinner Park Farm

HA2

Sports Gd

Headstone Lane
Parkfield Ho

Augustine Rd

Parkfield Ave

The Close
Pinner Park

The Rise

Tudor Gdns

HARROW

Whitefriars Trad Est

Belmont Fst & Mid Schs

90

A404 Harrow

London STREET ATLAS

A409 Harrow

TALBOT RD

A3
1 ASHWOOD HO
2 ROSEMARY CT
3 RANDOLPH CT
4 AVON CT
5 CHERRY CROFT GDNS
6 ALDEN MEAD

F3
1 CASTELLANE CL
F4
1 CYGNET HO
2 CORONET HO
3 AMBERDENE
4 KENNETH GDNS

Index

Church Rd **6** Beckenham BR2..........**53** C6

Place name
May be abbreviated on the map

Location number
Present when a number indicates the place's position in a crowded area of mapping

Locality, town or village
Shown when more than one place has the same name

Postcode district
District for the indexed place

Page and grid square
Page number and grid reference for the standard mapping

Public and commercial buildings are highlighted in magenta **Places of interest** are highlighted in blue with a star★

Abbreviations used in the index

Abbreviation	Meaning
Acad	Academy
App	Approach
Arc	Arcade
Ave	Avenue
Bglw	Bungalow
Bldg	Building
Bsns, Bus	Business
Bvd	Boulevard
Cath	Cathedral
Cir	Circus
Cl	Close
Cnr	Corner
Coll	College
Com	Community
Comm	Common
Cott	Cottage
Cres	Crescent
Cswy	Causeway
Ct	Court
Ctr	Centre
Ctry	Country
Cty	County
Dr	Drive
Dro	Drove
Ed	Education
Emb	Embankment
Est	Estate
Ex	Exhibition
Gd	Ground
Gdn	Garden
Gn	Green
Gr	Grove
H	Hall
Ho	House
Hospl	Hospital
HQ	Headquarters
Hts	Heights
Ind	Industrial
Inst	Institute
Int	International
Intc	Interchange
Junc	Junction
L	Leisure
La	Lane
Liby	Library
Mdw	Meadow
Meml	Memorial
Mkt	Market
Mus	Museum
Orch	Orchard
Pal	Palace
Par	Parade
Pas	Passage
Pk	Park
Pl	Place
Prec	Precinct
Prom	Prom
Rd	Road
Recn	Recreation
Ret	Retail
Sh	Shopping
Sq	Square
St	Street
Sta	Station
Terr	Terrace
TH	Town Hall
Univ	University
Wk, Wlk	Walk
Wr	Water
Yd	Yard

Index of localities, towns and villages

A

Abbots Langley 153 F7
Adeyfield 125 A3
Aimes Green 149 F2
Albury 57 A6
Albury End 56 F4
Aldbury 101 C5
Aldenham 155 B3
Aley Green 62 E1
Allen's Green 96 F6
Amwell 115 A6
Ansells End 65 F2
Anstey 29 B6
Apsley End 19 E7
Ardeley 38 F3
Arkley 171 A4
Arlesey 11 A4
Ashley Green 136 A7
Ashwell 4 D3
Ashwell End 4 A5
Aspenden 40 D5
Aston 51 E2
Aston Clinton 99 A3
Aston End 51 E5
Astrope 79 A3
Ayot Green 89 A1
Ayot St Lawrence 88 B6
Ayot St Peter 88 F3
Ayres End 107 E5

B

Babbs Green 94 E5
Baker's End 94 E7
Baldock 23 E8
Ballingdon Bottom 82 F1
Barkway 17 D4
Barley 8 F1
Barleycroft End 43 B4
Barnet 171 F4
Barnet Gate 170 F3
Barwick 73 C3
Bassus Green 52 F8
Batchworth 165 F1
Batford 86 D3
Bayford 132 F6
Bedmond 139 F4
Bedwell 50 E5
Bell Bar 145 A7
Belsize 151 E6
Bendish 66 A7
Bengeo 113 C8
Benington 52 E4
Bennetts End 139 A8
Bentfield Green 59 D8
Bentley Heath 158 F4
Berkhamsted 122 C6
Bernard's Heath 127 F6
Birchanger 59 E2
Birch Green 112 C3
Birchwood 130 B7
Biscot 45 C2
Bishop's Park 76 B6
Bishop's Stortford 76 D7
Blackmore End 87 C6
Blue Hill 70 D5
Borehamwood 170 B6
Botany Bay 160 D3
Botley 136 A1
Bourne End 123 E2
Bovingdon 137 B3
Boxmoor 124 B1
Bragbury End 69 D6
Bramfield 91 C4
Braughing 55 F6
Braughing Friars 56 C5
Breachwood Green 47 E1
Brent Pelham 30 A2
Brickendon 133 C4
Bricket Wood 140 F1
Broad Colney 142 D3
Broadgreen Wood 132 F8
Broadoak End 112 F8
Broadwater 51 A1
Broken Green 56 C2
Brookmans Park 144 F5
Broxbourne 134 F3
Buckland 27 D8
Buckland Common 120 B3
Bulbourne 100 C8
Bulls Cross 162 A3
Bull's Green 90 D7
Bullsmoor 162 D4
Bullstrode 137 E3
Buntingford 40 F7
Burge End 20 D5
Burnham Green 90 C6
Burns Green 52 F2
Bury Green
Bishop's Stortford 75 E7
Bury Green Cheshunt ...162 B8
Bury Park 45 B1
Bushey 168 A2
Bushey Heath 168 E2
Bygrave 13 C5

C

Caddington 62 D3
Cadwell 21 F5
Caldecote 3 C1
Capability Green 63 F4
Chalfont St Peter 172 A3
Chandler's Cross 152 F1
Chapel End 99 C8
Chapmore End 92 D5
Charlton 34 D5
Chatter End 58 C7
Chaulden 123 E2
Chaul End 62 C7
Cheapside 29 B7
Cheddington 80 A8
Chells 51 B6
Chenies 151 B1
Cherry Green 40 C1
Cheshunt 148 C1
Cheverell's Green 83 C4
Childwick Green 107 C2
Chiltern Green 65 B3
Chipperfield 152 B8
Chipping 27 D5
Chipping Barnet 171 F5
Chiswellgreen 141 A5
Cholesbury 120 C2
Chorleywood 164 E5
Chorleywood West 164 B5
Church End Arlesey 11 B7
Church End Little Hadham .57 D2
Church End Pitstone 80 D3
Church End Redbourn ..105 F4
Church End Sarratt 151 F1
Churchgate 148 A1
Churchgate Street 118 F3
Clapgate 57 C6
Clay End 52 F7
Clement's End 82 D3
Clothall 24 E4
Cockernhoe 46 F3
Codicote 67 E1
Codicote Bottom 88 D8
Cold Christmas 94 B6
Cole Green 112 A3
Colliers End 73 A6
Collins Cross 77 B8
Colney Heath 143 D8
Colney Street 141 E1
Commonwood 152 B5
Corey's Mill 36 B2
Cottered 39 C7
Counter's End 124 A3
Cow Roast 101 B1
Cradle End 75 F8
Crafton 60 F4
Crews Hill 161 B4
Cromer 38 D5
Croxley Green 166 A4
Cuckolds Cross 66 D3
Cuffley 146 E3
Cumberlow Green 25 E1
Cupid Green 125 B7

D

Dagnall 81 C6
Damask Green 37 B8
Dancers Hill 158 C3
Dane End 71 F8
Datchworth 69 E2
Datchworth Green 69 C1
Deacons Hill 170 A3
Dewes Green 30 F1
Digswell 89 F4
Digswell Park 89 D1
Drayton Beauchamp 99 C5
Duck End 59 E1
Dudswell 121 D7
Dunstable 44 A1
Dyer's Green 2 B8

E

Eastbury 174 F5
Eastend 116 E1
East End 43 E4
East End Green 112 D2

Easthall 49 B2
East Hyde 85 F8
Eastwick 117 A4
Edgware 170 E1
Edworth 3 A6
Ellenbrook 129 D5
Elstree 169 E3
Enfield 162 E1
Enfield Lock 162 F2
Enfield Wash 162 D1
Epping Green 132 D2
Essendon 131 F6
Eyeworth 1 A8

F

Farley Hill 63 B6
Farnham 58 D6
Farnham Green 58 B7
Felden 138 A8
Fields End 123 D4
Fishers Green 50 A8
Flamstead 84 B1
Flamstead End 148 B4
Flaunden 151 A6
Fleetville 128 B4
Ford End 30 E4
Freezy Water 162 E3
Frithsden 123 B8
Frogmore 141 E4
Frogmore End 138 E7
Furneux Pelham 43 A5
Further Ford End 30 D6

G

Gaddesden Row 104 C6
Gadebridge 124 A5
Ganwick Corner 159 B4
Garston 154 C4
Gaston Green 98 B7
Gilston 117 E5
Goff's Oak 147 C3
Gorhambury 126 C4
Graveley 36 C4
Gravesend 57 B8
Great Amwell 114 F5
Great Ashby 37 D3
Great Chishill 9 F2
Great Gaddesden 103 D3
Great Hallingbury 77 E4
Great Hormead 42 A8
Great Munden 54 C5
Great Offley 33 D2
Great Wymondley 35 F6
Green End Braughing 55 E7
Green End Buntingford 26 D7
Green End Dane End 53 E1
Green End
Hemel Hempstead 124 A2
Green Street
Bishop's Stortford 75 E8
Green Street
Borehamwood 157 B2
Green Tye 75 D1
Grovehill 124 E8
Gubblecote 79 D3
Guilden Morden 1 F4
Gustard Wood 87 D4

H

Hadham Cross 74 E2
Hadham Ford 75 B8
Hadley 171 F6
Hadley Wood 159 C2
Haldens 89 F1
Hall Grove 111 B4
Hammerfield 124 A3
Hammond Street 147 D5
Handside 110 C5
Hanscombe End 19 C8
Harefield 173 C1
Hare Street Buntingford 41 D7
Hare Street Cottered 38 F6
Harlow 117 D2
Harmer Green 90 B5
Harpenden 86 E2
Harpenden Common 107 B7
Harrow 176 E1
Harrow Weald 176 D2
Hart Hill 46 A1
Hastoe 119 F7
Hatch End 175 E3
Hatching Green 107 A6
Hatfield 130 B8
Hatfield Garden Village .129 E8
Hatfield Heath 98 E3
Hatfield Hyde 110 F3
Haultwick 53 F3
Hawridge 120 E1
Hay Green 15 F6

Hazel End 59 A6
Hebing End 53 A2
Hemel Hempstead 124 D6
Henlow 10 D8
Heronsgate 164 D2
Hertford 113 C5
Hertford Heath 114 B3
Hertingfordbury 112 E5
Hexton 19 B2
Higham Gobion 19 A6
High Barnet 171 E6
High Cross 72 F2
Highfield 124 F6
High Town 63 E8
High Wych 97 B1
Hill End 173 B4
Hinxworth 3 C5
Hitchen Hill 34 E5
Hitchin 34 E8
Hockerill 77 A6
Hoddesdon 135 C2
Hogpits Bottom 151 B7
Holdbrook 163 A5
Holwell 21 B7
Holwellbury 10 B1
Holyfield 149 D3
Holywell Watford 166 D3
Holywell Whipsnade 82 B6
Hoo End 66 E4
Hook's Cross 69 F6
Horn Hill 172 B6
Howe Green 77 D2
How Wood 141 B3
Hudnall 102 F7
Hudnall Corner 103 B7
Hunsdon 95 D1
Hunsdonbury 116 D7
Hunton Bridge 153 C6

I

Ickleford 21 E4
Ivinghoe 80 F5

J

Jockey End 103 F8

K

Kelshall 15 D5
Kemprow 155 D3
Kensworth Common 82 E8
Kensworth Lynch 62 A1
Kettle Green 74 C1
Keysers Estate 135 B1
Kimpton 66 C1
Kings Langley 139 A1
King's Walden 48 A3
Kinsbourne Green 85 C5
Kitt's End 158 E1
Knebworth 69 A5
Kneesworth 2 A5

L

Lanes End 119 C4
Langley 49 F1
Langleybury 153 B4
Latchford 73 F5
Latchmore Bank 77 B2
Latimer 150 E3
Leagrave 44 D5
Lea Valley 86 F2
Leavesden Green 153 E5
Ledburn 61 C8
Lemsford 110 A5
Letchmore Heath 168 E8
Letchworth 22 C5
Letty Green 112 B2
Level's End 58 C5
Levens Green 54 C1
Leverstock Green 125 C2
Ley Green 47 F5
Ley Hill 150 B8
Lilley 32 D2
Limbury 44 F5
Little Berkhamsted 132 C4
Little Chalfont 150 B1
Little Chishill 18 E7
Little Gaddesden 102 D7
Little Hadham 57 C2
Little Hallingbury 98 D8
Little Heath
Hemel Hempstead 123 B5
Little Heath Potters Bar . . .145 B2
Little Hormead 42 A6
Little Parndon 117 B1
Little Tring 99 F6
Little Wymondley 35 E3

London Colney 142 E5
Long Marston 79 B3
Loudwater 165 D6
Lower End 79 F3
Lower Green Ickleford 21 E5
Lower Green Meesden 29 E6
Lower Nazeing 149 E8
Lower Sheering 98 A1
Lower Stondon 10 A3
Lower Titmore Green 35 F1
Luffenhall 38 C7
Luton 45 C3

M

Mackerye End 86 F4
Mangrove Green 46 E4
Maple Cross 172 D6
Mardleybury 69 C2
Mark Hall North 118 A3
Mark Hall South 118 A1
Markyate 83 E6
Marshalls Heath 87 A2
Marshalswick 128 B6
Marsh Farm 44 E7
Marsworth 80 A1
Meesden 29 F6
Meldreth 2 F8
Mentmore 61 D4
Meriden 154 E3
Merry Hill 168 B1
Micklefield Green 152 B1
Mill End Buntingford 26 E6
Mill End Rickmansworth . .164 F1
Mill Green 130 E8
Moneyhill 165 B1
Monken Hadley 171 E7
Moor Green 39 D2
Moor Park 174 D6
Mount Pleasant 173 A2
Much Hadham 74 F3

N

Napsbury 142 B5
Nash Mills 139 A6
Nasty 54 D6
Nazeing Marsh 149 A8
Nether Street 95 E5
Nettleden 103 B1
Newgate Street 146 F7
New Greens 127 D7
New Ground 101 A2
New Mill 100 A6
Newmill End 64 D1
Newnham 12 E8
Newsells 17 D7
Newtown 40 F8
New Town
Bishop's Stortford 76 F6
New Town Luton 63 E5
Northaw 146 A1
North End 15 D6
North Mymms 144 A5
North Watford 154 B2
Northwood 174 E2
Northwood Hills 174 F1
Norton 12 C1
Norton Bury 12 C2
Norton Green 50 B3
Nup End 60 B3
Nuthampstead 18 A2

O

Oakfield 35 B6
Oaklands 89 F7
Odsey 5 C1
Old Hall Green 54 F1
Old Harlow 118 D4
Old Hatfield 130 D6
Old Knebworth 68 C6
Old Town 50 C8
Orchard Leigh 136 A3
Oxhey 167 E3
Oxlease 130 B5

P

Painter's Green 69 D2
Panshanger 111 B7
Park Street 141 D5
Patchetts Green 168 D8
Peartree 110 F5
Pegsdon 19 D1
Pepperstock 63 C1
Perry Green 96 B8
Peters Green 65 C3
Piccotts End 124 C7
Pimlico 139 E7

Pin Green 50 F8
Pinner 175 E1
Pinner Green 175 C1
Pirton 20 E4
Pitstone 80 D4
Poplars 51 D3
Potten End 123 C7
Potters Bar 159 D6
Potters Crouch 140 D7
Pottersheath 89 D7
Pouchen End 123 D2
Presdales 114 E7
Preston 48 D6
Puckeridge 55 D3
Pudds Cross 136 E2
Purwell 35 D8
Puttenham 78 E2

R

Rableyheath 68 D3
Radlett 156 C5
Radwell 12 C4
Redbourn 106 B6
Reed 16 F5
Reed End 16 B5
Rickmansworth 165 C1
Ridge 157 F5
Ringshall 81 B1
Roast Green 30 F6
Roe Green Hatfield 130 A6
Roe Green Sandon 26 B8
Roestock 143 E8
Rosedale 148 A3
Round Green 45 F2
Rowley Green 170 F5
Roydon 116 C1
Royston 7 C5
Rucklers Lane 138 E5
Rushden 25 F3
Rusling End 67 D7
Rye Park 135 B7

S

Sacombe 71 E3
Sacombe Green 72 A4
St Albans 127 F4
St Ibbs 35 B2
St Ippolyts 35 B3
St Julians 141 D8
St Leonards 119 E3
St Margarets 115 B4
St Michael's Mead 76 C5
St Nicholas 37 A2
St Paul's Walden 49 B1
St Stephens 127 D1
Sandon 15 B1
Sandridge 108 C1
Sarratt 152 A4
Sarratt Bottom 151 E2
Sawbridgeworth 97 C3
Sewardstone 163 D1
Shaftenhoe End 18 B8
Shaw Green 25 D5
Sheepcote Green 30 F6
Sheering 98 C1
Shenley 157 A5
Shenleybury 156 E8
Shephall 51 B3
Sherrardspark 110 C8
Shillington 19 F8
Shootersway 121 F4
Sleapshyde 129 C2
Slip End 63 C2
Smallford 129 B4
Smith's End 18 A8
Smug Oak 141 B1
Snailswell 21 E6
Sopwell 141 F8
South-end 96 B6
Southern Green 26 A4
South Hatfield 130 B2
South Mimms 158 A8
South Oxhey 175 B7
Spellbrook 97 E8
Spencerswood 119 C7
Spitalbrook 135 A4
Staines Green 112 D4
Stanborough 110 A3
Standon 55 E1
Standon Green End 72 E4
Stanmore 176 F5
Stanstead Abbotts 115 E4
Stansted Mountfitchet . .59 C6
Stapleford 92 A7
Starling's Green 30 F3
Startop's End 79 F1
Steeple Morden 5 B8
Stevenage 50 D8
Stocking Pelham 43 E7
Stopsley 46 B4
Stortford Park 76 C8
Stotfold 11 E7

Streatley 31 A5
Studham 82 C4
Sundon Park 44 E7
Swanley Bar 145 B2
Symonds Green 50 A7

T

Temple Fields 118 A4
Tewin 90 E2
Tewin Wood 90 D5
The Camp 128 B2
The Green 81 F8
Therfield 15 F7
The Rookery 167 B2
The Ryde 130 C8
The Swillett 164 B3
Thorley 76 C3
Thorley Park 76 D5
Thorley Street 76 F3
Throcking 26 F1
Thundridge 93 E7
Titmore Green 35 E2
Todd's Green 36 A2
Tonwell 92 F7
Totteridge 171 E1
Tower Hill 137 F2
Town Park 117 E2
Townsend 127 C6
Trims Green 97 C7
Tring 100 B3
Tringford 99 F7
Tring Wharf 100 B6
Trowley Bottom 105 B8
Turnford 148 E5
Two Waters 138 C8
Tylers Causeway 132 D1
Tyttenhanger 142 E8

U

Upper Dunsley 100 C4

W

Wadesmill 93 D8
Walkern 38 A1
Wallington 25 D8
Walsworth 22 A1
Waltham Abbey 163 D7
Waltham Cross 162 E5
Warden Hill 45 D7
Ware 93 F2
Wareside 94 E4
Warners End 123 F4
Warren's Green 37 D6
Washall Green 30 C1
Waterdale 140 C1
Waterford 92 A2
Watford 167 C3
Watford Heath 167 E2
Watton at Stone 70 D4
Welham Green 144 C7
Well End 157 C1
Wellpond Green 56 D1
Welwyn 89 B4
Welwyn Garden City 110 E7
West End 131 C5
Westland Green 56 E1
West Leith 99 F1
Westmill Buntingford 40 F3
Westmill Hitchin 21 C1
Weston 24 C1
West Watford 167 A4
Westwick Row 125 E2
Wheathampstead 108 C7
Whelpley Hill 136 D5
Whempstead 71 B7
Whippendell Bottom 138 C1
Whipsnade 82 A8
Whitwell 66 E6
Widford 95 E4
Wigginton 100 D1
Wigginton Bottom 120 D8
Wigmore 46 E2
Wildhill 131 D2
Willian 23 B2
Wilstone 79 D1
Wilstone Green 99 D8
Wingrave 60 C3
Winsdon Hill 63 B7
Woodcock Hill 173 D6
Wood End 53 D7
Woodhall 110 E4
Woodside Luton 63 A2
Woodside Watford 154 B7
Woodside 131 A2
Woodside Green 77 F1
Woolmer Green 69 B2
Wormley 148 E8
Wormley West End 147 F8
Wyddial 28 A3

A

Aashiana Ct WD18 167 A3
Abbey Ave AL3 127 B1
Abbey CE Prim Sch The AL1 127 D2
Abbey Ct St Albans AL1 127 D2
Waltham Abbey EN9 163 B5
Abbey Dr
Abbots Langley WD5 154 A7
Luton LU2 46 A1
Abbey Mead Ind Est EN9 163 C5
Abbey Mill End AL3 127 C2
Abbey Mill La AL3 127 C2
Abbey Rd EN8 162 E5
Abbey Sta AL1 127 D1
Abbey Theatre AL1 127 C1
Abbey View Radlett WD7 155 F4
St Albans AL1 127 D1
Watford WD25 154 D3
Abbey View Rd AL3 127 C3
Abbeygate Bsns Ctr The 6 LU2 63 F8
Abbeyview EN9 163 C6
Abbis Orch SG5 21 E5
Abbot John Mews 4 AL4 87 D1
Abbots Ave AL1 141 E8
Abbots Ave W AL1 141 D8
Abbots Cl SG3 69 D1
Abbots Ct LU2 46 A1
Abbots Gr SG1 50 F5
Abbots Langley Sch WD5 139 F1
Abbots Pk AL1 128 A1
Abbots Pl WD6 157 B2
Abbots Rd WD5 139 E1
Abbots Rise WD4 138 F5
Abbots View WD4 138 F4
Abbots Wood Rd LU2 64 A8
Abbotsbury Ct WD25 154 B7
Abbotsford Lodge 1 HA6 174 E5
Abbotswood Par LU2 46 A1
Abbotts Ct SG12 115 C4
Abbotts La SG12 95 D3
Abbotts Rd SG6 22 D6
Abbotts Rise SG12 115 D4
Abbotts Way
Bishop's Stortford CM23 76 E3
Stanstead Abbotts SG12 115 D4
Wingrave HP22 60 A4
Abbotts Yd 1 SG8 7 D6
Abbottsfield Cotts SG12 94 E5
Abdale La AL9 144 C4
Abel Cl HP2 125 A3
Abel Smith Sch SG13 113 D6
Aberdale Gdns EN6 158 F7
Aberdeen Rd HA3 176 F1
Aberford Rd WD6 170 A7
Abigail Cl LU3 45 D3
Abigail Ct LU3 45 D3
Abingdon Lodge EN5 171 E5
Abingdon Pl EN6 159 B7
Abingdon Rd LU4 44 C3
Abinger Cl SG1 50 E3
Aboyne Lodge Jun Mix Inf Sch AL3 127 D4
Abraham Cl WD19 175 B6
Abridge Cl EN8 162 D4
Abstacle Hill HP23 99 F3
Acacia Cl
Hammond Street EN7 147 E4
Stanmore HA7 176 E4
Acacia Gr HP4 122 B3
Acacia Rd EN2 161 D1
Acacia St AL10 130 A2
Acacia Wlk
Harpenden AL5 107 D6
Tring HP23 99 E3
Acacias Ct EN11 135 A6
Academy Ho 4 WD6 170 A5
Acers AL2 141 C3
Achilles Cl HP2 124 F5
Ackroyd Rd SG8 7 E8
Acme Rd WD24 154 B1
Acorn Cl LU2 45 F3
Acorn Ct EN8 162 D6
Acorn Glade AL6 89 F4
Acorn La EN6 146 E2
Acorn Pl WD24 154 A2
Acorn Rd HP3 125 A2
Acorns The AL4 128 D3
Acre Piece SG4 35 A6
Acre Way HA6 174 F2
Acre Wood HP2 124 E2
Acremore St SG11 75 C7
Acrewood Way AL4 128 F3
Acton Cl EN8 162 E8
Acworth Cres LU4 44 C5
Acworth Ct 2 LU4 44 C5
Adam's Yd 1 SG14 113 D6
Adams Ho CM20 117 D1
Adams Way HP23 100 B6
Adamsfield EN7 148 A5
Adderley Rd
Bishop's Stortford CM23 76 F7
Harrow HA3 176 F2
Addington Way LU4 44 D3
Addiscombe Rd WD18 167 B5
Addison Cl HA6 175 A2
Addison Way HA6 174 F2
Adelaide Cl EN1 161 F1
Adelaide Ct EN8 162 F5
Adelaide St Luton LU1 63 D7
St Albans AL3 127 D4
Adele Ave AL6 89 F3
Adeyfield Gdns HP2 124 F4
Adeyfield Rd HP2 124 F3
Adeyfield Sch HP2 125 A3
Adhara Rd HA6 175 A5
Adingtons CM20 117 F2
Adlington Ct LU4 44 C4
Admiral St SG13 114 A6
Admiral Way HP4 121 F6
Admirals Cl AL4 143 E8
Admirals Ct 6 HA6 174 F5
Admirals Wlk
Hoddesdon EN11 135 B4
St Albans AL1 142 A8
Adrian Cl Barnet EN5 171 D3
Harefield UB9 173 D2
Adrian Ho WD5 153 E8
Adrian Rd WD5 153 E8
Adstone Rd LU1 62 F3
Ailsworth Rd LU3 45 A7
Ainsdale Rd WD19 175 C7
Ainsland Ct LU4 44 B2
Aintree Rd SG8 7 F6
Aintree Way SG1 51 C8
Airedale HP2 124 E6
Airfield Ind Est HP23 79 E5
Airfield Way WD25 153 F5
Airport Approach Rd
Luton LU2 64 D7
Luton LU2 64 D8
Airport Executive Pk LU2 64 D8
Airport Way LU1,LU2 64 A5
Aitken Rd EN5 171 C4
Akeman Cl AL3 126 F1
Akeman St HP23 100 A3
Akrill Ho AL5 86 A3
Alamein Cl EN10 134 E3
Alan Dr EN5 171 E3
Alandale Dr HA5 175 B2
Alba Rd CM17 118 C1
Alban Ave AL3 127 D5
Alban Cres WD6 170 B8
Alban Ct Barnet EN5 171 D5
St Albans AL1 128 C3
Alban Ho WD6 170 B8
Alban Pk Ind Est AL4 128 F3
Alban Rd SG6 23 C3
Alban Wood Inf Sch WD25 154 B7
Alban Wood Jun Sch WD25 154 B6
Albanian Ct AL1 128 A2
Albans View WD25 154 B6
Albany Cl WD23 168 D3
Albany Ct Harpenden AL5 107 C8
Luton LU1 63 B8
Albany Mews
Chiswell Green AL2 141 A4
3 Ware SG12 93 E1
Albany Park Ave EN3 162 D1
Albany Pl AL7 110 E6
Albany Rd EN3 162 D1
Albany Sch EN3 162 D1
Albany Terr HP23 100 B6
Albatross Ct SG13 114 B7
Albemarle Ave
Cheshunt EN8 148 C3
Potters Bar EN6 159 B7
Albeny Gate AL1 127 D2
Albert Ct EN8 162 F5
Albert Rd Arlesey SG15 11 A4
Luton LU1 63 E6
Albert Rd N WD17 167 B6
Albert Rd S WD17 167 B6
Albert St Markyate AL3 83 E5
St Albans AL1 127 D2
Stevenage SG1 50 D7
Tring HP23 100 A3
Albion Cl SG13 113 E7
Albion Ct 4 LU2 63 E8
Albion Hill HP2 124 D2
Albion Rd Luton LU2 63 E8
Pitstone LU7 80 D5
St Albans AL1 127 F3
Albion The 9 SG12 93 D2
Albury CE Prim Sch SG11 57 A6
Albury Cl LU3 31 A1
Albury Dr Pinner HA5 175 D3
Pinner HA5 175 E3
Albury Grove Rd EN8 148 D1
Albury Rd SG11 57 C2
Albury Ride EN8 162 D8
Albury Wlk EN8 148 C1
Albyn Ho HP2 124 D3
Alconbury
Bishop's Stortford CM23 59 B1
Welwyn Garden City AL7 111 E6
Alcorns The CM24 59 E7
Aldbury CE Prim Sch HP23 101 C6
Aldbury Cl St Albans AL4 128 C8
Watford WD25 154 D3
Aldbury Gdns HP23 100 B6
Aldbury Gr AL7 111 B6
Aldbury Rd WD3 164 F2
Aldeburgh Cl SG1 36 A1
Alden Mead 6 HA5 176 A3
Aldenham Ave WD7 156 A3
Aldenham Ctry Pk* WD6 169 B4
Aldenham Gr WD7 156 B5
Aldenham Rd
Bushey WD23 168 A6
Elstree WD6,WD25 169 B5
Radlett WD7 156 A4
Watford WD23 167 E5
Aldenham Sch WD6 168 F7
Alder Cl Baldock SG7 23 F7
Bishop's Stortford CM23 76 D4
Chiswell Green AL2 141 C3
Hoddesdon EN11 135 B8
Alder Cres LU3 45 A3
Alder Ct LU3 45 B3
Alder Wlk WD25 154 B4
Alderbury Rd CM24 59 E8
Alderley Ct HP4 122 C3
Alderman Cl AL9 144 C7
Alderney Ho Enfield EN3 162 D1
7 Watford WD18 166 F3
Alders Ct AL7 111 A6
Alders End La AL5 85 F2
Alders Wlk CM21 97 E2
Aldersgrove EN9 163 E5
Alderton Cl 5 LU2 46 D1
Alderton Dr HP4 102 B8
Alderwood Ho 6 WD19 175 C7
Alderwood Mews EN4 159 C1
Aldhous Cl LU3 45 B5
Aldis Mews EN3 163 A2
Aldock AL7 111 A3
Aldock Rd SG1 50 E7
Aldridge Ave EN3 163 A1
Aldridge Ct SG7 12 E1
Aldwick AL1 128 B1
Aldwick Ct AL1 128 B1
Aldwick Rd AL5 107 E8
Aldwickbury Cres AL5 86 D1
Aldwickbury Sch AL5 107 E8
Aldwyck Ct HP1 124 C4
Aldwyke Rise SG12 93 C3
Aldykes AL10 129 F5
Alesia Rd LU3 44 F6
Alex Ct HP2 124 D4
Alexander Ct 2 EN8 148 D1
Alexander Gate SG1 51 C8
Alexander Rd
Hertford SG14 113 A6
London Colney AL2 142 D6
Stotfold SG5 11 F6
Alexandra Ave LU3 45 C2
Alexandra Ct
Cheshunt EN8 162 F5
11 Watford WD24 167 C7
Alexandra Mews WD17 167 A7
Alexandra Rd
Borehamwood WD6 170 D8
Chipperfield WD4 138 A1
Hemel Hempstead HP2 124 D4
Hitchin SG5 21 F1
Sarratt WD3 152 A3
St Albans AL1 127 E3
Watford WD17 167 A7
Kings Langley WD4 139 B1
Alexandra Way EN8 162 F5
Aleyn Way SG7 13 B1
Alfriston Cl LU2 46 C3
Algar Cl HA7 176 F5
Alington La SG6 22 F3
Alison Ct HP2 125 C4
All Saints CE Prim Sch
Bishop's Stortford CM23 77 B8
Datchworth SG3 69 D3
All Saints Cl CM23 77 A8
All Saints Cres WD25 154 D6
All Saints La WD3 166 A3
All Saints Mews HA3 176 E4
Allandale
Hemel Hempstead HP2 124 D5
St Albans AL3 141 B8
Allandale Cres EN6 158 E7
Allandale Rd EN3 162 D3
Allard Cl EN7 147 F4
Allard Cres WD23 168 C1
Allard Way EN10 134 E2
Alldicks Rd HP3 124 F1
Allen Cl Shenley WD7 156 E7
Wheathampstead AL4 108 D7
Allen Ct 2 AL10 130 B3
Allenby Ave LU5 44 A1
Allendale LU3 31 A1
Allerton Cl WD6 156 F1
Allerton Rd WD6 156 F1
Alleyns Rd SG1 50 D7
Allied Bsns Ctr AL5 86 C3
Allis Mews CM17 118 C1
Allison SG6 23 C5
Allton Rd SG16 10 A4
Allum La WD6 169 E5
Allwood Rd EN7 147 F4
Alma Ct
Borehamwood WD6 156 F1
Potters Bar EN6 145 C1
Alma Cut AL1 127 E2
Alma Link 4 LU1 63 D7
Alma Rd
Berkhamsted HP4 121 E6
St Albans AL1 127 E2
Alma Row HA3 176 D2
Alma St LU1 63 D7
Almond Cl LU3 45 B4
Almond Hill Jun Sch SG1 50 E8
Almond Way
Borehamwood WD6 170 B5
Harrow HA2 176 C1
Almond Wlk 1 AL10 130 A2
Almonds La SG1 50 E8
Almonds The AL1 142 B7
Alms La SG7 4 D4
Almshoe Bury Cotts SG4 49 D8
Almshouse La EN1 162 B2
Almshouses SG3 68 B5
Alnwick Dr HP23 78 F7
Alpha Bsns Pk AL9 144 C8
Alpha Pl 4 CM23 76 F8
Alpine Cl SG4 35 A5
Alpine Way LU3 44 D8
Alpine Wlk HA7 176 E8
Alsford Wharf 1 HP4 122 C4
Alsop Cl AL2 142 E3
Alston Ct 2 EN5 171 E6
Alston Rd Barnet EN5 171 E6
Hemel Hempstead HP1 124 A2
Alswick Hall Cotts SG9 41 B8
Altair Way HA6 174 F5
Altham Gdns WD19 175 D6
Altham Gr CM20 117 F3
Altham Rd HA5 175 E3
Althorp Cl EN5 171 A2
Althorp Rd LU3 45 C1
Althorpe Rd AL1 127 F4
Alton Ave HA7 176 F3
Alton Gdns LU1 63 F5
Alton Rd LU1 63 F5
Altwood AL5 86 D1
Alva Way WD19 175 D8
Alverton AL3 127 C6
Alwin Pl WD18 166 E5
Alwyn Cl
Borehamwood WD6 169 F3
Luton LU2 45 E2
Alyngton HP4 121 E7
Alzey Gdns AL5 107 D8
Amberdene 3 HA7 176 F4
Amberley Cl
Harpenden AL5 86 B2
Luton LU2 46 D4
Amberley Gn SG12 93 C4
Amberry Ct CM20 117 D1
Ambient Ho EN3 162 F3
Ambleside Harpenden AL5 86 D2
Luton LU3 44 F5
Ambrose La AL5 85 F4
Amenbury Ct AL5 86 A1
Amenbury La AL5 86 A1
Amersham Ho WD18 166 E2
Amersham Rd WD3 164 B8
Ames Cl Luton LU3 31 A1
Luton LU3 44 F8
Amor Way SG6 23 B6
Amwell Cl WD25 154 E4
Amwell Comm AL7 111 C5
Amwell Ct
Hoddesdon EN11 135 A7
Waltham Abbey EN9 163 E6
Amwell End SG12 93 D1
Amwell Hill SG12 114 F6
Amwell La
Stanstead Abbotts SG12 115 B5
Wheathampstead AL4 108 B7
Amwell Pl SG13 114 C4
Amwell St EN11 135 A7
Amwell View Sch SG12 115 B4
Anchor Cl EN8 148 D3
Anchor Cotts SG12 93 D7
Anchor La
Hemel Hempstead HP1 124 B1
Hemel Hempstead HP1 124 C2
Tonwell SG12 93 B6
Anchor Rd SG7 23 F7
Anchor St CM23 77 A6
Ancient Almhos 4 EN8 148 D1
Anderson Cl UB9 173 A2
Anderson Ho AL4 128 D2
Anderson Rd
Shenley WD7 157 A6
Stevenage SG2 51 D6
Anderson's Ho 3 SG5 34 F8
Anderson's La SG9 29 A1
Andover Cl LU4 44 C6
Andrew Cl WD7 156 F6
Andrew Reed Ct 10 WD24 167 C7
Andrew's La
Cheshunt EN7 148 B3
Goff's Oak EN7 147 F3
Andrews Cl HP2 124 D5
Andrews Lane Prim Sch EN7 148 B3
Andrewsfield AL7 111 C6
Anelle Rise HP3 138 F7
Anershall HP22 60 B3
Angel Cl LU4 44 D3
Angel Cotts SG5 33 D2
Angel Pavement 7 SG8 7 D6
Angell's Mdw SG7 4 D4
Angle Ways SG2 51 B1
Anglefield Rd HP4 122 A4
Anglesey Cl CM23 76 C7
Anglesey Rd WD19 175 C5
Anglian Bsns Pk SG8 7 C7
Anglian Cl WD24 167 C7
Angotts Mead SG1 50 B6
Angus Cl LU4 44 A3
Anmer Gdns LU4 44 B4
Annables La AL5 85 A4
Annette Cl HA3 176 E1
Anns Cl HP23 99 E3
Ansell Ct SG1 36 B1
Anselm Rd HA5 175 F3
Anson Cl Bovingdon HP3 136 F4
Sandridge AL4 108 C1
St Albans AL1 128 B1
Anson Wlk HA6 174 C6
Anstee Rd LU4 44 B6
Anstey Fst Sch SG9 29 A6
Anthony Cl WD19 167 D1
Anthony Gdns LU1 63 D6
Anthony Rd WD6 169 F7
Anthorne Cl EN6 159 B8
Anthus Mews HA6 174 E3
Antoinette Ct WD5 139 F2
Antoneys Cl HA5 175 D1
Antonine Gate AL3 127 A2
Anvil Cl HP3 137 B3
Anvil Ct Buntingford SG9 40 E8
Luton LU3 44 E5
Anvil Ho 8 AL5 86 A2
Apex Point AL9 130 C1
Aplins Cl AL5 86 A2
Apollo Ave HA6 175 A5
Apollo Way
Hemel Hempstead HP2 124 F5
Stevenage SG2 51 C8
Apple Cotts HP3 137 A4
Apple Orch The HP2 124 F5
Appleby St EN7 147 E5
Applecroft
Berkhamsted HP4 121 E6
Chiswell Green AL2 141 B3
Lower Stondon SG16 10 B3
Applecroft Rd Luton LU2 46 C4
Welwyn Garden City AL8 110 B6
Applecroft Sch AL8 110 B5
Appleford's Cl EN11 134 F8
Appleton Ave SG12 94 E5
Appleton Fields CM23 76 E4
Appletree Gr AL3 106 B6
Appletree Wlk WD25 154 B4
Appletrees SG5 34 D6
Applewood Cl AL5 85 E3
Appleyard Terr EN3 162 C2
Approach Rd AL1 127 E2
Approach The EN6 158 F7
Appspond La AL2 140 C8
April Pl CM21 97 F3
Apsley Cl CM23 76 F4
Apsley End Rd SG5 19 E6
Apsley Grange HP3 138 E6
Apsley Ind Est HP3 138 D7
Apsley Manor Farm Barns HP3 138 D5
Apsley Mills Ret Pk HP3 138 E7
Apsley Sta HP3 138 E6
Apton Ct CM23 76 F7
Apton Fields 7 CM23 76 F6
Apton Rd CM23 76 F7
Aquarius Way HA6 175 A6
Aragon Cl Enfield EN2 160 F1
Hemel Hempstead HP2 125 C8
Aran Cl AL5 107 D6
Arbour Cl LU3 31 A1
Arbour The SG13 113 D4
Arbroath Gn WD19 175 B7
Arcade 5 SG5 34 E7
Arcade The Hatfield AL10 130 B6
Letchworth SG6 22 F6
Luton LU4 45 C1
Arcade Wlk 4 SG5 34 E7
Arcadian Ct AL5 86 A2
Arch Rd SG4 35 E4
Archer Cl WD4 138 F2
Archer Rd SG1 51 A6
Archers SG9 40 F8
Archers Cl Hertford SG14 113 C7
Redbourn AL3 106 B5
Archers Fields AL1 127 F5
Archers Green La AL6 111 E8
Archers Ride AL7 111 B4
Archers Way SG6 22 D6
Arches Hall Cotts SG11 73 E5
Archfield AL7 89 E1
Archway Ho AL9 130 C6
Archway Par LU3 44 F4
Archway Rd LU3 44 E4
Arckle Ho EN10 148 F5
Ardeley St Lawrence CE Prim Sch SG2 38 F3
Arden Cl Bovingdon HP3 137 A3
Bushey WD23 168 F2
Arden Ct WD3 173 A8
Arden Gr AL5 86 B1
Arden Pl LU2 45 E1
Arden Press Way SG6 23 B6
Ardens Way AL4 128 D6
Ardentinny AL1 127 E2
Ardleigh Gn LU2 46 E1
Ardross Ave HA6 174 E5
Arena Par SG6 22 F6
Arena The EN3 162 F1
Argent Way EN7 147 D5
Argyle Ct WD18 166 F5
Argyle Rd EN5 171 C5
Argyle Way SG1 50 C5
Argyll Ave LU3 45 C2
Argyll Rd HP2 124 E8
Arkley Ct HP2 125 B8
Arkley Dr EN5 171 B4
Arkley La EN5 171 B5
Arkley Pk Cvn Pk EN5 170 D3
Arkley Rd HP2 125 B8
Arkley View EN5 171 B5
Arkwrights CM20 117 F1
Arlesey Ho SG15 11 A8
Arlesey New Rd SG15,SG6 22 B7
Arlesey Rd Henlow SG16 10 D8
Henlow SG16 10 E8
Ickleford SG5 21 F5
Stotfold SG5 11 E6
Arlesey Sta SG15 11 A8
Arlington Cotts EN6 158 A7
Arlingham Mews EN9 163 C6
Arlington Cres EN8 162 E5
Armand Cl WD17 153 F1
Armitage Cl WD3 165 D5
Armitage Gdns LU4 44 D1
Armour Rise SG4 22 B2
Armourers Cl CM23 76 B4

Armstrong Cl
Borehamwood WD6 .....170 C6
London Colney AL2 .....142 E4
Armstrong Gdns WD7 ..156 E7
Armstrong Pl 1 HP1 ...124 D4
Arncliffe Cres LU2 .....45 E1
Arndale Ctr LU1 ....63 E7
Arnett Cl WD3 ....165 A3
Arnett Hills Jun Mix Inf Sch
WD3 ....165 A3
Arnett Way WD3 ....165 A2
Arnold Ave E EN3 ....163 A1
Arnold Ave W EN3 ......162 F1
Arnold Cl Hitchin SG4 ....35 B8
Luton LU2 ....46 A3
Stevenage SG1 ....36 D2
Arnold Rd EN9 ....163 C4
Arnolds La SG7 ....3 D6
Arran Cl HP3 ....125 C1
Arran Ct LU1 ....63 D7
Arran Ho 15 WD18 .....166 F3
Arranmore Ct WD23 .....167 E5
Arretine Cl AL3 ....126 F1
Arrewig La HP5,HP23 ...119 D1
Arrow Cl LU3 ....44 E6
Art School Yd 6 AL1 ...127 D3
Arthur Gibbens Ct SG1 ..37 A1
Arthur Rd AL1 ....128 B3
Arthur St Luton LU1 ......63 E6
Watford WD23 ....167 D5
Artichoke Dell WD3 ....164 E4
Artillery Pl HA3 ....176 C3
Artisan Cres AL3 ....127 C4
Arts Educational Sch The
HP23 ....100 B3
Arundel Cl Aston SG2 ....51 E3
Cheshunt EN8 ....148 C3
Hemel Hempstead HP2 ...125 B4
Arundel Dr WD6 ....170 C5
Arundel Gr AL3 ....127 D7
Arundel Ho WD6 ....170 C5
Arundel Rd LU4 ....44 F2
Arundell Rd WD5 ....154 A7
Arwood Mews SG7 ....23 F7
Ascent Pk CM20 ....118 A4
Ascot Cl
Bishop's Stortford CM23 ...77 C8
Borehamwood WD6 .....170 A4
Ascot Cres SG1 ....37 B1
Ascot Gdns EN3 ....162 C2
Ascot Ind Est SG6 ....23 B7
Ascot Rd Luton LU3 ......45 B2
Royston SG8 ....7 F6
Watford WD18 ....166 E4
Ascot Terr SG12 ....114 F7
Ascots La AL7 ....110 F2
Ash Cl
Abbots Langley WD5 .....153 D7
Brookmans Park AL9 ....145 A6
Harefield UB9 ....173 D2
Harrow HA7 ....176 F4
Watford WD25 ....154 B4
Ash Copse AL2 ....154 F8
Ash Dr Hatfield AL10 ....130 A2
Hitchin SG4 ....35 A4
Ash Gr Harefield UB9 ....173 D2
Hemel Hempstead HP3 ...138 F7
Wheathampstead AL4 .....87 C1
Ash Groves CM21 ....98 A2
Ash Hill Cl WD23 ....168 B1
Ash Mdw SG10 ....74 F2
Ash Mill SG8 ....17 C3
Ash Rd Luton LU4 ....63 B8
Tring HP23 ....99 F4
Ware SG12 ....94 A3
Ash Ride EN2 ....161 A4
Ash Tree Field CM20 ....117 A2
Ash Tree Rd WD24 ......154 B3
Ash Vale WD3 ....172 D5
Ash Way SG8 ....7 F6
Ashanger La SG7 ....24 D4
Ashbourne Cl SG6 ....23 B3
Ashbourne Ct AL4 ....142 C8
Ashbourne Rd EN10 .....134 F2
Ashbourne Sq HA6 .....174 E4
Ashbrook La SG4 ....35 C3
Ashburnam Wlk SG2 .....50 F1
Ashburnham Cl WD19 ..175 A7
Ashburnham Dr WD19 ..175 A7
Ashburnham Rd LU1 ....63 C7
Ashbury Cl AL10 ....129 E5
Ashby Ct HP2 ....105 B1
Ashby Gdns AL1 ....141 D7
Ashby Rd
Berkhamsted HP4 ....121 D7
Watford WD24 ....154 A1
Ashby Rise CM23 ....59 B1
Ashcombe AL8 ....89 E2
Ashcroft HA5 ....176 A4
Ashcroft Cl AL5 ....107 E8
Ashcroft Ct EN10 ....134 F1
Ashcroft High Sch LU2 ..46 C2
Ashcroft Rd LU2 ....46 B3
Ashdale CM23 ....76 D4
Ashdale Gdns LU3 ....31 A1
Ashdale Gr HA7 ....176 F4
Ashdales AL1 ....141 D7
Ashdown SG6 ....11 F1
Ashdown Cres EN8 ......148 E3
Ashdown Dr WD6 ....169 F7
Ashdown Rd
Stevenage SG2 ....69 B8
Watford WD23 ....167 D6
Ashendene Rd SG13 ....132 F4
Ashfield Ave WD23 .....168 C2
Ashfield Jun Sch WD23 .168 B2
Ashfield Way LU3 ....45 A6
Ashfields WD24,WD25 ...153 F4
Ashford Gn WD19 ....175 D5
Ashfords SG9 ....40 E8
Ashleigh SG2 ....51 B4
Ashleigh Ct
Hoddesdon EN11 ....135 A5
2 Rickmansworth WD3 ...165 D2
Ashleigh Cvn Pk SG11 ...73 C3
Ashley Cl Cheddington LU7 80 A8
Hemel Hempstead HP3 ...124 F1
Pinner HA5 ....175 B1
Welwyn Garden City AL8 .110 C8
Ashley Ct AL10 ....130 B6
Ashley Dr WD6 ....170 D4
Ashley Gdns AL5 ....85 D3
Ashley Ho WD18 ....166 E2
Ashley Rd Hertford SG14 .113 B5
St Albans AL1 ....128 C2
Ashleys WD3 ....164 F2
Ashlyn Cl WD23 ....167 E5
Ashlyns Ct HP4 ....122 B3
Ashlyns Rd HP4 ....122 B3
Ashlyns Sch HP4 ....122 C2
Ashmore Gdns HP3 .....125 B2
Ashridge Cl HP3 ....137 A3
Ashridge College Gdns*
HP4 ....102 D5
Ashridge Cotts HP4 ....102 E5
Ashridge Dr
Bricket Wood AL2 ....140 F1
South Oxhey WD19 ......175 C5
Ashridge Estate Visitor Ctr*
HP4 ....101 E6
Ashridge Ho WD18 ......166 E2
Ashridge La HP5 ....150 D7
Ashridge Management Coll
HP4 ....102 C5
Ashridge Rise HP4 ......121 F5
Ashton Rd Enfield EN3 ..162 E3
Luton LU1 ....63 E5
Ashton's La SG7 ....23 F6
Ashtree Ct AL1 ....127 F3
Ashtree Prim Sch SG2 ...51 C4
Ashtree Way HP1 ....124 A2
Ashurst Cl HA6 ....174 E3
Ashville Way SG7 ....13 A1
Ashwell SG1 ....36 C2
Ashwell & Morden Sta
SG7 ....5 D2
Ashwell Ave LU3 ....44 C8
Ashwell Cl SG4 ....36 B4
Ashwell Comm SG4 ......36 B4
Ashwell Par LU3 ....44 C8
Ashwell Pk AL5 ....86 D1
Ashwell Prim Sch SG7 ....4 D4
Ashwell Rd Bygrave SG7 ..13 C4
Guilden Morden SG8 ....1 F1
Hinxworth SG7 ....3 E5
Newnham SG7 ....12 F8
Ashwell St Ashwell SG7 ....4 D4
Kneesworth SG8 ....2 A3
St Albans AL3 ....127 D4
Ashwell Village Mus*
SG7 ....4 D4
Ashwood Ho 1 HA5 ....176 A3
Ashwood Mews AL1 ....127 D1
Ashwood Pl SG4 ....35 A5
Ashwood Rd EN6 ....159 B6
Askew Rd HA6 ....174 D8
Aspasia Cl AL1 ....127 F2
Aspen Cl
Bricket Wood AL2 ....140 E1
Stevenage SG2 ....69 B7
Aspen Park Dr WD25 ....154 B4
Aspen Way Enfield EN3 ..162 D4
Welwyn Garden City AL7 ..111 C5
Aspenden Rd SG9 ....40 E6
Aspens The
Bishop's Stortford CM23 ...59 B3
Hitchin SG4 ....35 A6
Aspfield Row HP1 ......124 B5
Asquith Ct SG2 ....69 C7
Asquith Ho AL8 ....110 D7
Ass House La HA3 ......176 B6
Astall Cl HA3 ....176 E2
Aster Cl CM23 ....76 D6
Asters The EN7 ....147 D3
Astley Cooper Sch HP2 .125 A8
Astley Gn LU2 ....46 D2
Astley Rd HP1 ....124 C3
Aston Bury SG2 ....69 F8
Aston Cl Bushey WD23 ...168 C3
Stevenage SG1 ....36 C2
Watford WD24 ....167 C7
Aston End Rd SG2 ....51 E3
Aston Grange SG14 .....113 D8
Aston La SG2 ....69 E8
Aston Rd SG11 ....55 D2
Aston Rise SG4 ....35 B6
Aston St Mary's CE Prim Sch
SG2 ....51 E2
Aston View HP2 ....105 A1
Aston Way EN6 ....159 D7
Astonia Ho SG7 ....23 F7
Astons Rd HA6 ....174 C6
Astra Ct Luton LU2 ....45 F2
Watford WD18 ....166 F4
Astra Ctr CM20 ....117 F4
Astral Cl SG16 ....10 B3
Astrope La HP23 ....79 B3
Astwick Ave AL10 ....129 F8
Astwick Manor AL10 ...129 C8
Astwick Rd Stotfold SG5 ...11 F8
Stotfold SG5 ....3 A2
Athelstan Rd HP3 ....138 F8
Athelstan Wlk N AL7 ...110 E5
Athelstan Wlk S AL7 ...110 D5
Athelstone Rd HA3 .....176 D1
Athena Est CM20 ....118 B4
Athena Pl HA6 ....174 F2
Athenia Cl EN7 ....147 B2
Atherstone Rd LU4 ....44 D1
Atherton End CM21 ......97 E3
Athlone Cl WD7 ....156 B3
Athol Cl HA5 ....175 B2
Athol Gdns HA5 ....175 B2
Atholl Cl LU3 ....44 D8
Atria Rd HA6 ....175 A5
Attenborough Cl WD19 .175 E7
Attimore Cl AL8 ....110 B5
Attimore Rd AL8 ....110 B5
Aubretia Ho AL7 ....111 B4
Aubrey Ave AL2 ....142 C5
Aubrey Gdns LU4 ....44 B6
Aubrey La AL3 ....105 E2
Aubreys SG6 ....23 A2
Aubreys Rd HP1 ....123 E3
Aubries SG2 ....38 B1
Auckland Cl EN1 ....162 B2
Auckland Rd EN6 ....158 E7
Auden Dr WD6 ....170 A4
Audley Cl WD6 ....170 A6
Audley Ct HA5 ....175 C1
Audley Gdns EN9 ....163 C5
Audrey Gdns CM23 ......76 F4
Audwick Cl EN8 ....148 E3
Augustine Ct EN9 ....163 B6
Augustine Rd HA3 ......176 C2
Augustus Cl AL3 ....127 A1
Augustus Gate SG2 ......51 D8
Augustus Smith Ho 8
HP4 ....122 D4
Austen Paths SG2 ....51 C6
Austin Mews 6 HP1 .....124 D4
Austin Rd LU3 ....45 C4
Austins Mead HP3 .....137 B3
Austins Pl HP2 ....124 D4
Autumn Glades HP3 ....125 C1
Autumn Gr AL7 ....111 B4
Avalon Cl WD25 ....154 E7
Avebury Ave LU2 ....45 D4
Avebury Ct HP2 ....125 A5
Avenue App WD4 ....139 A1
Avenue Ct AL6 ....89 E7
Avenue Grimaldi LU3 ....45 A3
Avenue Mans EN5 ....171 F5
Avenue One SG6 ....23 C6
Avenue Pl CM23 ....77 A6
Avenue Rd
Bishop's Stortford CM23 ...77 B6
Hoddesdon EN11 ....135 D5
Pinner HA5 ....175 E1
St Albans AL1 ....127 E4
Avenue Rise WD23 ......168 A4
Avenue St Nicholas AL5 .86 A1
Avenue Terr WD19 ......167 E3
Avenue The Barnet EN5 ..171 E6
Bushey WD23 ....167 F5
Harrow HA3 ....176 F2
Hemel Hempstead HP1 ...123 E4
Hertford SG14 ....113 B8
Hitchin SG4 ....35 A7
Luton LU4 ....44 D5
Northwood HA6 ....174 C4
Oaklands AL6 ....89 D7
Pinner HA5 ....175 F4
Potters Bar EN6 ....145 A1
Radlett WD7 ....156 B5
Stevenage SG1 ....50 D8
Stotfold SG5 ....11 F6
Watford WD17 ....167 A7
Avey La EN9 ....163 E2
Avia Cl HP3 ....138 D7
Avior Dr HA6 ....174 F6
Avocet SG6 ....11 E1
Avon Chase SG16 ....10 C4
Avon Cl WD25 ....154 C5
Avon Cotts LU2 ....46 B3
Avon Ct 17 Harpenden AL5 .86 B1
Luton LU1 ....63 C8
4 Pinner HA5 ....176 A3
Avon Dr SG1 ....37 A3
Avon Mews HA5 ....175 F2
Avon Rd SG16 ....10 B4
Avon Sq HP2 ....124 F8
Avondale Ct AL1 ....127 E3
Avondale Rd LU1 ....63 C8
Axe Cl LU3 ....44 E6
Aycliffe Dr HP2 ....124 E7
Aycliffe Drive Prim Sch
HP2 ....124 E7
Aycliffe Rd WD6 ....156 F1
Aydon Rd LU3 ....45 B6
Aylands Rd EN3 ....162 D3
Aylands Sch EN3 ....162 C3
Aylesbury Rd HP23 ......99 E3
Aylott Ct SG14 ....70 D4
Aylotts Cl SG9 ....40 D8
Aylsham Rd EN11 ......135 C8
Aylward Dr SG2 ....51 B7
Aynho St WD18 ....167 B4
Aynsworth Ave CM23 ....59 B2
Ayot Gn Ayot St Peter AL6 .89 A1
Hatfield AL6 ....109 F8
Ayot Ho AL6 ....88 A6
Ayot Little Green La AL6 .88 F1
Ayot Path WD6 ....157 A1
Ayot St Peter Rd AL6 ....88 E3
Ayr Cl SG1 ....51 C8
Ayres End La AL3,AL5 ...107 E5
Aysgarth Cl AL5 ....107 B8
Aysgarth Rd AL3 ....106 A6
Azalea Cl AL2 ....142 B4
Azure Appartments
HA3 ....176 E2

B

Baas Hill EN10 ....134 D2
Baas Hill Cl EN10 ......134 E2
Baas La EN10 ....134 E3
Babbage Rd SG1 ....50 B5
Back La Buckland SG9 ....27 D8
Little Hallingbury CM22 ...98 B7
Preston SG4 ....48 D6
Radlett WD25 ....168 E8
Sheering CM22 ....98 B1
Tewin AL6 ....90 E2
Back St Ashwell SG7 ......4 C3
Luton LU2 ....63 E8
Back The HP4 ....123 B7
Bacon's Yd SG7 ....4 D4
Bacons Dr EN6 ....146 E2
Badburgham Ct EN9 ....163 F6
Baddeley Cl
Holdbrook EN3 ....163 A2
Stevenage SG2 ....51 B2
Bader Cl Stevenage SG1 ...36 F1
Welwyn Garden City AL7 .111 C6
Badger Cl SG3 ....69 A6
Badger Way AL10 ....130 B3
Badgers CM23 ....76 E5
Badgers Cl
Borehamwood WD6 .....169 F7
Hertford SG13 ....114 B6
Stevenage SG1 ....50 E4
Badgers Croft
Barnet HP2 ....171 E1
Hemel Hempstead HP2 ...125 D2
Hoddesdon EN10 ....134 E2
Badgers Ct WD25 ......154 A5
Badgers Wlk
Chorleywood WD3 ......164 F5
Tewin AL6 ....90 C5
Badingham Dr AL5 ....85 E1
Badminton Cl
3 Borehamwood WD6 ...170 A7
Stevenage SG2 ....69 B7
Badminton Ho 8 WD24 167 C7
Badminton Pl EN10 ....134 E3
Bagenal Ho WD5 ....153 F7
Bagwicks Cl LU3 ....44 E7
Bailey Hill Ct LU1 ....63 E5
Bailey St LU1 ....63 F6
Baines La SG3 ....69 C4
Baird Cl WD23 ....168 B3
Bairstow Cl WD6 ....169 E8
Baisley Ho EN7 ....148 A3
Baker Ct WD6 ....170 B7
Baker St Enfield EN1 ....161 E1
Hertford SG13 ....113 E6
Luton LU1 ....63 E5
Potters Bar EN6 ....158 E5
2 Stevenage SG1 ....50 C7
Baker's La SG4 ....67 F1
Bakers Ct 6 CM23 ....77 A7
Bakers Gr AL7 ....111 C7
Bakers La Barley SG8 ......8 F2
Kensworth Common LU6 ...82 E8
Bakers Rd EN7 ....148 B1
Bakers Wlk CM21 ....97 E2
Bakerscroft 1 EN8 .....148 E3
Bakery Ct CM24 ....59 D6
Bakery The 2 SG12 ......93 D2
Bakewell Cl LU4 ....44 C1
Balcary Gdns HP4 ......121 F4
Balcombe Cl LU2 ....46 D4
Balcon Way WD6 ....170 C8
Baldock Ind Est SG7 .....23 F7
Baldock La SG6 ....23 D4
Baldock Rd Aspenden SG9 40 B8
Letchworth SG6 ....23 B5
Royston SG8 ....6 C4
Stotfold SG5 ....12 A5
Baldock St Royston SG8 ....7 C6
Ware SG12 ....93 D2
Baldock Sta SG7 ....12 F1
Baldock Way WD6 ......169 F8
Baldways Cl HP22 ....60 C3
Baldwins AL7 ....111 C6
Baldwins La WD3 ......166 B5
Balfour Ct AL5 ....86 C3
Balfour Mews HP3 ......137 A4
Balfour St SG14 ....113 C7
Baliol Rd SG5 ....34 F8
Ballater Cl WD19 ....175 C6
Ballinger Ct
Berkhamsted HP4 ....122 B3
1 Watford WD18 ....167 B6
Balloon Cnr AL9 ....144 B8
Ballslough Hill SG4 ......66 D1
Balmoral Cl
Chiswell Green AL2 .....141 C3
Stevenage SG2 ....69 C7
Balmoral Dr WD6 ....170 D5
Balmoral Ho WD6 ....170 C5
Balmoral Rd
Abbots Langley WD5 .....154 A7
Enfield EN3 ....162 D3
Hitchin SG5 ....21 E1
Watford WD24 ....154 C1
Balmore Wood LU3 ....31 B1
Balsams Cl SG13 ....113 D4
Bampton Rd LU4 ....44 B2
Bamville Wood AL5 .....107 C5
Banbury Cl LU4 ....44 F4
Banbury St WD18 ....167 B4
Bancroft SG5 ....34 F7
Bancroft Gdns HA3 .....176 C2
Bancroft Rd Harrow HA3 176 C1
Bancroft Rd *continued*
Luton LU3 ....45 B5
Bandley Rise SG2 ....51 C3
Banes Down EN9 ....135 E1
Bank Cl LU4 ....44 C4
Bank Ct HP1 ....124 C2
Bank Mill HP4 ....122 E4
Bank Mill La HP4 ....122 E3
Banks Rd WD6 ....170 C7
Bankside Cl UB9 ....173 A4
Bankside Down WD3 ....165 D3
Bannister Gdns SG8 ......7 E8
Bantel Villas EN11 ......135 C8
Barbel Cl EN8 ....163 A5
Barberry Rd HP1 ....124 A3
Barbers La 2 LU1 ....63 E7
Barbers Wlk HP23 ....99 F3
Barchester Rd HA3 .....176 D1
Barclay Cl
Hertford Heath SG13 ....114 B4
Watford WD18 ....167 A3
Barclay Cres SG1 ....50 E7
Barclay Ct
Hoddesdon EN11 ....135 A5
Luton LU2 ....63 F8
Barclay Sch SG1 ....50 D8
Barden Cl UB9 ....173 C3
Bards Cnr HP1 ....124 B4
Bardwell Ct 6 AL1 ....127 D2
Bardwell Rd AL1 ....127 D2
Barfolds AL9 ....144 C8
Barford Rise LU2 ....46 D1
Barge Ho HP3 ....138 E7
Bargrove Ave HP1 ......124 A2
Barham Ave WD6 ....169 F5
Barham Rd SG2 ....51 C5
Barker Cl HA6 ....174 F3
Barkers Mead
Bishop's Stortford CM22 ...77 B1
Little Hallingbury CM22 ...98 B8
Barkham Cl LU7 ....79 F7
Barking Cl LU4 ....44 B6
Barkston Path WD6 .....157 A1
Barkway CE Fst Sch SG8 17 C4
Barkway Hill SG8 ....17 E6
Barkway Rd SG8 ....7 E5
Barkway St SG8 ....7 D5
Barley Brow WD25 ......154 C8
Barley CE Fst Sch SG8 ....9 A1
Barley Cl WD23 ....168 B4
Barley Croft
Hemel Hempstead HP2 ...125 C3
Hertford SG14 ....113 D8
Stapleford SG14 ....92 A3
Barley Ct EN7 ....148 B1
Barley Hills CM23 ....76 E4
Barley La LU4 ....44 C5
Barley Mow La AL4 .....142 F8
Barley Ponds Cl SG12 ....93 F1
Barley Ponds Rd SG12 ...93 F1
Barley Rd Barley SG8 ......9 A7
Great Chishill SG8 ....9 C2
Barley Rise Baldock SG7 ..24 B8
Harpenden AL5 ....86 C4
Barleycorn The 1 LU3 ..63 D8
Barleycroft
Buntingford SG9 ....40 E6
Stevenage SG2 ....51 D3
Tonwell SG12 ....92 F7
Barleycroft Gn AL8 .....110 C6
Barleycroft Rd AL8 .....110 C5
Barleyvale LU3 ....45 A8
Barlings Rd AL5 ....107 B5
Barmor Cl HA2 ....176 B1
Barmouth Row 6 HP2 .124 E6
Barn Cl
Hemel Hempstead HP3 ...138 F8
Radlett WD7 ....156 A4
Welwyn Garden City AL8 .110 C6
Barn Ct CM21 ....97 E3
Barn Lea WD3 ....165 A1
Barnack Cl SG8 ....7 C7
Barnacres Rd HP3 ......139 A8
Barnard Acres EN9 .....149 E8
Barnard Gn AL7 ....110 F5
Barnard Rd Luton LU1 ....63 A7
Sawbridgeworth CM21 ....97 E4
Barnard Way HP3 ....124 E1
Barncroft SG11 ....57 C7
Barncroft Prim Sch
HP2 ....124 D8
Barncroft Rd HP4 ....121 F3
Barncroft Way AL1 .....128 A2
Barndell Cl SG5 ....11 F6
Barndicott AL7 ....111 C6
Barndicott Ho AL7 ......111 C6
Barnes La WD4 ....138 D3
Barnes Rise WD4 ....138 F4
Barnet By-Pass
Borehamwood WD6 .....170 E5
Dancers Hill EN5 ....158 A3
Barnet Coll EN5 ....171 F5
Barnet Gate La EN5 .....170 F3
Barnet General Hospl
EN5 ....171 D5
Barnet Hill EN5 ....171 F5
Barnet Hill Jun Mix Inf Sch
EN5 ....171 F4
Barnet La
Borehamwood WD6 .....170 B3
Totteridge EN5,N20 .....171 F2
Barnet Mus* EN5 ....171 E5
Barnet Rd Barnet EN5 ...170 E3
Ganwick Corner EN6,EN5 .159 A4
London Colney AL2 ......142 F4
Barnet Stall Market
EN5 ....171 E6
Barnet Trad Est EN5 ....171 F6

Barnet Way (Barnet By-Pass) NW7 170 D2
Barnfield HP3 138 F8
Barnfield Ave LU2 45 D5
Barnfield Cl
Hoddesdon EN11 135 A8
Lower Nazeing EN9 135 F1
Barnfield Coll LU3 45 B8
Barnfield Coll (North)
Luton LU2 63 F8
Luton,Stopsley Common LU2 45 D5
Barnfield Coll (South) LU1 63 B5
Barnfield Ct AL5 107 C8
Barnfield Rd
Harpenden AL5 107 C8
St Albans AL4 128 C5
Welwyn Garden City AL7 110 E4
Barnhurst Path WD19 175 C5
Barns Dene AL5 85 E2
Barns The HP23 99 F1
Barnsdale Cl WD6 169 F8
Barnside Ct AL8 110 C6
Barnston Cl LU2 46 D1
Barnsway WD4 138 E3
Barnview Lo HA3 176 E2
Barnwell SG2 51 B2
Barnwell Sch SG2 51 B2
Barnwood Cl N20 171 F1
Baron Ct SG1 36 B1
Barons Ct 7 LU2 45 D1
Barons The CM23 76 D5
Baronsmere Ct 7 EN5 171 E5
Barr Rd EN6 159 C6
Barra Cl HP3 139 C8
Barra Ho 6 WD18 166 F3
Barrass Cl EN3 163 A2
Barratt Ind Pk LU2 64 C6
Barratt Way HA3 176 D1
Barrells Down Rd CM23 58 E1
Barrett La 5 CM23 76 F7
Barrington Dr UB9 173 A3
Barrington Mews AL7 111 B5
Barrington Rd SG6 22 F4
Barrons Row AL5 107 D7
Barrow La EN7 147 F1
Barrow Point Ave HA5 175 E1
Barrow Point La HA5 175 E1
Barrowby Cl LU2 46 D1
Barrowdene Cl HA5 175 E1
Barry Cl AL2 141 B6
Barry Ct SG1 50 B8
Bartel Cl HP3 125 D1
Bartholomew Court Sh Pavilion EN8 162 E6
Bartholomew Ho EN3 162 E2
Bartholomew Rd 8 CM23 76 F6
Bartletts Cotts 4 EN5 171 E6
Bartletts Mead SG14 92 D1
Barton Cl AL5 86 C3
Barton Rd Hexton SG5 19 A1
Luton LU3 45 C7
Wheathampstead AL4 108 C8
Barton Way
Borehamwood WD6 170 A7
Croxley Green WD3 166 B4
Bartons The WD6 169 D3
Bartrams La EN4 159 C1
Bartrop Cl EN7 147 D3
Bartrum Villas 4 HP4 122 D4
Barwick La SG11 73 C3
Basbow La 2 CM23 76 F7
Basil Mews CM17 118 C1
Basildon Cl WD18 166 C3
Basildon Sq HP2 124 F7
Basils Rd SG1 50 D7
Baslow Cl HA3 176 D2
Bassett Cl AL3 106 B5
Bassil Rd HP2 124 D2
Bassingbourne Cl EN10 134 F3
Bassingburn Wlk AL7 110 F5
Bassus Gn SG2 52 F8
Batchelors SG11 55 E2
Batchwood Dr AL3 127 C6
Batchwood Gdns AL3 127 D6
Batchwood Sch AL3 127 D6
Batchwood View AL3 127 D5
Batchworth Heath WD3 174 B5
Batchworth Heath Hill WD3 174 A6
Batchworth Hill London Rd WD3 173 F7
Batchworth La HA6 174 D5
Bateman Rd WD3 166 A3
Bates Ho 2 SG1 50 E6
Batford Cl AL7 111 B5
Batford Rd AL5 86 D3
Bath Pl EN5 171 F6
Bath Rd LU3 45 D2
Bathurst Rd HP2 124 E6
Batterdale AL9 130 C6
Battlefield Rd AL1 127 F5
Battlers Green Dr WD7 155 E3
Battleview AL4 108 E8
Baud Cl SG11 57 E2
Baulk The
Cheddington LU7 79 F7
Lilley LU2 32 D2
Pitstone LU7 80 F5
Bay Cl LU4 44 B6
Bay Ct HP4 122 B4
Bay Tree Cl
Chiswell Green AL2 141 C3
Hammond Street EN7 147 F4
Bay Tree Wlk WD17 154 A1
Bayford CE Prim Sch SG13 132 F5
Bayford Cl
Hemel Hempstead HP2 125 C8
Hertford SG13 113 C4
Bayford Gn SG13 133 A6
Bayford La SG13 132 F7
Bayford Sta SG13 133 B5
Bayfordbury Coll (Univ of Hertfordshire) SG13 113 B1
Bayhurst Dr HA6 174 F4
Baylam Dell LU2 46 E1
Bayley Hall Mews SG14 113 D5
Baylie Ct HP2 124 E4
Baylie La HP2 124 E4
Bayworth SG6 23 B5
Beacon Ct SG13 114 C3
Beacon Ho AL1 127 F3
Beacon Rd Ringshall HP4 81 A1
Ware SG12 94 A2
Beacon Way
Rickmansworth WD3 165 B3
Tring HP23 100 C5
Beacons The
Hatfield AL10 130 C6
Stevenage SG1 37 B3
Beaconsfield LU2 64 B8
Beaconsfield Rd
Enfield EN3 162 D2
Hatfield AL10 130 C6
St Albans AL1 127 E3
Tring HP23 99 E3
Beadles The CM22 98 B8
Beadlow Rd LU4 44 A4
Beagle Cl WD7 155 F2
Beale Cl SG2 51 C6
Beamish Dr WD23 168 C1
Beane Ave SG2 51 D6
Beane Rd Hertford SG14 113 B7
Watton at S SG14 70 D4
Beane River View SG14 113 C6
Beane Wlk SG2 51 D6
Beaneside The SG14 70 D4
Beanfield Rd CM21 97 A4
Beanley Cl LU2 46 E2
Bear La SG7 4 D4
Bearton Ave SG5 34 E8
Bearton Ct SG5 21 E1
Bearton Gn SG5 21 D1
Bearton Rd SG5 21 E1
Bearwood Cl EN6 159 D8
Beatty Rd EN8 162 F5
Beauchamp Gdns WD3 165 A1
Beauchamps AL7 111 B5
Beaulieu Cl WD19 167 C1
Beaulieu Dr EN9 163 B6
Beaumayes Cl HP1 124 B2
Beaumont Ave AL1 128 B4
Beaumont Cl 3 SG5 34 D8
Beaumont Ct 10 AL5 86 B1
Beaumont Gate WD7 156 A4
Beaumont Hall La AL3 106 C2
Beaumont Pl Barnet EN5 171 F8
Watford WD18 167 A4
Beaumont Rd
Hammond Street EN7 147 F7
Luton LU3 45 B2
Beaumont Sch AL4 128 C4
Beaumont View EN7 147 D5
Beazley Cl SG12 93 E2
Beckbury Cl LU2 46 E2
Becket Gdns AL6 89 C4
Beckets Sq HP4 122 A6
Beckets Wlk 14 SG12 93 D1
Beckett's Ave AL3 127 C6
Becketts SG14 113 A5
Beckfield La SG9 26 D7
Beckham Cl LU2 45 D7
Becks Cl AL3 83 D5
Bedale Rd EN2 161 C1
Bede Cl HA5 175 D2
Bede Ct HP4 102 C8
Bedford Almshouses 1 WD18 167 C5
Bedford Ave EN5 171 F4
Bedford Cl WD3 151 B1
Bedford Cres EN3 162 E4
Bedford Gdns 4 LU2 63 D8
Bedford Park Rd AL1 127 E3
Bedford Rd Hitchin SG5 34 E7
Ickleford SG5 21 D5
Letchworth SG6 22 D7
Lower Stondon SG16 10 B3
Moor Park HA6 174 D6
St Albans AL1 127 E2
Bedford St
Berkhamsted HP4 122 D4
Hitchin SG5 34 D7
Watford WD24 167 B8
Bedmond La
Bricket Wood AL3,WD5 140 B6
St Albans AL3 126 F1
Bedmond Rd
Abbots Langley WD5 139 F2
Hemel Hempstead HP3 125 D1
Pimlico HP3 139 E7
Bedmond Village Prim Sch WD5 139 F3
Bedwell Ave AL9,SG13 132 A7
Bedwell Cl AL7 110 E5
Bedwell Cres SG1 50 F5
Bedwell Prim Sch SG1 51 A5
Bedwell Rise SG1 50 E5
Beech Ave
Crews Hill EN2 161 A4
Radlett WD7 156 A5
Beech Bottom AL3 127 D6
Beech Cl Harpenden AL5 107 C5
Beech Cl *continued*
Hatfield AL10 130 A4
Beech Cres AL4 108 D7
Beech Ct Harpenden AL5 85 F3
Hoddesdon EN10 135 A3
Beech Dr
Berkhamsted HP4 122 C3
Borehamwood WD6 169 F7
Sawbridgeworth CM21 118 C8
Stevenage SG2 51 B3
Beech Farm Dr AL4 128 F7
Beech Gr HP23 100 C4
Beech Hill
Hadley Wood EN4 159 E1
Letchworth SG6 22 D7
Luton LU2 46 D8
Beech Hill Com Prim Sch LU4 45 B1
Beech Hill Ct HP4 122 D4
Beech Ho EN11 134 F6
Beech Hyde La AL4 108 F6
Beech Hyde Prim Sch AL4 108 D7
Beech Mews SG12 114 D7
Beech Pk HP6 150 B1
Beech Pl AL3 127 D6
Beech Rd Luton LU1 63 C8
St Albans AL3 127 E6
Watford WD24 154 B2
Beech Ridge Baldock SG7 23 F6
Harpenden AL5 85 B5
Beech Way AL4 87 B6
Beech Wlk HP23 100 C4
Beechcroft
Berkhamsted HP4 122 C3
Datchworth SG3 69 D1
Beechcroft Ave WD3 166 C4
Beechcroft Rd WD23 167 E4
Beechen Gr WD17 167 C6
Beeches The
Chorleywood WD3 164 F4
Hemel Hempstead HP1 124 B2
Hitchin SG4 35 A6
Park Street AL2 141 D4
Royston SG8 7 D6
Tring HP23 100 C4
2 Watford WD18 167 B6
Welwyn AL6 89 C4
Beechfield
Hoddesdon EN11 115 A2
Kings Langley WD4 138 F1
Sawbridgeworth CM21 97 F2
Beechfield Cl
Borehamwood WD6 169 E7
Redbourn AL3 106 B5
Beechfield Ct 5 WD17 167 A8
Beechfield Rd
Hemel Hempstead HP1 124 B2
Ware SG12 93 F2
Welwyn Garden City AL7 110 E5
Beechfield Sch WD24 154 A2
Beechfield Wlk EN9 163 D4
Beeching Cl AL5 86 B4
Beechlands CM23 76 F5
Beecholm Mews 5 EN8 148 E3
Beechpark Way WD17 153 E2
Beechtree La AL3 126 B2
Beechwood Ave
Chorleywood WD3 164 B5
Little Chalfont HP6 150 C1
Potters Bar EN6 159 B6
St Albans AL1 128 C4
Beechwood Cl
Baldock SG7 23 F5
Hammond Street EN7 147 E5
Hertford SG13 113 F6
Hitchin SG5 21 D2
Beechwood Cotts WD3 164 C3
Beechwood Ct HP22 99 A4
Beechwood Dr HP23 101 D5
Beechwood Park Sch AL3 83 B1
Beechwood Pk
Chorleywood WD3 164 F5
Hemel Hempstead HP3 137 F7
Beechwood Rd LU4 44 E3
Beechwood Rise WD24 154 B2
Beecroft La SG2 38 C2
Beehive Cl WD6 169 D3
Beehive Gn AL7 111 A4
Beehive La AL7 111 A3
Beehive Rd EN7 147 B3
Beesonend Cotts AL5 107 B4
Beesonend La AL3,AL5 106 E3
Beeston Cl WD19 175 D6
Beeston Dr EN8 148 D4
Beetham Ct SG12 92 E4
Beethoven Rd WD6 169 D3
Beeton Cl HA5 176 A3
Beggarman's La SG11 72 D8
Beggars Bush La WD18, WD3 166 D4
Beggars La HP23 101 A3
Beken Ct WD25 154 C4
Belcher Rd 6 EN11 135 A7
Beldam Ave SG8 7 E5
Beldams Gate CM23 77 B5
Beldams La CM23 77 B5
Belfairs WD19 175 D5
Belford Rd WD6 156 F1
Belfry Ave UB9 173 A2
Belfry The Luton LU2 45 E6
Watford WD24 167 D8
Belfry Villas UB9 173 A2
Belgrave Ave WD18 166 F4
Belgrave Cl AL4 128 C7
Belgrave Dr WD4 139 C3
Belgrave Ho 6 CM23 77 B8
Belgrave Mews SG2 69 A8
Belgrave Rd LU4 44 D5
Belgravia Cl EN5 171 F6
Belham Rd WD4 139 A3
Bell Acre SG6 23 B4
Bell Acre Gdns SG6 23 B4
Bell Cl Bedmond WD5 139 F4
Hitchin SG4 35 B6
Knebworth SG3 69 A5
7 Pinner HA5 175 C1
Bell Farm Ind Est SG8 18 A2
Bell Gn HP3 137 B4
Bell La
Abbots Langley WD5 140 A4
Berkhamsted HP4 121 E5
Brookmans Park AL9 145 A7
Enfield EN3 162 E1
Hertford SG14 113 D6
Hoddesdon EN11 135 A6
Hoddesdon, Broxbourne EN11 134 E2
Little Chalfont HP6 150 C1
Nuthampstead SG8 18 B2
Shenley AL2 142 E2
Stevenage SG1 50 C7
Widford SG12 95 D4
Bell Lane Comb Sch HP6 150 B1
Bell Leys HP22 60 B3
Bell Mead CM21 97 E2
Bell Rdbt The AL2 142 F4
Bell Row SG7 23 E7
Bell St CM21 97 E2
Bell View AL4 128 D3
Bell Wlk HP22 60 B3
Bellamy Cl Knebworth SG3 68 F5
Watford WD17 167 A8
Bellamy Rd EN8 148 E2
Bellchambers Cl AL2 142 C5
Belle Vue La WD23 168 D1
Belle Vue Rd SG12 93 F1
Bellerby Rise LU4 44 B6
Bellevue Terr UB9 173 A3
Bellfield Ave HA3 176 D4
Bellgate HP2 124 E6
Bellgate Prim Sch HP2 124 E5
Bellingdon WD19 175 E7
Bellis Ho AL7 111 B4
Bellmount Wood Ave WD17 166 E8
Bells Hill Barnet EN5 171 D5
Bishop's Stortford CM23 76 E7
Belmers Rd HP23 100 D1
Belmont Ct 7 AL1 127 D2
Belmont Fst Sch HA3 176 F1
Belmont Hill AL1 127 D2
Belmont Lodge HA3 176 D3
Belmont Mid Sch HA3 176 F1
Belmont Rd
Hemel Hempstead HP3 138 E8
Luton LU1 63 C7
Watford WD23 167 E4
Belmor WD6 170 A3
Belper Rd LU4 44 D2
Belsham Pl LU2 46 E2
Belsize Cl
Hemel Hempstead HP3 125 A2
St Albans AL4 128 C8
Belsize Cotts WD3 151 E6
Belsize Rd Harrow HA3 176 D3
Hemel Hempstead HP3 125 A2
Belswains Gn HP3 138 E8
Belswains La HP3 138 F7
Belswains Prim Sch HP3 138 F7
Belton Rd HP4 122 A5
Beltona Gdns EN8 148 D4
Belvedere Gdns AL2 141 A4
Belvedere Rd LU3 45 B5
Bembridge Gdns LU3 44 F7
Ben Austins AL3 106 A4
Benbow Cl AL1 128 B1
Benchley Hill SG4 35 C8
Benchleys Rd HP1 123 F2
Bencroft EN7 148 A5
Bencroft Rd HP2 124 E3
Bencroft Wood★ EN10 133 D1
Bendish La SG4 66 C7
Bendysh Rd WD23 167 E5
Benedict Ct HA5 175 F2
Benedictine Gate EN8 148 E4
Benford Rd EN11 134 F4
Bengarth Dr HA3 176 D1
Bengeo Ho SG14 92 C1
Bengeo Mdws SG14 92 C1
Bengeo Mews SG14 92 C1
Bengeo Prim Sch SG14 92 C1
Bengeo St SG14 113 C8
Benhooks Ave CM23 76 E5
Benhooks Pl 1 CM23 76 E5
Benington CE Prim Sch SG2 52 D4
Benington Cl LU2 45 F5
Benington Lordship Gdns★ SG2 52 D4
Benington Rd Aston SG2 51 F2
Benington SG2 52 A7
Benneck Ho WD18 166 E3
Bennett Cl
Northwood HA6 174 F3
Welwyn Garden City AL7 110 F2
Bennett Ct Letchworth SG6 22 F6
Letchworth SG6 23 A5
Bennetts Cl AL4 143 D8
Bennetts End Cl HP3 124 F1
Bennetts End Rd HP3 125 A1
Bennetts La SG9 25 F4
Bennettsgate HP3 139 A8
Benningfield Cl SG12 95 D5
Benningfield Gdns HP4 122 E6
Benningfield Rd SG12 95 D4
Benskin Rd WD18 167 A4
Benslow La SG4 35 A7
Benslow Rise SG4 35 A8
Benson Cl LU3 44 F7
Benson Ct EN3 163 A1
Benstede SG2 69 C8
Bentfield Bower CM24 59 C8
Bentfield End Cswy CM24 59 D7
Bentfield Gdns CM24 59 D7
Bentfield Gn CM24 59 D8
Bentfield Prim Sch CM24 59 D8
Bentfield Rd CM24 59 D7
Bentick Way SG4 67 F2
Bentley Cl CM23 76 F5
Bentley Ct 2 LU1 63 C8
Bentley Heath La EN5 158 F4
Bentley Lodge WD23 176 E8
Bentley Rd SG14 112 F7
Bentley Wood High Sch HA7 176 F5
Benton Rd WD19 175 D5
Bentons The HP4 121 F6
Bentsley Cl AL4 128 C7
Berceau Wlk WD17 166 E8
Berdan Ct EN3 163 A2
Berefeld HP2 124 D5
Beresford Rd Luton LU4 45 A1
Rickmansworth WD3 164 F1
St Albans AL1 128 C2
Bericot Way AL7 111 D6
Berkeley SG6 23 A4
Berkeley Cl
Abbots Langley WD5 153 F8
Borehamwood WD6 170 A4
6 Hitchin SG5 34 D8
Potters Bar EN6 158 F7
Stevenage SG2 69 A8
Ware SG12 93 C2
Berkeley Ct
Croxley Green WD3 166 D4
6 Harpenden AL5 86 A2
Berkeley Mews AL1 128 B2
Berkeley Path 2 LU2 63 E8
Berkeley Sq HP2 105 C1
Berkhamsted Castle★ HP4 122 D5
Berkhamsted Collegiate Sch
Berkhamsted HP4 122 B4
Berkhamsted HP4 122 C4
Berkhamsted Rd HP1 123 E5
Berkhamsted Sta HP4 122 C5
Berkley Ave EN8 162 D5
Berkley Cl Pitstone LU7 80 D3
St Albans AL4 128 C7
Berkley Ct 2 HP4 122 C4
Berkley Pl EN8 162 D5
Berks Hill WD3 164 C4
Bermer Rd WD24 167 C8
Bernard Gr EN9 163 B6
Bernard St AL3 127 D4
Bernard's Heath Inf Sch AL1 127 F5
Berners Dr AL1 141 E8
Berners Way EN10 148 F8
Bernhardt Cres SG2 51 C6
Berries The AL4 128 A7
Berrow Cl LU2 46 E2
Berry Ave WD24 154 B3
Berry Cl WD3 165 B2
Berry Grove La WD24, WD25 154 E1
Berry La WD3 165 A2
Berry Leys LU3 44 E7
Berry Way WD3 165 B2
Berryfield LU7 79 F7
Berrygrove La WD25 168 A8
Berrymead HP2 124 F5
Berthold Mews EN9 163 B6
Bertram Ho 4 SG1 50 E6
Berwick Cl Harrow HA7 176 F4
Holdbrook EN8 163 A5
Stevenage SG1 50 A8
Berwick Rd WD6 156 F1
Besant Ho 2 WD24 167 D7
Besford Cl LU2 46 E2
Bessemer Cl SG5 21 E2
Bessemer Dr SG1 50 B4
Bessemer Rd AL7,AL8 89 E2
Bethune Cl LU1 63 B6
Bethune Ct LU1 63 B6
Betjeman Cl
Cheshunt EN7 148 A3
Harpenden AL5 86 C1
Betjeman Rd SG8 2 D1
Betjeman Way HP1 124 B4
Betony Vale SG8 7 E5
Bettespol Mdws AL3 106 A6
Betty's La HP23 100 A4
Bevan Cl HP3 124 E1
Bevan Ho 3 WD24 167 D7
Beverley Cl SG8 7 B8
Beverley Gdns
Cheshunt EN7 148 A1
St Albans AL4 128 D7
Welwyn Garden City AL7 111 C6
Beverley Rd Luton LU4 44 F1
Stevenage SG1 37 B2
Beverly Cl EN10 134 E2
Bevil Ct EN11 115 A1
Bewdley Cl AL5 107 D6
Bewley Cl EN8 162 D8

Bexhill Rd LU2 ... 46 D2
Beyers Gdns EN11 ... 115 A1
Beyers Prospect EN11 ... 115 A1
Beyers Ride EN11 ... 115 A1
Bibbs Hall La SG4,AL6 ... 87 E6
Biddenham Turn WD25 ... 154 C4
Bideford Gdns LU3 ... 45 D4
Bideford Rd EN3 ... 162 F1
Bidwell Cl SG6 ... 23 B5
Biggin Hill SG9 ... 28 D7
Biggin La SG5 ... 34 F7
Biggs Grove Rd EN7 ... 147 E4
Bignells Cnr EN6 ... 158 B5
Billet La HP4 ... 122 A6
Billy Lows La EN6 ... 159 B8
Bilton Rd SG4 ... 21 F2
Bilton Way Enfield EN3 ... 162 F1
Luton LU1 ... 44 F1
Bingen Rd SG5 ... 21 C1
Bingham Cl HP1 ... 123 F5
Bingham's Park Childrens Farm★ HP1 ... 123 E8
Bingley Rd EN11 ... 135 C6
Binham Cl LU2 ... 45 D7
Binyon Cres HA7 ... 176 F5
Birch Copse AL2 ... 140 E1
Birch Ct HA6 ... 174 C4
Birch Dr Hatfield AL10 ... 130 A4
Maple Cross WD3 ... 172 D5
Birch Gn
Hemel Hempstead HP1 ... 123 F5
Hertingfordbury SG14 ... 112 C4
Birch Gr Oaklands AL6 ... 89 E8
Potters Bar EN6 ... 159 B7
Birch La HP3 ... 151 B7
Birch Leys HP2 ... 125 C8
Birch Link LU4 ... 45 C1
Birch Pk HA3 ... 176 C3
Birch Rd
Berkhamsted HP4 ... 121 D7
Woolmer Green SG3 ... 69 B1
Birch Tree Gr HP5 ... 136 B1
Birch Tree Wlk WD17 ... 153 F2
Birch Way
Harpenden AL5 ... 107 C8
London Colney AL2 ... 142 D4
Birch Wlk WD6 ... 170 A8
Birchall La SG14 ... 111 E4
Birchall Wood AL7 ... 111 C5
Birchalls CM24 ... 59 E8
Birchanger CE Prim Sch CM23 ... 59 D2
Birchanger Ind Est CM23 59 B2
Birchanger La CM23 ... 59 D2
Birchen Gr LU2 ... 45 F3
Bircherley Ct 14 SG14 ... 113 D6
Bircherley Green Ctr The 9 SG14 ... 113 D6
Bircherley St SG14 ... 113 D6
Birches The
Bushey WD23 ... 168 C4
Codicote SG4 ... 89 A8
Hemel Hempstead HP3 ... 137 F8
Letchworth SG6 ... 22 E8
Birchfield Rd EN8 ... 148 C2
Birchmead WD17 ... 153 F1
Birchmead Cl AL3 ... 127 D6
Birchway AL10 ... 130 B7
Birchwood
Birchanger CM23 ... 59 D2
Shenley WD7 ... 157 A5
Waltham Abbey EN9 ... 163 E5
Birchwood Ave AL10 ... 130 A7
Birchwood Avenue Prim Sch AL10 ... 130 B7
Birchwood Cl AL10 ... 130 A7
Birchwood High Sch CM23 ... 77 C8
Birchwood Way AL2 ... 141 B3
Birdcroft Rd AL8 ... 110 D5
Birdie Way SG13 ... 114 B7
Birds Cl AL7 ... 111 B4
Birds Hill SG6 ... 23 A6
Birdsfoot La LU3 ... 45 B6
Birkbeck Rd EN2 ... 161 D1
Birkdale Gdns WD19 ... 175 D7
Birken Ct HA6 ... 174 B5
Birklands AL1 ... 142 B7
Birklands La AL1 ... 142 B7
Birling Dr LU2 ... 46 C4
Birnbeck Ct 1 EN5 ... 171 D5
Birstal Gn WD19 ... 175 D6
Birtley Croft LU2 ... 46 E1
Biscot Rd LU3 ... 45 C2
Bishop Ct WD5 ... 153 F8
Bishop Ken Rd HA3 ... 176 F2
Bishop Sq AL10 ... 129 E5
Bishop Wood CE Jun Sch HP23 ... 100 A3
Bishop's Ave CM23 ... 76 F3
Bishop's Cl AL4 ... 128 A7
Bishop's Garth AL4 ... 128 A7
Bishop's Hatfield Girls' Sch AL10 ... 130 A5
Bishop's Palace (rem of)★ AL9 ... 130 D6
Bishop's Stortford Bsns Ctr CM23 ... 77 A6
Bishop's Stortford Coll CM23 ... 76 E7
Bishop's Stortford High Sch The CM23 ... 76 F4
Bishop's Stortford Sta CM23 ... 77 A6
Bishop's Wood Ctry Pk★ WD3 ... 173 F4
Bishops Ave
Borehamwood WD6 ... 169 F4
Moor Park HA6 ... 174 F7
Bishops Cl Barnet EN5 ... 171 D3
Hatfield AL10 ... 129 F5
Bishops Ct Cheshunt EN8 148 B1
6 Luton LU3 ... 45 D1
Bishops Field HP22 ... 99 A4
Bishops Mead HP1 ... 124 B1
Bishops Park Way CM23 ... 76 B7
Bishops Rd AL6 ... 90 E6
Bishops Rise AL10 ... 129 F2
Bishops Wood Hospl HA6 ... 174 B4
Bishopscote Rd LU3 ... 45 B3
Biskra WD17 ... 167 A8
Bisley Cl EN8 ... 162 D6
Bit The HP23 ... 100 D1
Bittern Cl
Hammond Street EN7 ... 147 C6
Hemel Hempstead HP3 ... 138 F6
Stevenage SG2 ... 51 D2
Bittern Way SG6 ... 11 E1
Black Boy Wood AL2 ... 141 A1
Black Cut AL1 ... 127 E2
Black Fan Rd
Welwyn Garden City AL7 ... 110 F7
Welwyn Garden City AL7 ... 111 B6
Black Green Wood Cl AL2 ... 141 B2
Black Lion Ct CM17 ... 118 C4
Black Lion Hill WD7 ... 156 F7
Black Smiths Cl SG12 ... 115 A7
Black Swan Ct 1 SG12 ... 93 D1
Black Swan La LU3 ... 45 A5
Blackadder Cotts EN9 ... 149 D8
Blackberry Mead SG2 ... 51 D3
Blackbirds La WD25 ... 155 C5
Blackbury Cl EN6 ... 159 C8
Blackbush Spring CM20 118 A1
Blackbushe CM23 ... 59 C1
Blackdale EN7 ... 148 A4
Blackdown Cl SG1 ... 37 B3
Blacketts Wood Dr WD3 ... 164 B5
Blackford Rd WD19 ... 175 D5
Blackhorse Cl SG4 ... 35 A5
Blackhorse La Hitchin SG4 35 A5
Redbourn AL3 ... 106 A6
Ridge EN6 ... 157 F8
Blackhorse Rd SG6 ... 23 C8
Blackley Cl WD17 ... 153 F2
Blackmoor La WD18 ... 166 D4
Blackmore SG6 ... 23 B3
Blackmore Gate HP22 ... 99 A4
Blackmore Manor AL4 ... 87 B6
Blackmore Way AL4 ... 87 B6
Blacksmith Cl SG5 ... 11 F7
Blacksmith's La
Reed SG8 ... 16 D5
St Albans AL3 ... 127 B3
Blacksmiths Cl CM23 ... 76 B5
Blacksmiths Hill SG2 ... 52 E4
Blacksmiths Way CM21 ... 97 B1
Blackthorn Cl
St Albans AL4 ... 128 C6
Watford WD25 ... 154 B7
Blackthorn Dr LU2 ... 46 C4
Blackthorn Rd AL7 ... 111 A5
Blackthorne Cl AL10 ... 129 F2
Blackwater La HP3 ... 125 E1
Blackwell Cl HA3 ... 176 D3
Blackwell Dr WD19 ... 167 C3
Blackwell Hall La HP5 ... 150 C6
Blackwell Rd WD4 ... 139 A2
Blackwood Ct EN7 ... 148 F5
Bladon Cl SG4 ... 35 F3
Blaine Cl HP23 ... 100 A6
Blair Cl
Bishop's Stortford CM23 ... 76 C7
Hemel Hempstead HP2 ... 105 B1
Stevenage SG2 ... 50 F1
Blairhead Dr WD19 ... 175 B7
Blake Cl Royston SG8 ... 2 D1
St Albans AL1 ... 142 A8
Blakedown LU2 ... 45 E1
Blakemere Rd AL8 ... 110 D8
Blakemore End Rd SG4 ... 35 D3
Blakeney Dr LU2 ... 45 C7
Blakeney Ho SG1 ... 50 A7
Blakeney Rd SG1 ... 50 A7
Blakes Ct
Rickmansworth WD3 ... 165 C1
Sawbridgeworth CM21 ... 97 E2
Blakes Way AL6 ... 89 C6
Blanchard Gr EN3 ... 163 B1
Blanche La EN6 ... 157 F5
Blandford Ave LU2 ... 45 D6
Blandford Rd AL1 ... 128 A3
Blanes The SG12 ... 93 C3
Blattner Cl WD6 ... 169 E5
Blaxland Terr 9 EN8 ... 148 D3
Blaydon Rd LU2 ... 64 A8
Blegberry Gdns HP4 ... 121 E4
Blenheim Cl
Cheddington LU7 ... 79 F8
Sawbridgeworth CM21 ... 118 C8
Watford WD19 ... 167 D2
Blenheim Cres LU3 ... 45 C2
Blenheim Ct
Bishop's Stortford CM23 ... 76 C7
Welwyn Garden City AL7 ... 110 F7
Blenheim Rd Barnet EN5 171 D5
St Albans AL1 ... 127 F4
Blenheim Way SG2 ... 69 D7
Blenhiem Rd WD5 ... 154 A7
Blenkin Cl AL3 ... 127 C7
Blind La SG2,SG9 ... 38 F5
Blindman's La EN8 ... 148 D2
Block 10 4 WD17 ... 167 A8
Block 13 3 WD17 ... 167 A8
Block 14 2 WD17 ... 167 A8
Bloomfield Ave LU2 ... 46 A1
Bloomfield Ho 6 SG1 ... 50 E6
Bloomfield Rd
Hammond Street EN7 ... 147 C6
Harpenden AL5 ... 85 F3
Blossom La EN2 ... 161 C1
Blue Bridge Rd AL9 ... 144 E4
Bluebell Cl
Hemel Hempstead HP1 ... 123 E2
Hertford SG13 ... 114 A6
Bluebell Dr
Bedmond WD5 ... 139 F4
Goff's Oak EN7 ... 147 D3
Bluebell Way AL10 ... 109 F1
Bluebell Wood Cl LU1 ... 63 A7
Bluebells AL6 ... 89 D7
Blueberry Cl AL3 ... 127 D7
Bluebird Way AL2 ... 140 E1
Bluebridge Ave AL9 ... 144 F4
Bluecoat Yd SG12 ... 93 D1
Bluecoats Ave SG14 ... 113 D6
Bluecoats Ct 18 SG14 ... 113 D6
Bluehouse Hill AL3 ... 127 A3
Bluett Rd AL2 ... 142 D4
Blundell Cl AL3 ... 127 D7
Blundell Rd LU3 ... 45 A4
Blunesfield EN6 ... 159 D8
Blunts La AL2 ... 140 D5
Blyth Cl
Borehamwood WD6 ... 170 A8
Stevenage SG1 ... 50 A7
Blyth Pl 13 LU1 ... 63 D6
Blythe Rd EN11 ... 135 D5
Blythway AL7 ... 89 F1
Blythway Ho AL7 ... 89 F1
Blythwood Gdns CM24 ... 59 D6
Blythwood Rd HA5 ... 175 D2
Boardman Cl EN5 ... 171 E4
Bockings SG2 ... 38 C1
Bodmin Rd LU4 ... 44 F3
Bodwell Cl HP1 ... 124 A4
Bogmoor Rd SG8 ... 18 A8
Bognor Gdns WD19 ... 175 C5
Bohemia HP2 ... 124 E4
Boissy Cl AL4 ... 128 E2
Boleyn Cl HP2 ... 125 C8
Boleyn Ct EN10 ... 134 E2
Boleyn Dr AL1 ... 127 D1
Boling Brook AL4 ... 128 A7
Bolingbroke Rd LU1 ... 63 B6
Bolney Gn LU2 ... 46 D3
Bolton Rd LU1 ... 63 F7
Boltons Park (Royal Veterinary Coll) EN6 ... 145 A2
Bond Ct AL5 ... 85 F3
Bondor Bsns Ctr SG7 ... 23 F7
Boniface Gdns HA3 ... 176 B3
Boniface Wlk HA3 ... 176 B3
Bonks Hill CM21 ... 97 D1
Bonney Gr EN7 ... 148 A1
Bonneygrove Prim Sch EN7 ... 148 A1
Bonnick Cl LU1 ... 63 C6
Booths Cl AL9 ... 144 D7
Boreham Holt WD6 ... 169 F5
Borehamwood Ent Ctr WD6 ... 169 F6
Borehamwood Ind Pk WD6 ... 170 D7
Bornedene EN6 ... 158 E8
Borodale AL5 ... 86 A1
Borough Way EN6 ... 158 E7
Borrell Cl EN10 ... 134 F3
Borrowdale Ct 4 HP2 ... 124 E6
Borton Ave SG16 ... 10 B4
Bosanquet Rd EN11 ... 135 C8
Boscombe Ct SG6 ... 23 B6
Bosmore Rd LU3 ... 44 F5
Boswell Cl WD7 ... 156 E7
Boswell Dr SG5 ... 21 E4
Boswell Gdns SG1 ... 36 D1
Boswick La HP4 ... 121 D8
Botley La HP5 ... 136 A1
Botley Rd Botley HP5 ... 136 A1
Hemel Hempstead HP2 ... 125 B8
Bottom House La HP23 ... 101 A1
Bottom La WD3,WD4 ... 152 C4
Bottom Rd HP23 ... 119 F3
Bough Beech Ct EN3 ... 162 D2
Boughton Way HP6 ... 150 C1
Boulevard Ctr The WD6 170 A6
Boulevard The
Watford WD18 ... 166 D4
Welwyn Garden City AL7 ... 110 F8
Boulton Rd SG1 ... 37 C2
Bounce The HP2 ... 124 D5
Boundary Cl EN5 ... 171 F8
Boundary Cotts HP3 ... 137 D2
Boundary Ct AL7 ... 110 F2
Boundary Dr SG14 ... 113 D8
Boundary Ho
Cheshunt EN8 ... 162 D7
Welwyn Garden City AL7 ... 110 D3
Boundary La AL7 ... 110 E2
Boundary Pk HP2 ... 125 C5
Boundary Rd
Bishop's Stortford CM23 ... 77 A5
St Albans AL1 ... 127 E5
Boundary Way
Hemel Hempstead HP2 ... 125 C5
Watford WD25 ... 154 C7
Bounds Field SG11 ... 75 F8
Bourne Apartments The 2 AL5 ... 85 F2
Bourne Cl
Hoddesdon EN10 ... 134 F3
Ware SG12 ... 93 D2
Bourne End Cotts HP1 ... 123 C1
Bourne End Rd HA6 ... 174 E6
Bourne Hall WD23 ... 168 A3
Bourne Honour SG12 ... 92 E7
Bourne La SG10 ... 96 A6
Bourne Rd
Berkhamsted HP4 ... 121 F5
Bushey WD23 ... 168 A4
Bourne The
Bishop's Stortford CM23 ... 77 A8
Bovingdon HP3 ... 137 A4
Clapgate SG11 ... 57 C6
3 Harpenden AL5 ... 85 F2
Ware SG12 ... 93 D2
Bournehall Ave WD23 ... 168 A4
Bournehall La WD23 ... 168 A4
Bournehall Prim Sch WD23 ... 168 B4
Bournehall Rd WD23 ... 168 A3
Bournemouth Rd 3 SG1 ... 50 B8
Bouvier Rd EN3 ... 162 C1
Bovingdon Cres WD25 ... 154 D5
Bovingdon Ct HP3 ... 137 A3
Bovingdon Prim Sch HP3 ... 137 B4
Bowbrookvale LU2 ... 46 F1
Bowcock Wlk SG1 ... 50 E3
Bower Heath La AL5 ... 86 C6
Bower's Par AL5 ... 86 A1
Bowers Way AL5 ... 86 A1
Bowershott SG6 ... 23 A4
Bowes Lyon Mews AL3 ... 127 D3
Bowgate AL1 ... 127 E4
Bowlers Mead SG9 ... 40 D7
Bowles Gn EN1 ... 162 B3
Bowling Cl
14 Bishop's Stortford CM23 76 F6
Harpenden AL5 ... 107 C7
Bowling Ct WD18 ... 167 A5
Bowling Gn SG1 ... 50 C8
Bowling Green La
Buntingford SG9 ... 40 D8
Luton LU2 ... 45 E2
Bowling Rd SG12 ... 93 E1
Bowman Trad Est SG1 ... 50 B5
Bowmans Ave SG4 ... 35 B6
Bowmans Cl
Potters Bar EN6 ... 159 D7
Welwyn AL6 ... 89 C6
Bowmans Ct HP2 ... 124 E5
Bowmans Gn WD25 ... 154 E3
Bowmansgreen Prim Sch AL2 ... 142 C4
Bowring Gn WD19 ... 175 C5
Bowyer Ct EN8 ... 162 F6
Bowyer's Cl SG5 ... 21 D1
Bowyers 6 HP2 ... 124 D5
Box La
Hemel Hempstead HP3 ... 137 E7
Hoddesdon EN11 ... 134 E6
Boxberry Cl SG1 ... 50 E6
Boxfield AL7 ... 111 B3
Boxfield Gn SG2 ... 51 D8
Boxgrove Cl LU2 ... 46 C5
Boxhill 3 HP2 ... 124 D5
Boxmoor House Sch HP3 ... 137 F8
Boxmoor Prim Sch HP1 124 A2
Boxted Cl LU4 ... 44 C5
Boxted Rd HP1 ... 123 F5
Boxtree La HA3 ... 176 D3
Boxtree Rd HA3 ... 176 D3
Boxwell Rd HP4 ... 122 B4
Boyce Cl WD6 ... 169 E8
Boyd Cl 1 CM23 ... 77 B8
Boyes Cres AL2 ... 142 B5
Boyle Cl LU2 ... 63 E8
Brace Cl EN7 ... 147 B6
Braceby Cl LU3 ... 44 F6
Braceys SG2 ... 52 F2
Brache Cl AL3 ... 106 A5
Brache Ct LU1 ... 63 F6
Bracken Cl WD6 ... 170 B8
Bracken La AL6 ... 89 F7
Brackendale EN6 ... 159 A6
Brackendale Gr
Harpenden AL5 ... 85 D3
Luton LU3 ... 45 B5
Brackendene AL2 ... 140 F1
Brackenhill HP4 ... 122 F5
Brackens The HP2 ... 124 D4
Bracklesham Gdns LU2 ... 46 D3
Bracknell Pl HP2 ... 124 F7
Bradbery WD3 ... 172 D5
Bradbury Cl WD6 ... 170 B8
Bradcot Cotts SG2 ... 39 C2
Bradden Cotts HP2 ... 103 F8
Bradden La HP1,HP2 ... 103 E7
Bradden Villas HP2 ... 103 F8
Braddon Ct 13 EN5 ... 171 E6
Bradford Rd WD3 ... 164 C2
Bradgate EN6 ... 146 D4
Bradgate Cl EN6 ... 146 D3
Bradgers Hill Rd LU2 ... 45 E4
Bradley Comm CM23 ... 59 C3
Bradley Rd Enfield EN3 ... 162 E2
Luton LU4 ... 44 D1
Waltham Abbey EN9 ... 163 C4
Bradleys Cnr SG4 ... 35 C8
Bradman Way SG1 ... 37 A1
Bradmore Gn AL9 ... 144 E5
Bradmore La AL9 ... 144 C5
Bradmore Way AL9 ... 144 E5
Bradshaw Rd WD24 ... 154 C1
Bradshaws AL10 ... 129 F1
Bradway SG4 ... 66 E6
Braemar Cl SG2 ... 69 B7
Braemar Ct WD23 ... 168 A3
Braemar Turn HP2 ... 105 B1
Braeside Cl HA5 ... 176 A3
Bragbury Cl SG2 ... 69 D7
Bragbury La SG2,SG3 ... 69 D5
Bragmans La WD3 ... 151 E6
Braham Ct 2 SG5 ... 34 E7
Brain Cl AL10 ... 130 B6
Braithwaite Ct 16 LU3 ... 45 D1
Brakynbery HP4 ... 121 E7
Bramble Cl Harpenden AL5 85 F3
Luton LU4 ... 44 C4
Watford WD25 ... 154 A5
Bramble Rd
Hatfield AL10 ... 129 D5
Luton LU4 ... 44 C4
Bramble Rise CM20 ... 117 C1
Brambles The
Bishop's Stortford CM23 ... 76 C6
Cheshunt EN8 ... 162 D8
Oaklands AL6 ... 89 E8
Royston SG8 ... 7 E5
St Albans AL1 ... 127 D1
Stevenage SG1 ... 36 D2
Ware SG12 ... 93 C3
Brambling Cl WD23 ... 167 E5
Brambling Rise HP2 ... 124 E6
Bramfield Hitchin SG4 ... 35 B6
Watford WD25 ... 154 E5
Bramfield Ct SG14 ... 113 A7
Bramfield La SG14 ... 91 F3
Bramfield Pl HP2 ... 105 A1
Bramfield Rd
Datchworth SG3 ... 90 E8
Hertford SG14 ... 112 F8
Bramham Ct HA6 ... 174 E4
Bramhanger Acre LU3 ... 44 D7
Bramingham Bsns Pk LU3 ... 45 B8
Bramingham Prim Sch LU3 ... 45 B8
Bramingham Rd LU3 ... 44 F6
Bramleas WD18 ... 166 F5
Bramley Cl SG7 ... 12 F1
Bramley Ct WD25 ... 154 B8
Bramley Gdns WD19 ... 175 C5
Bramley House Ct EN2 ... 161 D2
Bramley Shaw EN9 ... 163 F6
Bramley Way AL4 ... 128 C2
Brampton Cl
Cheshunt EN7 ... 148 A3
Harpenden AL5 ... 86 D1
Brampton Park Rd SG5 ... 21 E1
Brampton Rd Royston SG8 ... 7 F6
South Oxhey WD19 ... 175 A7
St Albans AL1 ... 128 A4
Brampton Terr WD6 ... 157 A1
Bramshaw Gdns WD19 ... 175 D5
Bramshot Way WD19 ... 175 A8
Bramshott Cl SG4 ... 34 F5
Branch Cl AL10 ... 130 C7
Branch Rd
Park Street AL2 ... 141 D4
St Albans AL3 ... 127 B4
Brand St SG5 ... 34 E7
Brandles Rd SG6 ... 23 A3
Brandles Sch SG7 ... 23 E7
Brandon Cl EN7 ... 147 F5
Brandon Ct HP23 ... 78 D7
Brandon Mobile Home Pk AL4 ... 128 D2
Branksome Cl HP2 ... 125 A4
Branscombe Ho WD24 ... 154 A2
Branton Cl LU2 ... 46 E2
Brantwood Rd LU1 ... 63 C7
Brawlings La SL9 ... 172 A6
Bray Cl WD6 ... 170 C8
Bray Dr SG1 ... 37 A3
Bray Lodge 2 EN8 ... 148 E3
Brayes Manor SG5 ... 11 F6
Brays Ct LU2 ... 46 B3
Brays Rd LU2 ... 46 B3
Braziers End HP5 ... 120 C1
Braziers Field SG13 ... 113 F6
Braziers Quay CM23 ... 77 A6
Breach Barns La EN9 ... 149 F1
Breachwood Green Jun Mix Inf Sch SG4 ... 47 E1
Bread & Cheese La EN7 147 D6
Breadcroft La AL5 ... 86 B1
Breakmead AL7 ... 111 B4
Breaks Rd AL10 ... 130 B6
Breakspear SG2 ... 51 C3
Breakspear Ave AL1 ... 127 F2
Breakspear Coll WD5 ... 139 F1
Breakspear Ct WD5 ... 139 F1
Breakspear Rd N UB9 ... 173 D1
Breakspear Way HP2 ... 125 C4
Breakspeare Cl WD24 ... 154 B1
Breakspeare Rd WD5 ... 153 E8
Breakspeare Sch WD5 ... 153 E8
Brecken Cl AL4 ... 128 A7
Brecon Cl 14 LU1 ... 63 D6
Breeze Terr 5 EN8 ... 148 D3
Bren Ct EN3 ... 163 A2
Brendon Ave LU2 ... 46 C1
Brent Ct SG1 ... 50 E5
Brent Pl EN5 ... 171 F4
Brett Pl WD24 ... 154 A2
Brett Rd EN5 ... 171 C4
Bretts Mead LU1 ... 63 C5
Bretts Mead Ct LU1 ... 63 C5
Brewers Cl CM23 ... 76 C5
Brewery Cotts SG7 ... 12 E1

Brewery La Baldock SG7 . .23 E8
Stansted Mountfitchet CM24 . . . .59 E7
Brewery Rd EN11 . . .135 A6
Brewery Yd CM24 . . .59 F7
Brewhouse Hill AL4 . .108 C8
Brewhouse La SG14 . .113 C6
Briants Cl HA5 . . .175 F1
Briar Cl Cheshunt EN8 . .148 C2
Luton LU2 . . .46 C4
Potten End HP4 . . .123 A7
Briar Patch La SG6 . . .22 D3
Briar Rd St Albans AL4 . .128 D6
Watford WD25 . . .154 B4
Briar Way HP4 . . .122 D3
Briarcliff HP1 . . .123 E4
Briardale Stevenage SG1 . .50 E4
Ware SG12 . . .93 C3
Briarley Cl EN10 . . .134 F1
Briars Cl AL10 . . .130 A5
Briars La AL10 . . .130 A5
Briars The Bushey WD23 .168 E2
Cheshunt EN8 . . .162 E8
Hertford SG13 . . .114 A6
Sarratt WD3 . . .152 A3
Briars Wood AL10 . . .130 A5
Briarswood EN7 . . .147 E3
Briarwood Dr HA6 . . .175 A1
Briary La SG8 . . .7 C5
Briary Wood End AL6 . . .89 F8
Briary Wood La AL6 . . .89 F8
Brick Cotts SG9 . . .27 D8
Brick Kiln Cl WD19 . . .167 E3
Brick Kiln La SG4 . . .34 E5
Brick Kiln Rd SG1 . . .50 C6
Brick Knoll Pk AL1 . . .128 C2
Brickcroft EN10 . . .148 E5
Brickenden Ct EN9 . . .163 F6
Brickendon Ct EN11 . . .135 A5
Brickendon La SG13 . . .133 D6
Bricket Rd AL1 . . .127 D3
Bricket Wood Sta AL2 . .141 A1
Brickfield AL10 . . .130 A2
Brickfield Ave HP3 . . .125 B2
Brickfield Cotts WD6 . . .169 F6
Brickfield Ct AL10 . . .130 B2
Brickfield La EN5 . . .170 F3
Brickfields Ind Est HP2 .125 B7
Brickfields The SG12 . . .93 B2
Brickly Rd LU4 . . .44 C5
Brickmakers La HP3 . . .125 B2
Brickwall Cl AL6 . . .110 A8
Brickyard La SG8 . . .16 E5
Bride Hall La AL6 . . .88 A5
Bridewell Cl SG9 . . .40 E8
Bridge Ct
1 Berkhamsted HP4 . . .122 D4
Harpenden AL5 . . .85 F3
Radlett WD7 . . .156 B4
Bridge End SG9 . . .40 E8
Bridge Foot SG12 . . .93 D1
Bridge Pk AL7 . . .110 E7
Bridge Pl WD17 . . .167 D4
Bridge Rd
Abbots Langley WD4 . . .153 C6
Letchworth SG6 . . .22 F6
Stevenage SG1 . . .50 C7
Welwyn Garden City AL8 . .110 C7
Woolmer Green SG3 . . .69 A2
Bridge Rd E AL7 . . .110 F6
Bridge Rd W SG1 . . .50 B7
Bridge St
Berkhamsted HP4 . . .122 D4
Bishop's Stortford CM23 . . .76 F7
Hemel Hempstead HP1 . . .124 C2
Hitchin SG5 . . .34 E6
Kneesworth SG8 . . .2 B8
Luton LU1 . . .63 E8
Bridgefields AL7 . . .110 F7
Bridgefoot SG9 . . .40 E7
Bridgefoot Cotts AL2 . . .155 F8
Bridgefoot La EN6 . . .158 D6
Bridgeford Ho
13 Bishop's Stortford CM23 76 F6
5 Watford WD18 . . .167 B6
Bridgegate Bsns Ctr AL7 . . .110 F7
Bridgend Rd EN1 . . .162 C4
Bridgenhall Rd EN1 . . .161 F1
Bridger Cl WD25 . . .154 E6
Bridges Ct SG14 . . .113 C6
Bridges Rd HA7 . . .176 F5
Bridgewater Ct HP4 . . .102 C8
Bridgewater Hill HP4 . . .121 F7
Bridgewater Mid Sch HP4 . . .122 A6
Bridgewater Monument The* HP4 . . .101 E7
Bridgewater Rd HP4 . . .122 B5
Bridgewater Way WD23 168 B3
Bridgeways EN11 . . .135 B5
Bridle Cl Enfield EN3 . . .162 F2
Hoddesdon EN11 . . .115 A2
St Albans AL3 . . .127 E5
Bridle La WD3 . . .165 D6
Bridle Path WD17 . . .167 B7
Bridle Way
Berkhamsted HP4 . . .122 A6
Great Amwell SG12 . . .115 A6
Hoddesdon EN11 . . .115 A1
Bridle Way (N) EN11 . . .115 B2
Bridle Way (S) EN11 . . .115 A1
Bridleway HP23 . . .119 E5
Bridlington Rd WD19 . . .175 D7
Brierley Cl LU2 . . .46 D2
Briery Ct WD3 . . .165 A5
Briery Field WD3 . . .165 A5
Briery Way HP2 . . .125 A4
Brigadier Ave EN2 . . .161 C1
Brigadier Hill EN2 . . .161 C1
Brightman Cotts 2 LU3 . .45 A7
Brighton Rd WD24 . . .154 A1
Brighton Way SG1 . . .50 A8
Brightview Cl AL2 . . .140 E2
Brightwell Ct WD18 . . .167 A4
Brightwell Rd WD18 . . .167 A4
Brill Cl LU2 . . .46 D2
Brimfield Cl LU2 . . .46 D2
Brimsdown Ave EN3 . . .162 E1
Brimstone Way HP4 . . .121 F6
Brindley Way HP3 . . .138 F6
Brinklow Ct AL3 . . .141 B8
Brinley Cl EN8 . . .162 D8
Brinsley Rd HA3 . . .176 D1
Brinsmead AL2 . . .141 E4
Briscoe Cl EN11 . . .134 F8
Briscoe Rd EN11 . . .134 F8
Bristol Ho 16 WD6 . . .170 A7
Bristol Rd LU3 . . .45 B4
Britannia SG11 . . .55 E2
Britannia Ave LU3 . . .45 B4
Britannia Bsns Pk EN8 .162 F5
Britannia Ests LU3,LU4 . .45 B2
Britannia Hall LU2 . . .64 C8
Britannia Pl 3 CM23 . . .76 E5
Britannia Rd EN8 . . .162 F5
Brittain Way SG2 . . .51 B4
Britten Cl WD6 . . .169 D3
Britton Ave AL3 . . .127 D3
Britwell Dr HP4 . . .122 E6
Brixham Cl SG1 . . .50 B7
Brixton Rd WD24 . . .167 B8
Broad Acre AL2 . . .140 E1
Broad Acres AL10 . . .129 F8
Broad Baulk SG9 . . .40 D8
Broad Ct AL7 . . .110 E6
Broad Gn SG13 . . .132 F8
Broad Green Wood SG13 . . .133 A8
Broad Mead LU3 . . .45 A3
Broad Oak Ct LU2 . . .46 D3
Broad Oak Way SG2 . . .50 F1
Broad St HP2 . . .124 D4
Broad Wlk CM20 . . .117 D1
Broadacres LU2 . . .45 D6
Broadcroft
2 Hemel Hempstead HP2 124 D5
Letchworth SG6 . . .22 F2
Broadfield
Bishop's Stortford CM23 . . .58 F2
Harlow CM20 . . .117 E1
Broadfield Cl SG10 . . .74 E1
Broadfield Ct WD23 . . .176 E8
Broadfield Inf Sch HP2 .124 F3
Broadfield Jun Sch HP2 124 F3
Broadfield Pl AL8 . . .110 B5
Broadfield Rd
Hemel Hempstead HP2 . . .124 F3
Woolmer Green SG3 . . .69 B1
Broadfield Way SG10 . . .74 F1
Broadfields
Goff's Oak EN7 . . .147 B2
Harpenden AL5 . . .85 F2
Harrow HA2 . . .176 B1
High Wych CM21 . . .97 B1
Broadfields La WD19 . . .167 B1
Broadfields Prim Sch CM20 . . .117 E1
Broadgate EN9 . . .163 F7
Broadgreen Rd EN7 . . .147 D5
Broadhall Way SG2 . . .51 B2
Broadlake Cl AL2 . . .142 D4
Broadlands WD7 . . .156 B4
Broadlands Cl EN8 . . .162 D5
Broadlawns Ct HA3 . . .176 F2
Broadleaf Ave CM23 . . .76 D4
Broadleaf Gr AL8 . . .89 B1
Broadley Gdns WD7 . . .156 E7
Broadmead SG4 . . .35 B5
Broadmead Cl HA5 . . .175 E3
Broadmead Ind Sch LU1 .63 E5
Broadmeadow Ride SG4 .35 A4
Broadmeads SG12 . . .93 D1
Broadoak Ave EN3 . . .162 D4
Broadstone Rd AL5 . . .107 D7
Broadview SG1 . . .50 E6
Broadview Ho EN3 . . .162 F3
Broadwalk The HA6 . . .174 C1
Broadwater
Berkhamsted HP4 . . .122 C5
Potters Bar EN6 . . .145 B1
Broadwater Ave SG6 . . .22 E5
Broadwater Cres
Stevenage SG2 . . .69 C8
Welwyn Garden City AL7 .110 D5
Broadwater Dale SG6 . . .22 E5
Broadwater La SG2 . . .51 D1
Broadwater Rd AL7 . . .110 E6
Broadway SG6 . . .22 F5
Broadway Ave CM17 . . .118 B4
Broadway Ct SG6 . . .22 E3
Broadway The
Harrow HA3 . . .176 F1
Hatfield AL9 . . .130 C6
Kimpton AL4 . . .87 B5
Pinner HA5 . . .175 F3
Watford WD17 . . .167 C6
Brocket Cnr AL8 . . .109 F4
Brocket Ct
Hoddesdon EN11 . . .135 A6
Luton LU4 . . .44 D5
Brocket Rd Hatfield AL8 .110 A3
Hoddesdon EN11 . . .135 A6
Brocket View AL4 . . .108 D8
Brockett Cl AL8 . . .110 B6
Brockhurst Cl HA7 . . .176 F4
Brocklesbury Cl WD24 .167 D7
Brockley Hill HA7 . . .169 C1
Brockley Hill Ho HA7 . . .169 C1
Brockswood La AL8 . . .110 B7
Brockswood Prim Sch HP2 . . .105 C1
Brockwell Shott SG2 . . .38 B1
Brodewater Rd WD6 . . .170 B7
Brodie Rd EN2 . . .161 C1
Broken Green Cotts SG11 . . .56 C2
Bromborough Gn WD19 175 C5
Bromet Cl WD17 . . .153 F1
Bromet Sch WD19 . . .167 D2
Bromleigh Cl EN8 . . .148 E3
Bromley HP23 . . .79 A4
Bromley La SG10,SG11 . . .74 D6
Brompton Cl LU3 . . .44 F8
Brompton Gdns LU3 . . .44 F8
Bronte Cres HP2 . . .105 B1
Bronte Paths SG2 . . .51 C6
Brook Bank EN1 . . .162 B2
Brook Cl WD6 . . .170 B7
Brook Cotts CM24 . . .59 E5
Brook Ct LU3 . . .45 D1
Brook Dr Radlett WD7 . . .155 F6
Stevenage SG2 . . .69 B8
Brook End CM21 . . .97 D2
Brook Field SG2 . . .51 E2
Brook Ho WD23 . . .168 C1
Brook La
Berkhamsted HP4 . . .122 B5
Sawbridgeworth CM21 . . .97 D2
Brook Rd
Borehamwood WD6 . . .170 A7
Cheshunt EN8 . . .162 F5
Sawbridgeworth CM21 . . .97 E1
Stansted Mountfitchet CM24 . . .59 E6
Brook St Luton LU3 . . .63 D8
Stotfold SG5 . . .11 E6
Tring HP23 . . .100 B4
Brook View Hitchin SG4 . . .35 C6
Stansted Mountfitchet CM24 . . .59 E5
Brookbridge La SG3 . . .69 D2
Brookdene Ave WD19 . . .167 C1
Brookdene Dr HA6 . . .174 F4
Brooke Cl WD23 . . .168 C2
Brooke End AL3 . . .106 A4
Brooke Gdns CM23 . . .77 C7
Brooke Rd SG8 . . .7 D8
Brooke Way WD23 . . .168 C2
Brooker Rd EN9 . . .163 C5
Brookfield Cl HP23 . . .100 B4
Brookfield Ct 14 EN8 . . .148 D3
Brookfield Ctr EN8 . . .148 D4
Brookfield Gdns EN8 . . .148 D4
Brookfield La SG2 . . .51 F3
Brookfield La E EN8 . . .148 D3
Brookfield La W EN8 . . .148 C4
Brookfield Ret Pk EN8 . .148 D5
Brookfields CM21 . . .97 D2
Brookhill SG2 . . .68 F8
Brookhouse Pl 3 CM23 . . .76 F8
Brookland Inf Sch EN8 .148 E3
Brookland Jun Sch EN8 148 E3
Brooklands Cl LU4 . . .44 C6
Brooklands Ct AL1 . . .127 E3
Brooklands Gdns EN6 . . .158 E7
Brookmans Ave AL9 . . .144 F5
Brookmans Park Prim Sch AL9 . . .144 E5
Brookmans Park Sta AL9 . . .144 E5
Brookmead Sch LU7 . . .80 E5
Brookmill Ct WD19 . . .167 B2
Brooks Ct SG14 . . .112 F7
Brooksfield AL7 . . .111 B7
Brookshill HA3 . . .176 D5
Brookshill Ave HA3 . . .176 E5
Brookshill Dr HA3 . . .176 D5
Brookside Buckland SG9 . .27 D5
Furneux Pelham SG9 . . .43 B4
Hatfield AL10 . . .129 D5
Hertford SG13 . . .113 E5
Hoddesdon EN11 . . .135 A6
Letchworth SG6 . . .22 F5
South Mimms EN6 . . .158 A7
Waltham Abbey EN9 . . .163 E7
Watford WD24 . . .154 D3
Brookside Cl EN5 . . .171 E3
Brookside Cotts WD4 . . .153 C5
Brookside Cres EN6 . . .146 E4
Brookside Gdns EN1 . . .162 C2
Brookside Rd WD19 . . .167 B2
Broom Barns Jun Mix Inf Sch SG1 . . .50 E5
Broom Cl
Hammond Street EN7 . . .148 A4
Hatfield AL10 . . .129 F2
Broom Cnr AL5 . . .107 C8
Broom Gr Knebworth SG3 .68 F5
Watford WD17 . . .154 A1
Broom Hill
Hemel Hempstead HP1 . . .123 E2
Welwyn AL6 . . .90 A8
Broom Wlk SG1 . . .50 E5
Broomer Pl EN8 . . .148 C2
Broomfield
Chiswell Green AL2 . . .141 C4
Harlow CM20 . . .118 B3
Broomfield Ave EN10 . . .148 E5
Broomfield Cl AL6 . . .89 C4
Broomfield Ct 2 AL10 . .130 A6
Broomfield Rd AL6 . . .89 C4
Broomfield Rise WD5 . . .153 D7
Broomhills AL7 . . .111 B7
Broomleys AL4 . . .128 D6
Brooms Cl AL8 . . .89 D1
Brooms Rd LU2 . . .64 A8
Broomstick Hall Rd EN9 . . .163 E6
Broomstick La HP5 . . .136 A1
Broughinge Rd WD6 . . .170 B7
Broughton Ave LU3 . . .45 C5
Broughton Hill SG6 . . .23 B6
Broughton Way WD3 . . .165 A2
Brow The WD25 . . .154 B6
Brown's Cl LU4 . . .44 D5
Brown's Cnr SG9 . . .27 F3
Brown's La HP23 . . .119 F7
Brown's Rise HP23 . . .119 F3
Brownfield Way AL4 . . .87 B6
Brownfields AL7 . . .110 F7
Brownfields Ct AL7 . . .111 A7
Browning Dr SG4 . . .35 B8
Browning Rd Enfield EN2 161 D1
Harpenden AL5 . . .86 C2
Luton LU4 . . .44 A2
Brownings La SG4 . . .47 D1
Brownlow Gate HP4 . . .81 B1
Brownlow La LU7 . . .80 A7
Brownlow Rd
Berkhamsted HP4 . . .122 C5
Borehamwood WD6 . . .170 A5
Browns Hedge LU7 . . .80 C3
Browns Spring HP4 . . .123 C7
Brownsea Ho 12 WD18 . .166 F3
Brox Dell SG1 . . .50 E6
Broxbourne CE Prim Sch EN10 . . .134 F2
Broxbourne Sch The EN10 . . .134 E1
Broxbourne Sta EN10 . .135 A3
Broxbournebury Mews EN10 . . .134 C3
Broxley Mead LU4 . . .44 D5
Bruce Gr WD24 . . .154 C1
Bruce Rd 9 Barnet EN5 . .171 E6
Harrow HA3 . . .176 E1
Bruce Way EN8 . . .162 D6
Brunel Rd SG2 . . .51 B7
Brunswick Ct EN11 . . .135 A5
Brunswick Rd EN3 . . .163 A1
Brunswick St LU2 . . .63 F8
Brushrise WD24 . . .154 A3
Brushwood Dr WD3 . . .164 C5
Brussels Way LU3 . . .44 D8
Bryan Rd CM23 . . .76 F8
Bryanstone Rd EN8 . . .162 F5
Bryant Cl EN5 . . .171 F4
Bryant Ct AL5 . . .86 A3
Bryce Cl SG12 . . .93 D3
Bryfield Cotts HP3 . . .137 C1
Bsns Ctr E SG6 . . .23 C6
Bsns Ctr The LU2 . . .64 B6
Bsns Ctr W SG6 . . .23 C6
Buchanan Ct
Borehamwood WD6 . . .170 C7
Luton LU2 . . .64 B8
Buchanan Dr LU2 . . .64 B8
Buckettsland La WD6 . . .157 D2
Buckingham Dr LU2 . . .46 D2
Buckingham Rd
Borehamwood WD6 . . .170 D5
Tring HP23 . . .99 E3
Watford WD24 . . .154 C2
Buckinghamshire Chilterns Unvi Coll (Chalfont Campus) HP8 . . .172 A8
Buckland Rd HP22 . . .99 A4
Buckland Rise HA5 . . .175 D2
Bucklands Croft HP23 . . .99 C8
Bucklands The WD3 . . .165 A2
Buckle Cl LU3 . . .44 F7
Bucklers Ct EN10 . . .134 F1
Bucklersbury SG5 . . .34 E6
Bucknalls Cl WD25 . . .154 E7
Bucknalls Dr AL2 . . .154 F8
Bucknalls La WD25 . . .154 E7
Bucks Alley SG13 . . .132 D4
Bucks Ave WD19 . . .167 E2
Bucks Hill WD4 . . .152 C5
Buckthorn Ave SG1 . . .50 E4
Buckton Rd WD6 . . .156 F1
Buckwood La LU6 . . .82 C7
Buckwood Rd AL3 . . .83 C6
Buddcroft AL7 . . .111 B7
Bude Cres SG1 . . .50 A7
Bulbourne Cl
Berkhamsted HP4 . . .121 F6
Hemel Hempstead HP1 . . .124 A2
Bulbourne Ct HP23 . . .100 A7
Bulbourne Rd HP23 . . .100 B7
Bull La Buckland SG9 . . .27 C8
Cottered SG9 . . .39 C8
Wheathampstead AL4 . . .108 A6
Bull Plain SG14 . . .113 D6
Bull Rd AL5 . . .107 B8
Bull Stag Gn AL9 . . .130 C7
Bull's Cross EN2 . . .162 A3
Bullace Cl HP1 . . .124 A4
Bullbeggars La HP4 . . .123 A4
Bullen's Green La AL4 . . .143 E8
Bullfields CM21 . . .97 E3
Bullhead Rd WD6 . . .170 C6
Bullock's Hill SG4 . . .49 B1
Bullock's La SG13 . . .113 C4
Bullrush Cl AL10 . . .130 B4
Bulls Cross Ride EN7 . . .162 A5
Bulls La AL9 . . .144 E7
Bullsland Gdns WD3 . . .164 B3
Bullsland La WD3 . . .164 B2
Bullsmoor Cl EN8 . . .162 C4
Bullsmoor Gdns EN8 . . .162 B4
Bullsmoor La EN1,EN3 . .162 C4
Bullsmoor Ride EN8 . . .162 C4
Bullsmoor Way EN8 . . .162 C4
Bullwell Cres EN8 . . .148 E2
Bulstrode Cl WD4 . . .137 E2
Bulstrode La
Chipperfield WD4 . . .137 F3
Hemel Hempstead HP3 . . .138 A5
Bulwer Link SG1 . . .50 E3
Buncefield La HP2 . . .125 C5
Bungalows The
Essendon AL9 . . .131 F7
Harpenden AL5 . . .86 C3
Bunker's Farm Cotts HP3 . . .139 D8
Bunkers La HP3 . . .139 B7
Bunnsfield AL7 . . .111 C7
Bunstrux HP23 . . .100 A4
Bunting Rd LU4 . . .44 A4
Buntingford Rd SG11 . . .55 D4
Bunyan Cl Pirton SG5 . . .20 D4
Tring HP23 . . .100 B5
Bunyan Rd SG5 . . .34 F8
Bunyans Cl LU3 . . .45 A5
BUPA Bushey Hospl WD23 . . .168 F1
Burbage Cl EN8 . . .162 F8
Burchell Ct WD23 . . .168 C2
Burfield Cl AL10 . . .130 A7
Burfield Ct LU2 . . .46 D3
Burfield Rd WD3 . . .164 C4
Burford Cl LU3 . . .31 A1
Burford Gdns EN11 . . .135 B7
Burford Mews 9 EN11 . .135 A7
Burford Pl 10 EN11 . . .135 A7
Burford St EN11 . . .135 A7
Burford Way SG5 . . .21 D2
Burgage Ct 12 SG12 . . .93 D1
Burgage La SG12 . . .93 D1
Burge End La SG5 . . .20 C5
Burgess Cl EN7 . . .147 C6
Burgess Ct WD6 . . .156 F1
Burghley Ave
Bishop's Stortford CM23 . . .76 C7
Borehamwood WD6 . . .170 C4
Burghley Cl SG2 . . .69 B8
Burgoyne Hatch CM20 . . .118 A1
Burgundy Croft AL7 . . .110 F4
Burhill Gr HA5 . . .175 E1
Burleigh Mead AL9 . . .130 C7
Burleigh Prim Sch EN8 .148 D1
Burleigh Rd
Cheshunt EN8 . . .162 E7
Hemel Hempstead HP2 . . .125 C2
Hertford SG13 . . .114 A7
St Albans AL1 . . .128 B3
Burleigh Way EN6 . . .146 E1
Burley SG6 . . .11 F2
Burley Ho WD5 . . .153 F7
Burley Rd CM23 . . .77 A4
Burn's Gn SG2 . . .52 F2
Burnell Rise SG6 . . .22 D5
Burnell Wlk SG6 . . .22 E5
Burnells Way CM24 . . .59 E7
Burnet Cl HP3 . . .124 E2
Burnett Ave SG16 . . .10 B4
Burnett Sq SG14 . . .112 F7
Burnham Cl
Datchworth AL6 . . .90 C6
Enfield EN1 . . .161 E1
Burnham Green Rd AL6, SG3 . . .90 D6
Burnham Rd Luton LU2 . . .46 B2
St Albans AL1 . . .128 B3
Burnley Cl WD19 . . .175 C5
Burns Cl Hitchin SG4 . . .35 B8
Stevenage SG2 . . .51 C8
Burns Dr HP2 . . .105 B1
Burns Rd SG8 . . .7 D8
Burnsall Pl AL5 . . .107 C6
Burnside Hertford SG14 .113 A5
Hoddesdon EN11 . . .134 F6
Sawbridgeworth CM21 . . .97 D2
St Albans AL1 . . .128 B1
Burnside Cl AL10 . . .130 A8
Burnside Terr CM17 . . .118 F3
Burnt Cl LU3 . . .44 F7
Burnt Mill CM20 . . .117 C3
Burnt Mill Comp Sch CM20 . . .117 F2
Burntfarm Ride EN2,EN7 161 B7
Burntmill Cl CM20 . . .117 C3
Burntmill Cnr CM20 . . .117 D4
Burntmill La CM20 . . .117 D3
Burr Cl AL2 . . .142 E4
Burr St LU2 . . .63 E8
Burr's Pl LU1 . . .63 E6
Burrowfield AL7 . . .110 D4
Burrows Chase EN9 . . .163 D3
Burrs La SG8 . . .17 C3
Bursland SG6 . . .22 D6
Burston Dr AL2 . . .141 C3
Burton Ave WD18 . . .167 A5
Burton Cl AL4 . . .87 C5
Burton Dr EN3 . . .163 A2
Burton Grange EN7 . . .147 E4
Burton La EN7 . . .147 E3
Burtons La WD3 . . .164 A4
Burtons Mill CM21 . . .97 F3
Burvale Ct 3 WD18 . . .167 B6
Burwell Rd SG2 . . .51 B4
Bury Cotts AL3 . . .105 E5
Bury End SG5 . . .20 D4
Bury Field SG9 . . .29 B7

Bury Gn
Hemel Hempstead HP1 ... 124 C4
Wheathampstead AL4 ... 108 C8
Bury Green Rd
Cheshunt EN7 ... 162 A7
Cheshunt EN7 ... 162 A8
Bury Hill HP1 ... 124 C4
Bury Hill Cl HP1 ... 124 C4
Bury Holme EN10 ... 148 F8
Bury La Bramfield SG14 ... 91 B4
Codicote SG4 ... 67 F2
Datchworth SG3 ... 69 D3
Rickmansworth WD3 ... 165 D1
Streatley LU3 ... 31 A5
Bury Mdws WD3 ... 165 D1
Bury Mead SG15 ... 11 A7
Bury Mead Rd SG5 ... 21 F1
Bury Park Rd LU1 ... 63 C8
Bury Plantation SG8 ... 7 F6
Bury Rd Harlow CM17 ... 118 D4
Hatfield AL10 ... 130 C6
Hemel Hempstead HP1 ... 124 C3
Bury Rise HP3 ... 137 D6
Bury The SG4 ... 67 F2
Burycroft AL8 ... 89 E1
Burydale SG2 ... 69 B8
Burydale Jun Sch SG2 ... 51 B1
Burydell La AL2 ... 141 D5
Buryfield Terr SG12 ... 93 C1
Buryfield Way SG12 ... 93 C1
Burymead SG1 ... 36 C1
Burywick AL5 ... 107 B5
Bush Hall La AL9 ... 130 D8
Bush Spring SG7 ... 13 A1
Bushbarns EN7 ... 148 A2
Bushby Ave EN10 ... 134 F1
Bushel Wharf HP23 ... 100 A6
Bushell Gn WD23 ... 176 D8
Bushey Cl AL7 ... 111 B5
Bushey Gn AL7 ... 111 B5
Bushey Grove Rd WD23 ... 167 E5
Bushey Hall Dr WD23 ... 167 E5
Bushey Hall Rd WD23 ... 167 E5
Bushey Hall Sch WD23 ... 167 F4
Bushey Heath Prim Sch
WD23 ... 168 D1
Bushey Ley AL7 ... 111 B5
Bushey Manor Jun Sch
WD23 ... 167 E4
Bushey Meads Sch
WD23 ... 168 C4
Bushey Mill Cres WD24 ... 154 C3
Bushey Mill La
Watford WD23 ... 167 E8
Watford,North Watford
WD24 ... 154 D1
Bushey Mus★ WD23 ... 168 A3
Bushey Pk WD23 ... 168 A3
Bushey Sta WD19 ... 167 D3
Bushfield Rd HP3 ... 137 C6
Bushmead Ct LU2 ... 45 E6
Bushmead Prim Sch LU2 ... 45 E5
Bushmead Rd LU2 ... 45 E5
Bushwood Cl AL9 ... 144 B8
Butchers La SG4 ... 48 D6
Bute Sq LU1 ... 63 E7
Bute St LU1 ... 63 E7
Butely Rd LU4 ... 44 B5
Butler's Hall La CM23 ... 76 B3
Butlers Ct EN8 ... 162 E7
Butlers Dr E4 ... 163 C1
Butlers Yd SG7 ... 12 E1
Butlin Rd LU1 ... 63 B7
Butt Field View AL1 ... 141 C7
Buttercup Cl AL10 ... 109 F1
Butterfield Cotts WD3 ... 172 E3
Butterfield Ct SG7 ... 23 E8
Butterfield Green Rd
LU2 ... 46 A6
Butterfield La AL1 ... 141 E7
Butterfield Rd AL4 ... 108 C7
Butterfly La WD6 ... 169 B7
Buttermere Cl AL1 ... 128 B2
Buttersweet Rise CM21 ... 97 E1
Butterwick WD25 ... 154 E3
Butterworth Path 1 LU2 ... 63 E8
Buttlehide WD3 ... 172 D5
Butts End HP1 ... 124 A5
Butts The EN10 ... 148 E7
Buttsmead HA6 ... 174 C3
Buxton Cl AL4 ... 128 D6
Buxton Path WD19 ... 175 C7
Buxton Rd LU1 ... 63 D7
Buxtons La SG8 ... 1 F3
Buzzard Rd LU4 ... 44 A4
By The Mount AL7 ... 110 D5
By The Wood WD19 ... 175 E8
By-Wood End SL9 ... 172 A5
Byde St SG14 ... 113 C7
Bye Way The HA3 ... 176 F2
Byers Cl EN6 ... 159 C5
Byewaters WD18 ... 166 C3
Byeway The WD3 ... 173 E8
Byfield AL8 ... 89 E1
Byfield Cl LU4 ... 44 B1
Byfleet Ind Est WD18 ... 166 B1
Byford Ho 5 EN5 ... 171 D5
Bygrave SG1 ... 36 C2
Bygrave Rd SG7 ... 12 F1
Bylands Cl CM23 ... 76 D6
Bylands Ho AL3 ... 106 A7
Byng Dr EN6 ... 159 A8
Byng Rd EN5 ... 171 D6
Byrd Wlk SG7 ... 23 F7
Byron Ave
Borehamwood WD6 ... 170 A4
Watford WD24 ... 167 D8
Byron Cl
Hammond Street EN7 ... 147 F4
Hitchin SG4 ... 35 B8
Stevenage SG2 ... 51 C7
Byron Ct EN8 ... 148 B3
Byron Pl HP2 ... 105 B1
Byron Rd Harpenden AL5 ... 86 A2
Harrow HA3 ... 176 F1
Luton LU4 ... 44 B2
Royston SG8 ... 7 E8
Byslips Rd LU6 ... 82 D5
Byway The EN6 ... 159 A6
Byways HP4 ... 122 E5

C

Cabot Cl SG2 ... 51 A7
Caddington Comm AL3 ... 83 E8
Caddis Cl HA7 ... 176 F3
Cade Cl SG6 ... 12 C1
Cades Cl LU1 ... 63 A6
Cades La LU1 ... 63 A6
Cadia Cl LU1 ... 62 E4
Cadmore Ct
12 Cheshunt EN8 ... 148 D3
Hertford SG14 ... 112 F7
Cadmore La EN8 ... 148 E2
Cadwell Ct SG4 ... 22 A2
Cadwell La SG4 ... 22 A2
Caernarvon Cl
Hemel Hempstead HP2 ... 124 D3
Stevenage SG2 ... 69 B7
Caernarvon Ct HP2 ... 124 D3
Caesars Rd AL4 ... 108 E8
Cage Pond Rd WD7 ... 156 F6
Cairn Way HA7 ... 176 F4
Cairns Cl AL4 ... 128 D2
Caishowe Rd WD6 ... 170 B8
Caister Cl
Hemel Hempstead HP2 ... 124 E2
Stevenage SG1 ... 36 A1
Calais Cl EN7 ... 147 D5
Calbury Cl AL1 ... 128 B2
Caldbeck EN9 ... 163 D5
Caldecot Ave EN7 ... 147 F2
Caldecot Way EN10 ... 134 F1
Caldecote Gdns WD23 ... 168 E2
Caldecote La WD23 ... 168 F3
Caldecote Rd SG7 ... 12 E8
Calder Ave AL9 ... 145 B5
Calder Way SG1 ... 37 A3
Caldwell Rd WD19 ... 175 D6
Caleb Cl LU4 ... 44 F2
Caledon Rd AL2 ... 142 D5
Caledonian Ct WD17 ... 167 B7
California SG7 ... 12 F1
California Ct 2 WD23 ... 168 D1
California La WD23 ... 168 D1
Callaghan Ct HP4 ... 122 D4
Callanders The WD23 ... 168 E1
Callisto Ct HP2 ... 124 F6
Callowland Pl WD24 ... 154 B1
Calnwood Rd LU4 ... 44 C3
Calton Ave SG14 ... 112 F7
Calton Ct SG14 ... 112 F6
Calton Ho SG14 ... 112 F6
Calverley Cl CM23 ... 76 E4
Calvert Rd EN5 ... 171 D7
Calverton Rd LU3 ... 45 A6
Cam Ctr SG4 ... 22 A3
Cam Sq SG4 ... 22 A3
Camberley Pl AL5 ... 107 D6
Camborne Dr HP2 ... 124 E7
Cambrian Way HP2 ... 124 F6
Cambridge Cl EN8 ... 148 C2
Cambridge Cotts SG11 ... 72 E2
Cambridge Cres SG8 ... 2 A8
Cambridge Ct EN5 ... 171 F6
Cambridge Dr EN6 ... 158 E8
Cambridge Rd
Barkway SG8 ... 17 D5
Barley SG8 ... 9 A3
Harlow CM20 ... 118 C6
Hitchin SG4 ... 22 C2
Sawbridgeworth CM21 ... 97 E4
St Albans AL1 ... 128 B2
Standon SG11 ... 55 C2
Stansted Mountfitchet
CM24 ... 59 E8
6 Watford WD18 ... 167 C5
Cambridge St LU1 ... 63 F6
Cambridge Terr 16 HP4 ... 122 D4
Cameron Ct 8 SG12 ... 93 D2
Cameron Dr EN8 ... 162 D5
Camfield AL7 ... 110 F2
Camford Way LU3 ... 44 A8
Camlet Way AL3 ... 127 B4
Camp Prim Sch AL1 ... 128 B2
Camp Rd AL1 ... 128 B2
Camp View Rd AL1 ... 128 B2
Campana Ct EN5 ... 171 D6
Campania Gr LU3 ... 45 A8
Campbell Cl
Buntingford SG9 ... 40 E7
Hitchin SG4 ... 35 B8
Campers Ave SG6 ... 22 E5
Campers Rd SG6 ... 22 E5
Campers Wlk SG6 ... 22 E5
Campfield Rd
Hertford SG14 ... 113 B5
St Albans AL1 ... 128 A3
Campfield Way SG6 ... 22 D5
Campine Cl 1 EN8 ... 148 D3
Campion Cl WD25 ... 154 A6
Campion Ct SG1 ... 50 C8
Campion Rd
Hatfield AL10 ... 129 F8
Hemel Hempstead HP1 ... 123 E2
Campion Way SG8 ... 7 E5
Campions CM17 ... 118 F5
Campions Ct HP4 ... 122 B3
Campions The
Borehamwood WD6 ... 157 A1
Stansted Mountfitchet
CM24 ... 59 E8
Campkin Mead SG2 ... 51 D3
Camps Hill Com Prim Sch
SG2 ... 51 C6
Campus Five SG6 ... 23 C7
Campus The AL8 ... 110 D7
Canada La EN10 ... 148 E6
Canadas The EN10 ... 148 E6
Canal Ct HP4 ... 122 E4
Canal Way UB9 ... 173 A4
Canalside HP4 ... 121 F6
Canberra Cl
Kneesworth SG8 ... 2 B5
St Albans AL3 ... 127 F7
Canberra Gdns LU3 ... 45 B6
Candlefield Cl HP3 ... 139 A8
Candlefield Rd HP3 ... 139 A8
Candlefield Wlk HP3 ... 139 A8
Caneland Ct EN9 ... 163 F5
Canfield CM23 ... 76 E8
Cangelis Cl HP1 ... 124 A1
Canham Cl SG4 ... 66 D1
Cannix Cl SG2 ... 51 A2
Cannon Ho 1 SG4 ... 34 F6
Cannon La LU2 ... 46 B5
Cannon Mews EN9 ... 163 B6
Cannon Rd WD18 ... 167 C4
Cannon St AL3 ... 127 D4
Cannon's Cl SG8 ... 1 F5
Cannons Cl CM23 ... 59 A1
Cannons Ct SG11 ... 55 D3
Cannons Mdw AL6 ... 90 E2
Cannons Mead CM24 ... 59 D7
Cannons Mill La CM23 ... 59 A1
Canons Cl WD7 ... 156 B4
Canons Field AL6 ... 87 D1
Canons Gate
Cheshunt EN8 ... 148 F5
Harlow CM20 ... 117 A2
Canons Rd SG12 ... 93 C2
Canonsfield AL6 ... 89 E8
Canonsfield Ct AL6 ... 89 E7
Canonsfield Rd AL6 ... 89 E8
Canopus Way HA6 ... 175 A6
Canopy La CM17 ... 118 C1
Cantelowes Ho EN5 ... 171 D4
Canterbury Cl Luton LU3 ... 44 F4
Northwood HA6 ... 174 F4
Canterbury Ct AL1 ... 127 F4
Canterbury Ho
10 Borehamwood WD6 ... 170 A7
4 Watford WD24 ... 167 C7
Canterbury Rd
Borehamwood WD6 ... 170 A7
Watford WD17 ... 167 B7
Canterbury Way
Croxley Green WD3 ... 166 C6
Stevenage SG1 ... 36 F2
Cape Rd AL1 ... 128 B3
Capel Ct SG11 ... 57 E2
Capel Ho WD19 ... 175 D6
Capel Manor Gdns★
EN1,EN7 ... 162 B4
Capel Manor Prim Sch
EN1 ... 162 B4
Capel Rd Enfield EN1 ... 162 B3
Watford WD19 ... 167 E3
Capell Ave WD3 ... 164 C4
Capell Rd WD3 ... 164 D4
Capell Way WD3 ... 164 D4
Capella Rd HA6 ... 174 F6
Capelvere Wlk WD17 ... 166 E8
Caponfield AL7 ... 111 B4
Capron Rd LU4 ... 44 E4
Captains Wlk HP4 ... 122 D3
Caractacus Cottage View
WD18 ... 167 A3
Caractacus Gn WD18 ... 166 F3
Caravan La WD3 ... 165 E2
Carbone Hill EN6,SG13 ... 146 D5
Carde Cl SG14 ... 112 F7
Cardiff Cl SG2 ... 69 B7
Cardiff Gr LU1 ... 63 D7
Cardiff Pl SG8 ... 2 A8
Cardiff Rd Luton LU1 ... 63 D7
Watford WD18 ... 167 B4
Cardiff Way WD5 ... 154 A7
Cardigan Ct 11 LU1 ... 63 D8
Cardigan Gdns 12 LU1 ... 63 D8
Cardigan St LU1 ... 63 D7
Cardinal Ave WD6 ... 170 B5
Cardinal Cl EN7 ... 147 F5
Cardinal Ct
Borehamwood WD6 ... 170 B6
3 Luton LU2 ... 45 D1
Cardinal Gr AL3 ... 127 B1
Cardinal Newman RC Sec Sch
LU2 ... 31 C1
Cardinals Gate SG8 ... 7 C6
Cardy Rd HP1 ... 124 B3
Careless Ct 21 CM23 ... 76 F7
Carew Lodge HA6 ... 174 E4
Carew Rd HA6 ... 174 F4
Carew Way WD19 ... 175 F7
Careys Croft HP4 ... 122 A7
Carisbrook Rd AL2 ... 141 B5
Carisbrooke Ave WD24 ... 167 D8
Carisbrooke Rd
Harpenden AL5 ... 86 C2
Luton LU4 ... 44 E1
Carleton Rd EN8 ... 148 E4
Carleton Rise AL6 ... 89 C6
Carlisle Ave AL3 ... 127 D4
Carlisle Ho 15 WD6 ... 170 A7
Carlton Bank 2 AL5 ... 86 B1
Carlton Cl
Borehamwood WD6 ... 170 D5
Luton LU3 ... 45 C2
Carlton Cres LU3 ... 45 C2
Carlton Ct
1 Harpenden AL5 ... 86 B1
Watford WD19 ... 167 C3
Carlton Pl HA6 ... 174 B5
Carlton Rd AL5 ... 86 B2
Carman Ct HP23 ... 99 F3
Carmelite Cl HA3 ... 176 C2
Carmelite Rd
Harrow HA3 ... 176 C1
Luton LU4 ... 44 A3
Carmelite Way HA3 ... 176 C1
Carmelite Wlk HA3 ... 176 C2
Carmen Ct WD6 ... 156 F1
Carnaby Rd EN10 ... 134 E3
Carnarvon Rd EN5 ... 171 E6
Carnegie Cl EN3 ... 163 B1
Carnegie Gdns LU3 ... 45 A8
Carnegie Rd AL3 ... 127 D7
Caro La HP3 ... 125 B1
Carol Cl LU3 ... 45 B4
Carole Ct LU1 ... 63 E5
Caroline Ho WD23 ... 168 A3
Caroline Pl WD19 ... 167 E3
Carolyn Ct LU3 ... 45 B4
Caroon Dr WD3 ... 152 B3
Carpenders Ave WD19 ... 175 E8
Carpenders Cl AL5 ... 85 D4
Carpenders Park Sta
WD19 ... 175 D7
Carpenter Way EN6 ... 159 D6
Carpenters Rd EN1 ... 162 C3
Carpenters The CM23 ... 76 B5
Carpenters Wood Dr
WD3 ... 164 B5
Carpenters Yd HP23 ... 100 A3
Carriden Ct SG14 ... 112 F8
Carrigans CM23 ... 76 E8
Carrington Ave WD6 ... 170 C4
Carrington Cl
Arkley EN5 ... 171 A4
Borehamwood WD6 ... 170 C4
Carrington Pl HP23 ... 100 C5
Carrington Sq HA3 ... 176 C3
Carsdale Cl LU3 ... 45 A6
Cart Path WD25 ... 154 C6
Cart Tk The HP3 ... 138 F6
Carteret Rd LU2 ... 46 C1
Carterhatch La EN1 ... 161 F1
Carters Cl Arlesey SG15 ... 11 A7
Aston SG2 ... 51 D4
Carters La (Wibbly Wobbly
La) SG5 ... 34 A6
Carters Leys CM23 ... 76 D8
Carters Way SG15 ... 11 A7
Carters Wlk SG15 ... 11 A7
Cartersfield Rd EN9 ... 163 C5
Carthagena Est EN9 ... 135 C3
Cartwright Rd Royston SG8 ... 7 D5
Stevenage SG1 ... 37 C2
Carve Ley AL7 ... 111 B5
Carvers Croft SG3 ... 69 B2
Cary Wlk WD7 ... 156 B5
Cashio La SG6 ... 23 A8
Caslon Way SG6 ... 11 F1
Cassandra Gate EN8 ... 148 F4
Cassio Ho WD18 ... 166 F5
Cassio Rd WD18 ... 167 B5
Cassiobridge Rd WD18 ... 166 E5
Cassiobridge Terr WD3 ... 166 D4
Cassiobury Dr WD17 ... 166 F7
Cassiobury Inf Sch
WD17 ... 166 E8
Cassiobury Jun Sch
WD17 ... 166 E8
Cassiobury Park Ave
WD18 ... 166 F6
Castano Ct WD5 ... 153 E8
Castellane Cl 1 HA7 ... 176 F3
Castile Ct EN8 ... 163 A5
Castile Gdns WD4 ... 138 F2
Castings Ho SG6 ... 23 A7
Castle Cl Bushey WD23 ... 168 B3
Hoddesdon EN11 ... 115 C1
Pitstone LU7 ... 80 D3
Castle Cotts SG9 ... 29 B7
Castle Croft Rd LU1 ... 63 A6
Castle Ct SG5 ... 21 D1
Castle Gate SG14 ... 113 C5
Castle Gate Way HP4 ... 122 C6
Castle Hill HP4 ... 122 C6
Castle Hill Ave HP4 ... 122 C5
Castle Hill Cl HP4 ... 122 C5
Castle Hill Ct HP4 ... 122 C6
Castle Mead HP1 ... 124 B1
Castle Mead Gdns SG14 ... 113 C6
Castle Mews 3 HP4 ... 122 D4
Castle Rd Enfield EN3 ... 162 E1
Hoddesdon EN11 ... 115 C1
St Albans AL1 ... 128 B3
Castle Rise AL4 ... 86 F2
Castle Row HP23 ... 100 A3
Castle St
Berkhamsted HP4 ... 122 C4
Bishop's Stortford CM23 ... 76 F6
Hertford SG14 ... 113 D5
Luton,High Town LU1 ... 63 E7
Castle St *continued*
Luton,New Town LU1 ... 63 E6
Wingrave HP22 ... 60 B3
Castle View CM23 ... 77 A7
Castle Wlk CM24 ... 59 E6
Castleford Cl WD6 ... 156 F1
Castles Cl SG5 ... 11 F8
Catalin Ct EN9 ... 163 D6
Caterham Ct EN9 ... 163 F5
Catesby Gn LU3 ... 31 A1
Catham Cl AL1 ... 128 B1
Cathedral & Abbey Church of
St Alban★ AL3 ... 127 D3
Cathedral Ct AL3 ... 127 B1
Catherall Rd LU3 ... 45 B6
Catherine Cl HP2 ... 125 B8
Catherine Cotts HP23 ... 120 E8
Catherine Ho WD19 ... 175 B7
Catherine Rd EN3 ... 162 E3
Catherine St AL3 ... 127 D4
Catherine Wheel Mews 20
SG12 ... 93 D1
Catisfield Rd EN3 ... 162 E2
Catkin Cl HP1 ... 124 B4
Catlin St HP3 ... 138 B8
Catsbrook Rd LU3 ... 45 B6
Catsdell Bottom HP3 ... 139 B8
Catsey La WD23 ... 168 C2
Catsey Wood WD23 ... 168 C2
Catterick Way WD6 ... 169 F8
Cattlegate Cotts EN6 ... 160 D8
Cattlegate Hill EN6 ... 160 D7
Cattlegate Rd
Crews Hill EN2 ... 161 A5
Northaw EN6 ... 160 D6
Cattley Cl EN5 ... 171 E5
Cattlins Cl EN7 ... 147 F2
Cattsdell HP2 ... 124 E5
Causeway Cl EN6 ... 159 D8
Causeway Ho WD5 ... 153 E8
Causeway The
1 Bishop's Stortford CM23 ... 77 A7
Braughing SG9,SG11 ... 42 D1
Brent Pelham SG9 ... 30 B1
Buntingford SG9 ... 40 F8
Furneux Pelham SG9 ... 43 A3
Kneesworth SG8 ... 2 A5
Potters Bar EN6 ... 159 D8
Therfield SG8 ... 15 F7
Cautherly La SG12 ... 115 A5
Cavalier SG1 ... 36 B1
Cavalier Cl LU3 ... 45 A5
Cavalier Ct 7 HP4 ... 122 C4
Cavan Ct AL10 ... 130 A4
Cavan Dr AL3 ... 127 D8
Cavan Rd AL3 ... 106 A6
Cave Gate SG9 ... 28 D6
Cavell Rd EN7 ... 148 A4
Cavell Wlk SG2 ... 51 C5
Cavendish Cres WD6 ... 170 A5
Cavendish Ct
Croxley Green WD3 ... 166 D4
Hemel Hempstead HP3 ... 138 E6
Cavendish Rd
Barnet EN5 ... 171 C6
Luton LU3 ... 45 B2
Markyate AL3 ... 83 D6
St Albans AL1 ... 127 F3
Stevenage SG1 ... 50 B5
Cavendish Sch The HP1 ... 124 B4
Cavendish Way AL10 ... 129 F5
Cawkell Cl CM24 ... 59 D7
Caxton Ct Enfield EN3 ... 162 E4
Luton LU3 ... 44 F4
Caxton Ctr AL3 ... 127 F8
Caxton Hill SG13 ... 113 F6
Caxton Rd EN11 ... 115 B2
Caxton Way
Stevenage SG1 ... 50 B4
Watford WD18 ... 166 D2
Cecil Cl CM23 ... 77 D7
Cecil Cres AL10 ... 130 B7
Cecil Ct EN5 ... 171 D6
Cecil Rd Brickendon SG13 ... 113 C3
Cheshunt EN8 ... 162 E7
Hoddesdon EN11 ... 135 C8
South Mimms EN6 ... 158 B7
St Albans AL1 ... 127 F3
Cecil St WD24 ... 154 B1
Cedar Ave Cheshunt EN8 ... 162 D6
Ickleford SG5 ... 21 E4
Cedar Cl Hertford SG14 ... 113 B6
Potters Bar EN6 ... 145 A1
Sawbridgeworth CM21 ... 97 E1
Ware SG12 ... 114 D8
Cedar Cres SG8 ... 7 B6
Cedar Ct
Bishop's Stortford CM23 ... 58 F1
St Albans AL4 ... 128 D3
Watford WD25 ... 154 D6
Cedar Dr HA5 ... 176 A4
Cedar Gn EN11 ... 135 A5
Cedar Grange HA6 ... 174 C3
Cedar Lawn Ave EN5 ... 171 E4
Cedar Lodge 8 EN8 ... 148 D3
Cedar Park Rd EN2 ... 161 C1
Cedar Pk CM23 ... 76 D4
Cedar Pl HA6 ... 174 C4
Cedar Rd
Berkhamsted HP4 ... 122 E3
Enfield EN2 ... 161 C1
Hatfield AL10 ... 130 A4
Watford WD19 ... 167 D3
Cedar Way HP4 ... 122 D3
Cedar Wlk
Hemel Hempstead HP3 ... 124 D1
Waltham Abbey EN9 ... 163 D5
Welwyn Garden City AL7 ... 111 B5

- Cedar Wood Dr WD25 154 B4
- Cedars Ave WD3 165 C1
- Cedars Cl WD6 170 B5
- Cedars Fst Sch HA3 176 C2
- Cedars Mid Sch HA3 176 C2
- Cedars The
  - Berkhamsted HP4 122 E4
  - 13 Harpenden AL5 86 B1
  - 5 Rickmansworth WD3 165 D2
  - St Albans AL3 127 C5
  - Stevenage SG2 69 B8
- Cedars Wlk WD3 164 F5
- Cedarwood Dr AL4 128 D3
- Celandine Dr LU3 45 A8
- Cell Barnes Cl AL1 128 B1
- Cell Barnes La AL1 128 B1
- Cemetery Hill HP1 124 C2
- Cemetery Rd CM23 76 F6
- Cemmaes Court Rd HP1 124 C3
- Cemmaes Mdw HP1 124 C3
- Centennial Ave WD6 169 C2
- Centennial Ct
  - Rickmansworth WD3 165 E2
  - Stanmore WD6 169 C2
- Centennial Pk WD6 169 C2
- Central App SG6 22 F6
- Central Ave
  - Cheshunt EN8 162 E6
  - Lower Stondon SG16 10 B3
  - Whipsnade LU6 81 E8
- Central Dr St Albans AL4 128 C4
  - Welwyn Garden City AL7 110 F8
- Central Hts WD18 166 F5
- Central Prim Sch WD18 167 C5
- Central Rd CM20 118 A4
- Central Way HA6 174 E3
- Centro HP2 125 C5
- Century Cl AL3 127 C4
- Century Ct WD18 166 C2
- Century Pk WD17 167 C4
- Century Rd
  - Hoddesdon EN11 135 A7
  - Ware SG12 93 D2
- Cervantes Ct HA6 174 F3
- Chace Ave EN6 159 D7
- Chace The SG2 50 F1
- Chad La AL3 84 C4
- Chadwell SG12 114 C8
- Chadwell Ave EN8 148 C3
- Chadwell Cl LU2 45 F1
- Chadwell Rd SG1 50 B3
- Chadwell Rise SG12 114 C8
- Chaffinch La WD18 166 F2
- Chaffinches Gn HP3 139 A7
- Chagny Cl SG6 22 E6
- Chalet Cl HP4 121 F4
- Chalfont Cl HP2 125 B8
- Chalfont Ho WD18 166 E2
- Chalfont La
  - Chorleywood WD3 164 B4
  - Maple Cross WD3 172 D3
- Chalfont Pl AL1 127 E3
- Chalfont Rd WD3,SL9, HP8 172 C7
- Chalfont Shire Ctr* HP8 172 A7
- Chalfont Way LU2 46 D2
- Chalfont Wlk 2 HA5 175 C1
- Chalgrove AL7 111 D7
- Chalk Dale AL7 111 B7
- Chalk Field SG6 23 C3
- Chalk Hill Great Offley LU2 47 A5
  - Watford WD19 167 E3
- Chalk Hills SG7 23 F5
- Chalkdell Fields AL4 128 A7
- Chalkdell Hill HP2 124 E3
- Chalkdell Path 8 SG5 34 D8
- Chalkdown Luton LU2 45 E6
  - Stevenage SG2 51 D7
- Chalks Ave CM21 97 D3
- Challney Boys High Sch & Com Coll LU4 44 D2
- Challney Cl LU4 44 D2
- Challney Girls High Sch LU4 44 D2
- Chalmers Ct WD3 165 F3
- Chalton Rd LU4 44 C5
- Chamberlaines AL5 85 A5
- Chambers Gate SG1 50 D7
- Chambers Gr AL7 110 E3
- Chambers La SG5 21 E4
- Chambers' St SG14 113 C6
- Chambersbury La HP3 139 A7
- Chambersbury Prim Sch HP3 139 B8
- Champions Cl WD6 157 B2
- Champions Gn EN11 115 A1
- Champions Way EN11 115 A1
- Champneys 3 WD19 175 E8
- Chancellor's Sch AL9 145 A6
- Chancellors SG15 11 B7
- Chancellors Rd SG1 36 D1
- Chancery Cl AL4 128 D8
- Chandler's La WD3 152 E2
- Chandlers Cl CM23 76 C4
- Chandlers Rd AL4 128 C6
- Chandlers Way SG14 113 A6
- Chandos Cl HP6 150 C1
- Chandos Rd
  - Borehamwood WD6 170 A7
  - Luton LU4 44 F1
- Channock's Farm Cotts CM20 117 C7
- Chantry Cl
  - Bishop's Stortford CM23 76 E8
  - Edgware NW7 170 F2
  - Enfield EN2 161 C1
- Chantry Cl *continued*
  - Kings Langley WD4 139 A2
- Chantry Ct AL10 130 A4
- Chantry La Hatfield AL10 129 F4
  - Hatfield AL10 130 A4
  - Little Wymondley SG4 35 F2
  - London Colney AL2 142 D5
- Chantry Mount CM23 76 E8
- Chantry Pl HA3 176 B2
- Chantry Rd
  - Bishop's Stortford CM23 76 E8
  - Harrow HA3 176 B2
- Chantry The
  - 6 Bishop's Stortford CM23 76 F8
  - Harlow CM20 118 A2
- Chaomans SG6 22 F3
- Chapel Cl
  - Brookmans Park AL9 145 D4
  - Little Gaddesden HP4 102 D6
  - Luton LU2 45 C8
  - St Albans AL1 141 D8
- Chapel Cotts HP2 124 D4
- Chapel Croft WD4 152 A8
- Chapel Crofts HP4 121 E6
- Chapel Dr SG15 11 A4
- Chapel End
  - Buntingford SG9 40 E7
  - Hoddesdon EN11 135 A5
- Chapel End La HP23 99 C8
- Chapel Fields HP23 99 C8
- Chapel Hill CM24 59 E6
- Chapel La
  - Letty Green SG14 112 B3
  - Little Hadham SG11 75 A8
  - Long Marston HP23 79 B4
- Chapel Pl SG5 11 F6
- Chapel Rd
  - Breachwood Green SG4 65 E8
  - Flamstead AL3 84 B2
- Chapel Row
  - 3 Bishop's Stortford CM23 76 F6
  - Harefield UB9 173 C2
  - Hitchin SG5 34 F8
  - Whitwell SG4 66 A8
- Chapel St
  - Berkhamsted HP4 122 D4
  - Hemel Hempstead HP2 124 D4
  - Hinxworth SG7 3 D6
  - Luton,High Town LU1 63 E7
  - Luton,New Town LU1 63 E6
  - Tring HP23 99 F3
- Chapel Viaduct LU1 63 E7
- Chapel Way WD5 139 F4
- Chapelfields SG12 115 D4
- Chapman Rd SG1 36 B1
- Chapmans End SG11 55 D3
- Chappel Mdw HP23 100 B6
- Chappell Ct SG12 92 E7
- Chapterhouse Rd LU4 44 A3
- Chard Dr LU3 31 B1
- Chardia Terr EN8 148 D1
- Charding Cres SG8 7 C7
- Chardins Cl HP1 123 F4
- Charkham Mews AL9 144 C7
- Charles St
  - Berkhamsted HP4 122 B4
  - Hemel Hempstead HP1 124 C2
  - Luton LU2 63 F8
  - Tring HP23 100 A3
- Charlesworth Cl 4 HP3 124 D1
- Charlock Way WD18 166 F3
- Charlotte Cl AL4 128 E3
- Charlottes Ct 2 LU1 63 D7
- Charlton Cl EN11 135 A6
- Charlton Mead La EN11 135 D5
- Charlton Rd SG5 34 D5
- Charlton Way EN11 135 B6
- Charlwood Cl HA3 176 E4
- Charlwood Rd LU4 44 B1
- Charmbury Rise LU2 46 A4
- Charmouth Ct AL1 128 A6
- Charmouth Rd AL1 128 A5
- Charndon Cl LU3 31 B1
- Charnwood Rd EN1 162 B3
- Charter Ho WD3 166 A4
- Charter Pl WD17 167 C6
- Chartley Ave HA7 176 F4
- Chartridge WD19 175 D8
- Chartridge Cl Arkley EN5 171 A4
  - Bushey WD23 168 C3
- Chartridge Way HP2 125 C3
- Chartwell Cl EN9 163 E6
- Chartwell Ct 8 EN5 171 E5
- Chartwell Dr LU2 45 E3
- Chartwell Rd HA6 174 F4
- Charwood Cl WD7 156 E6
- Chasden Rd HP1 123 F5
- Chase Cl SG15 11 A8
- Chase Farm Hospl EN2 161 A1
- Chase Hill Rd SG15 11 A7
- Chase St LU1 63 E6
- Chase The Arlesey SG15 11 A6
  - Bishop's Stortford CM23 76 F6
  - Goff's Oak EN7 147 B3
  - Great Amwell SG12 115 A6
  - Harlow CM17 118 C1
  - Hemel Hempstead HP2 124 E2
  - Hertford SG13 113 F6
  - Oaklands AL6 89 F7
  - Radlett WD7 155 F4
  - Watford WD18 166 E5
- Chaseside Cl LU7 80 A7
- Chaseways CM21 118 C8
- Chasten Hill SG6 22 D7
- Chater Inf Sch WD18 167 A5
- Chater Jun Sch WD18 167 B5
- Chatsworth Cl
  - Bishop's Stortford CM23 76 C7
- Chatsworth Cl *continued*
  - Borehamwood WD6 170 A6
- Chatsworth Ct
  - St Albans AL1 127 F3
  - Stevenage SG2 50 F1
- Chatsworth Mews WD24 154 A1
- Chatsworth Rd LU4 45 B1
- Chatter End CM23 58 C7
- Chatteris Cl LU4 44 D4
- Chatterton SG6 23 C5
- Chatton Cl LU2 46 E2
- Chaucer Cl HP4 121 F5
- Chaucer Ct EN11 115 A1
- Chaucer Ho 3 EN5 171 D5
- Chaucer Rd Luton LU3 45 C2
  - Royston SG8 7 C8
- Chaucer Way Hitchin SG4 35 C7
  - Hoddesdon EN11 115 A2
- Chaucer Wlk HP2 105 B1
- Chaul End La LU4 44 E1
- Chaul End Rd
  - Caddington LU1 62 D6
  - Luton LU4 44 B1
- Chaulden House Gdns HP1 123 F1
- Chaulden Jun & Inf Schs HP1 123 F2
- Chaulden La HP1 123 E1
- Chaulden Terr HP1 123 F2
- Chauncey Ho WD18 166 E3
- Chauncy Ave EN6 159 C6
- Chauncy Cl SG12 93 D3
- Chauncy Ct 19 SG14 113 D6
- Chauncy Gdns SG7 13 B1
- Chauncy Ho 3 SG1 50 E6
- Chauncy Rd SG1 50 E6
- Chauncy Sch The SG12 93 B2
- Chaworth Gn 1 LU4 44 C5
- Cheapside LU1 63 E7
- Cheapside Sq 4 LU1 63 E7
- Chedburgh AL7 111 D7
- Cheddington Comb Sch LU7 80 A7
- Cheddington La HP23 79 C5
- Cheddington Rd LU7 80 C4
- Cheffins Rd EN11 114 F1
- Chells Ent Village SG2 51 C6
- Chells La SG2 51 D7
- Chells Way SG2 51 B6
- Chelmsford Rd SG14 113 B5
- Chelsea Fields EN11 115 B2
- Chelsing Rise HP2 125 C2
- Chelsworth Cl 1 LU2 46 D1
- Cheltenham Ct AL1 128 A2
- Cheltenham Ho 2 WD24 167 C7
- Chelveston AL7 111 D7
- Chelwood Ave AL10 130 A8
- Chelwood Cl HA6 174 C3
- Chenduit Way HA7 176 F5
- Chene Dr AL3 127 D5
- Cheney Rd LU4 44 C5
- Chenies Ave HP6 150 D1
- Chenies Ct HP2 125 B8
- Chenies Gn CM23 76 D6
- Chenies Manor Ho* WD3 151 A1
- Chenies Rd WD3 164 D7
- Chenies Sch WD3 151 B1
- Chenies Way WD18 166 E2
- Chennells AL10 129 F4
- Chennells Cl SG4 22 B2
- Chennies The AL5 107 C7
- Chepstow AL5 85 F2
- Chepstow Cl SG1 51 B8
- Chequer Ct LU1 63 F6
- Chequer La AL3 106 B4
- Chequer St Luton LU1 63 F6
  - St Albans AL1 127 D3
- Chequers
  - Bishop's Stortford CM23 76 C8
  - Hatfield AL9 130 D8
  - Welwyn Garden City AL7 110 D3
- Chequers Bridge Rd SG1 50 C6
- Chequers Cl
  - Buntingford SG9 40 D8
  - Pitstone LU7 80 C4
  - Standon SG11 55 D4
  - Stotfold SG5 12 A6
- Chequers Cotts
  - Preston SG4 48 D6
  - Whipsnade LU6 82 A8
- Chequers End HP2 104 D5
- Chequers Field AL7 110 D3
- Chequers La
  - Abbots Langley WD2 140 C1
  - Pitstone LU7 80 C5
  - Preston SG4 48 D7
- Chequers Wlk EN9 163 F6
- Cheriton Cl AL4 128 D7
- Cherry Bank HP2 124 D5
- Cherry Blossom Cl 2 CM17 118 C4
- Cherry Cl SG3 68 F4
- Cherry Croft
  - Croxley Green WD3 166 B3
  - Welwyn Garden City AL8 89 D2
- Cherry Croft Gdns 4 HA5 175 F3
- Cherry Ct HA5 175 D2
- Cherry Dr SG8 7 E7
- Cherry Gdns
  - Bishop's Stortford CM23 77 A8
  - Sawbridgeworth CM21 97 E4
  - Tring HP23 99 F3
- Cherry Green La SG9 40 F3
- Cherry Hill
  - Chiswell Green AL2 141 A6
  - Harrow HA3 176 E4
  - Rickmansworth WD3 165 B6
- Cherry Hills WD19 175 E5
- Cherry Hollow WD5 153 F8
- Cherry Orch HP1 124 A5
- Cherry Orchard La SG9 28 A3
- Cherry Rd EN3 162 C1
- Cherry Tree Ave AL2 142 D5
- Cherry Tree Cl
  - Arlesey SG15 11 A4
  - Luton LU2 46 A1
- Cherry Tree Gn SG14 112 F7
- Cherry Tree La
  - Cholesbury HP23 120 A3
  - Chorleywood WD3 164 C1
  - Potters Bar EN6 159 B5
  - Wheathampstead AL4 87 A2
- Cherry Tree Prim Sch WD24 154 A3
- Cherry Tree Rd
  - Hoddesdon EN11 135 A7
  - Watford WD24 154 B3
- Cherry Tree Rise SG2 38 B1
- Cherry Trees SG16 10 B3
- Cherry Trees Dr SG2 51 B7
- Cherry Way AL10 130 A2
- Cherry Wlk WD3 165 C7
- Cherrydale WD18 166 F5
- Cherrytree La HP2 125 C7
- Chertsey Cl LU2 64 D8
- Chertsey Rise SG2 51 C4
- Cherwell Cl WD3 166 A4
- Cherwell Dr SG1 37 A3
- Chesfield Cl CM23 76 F5
- Chesford Rd LU2 46 C4
- Chesham Ct HA6 174 F4
- Chesham Prep Sch HP5 136 A4
- Chesham Rd
  - Berkhamsted HP4 122 C3
  - Bovingdon HP3,HP3 136 E3
  - Wigginton HP23 120 E7
- Chesham Way WD18 166 F3
- Cheshire Dr WD25 153 F5
- Cheshunt Centre The EN8 148 D3
- Cheshunt Folly EN8 148 B3
- Cheshunt Sch EN8 148 C1
- Cheshunt Sta EN8 148 F1
- Cheshunt Wash EN8 148 E4
- Cheslyn Cl LU2 46 E2
- Chess Cl Latimer HP5 150 D3
  - Rickmansworth WD3 165 D5
- Chess Hill WD3 165 D5
- Chess La WD3 165 D5
- Chess Vale Rise WD3 165 F3
- Chess Way WD3 165 A6
- Chesswood Ct WD3 165 D1
- Chesswood Way HA5 175 D1
- Chester Ave LU4 44 E3
- Chester Cl Luton LU4 44 F2
  - Potters Bar EN6 145 B2
- Chester Gibbons Gn AL2 142 D5
- Chester Ho HA6 174 F3
- Chester Pl 1 HA6 174 E3
- Chester Rd
  - Borehamwood WD6 170 D6
  - Northwood HA6 174 F3
  - Stevenage SG1 37 A1
  - Watford WD18 167 A5
- Chesterfield Flats EN5 171 D4
- Chesterfield Inf & Jun Schs EN3 162 E2
- Chesterfield Rd
  - Barnet EN5 171 D4
  - Enfield EN3 162 E2
- Chesterton Ave AL5 86 D1
- Chestnut Ave
  - Lower Stondon SG16 10 C3
  - Luton LU3 44 C8
  - Northwood HA6 174 F2
  - Rickmansworth WD3 165 A4
  - Ware SG12 93 F3
- Chestnut Cl
  - Bishop's Stortford CM23 76 E6
  - Dagnall HP4 81 C5
  - Hunsdon SG12 95 D1
  - Potten End HP4 123 B6
- Chestnut Ct
  - 4 Hitchin SG5 34 D8
  - Watford WD18 166 E5
- Chestnut Dr
  - Berkhamsted HP4 122 D3
  - Harrow HA3 176 F2
  - Hatfield Heath CM22 98 F3
  - St Albans AL4 128 C5
- Chestnut La
  - Kneesworth SG8 2 B6
  - Totteridge N20 171 E1
- Chestnut Rd EN3 162 E3
- Chestnut Rise WD23 168 B2
- Chestnut Wlk Hitchin SG4 35 A4
  - Royston SG8 7 E5
  - Stevenage SG1 36 D1
  - Watford WD24 154 A2
- Chestnuts The
  - Codicote SG4 67 F2
  - Hemel Hempstead HP3 137 F7
  - Hertford SG13 113 D5
- Cheverell's Gn AL3 83 C4
- Cheverells Cl AL3 83 D4
- Cheviot Cl Bushey WD23 168 C3
  - Luton LU3 44 D7
- Cheviot Rd LU3 44 D7
- Cheviots Hatfield AL10 130 A3
  - Hemel Hempstead HP2 124 F6
- Cheyne Cl Pitstone LU7 80 D4
  - Ware SG12 93 D3
- Cheynes Inf Sch LU3 44 D8
- Chicheley Gdns HA3 176 C3
- Chicheley Rd HA3 176 C3
- Chichester Way WD25 154 E6
- Chicken La AL2 142 D4
- Chidbrook Ho WD18 166 E3
- Chigwell Hurst Ct HA5 175 D1
- Chilcott Rd WD24 153 F3
- Chilcourt SG8 7 C6
- Childs Ave UB9 173 C1
- Childwick Ct HP3 139 B8
- Childwick Gn AL3 107 C2
- Chilham Cl HP2 124 E2
- Chiltern Ave WD23 168 C3
- Chiltern Cl
  - Borehamwood WD6 169 F7
  - Bushey WD23 168 B3
  - Goff's Oak EN7 147 B4
  - Ware SG12 93 D3
  - Watford WD18 166 F5
  - Berkhamsted HP4 121 F5
- Chiltern Cnr HP4 122 A5
- Chiltern Cotts HP23 120 A2
- Chiltern Ct
  - 19 Harpenden AL5 86 B1
  - St Albans AL4 128 D7
- Chiltern Dr WD3 165 A2
- Chiltern Gdns LU4 44 F3
- Chiltern Open Air Mus* HP8 164 A1
- Chiltern Park Ave HP4 122 A6
- Chiltern Rd Baldock SG7 23 F6
  - Hitchin SG4 35 A7
  - St Albans AL4 128 C7
  - Wingrave HP22 60 A3
- Chiltern Rise LU1 63 D6
- Chiltern View SG6 22 D5
- Chiltern Villas HP23 99 E3
- Chiltern Way HP23 100 C5
- Chilterns
  - Berkhamsted HP4 121 F6
  - Hatfield AL10 130 A2
  - Hemel Hempstead HP2 124 E5
- Chilterns The Hitchin SG4 35 A6
  - Kensworth Common LU6 82 F8
  - Stevenage SG1 37 B3
- Chilton Ct SG14 112 F8
- Chilton Gn AL7 111 C6
- Chilvers Bank SG7 23 E7
- Chilwell Gdns WD19 175 C6
- Chilworth Gate EN10 134 F1
- Chime Sq AL3 127 E4
- Chimneys The WD23 167 F4
- Chindit Cl EN10 134 E3
- Chinneck Ho 10 HP4 122 C4
- Chinnery Cl EN1 161 F1
- Chinnery Hill CM23 76 F5
- Chipperfield Rd
  - Bovingdon HP3 137 C3
  - Hemel Hempstead HP3 138 C7
  - Kings Langley WD4 138 D2
- Chipping Cl 8 EN5 171 E6
- Chipping Hall Cotts SG9 27 D4
- Chippingfield CM17 118 C3
- Chirdland Ho WD18 166 E3
- Chishill Rd Barley SG8 9 A2
  - Great Chishill SG8 9 F3
- Chishill Windmill* SG8 9 C2
- Chiswell Ct WD24 154 C1
- Chiswell Green La AL2 140 E6
- Chittenden Cl 5 EN9 115 B1
- Chivenor Pl AL4 128 C1
- Chobham Ct 8 LU1 63 F6
- Chobham St LU1 63 F6
- Chobham Wlk 5 LU1 63 E6
- Cholesbury 1 WD19 175 E8
- Cholesbury Ho WD18 166 E3
- Cholesbury La HP23 120 B2
- Cholesbury Rd HP23 120 D5
- Chorleywood Bottom WD3 164 D4
- Chorleywood Cl WD3 165 D2
- Chorleywood House Dr WD3 164 E6
- Chorleywood Prim Sch WD3 164 C3
- Chorleywood Rd WD3 165 C4
- Chorleywood Sta WD3 164 D5
- Chouler Gdns SG1 36 C2
- Chowns The AL5 107 A5
- Christ Church CE Prim Sch SG12 93 E1
- Christ Church CE Sch WD3 164 F5
- Christ Church La EN5 171 E7
- Christ Church Prim Sch EN5 171 D7
- Christchurch Cl AL3 127 D4
- Christchurch Cres WD7 156 A3
- Christchurch Ho HP23 100 A3
- Christchurch Pl SG14 113 C6
- Christchurch Rd
  - Hemel Hempstead HP2 124 D4
  - Tring HP23 99 F4
- Christie Cl EN10 134 F3
- Christie Rd Stevenage SG2 51 D5
  - Waltham Abbey EN9 163 B4
- Christina Ct AL3 83 E5
- Christopher Ct
  - Hemel Hempstead HP3 138 D8
  - 13 Ware SG12 93 D1
- Christopher Pl 3 AL3 127 D3
- Christy's Yd SG7 3 D6

Church Cl Codicote SG4 . . .67 F2
Cuffley EN6 . . . . .146 E2
Little Berkhamsted SG13 .132 C4
Northwood HA6 . . . . .174 F3
Radlett WD7 . . . . .156 A3
Reed SG8 . . . . .16 E4
Studham LU6 . . . . .82 B4
Church Cotts
Essendon AL9 . . . . .131 E6
Gilston CM20 . . . . .117 C7
Great Gaddesden HP1 . . .103 D3
Church Cres
Sawbridgeworth CM21 . . . .97 F2
St Albans AL3 . . . . .127 C4
Church Ct
Hoddesdon EN10 . . . . . . .135 A3
10 Ware SG12 . . . . .93 D2
Church End Arlesey SG15 .11 A8
Barley SG8 . . . . .9 A1
Braughing SG11 . . . . .55 F7
Markyate AL3 . . . . .83 D6
Redbourn AL3 . . . . .106 A4
Sandridge AL4 . . . . .108 C2
Walkern SG2 . . . . .38 C2
Church End Cotts WD3 .151 F1
Church Farm La HP23 . . .79 F3
Church Farm Way
WD25 . . . . .155 B1
Church Field SG12 . . . . . .93 B3
Church Field Path EN8 .148 C2
Church Gates 4 HP4 . . .122 C4
Church Gn Benington SG2 .52 D4
Great Wymondley SG4 . . . . .35 E6
Harpenden AL5 . . . . .86 A1
Church Green Row AL5 . .86 A1
Church Hill
Bedmond WD5 . . . . .139 F4
Cheddington LU7 . . . . .80 A8
Harefield UB9 . . . . .173 C1
Hertford Heath SG13 . . . .114 C4
Church La Arlesey SG15 . .11 A7
Ashwell SG7 . . . . .4 D4
Barkway SG8 . . . . .17 C4
Berkhamsted HP4 . . . . . . .122 C4
Bishop's Stortford CM23 . . .76 D3
Bovingdon HP3 . . . . .137 B4
Cheddington LU7 . . . . .80 A8
Cheshunt EN8 . . . . .148 C2
Colney Heath AL4 . . . . . . .143 B8
Dane End SG12 . . . . .71 F8
Graveley SG4 . . . . .36 C4
Guilden Morden SG8 . . . . . . .1 F5
Harrow HA3 . . . . .176 F2
Hatfield AL9 . . . . .130 C5
Hoddesdon EN10 . . . . .134 C1
Kimpton SG4 . . . . .66 D1
Kings Langley WD4 . . . . . .139 A2
Letchworth SG6 . . . . .12 C1
Marsworth HP23 . . . . .79 F1
Much Hadham SG10 . . . . . .74 F3
Northaw EN6 . . . . .146 A1
Preston SG4 . . . . .48 D6
Radlett WD25 . . . . .155 B1
Reed SG8 . . . . .16 E5
Rickmansworth WD3 . . . . .165 B1
4 Royston SG8 . . . . .7 D6
Sarratt WD3 . . . . .152 A2
Stapleford SG14 . . . . .92 A6
Stevenage SG1 . . . . .50 C7
Therfield SG8 . . . . .15 F7
Tring HP23 . . . . .120 A7
Weston SG4 . . . . .24 D1
Church Manor CM23 . . . .77 B8
Church Mead
Roydon CM19 . . . . .116 B1
Studham LU6 . . . . .82 B4
Church Meadow Cotts
HP1 . . . . .103 D3
Church Mill Grange
CM17 . . . . .118 E4
Church Path
Great Amwell SG12 . . . . . .114 F6
Little Wymondley SG4 . . . . .35 F3
Church Pl AL6 . . . . .89 C5
Church Rd Flamstead AL3 .84 B2
Great Hallingbury CM22 . . .77 D3
Hemel Hempstead HP3 . . .125 C2
Hertford SG14 . . . . .113 C7
King's Walden SG4 . . . . . . .47 F3
Little Berkhamsted SG13 .132 C4
Little Gaddesden HP4 . . . .102 D8
Northwood HA6 . . . . .174 F3
Pitstone, Church End LU7 . .80 E3
Pitstone, Ivinghoe LU7 . . . .80 F5
Potten End HP4 . . . . .123 B6
Potters Bar EN6 . . . . .145 B1
Slip End LU1 . . . . .63 C2
Stansted Mountfitchet CM24 59 F5
Stotfold SG5 . . . . .11 F6
Streatley LU3 . . . . .31 A6
Studham LU6 . . . . .82 B4
Watford WD17 . . . . .167 B8
Welwyn Garden City AL8 .110 D6
Church Row Mews 2
SG12 . . . . .93 D1
Church St Baldock SG7 . . .12 E1
Bishop's Stortford CM23 . . .76 F7
Bovingdon HP3 . . . . .137 B4
Buntingford SG9 . . . . .40 E8
Essendon AL9 . . . . .131 E6
Guilden Morden SG8 . . . . . . .1 F5
Hatfield AL9 . . . . .130 C5
Hemel Hempstead HP2 . . .124 D5
Hertford SG14 . . . . .113 D6
Luton LU2 . . . . .63 E7
Church St *continued*
Luton,High Town LU2 . . . . . .63 F8
Rickmansworth WD3 . . . . .165 E1
Sawbridgeworth CM21 . . . .97 E2
Shillington SG5 . . . . .19 E8
St Albans AL3 . . . . .127 D4
Waltham Abbey EN9 . . . . .163 C6
Ware SG12 . . . . .93 D1
Watford WD18 . . . . .167 C5
Welwyn AL6 . . . . .89 C5
Wheathampstead AL4 . . . .108 D8
Wingrave HP22 . . . . .60 B2
Church Street Ind Est
SG12 . . . . .93 D1
Church View
Hoddesdon EN10 . . . . .134 F3
Long Marston HP23 . . . . . .79 A4
Church Wlk
Bushey WD23 . . . . .168 A3
Sawbridgeworth CM21 . . . .97 F2
Church Yd Hitchin SG5 . . .34 E7
Tring HP23 . . . . .100 A3
Churchfield Barley SG8 . . . .9 A1
Harlow CM20 . . . . .118 B2
Harpenden AL5 . . . . .107 C8
Churchfield Ho AL8 . . . .110 C6
Churchfield Rd AL6 . . . . .90 C1
Churchfields
Hertford SG13 . . . . .113 D5
Hoddesdon EN10 . . . . . . .135 A3
Standon SG11 . . . . .55 E2
Stansted Mountfitchet CM24 59 F6
Churchfields La EN10 . . .135 A3
Churchfields Rd WD24 . .153 F3
Churchgate
Cheshunt EN8 . . . . .148 B1
7 Hitchin SG5 . . . . .34 E7
Churchgate CE Prim Sch
CM17 . . . . .118 F3
Churchgate Rd EN8 . . . .148 B2
Churchgate St CM17 . . . .118 E4
Churchill Cres AL9 . . . . .144 C8
Churchill Rd Luton LU4 . . .45 A1
St Albans AL1 . . . . .128 A4
Churchyard Wlk 6 SG5 . . .34 E7
Cicero Dr LU3 . . . . .45 A8
Cillocks Cl EN11 . . . . . . .135 A7
Claggy Rd SG4 . . . . .66 B2
Claire Ct Bushey WD23 . .168 D1
Cheshunt EN8 . . . . .162 D7
5 Pinner HA5 . . . . .175 F3
Clamp Hill HA7 . . . . .176 E5
Clapgate Rd WD23 . . . . .168 B3
Clare Cl WD6 . . . . .169 F3
Clare Cres SG7 . . . . .23 E6
Clare Ct Enfield EN3 . . . .162 E4
Northwood HA6 . . . . .174 E5
St Albans AL1 . . . . .127 F2
Claremont
Bricket Wood AL2 . . . . . . .155 A8
Goff's Oak EN7 . . . . .147 F2
Claremont Cres WD3 . . .166 C4
Claremont Rd
Hadley Wood EN4 . . . . . . .159 D2
Harrow HA3 . . . . .176 E1
Luton LU4 . . . . .45 B1
Clarence Cl WD23 . . . . . .168 F2
Clarence Rd
Berkhamsted HP4 . . . . . . .122 C4
Harpenden AL5 . . . . .86 A3
St Albans AL1 . . . . .128 A4
Stansted Mountfitchet
CM24 . . . . .59 E7
Clarendon Cl 1 HP2 . . .124 E4
Clarendon Ct
Harpenden AL5 . . . . .86 B3
7 Northwood HA6 . . . . . . .174 F5
Clarendon Mews WD6 . .170 A6
Clarendon Par EN8 . . . .148 D2
Clarendon Rd
Borehamwood WD6 . . . . .170 A6
Cheshunt EN8 . . . . .148 D2
Harpenden AL5 . . . . .86 B3
Luton LU2 . . . . .45 E1
Watford WD17 . . . . .167 B6
Clarion Cl SG5 . . . . .33 C2
Clarion Ho SG5 . . . . .33 C2
Clark Rd SG8 . . . . .7 D7
Clarke Way WD25 . . . . . .154 A4
Clarke's Rd AL10 . . . . . . .130 B7
Clarke's Spring HP23 . . .100 F5
Clarkfield WD3 . . . . .165 B1
Clarklands Ind Est★
CM21 . . . . .97 E5
Clarks Cl SG12 . . . . .93 D3
Clarks Mead WD23 . . . . .168 D2
Claudian Pl AL3 . . . . . . .127 A1
Claverhambury Rd EN9 .149 F2
Claverley Gn LU2 . . . . . . .46 E2
Claverton Cl HP3 . . . . . .137 A3
Clay End SG2 . . . . .52 F7
Clay Hill EN2 . . . . .161 D2
Clay La WD23 . . . . .168 E2
Claybury WD23 . . . . .168 B2
Claybush Rd SG7 . . . . .4 D3
Claycroft AL7 . . . . .111 B7
Claydon Cl LU3 . . . . .45 C7
Claydown Way LU1 . . . . .63 B1
Claygate Ave AL5 . . . . . . .85 E2
Clayhall Rd LU6 . . . . .82 F7
Clayhill HP23 . . . . .120 E7
Claymore HP2 . . . . .124 E7
Claymore Dr SG5 . . . . . . .21 F5
Claymores SG1 . . . . .50 E6
Claypons CM23 . . . . .77 B7
Clayton Hill Ctry Pk★
EN9 . . . . .149 D8
Clayton Par 7 EN8 . . . .148 D1
Cleall Ave EN9 . . . . .163 C5
Cleave The AL5 . . . . .86 D1
Clement Pl HP23 . . . . . .100 A3
Clement Rd EN8 . . . . . . .148 E4
Clements End Rd LU6,
HP2 . . . . .82 E2
Clements Rd WD3 . . . . .164 D4
Clements St SG12 . . . . . . .93 E1
Clementsbury SG13 . . . .133 C8
Clevedon Rd LU2 . . . . . . .46 B2
Cleveland Cres WD6 . . .170 C4
Cleveland Rd
Hemel Hempstead HP2 . . .125 B5
Markyate AL3 . . . . .83 E5
Cleveland Way
Hemel Hempstead HP2 . . .125 B5
Stevenage SG1 . . . . .37 C3
Cleves Rd HP2 . . . . .125 B8
Cleviscroft SG1 . . . . .50 E4
Clewer Cres HA3 . . . . . .176 D2
Clifford Cres LU4 . . . . . . .44 D5
Clifford Ct 10 CM23 . . . . .77 A7
Clifton Cl EN8 . . . . .148 E2
Clifton Rd Luton LU1 . . . . .63 B8
Watford WD18 . . . . .167 B4
Clifton St AL1 . . . . .127 E4
Clifton Way
Borehamwood WD6 . . . . .170 A8
Ware SG12 . . . . .93 D3
Climb The WD3 . . . . .165 B3
Clinton Ave LU2 . . . . .45 F3
Clinton End HP2 . . . . . . .125 C3
Clitheroe Gdns WD19 . .175 D7
Clive Cl EN6 . . . . .158 F8
Clive Ct LU2 . . . . .45 E1
Clive Par HA6 . . . . .174 E3
Clive Way WD24 . . . . . . .167 C8
Clock Ho The EN2 . . . . . .161 F2
Clockhouse Mews WD3 164 E6
Cloister Garth
Berkhamsted HP4 . . . . . . .122 C4
St Albans AL1 . . . . .141 E7
Cloister Lawns SG6 . . . . .22 F4
Cloister Wlk HP2 . . . . . .124 D5
Cloisters Rd
Letchworth SG6 . . . . .23 A4
Luton LU4 . . . . .44 B3
Cloisters The
Bushey WD23 . . . . .168 B3
Kings Langley WD4 . . . . . .139 A2
Rickmansworth WD3 . . . . .165 E2
3 Watford WD18 . . . . . . .167 C5
Welwyn Garden City AL8 .110 D6
Clonard Way HA5 . . . . . .176 A4
Clore Shalom Sch
London Colney WD7 . . . . .142 E1
Shenleybury WD7 . . . . . . .156 E8
Close The Baldock SG7 . . . .23 E7
Brookmans Park AL9 . . . . .144 E5
Bushey WD23 . . . . .168 A4
Codicote SG4 . . . . .67 F1
Harpenden AL5 . . . . .85 D4
Harrow HA2 . . . . .176 C1
Hinxworth SG7 . . . . .3 D6
Luton LU3 . . . . .45 A5
Markyate AL3 . . . . .83 E5
Potters Bar EN6 . . . . .159 A7
Radlett WD7 . . . . .155 F6
Rickmansworth WD3 . . . . .165 B1
Royston SG8 . . . . .7 F7
St Albans AL1 . . . . .141 C8
Wallington SG9 . . . . .25 E6
Ware SG12 . . . . .93 E1
Closemead Cl HA6 . . . . .174 C4
Clothall Rd Baldock SG7 . .23 F8
Clothall SG7 . . . . .24 C6
Clovelly Way SG1 . . . . . . .50 A7
Clover Ave CM23 . . . . . . .76 B6
Clover Cl LU4 . . . . .44 A3
Clover Field The WD23 .167 F3
Clover Way Hatfield AL10 129 F8
Hemel Hempstead HP1 . . .124 B4
Cloverfield AL7 . . . . .89 F1
Cloverland AL10 . . . . . . .129 F2
Clump The WD3 . . . . . . .165 B4
Cluny Way SG15 . . . . .11 A5
Clusterbolts SG14 . . . . . .92 A7
Clutterbucks WD3 . . . . .152 A3
Clyde Rd EN11 . . . . .135 D5
Clyde Sq HP2 . . . . .124 F8
Clyde Terr SG13 . . . . . . .114 A6
Clydesdale Cl WD6 . . . . .170 D4
Clydesdale Ct LU4 . . . . . .44 A3
Clydesdale Path WD6 . .170 D4
Clydesdale Rd Luton LU4 .44 A3
Royston SG8 . . . . .7 E6
Clydesdale Wlk EN10 . . .148 F6
Clyfton Cl EN10 . . . . . . .148 F8
Clyston Rd WD18 . . . . . .166 F3
Coach Dr SG4 . . . . .34 F5
Coach House Cloisters
SG7 . . . . .23 E7
Coach Mews AL1 . . . . . .128 B3
Coachman's La SG7 . . . . .23 D8
Coanwood Cotts SG12 . . .94 E4
Coates Dell WD25 . . . . .154 E6
Coates Rd WD6 . . . . . . .169 D2
Coates Way WD25 . . . . .154 E6
Coates Way Jun Mix Inf Sch
WD25 . . . . .154 E6
Cob Lane Cl AL6 . . . . .89 F4
Cobb Cl WD6 . . . . .170 C4
Cobb Gn WD25 . . . . .154 B7
Cobb Rd HP4 . . . . .121 F4
Cobbett Cl EN3 . . . . .162 C3
Cobbetts Ride HP23 . . . . .99 F3
Cobbins The EN9 . . . . . .163 E6
Cobbins Way CM17 . . . . .118 E4
Cobbinsbank EN9 . . . . . .163 D6
Cobblers Wick HP22 . . . .60 B3
Cobden Hill WD7 . . . . . .156 B2
Cobden St LU2 . . . . .45 F1
Cobham Rd SG12 . . . . . . .93 F2
Cobmead AL10 . . . . .130 B7
Cock Gr HP23 . . . . .121 C4
Cock La Brent Pelham CB11 30 F3
Hoddesdon EN11 . . . . . . .134 D4
Cockbush Ave SG13 . . . .114 B7
Cocker Rd EN1 . . . . .162 C3
Cockernhoe Endowed Prim Sch LU2 . . . . .46 E3
Cockfosters Rd EN4 . . . .159 E1
Cockle Way WD7 . . . . . .156 E6
Cockrobin La CM20 . . . .117 A7
Codicote CE Prim Sch
SG4 . . . . .67 E1
Codicote Dr WD25 . . . . .154 D5
Codicote Ho SG1 . . . . . . .36 C1
Codicote Hts SG4 . . . . . . .68 B1
Codicote Innovation Ctr
SG4 . . . . .88 E8
Codicote Rd
Ayot St Lawrence AL4,AL6,
SG4 . . . . .88 C3
Welwyn AL6 . . . . .89 B7
Wheathampstead AL4 . . . . .87 D1
Whitwell SG4 . . . . .66 F6
Codicote Row HP2 . . . . .105 B1
Codmore Wood Rd HP5 150 D6
Cohen Cl EN8 . . . . .162 E8
Colborne Ho WD18 . . . . .166 E3
Colbron Cl SG7 . . . . .4 C4
Colburn Ave HA5 . . . . . .175 E4
Colchester Rd HA6 . . . . .175 A1
Cold Christmas La SG12 .93 E6
Coldham Gr EN3 . . . . . . .162 E2
Coldharbour La
Bushey WD23 . . . . .168 C4
Harpenden AL5 . . . . .86 C4
Cole Green La AL7 . . . . .111 B4
Cole Green Way SG14 . . .113 A4
Cole Rd WD17 . . . . .167 B8
Colebrook Ave LU3 . . . . . .44 C7
Coleman Green La
Sandridge AL4 . . . . .108 E4
Wheathampstead AL4 . . . .109 A7
Coleman's La EN9 . . . . . .149 E5
Colemans Cl SG5 . . . . . . .20 D4
Colemans Rd SG4 . . . . . . .47 D1
Coleridge Cl
Hammond Street EN7 . . . .147 F4
Hitchin SG4 . . . . .35 B8
Coleridge Cres HP2 . . . .105 B1
Coleridge Ct 9 AL5 . . . . .86 B1
Coleridge Way WD6 . . . .170 A5
Coles Gn WD23 . . . . .168 C1
Coles Hill HP1 . . . . .124 A5
Colesdale EN6 . . . . .146 E1
Colestrete SG1 . . . . .50 F5
Colestrete Cl SG1 . . . . . . .51 A5
Coleswood Rd AL5 . . . . .107 C7
Colgate Ct EN5 . . . . .171 E4
Colgate Pl EN3 . . . . .163 A2
Colgrove AL8 . . . . .110 C5
Colin Rd LU2 . . . . .45 F2
Colindale Ave AL1 . . . . .127 F1
College Ave HA3 . . . . . .176 E2
College Cl
Bishop's Stortford CM23 . . .76 D7
Flamstead AL3 . . . . .84 B1
Harrow HA3 . . . . .176 E3
Ware SG12 . . . . .114 D8
College Ct Cheshunt EN8 148 C1
Hoddesdon EN11 . . . . . . .134 F8
College Hill Rd HA3 . . . .176 E3
College Ho LU1 . . . . .63 F7
College La AL10 . . . . . . .129 E4
College Lake Wildlife Ctr★
HP23 . . . . .100 C8
College Pl AL3 . . . . .127 C3
College Rd
Abbots Langley WD5 . . . . .154 A8
Aston Clinton HP22 . . . . . . .78 C1
Cheshunt EN8 . . . . .148 D1
Harrow HA3 . . . . .176 E2
Hertford Heath SG13 . . . .114 D2
Hitchin SG5 . . . . .34 F8
Hoddesdon EN11 . . . . . . .134 F8
St Albans AL1 . . . . .128 B2
College St AL3 . . . . .127 D3
College Way
Northwood HA6 . . . . .174 D4
Welwyn Garden City AL8 .110 D7
College Yd WD24 . . . . . .154 B1
Collens Rd AL5 . . . . .107 B5
Collenswood Rd SG2 . . . .51 B4
Collenswood Sch SG2 . . . .51 C4
Collet Cl EN8 . . . . .148 D3
Collet Gdns EN8 . . . . . . .148 D3
Collett Rd
Hemel Hempstead HP1 . . .124 C3
Ware SG12 . . . . .93 D2
Collett Sch The HP1 . . . .124 B4
Colleyland WD3 . . . . . . .164 D5
Collingdon Ct 10 LU1 . . . .63 D8
Collingdon St LU1 . . . . . .63 D8
Collings Wells Cl LU1 . . . .62 E4
Collingtree LU2 . . . . .46 B4
Collingwood Cl LU4 . . . . .44 D3
Collingwood Ct SG8 . . . . . .7 D7
Collingwood Dr AL2 . . . .142 D6
Collins Cross CM23 . . . . .59 B1
Collison Cl SG4 . . . . .22 C2
Collyer Rd AL2 . . . . .142 D4
Colmer Pl HA3 . . . . .176 D3
Colnbrook Cl AL2 . . . . . .142 E4
Colnbrook Sch WD19 . . .175 C7
Colne Ave
Rickmansworth WD3 . . . . .173 A8
Watford WD19 . . . . .167 C3
Colne Bridge Ret Pk
WD17 . . . . .167 D4
Colne Gdns AL2 . . . . . . .142 E4
Colne Lo WD3 . . . . .165 A1
Colne Lodge WD23 . . . . .167 D5
Colne Mead WD3 . . . . . .173 A8
Colne Valley Ret Pk
WD17 . . . . .167 D4
Colne Way
Hemel Hempstead HP2 . . .124 F8
Watford WD24,WD25 . . . . .154 E2
Colne Way Ct WD24 . . . .154 D3
Colney Heath Jun & Inf Sch
AL4 . . . . .129 C1
Colney Heath La AL4 . . .128 E2
Colonial Bsns Pk WD24 167 C8
Colonial Way WD24 . . . .167 D8
Colonnade The 7 EN8 . . .148 D3
Colonsay HP3 . . . . .125 C1
Colston Cres EN7 . . . . . .147 B4
Colt Hatch CM20 . . . . . .117 B1
Colt Mews EN3 . . . . .163 A2
Colthurst Gdns EN11 . . .135 D8
Colts Cnr SG2 . . . . .51 B4
Colts Croft SG8 . . . . .9 E2
Colts The CM23 . . . . .76 E4
Coltsfield CM24 . . . . .59 E8
Coltsfoot AL7 . . . . .111 B4
Coltsfoot Dr SG8 . . . . .7 E6
Coltsfoot Gn LU4 . . . . . . .44 A5
Coltsfoot La SG3 . . . . . . .90 D7
Coltsfoot Rd SG12 . . . . . .93 E3
Coltsfoot The HP1 . . . . .123 E2
Columbus Cl SG2 . . . . . . .51 A7
Columbus Gdns HA6 . . .175 A2
Colvin Gdns EN8 . . . . . .162 D4
Colwell Rd SG2 . . . . .51 C3
Colwell Rise LU2 . . . . . . .46 E2
Colwyn Cl SG1 . . . . .50 B7
Colyer Cl AL6 . . . . .89 F3
Combe Ho WD18 . . . . . . .166 E3
Combe Rd WD18 . . . . . . .166 F3
Combe St HP1 . . . . .124 C3
Combewood WD25 . . . . .154 C7
Comet Cl WD25 . . . . . . .153 F5
Comet Rd AL10 . . . . .129 F6
Comet Way AL10 . . . . . .129 E5
Commerce Way SG6 . . . . .22 F6
Common Field HP23 . . .100 D1
Common Gate Rd WD3 .164 E4
Common Gdns HP4 . . . .123 B6
Common La Ashwell SG7 . . .4 B6
Harpenden AL5 . . . . .86 D5
Kimpton SG4 . . . . .66 B1
Kings Langley WD4 . . . . . .138 F3
Radlett WD7,WD25 . . . . . .155 E1
Common Rd
Chorleywood WD3 . . . . . .164 D5
Kensworth Common LU6 . . .82 F8
Stanmore HA7 . . . . .176 D7
Stotfold SG5 . . . . .11 F7
Studham LU6 . . . . .82 B3
Common Rise SG4 . . . . . .22 A1
Common The
Chipperfield WD4 . . . . . . .152 B8
Harpenden AL5 . . . . .85 C4
Hatfield AL10 . . . . .130 A6
London Colney WD7 . . . . .156 B8
Potten End HP4 . . . . .123 A6
Stanmore HA7 . . . . .176 F8
Common View SG6 . . . . . .23 B8
Common View Sq SG6 . . .23 A8
Common Wharf SG12 . . . .93 E1
Commonfields CM20 . . .117 E1
Commons La HP2 . . . . . .124 E4
Commons The AL7 . . . . .111 B3
Commonswood Sch
AL7 . . . . .111 B3
Community Way WD3 . . .166 B4
Compass Point HP4 . . . .121 E6
Compton Ave LU4 . . . . . . .44 D4
Compton Gdns AL2 . . . . .141 B5
Compton Pl WD19 . . . . . .175 E6
Comroston EN11 . . . . . . .135 A6
Comyne Rd WD24 . . . . . .153 F3
Comyns The WD23 . . . . .168 C1
Concorde Dr HP2 . . . . . .124 D3
Concorde St LU2 . . . . . . .63 F8
Conduit La
Great Hormead SG9 . . . . . .29 B1
Hoddesdon EN11 . . . . . . .135 A6
Conduit La E EN11 . . . . .135 B6
Conemara Ct EN10 . . . . .148 F5
Coney Cl AL10 . . . . .130 B3
Coney Gree CM21 . . . . . . .97 D3
Coneydale AL8 . . . . .110 D8
Congreve Rd EN9 . . . . . .163 E6
Conifer Cl
Goff's Oak EN7 . . . . .147 F2
Stevenage SG2 . . . . .51 D7
Conifer Ct 7 CM23 . . . . . .76 F8
Conifer Wlk SG2 . . . . .51 C7
Conifers The WD25 . . . . .154 C4
Coningesby Dr WD17 . . .166 E7
Coningsby Bank AL1 . . .141 D7
Coningsby Cl AL9 . . . . . .144 D7
Coningsby Ct WD7 . . . . .156 A3
Coningsby Dr EN6 . . . . .159 D6
Coniston Cl HP3 . . . . . . .125 C2
Coniston Lodge 3
WD17 . . . . .167 A7
Coniston Rd
Kings Langley WD4 . . . . . .138 F3
Luton LU3 . . . . .44 F5

Connaught Cl HP2 ....125 A5
Connaught Gdns HP4 ....121 F7
Connaught Rd
Barnet EN5 ....171 D3
Harpenden AL5 ....86 B2
Harrow HA3 ....176 F2
Luton LU4 ....44 F1
St Albans AL3 ....127 C6
Connemara Cl WD6 ....170 D3
Connop Rd EN3 ....162 D1
Connor's Cl SG8 ....1 F4
Conquerors Hill AL4 ....108 E8
Conquest Cl SG4 ....34 F5
Constable Ct LU4 ....45 A1
Constantine Cl SG1 ....36 F1
Constantine Pl SG7 ....13 B1
Convent Cl SG5 ....34 F8
Convent Ct HP23 ....99 F3
Conway Gdns EN2 ....161 E1
Conway Ho WD6 ....170 C5
Conway Rd LU4 ....45 B1
Cony Cl [7] EN7 ....147 E5
Conyers CM20 ....117 C2
Cook Rd SG2 ....51 B7
Cook's Hole Rd EN2 ....161 C1
Cooks Mead WD23 ....168 B3
Cooks Spinney CM20 ....118 A2
Cooks Vennel HP1 ....124 B5
Cooks Way Hatfield AL10 130 B3
Hitchin SG4 ....22 A1
Coombe Gdns HP4 ....121 F5
Coombe Hill Rd WD3 ....165 A2
Coombe Rd
Bushey WD23 ....168 D2
Kelshall SG8 ....6 A1
Coombelands Rd SG8 ....2 E1
Coombes Rd AL2 ....142 C5
Cooper Way [10] HP4 ....122 D4
Cooper's Cl SG4 ....66 B1
Cooper's Ct SG12 ....114 E8
Cooper's Hill SG4 ....87 B8
Coopers Cl Aston SG2 ....51 D4
Bishop's Stortford CM23 ....76 B4
Coopers Cres WD6 ....170 C8
Coopers Ct SG14 ....113 D6
Coopers Field SG6 ....22 D7
Coopers Gate AL4 ....129 B1
Coopers Green La AL4, AL10 ....109 D1
Coopers La EN6 ....145 E1
Coopers Lane Rd EN6 ....160 B6
Coopers Mdw AL3 ....106 A6
Coopers Mews
Harpenden AL5 ....107 A8
Watford WD25 ....154 C8
Coopers Rd EN6 ....145 C1
Coopers Wlk [10] EN8 ....148 D3
Cooters End La AL5 ....85 F5
Copenhagen Cl LU3 ....44 D8
Copmans Wick WD3 ....164 D4
Coppens The SG5 ....12 A5
Copper Beech Cl HP3 ....137 F8
Copper Beech Ct [4] HA6 ....174 E3
Copper Beeches
[11] Harpenden AL5 ....86 B1
Oaklands AL6 ....89 D7
Copper Ct CM21 ....97 E2
Copperfields Luton LU4 ....44 C3
Royston SG8 ....7 C6
Welwyn Garden City AL7 ....111 C5
Coppermill La WD3,UB9 .172 F3
Copperwood SG13 ....113 F6
Coppice Cl Harrow HA7 .176 F4
Hatfield AL10 ....129 F1
Coppice Farm Pk HP23 .119 D4
Coppice Mead SG5 ....11 E5
Coppice The
Bishop's Stortford CM23 ....76 D5
[1] Harpenden AL5 ....85 F2
Hemel Hempstead HP2 ....125 B4
Watford WD19 ....167 C3
Wigginton HP23 ....100 C1
Coppings The EN11 ....115 A1
Coppins Cl HP4 ....121 F4
Coppins The
Harrow HA3 ....176 E4
Markyate AL3 ....83 D5
Copse Cl HA6 ....174 C1
Copse Hill AL6 ....90 A8
Copse The
Bishop's Stortford CM23 ....77 C8
Hemel Hempstead HP1 ....123 E5
Hertford SG13 ....114 A6
Copse Way LU3 ....44 D8
Copse Wood Way HA6 .174 C2
Copsewood Rd WD24 ....167 B8
Copt Hall Cotts LU2 ....64 E4
Copthall Cl CM22 ....77 F4
Copthorne LU2 ....46 D3
Copthorne Ave EN10 ....134 F3
Copthorne Cl WD3 ....165 F4
Copthorne Rd WD3 ....165 F4
Coral Gdns HP2 ....124 F3
Coral Ho CM20 ....117 A1
Corals Mead AL7 ....110 D5
Coram Cl HP4 ....122 C3
Corbridge Dr LU2 ....46 E1
Corby Cl AL2 ....141 A6
Cordell Cl EN8 ....148 E3
Corder Cl AL3 ....141 A8
Coreys Mill La SG1 ....36 C1
Corfe Cl
Borehamwood WD6 ....170 D6
[4] Hemel Hempstead HP2 124 E2
Corinium Gate AL3 ....127 A1
Corinium Gdns LU3 ....45 A8
Corncastle Rd LU1 ....63 D6
Corncrake Cl LU2 ....46 C5
Corncroft AL10 ....130 B7
Cornel Cl LU1 ....63 A7
Cornel Ct LU1 ....63 A7
Cornelia Ct [3] AL5 ....86 A2
Cornelious Ho WD18 ....166 F5
Corner Cl SG6 ....22 E6
Corner Hall HP3 ....124 D1
Corner Hall Ave HP3 ....124 D1
Corner View AL9 ....144 C7
Corner Wood AL3 ....83 D5
Cornerfield AL10 ....130 B8
Corners AL7 ....111 A7
Cornfield Cres HP4 ....121 D7
Cornfield Rd WD23 ....168 B5
Cornfields
Hemel Hempstead HP1 ....124 B2
Stevenage SG2 ....51 C7
Cornflower Way AL10 ....129 E8
Cornhill Dr EN3 ....162 E2
Cornmead AL8 ....89 C1
Cornmill EN9 ....163 C6
Cornwall Cl EN8 ....162 E6
Cornwall Ct [6] HA6 ....175 F3
Cornwall Ho CM23 ....76 E4
Cornwall Rd
Harpenden AL5 ....86 B2
Pinner HA5 ....175 F3
St Albans AL1 ....127 E1
Coronation Ave SG8 ....7 C5
Coronation Rd
Bishop's Stortford CM23 ....76 E5
Ware SG12 ....93 D2
Coronet Ho [2] HA7 ....176 F4
Corringham Ct AL1 ....127 F4
Corton Cl SG1 ....50 B8
Corvus Cl SG8 ....7 E8
Cory-Wright Way AL4 ....87 E1
Cosgrove Way LU1 ....44 D1
Cosne Mews AL5 ....107 C7
Costins Wlk [12] HP4 ....122 D4
Cotefield LU4 ....44 C3
Cotesmore Rd HP1 ....123 E2
Cotlandswick AL2 ....142 C5
Cotney Croft SG2 ....51 D3
Cotsmoor AL1 ....127 F3
Cotswold HP2 ....124 E6
Cotswold Ave WD23 ....168 C3
Cotswold Bsns Pk LU1 ....62 D2
Cotswold Cl AL4 ....128 C8
Cotswold Gdns LU3 ....44 C7
Cotswolds AL10 ....130 A3
Cottage Cl
Croxley Green WD3 ....165 F3
Watford WD17 ....166 F7
Cottage Gdns EN8 ....148 D2
Cotter Ho SG1 ....37 A3
Cottered Rd SG9 ....26 F1
Cotterells HP1 ....124 C2
Cotterells Hill HP1 ....124 C3
Cotton Dr SG13 ....114 B7
Cotton Field AL10 ....130 B7
Cotton Rd EN6 ....159 C8
Cottonmill Cres AL1 ....127 D2
Cottonmill La AL1 ....127 D1
Coulser Cl HP1 ....124 A6
Coulson Ct
London Colney AL2 ....142 D4
Luton LU1 ....62 F8
Coulter Cl EN6 ....146 D4
Council Cotts
Great Wymondley SG4 ....35 F6
Letchworth SG6 ....23 B2
Radwell SG7 ....12 C4
Counters Cl HP1 ....124 A3
Countess Anne CE Prim Sch AL9 ....130 C6
Countess Cl UB9 ....173 C1
Countess Ct [4] LU2 ....45 D1
Couper Ho WD18 ....166 E3
Coursers Farm Cotts AL4 ....143 C6
Coursers Rd AL2,AL4 ....143 C6
Court Cl CM23 ....76 E5
Court Needham EN3 ....163 A2
Courtaulds WD4 ....138 B1
Courtenay Ave HA3 ....176 C2
Courtenay Gdns HA3 ....176 C1
Courtfield Cl EN10 ....135 A3
Courtfields AL5 ....86 D1
Courtlands Cl WD24 ....153 E4
Courtlands Dr WD17 ....153 E3
Courtleigh Ave EN4 ....159 D1
Courtway The WD19 ....175 E8
Courtyard Mews SG12 ....92 E4
Courtyard The
Hemel Hempstead HP3 ....138 D5
Hertingfordbury SG14 ....112 F5
St Albans AL4 ....128 F3
Courtyards The WD18 ....166 D2
Covent Garden Cl LU4 ....44 F3
Coventry Cl SG1 ....37 B1
Coverdale
Hemel Hempstead HP2 ....124 E6
Luton LU4 ....44 B6
Coverdale Ct EN3 ....162 E2
Covert Cl HP4 ....121 D6
Covert Rd HP4 ....121 D6
Covert The HA6 ....174 C2
Cow La Bushey WD23 ....168 A3
Tring HP23 ....100 D4
Watford WD25 ....154 C3
Cowards La SG4 ....88 F8
Cowbridge SG14 ....113 C6
Cowdray Cl LU2 ....46 C3
Cowles EN7 ....147 F4
Cowley Hill WD6 ....157 B1
Cowley Hill Sch WD6 ....170 A8
Cowlins CM17 ....118 D4
Cowper Cres SG14 ....92 B1
Cowper Ct Markyate AL3 ....83 D5
Watford WD24 ....154 A2
Cowper Rd
Berkhamsted HP4 ....122 B4
Harpenden AL5 ....86 C1
Hemel Hempstead HP1 ....124 B2
Markyate AL3 ....83 D5
Welwyn Garden City AL7 ....110 F4
Cowper Rise AL3 ....83 D5
Cowper St LU1 ....63 E5
Cowpers Way AL6 ....90 D5
Cowridge Cres LU2 ....64 A8
Cowslip Cl SG8 ....7 F5
Cowslip Hill SG6 ....22 E7
Cowslips AL7 ....111 C5
Cox Cl WD7 ....156 F7
Cox's Way SG15 ....11 A6
Coxfield Cl HP2 ....124 E2
Coyney Gn LU3 ....45 C1
Cozens La E EN10 ....134 F1
Cozens La W EN10 ....134 F1
Cozens Rd SG12 ....94 A2
Crab La WD25 ....155 B4
Crab Tree La SG5 ....20 D4
Crab Tree Rd SG3 ....68 F4
Crabb's La SG9 ....43 F6
Crabbes Cl SG5 ....34 E7
Crabtree Cl
Bushey WD23 ....168 B4
Hemel Hempstead HP3 ....124 D1
Crabtree Ct [3] HP3 ....124 E1
Crabtree Dell SG6 ....23 B3
Crabtree Inf Sch AL5 ....86 C1
Crabtree La
Harpenden AL5 ....86 C1
Hemel Hempstead HP3 ....124 D1
Crabtree Wlk EN10 ....134 E4
Crackley Mdw HP2 ....125 B8
Cradock Rd LU4 ....44 B1
Crafton Gn CM24 ....59 E7
Cragg Ave WD7 ....155 F3
Cragside SG2 ....69 C7
Craig Mount WD7 ....156 B4
Craigavon Rd HP2 ....124 F7
Craiglands AL4 ....128 D7
Craigmore Ct [5] HA6 ....174 E3
Craigs Wlk [4] EN8 ....148 D3
Craigweil Ave WD7 ....156 B4
Crakers Mead [4] WD18 .167 B6
Cranborne Ave
Hitchin SG5 ....34 D6
Potters Bar EN6 ....144 E1
Cranborne Cl
Brickendon SG13 ....113 C3
Potters Bar EN6 ....158 E8
Cranborne Cres EN6 ....158 E8
Cranborne Ct EN3 ....162 D3
Cranborne Gdns AL7 ....110 F5
Cranborne Ind Est EN6 .144 E1
Cranborne Par EN6 ....158 D8
Cranborne Prim Sch EN6 ....158 F8
Cranborne Rd
Cheshunt EN8 ....162 D7
Hatfield AL10 ....130 B6
Hoddesdon EN11 ....135 C7
Potters Bar EN6 ....144 E1
Cranbourne SG1 ....36 B1
Cranbourne Dr
Harpenden AL5 ....107 D6
Hoddesdon EN11 ....115 C2
Cranbourne Ho EN11 ....115 C2
Cranbourne Prim Sch The EN11 ....115 B2
Cranbourne Rd HA6 ....174 F1
Cranbrook Cl SG12 ....93 D3
Cranbrook Dr Luton LU3 ..44 D8
St Albans AL4 ....128 E3
Crane Mead SG12 ....114 E8
Crane Mead Bsns Pk SG12 ....114 E8
Cranefield Dr WD25 ....154 E6
Cranes Way WD6 ....170 C4
Cranfield Cres EN6 ....146 E2
Cranford Ct
Harpenden AL5 ....86 C1
Hertford SG14 ....112 F7
Cranleigh Cl EN7 ....148 A3
Cranleigh Gdns LU3 ....45 D3
Cranmer Cl EN6 ....145 C1
Cranmore Ct AL1 ....127 F4
Cranwell Cl AL4 ....128 C1
Cranwell Gdns CM23 ....59 C1
Cravells Ct AL5 ....107 C7
Cravells Rd AL5 ....107 C7
Crawford Rd AL10 ....130 A7
Crawley Cl LU1 ....63 C1
Crawley Dr HP2 ....124 F7
Crawley Green Inf Sch LU2 ....64 B8
Crawley Green Rd
Luton, Hart Hill LU2 ....64 A8
Luton, Wigmore LU2 ....46 D1
Crawley Rd LU1 ....63 D8
Crawley's La HP23 ....120 F7
Creamery Ct SG6 ....23 C3
Creasy Cl WD5 ....153 F8
Crecy Gdns AL3 ....106 A6
Creighton Ave AL1 ....141 D8
Crescent E EN4 ....159 C1
Crescent Rd
Bishop's Stortford CM23 ....77 A6
Hemel Hempstead HP2 ....124 D3
Luton LU2 ....63 F8
Crescent Rise LU2 ....63 F8
Crescent The
Abbots Langley WD5 ....139 F1
Ardeley SG2 ....38 F2
Bricket Wood AL2 ....141 A1
Caddington LU1 ....62 E3
Cottered SG9 ....39 D7
Croxley Green WD3 ....166 B3
Harlow CM17 ....118 C6
Hitchin SG5 ....21 D1
Letchworth SG6 ....23 A5
Lower Stondon SG16 ....10 C4
Marsworth HP23 ....80 A1
Pitstone LU7 ....80 C4
Radlett WD25 ....155 B1
St Ippolyts SG4 ....35 A3
Watford WD18 ....167 C5
Welwyn AL6 ....89 C4
Crescent W EN4 ....159 C1
Cress End WD3 ....165 A1
Cresset Cl SG12 ....115 C3
Cresswick SG4 ....66 E7
Crest Dr EN3 ....162 C1
Crest Pk HP2 ....125 C4
Crest The
Goff's Oak EN7 ....147 B4
Luton LU3 ....45 B7
Oaklands AL6 ....89 D8
Sawbridgeworth CM21 ....97 D2
Ware SG12 ....93 D3
Cresta Cl LU5 ....44 A2
Cresta Ho [3] LU1 ....63 D7
Creswick Ct AL7 ....110 D5
Creswick Jun Mix Inf Sch AL7 ....110 D3
Crew Curve HP4 ....121 F7
Crews Hill EN2 ....160 F5
Crews Hill Sta EN2 ....160 F5
Crib St SG12 ....93 D2
Cricketer's Rd SG15 ....11 A4
Cricketers Cl AL3 ....127 E4
Cricketfield La CM23 ....76 E8
Cringle Ct EN6 ....145 C1
Crispin Field LU7 ....80 C4
Croasdaile Rd CM24 ....59 E8
Croasdale Cl CM24 ....59 E8
Crocus Field EN5 ....171 F3
Croft Cl WD4 ....138 A1
Croft Ct
Borehamwood WD6 ....170 D6
[4] Harpenden AL5 ....86 B1
Hitchin SG5 ....34 E7
Croft End Rd WD4 ....138 A1
Croft Field
Chipperfield WD4 ....138 A1
Hatfield AL10 ....130 A5
Croft La
Chipperfield WD4 ....138 A1
Letchworth SG6 ....12 B1
Croft Mdw WD4 ....138 A1
Croft Mdws LU7 ....80 A7
Croft Rd Luton LU2 ....46 B3
Ware SG12 ....93 C2
Croft The Barnet EN5 ....171 E5
Chiswell Green AL2 ....141 A6
Hoddesdon EN10 ....148 E8
Luton LU3 ....44 D8
Wareside SG12 ....94 E4
Welwyn Garden City AL7 ....110 F3
Croft Wlk EN10 ....148 E8
Crofters CM21 ....97 E3
Crofters End CM21 ....97 E3
Crofters Rd HA6 ....174 E6
Crofts Path HP3 ....125 B1
Crofts The
Hemel Hempstead HP3 ....125 B2
Stotfold SG5 ....11 F6
Croftwell AL5 ....107 F8
Cromer Cl HP4 ....102 E5
Cromer Rd WD24 ....154 C1
Cromer Way
Luton, Stopsley Common LU2 ....45 E6
Luton, Warden Hill LU2 ....45 D7
Cromer Windmill* SG2 .38 E6
Crompton Pl EN3 ....163 A1
Crompton Rd SG1 ....50 A6
Cromwell Ave EN7 ....148 B1
Cromwell Cl
Bishop's Stortford CM23 ....76 B7
St Albans AL4 ....128 D8
Cromwell Gn SG6 ....23 B8
Cromwell Hill LU2 ....45 D1
Cromwell Rd
Borehamwood WD6 ....169 E8
Cheshunt EN7 ....148 B3
Hertford SG13 ....114 A7
Letchworth SG6 ....23 B8
Luton LU3 ....45 D1
Stevenage SG2 ....51 C5
Ware SG12 ....93 F2
Cromwell Way SG5 ....20 D4
Crooked Mile
Waltham Abbey EN9 ....163 C6
Waltham Abbey EN9 ....163 C7
Crooked Way EN9 ....135 E1
Crookhams AL7 ....90 A1
Crop Comm AL10 ....130 B7
Crosby Cl Luton LU4 ....45 A2
St Albans AL4 ....142 C8
Crosfield Ct WD17 ....167 D4
Cross Farm Mews HP3 .137 D2
Cross La Harpenden AL5 .107 C5
Hertford SG14 ....113 B6
Cross Oak Rd HP4 ....122 A4
Cross Rd Cheshunt EN8 .162 E6
Hertford SG14 ....113 C7
Watford WD19 ....167 E3
Cross St Letchworth SG6 ..22 F7
Cross St *continued*
Luton LU2 ....63 E8
[2] St Albans AL3 ....127 D3
Ware SG12 ....93 E1
Watford WD17 ....167 C6
Cross Way AL5 ....86 C3
Cross Way The
Harrow HA3 ....176 E1
Luton LU1 ....63 C5
Crossbrook AL10 ....129 E4
Crossbrook St EN8 ....162 D8
Crossett Gn HP3 ....125 C1
Crossfell Rd HP3 ....125 C2
Crossfield Rd EN11 ....135 B8
Crossfields AL3 ....141 B8
Crossfields Cl HP4 ....121 F4
Crossgates SG1 ....50 E5
Crosslands LU1 ....62 E3
Crossleys SG6 ....11 F2
Crossmead WD19 ....167 B3
Crossoaks La EN6 ....157 F5
Crosspath The WD7 ....156 A4
Crosspaths AL5 ....85 C4
Crossway Harlow CM17 ..118 D1
Pinner HA5 ....175 B1
Welwyn Garden City AL8 ..89 C2
Crossways Barley SG8 ....8 F1
Berkhamsted HP4 ....121 F3
Hemel Hempstead HP3 ....125 B3
Crouch Ct CM20 ....117 C3
Crouch Hall Gdns AL3 ..106 A6
Crouch Hall La AL3 ....106 A6
Crouch La EN7 ....147 C4
Crouchfield
Hemel Hempstead HP1 ....124 B2
Hertford SG14 ....92 C1
Crouchfield La SG12 ....92 E4
Crow Furlong SG5 ....34 D7
Crow La SG8 ....16 F5
Crowborough Path WD19 ....175 D6
Crowland Rd LU2 ....46 C5
Crown Cl CM22 ....98 C1
Crown Cotts Botley HP5 .150 B8
King's Walden SG4 ....48 A6
Crown Lodge SG15 ....11 A4
Crown Rd WD6 ....170 B8
Crown Rise WD25 ....154 D5
Crown Rose Ct HP23 ....100 A3
Crown St AL3 ....106 B5
Crown Terr CM23 ....77 A7
Crown Wlk HP3 ....138 E7
Crown Yd AL3 ....106 D2
Crownfield EN10 ....135 A2
Croxdale Rd WD6 ....170 A7
Croxley Ctr WD18 ....166 D4
Croxley Sta WD3 ....166 B3
Croxley View WD18 ....166 E3
Croxton Cl [3] LU3 ....45 A7
Crozier Ave CM23 ....76 C8
Crunnell's Gn SG4 ....48 E5
Crusader Way WD18 ....166 F3
Cubbington Cl LU3 ....45 A7
Cubitt Cl SG4 ....35 C7
Cubitts Cl AL6 ....89 F3
Cublands SG13 ....114 B6
Cuckmans Dr AL2 ....141 A6
Cuckoo's Nest LU2 ....64 A7
Cucumber La AL9,SG13 .132 A1
Cuffley Ave WD25 ....154 D5
Cuffley Cl LU3 ....44 F4
Cuffley Ct HP2 ....125 C8
Cuffley Hill EN7 ....147 B2
Cuffley Sch EN6 ....146 F1
Cuffley Sta EN6 ....146 F2
Cullera Cl HA6 ....174 F4
Cullings Ct EN9 ....163 F6
Culver Ct SG10 ....74 F1
Culver Lo AL1 ....127 E5
Culver Rd AL1 ....127 E5
Culverden Rd WD19 ....175 B7
Culverhouse Rd LU3 ....45 C3
Culworth Cl LU1 ....62 E3
Cumberland Cl
Hertford SG14 ....113 C8
Pimlico HP3 ....139 E7
Cumberland Ct
[2] Hoddesdon EN11 ....135 A7
St Albans AL3 ....127 E4
Cumberland Dr AL3 ....106 B6
Cumberland St LU1 ....63 E6
Cumberlow Pl HP2 ....125 C2
Cumcum Hill AL9 ....131 E2
Cundalls Rd SG12 ....93 E2
Cunningham Ave
Enfield EN3 ....162 E3
Hatfield AL10 ....129 D6
St Albans AL1 ....127 F1
Cunningham Ct [3] EN8 .148 E3
Cunningham Hill Inf Sch AL1 ....128 A1
Cunningham Hill Jun Sch AL1 ....128 A1
Cunningham Hill Rd AL1 ....128 A1
Cunningham Rd EN8 ....148 E4
Cupid Green La
Flamstead HP2 ....104 E3
Hemel Hempstead HP2 ....105 A1
Curlew Cl
Berkhamsted HP4 ....122 C3
Letchworth SG6 ....11 E1
Curlew Cres SG8 ....7 E8
Curlew Ct EN10 ....148 F8
Curlew Rd LU2 ....46 C5

Curo Pk AL2 141 E4
Currie St SG13 113 E6
Curteys CM17 118 D5
Curtis Cl WD3 165 A1
Curtis Rd HP3 125 D2
Curtis Way HP4 122 D3
Curtiss Dr WD25 153 F5
Curzon Gate Ct 1 WD17 167 A8
Curzon Rd LU3 45 C1
Cussans Ho WD18 166 E3
Cussons Cl EN7 148 A2
Cut Throat Ave HP4,LU6 81 E7
Cutenhoe Rd LU1 63 E4
Cutforth Rd CM21 97 E3
Cuthbert Cl EN7 147 F2
Cutlers Gn LU2 46 F2
Cutmore Dr AL4 129 B1
Cutts La SG4 66 D1
Cuttsfield Terr HP1 123 F2
Cuttys La SG1 50 E5
Cwmbran Ct HP2 124 F7
Cygnet Cl
Borehamwood WD6 170 C8
Northwood HA6 174 C4
Cygnet Ct 11 CM23 76 F6
Cygnet Ho
Hemel Hempstead HP3 138 F6
1 Stanmore HA7 176 F4
Cygnet Way CM19 116 A1
Cylers Thicket AL6 89 C6
Cymbeline Ct AL3 127 C4
Cypress Ave
Crews Hill EN2 161 A4
Welwyn Garden City AL7 111 C5
Cypress Cl EN9 163 D5
Cypress Rd HA3 176 D1
Cypress Wlk WD25 154 B4
Cyrils Way AL1 141 D8

D

Dacorum Way HP1 124 C3
Dacre Bldgs EN8 148 F2
Dacre Cres SG4 66 C1
Dacre Gdns WD6 170 D4
Dacre Gn SG8 7 F6
Dacre Ind Est EN8 148 F3
Dacre Rd SG5 35 A8
Daffodil Cl AL10 109 F1
Dagger La WD6 169 B4
Daggs Dell Rd HP1 123 E5
Dagnall Rd
Great Gaddesden HP1 103 C5
Whipsnade HP4,LU6 81 D8
Dagnall Sch HP4 81 C5
Dagnalls SG6 22 F2
Dahlia Cl
Hammond Street EN7 147 C6
Luton LU2 46 B4
Dailmead EN6 157 F5
Daintrees SG12 95 E4
Daintry Lodge HA6 174 F3
Dairy Cotts SG5 19 B2
Dairy Mews WD18 167 A4
Dairy Way WD5 139 F2
Dairyglen Ave EN8 162 E7
Daisy Ct SG6 23 A8
Daisy Dr AL10 129 F8
Dalby Cl LU4 44 B3
Dale Ave AL4 87 B5
Dale Cl Hitchin SG4 34 F4
Pinner HA5 175 B2
Dale Ct CM21 97 D1
Dale Rd LU1 63 C7
Dale The Letchworth SG6 22 E5
Waltham Abbey EN9 163 E5
Dales Path WD6 170 D4
Dales Rd WD6 170 D4
Daleside Dr EN6 158 F6
Dalewood Harpenden AL5 86 D1
Welwyn Garden City AL7 111 D5
Dalkeith Rd AL5 86 C1
Dallow Prim Sch LU1 63 C8
Dallow Rd LU1 63 B8
Dalroad Ent Est LU1 63 B8
Dalton Cl LU3 31 B1
Dalton Gdns CM23 76 E4
Dalton St AL3 127 D4
Dalton Way
Watford WD17 167 D4
Whitwell SG4 66 E7
Daltry Cl SG1 36 C2
Daltry Rd SG1 36 C2
Damask Cl Tring HP23 100 C4
Weston SG4 37 B8
Damask Gn HP1 123 E2
Damask Green Rd SG4 37 B8
Dame Alice Owen's Sch EN6 158 E6
Dammersey Cl AL3 83 F4
Damson Way AL4 128 C5
Dancers End La HP23 99 C2
Dancers Hill Rd EN5 158 E3
Dancers La EN5 158 C4
Dancote SG3 68 F5
Dane Acres CM23 76 D8
Dane Bridge La SG10 75 B2
Dane Cl Harpenden AL5 86 C4
Stotfold SG5 11 F8
Dane Ct AL1 128 B2
Dane End SG8 16 B4
Dane End Ho SG1 36 C1
Dane End La SG4 37 E5
Dane End Rd SG11 72 E3
Dane Ho CM23 76 D8
Dane O'Coys Rd CM23 58 E1
Dane Pk CM23 76 D8
Dane Rd LU3 45 C2
Dane St CM23 77 A7
Danebridge Rd SG10 75 B2
Danefield Rd SG5 20 C4
Danemead EN11 115 A1
Danes The AL2 141 C3
Danesbury La AL6 89 D8
Danesbury Park Rd AL6 89 D8
Danesbury Pk
Hertford SG14 113 D7
Welwyn AL6 89 C7
Danesbury Pk Cvn Site AL6 89 D8
Danescroft SG6 12 A1
Danesgate SG1 50 D4
Danestrete SG1 50 D5
Daniel Ho 4 HA5 175 C1
Daniells AL7 111 A7
Danvers Croft HP23 100 C5
Danvers Dr LU3 31 C1
Danziger Way WD6 170 C8
Darblay Cl AL4 108 F5
Darby Dr
Waltham Abbey EN9 163 C6
Welwyn AL6 68 E3
Darcy Cl EN8 162 E8
Dark La
Cheshunt EN7 148 A1
Codicote SG4 88 E8
Harpenden AL5 107 D7
Sandon SG9 15 B1
Wingrave HP22 60 C3
Darkes La EN6 159 A8
Darlands Dr EN5 171 D4
Darley Hall LU2 47 C1
Darley Rd LU2,SG4 47 C2
Darnhills WD7 155 F4
Darnicle Hill EN7 147 A6
Darr's La HP4 121 D6
Darrington Rd WD6 169 E8
Dart The HP2 125 A8
Dartmouth Mews LU4 44 D3
Darwin Cl
Hemel Hempstead HP2 105 B1
St Albans AL3 127 E7
Darwin Gdns WD19 175 C5
Darwin Rd SG2 51 B6
Dashes The CM20 117 E1
Datchet Cl HP2 125 B8
Datchworth Turn HP2 125 C3
Dauphin Ct 5 LU2 45 D1
Dauphine Ct HA3 176 E1
Davenham Ave HA6 174 F5
Daventer Dr HA7 176 F3
David Evans Ct SG6 22 D7
Davies St SG13 113 E6
Davis Cres SG5 20 D4
Davis Ct AL1 127 E3
Davis Ho 11 HP4 122 C4
Davis' Row SG15 11 A4
Davison Cl EN8 148 D3
Davison Dr EN8 148 D3
Davys Cl AL4 108 E7
Dawes La Sarratt WD3 151 F3
Wheathampstead AL4 87 D1
Dawley AL7 89 F1
Dawley Ct HP2 125 A7
Dawlish Cl SG2 69 C7
Dawlish Rd LU4 44 F3
Dawson Cl SG16 10 C5
Day's Cl SG8 7 C5
Dayemead AL7 111 B3
Days Cl AL10 129 F5
Days Mead AL10 129 F5
De Haviland Cl AL10 129 F6
De Havilland Aircraft Heritage Mus The★ AL2 143 B2
De Havilland Ct WD7 156 E7
De Havilland Way WD5 153 F7
De Tany Ct AL1 127 D2
De Vere Wlk WD17 166 E7
Deacon Cl AL1 141 D7
Deacon's Hill Rd WD6 170 A4
Deacons Cl
Borehamwood WD6 170 A5
Pinner HA5 175 B1
Deacons Ct 7 LU2 63 D8
Deacons Hill WD19 167 C3
Deacons Hts WD6 170 A3
Deacons Way SG5 21 D1
Deaconsfield Rd HP3 138 E8
Dead Woman's La SG4 48 C7
Deadman's Ash La WD3 152 B3
Deakin Cl WD18 166 E2
Dean Ct WD25 154 D6
Dean Field HP3 137 A4
Dean Moore Cl AL1 127 D2
Dean The HP22 60 B3
Dean's Gdns AL4 128 A7
Deane Ct HA6 174 E2
Deans Cl
Abbots Langley WD5 153 D7
Tring HP23 100 A4
Deans Furlong HP23 100 A4
Deans Lawn 8 HP4 122 C4
Deans Mdw HP4 81 C5
Deanscroft SG3 68 F5
Deansway HP3 138 F8
Deard's End La SG3 68 F6
Deards Wood SG3 68 F5
Debenham Ct EN5 171 C4
Debenham Rd EN7 148 B4
Dee The HP2 124 F8
Deep Denes LU2 46 A2
Deepdene EN6 158 D8
Deeping Cl SG3 68 F4
Deer Cl SG13 113 F6
Deer Park Way EN9 163 B4
Deerfield Cl SG12 93 D2
Deerings The AL5 107 A4
Deerswood Ave AL10 130 B3
Deeves Hall La EN6 157 E6
Deimos Dr HP2 125 A6
Delahay Rise HP4 122 B6
Delamare Rd EN8 148 F2
Delamere Rd WD6 170 B8
Delfcroft SG12 93 C2
Delfield Gdns LU1 62 E4
Delius Cl WD6 169 C3
Dell Cl AL5 86 B3
Dell Ct WD3 173 A8
Dell Field Ave HP4 122 B6
Dell La
Bishop's Stortford, Hockerill CM23 77 A7
Bishop's Stortford, Latchmore Bank CM22 77 B1
Spellbrook CM22 98 A8
Dell Mdw HP3 138 E7
Dell Rd
Berkhamsted HP4 121 D7
Enfield EN3 162 C1
Watford WD24 154 A2
Dell Rise AL2 141 B5
Dell Side WD24 154 A2
Dell Springs SG9 40 E8
Dell The
Baldock SG7 23 E6
Brickendon SG13 113 C3
Caddington LU1 62 E3
Luton LU2 46 F1
Markyate AL3 83 D5
Moor Park HA6 174 E8
Pinner HA5 175 D1
Radlett WD7 156 A4
Royston SG8 7 C5
St Albans AL1 128 A4
Stevenage SG1 50 E5
Waltham Abbey EN9 163 C3
Welwyn AL6 90 A4
Dellcot Cl LU2 46 B4
Dellcott Cl AL8 110 C7
Dellcroft Way AL5 107 A5
Dellcut Rd HP2 125 A5
Dellfield St Albans AL1 127 F2
Thundridge SG12 93 D8
Dellfield Cl
Berkhamsted HP4 122 A6
Radlett WD7 155 F4
Watford WD17 167 A7
Dellfield Ct
1 Harlow CM17 118 C4
Luton LU2 46 D2
Dellfield Rd AL10 130 A5
Dellmeadow WD5 139 E1
Dellors Cl EN5 171 D4
Dells The
11 Bishop's Stortford CM23 76 F7
Hemel Hempstead HP3 125 B2
Dells Wood Cl EN11 114 F1
Dellsome La
Colney Heath AL4 143 E8
Welham Green AL9 144 B8
Dellswood Cl SG13 113 E5
Dellwood WD3 165 B1
Delmar Ave HP2 125 D2
Delmer Ct WD6 156 F1
Delmerend La AL3 84 C1
Delphine Cl LU1 63 B6
Delrow Cotts WD25 168 C8
Delta Gain WD19 175 D7
Demontfort Rise SG12 93 C3
Denbigh Cl 2 HP2 124 E2
Denbigh High Sch LU3 45 C2
Denbigh Inf Sch LU3 45 B2
Denbigh Jun Sch LU3 45 B2
Denbigh Rd LU3 45 B2
Denby SG6 23 B4
Dencora Ctr The AL1 128 A3
Dencora Way LU3 44 B8
Dendridge Cl EN1 162 B2
Dene La SG2 51 E2
Dene Rd HA6 174 D4
Denes The HP3 138 F7
Denewood Cl WD17 153 F2
Denham Cl
Hemel Hempstead HP2 125 A8
Luton LU3 44 E8
Denham La SL9 172 A2
Denham Way WD6 170 C8
Denham Way (North Orbital Rd) WD3 172 E4
Denmark Cl LU3 44 E8
Denmark St WD17 167 B7
Dennis Cl HP22 99 A4
Dennis Ct 1 AL3 127 D4
Denny Ave EN9 163 D5
Denny Ct CM23 59 B2
Denny Gate EN8 148 F4
Denny's La HP4 121 F3
Densley Cl AL8 110 D8
Denton Cl
Barnet EN5 171 C4
Luton LU4 44 B3
Denton Ho 10 WD19 175 C7
Denton Rd SG1 50 E4
Dents Cl SG6 23 C3
Derby Ave HA3 176 D2
Derby Ho HA5 175 D1
Derby Rd
Hoddesdon EN11 135 D5
Luton LU4 44 C2
Watford WD18 167 C5
Derby Way SG1 51 B8
Derry Leys AL10 129 E7
Derwent Ave Luton LU3 45 B7
Pinner HA5 175 E4
Derwent Cl WD25 154 C5
Derwent Lower Sch SG16 10 B5
Derwent Rd
Harpenden AL5 85 C4
Hemel Hempstead HP3 125 C2
Lower Stondon SG16 10 B4
Luton LU2 64 A8
Des Fuller Ct 3 LU1 63 F6
Desborough Cl
Hertford SG14 92 C1
Welwyn Garden City AL7 111 B3
Desborough Dr AL6 90 D5
Desborough Rd SG4 35 C8
Desmond Rd WD24 153 F3
Deva Cl AL3 127 A1
Devereux Dr WD17 153 E1
Devoils La 9 CM23 76 F7
Devon Ct AL1 127 E2
Devon Rd Luton LU2 64 B8
Watford WD24 167 D8
Devonshire Bsns Pk WD6 170 D6
Devonshire Cl SG2 69 A8
Devonshire Ct HA5 175 F2
Devonshire Rd
5 Harpenden AL5 86 B1
Pinner HA5 175 F2
Dewars Cl AL6 89 C6
Dewes Green Rd CM23 30 F1
Dewgrass Gr EN8 162 D4
Dewhurst Rd EN8 148 C2
Dewhurst St Mary CE Prim Sch EN8 148 C2
Dewpond Cl SG1 50 C8
Dewsbury Rd LU3 45 C6
Dexter Cl Luton LU3 31 B1
St Albans AL1 128 A2
Dexter Rd Barnet EN5 171 D3
Harefield UB9 173 C1
Diamond Ind Ctr SG6 23 C7
Diamond Rd WD24 154 A1
Dickens Cl AL3 127 D4
Dickens Ct HP2 105 B1
Dickenson Way 19 SG12 93 D1
Dicker Mill SG13 113 D7
Dicket Mead AL6 89 C5
Dickins Cl EN7 148 A5
Dickinson Ave WD3 166 A3
Dickinson Quay HP3 138 F7
Dickinson Sq WD3 166 A3
Dickinsons Field AL5 107 C7
Dickson EN7 147 F4
Dig Dag Hill EN7 147 F4
Digswell Cl WD6 157 A1
Digswell Ct AL8 110 E8
Digswell Hill AL6 89 B2
Digswell Ho AL8 89 D2
Digswell House Mews AL8 89 D2
Digswell La AL7 89 F2
Digswell Park Rd
Welwyn Garden City AL8 89 D3
Welwyn Garden City AL8 89 E3
Digswell Pl AL8 89 C1
Digswell Rd AL8 89 E1
Digswell Rise AL8 110 E8
Dimmocks La WD3 152 B3
Dimsdale Cotts SG9 29 B7
Dimsdale Cres CM23 77 B6
Dimsdale St SG14 113 C6
Dinant Link Rd EN11 135 B7
Dingle Cl EN5 170 F3
Dinmore HP3 136 F3
Ditchfield Rd EN11 115 A1
Ditchling Cl LU2 46 C3
Ditchling Ct 1 AL1 127 E3
Ditchmore La SG1 50 D6
Ditton Gn LU2 46 E3
Divine Saviour RC Prim Sch WD5 153 D7
Divot Pl SG13 114 B7
Dixies Cl SG7 4 D3
Dixon Pl SG9 40 E7
Dixon's Ct SG12 114 E8
Dixons Hill Cl AL9 144 B6
Dixons Hill Rd AL9 144 C7
Dobb's Weir Rd EN11, CM19 135 D5
Docklands SG5 20 D4
Doctor's Commons Rd HP4 122 B4
Dodds La HP2 104 E1
Dodwood AL7 111 B5
Dog Kennel La
Chorleywood WD3 164 F5
Hatfield AL10 130 A6
Royston SG8 7 D6
Doggetts Way AL1 127 C1
Dognell Gn AL8 110 B7
Dolesbury Dr AL6 89 E8
Dollimore Cl SG4 67 F1
Dollis Brook Wlk EN5 171 E3
Dollis Valley Dr EN5 171 F4
Dollis Valley Way EN5 171 F3
Dolphin Sq HP23 100 A3
Dolphin Way CM23 77 A8
Dolphin Yd
2 Hertford SG14 113 D6
St Albans AL1 127 D3
7 Ware SG12 93 D1
Dominic Ct EN9 163 B6
Doncaster Cl SG1 51 C8
Doncaster Gn WD19 175 C5
Donkey La HP23 99 E2
Donne Cl SG8 7 C8
Dorant Ho AL3 127 D7
Dorcas Ct AL1 127 E2
Dorchester Ave EN11 135 A8
Dorchester Ct
Croxley Green WD3 166 D4
St Albans AL1 128 A2
Watford WD19 167 E3
Dordans Rd LU4 44 F4
Dorel Cl LU2 45 F2
Dormans Cl HA6 174 D3
Dormer Cl EN5 171 D4
Dormie Cl AL3 127 C5
Dornan Ct LU1 63 E5
Dorrien's Croft HP4 121 F7
Dorrington Cl LU3 45 C1
Dorrofield Cl WD3 166 D4
Dorset Cl HP4 121 F5
Dorset Ct 4 LU1 63 F6
Dorset Ho 13 CM23 76 F7
Douglas Ave WD24 154 E2
Douglas Cl AL6 89 E3
Douglas Dr SG1 51 A8
Douglas Ho 11 EN8 148 D3
Douglas Rd
Harpenden AL5 85 F2
Luton LU4 45 A2
Douglas Way AL7 111 C6
Dove Cl
Bishop's Stortford CM23 76 E3
Stansted Mountfitchet CM24 59 E8
Dove Ct AL10 130 A3
Dove La EN6 159 C5
Dove Pk
Chorleywood WD3 164 C4
Pinner HA5 176 A3
Dove Rd SG1 36 F3
Dovecote The SG7 4 D4
Dovedale
Luton LU2 45 E6
Stevenage SG2 51 B4
Ware SG12 93 C3
Dovedale Cl UB9 173 C1
Dovehouse Croft CM20 118 A2
Dovehouse Hill LU2 46 B1
Dovehouse La LU6 82 D8
Dover Cl Luton LU3 45 A3
Pitstone LU7 80 D2
Dover Way WD3 166 C5
Doverfield EN7 147 C2
Dowding Way WD25 153 F5
Dower Ct SG4 34 F5
Dower Mews 5 HP4 122 C4
Dowland Ho EN1 161 F1
Dowling Ct HP3 138 D8
Down Edge AL3 105 F5
Down Green La AL4 108 B7
Downalong WD23 168 D1
Downedge AL3 127 B4
Downer Dr WD3 152 A3
Downes Rd AL4 128 B7
Downfield Cl SG13 114 C4
Downfield Ct SG12 93 B5
Downfield Jun Mix Inf Sch EN8 162 E8
Downfield Rd
Cheshunt EN8 162 E8
Hertford Heath SG13 114 C5
Downfields AL8 110 B4
Downhall Ley SG9 40 E7
Downings Wood WD3 172 D5
Downlands
Baldock SG7 13 A1
Luton LU3 44 C7
Royston SG8 7 C6
Stevenage SG2 51 D7
Waltham Abbey EN9 163 E5
Downlands Cvn Pk LU1 84 C8
Downs La AL10 130 A3
Downs Rd LU1 63 C7
Downs The AL10 130 A3
Downs View LU4 44 D4
Downsfield AL10 130 B2
Downside HP2 124 E4
Downside Inf Sch LU4 44 E1
Downside Jun Sch LU4 44 E1
Downsway Ct SG8 7 C6
Downton Ct 3 LU3 63 D8
Downview LU4 44 B2
Dowry Wlk WD17 153 F1
Dragon Moth Rd AL10 129 D6
Drakes Cl EN8 148 D3
Drakes Dr
Northwood HA6 174 B2
St Albans AL1 128 C1
Stevenage SG2 51 B7
Drakes Mdw CM17 118 E4
Drakes Way AL10 130 B3
Drapers Mews LU3 45 C1
Drapers Way SG1 50 C7
Drayman's Cl CM23 76 B5
Drayson Cl EN9 163 E7
Drayton Ave EN6 158 E7
Drayton Rd
Borehamwood WD6 170 A5
Luton LU4 44 A3
Driftway SG8 16 E4
Driftway The HP2 124 F3
Driftwood Ave AL2 141 B5
Drive The
Barnet EN5 171 E6
Brookmans Park AL9 145 B6

Drive The *continued*
Cheshunt EN7 148 B3
Goff's Oak EN7 147 B3
Harlow CM20 117 E1
Harpenden AL5 86 A1
Hertford SG14 113 C8
Hoddesdon EN11 135 A8
Kimpton AL4 87 B7
London Colney AL2 142 A5
Northwood HA6 174 E2
Oaklands AL6 69 A1
Potters Bar EN6 158 F7
Radlett WD7 156 A5
Rickmansworth WD3 165 C3
Sawbridgeworth CM21 97 E2
Watford WD17 153 E2
Driver's End SG4 68 A4
Driver's End La SG4,SG3 68 A4
Driveway The
Cuffley EN6 146 E3
Hemel Hempstead HP1 124 B1
Dromey Gdns HA3 176 F3
Drop La AL2 155 C7
Drovers Way
Bishop's Stortford CM23 76 C5
Hatfield AL10 130 B8
St Albans AL1 127 D3
Drummond Dr HA7 176 F3
Drummond Ride HP23 100 A5
Drummonds The LU4 44 C2
Drury La SG12 95 E1
Drycroft AL7 110 E2
Dryden Cres SG2 51 C8
Dryden Rd HA3 176 F2
Drysdale Cl 7 HA6 174 E3
Dubbs Knoll Rd SG8 1 F5
Dubrae Cl AL3 127 A1
Duchess Cl CM23 76 C7
Duchy Rd EN4 159 D1
Duck End CM23 59 E1
Duck La SG2 52 E4
Duck's Hill Rd HA6 174 B1
Ducketts La SG10 75 D1
Ducketts Mead CM19 116 B1
Ducketts Wharf 10 CM23 76 F6
Ducketts Wood SG12 93 E6
Duckling La CM21 97 E2
Duckmore La HP23 99 E2
Dudley Ave EN8 162 D7
Dudley Hill Cl AL6 89 E8
Dudley St LU2 63 E8
Dudswell La HP4 121 D7
Dugdale Ct SG5 21 C1
Dugdale Hill La EN6 158 E7
Dugdales WD3 166 A5
Duke St Hoddesdon EN11 135 A7
Luton LU2 63 E8
Watford WD17 167 C6
Duke's La SG5 34 F8
Dukes Ave LU6 81 E8
Dukes Ct 4 LU1 63 D6
Dukes Ride
Bishop's Stortford CM23 76 C7
13 Luton LU2 45 D1
Dukes Way HP4 122 A6
Dulwich Way WD3 166 A4
Dumbarton Ave EN8 162 D5
Dumbletons WD3 172 E6
Dumfries Cl WD19 175 A7
Dumfries Ct 9 LU1 63 D6
Dumfries St LU1 63 D6
Duncan Cl AL7 110 E5
Duncan Ct AL1 127 F1
Duncan Way WD23 167 F7
Duncombe Cl
Hertford SG14 113 C8
Luton LU3 45 C6
Duncombe Rd
Berkhamsted HP4 121 E6
Hertford SG14 113 C8
Duncombe Sch SG14 113 C7
Duncots Cl SG5 21 E3
Dundale Prim Sch
HP23 100 A5
Dundale Rd HP23 100 A4
Dundas Mews EN3 163 A2
Dunedin Ho SG8 7 C6
Dunfermline Ho 9
WD19 175 C7
Dunford Ct 7 HA5 175 F3
Dunham's La SG6 23 C6
Dunkirks Mews SG13 113 D4
Dunlin SG6 11 E1
Dunlin Rd HP2 124 E8
Dunmow Ct LU3 45 D2
Dunmow Rd CM23 77 C7
Dunn Cl SG1 50 E3
Dunnock Cl WD6 170 A5
Dunny La WD4 151 F7
Dunraven Ave LU1 63 A8
Dunsby Rd LU3 45 A6
Dunsley Pl HP23 100 B3
Dunsmore WD19 175 D8
Dunsmore Cl WD23 168 D3
Dunsmore Rd LU1 63 C6
Dunsmore Way WD23 168 D3
Dunstable Cl LU4 45 A1
Dunstable Ct LU4 44 F2
Dunstable Pl 5 LU1 63 D7
Dunstable Rd
Caddington LU1,LU6 62 C3
Dagnall HP4,LU6 81 C7
Luton LU4 44 D2
Luton,Bury Park LU1,LU4 45 B1
Redbourn AL3 106 A7
Studham LU6 82 B6
Dunster Cl Barnet EN5 171 D5
Harefield UB9 173 B2
Dunster Ct WD6 170 D6
Dunster Rd HP2 105 B1
Dunsters Mead AL7 111 B4
Dunston Hill HP23 100 A4
Durban Rd E WD18 167 A5
Durban Rd W WD18 167 A5
Durbar Rd LU4 45 B1
Durham Cl
Sawbridgeworth CM21 97 C1
Stanstead Abbotts SG12 115 B5
Durham Ct EN5 171 F6
Durham Ho 14 WD6 170 A7
Durham Rd
Borehamwood WD6 170 C6
Luton LU2 64 A7
Stevenage SG1 37 A1
Durley Gdns LU1 63 D5
Durrant Ct HA3 176 E2
Durrants Dr WD3 166 C5
Durrants Hill Rd HP3 138 D8
Durrants La HP4 121 F5
Durrants Rd HP4 121 F5
Dury Rd EN5 171 F7
Duxford Cl LU3 45 B7
Duxons Turn HP2 125 B4
Dwight Rd WD18 166 D2
Dyer Ct EN3 163 A2
Dyers Ct CM23 76 C5
Dyes La SG4 49 F3
Dyke La AL4 108 E7
Dylan Cl WD6 169 D2
Dymoke Gn AL4 128 A7
Dymokes Way EN11 115 A1
Dyrham La EN5 158 A3
Dyson Ct WD17 167 C5
Dysons Cl EN8 162 D6

E

Eagle Centre Way LU4 44 B7
Eagle Cl LU4 44 A4
Eagle Ct Baldock SG7 12 E1
Hertford SG13 114 B7
Eagle Way AL10 130 A3
Ealing Cl WD6 170 D8
Earl St WD17 167 C6
Earls Cl CM23 76 D6
Earls Hill Gdns SG8 7 C6
Earls La EN6 157 F6
Earls Meade LU2 45 D1
Earlsmead SG6 22 F3
Easington Rd SG12 71 E7
Easingwold Gdns LU1 62 F8
East Burrowfield AL7 110 D4
East Cl
Chiswell Green AL2 141 B6
Hitchin SG4 22 B1
Stevenage SG1 50 F5
East Comm
Harpenden AL5 107 C7
Redbourn AL3 106 A4
East Dr Moor Park WD1 174 E8
Sawbridgeworth CM21 97 E1
St Albans AL4 128 F4
Watford WD25 154 B3
East End Way HA5 175 F1
East Flint HP1 123 F4
East Gate CM20 117 D1
East Gn HP3 139 A6
East Hertfordshire Sec Ctr
(PRU) EN8 162 D5
East Hill LU3 45 B6
East La
Abbots Langley WD5 140 A2
Wheathampstead AL4 87 D1
East Lodge La EN2 160 E4
East Mead AL7 111 B3
East Mimms 4 HP2 124 E4
East Mount AL4 87 D1
East Pk Harlow CM17 118 C3
Sawbridgeworth CM21 97 E1
East Rd
Bishop's Stortford CM23 77 B7
Enfield EN3 162 C1
Harlow CM20 118 B4
East Reach SG2 51 A2
East Ridgeway EN6 146 E3
East Riding AL6 90 D5
East St
Hemel Hempstead HP2 124 D3
Lilley LU2 32 D2
Ware SG12 93 D1
East View Barnet EN5 171 F6
Essendon AL9 131 F6
St Ippolyts SG4 35 C2
East Wlk CM20 117 D1
Eastbourne Ave SG1 50 A6
Eastbrook Prim Sch
HP2 125 A8
Eastbrook Rd EN9 163 E6
Eastbrook Way HP2 124 E3
Eastbury Ave HA6 174 F5
Eastbury Ct
St Albans AL1 127 F4
Watford WD19 167 C2
Eastbury Farm Jun Mix Inf
Sch HA6 174 F6
Eastbury Pl HA6 174 F5
Eastbury Rd
Northwood HA6 174 E4
Watford WD19 167 C3
Eastcheap SG6 22 F6
Eastcote Dr AL5 107 D6
Eastcott Cl LU2 46 D1
Eastend Cotts CM19 116 D1
Eastern Ave
Cheshunt EN8 162 F6
Eastern Ave *continued*
Lower Stondon SG16 10 C3
Eastern Way SG6 12 A1
Eastfield Ave WD24 167 D8
Eastfield Cl LU2 46 C4
Eastfield Ct AL4 128 D6
Eastfield Prim Sch EN3 162 D1
Eastfield Rd
Cheshunt EN8 162 F7
Enfield EN3 162 D1
Royston SG8 7 E6
Eastgate SG1 50 D5
Eastglade HA6 174 F5
Easthall Cotts SG4 67 C8
Easthall Ho SG1 36 C1
Eastham Cl EN5 171 F4
Eastholm SG6 23 A8
Eastholm Gn SG6 23 A8
Eastlea Ave WD25 154 E2
Eastman Way HP2 125 A6
Eastmoor Ct AL5 107 C6
Eastmoor Pk AL5 107 C6
Eastnor HP3 137 A3
Easton Gdns WD6 170 E5
Eastor AL7 90 A1
Eastwick Cres WD3 172 F8
Eastwick Hall La CM20 117 A5
Eastwick Rd
Eastwick CM20 117 B4
Gilston CM20 117 E6
Eastwick Row HP2 125 A2
Eastwood Ct HP2 125 A4
Eaton Gate HA6 174 C4
Eaton Green Ct LU2 64 C8
Eaton Green Rd LU2 64 C8
Eaton Ho 5 CM23 77 B8
Eaton Pl LU2 46 D1
Eaton Rd
Hemel Hempstead HP2 125 B6
St Albans AL1 128 B3
Eaton Valley Rd LU2 64 B8
Ebberns Rd HP3 138 E8
Ebenezer St 7 LU1 63 D6
Ebury App WD3 165 D1
Ebury Cl HA6 174 C5
Ebury Ct WD3 165 D1
Ebury Rd
Rickmansworth WD3 165 D1
Watford WD17 167 C6
Ebury Rdbt WD3 165 D1
Echo Hill SG8 7 C5
Eddy St HP4 122 A5
Eden Cl EN3 163 A1
Edenhall Cl HP2 125 D2
Edens Cl CM23 77 B7
Edens Mount CM21 97 F4
Edenvale EN7 148 B2
Edgars Ct AL7 110 E5
Edgbaston Dr WD7 156 E7
Edgbaston Rd WD19 175 B7
Edgcott Cl LU3 31 B1
Edgecote Cl LU1 62 E3
Edgehill Gdns LU3 44 C8
Edgewood Dr LU2 46 C6
Edgeworth Cl SG2 51 C1
Edgware Way HA8 169 D1
Edgwarebury La WD6,
HA8 169 F1
Edinburgh Ave WD3 165 A2
Edinburgh Cres EN8 162 E6
Edinburgh Dr WD5 154 A7
Edinburgh Gdns CM23 76 E6
Edinburgh Pl CM20 118 A4
Edinburgh Sq SG8 2 A6
Edinburgh Way CM20 117 E3
Edison Cl AL4 128 C2
Edison Rd SG2 51 B6
Edkins Cl LU2 45 E5
Edlyn Cl HP4 121 F5
Edmonds Dr SG2 51 D4
Edmund Beaufort Dr
AL3 127 E5
Edmund Mews WD4 139 A2
Edmunds Rd SG14 112 F7
Edridge Cl WD23 168 C4
Edulf Rd WD6 170 B8
Edward Amey Cl WD25 154 C3
Edward Cl
Abbots Langley WD5 153 F7
St Albans AL1 127 F2
Edward Cotts SG11 54 C3
Edward Ct
Hemel Hempstead HP3 138 D7
Waltham Abbey EN9 163 F6
Edward St LU2 45 F1
Edwards Ho 5 SG1 50 E6
Edwick Ct EN8 148 D2
Edwin Ware Ct 1 HA5 175 C1
Edwinstree CE Mid Sch
SG9 40 D8
Edwyn Cl EN5 171 D3
Egdon Dr LU2 45 D6
Egerton Rd HP4 122 B6
Egerton-Rothesay Sch
HP4 121 E4
Egg Farm La WD4 139 B1
Egglesfield Cl HP4 121 E6
Eggleton Dr HP23 100 A5
Eight Acres HP23 100 A4
Eighth Ave LU3 44 D7
Eisenberg Cl SG7 13 B1
Elaine Gdns LU1 63 A1
Elbow La
Hertford Heath SG13 134 B7
Stevenage SG2 51 B1
Eldefield SG6 22 D7
Elder Ct WD23 176 E8
Elder Rd SG12 93 F3
Elder Way SG1 50 E3
Elderbeck Cl EN7 148 A2
Elderberry Cl LU2 46 B4
Elderberry Dr SG4 35 A4
Elderberry Way WD25 154 B4
Elderfield CM17 118 D4
Eldon Ave WD6 170 B7
Eldon Rd
Hoddesdon EN11 135 D4
Luton LU4 44 C1
Eldrig Turn HP2 124 E7
Eleanor Ave AL3 127 D5
Eleanor Cross Rd EN8 162 F5
Eleanor Gdns EN5 171 D4
Eleanor Rd Cheshunt EN8 162 E6
Hertford SG14 113 C7
Eleanor Way EN8 162 F5
Electric Ave EN3 162 F3
Element Ho EN3 162 F3
Eleni Ho EN8 162 D6
Elfrida Rd WD18 167 C4
Elgar Cl WD6 169 D2
Elgar Path LU2 63 E8
Elgin Dr HA6 174 E3
Elgin Ho SG4 35 A6
Elgin Rd Cheshunt EN8 148 C1
Hoddesdon EN10 148 F8
Elgood Ave HA6 175 A3
Eliot Rd Royston SG8 7 D8
Stevenage SG2 51 C6
Elizabeth Cl Barnet EN5 171 D6
Lower Nazeing EN9 149 D8
Welwyn Garden City AL7 111 C6
Elizabeth Ct 10 Luton LU1 63 D6
St Albans AL4 128 D6
Watford WD17 153 F1
Elizabeth Dr HP23 100 B6
Elizabeth Ho
7 Watford WD24 167 C7
Welwyn Garden City AL7 111 C6
Elizabeth Rd CM23 76 E5
Elizabeth St LU1 63 D6
Elizabeth Way CM20 117 B2
Ellen Cl HP2 124 F4
Ellenborough Cl CM23 76 D5
Ellenbrook Cl WD24 167 C8
Ellenbrook Cres AL10 129 D5
Ellenbrook La AL10 129 D4
Ellenhall Cl LU3 45 C1
Ellerdine Cl LU3 45 B4
Ellesborough Cl WD19 175 C5
Ellesfield AL6 89 B5
Ellesmere Gr EN5 171 F4
Ellesmere Rd HP4 122 D4
Ellice SG6 23 B4
Ellingham Cl HP2 125 A5
Ellingham Rd HP2 124 F4
Elliott Cl AL7 110 D3
Elliott Ct CM23 77 A8
Ellis Ave SG1 50 E8
Ellis Fields AL3 127 E6
Elliswick Rd AL5 86 B2
Ells Ct LU2 45 F1
Ellwood Gdns WD25 154 C5
Ellwood Terr WD3 164 D4
Elm Ave Caddington LU1 62 E3
Watford WD19 167 E2
Elm Cl EN9 163 D5
Elm Cotts Holdbrook EN9 163 D1
Meesden SG9 29 F6
Elm Dr Cheshunt EN8 148 E3
Hatfield AL10 130 A4
St Albans AL4 128 C3
Elm Gdns Enfield EN2 161 D1
Welwyn Garden City AL8 110 B6
Elm Gn HP1 123 E5
Elm Gr Berkhamsted HP4 122 C4
Bishop's Stortford CM23 77 B7
Watford WD24 154 A2
Elm Hatch HA5 175 F3
Elm Park Rd HA5 175 D1
Elm Pk SG7 23 F8
Elm Rd Barnet EN5 171 F5
Bishop's Stortford CM23 76 F8
Elm Terr HA3 176 D2
Elm Tree Wlk
Chorleywood WD3 164 F5
Tring HP23 100 A5
Elm Way WD3 165 B1
Elm Wlk Radlett WD7 155 F3
Royston SG8 7 F7
Stevenage SG2 51 B3
Elmbank Ave EN5 171 C5
Elmbridge CM17 118 F3
Elmbrook Dr CM23 76 E3
Elmcote HA5 175 D1
Elmcote Way WD3 165 F3
Elmfield Cl EN6 158 E6
Elmfield Ct LU2 46 A1
Elmfield Rd EN6 158 E6
Elmhurst EN10 135 A4
Elmhurst Cl WD23 167 E5
Elmhurst Rd EN3 162 C2
Elmoor Ave AL6 89 B5
Elmoor Cl AL6 89 B4
Elmore Rd Enfield EN3 162 D1
Luton LU2 46 A1
Elmroyd Ave EN6 158 F6
Elmroyd Cl EN6 158 F6
Elms Cl SG4 35 E3
Elms Rd Harrow HA3 176 E3
Ware SG12 94 A2
Elms The Codicote SG4 67 F2
Hertford SG13 114 A6
Stevenage SG2 69 B8
Elmscroft Gdns EN6 158 F7
Elmside LU6 82 E8
Elmside Wlk SG5 34 E7
Elmswell Ct SG14 112 F7
Elmtree Ave LU2 46 E3
Elmwood
Sawbridgeworth CM21 97 F1
Welwyn Garden City AL8 110 B5
Elmwood Ave Baldock SG7 23 F7
Borehamwood WD6 170 B5
Elmwood Cres LU2 45 E3
Elmwood Ct SG7 23 F8
Elppin Ct EN10 134 F3
Elsinge Rd EN1 162 C3
Elstree & Borehamwood Sta
WD6 170 A5
Elstree Distribution Pk
WD6 170 D6
Elstree Hill N WD6 169 D4
Elstree Hill S WD6 169 D2
Elstree Pk WD6 170 D3
Elstree Rd Bushey WD23 168 E2
Elstree WD6 169 A3
Hemel Hempstead HP2 105 A1
Elstree Way WD6 170 C7
Elton Ave EN5 171 F4
Elton Ct SG14 113 C7
Elton Pk WD17 167 B7
Elton Rd SG14 113 C7
Elton Way WD25 168 B7
Elvaston Ct EN5 171 C4
Elveden Cl LU2 45 E6
Elvington Gdns LU3 31 B1
Ely Cl Hatfield AL10 129 F6
Stevenage SG1 37 B1
Ely Gdns WD6 170 D4
Ely Rd AL1 128 B2
Ely Way LU4 44 D4
Embleton Rd WD19 175 A7
Emerald Ct WD6 156 F1
Emerald Rd LU4 44 A3
Emerton Ct HP4 121 E7
Emerton Garth HP4 121 E7
Emma Rothschild Ct
HP23 100 A5
Emma's Cres SG12 115 B4
Emmanuel Lodge EN8 148 C1
Emmanuel Rd HA6 174 F3
Emmer Gn LU2 46 F2
Emmitt Cl WD7 156 E6
Emperor Cl HP4 121 F7
Emperors Gate SG2 51 D8
Empire Ctr WD24 167 C8
Empire Pl WD18 166 F5
Empress Rd LU3 44 E4
Endeavour Rd EN8 148 E4
Enderby Rd LU3 45 C6
Enderley Cl HA3 176 E2
Enderley Rd HA3 176 E2
Endersby Rd EN5 171 C4
Endymion Ct AL10 130 C6
Endymion Mews AL10 130 C6
Endymion Rd AL10 130 C6
Enfield Cty Lower Sch
EN2 161 E1
Enfield Lock Sta EN3 162 E2
Englefield LU2 45 F3
Englehurst AL5 86 D1
Enid Cl AL2 154 F8
Enjakes Cl SG2 69 B7
Ennerdale Cl AL1 128 B1
Ennis Cl AL5 107 D6
Ennismore Cl SG6 23 C3
Ennismore Gn LU2 46 F1
Enslow Cl LU1 62 E3
Enterprise Ctr Luton LU2 64 B6
1 Luton,High Town LU2 63 F8
Enterprise Ctr The
Potters Bar EN6 144 E1
Stevenage SG1 50 B7
Enterprise Pk SG4 66 C2
Enterprise Way
Hemel Hempstead HP2 125 C5
Luton LU3 45 B8
Enville Ho 8 WD19 175 C7
Epping Forest District Mus*
EN9 163 C6
Epping Gn HP2 125 B8
Epping Way LU3 44 C8
Epsom Ct WD3 165 B1
Ereswell Rd LU3 45 A7
Erin Cl LU4 45 A2
Erin Ct LU4 45 A2
Ermine Cl Cheshunt EN7 162 B8
Royston SG8 7 D8
St Albans AL3 127 A2
Ermine Ct SG9 40 E8
Ermine Pl 8 LU2 45 D1
Ermine Point Bsns Pk
SG12 93 B3
Ermine St Buckland SG9 27 D6
Thundridge SG12 93 D7
Erskine Ho 5 WD19 175 D7
Escarpment Ave HP4,LU6 81 D8
Escot Way EN5 171 C4
Esdaile La EN11 135 A5
Eskdale
London Colney AL2 142 F4
Luton LU4 44 C5
Eskdale Ct 3 HP2 124 E6
Essendon CE Prim Sch
AL9 131 F6
Essendon Gdns AL7 110 F6
Essendon Hill AL9 131 F7
Essex Cl LU1 63 F6
Essex Ct 7 LU1 63 E6
Essex La WD4 153 D6
Essex Mead HP2 105 A1

Essex Rd
Borehamwood WD6 .....170 A6
Hoddesdon EN11 ....135 C6
Stevenage SG1 ....50 B8
Watford WD17 ....167 B7
Essex St AL1 ....127 E4
Essex Yd HP22 ....60 C3
Estcourt Rd WD17 .....167 C6
Estfeld Cl 4 EN11 .....115 B1
Ethelred Cl AL7 ....110 F5
Etna Rd AL3 ....127 D4
Eton Ho 9 WD24 ......167 C7
Etonbury Mid Sch SG15 ..11 C7
Europa Rd HP2 ....124 F6
Euston Ave WD18 ......166 F4
Evan's Cl WD3 ....166 A4
Evans Ave WD25 ....153 F4
Evans Cl SG8 ....7 D7
Evans Gr AL4 ....128 C7
Evans Way HP23 ....100 B4
Evans Wharf HP3 ......138 E7
Evedon Cl LU3 ....44 F6
Evelyn Dr HA5 ....175 D3
Evelyn Rd LU5 ....44 A1
Evelyn Sharp Ho HP2 ..125 A2
Evensyde WD18 ....166 D3
Everard Cl AL1 ....127 D1
Everest Cl SG15 ....11 B5
Everest Gdns CM23 ......76 E6
Everest Way HP2 ....125 A3
Everett Cl Bushey WD23 .168 E1
Hammond Street EN7 ....147 C6
Everett Ct WD7 ....156 A5
Evergreen Cl SG3 ....69 A2
Evergreen Rd SG12 ......93 F3
Evergreen Way LU3 ......45 A8
Evergreen Wlk 2 HP3 ..124 E1
Everlasting La AL3 .....127 C5
Eversden Ct HP2 ....105 B1
Eversley Lodge EN11 ...135 A6
Evron Pl 4 SG14 ......113 D6
Exchange Bldgs 7 EN5 .171 E6
Exchange Rd
Stevenage SG1 ....50 F5
Watford WD18 ....167 B5
Executive Pk Ind Est
AL1 ....128 B3
Exeter Cl Stevenage SG1 ..37 B2
Watford WD24 ....167 C7
Exeter Ho 7 WD6 ....170 A7
Exhims Mews HP4 ......121 E6
Explorer Dr WD18 ....166 F3
Extension Rd SG13 ......113 F6
Exton Ave LU2 ....46 A1
Eynsford Ct SG4 ....34 F6
Eynsford Rd LU4 ....44 D3

F

Faggots Cl WD7 ....156 C4
Faints Cl EN7 ....147 F2
Fair Cl WD23 ....168 B2
Fair Oak Ct LU2 ....45 F3
Fair Oak Dr LU2 ....45 F3
Fair View EN6 ....145 B2
Fairacre HP3 ....138 F7
Fairacre Ct 2 HA6 .....174 E3
Fairacres Cl EN6 ....158 F6
Fairburn Cl WD6 ....170 A8
Faircross Ho 6 WD17 ..167 B6
Faircross Way AL1 ......128 A5
Fairfax Ave LU3 ....44 D7
Fairfax Rd SG13 ....113 F7
Fairfield Buntingford SG9 ..40 F6
Northwood HA6 ....175 A1
Pinner HA6 ....175 A1
Fairfield Ave WD19 .....175 D7
Fairfield Cl
Harpenden AL5 ....86 D1
Hatfield AL10 ....130 C8
Northwood HA6 ....174 B4
Radlett WD7 ....155 E2
Fairfield Dr EN10 ....148 F7
Fairfield Jun Sch WD7 .155 E3
Fairfield Rd EN11 ....135 A8
Fairfield Way Hitchin SG4 .35 D8
Stevenage SG1 ....37 C3
Fairfield Wlk 6 EN8 ....148 E3
Fairfields Prim Sch
EN7 ....148 A4
Fairfolds WD25 ....154 E4
Fairford Ave LU2 ....45 E4
Fairgreen Rd LU1 ....62 F3
Fairhaven AL2 ....141 D4
Fairhaven Cres WD19 ..175 A7
Fairhill HP3 ....138 F7
Fairlands Lo WD6 ......170 A5
Fairlands Lodge 6
WD6 ....170 A5
Fairlands Prim Sch SG1 .50 D6
Fairlands Way SG1 ....51 A7
Fairlawns Pinner HA5 ...175 D1
Watford WD17 ....153 F1
Fairley Way EN7 ....148 B3
Fairmead Ave AL5 ......107 C8
Fairoaks Gr EN3 ....162 D2
Fairseat Cl WD23 ....176 E8
Fairshot Ct AL4 ....108 D2
Fairthorn Cl HP23 ....99 E3
Fairview Dr WD17 ......153 E3
Fairview Est EN11 ......135 C7
Fairview Rd SG1 ....50 B7
Fairway
Bishop's Stortford CM23 ...77 C6

Fairway *continued*
Hemel Hempstead HP3 ...138 F7
Sawbridgeworth CM21 ....97 F2
Ware SG12 ....114 C8
Fairway Ave WD6 ....170 B7
Fairway Cl
Chiswell Green AL2 ......141 C4
Harpenden AL5 ....107 A5
Fairway Ct HP3 ....138 F7
Fairway Ho WD6 ....170 B6
Fairway The
Abbots Langley WD5 .....153 D7
Moor Park HA6 ....174 E6
Fairways Cheshunt EN8 ..148 D5
Waltham Abbey EN9 .....163 E5
Faithfield WD19 ....167 E3
Falcon Cl Hatfield AL10 ..130 A3
Northwood HA6 ....174 E3
Sawbridgeworth CM21 ....97 C1
Stevenage SG2 ....51 D2
Falcon Ct 2 SG12 ....93 C3
Falcon Ridge HP4 ....122 C3
Falcon Way
Watford WD25 ....154 E5
Welwyn Garden City AL7 ..110 E8
Falconer Rd WD23 ......168 A3
Falconer Sch WD23 ......168 A4
Falconer St CM23 ....76 C5
Falconers Field AL5 ......85 E3
Falconers Pk CM21 ....97 D1
Falconers Rd LU2 ....46 B1
Falkirk Gdns WD19 .....175 D5
Falkland Rd EN5 ....171 E7
Fallow End AL6 ....68 D1
Fallow Rise SG13 ....113 F6
Fallowfield Luton LU3 ....45 C4
Stevenage SG2 ....51 C3
Welwyn Garden City AL7 ...89 F1
Fallowfield Cl UB9 ......173 C2
Fallowfield Wlk HP1 ....124 A6
Fallows Gn AL5 ....86 B3
Falmouth Ct AL3 ....127 D5
Falstaff Gdns AL1 ....141 C8
Falstone Gn LU2 ....46 E1
Fanhams Hall Rd SG12 ..93 F3
Fanhams Rd SG12 ....93 E2
Fanshaw Ct SG14 ....113 C7
Fanshawe Cres SG12 .....93 C2
Fanshawe St SG14 ....113 B7
Fanshaws La SG13 ......133 C5
Fantail La HP23 ....99 F4
Far End AL10 ....130 B2
Faraday Cl Luton LU4 ....44 C1
Watford WD18 ....166 D3
Faraday Rd SG2 ....51 B6
Faringdon Rd LU4 ....44 C3
Faringford Cl EN6 ......159 D8
Farland Rd HP2 ....125 B3
Farley Ct LU1 ....63 C5
Farley Farm Rd LU1 ......63 B5
Farley Hill LU1 ....63 C5
Farley Jun Sch LU1 ....63 C6
Farley Lodge LU1 ....63 D5
Farm Ave AL5 ....85 D4
Farm Cl Barnet EN5 .....171 C4
Borehamwood WD6 ......156 E1
Cheshunt EN8 ....148 C1
Cuffley EN6 ....146 E4
Harpenden AL5 ....85 D4
Hertford SG14 ....113 A6
Letchworth SG6 ....12 A1
London Colney WD7 .....142 E1
Roydon CM19 ....116 B1
Shenleybury WD7 ....156 E8
Stevenage SG1 ....50 E4
Welwyn Garden City AL8 ..110 C6
Farm Cotts SG12 ....93 D5
Farm Cres AL2 ....142 A5
Farm End HA6 ....174 B2
Farm Field WD17 ....153 E1
Farm Gn LU1 ....63 C5
Farm Hill Rd EN9 ....163 D6
Farm La Hoddesdon EN11 135 C8
Rickmansworth WD3 .....165 C6
Standon SG11 ....73 A8
Farm Pl HP4 ....121 F5
Farm Rd
Little Chalfont WD3 .....164 A5
Northwood HA6 ....174 C5
Slip End LU1 ....85 B7
St Albans AL1 ....128 B4
Farm Way Bushey WD23 .168 B5
Moor Park HA6 ....174 F6
Farmbrook LU2 ....45 D7
Farmers Cl WD25 ....154 B6
Farmery Ct HP4 ....122 E6
Farmhouse Cl EN10 ......148 F6
Farmhouse La HP2 ......125 A5
Farmhouse The HP2 .....125 A5
Farmstead Rd HA3 ......176 D1
Farne Ho 5 WD18 ....166 F3
Farnham CE Prim Sch
CM23 ....58 D6
Farnham Cl
Bovingdon HP3 ....137 A3
Sawbridgeworth CM21 ....97 C1
Farnham Gn CM23 ....58 B7
Farnley Gr LU2 ....64 A7
Farquhar St SG14 ....113 C7
Farr's La LU2 ....65 B1
Farraline Rd WD18 ......167 B5
Farrant Way WD6 ....169 E8
Farrer Top AL3 ....83 E5
Farriday Cl AL3 ....127 E7
Farrier Ct SG8 ....7 C7
Farriers SG12 ....115 A6
Farriers Cl Baldock SG7 ...12 E1
Bovingdon HP3 ....137 B3

Farriers Cl *continued*
Codicote SG4 ....67 F1
Farriers Ct WD25 ....154 B7
Farriers End EN10 ....148 F5
Farriers Way WD6 ......170 D4
Farringford Cl AL2 ......141 B5
Farrington Cotts EN5 ...171 F6
Farrington Pl HA6 ......174 F6
Farrow Cl LU3 ....31 C1
Farthing Cl WD18 ......167 C4
Farthing Dr SG6 ....23 C3
Farthings The HP1 ......124 B3
Faulkner Ct AL1 ....127 E5
Faverolle Gn EN8 ....148 D3
Faversham Cl HP23 .....100 A4
Fawbert & Barnard Inf Sch
CM21 ....97 E2
Fawbert & Barnard Sch
CM17 ....118 C3
Fawcett Rd SG2 ....51 B8
Fawkon Wlk EN11 ......135 A6
Fawn Ct AL9 ....130 C7
Fay Gn WD5 ....153 D6
Fayerfield EN6 ....159 D8
Fayland Cotts SG9 ....41 E7
Feacey Down HP1 ....124 B5
Fearney Mead WD3 .....165 A1
Fearnhill Sch SG6 ....22 C5
Fearnley Rd AL8 ....110 C5
Fearnley St WD18 ......167 B5
Feather Dell AL10 ....130 A5
Featherbed La HP3 .....138 B7
Featherston Rd SG2 ......51 C3
Featherstone Gdns
WD6 ....170 C5
Featherstone Wood Prim Sch
SG2 ....51 C3
Federal Way WD24 ......167 C8
Felbrigg Cl LU2 ....46 F2
Felden Cl Pinner HA5 ...175 E3
Watford WD25 ....154 D5
Felden Dr HP3 ....138 A7
Felden La HP3 ....138 A7
Felden Lawns HP3 ......138 A7
Felix Ave LU2 ....46 A2
Fell Path WD6 ....170 D4
Fellowes La AL4 ....143 E8
Fellowes Way SG2 ....51 A2
Fells Cl SG5 ....34 F8
Felmersham Ct LU1 ......63 B7
Felmersham Rd LU1 .....63 A7
Felmongers CM20 ....118 B2
Felstead Cl LU2 ....45 F3
Felstead Rd EN8 ....162 E7
Felstead Way LU2 ....45 F3
Felton Cl
Borehamwood WD6 ......156 E1
Cheshunt EN10 ....148 F6
Luton LU2 ....46 D1
Fen End SG5 ....11 F8
Fennycroft Rd HP1 .....124 A6
Fensom's Cl HP2 ....124 D4
Fensomes Alley HP2 ...124 D4
Fenwick Cl LU3 ....45 B5
Fenwick Path WD6 ......156 F1
Ferguson Gr EN8 ....148 D2
Fermor Cres LU2 ....46 C1
Fern Cl EN10 ....148 F8
Fern Ct HP4 ....122 B4
Fern Dells AL10 ....129 F4
Fern Dr HP3 ....124 E2
Fern Gr AL8 ....89 D2
Fern Ho HA7 ....176 F4
Fern Way WD25 ....154 B4
Ferndale
7 Harpenden AL5 ....86 A2
Much Hadham SG10 ......74 F2
Ferndale Rd Enfield EN3 .162 E2
Luton LU1 ....63 B7
Ferndene AL2 ....154 F8
Ferndown HA6 ....175 A1
Ferndown Cl HA5 ....175 E3
Ferndown Rd WD19 ....175 C6
Fernecroft AL1 ....141 D8
Ferney Rd EN7 ....147 D5
Fernheath LU3 ....31 A1
Fernhills WD4 ....153 D6
Fernleigh Ct HA2 ....176 B1
Fernleys AL4 ....128 C5
Ferns Cl EN3 ....162 E3
Fernville La HP2 ....124 D3
Ferny Hill EN4 ....159 F1
Ferrars Cl LU4 ....44 B1
Ferrars Inf Sch LU4 ....44 B3
Ferrars Jun Sch LU4 ......44 B3
Ferrers La AL4 ....108 B5
Ferrier Rd SG2 ....51 C6
Ferryhills Cl WD19 .....175 C7
Feryngs Cl CM17 ....118 D4
Fesants Croft CM20 .....118 B3
Fetherstone Cl EN6 .....159 D7
Fiddle Bridge La AL10 ..129 F6
Fiddlebridge Ind Ctr
AL10 ....129 F6
Fidler Pl WD23 ....168 B3
Field Cl Harpenden AL5 ..107 D7
St Albans AL4 ....128 A7
Field Cres SG8 ....7 F7
Field End EN5 ....171 B5
Field End Cl Luton LU2 ...46 C4
Watford WD19 ....167 E2
Wigginton HP23 ....100 D1
Field Fare Gn LU4 ....44 A5
Field Inf Sch WD18 ......167 C4
Field Jun Sch WD18 .....167 C4
Field La SG6 ....22 F4
Field Rd
Hemel Hempstead HP2 ...125 A3

Field Rd *continued*
Watford WD19 ....167 E3
Field View Rd EN6 ......159 A6
Field View Rise AL2 .....140 E2
Field Way Bovingdon HP3 137 A4
Hoddesdon EN11 ....115 C2
Rickmansworth WD3 .....165 B1
Field's Ct EN6 ....159 D6
Fielder Ctr (Univ of Herts)
AL10 ....129 D8
Fielders Way WD7 ......156 E6
Fieldfare Letchworth SG6 ..11 E1
Stevenage SG2 ....51 D3
Fieldfare Way SG8 ....7 E8
Fieldfares AL2 ....142 D4
Fieldgate Ho SG1 ....50 F5
Fieldgate Rd LU4 ....44 D2
Fieldings Rd EN8 ....148 F2
Fields End HP23 ....100 A6
Fields End La HP1 ....123 E5
Fieldway
Berkhamsted HP4 ....122 E2
Stanstead Abbotts SG12 ..115 B4
Wigginton HP23 ....100 D1
Fifth Ave Letchworth SG6 ..23 C6
Watford WD25 ....154 D4
Fifth Avenue / Allende Ave
CM20 ....117 C3
Figtree Hill HP2 ....124 D4
Filey Cl SG1 ....50 A7
Fillingham Way AL10 ...129 E7
Filmer Rd LU4 ....44 E4
Filton Ho 6 WD19 ......175 D7
Finch Cl Hatfield AL10 ..130 A3
Luton LU4 ....44 A4
Finch Gn WD3 ....164 F5
Finch La WD23 ....168 A5
Finch Rd HP4 ....122 A4
Finchdale HP1 ....124 A3
Finche's End SG2 ....52 B8
Finches The
Hertford SG13 ....114 B6
Hitchin SG4 ....35 A7
Finley Rd AL5 ....86 D3
Finsbury Ct EN8 ....162 E5
Finsbury Rd LU4 ....44 D5
Finucane Rise WD23 ....176 C8
Finway LU1 ....63 A8
Finway Ct WD18 ....166 F4
Finway Rd HP2 ....125 B7
Fir Cl SG2 ....50 F1
Fir Tree Cl HP3 ....125 B2
Fir Tree Ct WD6 ....169 F5
Fir Tree Hill WD3 ....153 A2
Firbank Dr WD19 ....167 E2
Firbank Rd AL3 ....127 F7
Firbank Trad Est LU1 ....63 A8
Fire Station Alley EN5 ..171 E7
Firecrest SG6 ....11 E1
Firlands CM23 ....76 E6
Firlands Ho CM23 ....76 E6
Firs Cl Hatfield AL10 ....130 B4
Hitchin SG5 ....34 D8
Firs Dr AL4 ....87 C5
Firs Jun Sch The CM23 ..76 E6
Firs La EN6 ....159 B6
Firs The
Hammond Street EN7 ....147 E4
Harpenden AL5 ....86 D2
St Albans AL1 ....142 B7
Welwyn Garden City AL8 ..89 C2
Wigginton HP23 ....100 D1
Firs Wlk Northwood HA6 .174 D4
Tewin AL6 ....90 E5
Firs Wood Cl EN6 ....159 F7
First Ave WD25 ....154 D4
First Avenue / Mandela Ave
CM20 ....117 F2
First Garden City Heritage
Mus★ SG6 ....23 A5
Firthesden Vinyard★
HP4 ....123 B8
Firway AL6 ....89 F7
Firway Cl AL6 ....89 F7
Firwood Ave AL4 ....128 E3
Fish Hill SG8 ....7 D6
Fish St AL3 ....106 B5
Fish Street Farm AL3 ..106 B5
Fisher Cl Holdbrook EN3 .163 A2
Kings Langley WD4 ......139 A2
Fisher Rd HA3 ....176 F1
Fisher's Green Rd SG1 ..50 B8
Fisher's Ind Est WD18 ..167 C4
Fishermans Way EN11 ..135 D8
Fishers Cl Holdbrook EN8 163 A5
Standon SG11 ....55 D3
Watford WD23 ....167 E6
Fishers Gn SG1 ....36 A1
Fishers Hatch CM20 .....117 E1
Fishers Mead SG11 ....55 D3
Fishery Cotts HP1 ....124 A1
Fishery Pas HP1 ....124 B1
Fishery Rd HP1 ....124 A1
Fishponds Rd SG5 ....34 E8
Fishpool St AL3 ....127 C3
Fitzjohn Ave EN5 ....171 F5
Fitzroy Ave LU3 ....45 B3
Fitzwarin Cl LU3 ....44 E8
Fitzwilliam Ct CM17 ....118 E4
Five Acres
Kings Langley WD4 ......138 F2
London Colney AL2 ......142 D6
Stansted Mountfitchet
CM24 ....59 E8
Five Acres Ave AL2 .....140 F2
Five Fields Cl WD19 ....175 F7
Five Oaks Caddington LU1 .62 F4
Hatfield AL10 ....130 B2

Five Oaks Mid Sch LU1 ..62 F3
Five Oaks Prim Sch
AL10 ....130 A3
Five Springs LU3 ....44 E6
Five Springs Ct LU3 .....44 E6
Flackwell Ho WD18 .....166 E3
Flags The HP2 ....125 B3
Flagstaff Cl EN9 ....163 B6
Flagstaff Rd EN9 ....163 B6
Flamstead End Prim Sch
EN7 ....148 A4
Flamstead End Rd EN8 .148 B3
Flamstead Sch AL3 ....84 B1
Flamsteadbury La AL3 .106 A4
Flandrian Cl EN3 ....163 B1
Flash La EN2 ....161 C3
Flatfield Rd HP3 ....125 A1
Flaunden Bottom HP3,
HP5 ....150 E4
Flaunden Hill HP3 ....151 A6
Flaunden Ho WD18 .....166 E2
Flaunden La
Bovingdon HP3 ....137 D3
Sarratt WD3 ....151 E6
Flavian Cl AL3 ....126 F1
Flax Mews AL3 ....83 E5
Flecker Cl HA7 ....176 F5
Fleet The SG8 ....7 C6
Fleetville Inf Sch AL1 ...128 B3
Fleetville Jun Sch AL1 ..128 A3
Fleetwood SG6 ....23 B4
Fleetwood Cres SG1 .....50 B7
Fleetwood Way WD19 ..175 C6
Fleming Cl EN7 ....148 A5
Fleming Cres SG14 ......113 A6
Fletcher Way HP2 ....124 D6
Flete Ho WD18 ....166 E3
Flexley Wood AL7 ....90 A1
Flight Path SG16 ....10 B3
Flinders Cl St Albans AL1 128 A1
Stevenage SG2 ....51 D5
Flint Cl LU3 ....44 E7
Flint Copse AL3 ....106 C6
Flint Ct LU1 ....63 D5
Flint Rd SG6 ....23 C8
Flint Way AL3 ....127 C7
Flintings The HP2 ....103 F8
Flora Gr AL1 ....127 F2
Floral Dr AL2 ....142 D5
Florence Ave LU3 ....44 D6
Florence Cl WD25 ....154 A4
Florence Ct HA6 ....174 E4
Florence St SG5 ....34 F8
Florence Wlk 8 CM23 ...76 F8
Florida Cl WD23 ....176 D8
Flowers Ind Est 11 LU1 ..63 E6
Flowers Way LU1 ....63 E7
Flowton Gr AL5 ....107 A7
Floyds Barns HP22 ....60 C2
Fog Cotts HP23 ....101 A5
Fogerty Cl EN3 ....163 B2
Fold Croft CM20 ....117 A1
Foldingshott SG3 ....69 D3
Follett Dr WD5 ....153 F8
Folly Ave AL3 ....127 C4
Folly Cl Hitchin SG4 ......35 A5
Radlett WD7 ....155 F3
Folly Fields AL4 ....87 B2
Folly La Caddington LU1 ..62 E4
St Albans AL3 ....127 C4
Folly Path SG4 ....35 A5
Folly Pathway WD7 .....155 F3
Folly The Buntingford SG9 .40 D7
Hertford SG14 ....113 D6
Folly View SG12 ....115 B4
Fontmell Cl AL3 ....127 E5
Fontwell Cl HA3 ....176 E3
Football Cl SG7 ....12 E1
Forbes Ave EN6 ....159 D7
Ford Cl WD23 ....168 C5
Ford Cotts SG11 ....75 B8
Ford Field SG11 ....75 A8
Ford Hill SG11 ....75 B8
Ford St SG11 ....55 E6
Fordham Cl SG7 ....4 D4
Fordham Rd SG8 ....7 E5
Fordhams Terr SG8 ....15 F7
Fordhams Wood (Nature
Reserve)★ SG8 ....6 E4
Fordwich Cl SG14 ....113 A6
Fordwich Hill SG14 ......113 A6
Fordwich Rd AL8 ....110 C5
Fordwich Rise SG14 .....113 A6
Fore St Harlow CM17 ....118 C4
Hatfield AL9 ....130 C6
Hertford SG14 ....113 D6
Weston SG4 ....24 B1
Forebury Ave CM21 ......97 F2
Forebury Cres CM21 .....97 F2
Forebury The CM21 ......97 F2
Forefield AL2 ....141 A4
Forelands Pl CM21 ....97 E2
Forest Ave 5 HP3 ......124 D1
Forest La WD7 ....156 B8
Forest Rd Cheshunt EN8 .148 D2
Enfield EN3 ....162 E3
Watford WD25 ....154 B6
Forest Row SG2 ....50 F1
Forest Wlk WD23 ....167 F8
Foresters Cl EN7 ....147 E4
Foresthall Rd CM24 ......59 E4
Forfar Ho 7 WD19 .....175 C7
Forge Cl
Chipperfield WD4 ....152 A8
5 Hitchin SG5 ....34 F8
Forge Cotts
Essendon AL9 ....131 E6
Hatfield Heath CM22 ......98 F3

For – Gle 191

Forge End AL2 141 A5
Forge La Northwood HA6 174 E3
Welwyn AL6 89 C5
Forres Cl EN11 135 A8
Forres Prim Sch EN11 115 B1
Forrest Cres LU2 46 A3
Forresters Dr AL7 111 C5
Fortnums Acre HA7 176 F4
Fortuna Cl SG1 51 C8
Fortune La WD6 169 D3
Forty Hall★ EN2 161 F2
Forty Hill EN2 161 F1
Forty Hill CE Prim Sch EN2 162 A2
Forty Hill Ho EN2 161 F1
Forum The SG1 50 D5
Fosbery Ct EN3 163 A2
Fosman Cl 7 SG5 34 D8
Foster Cl Cheshunt EN8 148 E1
Stevenage SG1 36 D1
Foster Dr SG4 35 A5
Foster Rd HP1 124 B1
Foston Cl LU3 44 F6
Fotherley Rd WD3 172 F8
Foulds Sch EN5 171 D6
Founceley Ave SG12 71 F8
Founders Rd EN11 115 B1
Fountain Ct
Borehamwood WD6 170 A7
Cheshunt EN8 148 D1
Fountain Dr SG13 113 F7
Fountain Pl EN9 163 C5
Fountains Rd LU3 45 D3
Four Acres Stevenage SG1 50 D7
Welwyn Garden City AL7 110 F4
Four Acres The CM21 98 A2
Four Limes AL4 108 D8
Four Swannes Prim Sch EN8 162 E6
Four Tubs The WD23 168 D2
Fouracres SG6 23 A3
Fouracres Dr HP3 124 F1
Fouracres Wlk HP3 124 F1
Fourdrinier Way HP3 138 D8
Fourth Ave Harlow CM20 117 C1
Letchworth SG6 23 C7
Luton LU3 44 D7
Watford WD25 154 D4
Fourways SG13 133 A5
Fourways Ct 1 EN11 135 A7
Fourways Market AL9 144 C7
Fovant SG1 36 B1
Fovant Cl AL5 107 C6
Fowley Cl EN8 162 F5
Fowlmere Rd SG8 9 F8
Fox Cl Bushey WD23 168 B5
Elstree WD6 169 D3
Wigginton HP23 100 D1
Fox Cnr SG8 1 F5
Fox Hill SG8 1 F5
Fox Hill Rd SG8 1 F5
Fox La SG8 15 F7
Fox Rd Stevenage SG1 50 E4
Wigginton HP23 100 C2
Fox's La AL9 144 F7
Foxbury Cl LU2 45 D6
Foxcroft AL1 128 A1
Foxdell HA6 174 D4
Foxdell Inf Sch LU1 63 A8
Foxdell Jun Sch LU1 62 E8
Foxdells SG14 112 C3
Foxdells La CM23 58 F2
Foxes Cl SG13 114 B6
Foxes Dr EN7 148 A2
Foxes La EN6 146 E3
Foxes Par EN9 163 C6
Foxfield SG2 51 C3
Foxfield Cl HA6 174 F4
Foxglove Bank SG8 7 F5
Foxglove Cl
Bishop's Stortford CM23 76 C6
Hatfield AL10 130 B4
Hoddesdon EN11 115 C1
Foxglove Way Luton LU3 45 D2
Oaklands AL6 89 E8
Foxgloves The HP1 123 E2
Foxgrove Path WD19 175 D5
Foxhill Luton LU2 45 E5
Watford WD24 154 A3
Foxholes Ave SG13 113 F6
Foxhollows AL10 130 B7
Foxlands Cl WD25 154 A5
Foxley Dr CM23 77 B8
Foxley Gr AL6 89 F4
Foxleys WD19 175 E7
Foxton Rd EN11 135 A6
Foxtree Ho WD25 154 E3
Foxwood Chase EN9 163 C4
Foyle Cl SG1 37 C3
Frampton Rd EN6 145 C1
Frampton St SG14 113 D6
Francis Ave AL3 127 D6
Francis Bacon Sch AL1 142 B8
Francis Cl Hitchin SG4 35 A5
Stotfold SG5 11 E6
Francis Combe Sch & Com Coll WD25 154 C7
Francis Ct Harlow CM20 117 B2
St Albans AL1 127 E2
Francis Green Ho EN9 163 B6
Francis House Prep Sch HP23 99 F3
Francis Rd Hinxworth SG7 3 C6
Ware SG12 93 D2
Watford WD18 167 B5
Francis St LU1 63 D8
Francis Wks EN11 135 B6
Frank Lester Way LU2 64 D8
Frank Martin Ct EN7 148 B1
Frankland Cl WD3 166 A2
Frankland Rd WD3 166 B3
Franklin Ave EN7 148 B1
Franklin Cl
Colney Heath AL4 129 E1
Hemel Hempstead HP3 138 E8
Pirton SG5 20 D4
Franklin Gdns SG4 22 B1
Franklin Rd WD17 167 B7
Franklin's Rd SG1 50 C8
Franks Cl SG16 10 B5
Franshams WD23 176 D8
Fraser Rd EN8 148 E3
Fred Millard Ct SG1 50 E5
Frederick St LU2 45 E1
Frederick Street Pas LU2 45 E1
Freeman Ave LU3 45 B8
Freemans Cl SG5 21 D1
Freewaters Cl SG5 21 E4
Freezywater St George's Prim Sch EN3 162 D3
Freman Coll SG9 40 D8
Freman Dr SG9 40 D8
French Horn Ct 5 SG12 93 D1
French Horn La AL10 130 B6
French Lodge SG5 34 F8
French Row 4 AL3 127 D3
French's Cl SG12 115 B4
Frenches Yd 21 SG12 93 D1
Frensham EN7 148 A4
Frensham Dr SG4 22 C2
Frere Ct CM23 58 F1
Freshwater Cl LU3 44 F7
Freshwaters CM20 117 E1
Fretherne Rd AL8 110 D6
Friars Cl LU1 63 B5
Friars Ct LU1 63 B5
Friars Field HP4 121 E7
Friars Rd Braughing SG11 56 A7
Weston SG4 24 B1
Friars Way
Kings Langley WD4 139 A1
Luton LU1 63 B5
Watford WD23 167 F8
Friars Wlk HP23 100 A4
Friars Wood CM23 77 C8
Friarscroft EN10 135 A3
Friday Furlong SG5 34 C8
Friedberg Ave CM23 76 D4
Friendless La AL3 83 F2
Friends Ave EN8 162 D7
Friern Cl 6 EN7 147 E5
Friesian Cl LU4 44 A3
Frimley Rd HP1 123 E4
Fringewood Cl HA6 174 B2
Frinton Cl WD19 175 B8
Friston Gn LU2 46 D1
Frithsden Copse HP4 122 F8
Frithwood Ave HA6 174 F4
Frithwood Prim Sch HA6 174 F4
Frobisher Cl WD23 168 A3
Frobisher Dr SG2 51 B7
Frobisher Rd AL1 128 C1
Frobisher Way AL10 129 D8
Froghall Cotts WD6 170 D3
Froghall La SG2 38 B1
Frogmoor Ct WD3 173 D8
Frogmoor La WD3 173 D8
Frogmore AL2 141 E4
Frogmore Hill SG14 70 B7
Frogmore Ho SG1 36 C1
Frogmore Home Pk AL2 141 D4
Frogmore Rd HP3 138 D8
Frogmore Road Ind Est HP3 138 D8
Frogmore St HP23 100 A3
Frogs Hall La SG11 53 F3
Frome Cl LU4 44 E4
Frome Sq HP2 125 A8
Front St LU1 63 C1
Front The HP4 123 B7
Frost Ho HP4 122 C3
Frowick Cl AL9 144 B8
Frowyke Cres EN6 158 A7
Fry Rd SG2 51 C5
Fryth Mead AL3 127 B4
Fulbeck Way HA2 176 C1
Fulbourne Cl LU4 44 E2
Fulford Gr WD19 175 B8
Fuller Ct 3 CM23 77 A7
Fuller Gdns WD24 154 B2
Fuller Rd WD24 154 B2
Fuller Way WD3 166 A4
Fuller's Almshouses CM24 59 F6
Fullers Cl EN9 163 F6
Fullers Ct SG6 22 E7
Fulling Mill La AL6 89 B6
Fulmar Cres HP1 124 A3
Fulmore Cl AL5 86 D4
Fulton Cl SG1 50 C5
Fulton Cres CM23 77 C8
Fulton Ct
Borehamwood WD6 156 F1
Holdbrook EN3 163 A1
Furham Field HA5 176 A3
Furlay Cl SG6 22 D7
Furlong The HP23 100 A3
Furlong Way SG12 115 A7
Furlongs HP1 124 A4
Furmston Ct SG6 23 A7
Furneux Pelham CE Sch SG9 43 A4
Furriers Cl CM23 76 C5
Furrowfield AL10 130 B7
Furrows The LU3 45 B7
Furse Ave AL4 128 A7
Furtherfield WD5 153 E7
Furtherground 1 HP2 124 E2
Furze Cl Luton LU2 45 D7
South Oxhey WD19 175 C5
Furze Gr SG8 7 E5
Furze Rd HP1 123 E2
Furze View WD3 164 C4
Furzebushes La AL2 140 F6
Furzedown SG2 51 B4
Furzedown Ct 18 AL5 86 B1
Furzefield EN8 148 B3
Furzefield Ct EN6 158 E8
Furzefield Ctr The EN6 158 D8
Furzefield Rd AL7 110 E4
Furzehill Mid Sch WD6 170 A5
Furzehill Par WD6 170 A6
Furzehill Rd WD6 170 B5
Furzen Cres AL10 129 F2

G

Gable Cl
Abbots Langley WD5 153 E7
Pinner HA5 176 A3
Gables Ave WD6 169 F6
Gables Lodge EN4 159 C1
Gables The
3 Hemel Hempstead HP1 124 D4
Sawbridgeworth CM21 97 E2
Watford WD19 167 C2
Watford,Woodside WD25 154 D6
Gaddesden Cres WD25 154 E5
Gaddesden Gr AL7 111 B6
Gaddesden La AL3 105 C4
Gaddesden Row HP2 104 C6
Gaddesden Row Jun Mix Inf Sch HP2 104 B6
Gade Ave WD18 166 E5
Gade Bank WD1 166 D5
Gade Cl
Hemel Hempstead HP1 124 B6
Watford WD18 166 E5
Gade Twr HP3 138 F6
Gade Valley Cl WD4 139 A3
Gade Valley Cotts HP1 103 E4
Gade Valley Jun Mix Inf Sch HP1 124 B4
Gade View Gdns WD4 153 C7
Gadebridge Ct HP1 124 C4
Gadebridge La
Hemel Hempstead HP1 124 B5
Hemel Hempstead HP1 124 C5
Gadebridge Rd HP1 124 B4
Gadeside WD24,WD25 153 E4
Gadeview HP1 124 C3
Gadeview Rd HP3 138 D7
Gadmore La HP23 119 F7
Gadswell Cl WD25 154 E3
Gage Cl SG8 7 D7
Gainsborough Ave AL1 127 F4
Gainsford Cres SG4 22 C2
Gainswood AL7 110 E5
Gaitskell Ho WD6 170 D5
Gall End La CM24 59 F7
Galleria The AL10 129 F5
Gallery The
Letchworth SG6 22 F6
7 Luton LU1 63 E7
Galley Gn SG13 115 A2
Galley Hill HP1 124 B6
Galley La EN5 171 B7
Galleycroft Ct 4 AL10 130 A6
Galleyhill Rd EN9 163 E7
Galleywood SG5 21 D4
Galliard Cl LU3 45 B4
Galloway Cl
1 Bishop's Stortford CM23 76 F8
Cheshunt EN10 148 F5
Galloway Rd CM23 58 F1
Gallows Hill WD4 153 C7
Gallows Hill La WD5 153 D8
Galston Rd LU3 44 D8
Gammon Cl HP3 125 A2
Gammons La WD17, WD24 154 A2
Gamnel Mews HP23 100 B7
Ganders Ash WD25 154 A6
Gandhi Ct 1 WD24 167 D7
Gangies Hill CM21 97 A4
Gant Ct EN9 163 F5
Ganton Wlk WD19 175 E6
Ganymede Pl HP2 124 F6
Gaping La SG5 34 D7
Garden Ave AL10 130 A2
Garden Cl Barnet EN5 171 C5
Harpenden AL5 107 A5
Royston SG8 7 E7
St Albans AL1 128 B4
Watford WD17 166 F7
Woolmer Green SG3 69 B2
Garden Cott AL2 141 E4
Garden Cotts SG11 73 A8
Garden Ct
Hoddesdon EN10 134 F4
Welwyn Garden City AL7 110 E7
Wheathampstead AL4 87 D1
Garden Field SG2 51 E2
Garden Field La HP4 122 F2
Garden Fields Jun Mix Inf Sch AL3 127 D6
Garden Ho SG13 113 C5
Garden Hos The CM21 98 B3
Garden La SG8 7 D5
Garden Rd
Abbots Langley WD5 153 E8
Garden Rd *continued*
Buntingford SG9 40 E8
Woolmer Green SG3 69 B2
Garden Row 6 SG5 34 F8
Garden Terr SG12 92 E4
Garden Terrace Rd CM17 118 C4
Garden Wlk Royston SG8 7 E7
Stevenage SG1 50 E5
Gardenia Ave LU3 45 A4
Gardens of the Rose The★ AL2 140 F5
Gardens The Baldock SG7 23 E8
Brookmans Park AL9 144 E4
Henlow SG16 10 D8
Stotfold SG5 11 E6
Watford WD17 166 F7
Gardiners La SG7 4 D4
Gardner Ct Luton LU1 63 E4
Watford WD25 154 C4
Gareth Ct WD6 156 F1
Garfield Ct LU2 46 D3
Garfield St WD24 154 B1
Garland Cl Cheshunt EN8 162 E8
Hemel Hempstead HP2 124 D4
Garland Ct 4 AL1 127 E3
Garland Rd SG12 93 E1
Garnault Rd EN1 161 F1
Garner Dr EN10 148 E5
Garnett Cl WD24 154 D3
Garnett Dr AL2 140 F2
Garrard Way AL4 108 D8
Garratts Rd WD23 168 C2
Garretts Cl SG14 113 C6
Garretts Mead LU2 46 B3
Garrison Ct 2 SG4 34 F7
Garrowsfield EN5 171 F4
Garsmouth Way WD25 154 D3
Garston Cres WD25 154 C5
Garston Dr WD25 154 C5
Garston Inf Sch WD25 154 D4
Garston La WD25 154 D5
Garston Manor Sch WD25 154 C7
Garston Park Par WD25 154 D5
Garston Sta WD25 154 D4
Garter Ct 10 LU2 45 D1
Garth Rd SG6 22 E3
Garth The WD5 153 D6
Garthland Dr EN5 171 C4
Gartlet Rd WD17 167 C6
Gas La SG8 17 C3
Gascoyne Cl EN6 158 A7
Gascoyne Way SG13, SG14 113 D5
Gatcombe Ct AL1 128 A2
Gate Cl WD6 170 C8
Gate Cotts WD3 164 D5
Gate End HA6 175 A3
Gatecroft HP3 139 A8
Gatehill Gdns LU3 31 B1
Gatehill Rd HA6 175 A3
Gatehouse Mews SG9 40 E8
Gates Way SG1 50 C6
Gatesbury Way SG11 55 D3
Gatesdene Cl HP4 102 C8
Gateshead Rd WD6 170 A8
Gateway Cl HA6 174 C4
Gateways The EN7 147 E3
Gatwick Cl CM23 59 B1
Gauldie Way SG11 55 D2
Gaumont App WD17 167 B6
Gaunts Way SG6 12 A2
Gaveston Dr HP4 122 B6
Gayland Ave LU2 64 B8
Gayton Cl LU3 45 B4
Gaywood Ave EN8 148 D1
Gazelda Ind Est WD17 167 D4
Gean Wlk 3 AL10 130 A2
Geddes Rd WD23 168 C5
Geddings Rd EN11 135 B6
Geddington Ct EN8 163 A5
Generals Wlk The EN3 162 E2
Gentle Ct SG7 23 E8
Gentlemens Field SG12 93 B3
George Field Ho 4 WD3 165 D2
George Gn CM22 77 B1
George Green Villas CM22 98 B8
George La 5 SG8 7 D6
George Leighton Ct SG2 51 B4
George Lovell Dr EN3 163 A2
George St
Berkhamsted HP4 122 D4
Hemel Hempstead HP2 124 D4
Hertford SG14 113 C6
Luton LU1 63 E7
Markyate AL3 83 E5
St Albans AL3 127 D3
Watford WD18 167 C5
George St W LU1 63 E7
George Street Prim Sch HP2 124 D4
George V Ave HA5 175 F1
George V Way WD3 152 B3
George Wlk 9 SG12 93 D1
George's Wood Rd AL9 145 B5
Georges Mead WD6 169 E3
Georgewood Rd HP3 139 A7
Georgina Ct SG15 11 A3
Gerard Ave CM23 76 E4
Gerard Ct 2 AL5 86 A2
Gernon Rd SG6 22 F5
Gernon Wlk SG6 22 F5
Gew's Cnr EN8 148 D2
Giant Tree Hill WD23 168 D1
Gibbons Cl
Borehamwood WD6 169 E8
Sandridge AL4 108 C1
Gibbons Way SG3 68 F5
Gibbs Cl EN8 148 D2
Gibbs Couch WD19 175 D7
Gibbs Field CM23 76 D5
Gibraltar Lodge AL5 86 D3
Gibson Cl SG4 35 B7
Gidian Ct AL2 141 D4
Gifford's La SG11 54 A2
Gilbert Ct AL5 86 B4
Gilbert Rd UB9 173 D1
Gilbert St EN3 162 C2
Gilbert Way HP4 122 A4
Gilbert's Hill HP23 119 E3
Gilbey Ave CM23 77 B6
Gilbey Cres CM24 59 E8
Gildea Cl HA5 176 A3
Gilden Cl CM17 118 E4
Gilden Way CM17 118 D3
Gilder Cl LU3 45 A8
Gilderdale LU4 44 B6
Gilders CM21 97 D2
Giles Cl AL4 108 C1
Giles Inf Sch The SG1 37 A1
Giles Jun Sch SG1 37 A1
Gill Cl WD18 166 C3
Gillam St LU2 63 E8
Gillan Gn WD23 176 C8
Gillian Ave AL1 141 C7
Gillian Ho HA3 176 E4
Gilliat's Gn WD3 164 D5
Gilliflower Ho EN11 135 A5
Gillings Ct EN5 171 E5
Gillison Cl SG6 23 B5
Gills Hill WD7 155 F4
Gills Hill La WD7 155 F3
Gills Hollow WD7 155 F3
Gilmour Cl EN2 162 A4
Gilpin Gn AL5 86 C1
Gilpin Rd SG12 114 E8
Gilpin's Gallop SG12 115 B4
Gilpin's Ride HP4 122 E5
Gilsland EN9 163 E4
Gilston Mews CM20 117 C6
Gilston Pk CM20 117 C7
Ginns Rd SG9 43 D6
Gippeswyck Cl HA5 175 D2
Gipsy La
Bishop's Stortford CM23, CM24 59 C4
Knebworth AL6,SG3 68 E4
Luton LU1 64 A6
Girdle Rd SG4 22 A2
Girons Cl SG4 35 B7
Girtin Rd WD23 168 C5
Girton Ct EN8 148 E1
Girton Way WD3 166 C4
Gisburne Way WD24 154 A2
Gladding Rd EN7 147 B6
Glade The Baldock SG7 23 F7
Letchworth SG6 22 F3
Welwyn Garden City AL8 110 C8
Glades The HP1 123 E4
Gladeside AL4 128 D6
Gladesmere Ct WD24 154 B2
Gladeway The EN9 163 D6
Gladsmuir Rd EN5 171 E7
Gladstone Ave LU1 63 C7
Gladstone Ct SG2 69 A8
Gladstone Pl EN5 171 D5
Gladstone Rd
Dane End SG12 71 F8
Hoddesdon EN11 135 B7
Ware SG12 93 C2
Watford WD17 167 C6
Glaisdale LU4 44 C5
Glamis Cl Cheshunt EN7 148 A2
Hemel Hempstead HP2 105 B1
Glanfield HP2 124 E6
Glassmill Ho 6 HP4 122 D4
Gleave Cl AL1 128 B4
Glebe Ave SG15 11 A7
Glebe Cl Essendon AL9 131 F6
Hemel Hempstead HP3 138 E7
Hertford SG14 113 D8
Pitstone LU7 80 D5
Watton at S SG14 70 D3
Glebe Cotts AL9 131 F6
Glebe Ct
Bishop's Stortford CM23 77 B8
Hatfield AL10 130 C6
Watford WD25 154 D6
Watton at S SG14 70 E3
Glebe Ho AL9 131 F6
Glebe La EN5 171 A3
Glebe Rd Hertford SG14 113 D8
Letchworth SG6 23 B8
Welwyn AL6 89 B5
Glebe The Ardeley SG2 38 F3
Harlow CM20 117 E1
Kings Langley WD4 139 A2
St Ippolyts SG4 35 C2
Stevenage SG2 51 B6
Watford WD25 154 D6
Glebe View SG2 38 C2
Glebeland AL10 130 C5
Glebelands CM20 117 F3
Gleed Ave WD23 176 D8
Glemsford Cl LU4 44 B6
Glemsford Dr AL5 86 D2
Glen Chess WD3 165 C5
Glen Faba Rd CM19 135 F6
Glen The Caddington LU1 62 E3

Glen The *continued*
Hemel Hempstead HP2 . . .124 F8
Northwood HA6 . . . . .174 D3
Glen Way WD17 . . . . . . .153 E1
Glenblower Ct AL4 . . . . .128 D3
Glenbourne SG4 . . . . .67 F1
Glencoe Rd WD23 . . . . .168 A3
Glencorse Gn WD19 . . . .175 D6
Glendale HP1 . . . . .124 B3
Glendale Wlk EN8 . . . . . .148 E1
Glendean Ct EN3 . . . . . .162 F3
Gleneagles Cl WD19 . . . .175 D6
Gleneagles Dr LU2 . . . . . .45 E6
Glenester Cl EN11 . . . . .115 A1
Glenferrie Rd AL1 . . . . .128 A3
Glenfield Ct SG14 . . . . .112 F7
Glenfield Rd LU3 . . . . . . .45 C6
Glengall Pl AL1 . . . . . . .141 E8
Glenhaven Ave WD6 . . . .170 A6
Glenlyn Ave AL1 . . . . . .128 B2
Glenmire Terr SG12 . . . .115 D4
Glenmore Gdns WD5 . . . .154 A7
Glenshee Cl HA6 . . . . . .174 C4
Glenview Gdns HP1 . . . .124 B3
Glenview Rd HP1 . . . . . .124 B3
Glenville Ave EN2 . . . . . .161 D1
Glenwood
Hoddesdon EN10 . . . . .134 F4
Welwyn Garden City AL7 . .111 D5
Glenwood Cl SG2 . . . . . . .51 C2
Glevum Cl AL3 . . . . .126 F1
Globe Cl AL5 . . . . .86 B1
Globe Cres CM23 . . . . . . .58 D6
Globe Ct Hertford SG14 . .113 C8
Hoddesdon EN10 . . . . .148 F8
Glossop Way SG15 . . . . . .11 B7
Gloucester Ave EN8 . . . .162 E6
Gloucester Cl SG1 . . . . . .36 E2
Gloucester Ho 6 WD6 . .170 A7
Gloucester Rd
Enfield EN2 . . . . .161 C1
1 Luton LU1 . . . . .63 F6
Glover Cl EN7 . . . . .147 F4
Glovers Cl SG13 . . . . . . .113 C4
Glovers Ct SG5 . . . . .21 F1
Glynde The SG2 . . . . .69 B8
Goat La EN1 . . . . .161 F1
Gobions Way EN6 . . . . . .145 B3
Goblins Gn AL7 . . . . . . .110 D5
Goddard End SG2 . . . . . . .69 C8
Goddards Cl SG13 . . . . .132 C4
Godfrey Cl SG2 . . . . .51 B3
Godfreys Cl LU1 . . . . .63 B6
Godfreys Ct LU1 . . . . .63 B6
Godfries Cl AL6 . . . . .90 E3
Godsafe CM17 . . . . .118 E4
Godwin Cl E4 . . . . .163 C1
Goff's La EN7 . . . . .147 E2
Goff's Oak Ave EN7 . . . .147 C3
Goffs Cres EN7 . . . . .147 C2
Goffs La EN7 . . . . .148 A2
Goffs Oak Jun Mix Inf Sch
EN7 . . . . .147 B3
Goffs Sch EN7 . . . . .148 A2
Gold Cl EN10 . . . . .134 E3
Gold Crest Cl LU4 . . . . . . .44 A5
Golda Cl EN5 . . . . .171 D3
Goldcrest Way WD23 . . .168 C1
Goldcroft HP3 . . . . .125 A1
Golden Dell AL7 . . . . . . .110 F2
Goldfield Inf Sch HP23 . . .99 F3
Goldfield Rd HP23 . . . . . .99 F3
Goldfinch Way WD6 . . . .170 A5
Goldings
Bishop's Stortford CM23 . . .77 B8
Hertford SG14 . . . . .92 A1
Goldings Cres AL10 . . . . .130 B6
Goldings Ho AL10 . . . . . .130 B6
Goldings La SG14 . . . . . . .92 A2
Goldington Cl EN11 . . . . .114 F1
Goldon SG6 . . . . .23 C4
Goldring Way AL2 . . . . . .142 B5
Goldsmith Way AL3 . . . . .127 C4
Goldstone Cl SG12 . . . . . .93 D2
Golf Cl WD23 . . . . .167 D6
Golf Club Rd AL9 . . . . . .145 A6
Golf Ride EN2 . . . . .161 A4
Gombards AL3 . . . . .127 D4
Gomer Cl SG4 . . . . .67 E2
Gonnerston AL3 . . . . . . .127 B4
Gonville Ave WD3 . . . . . .166 B3
Gonville Cres SG2 . . . . . . .51 C2
Goodacre Cl EN6 . . . . . .159 C7
Goodey Meade SG2 . . . . . .52 F2
Goodison Cl WD23 . . . . .168 C4
Goodliffe Pk CM23 . . . . . .59 B2
Goodrich Cl WD25 . . . . .154 A4
Goodwin Ct 4 EN8 . . . . .148 E3
Goodwin Ho WD18 . . . . .166 E3
Goodwin Stile CM23 . . . . .76 D5
Goodwins Mead LU7 . . . . .80 A7
Goodwood Ave
Enfield EN3 . . . . .162 C2
Watford WD24 . . . . .153 E3
Goodwood Cl EN11 . . . . .135 A7
Goodwood Par WD24 . . . .153 E3
Goodwood Path 2
WD6 . . . . .170 A7
Goodwood Rd SG8 . . . . . . .7 F6
Goodyers Ave WD7 . . . . .155 F5
Goose Acre Botley HP5 . .136 A1
Cheddington LU7 . . . . .80 A7
Goose La CM22 . . . . .98 E7
Gooseacre AL7 . . . . .110 F4
Gooseberry Hill LU3 . . . . .45 B7
Goosecroft HP1 . . . . .123 F4
Goosefields WD3 . . . . . . .165 C3
Goral Mead WD3 . . . . . .165 D1
Gordian Way SG2 . . . . . . .37 C1
Gordon Ave HA7 . . . . . . .176 F4
Gordon Cl AL1 . . . . .128 B2
Gordon Ct SG3 . . . . .69 A5
Gordon Ho AL1 . . . . .128 B2
Gordon Mans EN5 . . . . . .171 F5
Gordon Rd EN9 . . . . .163 A5
Gordon St LU1 . . . . .63 D7
Gordon Way EN5 . . . . . . .171 F5
Gordon's Wlk AL5 . . . . . .107 C8
Gore La SG11 . . . . .73 D3
Gorelands La HP8 . . . . . .172 A7
Gorham Dr AL1 . . . . .141 E8
Gorhambury★ AL3 . . . . . .126 C4
Gorle Cl WD25 . . . . .154 A4
Gorleston Cl SG1 . . . . . . .36 A1
Gorse Cl AL10 . . . . .129 F2
Gorse Cnr
Harpenden AL5 . . . . .107 C8
St Albans AL3 . . . . .127 D5
Gorselands AL5 . . . . .107 B7
Gorst Cl SG6 . . . . .22 E5
Gosford Ho WD18 . . . . . .166 E3
Gosforth La
South Oxhey WD19 . . . . . .175 B7
5 South Oxhey WD19 . . . .175 C7
Gosforth Path WD19 . . . .175 A7
Goshawk Cl LU4 . . . . .44 A4
Goslett Ct WD23 . . . . . . .168 A4
Gosling Ave SG5 . . . . .33 C2
Gosling Ski Ctr★ AL8 . . .110 C4
Gosmore SG1 . . . . .36 C2
Gosmore Ley Cl SG4 . . . . .34 F3
Gosmore Rd SG4 . . . . .34 F5
Gossamers The WD25 . . .154 E4
Gosselin Ho SG14 . . . . . .113 D8
Gosselin Rd SG14 . . . . . .113 C8
Gossom's End HP4 . . . . .122 A5
Gossoms Ryde HP4 . . . . .122 A5
Gothic Mede Lower Sch
SG15 . . . . .11 A5
Gothic Way SG15 . . . . .11 B5
Gould Cl AL9 . . . . .144 B7
Government Row EN3 . . .163 A2
Gowar Field EN6 . . . . . . .158 A7
Gower Rd SG8 . . . . .7 C7
Gowers The CM20 . . . . . .118 B2
Grace Ave WD7 . . . . .156 E6
Grace Cl WD6 . . . . .170 D8
Grace Gdns CM23 . . . . . . .76 F4
Grace Way SG1 . . . . .50 E7
Graces Maltings HP23 . . .100 A3
Graemesdyke Rd HP4 . . .122 A3
Grafton Cl AL4 . . . . .128 D2
Grafton Pl SG11 . . . . .55 F1
Graham Ave EN10 . . . . . .134 E2
Graham Cl AL1 . . . . .127 D1
Graham Ct 2 AL3 . . . . . .127 D4
Graham Gdns LU3 . . . . . . .45 C4
Graham Rd HA3 . . . . .176 E1
Grailands CM23 . . . . .76 D8
Grammar School Wlk
SG5 . . . . .34 E7
Grampian Way LU3 . . . . . .44 C8
Granaries The EN9 . . . . .163 E5
Granary Cl AL4 . . . . .108 D8
Granary Ct CM21 . . . . .97 E2
Granary La AL5 . . . . .86 C1
Granary The
Flamstead HP2 . . . . .104 F4
Roydon CM19 . . . . .116 B1
Stanstead Abbotts SG12 . .115 C3
Granby Ave AL5 . . . . .86 D2
Granby Ct AL5 . . . . .86 D2
Granby Rd Luton LU4 . . . . .44 E2
Stevenage SG1 . . . . .36 C2
Grandfield Ave WD17 . . . .167 A8
Grange Ave Luton LU4 . . . .44 D4
Totteridge N20 . . . . .171 E2
Grange Bottom SG8 . . . . . . .7 E5
Grange Cl
Hemel Hempstead HP2 . . .125 A2
Hertford SG14 . . . . .113 B6
Hitchin SG4 . . . . .35 A4
Markyate AL3 . . . . .83 D6
Watford WD17 . . . . .167 A8
Grange Court Rd AL5 . . . .107 C6
Grange Ct Hertford SG14 113 C7
Letchworth SG6 . . . . .12 A1
3 St Albans AL3 . . . . .127 D4
Waltham Abbey EN9 . . . . .163 C5
Grange Dr SG5 . . . . .11 F5
Grange Gdns SG12 . . . . . .114 E8
Grange Hill AL6 . . . . .89 C6
Grange Jun Sch SG6 . . . . . .12 A2
Grange La WD25 . . . . . . .168 D8
Grange Pk CM23 . . . . .58 F1
Grange Rd
Bishop's Stortford CM23 . . .77 A7
Borehamwood WD6 . . . . . .169 F4
Letchworth SG6 . . . . .22 F8
Pitstone LU7 . . . . .80 D5
Tring HP23 . . . . .100 C5
Watford WD23 . . . . .167 F4
Wilstone HP23 . . . . .79 D1
Grange Rise SG4 . . . . .67 F1
Grange St AL3 . . . . .127 D4
Grange The
Abbots Langley WD5 . . . . .153 E8
Bishop's Stortford CM23 . . .58 F1
Hoddesdon EN11 . . . . .135 A5
Rickmansworth WD3 . . . . .165 D2
Sewardstone EN9 . . . . . . .163 D2
Standon SG11 . . . . .55 D3
Therfield SG8 . . . . .15 F6
Grange Wlk CM23 . . . . . . .77 A7
Grangedale Cl HA6 . . . . .174 E2
Grangeside CM23 . . . . .59 A2
Grangewood EN6 . . . . . . .145 B1
Gransden Cl LU3 . . . . .45 A7
Grant Gdns AL5 . . . . .86 B2
Grantham Cl SG8 . . . . .7 B8
Grantham Gdns SG12 . . . . .93 E2
Grantham Gn WD6 . . . . . .170 C4
Grantham Mews HP4 . . . .122 D4
Grantham Rd LU4 . . . . .45 B1
Granville Ct AL1 . . . . . . .127 F3
Granville Dene HP3 . . . . .137 A4
Granville Gdns EN11 . . . .115 A2
Granville Rd Barnet EN5 .171 D6
Hitchin SG4 . . . . .22 C1
Luton LU1 . . . . .63 B8
St Albans AL1 . . . . .127 F3
Watford WD18 . . . . .167 C5
Berkhamsted HP4 . . . . . . .121 E6
Grasmere SG1 . . . . .37 C3
Grasmere Ave
Harpenden AL5 . . . . .86 C1
Luton LU3 . . . . .45 B7
Grasmere Cl
Hemel Hempstead HP3 . . .125 B1
Watford WD25 . . . . .154 B7
Grasmere Rd Luton LU3 . . .45 C7
St Albans AL1 . . . . .128 B1
Ware SG12 . . . . .93 E3
Grass Mdws SG2 . . . . .51 D7
Grass Warren AL6 . . . . . . .90 E1
Grassington Cl AL2 . . . . .141 A1
Grassy Cl HP1 . . . . .124 A4
Gravel Dr HP23 . . . . .99 B3
Gravel La HP1 . . . . .124 A3
Gravel Path
Berkhamsted HP4 . . . . . . .122 E5
Hemel Hempstead HP1 . . .124 A3
Graveley Ave WD6 . . . . . .170 C4
Graveley Cl SG1 . . . . .36 C2
Graveley Dell AL7 . . . . . .111 B5
Graveley La SG4 . . . . .36 B5
Graveley Prim Sch SG4 . . .36 B4
Graveley Rd Graveley SG1 .36 B3
Great Wymondley SG4 . . . . .35 F6
Gravelhill Terr HP1 . . . . .124 A2
Gravelly Dell SG11 . . . . . .55 F8
Gravelly La SG11 . . . . . . .55 F8
Gravely Ct HP2 . . . . .125 C2
Gray's La SG5 . . . . .34 D7
Grayling Ct HP4 . . . . . . .121 F6
Graylings The WD5 . . . . .153 D6
Grays Cl SG8 . . . . .7 C8
Grays Ct CM23 . . . . .76 E8
Graysfield AL7 . . . . .111 A3
Grazings The HP2 . . . . . .124 F5
Great Ashby Way SG1 . . . .37 B3
Great Braitch La AL10 . . .109 F1
Great Bramingham La
LU3 . . . . .31 B2
Great Break AL7 . . . . . . .111 B5
Great Cambridge Rd
Cheshunt EN8 . . . . .148 D4
Enfield EN1 . . . . .162 C6
Great Conduit AL7 . . . . . .111 C7
Great Dell AL8 . . . . .89 D1
Great Eastern Cl CM23 . . .77 A6
Great Elms Rd HP3 . . . . .138 F7
Great Gaddesden CE Prim
Sch HP1 . . . . .103 D3
Great Ganett AL7 . . . . . .111 C4
Great Gn SG5 . . . . .20 D4
Great Gr WD23 . . . . .168 B5
Great Groves EN7 . . . . . .147 E3
Great Hadham Rd CM23 . .76 C5
Great Heart HP2 . . . . . . .124 E5
Great Heath AL10 . . . . . .130 B8
Great Hyde Hall CM21 . . . .98 B3
Great Innings N SG14 . . . .70 D4
Great Innings S SG14 . . . .70 D3
Great Lawne SG3 . . . . . . .69 D2
Great Ley AL7 . . . . .110 E4
Great Mdw EN10 . . . . . . .135 A1
Great Molewood SG14 . . . .92 B1
Great North Rd
Barnet EN5 . . . . .171 E6
Brookmans Park AL9,EN6 .145 B5
Hatfield AL9 . . . . .130 C5
Oaklands AL6 . . . . .89 E7
Radwell SG7 . . . . .12 D3
Welwyn Garden City AL8 . .110 A7
Great Palmers HP2 . . . . .124 F8
Great Pk WD4 . . . . .139 A1
Great Plumtree CM20 . . .117 F2
Great Rd HP2 . . . . .124 F4
Great Slades EN6 . . . . . .158 F6
Great Stockwood Rd
EN7 . . . . .147 D5
Great Sturgess Rd HP1 . .123 F3
Great Whites Rd HP3 . . . .124 F1
Great Wood Ctry Pk★
EN6 . . . . .146 B5
Greatfield Cl AL5 . . . . . . .85 C4
Greatham Rd WD23 . . . . .167 D6
Green Acres Lilley LU2 . . .32 D2
Stevenage SG2 . . . . .51 C1
Welwyn Garden City AL7 . .110 F3
Green Banks AL1 . . . . . . .127 F1
Green Bushes LU4 . . . . . . .44 D6
Green Cl
Brookmans Park AL9 . . . . .144 E5
Cheshunt EN8 . . . . .162 E8
Luton LU4 . . . . .44 C5
Stevenage SG2 . . . . .50 F2
Green Croft AL10 . . . . . .130 A8
Green Ct 6 LU4 . . . . .44 C5
Green Dell Way HP3 . . . .125 C3
Green Dragon Ct LU1 . . . .63 F6
Green Drift SG8 . . . . .7 C7
Green Edge WD25 . . . . . .154 A4
Green End Braughing SG11 55 E8
Welwyn AL6 . . . . .89 B4
Green End Bsns Ctr
WD3 . . . . .152 A2
Green End Gdns HP1 . . . .124 A2
Green End La HP1 . . . . . .123 F3
Green End Rd HP1 . . . . . .124 A2
Green Hill Cl SG11 . . . . . .55 F7
Green La Ashwell SG7 . . . . .4 E5
Bovingdon HP3 . . . . .137 A3
Bovingdon,Pudds Cross
HP3 . . . . .136 F3
Braughing SG11 . . . . .55 F7
Croxley Green WD3 . . . . . .165 F4
Hemel Hempstead HP2 . . .125 D4
Hitchin SG4 . . . . .22 B1
Hoddesdon EN10 . . . . .149 B8
Kensworth Common LU6 . . .82 E8
Latimer HP5 . . . . .150 C6
Letchworth SG6 . . . . .23 C8
Luton LU2 . . . . .46 C4
Markyate AL3 . . . . .83 F5
Northwood HA6 . . . . .174 E3
Pitstone LU7 . . . . .80 E5
St Albans, New Greens
AL3 . . . . .127 D7
St Albans, Sopwell AL1 . . .142 A7
Watford WD19 . . . . .167 C2
Welwyn Garden City AL7 . .111 D5
Green Lane Cl AL5 . . . . . .107 E8
Green Lanes AL10 . . . . . .109 F2
Green Lanes Prim Sch
AL10 . . . . .109 F1
Green Leys Cotts SG11 . . . .55 F1
Green Man Ct CM20 . . . . .117 A4
Green Mdw EN6 . . . . .145 A1
Green Milverton LU3 . . . . .45 A7
Green Oaks LU2 . . . . .45 F3
Green Path HP22,HP23 . . .99 D4
Green St
Chorleywood WD3 . . . . . .164 C6
Harlow CM17 . . . . .118 D1
Royston SG8 . . . . .7 D8
Shenley WD6,WD7 . . . . . .157 A3
Stevenage SG1 . . . . .50 C7
Green The
Bishop's Stortford CM23 . . .76 F4
Cheddington LU7 . . . . .80 A7
Cheshunt EN8 . . . . .148 C3
Codicote SG4 . . . . .67 F1
Kimpton SG4 . . . . .66 D1
Knebworth SG3 . . . . .68 C5
London Colney AL2 . . . . . .142 D4
Luton LU4 . . . . .44 C5
Mentmore LU7 . . . . .61 D4
Newnham SG7 . . . . .12 E7
Peters Green LU2 . . . . .65 C3
Pitstone LU7 . . . . .80 D4
Potten End HP4 . . . . .123 B6
Royston SG8 . . . . .7 D6
Sarratt WD3 . . . . .152 A3
Stotfold SG5 . . . . .11 F7
Waltham Abbey EN9 . . . . .163 C5
Ware SG12 . . . . .93 D3
Welwyn AL6 . . . . .89 B5
Welwyn Garden City AL7 . .111 A4
Green Vale AL7 . . . . .111 A5
Green View Cl HP3 . . . . . .137 A2
Green Way Gdns HA3 . . . .176 E1
Green Way The HA3 . . . . .176 E2
Greenacre Cl EN5 . . . . . .158 F1
Greenacres
Bushey WD23 . . . . .176 D8
Hemel Hempstead HP2 . . .125 D2
Pitstone LU7 . . . . .80 C4
Greenall Cl EN8 . . . . . . .148 E1
Greenbank EN8 . . . . .148 B3
Greenbank Rd WD17 . . . .153 D3
Greenbury Cl Barley SG8 . . .8 F1
Chorleywood WD3 . . . . . .164 C5
Greencoates SG13 . . . . . .113 E5
Greene Field Rd HP4 . . . .122 C4
Greene Wlk HP4 . . . . . . .122 D3
Greener Ct EN3 . . . . .163 A2
Greenes Ct HP4 . . . . .122 C5
Greenfield Hatfield AL9 . . .130 D8
Royston SG8 . . . . .7 B7
Welwyn Garden City AL8 . . .89 D1
Greenfield Ave
Ickleford SG5 . . . . .21 D4
South Oxhey WD19 . . . . . .175 E8
Greenfield La SG5 . . . . . . .21 E4
Greenfield Rd SG1 . . . . . . .50 E7
Greenfield St EN9 . . . . . .163 C5
Greenfields Cuffley EN6 . .146 E1
Stansted Mountfitchet
CM24 . . . . .59 E7
Greenfields Prim Sch
WD19 . . . . .175 C5
Greengate LU3 . . . . .44 C8
Greenheys Cl HA6 . . . . . .174 E2
Greenhill Ave LU2 . . . . . . .45 E3
Greenhill Cres WD18 . . . .166 E3
Greenhill Ct HP1 . . . . . . .124 B2
Greenhill Pk CM23 . . . . . .76 D5
Greenhills SG12 . . . . .93 C3
Greenhills Cl WD3 . . . . . .165 B4
Greenland Rd EN5 . . . . . .171 C3
Greenlands WD6 . . . . . . .170 D3
Greenlane Ind Est SG6 . . . .23 C7
Greenleas EN9 . . . . .163 E5
Greenriggs LU2 . . . . .46 F2
Greenside WD6 . . . . .157 A1
Greenside Dr SG5 . . . . . . .34 D8
Greenside Pk LU2 . . . . . . .45 E3
Greenside Sch SG2 . . . . . . .51 B2
Greensleeves Cl AL4 . . . .128 C2
Greenstead CM21 . . . . .97 E1
Greensward WD23 . . . . . .168 B3
Greenway
Berkhamsted HP4 . . . . . . .122 A4
Bishop's Stortford CM23 . . .77 C6
Harpenden AL5 . . . . .107 E8
Hemel Hempstead HP2 . . .125 B3
Letchworth SG6 . . . . .23 A2
Pinner HA5 . . . . .175 B1
Walkern SG2 . . . . .52 B8
Greenway Fst Sch HP4 . .121 F4
Greenway The
Enfield EN3 . . . . .162 D4
Potters Bar EN6 . . . . .159 A6
Rickmansworth WD3 . . . . .165 A2
Tring HP23 . . . . .99 F5
Greenways
Abbots Langley WD5 . . . . .153 E7
Buntingford SG9 . . . . .40 D8
Goff's Oak EN7 . . . . .147 B2
Hertford SG14 . . . . .113 B6
Luton LU2 . . . . .46 B5
Stevenage SG1 . . . . .50 E6
Welwyn AL6 . . . . .89 E3
Greenwich Ct
Cheshunt EN8 . . . . .162 E5
St Albans AL1 . . . . .128 A2
Greenwich Way EN9 . . . . .163 C4
Greenwood Ave EN7 . . . .162 B8
Greenwood Cl EN7 . . . . . .162 B8
Greenwood Dr WD25 . . . .154 B5
Greenwood Gdns WD7 . . .156 E6
Greenyard EN9 . . . . .163 C6
Greer Rd HA3 . . . . .176 C2
Gregories Cl LU3 . . . . .45 D1
Gregory Ave EN6 . . . . . . .159 C6
Gregory Mews EN9 . . . . .163 B7
Gregson Cl WD6 . . . . . . .170 C8
Grenadier Cl AL4 . . . . . .128 C2
Grenadine Cl EN7 . . . . . .147 F4
Grenadine Way HP23 . . . .100 A5
Greneway Sch The SG8 . . . .7 E7
Grenfell Cl WD6 . . . . . . .170 C8
Grenville Ave EN10 . . . . .134 F2
Grenville Cl EN8 . . . . . . .162 D7
Grenville Ct WD3 . . . . . . .164 C5
Grenville Way SG2 . . . . . . .51 A1
Gresford Cl AL4 . . . . . . .128 D3
Gresham Cl LU2 . . . . .64 D8
Gresham Ct HP4 . . . . .122 B3
Gresley Cl AL8 . . . . .110 E8
Gresley Ct Enfield EN1 . . .162 C4
Potters Bar EN6 . . . . .145 C1
Gresley Way SG2 . . . . .51 D5
Greville Cl AL9 . . . . .144 C7
Grey House The 4
WD17 . . . . .167 A7
Greycaine Rd WD24 . . . . .154 D2
Greydells Rd SG1 . . . . . . .50 E6
Greyfriars SG12 . . . . .93 B3
Greyfriars La AL5 . . . . . .107 A7
Greyhound La EN6 . . . . . .158 A6
Greystoke Cl HP4 . . . . . .122 A3
Griffiths Way AL1 . . . . . .127 C1
Griffon Way WD25 . . . . . .153 F5
Grimsdyke Cres EN5 . . . .171 C6
Grimsdyke Fst & Mid Sch
HA5 . . . . .175 F4
Grimsdyke Lo AL1 . . . . . .128 A3
Grimsdyke Rd
Pinner HA5 . . . . .175 E3
Wigginton HP23 . . . . .100 D1
Grimston Rd AL1 . . . . . . .127 F2
Grimstone Rd SG4 . . . . . . .35 E4
Grimthorpe Cl AL3 . . . . . .127 D6
Grindcobbe AL1 . . . . . . .141 D8
Grinders End SG4 . . . . . . .36 B4
Grinstead La CM22 . . . . . .98 C6
Groom Rd EN10 . . . . .148 F5
Grooms Cotts HP5 . . . . . .136 B1
Groomsby Dr LU7 . . . . . . .80 E5
Grosvenor Ave WD4 . . . . .139 C3
Grosvenor Cl CM23 . . . . . .76 D4
Grosvenor Ct
Croxley Green WD3 . . . . . .166 D4
Stevenage SG1 . . . . .50 A7
Grosvenor Ho 4 CM23 . . .77 B8
Grosvenor Rd Baldock SG7 12 F1
Borehamwood WD6 . . . . . .170 B6
Hoddesdon EN10 . . . . .134 F3
Luton LU3 . . . . .45 B5
Moor Park HA6 . . . . .174 F5
St Albans AL1 . . . . .127 E2
Watford WD17 . . . . .167 C6
Grosvenor Rd W SG7 . . . . .12 F1
Grosvenor Terr HP1 . . . . .124 A2
Grotto The SG12 . . . . . . .114 D8
Ground La AL10 . . . . .130 B7
Grove Ave AL5 . . . . .107 D7
Grove Cotts WD23 . . . . . .168 A3
Grove Cres WD3 . . . . . . .166 A5
Grove Ct Arlesey SG15 . . . .11 A8
Barnet EN5 . . . . .171 F6
Waltham Abbey EN9 . . . . .163 B6
Grove Cvn Pk The LU1 . . . .63 B3
Grove End LU1 . . . . .63 B5
Grove Farm Pk HA6 . . . . .174 D5
Grove Gdns Enfield EN3 . .162 D1
Tring HP23 . . . . .100 B5
Grove Hall Rd WD23 . . . . .167 E5
Grove Hill CM24 . . . . .59 E7
Grove Ho Bushey WD23 . . .167 F3
Cheshunt EN8 . . . . .148 B1
Hitchin SG4 . . . . .22 A2
Grove Inf Sch The AL5 . . .107 D7
Grove Jun Sch The AL5 . .107 D7

Grove La HP5 .... 136 B5
Grove Lea AL10 .... 130 A2
Grove Mdw AL7 .... 111 C6
Grove Mead AL10 ...... 129 F5
Grove Mill La WD3,
WD17 .... 153 C1
Grove Park Rd LU1 ...... 63 B3
Grove Path EN7 .... 162 A8
Grove Pk
Bishop's Stortford CM23 .. 76 C8
Tring HP23 .... 100 C5
Grove Pl
19 Bishop's Stortford CM23 76 F7
Bushey WD25 .... 168 B8
Welham Green AL9 ...... 144 C7
Grove Rd
Borehamwood WD6 ..... 170 A8
Harpenden AL5 .... 107 D7
Hemel Hempstead HP1 .. 124 A1
Hitchin SG4 .... 21 F1
Luton LU1 .... 63 D7
Northwood HA6 .... 174 D5
Rickmansworth WD3 .... 173 A8
Slip End LU1 .... 63 B2
St Albans AL1 .... 127 D2
Stevenage SG1 .... 50 D7
Tring HP23 .... 100 C5
Ware SG12 .... 93 F2
Grove Rd W EN3 .... 162 C2
Grove Road Prim Sch
HP23 .... 100 C5
Grove The
Brookmans Park AL9 .... 145 A4
Chipperfield WD4 ...... 138 C1
Great Hallingbury CM22 ... 77 F4
Latimer HP5 .... 150 D3
Little Hadham SG11 ..... 75 E7
Luton LU1 .... 63 B5
Potters Bar EN6 .... 159 C7
Radlett WD7 .... 156 A5
Tring HP23 .... 100 C5
Grove Way WD3 .... 164 B4
Grove Wlk SG14 .... 113 C8
Grovebury Gdns AL2 ... 141 C4
Grovedale Cl EN7 ..... 147 F1
Groveland Way SG5 ..... 12 A5
Grovelands
Chiswell Green AL2 ..... 141 B4
Hemel Hempstead HP2 .. 125 C5
Grovelands Ave SG4 .... 22 C2
Grovelands Bsns Ctr
HP2 .... 125 C5
Grover Cl HP2 .... 124 D4
Grover Rd WD19 .... 167 D3
Grovewood Cl WD3 ..... 164 B4
Grubbs La AL9 .... 145 C8
Gryphon Ind Pk The
AL3 .... 127 F8
Guardian Ind Est LU1 .... 63 C8
Guernsey Cl LU4 .... 44 A3
Guernsey Ho Enfield EN3 162 D1
Watford WD18 .... 167 A3
Guessens Ct AL8 .... 110 C6
Guessens Gr AL8 .... 110 C6
Guessens Rd AL8 .... 110 C6
Guessens Wlk AL8 ..... 110 C7
Guilden Morden CE Prim Sch
SG8 .... 1 F5
Guildford Cl SG1 .... 36 F2
Guildford Rd AL1 ...... 128 B2
Guildford St LU1 .... 63 E7
Guildhouse The WD3 ... 166 B3
Guilfords CM17 .... 118 D5
Guinevere Gdns EN8 ... 162 E8
Gulland Cl WD23 .... 168 C4
Gullbrook HP1 .... 124 A3
Gullet Wood Rd WD25 . 154 A4
Gullicot Way LU7 .... 80 D4
Gulphs The SG13 ...... 113 D5
Gun La SG3 .... 68 F4
Gun Meadow Ave SG3 ... 69 A4
Gun Rd SG3 .... 69 A4
Gun Road Gdns SG3 ..... 68 F4
Gunnels Wood Ind Est
SG1 .... 50 D3
Gunnels Wood Rd SG1 .. 50 B5
Gunner Dr EN3 .... 163 A2
Gurney Court Rd AL1 .. 127 F5
Gurney's La SG5 .... 21 B7
Gwent Cl WD25 .... 154 D5
Gwynfa Cl AL6 .... 89 D7
Gwynne Cl HP23 .... 100 A5
Gwynns Wlk SG13 ..... 113 E6
Gyfford Wlk EN7 ...... 162 B8
Gypsy Cl SG12 .... 114 F4
Gypsy La
Abbots Langley WD4 .... 153 D5
Great Amwell SG12 ..... 114 F4
Welwyn Garden City AL7 .. 110 F1
Gypsy Moth Ave AL10 .. 129 E7

H

Haberdashers' Aske's Sch
for Boys WD6 .... 169 B6
Haberdashers' Aske's Sch
for Girls WD6 .... 169 B5
Hackforth Cl EN5 ...... 171 B4
Hackney Cl WD6 .... 170 D4
Haddam Hall SG11 ...... 57 E2
Haddenham Ct HP2 .... 105 B1
Haddestoke Gate EN8 .. 148 F5
Haddon Cl
Borehamwood WD6 ..... 170 A6
Hemel Hempstead HP3 .. 125 A2
Stevenage SG2 .... 69 C7
Haddon Ct 20 AL5 .... 86 B1
Haddon Rd
Chorleywood WD3 ..... 164 C4
Luton LU2 .... 63 F8
Hadham Ct CM23 .... 76 E8
Hadham Gr CM23 .... 76 C8
Hadham Ho CM23 .... 76 D8
Hadham Rd
Bishop's Stortford CM23 .. 76 D8
Little Hadham SG11 ..... 57 F1
Standon SG11 .... 55 F1
Hadland Cl HP3 .... 137 A5
Hadleigh SG6 .... 23 B4
Hadleigh Ct
Hoddesdon EN10 .... 134 F1
Wheathampstead AL5 ... 107 E6
Hadley Cl WD6 .... 169 F3
Hadley Ct LU3 .... 45 D1
Hadley Gn EN5 .... 171 F7
Hadley Gn W EN5 ...... 171 F7
Hadley Gr EN5 .... 171 E7
Hadley Green Rd EN5 .. 171 F7
Hadley Highstone EN5 . 171 F8
Hadley Par 6 EN5 ...... 171 E6
Hadley Rd EN2,EN4 .... 160 C1
Hadley Ridge EN5 ..... 171 F6
Hadley Wood Prim Sch
EN4 .... 159 C1
Hadley Wood Sta EN4 . 159 C1
Hadlow Down Cl LU3 ... 45 A5
Hadrian Cl AL3 .... 127 A1
Hadrian Way SG7 .... 23 D7
Hadrians Wlk SG1 ...... 51 C8
Hadwell Cl SG2 .... 51 A3
Hagdell Rd LU1 .... 63 C5
Hagden La WD18 ...... 167 A4
Haggerston Rd WD6 ... 156 E1
Hagsdell Rd SG13 ..... 113 D5
Haig Cl AL1 .... 128 B2
Haig Ho AL1 .... 128 B2
Hailey Ave EN11 ...... 115 A2
Hailey Cl SG13 .... 114 E2
Hailey Hall Sch SG13 .. 114 F2
Hailey La SG13 .... 114 E2
Haileybury & Imperial
Service Coll SG13 .... 114 D2
Haines Way WD25 ..... 154 A5
Haldane Cl EN3 .... 163 B1
Haldens AL7 .... 89 F1
Haldens Ho 3 AL7 ...... 89 F1
Hale Ct SG13 .... 113 D5
Hale Ho EN3 .... 162 D2
Hale La HP22 .... 119 A3
Hale Rd SG13 .... 113 D5
Hales Mdw AL5 .... 86 A2
Hales Park Cl HP2 .... 125 C4
Hales Pk HP2 .... 125 C4
Haleswood Rd HP2 .... 125 B4
Half Acre SG5 .... 34 D6
Half Acres CM23 .... 76 F8
Half Moon Cotts CM21 .. 97 B1
Half Moon La LU1 .... 84 C8
Half Moon Mdw HP2 ... 125 C8
Half Moon Mews 5
AL1 .... 127 D3
Halfhide La EN8 ...... 148 D5
Halfhides EN9 .... 163 D6
Halfway Ave LU4 .... 44 D1
Halifax Cl
Bricket Wood AL2 ...... 154 F8
Watford WD25 .... 153 F5
Halifax Rd WD3 .... 164 C2
Halifax Way AL7 ...... 111 E6
Hall Barns SG9 .... 42 F4
Hall Cl WD3 .... 165 A1
Hall Cotts SG9 .... 29 A1
Hall Dr UB9 .... 173 C2
Hall Gdns AL4 .... 143 D8
Hall Gr AL7 .... 111 B4
Hall Heath Cl AL1 .... 128 B5
Hall La Great Chishill SG8 .. 9 F2
Great Hormead SG9 ...... 29 A1
Kimpton SG4 .... 87 C8
Woolmer Green SG3 ..... 69 A2
Hall Mead SG6 .... 22 D6
Hall Park Gate HP4 ... 122 E3
Hall Park Hill HP4 .... 122 E3
Hall Pk HP4 .... 122 E3
Hall Place Cl AL1 .... 127 E4
Hall Place Gdns AL1 .. 127 E4
Hall Rd HP2 .... 125 B5
Hallam Cl WD24 ...... 167 C7
Hallam Gdns HA5 ..... 175 E3
Halland Way HA6 ..... 174 D4
Halley Rd EN9 .... 163 B3
Halleys Ridge SG14 ... 113 A5
Halliday Cl WD7 ...... 156 E7
Halling Hill CM20 ..... 117 F2
Hallingbury Cl CM22 ... 77 B1
Hallingbury Rd
Bishop's Stortford CM22 .. 77 B4
Sawbridgeworth CM21 .... 98 A4
Hallmores EN10 ...... 135 A4
Hallowell Rd HA6 ..... 174 E3
Hallowes Cres WD19 .. 175 A7
Halls Cl AL6 .... 89 C4
Hallside Rd EN1 ...... 161 F1
Hallwicks Rd LU2 .... 46 B3
Hallworth Dr SG5 .... 11 E6
Hallworth Ho SG5 ...... 11 E6
Halsey Dr
Hemel Hempstead HP1 .. 123 F5
Hitchin SG4 .... 35 B7
Halsey Pk AL2 .... 142 F4
Halsey Pl WD24 ...... 154 B1
Halsey Rd WD18 ...... 167 B6
Halstead Hill EN7 .... 147 E1
Halter Cl WD6 .... 170 D4
Halton Cl AL2 .... 141 C3
Halton Wood (Forest Wlks)★
HP23 .... 119 A5
Haltside AL10 .... 129 E4
Halwick Cl HP1 ...... 124 B1
Halyard Cl LU3 .... 45 B6
Halyard High Sch LU4 .. 44 A3
Hamberlins La HP4 ... 121 C7
Hamble Ct WD18 ..... 167 A5
Hambleden Pl WD7 .... 155 F4
Hambledon Ct EN4 .... 159 D1
Hamblings Cl WD7 .... 156 D6
Hambridge Way SG5 .... 20 D4
Hambro Cl LU2 .... 85 F7
Hamburgh Ct EN8 ..... 148 D3
Hamels Dr SG13 ...... 114 B7
Hamels La SG9 .... 55 B7
Hamer Cl HP3 .... 137 A3
Hamer Ct LU2 .... 45 D8
Hamilton Ave EN11 ... 135 A8
Hamilton Cl
Bricket Wood AL2 ...... 155 A8
Dagnall HP4 .... 81 C5
South Mimms EN6 ..... 158 A6
Hamilton Ct 3 AL10 ... 130 B3
Hamilton Mead HP3 ... 137 A4
Hamilton Rd
Abbots Langley WD4 .... 153 C6
Berkhamsted HP4 ...... 122 B4
South Oxhey WD19 ..... 175 B7
St Albans AL1 .... 128 A4
Hamilton St WD18 .... 167 C4
Hamlet Cl AL2 .... 140 F1
Hamlet The HP4 ...... 123 A7
Hammarskjold Rd
CM20 .... 117 D2
Hammer La HP2 ...... 124 F4
Hammer Par WD25 .... 154 A6
Hammerdell SG6 .... 22 D7
Hammers Gate AL2 .... 141 A5
Hammond Cl Barnet EN5 171 E4
Hammond Street EN7 .... 147 F5
Stevenage SG1 .... 50 D6
Hammond Ct LU1 .... 63 C1
Hammond End La AL5 . 106 F5
Hammond Prim Sch The
HP2 .... 124 F6
Hammonds Hill AL5 ... 106 F4
Hammonds La AL10 ... 109 B3
Hammondstreet Rd
EN7 .... 147 D5
Hammondswick AL5 ... 106 F4
Hamonte SG6 .... 23 C4
Hampden SG4 .... 66 C1
Hampden Cl SG6 .... 23 B8
Hampden Cres EN7 .... 162 B8
Hampden Hill SG12 ..... 93 F2
Hampden Hill Cl SG12 .. 93 F2
Hampden Pl AL2 ...... 141 E2
Hampden Rd
Harrow HA3 .... 176 C1
Hitchin SG4 .... 22 C1
Hampden Rise SG8 .... 7 D4
Hampden Way WD17 .. 153 E3
Hampermill La WD19 . 167 A1
Hampton Cl SG2 .... 69 C7
Hampton Gdns CM21 .. 118 C7
Hampton Rd LU4 .... 63 B8
Hamstel Rd CM20 ..... 117 C1
Hamsworth Ct SG14 .. 112 F7
Hanaper Dr SG8 .... 8 F2
Hanbury Cl Cheshunt EN8 148 E2
Ware SG12 .... 93 E1
Hanbury Cotts AL9 ... 131 E6
Hanbury Dr SG12 .... 93 C6
Hanbury Mews SG12 .... 93 C5
Hancock Ct WD6 ...... 170 C8
Hancock Dr LU2 .... 45 E5
Hancroft Rd HP3 ..... 124 F1
Hand La CM21 .... 97 C1
Handa Cl HP3 .... 139 B8
Handcross Rd LU2 ...... 46 D2
Handley Gate AL2 .... 140 F2
Handpost Lodge Gdns
HP2 .... 125 D2
Handside Cl AL8 ..... 110 C6
Handside Gn AL8 ..... 110 C7
Handside La AL8 ..... 110 C6
Handsworth Way WD19 175 A7
Hangar Ruding WD19 .. 175 F7
Hanger Cl HP1 .... 124 B2
Hangmans La AL6 .... 89 F8
Hanover Cl SG2 .... 50 F1
Hanover Ct
Croxley Green WD3 .... 166 A4
Hoddesdon EN11 .... 135 A7
Luton LU4 .... 44 D5
9 Pinner HA5 .... 175 F3
Waltham Abbey EN9 .... 163 C6
Hanover Gdns WD5 ... 139 F1
Hanover Gn HP1 ..... 124 A1
Hanover Ho AL7 ..... 110 F4
Hanover Wlk AL10 ... 129 F2
Hanross Cl AL2 ...... 140 E1
Hanscombe End Rd SG5 . 19 D7
Hanselin Cl HA7 ..... 176 F5
Hanswick Cl LU2 .... 46 B2
Hanworth Cl LU2 .... 45 D7
Hanyards End EN6 .... 146 E3
Hanyards La EN6 ..... 146 D3
Happy Valley Ind Pk
WD4 .... 139 B3
Harbert Gdns AL2 .... 141 C2
Harborne Cl WD19 ... 175 C5
Harbour Ct WD23 .... 168 B4
Harbury Dell LU3 ...... 45 B7
Harcourt Rd
Bushey WD23 .... 168 C4
Tring HP23 .... 100 C4
Harcourt St LU1 .... 63 E5
Hardenwick Ct 4 AL5 .. 86 A2
Harding Cl Luton LU3 ... 44 E7
Redbourn AL3 .... 106 B5
Watford WD25 .... 154 C6
Harding Ct AL5 .... 86 B4
Harding Par 8 AL5 ..... 86 B1
Hardings AL7 .... 111 C7
Hardingstone Ct EN8 .. 162 F5
Hardwick Cl SG2 .... 69 C7
Hardwick Gn LU3 ...... 45 B7
Hardwicke Pl AL2 .... 142 D4
Hardy Cl Barnet EN5 .. 171 E4
Hitchin SG4 .... 35 C7
Hardy Dr SG8 .... 7 D8
Hardy Rd HP2 .... 124 F4
Hare Cres WD25 ...... 154 A7
Hare La AL10 .... 130 B3
Hare Street Rd SG9 .... 41 B8
Harebell AL7 .... 110 E3
Harebell Cl SG13 ..... 114 B6
Harebreaks The WD24 . 154 B2
Harefield Harlow CM20 . 118 A1
Stevenage SG2 .... 51 C3
Harefield Ct LU1 .... 62 F8
Harefield Hospl UB9 .. 173 C2
Harefield Inf Sch UB9 . 173 C2
Harefield Jun Sch UB9 . 173 C2
Harefield Pl AL4 ..... 128 D6
Harefield Rd Luton LU1 .. 62 F8
Rickmansworth WD3 .... 173 D7
Harefield Road Ind Est
WD3 .... 173 E6
Harepark Cl HP1 ..... 123 F4
Haresfoot Sch HP4 ... 122 B1
Harewood WD3 .... 165 C4
Harewood Ct HA3 .... 176 E2
Harewood Rd WD19 ... 175 B7
Harford Dr WD17 .... 166 E8
Harforde Ct SG13 .... 114 A6
Hargrave Cl CM24 ...... 59 E8
Hargreaves Ave EN7 .. 162 B8
Hargreaves Cl EN7 ... 162 B8
Hargreaves Rd SG8 ...... 7 D5
Harkett Cl HA3 ...... 176 F1
Harkett Ct HA3 ...... 176 F1
Harkness EN7 .... 148 B2
Harkness Ct SG4 .... 22 B1
Harkness Ind Est WD6 . 170 A5
Harkness Way SG4 ...... 22 C2
Harland Ct UB9 ...... 173 C1
Harlech Rd WD5 ..... 154 A8
Harlequin The WD17 .. 167 C5
Harlesden Rd AL1 ... 128 A3
Harlestone Cl LU3 ..... 31 A1
Harley Ct AL4 .... 128 D7
Harlings The SG13 ... 114 C2
Harlow Coll CM20 .... 117 D1
Harlow Ct HP2 .... 125 A7
Harlow Mill Sta CM20 . 118 C5
Harlow Rd Roydon CM19 116 C1
Sawbridgeworth CM21 ... 118 C8
Harlow Sports Ctr
CM20 .... 117 D2
Harlow Stad (Greyhounds)
CM19 .... 116 E1
Harlow Town Sta CM20 117 D3
Harlowbury Prim Sch
CM17 .... 118 D4
Harlton Ct EN9 ...... 163 F5
Harmer Dell AL6 .... 89 F4
Harmer Green La AL6 .. 90 B5
Harmony Cl AL10 .... 130 A7
Harmsworth Way N20 . 171 F1
Harness Way AL4 .... 128 D6
Harold Cres EN9 .... 163 C7
Harold Ct EN8 .... 162 F5
Harpenden Hospl (private)
AL5 .... 86 A4
Harpenden La AL3 ... 106 B6
Harpenden Meml Hospl
AL5 .... 86 B2
Harpenden Prep Sch AL5 85 F2
Harpenden Rd
Wheathampstead AL5,AL4 . 108 B8
St Albans AL3 .... 127 E6
Harpenden Rise AL5 ... 85 F3
Harpenden Sta AL5 .... 86 B1
Harper Ct SG1 .... 50 F5
Harper La WD7 ...... 156 B8
Harperbury Hospl WD7 . 156 C8
Harps Hill AL3 .... 83 E5
Harpsfield Broadway
AL10 .... 129 F6
Harptree Way AL1 ... 128 A5
Harriet Walker Way
WD3 .... 164 F2
Harriet Way WD23 ... 168 D2
Harrington Cl 8 CM23 .. 77 A7
Harrington Ct SG13 .. 114 C3
Harriot Hts AL3 ..... 127 C4
Harris Ho 14 WD18 .. 166 F3
Harris La Great Offley SG5 33 D2
Shenley WD7 .... 157 A6
Harris Rd WD25 ..... 154 A4
Harris's La SG12 ...... 93 C1
Harrison Cl Hitchin SG4 . 34 F7
Northwood HA6 .... 174 C4
Harrison Rd EN9 .... 163 C4
Harrison Wlk EN8 ... 148 D1
Harrisons CM23 .... 59 D2
Harrogate Rd 2 WD19 . 175 C7
Harrow Coll, Harrow Weald
Campus HA3 .... 176 E4
Harrow Ct SG1 .... 50 E5
Harrow View HA2 .... 176 C1
Harrow Way WD19 ... 175 E6
Harrow Weald Pk HA3 . 176 D4
Harrow Yd HP23 ..... 100 A3
Harrowbond Rd CM17 . 118 C1
Harrowden Ct LU2 ..... 64 C8
Harrowden Rd LU2 .... 64 B8
Harrowdene SG2 .... 51 C4
Harry Scott Ct LU4 ... 44 C6
Harston Dr EN3 ...... 163 A1
Hart Hill Dr LU2 ...... 63 F8
Hart Hill La LU2 ...... 63 F8
Hart Hill Path LU2 .... 63 F8
Hart Hill Prim Sch LU2 . 63 F8
Hart La LU2 .... 64 A8
Hart Lodge 10 EN5 ... 171 E6
Hart Rd Harlow CM17 .. 118 C6
St Albans AL1 .... 127 D2
Hart Wlk LU2 .... 46 A1
Hartcran Ho 7 WD19 .. 175 D7
Hartfield Ave WD6 ... 170 A4
Hartfield Cl WD6 .... 170 A4
Hartfield Ct 6 SG12 ... 93 D2
Hartforde Rd WD6 ... 170 B8
Harthall La WD4,HP3 . 139 D4
Hartham La SG14 .... 113 D6
Hartham Villas SG14 . 113 C7
Hartland Ct SG5 .... 34 D7
Hartland Rd EN8 .... 148 D1
Hartley Rd LU2 .... 63 F8
Hartmoor Mews EN3 .. 162 D2
Harts Cl WD23 ...... 168 A8
Hartsbourne Ave WD23 . 176 D8
Hartsbourne Cl WD23 . 176 D8
Hartsbourne Pk WD23 . 176 E8
Hartsbourne Prim Sch
WD23 .... 176 D8
Hartsbourne Rd WD23 . 176 D8
Hartsbourne Way HP2 . 125 C2
Hartsfield Jun Mix Inf Sch
SG7 .... 12 F1
Hartsfield Rd LU2 ..... 46 B2
Hartspring La WD23,
WD25 .... 168 A8
Hartswood Gn WD23 .. 176 D8
Hartwell Gdns AL5 .... 85 E1
Hartwood 3 LU2 .... 63 F8
Harvest Cl LU4 .... 44 A3
Harvest Ct Letchworth SG6 23 A2
Oaklands AL6 .... 89 E7
St Albans AL4 .... 128 D7
Harvest End WD25 ... 154 D3
Harvest La SG2 .... 51 D7
Harvest Mead AL10 .. 130 B7
Harvest Rd WD23 .... 168 B5
Harvey Rd
Croxley Green WD3 .... 166 A3
London Colney AL2 .... 142 C5
Stevenage SG2 .... 51 B6
Harvey Road Prim Sch
WD3 .... 166 A3
Harvey's Hill LU2 ..... 45 F5
Harveyfields EN9 ... 163 C5
Harvingwell Pl HP2 . 125 B5
Harwood Cl Tewin AL6 .. 90 E2
Welwyn Garden City AL8 .. 89 E2
Harwood Hill AL8 ...... 89 E1
Harwood Hill Jun Mix Inf Sch
AL8 .... 89 E2
Harwoods Rd WD18 .. 167 A5
Hasedines Rd HP1 ... 124 A4
Haseldine Mdws AL10 . 129 F4
Haseldine Rd AL2 ... 142 D5
Haselfoot SG6 .... 22 E6
Hasketon Dr LU4 ...... 44 B6
Haslemere CM23 ...... 77 A4
Haslemere Est The
EN11 .... 135 D6
Haslemere Ind Est AL7 . 110 F7
Haslewood Ave EN11 . 135 A6
Haslingden Cl AL5 .... 85 D3
Hastings Cl SG1 ...... 50 A8
Hastings St LU1 .... 63 D6
Hastings Way
Croxley Green WD3 .... 166 C5
Watford WD23 .... 167 E5
Hastoe Farm Barns
HP23 .... 119 F7
Hastoe La HP23 ..... 100 A2
Hatch End High Sch
HA3 .... 176 B2
Hatch End Sta HA5 .. 176 A3
Hatch Gn CM22 .... 98 B8
Hatch La SG4 .... 24 A3
Hatching Gn AL5 .... 107 A6
Hatching Green Cl AL5 107 A6
Hatfield Ave AL10 .. 129 E8
Hatfield Bsns Ctr AL10 . 129 D8
Hatfield Cres HP2 .... 124 F7
Hatfield House & Gdns★
AL9 .... 130 D5
Hatfield Rd
Essendon AL9 .... 111 E1
Potters Bar EN6 .... 159 C8
St Albans AL1,AL4 ..... 128 C3
Watford WD24 .... 167 B8
Hatfield Sta AL9 ... 130 C6
Hatfield Tunnel AL10 . 129 F6
Hathaway Cl LU4 ...... 44 B2
Hathaway Ct AL4 .... 128 E3
Hatherleigh Gdns EN6 . 159 D7
Hatters La WD18 .... 166 D3
Hatters Way LU1,LU4 .. 44 D1
Hatton Rd EN8 ...... 148 D2
Havelock Rd
Kings Langley WD4 .... 138 F3
Luton LU2 .... 45 E1
Havelock Rise LU2 .... 45 E1

Haven Cl AL10 ....129 F6
Haven The SG5 ....11 F6
Havensfield WD4 ....152 B8
Haverdale LU4 ....44 C4
Havercroft Cl AL3 ....127 C1
Havers La CM23 ....76 E5
Havers Inf Sch CM23 ....76 F5
Havers Par CM23 ....76 F5
Haward Rd EN11 ....135 C8
Hawbush Cl AL6 ....89 B4
Hawbush Rise AL6 ....89 B5
Hawes Cl HA6 ....174 F3
Hawes La E4 ....163 C1
Haweswater Dr WD25 ...154 C6
Hawfield Gdns AL2 ......141 D5
Hawkesworth Cl HA6 ....174 E3
Hawkfield SG6 ....22 E8
Hawkfields LU2 ....45 E6
Hawkings Way HP3 .....137 A5
Hawkins Cl WD6 ....170 C7
Hawkins Hall La SG7 .....69 E2
Hawkshead Ct EN8 ......162 F5
Hawkshead La AL9 ......144 D3
Hawkshead Rd EN6 .....145 B2
Hawkshill AL1 ....128 A2
Hawkshill Dr HP3 ....137 F8
Hawksmead Cl EN3 ......162 D3
Hawksmoor WD7 ....157 A6
Hawksmoor Sch WD6 ...170 C8
Hawkwell Dr HP23 ......100 C4
Hawridge & Cholesbury CE
  Sch HP5 ....120 E2
Hawridge La HP5 ....120 F1
Hawridge Vale HP5 .....120 F1
Hawsley Rd AL5 ....107 A4
Hawthorn Ave LU2 ......46 B4
Hawthorn Cl
  Abbots Langley WD5 ..154 A7
  Harpenden AL5 ......107 D7
  Hertford SG14 ......113 A7
  Hitchin SG4 ....34 E6
  Royston SG8 ....7 F7
  Watford WD17 ......153 F1
Hawthorn Cres LU1 ......62 E3
Hawthorn Gr Barnet EN5 170 F3
  Enfield EN2 ....161 D1
Hawthorn Hill SG6 ......22 F7
Hawthorn La HP1 ....123 F4
Hawthorn Rd EN11 .....135 B8
Hawthorn Rise CM23 ....76 F3
Hawthorn Way
  Chiswell Green AL2 ....141 A7
  Royston SG8 ....7 F7
Hawthorne Ave EN7 ....162 B8
Hawthorne Cl EN7 ......162 B8
Hawthorne Ct HA6 .....175 A1
Hawthorne Rd WD7 ....156 A5
Hawthornes AL10 ....129 F3
Hawthorns The
  Berkhamsted HP4 ....122 A5
  Hemel Hempstead HP3 .137 F7
  Maple Cross WD3 ....172 D5
  Ridge EN6 ....157 E6
  Stevenage SG1 ......51 A4
  Ware SG12 ....93 C3
Hawtrees WD7 ....155 F4
Hay Cl WD6 ....170 C7
Hay Gn SG8 ....15 F6
Hay La AL5 ....86 A1
Hay Wains SG3 ....69 B2
Haybourn Mead HP4 ...124 B2
Haycroft
  Bishop's Stortford CM23 .77 C6
  Luton LU2 ....45 E6
Haycroft Rd SG1 ....50 E7
Hayden Rd EN9 ....163 C4
Haydock Rd SG8 ....7 F6
Haydon Dell WD23 .....167 F3
Haydon Hill Ho WD23 ..167 F2
Haydon Rd WD19 ......167 E3
Hayes Cl LU2 ....46 C5
Hayes Hill Farm★ EN9 .149 C3
Hayfield SG2 ....51 D7
Hayfield Cl WD23 ......168 B5
Haygarth SG3 ....69 A4
Hayhurst Rd LU4 ....44 B1
Hayley Bell Gdns CM23 ..76 F3
Hayley Comm SG2 ......51 C3
Hayling Dr LU2 ....46 D3
Hayling Rd WD19 ......175 B8
Haymeads AL8 ....89 E1
Haymeads La CM23 .....77 C6
Haymoor SG6 ....22 E7
Haynes Cl AL7 ....111 A5
Haynes Mead HP4 .....122 A6
Haysman Cl SG6 ....23 B7
Hayton Cl LU3 ....31 B2
Haywood Cl HA5 ......175 D1
Haywood Crn EN6 .....163 F5
Haywood Dr WD3 .....164 F4
Haywood La SG8 ....16 A6
Haywood Pk WD3 .....164 F4
Haywoods Dr HP3 .....137 F8
Haywoods La SG8 ......7 E7
Hazel Cl
  3 Hammond Street EN7 .147 F5
  Welwyn AL6 ....89 E3
Hazel Ct Hitchin SG4 ...35 A7
  Shenley WD7 ....156 F6
Hazel End CM23 ....59 A5
Hazel Gdns CM21 ......97 F1

Hazel Gr Hatfield AL10 ..129 F2
  Stotfold SG5 ....11 E5
  Watford WD25 ......154 B4
  Welwyn Garden City AL7 .111 C7
Hazel Grove Ho AL10 ...129 F3
Hazel Mead EN5 ....171 B4
Hazel Rd
  Berkhamsted HP4 ....122 D3
  Chiswell Green AL2 ...141 B3
Hazel Tree Rd WD24 ...154 B3
Hazelbury Ave WD5 ....153 C7
Hazelbury Cres LU1 .....63 C8
Hazelbury Ct 3 LU1 ....63 C8
Hazelcroft HA5 ....176 B4
Hazeldell AL5 ....70 D3
Hazeldell Link HP1 ......123 E2
Hazeldell Rd HP1 ......123 F2
Hazeldene EN8 ....162 F1
Hazelend Rd CM23 ......59 B4
Hazelgrove Prim Sch
  AL10 ....129 F2
Hazelmere Rd
  St Albans AL4 ......128 C6
  Stevenage SG1 ......69 A8
Hazels The AL6 ....90 E2
Hazelwood Cl Hitchin SG5 .34 F8
  Luton LU2 ....46 B4
Hazelwood Dr
  Pinner HA5 ....175 B1
  St Albans AL4 ......128 C4
Hazelwood La WD5 ....153 D7
Hazelwood Rd WD3 ....166 C3
Hazely HP23 ....100 C4
Heacham Cl LU4 ....44 B4
Headingley Cl
  Hammond Street EN7 ..147 F5
  Shenley WD7 ....156 F7
  Stevenage SG1 ......50 E8
Headlands Dr HP4 ......122 C5
Headstone La HA3 .....176 B2
Headstone Lane Sta
  HA3 ....176 B2
Healey Rd WD18 ......166 F3
Healy Ct EN5 ....171 D3
Hearle Way AL10 ......129 E7
Heath Ave Royston SG8 ...7 C6
  St Albans AL3 ......127 D5
Heath Brow HP1 ....124 C1
Heath Cl Harpenden AL5 .107 C7
  Hemel Hempstead HP1 .124 C2
  Luton LU1 ....63 B6
  Potters Bar EN6 ....145 B1
Heath Cotts EN6 ......145 B1
Heath Dr Potters Bar EN6 145 A1
  Ware SG12 ....93 D3
Heath Farm Ct WD17 ..153 D2
Heath Farm La AL1,AL3 .127 E5
Heath Hall SG7 ....23 F7
Heath Hill SG4 ....67 D1
Heath La Codicote SG4 ..67 E5
  Hemel Hempstead HP1 .124 C2
  Hertford Heath SG13 ..114 C2
Heath Lodge WD23 ....168 D1
Heath Mount Sch SG14 ..71 B2
Heath Rd
  Breachwood Green SG4 .47 D1
  Oaklands AL6 ....68 C4
  Potters Bar EN6 ....145 B1
  St Albans AL1 ......127 C5
  Watford WD17 ......167 C2
Heath Row CM23 ....59 B1
Heath The
  Breachwood Green SG4 .47 D2
  Radlett WD7 ....156 A6
Heath Way WD7 ....156 C8
Heathbourne Rd WD23 ..168 F1
Heathbrow Rd AL6 ......89 F8
Heathcote Ave AL10 ...130 A7
Heathcote Sch The SG2 .51 A2
Heathcroft AL7 ....111 C6
Heathdene Manor
  WD17 ....166 F8
Heather Cl
  Abbots Langley WD5 ..154 A7
  Bishop's Stortford CM23 ..76 D6
Heather Ct AL2 ....142 D4
Heather Gdns EN9 .....163 C4
Heather Rd AL8 ....110 C4
Heather Rise WD23 ....167 F7
Heather Way
  Harrow HA7 ....176 A1
  Hemel Hempstead HP2 .124 D4
  Potters Bar EN6 ....158 F7
Heathermere SG6 ....11 F1
Heathfield SG8 ....7 B6
Heathfield Cl
  Caddington LU1 ......62 F4
  Potters Bar EN6 ....145 B1
  Watford WD19 ......167 C2
Heathfield Ct 2 AL1 ...127 E4
Heathfield Lower Sch
  LU1 ....62 E4
Heathfield Rd Hitchin SG5 .21 F1
  Luton LU3 ....45 C4
  Watford WD23 ......167 C2
Heathgate SG13 ......114 B2
Heathlands AL6 ....68 F1
Heathlands Dr AL3 ....127 C5
Heathlands Sch AL3 ...127 C5
Heathside
  Colney Heath AL4 ....143 B8
  St Albans AL1 ......127 E5
Heathside Cl HA6 .....174 D5
Heathside Rd HA6 .....174 D6
Heathview AL5 ....107 B8
Heaton Ct EN8 ....148 D2
Heaton Dell LU2 ....46 E1
Heay Fields AL7 ....111 C7

Hebden Cl LU4 ....44 B4
Hebing End SG2 ....52 F2
Heckford Cl WD18 .....166 C3
Hedge Row HP1 ....124 A5
Hedgebrooms AL7 .....111 C7
Hedgerow Cl SG2 ......51 D8
Hedgerow La EN5 .....171 B4
Hedgerow The LU4 .....44 D6
Hedgerow Wlk EN8 ...148 D1
Hedgerows CM21 ......97 F2
Hedgerows The
  Bishop's Stortford CM23 ..77 B6
  Stevenage SG2 ......51 D8
Hedges Cl AL10 ....130 B6
Hedges The AL3 ....127 C7
Hedgeside HP4 ....123 A7
Hedgeside Rd HA6 ....174 C5
Hedley Cl HP22 ....99 A4
Hedley Rd AL1 ....128 B3
Hedley Rise LU2 ....46 F2
Hedley Villas AL1 .....128 B3
Hedworth Ave EN8 ....162 D6
Heights The
  Hemel Hempstead HP2 .124 F6
  Luton LU3 ....44 E5
Helena Cl EN4 ....159 D1
Helena Pl 5 HP2 ......124 D5
Helens Gate EN8 .....148 F5
Helham Gn SG12 ....94 F4
Hellards Rd SG1 ....50 D7
Hellebore Ct SG1 ......51 B8
Helmsley Cl LU4 ....44 C5
Helston Cl HA5 ....175 F3
Helston Gr HP2 ....124 D8
Helston Pl WD5 ....153 F7
Hemel Hempstead General
  Hospl HP2 ....124 D3
Hemel Hempstead Rd
  Great Gaddesden HP4 ..81 F1
  Hemel Hempstead HP2,
    HP3 ....125 C1
  Redbourn AL3,HP2 ...105 E2
  St Albans HP3,AL2,AL3 .126 D1
Hemel Hempstead Sch The
  HP1 ....124 C2
Hemel Hempstead Sta
  HP3 ....138 A8
Hemingford Dr LU2 .....45 D6
Hemingford Rd WD17 ..153 E3
Hemming Way WD25 ..154 A4
Hemmings The HP4 ...121 F4
Hemp La HP23 ....100 F1
Hempstall AL7 ....111 B4
Hempstead La HP4 ....123 C6
Hempstead Rd
  Bovingdon HP3 ......137 B5
  Kings Langley WD4 ..139 A3
  Watford WD17 ......153 E2
Henbury Way WD19 ...175 D7
Henderson Cl AL3 ....127 C7
Henderson Pl
  Bedmond WD5 ......139 F4
  Little Berkhamsted SG13 .132 C2
Hendon Wood La NW7 .171 A1
Hendren Ct SG1 ....51 A8
Henge Way LU3 ....44 E7
Henlow Ind Est SG16 ...10 B4
Henry Cl EN2 ....161 E1
Henry St
  Hemel Hempstead HP3 .138 D7
  Tring HP23 ....100 A3
Hensley Ct Hitchin SG4 ..35 B6
  Welwyn AL6 ....89 C6
Henstead Pl LU2 ....46 D1
Hepburn Ct EN6 ......158 A7
Heracles Cl AL2 ......141 C3
Herald Cl CM23 ....76 D6
Herbert St HP2 ....124 D7
Hereford Rd LU4 ....44 A3
Hereward Cl EN9 .....163 C7
Herga Ct WD17 ......167 A7
Heritage Cl AL3 ......127 D3
Heritage Wlk WD3 ....164 E6
Herkomer Cl WD23 ....168 B3
Herkomer Rd WD23 ...168 A3
Herm Ho EN3 ....162 D1
Hermitage Ct
  Potters Bar EN6 ....159 C6
Hermitage Ho CM24 ...59 D7
Hermitage Rd SG5 .....34 F7
Hermitage The SG15 ...11 B8
Herne Ct WD23 ......168 C2
Herne Rd Bushey WD23 .168 B3
  Stevenage SG1 ......36 B1
Herneshaw AL10 ......129 F3
Herns La AL7 ....111 B8
Herns Way AL7 ....111 A7
Heron Cl
  Hemel Hempstead HP3 .138 F6
  Rickmansworth WD3 ..173 D8
  Sawbridgeworth CM21 ..97 D1
Heron Ct CM23 ....77 A7
Heron Dr Luton LU2 .....45 E6
  Stansted Abbotts SG12 ..115 C3
Heron Mead EN3 .....163 A1
Heron Pl HP9 ....173 A4
Heron Trad Est LU3 ....44 C7
Heron Way Hatfield AL10 130 A3
  Stotfold SG5 ....11 E6
Heron Wlk HA6 ....174 E6
Heronfield SG6 ....145 C1
Herongate Rd EN8 ....148 E4
Herons Elm HP4 ......121 E7
Herons Way AL1 .....142 B8
Herons Wood CM20 ...117 B2
Heronsgate Rd WD3 ..164 B3

Heronslea WD25 ......154 C3
Heronswood EN9 .....163 E5
Heronswood Rd AL7 ...111 A5
Heronswood Rd AL7 ...111 A5
Hertford Castle★ SG14 .113 C5
Hertford County Hospl
  SG14 ....113 B6
Hertford East Sta SG13 .113 E6
Hertford Heath Jun Mix Inf
  Sch SG13 ....114 C4
Hertford Mews EN6 ...159 C8
Hertford Mus★ SG14 ..113 D6
Hertford North Sta
  SG14 ....113 B6
Hertford Rd Enfield EN3 .162 D1
  Great Amwell SG12 ..114 F4
  Hatfield AL9 ....111 B1
  Hoddesdon EN11 ....134 E8
  Stevenage SG2 ......69 B7
  Tewin AL6 ....90 F2
  Welwyn AL6 ....89 D3
Hertford Regional Coll
  Cheshunt EN10 .....148 F6
  Ware SG12 ....114 C8
Hertford St Andrew CE Prim
  Sch SG14 ....112 F7
Hertfordshire & Essex High
  Sch The CM23 ....77 B7
Hertfordshire Bsns Ctr
  AL2 ....142 D5
Hertfordshire Theatre Sch
  SG14 ....34 F6
Hertingfordbury Prim Sch
  SG14 ....112 C4
Hertingfordbury Rd
  Hertford SG14 ......113 B5
  Hertingfordbury SG14 .112 C4
Herts & Essex Com Hospl
  CM23 ....77 B6
Hertsmere Ind Pk WD6 .170 D6
Hertswood 1 EN5 ....171 E5
Hertswood Sch WD6 ..170 C7
Hester Ho CM20 ......117 C2
Heswall Ct 5 LU1 ......63 F6
Heswell Gn WD19 .....175 A7
Hetchleys HP1 ....124 A6
Hever Cl LU7 ....80 D2
Hewins Cl EN9 ....163 E7
Hewitt Cl AL4 ....108 D7
Hewlett Rd LU3 ....44 E5
Hexton Jun Mix Inf Sch
  SG5 ....19 A1
Hexton Rd
  Great Offley SG5 .....33 E8
  Lilley LU2 ....32 C4
Heybridge Ct SG14 ....112 F7
Heydon Rd SG8 ....9 E3
Heydons Cl AL3 ......127 D5
Heyford End AL2 .....141 C3
Heyford Rd WD7 .....155 F2
Heyford Way AL10 ....130 C7
Heysham Dr WD19 ....175 D5
Heywood Dr LU2 ....45 F2
Hibbert Ave WD24 ....154 D3
Hibbert Rd HA3 ......176 F1
Hibbert St LU1 ....63 E6
Hibbert Street Almshouses 13
  LU1 ....63 E6
Hibberts Ct SG6 ....22 E7
Hickling Cl LU2 ....46 D1
Hickling Way AL5 ......86 C3
Hickman Cl EN10 .....134 D3
Hickman Ct LU3 ....44 D8
Hickman's Hill SG7 .....24 D4
Hicks Rd AL3 ....83 F6
Hidalgo Ct HP2 ....124 F6
Hideaway The WD5 ...153 F8
Hides The CM20 ......117 C1
Higgins Rd EN7 ......147 D4
Higgins Wlk SG1 ......36 C1
High Acres WD5 .....153 D7
High Ash Rd AL4 .....108 C4
High Ave SG6 ....22 E4
High Barnet Sta EN5 ..171 C5
High Beech Rd LU3 ....44 D7
High Beeches Prim Sch
  AL5 ....86 D1
High Canons WD6 ....157 D2
High Cl WD3 ....165 C4
High Cross WD25 ....155 D2
High Dane SG4 ....22 A2
High Dells AL10 ......129 F4
High Elms
  Harpenden AL5 .....107 A6
  Watford WD25 .....154 B8
High Elms Cl HA6 ....174 D4
High Elms La
  Abbots Langley WD25,
    WD5 ....154 C8
  Benington SG2 ......52 F1
High Firs Radlett WD7 ..155 F4
  Radlett WD7 ....156 A4
High Firs Cres AL5 ....107 D8
High Gr St Albans AL3 .127 D5
  Welwyn Garden City AL8 .110 C7
High House Est CM17 ..118 F4
High La CM24 ....59 F8
High Mead LU3 ....45 A3
High Meads AL4 ......108 C4
High Oak Rd SG12 ....93 E3
High Oaks Enfield EN2 .160 F1
  4 Northwood HA6 ...174 F5
  St Albans AL3 ......127 D7
High Oaks Rd AL8 ....110 B7
High Pastures CM22 ...98 D1
High Plash SG1 ....50 E5
High Point 16 LU1 ......63 D6
High Rd Bushey WD23 ..168 D1

High Rd continued
  Essendon AL9 ......131 E5
  Harrow HA3 ....176 E3
  Hoddesdon EN10 ...134 F4
  Shillington SG5 ......19 E8
  Stapleford SG14 .....92 A2
  Watford WD25 .....154 A7
High Ridge Cuffley EN6 .146 E4
  Harpenden AL5 .....85 E3
  Luton LU2 ....46 C1
High Ridge Cl HP3 ....138 D6
High Ridge Rd HP3 ...138 D7
High Road Broxbourne
  EN10 ....134 F1
High Road Turnford
  EN10 ....148 E6
High Road Wormley
  EN10 ....148 F8
High St
  Abbots Langley WD5 .139 F1
  Arlesey SG15 ....11 A5
  Ashwell SG7 ....4 D4
  Baldock SG7 ....23 F8
  Barkway SG8 ....17 C3
  Barley SG8 ....8 F2
  Barnet EN5 ....171 F5
  Bedmond WD5 ......139 F4
  Berkhamsted HP4 ..122 B4
  Berkhamsted, Northchurch
    HP4 ....121 C6
  Bishop's Stortford CM23 .76 E1
  Bovingdon HP3 .....137 A4
  Buntingford SG9 .....40 E8
  Bushey WD23 ......168 A3
  Cheddington LU7 ....80 D7
  Cheshunt EN8 .....148 D2
  Cheshunt, Theabald's Grove Sta
    EN8 ....162 D7
  Cheshunt, Waltham Cross
    EN8 ....162 E5
  Codicote SG4 ....67 F1
  Colney Heath AL4 ...129 B1
  Elstree WD6 ....169 D3
  Eyeworth SG19 ......1 A8
  Flamstead AL3 ....84 B2
  Graveley SG4 ....36 C4
  Great Offley SG5 .....33 C3
  Guilden Morden SG8 ...1 F4
  Harefield UB9 ......173 C1
  Harlow CM17 ......118 D4
  Harpenden AL5 .....86 A1
  Harrow HA3 ....176 E1
  Hemel Hempstead HP1,
    HP3 ....124 D3
  Hinxworth SG7 ....3 D6
  Hitchin SG5 ....34 E7
  Hitchin, Gosmore SG4 ..34 F3
  Hoddesdon EN11 ...135 A5
  Hunsdon SG12 ......95 D1
  Kimpton SG4 ....66 C1
  Kings Langley WD4 ..139 A2
  London Colney AL2 ..142 D5
  Luton LU4 ....44 C4
  Markyate AL3 ....83 E5
  Much Hadham SG10 ..74 F3
  Northwood HA6 ....174 F2
  Pirton SG5 ....20 D4
  Pitstone LU7 ....80 E5
  Potters Bar EN6 ....159 C7
  Redbourn AL3 ......106 B5
  Reed SG8 ....16 E5
  Rickmansworth WD3 ..165 E1
  Roydon CM19 ......116 B1
  Royston SG8 ....7 D6
  Sandridge AL4 .....108 C2
  St Albans AL3 ......127 D3
  Standon SG11 ....55 F1
  Standon, Puckeridge SG11 .55 D3
  Stanstead Abbotts SG12 .115 C4
  Stevenage SG1 ......50 C7
  Stotfold SG5 ....11 F6
  Tring HP23 ....100 A3
  Walkern SG2 ....38 B1
  Ware SG12 ....93 D1
  Watford WD17 ......167 B6
  Watford WD17 ......167 C5
  Watton at S SG14 ....70 C3
  Welwyn AL6 ....89 C5
  Wheathampstead AL4 .87 D1
  Whitwell SG4 ....66 F7
  Widford SG12 ....95 E5
High Street Bsns Pk
  EN8 ....162 E7
High Street Gn HP2 ...125 A5
High Town Rd LU2 .....45 F1
High Tree Cl CM21 ....97 D1
High View
  Birchanger CM23 .....59 D3
  Chorleywood WD3 ...165 A5
  Hatfield AL10 ......130 A2
  Hitchin SG5 ....34 D7
  Markyate AL3 ....83 E5
  Watford WD18 .....166 F3
High View Ct HA3 ....176 E3
High Wickfield AL7 ...111 C5
High Wood Cl LU1 .....62 F7
High Wood Rd EN11 ..114 F1
High Wych CE Prim Sch
  CM21 ....97 A1
High Wych La CM21 ...97 A2
High Wych Rd
  Gilston CM21 ......117 C2
  High Wych CM21 .....97 B1
High Wych Way HP2 ..105 C2
Higham Dr LU2 ....46 D1
Highbanks Rd HA5 ...176 B4
Highbarns HP3 ......139 A6
Highbridge Ct EN9 ...163 B6

Highbridge Ho EN9 .... 163 B6
Highbridge Ret Pk EN9 . 163 B5
Highbridge St EN9 ..... 163 B6
Highbury Ho (North Herts Music Sch) SG4 .... 35 A7
Highbury Inf Sch SG4 ... 34 F6
Highbury Rd Hitchin SG4 . 35 A7
Luton LU3 .... 45 C1
Highbush Rd SG5 .... 11 E5
Highclere Ct 4 AL1 .... 127 E4
Highclere Dr HP3 ...... 139 B7
Highcroft 2 SG2 .... 50 F1
Highcroft Rd HP3 ...... 138 B6
Highfield Bushey WD23 .. 176 E8
Kings Langley WD4 ...... 138 E3
Letchworth SG6 .... 22 E4
Little Hadham SG11 ...... 57 C3
Sawbridgeworth CM21 .... 97 E3
South Oxhey WD19 ...... 175 F7
Watford WD25 .... 153 F5
Highfield Ave
Bishop's Stortford CM23 ... 77 C6
Harpenden AL5 .... 107 C8
Highfield Cl HA6 .... 174 E2
Highfield Cres HA6 ..... 174 E2
Highfield Ct
Hertford SG13 .... 113 D4
Stevenage SG1 .... 50 F7
Highfield Dr EN10 ...... 134 E2
Highfield Hall AL4 ..... 142 E7
Highfield Ho HP2 .... 124 F5
Highfield La
Colney Heath AL4 .... 142 E8
Hemel Hempstead HP2 ... 124 F5
Highfield Oval AL5 ...... 86 A4
Highfield Park Dr AL4 .. 142 C8
Highfield Rd
Berkhamsted HP4 .... 122 D4
Hammond Street EN7 .... 147 E5
Hertford SG13 .... 113 D4
Luton LU4 .... 45 B1
Northwood HA6 .... 174 E2
Sandridge AL4 .... 108 B1
Tring HP23 .... 99 E3
Watford WD23 .... 167 E4
Wigginton HP23 .... 100 D1
Highfield Sch The SG6 .. 22 D4
Highfield Way WD3 .... 165 B3
Highfields Cuffley EN6 .. 146 E3
Radlett WD7 .... 155 F4
Highfields Cl LU5 ...... 44 A2
Highfiled Way EN6 ..... 159 B7
Highgate Gr CM21 ...... 97 D2
Highgrove Ct EN8 ..... 162 D5
Highland Dr
Bushey WD23 .... 168 C2
Hemel Hempstead HP3 .. 125 B3
Highland Rd
Bishop's Stortford CM23 .. 76 F3
Lower Nazeing EN9 .... 135 E1
Northwood HA6 .... 175 A1
Highlands Hatfield AL9 .. 130 C8
Royston SG8 .... 7 E6
Watford WD19 .... 167 C1
Highlands The
Potters Bar EN6 .... 145 C1
Rickmansworth WD3 .... 165 B2
Highmead CM24 .... 59 E8
Highmill SG12 .... 93 D3
Highmoor AL5 .... 86 A4
Highover Cl LU2 .... 46 B1
Highover Jun Mix Inf Sch SG4 .... 22 C1
Highover Rd SG6 .... 22 D5
Highover Way SG4 ...... 22 B1
Highridge Pl EN2 ...... 160 F1
Highview Cl EN6 ...... 159 C6
Highview Gdns
Potters Bar EN6 .... 159 C6
St Albans AL4 .... 128 C8
Highway The HA7 ..... 176 F2
Highwood Ave WD23 ... 167 F8
Highwood Prim Sch WD23 .... 167 E8
Highwoodhall La HP3 .. 139 C7
Hilbury AL10 .... 129 F4
Hilfield La WD25 ...... 168 D6
Hilfield La S WD23 .... 168 F3
Hill Cl Barnet EN5 ..... 171 C4
Harpenden AL5 .... 86 C4
Luton LU3 .... 45 C7
Hill Comm HP3 .... 139 A8
Hill Crest
Potters Bar EN6 .... 159 C5
Whitwell SG4 .... 66 E6
Hill Crest Lodge WD6 .. 169 F5
Hill Croft Cl LU4 .... 44 C6
Hill Ct EN6 .... 159 C5
Hill Dyke Rd AL4 ...... 108 E7
Hill End La AL4 .... 128 C2
Hill End Rd UB9 .... 173 C3
Hill Farm Ave WD25 ... 154 A6
Hill Farm Cl WD25 .... 154 A6
Hill Farm La
Ayot St Lawrence AL6 .... 88 C5
Redbourn AL3 .... 106 C1
Hill Head Cotts SG10 ... 75 B1
Hill Ho Harefield UB9 .. 173 C1
Hertford SG13 .... 113 C5
Hill House Ave HA7 .... 176 F3
Hill Ley AL10 .... 129 F5
Hill Leys EN6 .... 146 E3
Hill Mead HP4 .... 122 A3
Hill Milford AL5 .... 86 D3
Hill Pickford AL5 .... 86 D4
Hill Rd Codicote SG4 ..... 67 E1
Northwood HA6 .... 174 D4
Hill Rise Cuffley EN6 .... 146 E3
Hill Rise *continued*
Luton LU3 .... 44 D7
Potters Bar EN6 .... 159 C5
Rickmansworth WD3 .... 165 B2
Hill Side LU7 .... 79 F7
Hill St AL3 .... 127 C3
Hill The Harlow CM17 .. 118 C4
Wheathampstead AL4 ... 108 D8
Hill Top SG7 .... 23 E7
Hill View
Berkhamsted HP4 ...... 122 A6
Buckland SG9 .... 27 D8
Whitwell SG4 .... 66 E6
Hillary Cl LU3 .... 44 D7
Hillary Cres LU1 .... 63 C6
Hillary Ho WD6 .... 170 B6
Hillary Rd HP2 .... 125 A4
Hillary Rise SG15 .... 11 B5
Hillberry Ct WD23 ..... 168 B2
Hillborough Inf Sch LU1 . 63 C6
Hillborough Jun Sch LU1 63 C6
Hillborough Rd LU1 ..... 63 D6
Hillbrow SG6 .... 22 D5
Hillcrest Baldock SG7 .... 23 F7
Hatfield AL10 .... 130 A5
St Albans AL3 .... 127 B1
Stevenage SG1 .... 50 F5
Hillcrest Ave LU2 .... 45 C8
Hillcrest Cl EN7 .... 147 C2
Hillcrest Rd WD7 ...... 157 A6
Hillcroft Cres WD19 ... 175 B8
Hilldown Rd HP1 ...... 124 A5
Hille Bsns Ctr WD24 ... 167 B8
Hillfield AL10 .... 130 C8
Hillfield Ave SG4 .... 22 A2
Hillfield Ct HP2 .... 124 E3
Hillfield Rd HP2 ...... 124 D3
Hillgate SG4 .... 22 A3
Hillgrove Bsns Pk EN9 . 135 C1
Hillhouse EN9 .... 163 F6
Hillhouse CE Prim Sch EN9 .... 163 F6
Hilliard Rd HA6 .... 174 F2
Hillingdon Rd WD25 ... 154 B5
Hillmead SG1 .... 51 A6
Hillmead Prim Sch CM23 76 C7
Hillpath SG6 .... 23 B6
Hillpoint WD3 .... 165 C4
Hillrise Ave WD24 .... 154 D2
Hills La HA6 .... 174 E2
Hillsborough Gn WD19 . 175 A7
Hillshott SG6 .... 23 A6
Hillshott Inf Sch SG6 ... 23 A6
Hillside Codicote SG4 .... 67 F1
Hatfield AL10 .... 130 A5
Hoddesdon EN11 ...... 134 F7
Royston SG8 .... 7 D5
St Albans AL4 .... 128 C2
Stevenage SG1 .... 50 F5
Ware SG12 .... 114 D8
Welwyn Garden City AL7 . 111 B3
Hillside Ave
Bishop's Stortford CM23 .. 77 A7
Borehamwood WD6 ..... 170 B5
Cheshunt EN8 .... 162 D8
Hillside Cl WD5 .... 153 E7
Hillside Cotts
Birchanger CM23 .... 59 C3
Wareside SG12 .... 94 F4
Hillside Cres Enfield EN2 161 D1
Northwood HA6 .... 175 A2
Stanstead Abbotts SG12 . 115 B4
Watford WD19 .... 167 D3
Hillside Ct Cheshunt EN8 162 D8
8 St Albans AL1 .... 127 E4
Hillside End CM23 ...... 59 C3
Hillside Gate 6 AL1 ... 127 E4
Hillside Gdns
Barnet EN5 .... 171 E5
Berkhamsted HP4 ...... 122 D3
Pinner HA6 .... 175 B2
Hillside Ho SG1 .... 50 F5
Hillside Jun & Inf Schs HA6 .... 175 A3
Hillside La SG12 .... 115 A5
Hillside Mans EN5 ..... 171 F5
Hillside Rd
Chorleywood WD3 ..... 164 C4
Harpenden AL5 .... 85 F3
Luton LU3 .... 45 D1
Pinner HA5 .... 175 B3
Radlett WD7 .... 156 B4
St Albans AL1 .... 127 E4
Watford WD23 .... 167 E4
Hillside Rise HA6 ..... 175 A3
Hillside Sch The WD6 ... 170 C5
Hillside Terr SG13 ..... 113 C4
Hillside Way AL6 .... 90 A8
Hilltop AL3 .... 105 F6
Hilltop Cl EN7 .... 147 F5
Hilltop Cotts
Great Munden SG11 ..... 54 D4
Great Offley SG5 .... 33 C3
Hilltop Ct LU1 .... 63 C7
Hilltop Rd Bedmond WD4 139 D4
Berkhamsted HP4 ...... 122 C3
Hilltop View AL4 ...... 108 C7
Hilltop Wlk AL5 .... 107 D8
Hillview Cl HA5 .... 175 F4
Hillview Cres LU2 .... 45 C8
Hillview Gdns EN8 .... 148 E4
Hillview Rd HA5 ...... 175 F4
Hilly Fields AL7 .... 111 C7
Hilmay Dr HP1 .... 124 C2
Hilton Cl SG1 .... 50 B7
Himalayan Way WD18 .. 166 F3
Hindhead Gn WD19 ... 175 C5
Hine Ho AL4 .... 128 D2
Hine Way SG5 .... 21 C1
Hinwick Cl SG15 .... 11 B7
Hinxworth Rd Ashwell SG7 . 4 B4
Hinxworth SG7 .... 3 C3
Hipkins CM23 .... 76 E4
Hipkins Pl EN10 .... 134 E3
Hispano Mews EN3 .... 163 A2
Hitchen Hill Path SG4 ... 34 F5
Hitchens Cl HP1 .... 123 F4
Hitchin Boys' Sch SG5 ... 34 E8
Hitchin British Schools Mus★ SG5 .... 34 F6
Hitchin Bsns Ctr The SG4 .... 22 A3
Hitchin Girls' Sch SG4 ... 34 F7
Hitchin Hill SG4 .... 34 F5
Hitchin Hospl SG5 .... 34 D8
Hitchin Mus★ SG5 .... 34 E7
Hitchin Rd Arlesey SG15 .. 11 A2
Great Wymondley SG4 .... 35 D6
Hexton SG5 .... 19 E1
Hitchin SG4 .... 34 F3
Kimpton SG4 .... 66 D2
Letchworth SG6 .... 22 E3
Lower Stondon SG16 ..... 10 C6
Luton LU2 .... 46 A4
Pirton SG5 .... 20 E2
Stevenage SG1 .... 36 B1
Stotfold SG5 .... 11 E5
Weston SG4 .... 24 B1
Hitchin Road Ind & Bsns Ctr SG15 .... 11 A3
Hitchin St SG7 .... 23 E8
Hitchin Sta SG4 .... 35 A8
Hitchwood Cotts SG4 .... 48 F5
Hither Field SG12 .... 93 E3
Hitherbaulk AL7 .... 110 E4
Hitherfield La AL5 ...... 86 A2
Hitherway AL8 .... 89 D2
Hitherwell Dr HA3 ..... 176 D2
Hive Cl WD23 .... 176 D8
Hive Rd WD23 .... 176 E8
Hixberry La AL4 .... 128 E1
Hobart Wlk AL3 .... 127 F7
Hobbs Cl Cheshunt EN8 .. 148 D2
St Albans AL4 .... 128 E2
Hobbs Cross Rd CM17 .. 118 F3
Hobbs Ct SG1 .... 51 A8
Hobbs Hayes SG8 .... 16 E5
Hobbs Hill AL6 .... 89 C4
Hobbs Hill Rd HP3 ..... 138 F8
Hobbs Hill Wood Prim Sch HP3 .... 125 B1
Hobbs Way AL8 .... 110 C5
Hobby Horse Cl EN7 ... 147 D5
Hobletts Manor Inf Sch HP2 .... 125 A4
Hobletts Manor Jun Sch HP2 .... 125 A4
Hobletts Rd HP2 .... 124 F4
Hobsons Cl EN11 ...... 114 F1
Hobsons Wlk HP23 ...... 99 F5
Hobtoe Rd CM20 .... 117 A1
Hockerill SG14 .... 70 E3
Hockerill Anglo-European Coll CM23 .... 77 B7
Hockerill Ct 7 CM23 .... 77 A7
Hockerill St CM23 .... 77 A7
Hocklands AL7 .... 111 C7
Hockwell Ring LU4 ...... 44 C4
Hoddesdon Ind Ctr EN11 .... 135 C7
Hoddesdon Rd SG12 .... 115 C3
Hodges Way WD18 .... 167 A3
Hodings Rd CM20 ...... 117 C2
Hodson Pl EN3 .... 163 A1
Hodwell SG7 .... 4 D4
Hoe La Enfield EN1,EN3 .. 162 B1
Lower Nazeing EN9 .... 135 F1
Ware SG12 .... 114 D7
Hoe The WD19 .... 175 D8
Hoecroft EN9 .... 135 F1
Hoecroft Ct EN3 ...... 162 C1
Hoestock Rd CM21 ...... 97 D2
Hog Hall La HP4 .... 81 A5
Hog La HP5 .... 121 C1
Hogarth Ct WD23 ..... 168 B2
Hogg End La AL3 ...... 126 C6
Hogg La WD6 .... 169 A5
Hogges Cl EN11 .... 135 A6
Hogpits Bottom HP3 ... 151 A7
Hogsdell La SG13 ..... 114 B4
Holbeck La EN7 .... 147 F5
Holbein Gate HA6 ..... 174 E5
Holborn Cl AL4 .... 128 D8
Holbrook Cl EN1 ...... 162 A1
Holcroft Rd AL5 .... 86 D3
Holdbrook SG4 .... 35 B7
Holdbrook Ct EN8 ..... 162 F5
Holdbrook Prim Sch EN8 .... 162 F5
Holden Cl Hertford SG13 . 113 E7
Hitchin SG4 .... 35 C7
Holders La SG2 .... 51 E5
Holdings The AL9 ...... 130 D7
Holecroft EN9 .... 163 E5
Holford Way LU3 .... 31 B1
Holgate Dr LU4 .... 44 B3
Holkham Cl LU4 .... 44 A4
Holkham Ho 11 EN5 ..... 171 E6
Holland Ct LU3 .... 45 C2
Holland Gdns WD25 ... 154 C4
Holland Rd LU3 .... 45 B2
Holland Way CM17 ..... 118 C1
Holland's Croft SG12 .... 95 D1
Holliday St HP4 .... 122 D4
Hollier Ct AL10 .... 130 B6
Holliers Way AL10 ..... 130 A5
Hollies Cl SG8 .... 7 E6
Hollies The
Bovingdon HP3 .... 137 A2
St Albans AL3 .... 127 E4
St Albans, Townsend AL3 . 127 C5
Watford WD18 .... 166 F5
Welwyn Garden City AL8 . 110 B2
Wigginton HP23 .... 100 D1
Hollies Way EN6 .... 159 C8
Hollow La SG4 .... 34 F7
Holloway La WD3 ...... 151 C2
Holloway The HP23,HP22 . 99 C4
Holloways La AL9 ...... 144 D7
Holly Cl AL10 .... 129 F4
Holly Copse SG1 .... 50 F4
Holly Croft SG14 ...... 113 A7
Holly Dell SG13 .... 113 C4
Holly Dr
Berkhamsted HP4 ...... 122 D3
Potters Bar EN6 .... 159 B6
Holly Farm Cl LU1 ...... 62 E3
Holly Gr HA5 .... 175 E2
Holly Grove Rd SG14 .... 91 C3
Holly Hall Ct AL6 .... 89 C5
Holly Hedges La HP3 .. 151 C8
Holly Ind Est WD24 .... 167 C8
Holly La AL5 .... 86 E6
Holly Leys SG2 .... 69 C8
Holly Rd Enfield EN3 ... 162 D3
Woolmer Green SG3 ..... 69 B1
Holly Shaws SG2 .... 51 B1
Holly St LU1 .... 63 E6
Holly Street Trad Est 12 LU1 .... 63 E6
Holly Tree Ct HP2 ...... 125 B3
Holly Wlk Harpenden AL5 . 86 D1
Welwyn Garden City AL8 .. 89 C2
Hollybush Ave AL2 ..... 141 A7
Hollybush Cl
Harrow HA3 .... 176 E2
Oaklands AL6 .... 89 E8
Potten End HP4 .... 123 D7
Watford WD19 .... 167 C2
Hollybush Hill LU2,SG5 ... 32 F1
Hollybush Ho AL7 ..... 110 E4
Hollybush La
Datchworth SG3 .... 69 C3
Flamstead AL3 .... 84 B3
Harpenden AL5 .... 86 A3
Hemel Hempstead HP1 .. 123 F4
Welwyn Garden City AL7 . 110 E3
Whitwell SG4 .... 66 B8
Hollybush Prim Sch SG14 .... 113 A6
Hollybush Rd LU2 .... 46 C1
Hollybush Row HP23 ... 120 D8
Hollybush Way EN7 .... 148 A3
Hollycross Rd SG12 .... 115 B7
Hollyfield Hatfield AL10 .. 130 A2
Tring HP23 .... 100 C5
Hollyfield Cl HP23 .... 100 C5
Hollyfields EN10 ...... 148 E5
Hollygrove WD23 ...... 168 D2
Hollyhock Cl HP1 ...... 123 E4
Hollytree Cl HP5 ...... 150 B8
Hollytree Ho WD24 .... 153 E3
Hollywood Ct WD6 ..... 169 F5
Holm Oak Pk WD18 .... 167 A4
Holmbrook Ave LU3 ..... 45 C5
Holmbury Cl WD23 .... 176 E8
Holmbury St Mary Ct AL1 .... 128 B2
Holmdale SG6 .... 23 B5
Holmdale Cl WD6 ...... 169 F7
Holme Cl Cheshunt EN8 .. 162 E8
Hatfield AL10 .... 129 F8
Holme Lea WD25 ...... 154 C5
Holme Pk WD6 .... 169 F7
Holme Pl HP2 .... 125 C4
Holme Rd AL10 .... 129 F8
Holme Way HA7 .... 176 F4
Holmes Ct AL3 .... 127 E4
Holmesdale EN8 .... 162 D4
Holmfield Cl LU1 .... 63 D5
Holmscroft Rd LU3 ...... 44 F6
Holmshill La EN5,WD6 .. 157 F2
Holmside Rise WD19 ... 175 B7
Holmwood Rd EN3 ..... 162 D3
Holroyd Cres SG7 .... 23 F7
Holt Cl WD6 .... 169 F5
Holt Cotts The SG4 ...... 66 C4
Holt Ho EN8 .... 148 B3
Holt The
Hemel Hempstead HP2 .. 124 E2
Welwyn Garden City AL7 . 111 D5
Holts Mdw AL3 .... 106 B6
Holtsmere Cl Luton LU2 .. 46 D1
Watford WD25 .... 154 C4
Holtsmere End Inf Sch HP2 .... 125 B8
Holtsmere End Jun Sch HP2 .... 125 B8
Holtsmere End La HP2 . 105 C1
Holwell SG1 .... 36 C2
Holwell Ct AL9 .... 111 F1
Holwell Hyde AL7 ...... 111 C4
Holwell Hyde La AL7 ... 111 C3
Holwell La AL9 .... 131 F8
Holwell Prim Sch AL7 ... 110 F5
Holwell Rd Holwell SG5 .. 21 C7
Pirton SG5 .... 20 E6
Welwyn Garden City AL7 . 110 E5
Holy Acre CM19 .... 116 A1
Holy Cross Hill EN10 ... 148 A8
Holy Family RC Jun Mix Inf Sch AL7 .... 90 A1
Holy Rood RC Inf Sch WD17 .... 153 D3
Holy Rood RC Jun Sch WD17 .... 153 D3
Holy Trinity CE Prim Sch
Cheshunt EN8 .... 162 D7
Northwood HA6 .... 174 C4
Holyfield Hall Farm★ EN9 .... 149 C4
Holyfield Rd EN9 ...... 149 D2
Holyrood Cres AL1 ..... 141 D7
Holyrood Ct WD18 ..... 167 B5
Holywell Cl LU6 .... 82 C6
Holywell Ct LU3 .... 45 B4
Holywell Hill AL1 ...... 127 D2
Holywell Jun Mix Inf Sch WD18 .... 166 F3
Holywell Rd Studham LU6 . 82 B6
Watford WD18 .... 167 A4
Home Cl Cheshunt EN10 . 148 F7
Luton LU4 .... 44 C4
Stotfold SG5 .... 11 F7
Home Farm Cotts
Newgate Street SG13 ... 146 F8
Slip End LU1 .... 85 A8
Home Farm Ct
Bovingdon HP3 .... 136 F1
Cockernhoe LU2 .... 46 D5
Standon SG11 .... 55 D3
Home Farm Ind Pk SG12 .... 115 F5
Home Farm Rd
Berkhamsted HP4 ...... 121 D7
Rickmansworth WD3 .... 174 A6
Home Field EN5 .... 171 F4
Home Ley AL7 .... 110 E6
Home Mdw AL7 .... 110 F6
Home Park Ind Est WD4 .... 139 B1
Home Park Mill Link Rd WD4 .... 139 B1
Home Way WD3 .... 164 F1
Homedale Dr LU4 .... 44 D2
Homedell Ho AL5 .... 85 E3
Homefield
Bovingdon HP3 .... 137 B3
Hinxworth SG7 .... 3 D6
Potten End HP4 .... 123 B7
Homefield La SG4 .... 49 F2
Homefield Rd
Bushey WD23 .... 168 A4
Chorleywood WD3 ..... 164 D5
Hemel Hempstead HP2 .. 125 A2
Radlett WD7 .... 155 F2
Ware SG12 .... 93 E2
Homeleigh Ct EN8 ..... 148 B1
Homeleigh St EN8 ..... 148 B1
Homepark Cotts WD4 .. 139 B1
Homerfield AL8 .... 110 C7
Homerswood La AL6 .... 89 A2
Homerswood Prim Sch AL8 .... 89 D2
Homerton Rd LU3 .... 45 A6
Homestead Cl AL2 ..... 141 C4
Homestead Ct AL7 ..... 110 F4
Homestead La AL7 ..... 110 F4
Homestead Moat SG1 .... 50 E4
Homestead Rd
Hatfield AL10 .... 130 B8
Rickmansworth WD3 .... 165 D2
Homestead Way LU1 ..... 63 C5
Homesteads The SG12 . 116 D8
Homewood Ave EN6 .... 146 E4
Homewood Ct WD3 .... 164 F5
Homewood Ind Sch AL2 141 B3
Homewood La EN6 ..... 146 C4
Homewood Rd AL1 ..... 128 B5
Honey Brook EN9 ...... 163 E6
Honey La
Brent Pelham CB11 ...... 30 F3
Buntingford SG9 .... 40 E8
5 Hertford SG14 ...... 113 D6
Waltham Abbey EN9 .... 163 E5
Honeybourne CM23 ...... 76 E4
Honeycroft AL8 .... 110 C5
Honeycroft Dr AL4 ..... 142 C8
Honeycross Rd HP1 .... 123 E2
Honeygate LU2 .... 45 E4
Honeymead AL6 .... 89 F3
Honeymeade CM21 ..... 118 C7
Honeysuckle Cl
Bishop's Stortford CM23 .. 76 C6
Hertford SG13 .... 114 A6
Honeysuckle Gdns AL10 130 B4
Honeyway SG8 .... 7 E6
Honeywood Cl EN6 .... 159 D6
Honilands Prim Sch EN1 .... 162 B3
Honiton Mews LU3 ...... 44 E6
Honours Mead HP3 .... 137 A4
Hoo Cotts SG5 .... 33 D1
Hoo Farm Cotts SG5 .... 33 D1
Hoo St LU1 .... 63 E5
Hoo The CM17 .... 118 C5
Hook Gate EN1 .... 162 B3
Hook La Northaw EN6 ... 159 F7
Northaw EN6 .... 160 A8
Hook's Cross SG14 ...... 69 F6
Hoopers Mews WD23 ... 168 B1
Hoops La SG8 .... 15 F6
Hop Garden Way WD25 . 154 C8
Hope Gn WD25 .... 154 A6
Hopewell Rd SG7 .... 23 D8
Hopground Cl AL1 ..... 128 A1
Hopkins Cres AL4 ..... 108 B1
Hopkins Yd AL1 .... 127 E2
Hoppit Rd EN9 .... 163 B7

Hopton Rd SG1 ....50 A8
Hopwood Cl WD17 .....153 E3
Horace Brightman Cl
LU3 ....45 A7
Horace Gay Gdns SG6 ...22 E6
Horbeam Cl WD6 ......170 A8
Hordle Gdns AL1 ....127 F2
Horizon Ho EN3 ....162 F3
Hormead CE Prim Sch
SG9 ....41 F8
Horn Hill SG4 ....66 E6
Hornbeam Cl SG14 .....113 B7
Hornbeam Ct SG4 ....35 E5
Hornbeam La AL9 ......131 E2
Hornbeam Spring SG3 ...68 F4
Hornbeam Way EN7 ....147 F2
Hornbeams
Bricket Wood AL2 ....140 F1
Welwyn Garden City AL7 ..111 B5
Hornbeams Ave EN1 ...162 C4
Hornbeams The
Harlow CM20 ....117 C2
Stevenage SG2 ....51 B4
Hornets The WD18 .....167 B5
Hornhill Rd WD3 ......172 D5
Horns Cl SG13 ....113 C4
Horns Mill Rd SG13 ....113 C3
Horns Rd SG13 ....113 C5
Hornsby Cl LU2 ....46 C1
Hornsfield AL7 ....111 C7
Horrocks Cl SG12 ....93 D3
Horsa Gdns AL10 ......129 E7
Horse Cross SG11 ....56 D3
Horse Hill HP5 ....150 D7
Horsecroft Rd HP1 .....124 A1
Horselers HP3 ....139 A8
Horsemans Dr AL2 .....141 B6
Horseshoe Bsns Pk AL2 141 B1
Horseshoe Cl Barley SG8 ..8 F1
Cheddington LU7 ....80 A7
Horseshoe Ct Hitchin SG4 .34 E6
Stanstead Abbotts SG12 ..115 D4
Horseshoe Hill SG9 .....42 A8
Horseshoe La
Great Hormead SG9 ......42 A8
Totteridge N20 ....171 D1
Watford WD25 ....154 C7
Horseshoe The HP3 .....125 C1
Horsham Cl LU2 ....46 D2
Horsleys WD3 ....172 D5
Horton Gdns HP2 ......105 A1
Horwood Cl WD3 ......165 A2
Horwood Cotts WD25 ...168 E8
Horwood Ct WD24 .....154 E2
Hospital Rd SG15 ....11 A4
Houghton Mews 12 LU1 .63 D6
Housden Cl AL4 ....108 E7
House La Arlesey SG15 ...11 A7
Sandridge AL4 ....108 C1
St Albans AL4 ....128 D7
House On The Hill Toy Mus★
CM24 ....59 F6
Housefield Way AL4 ....142 C8
Housewood End HP1 ...124 B6
Housman Ave SG8 ....2 C1
How Field AL5 ....85 E3
How Wood AL2 ....141 B3
How Wood Prim Sch
AL2 ....141 C4
How Wood Sta AL2 ....141 C3
Howard Agne Cl HP3 ...137 A4
Howard Cl Bushey WD23 .168 E2
Luton LU3 ....45 A4
St Albans AL1 ....128 C1
Stotfold SG5 ....11 E5
Waltham Abbey EN9 .....163 D5
Watford WD24 ....154 A2
Howard Ct Enfield EN1 ..161 E1
Letchworth SG6 ....23 B4
Howard Ctr The AL8 ...110 D6
Howard Dr
Borehamwood WD6 .....170 D5
Letchworth SG6 ....23 B3
Howard Gate SG6 ....23 B4
Howard Park Cnr SG6 ...23 A6
Howard Way Barnet EN5 171 D4
Harlow CM20 ....117 F2
Howards Cl HA5 ....175 B1
Howards Dr HP1 ....124 A5
Howards Wood SG6 .....23 B3
Howardsgate AL8 ......110 D6
Howberry Gn SG15 ......11 A3
Howe Cl WD7 ....156 E7
Howe Dell AL10 ....130 B5
Howe Dell Prim Sch
AL10 ....130 B5
Howe Green House Sch
CM22 ....77 D2
Howe Rd HP3 ....125 A1
Howell Hill Cl LU7 ......61 D5
Howfield Gn EN11 .....115 A1
Howicks Gn AL7 ....111 A3
Howland Garth AL1 ....141 C7
Howlands AL7 ....111 B3
Howlands Ho AL7 ......111 A3
Howse Rd EN9 ....163 B4
Howton Pl WD23 ......168 D1
Hoylake Ct LU1 ....63 F5
Hoylake Gdns WD19 ...175 D6
Hubbards Rd WD3 .....164 D4
Huckleberry Cl LU3 .....45 A8
Hudnall La HP4 ....102 E7
Hudson Cl St Albans AL1 .141 D8
Watford WD24 ....153 F3
Hudson Rd SG2 ....51 B7
Hudsons Ct EN6 ....159 A8
Huggins La AL9 ....144 C8
Hugh Villas CM23 ....77 A5
Hughenden Rd AL4 ....128 C6
Hugo Gryn Way WD7 ...156 E8
Hull Cl EN7 ....147 D5
Hull La SG11 ....55 E7
Humber Ct SG1 ....36 F3
Humberstone Cl LU4 ....44 E2
Humberstone Rd LU4 ...44 E2
Humphrey Talbot Ave
LU6 ....81 F7
Hunsdon AL7 ....111 D6
Hunsdon Jun Mix Inf Sch
SG12 ....95 D1
Hunsdon Rd
Stanstead Abbotts SG12 ..115 E5
Widford SG12 ....95 E3
Hunsdon Road Cotts
SG12 ....115 E5
Hunston Cl LU4 ....44 B5
Hunt Cl AL4 ....128 D6
Hunter Cl
Borehamwood WD6 .....170 C4
Potters Bar EN6 ....159 B6
Hunter Wlk WD6 ......170 D4
Hunter's La WD25 .....153 F6
Huntercrombe Gdns
WD19 ....175 C5
Hunters Cl
Bovingdon HP3 ....137 A2
Stevenage SG2 ....51 D7
Stotfold SG5 ....11 E6
Tring HP23 ....100 B5
Hunters Gate WD25 ....154 A6
Hunters Oak HP2 ......125 B8
Hunters Pk HP4 ....122 E5
Hunters Reach EN7 ....147 F2
Hunters Ride AL2 ......155 A8
Hunters Way Royston SG8 ..7 E6
Welwyn Garden City AL7 ..110 F3
Hunting Gate
Hemel Hempstead HP2 ...124 E7
Hitchin SG4 ....22 A3
Hunting Hall LU2 ....64 C8
Huntingdon Cl EN10 ...148 E7
Huntingdon Ct EN5 ....171 F6
Huntingdon Rd SG1 .....50 B8
Hunton Bridge Hill
WD4 ....153 C6
Hunts Cl LU1 ....63 C6
Huntsman Cl SG11 ......55 D3
Huntsmans Ct HP4 ......81 C5
Huntsmill Rd HP1 .....123 E2
Hurlock Way LU4 ....44 C5
Hurn Gr CM23 ....59 C1
Hurricane Way WD5 ...154 A7
Hurst Cl Baldock SG7 ....13 A1
Bishop's Stortford CM23 ...76 E7
Welwyn Garden City AL7 ..111 C5
Hurst Dr EN8 ....162 D5
Hurst Drive Prim Sch
EN8 ....162 D5
Hurst Pl HA6 ....174 B2
Hurst Way LU3 ....44 F5
Hurstlings AL7 ....111 B5
Hutchings Lo WD3 .....165 E1
Hutton Cl Hertford SG14 .113 A6
Luton LU4 ....44 E3
Hutton Gdns HA3 ......176 C3
Hutton La HA3 ....176 D3
Hutton Wlk HA3 ....176 C3
Hyatt Ind Est SG1 ....50 A5
Hyburn Cl
Bricket Wood AL2 ....140 F1
Hemel Hempstead HP3 ...125 B2
Hyde Ave
Potters Bar EN6 ....159 B6
Stotfold SG5 ....11 E5
Hyde Cl Barnet EN5 .....171 F6
Harpenden AL5 ....86 B4
Hyde Ct EN8 ....162 E5
Hyde Gn E SG2 ....51 B3
Hyde Gn N SG2 ....51 B3
Hyde Gn S SG2 ....51 B3
Hyde Ho 5 LU2 ....63 F8
Hyde La Bedmond HP3 ..139 D5
Bovingdon HP3 ....137 A3
Park Street AL2 ....141 D3
Peters Green LU2 ....65 C2
Hyde Mdws HP3 ....137 A4
Hyde Mead EN9 ....149 E8
Hyde Mead Ho EN9 ....149 E8
Hyde Rd Caddington LU1 ..62 F4
Watford WD17 ....167 A7
Hyde Terr HP3 ....139 E7
Hyde The Stevenage SG2 ..51 C3
Ware SG12 ....93 B2
Hyde Valley AL7 ....110 F4
Hyde View Rd AL5 ......86 B4
Hyde Way AL7 ....110 E6
Hydean Way SG2 ....51 B3
Hyperion Ct HP2 ......124 F6
Hyver Hill NW7 ....170 D2

I

Ibberson Way SG4 ......35 A7
Iceni Ct SG6 ....23 B7
Ickleford Bury SG5 ......21 E3
Ickleford Gate SG5 ......21 D3
Ickleford Prim Sch SG5 ..21 E4
Ickleford Rd SG5 ....34 F8
Ickley Cl LU4 ....44 B5
Icknield Cl Ickleford SG5 .21 E4
St Albans AL3 ....126 F1
Icknield Gn
Letchworth SG6 ....22 E6
Tring HP23 ....100 A6
Icknield High Sch LU3 ..45 C5
Icknield Inf Sch SG6 ....22 D6
Icknield Prim Sch LU3 ..45 B5
Icknield Rd LU3 ....44 F4
Icknield Walk Fst Sch SG8 7 E7
Icknield Way Baldock SG7 .12 E1
Dagnall LU6 ....81 A8
Letchworth SG6 ....22 E6
Luton LU3 ....45 B7
Tring HP23 ....99 E4
Icknield Way E SG7 .....12 F1
Icknield Wlk SG8 ....7 F7
Idenbury Ct LU1 ....63 C7
Ilex Ct HP4 ....122 B4
Ilford Cl LU2 ....46 D3
Ilkley Rd WD19 ....175 D5
Imberfield LU4 ....44 C3
Immanuel Coll WD23 ...168 E2
Imperial Pk WD24 .....167 C8
Imperial Way
Hemel Hempstead HP3 ...138 E7
Watford WD24 ....167 C8
Impresa Pk EN11 ......135 C7
Indells AL10 ....129 F4
Ingelheim Ct SG1 ....50 D7
Ingersoll Rd EN3 ......162 C1
Inglefield EN6 ....145 A1
Ingles AL8 ....89 E2
Ingleside Dr SG1 ....36 B1
Ingram Gdns LU2 ....45 D7
Inkerman Rd AL1 ......127 E2
Inkerman St LU1 ....63 D7
Inn's Cl SG1 ....50 D6
Innes Ct HP3 ....138 D8
Innova Way Enfield EN3 ..162 F3
Holdbrook EN3 ....163 A3
Inskip Cres SG1 ....50 E5
Iona Cl SG1 ....36 F2
Iredale View SG7 ....13 A1
Irene Stebbings Ho AL4 128 C4
Iron Dr SG13 ....114 B7
Irving Cl CM23 ....76 D4
Irving Cres LU7 ....80 A8
Isabel Gate EN8 ....148 F5
Isabella Ho EN8 ....163 A5
Isabelle Cl EN7 ....147 C2
Isenburg Way HP2 .....124 D8
Isherwood Cl SG8 ....7 C8
Island Centre Way EN3 .163 A2
Island Ct CM23 ....77 A5
Islay Ho 4 WD18 ......166 F3
Islington Way SG1 ......36 F2
Italstyle Bldgs CM20 ...118 C6
Itaska Cotts WD23 .....168 E1
Ivatt Ct SG4 ....35 C7
Iveagh Cl HA6 ....174 B2
Iveagh Ct HP2 ....124 D4
Ivel Ct SG6 ....23 C4
Ivel Rd SG1 ....50 C7
Ivel Way Baldock SG7 .....24 A6
Stotfold SG5 ....11 F8
Ives Rd SG14 ....113 B7
Ivinghoe Cl
St Albans AL4 ....128 C8
Watford WD25 ....154 D4
Ivinghoe Rd
Bushey WD23 ....168 D2
Rickmansworth WD3 .....165 A2
Ivory Cl AL4 ....128 C1
Ivory Ct HP3 ....138 E8
Ivy Ct LU1 ....63 B8
Ivy Ho WD19 ....167 D3
Ivy House La HP4 .....122 E4
Ivy Lea WD3 ....165 A1
Ivy Rd LU1 ....63 C8
Ivy Terr EN11 ....135 C8
Ivy Wlk AL10 ....129 F8
Ivybridge EN10 ....135 A4

J

J Ct CM20 ....117 F1
Jackdaw Cl SG2 ....51 D4
Jackdaws AL7 ....111 C6
Jackets La HA6 ....174 B3
Jacketts Field WD5 ....153 F8
Jackman's Pl SG6 ....23 B5
Jacks La UB9 ....173 A2
Jackson Sq 10 CM23 .....76 F7
Jackson St SG7 ....12 E1
Jackson's La SG8 ....16 E5
Jacksons Dr EN7 ......148 A3
Jacob Ct EN3 ....163 A2
Jacobs Ladder AL9 .....130 C5
James Bedford Cl HA5 .175 C1
James Cl WD23 ....167 E4
James Ct Luton LU4 ......44 B2
14 Luton,New Town LU1 ....63 E6
James Foster Ho SG5 ....21 E1
James Lee Sq EN3 .....163 A1
James Marshall Commercial
Ctr AL5 ....86 A1
James Way
South Oxhey WD19 ......175 D6
Stevenage SG1 ....50 C7
Jameson Ct AL1 ....127 F4
Jameson Rd AL5 ....86 B3
Jane Cl HP2 ....125 B8
Jansel Ho LU2 ....46 B4
Jarden SG6 ....23 C4
Jardine Ct SG1 ....51 A8
Jarman Cl HP3 ....124 E1
Jarman Way
Hemel Hempstead HP2 ...124 F2
Jarman Way *continued*
Royston SG8 ....7 B7
Jarvis Cl EN5 ....171 D4
Jarvis Cleys EN7 ......147 F5
Jasmin Cl
Bishop's Stortford CM23 ...76 C6
Northwood HA6 ....174 F2
Jasmin Way HP1 ....123 E4
Jasmine Ct SG5 ....11 F7
Jasmine Dr SG13 ......114 A6
Jasmine Gdns AL10 ....130 A7
Jasons Hill HP5 ....136 B2
Jasper Cl EN3 ....162 C1
Jay Cl SG6 ....22 E8
Jaywood LU2 ....46 C6
Jeans La CM23 ....76 E7
Jeans Way LU5 ....44 A1
Jeeves Yd 5 SG4 ....34 F6
Jeffrey Cl SG8 ....7 C8
Jeffries Rd SG12 ....93 E1
Jellicoe Gdns HA7 .....176 F4
Jellicoe Rd WD18 .....167 A3
Jenkins Ave AL2 ......140 E1
Jenkins Ct HP22 ....60 C3
Jenkins La
Bishop's Stortford CM22 ...77 C5
St Leonards HP23 ....119 E3
Jenning Wood AL6 ......89 F7
Jennings Cl SG1 ....50 E3
Jennings Rd AL1 ......128 A4
Jennings Way
Barnet EN5 ....171 C6
Hemel Hempstead HP3 ...124 E1
Jenningsbury Ct SG13 ..114 A4
Jenyns Sch SG11 ....55 F7
Jepps Cl EN7 ....147 E4
Jepps La SG8 ....7 D6
Jerome Dr AL3 ....127 A1
Jersey Cl EN11 ....135 A7
Jersey Ho Enfield EN3 ...162 D1
9 Watford WD18 ....166 F3
Jersey La
St Albans, Marshalswick
AL4 ....128 B5
St Albans, Sandridge AL4 .128 C8
Jersey Rd LU4 ....44 A3
Jervis Ave EN3 ....162 E4
Jervis Rd CM23 ....76 F6
Jessop Rd SG1 ....37 A1
Jeve Cl SG7 ....13 A1
Jewell Ct WD25 ....154 D5
Jill Grey Pl SG4 ....34 F6
Jillifer Rd LU4 ....44 A2
Jim Desormeaux Bglws
CM20 ....117 E2
Jinnings The AL7 ......111 B3
Jocelyns CM17 ....118 C4
Jocketts Hill HP1 ......123 F3
Jocketts Rd HP1 ....123 F2
Jodies Ct AL4 ....128 C5
Joel St HA6 ....175 A1
John Barker Pl SG5 ......21 C1
John Ct EN11 ....115 A1
John Eliot Cl EN9 .....135 E2
John F Kennedy RC Sch
HP1 ....123 F4
John Henry Newman RC Sch
The SG1 ....36 B1
John Lamb Ct HA3 .....176 E2
John Penrose Sch UB9 .173 D2
John Sale Cl SG7 ....4 C4
John St Luton LU1 ....63 E7
3 Royston SG8 ....7 D6
John Tate Rd SG13 ....113 F6
John Warner Sch The
EN11 ....115 B1
Johnby Cl EN3 ....162 E2
Johns La HP5 ....121 E1
Johns Rd CM23 ....59 A1
Johnson Ct HP3 ....124 E1
Joiner's Cl HP5 ....136 B1
Joint The SG8 ....16 E6
Jones Rd EN7 ....147 B1
Jonquil Cl AL7 ....111 B4
Jordan Cl WD25 ....153 F4
Jordan's Way AL2 .....140 F1
Jordans AL7 ....111 C7
Jordans Rd WD3 ......165 A1
Joslyn Cl EN3 ....163 A1
Jowitt Ho 1 SG1 ....50 E6
Joyce Ct EN9 ....163 D5
Jubilee Ave
London Colney AL2 ......142 D5
Ware SG12 ....93 F2
Jubilee Cl
Lower Stondon SG16 ......10 B3
Pinner HA5 ....175 C1
Jubilee Cotts
Aspenden SG9 ....40 D5
Great Hormead SG9 ......42 A8
Jubilee Cres SG15 ....11 A2
Jubilee Ct Harpenden AL5 .86 C3
Hatfield AL10 ....130 B8
Waltham Abbey EN9 .....163 F6
Jubilee Meml Ave SG1 ..50 D8
Jubilee Rd
Letchworth SG6 ....23 D7
Stevenage SG1 ....50 B8
Watford WD24 ....154 A1
Jubilee St LU2 ....45 F1
Jubilee Trad Ctr SG6 ....23 D7
Jubilee Wlk WD4 ......139 A1
Judge St WD24 ....154 B1
Judge's Hill EN6 ......145 F2
Julia Ct LU3 ....45 B4
Julia Gate SG2 ....51 C8
Julian's Ct SG1 ....50 C8
Julian's Rd SG1 ....50 B8
Julie Ho EN11 ....135 C8
Julius Gdns LU3 ....44 F7
Junction Cotts AL8 ....110 D7
Juniper Ave AL2 ......155 A8
Juniper Cl Barnet EN5 ...171 D4
Cheshunt EN10 ....148 F6
Luton LU4 ....44 E2
Rickmansworth WD3 .....173 D7
Juniper Ct HA3 ....176 F2
Juniper Gate WD3 .....173 D8
Juniper Gdns
Oaklands AL6 ....89 E7
Shenley WD7 ....156 E6
Juniper Gn HP1 ....123 E3
Juniper Gr WD17 ......154 A1
Juniper Ho EN10 ......148 F6
Juno Rd HP2 ....124 F6
Jupiter Dr HP2 ....124 F5
Jupiter Drive Jun Mix & Inf
Sch HP2 ....124 F5
Jupiter Gate SG2 ....51 D8
Juxon Cl HA3 ....176 B2

K

Kaida Ho 6 WD3 ......165 D2
Kardwell Cl SG4 ....35 A6
Karen Ho SG16 ....10 A4
Karens Ct EN3 ....162 D2
Katemon Ct SG12 ......115 D4
Kates Cl EN5 ....171 A4
Katescroft AL7 ....110 E2
Katherine Cl HP3 ......138 E8
Katherine Pl WD5 ......154 A7
Katrine Sq HP2 ....124 E7
Kay Cl HP23 ....100 A5
Kay Wlk AL4 ....128 D3
Keats Cl
Hemel Hempstead HP2 ...105 B1
Royston SG8 ....7 C8
Stevenage SG2 ....51 C7
Keats Ho 15 AL5 ....86 B1
Keats Way SG4 ....35 C7
Keble Terr WD5 ....153 F7
Kecksy's CM21 ....97 F4
Keeble Cl LU2 ....46 E1
Keele Cl WD24 ....167 C7
Keepers Cl
Cheddington LU7 ....80 A7
Luton LU2 ....46 C2
Keiths Rd HP3 ....125 A2
Keiths Wood SG3 ....68 F5
Kelbys AL7 ....111 C7
Keller Cl SG2 ....51 B4
Kelling Cl LU2 ....45 C8
Kelly Cl WD6 ....170 D7
Kelly Ct WD6 ....170 C7
Kelman Cl EN8 ....162 D8
Kelmscott Cl WD18 ....167 A4
Kelmscott Cres WD18 ..167 A4
Kelshall WD25 ....154 E3
Kelshall St SG8 ....15 E5
Kelvin Cl LU1 ....63 E6
Kelvin Cres HA3 ......176 E3
Kemble Cl EN6 ....159 D6
Kemble Ho HA7 ....176 F5
Kemp Pl WD23 ....168 A3
Kempe Cl AL1 ....141 C7
Kempe Rd EN1 ....162 C3
Kemprow WD25 ....155 D3
Kemps Dr HA6 ....174 F3
Kempsey Cl LU2 ....46 D2
Ken Davies Ct AL3 .....127 F7
Kendal Cl LU3 ....44 D7
Kendal Rd EN9 ....163 C4
Kendale HP3 ....125 B2
Kendale Rd 3 Hitchin SG4 34 F6
Luton LU4 ....44 B2
Kendall Cl AL7 ....110 F2
Kendall Ct WD6 ....170 C8
Kendals Cl WD7 ....155 E3
Kenerne Dr EN5 ....171 E4
Kenford Cl WD25 .....154 B7
Kenilworth Cl
Borehamwood WD6 .....170 C6
Hemel Hempstead HP2 ...124 E2
Stevenage SG2 ....69 C7
Kenilworth Cres EN1 ...161 E1
Kenilworth Ct WD17 ...167 A8
Kenilworth Dr
Borehamwood WD6 .....170 D6
Croxley Green WD3 ......166 B5
Kenilworth Gdns WD19 .175 C5
Kenilworth Ho WD6 ....170 C6
Kenilworth Prim Sch
WD6 ....170 D6
Kenilworth Rd LU1 ......63 C8
Kenmare Cl SG1 ....36 F3
Kennedy Ave EN11 ....134 F6
Kennedy Cl
Cheshunt EN8 ....148 E3
London Colney AL2 ......142 D5
Pinner HA5 ....175 F4
Kennedy Rd SG12 ....71 E7
Kennel La AL5 ....85 A5
Kennelwood La AL10 ...130 B6
Kennesbourne Ct AL5 ...85 D4
Kenneth Gdns 4 HA7 ..176 F4
Kenneth Rd LU2 ....46 A1
Kennett Way SG1 ....36 F3
Kenning Rd EN11 ......135 B8
Kennington Rd LU3 .....45 B3
Kensington Ave WD18 .166 F5
Kensington Cl AL1 .....128 A1
Kensington Ct EN1 ....161 E1
Kensington Mews
WD18 ....167 A5

Kensington Way WD6 170 D6
Kensworth Lower Sch
LU6 82 F8
Kensworth Rd LU6 82 D4
Kent Cl WD6 157 D1
Kent Cres CM23 76 E4
Kent Pl SG5 34 D8
Kent Rd LU1 62 F8
Kentish La AL9 145 C7
Kenton Gdns AL1 127 F2
Kenton La HA3 176 F3
Kents Ave HP3 138 D7
Kents La SG11 55 E2
Kenwood Dr WD3 172 F8
Kenworth Cl EN8 162 D6
Kenyon Pl AL7 110 E3
Kerdistone Cl EN6 145 B1
Kernow Ct LU2 46 A1
Kerr Cl SG3 68 F5
Kerri Cl EN5 171 C5
Kerril Croft CM20 117 A1
Kershaw Cl LU3 45 A8
Kershaw's Hill SG4 34 F6
Kessingland Ave SG1 36 A1
Keston Mews WD17 167 B7
Kestrel Cl
Berkhamsted HP4 122 C3
Stevenage SG2 51 D2
Watford WD25 154 E5
Kestrel Ct 4 SG12 93 C3
Kestrel Gdns CM23 76 C6
Kestrel Gn AL10 130 A4
Kestrel Way Luton LU4 44 A5
Royston SG8 7 E8
Welwyn Garden City AL7 110 F8
Kestrel Wlk SG6 23 B3
Kestrels The AL2 154 F8
Keswick Cl AL1 128 B1
Keswick Dr EN3 162 C3
Kettering Rd EN3 162 D2
Kettle Green Rd SG10 74 E2
Ketton Cl LU2 64 A7
Ketton Ct LU2 64 A7
Kevere Ct HA6 174 B5
Kewferry Dr HA6 174 C5
Kewferry Rd HA6 174 C5
Keyfield AL1 127 D2
Keymer Cl LU2 46 C3
Keynton Cl SG14 112 F7
Keysers Rd EN10 135 B1
Kibes La SG12 93 E1
Kidner Cl LU2 45 E5
Kilbride Ct HP2 124 F7
Kilby Cl WD25 154 D4
Kildonan Cl WD17 166 F8
Kilfillan Gdns HP4 122 A4
Kilfillan Pk HP4 122 A4
Killigrew Inf Sch AL2 141 B6
Killigrew Jun Sch AL2 141 B6
Kilmarnock Dr LU2 45 E5
Kilmarnock Rd WD19 175 D6
Kiln Ave HP6 150 C1
Kiln Cl HP4 123 B6
Kiln Cotts HP2 125 B4
Kiln Ground HP3 125 A1
Kiln House Cl SG12 93 E2
Kiln House Yd SG8 7 C6
Kiln La HP5 150 B8
Kiln Way HA6 174 E4
Kilncroft HP3 125 B1
Kilnfield AL7 89 F1
Kilsmore La EN8 148 D2
Kilvinton Dr EN2 161 D1
Kilworth Cl AL7 111 B4
Kimberley SG6 11 F2
Kimberley Cl CM23 77 A5
Kimberley Rd AL3 127 D4
Kimble Cl WD18 166 E2
Kimble Cres WD23 168 C2
Kimblewick WD19 167 E1
Kimbolton Cres SG2 69 A7
Kimbolton Gn WD6 170 C5
Kimps Way HP3 139 A8
Kimpton Bottom AL5,SG4 86 E7
Kimpton Cl HP2 125 B8
Kimpton Pl WD25 154 D5
Kimpton Prim Sch SG4 66 C1
Kimpton Rd
Ayot St Peter AL6 89 A6
Codicote SG4 67 B1
Kimpton SG4,AL4 87 C7
Luton LU1,LU2 64 A6
Peters Green LU2,SG4 65 E2
Kimptons Cl EN6 158 D7
Kimptons Mead EN6 158 D7
Kinderscout HP3 125 A1
Kindersley Cl AL6 89 C6
Kindersley Way WD5 153 D8
Kinetic Bsns Ctr WD6 170 A6
King Arthur Ct EN8 162 E8
King Charles Rd WD7 156 E7
King Edward Rd
Cheshunt EN8 162 E6
Shenley WD7 156 F6
Watford WD19 167 E3
King Edward St HP3 138 D7
King Edward's Rd SG12 93 E2
King George Ave WD23 168 B3
King George Cl SG1 50 E6
King George Rd
Waltham Abbey EN9 163 C5
Ware SG12 93 E2
King George's Way SG4 66 E6
King Georges Ave
WD18 166 E5
King Georges Cl SG5 21 D1
King Harold Ct EN9 163 C6
King Harold Sch EN9 163 E6
King Harry La AL3 127 B1
King Harry St HP2 124 D2
King Henry Ct LU3 45 B2
King Henry's Mews
EN3 163 A2
King Henrys Ct EN9 163 C3
King James Ave EN6 146 E2
King James Way SG8 7 D6
King St
Bishop's Stortford CM23 76 F7
Luton LU1 63 E7
Markyate AL3 83 E5
2 Royston SG8 7 D6
Tring HP23 100 A3
Watford WD18 167 C5
King Street Mews 1
CM23 76 F7
King Williams Ct EN9 163 C4
King's Cotts CM23 77 A6
King's La WD4 152 B8
King's Mews 7 HP2 124 D4
King's Rd Cheshunt EN8 162 E5
Hertford SG13 114 A7
Hitchin SG5 34 F8
London Colney AL2 142 C5
St Albans AL3 127 C3
King's Walden Rd SG5 33 D2
King's Wlk SG8 7 D5
Kingcroft Rd AL5 107 D7
Kingfisher Cl
Harrow HA3 176 F3
Northwood HA6 174 B2
Stanstead Abbotts SG12 115 C3
Wheathampstead AL4 87 D1
Kingfisher Ct Enfield EN2 160 F1
Hitchin SG4 35 A6
Kingfisher Dr HP3 138 F6
Kingfisher Lure
Kings Langley WD4 139 B2
Rickmansworth WD3 165 B5
Kingfisher Rise SG2 51 D2
Kingfisher Way
Bishop's Stortford CM23 77 A7
Roydon CM19 116 A1
Kingham Rd SG12 94 E5
Kinghamway LU2 45 E1
Kings Ave
Hemel Hempstead HP3 138 F7
Watford WD18 167 A5
Kings Cl
Chipperfield WD4 152 B8
Northwood HA6 174 F4
5 Watford WD18 167 C5
Kings Ct
Berkhamsted HP4 122 C5
Bishop's Stortford CM23 77 A8
Harpenden AL5 107 B8
Kings Farm Rd WD3 164 D3
Kings Field Cotts WD5 153 F8
Kings Heath Pk AL5 86 C6
Kings Hedges SG5 34 C8
Kings Langley Prim Sch
WD4 138 F3
Kings Langley Sch WD4 138 E3
Kings Langley Sta WD4 139 C1
Kings Mdw WD4 139 A3
Kings Oak WD3 166 A5
Kings Oak Private Hospl The
EN2 161 A1
Kings Park Ind Est WD4 139 B2
Kings Rd Barnet EN5 171 C6
Berkhamsted HP4 122 B3
Stevenage SG1 50 D4
Kings Sch The AL5 85 F4
Kings Walden Rise SG2 51 C8
Kingsbridge Rd CM23 77 A8
Kingsbury Ave AL3 127 C4
Kingsbury Watermill★
AL3 127 B4
Kingscroft AL7 111 B7
Kingsdale Ho AL6 89 B3
Kingsdale Rd HP4 122 A3
Kingsdown SG4 35 B6
Kingsdown Ave LU2 45 D5
Kingsfield EN11 135 A8
Kingsfield Ct WD19 167 D2
Kingsfield Dr EN3 162 D4
Kingsfield Rd
Dane End SG12 71 E8
Watford WD19 167 D3
Kingsfield Way EN3 162 D4
Kingsgate AL3 127 B1
Kingshill Ave AL4 128 B6
Kingshill Ct 6 EN5 171 E5
Kingshill Inf Sch SG12 93 D3
Kingshill Way HP4 122 B2
Kingshott Sch SG4 35 B5
Kingsland Ct 7 LU1 63 F6
Kingsland Rd
Hemel Hempstead HP1 124 A1
Luton LU1 63 F6
Kingsland Way SG7 4 D4
Kingsley Ave
Borehamwood WD6 169 F7
Cheshunt EN8 148 C2
Kingsley Ct AL7 110 F2
Kingsley Rd LU3 45 A5
Kingsley Wlk HP23 100 A4
Kingsmead
Cheshunt EN8 148 D3
Cuffley EN6 146 E3
Lower Nazeing EN9 135 C1
Sawbridgeworth CM21 97 E1
St Albans AL4 128 D6
Kingsmead Rd CM23 77 A8
Kingsmill Ct 1 AL10 130 B3
Kingston Pl HA3 176 F3
Kingston Rd LU2 45 F1
Kingston Vale SG8 7 E5
Kingsway Cuffley EN6 146 E1
Luton LU4 45 A1
Royston SG8 7 C8
Stotfold SG5 11 F7
Ware SG12 93 D3
Kingsway Gdns SG5 11 F7
Kingsway Ind Est LU1 63 A8
Kingsway Inf Sch WD25 154 A5
Kingsway Jun Sch
WD25 154 A5
Kingsway North Orbital Rd
WD25 154 B5
Kingswell Ride EN6 146 E1
Kingswood Ave SG4 35 D8
Kingswood Rd WD25 154 B5
Kingwell Rd EN4 159 D1
Kinloch Ct 6 AL5 86 B1
Kinross Cres LU3 44 D8
Kinsbourne Cl AL5 85 C4
Kinsbourne Cres AL5 85 D4
Kinsbourne Ct AL5 85 F3
Kinsbourne Green La
AL5 85 B3
Kintyre Ho 2 WD18 166 F3
Kipling Cl SG4 35 C7
Kipling Gr HP2 105 B1
Kipling Pl HA7 176 F4
Kipling Rd SG8 2 E1
Kipling The LU3 45 B6
Kipling Way AL5 86 B1
Kirby Cl HA6 174 F4
Kirby Dr LU3 45 A8
Kirkcaldy Gn 1 WD19 175 C7
Kirkdale Ct 8 LU1 63 E6
Kirkdale Rd AL5 86 A2
Kirklands AL8 89 D2
Kirkwick Ave AL5 86 A1
Kit's La SG7 25 C8
Kitchener Cl AL1 128 B2
Kitcheners La SG2 38 B1
Kitching La
St Ippolyts SG4 49 F5
Stevenage SG1 50 A5
Kite Field HP4 121 E7
Kite Way SG6 22 E8
Kitsbury Ct HP4 122 B4
Kitsbury Rd HP4 122 B4
Kitsbury Terr HP4 122 B4
Kitson Way CM20 117 C1
Kitswell Rd WD7 156 A6
Kitswell Way WD7 155 F6
Kitt's End Rd EN5 158 E2
Kiwi Ct SG5 21 F1
Klondyke AL5 85 D4
Knap Cl SG6 23 D8
Knebworth Ct CM23 76 D6
Knebworth Ctry Pk★
SG3 68 C7
Knebworth Ho★ SG3 68 B6
Knebworth Path WD6 170 D5
Knebworth Prim Sch
SG3 69 A5
Knebworth Sta SG3 68 F5
Kneesworth House Hospl
SG8 2 C5
Kneesworth Rd SG8 2 F8
Kneesworth St SG8 7 C6
Knella Gn AL7 111 A6
Knella Rd AL7 111 A6
Knella Road Workshops
AL7 111 A6
Knight St CM21 97 E2
Knight's Ct CM21 97 E2
Knights Cl
Bishop's Stortford CM23 76 C8
Buntingford SG9 40 E6
Knights Ct Bushey WD23 168 D1
Standon SG11 55 F1
Knights Field LU2 45 D1
Knights Orch
Hemel Hempstead HP1 123 F5
St Albans AL3 127 C3
Knights Templar Sch The
SG7 23 E8
Knights Templars Gn
SG2 51 C8
Knightsbridge Way HP2 124 E4
Knightscote Cl UB9 173 D1
Knightsfield AL8 89 D2
Knightsfield Sch AL8 89 D3
Knoll Cres HA6 174 F2
Knoll Gn HP2 124 E5
Knoll Rise LU2 45 E4
Knoll The SG13 114 B7
Knolles Cres AL9 144 B7
Knolls Cl HP22 60 B3
Knowl Piece SG4 22 A3
Knowl Pk WD6 169 E4
Knowl Way WD6 169 F4
Knowle SG1 36 B1
Knowle Dr AL5 107 D7
Knowle Ho EN11 135 A5
Knowle The EN11 135 A5
Knutsford Ave WD24 154 D1
Knutsford Sch WD24 154 D1
Koh-I-Noor Ave WD23 168 A3
Kristiansand Way SG6 23 C8
Kymswell Rd SG2 51 C3
Kynance Cl LU2 46 A2
Kynaston Cl HA3 176 D3
Kynaston Wood HA3 176 D3
Kyrkeby SG6 23 C4
Kytes Dr WD25 154 D6

L

Laburnum Cl
Cheshunt EN8 162 D8
Luton LU3 45 C7
Laburnum Gr
Chiswell Green AL2 141 B6
Luton LU3 45 B7
Laburnum Rd EN11 135 B8
Lachbury Cl LU1 63 A6
Lackmore Rd EN1 162 C4
Lacre Way SG6 23 C7
Ladbrooke Cl EN6 159 A7
Ladbrooke Dr EN6 159 A7
Ladbrooke JMI Sch EN6 159 B7
Ladies Gr AL3 127 C5
Lady Cooper Ct HP4 122 E6
Lady Gr AL7 110 E2
Lady Spencer's Gr AL1 127 C2
Lady St John Sq SG14 92 A1
Lady Zia Wernher Sch
LU2 46 B3
Lady's Cl WD18 167 C5
Ladygrove Cotts SG4 48 F5
Ladygrove Ct SG4 48 F5
Ladyhill LU4 44 B6
Ladymeadow HP3 138 D4
Ladyshot CM20 118 B1
Ladysmith Rd
Harrow HA3 176 E1
Pitstone LU7 80 E5
St Albans AL3 127 D4
Ladywalk WD3 172 E6
Ladywell Prospect CM21 98 A1
Ladywood Cl WD3 165 C6
Ladywood Rd SG14 112 F6
Laguna Ct 2 AL1 127 E3
Laidon Sq HP2 124 D7
Lake Dr WD23 176 D8
Lake Rd EN9 135 E2
Lake The WD23 168 D1
Lake View
Bishop's Stortford CM23 76 B3
Potters Bar EN6 159 C6
Lake Villas SG9 43 B4
Lakeland Cl HA3 176 D4
Lakes Ct SG12 115 B4
Lakeside
Borehamwood WD6 170 A4
Tring HP23 100 A5
Lakeside Pl AL2 142 D4
Lakeside Rd EN8 148 C3
Lakeside Sch AL8 110 B4
Lalleford Rd LU2 46 D1
Lalsham Ho 4 WD19 175 C7
Lamb Cl Hatfield AL10 130 B4
Watford WD25 154 C5
Lamb Ct AL4 108 E7
Lamb La AL3 106 B5
Lamb Mdw SG15 11 A3
Lambert Ct WD23 167 D5
Lamberton Ct WD6 170 A8
Lambourn Chase WD7 155 F3
Lambourn Dr LU2 45 E6
Lambourn Gdns AL5 85 F3
Lambs Cl Cuffley EN6 146 F2
Dunstable LU5 44 A1
Lambs Gdns SG12 95 D4
Lambton Ave EN8 162 D6
Lamer La AL4 87 D3
Lamers Rd LU2 46 B2
Lammas Mead SG5 21 E2
Lammas Path SG2 51 B4
Lammas Rd
Cheddington LU7 80 A7
Watford WD18 167 C4
Watton at S SG14 70 D4
Lammas Way SG6 22 F8
Lammasmead EN10 148 F8
Lamorna Cl Luton LU3 44 F6
Radlett WD7 156 B5
Lamorna Ct HA3 176 E1
Lampits EN11 135 B6
Lamsey Rd HP3 124 D1
Lancaster Ave
Hadley Wood EN4 159 D1
Hitchin SG5 34 E8
Luton LU2 45 C8
Lancaster Cl SG1 36 E2
Lancaster Dr HP3 136 F4
Lancaster Rd Hitchin SG5 34 E8
St Albans AL1 127 F5
Lancaster Way
Abbots Langley WD5 153 F8
Bishop's Stortford CM23 76 C8
Welwyn AL6 89 C3
Lancing Ho 5 WD24 167 C7
Lancing Rd LU2 46 D3
Lancing Way WD3 166 B4
Landau Way EN10 148 F5
Landford Cl WD3 173 E8
Landmead Rd EN8 148 E2
Landridge Dr EN1 162 B1
Lands' End WD6 169 D3
Lane End
Berkhamsted HP4 121 F4
Hatfield AL10 129 F2
Lane Gdns WD23 168 E2
Lanefield Wlk AL8 110 C6
Lanercost Cl AL6 90 A7
Langbridge Cl SG4 35 A4
Langdale Ave AL5 86 D2
Langdale Ct 2 HP2 124 E6
Langdale Gdns EN3 162 D4
Langdale Terr WD6 170 C6
Langdon St HP23 100 A3
Langfield Cl EN9 135 E1
Langford Cl AL4 128 C5
Langford Dr LU2 46 A3
Langham Cl Luton LU2 45 D7
St Albans AL4 128 D8
Langham Ho 9 LU1 63 D8
Langholme WD23 168 C1
Langland Ct HA6 174 D3
Langland Dr HA5 175 E3
Langleigh SG6 11 F1
Langley Ave HP3 138 F8
Langley Cres
Kings Langley WD4 139 A1
St Albans AL3 127 C5
Langley Ct EN7 147 C3
Langley Gn EN9 135 D1
Langley Gr AL4 108 C2
Langley Hill WD4 138 F2
Langley Hill Cl WD4 139 A2
Langley La
Abbots Langley WD5 153 F7
Langley SG4 49 E2
Langley Lodge La WD4 153 A8
Langley Rd
Abbots Langley WD5 153 F8
Chipperfield WD4 138 B1
Watford WD17 167 A8
Langley Row EN5 171 F8
Langley St LU1 63 E6
Langley Terrace Ind Pk 10
LU1 63 E6
Langley Way WD17 166 F8
Langley Wharf WD4 139 A4
Langleybury La WD4 153 B4
Langmead Dr WD23 168 D1
Langstone Ley AL7 111 B5
Langthorne Ave SG1 50 E6
Langton Gr HA6 174 C5
Langton Ho EN11 134 F6
Langton Rd Harrow HA3 176 C3
Hoddesdon EN11 134 F6
Langwood 6 WD17 167 A8
Langwood Gdns WD17 167 A8
Langworthy HA5 176 A4
Lankester Rd SG8 7 C5
Lannock SG6 23 D4
Lannock Hill SG4 23 E1
Lannock Prim Sch SG6 23 C4
Lanrick Copse HP4 122 E5
Lansdowne Cl WD25 154 D4
Lansdowne Ct EN10 135 A3
Lansdowne Rd LU3 45 D1
Lanterns La SG2 51 D5
Lanthony Ct SG15 11 A4
Lanthorn Cl EN10 134 E4
Laporte Way LU4 44 F1
Lapwing Cl HP2 124 E6
Lapwing Dell SG6 23 B3
Lapwing Rd LU4 44 A4
Lapwing Rise SG2 51 D3
Lapwing Way WD5 154 A8
Larch Ave
Bricket Wood AL2 140 E1
Hitchin SG4 35 A4
Larch Cl EN7 147 E4
Larch La AL6 89 F8
Larch Rise HP4 122 A5
Larch View HP1 124 B2
Larches Ave EN1 162 C4
Larches The
Berkhamsted HP4 121 D5
Little Chalfont HP6 150 B1
Luton LU2 45 D1
Northwood HA6 174 C4
St Albans AL4 128 D7
Ware SG12 93 C4
Watford WD23 167 E4
Larchwood CM23 76 D5
Lark Rise AL10 130 A3
Larken Cl WD23 168 C1
Larken Dr WD23 168 C1
Larkens Cl SG11 55 D3
Larkin Pl SG8 2 D1
Larkins Cl SG7 12 F1
Larkinson SG1 50 C7
Larks Ridge AL2 141 A4
Larksfield SG12 93 E3
Larkspur Cl
Bishop's Stortford CM23 76 D6
Hemel Hempstead HP1 123 E4
Larkspur Gdns LU4 44 F2
Larksway CM23 76 C6
Larkswood Rise AL4 128 C8
Larmans Rd EN3 162 D3
Larsen Dr EN9 163 D5
Larwood Gr SG1 51 A8
Larwood Sch SG1 50 F7
Latchford Mews 8 AL4 87 D1
Latchford Pl HP1 124 A2
Latchmore Bank CM22 77 B2
Latchmore Cl SG4 34 F5
Latimer Cl
Hemel Hempstead HP2 125 B8
Pinner HA5 175 C2
Watford WD18 166 E2
Latimer Ct EN8 162 F5
Latimer Gdns
Pinner HA5 175 C2
Welwyn Garden City AL7 111 B6
Latimer Rd
Little Chalfont HP6,HP5 150 C2
Luton LU1 63 E6
Latium Cl AL1 127 D2
Lattimore Rd
St Albans AL1 127 E3
Wheathampstead AL4 108 C8

Latton Hall Cl CM20 118 A1
Lauderdale Rd WD4 153 C6
Laughton Ct WD6 170 D7
Launceston WD3 164 B3
Laundry La EN9 149 E6
Launton Cl LU3 31 B1
Laura Ct HA2 176 C1
Laural Ct EN6 146 E2
Laurance Haines Prim Sch The WD18 167 A3
Laureate Way HP1 124 B5
Laurel Ave EN6 158 F7
Laurel Bank HP3 137 F8
Laurel Cl
Hemel Hempstead HP2 124 F4
Watford WD19 167 D2
Laurel Ct EN6 146 F1
Laurel Fields EN6 158 F8
Laurel Mews SG7 12 F1
Laurel Pk HA3 176 F3
Laurel Rd AL1 127 F3
Laurel Way SG5 21 E3
Laureldene SG10 74 F1
Laurels Cl AL3 141 B8
Laurels The
Bushey WD23 176 E8
Hammond Street EN7 147 E5
Potten End HP4 123 C6
Laurelside Wlk LU5 44 A2
Lauries Cl HP1 123 C1
Laurino Pl WD23 176 C8
Lavender Cl
Bishop's Stortford CM23 76 D6
Hammond Street EN7 147 F4
Harlow CM20 117 E1
Hatfield AL10 129 F8
Luton LU2 45 E7
Lavender Cres AL3 127 C5
Lavender Ct Baldock SG7 12 E1
Hitchin SG4 35 B6
Lavender Gdns
Enfield EN2 161 B1
Harrow HA3 176 E4
Lavender Prim Sch EN2 161 E1
Lavender Rd EN2 161 D1
Lavender Way SG5 34 D7
Lavender Wlk HP2 124 D5
Lavinia Ave WD25 154 D5
Lavrock La WD3 165 F2
Law Hall La SG4 66 A8
Law Hall Lane Cotts SG4 66 A8
Lawford Ave WD3 164 C3
Lawford Cl
Chorleywood WD3 164 C3
Luton LU1 63 C7
Lawn Ave SG4 66 C1
Lawn Gdns LU1 63 D5
Lawn La HP3 138 D8
Lawn Mans EN5 171 F5
Lawn The CM20 118 B3
Lawn Vale HA5 175 E1
Lawns Cl SG5 33 C2
Lawns Ct SG8 7 D5
Lawns Dr The EN10 134 F2
Lawns The Harrow HA5 176 B3
Hemel Hempstead HP1 123 E4
Shenley WD7 156 E6
St Albans AL3 127 C4
Stevenage SG2 51 D4
Welwyn Garden City AL8 89 D1
Lawnswood EN5 171 E4
Lawrance Gdns EN8 148 D3
Lawrance Rd AL3 127 C7
Lawrence Ave
Letchworth SG6 23 A4
Sawbridgeworth CM21 97 E4
Stanstead Abbotts SG12 115 C3
Stevenage SG1 50 E7
Lawrence Cl SG14 112 E7
Lawrence Ct [4] WD19 175 D7
Lawrence End Rd LU2 65 D4
Lawrence Hall End AL7 110 E3
Lawrence Moorings CM21 97 F2
Lawrie Ct HA3 176 F3
Laxton Cl LU2 46 E1
Laxton Gdns Baldock SG7 24 A7
Shenley WD7 156 E7
Lay Brook AL4 128 A7
Layard Rd EN1 161 F1
Layham Dr LU2 46 E1
Layhill HP2 124 D5
Layston CE Fst Sch SG9 40 F8
Layston Mdw SG9 40 F6
Layston Pk SG8 7 D5
Layton St AL7 110 E3
Le Corte Cl WD4 138 F2
Lea Bank LU3 44 E6
Lea Bank Ct LU3 44 E6
Lea Bushes WD25 154 E4
Lea Cl
Bishop's Stortford CM23 59 B1
Bushey WD23 168 B4
Lea Ct AL5 86 A3
Lea Farm Jun Sch WD25 154 D4
Lea Gn AL9 130 E8
Lea Gr CM23 59 B1
Lea Manor High Sch LU3 44 F8
Lea Manor Recn Ctr LU3 44 F8
Lea Mount EN7 147 E3
Lea Prim Sch The AL5 86 B4
Lea Rd Harpenden AL5 86 B3
Hoddesdon EN11 135 C8
Holdbrook EN9 163 A5
Lea Rd *continued*
Luton LU1 63 F7
Watford WD24 154 B1
Lea Road Ind Pk EN9 163 A5
Lea Valley High Sch EN3 162 C4
Lea Valley Park Visitor Ctr★ EN9 163 C6
Lea Wlk AL5 86 C4
Leacroft AL5 86 D3
Leaders Cl HP22 60 B3
Leaf Cl HA6 174 D3
Leaf Way AL1 141 D8
Leafield LU3 44 F4
Leaford Cres WD24 153 F2
Leaford Ct WD24 153 F3
Leaforis Rd EN7 148 A3
Leafy La HP23 99 E1
Leagrave High St LU4 44 B3
Leagrave Prim Sch LU4 44 C4
Leagrave Rd LU4 45 B2
Leagrave Sta LU4 44 E5
Leahoe Gdns SG13 113 C5
Lealands High Sch LU3 44 C8
Leamington Rd LU3 45 A7
Leander Gdns WD25 154 E2
Leas The Baldock SG7 23 E7
Hemel Hempstead HP3 139 A7
Watford WD23 167 F7
Leasey Bridge La AL4 87 A1
Leasey Dell Dr AL4 87 A2
Leaside HP2 125 C2
Leaside Ct AL5 86 C3
Leaside Wlk [6] SG12 93 D1
Leat Cl CM21 97 F3
Leathersellers Cl [12] EN5 171 E6
Leathwaite Cl LU3 45 A6
Leaves Spring SG2 51 A2
Leavesden Ct WD5 154 A8
Leavesden Film Studios WD4 153 E5
Leavesden Green Jun Mix Inf Sch WD25 154 A5
Leavesden Rd WD24 154 B1
Leaview EN9 163 B6
Lebanon Cl WD17 153 D3
Lectern La AL1 141 E7
Leda Ave EN3 162 D1
Ledgemore La HP1,HP2 103 F5
Ledwell Rd LU1 62 F3
Lee Bridge Cnr LU2 85 F7
Lee Cl Hertford SG13 113 C4
Stanstead Abbotts SG12 115 C4
Lee Farm Cl HP5 136 A1
Lee The HA6 174 F5
Lee Valley Ctry Pk★ EN10 135 B2
Leeches Way LU7 80 A7
Leecroft Rd EN5 171 E5
Leefe Way EN6 146 D3
Leeming Rd WD6 169 F8
Lees Ave HA6 174 F2
Leeside Barnet EN5 171 E3
Potters Bar EN6 159 D7
Leeswood Ct SG14 112 F7
Leete Pl SG8 7 D7
Leeway Cl HA5 175 F3
Leggatts Cl WD24 153 F3
Leggatts Rise WD25 154 A4
Leggatts Way WD24 154 A3
Leggatts Wood Ave WD24 154 B3
Leggett Gr SG1 50 E8
Leggfield Terr HP1 123 F3
Leghorn Cres LU4 44 A3
Legions Way CM23 77 A8
Legra Ave EN11 135 A6
Leicester Rd LU4 44 E1
Leigh Comm AL7 110 F4
Leigh Ct WD6 170 D7
Leigh Rodd WD19 175 F7
Leighton Buzzard Rd
Great Gaddesden HP1 103 E2
Hemel Hempstead HP1 124 C5
Leighton Ct EN8 148 D2
Leighton Rd Harrow HA3 176 D1
Wingrave HP22 60 C3
Lemonfield Dr WD25 154 E6
Lemsford Ct WD6 170 C5
Lemsford La AL8 110 B4
Lemsford Rd
Hatfield AL10 130 A6
St Albans AL1 127 F4
Lemsford Springs (Nature Reserve)★ AL8 110 A5
Lemsford Village AL8 109 F5
Lennon Ct LU1 63 D7
Lennox Gn LU2 46 F2
Lensbury Cl EN8 148 E3
Leonard Ct HA3 176 E3
Leonard's Cl AL6 89 E8
Lesbury Cl LU2 46 E1
Leslie Cl SG2 51 C2
Letchfield HP5 150 B8
Letchmore Cl SG1 50 D6
Letchmore Inf Sch SG1 50 D7
Letchmore Rd
Radlett WD7 156 A3
Stevenage SG1 50 D7
Letchworth Bsns & Ret Pk SG6 23 C6
Letchworth Cl WD19 175 D5
Letchworth Gate SG6 23 B4
Letchworth La SG6 22 F3
Letchworth Mus & Art Gall★ SG6 22 F5
Letchworth Rd
Baldock SG7 23 D7
Luton LU3 45 A4
Letchworth Sta SG6 22 F6
Letter Box Row SG4 34 F3
Level's Gn CM23 58 C5
Leven Cl Cheshunt EN8 162 D6
South Oxhey WD19 175 D5
Leven Dr EN8 162 D6
Leven Way HP2 124 D7
Levenage La SG12 95 E3
Levendale LU4 44 C5
Leventhorpe Sch The CM21 97 E4
Leveret Cl WD25 154 A5
Leverstock Green CE Prim Sch HP2 125 D2
Leverstock Green Rd
Hemel Hempstead HP2 125 B3
Hemel Hempstead HP2, HP3 125 C2
Leverstock Green Way HP2,HP3 125 C3
Leverton Jun & Inf Sch The EN9 163 F5
Leverton Way EN9 163 C6
Lewes Way WD3 166 C5
Lewington Ct EN3 162 D2
Lewis Cl UB9 173 C1
Lewis Ho [3] WD18 166 F3
Lewis La SG15 11 A6
Lewsey Park Ct LU4 44 A4
Lewsey Rd LU4 44 B2
Lexington Cl WD6 169 F6
Lexington Ct EN6 158 D8
Lexington Way EN5 171 D5
Ley Hill Rd HP3 136 E2
Ley Hill Sch HP5 136 B1
Ley Ho AL7 111 C6
Ley Park Prim Sch EN10 134 F1
Ley Wlk AL7 111 C6
Leyburne Cl LU7 61 C8
Leyburne Rd LU3 45 B6
Leycroft Way AL5 107 E7
Leyden Rd SG1 50 D2
Leygreen Cl LU2 64 A8
Leyhill Dr LU1 63 B4
Leyland Ave AL1 127 D1
Leyland Cl EN8 148 C2
Leys Ave SG6 22 F6
Leys Cl UB9 173 D2
Leys Prim Sch The SG1 37 A2
Leys Rd HP3 124 F1
Leys The St Albans AL4 128 D6
Tring HP23 100 B4
Leysdown AL7 111 D6
Leyton Gn AL5 86 A1
Leyton Rd AL5 86 A1
Liberty Cl SG13 113 C3
Liberty Wlk AL1 128 C2
Library Rd LU1 63 E7
Lichfield Ho [4] WD6 170 A7
Lichfield Rd HA6 175 A1
Lichfield Way EN10 134 F1
Liddel Cl LU3 45 B3
Lidgate Cl LU4 44 B6
Lieutenant Ellis Way EN7,EN8 162 A7
Lighthorne Rise LU3 45 A7
Lightswood Cl EN7 147 D4
Lilac Ave EN1 162 C3
Lilac Cl EN7 162 B8
Lilac Gr LU3 44 C8
Lilac Rd EN11 135 B8
Lilac Way AL5 107 D6
Lilbourne Dr SG13 114 A7
Lilley Bottom LU2,SG4 47 C5
Lilley Bottom Rd SG4 48 B1
Lilleyhoo La LU2,SG5 32 F2
Lilliard Cl EN11 115 B2
Lilly La HP2 125 D7
Limberlost The AL6 89 B7
Limbrick Rd AL5 107 C6
Limbury Rd LU3 44 F4
Lime Ave Kimpton AL4 87 B7
Luton LU4 44 C3
Lime Cl Aston SG2 51 D4
Harrow HA3 176 F1
Ware SG12 93 E2
Watford WD19 167 D2
Lime Gr Royston SG8 7 E8
Totteridge N20 171 F1
Lime Tree Pl AL1 127 E2
Lime Tree Wlk
Bushey WD23 176 E8
Enfield EN2 161 C1
Rickmansworth WD3 165 B4
Lime Walk Prim Sch HP2 124 F1
Lime Way WD7 156 C8
Lime Wlk HP3 124 F1
Limedene Cl HA5 175 D2
Limekiln Cl SG8 7 E5
Limekiln La Baldock SG7 23 F7
Stansted Mountfitchet CM24 59 C5
Limes Cres [4] CM23 77 A7
Limes Ct Cheshunt EN8 162 D7
Hoddesdon EN11 135 A6
Limes Rd EN8 162 E7
Limes The Buckland SG9 27 D8
Cheshunt EN10 148 F7
Hertford SG14 113 C6
Hitchin SG5 34 D6
Luton LU1 63 E5
[2] Northwood HA6 174 E5
St Albans AL1 127 E5
Limes The *continued*
Welwyn Garden City AL7 111 A4
Limetree Ave LU1 85 A7
Limetree Ct HA5 176 A3
Limit Home Pk HP4 121 D7
Linacres LU4 44 D4
Linbridge Way LU2 46 E2
Linces Way AL7 111 B4
Lincoln Cl
Bishop's Stortford CM23 76 D5
Welwyn Garden City AL7 111 D6
Lincoln Ct
Berkhamsted HP4 122 B4
Borehamwood WD6 170 D4
Lincoln Dr
Croxley Green WD3 166 B6
South Oxhey WD19 175 C7
Lincoln Hill SG9 29 A5
Lincoln Mews AL3 127 C2
Lincoln Rd Luton LU4 45 B1
Stevenage SG1 37 B2
Lincoln Way WD3 166 B5
Lincoln's Cl AL4 128 D8
Lincot La SG4 67 C7
Lindbergh AL7 111 C6
Linden Ave WD18 166 F5
Linden Cl EN7 148 B1
Linden Cres AL1 128 C3
Linden Ct Harpenden AL5 107 B8
[4] Luton LU2 63 F8
Linden Glade HP1 124 A2
Linden Gn SG6 23 A8
Linden Lea WD25 154 A6
Linden Rd Luton LU4 44 E4
Redbourn AL3 106 A6
Linden Sq UB9 173 A4
Lindencroft SG6 12 A1
Lindens The
Bishop's Stortford CM23 76 F6
Hatfield AL10 129 F6
Hemel Hempstead HP3 137 F8
Stevenage SG1 50 E4
Lindley Cl AL5 86 A4
Lindlings HP1 123 E2
Lindrick Ho [11] WD19 175 C7
Lindsay Ave SG4 35 B5
Lindsay Cl SG8 2 C1
Lindsay Pl EN7 148 B1
Lindsay Rd LU2 46 D1
Lindsey Cl CM23 58 F1
Lindsey Rd CM23 58 F1
Lindum Pl AL3 127 A1
Linfield Ct SG14 112 F7
Lingfield Cl HA6 174 E3
Lingfield Rd Royston SG8 7 F6
Stevenage SG1 37 C1
Lingfield Way WD17 153 F1
Lingholm Way EN5 171 D4
Lingmoor Dr WD25 154 C6
Linington Ave HP5 136 A1
Link Cl AL10 130 B5
Link Dr AL10 130 B5
Link Rd
Bishop's Stortford CM23 76 F8
Hemel Hempstead HP1 124 C6
Oaklands AL6 89 F8
Watford WD24 167 D7
Link The SG6 12 A1
Link Way CM23 76 E6
Link Wlk AL10 130 B6
Linkfield AL7 110 E2
Links Ave SG13 114 B7
Links Bsns Ctr The CM23 77 C7
Links Dr
Borehamwood WD6 169 F5
Radlett WD7 155 F6
Links The Cheshunt EN8 148 D5
Welwyn Garden City AL8 110 B6
Links View AL3 127 C5
Links Way
Croxley Green WD3 166 C5
Luton LU2 45 D8
Linkside Rd CM23 77 C6
Linksway HA6 174 C2
Linkway HA5 175 D2
Linkways E SG1 50 F5
Linkways W SG1 50 F5
Linley Ct AL3 127 F6
Linley Dell LU2 46 D2
Linnet Cl Bushey WD23 168 C1
Letchworth SG6 22 E8
Luton LU4 44 A4
Linnet Rd WD5 154 A8
Linnet Wlk [1] AL10 130 A3
Linning Pond AL3 84 B1
Linsey Cl HP3 139 A7
Linster Gr WD6 170 C4
Linten Cl SG4 35 C6
Linton Ave WD6 169 F7
Lintott Cl SG1 50 D6
Linwood CM21 97 E2
Linwood Rd
Harpenden AL5 107 C7
Ware SG12 93 F3
Lion Ct WD6 170 C8
Lion Yd SG4 66 D1
Liphook Rd WD19 175 D6
Lippitts Hill LU2 45 E5
Lismirrane Ind Pk WD6 169 B3
Lismore
Hemel Hempstead HP3 125 C1
Stevenage SG2 51 C1
Lister Ave SG4 34 F5
Lister Cl SG1 36 C2
Lister Cotts WD6 169 A4
Lister Hospl SG1 36 B2
Liston Cl LU4 44 B5
Little Acre AL3 127 D6
Little Acres SG12 114 D8
Little Beechill EN2 160 D3
Little Berkhamsted La AL9,SG13 132 B3
Little Berries LU3 44 E7
Little Bridge Rd [17] HP4 122 D4
Little Burrow AL7 110 D4
Little Bushey La WD23 168 C5
Little Catherells HP1 123 F5
Little Chishill Rd SG8 18 C8
Little Dell AL8 110 D8
Little Furze Jun Mix & Inf Sch WD19 175 B7
Little Gaddesden CE Prim Sch HP4 102 C8
Little Gaddesden Ho HP4 102 E6
Little Ganett AL7 111 C4
Little Gr WD23 168 B5
Little Graylings WD5 153 E6
Little Green Jun Sch WD3 166 B6
Little Green La WD3 166 B6
Little Grove Ave EN7 147 E4
Little Hadham Prim Sch SG11 57 C2
Little Hallingbury CE Prim Sch CM22 98 C7
Little Hardings AL7 111 C7
Little Hayes WD4 139 A2
Little Heath CM22 98 F3
Little Heath La HP4 123 B4
Little Heath Prim Sch EN6 145 C1
Little Heath Spinney AL3 127 E5
Little Henleys SG12 95 D1
Little Hill WD3 164 C3
Little Hoo HP23 99 F4
Little How Croft WD5 153 C8
Little Hyde SG2 51 B4
Little La Harpenden AL5 107 C6
Pirton SG5 20 D5
Little Lake AL7 111 B3
Little Larkins EN5 171 E3
Little Ley AL7 110 E3
Little Martins WD23 168 B4
Little Mead AL10 130 B8
Little Mimms [2] HP2 124 E4
Little Mollards HP22 60 A3
Little Moss La HA5 175 E1
Little Mundells AL7 110 F8
Little Munden CE Prim Sch SG12 71 E8
Little Orch HP2 125 A5
Little Orchard Cl
Abbots Langley WD5 153 D7
Pinner HA5 175 E1
Little Oxhey La WD19 175 E6
Little Parndon Sch CM20 117 B1
Little Piper's Cl EN7 147 B2
Little Pk HP3 137 A3
Little Potters WD23 168 E2
Little Rd HP2 124 F4
Little Reddings Prim Sch WD23 168 B4
Little Ridge AL7 111 A6
Little Rivers AL7 111 A7
Little St EN9 163 C3
Little Stock Rd EN7 147 D5
Little Stream Cl HA6 174 E5
Little Thistle AL7 111 C4
Little Tring Rd HP23 99 F6
Little Twye HP23 119 F3
Little Twye Rd HP23 119 F3
Little Wade AL7 110 F3
Little Widbury SG12 93 F1
Little Widbury La SG12 93 F1
Little Windmill Hill WD4 151 F7
Little Wood Croft LU3 44 E7
Little Youngs AL8 110 C6
Littlebrook Gdns EN8 148 D1
Littlebury Cl SG5 12 A5
Littlechurch Rd LU2 46 B3
Littlecote Pl HA5 175 E2
Littlefield Rd LU2 46 B2
Littlegreen La LU1 62 E3
Liverpool Rd Luton LU1 63 D7
St Albans AL1 127 E3
Watford WD18 167 B4
Livingstone Ct EN5 171 E7
Livingstone Link SG2 51 B8
Livingstone Wlk HP2 124 F7
Lloyd Mews EN3 163 A1
Lloyd Way SG4 66 C1
Lloyd-Taylor Cl SG11 57 B2
Loates La WD17 167 C6
Loates Pasture CM24 59 D8
Local Board Rd WD17 167 D4
Locarno Ave LU4 44 C6
Lochinver House Sch EN6 145 B1
Lochnell Rd HP4 121 F6
Lock Ho HP3 138 E7
Lock View CM21 97 F2
Lockers Park La HP1 124 B3
Lockers Park Sch HP1 124 B3
Locket Rd HA3 176 F1
Lockley Cres AL10 130 B7
Lockleys Dr AL6 89 C5
Lockyer Cl EN3 163 B1
Lodge Ave WD6 169 F4
Lodge Cl Cheddington LU7 80 A7
Hertford SG14 113 C8
Lodge Cres EN8 162 D5

Lodge Ct
Abbots Langley WD25 ....154 A7
Ickleford SG5 ....21 E3
Lodge Dr Hatfield AL9 ..130 D8
Rickmansworth WD3 .....165 C5
Lodge End
Croxley Green WD3 .....166 D5
Radlett WD7 ....156 B5
Lodge Farm SG4 ....67 E1
Lodge Farm Prim Sch
SG2 ....51 C7
Lodge Gdns AL5 ....86 A2
Lodge La EN9 ....163 D4
Lodge The Harefield UB9 173 C3
Watford WD24 ....167 C7
Lodge Way SG2 ....51 A1
Lodgefield AL7 ....89 E1
Loftus Cl LU4 ....44 B3
Logans EN5 ....171 D6
Loire Mews AL5 ....107 C7
Lombardy Cl HP2 ......125 D2
Lombardy Dr HP4 ......122 D3
Lombardy Way WD6 ....169 E7
Lomond Rd HP2 ....124 D7
Lomond Way SG1 ....37 C3
London Bible Coll HA6 .174 D4
London Coll of Professional
Studies LU1 ....63 E7
London Colney Jun Mix Inf
Sch AL2 ....142 D6
London Luton Airport
LU2 ....64 D7
London Rd
Aston Clinton HP22 ......99 A4
Baldock SG7 ....23 F6
Barkway SG8 ....17 D1
Barley SG8 ....8 F1
Berkhamsted HP4 ....122 E3
Bishop's Stortford CM23 ...77 A5
Buntingford SG9 ....40 F6
Bushey WD23 ....167 F3
Harlow CM17 ....118 C2
Hemel Hempstead HP1,
HP3 ....124 A1
Hertford SG13 ....113 E5
Hertford Heath SG13 ....114 B3
Hitchin SG4 ....34 F5
Knebworth SG3 ....69 A3
Langley SG4 ....49 D5
Luton LU1 ....84 F7
Luton,New Town LU1 ......63 E4
Markyate AL3 ....83 F5
Rickmansworth WD3 .....173 E8
Royston SG8 ....7 D5
Sawbridgeworth CM21 ....97 E2
Shenley WD7 ....157 A5
St Albans AL1 ....142 C7
Stevenage SG1,SG2 ......50 D3
Stotfold SG5 ....3 A2
Tring HP23 ....100 C3
Ware SG12 ....114 E7
Welwyn AL6 ....89 C4
London Row SG15 ....11 A3
Londrina Ct 14 HP4 ....122 D4
Londrina Terr 15 HP4 ..122 D4
Long Arrotts HP1 ......124 B5
Long Barn Cl WD25 .....154 A7
Long Buftlers AL5 .....107 F8
Long Chaulden HP1 ....123 E3
Long Cl LU2 ....46 C3
Long Croft CM24 ....59 D8
Long Croft Dr EN8 .....163 A5
Long Croft Rd Luton LU1 .63 A7
Maple Cross WD3 ......172 D5
Long Cutt AL3 ....106 A6
Long Elmes HA3 ....176 C2
Long Elms WD5 ....153 D6
Long Elms Cl WD5 ......153 D6
Long Fallow AL2 ....141 A4
Long Grove Cl EN10 ....134 E4
Long Hale LU7 ....80 C3
Long Hedge LU7 ....80 C4
Long Hyde SG2 ....51 B4
Long John HP3 ....124 F1
Long La Aston SG2 ....51 E5
Bovingdon HP3 ....150 F8
Chorleywood WD3 ......164 D2
Rickmansworth WD3 .....172 F8
Whitwell SG4 ....66 A7
Long Leaves SG2 ....51 A2
Long Ley Cheddington LU7 .80 A7
Harlow CM20 ....117 F1
Welwyn Garden City AL7 .111 C6
Long Marston CE Prim Sch
HP23 ....79 B4
Long Marston Rd
Cheddington HP23,LU7 ....79 E7
Marsworth HP23 ....79 F2
Long Mdw
Bishop's Stortford CM23 ...76 D6
Markyate AL3 ....83 F5
Watton at S SG14 ....70 D4
Long Mimms 3 HP2 .....124 E4
Long Moor EN8 ....148 E2
Long Pightle Mobile Home
Pk WD3 ....152 F2
Long Ridge SG2 ....51 D1
Long Room UB9 ....173 A3
Long Row SG5 ....19 D1
Long Spring AL3 ....127 F7
Long View HP4 ....122 A6
Longacre CM17 ....118 B4
Longacres AL4 ....128 D3
Longbridge Cl HP23 ....100 A6
Longcliffe Path WD19 ..175 A7
Longcroft WD19 ....167 B2
Longcroft Ave AL5 ......85 F1
Longcroft Gdns AL8 ....110 D5
Longcroft Gn AL8 ......110 D5
Longcroft La
Bovingdon HP3 ....137 D5
Welwyn Garden City AL8 .110 D5
Longcroft Rd SG1 ....50 E7
Longcrofts EN9 ....163 E5
Longdean Pk HP3 ....139 A7
Longdean Sch HP3 .....139 B8
Longfield HP3 ....125 B1
Longfield Ave EN3 ......162 C1
Longfield Ct SG6 ....22 D7
Longfield Dr LU4 ....44 D1
Longfield Gdns HP23 ....99 E3
Longfield La EN7 ....148 A4
Longfield Rd
Harpenden AL5 ....107 C7
Tring HP23 ....99 F3
Longfields SG2 ....51 C1
Longlands HP2 ....125 A3
Longlands Cl EN8 ......162 D7
Longlands Prim Sch
EN10 ....148 F6
Longlands Rd AL7 ......110 F5
Longlees WD3 ....172 D5
Longman Ct HP3 ....138 E6
Longmans SG11 ....55 F7
Longmans Cl WD18 .....166 C3
Longmead
Buntingford SG9 ....40 D7
Hatfield AL10 ....130 B8
Letchworth SG6 ....22 E7
Woolmer Green SG3 ......69 A2
Longmeadow Dr SG5 ......21 F5
Longmeadow Gn SG2 ......51 C1
Longmeadow Jun & Inf Schs
SG2 ....51 B1
Longmore Cl WD3 ....172 F6
Longmore Gdns AL7 .....110 F6
Longridge WD7 ....156 B5
Longspring WD24 ....154 B2
Longstanton Ct HP2 ....105 B1
Longwood Rd SG14 ......112 F8
Longwood Sch WD23 ....167 F5
Loning The EN3 ....162 C1
Lonsdale HP2 ....124 E6
Lonsdale Cl Luton LU3 ...45 B5
Pinner HA5 ....175 E2
Lonsdale Ct SG1 ....50 F7
Lonsdale Rd SG1 ....50 F7
Lonsdale Sch SG1 ....50 F7
Loom La WD7 ....156 A2
Loom Pl WD7 ....156 A3
Loop Rd EN9 ....163 B7
Loppys Hill CM24 ....59 E6
Lorane Ct WD17 ....167 A7
Lord Mead La AL6,SG4 ...88 C7
Lord St Hoddesdon EN11 .134 D6
Watford WD17 ....167 C6
Lords Ave CM23 ....76 B7
Lords Cl WD7 ....156 E7
Lords Mdw AL3 ....106 A5
Lords Pl 12 LU2 ....45 D1
Lords Wood AL7 ....111 C6
Lordship Ctr SG6 ....23 A3
Lordship Farm SG6 ......23 B2
Lordship Farm Prim Sch
SG6 ....23 A3
Lordship La SG6 ....23 B4
Lordship Rd EN7 ....148 B1
Loreto Coll AL1 ....127 E3
Loring Rd HP4 ....122 C3
Lorne Rd HA3 ....176 F1
Lorraine Pk HA3 ....176 E3
Lorrimer Cl LU2 ....45 E6
Lothair Ct 3 AL10 ......130 A6
Lothair Rd LU2 ....46 A4
Loudwater Dr WD3 ......165 C5
Loudwater Ho WD3 ......165 C5
Loudwater Hts WD3 .....165 C6
Loudwater La WD3 ......165 E5
Loudwater Ridge WD3 ...165 C5
Louisa Cotts HP23 .....100 A3
Louise Wlk HP3 ....137 A3
Louisville Cl SG12 .....115 C4
Louvain Way WD25 .....154 B7
Lovatts WD3 ....166 A5
Love La
Abbots Langley WD5 .....139 F1
Ashwell SG7 ....4 A4
Kings Langley WD4 .....138 E3
Pinner HA5 ....175 E1
Lovel Cl HP1 ....124 A3
Lovell Cl SG4 ....35 A6
Lovell Rd EN1 ....162 B3
Lovering Rd EN7 ....147 C6
Lovett Rd AL2 ....142 A5
Low Hill Rd CM19 ......135 F6
Low Rd AL9 ....131 F8
Lowbell La AL2 ....142 E4
Lower Adeyfield Rd
HP2 ....124 D4
Lower Barn HP3 ....138 F8
Lower Bourne Cl 5
SG12 ....93 C3
Lower Bourne Gdns
SG12 ....93 C3
Lower Clabdens SG12 ....93 F1
Lower Cotts SG9 ....30 B2
Lower Dagnall St AL3 ..127 C3
Lower Derby Rd 4
WD17 ....167 C5
Lower Emms HP2 ....125 C8
Lower End HP22 ....60 B2
Lower Farm Cotts SG7 ....3 B7
Lower Gn AL6 ....90 E2
Lower Gower Rd SG8 .....7 D8
Lower Harpenden Rd
LU1,LU2 ....64 C3
Lower Hatfield Rd SG13 112 F1
Lower High St WD17 ...167 D4
Lower Icknield Way
Marsworth HP23 ....80 A1
Wilstone HP22,HP23 ......99 C7
Lower Innings SG5 ....34 D8
Lower King St SG8 ....7 D6
Lower Kings Rd HP4 ...122 C5
Lower Luton Rd AL4,AL5 .86 C3
Lower Mardley Hill AL6 ..89 F8
Lower Mdw EN8 ....148 D4
Lower Paddock Rd
WD19 ....167 E3
Lower Park Cres CM23 ...76 F5
Lower Paxton Rd AL1 ..127 E2
Lower Plantation WD3 .165 C6
Lower Rd
Breachwood Green SG4 ....47 F1
Chorleywood WD3 ......164 D5
Great Amwell SG12 .....114 F6
Hemel Hempstead HP3 ...139 A5
Little Hallingbury CM22 ....98 C7
Lower Sales HP1 ....123 F2
Lower Sean SG2 ....51 A3
Lower Shott EN7 ....147 F5
Lower St CM24 ....59 F7
Lower Tail WD19 ....175 E7
Lower Tub WD23 ....168 D2
Lower Yott HP2 ....124 F2
Lowerfield AL7 ....111 A5
Lowes Cl SG1 ....37 C2
Lowestoft Rd WD24 .....167 B8
Loweswater Cl WD25 ...154 C6
Lowfield CM21 ....97 E1
Lowfield Ct EN11 ....135 A6
Lowfield La EN11 ....135 A6
Lowgate La
Dane End SG12 ....72 A4
Thundridge SG12 ....72 C5
Lowlands AL9 ....130 C8
Lowson Gr WD19 ....167 E2
Lowswood Cl HA6 ....174 C2
Lowther Cl WD6 ....169 F4
Loxley Ct SG12 ....93 E1
Loxley Rd HP4 ....121 F6
Loxwood Cl HP3 ....137 F8
Lucan Rd EN5 ....171 E6
Lucas Ct EN9 ....163 F6
Lucas Gdns LU3 ....45 B8
Lucas La Ashwell SG7 .....4 E4
Hitchin SG5 ....34 D7
Lucern Cl EN7 ....147 E4
Lucerne Way LU3 ....45 C4
Lucks Hill HP1 ....123 E3
Ludgate HP23 ....99 F4
Ludlow Ave LU1 ....63 E4
Ludlow Mead WD19 .....175 B7
Ludlow Way WD3 ....166 C5
Ludwick Cl AL7 ....110 F4
Ludwick Gn AL7 ....110 F5
Ludwick Way AL7 ....110 F5
Luffenham Ho 1 WD19 175 D7
Lukes La HP23 ....79 D3
Lukes Lea HP23 ....80 A1
Lullington Cl LU2 ....46 C3
Lullington Garth WD6 ..170 B4
Lulworth Ave EN7 ......147 B2
Lumbards AL7 ....90 A1
Lumen Rd SG8 ....7 D7
Lunardi Ct SG11 ....55 C3
Lundin Wlk WD19 ......175 D6
Lundy Ho WD18 ....166 F4
Luton & Dunstable Hospl
LU4 ....44 C2
Luton & Dunstable Hospl
(Faringdon Wing) LU4 .44 C3
Luton Airport Parkway Sta
LU1 ....64 B5
Luton Dr The LU1 ....64 B3
Luton Ent Pk LU3 ....44 B8
Luton La Harpenden AL3 ..85 B1
Redbourn AL3 ....106 A8
Luton Maternity Hospl
LU4 ....44 C2
Luton Mus & Art Gall★
LU3 ....45 D2
Luton Rd Caddington LU1 .63 A4
Cockernhoe LU2 ....46 E3
Dunstable LU5 ....44 A1
Great Offley SG5 ....33 B2
Harpenden AL5 ....85 D4
Kimpton SG4 ....66 B2
Luton LU4 ....44 A7
Markyate AL3 ....83 F7
Streatley LU3 ....31 A6
Luton Regional Sports Ctr
LU2 ....46 A5
Luton Ret Pk LU1 ....64 A6
Luton Sixth Form Coll
LU2 ....45 E4
Luton Sta LU2 ....63 E8
Luton Town FC LU1 ....63 C8
Luton Univ LU1 ....63 F7
Luton Univ, Putteridge Bury
LU2 ....46 D6
Luton White Hill
Great Offley SG5 ....33 B2
Lilley LU2 ....46 F8
Luxembourg Cl LU3 .....44 D8
Luxford Pl CM21 ....97 F1
Luynes Rise SG9 ....40 E6
Lybury La AL3 ....105 F7
Lycaste Cl AL1 ....128 A2
Lych Gate WD25 ....154 D6
Lychgate Cotts HP3 ....137 B4
Lydekker Mews 1 AL5 ....86 A2
Lydia Ct AL9 ....144 C7
Lydia Mews AL9 ....144 C7
Lye Hill SG4 ....65 D7
Lye La AL2 ....141 A2
Lye The HP4 ....102 D6
Lygean Ave SG12 ....93 E1
Lygetun Dr LU3 ....44 F7
Lygrave SG2 ....69 C8
Lyle's Row SG4 ....34 F6
Lyles La AL8 ....110 E8
Lymans Rd SG15 ....11 A6
Lyme Ave HP4 ....121 D7
Lymington Ct WD25 .....154 A5
Lymington Rd SG1 ....50 B8
Lynbury Ct WD18 ....167 A6
Lynch Ct AL4 ....128 D2
Lynch Hill LU6 ....83 A8
Lynch The EN11 ....135 B6
Lyndale SG1 ....50 E4
Lyndhurst Ave HA5 .....175 B2
Lyndhurst Cl AL5 ....86 C2
Lyndhurst Dr AL5 ....86 C2
Lyndhurst Gdns HA5 ....175 B2
Lyndhurst Rd LU1 ....63 C7
Lyndon Ave HA5 ....175 E4
Lyndon Mead AL4 ....108 C2
Lyne Way HP1 ....123 F5
Lyneham Rd LU2 ....46 C1
Lynford Cl EN5 ....170 F4
Lynmouth Rd AL7 ....110 F6
Lynn Cl HA3 ....176 D1
Lynsey Cl AL3 ....106 A6
Lynton Ave Arlesey SG15 ..11 A5
St Albans AL1 ....128 C2
Lynton Crest EN6 ......159 A7
Lynton Ct CM23 ....76 E4
Lynton Par EN8 ....148 D1
Lynwood Ave LU2 ....46 A3
Lynwood Dr HA6 ....174 F2
Lynwood Hts WD3 ....165 C4
Lyon Way AL4 ....129 A3
Lyrical Way HP1 ....124 B5
Lys Hill Gdns SG14 .....113 B8
Lysander Cl HP3 ....137 A4
Lysander Way
Abbots Langley WD5 .....154 A7
Welwyn Garden City AL7 .111 D7
Lysley Pl AL9 ....145 C4
Lytham Ave WD19 ....175 D5
Lytton Ave Enfield EN3 ..162 E1
Letchworth SG6 ....22 F5
Lytton Fields SG3 ....68 F5
Lytton Gdns AL8 ....110 D6
Lytton Rd HA5 ....175 E3
Lytton Way SG1 ....50 C6
Lyttons Way EN11 ......115 A1

M

Mabbutt Cl AL2 ....140 E1
Mabey's Wlk CM21 ....97 B1
Macaulay Rd LU4 ....44 A2
Macdonnell Gdns WD25 153 F4
Macer's La EN10 ....148 F7
Macers Ct EN10 ....148 F7
Macfadyen Webb Ho
SG6 ....23 A7
Macintosh Cl EN7 ......147 D5
Macintyre Sch HP22 ......60 C3
Mackenzie Sq SG2 ....51 B3
Mackerel Hall SG8 ....7 B6
Maddesfield Ct WD7 ....156 E6
Maddison Hts WD18 .....166 F5
Maddles SG6 ....23 D4
Maddox Rd Harlow CM20 117 E1
Hemel Hempstead HP2 ...125 B3
Made Feld SG1 ....50 F5
Madford Ret Pk LU4 ......44 F2
Madgeways Cl SG12 .....114 F5
Madgeways La SG12 .....114 F5
Magdalene Ct SG7 ....12 F1
Magellan Cl SG2 ....51 D5
Magisters Lodge WD3 ..166 A3
Magna Cl AL5 ....107 D6
Magnaville Rd
Bishop's Stortford CM23 ...76 E4
Bushey WD23 ....168 F2
Magnolia Ave WD5 ......154 A7
Magnolia Cl
Hertford SG13 ....114 A6
Park Street AL2 ....141 D5
Magpie Cl EN1 ....162 A1
Magpie Cres SG2 ....51 D4
Magpie Hall Rd WD23 ..176 E8
Magpie Wlk 2 AL10 .....130 A3
Magpies The LU2 ....45 E6
Maiden St SG4 ....24 C1
Maidenhall Inf Sch LU4 .45 A2
Maidenhall Jun Sch LU4 .45 A2
Maidenhall Rd LU4 ....45 A2
Maidenhead St 3 SG14 113 D6
Maidenhead Yd SG14 ...113 D6
Main Ave HA6 ....174 C7
Main Par WD3 ....164 C5
Main Rd SG14 ....91 D3
Main Rd N HP4 ....81 A6
Main Rd S HP4 ....81 D4
Maison Alfont HA3 .....176 E2
Maitland Rd CM24 ....59 E6
Major Haddock Cl SG8 ....7 C4
Malden Fields WD23 ....167 D4
Malden Ho 15 WD19 .....175 C7
Malden Lodge 2 WD17 167 A7
Malden Rd
Borehamwood WD6 ......170 A6
Watford WD17 ....167 B7
Maldon Ct AL5 ....86 B2
Malham Cl LU4 ....44 F2
Malins Cl EN5 ....171 C4
Mall The AL2 ....141 C4
Mallard Gdns LU3 ....45 A5
Mallard Rd Royston SG8 ...7 C6
Stevenage SG2 ....51 D2
Watford WD5 ....154 A8
Mallard Way
Northwood HA6 ....174 C3
Roydon CM19 ....116 A1
Watford WD25 ....154 E3
Mallards Ct WD19 ......175 F7
Mallards The HP3 ......138 F6
Mallion Ct EN9 ....163 F6
Mallories CM20 ....117 F2
Mallow The LU3 ....44 F3
Mallow Wlk
Goff's Oak EN7 ....147 D3
Royston SG8 ....7 E5
Malm Cl WD3 ....173 D8
Malmes Croft HP3 ......125 C1
Malmsdale AL8 ....89 D2
Maltby Dr EN1 ....162 B1
Malthouse Ct 5 AL1 ....127 D2
Malthouse Gn LU2 ....46 F1
Malthouse La SG5 ....12 A7
Malthouse Pl WD7 ......156 A5
Malthouse The 15 SG14 .113 D6
Malting Cotts SG9 ....40 D5
Malting La Aldbury HP23 101 D5
Braughing SG11 ....55 E7
Dagnall HP4 ....81 C5
Much Hadham SG10 ......74 F2
Malting Mead AL10 .....130 C6
Maltings Cl Baldock SG7 ..13 B1
Royston SG8 ....7 C7
Maltings Ct 2 SG7 ....23 F8
Maltings Dr AL4 ....108 C8
Maltings Ind Est The
SG12 ....115 D4
Maltings La SG8 ....9 E2
Maltings Mews SG13 ....113 C5
Maltings Orch SG5 ....20 D3
Maltings The
Abbots Langley WD4 .....153 C5
Hemel Hempstead HP2 ...124 D4
Letchworth SG6 ....12 C1
Royston SG8 ....7 C7
St Albans AL1 ....127 D3
Walkern SG2 ....52 B8
Malus Cl HP2 ....125 A4
Malvern Cl Bushey WD23 168 C3
Hatfield AL10 ....129 F6
St Albans AL4 ....128 C7
Malvern Rd Enfield EN3 .162 E2
Luton LU1 ....63 B7
Malvern Way
Croxley Green WD3 .....166 B4
Hemel Hempstead HP2 ...124 F6
Malvern Way Inf Sch
WD3 ....166 C4
Malzeard Ct 17 LU3 .....45 D1
Malzeard Rd LU3 ....45 D1
Manan Cl HP3 ....125 C1
Manchester Cl SG1 ....36 F3
Manchester St LU1 ....63 E7
Mancroft Rd LU1 ....62 E2
Mandela Pl 4 WD24 .....167 D7
Mandelyns HP4 ....121 E7
Mandeville SG2 ....69 C8
Mandeville Cl
Hertford SG13 ....113 C3
Hoddesdon EN10 ....134 F3
Watford WD17 ....153 F1
Mandeville Dr AL1 .....141 D8
Mandeville Prim Sch
Sawbridgeworth CM21 ....97 D3
St Albans AL1 ....141 D8
Mandeville Rd
Enfield EN3 ....162 E3
Hertford SG13 ....113 C3
Potters Bar EN6 ....159 C7
Mandeville Rise AL8 ...110 D8
Mangrove Dr SG13 ......113 E4
Mangrove Gn LU2 ....46 E4
Mangrove La SG13 ......113 E2
Mangrove Rd
Cockernhoe LU2 ....46 E4
Hertford SG13 ....113 E5
Luton LU2 ....46 C2
Manhattan Ave WD18 ...166 F5
Manland Ave AL5 ....86 C2
Manland Prim Sch AL5 ...86 B3
Manland Way AL5 ....86 C3
Manley Highway SG5 ......34 B7
Manley Highway Cotts
SG5 ....34 A7
Manley Rd HP2 ....124 E4
Manly Dixon Dr EN3 ....162 E2
Mannicotts AL8 ....110 B6
Manning Ct WD19 ....167 D3
Manning Pl LU2 ....46 E2
Manor Ave HP3 ....138 D8
Manor Cl Barnet EN5 ....171 E5
Berkhamsted HP4 ....122 C4
Hatfield AL10 ....129 F8
Hertford SG14 ....113 D8
Ickleford SG5 ....21 E3
Letchworth SG6 ....22 F3
Manor Cotts
Chorleywood WD3 ......164 B3
Northwood HA6 ....174 F2
Manor Cres SG4 ....35 B6
Manor Ct Caddington LU1 .62 F4
Cheshunt EN8 ....162 D8
Enfield EN1 ....162 B3
Harefield UB9 ....173 C1

Manor Ct *continued*
Potters Bar EN6 .....158 F7
Radlett WD7 .....155 F1
Waltham Abbey EN9 .....163 D6
Manor Dr AL2 .....141 A4
Manor Farm Bsns Pk SG5 .....19 A6
Manor Farm Cl LU4 .....44 C3
Manor Farm La LU7 .....61 C8
Manor Farm Rd EN1 .....162 B4
Manor Farm Stables SG3 68 C5
Manor Fields Prim Sch CM23 .....76 D5
Manor Ho The 2 HA6 .....174 F5
Manor House Dr
Northwood HA6 .....174 B3
Stevenage SG2 .....51 D7
Manor House Gdns WD5 .....153 D8
Manor Links CM23 .....77 C7
Manor Lodge Sch WD7 .143 C1
Manor Par AL10 .....129 F8
Manor Place Ind Est WD6 .....170 C6
Manor Pound Rd LU7 ...80 A7
Manor Rd Barnet EN5 ...171 E5
Bishop's Stortford CM23 ...77 A7
Caddington LU1 .....62 F2
Cheddington LU7 .....79 F7
Harlow CM17 .....118 C5
Hatfield AL10 .....129 F8
Hoddesdon EN11 .....135 A7
Lea Valley AL4 .....86 F2
London Colney AL2 .....142 C5
Luton LU1 .....63 F6
Potters Bar EN6 .....159 A8
St Albans AL1 .....127 E4
Stansted Mountfitchet CM24 .....59 E5
Tring HP23 .....100 A4
Waltham Abbey EN9 .....163 D6
Watford WD17 .....167 B8
Manor St HP4 .....122 D4
Manor View SG2 .....51 B1
Manor Way
Borehamwood WD6 .....170 C6
Cheshunt EN8 .....148 E1
Croxley Green WD3 .....166 B5
Letchworth SG6 .....22 F3
Potters Bar EN6 .....145 A1
Manorcroft Par 6 EN8 .148 D1
Manorside EN5 .....171 E5
Manorville Rd HP3 .....138 C7
Mansard Cl HP23 .....100 A3
Mansards The AL1 .....127 F4
Manscott Ho 8 WD19 ..175 D7
Manscroft Rd HP1 .....124 B5
Mansdale Rd AL3 .....105 F4
Manse Ct AL3 .....83 F5
Mansells La SG4 .....67 F3
Mansfield CM21 .....97 A1
Mansfield Ct SG14 .....113 C8
Mansfield Gdns SG14 ..113 C8
Mansfield Mews 1 SG7 .23 F8
Mansfield Rd Baldock SG7 23 E8
Luton LU4 .....45 B1
Mansion Dr HP23 .....100 B3
Mansion The HP4 .....122 E6
Manston Cl EN8 .....148 C1
Manston Dr CM23 .....59 B1
Manston Way AL4 .....128 D2
Manton Dr LU2 .....45 D3
Manton Rd Hitchin SG4 ...35 B6
Holdbrook EN3 .....163 A1
Manx Cl LU4 .....45 A2
Maple Ave
Bishop's Stortford CM23 ...76 D8
St Albans AL3 .....127 C7
Maple Cl
Bishop's Stortford CM23 ...76 D8
Hatfield AL10 .....130 A4
Watford WD23 .....167 E7
Maple Cotts AL5 .....107 B5
Maple Cross Jun Mix Inf Sch WD3 .....172 E5
Maple Ct
5 Borehamwood WD6 ...170 A5
16 Luton LU1 .....63 D6
5 Pinner HA5 .....175 C1
Stanstead Abbotts SG12 ..115 D3
Watford WD25 .....154 D3
Maple Flats AL5 .....86 A3
Maple Gn HP1 .....123 E5
Maple Gr
Bishop's Stortford CM23 ...76 D8
Watford WD17 .....167 A8
Welwyn Garden City AL7 ...89 F1
Maple Leaf Cl WD5 .....154 A7
Maple Lodge SG14 .....113 C5
Maple Lodge Cl WD3 ...172 E6
Maple Pk EN11 .....135 C6
Maple Rd AL5 .....85 F1
Maple Rd E LU4 .....63 B8
Maple Rd W LU4 .....63 B8
Maple River Ind Est CM20 .....118 B6
Maple Sch AL1 .....127 E4
Maple Spring CM23 .....76 D8
Maple Way
Kensworth Common LU6 ...82 E8
Royston SG8 .....7 E8
Maplecroft La EN9 .....135 E2
Maplefield AL2 .....141 C2
Mapleleaf Villas EN8 ...148 D4
Maples Ct 1 SG5 .....34 E7
Maples The
Goff's Oak EN7 .....147 E3
Hitchin SG4 .....34 F5
Maplethorpe Ct SG12 ...93 C1
Mapleton Cres EN3 .....162 C1
Maplewood SG12 .....93 C3
Maplewood Ct 3 HA6 ..174 F5
Maran Ave AL6 .....89 C4
Marbury Pl LU3 .....44 F4
Marchmont Gn HP2 .....124 D5
Marconi Way AL4 .....128 D3
Marcus Cl 1 SG1 .....51 C8
Marden Hill Ho AL6 .....111 F8
Mardle Cl LU1 .....62 E2
Mardlebury Rd SG3 .....69 B1
Mardley Ave AL6 .....90 A8
Mardley Dell AL6 .....68 F1
Mardley Hill AL6 .....69 A1
Mardley Hts AL6 .....69 A1
Mardley Wood AL6 .....68 F1
Mardleybury Ct SG3 .....69 A1
Mardon 1 HA5 .....175 F3
Mardyke Rd CM20 .....118 A2
Marford Rd
Hatfield AL4,AL6 .....109 C7
Wheathampstead AL4 .....108 E8
Margaret Ave AL3 .....127 D5
Margaret Cl
Abbots Langley WD5 .....153 F7
Potters Bar EN6 .....159 C6
Waltham Abbey EN9 .....163 D6
Margaret Cotts WD7 ...156 C8
Margaret Wix Prim Sch AL3 .....127 C7
Margeholes WD19 .....175 E8
Margery Wood AL7 .....90 A1
Margherita Pl EN9 .....163 F5
Margrave Gdns 4 CM23 .76 E5
Marguerite Way CM23 ...76 C6
Marian Gdns WD25 .....154 B6
Maricas Ave HA3 .....176 D2
Marigold Pl CM17 .....118 B4
Marina Gdns EN8 .....148 C1
Mariner Way 2 HP2 .....125 A2
Marion Cl WD23 .....167 F8
Marion Wlk 4 HP2 .....124 F8
Mark Hall Comp Sch CM17 .....118 C3
Mark Hall Cycle Mus & Gdns★ CM20 .....118 B3
Mark Hall Moors CM20 .118 B3
Mark Rd HP2 .....125 B5
Markab Rd HA6 .....175 A5
Markeston Gn WD19 ...175 D6
Market Hill
Buntingford SG9 .....40 E7
6 Royston SG8 .....7 D6
Royston SG8 .....7 D5
Market Ho CM20 .....117 D1
Market Oak La HP3 .....139 A7
Market Pl Hatfield AL10 ..130 B6
6 Hertford SG14 .....113 D6
Hitchin SG5 .....34 E7
St Albans AL3 .....127 D3
Stevenage SG1 .....50 D5
Watford WD17 .....167 C5
Market Sq
6 Bishop's Stortford CM23 76 F7
Luton LU1 .....63 B6
Stevenage SG1 .....50 D5
Waltham Abbey EN9 .....163 C6
Market St
7 Bishop's Stortford CM23 76 F7
Harlow CM17 .....118 C4
Hertford SG14 .....113 D6
Watford WD18 .....167 B5
Markfield Cl LU3 .....45 C7
Markham Cl WD6 .....169 F6
Markham Rd
Hammond Street EN7 .....147 C6
Luton LU3 .....45 C8
Markyate Rd LU1 .....63 B1
Markyate Village Sch AL3 .....83 D6
Marlborough Cl
Bishop's Stortford CM23 ...76 F5
Oaklands AL6 .....89 F8
Weston SG4 .....37 B8
Marlborough Ct
Luton LU1 .....63 D7
Northwood HA6 .....174 F3
Marlborough Gate AL1 ..127 E3
Marlborough Ho HP4 ..122 B3
Marlborough Pk AL5 ..107 C7
Marlborough Rd
Luton LU3 .....45 D1
St Albans AL1 .....127 E3
Stevenage SG2 .....51 C5
Watford WD18 .....167 B5
Marlborough Rise HP2 .124 E6
Marlborough Sch AL1 ..141 C8
Marle Gdns EN9 .....163 C7
Marley Ct EN10 .....148 F8
Marley Rd AL7 .....111 A4
Marlin Cl HP4 .....121 F5
Marlin Copse HP4 .....122 A3
Marlin Hill HP23 .....120 A8
Marlin Sq WD5 .....153 F8
Marlins Cl WD3 .....164 E7
Marlins End HP4 .....121 F3
Marlins Mdw WD18 .....166 D3
Marlins The HA6 .....174 F5
Marlins Turn HP1 .....124 B6
Marlow Ave LU1 .....63 A8
Marlowe Cl SG2 .....51 C8
Marlowes HP1 .....124 D3
Marmet Ave SG6 .....22 E6
Marnham Rise HP1 .....124 A5
Marquis Cl
Bishop's Stortford CM23 ...76 B7
Harpenden AL5 .....86 D2
Marquis Ct 9 LU2 .....45 D1
Marquis La AL5 .....86 D2
Marrilyne Ave EN3 .....162 F1
Marriott Rd Barnet EN5 .171 D6
Luton LU3 .....45 B6
Marriott Terr WD3 .....164 F5
Marriotts CM17 .....118 C5
Marriotts Sch SG2 .....51 A6
Marriotts Way HP3 .....124 D1
Marryat Rd EN1 .....162 B4
Marschefield SG5 .....11 E6
Marsden Cl AL8 .....110 B4
Marsden Gn AL8 .....110 B4
Marsden Rd AL8 .....110 C5
Marsh Cl EN8 .....162 F6
Marsh Hill EN9 .....149 E4
Marsh Ho LU3 .....44 F4
Marsh La Harlow CM17 ..118 E5
Stanstead Abbotts SG12 ..115 D4
Ware SG12 .....114 E8
Marsh Rd LU3 .....44 F4
Marshal's Dr AL1 .....128 A6
Marshall Ave AL3 .....127 F6
Marshall Rd LU2 .....46 C2
Marshall's La SG12,SG11 .72 C2
Marshalls Heath La AL4, AL5 .....87 A4
Marshalls Way AL4 .....86 F2
Marshals Ct AL1 .....128 B5
Marshalswick La AL1 ...128 B6
Marshbarns CM23 .....76 C8
Marshcroft Dr EN8 .....148 F1
Marshcroft La HP23 ....100 D6
Marshe Cl EN6 .....159 D7
Marshgate Harlow CM20 .117 E3
Stevenage SG1 .....50 D5
Marshgate Dr SG13 .....113 E7
Marshgate Trad Est SG13 .....113 E7
Marshmoor Cres AL9 ..130 D1
Marshmoor La AL9 .....144 D8
Marsom Gr LU3 .....45 B8
Marston Cl HP3 .....125 A2
Marston Ct HP23 .....79 B4
Marston Gdns LU2 .....45 D4
Marston Rd EN11 .....135 B7
Marsworth Ave HA5 ....175 D2
Marsworth CE Inf Sch HP23 .....80 A2
Marsworth Cl WD18 ....166 E2
Marsworth Rd LU7 .....80 D4
Marsworth Resr Nature Reserve★ HP23 .....100 A8
Marten Gate AL4 .....128 A7
Martham Ct AL5 .....86 C3
Marthorne Cres HA3 ...176 D1
Martian Ave HP2 .....124 F6
Martin Cl AL10 .....130 A3
Martin Way SG6 .....22 D5
Martindale Ct SG7 .....23 F6
Martindale Prim Sch HP1 .....123 F4
Martindale Rd HP1 .....123 F4
Martindales The LU2 ....63 F7
Martinfield AL7 .....110 F7
Martinfield Bsns Ctr AL7 .....110 F7
Martingale Rd SG8 .....7 E6
Martini Dr EN3 .....163 A2
Martins Cl WD7 .....155 E3
Martins Dr Cheshunt EN8 148 E3
Hertford SG13 .....114 B6
Martins Way SG1 .....36 E1
Martins Wlk WD6 .....170 A5
Martins Wood Prim Sch SG1 .....37 B1
Martlesham AL7 .....111 E6
Martyr Cl AL1 .....141 D7
Marwood Cl WD4 .....138 F2
Mary Brash Ct LU2 .....46 C3
Mary Cross Cl HP23 ....100 D1
Mary Exton Jun Mix Inf Sch SG4 .....35 C7
Mary McArthur Pl CM24 .59 E8
Mary Park Gdns CM23 ...76 F4
Mary Proud Ct AL6 .....89 E7
Maryland AL10 .....129 F5
Marymead Ct SG2 .....69 A8
Marymead Dr SG2 .....69 A8
Marymead Ind Est SG2 ..69 B8
Maryport Rd LU4 .....45 A2
Masefield SG4 .....35 C7
Masefield Ave
Borehamwood WD6 .....170 B4
Stanmore HA7 .....176 F5
Masefield Ct AL5 .....86 B4
Masefield Rd AL5 .....86 B4
Masefield Way SG8 .....2 D1
Maslen Rd AL4 .....128 C1
Mason Cl WD6 .....170 D7
Mason Way EN9 .....163 F6
Mason's Yd 2 HP4 .....122 D4
Masons Ct CM23 .....76 E7
Masons Rd Enfield EN1 ..162 C3
Hemel Hempstead HP2 ...125 B4
Masterman Wharf 12 CM23 .....76 F7
Masters Cl LU1 .....63 B5
Matching La CM23 .....76 D8
Mathams Dr CM23 .....76 D5
Mathews Cl SG1 .....36 D1
Matlock Cl EN5 .....171 D4
Matlock Cres Luton LU4 ..44 C1
South Oxhey WD19 .....175 C7
Matthew Gate SG4 .....35 A5
Mattocke Rd SG5 .....21 C1
Maud Jane's Cl LU7 .....80 E5
Maude Cres WD24 .....154 B1
Maulden Cl LU2 .....46 C1
Maxted Cl HP2 .....125 C5
Maxted Cnr HP2 .....125 B6
Maxted Rd HP2 .....125 C6
Maxwell Cl WD3 .....173 A8
Maxwell Rd
Borehamwood WD6 .....170 B6
Northwood HA6 .....174 E3
St Albans AL1 .....128 B2
Stevenage SG1 .....50 B5
Maxwell Rise WD19 .....167 E2
Maxwell's Path SG5 .....34 D8
May Cl AL3 .....127 D5
May Cotts WD18 .....167 C4
May Gdns WD6 .....169 D3
May St Great Chishill SG8 ...9 E2
Luton LU1 .....63 E5
Mayall Cl EN3 .....163 A1
Maybury Ave EN8 .....148 B3
Maybury Cl EN1 .....162 B1
Maycock Gr HA6 .....174 F4
Maycroft Letchworth SG6 ..12 A1
Pinner HA5 .....175 B1
Maycroft Rd EN7 .....147 E5
Maydencroft La SG4 .....34 E3
Maydwell Lodge WD6 ..169 F7
Mayer Rd EN9 .....163 B3
Mayes Cl CM23 .....77 D8
Mayfair Cl AL4 .....128 C8
Mayfare WD3 .....166 D4
Mayfield
Waltham Abbey EN9 .....163 D5
Welwyn Garden City AL8 ...89 C2
Mayfield Cl Harlow CM17 118 F4
Harpenden AL5 .....85 E3
Mayfield Inf Sch EN8 ...148 E4
Mayfield Pk CM23 .....76 D3
Mayfield Rd LU2 .....46 B4
Mayflower Ave HP2 ....124 D3
Mayflower Cl
Codicote SG4 .....67 F1
Hertingfordbury SG14 ....112 E4
Lower Nazeing EN9 .....149 E8
Mayflower Gdns CM23 ...76 B6
Mayflower Rd AL2 .....141 B4
Mayhill Rd EN5 .....171 E3
Maylands Ave HP2 .....125 B5
Maylands Ct HP2 .....125 B4
Maylands Rd WD19 .....175 C6
Mayles Cl SG1 .....50 B7
Maylin Cl SG4 .....35 C8
Maylins Dr CM21 .....97 D2
Maynard Ct
Holdbrook EN3 .....163 A1
Waltham Abbey EN9 .....163 F5
Maynard Dr AL1 .....141 D8
Maynard Pl EN6 .....146 E2
Maynard Rd HP2 .....124 D2
Mayne Ave Luton LU4 ....44 C4
St Albans AL3 .....127 A2
Mayo Cl EN8 .....148 C3
Mayo Gdns HP1 .....124 B2
Maypole St CM17 .....118 C1
Mays La EN5 .....171 D3
Mayshades Cl SG3 .....69 A2
Maythorne Cl WD18 ....166 E5
Maytree Cres WD24 ....153 F4
Maytree La HA7 .....176 F3
Maytrees Hitchin SG4 .....35 A6
Radlett WD7 .....156 A2
Maze Green Hts CM23 ...76 C7
Maze Green Rd CM23 ...76 D7
Mazoe Cl CM23 .....76 F5
Mazoe Rd CM23 .....76 F5
McAdam Cl EN11 .....135 A8
Mcclintock Pl EN3 .....163 B2
McDonald Ct AL10 .....130 A3
McDougall Rd 13 HP4 ..122 D4
McGredy EN7 .....148 B2
McKellar Cl WD23 .....176 C8
McKenzie Rd EN10 .....135 A3
Mead Bsns Ctr SG13 ....113 E7
Mead Cl Harrow HA3 ....176 D2
Stevenage SG1 .....50 F6
Mead Ct
Stansted Mountfitchet CM24 .....59 D7
Waltham Abbey EN9 .....163 B5
Mead Ho AL10 .....130 B8
Mead La SG13 .....113 E7
Mead Park Ind Est CM20 .....117 F4
Mead Pl WD3 .....165 B1
Mead Rd WD7 .....157 A6
Mead The Cheshunt EN8 .148 C2
Hitchin SG5 .....21 F2
Hoddesdon EN10 .....135 B2
South Oxhey WD19 .....175 E7
Mead View SG9 .....43 E6
Mead Way WD23 .....167 E7
Meadgate Rd EN9 .....135 C3
Meadow Ave WD7 .....156 C8
Meadow Cl Barnet EN5 ..171 F3
Bricket Wood AL2 .....141 A2
Datchworth SG3 .....69 D1
Enfield EN3 .....162 E1
Hertford SG13 .....113 F7
London Colney AL2 .....142 D4
St Albans AL4 .....128 C6
Tring HP23 .....100 A4
Welham Green AL9 .....144 D7
Meadow Croft
Caddington LU1 .....62 F4
Hatfield AL10 .....129 F5
Meadow Dell AL10 .....129 F5
Meadow Gn AL8 .....110 C6
Meadow La LU7 .....80 E3
Meadow Rd
Berkhamsted HP4 .....122 B6
Borehamwood WD6 .....170 B7
Bushey WD23 .....168 B4
Hemel Hempstead HP3 ...139 A7
Luton LU3 .....45 B4
Watford WD25 .....154 B5
Meadow The
Hertford Heath SG13 .....114 E2
Welwyn Garden City AL7 ..111 C6
Meadow View
Buntingford SG9 .....40 D6
Whitwell SG4 .....66 E6
Meadow Way
Bedmond WD5 .....139 F4
Caddington LU1 .....62 E4
Codicote SG4 .....67 E1
Great Offley SG5 .....33 C3
Hitchin SG5 .....34 D6
Kings Langley WD4 .....139 A1
Letchworth SG6 .....22 F5
Potters Bar EN6 .....159 A5
Rickmansworth WD3 .....165 C2
Sawbridgeworth CM21 .....98 A1
Stevenage SG1 .....50 F5
Stotfold SG5 .....11 F6
Therfield SG8 .....16 A6
Meadow Way The HA3 ..176 E2
Meadow Wlk
Harpenden AL5 .....107 C8
Standon SG11 .....55 E2
Meadow Wood Sch WD23 .....168 C4
Meadowbank Hitchin SG4 .22 B1
Kings Langley WD4 .....139 A1
Watford WD19 .....167 C2
Meadowbanks EN5 .....171 A4
Meadowbrook HP23 .....100 B6
Meadowcroft
Berkhamsted HP4 .....121 D7
Bushey WD23 .....168 B3
St Albans AL1 .....142 A8
Stansted Mountfitchet CM24 .....59 E7
Meadowcross EN9 .....163 E5
Meadowlands CM23 .....59 A2
Meadows The
Bishop's Stortford CM23 ...76 E5
Breachwood Green SG4 ....47 E1
Hemel Hempstead HP1 ...123 E4
Sawbridgeworth CM21 .....98 A2
Meadows View Cotts SG12 .....94 C7
Meadowside WD25 .....154 B8
Meadowsweet Cl CM23 ..76 C6
Meads La AL4 .....87 D1
Meads Prim Sch The LU3 .....45 A6
Meads The
Berkhamsted HP4 .....121 F6
Bricket Wood AL2 .....140 F2
Letchworth SG6 .....22 E6
Luton LU3 .....45 A3
Stansted Mountfitchet CM24 59 F6
Tring HP23 .....100 B4
Meadview Rd SG12 .....114 D8
Meadway Barnet EN5 ....171 F5
Berkhamsted HP4 .....122 E5
Colney Heath AL4 .....143 D8
Enfield EN3 .....162 D3
Harpenden AL5 .....107 E8
Hoddesdon EN11 .....135 A4
Knebworth SG3 .....68 F4
Stevenage SG1 .....50 A6
Welwyn Garden City AL7 ..110 F4
Stevenage SG1 .....50 B7
Meadway Cl HA5 .....176 B4
Meadway The EN6 .....146 F2
Meautys AL3 .....127 A1
Medalls Link SG2 .....51 A3
Medalls Path SG2 .....51 A3
Medcalf Rd EN3 .....162 F2
Medina Rd LU4 .....45 A1
Medlows AL5 .....85 E2
Medow Mead WD7 .....155 F6
Medway Cl WD25 .....154 C5
Medway Rd HP2 .....124 F8
Medwick Mews HP2 ....125 B8
Mees Cl LU3 .....31 A1
Meeting Alley WD17 ...167 C5
Meeting House La
Baldock SG7 .....12 E1
Buntingford SG9 .....40 E7
Megg La WD4 .....138 B1
Melbourn Rd SG8 .....7 D7
Melbourn St SG8 .....7 D6
Melbourne Cl
St Albans AL3 .....127 F7
Stotfold SG5 .....11 F6
Melbourne Ct
Cheshunt EN8 .....162 F5
Welwyn Garden City AL8 ..110 B5
Melbourne Rd WD23 ...168 B3
Melford Cl 3 LU2 .....46 D1
Melings The HP2 .....125 B8
Melne Rd SG2 .....69 B8
Melrose Ave
Borehamwood WD6 .....170 B4
Potters Bar EN6 .....159 B7
Melrose Ct EN8 .....148 D2
Melrose Pl WD17 .....153 F1
Melson Sq 8 LU1 .....63 E7
Melson St LU1 .....63 E7
Melsted Rd HP1 .....124 B3
Melvern Cl SG2 .....69 B7
Melvyn Cl EN7 .....147 B3

Memorial Rd LU3 44 F4
Mendip Cl AL4 128 C8
Mendip Rd WD23 168 C3
Mendip Way
Hemel Hempstead HP2 124 E6
Luton LU3 44 C8
Mendlesham AL7 111 E6
Mentley La SG11 54 E4
Mentley La E SG11 55 D4
Mentley La W SG11 55 C4
Mentmore★ LU7 61 C4
Mentmore Cross Rds
LU7 60 F6
Mentmore Rd
Cheddington LU7 79 F8
St Albans AL1 127 E1
Mentmore View HP23 99 F5
Mepham Cres HA3 176 C3
Mepham Gdns HA3 176 C3
Mercer Pl HA5 175 C1
Mercers HP2 124 E5
Mercers Ave CM23 76 B4
Mercers Row AL1 127 C1
Merchant Dr SG13 113 F7
Merchant Taylors' Sch
HA6 166 E1
Merchants Wlk SG7 13 B1
Mercia Rd SG7 24 A8
Mercury Ho WD18 166 E5
Mercury Wlk 1 HP2 124 F6
Mereden Ct AL1 141 C8
Meredews SG6 23 B7
Meredith Cl HA5 175 D3
Meredith Rd SG1 51 A8
Merefield CM21 97 E1
Meriden Ho 3 EN5 171 E5
Meriden Prim Sch
WD25 154 D3
Meriden Way WD25 154 E2
Meridian Sch SG8 7 E7
Meridian Way SG12 115 B5
Merle Ave UB9 173 C1
Merlin Ctr The AL4 128 F3
Merlin Way WD25 153 F5
Merling Croft HP4 121 E7
Mermaid Cl SG4 35 B7
Merrill Pl 2 CM23 76 E5
Merritt Wlk AL9 144 B8
Merrow Dr HP1 123 E4
Merrows Cl HA6 174 C4
Merry Hill Inf Sch
WD23 168 B2
Merry Hill Mount WD23 168 B1
Merry Hill Rd WD23 168 B1
Merryfield WD17 154 A1
Merryfields AL4 128 E3
Mersey Pl
Hemel Hempstead HP2 124 F8
1 Luton LU1 63 D7
Merton Rd Enfield EN2 161 D1
Watford WD18 167 B5
Meryfield Cl WD6 169 F7
Meryfield Prim Sch
WD6 169 F8
Metford Cres EN3 163 A1
Metro Ctr St Albans AL4 127 F7
Watford WD18 166 D2
Metropolis Ctr WD6 170 A6
Metropolitan Mews
WD18 166 E5
Metropolitan Pl WD18 166 F5
Metropolitan Station App
WD18 166 F5
Meux Cl EN7 162 A8
Mews The
Bishop's Stortford CM22 77 A3
3 Harpenden AL5 86 B1
Letchworth SG6 12 C1
Sawbridgeworth CM21 97 E3
Stansted Mountfitchet CM24 59 F7
Meyer Gn EN1 162 A1
Meyrick Ave LU1 63 C6
Meyrick Ct LU1 63 D6
Mezen Cl HA6 174 D5
Michael Muir Ho SG5 21 D1
Michaels Rd CM23 59 A2
Micklefield Rd HP2 125 C3
Micklefield Way WD6 156 E1
Micklem Dr HP1 123 F4
Micklem Prim Sch HP1 124 A4
Midcot Way HP4 121 F6
Middle Drift SG8 7 C6
Middle Furlong WD23 168 B5
Middle Hill HP1 123 E3
Middle La HP3 137 A1
Middle Ope WD24 154 B2
Middle Rd
Berkhamsted HP4 122 B4
Waltham Abbey EN9 163 B7
Middle Row
5 Bishop's Stortford CM23 76 F6
1 Stevenage SG1 50 C7
Middle St EN9 149 F8
Middle Way WD24 154 B2
Middle Way The HA3 176 F1
Middlefield
Hatfield AL10 130 A6
Welwyn Garden City AL7 110 E3
Middlefield Ave EN11 135 A8
Middlefield Cl
Hoddesdon EN11 135 A8
St Albans AL4 128 C6
Middlefield La SG16 10 C7
Middlefield Rd EN11 135 A8
Middlefields SG6 11 F1
Middlefields Ct SG6 11 F1
Middleknights Hill HP1 124 A6
Middlesborough Cl SG1 36 F2
Middleton Mid Sch
SG12 114 D7
Middleton Rd Luton LU2 46 D4
Rickmansworth WD3 165 A1
Midhurst SG6 22 F8
Midhurst Gdns LU3 45 C4
Midland Cotts SG5 22 A1
Midland Ho 5 AL1 127 E3
Midland Rd
Hemel Hempstead HP2 124 D3
Luton LU2 63 E8
Midland Way SG16 10 B3
Midway AL3 141 B8
Mike Mably Ho AL10 129 F7
Milbourne Ct 1 WD17 167 A7
Milburn Cl LU3 31 B1
Milby Ct WD6 169 F8
Mildmay Rd SG1 37 B1
Mildred Ave
Borehamwood WD6 170 B5
Watford WD18 167 A5
Mile Cl EN9 163 C6
Mile House Cl AL1 142 A8
Mile House La AL1 142 A8
Milestone Cl SG2 51 D4
Milestone Rd Hitchin SG5 21 D2
Knebworth SG3 69 A5
Milford Cl AL4 128 D7
Milford Hill AL5 86 D4
Milksey La SG4 36 C5
Mill Bridge Barnet EN5 171 F3
Hertford SG14 113 C6
Mill Cl Buntingford SG9 40 E7
Hatfield AL8 110 A5
Hemel Hempstead, Nash Mills
HP3 139 A6
Hemel Hempstead, Piccotts End
HP1 124 B7
Hitchin SG4 35 C8
Stotfold SG5 12 A6
Ware SG12 93 D1
Wingrave HP22 60 A3
Mill Cnr EN5 171 F8
Mill Cotts LU7 60 D8
Mill End SG11 55 F2
Mill Farm Cl HA5 175 C1
Mill Gdns HP23 100 A4
Mill Green La AL9 110 E1
Mill Green Mus & Mill★
AL9 130 E8
Mill Green Rd AL7 110 E5
Mill Ground Cotts SG4 24 C1
Mill Hill Farnham CM23 58 E5
Royston SG8 7 E4
Stansted Mountfitchet
CM24 59 E6
Mill La Albury SG11 57 C6
Arlesey SG15 10 F4
Cheshunt EN8 148 E3
Flamstead AL3 84 A1
Harlow CM17 118 E4
Hatfield Heath CM22 98 F3
Hexton SG5 19 C3
Hitchin SG4 34 F3
Hoddesdon EN10 135 A2
Kings Langley WD4 139 A2
Meesden SG9 30 A5
Sawbridgeworth CM21 97 F3
Stotfold SG5 12 A6
Therfield SG8 15 F8
Watton at S SG12 71 A6
Welwyn AL6 89 C5
Weston SG4 24 C1
Wingrave HP22 60 C2
Mill Lane Cl EN10 134 F2
Mill Mead Prim Sch
SG14 113 C6
Mill Race SG12 115 D4
Mill Rd Hertford SG14 113 D6
Royston SG8 7 D7
St Ippolyts SG4 35 A3
Mill Side CM24 59 E6
Mill St Ashwell SG7 4 D4
Berkhamsted HP4 122 C4
Bishop's Stortford CM23 77 A5
Hemel Hempstead HP3 138 D8
Luton LU1 63 D8
Mill Stream Lodge WD3 173 A8
Mill View AL2 141 D4
Mill View Rd HP23 99 F4
Mill Way
Breachwood Green SG4 47 D2
Rickmansworth WD3 164 F1
Watford WD23 167 E8
Millacres 1 SG12 93 E1
Milland Ct WD6 170 D8
Millard Way SG4 22 C1
Millbank HP3 138 D7
Millbridge Mews 2
SG14 113 C6
Millbrook Ct SG12 93 D2
Millbrook Rd WD23 167 F8
Millbrook Sch EN8 148 E2
Millcrest Rd EN7 147 B3
Millcroft CM23 59 A1
Millennium Ct WD3 165 E2
Millennium Wharf WD3 165 E1
Miller Ave EN3 163 A1
Miller Cl HA5 175 C1
Millers Cl CM23 76 C5
Millers Ct SG14 113 D5
Millers La SG12 115 C4
Millers Rise AL1 127 E2
Millers View SG10 74 E1
Millfield
Berkhamsted HP4 122 D5
Harlow CM17 118 C4
Thundridge SG12 93 E8
Millfield *continued*
Welwyn Garden City AL7 111 C7
Millfield Fst Sch SG9 40 E7
Millfield Ho WD18 166 D3
Millfield La
Caddington LU1 62 D2
Hitchin SG4 34 F4
Little Hadham SG11 75 D8
Millfield Rd LU3 45 B3
Millfield Way LU1 62 D3
Millfield Wlk HP3 139 A8
Millfields
Sawbridgeworth CM21 97 F3
Stansted Mountfitchet
CM24 59 E6
Millgreen Cotts AL9 131 F8
Millhoo Ct EN9 163 F5
Millhouse La WD5 140 A4
Millhurst Mews CM17 118 E4
Milliners Ct AL1 127 E3
Milliners Way
Bishop's Stortford CM23 76 C4
Luton LU3 45 C1
Millmead Way SG14 113 B6
Millside CM23 77 A5
Millstream Cl
Hertford SG14 113 B6
Hitchin SG4 22 A1
Millthorne Cl WD3 165 F4
Millwards AL10 130 B2
Millwood Ct SG5 11 F6
Millwright Wlk HP3 138 F6
Milne Cl SG6 23 B3
Milne Field HA5 176 A3
Milner Cl WD25 154 B6
Milner Ct Bushey WD23 168 B3
Luton LU2 63 E8
Milneway UB9 173 B2
Milton Ave EN5 171 F4
Milton Cl SG8 2 C1
Milton Ct
Hammond Street EN7 147 F5
12 Harpenden AL5 86 B1
Hemel Hempstead HP2 105 B1
Waltham Abbey EN9 163 C5
Milton Dene HP2 125 B8
Milton Dr WD6 170 B4
Milton Rd Harpenden AL5 86 B1
Luton LU1 63 C6
Ware SG12 93 D2
Milton St
Waltham Abbey EN9 163 C5
Watford WD24 167 B8
Milton View SG4 35 C7
Milverton Gn LU3 45 A7
Mimms Hall Rd EN6 158 D7
Mimms La EN6,WD7 157 C6
Mimram Cl SG4 66 E7
Mimram Pl AL6 89 C5
Mimram Rd
Hertford SG14 113 B5
Welwyn AL6 89 C5
Mimram Wlk AL6 89 C5
Minchen Rd CM20 118 A1
Minderhall Ct SG1 50 C7
Minehead Way SG1 50 A7
Minerva Cl 3 SG1 51 C8
Minerva Dr WD24 153 E3
Minims The AL10 130 A7
Minister Ct AL2 141 E3
Minoan Dr HP3 138 E7
Minorca Way LU4 44 A3
Minsden Rd SG2 51 D3
Minster Cl AL10 130 A3
Minster Ho AL10 130 A3
Minster Rd SG8 7 C8
Minstrel Cl HP1 124 B4
Minstrel Ct HA3 176 E1
Miss Joans Ride HP4,LU6 81 E7
Missden Dr HP3 125 C1
Missenden Ho WD18 166 E2
Mistletoe Ct LU2 64 C8
Mistletoe Hill LU2 64 C8
Mistley Rd CM20 118 A2
Misswell La HP23 99 F3
Mitchell Cl
Abbots Langley WD5 154 A7
Bovingdon HP3 136 F4
St Albans AL1 141 D7
Welwyn Garden City AL7 111 C6
Mitre Bldgs CM20 117 C1
Mitre Ct 20 SG14 113 D6
Mitre Gdns CM23 77 A4
Mixes Hill Ct LU2 46 A4
Mixes Hill Rd LU2 45 F4
Mixies The SG5 11 E6
Moakes The LU3 44 E7
Moat Cl WD23 168 B4
Moat La Luton LU3 45 B4
Wingrave HP22 60 B2
Moat The SG11 55 D3
Moatfield Rd WD23 168 B4
Moatside SG9 29 B7
Moatview Ct WD23 168 B4
Moatwood Gn AL7 110 E5
Mobbsbury Way SG2 51 C7
Mobley Gn LU2 46 B3
Moffats Cl AL9 145 A5
Moffats La AL9 144 F5
Moira Cl LU3 44 D7
Moles La SG9 28 A3
Molescroft AL5 85 D4
Molesworth EN11 115 A2
Molewood Rd SG14 113 B7
Mollison Ave EN3 163 A3
Molteno Rd WD17 167 A8
Molyneaux Ave HP3 136 F4
Momples Rd CM20 118 B1
Monarch Hall LU2 64 C8
Monarch Wlk WD7 156 F6
Monarch's Way EN8 162 E6
Monastery Cl AL3 127 C3
Money Hole La AL6 111 E7
Moneyhill Ct WD3 165 B1
Moneyhill Par WD3 165 C1
Moneyhill Rd WD3 165 C1
Monica Cl WD24 167 D7
Monkhams Hall EN9 149 C2
Monklands SG6 22 D6
Monks Cl
Hoddesdon EN10 135 A3
Letchworth SG6 22 C6
Redbourn AL3 106 B5
St Albans AL1 127 E1
Monks Horton Way AL1 128 A4
Monks Rise AL8 89 D2
Monks Row 7 SG12 93 D2
Monks View SG2 50 F2
Monks Walk Sch AL8 89 C3
Monks Wlk SG9 40 E7
Monksmead WD6 170 C5
Monksmead Sch WD6 170 C6
Monkswick Rd CM20 117 F1
Monkswood AL8 89 C2
Monkswood Ave EN9 163 D6
Monkswood Dr CM23 76 D6
Monkswood Gdns WD6 170 D6
Monkswood Ret Pk SG1 50 E3
Monkswood Way SG1 50 E3
Monmouth Rd WD17 167 B6
Monro Gdns HA3 176 E3
Monro Ind Est EN8 162 E5
Mons Ave SG7 23 F6
Mons Cl AL5 107 D6
Monson Rd EN10 134 F3
Montacute Rd WD23 168 E2
Montague Ave LU4 44 C6
Montague Hall Pl WD23 168 A3
Montague Rd HP4 122 B4
Montayne Rd EN8 162 D7
Monterey Lodge HA6 174 E4
Montesole Ct 6 HA5 175 C1
Montessori At Little
Cheverells (Sch) AL3 83 D4
Montfitchet Wlk SG2 51 D7
Montgomerie Cl HP4 122 A6
Montgomery Ave HP2 125 A4
Montgomery Dr EN8 148 E3
Monton Cl LU3 44 F6
Montrose Ave LU3 45 C3
Montrose Rd HA3 176 F1
Monument Pl AL3 127 D4
Moon La EN5 171 F6
Moor End Rd HP1 124 C2
Moor Hall La CM23 76 B3
Moor Hall Rd CM17 118 F4
Moor La Moor Park WD3 174 A8
Sarratt WD3 151 E3
Moor Lane Crossing
WD18 166 C2
Moor Mill La AL2 141 E2
Moor Park Rd HA6 174 D4
Moor Park Sta HA6 174 D7
Moor Pk Ind Ctr WD18 166 C2
Moor St LU1 63 C8
Moor View WD18 167 A3
Moore Rd HP4 121 F6
Moorend AL7 111 A3
Moorfields SG9 41 E8
Moorhen Way CM19 116 A1
Moorhurst Ave EN7 147 B2
Moorings The
Bishop's Stortford CM23 77 A5
St Albans AL1 127 F4
Watford WD23 167 E5
Moorland Gdns LU2 63 D8
Moorland Rd
Harpenden AL5 86 B4
Hemel Hempstead HP1 124 A1
Moorlands
Park Street AL2 141 E3
Welwyn Garden City AL7 111 A3
Moorlands Reach CM21 98 A1
Moorlands Sch LU4 44 C3
Moormead Cl SG5 34 D6
Moormead Hill SG5 34 D6
Moors Farm Cotts HP5 136 B4
Moors Ley SG2 38 B1
Moors The AL7 111 A7
Moors Wlk AL7 111 C6
Moorside
Hemel Hempstead HP3 138 B8
Welwyn Garden City AL7 111 A3
Moortown Rd WD19 175 C6
Moorymead Cl SG14 70 D3
Moran Cl AL2 154 F8
Morecambe Cl Luton LU4 44 B3
Stevenage SG1 50 B7
Morefields HP23 100 A6
Moremead EN9 163 D6
Moreton Ave AL5 85 F2
Moreton Cl EN7 148 B4
Moreton End Cl AL5 85 F2
Moreton End La AL5 85 F2
Moreton Pk Ind Est LU2 46 A2
Moreton Pl AL5 85 F3
Moreton Rd N LU2 46 A2
Moreton Rd S LU2 46 A2
Morgan Cl
Northwood HA6 174 F4
Stevenage SG1 36 D1
Morgan Gdns WD25 155 B2
Morgan's Rd SG13 113 D4
Morgan's Wlk SG13 113 D3
Morgans Cl SG13 113 D4
Morgans Jun Mix Inf Sch
SG13 113 D4
Morice Rd EN11 134 F8
Morland Way EN8 148 E3
Morley Gr CM20 117 C2
Morley Hill EN2 161 D1
Morley La SG11 73 F5
Morningside WD3 165 C1
Mornington AL6 90 A4
Mornington Rd WD7 156 B5
Morpeth Ave WD6 156 F1
Morpeth Cl 3 HP2 124 E2
Morrell Cl LU3 45 A7
Morrell Ct AL7 110 F7
Morrello Gdns SG4 35 A5
Morris Cl
Lower Stondon SG16 10 C5
Luton LU3 44 E8
Morris Ct Holdbrook EN3 163 A2
Waltham Abbey EN9 163 F5
Morris Way AL2 142 D5
Morrison Ct 5 EN5 171 E5
Morriston Cl WD19 175 C5
Morse Cl UB9 173 C1
Mortain Dr HP4 121 F6
Mortimer Cl
Bushey WD23 168 B3
Luton LU1 63 A7
Mortimer Gate EN8 148 F4
Mortimer Hill HP23 100 B4
Mortimer Rd SG8 7 E7
Mortimer Rise HP23 100 B4
Morton Cl LU7 80 C4
Morton St SG8 7 D7
Morven Cl EN6 159 C8
Mosquito Way AL10 129 E7
Moss Bury Prim Sch SG1 51 A7
Moss Cl Pinner HA5 175 F1
Rickmansworth WD3 173 D8
Moss Gn AL7 110 E4
Moss La HA5 175 E1
Moss Rd WD25 154 B5
Moss Side AL2 140 F1
Moss Way SG5 21 C1
Mossbank Ave LU2 64 C8
Mossdale Ct 3 LU4 44 C5
Mossendew Cl UB9 173 D2
Mossman Dr LU1 62 E4
Mostyn Rd Bushey WD23 168 C4
Luton LU3 44 E4
Mott St E4 163 D1
Motts Cl SG14 70 D4
Moulton Rise LU2 63 F8
Mount Cl HP1 123 F3
Mount Dr
Park Street AL2 141 D6
Stansted Mountfitchet
CM24 59 E5
Mount Garrison SG4 34 F7
Mount Grace Rd EN6 159 B8
Mount Grace Sch EN6 159 B8
Mount Keen SG1 37 C3
Mount Pleasant
Harefield UB9 173 A2
Hertford Heath SG13 114 C4
Hitchin SG5 34 D6
St Albans AL3 127 C3
Mount Pleasant Cl AL9 130 D8
Mount Pleasant Flats
SG1 50 E8
Mount Pleasant La
Bricket Wood AL2 140 E1
Hatfield AL9 130 C8
Mount Pleasant Lane Jun Mix
& Inf Sch AL2 140 E1
Mount Pleasant Rd LU3 44 E5
Mount Rd Hertford SG14 113 A5
Wheathampstead AL4 87 D1
Mount The Barley SG8 8 F1
Hammond Street EN7 147 D5
5 Luton LU3 63 D8
Potters Bar EN6 145 B1
Rickmansworth WD3 165 C3
Mount Vernon Hospl
HA6 174 B4
Mount View Enfield EN2 160 F1
London Colney AL2 142 F4
Rickmansworth WD3 165 B1
Mount Way AL7 110 F3
Mountbatten Cl AL1 142 B8
Mounteagle SG8 7 D5
Mountfield Rd
Hemel Hempstead HP2 124 E3
Luton LU2 45 E2
Mountfitchet Castle &
Norman Village★ CM24 59 F6
Mountfitchet High Sch
CM24 59 F4
Mountfitchet Rd CM24 59 E5
Mountgrace Rd LU2 46 C6
Mountjoy SG4 22 C1
Mountside HA7 176 F2
Mountsorrel SG13 113 F6
Mountview HA6 174 F4
Mountview Rd EN7 147 E5
Mountway EN6 145 A1
Mountway Cl AL7 110 F3
Mowat Ind Est WD24 154 C1
Mowbray Cres SG5 11 F7
Mowbray Gdns SG4 35 A5
Mowbray Rd CM20 118 A3
Mowbrays The SG5 11 F7
Moxes Wood LU3 44 E7
Moxom Ave EN8 148 E1
Moxon St EN5 171 F6

Mozart Ct SG1 ....50 C5
Muddy La SG6 ....22 F3
Muirfield LU2 ....45 E6
Muirfield CI WD19 ....175 C6
Muirfield Gn WD19 ...175 C6
Muirfield Rd WD19 ...175 B6
Muirhead Way SG3 ....68 F5
Mulberry CI
  Cheshunt EN10 ......148 F7
  Chiswell Green AL2 ..141 B3
  Luton LU1 ....63 B7
  Stotfold SG5 ....11 A5
  Tring HP23 ....100 A3
  Watford WD17 ....153 E3
Mulberry Ct
  Bishop's Stortford CM23 ...77 A5
  5 Hemel Hempstead HP1 124 D4
  Royston SG8 ....7 D5
Mulberry Gdns WD7 ...156 E6
Mulberry Gn CM17 ....118 D4
Mulberry Lodge WD19 .167 D3
Mulberry Mead AL10 ...109 F1
Mulberry PI AL3 ....106 B4
Mulberry Terr CM17 ...118 B4
Mulberry Way SG5 .....21 D2
Mull Ho WD18 ....166 F4
Mullion CI Harrow HA3 .176 B2
  Luton LU2 ....46 B5
Mullion Wlk WD19 ....175 C6
Mullway SG6 ....22 C6
Mulready Wlk HP3 ....138 E7
Mundells
  Hammond Street EN7 .148 A4
  Welwyn Garden City AL7 .111 A8
Mundells Ct AL7 ......110 F8
Munden Gr WD24 .....154 D1
Munden Rd SG12 ......71 E7
Munden View WD25 ...154 D3
Mundesley CI
  South Oxhey WD19 ..175 C6
  Stevenage SG1 ....36 B1
Mungo-Park CI WD23 .176 C8
Munro Rd WD23 ......168 C4
Muntings The SG2 ....51 A3
Munts Mdw SG4 ......24 C1
Murchison Rd EN11 ...115 B3
Muriel Ave WD18 .....167 C4
Murray Cres HA5 .....175 D2
Murray Rd
  Berkhamsted HP4 ....122 C6
  Northwood HA6 ......174 E3
Murrell La SG5 ....12 A1
Murton Ct AL1 ....127 E4
Museum St HP23 .....100 A3
Museum of St Albans★
  AL1 ....127 E3
Musgrave CI EN7 .....147 F3
Musk Hill HP1 ....123 E2
Muskalls CI EN7 ......148 A4
Muskham Rd CM20 ...118 B3
Musleigh Manor SG12 ..93 F1
Musley Hill SG12 ......93 E2
Musley Inf Sch SG12 ..93 E2
Musley La SG12 ....93 E2
Mussons Path LU2 ....45 E1
Muswell CI LU3 ......45 B6
Mutchetts CI WD25 ...154 E6
Mutford Croft **2** LU2 .46 D1
Mutton La EN6 ....158 E8
Myddelton Ave EN1 ...161 E1
Myddelton House Gdns★
  EN2 ....162 A3
Myddelton Path SG12 ..162 B8
Myddleton Rd SG12 ...114 D8
Myers CI WD7 ....156 E7
Myles Ct EN7 ....147 C2
Mylne CI EN8 ....148 C4
Mylne Ct EN11 ....115 A1
Mymms Dr AL9 ....145 B4
Mymwood CI AL9 .....145 C4
Myrtle Cotts
  Sarratt WD3 ....152 A3
  Tring HP23 ....100 C8
Myrtle Gn HP1 ....123 E4
Myrtle Gr EN2 ....161 D1
Myrtleside CI HA6 ....174 D3
Myson Way CM23 .....77 B7

N

Nags Head CI SG13 ...114 B7
Nails La **15** CM23 .....76 F7
Nairn CI AL5 ....107 D6
Nairn Gn WD19 ......175 C6
Nan Aires HP22 ......60 A3
Nancy Downs WD19 ..167 C2
Nap The WD4 ....139 A2
Napier CI AL2 ....142 D6
Napier Ct Cheshunt EN8 .148 B3
  Luton LU1 ....63 D7
Napier Dr WD23 .....167 E5
Napier Hall LU2 ......64 C8
Napier Rd LU1 ....63 D7
Nappsbury Rd LU4 ...44 D5
Napsbury Ave AL2 ...142 C5
Napsbury La AL1 .....142 A7
Nascot PI WD17 .....167 B7
Nascot Rd WD17 .....167 B7
Nascot St WD17 .....167 B7
Nascot Wood Inf Sch
  WD17 ....154 A1
Nascot Wood Jun Sch
  WD17 ....154 A1
Nascot Wood Rd WD17 .153 F1

Naseby Rd LU1 ....63 B7
Nash CI
  Borehamwood WD6 ..169 F5
  Datchworth SG3 .....69 E2
  Stevenage SG2 ......51 B6
  Welham Green AL9 ...144 D8
Nash Gn HP3 ....138 F6
Nash Mills CE Prim Sch
  HP3 ....138 F6
Nash Mills La HP3 ....138 F5
Nash Rd SG8 ....7 D5
Nathaniel Wlk HP23 ..100 A5
Nathans CI AL6 ......89 C6
Nayland CI LU2 ......46 E1
Nazeing New Rd EN10 .135 B2
Nazeing Prim Sch EN9 .149 E8
Nazeing Rd EN9 .....135 D1
Nazeingbury CI EN9 ..135 D1
Nazeingbury Par EN9 .135 D1
Neagh CI SG1 ....37 C3
Neagle CI WD6 ......170 C8
Neal CI HA6 ....175 A2
Neal Ct Hertford SG14 .113 C6
  Waltham Abbey EN9 .163 F6
Neal St WD18 ....167 C4
Necton Rd AL4 ......108 E8
Needham Rd LU4 ....44 B6
Neild Way WD3 ......164 F2
Nell Gwynn CI WD7 ..156 E7
Nelson Ave AL1 .....142 B8
Nelson Rd
  Bishop's Stortford CM23 ..77 A5
  Dagnall HP4 ....81 C5
Nelson St LU3 ....113 B7
Nene Rd SG16 ....10 A4
Neptune Ct WD6 .....170 A6
Neptune Dr HP2 .....124 E5
Neptune Gate SG2 ...51 D8
Neston Rd WD24 ....154 C2
Netherby CI HP23 ...100 C6
Nether St SG12 ......95 E4
Netherby CI HP23 ...100 C6
Nethercott CI LU2 ...46 C1
Netherfield Ct SG12 .115 D3
Netherfield La SG12 .115 E3
Netherfield Rd AL5 ..107 B4
Netherhall Rd CM19 .135 F5
Netherstones SG5 ...11 F7
Netherway AL3 ......141 A8
Netley Dell SG6 .....23 B3
Nettleswell Cross CM20 .117 D1
Nettleswell Orch CM20 .117 D1
Nettleswell Rd CM20 .117 F3
Nettleswell Twr CM20 .117 F3
Nettlecroft
  Hemel Hempstead HP1 .124 B2
  Welwyn Garden City AL7 .111 B7
Nettleden Rd
  Little Gaddesden HP4 .102 E4
  Nettleden HP1 ....103 C1
  Potten End HP4 .....123 B8
Nevell's Gn SG6 .....22 F6
Nevells Rd SG6 ......22 F6
Nevil CI HA6 ....174 D5
Nevill Gr WD24 .....167 B8
Neville CI EN6 ......158 F8
Neville Rd LU3 ......45 A5
Neville Road Pas LU3 .45 A5
Neville's Ct SG6 ....23 B7
New Barn La CM22 ..77 D1
New Barnes Ave AL1 .142 A8
New Barns La SG10 ..74 F4
New Bedford Rd
  Luton LU3 ....45 D3
  Luton,High Town LU1 .63 D8
New Briars Prim Sch
  AL10 ....130 A5
New CI SG3 ....68 F6
New Cotts
  Brookmans Park AL9 .144 D3
  Cheshunt EN8 ......162 C5
  Markyate AL3 ....83 E6
  Whitwell SG4 ....66 A7
New Ct SG3 ....69 A2
New England CI SG4 ..34 F4
New England St AL3 ..127 C3
New Farm La HA6 ...174 E2
New Farm Traveller's Site
  SG8 ....2 A8
New Ford Bsns Pk EN8 .162 F5
New Ford Rd EN8 ....162 F5
New Forge PI AL3 ...106 B5
New Greens Ave AL3 ..127 D7
New Hall CI HP3 .....137 A4
New House Pk AL1 ...142 B7
New Inn Rd SG7 .....3 D5
New Kent Rd AL1 ....127 C4
New Mill Terr HP23 ...100 B6
New Par WD3 ....164 C5
New Park Dr HP2 ....125 B3
New Park La SG2 ....51 E2
New Park Rd
  Harefield UB9 ......173 C2
  Newgate Street SG13 ..146 D7
New Path CM23 .....76 E8
New PI AL6 ....89 B4
New Provident PI **7**
  HP4 ....122 D4
New Rd
  Berkhamsted HP4 ...122 D6
  Berkhamsted,Northchurch
    HP4 ....121 F7
  Chipperfield WD4 ...137 F1
  Croxley Green WD3 ..166 A4
  Elstree WD6 ....169 D3
  Great Chishill SG8 ..9 D6
  Harlow CM17 ....118 D4
  Hatfield AL8 ....110 A3
  Hertford SG14 ......113 D8

New Rd continued
  Hoddesdon EN10 ....135 A4
  Little Hadham SG11 ..75 A7
  Lower Stondon SG17 .10 A8
  Radlett WD7 ....155 E2
  Radlett, Letchmore Heath
    WD25 ....168 E8
  Sarratt WD3 ....151 F1
  Shenley WD7 ....157 A5
  South Mimms EN6 ...158 A6
  Tring HP23 ....100 B6
  Ware SG12 ....93 D1
  Welwyn AL6 ....89 F3
  Woolmer Green SG3 ..69 B3
New River Ave SG12 ..115 B4
New River CI EN11 ...135 B7
New River Ct EN7 ...162 B8
New River Trad Est
  EN8 ....148 D5
New St Berkhamsted HP4 .122 D4
  Cheddington LU7 ....79 F7
  5 Luton LU1 ....63 D6
  Sawbridgeworth CM21 ..97 E3
  Slip End LU1 ....63 C1
  Watford WD18 ......167 C5
New Station Cotts EN10 .135 A3
New Town SG4 ......67 F1
New Town Rd **9** LU1 ..63 E6
New Town St LU1 ...63 E6
New Wood AL7 ......111 C7
Newark CI SG8 ......7 C8
Newark Gn WD6 ....170 C6
Newark Rd AL5 .....45 A2
Newberries Ave WD7 .156 B4
Newberries Prim Sch
  WD7 ....156 C4
Newbiggin Path WD19 .175 C6
Newbold La LU3 ....45 B7
Newbolt SG8 ....7 D8
Newbolt Rd HA7 ....176 F5
Newbury Ave EN3 ...162 F2
Newbury CI
  Bishop's Stortford CM23 ..76 E8
  Luton LU2 ....44 E2
  Stevenage SG1 ......36 D1
Newcastle CI SG1 ...36 F2
Newcombe Rd LU1 ..63 C7
Newcome Path WD7 .157 A5
Newcome Rd WD7 ..157 A5
Newdigate Gn UB9 ..173 D2
Newdigate Rd UB9 ..173 C2
Newdigate Rd E UB9 .173 D2
Newell La SG12 .....38 D7
Newell Rd HP3 ......138 E8
Newell Rise HP3 ....138 E8
Newells SG6 ....23 D4
Newells Hedge LU7 ..80 D5
Newfield La HP2 ....124 F3
Newfield Way AL4 ...128 D1
Newfields AL5 ......110 B5
Newford CI HP2 ....125 B4
Newgate SG2 ....51 A4
Newgate CI AL4 ....128 D6
Newgate St SG2 ....146 E7
Newgate Street Village
  SG13 ....146 E6
Newgatestreet Rd EN7 .147 B4
Newground Rd HP23 .101 B3
Newhall Dr WD6 ....163 F6
Newhouse Cres WD25 .154 B6
Newhouse Rd HP3 ...137 A4
Newland CI Pinner HA5 .175 F4
  St Albans AL1 ....142 A8
Newland Gdns SG13 .113 E6
Newlands Hatfield AL9 .130 C7
  Letchworth SG6 ....23 A3
Newlands Ave WD7 ..155 F5
Newlands CI E SG4 ..34 F4
Newlands CI W SG4 ..34 F4
Newlands Cvn Site WD5 .139 F5
Newlands La SG4 ...34 F4
Newlands PI EN5 ...171 D4
Newlands Rd
  Hemel Hempstead HP1 .123 E4
  Luton LU1 ....63 C3
Newlands Way EN6 ..145 B1
Newlands Wlk WD25 ..154 D6
Newlyn CI
  Bricket Wood AL2 ...140 E1
  Stevenage SG1 .....50 A6
Newlyn Rd EN5 .....171 F5
Newman Ave SG8 ...7 F6
Newmans CI SG14 ...70 D3
Newmans Dr AL5 ...85 F2
Newmarket Ct AL3 ..127 C4
Newmarket Rd
  Royston SG8 ....7 E6
  Royston SG8 ....7 F6
Newnham CI LU2 ...46 D1
Newnham Par **5** EN8 .148 D1
Newnham Rd SG12 ..12 E6
Newnham Way SG7 ..4 B2
Newport CI EN3 ....162 E2
Newport Mead WD19 .175 D6
Newports CM21 ....97 C1
Newquay Gdns WD19 .175 B8
Newstead AL10 .....129 F2
Newstead Ho UB9 ..173 C1
Newteswell Dr EN9 ..163 D7
Newton CI
  Harpenden AL5 .....107 D6
  Hoddesdon EN11 ...115 B2
Newton Cres WD6 ..170 D6
Newton Dr CM21 ...97 D1
Newton Rd Harrow HA3 .176 E1
  Stevenage SG2 .....51 B6
Newtondale LU4 ....44 C5

Newtons Way SG4 ...34 F6
Newtown Rd CM23 ..76 F6
Niagara CI EN8 .....148 D2
Nicholas Breakspear RC Sch
  AL4 ....128 C2
Nicholas CI
  St Albans AL3 ......127 D6
  Watford WD24 .....154 B2
Nicholas La SG14 ...113 C6
Nicholas PI SG1 ....36 D1
Nicholas Rd WD6 ...169 F4
Nicholas Way
  Hemel Hempstead HP2 .124 F5
  Northwood HA6 ....174 C2
Nicholls CI Luton LU2 .46 C2
  Redbourn AL3 ......105 F5
Nicholson Court Ind Ctr
  EN11 ....135 B6
Nicola CI HA3 ......176 D1
Nicoll Way WD6 ....170 D5
Nicolson Dr WD23 ..176 C8
Nidderdale HP2 .....124 F6
Nightingale Ave SG8 ..2 A5
Nightingale CI Luton LU2 .46 C6
  Radlett WD7 ....155 F3
  Watford WD5 ......154 A8
Nightingale Ct
  Hertford SG14 ......113 C6
  Hitchin SG5 ....35 A8
  1 Luton LU3 ....63 C8
  Radlett WD7 ....156 A4
  Rickmansworth WD3 .165 C2
Nightingale La AL1,AL4 .142 C7
Nightingale Lodge HP4 .122 B4
Nightingale PI WD3 ..165 D2
Nightingale Rd
  Bushey WD23 ......168 A4
  Hammond Street EN7 .147 C6
  Hitchin SG5 ....34 F8
  Rickmansworth WD3 .165 C2
Nightingale Terr SG15 ..11 A3
Nightingale Way
  Baldock SG7 ....23 F6
  Royston SG8 ....7 E8
Nightingale Wlk
  Hemel Hempstead HP2 .105 C1
  Stevenage SG2 .....51 C5
Nightingales EN9 ...163 E5
Nimbus Way SG4 ...35 C7
Nimmo Dr WD23 ...168 D2
Nimrod CI AL4 .....128 C5
Nimrod Dr AL10 ....129 D6
Nine Ashes SG12 ...116 D7
Ninefields EN9 .....163 F6
Ninesprings Way SG4 .35 B6
Ninfield Ct LU2 .....46 C3
Ninian Rd HP2 .....124 E8
Ninning's La AL6 ...68 D2
Ninnings Cotts AL5 .107 A8
Ninth Ave LU3 .....44 D7
Niton CI EN5 ....171 D3
Niven CI WD6 ......170 C8
Noake Mill La HP1 ..124 A8
Nobel Sch The SG2 ..51 C7
Nobel Villas SG1 ...163 D5
Nobles The CM23 ...76 D6
Node Way Gdns AL6 ..89 C3
Nodes Dr SG2 ......51 A1
Noke La AL2 ....140 E4
Noke Lane Bsns Ctr AL2 .140 F4
Noke Shot AL5 .....86 C4
Noke Side AL2 .....141 A4
Noke The SG2 ......69 B8
Nokes The HP1 ....124 A5
Nokeside SG2 ......69 B8
Nook The SG2 .....115 B4
Norbury Ave WD24 .167 C4
Norfolk Ave WD24 ..154 C1
Norfolk CI E **4** EN5 ..171 E5
Norfolk Gdns WD6 ..170 D5
Norfolk Rd
  Buntingford SG9 ...40 E8
  Luton LU2 ....64 A7
  Rickmansworth WD3 .165 A1
Norfolk Way CM23 ..76 F5
Norman Ave CM23 ..76 D6
Norman CI St Albans AL1 .141 E8
  Waltham Abbey EN9 .163 D6
Norman Cres HA5 ...175 C2
Norman Ct
  Potters Bar EN6 ....145 C1
  Stansted Mountfitchet
    CM24 ....59 E7
  Stevenage SG1 .....36 F1
Norman Rd Luton LU3 .45 B2
  Welwyn AL6 ....89 B3
Norman's La SG8 ...7 D5
Norman's Way CM24 ..59 E7
Normandy Ave EN5 ..171 F5
Normandy Ct HP1 ..124 D4
Normandy Dr HP4 ..122 B6
Normandy Rd AL3 ..127 C4
Normandy Way EN11 .135 D8
Normans CI SG6 ...11 F1
Normans La AL6 ...68 C2
Normansfield CI WD23 .168 B2
Norris CI CM23 .....77 C7
Norris Gr EN10 ....134 E3
Norris La EN11 .....135 A7
Norris Rd EN11 ....135 A6
Norris Rise EN11 ...134 F7
North App
  Moor Park HA6 .....174 C8
  Watford WD25 ....154 A5
North Area Pupil Referral
  Unit SG6 ....22 D3
North Ave Letchworth SG6 .23 B8
  Shenley WD7 ....156 E7

North Barn EN10 ....135 B1
North CI Barnet EN5 ..171 C4
  Chiswell Green AL2 ..141 B6
  Royston SG8 ....7 C7
North Comm AL3 ...106 A5
North Common Rd AL3 .106 A4
North Cotts AL2 ....142 A6
North CI AL3 ....83 E5
North Dr St Albans AL4 .128 E5
  Thundridge SG11 ...72 E1
North Drift Way LU1 ..63 B6
North End SG6 .....15 D6
North Gate CM20 ...117 C1
North Hertfordshire Coll
  Letchworth SG6 ....22 F5
  Stevenage SG1 .....50 D4
North Hertfordshire Coll
  (Hitchin Ctr) SG4 ...35 B8
North Hill WD3 .....164 E8
North Luton Ind Est LU4 .44 B7
North Orbital Commercial Pk
  AL1 ....142 A7
North Orbital Rd
  Bricket Wood AL2 ..140 E2
  Chiswell Green AL2 ..141 B5
  Colney Heath AL4 ..129 C2
  London Colney AL1,AL2,
    AL4 ....142 D6
  Park Street AL2 ....141 E6
  Watford WD25 .....154 D7
North PI Harlow CM20 .118 B5
  Hitchin SG5 ....21 D1
  Waltham Abbey EN9 .163 B6
North Rd Baldock SG7 ..12 C2
  Berkhamsted HP4 ..122 B4
  Cheshunt EN8 .....162 E6
  Chorleywood WD3 ..164 D4
  Hertford SG14 ......113 A7
  Hertford SG14 ......113 C6
  Hoddesdon EN11 ...135 A7
  Stevenage SG1 .....36 C2
North Ride AL6 .....89 C6
North Riding AL2 ...141 A1
North Road Ave SG14 .113 A7
North Road Gdns SG14 .113 B6
North St
  4 Bishop's Stortford CM23 .76 F7
  Lower Nazeing EN9 .135 E1
  Luton, Hart Hill LU2 .45 E1
  Luton,High Town LU1 .63 E8
North Terr **5** CM23 ..76 F8
North View Cotts SG1 ..95 D4
North Western Ave
  Stanmore WD6 .....169 A2
  Watford,Garston WD24 .154 C3
  Watford,Leavesden Green
    WD2 ....153 D4
  Bushey WD23,W25 .168 C6
Northaw CE Prim Sch
  EN6 ....146 A1
Northaw CI HP2 ....125 B8
Northaw Pk EN6 ...159 F7
Northaw Rd E EN6 ..146 E1
Northaw Rd W EN6 ..160 C8
Northbridge Rd HP4 ..122 A6
Northbrook Dr HA6 ..174 E3
Northbrook Rd EN5 ..171 E3
Northchurch La HP4,
  HP5 ....121 D2
Northchurch St Mary's CE
  Fst Sch HP4 ....121 E6
Northcliffe Dr N20 ...171 F1
Northcote **3** HA5 ...175 C1
Northcotts AL9 .....130 C6
Northcourt WD3 ....165 A1
Northdown Rd AL10 .130 A2
Northend HP3 ......125 C9
Northern Ave SG16 ..10 C3
Northern Ho EN8 ...54 A6
Northfield Braughing SG11 .55 F7
  Hatfield AL10 ......130 B8
  Standon SG11 .....55 E2
Northfield Gdns WD24 .154 C2
Northfield Rd
  Aldbury HP23 ......100 F7
  Borehamwood WD6 .170 B8
  Cheshunt EN8 .....162 E7
  Guilden Morden SG7 ..1 C2
  Harpenden AL5 .....86 C4
  Sawbridgeworth CM21 ..97 E4
Northfields SG6 ....11 F1
Northfields Inf Sch SG6 .11 F1
Northgate HA6 .....174 C3
Northgate End CM23 ..76 E8
Northgate Ho EN8 ..148 D2
Northgate Path WD6 .169 F8
Northgate Prim Sch
  CM23 ....76 E8
Northlands EN6 .....159 D8
Northolt Ave CM23 ..59 B1
Northridge Way HP1 .124 A3
Northside AL4 ......108 B4
Northumberland Ave
  EN1 ....162 B1
Northview Rd LU2 ..45 F2
Northway
  Rickmansworth WD3 .165 D2
  1 Welwyn Garden City AL7 .89 F1
Northwell Dr LU3 ...44 F7
Northwick Rd WD19 .175 C6
Northwood AL7 ....111 D6
Northwood & Pinner District
  Hospl HA6 ....175 A2
Northwood CI EN7 ..147 F4
Northwood Coll HA6 .174 D3
Northwood Hills Cir
  HA6 ....175 A2

Northwood Hills Sta HA6 175 A1
Northwood Prep Sch WD3 174 C8
Northwood Rd UB9 173 E3
Northwood Sch HA6 175 B2
Northwood Sta HA6 174 E3
Northwood Way
Harefield UB9 173 D2
Northwood HA6 175 A3
Norton Bury La SG6 12 C2
Norton Cl WD6 170 A8
Norton Cres SG7 23 E8
Norton Gn SG1 50 B3
Norton Green Rd SG1 50 C4
Norton Mill La SG6 12 D3
Norton Rd
Letchworth SG5,SG6,SG7 12 C2
Luton LU3 44 F4
Stevenage SG1 50 D4
Norton Road Prim Sch LU3 44 F4
Norton Way N SG6 23 A7
Norton Way S SG6 23 A5
Nortonstreet La SG4 67 B7
Norvic Rd HP23 80 A1
Norwich Cl SG1 37 B1
Norwich Ho 5 WD6 170 A7
Norwich Way WD3 166 B5
Norwood Cl SG14 112 F7
Norwood Rd EN8 148 E1
Nottingham Cl WD25 154 A6
Nottingham Rd WD3 164 C1
Novello Way WD6 170 D8
Nugent's Pk HA5 175 F2
Nugents Ct HA5 175 E2
Numbers Farm WD4 139 C2
Nun's Cl SG5 34 E7
Nunfield WD4 152 B8
Nunnery Cl AL1 127 E1
Nunnery La LU3 45 B5
Nunnery Stables AL1 127 D1
Nuns La AL1 141 E8
Nunsbury Dr EN10 148 E6
Nunsbury Drive Cotts EN10 148 E6
Nup End Cl HP22 60 B3
Nup End La HP22 60 B3
Nupton Dr EN5 171 C3
Nurseries Rd AL4 108 E7
Nursery Cl
Bishop's Stortford CM23 76 F6
Stevenage SG2 69 A8
Nursery Cotts SG1 50 A6
Nursery Fields CM21 97 D2
Nursery Gdns
Goff's Oak EN7 147 D3
Tring HP23 100 B4
Ware SG12 93 E1
Welwyn Garden City AL7 89 E1
Nursery Hill AL7 89 E1
Nursery Par LU3 44 E5
Nursery Rd
Bishop's Stortford CM23 76 F6
Cheshunt EN10 148 F6
Hoddesdon EN11 115 B1
Lower Nazeing EN9 135 D2
Luton LU3 44 F5
Nursery Row 5 EN5 171 E6
Nursery Terr HP4 123 B7
Nut Gr AL8 89 D1
Nut Slip SG9 40 E6
Nutcroft SG3 69 D2
Nutfield AL7 90 A1
Nuthampstead Rd SG8 17 E2
Nutleigh Gr SG5 21 D1
Nuttfield Cl WD3 166 B3
Nutwood Gdns 5 EN7 147 E5
Nye Way HP3 137 A3
Nymans Cl LU2 46 D3

O

Oak Ave
Bricket Wood AL2 141 A1
Enfield EN2 160 F1
Oak Cl
Hemel Hempstead HP3 138 F7
Waltham Abbey EN9 163 D5
Oak Ct HA6 174 D4
Oak Dr Berkhamsted HP4 122 D3
Sawbridgeworth CM21 118 C8
Oak End SG9 40 D7
Oak Farm WD6 170 C4
Oak Glade HA6 174 B2
Oak Gn WD5 153 E7
Oak Gr Hatfield AL10 129 F5
Hertford SG13 113 E4
Oak Green Way WD5 153 E7
Oak Hall CM23 76 E8
Oak La Cholesbury HP23 120 B2
Cuffley EN6 146 F3
Graveley SG4 36 C4
Oak Path WD23 168 B3
Oak Piece AL6 89 E7
Oak Piece Ct AL6 89 E7
Oak Pk SG12 95 B1
Oak Rd Luton LU4 63 C8
Woolmer Green SG3 69 B1
Oak St
Bishop's Stortford CM23 76 F6
Hemel Hempstead HP3 138 F7
Oak Tree Cl
Abbots Langley WD5 153 D7
Benington SG2 52 F4
Hatfield AL10 130 A6
Hertford Heath SG13 114 C3
Oak Tree Cl *continued*
Letchworth SG6 22 E4
Oak Tree Ct Elstree WD6 169 D3
Oaklands AL6 89 E8
Oak Way AL5 107 A5
Oakbank WD7 156 B3
Oakcroft Cl HA5 175 B1
Oakdale AL8 89 D1
Oakdale Ave HA6 175 A1
Oakdale Cl WD19 175 C6
Oakdale Rd WD19 175 C6
Oakdene EN8 148 E1
Oakdene Cl HA5 175 F3
Oakdene Rd
Hemel Hempstead HP3 138 F7
Watford WD24 154 B3
Oakdene Way AL1 128 C3
Oaken Gr AL7 110 E3
Oakfield WD3 165 A2
Oakfield Ave SG4 35 B5
Oakfield Cl EN6 158 F8
Oakfield Rd AL5 107 A5
Oakfields SG2 51 C1
Oakfields Ave SG3 69 A6
Oakfields Cl SG2 51 C1
Oakfields Rd SG3 69 A6
Oakhill SG6 23 D4
Oakhill Ave HA5 175 E1
Oakhill Cl WD3 172 E6
Oakhill Ct EN5 171 D5
Oakhill Dr AL6 89 A6
Oakhill Rd WD3 172 D6
Oakhurst Ave AL5 107 A5
Oakhurst Pl WD18 166 F5
Oakhurst Rd EN3 162 D3
Oakington AL7 111 D6
Oaklands HP4 122 A4
Oaklands (Herts Coll of Agriculture & Hort) AL4 128 E4
Oaklands Ave
Brookmans Park AL9 144 E4
Watford WD19 167 B1
Oaklands Cl CM23 59 B2
Oaklands Coll
St Albans AL1 127 E3
St Albans,The Camp AL4 128 D1
Oaklands Coll (Boreham Wood Campus) WD6 170 C7
Oaklands Coll (Harpenden Campus) AL5 86 B1
Oaklands Coll (Lemsford Lane Campus) AL8 110 B4
Oaklands Coll (Welwyn Garden City Campus) AL8 110 D7
Oaklands Ct Oaklands AL6 89 E7
Watford WD17 167 A8
Oaklands Dr CM23 59 B2
Oaklands Gate HA6 174 E4
Oaklands Gr EN10 148 E7
Oaklands La Arkley EN5 171 B5
St Albans AL4 128 F5
Oaklands Pk CM23 59 B2
Oaklands Prim Sch AL6 89 E7
Oaklands Rd
Hammond Street EN7 147 E5
Totteridge N20 171 F2
Oaklands Rise AL6 89 F7
Oaklands Wood AL10 130 A5
Oaklawn HP23 100 A3
Oaklea AL6 89 E7
Oaklea Cl AL6 89 E8
Oaklea Wood AL6 89 E7
Oakleigh Ct CM23 76 D8
Oakleigh Dr WD3 166 C3
Oakleigh Rd HA5 175 F4
Oakley Cl LU4 44 D4
Oakley Ct SG8 7 D7
Oakley Rd
Harpenden AL5 107 D7
Luton LU4 44 E3
Oakmeade HA5 176 A4
Oakmede 6 EN5 171 D5
Oakmere Ave EN6 159 C6
Oakmere Cl EN6 159 D8
Oakmere La EN6 159 C7
Oakmere Prim Sch EN6 159 D7
Oakridge AL2 140 F2
Oakridge Ave WD7 155 F6
Oakridge La WD7 155 E5
Oakroyd Ave EN6 158 F6
Oakroyd Cl EN6 158 F6
Oaks Cl Hitchin SG4 34 F5
Radlett WD7 155 F4
Oaks Cross SG2 51 B1
Oaks Ret Pk CM20 117 F3
Oaks The
Berkhamsted HP4 122 A4
Slip End LU1 63 C1
Watford WD19 167 C1
Oaktree Cl
14 Bishop's Stortford CM23 76 F7
Goff's Oak EN7 147 B3
Oaktree Cotts SG12 114 F6
Oaktree Garth AL7 110 E5
Oakview Cl Cheshunt EN7 148 B3
Harpenden AL5 106 F5
Oakway LU6 82 B7
Oakway Pl WD7 156 A5
Oakwell Cl SG2 69 D7
Oakwell Dr EN6 160 B7
Oakwood
Berkhamsted HP4 121 F3
Waltham Abbey EN9 163 E5
Oakwood Ave WD6 170 B5
Oakwood Cl SG2 51 C2
Oakwood Dr
Harpenden AL5 106 F5
Luton LU3 44 C8
St Albans AL4 128 C4
Oakwood Est CM20 118 B4
Oakwood Prim Sch AL4 128 C4
Oakwood Rd
Bricket Wood AL2 140 F2
Pinner HA5 175 B1
Oban Terr LU1 63 B8
Oberon Cl WD6 170 C8
Obrey Way CM23 76 E3
Occupation Rd WD18 167 B4
Octagan The SG12 93 D2
Octavia Ct WD24 167 C7
Oddfellows Ct 10 SG14 113 D6
Oddy Hill Tring HP23 100 C3
Wigginton HP23 100 C2
Odeon Par WD24 154 B3
Odyssey Rd WD6 170 B8
Offa Rd AL3 127 C3
Offas Way AL4 108 D8
Offerton Ho 13 WD19 175 C7
Offley Cross SG5 34 B5
Offley Endowed Prim Sch SG5 33 C3
Offley Hill SG5 33 C3
Offley Rd SG5 34 D6
Ogard Rd EN11 135 C8
Okeford Cl HP23 99 F4
Okeford Dr HP23 99 F4
Okeley La HP23 99 E3
Old Bakery SG5 34 E7
Old Barn La WD3 165 F4
Old Barn Mews WD3 165 F4
Old Bedford Rd Luton LU2 45 E4
Luton, Warden Hill LU2 45 D6
Old Bell Cl CM24 59 D6
Old Bourne Way SG1 37 A3
Old Brewery Cl SG5 11 F7
Old Brewery Pl SG4 66 D1
Old Chantry La SG4 35 F2
Old Charlton Rd SG5 34 E6
Old Chorleywood Rd WD3 165 D3
Old Church La SG12 93 E7
Old Coach Rd The SG14 112 C4
Old Common The SG9 43 B4
Old Crabtree La HP2 124 E2
Old Cross SG14 113 C6
Old Dean HP3 137 A4
Old Dr The AL8 110 B5
Old Farm LU7 80 D4
Old Fishery La
Hemel Hempstead HP1 123 F1
Hemel Hempstead HP1 137 F8
Old Fold Cl EN5 171 F8
Old Fold La EN5 171 F8
Old Fold View EN5 171 C6
Old Forge Cl
Abbots Langley WD25 154 A6
Welwyn Garden City AL7 89 F2
Old Forge Rd EN1 161 F1
Old Forge Row SG13 114 B3
Old Forge The HP23 79 B4
Old French Horn La AL10 130 B6
Old Gannon Cl HA6 174 C5
Old Garden Ct AL3 127 C3
Old Gorhanbury Ho★ AL3 126 C4
Old Granary The SG7 4 D4
Old Grove Cl EN7 147 D5
Old Hale Way SG5 21 E2
Old Hall Cl HA5 175 E2
Old Hall Dr HA5 175 E2
Old Harpenden Rd AL3 127 E6
Old Hat Factory The 1 LU2 45 D1
Old Herns La AL7 111 C8
Old Hertford Rd AL9 130 C7
Old Highway EN11 135 C8
Old House Ct HP2 124 F3
Old House La
Lower Nazeing EN9 149 F8
Sarratt WD4 152 F4
Old House Rd HP2 124 F3
Old Knebworth La SG3, SG2 68 D8
Old La SG3 69 B5
Old Leys AL10 130 A2
Old London Rd
Hertford SG13 113 E6
St Albans AL1 127 E2
Old Maltings The 2 CM23 77 A7
Old Maple HP2 104 F1
Old Meadow Cl HP4 122 A2
Old Mill Gdns HP4 122 D4
Old Mill La CM22 98 B6
Old Mill Rd WD4 153 C5
Old Nazeing Rd EN9, EN10 135 C1
Old North Rd
Kneesworth SG8 2 B4
Royston SG8 7 C8
Old Oak AL1 141 E8
Old Oak Cl SG15 11 A8
Old Oak Close Ind Est SG15 11 A8
Old Oak Gdns HP4 121 E7
Old Oaks EN9 163 E7
Old Orch Luton LU1 63 D5
Park Street AL2 141 D5
Old Orchard Cl EN4 159 D1
Old Orchard Mews HP4 122 C3
Old Park Rd SG5 34 E7
Old Parkbury La AL2 141 F1
Old Parkway Sch AL8 110 C5
Old Priory Pk AL1 127 E2
Old Rd CM17 118 D5
Old Rectory Cl AL5 86 A2
Old Rectory Dr AL10 130 B5
Old Rectory Gdns AL4 108 D8
Old Redding HA3 176 C6
Old River La CM23 76 F7
Old School Cl SG4 67 F1
Old School Cotts HP5 136 D5
Old School Flats The HP23 99 D8
Old School Gn SG2 52 E5
Old School Orch SG14 70 E3
Old School The
Hertford Heath SG13 114 C4
Shillington SG5 19 E8
Old School Wlk
Arlesey SG15 11 A4
Slip End LU1 63 C1
Old Shire La WD3 164 A2
Old Solesbridge La WD3 165 A6
Old Sopwell Gdns AL1 127 E1
Old South Cl HA5 175 D2
Old Uxbridge Rd WD3 172 E3
Old Vicarage Gdns AL3 83 D6
Old Waddling La 5 AL4 87 D1
Old Walled Gdn The SG1 36 C1
Old Watford Rd AL2 140 E2
Old Watling St AL3 84 B3
Old Works The AL1 127 E2
Old's App WD18 166 C1
Old's Cl WD18 166 B1
Olde Ct HA6 174 E4
Olde Swann Ct SG1 50 C8
Olden Mead SG6 23 B3
Oldfield Cl EN8 148 E3
Oldfield Ct AL1 127 E3
Oldfield Dr EN8 148 E3
Oldfield Farm Rd
Lower Stondon SG16 10 B4
Lower Stondon SG16 10 C4
Oldfield Rd
Hemel Hempstead HP1 123 E2
London Colney AL2 142 D6
Oldfield Rise SG4 66 E7
Oldhall Ct SG4 66 E7
Oldhall St SG14 113 D6
Oldhams Trad Est WD24 154 C2
Oldhill Wood LU6 82 D6
Oldhouse Croft CM20 117 E2
Oldings Cnr AL9 110 B1
Oldpark Ride EN7 161 D7
Oldwood AL6 89 D7
Olive Taylor Ct HP2 124 F7
Oliver Cl
Hemel Hempstead HP3 138 E7
Park Street AL2 141 D4
Oliver Ct SG12 92 E4
Oliver Rd HP3 138 F7
Oliver Rise HP3 138 E7
Oliver's La SG5 11 F7
Olivers Cl HP4 123 C7
Olivia Gdns UB9 173 C2
Olleberrie La HP3,WD3 151 D7
Olwen Mews HA5 175 D1
Olyard Ct LU1 63 B6
Olympus Rd SG16 10 B4
Omega Ct 4 SG12 93 D1
Omega Maltings 2 SG12 93 E1
On The Hill WD19 175 E8
Onslow Cl AL10 130 B5
Onslow Rd LU4 44 D5
Onslow St Audrey's Sch AL10 130 B5
Ontario Cl EN10 148 E6
Opening The SG4 88 F8
Openshaw Way SG6 23 A6
Optima Bsns Pk EN11 135 C7
Opus Ct WD6 170 A6
Oram Pl HP3 138 D8
Orbital Cres WD25 153 F4
Orchard Ave
Berkhamsted HP4 122 A4
Harpenden AL5 85 F1
Watford WD25 154 B8
Orchard Cl
Borehamwood WD6 169 F6
Bushey WD23 168 D1
Caddington LU1 62 E4
Chorleywood WD3 164 D5
Cuffley EN6 146 E3
Hemel Hempstead HP2 124 F5
Kneesworth SG8 2 A5
Letchworth SG6 22 F8
Little Berkhamsted SG13 132 C4
Radlett WD7 155 E3
St Albans AL1 127 F2
St Ippolyts SG4 34 F3
Stanstead Abbotts SG12 115 C4
Ware SG12 93 D2
Watford WD17 166 F7
Wingrave HP22 60 B3
Orchard Cres SG1 50 C7
Orchard Croft CM20 118 A2
Orchard Ct HP9 137 A4
Orchard Dr
Chiswell Green AL2 141 B5
Chorleywood WD3 164 D5
Standon SG11 55 E2
Watford WD17 166 F8
Orchard Gdns EN9 163 C5
Orchard Ho SG11 55 F7
Orchard House La AL1 127 D2
Orchard Lea CM21 97 C1
Orchard Mead AL10 129 F5
Orchard On The Green The WD3 165 F4
Orchard Pl EN8 148 D1
Orchard Prim Sch The WD24 153 F3
Orchard Rd Baldock SG7 12 E1
Barnet EN5 171 F5
Bishop's Stortford CM23 59 B1
Hitchin SG4 22 B1
Royston SG8 7 B7
Stevenage SG1 50 C7
Tewin AL6 90 C5
Welwyn AL6 89 C5
Orchard Sq EN10 148 F7
Orchard St
Hemel Hempstead HP3 138 D8
St Albans AL3 127 C2
Orchard The Baldock SG7 23 F8
Codicote SG4 67 F1
Hertford SG14 92 C1
Kings Langley WD4 139 A2
Radlett WD6 168 F7
Tonwell SG12 92 E7
Welwyn Garden City AL8 110 D8
Orchard View AL6 89 F7
Orchard Way
Bovingdon HP3 137 A3
Breachwood Green SG4 47 E1
Goff's Oak EN7 147 B3
Knebworth SG3 68 E5
Letchworth SG6 22 F8
Lower Stondon SG16 10 B3
Luton LU4 44 C4
Pitstone LU7 80 E5
Potters Bar EN6 145 B2
Rickmansworth WD3 165 A2
Royston SG8 7 C8
Orchards The
Sawbridgeworth CM21 97 E3
Slip End LU1 63 C2
Tring HP23 99 F3
Orchid Cl
Goff's Oak EN7 147 C1
Hatfield AL10 109 F1
Orchid Ho AL1 127 F3
Ordelmere SG6 11 F1
Ordnance Rd EN3 162 E2
Oregon Way LU3 45 A8
Organ Hall Rd WD6 169 E8
Orient Cl AL1 127 E1
Orient Ctr The WD24 154 D2
Oriole Cl WD5 154 A8
Oriole Way CM23 76 C6
Orion Gate SG1 50 F5
Orion Way HA6 175 A6
Orkney Ho WD18 166 F4
Orlando Cl SG4 35 A6
Ormesby Dr EN6 158 D7
Ormonde Rd HA6 174 D6
Ormsby Cl LU1 63 E5
Ormskirk Rd WD19 175 D5
Oronsay HP3 125 B1
Orphanage Rd WD17, WD24 167 C7
Orpington Cl LU4 44 A3
Orton Cl AL4 128 A7
Orwell Ave SG1 36 F3
Orwell Ct 5 WD24 167 D7
Orwell View SG7 13 B1
Osborn Way AL8 110 D6
Osborne Ct 9 Luton LU1 63 F6
Potters Bar EN6 145 B1
Osborne Gdns EN6 145 B1
Osborne Rd
Cheshunt EN8 148 E4
Hoddesdon EN10 135 A4
Luton LU1 63 F6
Potters Bar EN6 145 B1
Watford WD24 154 C1
Osborne Way HP23 100 D1
Osbourne Ave WD4 138 F3
Osbourne Gdns 5 CM23 76 E5
Osier Ct 8 SG5 34 F8
Osiers The WD3 166 C4
Osmington Pl HP23 99 F4
Osprey Cl WD25 154 E5
Osprey Gdns SG2 51 D2
Osprey Ho 3 SG12 93 C3
Osprey Wlk LU4 44 A5
Ostell Cres EN3 163 A1
Oster St AL3 127 C4
Osterley Cl SG2 69 C7
Ostler Cl CM23 76 C4
Oswald Rd AL1 127 E2
Otley Way WD19 175 C7
Otter Gdns AL10 130 B4
Otterspool La WD25 154 E1
Otterspool Way WD25 154 F1
Otterton Cl AL5 85 F3
Ottoman Terr WD17 167 C6
Ottway Wlk AL6 89 C4
Otway Gdns WD23 168 E2
Otways Cl EN6 159 B6
Oudle La SG10 74 F2
Oughton Cl SG5 34 C8
Oughton Head Way SG5 34 D8
Oughton Prim Sch SG5 21 C1
Oughtonhead La SG5 34 C8
Oughtonhead Prim Sch SG5 34 C8
Oulton Cres EN6 158 D7
Oulton Rise AL5 86 C3
Oulton Way WD19 175 F6
Oundle Ave WD23 168 C3
Oundle Ct SG2 69 C8

Oundle Path SG2 .69 C8
Oundle The SG2 .69 C8
Our Lady RC Prim Sch
AL7 .110 E4
Our Lady's RC Prim Sch
SG5 .21 E2
Ousden Cl EN8 .148 E1
Ousden Dr EN8 .148 E1
Ouseley Cl LU4 .44 D3
Outlook Ho EN3 .162 F3
Oval The Cheshunt EN10 .148 E7
Lower Stondon SG16 .10 C3
Stevenage SG1 .37 A1
Overfield Rd LU2 .46 C1
Overlord Cl EN10 .134 E3
Overstone Rd
Harpenden AL5 .86 C1
Luton LU4 .44 D1
Overstream WD3 .165 B5
Overtrees AL5 .85 F3
Oving Cl LU2 .46 D2
Owen Dr SG8 .2 D1
Owen Jones Cl SG16 .10 C5
Owens Way WD3 .166 A5
Owles La SG9 .41 A6
Ox La AL5 .86 B3
Oxcroft CM23 .76 F3
Oxen Ind Est LU2 .45 F1
Oxen Rd LU2 .45 F1
Oxendon Dr EN11 .135 A5
Oxfield Cl HP4 .122 A3
Oxford Ave AL1 .128 C2
Oxford Cl Cheshunt EN8 .148 D2
Kneesworth SG8 .2 A7
Moor Park HA6 .174 D6
Oxford Ho 8 WD6 .170 A7
Oxford Pl AL10 .129 E7
Oxford Rd
Breachwood Green SG4 .47 E1
2 Luton LU1 .63 E6
Oxford St WD18 .167 B4
Oxhey Ave WD19 .167 D2
Oxhey Dr S WD19 .175 B7
Oxhey Inf Sch WD23 .167 E4
Oxhey La Pinner HA5 .176 A5
South Oxhey WD19 .175 F7
Watford WD19 .167 D2
Oxhey Rd WD19 .167 D2
Oxhey Ridge Cl HA6 .175 B5
Oxhey Wood Prim Sch
WD19 .175 C7
Oxlease Dr AL10 .130 B4
Oxleys Rd SG2 .51 B3
Oxleys The CM17 .118 E4
Oysterfields AL3 .127 C4

P

Pacatian Way SG1 .51 C8
Packhorse Cl AL4 .128 C6
Packhorse La EN6 .157 D8
Paddick Cl EN11 .134 F7
Paddock Cl Hunsdon SG12 95 D1
Letchworth SG6 .23 A5
Watford WD19 .167 E3
Paddock Ho AL7 .111 B6
Paddock Rd SG9 .40 E8
Paddock The
Bishop's Stortford CM23 .76 D3
Hatfield AL10 .130 A6
Hitchin SG4 .35 A5
Hoddesdon EN10 .135 A3
Paddock Way HP1 .123 E3
Paddock Wood AL5 .107 E7
Paddocks Cl SG2 .51 B4
Paddocks The
Chorleywood WD3 .164 F5
Codicote SG4 .68 A1
Hertford Heath SG13 .114 B3
Kimpton AL4 .87 B6
Stevenage SG2 .51 B3
Welwyn Garden City AL7 .111 B7
Padgate Ho 12 WD19 .175 C7
Padgets The EN9 .163 E5
Page Cl SG7 .23 F6
Page Hill SG12 .93 C2
Page Rd SG13 .114 A6
Pageant Rd AL1 .127 D2
Pages Cl CM23 .76 D5
Pages Croft HP4 .122 A6
Paget Cotts SG12 .71 F7
Paignton Cl LU4 .44 D4
Paine's La HA5 .175 E1
Paines Orch LU7 .80 A8
Painters La EN3 .162 E4
Palace Cl WD4 .139 A1
Palace Gdns
Bishop's Stortford CM23 .76 E5
Royston SG8 .7 C6
Palfrey Cl AL3 .127 D5
Pallas Rd HP2 .124 F5
Pallett Ct EN11 .135 B4
Palmer Ave WD23 .168 B4
Palmer Cl SG14 .113 C8
Palmer Ct SG12 .92 E4
Palmer Gdns EN5 .171 D4
Palmer Rd SG14 .113 D8
Palmers Gr EN9 .135 F1
Palmers La 8 CM23 .76 F7
Palmers Rd WD6 .170 B8
Palmers Way EN8 .148 E2
Palmerston Cl AL8 .110 C6
Palmerston Ct SG2 .51 B7
Palmerston Dr 7 AL4 .87 D1
Pamela Ave HP3 .138 F8
Pamela Gdns CM23 .76 F3
Pams La SG4 .66 D1
Pancake La HP2 .125 D2
Pankhurst Cres SG2 .51 C5
Pankhurst Pl WD24 .167 C6
Pankridge WD19 .175 D8
Panshanger Aerodrome
AL6,AL7 .111 D7
Panshanger Dr AL7 .111 C6
Panshanger Prim Sch
AL7 .111 A7
Pantiles The WD23 .168 D1
Panxworth Rd 1 HP3 .124 D1
Paper Mill La SG11 .55 E1
Par Cl SG13 .114 B7
Parade The
Hatfield AL10 .130 C7
Letchworth SG6 .11 F1
Luton LU3 .44 C7
South Oxhey WD19 .175 D7
South Oxhey WD19 .175 E7
Watford WD17 .167 B6
Paradise HP2 .124 D2
Paradise Cl EN7 .148 B3
Paradise Rd EN9 .163 C5
Paradise Wildlife Pk*
EN10 .133 F2
Paramount Ind Est
WD24 .154 C1
Parish Cl WD25 .154 C5
Parishes Mead SG2 .51 D4
Park Ave
Bishop's Stortford CM23 .76 F3
Luton LU3 .44 C7
Potters Bar EN6 .159 D6
Radlett WD7 .156 B6
Rickmansworth WD3 .165 A5
St Albans AL1 .128 A4
Watford WD23 .167 E7
Watford,West Watford
WD18 .167 A5
Park Ave N AL5 .85 F1
Park Ave S AL5 .85 F1
Park Avenue Maisonettes
WD23 .167 F7
Park Avenue Trad Est
LU3 .44 C7
Park Cl Baldock SG7 .23 F7
Brookmans Park AL9 .145 A5
Harrow HA3 .176 E2
Hatfield AL9 .130 C6
Markyate AL3 .83 D5
Rickmansworth WD3 .174 B6
Stevenage SG2 .51 B1
Watford WD23 .167 D6
Park Cnr AL4 .143 B8
Park Cres Baldock SG7 .23 E7
Borehamwood WD6 .169 F6
Harrow HA3 .176 E2
Park Ct Harlow CM20 .117 D2
Letchworth SG6 .23 A6
Luton LU2 .45 D1
Northwood HA6 .174 F4
Park Dr Baldock SG7 .23 E7
Potters Bar EN6 .159 B8
Standon SG11 .55 D3
Stanmore HA3 .176 E4
Park Farm Cl SG16 .10 D8
Park Farm Ind Est SG9 .40 D8
Park Farm Ind Pk SG8 .18 F2
Park Farm La SG8 .18 C2
Park Gate SG4 .34 F6
Park Gdns SG7 .23 E7
Park Hill Harlow CM17 .118 B4
Harpenden AL5 .85 F2
Park Hill Rd HP1 .124 B3
Park Ho
Berkhamsted HP4 .122 B5
Welwyn Garden City AL8 .110 D7
Park Ind Est AL2 .141 E4
Park La
Bishop's Stortford CM23 .76 F4
Cheshunt EN7 .162 D6
Colney Heath AL4 .129 C1
Hammond Street EN7 .148 A4
Harefield UB9 .173 B2
Harlow CM20 .117 D2
Hemel Hempstead HP2 .124 D2
Hoddesdon EN10 .134 F3
Kimpton SG4 .66 C1
Knebworth SG3 .68 D5
Standon SG11 .55 D3
Park Lane Paradise
EN7 .148 A6
Park Lodge WD25 .154 D5
Park Mans HA6 .174 C7
Park Mdw AL9 .130 C6
Park Mead CM20 .117 B1
Park Mews AL9 .130 C6
Park Mount AL5 .85 F3
Park Nook Gdns EN2 .161 D2
Park Pl Park Street AL2 .141 D4
Stevenage SG1 .50 D5
Park Place Chambers
SG1 .50 D5
Park Rd Barnet EN5 .171 F5
Bushey WD23 .168 A3
Cheshunt EN8 .162 D6
Enfield EN3 .162 E3
Hemel Hempstead HP1 .124 C1
Hertford SG13 .113 E6
Hoddesdon EN11 .135 A6
Northaw EN6 .146 A1
Radlett WD7 .156 A4
Rickmansworth WD3 .165 E2
Stansted Mountfitchet
CM24 .59 E6
Park Rd *continued*
Tring HP23 .100 A3
Ware SG12 .93 B2
Watford WD17 .167 B8
Park Rise
Berkhamsted HP4 .121 E6
Harpenden AL5 .85 E3
Harrow HA3 .176 E2
Park Rise Cl AL5 .85 E3
Park Sq LU1 .63 E7
Park St Baldock SG7 .23 E8
Berkhamsted HP4 .122 B5
Hatfield AL9 .130 C6
Hitchin SG4 .34 E6
Luton LU1 .63 F6
Park Street AL2 .141 D5
Tring HP23 .100 A3
Park St W LU1 .63 E7
Park Street CE Sch AL2 141 D4
Park Street La AL2 .141 C3
Park Street Sta AL2 .141 D5
Park Terr Enfield EN3 .162 E1
2 Luton LU1 .63 F6
Much Hadham SG10 .74 F3
Park The Redbourn AL3 .106 B5
St Albans AL1 .128 A5
Park Viaduct LU1 .63 F6
Park View
Great Hormead SG9 .42 A7
Hatfield AL9 .130 C7
Hoddesdon EN11 .135 A5
Pinner HA5 .175 F2
Potters Bar EN6 .159 C6
Stevenage SG2 .51 B1
Park View Cl Luton LU3 .44 D6
St Albans AL1 .128 A2
Park View Cotts CM23 .76 F3
Park View Ct HP4 .122 B4
Park View Dr AL3 .83 D6
Park View Rd
Berkhamsted HP4 .122 B4
Pinner HA5 .175 B3
Park Way Hitchin SG5 .34 E6
Rickmansworth WD3 .165 C1
Parker Ave SG14 .113 D8
Parker Cl SG6 .22 E4
Parker St WD24 .167 B8
Parker's Field SG2 .51 C4
Parkers La SG7 .3 D5
Parkfield
Chorleywood WD3 .164 F5
Letchworth SG6 .23 D4
Markyate AL3 .83 D5
Parkfield Ave HA2 .176 C1
Parkfield Cres
Harrow HA2 .176 C1
Kimpton SG4 .66 D1
Parkfield Ho HA2 .176 B2
Parkfield View EN6 .159 B7
Parkfields AL8 .110 D6
Parkgate Inf Sch WD24 .154 C2
Parkgate Jun Sch
WD24 .154 C2
Parkgate Rd WD24 .154 C2
Parkhurst Rd SG14 .113 C7
Parkins Cl SG11 .73 A6
Parkinson Cl AL4 .108 D8
Parkland Cl 3 EN11 .115 B1
Parkland Dr LU1 .63 D5
Parklands Bushey WD23 .168 C3
Hemel Hempstead HP1 .123 F5
Royston SG8 .7 E6
Waltham Abbey EN9 .163 D7
Parklands Cl EN4 .159 D1
Parklands Dr AL3 .127 A2
Parkmead 6 LU1 .63 F6
Parkside Cheshunt EN8 .162 E5
Potters Bar EN6 .159 C7
Watford WD19 .167 C3
Welwyn AL6 .89 C5
Wyddial SG9 .27 D2
Parkside Com Prim Sch
WD6 .156 F1
Parkside Ct EN7 .148 B3
Parkside Dr WD17 .166 F7
Parkside Rd HA6 .174 F5
Parkview Ct HA3 .176 E3
Parkview Ho WD19 .167 D3
Parkway
Sawbridgeworth CM21 .97 F1
Stevenage SG2 .51 A1
Welwyn Garden City AL8 .110 C6
Parkway Cl AL8 .110 C6
Parkway Ct AL1 .142 B8
Parkway Gdns AL8 .110 D5
Parkway Rd LU1 .64 B5
Parkwood Cl EN10 .134 F4
Parkwood Dr HP1 .123 F3
Parliament Sq SG14 .113 D6
Parmiter's Sch WD25 .154 C8
Parndon Mill La CM20 .117 B3
Parnel Rd SG12 .93 F2
Parnell Cl WD5 .139 F1
Parr Cres HP2 .125 B8
Parrott's La HP23 .120 A4
Parrotts Cl WD3 .166 A4
Parrotts Field EN11 .135 B7
Parson's Cl AL3 .84 B1
Parsonage Cl
Abbots Langley WD5 .139 E1
Tring HP23 .100 A4
Parsonage Ct HP23 .100 A3
Parsonage Farm
Rickmansworth WD3 .165 C2
Wingrave HP22 .60 B3
Parsonage Farm Trad Est
CM24 .59 F3
Parsonage La Albury SG11 57 A6
Parsonage La *continued*
Bishop's Stortford CM23 .77 C8
Spellbrook CM21 .97 D6
Stansted Mountfitchet CM24 59 F4
Welham Green AL9 .144 B8
Parsonage Pl HP23 .100 A3
Parsonage Rd
Rickmansworth WD3 .165 D2
Welham Green AL9 .144 B8
Parsons Green Est SG1 .37 C2
Parthia Cl SG8 .7 E6
Partridge Cl Barnet EN5 .171 C3
Bushey WD23 .168 C1
Luton LU4 .44 A5
Partridge Hill SG7 .4 C3
Partridge Rd AL3 .127 D7
Parva Cl AL5 .107 D6
Parvills EN9 .163 D7
Parys Rd LU3 .45 B6
Pascal Way SG6 .23 B8
Pasfield EN9 .163 D6
Passfield Cotts SG11 .72 F1
Passingham Ave SG4 .35 A6
Paston Rd HP2 .124 E5
Pasture Cl WD23 .168 C2
Pasture La SG4 .65 E8
Pasture Rd SG6 .22 E3
Pastures Ct LU4 .44 A3
Pastures The
Chiswell Green AL2 .141 A7
Hatfield AL10 .130 B4
Hemel Hempstead HP1 .123 E4
Stevenage SG2 .51 D8
Totteridge N20 .171 F1
Ware SG12 .93 C3
Watford WD19 .167 C2
Welwyn Garden City AL7 .111 B4
Pastures Way LU4 .44 A4
Pat Larner Ho 9 AL1 .127 D2
Paternoster Cl EN9 .163 F6
Paternoster Hill EN9 .163 F7
Pathway The
Radlett WD7 .155 F3
Watford WD19 .167 D1
Patmore Cl CM23 .76 C8
Patmore Heath (Nature
Reserve)* SG11 .57 D8
Patmore Link Rd HP2 .125 C2
Patmore Rd EN9 .163 E5
Patricia Gdns CM23 .76 E5
Patrick Gr EN9 .163 B6
Paul's Gn EN8 .162 E6
Pauls La EN11 .135 A6
Paxton Rd
Berkhamsted HP4 .122 D4
St Albans AL1 .127 E2
Payne End SG9 .15 B1
Payne's Pk SG5 .34 E7
Paynes Cl SG6 .12 A1
Paynes Field Cl HP4 .121 D7
Paynes La EN9 .149 C7
Paynesfield Rd WD23 .168 F2
Pea La HP4 .121 D7
Peabody Ct EN3 .163 A2
Peace Cl EN7 .148 B2
Peace Dr WD17 .167 A6
Peace Gr AL6 .90 A7
Peace Prospect WD17 .167 A6
Peach Ct LU1 .63 F6
Peacock Wlk WD5 .154 A8
Peacocks Cl HP4 .121 F6
Peakes La EN7 .147 F4
Peakes Pl AL1 .127 F3
Peakes Way EN7 .147 F4
Pear Tree Cl SG16 .10 B3
Pear Tree Dell SG6 .23 B3
Pear Tree Wlk EN7 .147 E5
Pearces Wlk 4 AL1 .127 D2
Pearl Ct Baldock SG7 .12 F1
Hoddesdon EN11 .135 A6
Pearman Dr SG12 .71 E7
Pearsall Cl SG6 .23 B5
Pearson Ave SG13 .113 C4
Pearsons Cl SG13 .113 C4
Peartree Cl
Hemel Hempstead HP1 .124 A4
Welwyn Garden City AL7 .110 E6
Peartree Ct
Watford WD24 .154 D3
Welwyn Garden City AL7 .110 E5
Peartree Farm AL7 .110 E6
Peartree La AL7 .110 E6
Peartree Prim Sch AL7 .110 E5
Peartree Rd
Hemel Hempstead HP1 .124 A4
Luton LU2 .46 C4
Peartree Spring Inf Sch
SG2 .51 B3
Peartree Spring Jun Sch
SG2 .51 B3
Peartree Way SG2 .51 A3
Peascroft Rd HP3 .125 B1
Peasecroft SG9 .39 C7
Peasmead SG9 .40 E6
Pebbles The SG7 .12 C4
Peck's Hill EN9 .135 E2
Peckworth Ind Est SG16 .10 A4
Pedlars La SG8 .15 E7
Pedley Hill HP4,LU6 .82 C1
Peel Cres SG14 .113 C8
Peel Pl 6 LU1 .63 D7
Peel St LU1 .63 D7
Peerglow Ctr SG12 .114 E8
Peerglow Ind Est WD18 166 B1
Peg's La SG13 .113 D5
Pegasus Ct WD5 .153 F7
Pegasus Pl AL3 .127 D5
Pegmire La WD25 .168 C8
Pegrum Dr AL2 .142 B5
Pegs La SG12 .95 D5
Pegsdon Cl LU3 .45 B7
Pegsdon Way SG5 .19 E1
Peitley Cotts AL3 .84 A1
Pelham Ct
Hemel Hempstead HP2 .125 C3
Welwyn Garden City AL7 .111 C5
Pelham Rd SG11 .55 F7
Pelhams The WD25 .154 D4
Pelican Way SG6 .11 F1
Pemberton Almshouses 4
AL3 .127 D4
Pemberton Cl AL1 .141 D8
Pembridge Chase HP3 .137 A3
Pembridge La EN10 .133 E2
Pembridge Rd HP3 .137 A3
Pembroke Ave
Enfield EN1 .162 B1
Luton LU4 .44 F3
Pembroke Cl EN10 .148 E8
Pembroke Dr EN7 .147 B2
Pembroke Ho 3 WD6 .170 A5
Pembroke Rd Baldock SG7 23 F8
Moor Park HA6 .174 C7
Pemsel Ct HP3 .124 E1
Penda Cl LU3 .44 F7
Pendennis Ct AL5 .107 D7
Penfold Cl SG7 .24 A7
Penfold Trad Est WD24 .167 C8
Pengelly Cl EN7 .148 B1
Penhill LU3 .44 E6
Penhill Ct LU3 .44 E6
Penman Cl AL2 .141 A4
Penn Cl WD3 .164 D3
Penn Ho Moor Park HA6 .174 C7
14 South Oxhey WD19 .175 C7
Penn Pl 1 WD3 .165 D2
Penn Rd
Chiswell Green AL2 .141 C4
Rickmansworth WD3 .165 A1
Stevenage SG1 .50 E4
Penn Way
Chorleywood WD3 .164 D3
Letchworth SG6 .23 B3
Pennard Ho 8 WD19 .175 D7
Penne Cl WD7 .156 A5
Pennine Ave LU3 .44 D8
Pennine Way HP2 .125 A7
Pennington La CM24 .59 D8
Penningtons CM23 .76 C5
Penns The SG8 .17 E6
Penny Croft AL5 .107 A4
Penny Ct WD17 .167 B7
Pennyfather Cl SG3 .69 E2
Pennyfathers La AL6 .90 B4
Pennymead CM20 .118 A1
Penray EN5 .171 E6
Penrose Ave WD19 .175 E8
Penrose Ct HP2 .124 E7
Penscroft Gdns WD6 .170 D5
Penshurst CM17 .118 C3
Penshurst Cl AL5 .85 D4
Penshurst Rd EN6 .159 D7
Penta Ct WD6 .170 A5
Pentagon Pk HP2 .125 C5
Pentland HP2 .124 F6
Pentland Rd WD23 .168 C3
Pentland Rise SG1 .37 C3
Pentley Cl AL8 .89 D1
Pentley Pk AL8 .89 D1
Penton Dr EN8 .148 D2
Pentrich Ave EN1 .162 A1
Penzance Cl UB9 .173 D1
Peplins Cl AL9 .144 E5
Peplins Way AL9 .144 E5
Peppard Cl AL3 .106 A6
Pepper Ct SG7 .23 F8
Pepper Hill SG12 .114 F4
Peppercorn Wlk SG4 .35 B7
Peppett's Gn HP5 .120 D1
Pepsal End SG2 .69 B8
Pepsal End Rd LU1 .84 C7
Pepys Cres EN5 .171 C4
Pepys Way SG7 .23 E8
Percheron Dr LU4 .44 A3
Percheron Rd WD6 .170 D3
Percival Ct EN8 .148 E1
Percival Way LU2 .64 C7
Percy Rd WD18 .167 B5
Peregrine Cl
Bishop's Stortford CM23 .76 D6
Watford WD25 .154 E5
Peregrine Ho 1 SG12 .93 C3
Peregrine Rd LU4 .44 A4
Perham Way AL2 .142 D6
Perivale Gdns WD25 .154 B5
Periwinkle Cl SG8 .17 C5
Periwinkle La SG5 .21 F1
Permain Cl WD7 .156 E6
Perowne Way SG11 .55 E3
Perram Cl EN10 .148 E5
Perriors Cl EN7 .148 A4
Perry Dr SG8 .7 E7
Perry Gn HP2 .105 A1
Perry Hill EN9 .149 F8
Perry Mead WD23 .168 C3
Perrycoste Ct AL4 .128 A8
Perrymead LU2 .46 F2
Perrysfield Rd EN8 .148 E5
Perrywood AL8 .110 D8
Perrywood La SG14 .91 B7
Perspective Ho EN3 .162 E3
Pescot Hill HP1 .124 B5
Petard Cl LU4 .44 A2
Peter's Pl HP4 .121 E6
Peterborough Ho 9
WD6 .170 A7

Peterlee Ct 2 HP2 ...124 F7
Peters Ave AL2 ...142 C5
Peters Way SG3 ...68 F6
Peters Wood Hill SG12 .114 E7
Petersfield AL3 ...127 E7
Peterslea WD4 ...139 B2
Pettys Cl EN8 ...148 D3
Petunia Ct LU3 ...45 C1
Petworth Cl SG2 ...69 C7
Pevensey Cl LU2 ...46 D4
Pewterers Ave CM23 ...76 C4
Pheasant Cl
Berkhamsted HP4 ...122 C3
Tring HP23 ...100 B6
Pheasants Way WD3 ...165 B2
Phillimore Ct WD7 ...155 E3
Phillimore Pl WD7 ...155 E3
Phillipers WD25 ...154 E4
Phillips Ave SG8 ...7 C8
Phipps Hatch La EN2 ...161 C1
Phoenix Cl HA6 ...174 F6
Phoenix Ct EN3 ...162 C1
Phyllis Courtnage Ho 4
HP2 ...124 D5
Piccotts End La HP2 ...124 D7
Piccotts End Rd HP1 ...124 C7
Pick Hill EN9 ...163 F7
Pickets Cl WD23 ...168 E1
Picketts AL8 ...89 D1
Pickford Hill AL5 ...86 C3
Pickford Rd Markyate AL3 83 D5
St Albans AL1 ...128 B2
Picknage Cnr SG8 ...9 A2
Picknage Rd SG8 ...9 A2
Pie Cnr AL3 ...84 C1
Pie Gdn AL3 ...84 C1
Pierian Spring HP1 ...124 B5
Pietley Hill AL3 ...84 A1
Pig La CM22 ...77 A3
Pigeonwick AL5 ...86 B3
Piggotts La LU4 ...44 D4
Piggotts Way CM23 ...76 E5
Piggottshill La AL5 ...107 D8
Pightle Cl SG8 ...7 D7
Pightle The LU7 ...80 D3
Pike End SG1 ...50 D6
Pikes Cotts EN5 ...171 C5
Pikes Leap 6 AL4 ...87 D1
Pilgrim Cl
Chiswell Green AL2 ...141 C4
Watford WD25 ...154 D6
Pilgrims Row SG9 ...40 F3
Pilgrims Way SG1 ...37 B2
Piltdown Rd WD19 ...175 D6
Pin Green Ind Est SG1 ...37 C2
Pin Green Prim Sch SG1 .50 F6
Pinchfield WD3 ...172 D5
Pindar Rd EN11 ...135 C7
Pine Cl Berkhamsted HP4 122 B4
Cheshunt EN8 ...148 D3
Pine Crest AL6 ...89 E8
Pine Gr
Bishop's Stortford CM23 ...77 B6
Bricket Wood AL2 ...140 F1
Brookmans Park AL9 ...145 B6
Totteridge N20 ...171 F1
Watford WD23 ...167 F8
Pine Ridge AL1 ...142 A8
Pine Tree Cl HP2 ...124 D4
Pine Wlk HP4 ...121 D7
Pinecroft HP3 ...138 F7
Pinecroft Cres EN5 ...171 E5
Pinecroft Ct HP3 ...138 F7
Pinehill Hospl SG4 ...35 A7
Pinehurst Cl WD5 ...153 E7
Pinelands CM23 ...58 F1
Pineridge Ct 4 EN5 ...171 D5
Pines Ave EN1 ...162 B3
Pines Cl HA6 ...174 E4
Pines Hill CM24 ...59 D5
Pines The
Borehamwood WD6 ...169 F7
Hemel Hempstead HP3 ...137 F7
Pinetree Gdns 5 HP2 ...124 E2
Pinetree Ho WD25 ...154 E3
Pinewood AL7 ...110 E4
Pinewood Ave HA5 ...176 B4
Pinewood Cl
Borehamwood WD6 ...170 D7
Pinner HA5 ...176 B4
South Oxhey WD19 ...175 B5
St Albans AL4 ...128 C3
Watford WD17 ...167 A8
Pinewood Dr EN6 ...158 F8
Pinewood Gdns HP1 ...124 B3
Pinewood Lodge 1
WD23 ...168 D1
Pinewood Sch SG12 ...114 D7
Pinewoods 4 SG2 ...50 F1
Pinfold Rd WD23 ...167 F7
Pinford Dell 4 LU2 ...46 D1
Pinks Farm WD7 ...157 C8
Pinnacles EN9 ...163 E5
Pinnate Pl AL7 ...110 E2
Pinner Gn HA5 ...175 C1
Pinner Hill HA5 ...175 B3
Pinner Hill Rd HA5 ...175 C1
Pinner Park Ave HA2 ...176 C1
Pinner Park Gdns HA2 .176 C1
Pinner Rd
Northwood HA6 ...175 A1
Watford WD19 ...167 E2
Pinner Wood Fst & Mid Schs
HA5 ...175 C2
Pinnocks Cl SG7 ...23 F7
Pinnocks La SG7 ...23 F8
Pinto Cl WD6 ...170 D3
Pioneer Way WD18 ...166 F3
Pipers Ave AL5 ...107 D7
Pipers Cl AL3 ...106 A6
Pipers Hill HP1 ...103 D3
Pipers La
Caddington AL3,LU1 ...62 F1
Wheathampstead AL5 ...107 F7
Pipit Cl SG8 ...7 E8
Pippens AL8 ...89 E1
Pippin Cl WD7 ...156 E6
Pippin Gr SG8 ...7 C7
Pippins The WD25 ...154 C5
Pirton Cl Hitchin SG5 ...34 D6
St Albans AL4 ...128 C8
Pirton Cross SG5 ...34 A7
Pirton Ct HP2 ...124 F4
Pirton Hill Inf Sch LU4 .44 B6
Pirton Hill Jun Sch LU4 .44 B6
Pirton Rd Hitchin SG5 ...34 C6
Holwell SG5 ...21 A7
Luton LU4 ...44 D5
Pirton Sch SG5 ...20 D4
Pishiobury Dr CM21 ...118 D8
Pitsfield AL8 ...89 D1
Pitsford Terr LU2 ...46 A1
Pitstone Cl AL4 ...128 C8
Pitstone Common Forest
Trails★ HP4 ...101 E7
Pitstone Green Farm Mus★
LU7 ...80 D4
Pitstone Windmill★ LU7 .80 F4
Pitt Ct SG2 ...51 B1
Pitt Dr AL4 ...142 C8
Pitteway Wlk SG14 ...113 C6
Pittmans Field CM20 ...117 F1
Pix Ct SG15 ...11 A8
Pix Farm La HP1 ...123 C2
Pix Rd Letchworth SG6 ...23 A6
Stotfold SG5 ...11 E5
Pixies Hill Cres HP1 ...123 F2
Pixies Hill Jun Mix Inf Sch
HP1 ...123 F2
Pixies Hill Rd HP1 ...123 F2
Pixmore Ave SG6 ...23 B6
Pixmore Ind Est SG6 ...23 A6
Pixmore Jun Sch SG6 ...23 A5
Pixmore Way SG6 ...23 A5
Plaistow Way SG8 ...9 E2
Plaiters Cl HP23 ...100 B4
Plaitford Cl WD3 ...173 E8
Plantaganet Pl EN9 ...163 B6
Plantation Rd LU3 ...44 D7
Plantation Wlk HP1 ...124 A6
Plash Dr SG1 ...50 E5
Plashes Cl SG11 ...55 D2
Plashes Dr SG9 ...40 F6
Plashets CM22 ...98 D1
Platt Cl LU4 ...44 D4
Plaw Hatch Cl CM23 ...77 B8
Plaw Hatch Cnr CM23 ...77 D8
Playford Sq LU4 ...44 D5
Pleasance The AL5 ...85 D4
Pleasant Pl WD3 ...172 E3
Pleasant Rd CM23 ...76 E8
Pleasant Rise AL9 ...130 C8
Plewes Cl LU6 ...82 E8
Plough Cl SG8 ...5 B8
Plough Hill EN6 ...146 E2
Plough La Harefield UB9 .173 C4
King's Walden SG4 ...48 A5
Potten End HP4 ...123 B7
Sarratt WD3 ...151 F6
Ploughmans Cl CM23 ...76 C5
Ploughmans End AL7 ...111 C5
Plover Cl HP4 ...122 C3
Plum Tree Rd SG16 ...10 B2
Plummers La LU2 ...65 C2
Plumpton Cl LU2 ...46 D3
Plumpton Rd EN11 ...135 C8
Pluto Rise HP2 ...124 F5
Plymouth Cl LU2 ...46 B1
Poets Chase HP1 ...124 B5
Poets Cl HP1 ...124 B4
Poets Ct AL5 ...86 B1
Poets Gate
Goff's Oak EN7 ...147 E3
Widford SG12 ...95 D4
Poets Gn LU4 ...44 A2
Polayn Garth AL8 ...110 C7
Polegate LU2 ...46 D2
Polehanger La HP1 ...123 E5
Poles Hill WD3 ...151 E6
Poles La Thundridge SG12 .93 C6
Ware SG12 ...93 C3
Poles Pk SG12 ...93 C6
Police Row SG8 ...15 F7
Police Station La WD23 168 B2
Pollard Gdns SG1 ...50 F8
Pollards WD3 ...172 D5
Pollards Cl EN7 ...147 C2
Pollards Way SG5 ...20 D4
Pollicott Cl AL4 ...128 C8
Pollywick Rd HP23 ...100 D1
Polsten Mews EN3 ...163 A2
Polzeath Cl LU2 ...64 C8
Pomeroy Cres WD24 ...154 B3
Pomeroy Gr LU2 ...45 E6
Pomfret Ave LU2 ...45 F1
Pond Cl Harefield UB9 ...173 C1
Luton LU4 ...44 B5
Stevenage SG1 ...50 C7
Tring HP23 ...100 A4
Pond Croft Hatfield AL10 .129 F5
Welwyn Garden City AL7 ...110 E5
Pond Ct SG4 ...67 F1
Pond Field AL7 ...90 A1
Pond La Baldock SG7 ...23 E8
Little Gaddesden HP4 ...102 E7
Pond La *continued*
Stansted Mountfitchet
CM24 ...59 D7
Pond Rd HP3 ...139 A6
Pondcroft Rd SG3 ...69 A4
Pondfield Cres AL4 ...128 B7
Pondside SG4 ...36 C4
Pondsmeade AL3 ...106 B5
Pondwick Rd AL5 ...85 E2
Pondwicks Cl AL1 ...127 C2
Pondwicks Rd LU1 ...63 F7
Ponsbourne St Mary's CE
Prim Sch SG13 ...146 E7
Pooleys La AL9 ...144 C8
Pope Paul RC Prim Sch
EN6 ...158 F6
Pope's Rd WD5 ...153 E8
Popes Ct LU2 ...45 D1
Popes La WD24 ...154 B1
Popes Row SG12 ...93 D3
Popis Gdns SG12 ...93 E2
Poplar Ave Hatfield AL10 129 D5
Luton LU3 ...45 C8
Poplar Cl Hitchin SG4 ...35 B6
Pinner HA5 ...175 D2
Royston SG8 ...7 E7
Thundridge SG11 ...72 F2
Poplar Dr Royston SG8 ...7 E7
Stotfold SG5 ...11 F8
Poplar Rd LU6 ...82 E8
Poplar Shaw EN9 ...163 F6
Poplar View SG12 ...92 E4
Poplars AL7 ...111 B7
Poplars Cl Hatfield AL10 .129 D5
Luton LU2 ...46 B3
Watford WD25 ...154 B7
Poplars The Arlesey SG15 .11 A8
Borehamwood WD6 ...170 A8
Great Hallingbury CM22 ...77 F4
2 Hammond Street EN7 .147 E5
Harefield UB9 ...173 C2
Hemel Hempstead HP1 ...124 B2
Ickleford SG5 ...21 F5
St Albans AL1 ...142 B7
Popple Way SG1 ...50 E6
Poppy Cl
Hemel Hempstead HP1 ...123 E4
Luton LU3 ...45 D2
Poppy Mead SG1 ...50 F4
Poppy Wlk
Goff's Oak EN7 ...147 D3
Hatfield AL10 ...129 F8
Poppyfields AL7 ...111 C5
Porlock Dr LU2 ...46 C1
Port Hill SG14 ...113 C7
Port La CM22 ...77 B2
Port Vale SG14 ...113 C6
Porter's Mews SG4 ...67 F1
Porters Cl SG9 ...40 E8
Porters Hill AL5 ...86 C4
Porters Park Dr WD7 ...156 E7
Porters Wood AL3 ...127 F7
Portland Ct LU4 ...45 A1
Portland Dr
Cheshunt EN7 ...162 A8
Enfield EN2 ...161 E1
Portland Hts HA6 ...174 F6
Portland Ind Est SG15 ...11 A3
Portland Pl
17 Bishop's Stortford CM23 76 F7
Hertford Heath SG13 ...114 C4
Portland Rd
Bishop's Stortford CM23 ...76 F7
Luton LU4 ...45 A1
Portland St AL3 ...127 C4
Portman Cl Hitchin SG5 ...21 D2
St Albans AL4 ...128 C7
Portman Ho AL3 ...127 D6
Portmill La SG5 ...34 F7
Post Office Cotts CM22 ...98 C8
Post Office Rd CM20 ...117 D1
Post Office Row SG4 ...24 B1
Post Office Wlk 8
SG14 ...113 D6
Post Wood Rd SG12 ...114 E7
Postfield AL7 ...90 A1
Posting Ho HP23 ...101 A5
Postwood Gn SG13 ...114 C3
Potash La HP23 ...79 A5
Potten End CE Fst Sch
HP4 ...123 B6
Potten End Hill HP1 ...123 E8
Potter St
Bishop's Stortford CM23 ...76 F7
Pinner HA5 ...175 B2
Potter Street Hill HA5 ...175 B3
Potters Bar Com Hospl
EN6 ...159 C5
Potters Bar Mus★ EN6 .158 F7
Potters Bar Sta EN6 ...158 F7
Potters Ct EN6 ...159 A7
Potters Field AL3 ...127 E7
Potters Heights Cl HA5 .175 B3
Potters La
Borehamwood WD6 ...170 C8
Stevenage SG1 ...50 B4
Potters Mews WD6 ...169 D3
Potterscrouch La AL2,
AL3 ...140 E7
Pottersheath Rd AL6 ...68 D1
Pottery Cl LU3 ...44 F7
Potton Rd SG8 ...1 F6
Pouchen End La HP1 ...123 D3
Poulteney Rd CM24 ...59 E8
Poultney Cl WD7 ...156 F7
Pound Ave SG1 ...50 D6
Pound Cl
Lower Nazeing EN9 ...149 E8
Pound Cl *continued*
Sandridge AL4 ...108 C2
Pound Gn SG8 ...1 F5
Pound La WD7 ...156 F6
Poundfield WD25 ...153 F4
Poundwell AL7 ...111 A5
Powdermill La EN9 ...163 B6
Powdermill Mews EN9 .163 B6
Powdermill Way EN9 ...163 B6
Power Ct LU1 ...63 F7
Power Dr EN3 ...162 F3
Powis Ct Bushey WD23 ...168 D1
Potters Bar EN6 ...159 C5
Powys Ct WD6 ...170 D6
Poynders Hill HP2 ...125 C3
Poynders Mdw SG4 ...88 F8
Poynings Cl AL5 ...107 F8
Poynters Rd LU5 ...44 A2
Prae Cl AL3 ...127 B3
Prae Wood Prim Sch
AL3 ...127 A1
Praetorian Ct AL1 ...141 C8
Prebendal The LU1 ...63 B2
Precinct The EN10 ...134 F3
Premier Ct EN3 ...162 D1
Premier Pl WD18 ...166 F4
Prentice Way LU2 ...64 D7
Prescott Rd EN8 ...148 E4
Presdales Ct SG12 ...114 D8
Presdales Dr SG12 ...114 E8
Presdales Sch SG12 ...114 D7
Presentation Ct LU1 ...63 F6
President Way LU2 ...64 D8
Prestatyn Cl SG1 ...50 B8
Preston Ct HA6 ...175 A1
Preston Gdns
Enfield EN3 ...162 E2
Luton LU2 ...45 F2
Preston Path LU2 ...45 F2
Preston Prim Sch SG4 ...48 D6
Preston Rd Preston SG4 ...48 E7
St Ippolyts SG4 ...34 F1
Prestwick Cl LU2 ...45 E5
Prestwick Dr CM23 ...59 B1
Prestwick Rd WD19 ...175 D6
Prestwood 2 WD19 ...175 E8
Prestwood Gate AL1 ...127 E5
Pretoria Rd WD18 ...167 A5
Pretty Cnr HA6 ...175 A5
Priestland Gdns HP4 ...122 E6
Priestleys LU1 ...63 A7
Primary Way SG15 ...11 A4
Primett Rd SG1 ...50 C7
Primley La CM22 ...98 C1
Primrose Cl Arlesey SG15 .11 A4
Bishop's Stortford CM23 ...76 C6
Hatfield AL10 ...130 B4
Hemel Hempstead HP1 ...123 E2
Luton LU3 ...45 D2
Primrose Cotts WD7 ...156 A4
Primrose Ct SG1 ...50 D7
Primrose Dr SG13 ...114 B6
Primrose Gdns
Bushey WD23 ...168 B2
Radlett WD7 ...156 A4
Primrose Hill WD4 ...139 B3
Primrose Hill Rd SG1 ...50 D7
Primrose La Arlesey SG15 11 A4
Radlett WD25 ...155 D1
Primrose Path EN7 ...162 A8
Primrose View SG8 ...7 F5
Prince Andrew's Cl SG8 ..7 D5
Prince Edward St 6
HP4 ...122 C4
Prince Eugene Pl AL1 ...141 C8
Prince of Wales Prim Sch
EN3 ...162 F2
Prince Pk HP1 ...124 A2
Prince St WD17 ...167 C6
Prince Way LU2 ...64 D8
Prince's St SG5 ...11 F7
Princes Ave Enfield EN3 .162 E4
Watford WD18 ...167 A5
Princes Cl HP4 ...122 A6
Princes Ct
Bishop's Stortford CM23 ...76 C7
Hemel Hempstead HP3 ...138 B8
Princes Gate
Bishop's Stortford CM23 ...76 C7
Harlow CM20 ...117 E3
Princes Mews SG8 ...7 C6
Princes Pl 15 LU2 ...45 D1
Princes St SG12 ...93 D2
Princess Alexandra Hospl
CM20 ...117 C1
Princess Diana Dr AL4 .128 D2
Princess Helena Coll The
SG4 ...48 E6
Princess St LU1 ...63 D7
Printers Ct AL1 ...127 D2
Printers Way CM20 ...118 A5
Priors 9 CM23 ...77 A7
Priors Cl SG13 ...114 B3
Priors Ct CM22 ...98 A2
Priors Hill SG5 ...20 C4
Priors Wood Prim Sch
SG12 ...94 A3
Priors Wood Rd SG13 ...114 C3
Priory Ave CM17 ...118 C5
Priory Cl Cheshunt EN10 .148 E7
Hoddesdon EN11 ...135 A5
Royston SG8 ...7 E6
Stanmore HA7 ...176 F7
Totteridge N20 ...171 F2
Priory Ct
9 Berkhamsted HP4 ...122 C4
Bishop's Stortford CM23 ...76 F7
Bushey WD23 ...168 C1
Priory Ct *continued*
13 Hertford SG14 ...113 D6
Hitchin SG4 ...34 F5
St Albans AL1 ...127 E2
Priory Dell SG1 ...50 F5
Priory Dr Stanmore HA7 .176 F7
Stansted Mountfitchet
CM24 ...59 E5
Priory End SG4 ...34 F5
Priory Gate EN8 ...148 F4
Priory Gdns
Berkhamsted HP4 ...122 C4
Luton LU2 ...45 D4
Priory La
Great Wymondley SG4 ...35 F4
Royston SG8 ...7 D6
Priory Lo WD3 ...165 D2
Priory Orch AL3 ...84 B2
Priory Row SG12 ...95 E4
Priory Sch The SG5 ...21 E2
Priory St Hertford SG14 .113 D6
Ware SG12 ...93 C1
Priory View
Bushey WD23 ...168 E2
Little Wymondley SG4 ...35 E4
Priory Way SG4 ...34 F4
Priory Wharf 12 SG14 ...113 D6
Priory Wlk AL1 ...141 E8
Pritchett Cl EN3 ...163 A2
Proctor Way LU2 ...64 C7
Proctors Way CM23 ...77 A4
Progress Way LU4 ...44 B7
Progression Ctr HP2 ...125 A6
Prospect La AL5 ...107 A4
Prospect Pl AL6 ...89 C5
Prospect Rd
Cheshunt EN8 ...148 C2
St Albans AL1 ...127 D1
Prospect Way LU2 ...64 C7
Protea Way SG6 ...23 B6
Providence Gr SG1 ...50 E8
Providence Pl 17 SG14 .113 D6
Providence Way SG7 ...23 F7
Provost Way LU2 ...64 C8
Prowse Ave WD23 ...176 C8
Pryor Cl WD5 ...153 F7
Pryor Rd SG7 ...23 F6
Pryor Way SG6 ...23 D5
Pryors Cl CM23 ...77 A6
Pryors Ct SG7 ...12 F1
Puddephat's La AL3 ...104 D7
Pudding La Barley SG8 ...9 A1
Hemel Hempstead HP1 ...124 A5
Puddingstone Dr AL4 ..128 C1
Pudgell The SG8 ...9 E2
Pulham Ave EN10 ...134 E3
Pullar Meml Prim Sch
SG11 ...72 E2
Puller Rd Barnet EN5 ...171 E7
Hemel Hempstead HP1 ...124 A2
Pulleys Cl HP1 ...123 F4
Pulleys La HP1 ...123 F4
Pullman Cl AL1 ...127 E1
Pullman Dr SG4 ...35 B7
Pulter's Way SG4 ...35 A6
Pump Hill SG9 ...30 A2
Pump Ho The 12 CM23 ...77 A7
Pumphouse The SG8 ...7 D7
Punch Bowl La AL3 ...126 B8
Punchard Cres EN3 ...163 B1
Purbeck Ho 8 WD18 ...166 F3
Purbrock Ave WD25 ...154 C3
Purcell Cl Datchworth AL6 .90 E6
Radlett WD6 ...169 D8
Purcell Ct SG1 ...50 C8
Purcell Sch WD23 ...168 A7
Purkiss Rd SG13 ...113 C3
Purley Ctr LU3 ...44 E7
Purlings Rd WD23 ...168 B4
Pursley Gdns WD6 ...157 A1
Purway Cl LU3 ...44 E7
Purwell La SG4 ...35 C8
Purwell Prim Sch SG4 ...35 D8
Putney Rd EN3 ...162 D3
Puttenham Cl WD19 ...175 D8
Puttenham Ct HP23 ...78 F2
Putteridge High Sch LU2 46 C5
Putteridge Inf Sch LU2 ..46 C5
Putteridge Jun Sch LU2 46 C5
Putteridge Par LU2 ...46 B4
Putteridge Rd LU2 ...46 C4
Putteridge Recn Ctr LU2 46 C5
Putterills The AL5 ...86 A1
Putters Croft HP2 ...124 F8
Puttocks Cl AL9 ...144 C8
Puttocks Dr AL9 ...144 C8
Pye Cnr CM20 ...117 D5
Pyghtle Ct LU1 ...63 A7
Pyghtle The
Buntingford SG9 ...40 D7
Luton LU1 ...63 A7
Pyms Cl SG6 ...23 B8
Pynchbek CM23 ...76 E3
Pynchon Paddocks CM22 98 D7
Pynefield Ho WD3 ...164 F2
Pytchley Cl LU2 ...45 E5

Q

Quadrangle The AL8 ...110 C7
Quadrant The
Letchworth SG6 ...22 F6
Royston SG8 ...7 C8
St Albans AL4 ...128 B6

Quadrant The *continued*
Stevenage SG1 ... 50 D4
Quail Wlk SG8 ... 7 E8
Quaker La EN9 ... 163 C5
Quaker Rd SG12 ... 93 E3
Quakers La EN6 ... 159 B8
Quantock Cl Luton LU3 ... 45 B8
St Albans AL4 ... 128 C7
Stevenage SG1 ... 37 D3
Quantock Rise LU3 ... 31 B1
Quantocks HP2 ... 124 F6
Quartermass Cl HP1 ... 124 A4
Quartermass Rd HP1 ... 124 A4
Queen Anne's Cl SG5 ... 11 F5
Queen Elizabeth Ct
Barnet EN5 ... 171 F5
Waltham Abbey EN9 ... 163 C3
Queen Elizabeth II Hospl AL7 ... 111 A2
Queen Elizabeth's Girls Sch EN5 ... 171 F5
Queen Elizabeth's Sch EN5 ... 171 D6
Queen Hoo La AL6 ... 90 F6
Queen Mary's Ave WD18 ... 166 E5
Queen Marys Ct EN9 ... 163 C4
Queen St
Chipperfield WD4 ... 152 A7
Hitchin SG4,SG5 ... 34 F7
Pitstone LU7 ... 80 D4
St Albans AL3 ... 127 C3
Stotfold SG5 ... 12 A6
Tring HP23 ... 100 A3
Queen Victoria Meml Hospl AL6 ... 89 B4
Queen's Cl CM21 ... 97 F4
Queen's Ct
Aspenden SG9 ... 40 D5
Hertford SG13 ... 113 D5
St Albans AL1 ... 128 B3
Queen's Dr EN8 ... 163 A5
Queen's Dr The WD3 ... 165 A3
Queen's Pl WD17 ... 167 C6
Queen's Rd
Cheshunt EN8 ... 162 E6
Harpenden AL5 ... 107 B7
Hertford SG13 ... 113 D5
Watford WD17 ... 167 C6
Queen's Sq The HP2 ... 124 F4
Queens Ave WD18 ... 166 F5
Queens Cl 4 Luton LU1 ... 63 E6
Stansted Mountfitchet CM24 ... 59 E8
Queens Cres
Bishop's Stortford CM23 ... 76 E5
St Albans AL4 ... 128 B6
Queens Ct Cheshunt EN8 ... 162 F5
14 Luton LU2 ... 45 D1
Watford WD17 ... 167 C6
Queens Dr WD5 ... 153 F7
Queens Head Wlk EN10 ... 148 E8
Queens Rd Barnet EN5 ... 171 D6
Berkhamsted HP4 ... 122 A5
Royston SG8 ... 7 D7
Ware SG12 ... 93 F2
Queens Road Est EN5 ... 171 D6
Queens Silver Ct HA6 ... 174 E2
Queens Way
Cheshunt EN8 ... 162 F5
Shenley WD7 ... 156 E7
Queens' Sch WD23 ... 168 A6
Queensgate EN8 ... 162 F5
Queensgate Ctr CM20 ... 117 F4
Queensway
Hemel Hempstead HP1, HP2 ... 124 E4
Royston SG8 ... 7 D7
Stevenage SG1 ... 50 D5
Queensway Ho 1 AL10 ... 130 A6
Queenswood Cres WD25 ... 154 A6
Queenswood Dr SG4 ... 22 C1
Queenswood Sch AL9 ... 145 D3
Quendell Wlk HP2 ... 124 E3
Quendon Dr EN9 ... 163 D6
Quickbeams AL7 ... 90 A1
Quickbury Farm CM21 ... 98 B2
Quickley La WD3 ... 164 C4
Quickley Rise WD3 ... 164 C3
Quickly Brow WD3 ... 164 B3
Quickmoor La WD4 ... 152 C6
Quickswood LU3 ... 45 A7
Quickwood Cl WD3 ... 165 A3
Quills SG6 ... 23 D4
Quilter Cl LU3 ... 44 F4
Quin Ct SG11 ... 55 F7
Quinces Croft HP1 ... 124 A5
Quincey Rd SG12 ... 93 C4
Quinn Way SG6 ... 23 C5
Quinta Dr EN5 ... 171 C4

R

Raans Rd HP6 ... 150 A1
Raban Cl SG2 ... 51 C1
Raban Ct SG7 ... 12 F1
Rabley Heath Rd AL6 ... 68 B2
Rackman Dr LU3 ... 45 C5
Radburn Cnr SG6 ... 23 C5
Radburn Prim Sch SG6 ... 23 C5
Radburn Way SG6 ... 23 C4
Radcliffe Rd SG5 ... 35 A8
Radlett Inf Sch WD7 ... 156 B3
Radlett La WD7 ... 156 E6
Radlett Lodge Sch WD7 ... 156 B8
Radlett Park Rd WD7 ... 156 A4
Radlett Prep Sch WD7 ... 156 C1
Radlett Rd
London Colney AL2 ... 141 E2
Watford WD24 ... 167 D7
Radlett Sta WD7 ... 156 A4
Radnor Ct HA3 ... 176 F2
Radstone Pl LU2 ... 46 E1
Radwell La SG7 ... 12 C4
Raebarn Gdns EN5 ... 171 B4
Raffin Cl SG3 ... 69 E3
Raffin Green La SG3 ... 69 F4
Raffin Pk SG3 ... 69 E3
Ragged Hall La AL2 ... 140 E7
Raglan Ave EN8 ... 162 D5
Raglan Gdns WD19 ... 167 B1
Raglan Ho HP4 ... 122 A4
Rags La EN7 ... 147 E4
Railway Pl SG13 ... 113 E6
Railway Rd EN8 ... 162 F6
Railway St SG13,SG14 ... 113 D6
Railway Terr WD4 ... 139 A4
Rainbow Cl AL3 ... 105 F6
Rainbow Ct WD19 ... 167 C3
Rainer Cl EN8 ... 148 D2
Rainsborough Ct SG13 ... 114 A7
Rainsford Rd CM24 ... 59 E8
Raleigh Cres SG2 ... 51 B8
Raleigh Gr LU4 ... 44 D1
Rally The SG15 ... 11 A7
Ralph Sadleir Mid Sch SG11 ... 55 E3
Ralston Way WD19 ... 175 D8
Ram Gorse CM20 ... 117 B2
Ram Yard (Ind Est) SG15 ... 11 A4
Ramblers Way AL7 ... 111 C5
Rambling Way HP4 ... 123 C6
Ramerick Gdns SG15 ... 11 A2
Ramney Dr EN3 ... 162 E2
Ramparts The AL3 ... 127 B2
Ramridge Prim Sch LU2 ... 46 B2
Ramridge Rd LU2 ... 46 A2
Ramryge Ct AL1 ... 127 D1
Ramsay Cl EN10 ... 134 E2
Ramsbury Rd AL1 ... 127 E2
Ramsdell SG1 ... 50 F5
Ramsey Cl
Brookmans Park AL9 ... 145 D4
St Albans AL1 ... 128 A1
Ramsey Lodge Ct 7 AL1 ... 127 E4
Ramson Rise HP1 ... 123 E2
Rand's Cl SG5 ... 21 B7
Rand's Cotts SG5 ... 21 B7
Rand's Mdw SG5 ... 21 B7
Randalls Ride HP2 ... 124 E5
Randalls Wlk AL2 ... 140 F1
Randals Hill SG2 ... 51 C3
Randolph Ct 3 HA5 ... 176 A3
Randon Cl HA2 ... 176 B1
Ranelagh Rd HP2 ... 125 B3
Ranleigh Wlk AL5 ... 107 D6
Rannoch Wlk HP2 ... 124 D7
Ranock Cl LU3 ... 44 D8
Ranskill Rd WD6 ... 170 A8
Ransom Cl Hitchin SG4 ... 34 F4
Watford WD19 ... 167 C2
Rant Mdw
Hemel Hempstead HP3 ... 125 A1
Hemel Hempstead HP3 ... 125 A2
Ranulf Cl CM17 ... 118 C6
Ranworth Ave
Hoddesdon EN11 ... 115 B2
Stevenage SG2 ... 69 C7
Ranworth Cl 2 HP3 ... 124 D1
Ranworth Gdns EN6 ... 158 D8
Raphael Cl WD7 ... 156 E7
Raphael Dr WD24 ... 167 D7
Rapper Ct LU3 ... 63 D8
Rasehill Cl WD3 ... 165 C4
Rathlyn HP3 ... 139 B8
Ratty's La EN11,CM19 ... 135 D6
Raven Cl WD3 ... 165 D2
Raven Ct AL10 ... 130 A4
Ravenbank Rd LU2 ... 46 C5
Ravenfield Rd AL7 ... 110 F6
Ravenhill Way LU4 ... 44 B4
Ravens Ct HP4 ... 122 E6
Ravens La HP4 ... 122 D4
Ravens Wharf 5 HP4 ... 122 D4
Ravenscroft Barnet EN5 ... 171 E5
Harpenden AL5 ... 107 D6
Hoddesdon EN10 ... 134 F3
Watford WD25 ... 154 E4
Ravenscroft Pk EN5 ... 171 D5
Ravenscroft Sch & Tech Coll The N20 ... 171 F2
Ravensdell HP1 ... 123 F4
Ravensthorpe LU2 ... 46 B4
Ravenswood Pk HA6 ... 175 A4
Rawdon Dr EN11 ... 135 A5
Ray's Hill HP5 ... 120 C2
Rayburn Rd HP1 ... 124 A5
Raydon Rd EN8 ... 162 D7
Rayfield AL8 ... 89 D1
Rayleigh Ho WD5 ... 153 F7
Raymer Cl AL1 ... 127 E4
Raymer Ct 1 AL1 ... 127 E4
Raymond Cl WD5 ... 153 D7
Raymond Cotts SG5 ... 21 E4
Raymond Ct EN6 ... 159 C5
Raymonds Cl AL7 ... 110 E4
Raymonds Plain AL7 ... 110 E4
Raynham Cl CM23 ... 77 C8
Raynham Rd CM23 ... 77 B8
Raynham St SG13 ... 113 E6
Raynham Way LU2 ... 46 D1
Raynsford Rd SG12 ... 93 E1
Raynton Rd EN3 ... 162 D2
Readings The WD3 ... 164 F6
Recreation Ground CM24 ... 59 E6
Rectory Cl
Bishop's Stortford CM23 ... 76 D3
Essendon AL9 ... 131 F6
Hunsdon SG12 ... 116 D8
Rectory Dr CM23 ... 58 D6
Rectory Gdns AL10 ... 130 B5
Rectory La
Berkhamsted HP4 ... 122 C4
Datchworth SG3 ... 69 C2
Farnham CM23 ... 58 D6
Kings Langley WD4 ... 139 A3
Lilley LU2 ... 32 D2
Rickmansworth WD3 ... 165 D1
Shenley WD7 ... 157 B7
Stevenage SG1 ... 36 D1
Watton at S SG14 ... 70 D3
Rectory Rd
Rickmansworth WD3 ... 165 D2
Welwyn Garden City AL8 ... 89 B1
Rectory Wood CM20 ... 117 C1
Red Brick Cotts SG11 ... 57 B1
Red Cottage HP23 ... 100 D1
Red Cow Cotts LU6 ... 83 C8
Red House Cl SG12 ... 114 E8
Red Lion Cl WD25 ... 155 C2
Red Lion Cotts SG5 ... 33 D2
Red Lion Ct 5 CM23 ... 77 A7
Red Lion La
Hemel Hempstead HP3 ... 139 A5
Sarratt WD3 ... 152 A4
Red Lodge WD6 ... 169 F6
Red Lodge Gdns HP4 ... 122 A3
Red Rails LU1 ... 63 C5
Red Rails Ct LU1 ... 63 C5
Red Rd WD6 ... 169 F6
Redan Rd SG12 ... 93 E3
Redbourn Ind Ctr AL3 ... 106 B5
Redbourn Inf Sch AL3 ... 106 A6
Redbourn Jun Sch AL3 ... 106 A6
Redbourn La AL3,AL5 ... 106 E6
Redbourn Rd
Hemel Hempstead HP2 ... 125 B8
St Albans AL3 ... 126 E7
Redbourn Village Mus★ AL3 ... 106 A5
Redbournbury La AL3 ... 106 D2
Redbournbury Water Mill★ AL3 ... 106 D2
Redbrick Row CM22 ... 98 B8
Redcar Dr SG1 ... 50 A6
Redcote La AL5 ... 107 A7
Redding Ho WD18 ... 166 E3
Redding La AL3 ... 105 F8
Reddings
Hemel Hempstead HP3 ... 125 A1
Welwyn Garden City AL8 ... 110 C7
Reddings Ave WD23 ... 168 B4
Reddings Prim Sch The HP3 ... 125 A1
Reddings The WD6 ... 169 F6
Redditch Ct HP2 ... 124 F7
Redferns Cl LU1 ... 63 A6
Redferns Ct LU1 ... 63 A6
Redgrave Gdns LU3 ... 44 F7
Redhall Cl AL10 ... 129 F1
Redhall Dr AL10 ... 129 F1
Redhall La
Colney Heath AL4 ... 129 E1
Sarratt WD3 ... 165 E8
Redheath Cl WD25 ... 153 F4
Redhill Rd SG5 ... 34 D8
Redhoods Way E SG6 ... 22 E7
Redhoods Way W SG6 ... 22 E6
Redhouse The EN10 ... 134 F1
Redlands Rd EN3 ... 162 E1
Redmire Cl LU4 ... 44 B6
Redoubt Cl SG4 ... 22 A1
Redpole Ct WD3 ... 165 E1
Redricks La CM21 ... 118 A6
Redvers Cl CM23 ... 59 A2
Redwell Ct EN8 ... 162 F5
Redwing Cl SG2 ... 51 D4
Redwing Gr WD5 ... 154 A8
Redwing Rise SG8 ... 7 E8
Redwood Cl WD19 ... 175 D6
Redwood Dr
Hemel Hempstead HP3 ... 124 E1
Luton LU3 ... 44 C8
Redwood Rise WD6 ... 157 B2
Redwood Way EN5 ... 171 D4
Redwoods Hertford SG14 ... 113 C7
Welwyn Garden City AL8 ... 89 D3
Reed Cl AL2 ... 142 E4
Reed Fst Sch SG8 ... 16 E5
Reed Pl AL5 ... 85 F3
Reedham Cl AL2 ... 141 A2
Reedings Jun Sch CM21 ... 97 F4
Reedings Way CM21 ... 97 E3
Reeds Chapel 12 WD24 ... 167 C7
Reeds Cres WD24 ... 167 C7
Reeds Dale LU2 ... 46 F2
Reeds The AL7 ... 110 D5
Reeves Ave LU3 ... 45 B4
Reeves Pightle SG8 ... 9 F3
Regal Cl SG11 ... 55 E2
Regal Ct 4 Hitchin SG5 ... 34 F8
Tring HP23 ... 100 A3
Regal Way WD24 ... 154 C1
Regency Cl CM23 ... 76 E7
Regency Ct
Hemel Hempstead HP2 ... 124 D3
Hoddesdon EN10 ... 148 F8
St Albans AL1 ... 128 B3
Regency Ct *continued*
Watford WD17 ... 167 A8
Regency Ho WD7 ... 156 A4
Regent Cl
Kings Langley WD4 ... 139 A3
St Albans AL4 ... 128 C7
Welwyn Garden City AL7 ... 110 E5
Regent Ct SG5 ... 11 F7
Regent Gate EN8 ... 162 E5
Regent St Luton LU1 ... 63 E7
Stotfold SG5 ... 11 F7
Watford WD24 ... 154 B1
Regent's Ct HA5 ... 175 D1
Regents Cl WD7 ... 156 A5
Regina Cl EN5 ... 171 D6
Reginald Mews CM17 ... 118 C1
Reginald Rd HA6 ... 174 F3
Reginald St LU2 ... 45 E1
Remus Cl AL1 ... 141 D7
Rendlesham Ave WD7 ... 155 F2
Rendlesham Cl SG12 ... 93 B2
Rendlesham Rd EN2 ... 161 B1
Rendlesham Way WD3 ... 164 C3
Rennie Ct EN3 ... 163 A1
Rennison Cl EN7 ... 147 F4
Renshaw Cl LU2 ... 46 E2
Repton Cl LU3 ... 44 F6
Repton Gn AL3 ... 127 D6
Repton Way WD3 ... 166 A4
Reson Way HP1 ... 124 B2
Reston Cl WD6 ... 157 B1
Reston Path
Borehamwood WD6 ... 157 A1
Luton LU2 ... 46 E2
Retford Cl WD6 ... 157 A1
Retreat The WD5 ... 153 C8
Revels Cl SG14 ... 113 D8
Revels Rd SG14 ... 113 D8
Reynard Copse CM23 ... 58 F1
Reynard Way SG13 ... 114 B6
Reynard's Way AL2 ... 140 F2
Reynards Rd AL6 ... 89 C7
Reynolds SG6 ... 11 F1
Reynolds Cl HP1 ... 124 A4
Reynolds Cres AL4 ... 128 B8
Rhee Spring SG7 ... 13 B1
Rhodes Ave CM23 ... 76 F5
Rhodes Meml Mus & Commonwealth Ctr★ CM23 ... 77 A6
Rhodes Way WD24 ... 167 D8
Rhymes HP1 ... 124 B5
Rib Cl SG11 ... 55 E2
Rib Vale SG14 ... 92 D1
Rib Way SG9 ... 40 E7
Ribbledale AL2 ... 142 F4
Ribblesdale HP2 ... 124 E6
Ribocon Way LU4 ... 44 B7
Ribston Cl WD7 ... 156 D6
Riccat La SG1 ... 36 F3
Rice Cl HP2 ... 124 F4
Richard Ct 1 EN5 ... 171 E6
Richard Hale Sch SG13 ... 113 D5
Richard Stagg Cl AL1 ... 128 C1
Richard Wittington Prim Sch The CM23 ... 76 E4
Richards Cl
Bushey WD23 ... 168 D2
Luton LU1 ... 63 B6
Richards Ct LU1 ... 63 B5
Richards St AL10 ... 129 E7
Richardson Cl AL2 ... 142 E4
Richardson Cres EN7 ... 147 B6
Richardson Pl AL4 ... 129 B1
Richfield Rd WD23 ... 168 C2
Richmond Cl
Bishop's Stortford CM23 ... 76 C7
Borehamwood WD6 ... 170 D4
Cheshunt EN8 ... 148 C2
Ware SG12 ... 93 B3
Richmond Ct
4 Hatfield AL10 ... 130 B3
Hoddesdon EN10 ... 134 F3
Luton LU2 ... 45 F1
Potters Bar EN6 ... 159 C8
St Albans AL1 ... 128 A3
Richmond Dr WD17 ... 166 E7
Richmond Gdns HA3 ... 176 F3
Richmond Hill LU2 ... 45 F2
Richmond Hill Sch LU2 ... 45 E2
Richmond Rd EN6 ... 159 C8
Richmond Way WD3 ... 166 C5
Richmond Wlk AL4 ... 128 D7
Rickfield Cl AL10 ... 130 A3
Rickmansworth La SL9 ... 172 A5
Rickmansworth Park Jun Mix Inf Sch WD3 ... 165 E2
Rickmansworth Rd
Chorleywood WD3 ... 164 F6
Harefield UB9 ... 173 D3
Northwood HA6 ... 174 D3
Pinner HA5 ... 175 C1
Watford WD18 ... 166 E5
Rickmansworth Sch WD3 ... 165 F3
Rickmansworth Sta WD3 ... 165 D2
Rickyard Cl LU2 ... 46 B3
Rickyard Mdw AL3 ... 106 A5
Rickyard The Ashwell SG7 ... 4 D3
Letchworth SG6 ... 12 C1
Riddell Gdns SG7 ... 23 F8
Riddy Hill Cl SG4 ... 35 A6
Riddy La Hitchin SG4 ... 35 A6
Luton LU3 ... 45 C5
Riddy The SG4 ... 88 F8
Ridge Ave Harpenden AL5 ... 85 E4
Letchworth SG6 ... 23 A6
Ridge Ct LU2 ... 46 A1
Ridge La WD17 ... 153 F2
Ridge Lea HP1 ... 123 F2
Ridge Rd SG6 ... 23 A6
Ridge St WD24 ... 154 B1
Ridge The Barnet EN5 ... 171 F4
Letchworth SG6 ... 23 A6
Northwood HA6 ... 174 F3
Ridge View HP23 ... 100 C5
Ridge Way WD3 ... 165 B2
Ridgedown AL3 ... 106 A5
Ridgefield WD17 ... 153 E2
Ridgehurst Ave WD25 ... 153 F5
Ridgeleigh Ct 3 EN5 ... 171 E6
Ridgeview Cl EN5 ... 171 D3
Ridgeway
Berkhamsted HP4 ... 121 F4
Harpenden AL5 ... 85 E4
Kensworth Common LU6 ... 82 E8
Little Hadham SG11 ... 57 B1
London Colney WD7 ... 156 C8
Stevenage SG1 ... 50 F5
Welwyn Garden City AL7 ... 111 B6
Ridgeway Cl HP3 ... 138 F5
Ridgeway Ct HA5 ... 176 A3
Ridgeway The
Codicote SG4 ... 67 F1
Cuffley EN6 ... 146 A4
Hadley Wood EN2,EN4 ... 160 D3
Hertford SG14 ... 112 F7
Hitchin SG5 ... 34 D6
Radlett WD7 ... 155 F2
St Albans AL4 ... 128 C7
Ware SG12 ... 93 C3
Watford WD17 ... 153 E2
Ridgewood Dr AL5 ... 85 E4
Ridgewood Gdns AL5 ... 85 E4
Ridgmont Rd AL1 ... 127 E2
Ridgway Rd LU2 ... 45 F1
Ridings The
Bishop's Stortford CM23 ... 76 D4
Hertford SG14 ... 113 A5
Latimer HP5 ... 150 D3
Luton LU3 ... 45 C1
Markyate AL3 ... 83 E6
Stevenage SG2 ... 51 B3
Ridler Rd EN1 ... 161 E1
Ridlins End SG2 ... 51 C2
Rigby Pl EN3 ... 163 A2
Rigery La SG11 ... 73 A7
Riley Rd EN3 ... 162 C1
Ringmer Ct LU2 ... 46 C3
Ringshall Dr HP4 ... 102 C8
Ringshall Rd HP4 ... 81 B3
Ringtale Pl SG7 ... 13 B1
Ringway Rd AL2 ... 141 C4
Ringwood Rd LU2 ... 45 D7
Ripley Rd Enfield EN2 ... 161 C1
Luton LU4 ... 44 C1
Ripley Way Cheshunt EN7 ... 148 B1
Hemel Hempstead HP1 ... 123 E4
Ripon Rd SG1 ... 37 A2
Ripon Way
Borehamwood WD6 ... 170 D4
St Albans AL4 ... 128 D7
Rise Cotts SG12 ... 95 D2
Rise The Baldock SG7 ... 23 E7
Borehamwood WD6 ... 169 F4
Harrow HA3 ... 176 C1
Park Street AL2 ... 141 D6
Risedale Cl HP3 ... 138 E8
Risedale Hill HP3 ... 138 E8
Risedale Rd HP3 ... 138 E8
Rising Hill Cl HA6 ... 174 C4
Risingholme Cl
Bushey WD23 ... 168 B2
Harrow HA3 ... 176 E2
Risingholme Rd HA3 ... 176 E1
Ritcroft Cl HP3 ... 125 B2
Ritcroft Dr HP3 ... 125 B2
Ritcroft St HP3 ... 125 B2
Ritz Ct EN6 ... 159 A8
Rivenhall End AL7 ... 111 C6
River Ave EN11 ... 135 B7
River Cl EN8 ... 163 A5
River Ct Ickleford SG5 ... 21 F4
Sacombe SG12 ... 92 E4
Sawbridgeworth CM21 ... 97 F3
River Gn SG9 ... 40 E8
River Hill AL3 ... 84 B2
River Lee Ctry Pk★ EN9 ... 149 B1
River Mead SG5 ... 21 C2
River Meads SG12 ... 115 C4
River Park Ind Est HP4 ... 122 A5
River Pk HP1 ... 124 A1
River St SG12 ... 93 E1
River View AL7 ... 89 F2
River Way Harlow CM20 ... 118 B5
Luton LU3 ... 44 E5
Riverbank HP1 ... 124 B7
Riverbanks Cl AL5 ... 86 C4
Riverfield La CM21 ... 97 E3
Riverford Cl AL5 ... 86 B4
Rivermill CM20 ... 117 C2
Rivermill Ct SG8 ... 7 C7
Rivers Hospl The CM21 ... 97 C1
Riversend Rd HP3 ... 138 C8
Rivershill SG14 ... 70 E3
Riverside
Bishop's Stortford CM23 ... 76 F7
Buntingford SG9 ... 40 E7
Hemel Hempstead HP3 ... 138 F6
Hertford SG14 ... 113 D6
London Colney AL2 ... 142 E4
Welwyn AL6 ... 89 B5
Riverside Ave EN10 ... 135 A1
Riverside Bsns Pk CM24 ... 59 E6

Riverside Cl
Kings Langley WD4 139 B2
St Albans AL1 127 E1
Riverside Club (Tennis Ctr) The HA6 174 B3
Riverside Cotts SG12 115 C4
Riverside Ct
Harlow CM20 118 C6
St Albans AL1 127 E1
Riverside Dr WD3 165 D1
Riverside Est AL5 86 C4
Riverside Gdns HP4 122 A5
Riverside Mews
Hoddesdon EN10 148 E8
10 Ware SG12 93 D1
Riverside Path EN8 148 C2
Riverside Rd Luton LU3 45 A5
St Albans AL1 127 E2
Watford WD19 167 B3
Riverside Wlk 16 CM23 76 F7
Riversmead EN11 135 A5
Riversmeet SG14 113 B5
Rivett Cl SG7 13 A1
Roan Wlk SG8 7 E6
Roaring Meg Ret Pk SG1 50 E3
Robbery Bottom La AL6 90 A8
Robbs Cl HP1 124 A5
Robe End HP1 123 F5
Robert Allen Ct 3 LU1 63 E6
Robert Ave AL1 141 C7
Robert Cl EN6 158 E6
Robert Humbert Ho SG6 23 A5
Robert Saunders Ct SG6 22 E4
Robert Tebbutt Ct SG5 34 E6
Robert Wallace Cl CM23 58 F1
Roberts Cl EN8 148 E1
Roberts La SL9 172 B5
Roberts Rd WD18 167 C4
Roberts Way AL10 129 F3
Roberts Wood Dr SL9 172 A5
Robertson Cl EN10 148 E5
Robertson Rd 11 HP4 122 D4
Robeson Way WD6 170 C8
Robin Cl SG12 115 C3
Robin Ct AL5 86 B4
Robin Hill HP4 122 C3
Robin Hood Dr
Harrow HA3 176 F3
Watford WD23 167 F8
Robin Hood La AL10 130 A6
Robin Hood Mdw HP2 124 F8
Robin Mead AL7 90 A1
Robin Way EN6 146 E3
Robina Cl HA6 174 F2
Robins Cl AL2 142 E4
Robins Nest Hill SG13 132 C6
Robins Rd HP3 125 A1
Robins The CM17 118 C6
Robins Way AL10 129 F2
Robinsfield HP1 124 A3
Robinson Ave EN7 147 B3
Robinson Cl CM23 76 F5
Robinson Cres WD23 168 C1
Robinsway EN9 163 E5
Robinswood LU2 45 E5
Robsons Cl EN8 148 C2
Rochdale Ct 6 LU1 63 E6
Rochester Ave LU2 46 C4
Rochester Dr WD25 154 C4
Rochester Way
Croxley Green WD3 166 B5
Royston SG8 7 D8
Rochford Ave EN9 163 D5
Rochford Cl
Cheshunt EN10 148 E5
Stansted Mountfitchet CM24 59 E5
Rochford Dr LU2 46 E2
Rochford Ho EN9 163 D6
Rochford Rd CM23 59 C1
Rock Rd SG8 7 C8
Rockfield Ave SG12 93 D3
Rockingham Gate WD23 168 C3
Rockingham Way SG1 50 E4
Rockleigh SG14 113 C6
Rockley Rd LU1 63 A7
Rockliffe Ave WD4 139 A1
Rockways EN5 170 F3
Rodeheath LU4 44 D3
Roden Cl CM17 118 F4
Rodgers Cl WD6 169 D3
Rodings Row EN5 171 E5
Rodney Ave AL1 128 A1
Rodney Cres EN11 135 A8
Rodwell Yd HP23 100 A3
Roe Cl SG5 11 E5
Roe End La AL3 83 B4
Roe Green Cl AL10 129 F4
Roe Green Ctr AL10 129 F4
Roe Green La AL10 129 F5
Roe Hill Cl AL10 129 F4
Roebuck Cl
Hertford SG13 114 A6
Luton LU1 63 B6
Roebuck Ct 1 SG2 50 F1
Roebuck Gate SG2 50 F1
Roebuck Prim Sch SG2 50 F2
Roebuck Ret Pk SG1 50 E2
Roecroft Lower Sch SG5 11 F6
Roedean Ave EN3 162 C1
Roedean Cl LU2 46 D3
Roedean Ho 3 WD24 167 C7
Roefields Cl HP3 138 A7
Roehyde Way AL10 129 E2
Roestock Gdns AL4 129 E1
Roestock La AL4 129 E1
Rofant Rd HA6 174 E4
Rogate Rd LU2 46 C5
Roger de Clare Sch SG11 55 E2
Roger's La SG9 29 A5
Rogers Ct EN7 147 D4
Rogers Ruff HA6 174 C2
Rokewood Mews 3 SG12 93 D2
Roland St AL1 128 B2
Rolleston Cl SG12 93 C3
Rollswood AL7 110 E3
Rollswood Rd AL6 89 B8
Rollys La SG7 4 D4
Roman Cl UB9 173 B2
Roman Gdns WD4 139 B1
Roman Ho
London Colney AL2 142 D4
Watford WD18 166 E5
Roman La SG7 24 A8
Roman Mews 7 EN11 135 A7
Roman Rd LU4 44 E3
Roman Rise CM21 97 D2
Roman St 8 EN11 135 A7
Roman Vale CM17 118 C5
Roman Way Markyate AL3 83 E6
Standon SG11 55 D3
Waltham Abbey EN9 163 B4
Welwyn AL6 89 C6
Roman Way Fst Sch SG8 7 C8
Romans End AL3 127 C1
Romany Cl SG6 22 C6
Romany Ct HP2 125 C4
Romeland Elstree WD6 169 D3
St Albans AL3 127 C3
Waltham Abbey EN9 163 C6
Romeland Hill AL3 127 C3
Romilly Dr WD19 175 F6
Rondini Ave LU3 45 B3
Ronsons Way AL4 127 F7
Rook Tree Cl SG5 12 A6
Rook Tree La SG5 12 A6
Rookery Dr LU2 45 E6
Rookery The
Hatfield AL9 144 D8
Stansted Mountfitchet CM24 59 E8
Westmill SG9 40 F3
Rookery Yd SG1 50 C7
Rookes Cl SG6 23 B3
Rooks Cl AL8 110 D5
Rooks Hill
Rickmansworth WD3 165 D5
Welwyn Garden City AL8 110 C5
Rooks Nest Cotts SG1 36 E2
Rooks Nest Farm SG1 36 E2
Rooks Nest La SG8 16 A5
Rookwood Dr SG2 51 B1
Rosary Ct EN6 145 B1
Rosary Gdns WD23 168 E2
Rose Acre Pimlico HP3 139 E6
Redbourn AL3 105 F6
Rose Cotts Arlesey SG15 11 A6
Bricket Wood AL2 141 B1
Meesden SG9 30 A5
Wyddial SG9 28 A3
Rose Ct
Hammond Street EN7 148 A4
St Albans AL4 128 C5
Rose Garden Mews WD3 165 B5
Rose Gdns WD18 167 A4
Rose La Essendon AL9 131 C5
Wheathampstead AL4 87 C2
Rose Lawn WD23 168 C1
Rose Mdw SG11 41 E4
Rose Mead EN6 145 C1
Rose Vale EN11 135 A6
Rose Wlk Royston SG8 7 C7
St Albans AL4 128 C5
Rose Wlk The WD7 156 B3
Rose Wood Cl LU2 45 F3
Roseacre Gdns AL7 111 D6
Roseacres CM21 97 D3
Rosebank EN9 163 E6
Rosebarn La HP23 79 D1
Roseberry Ct WD17 167 A8
Rosebery CM23 77 C6
Rosebery Ave AL5 85 F1
Rosebery Mews LU7 61 D4
Rosebery Rd WD23 168 B2
Rosebery Way HP23 100 B5
Rosebriar Wlk WD24 153 F3
Rosecroft Ct HA6 174 C4
Rosecroft Dr WD17 153 E3
Rosecroft La AL6 90 A8
Rosedale AL7 89 F2
Rosedale Ave EN7 147 F2
Rosedale Cl
Bricket Wood AL2 140 E1
Luton LU3 44 C7
Rosedale Way EN7 148 A3
Roseheath HP1 123 E4
Rosehill HP4 122 B4
Rosehill Cl EN11 134 F6
Rosehill Ct HP1 124 A1
Rosehill Gdns WD5 153 C7
Roselands Ave EN11 114 F1
Roselands Prim Sch EN11 114 F1
Roseley Cotts CM20 117 B4
Rosemary Cl 3 CM17 118 C4
Rosemary Ct 2 HA5 176 A3
Rosemont Cl SG6 22 E6
Rosemoor Cl AL7 110 F5
Rosewood Ct HP1 123 E4
Rosewood Dr EN2 161 A4
Roslyn Cl EN10 134 E2
Ross Cl Hatfield AL10 130 A8
Luton LU1 63 B6
Ross Cl *continued*
Stanmore HA3 176 C3
Ross Cres WD25 154 A4
Ross Ct SG2 51 B7
Ross Haven Pl HA6 174 F2
Ross Way HA6 174 F6
Rossendale Cl EN2 161 B3
Rossfold Rd LU3 44 D8
Rossgate HP1 124 A5
Rossgate Prim Sch HP1 124 A5
Rossington Ave WD6 156 E1
Rossington Cl EN1 162 B1
Rossiter Fields EN5 171 F3
Rosslyn Cres LU3 45 C5
Rosslyn Rd WD18 167 B6
Rossway LU1 63 B1
Rossway Dr WD23 168 D4
Rossway La HP4 121 A7
Roswell Cl EN8 148 E1
Rothamsted Ave AL5 86 A1
Rothamsted Ct AL5 86 A1
Rothamsted Experimental Sta AL5 107 A8
Rother Cl WD25 154 C5
Rotheram Ave LU1 63 B5
Rotherfield LU2 46 D3
Rotherfield Rd EN3 162 D2
Rothesay Ct HP4 122 A4
Rothesay Rd LU1 63 D7
Roughdown Ave HP3 138 A8
Roughdown Rd HP3 138 B8
Roughdown Villas HP3 138 A8
Roughdown Villas Rd HP3 138 A8
Roughs The HA6 174 E7
Roughwood Cl WD17 153 E1
Round Diamond Prim Sch SG1 37 B3
Round Mead SG2 51 D3
Roundabout Ho HA6 175 A2
Roundabout La AL6 89 F8
Roundbush La WD25 155 C1
Roundcroft EN7 147 F5
Roundfield Ave AL5 86 D3
Roundhaye SG11 55 D3
Roundhedge Way EN2 160 F1
Roundhills EN9 163 E4
Roundings The SG13 114 C2
Roundmoor Dr EN8 148 E2
Roundway The WD18 166 F2
Roundwood HP3 138 E4
Roundwood Cl
Hitchin SG4 22 C2
Oaklands AL6 89 D8
Roundwood Ct AL5 85 F3
Roundwood Dr AL8 110 C7
Roundwood Gdns AL5 85 E2
Roundwood La AL5 85 D3
Roundwood Park Sch AL5 85 E2
Roundwood Pk AL5 85 E3
Roundwood Prim Sch AL5 85 E2
Rounton Rd EN9 163 E6
Rousebarn La WD3 166 C7
Row The HP5 120 D2
Rowan Cl
Bricket Wood AL2 155 A8
Harrow HA7 176 F4
Luton LU1 63 B7
Shenley WD7 156 E6
St Albans AL4 128 E3
Weston SG4 37 B8
Rowan Cres
Letchworth SG6 22 E7
Stevenage SG1 50 E7
Rowan Dr EN10 148 F6
Rowan Gr SG4 35 A4
Rowan Way AL5 107 C8
Rowan Wlk
2 Hatfield AL10 130 A2
Sawbridgeworth CM21 97 E2
Rowans AL7 90 A1
Rowans Prim Sch The AL7 90 A1
Rowans The Baldock SG7 23 E7
Hemel Hempstead HP1 124 A3
Hoddesdon EN10 134 F4
Rowbeech Cotts LU6 83 C8
Rowbourne Pl EN6 146 D3
Rowcroft HP1 123 E2
Rowel Field LU2 46 C1
Rowington Cl LU2 46 E2
Rowland Pl HA6 174 E3
Rowland Rd SG1 50 F4
Rowland Way SG6 22 F6
Rowlands Ave HA5 176 B4
Rowlands Cl EN8 148 D1
Rowlands Ct 3 EN8 148 D1
Rowlatt Ct AL1 127 E4
Rowlatt Dr AL3 127 A1
Rowley Cl WD19 167 E3
Rowley Gdns EN8 148 D3
Rowley Green Rd EN5 171 A4
Rowley La Barnet EN5 170 F5
Borehamwood WD6 170 D7
Rowley Wlk HP2 125 C8
Rowley's Rd SG13 113 F7
Rowney Gdns CM21 118 C8
Rowney La SG12 72 B5
Rowney Wood CM21 97 C1
Rows The CM20 117 D1
Roxley Cotts SG6 23 B2
Roxley Manor SG6 36 B8
Roy Rd HA6 174 F3
Royal Ave EN8 162 E6
Royal Ct Aldbury HP23 101 A5
Hemel Hempstead HP3 138 E8
Royal Masonic Sch for Girls WD3 165 D4
Royal National Orthopaedic Hospl HA7 169 B1
Royal Oak Cl SG9 27 D5
Royal Oak Gdns 6 CM23 76 F6
Royal Oak La SG5 20 D4
Royal Rd AL1 128 B3
Royal Veterinary Coll AL9 144 D3
Royce Cl EN10 134 F2
Royce Gr WD25 153 F5
Roydon Cl LU4 44 A4
Roydon Ct HP2 105 A1
Roydon Lodge Chalet Est CM19 116 C1
Roydon Mill CM19 116 A1
Roydon Mill Leisure Pk CM19 116 A1
Roydon Rd Harlow CM19 116 E1
Stanstead Abbotts SG12 115 E4
Roydon Sta CM19 116 B2
Royse Gr SG8 7 D4
Roysia Mid Sch SG8 7 D8
Royston & District Mus★ SG8 7 C6
Royston Cl SG14 113 B6
Royston Gr HA5 176 A4
Royston Hospl SG8 7 D4
Royston Park Rd HA5 176 A5
Royston Rd Baldock SG7 13 D2
Barkway SG8 17 C5
Barley SG8 8 F3
St Albans AL1 128 B2
Royston Sta SG8 7 C7
Rubin Pl EN3 163 A2
Rucklers La WD4 138 C4
Ruckles Cl SG1 50 E5
Rudd Cl SG2 51 B3
Rudham Gr SG6 23 C3
Rudolf Steiner Sch WD4 138 E2
Rudolph Rd WD23 168 A3
Rudyard Cl LU4 44 D3
Rue de St Lawrence EN9 163 C5
Rueley Dell Rd LU2 32 D2
Rufford Cl WD17 153 F2
Rugby Way WD3 166 B4
Ruins The AL3 106 B5
Rumballs Cl HP3 139 A8
Rumballs Ct CM23 76 C4
Rumballs Rd HP3 139 A8
Rumbold Rd EN11 135 C8
Rumsley EN7 148 A4
Runcie Cl AL4 128 A7
Runcorn Cres HP2 124 F7
Rundells SG6 23 D4
Runfold Ave LU3 45 A5
Runham Cl LU4 44 A4
Runham Rd HP3 124 E1
Runley Rd LU1 62 F7
Runnalow SG6 22 E7
Runsley AL7 90 A1
Runswick Ct SG1 50 A7
Runway The AL10 129 E7
Ruscombe Dr AL2 141 C5
Rush Cl SG12 115 C4
Rush Dr EN9 163 C3
Rushall Gn LU2 46 E2
Rushby Mead SG6 23 A5
Rushby Pl SG6 23 A5
Rushby Wlk SG6 23 A6
Rushden Rd SG9 26 A8
Rushen Dr SG13 114 C3
Rushendon Furlong LU7 80 E5
Rushes Ct CM23 77 A5
Rushfield
Potters Bar EN6 158 E6
Sawbridgeworth CM21 97 E2
Rushfield Rd SG12 93 F3
Rushleigh Ave EN8 148 D1
Rushleigh Gn CM23 76 D4
Rushmead Villas CM20 117 E3
Rushmere Ct HP3 138 E7
Rushmere La HP5 136 B3
Rushmoor Cl WD3 173 D8
Rushmore Cl LU1 62 E4
Rushton Ave WD25 154 A4
Rushton Ct EN8 148 D2
Ruskin Ave EN9 163 E5
Ruskin Cl EN7 147 E5
Ruskin La SG4 35 C7
Rusper Gn LU2 46 D3
Russell Ave AL3 127 D3
Russell Cl
Kensworth Common LU6 82 E8
Moor Park HA6 174 C5
Stevenage SG2 51 B2
Russell Cres WD25 153 F4
Russell Ct AL2 141 A1
Russell La WD17 153 D3
Russell Mead HA3 176 F2
Russell Pl HP3 138 B8
Russell Rd Enfield EN1 161 F1
Moor Park HA6 174 C6
Russell Rise LU1 63 D6
Russell Sch The WD3 164 B5
Russell St Hertford SG14 113 C6
Luton LU1 63 D6
Russell Way WD19 167 B2
Russell's Ride EN8 162 E8
Russell's Slip SG5 34 D6
Russellcroft Rd AL8 110 C7
Russet Cl EN7 147 E5
Russet Dr Shenley WD7 156 E7
St Albans AL4 128 C2
Russett Ho AL7 111 D6
Russett Wood AL7 111 D5
Russettings 2 HA5 175 F3
Rutherford Cl
Borehamwood WD6 170 C7
Stevenage SG1 50 A6
Rutherford Way WD23 168 E1
Ruthin Cl LU1 63 D5
Ruthven Ave EN8 162 D6
Rutland Cres LU2 64 A7
Rutland Ct LU2 64 A7
Rutland Gdns HP2 124 F4
Rutland Hall LU2 64 A7
Rutland Pl WD23 168 D1
Rutts The WD23 168 D1
Ryall Cl AL2 140 E2
Ryan Way WD24 167 C8
Ryans Ct LU2 45 F1
Rydal Ct WD25 154 B7
Rydal Mount EN6 158 E6
Rydal Way LU3 44 F5
Ryde Sch The AL9 130 C8
Ryde The AL9 130 C8
Ryder Ave SG5 21 D3
Ryder Cl Bovingdon HP3 137 A4
Bushey WD23 168 B3
Hertford SG13 114 B7
Ryder Seed Mews 3 AL1 127 D2
Ryder Way SG5 21 D3
Ryders Ave AL4 129 E3
Ryders Hill SG1 37 C3
Rye Cl Harpenden AL5 86 B4
Stevenage SG1 36 F3
Rye Gdns SG7 13 B1
Rye Hill Harpenden AL5 86 B4
2 Luton LU2 45 D1
Rye House Gatehouse★ EN11 135 D8
Rye House Sta EN11 135 C8
Rye Mead Cotts EN11 135 C8
Rye Rd EN11 135 C8
Rye St CM23 58 F1
Ryecroft Hatfield AL10 129 F3
Stevenage SG1 50 E7
Ryecroft Cl HP2 125 C2
Ryecroft Cres EN5 171 B4
Ryecroft Ct AL4 128 F3
Ryecroft Way LU2 46 A4
Ryefeld Cl EN11 115 B2
Ryefield LU3 31 A1
Ryefield Cres HA6 175 A1
Ryelands AL7 110 F3
Ryelands Prim Sch EN11 135 B7
Rylands Heath LU2 46 F2
Ryley Cl SG16 10 B5
Ryman Ct WD3 164 C3
Rymill Cl HP3 137 A3
Ryton Cl LU1 63 B6

S

Saberton Cl AL3 105 F4
Sabine Ho WD5 153 F7
Sacombe Gn LU3 31 B1
Sacombe Green Rd SG12 71 E4
Sacombe Pound SG12 71 E3
Sacombe Rd
Hemel Hempstead HP1 123 F5
Hertford SG14 92 C1
Stapleford SG14 92 B4
Sacombs Ash La CM21 96 E7
Sacred Heart Language Coll The HA3 176 E1
Sacred Heart Prim Sch LU2 46 A3
Sacred Heart RC Prim Sch
Bushey WD23 167 F3
Ware SG12 93 D1
Saddlers Cl Arkley EN5 171 B4
Baldock SG7 23 E8
Bishop's Stortford CM23 76 C4
Borehamwood WD6 170 D3
Pinner HA5 176 A4
Saddlers Mews AL3 83 E5
Saddlers Path WD6 170 D4
Saddlers Pl SG8 7 C7
Saddlers Wlk WD4 139 A2
Sadleir Rd AL1 127 E1
Sadler Cl EN7 147 C6
Sadlers Way SG14 113 A6
Sadlier Rd SG11 55 E2
Saffron Cl Arlesey SG15 11 A7
Hoddesdon EN11 134 F7
Luton LU2 45 D7
Saffron Green Prim Sch WD6 170 E5
Saffron Hill SG6 22 E6
Saffron La HP1 124 B4
Saffron Mdw SG11 55 E2
Saffron St SG8 7 F5
Sainfoin End HP2 125 A5
St Adrian's RC Prim Sch AL1 141 C8
St Agnell's Farm Mews HP2 105 A1
St Agnells Ct HP2 125 A7
St Agnells La HP2 125 A8
St Alban & St Stephen RC Inf Sch AL1 127 F2
St Alban & St Stephen RC Jun Sch AL1 128 A3
St Alban's RC Prim Sch CM20 117 F2

St Albans City Hospl AL3 127 C5
St Albans Dr SG1 36 E1
St Albans Girls' Sch AL3 127 E7
St Albans High Sch for Girls AL1 127 E4
St Albans Hill HP3 124 F1
St Albans La WD5 140 A5
St Albans Link SG1 36 E1
St Albans Music Sch AL3 127 D6
St Albans Rd Barnet EN5 171 E7
  Codicote SG4 88 F7
  Dancers Hill EN5 158 C3
  Harpenden AL5 107 B6
  Hemel Hempstead HP2, HP3 124 E2
  Redbourn AL3 106 C3
  Ridge EN6 157 F8
  Sandridge AL4 108 B1
  St Albans AL4 128 A8
St Albans Rd E AL10 130 B6
St Albans Rd W AL10 129 D5
St Albans Ret Pk AL1 127 D1
St Albans Roman Theatre* AL3 127 A3
St Albans Sch AL3 127 C3
St Albans Sta AL1 127 F3
St Albert the Great RC Prim Sch HP3 125 A2
St Aldates Ct LU3 45 B3
St Andrew Mews [1] SG14 113 C6
St Andrew St SG14 113 C6
St Andrew's Ave AL5 85 F1
St Andrew's CE Prim Sch SG4 35 A7
St Andrew's CE Prim Sch SG10 74 F2
St Andrew's Cl LU1 63 B1
St Andrew's Ho CM20 117 F2
St Andrew's Pl [2] SG4 34 F6
St Andrew's Rd HP3 138 D7
St Andrews CE Prim Sch SG12 115 D4
St Andrews Dr SG1 36 F2
St Andrews Mews LU3 45 A4
St Andrews Montessori Prep Sch WD25 154 C8
St Andrews Rd [2] WD19 175 D7
St Andrews Terr WD19 175 C5
St Andrews Wlk LU1 63 C1
St Ann's La LU1 63 F7
St Ann's Rd LU1 63 F7
St Anna Rd EN5 171 D4
St Anne's Cl EN7 148 A3
St Anne's Ct [7] SG5 34 F8
St Anne's Pk EN10 135 A4
St Anne's Rd Hitchin SG5 34 F8
  London Colney AL2 142 D4
St Annes Cl WD19 175 C6
St Anthonys Ave HP3 125 B1
St Anthonys RC Prim Sch WD18 166 E4
St Audreys Cl AL10 130 B2
St Audreys Gn AL7 110 F5
St Augusta Ct AL3 127 D5
St Augustine Ave LU3 45 C3
St Augustine Cl [1] SG5 34 F8
St Augustine RC Prim Sch EN11 135 B6
St Augustines Cl EN10 134 F3
St Augustines Dr EN10 134 F3
St Barnabas Ct
  Harrow HA3 176 C2
  Hemel Hempstead HP2 125 A3
St Bartholomew's CE Prim Sch HP23 100 D1
St Barts Cl AL4 128 D2
St Bernadette RC Prim Sch AL2 142 D4
St Bernard's Cl LU3 45 C3
St Bernard's Rd AL3 127 E4
St Brelades Pl AL4 128 D7
St Catharine's Rd EN10 135 A4
St Catherine of Siena RC Prim Sch WD25 154 D6
St Catherine's CE Prim Sch SG12 93 B2
St Catherines Ave LU3 45 B3
St Catherines Ct CM23 76 E7
St Christopher Sch SG6 22 F3
St Christophers Ct WD3 164 D5
St Clement Danes Sch WD3 164 D7
St Clement's CE Jun Sch EN8 148 E4
St Clements Ct EN9 163 C6
St Columba's Coll AL3 127 C1
St Cross Chambers EN11 135 A4
St Cross Ct EN11 135 A4
St Cross RC Prim Sch EN11 135 A4
St Cuthbert Mayne RC Jun Sch HP1 124 B4
St Cuthberts Gdns [3] HA5 175 F3
St Cuthberts Rd EN11 115 C1
St David's Cl HP2 125 D2
St David's Dr EN10 134 F4
St Davids Cl SG1 36 F2
St Dominic RC Prim Sch AL5 107 B8
St Dunstan's Rd SG12 116 D8
St Edmund's Coll SG11 55 A1
St Edmund's Way CM17 118 C4
St Edmunds HP4 122 C3
St Edmunds Wlk AL4 128 D2
St Elizabeth's Sch & Home SG10 96 C6
St Elmo Ct SG4 34 F5
St Ethelbert Ave LU3 45 C4
St Etheldreda's Dr AL10 130 C5
St Evroul Ct [5] SG12 93 D2
St Faiths Cl SG4 22 B1
St Francis Cl
  Buntingford SG9 40 F6
  Potters Bar EN6 159 C5
  Watford WD19 167 B1
St Francis' Coll SG6 22 E4
St George's Dr WD19 175 E6
St George's Rd
  Enfield EN1 161 F1
  Hemel Hempstead HP3 138 C7
  Watford WD24 154 B1
St George's Sch AL5 86 B2
St George's Way SG1 50 D5
St Georges End SG9 29 A6
St Georges Works EN8 148 F1
St Giles Ct EN8 162 C4
St Giles Rd SG4 67 F2
St Giles' Ave EN6 158 B7
St Giles' CE Prim Sch EN6 158 A7
St Helen's CE Prim Sch AL4 108 D8
St Helen's Cl AL4 108 D8
St Helen's Sch HA6 174 E4
St Heliers Rd AL4 128 B8
St Hilda's Sch
  Bushey WD23 168 B2
  Harpenden AL5 85 F2
St Hugh's Sch SG11 73 A8
St Ignatius Coll EN1 162 B2
St Ippolyts CE Prim Sch SG4 35 B3
St Ives Cl Luton LU3 45 B3
  Welwyn AL6 89 F3
St James Ctr CM20 118 A4
St James Rd
  Harpenden AL5 86 B4
  Watford WD18 167 B4
St James Way CM23 76 C3
St James' Rd LU3 45 B3
St James's Ct AL5 86 B3
St James's Rd EN7 147 D3
St Joan of Arc RC Sch WD3 165 E2
St John Cl LU1 63 B5
St John Fisher RC Prim Sch AL4 128 C6
St John RC Prim Sch SG7 23 F7
St John The Baptist CE Prim Sch SG12 115 A5
St John's Ave CM17 118 D4
St John's CE Prim Sch
  Crews Hill EN2 161 B2
  Hatfield AL8 109 F5
  Welwyn Garden City AL6 89 F2
St John's Cl EN6 159 C6
St John's Cres CM24 59 E7
St John's Ct
  Harpenden AL5 107 C7
  [21] Hertford SG13 113 D6
  [6] Northwood HA6 174 E3
St John's La CM24 59 E7
St John's Path SG4 34 F5
St John's RC Prim Sch WD3 165 B1
St John's Rd
  Arlesey SG15 11 A4
  Harpenden AL5 107 C7
  Hemel Hempstead HP1 124 B1
  Hitchin SG4 34 F6
  Stansted Mountfitchet CM24 59 E7
  Watford WD17 167 B7
St John's Sch HA6 175 B4
St John's St SG13 113 D6
St John's Terr EN2 161 D2
St John's Well Ct HP4 122 B5
St John's Well La HP4 122 B5
St Johns SG11 55 E3
St Johns CE Inf Sch WD7 155 F4
St Johns Cl AL6 89 C6
St Johns Ct Luton LU1 63 B5
  Rickmansworth WD3 165 B1
  St Albans AL1 128 B5
St Johns La SG12 115 A6
St Johns Wlk CM17 118 C4
St Joseph RC Prim Sch WD19 175 C7
St Joseph's Cl LU3 45 A4
St Joseph's in the Park Sch SG14 113 A4
St Joseph's RC Inf Sch LU3 45 A4
St Joseph's RC Jun Sch LU3 45 A4
St Joseph's RC Prim Sch
  Bishop's Stortford CM23 76 E6
  Cheshunt EN8 162 E7
  Hertford SG14 113 A7
St Joseph's Rd EN8 162 E6
St Josephs Court La AL5 107 B8
St Julian's Rd AL1 127 D1
St Katharines Cl SG5 21 D3
St Katherine's Way HP4 121 F7
St Laurence Dr EN10 148 F8
St Lawrence Cl
  Abbots Langley HP3 139 E1
  Bovingdon HP3 137 A4
St Lawrence Way AL2 140 F1
St Lawrences Ave LU3 45 C3
St Leonard's Ct AL4 108 C1
St Leonard's Rd SG14 113 D8
St Leonards Cl
  Hertford SG14 113 E8
  Watford WD23 167 E5
St Leonards Cres AL4 108 C1
St Leonards Rd EN9 149 D6
St Luke's Ave EN2 161 D1
St Luke's Cl LU4 44 E2
St Luke's Sch AL3 106 A6
St Magnus Ct HP3 125 C1
St Margaret Clitheroe RC Prim Sch SG2 50 F2
St Margaret of Scotland Jun Sch LU1 63 B5
St Margaret of Scotland RC Inf Sch LU1 63 B5
St Margaret's Cl HP4 122 D3
St Margaret's Rd SG12 115 B2
St Margaret's Sch WD23 168 A2
St Margarets SG2 50 F2
St Margarets Ave LU3 45 B3
St Margarets Cl LU3 31 A6
St Margarets Sta SG12 115 C4
St Margarets Way HP2 125 D3
St Mark's Cl SG5 21 D1
St Marks Cl AL4 129 B1
St Martha's Convent Jun Sch EN5 171 E5
St Martin de Porres RC Prim Sch LU4 44 A4
St Martin's Ave LU2 45 F2
St Martin's Rd SG3 69 A5
St Martin's Sch HA6 174 D5
St Martins HA6 174 D5
St Martins Cl
  Harpenden AL5 86 C4
  South Oxhey WD19 175 C6
St Mary RC Prim Sch SG8 7 D7
St Mary's Ave
  Berkhamsted UB2 121 D6
  Moor Park HA6 174 E5
  Stotfold SG5 11 F6
St Mary's CE High Sch EN8 148 B1
St Mary's CE Jun Sch SG12 93 D3
St Mary's CE Prim Sch WD3 173 D7
St Mary's CE Prim Sch
  Stansted Mountfitchet CM24 59 E7
  Welham Green AL9 144 B8
St Mary's Cl
  Letchworth SG6 22 F2
  Pirton SG5 20 D4
  Redbourn AL3 106 A4
St Mary's Ct
  [8] Hemel Hempstead HP2 124 D4
  Potters Bar EN6 159 B7
  Welwyn AL6 89 C4
St Mary's Ctyd [3] SG12 93 D1
St Mary's Dr CM24 59 F5
St Mary's Inf Sch SG7 23 E6
St Mary's Jun Mix Sch SG7 23 E6
St Mary's La SG14 112 F3
St Mary's Lower Sch SG5 12 A6
St Mary's Prim Sch AL6 89 B4
St Mary's RC Sch CM23 76 E7
St Mary's Rd
  Cheshunt EN8 148 C2
  Hemel Hempstead HP2 124 D4
  Luton LU1 63 F7
  Standon SG11 55 D2
  Watford WD18 167 B5
St Mary's Rise SG4 47 D1
St Mary's Way SG7 23 E6
St Marys Cl SG2 51 E2
St Marys Pk SG8 7 D6
St Marys Rd AL6 89 C5
St Marys Wlk AL4 128 B7
St Matthew's Inf Sch LU2 45 E1
St Matthews Cl Luton LU2 63 E8
  Watford WD19 167 D3
St Meryl Sch WD19 175 E7
St Michael's CE Prim Sch
  Bishop's Stortford CM23 76 F7
  St Albans AL3 127 B3
St Michael's Cres LU3 45 D3
St Michael's Ct AL3 127 B3
St Michael's Mount SG4 35 A8
St Michael's RC High Sch WD25 154 D7
St Michael's Rd EN10 135 A3
St Michael's St AL3 127 B3
St Michael's Woolmer Green CE Prim Sch Woolmer Green CE Prim Sch
Woolmer Green CE Prim Sch SG3 69 A1
St Michaels Ave HP3 125 B1
St Michaels Cl
  Harlow CM20 117 E1
  Harpenden AL5 107 D7
St Michaels Ct SG1 51 B8
St Michaels Dr WD25 154 B6
St Michaels Rd SG4 35 B7
St Michaels View AL10 130 B7
St Michaels Way EN6 145 B1
St Mildreds Ave LU3 45 C3
St Monicas Ave LU3 45 B3
St Neots Cl WD6 157 A1
St Nicholas CE Prim Sch
  Harpenden AL5 86 A1
  Letchworth SG6 12 C1
  Stevenage SG2 50 F4
St Nicholas Cl WD6 169 D3
St Nicholas Ct AL5 85 F3
St Nicholas Elstree CE Prim Sch WD6 169 D3
St Nicholas Gn CM17 118 C1
St Nicholas House Prep Sch HP3 139 B6
St Nicholas Mount HP1 123 F3
St Nicholas Sch CM17 118 F3
St Ninian's Ct [8] LU2 63 D8
St Olam's Cl LU3 45 B6
St Olives SG5 11 E6
St Pancras Ho SG8 2 D1
St Paul's CE Prim Sch WD4 152 A8
St Paul's Gdns LU1 63 E5
St Paul's Rd
  Hemel Hempstead HP2 124 E4
  Luton LU1 63 E5
St Paul's Walden SG4 49 A1
St Paul's Walden Prim Sch SG4 66 D7
St Pauls CE Prim Sch WD4 153 C5
St Pauls Cl AL5 107 D8
St Pauls Ct [3] SG2 50 F1
St Pauls Pl AL1 128 A3
St Pauls RC Prim Sch EN7 148 B4
St Pauls Way
  Waltham Abbey EN9 163 D6
  Watford WD24 167 C7
St Peter's Ave SG15 11 A7
St Peter's CE Prim Sch WD3 165 B1
St Peter's Cl
  Barnet EN5 171 B4
  Bushey WD23 168 D1
  Rickmansworth WD3 165 B1
  St Albans AL1 127 D4
St Peter's Rd AL1 127 E4
St Peter's Sch AL1 127 E2
St Peter's St AL1 127 D4
St Peters Cl AL10 130 A6
St Peters Hill HP23 100 A4
St Peters Rd LU1 63 B7
St Peters Way WD3 164 B5
St Philip Howard RC Prim Sch AL10 130 B5
St Raphaels Ct [5] AL1 127 E4
St Ronans Cl EN4 159 D1
St Rose's RC Inf Sch HP1 124 A1
St Saviors View AL1 127 F4
St Saviour's Cres LU1 63 D6
St Stephen's Ave AL3 141 B8
St Stephen's Cl AL3 141 B8
St Stephen's Hill AL1 127 C1
St Stephen's Rd EN3 162 D2
St Stephens Rd EN5 171 D4
St Teresa RC Prim Sch WD6 170 B7
St Teresa's RC Fst & Mid Sch HA3 176 C2
St Thomas Ct HA5 175 E2
St Thomas More RC Prim Sch
  Berkhamsted HP4 122 A4
  Letchworth SG6 22 D4
St Thomas of Canterbury RC Prim Sch SG11 55 C3
St Thomas Pl AL4 108 D8
St Thomas' Dr HA5 175 E2
St Thomas's Cl LU2 46 A4
St Thomas's Rd LU2 46 A4
St Vincent de Paul RC Prim Sch SG1 51 A6
St Vincent Dr AL1 128 A1
St Vincent Gdns LU4 44 D3
St Vincent's Way EN6 159 C6
St Winifreds Ave LU3 45 C3
St Yon Ct AL4 128 E3
Sale Dr SG7 12 F1
Salisbury Ave
  Harpenden AL5 86 A1
  St Albans AL1 128 B4
Salisbury Cl
  Bishop's Stortford CM23 76 F5
  Potters Bar EN6 159 C7
Salisbury Cres EN8 162 D7
Salisbury Gdns AL7 110 F5
Salisbury Hall Dr AL10 129 E7
Salisbury Ho AL3 127 C2
Salisbury Rd Baldock SG7 12 F1
  Barnet EN5 171 E6
  Enfield EN3 162 F2
  Harpenden AL5 86 D3
  Hoddesdon EN11 135 C8
  Luton LU1 63 D6
  Stevenage SG1 37 A2
  Watford WD24 154 C1
  Welwyn Garden City AL7 111 A5
Salisbury Sq
  Hatfield AL9 130 C6
Salisbury Sq *continued*
  [7] Hertford SG14 113 D6
Sally Deards La AL6 68 B3
Salmon Cl AL7 90 A1
Salmons Cl SG12 93 D4
Saltdean Cl LU2 46 D4
Salter's Cl HP4 121 F6
Salters CM23 76 C4
Salters Cl WD3 165 E1
Salters Gdns WD17 167 A8
Saltfield Cres LU4 44 C4
Salusbury La SG5 33 C2
Salvatorian Coll HA3 176 E1
Salwey Cres EN10 134 F3
Samian Gate AL3 126 F1
Sampson Ave EN5 171 D4
Samuel Lucas Jun Mix Inf Sch SG5 34 D7
Samuel Sq [2] AL1 127 D2
Sancroft Rd HA3 176 F1
Sanctuary Cl UB9 173 C3
Sandalls Spring HP1 123 F5
Sandalwood Cl LU3 45 B7
Sanday Cl HP3 125 B1
Sandbrook La HP23 79 C1
Sandell Cl LU2 45 F2
Sandeman Gdns SG12 93 E2
Sander's Cnr EN2 161 B5
Sanderling Cl SG6 22 E8
Sanders Cl
  Hemel Hempstead HP3 138 F7
  London Colney AL2 142 D4
  Stansted Mountfitchet CM24 59 D6
Sanders Rd HP3 139 A7
Sandfield Rd AL1 128 A3
Sandgate Rd LU4 44 D2
Sandhurst Ct AL5 107 D6
Sandifield AL10 130 B2
Sandle Rd CM23 77 A7
Sandmere Cl HP2 125 A2
Sandon Cl HP23 99 F4
Sandon Jun Mix Inf Sch SG9 15 C1
Sandon Rd EN8 148 C1
Sandover Cl SG4 35 B6
Sandown Rd
  Stevenage SG1 37 C1
  Watford WD24 154 C1
Sandown Road Ind Est WD24 154 C2
Sandpit Hill Cotts HP23 120 B3
Sandpit La AL1,AL4 128 C5
Sandpit Rd AL7 110 E4
Sandridge Cl HP2 105 A1
Sandridge Ct AL4 128 D7
Sandridge Gate Bsns Ctr AL1 127 F7
Sandridge Pk AL3 127 F8
Sandridge Rd AL1 127 F5
Sandridge Sch AL4 108 D1
Sandridgebury La
  Sandridge AL3,AL4 108 A2
  St Albans AL3 127 E8
Sandringham Cres AL4 128 C8
Sandringham Gdns [6] CM23 76 E5
Sandringham Rd
  Potters Bar EN6 145 B1
  Watford WD24 154 C2
Sandringham Sch AL4 128 B7
Sandringham Way EN8 162 D5
Sandy Cl SG14 113 B6
Sandy Gr SG4 34 F6
Sandy La Bushey WD25 168 C6
  Moor Park HA6 175 A5
Sandy Lane Cvn Site WD25 168 C6
Sandy Lodge HA6 174 E8
Sandy Lodge Ct HA6 174 E5
Sandy Lodge La HA6 174 E8
Sandy Lodge Rd WD3 174 C8
Sandy Lodge Way HA6 174 E4
Sandycroft Rd HP6 150 C1
Sanfoin Rd LU4 44 A4
Sanfoine Cl SG4 35 C8
Santers La EN6 158 E6
Santingfield N LU1 63 B6
Santingfield S LU1 63 B6
Sappers Cl CM21 97 F2
Saracen Est HP2 125 B5
Saracens Head HP2 125 A4
Saracens Head Yd [1] AL1 127 D2
Sargents SG11 55 F1
Sarita Cl HA3 176 D1
Sark Ho Enfield EN3 162 D1
  [10] Watford WD18 166 F3
Sarratt Ave HP2 125 A8
Sarratt CE Prim Sch WD3 152 A3
Sarratt La
  Rickmansworth WD3 165 C6
  Sarratt WD3 165 D8
Sarratt Rd WD3 165 C8
Sarum Pl HP2 124 E7
Sarum Rd LU3 44 F4
Satinwood Ct [1] HP3 124 E1
Saturn Way HP2 124 F6
Sauncey Ave AL5 86 B3
Sauncey Wood AL5 86 E4
Sauncey Wood La AL5 86 E6
Sauncey Wood Prim Sch AL5 86 D4
Saunders Cl
  Cheshunt EN8 148 D4
  Letchworth SG6 23 C7
Savanna Ct WD18 166 F5

Savill Cl EN7 . . . . .147 C6
Savoy Cl UB9 . . . . .173 D1
Sawbridgeworth Rd
 Hatfield Heath CM22 . . . . .98 E3
 Little Hallingbury CM22 . . .98 B6
Sawbridgeworth Sta
 CM21 . . . . .98 A3
Sawells EN10 . . . . .134 F2
Sawtry Cl LU3 . . . . .45 A6
Sawtry Way WD6 . . . . . . .157 A1
Sawyers La EN6 . . . . .158 D5
Sawyers Way HP2 . . . . . .124 E3
Sax Ho SG1 . . . . .11 E1
Saxon Ave SG5 . . . . .11 E8
Saxon Cl Harpenden AL5 . .86 C4
 Letchworth SG6 . . . . .11 F1
Saxon Ct
 Borehamwood WD6 . . . . .169 E8
 6 Hitchin SG4 . . . . .34 F6
Saxon Rd Luton LU3 . . . . . .45 C2
 Welwyn AL6 . . . . .89 B3
 Wheathampstead AL4 . . .108 D7
Saxon Way Baldock SG7 . . .13 B1
 Waltham Abbey EN9 . . . . .163 C6
Saxted Cl LU2 . . . . .46 D1
Saxton Mews WD17 . . . . .167 A7
Sayer Way SG1 . . . . .68 F4
Sayers Gdns HP4 . . . . . . .122 A6
Sayes Ct CM21 . . . . .97 F2
Sayesbury Ave CM21 . . . . .97 E3
Sayesbury Rd CM21 . . . . . .97 F3
Sayfield Cotts SG9 . . . . . . .26 B8
Saywell Rd LU2 . . . . .46 B1
Scammell Way WD18 . . . .166 F3
Scarborough Ave SG1 . . . . .50 B7
Scatterdells La WD4 . . . . .138 A2
Scholar's Hill SG12 . . . . . . .95 A4
Scholars Cl AL4 . . . . .143 C8
Scholars Mews AL8 . . . . .110 D8
Scholars The WD18 . . . . . .167 B2
Scholars Wlk 4 AL10 . . . .130 A2
School Cl Essendon AL9 . . .131 F6
 Stevenage SG2 . . . . .51 B3
School Cotts SG4 . . . . .47 F6
School Gdns HP4 . . . . . . .123 B6
School Ho The 1 SG7 . . . .23 F7
School La Ardeley SG2 . . . .38 F3
 Aston SG2 . . . . .51 E2
 Barley SG8 . . . . .9 A1
 Bricket Wood AL2 . . . . . .155 A7
 Bushey WD23 . . . . .168 B2
 Essendon AL9 . . . . .131 F6
 Great Offley SG5 . . . . .33 C3
 Harlow CM20 . . . . .117 C4
 Hatfield AL10 . . . . .130 C6
 Luton LU4 . . . . .44 D4
 Preston SG4 . . . . .48 E5
 Tewin AL6 . . . . .90 E2
 Watton at S SG14 . . . . . . .70 E3
 Welwyn AL6 . . . . .89 B4
 Weston SG4 . . . . .24 C1
School Mead WD5 . . . . . .153 D7
School Rd EN6 . . . . .145 C4
School Row HP1 . . . . .123 F2
School Wlk SG6 . . . . .23 B6
Schoolfields SG6 . . . . .23 C5
Schubert Rd WD6 . . . . . . .169 D3
Scot Gr HA5 . . . . .175 D3
Scotfield Ct LU2 . . . . .46 D3
Scots Hill WD3 . . . . .165 F3
Scots Hill Cl WD3 . . . . . . .165 F3
Scots Mill La WD3 . . . . . .165 F3
Scotscraig WD7 . . . . .155 F4
Scotswood EN5 . . . . .171 B4
Scott Ave SG12 . . . . .115 B4
Scott Cl SG8 . . . . .2 D1
Scott Rd
 Bishop's Stortford CM23 . . .76 E6
 Luton LU3 . . . . .44 C7
 Stevenage SG2 . . . . .51 C6
Scott's Grotto ★ SG12 . . .114 D8
Scott's Rd SG12 . . . . .114 D8
Scotts Cl SG12 . . . . .114 D8
Scotts View AL8 . . . . .110 C5
Scottswood Cl WD23 . . . .167 E7
Scottswood Rd WD23 . . . .167 E7
Scratchwood Nature Trail ★
 NW7 . . . . .170 D2
Scriveners Ct HP2 . . . . . .124 E3
Scrubbits Sq WD7 . . . . . .156 A4
Scrubbitts Park Rd
 WD7 . . . . .156 A4
Seabrook LU4 . . . . .44 B3
Seabrook Rd WD4 . . . . . .139 D4
Seacroft Gdns WD19 . . . .175 D7
Seaford Cl LU2 . . . . .46 C3
Seaforth Ct EN11 . . . . . . .135 B4
Seaforth Dr EN8 . . . . .162 D6
Seal Cl LU4 . . . . .44 D3
Seaman Cl AL2 . . . . .141 D6
Searches La WD5 . . . . . . .140 C4
Seaton Rd
 Hemel Hempstead HP3 . . .124 E1
 London Colney AL2 . . . . .142 D5
 Luton LU4 . . . . .44 D4
Sebright Rd Barnet EN5 . . .171 E6
 Hemel Hempstead HP1 . . .124 A1
 Markyate AL3 . . . . .83 E5
Secker Cres HA3 . . . . . . .176 C2
Second Ave
 Letchworth SG6 . . . . .23 C6
 Watford WD25 . . . . .154 D4
Sedbury Cl LU3 . . . . .45 A6
Sedge Gn EN9,CM19 . . . .135 E6
Sedgewick Ct HP2 . . . . . .105 B1
Sedgwick Rd LU4 . . . . .44 B7
Sedley Cl EN1 . . . . .162 B1
Seebohm Cl SG5 . . . . .21 C1

Seeleys The CM17 . . . . . .118 C4
Sefton Ave HA3 . . . . .176 D2
Sefton Cl AL1 . . . . .127 F4
Sefton Rd SG1 . . . . .37 B1
Selbourne Rd LU4 . . . . . . .45 A2
Selby Ave AL3 . . . . .127 D3
Selden Hill HP2 . . . . .124 D2
Sele Mill SG14 . . . . .113 B6
Sele Rd SG14 . . . . .113 B6
Sele Sch The SG14 . . . . . .112 F6
Selina Cl LU3 . . . . .44 C7
Sell Cl EN7 . . . . .147 B5
Sellers Cl WD6 . . . . .170 C8
Sells Rd SG12 . . . . .93 C2
Sellwood Dr EN5 . . . . . . .171 D4
Selsey Dr LU2 . . . . .46 D4
Selwyn Ave AL10 . . . . . . .129 E4
Selwyn Cres AL10 . . . . . .129 E5
Selwyn Dr AL10 . . . . .129 E5
Sempill Rd HP3 . . . . .124 E1
Senate Pl SG1 . . . . .37 B3
Sentis Ct HA6 . . . . .174 F4
Sequoia Cl WD23 . . . . . . .168 D1
Sequoia Pk HA5 . . . . .176 B4
Serby Ave SG8 . . . . .7 D8
Sergehill La WD5 . . . . . . .140 A5
Serpentine Cl SG1 . . . . . . .37 C2
Service Industry Bays
 CM20 . . . . .117 F2
Service Rd The EN6 . . . . .159 A7
Seven Acres HA4 . . . . .86 F1
Seven Roe's Malting SG7 . .23 E8
Sevenoaks Ct HA6 . . . . . .174 C3
Severalls The LU2 . . . . . . .46 B3
Severn Dr EN1 . . . . .162 A1
Severn Way
 Stevenage SG1 . . . . .36 F3
 Watford WD25 . . . . .154 C5
Severnmead HP2 . . . . . . .124 E6
Severnvale AL2 . . . . .142 F4
Sewardstone Rd EN9 . . . .163 D3
Sewardstone St EN9 . . . . .163 C5
Sewell Cl AL4 . . . . .128 E3
Sewell Harris Cl CM20 . . .117 B2
Sewells AL8 . . . . .89 E1
Sexton Cl EN7 . . . . .147 B6
Seymour Ave LU1 . . . . . . .63 F5
Seymour Cl HA5 . . . . .175 F2
Seymour Cres HP2 . . . . . .124 E3
Seymour Ct HP4 . . . . .121 E6
Seymour Mews CM21 . . . .118 C2
Seymour Rd
 Berkhamsted HP4 . . . . . .121 E6
 Luton LU1 . . . . .63 F5
 St Albans AL3 . . . . .127 E6
Shackledell SG2 . . . . .50 F2
Shacklegate La SG4 . . . . . .66 E5
Shackleton Gdns CM23 . . .76 E6
Shackleton Spring SG2 . . . .51 A3
Shackleton Way
 Abbots Langley WD5 . . . .154 A7
 Welwyn Garden City AL7 . .110 D6
Shady Bush Cl WD23 . . . .168 C2
Shady La WD17 . . . . .167 B7
Shafford Cotts
 Hemel Hempstead HP3 . . .139 A5
 St Albans AL3 . . . . .126 F6
Shaftenhoe End Rd
 Barley SG8 . . . . .9 A1
 Nuthampstead SG8 . . . . . .18 B8
Shaftesbury Ct
 Croxley Green WD3 . . . . .166 C4
 Stevenage SG1 . . . . .50 E4
Shaftesbury High Sch
 HA3 . . . . .176 B2
Shaftesbury Ind Ctr SG6 . .23 B7
Shaftesbury Quay 11
 SG14 . . . . .113 D6
Shaftesbury Rd Luton LU4 . .45 B1
 Watford WD17 . . . . .167 C6
Shaftesbury Way
 Bedmond WD4 . . . . .139 C3
 Royston SG8 . . . . .7 E5
Shakespeare SG8 . . . . .7 D8
Shakespeare Ct EN11 . . . .115 A2
Shakespeare Ind Est
 WD24 . . . . .154 A1
Shakespeare Rd
 Harpenden AL5 . . . . .86 C1
 Luton LU4 . . . . .44 B2
Shakespeare St WD24 . . . .154 B1
Shalcross Dr EN8 . . . . . . .148 F1
Shallcross Cres 6 AL10 . .130 A2
Shambrook Rd EN7 . . . . . .147 B6
Shangani Rd CM23 . . . . . . .76 F5
Shanklin Cl
 Goff's Oak EN7 . . . . .147 F2
 Luton LU3 . . . . .45 A7
Shanklin Gdns WD19 . . . .175 C6
Shantock Hall La HP3 . . . .136 E1
Shantock La HP3 . . . . . . .136 E1
Sharmans Cl AL6 . . . . .89 F4
Sharose Ct AL3 . . . . .83 E5
Sharpcroft 1 HP2 . . . . . . .124 D5
Sharpenhoe Rd LU3 . . . . . .31 A5
Sharples La HP1 . . . . .123 B1
Sharples Cl LU2 . . . . .46 D4
Sharps Way Hitchin SG4 . . .22 A1
 Hitchin SG4 . . . . .35 A8
Shaw Cl Bushey WD23 . . . .176 E8
 Cheshunt EN8 . . . . .148 C3
Shaw's Cnr ★ AL6 . . . . . . .88 A6
Shaws The AL7 . . . . .111 C5
Shearers The CM23 . . . . . . .76 C4
Sheares Hoppit SG12 . . . . .95 D2
Shearwater Cl SG1 . . . . . . .50 D4
Sheepcot Dr WD25 . . . . . .154 C5
Sheepcot La WD25 . . . . . .154 B6

Sheepcot Villas WD25 . . . .154 C5
Sheepcote AL7 . . . . .111 A3
Sheepcote La AL4 . . . . .87 F1
Sheepcote Rd HP2 . . . . . .124 F3
Sheepcroft Hill SG2 . . . . . .51 D3
Sheephouse Rd HP3 . . . . .124 F1
Sheering CE Prim Sch
 CM22 . . . . .98 D1
Sheering Dr CM22 . . . . . .118 E4
Sheering Lower Rd
 CM21 . . . . .98 A2
Sheering Mill La CM21 . . . .97 F2
Sheering Rd
 Harlow CM17 . . . . .118 F4
 Harlow CM17 . . . . .118 F5
Sheethanger La HP3 . . . . .138 A7
Shefton Rise HA6 . . . . . . .175 A3
Sheldon Cl EN5 . . . . .147 E5
Shelford Rd EN5 . . . . .171 C3
Shelley Cl Hitchin SG4 . . . .35 C7
 Moor Park HA6 . . . . .174 F5
 Royston SG8 . . . . .2 D1
Shelley Ct Cheshunt EN7 . .148 A3
 16 Harpenden AL5 . . . . . .86 B1
 Waltham Abbey EN9 . . . . .163 F6
Shelley La UB9 . . . . .173 A3
Shelley Rd LU4 . . . . .44 B2
Shelton Way LU2 . . . . .46 A3
Shendish Edge HP3 . . . . . .138 F6
Shenley Ct HP2 . . . . .125 B8
Shenley Hill WD7 . . . . . . .156 B4
Shenley La AL2 . . . . .142 A4
Shenley Prim Sch WD7 . . .156 F5
Shenley Rd
 Borehamwood WD6 . . . . .170 B6
 Hemel Hempstead HP2 . . .105 B1
 Radlett WD7 . . . . .156 C4
Shenleybury WD7 . . . . . . .156 E8
Shenleybury Cotts WD7 . .156 E8
Shenleybury Villas WD7 . .156 E8
Shenstone Hill HP4 . . . . . .122 E5
Shenval Ho CM20 . . . . . . .118 A4
Shephall Gn SG2 . . . . .51 B2
Shephall Green Inf Sch
 SG2 . . . . .51 B2
Shephall La SG2 . . . . .50 F1
Shephall View SG1 . . . . . . .51 A5
Shephall Way SG1 . . . . . . .51 C3
Shepherd Cl
 Abbots Langley WD5 . . . .153 F8
 Royston SG8 . . . . .7 E5
Shepherd Inf Sch WD3 . . .165 A1
Shepherd Prim Sch
 WD3 . . . . .165 A1
Shepherd's La WD3 . . . . . .164 E2
Shepherd's Row AL3 . . . . .106 B5
Shepherds Cl CM23 . . . . . . .76 C4
Shepherds Gn SG1 . . . . . . .92 C1
Shepherds La SG1 . . . . .50 A6
Shepherds Mead SG5 . . . . .21 C7
Shepherds Rd WD18 . . . . .166 F5
Shepherds Way
 Brookmans Park AL9 . . . .145 D4
 Harpenden AL5 . . . . .85 D4
 Rickmansworth WD3 . . . .165 B2
Shepherds Wlk WD3 . . . . .176 D8
Shepley Mews EN3 . . . . . .163 A2
Sheppard Cl EN1 . . . . .162 B1
Sheppards Cl AL3 . . . . . . .127 E6
Sheppards Yd 4 HP1 . . . .124 D4
Shepperton Dr WD6 . . . . .170 D8
Sheppey's La WD5 . . . . . .139 E3
Sheraton Cl WD6 . . . . . . .169 F4
Sheraton Ho WD3 . . . . . . .164 C5
Sheraton Mews WD18 . . . .166 E5
Sherborne Ave LU2 . . . . . .45 D6
Sherborne Cotts WD18 . . .167 D4
Sherborne Pl HA6 . . . . . . .174 D4
Sherborne Way WD3 . . . . .166 B5
Sherbourne Cl HP2 . . . . . .124 E6
Sherbourne Ct AL1 . . . . . .127 F3
Sherd Cl LU3 . . . . .44 F7
Sheredes Dr EN11 . . . . . . .134 F4
Sheredes Prim Sch
 EN11 . . . . .134 F4
Sheredes Sch EN11 . . . . . .134 F5
Sherfield Ave WD3 . . . . . .173 E8
Sheridan Cl HP1 . . . . .124 B2
Sheridan Rd Luton LU3 . . . .45 C2
 Watford WD19 . . . . .167 D2
Sheriden Wlk EN10 . . . . . .134 E3
Sheriff Way WD25 . . . . . .154 A5
Sheringham Ave SG1 . . . . .36 B1
Sheringham Cl LU2 . . . . . . .45 C7
Sherington Ave HA5 . . . . .176 A3
Sherland Ct WD7 . . . . . . .156 A4
Shernbroke Rd EN9 . . . . . .163 F5
Sherrards Mans AL8 . . . . . .89 B1
Sherrards Mews AL8 . . . . . .89 B1
Sherrardspark Rd AL8 . . . .110 D8
Sherrardswood Sch AL6 . . .89 D4
Sherwood SG6 . . . . .22 F8
Sherwood Ave
 Potters Bar EN6 . . . . .158 E7
 St Albans AL4 . . . . .128 B6
Sherwood Ct
 20 Bishop's Stortford CM23 . .76 F7
 Watford WD25 . . . . .154 A5
Sherwood Ho WD5 . . . . . .153 F8
Sherwood Pl 1 HP2 . . . . . .124 F7
Sherwood Rd Luton LU4 . . .45 A2
 Watford WD25 . . . . .154 B6
Sherwoods Rd WD19 . . . .167 F4
Sherwoods Rise AL5 . . . . .107 D8
Shetland Cl WD6 . . . . .170 D3
Shetland Ho 13 WD18 . . . .166 F3
Shillington Rd SG5 . . . . . . .20 B5
Shillitoe Ave EN6 . . . . . . .158 E7

Shingle Cl LU3 . . . . .45 A8
Ship La LU7 . . . . .80 D3
Shire Cl EN10 . . . . .148 F5
Shire Ct HP2 . . . . .125 D4
Shire La
 Chalfont St Peter,Horn Hill
  WD3 . . . . .172 A1
 Chalfont St Peter,West Hyde
  WD3 . . . . .172 C4
 Chorleywood WD3 . . . . . .164 C4
 Maple Cross WD3 . . . . . .172 B5
 Tring HP23 . . . . .120 B4
Shiremeade WD6 . . . . . . .169 F4
Shires The Luton LU2 . . . . .45 D1
 Royston SG8 . . . . .7 E6
 Watford WD25 . . . . .154 D4
Shirley Cl Cheshunt EN8 . .148 C2
 Cheshunt,Wormley EN10 . .148 F7
 Stevenage SG2 . . . . .51 C8
Shirley Rd
 Abbots Langley WD5 . . . .153 F7
 Luton LU1 . . . . .63 C8
 St Albans AL1 . . . . .127 C4
Shootersway AL5 . . . . . . .121 E4
Shootersway La HP4 . . . . .121 E4
Shootersway Pk HP4 . . . . .121 F3
Shoplands AL8 . . . . .89 D2
Shoreham Cl SG1 . . . . .50 A8
Short Hale LU7 . . . . .80 D3
Short La Aston SG2 . . . . . . .51 E4
 Bricket Wood AL2 . . . . . .140 E2
Shortcroft CM23 . . . . .77 D7
Shortlands Gn AL7 . . . . . .110 F5
Shortlands Pl CM23 . . . . . .76 F8
Shortmead Dr EN8 . . . . . .162 E8
Shothanger Way HP3 . . . .137 D6
Shott La SG6 . . . . .23 C6
Shottfield Cl AL4 . . . . .108 D2
Shrevington Gr LU3 . . . . . .45 C3
Shrubbery Gr SG8 . . . . .7 D4
Shrubbery The HP1 . . . . . .123 E4
Shrubhill Rd HP1 . . . . .123 F2
Shrublands AL9 . . . . .145 B5
Shrublands Ave HP4 . . . . .122 A4
Shrublands Rd HP4 . . . . . .122 A5
Shrublands The EN6 . . . . .158 A5
Shrubs UB9 . . . . .173 F4
Shrubs Rd UB9 . . . . .173 F4
Shugars Gn HP23 . . . . . . .100 B5
Sibley Ave AL5 . . . . .107 E7
Sibley Cl LU2 . . . . .46 B3
Sibthorpe Rd AL9 . . . . . . .144 D7
Siccut Rd SG4 . . . . .35 C4
Sicklefield Cl EN7 . . . . . . .147 F5
Siddons Rd SG2 . . . . .51 C6
Sidford Cl HP1 . . . . .123 F3
Sidings Ct SG14 . . . . .113 C7
Sidings The
 Hatfield AL10 . . . . .129 E4
 Hemel Hempstead HP2 . . .124 D3
 Hoddesdon EN10 . . . . . .135 A1
Sidmouth Cl WD19 . . . . . .175 B8
Sidney Ct EN8 . . . . .162 F5
Sidney Terr SG14 . . . . .76 F6
Signal Cl SG16 . . . . .10 B3
Silam Rd SG1 . . . . .50 E5
Silecroft Rd LU2 . . . . .64 B8
Silk Mill Ct WD19 . . . . . . .167 B2
Silk Mill Rd
 Redbourn AL3 . . . . .106 B4
 Watford WD19 . . . . .167 B2
Silk Mill Way HP23 . . . . . .100 A5
Silkin Ct SG2 . . . . .51 D3
Silver Birch Ct EN8 . . . . . .162 D8
Silver Ct HA3 . . . . .176 D3
Silver Ct Ashwell SG7 . . . . .4 D4
 Hitchin SG5 . . . . .34 F8
Silver Dell WD24 . . . . . . .153 F4
Silver Hill WD6,WD7 . . . . .157 B3
Silver Pl WD18 . . . . .166 F5
Silver St Anstey SG9 . . . . .29 A5
 Ashwell SG7 . . . . .4 D4
 Goff's Oak EN7 . . . . .147 D1
 Guilden Morden SG8 . . . . . .1 F4
 Luton LU2 . . . . .63 E7
 Stansted Mountfitchet
  CM24 . . . . .59 D6
 Waltham Abbey EN9 . . . .163 C6
Silver Trees AL2 . . . . .140 F1
Silverbirch Ave SG5 . . . . . .11 F8
Silverdale Ho HA6 . . . . . . .174 F4
Silverdale Rd WD23 . . . . .167 E4
Silverfield EN10 . . . . .134 F1
Silverthorn Dr HP3 . . . . . .139 B7
Silverwood Cl HA6 . . . . . .174 C4
Simmonds Rise HP3 . . . . .124 D1
Simon Balle Sch SG13 . . .113 E6
Simon Dean HP3 . . . . .137 A4
Simpson Cl LU4 . . . . .44 D2
Simpson Dr SG7 . . . . .23 F8
Simpsons Ct 3 SG7 . . . . . .23 F8
Sinderby Cl WD6 . . . . .169 E8
Sinfield Cl SG1 . . . . .51 A5
Singlets La AL3 . . . . .84 C2
Sir Frederic Osborn Sch
 AL7 . . . . .111 B7
Sir Herbert Janes Village The
 LU4 . . . . .44 D4
Sir John Lawes Sch AL5 . . .86 C4
Sir John Newsom Way
 AL7 . . . . .110 E3
Sir Joseph's Wlk AL5 . . . .107 A8
Sir Peter's Way HP4 . . . . . .81 D7
Sirus Rd HA6 . . . . .175 A5
Sish Cl SG1 . . . . .50 D6
Sish La SG1 . . . . .50 D6
Siskin Cl
 Borehamwood WD6 . . . . .170 A5

Siskin Cl continued
 Royston SG8 . . . . .7 E8
 Watford WD23 . . . . .167 E5
Sisson Cl SG2 . . . . .51 C2
Sitwell Gr HA7 . . . . .176 F5
Six Acres HP3 . . . . .139 A8
Six Cotts SG11 . . . . .57 C6
Six Hills Way SG1,SG2 . . . .50 F5
Sixth Ave Letchworth SG6 . .23 C6
 Watford WD25 . . . . .154 D4
Skegness Rd SG1 . . . . .50 A8
Skegsbury La SG4 . . . . .65 F1
Skelton Cl LU3 . . . . .31 B1
Skidmore Way WD3 . . . . .165 E1
Skimpans Cl AL9 . . . . .144 D7
Skimpot Rd LU4 . . . . .44 A1
Skinners St CM23 . . . . .76 C4
Skipton Cl SG2 . . . . .68 F8
Skua Cl LU4 . . . . .44 A5
Skye Ho 11 WD18 . . . . . . .166 F3
Skylark Cnr SG2 . . . . .51 D3
Skylark Pl SG8 . . . . .7 E8
Skys Wood Rd AL4 . . . . . .128 B7
Skyswood Prim Sch
 AL4 . . . . .128 C6
Slade Ct WD7 . . . . .156 A4
Sleaford Gn WD19 . . . . . .175 D7
Sleapcross Gdns AL4 . . . .129 C2
Sleaps Hyde SG2 . . . . .51 C1
Sleapshyde La AL4 . . . . . .129 C2
Sleddale HP2 . . . . .124 E6
Sleets End HP1 . . . . .124 B5
Slimmons Dr AL4 . . . . . . .128 A7
Slip End SG7 . . . . .14 B6
Slip End Lower Sch LU1 . . .63 B1
Slip La SG3,AL6 . . . . .68 C3
Slipe La EN10 . . . . .148 F7
Slipe The LU7 . . . . .80 A7
Slippers Hill HP2 . . . . .124 D4
Sloan Cl SG1 . . . . .50 F6
Sloansway AL7 . . . . .90 A1
Slowmans Cl AL2 . . . . . . .141 C3
Slype The AL4 . . . . .87 B5
Small Acre HP1 . . . . .123 F3
Smallcroft AL7 . . . . .111 B7
Smallford La AL4 . . . . .129 B2
Smallwood Cl AL4 . . . . . . .108 E7
Smarts Gn EN7 . . . . .147 F5
Smeaton Cl EN9 . . . . .163 E7
Smeaton Rd EN3 . . . . .163 A2
Smith St WD18 . . . . .167 C5
Smith's End La
 Barley SG8 . . . . .17 F8
 Nuthampstead SG8 . . . . . .18 A8
Smithfield HP2 . . . . .124 D5
Smiths Cres AL4 . . . . .129 C2
Smiths La HP17 . . . . .147 D5
Smiths Lane Mall 5 LU1 . .63 E7
Smiths Sq 6 LU1 . . . . .63 E7
Smithy The
 Little Hadham SG11 . . . . . .57 B2
 Sawbridgeworth CM21 . . . .97 E3
Smug Oak Bsns Ctr AL2 . .141 B1
Smug Oak La AL2 . . . . . . .141 D1
Snailswell La SG5 . . . . .21 C5
Snatchup AL3 . . . . .106 A5
Snells Mead SG9 . . . . .40 F7
Snipe The SG8 . . . . .24 B1
Snowdrop Cl CM23 . . . . . . .76 C6
Snowford Cl 7 LU3 . . . . . .45 A7
Snowley Par CM23 . . . . . . .59 B1
Soham Rd EN3 . . . . .162 F2
Solar Ct WD18 . . . . .166 F4
Solar Way EN3 . . . . .162 F3
Solesbridge Cl WD3 . . . . .164 F6
Solesbridge La WD3 . . . . .165 B7
Sollershott E SG6 . . . . .22 F4
Sollershott Hall SG6 . . . . . .22 F4
Sollershott W SG6 . . . . . . .22 E4
Solomon's Hill WD3 . . . . .165 D2
Solway HP2 . . . . .124 F5
Solway Rd N LU3 . . . . .45 A4
Solway Rd S LU3 . . . . .45 A3
Somerby Cl EN10 . . . . . . .135 A2
Someries Inf Sch LU2 . . . . .46 C3
Someries Jun Sch LU2 . . . .46 C3
Someries
 Harpenden AL5 . . . . .86 C4
 Hemel Hempstead HP1 . . .123 F4
Somers Rd AL9 . . . . .144 C7
Somers Sq AL9 . . . . .144 C8
Somers Way WD23 . . . . . .168 C2
Somersby Cl LU1 . . . . .63 E5
Somerset Ave LU2 . . . . . . .46 A1
Somerset Rd EN3 . . . . . . .163 A1
Somersham AL7 . . . . .111 D6
Sommer's Ct SG12 . . . . . .114 E8
Sonia Ct WD18 . . . . .167 C2
Soothouse Spring AL3 . . . .127 F7
Soper Mews EN3 . . . . .163 A1
Soper Sq CM17 . . . . .118 C1
Sopers Rd EN6 . . . . .146 F2
Sopwell La AL1 . . . . .127 D2
Sorrel Cl Luton LU3 . . . . . .45 B8
 Royston SG8 . . . . .7 F5
Sorrel Garth SG4 . . . . .35 A6
Sotheron Rd WD17 . . . . . .167 C6
Souberie Ave SG6 . . . . . . .22 F5
Souldern St WD18 . . . . . . .167 B4
South App HA6 . . . . .174 D7
South Bank Rd HP4 . . . . . .121 F6
South Block CM21 . . . . . . .97 F2
South Charlton Mead La
 EN11 . . . . .135 D5
South Cl Baldock SG7 . . . . .23 F7

South Cl *continued*
Barnet EN5 .....171 F6
Chiswell Green AL2 .....141 B6
Royston SG8 .....7 B7
South Comm AL3 .....106 B5
South Cottage Dr WD3 .164 F4
South Cottage Gdns
WD3 .....164 F4
South Dene HP2 .....104 A8
South Dr Cuffley EN6 ....146 E1
St Albans AL4 .....128 E4
South Drift Way LU1 .....63 B5
South Farm Cotts AL2 ..142 C3
South Hill Cl SG4 .....35 A6
South Hill Prim Sch
HP1 .....124 C2
South Hill Rd HP1 .....124 C3
South Ley AL7 .....110 E3
South Ley Ct AL7 .....110 E3
South Lodge Mews 2
SG7 .....23 F7
South Luton High Sch
LU1 .....63 F5
South Ordnance Rd
EN3 .....163 A2
South Park Ave WD3 ....164 F4
South Park Gdns HP4 ..122 B5
South Pl Harlow CM20 ....118 A4
Hitchin SG5 .....34 D8
Waltham Abbey EN9 .....163 C6
South Rd Baldock SG7 .....24 A7
Bishop's Stortford CM23 ...77 A5
Chorleywood WD3 .....164 C4
Harlow CM20 .....118 A4
Luton LU1 .....63 D6
Standon SG11 .....55 D2
South Riding AL2 .....141 A1
South St
Bishop's Stortford CM23 ...76 F6
Hertford SG14 .....113 D6
Stanstead Abbotts SG12 ..115 C4
South Street Commercial Ctr
1 CM23 .....76 F6
South View SG6 .....22 F5
South View Rd HA5 ....175 B4
South Way
Abbots Langley WD5,
WD25 .....153 E6
Hatfield AL10 .....130 B2
Waltham Abbey EN9 .....163 C3
South Weald Dr EN9 ....163 D6
Southacre Way HA5 .....175 C2
Southall Cl SG12 .....93 D2
Southbrook CM21 .....97 E1
Southbrook Dr 2 EN8 .148 D3
Southdown Ct AL10 .....130 A2
Southdown Ho AL5 .....107 C8
Southdown Ind Est AL5 107 C8
Southdown Rd
Harpenden AL5 .....107 B8
Hatfield AL10 .....130 A2
Southend Cl SG1 .....50 D7
Southern Ave SG16 .....10 C3
Southern Gn SG9 .....26 A4
Southern Rise LU2 .....85 F7
Southern Terr 2 EN11 ..115 B1
Southern Way
Letchworth SG6 .....22 E8
Studham LU6 .....82 C4
Southernwood Cl HP2 ..125 A4
Southerton Way WD7 ...156 E6
Southfield Barnet EN5 ...171 D3
Braughing SG11 .....55 F7
Welwyn Garden City AL7 .110 D4
Southfield Ave WD24 ...154 C1
Southfield Rd
Cheshunt EN8 .....162 E7
Hoddesdon EN11 .....135 A7
Southfield Sch AL10 ...130 B1
Southfield Way AL4 ....128 D6
Southfields
Letchworth SG6 .....11 F1
Standon SG11 .....55 E2
Southgate SG1 .....50 D4
Southgate Cotts WD3 ..165 E2
Southgate Ct 5 AL5 .....86 A2
Southgate Ho 1 EN8 ....148 D1
Southgate Rd EN6 .....159 C6
Southhill HA6 .....174 E2
Southlynn Ho 2 LU2 .....63 F8
Southmead Cres EN8 ...148 F1
Southmill Ct CM23 .....77 A6
Southmill Rd CM23 .....77 A5
Southmill Trad Ctr CM23 .77 A6
Southsea Ave WD18 ....167 A5
Southsea Rd SG1 .....50 B8
Southside SG9 .....28 A3
Southview Cl 1 EN7 ....147 E5
Southview Rd AL5 .....86 D3
Southwark Cl SG1 .....37 B2
Southwark Ho 11 WD6 .170 A7
Southwold Cl SG1 .....50 A6
Southwold Rd WD24 ....154 C2
Soval Ct HA6 .....174 D3
Sovereign Ct WD18 .....167 A5
Sovereign Pk
Hemel Hempstead HP2 ...125 B5
Luton LU4 .....44 F1
St Albans AL4 .....128 D2
Sowerby Ave LU2 .....46 C3
Sparhawke SG6 .....12 A1
Sparrow Cl LU4 .....44 A4
Sparrow Dr SG2 .....51 D4
Sparrows Herne WD23 .168 C2
Sparrows Way WD23 ...168 C1
Sparrowswick Ride AL3 127 C8
Spayne Cl LU3 .....45 B8
Spear Cl LU3 .....44 E6
Spectrum Ho EN3 .....162 E3
Speedwell Cl
Hemel Hempstead HP1 ...123 E2
Luton LU3 .....45 A8
Speke Cl SG2 .....51 D5
Spellbrook La E CM22 ...97 F8
Spellbrook La W CM23 ..97 E7
Spellbrook Prim Sch
CM23 .....97 F7
Spellbrooke 5 SG5 .....34 D8
Spencer Ave EN7 .....147 E5
Spencer Cl CM24 .....59 E6
Spencer Gate AL1 .....127 E5
Spencer Ho SG5 .....11 F6
Spencer Jun Sch AL3 ..127 E6
Spencer Mews AL1 .....127 E4
Spencer Pl AL4 .....108 C2
Spencer Rd Harrow HA3 .176 E1
Luton LU3 .....45 C2
Spencer St
Hertford SG13 .....113 E7
St Albans AL3 .....127 D3
Spencer Way HP1 .....124 A6
Spencer Wlk WD3 .....165 C4
Spenser Cl SG8 .....2 D1
Spenser Rd AL5 .....86 C1
Sperberry Hill SG4 .....35 B2
Speyhawk Pl EN6 .....145 B1
Sphere Ind Est The AL1 128 A2
Spicer St AL3 .....127 C3
Spicersfield EN7 .....148 A4
Spindleberry Cl AL6 .....90 A7
Spinney Cl SG4 .....35 B6
Spinney Ct CM21 .....97 E2
Spinney Jun & Inf Schs The
CM20 .....118 A1
Spinney La AL6 .....68 E3
Spinney Rd LU3 .....44 D7
Spinney St SG13 .....114 A6
Spinney The Baldock SG7 ..23 E7
Berkhamsted HP4 .....121 F3
Cheshunt EN7 .....148 B1
Harpenden AL5 .....85 E3
Hertford SG13 .....113 F6
Hoddesdon EN10 .....134 F4
Potters Bar EN6 .....159 D8
Radlett WD25 .....155 D1
Stansted Mountfitchet
CM24 .....59 E6
Stevenage SG2 .....51 D7
Watford WD17 .....167 A8
Welwyn Garden City AL7 ..110 E5
Spinneys Dr AL3 .....127 B1
Spires Sh Ctr The EN5 ..171 E6
Spires The
Bishop's Stortford CM23 ...76 D7
Hemel Hempstead HP2 ...124 D2
Spittlesea Rd LU2 .....64 C7
Spooners Dr AL2 .....141 C4
Spratts La LU6 .....82 F8
Spreckley Cl SG16 .....10 B5
Spring Cl Barnet EN5 ....171 D4
Borehamwood WD6 .....170 A8
Harefield UB9 .....173 D2
Latimer HP5 .....150 D3
Spring Court Rd EN2 ...161 A1
Spring Crofts WD23 ....168 A4
Spring Dr SG2 .....69 B8
Spring Field Rd HP4 ...122 A6
Spring Gdns WD25 .....154 C3
Spring Glen AL10 .....129 F4
Spring Hills CM20 .....117 B1
Spring Hills Twr CM20 ..117 A1
Spring La Cottered SG9 ..39 C5
Hemel Hempstead HP1 ...124 A4
Spring Mews CM21 .....97 E2
Spring Pl 6 LU1 .....63 D6
Spring Rd Harpenden AL5 .85 A4
Letchworth SG6 .....22 E4
Letchworth SG6 .....22 E6
Spring Valley Ent Ctr
AL3 .....127 E7
Spring View Rd SG12 ...114 C8
Spring Way HP2 .....125 C5
Spring Wlk EN10 .....134 C2
Springfield WD23 .....168 D1
Springfield Cl
Croxley Green WD3 .....166 B4
Potters Bar EN6 .....159 E8
Springfield Cres AL5 ....86 B5
Springfield Ct
Bishop's Stortford CM23 ...76 E8
Rickmansworth WD3 .....165 B1
Springfield Lodge SG13 113 E5
Springfield Rd
Cheshunt EN8 .....162 E7
Hemel Hempstead HP2 ...124 F4
Luton LU3 .....45 C6
St Albans AL4 .....129 B3
St Albans, The Camp AL1 .128 A2
Watford WD25 .....154 B6
Springfields
Hoddesdon EN10 .....134 F4
Waltham Abbey EN9 .....163 E5
Welwyn Garden City AL8 ..110 B4
Springfields Ho AL8 ....110 C4
Springhall Ct CM21 .....97 E2
Springhall La CM21 .....97 E1
Springhall Rd CM21 .....97 E2
Springhead SG7 .....4 D4
Springle La SG13 .....114 F2
Springmead Jun Mix Inf Sch
AL7 .....111 C7
Springs Cotts EN10 .....148 E7
Springs The
Cheshunt EN10 .....148 E6
Hertford SG13 .....113 F7
Springshott SG6 .....22 E5
Springwell Ave WD3 ....173 A8
Springwell Ct
Rickmansworth WD3 .....173 A8
Stanstead Abbotts SG12 ..115 C4
Springwell La WD3 .....173 A6
Springwood EN7 .....148 A5
Springwood Cl UB9 ....173 D2
Springwood Wlk AL4 ...128 D6
Spruce Way AL2 .....141 B4
Spur Cl WD5 .....153 D6
Spur The
3 Cheshunt EN8 .....148 D3
Stevenage SG1 .....50 E4
Spurcroft LU3 .....31 C1
Spurrs Cl SG4 .....35 B7
Square St CM17 .....118 C1
Square The
Braughing SG11 .....55 F7
Buckland SG9 .....27 D5
Hemel Hempstead HP1 ...124 C3
Hoddesdon EN10 .....148 E8
Much Hadham SG10 .....74 F3
Potten End HP4 .....123 B7
Redbourn AL3 .....105 F6
Sawbridgeworth CM21 ...97 E2
Watford WD24 .....154 B2
Squires Cl CM23 .....76 C8
Squires Ct EN11 .....135 A5
Squires Ride HP2 .....104 F1
Squirrel Chase HP1 ....123 E4
Squirrels Cl 2 CM23 ....76 F8
Squirrels The
Bushey WD23 .....168 D3
Hertford SG13 .....114 B6
Welwyn Garden City AL7 ..111 C5
Stable Block The AL6 ....90 B2
Stable Cotts SG11 .....57 E2
Stable Ct AL1 .....127 E5
Stable Mews
Northaw AL9 .....145 E3
St Albans AL1 .....127 E4
Stables The CM21 .....98 B3
Stacey Ct 9 CM23 .....76 F6
Stackfield CM20 .....118 A3
Stacklands AL8 .....110 B4
Staddles CM22 .....98 B8
Stadium Est The LU4 ....44 B1
Stadium Way CM19 .....116 F1
Staff Cotts UB9 .....173 B2
Stafford Cl EN8 .....148 B2
Stafford Ct EN10 .....135 A3
Stafford Dr EN10 .....135 A3
Stafford Ho
Bishop's Stortford CM23 ...76 F5
Hoddesdon EN10 .....135 A3
Stafford Rd HA3 .....176 C3
Staffords CM17 .....118 E4
Stag Ct WD3 .....164 C5
Stag Green Ave AL9 ....130 C7
Stag La Berkhamsted HP4 122 B5
Chorleywood WD3 .....164 C3
Stagg Hill EN4 .....159 E3
Stainer Rd
Borehamwood WD6 .....156 D1
Radlett WD6 .....169 D8
Stainers CM23 .....76 C5
Stains Cl EN8 .....148 F3
Stake Piece Rd SG8 .....7 C5
Stakers Ct AL5 .....86 B1
Stamford Ave SG8 .....7 D7
Stamford Cl Harrow HA3 176 E3
Potters Bar EN6 .....159 D7
Stamford Ct SG8 .....7 D7
Stamford Rd WD17 .....167 B7
Stamford Yd SG8 .....7 C6
Stanborough Ave WD6 .157 B1
Stanborough Cl
Borehamwood WD6 .....157 A1
Welwyn Garden City AL8 ..110 C5
Stanborough Gn AL8 ...110 C4
Stanborough La AL8 ...110 C4
Stanborough Mews
AL8 .....110 D4
Stanborough Prim Sch
WD25 .....154 C4
Stanborough Rd AL8 ...110 C4
Stanborough Sch AL8 ..110 B4
Stanborough Sec Sch
WD25 .....154 B4
Stanbury Ave WD17 ....153 E2
Standalone Farm★ SG6 .22 D8
Standard Rd EN3 .....162 E2
Standfield WD5 .....139 E1
Standhill Cl SG4 .....34 F6
Standhill Rd SG4 .....34 F6
Standon Bsns Pk SG11 ..55 E1
Standon Ct SG11 .....55 F1
Standon Hill SG11 .....55 D2
Standon Rd SG11 .....56 E3
Standring Rise HP3 ....138 B8
Stane Cl CM23 .....58 F1
Stane Field SG6 .....23 B3
Stane St SG7 .....13 A1
Stanelow Cres SG11 ....55 D2
Stanfields Ct CM20 ....117 E1
Stanford Rd LU2 .....46 A1
Stangate Cres WD6 ....170 E4
Stanhope Ave HA3 .....176 D2
Stanhope Rd Barnet EN5 171 D3
Cheshunt EN8 .....162 E6
St Albans AL1 .....127 F3
Stanier Rise HP4 .....121 F7
Stanley Ave AL2 .....141 A6
Stanley Dr AL10 .....130 B3
Stanley Gdns
Borehamwood WD6 .....169 E8
Tring HP23 .....99 F3
Stanley Livingstone Ct 2
LU1 .....63 D6
Stanley Rd Hertford SG13 113 E5
Northwood HA6 .....175 A2
Stevenage SG2 .....51 B7
Streatley LU3 .....31 A5
Watford WD18 .....167 C5
Stanley St LU1 .....63 D6
Stanmore Chase AL4 ...128 D2
Stanmore Cres LU3 .....44 F4
Stanmore Rd
Stevenage SG1 .....50 D7
Watford WD24 .....167 B8
Stanmount Rd AL2 .....141 A6
Stannington Path WD6 .170 A8
Stanstead Dr EN11 .....135 B8
Stanstead Rd
Hertford SG13 .....114 A6
Hertford Heath SG13 ....114 D5
Hoddesdon EN11 .....115 B1
Stansted Hill SG10 .....75 A1
Stansted Mountfitchet Sta
CM24 .....59 E6
Stansted Mountfitchet
Windmill★ CM24 .....59 D6
Stansted Rd
Birchanger CM23,CM24 ....59 C4
Bishop's Stortford CM23 ...59 B2
Stanton Cl AL4 .....128 D7
Stanton Rd LU4 .....44 C1
Stantons CM20 .....117 B1
Staplefield Cl HA5 .....175 E3
Stapleford AL7 .....111 D6
Stapleford Prim Sch
SG14 .....92 A6
Stapleford Rd LU2 .....46 C4
Stapleton Cl EN6 .....159 D8
Stapleton Rd WD6 .....157 A2
Stapley Rd AL3 .....127 D4
Stapylton Rd EN5 .....171 E6
Star Holme Ct SG12 .....93 E1
Star St SG12 .....93 E1
Starkey Cl EN7 .....147 C6
Starlight Way AL4 .....128 C1
Starling La EN6 .....146 F3
Startpoint LU1 .....63 C7
Stately Ct LU3 .....45 D1
Statham Cl LU3 .....31 B1
Stathams Ct AL3 .....106 A3
Station App
Cheshunt EN8 .....162 E5
Chorleywood WD3 .....164 D5
Harlow CM20 .....118 C5
Harpenden AL5 .....86 B1
Hitchin SG4 .....35 A8
Kings Langley WD4 .....139 B1
Knebworth SG3 .....68 F5
Northwood HA6 .....174 E3
Radlett WD7 .....156 A4
South Oxhey WD19 .....175 D7
Station Cl
Brookmans Park AL9 .....144 E5
Potters Bar EN6 .....158 F8
Station Ct 15 SG12 .....93 D1
Station Footpath WD4 ..139 B1
Station Mews EN6 .....159 A8
Station Par SG6 .....22 F6
Station Pl SG6 .....22 F6
Station Rd Aldbury HP23 .101 B5
Arlesey SG15 .....11 A4
Ashwell SG7 .....4 F4
Baldock SG7 .....12 F1
Berkhamsted HP4 .....122 D4
Bishop's Stortford CM23 ...77 A7
Borehamwood WD6 .....170 A5
Braughing SG11 .....55 E5
Bricket Wood AL2 .....155 A8
Brookmans Park AL9 .....144 D6
Buntingford SG9 .....40 E7
Cheddington LU7 .....79 F8
Cuffley EN6 .....146 F2
Harlow CM17 .....118 C4
Harpenden AL5 .....86 C2
Hemel Hempstead HP1 ...124 C1
Hoddesdon EN10 .....135 A3
Holdbrook EN9 .....163 A5
Kings Langley WD4 .....139 B1
Knebworth SG3 .....69 A5
Letchworth SG6 .....22 F6
Letty Green SG14 .....112 B3
Long Marston HP23 .....79 B4
Lower Stondon SG16 .....10 A4
Luton, Leagrave LU4 .....44 E5
Luton,High Town LU1 .....63 E8
Much Hadham SG10 .....74 E1
Pitstone LU7 .....80 E5
Radlett WD7 .....156 A4
Rickmansworth WD3 .....165 D2
Sawbridgeworth CM21 .....97 F3
St Albans AL4 .....129 B3
Standon SG11 .....55 E2
Stanstead Abbotts SG12 ..115 C4
Stansted Mountfitchet
CM24 .....59 E6
Steeple Morden SG7,SG8 ...5 C5
Tring HP23 .....100 D4
Ware SG12 .....93 E1
Watford WD17 .....167 B7
Watton at S SG14 .....70 D3
Welwyn AL6 .....89 E3
Wheathampstead AL4 .....87 D1
Station Rdbt WD3 .....165 D2
Station Terr Hitchin SG4 ..35 A8
Park Street AL2 .....141 D5
Station Way
Letchworth SG6 .....22 E6
St Albans AL1 .....127 F3
Stationers Pl HP3 .....138 E6
Staveley Rd LU4 .....44 C1
Steeplands WD23 .....168 B2
Steeple View CM23 .....76 F8
Sten Cl EN3 .....163 A2
Stephens Cl LU2 .....46 A3
Stephens Gdns LU2 .....46 A2
Stephens Way AL3 .....105 F5
Stephenson Cl SG8 .....7 B7
Stephenson Way WD23,
WD24 .....167 D7
Stephenson Wharf HP3 .138 F6
Stephyns Chambers
HP1 .....124 C2
Stepnells HP23 .....80 A1
Stepping Stones The
LU3 .....44 E5
Sterling Ave EN8 .....162 D5
Sterling Rd EN2 .....161 D1
Stevenage Cres WD6 ...169 E8
Stevenage Mus★ SG1 ...50 E5
Stevenage Rd Hitchin SG4 34 F5
Knebworth SG2,SG3 .....68 F7
Little Wymondley SG4 .....35 E3
Little Wymondley, Titmore Green
SG4 .....35 E2
St Ippolyts SG4 .....35 C2
Walkern SG2 .....51 E8
Stevenage Rise HP2 ....124 F7
Stevenage Sta SG1 .....50 C5
Stevens Cl EN6 .....158 D6
Stevens Gn WD23 .....168 C1
Steward Cl EN8 .....148 E1
Stewart Cl WD5 .....154 A7
Stewart Rd AL5 .....86 B2
Stewarts The CM23 .....76 E6
Stile Plantation SG8 .....7 E6
Stilton Path WD6 .....157 A1
Stirling Bsns Pk EN8 ...162 F5
Stirling Cl Hitchin SG4 ...35 C7
Stevenage SG2 .....69 D7
Stirling Cnr EN5 .....170 D3
Stirling Ho WD6 .....170 C5
Stirling Way
Borehamwood WD6 .....170 D4
Watford WD5 .....154 A7
Welwyn Garden City AL7 ..111 E6
Stirling Way Ret Pk
WD6 .....170 D3
Stoat Cl SG13 .....114 A6
Stobarts Cl SG3 .....68 F6
Stock Bank SG8 .....8 D1
Stockbreach Cl AL10 ...130 A6
Stockbreach Rd AL10 ...130 A6
Stockens Dell SG3 .....68 F4
Stockens Gn SG3 .....68 F4
Stockers Farm Rd WD3 173 D8
Stockfield Ave EN11 ....135 B8
Stockholm Way LU3 .....44 E8
Stocking Hill SG9 .....39 B8
Stocking La SG8 .....18 C1
Stockings La SG13 .....132 D6
Stockingstone Rd LU2 ..45 E3
Stockmen Field CM23 ...76 C5
Stockport Rd WD3 .....164 C2
Stocks Mdw HP2 .....125 A4
Stocks Rd HP23 .....101 D7
Stockwell Cl EN7 .....148 E3
Stockwell La EN7 .....148 B3
Stockwood Craft Mus &
Gdns★ LU1 .....63 D4
Stockwood Cres LU1 ....63 D6
Stockwood Ct 17 LU1 ...63 D6
Stockwood Pk★ LU1 ....63 D3
Stone Cross CM20 .....117 D1
Stonecroft SG3 .....68 F5
Stonecroft Cl EN5 .....171 B5
Stonecross AL1 .....127 E4
Stonecross Rd AL10 ....130 B7
Stonehill Jun Mix Inf Sch
SG6 .....11 E1
Stonehills AL8 .....110 D7
Stonelea Rd HP3 .....138 F8
Stoneleigh CM21 .....97 D3
Stoneleigh Ave EN1 ....162 B1
Stoneleigh Cl
Cheshunt EN8 .....162 D6
Luton LU3 .....45 B7
Stoneleigh Dr EN11 ....115 B1
Stoneley SG6 .....11 F1
Stonemason Cl AL5 .....86 A3
Stonemead AL8 .....89 D3
Stonesdale LU4 .....44 C4
Stoneways Cl LU4 .....44 C6
Stoney Brook CM24 .....59 E5
Stoney Cl HP4 .....121 F6
Stoney Comm CM24 .....59 E5
Stoney Common Rd
CM24 .....59 D5
Stoney La Bovingdon HP3 137 C5
Chipperfield WD4 .....137 E1
Hemel Hempstead HP1 ...137 B8
Stoney Pl CM24 .....59 E5
Stoneycroft
Aldbury HP23 .....101 C5
Hemel Hempstead HP1 ...124 A3
Welwyn Garden City AL7 ..111 A7
Stoneyfield Dr CM24 ....59 E6
Stoneygate Rd LU4 .....44 D3
Stonnells Cl SG6 .....22 F8
Stony Croft SG1 .....50 E6
Stony Hills SG12 .....92 C7
Stony La
Chenies HP5,HP6 .....150 E1
Great Offley LU2,SG4 .....47 C4

Stonyshotts EN9 163 E6
Stookslade HP22 60 A3
Stopsley High Sch LU2 45 F4
Stopsley Prim Sch LU2 46 A4
Stopsley Way LU2 46 A3
Storehouse La SG4 34 F6
Storey Ct WD23 168 B4
Storey St HP3 138 D7
Stormont Rd SG5 21 F1
Stormont Sch EN6 159 D8
Stornoway HP3 125 B1
Stort Lodge CM23 76 D8
Stort Mill CM20 118 B6
Stort Rd CM23 76 F6
Stort Valley Ind Pk CM23 59 B2
Stortford Hall Ind Pk CM23 77 B7
Stortford Hall Pk CM23 77 B8
Stortford Hall Rd 3 CM23 77 B8
Stortford Rd
Hatfield Heath CM22 98 E4
Hoddesdon EN11 135 C7
Little Hadham SG11 57 C2
Standon SG11 55 F2
Stotfold Ho SG5 11 F6
Stotfold Rd Arlesey SG15 11 C7
Hinxworth SG7 3 C1
Hitchin SG4,SG6 22 C4
Letchworth SG6 11 D1
Stow The CM20 117 F2
Stox Mead HA3 176 D2
Strafford Cl EN6 159 A7
Strafford Ct SG3 69 A5
Strafford Gate EN6 159 A7
Strafford Rd EN5 171 E6
Straits The EN9 163 B7
Strandburgh Pl HP3 125 B1
Strangers Way LU4 44 C4
Strangeways WD17 153 E3
Stratfield Dr EN10 134 E4
Stratfield Rd WD6 170 A7
Stratford Lodge WD17 167 B8
Stratford Rd Luton LU4 45 B1
Watford WD17 167 A7
Stratford Way
Bricket Wood AL2 140 F2
Hemel Hempstead HP3 138 B8
Watford WD17 167 A7
Strathmore Ave
Hitchin SG5 21 F1
Luton LU1 63 F5
Strathmore Ct SG5 21 F1
Strathmore Inf Sch SG5 21 E2
Strathmore Rd SG4 66 E6
Strathmore Wlk LU1 63 F6
Stratton Ave EN2 161 D2
Stratton Ct 8 HA5 175 F3
Stratton Gdns LU2 45 D4
Straw Plait Way SG15 10 F4
Strawberry Field
8 Hatfield AL10 130 A2
Luton LU3 44 E7
Strawberry Fields SG12 93 B2
Strawfields AL7 111 B7
Strawmead AL10 130 B7
Strawplaiters Cl SG3 69 A2
Straws Hadley Ct HP22 60 B2
Strayfield Rd EN2 161 B2
Stream Woods Jun & Inf Sch AL10 130 B4
Street The Braughing SG11 55 F7
Chipperfield WD4 152 A8
Dane End SG11 53 F3
Furneux Pelham SG9 43 A4
Sheering CM22 98 E1
Wallington SG7 25 C8
Stretton Way WD6 156 E1
Stringers La SG2 51 E2
Stripling Way WD18 167 A3
Stroma Cl HP3 125 C1
Stronnell Cl LU2 46 B3
Stronsay Cl HP3 125 C1
Stroud Wood Bsns Ctr AL2 141 E4
Stuart Ct WD6 169 D3
Stuart Dr Hitchin SG4 35 B7
Royston SG8 7 D8
Stuart Ho EN9 163 F6
Stuart Rd AL6 89 B3
Stuart St LU1 63 D7
Stuart St Pas 7 LU1 63 D7
Stuart Way EN7 162 B8
Stuarts Cl 3 HP3 124 D1
Stud Gn WD25 154 B7
Studham CE Lower Sch LU6 82 B4
Studham La Dagnall HP4 81 D4
Whipsnade LU6 82 A7
Studio Way WD6 170 C8
Studios The WD23 168 A3
Studlands Rise SG8 7 E6
Studlands Rise Fst Sch SG8 7 E5
Studley Rd LU3 45 D1
Stump Cross SG8 15 C6
Sturgeon's Way SG4 22 B2
Sturla Cl SG14 113 B7
Sturlas Way EN8 162 D6
Sturmer Cl AL4 128 C2
Sturrock Way SG4 35 C6
Styles Cl LU2 46 C2
Such Cl SG6 23 B7
Sudbury Ct AL1 127 E2
Sudbury Rd LU4 44 B6
Suffolk Cl
Borehamwood WD6 170 D4
London Colney AL2 142 C6
Suffolk Cl *continued*
Luton LU4 44 A3
Suffolk Rd
Potters Bar EN6 158 E7
Royston SG8 7 E6
Sugar La HP1 123 B1
Sulgrave Cres HP23 100 C5
Sullivan Cres UB9 173 D1
Sullivan Way WD6 169 C3
Summer Ct HP2 124 D5
Summer Dale AL8 89 D1
Summer Gr WD6 169 D3
Summer Hill WD6 170 A4
Summer St LU1 63 C1
Summer Wlk AL3 83 E5
Summercroft Jun & Inf Schs CM23 77 C8
Summerfield AL10 130 A2
Summerfield Cl AL2 142 C5
Summerfield Rd
Luton LU1 62 F8
Watford WD25 154 A4
Summerhill Ct AL1 127 F4
Summerhouse La
Harefield UB9 173 A3
Radlett WD25 168 C8
Summerhouse Way WD5 139 F1
Summerlands Rd AL4 128 C7
Summers Lodge SG6 22 D6
Summers Rd LU2 46 C1
Summers Way AL2 142 E4
Summerswood La EN6, WD6 157 E4
Summerswood Prim Sch WD6 170 B5
Summit Ct EN5 171 F6
Summit Rd EN6 144 E1
Sumpter Yd AL1 127 D3
Sun Hill SG8 7 C5
Sun La AL5 86 A2
Sun Sq 2 HP1 124 D4
Sun St Baldock SG7 23 E8
Hitchin SG5 34 E6
Sawbridgeworth CM21 97 F1
Waltham Abbey EN9 163 C6
Sunbury Ct
2 Barnet EN5 171 E5
St Albans AL1 128 B2
Sunderland Ave AL1 128 A4
Sunderland Est WD4 139 B2
Sunderland Gr WD25 153 F5
Sundew Rd HP1 123 E2
Sundon Park Jun Sch LU3 44 C8
Sundon Park Rd LU3 44 C7
Sunmead Rd HP2 124 D5
Sunningdale
Bishop's Stortford CM23 76 E6
Luton LU2 45 F3
Sunningdale Mews AL7 89 F2
Sunny Bank Prim Sch EN6 159 A5
Sunny Hill SG9 40 F7
Sunnybank LU7 79 F7
Sunnybank Rd EN6 159 A6
Sunnydell AL2 141 B5
Sunnyfield AL9 130 D8
Sunnyhill Rd
Hemel Hempstead HP1 124 B3
Maple Cross WD3 172 D4
Sunnyside
Lower Nazeing EN9 135 F1
Stansted Mountfitchet CM24 59 E6
Sunnyside Cotts HP5 136 A5
Sunnyside Rd SG4 35 A5
Sunridge Ave LU2 45 E2
Sunrise Cres HP3 138 F8
Sunrise Ind Est LU2 46 A2
Sunset Dr LU2 45 F3
Sunset View EN5 171 E7
Sunshine House Sch HA6 174 D4
Surrey Pl HP23 100 A3
Surrey St LU1 63 E6
Surrey Street Prim Sch LU1 63 F6
Sursham Ct AL3 83 E5
Sussex Ct EN11 135 A7
Sussex Pl LU2 46 D2
Sussex Rd WD24 154 A1
Sutcliffe Cl
Bushey WD23 168 C5
Stevenage SG1 51 A8
Sutherland Ave EN6 146 D3
Sutherland Cl EN5 171 E5
Sutherland Ct
Watford WD18 166 C2
Welwyn Garden City AL7 110 F7
Sutherland Pl LU1 63 D5
Sutherland Way EN6 146 E3
Sutton Acres CM22 98 D7
Sutton Cl
Hoddesdon EN10 134 E4
Tring HP23 100 B6
Sutton Cres EN5 171 D4
Sutton Ct SG12 114 E8
Sutton Gdns
Caddington LU1 62 E3
Luton LU3 44 D6
Sutton Path WD6 170 A6
Sutton Rd St Albans AL1 128 B3
Watford WD17 167 C6
Swale Cl SG1 37 A3
Swallow Cl
Bushey WD23 168 C1
Luton LU4 44 A4
Swallow Cl *continued*
Rickmansworth WD3 165 C2
Swallow Ct Enfield EN3 162 C2
Hertford SG14 113 C6
Welwyn Garden City AL7 110 F6
Swallow Dell Prim Sch AL7 111 A5
Swallow End AL7 110 F6
Swallow Gdns AL10 130 A3
Swallow La AL1 142 B8
Swallow Oaks WD5 153 F7
Swallow Pk HP2 125 B7
Swallowdale La HP2 125 B6
Swallowfields AL7 110 F6
Swallows CM17 118 C4
Swallows The AL7 89 F2
Swan & Pike Rd EN3 163 A1
Swan Cl WD3 165 D2
Swan Ct
2 Bishop's Stortford CM23 76 F6
Chorleywood WD3 164 C5
Swan Field Ho 3 WD3 165 D2
Swan La SG8 1 F4
Swan Mead
Hemel Hempstead HP3 138 F6
Luton LU4 44 B4
Swan Rd EN8 162 E5
Swan St SG7 4 D4
Swanfield Rd EN8 162 E6
Swangley's La SG3 69 B4
Swanhill AL7 90 A1
Swanland Rd AL9,EN6 144 B3
Swanley Bar La EN6 145 B3
Swanley Cres EN6 145 B2
Swanley Ct WD24 154 C2
Swannells Wood LU6 82 C4
Swans Cl AL4 128 E2
Swans Ct EN8 162 E5
Swanstand SG6 23 D4
Swanston Grange LU4 44 B2
Swanston Path 3 WD19 175 C7
Swasedale Rd LU3 45 A6
Sweet Briar
Bishop's Stortford CM23 76 B6
Welwyn Garden City AL7 111 A5
Sweetbriar Cl HP1 124 A6
Sweyns Mead SG2 51 C7
Swift Cl Letchworth SG6 22 E8
Royston SG8 2 D1
Stanstead Abbotts SG12 115 C3
Swiftfields AL7 111 A7
Swifts Green Cl LU2 46 B5
Swifts Green Rd LU2 46 B5
Swinburne Ave SG5 21 C1
Swinburne Ct SG8 2 D1
Swing Gate Fst Sch HP4 122 D3
Swing Gate La HP4 122 D2
Swingate SG1 50 D5
Swinnell Cl SG8 2 B5
Swiss Ave WD18 166 E6
Swiss Cl WD18 166 E6
Sword Cl EN10 134 D3
Sworders Yd 3 CM23 76 F7
Sycamore App WD3 166 C4
Sycamore Ave AL10 130 A4
Sycamore Cl
Hammond Street EN7 147 F4
Hitchin SG4 35 A4
Watford WD23 167 E7
Watford,Garston WD25 154 B4
Sycamore Dr
Park Street AL2 141 D4
Tring HP23 100 B4
Sycamore Ho HP2 124 E4
Sycamore Rd WD3 166 D4
Sycamore Rise HP4 122 D3
Sycamores The
Baldock SG7 23 E8
Bishop's Stortford CM23 77 B6
Hemel Hempstead HP3 137 F8
Radlett WD7 156 B5
8 St Albans AL1 127 D2
Sydney Rd WD18 166 F4
Sylam Cl LU3 44 E7
Sylvan Cl HP3 125 A2
Sylvan Hts AL1 128 A1
Sylvan Way AL7 111 C5
Sylvandale AL7 111 C5
Sylvia Ave HA5 175 F4
Symonds Ct 13 EN8 148 D3
Symonds Green La SG1 50 A6
Symonds Green Rd SG1 50 A7
Symonds Rd SG5 34 D8

T

Tabbs Cl SG6 23 B7
Tacitus Cl 2 SG1 51 C8
Tailors CM23 76 B5
Takeley Cl EN9 163 D6
Talbot Ave WD19 167 E2
Talbot Ct HP3 124 D1
Talbot Rd Harrow HA3 176 F1
Hatfield AL10 130 A8
Luton LU2 45 F2
Rickmansworth WD3 165 E1
Talbot St Hertford SG13 113 E6
Hitchin SG5 34 C8
Talbot Way SG6 12 B1
Talisman St SG4 35 C6
Tall Trees Hitchin SG4 35 A4
Royston SG8 7 E6
Tallack Cl HA3 176 E3
Tallents Cres AL5 86 D3
Tallis Way WD6 169 E8
Tamar Cl SG1 37 A3
Tamar Gn HP2 124 F8
Tamarisk Cl AL3 127 D7
Tameton Cl LU2 46 F2
Tamworth Rd SG13 113 F7
Tancred Rd LU2 46 A4
Tanfield Cl EN7 148 A4
Tanfield Gn LU2 46 E1
Tanglewood
Harpenden AL5 85 F2
Welwyn AL6 90 A7
Tanglewood Cl HA7 176 E8
Tankerfield Pl AL3 127 C3
Tanner Ho WD19 167 B2
Tanners Cl AL3 127 C4
Tanners Cres SG13 113 C4
Tanners Hill WD5 154 A8
Tanners Way SG12 116 D8
Tanners Wood Cl WD5 153 E7
Tanners Wood Ct WD5 153 E7
Tanners Wood Jun Mix Inf Sch WD5 153 E7
Tanners Wood La WD5 153 E7
Tannery Cl SG8 7 C6
Tannery Drift SG8 7 C6
Tannery Drift Sch SG8 7 C6
Tannery The SG9 40 E7
Tannery Yd SG4 66 F6
Tannsfield Dr 1 HP2 124 F5
Tannsmore Cl 2 HP2 124 F5
Tansycroft AL7 111 B7
Tanworth Cl HA6 174 C4
Tanworth Gdns HA5 175 C1
Tany's Dell CM20 118 A3
Tany's Dell Com Prim Sch CM20 118 A3
Tanyard La AL6,SG4 88 B8
Tapster St EN5 171 F6
Taransay HP3 125 B1
Tarlings CM20 117 F3
Tarpan Way EN10 148 F6
Tarrant SG1 36 B1
Tarrant Dr AL5 107 D7
Tassell Hall AL3 105 F6
Tate Gdns WD23 168 E2
Tates Way SG1 36 B2
Tatlers La SG2 51 E4
Tatsfield Ave EN9 149 E8
Tatsford Villas EN9 135 C1
Tattershall Dr HP2 105 B1
Tattle Hill SG14 91 E2
Tattlers Hill HP22 60 B3
Tatton St CM17 118 C1
Tauber Cl WD6 169 F5
Taunton Ave LU2 46 B1
Taverners HP2 124 E5
Taverners Way EN11 135 A6
Tavistock Ave AL1 141 D8
Tavistock Cl
Potters Bar EN6 159 D8
St Albans AL1 141 D8
Tavistock Cres LU1 63 E5
Tavistock Rd WD24 167 D8
Tavistock St LU1 63 E6
Taylers Cotts EN6 157 F5
Taylor Cl Harefield UB9 173 C1
St Albans AL4 128 A8
Taylor St LU2 63 F8
Taylor Trad Est SG13 114 B7
Taylor's Hill SG4 34 F6
Taylor's La EN5 171 F8
Taylor's Rd SG5 11 F8
Taylors Ave EN11 135 A5
Taylors La HP23 119 C3
Taywood Cl SG2 51 B2
Teal Dr HA6 174 C3
Teal Ho WD25 154 E3
Teal Way HP3 138 F6
Teasdale Cl SG8 2 D1
Teasel Cl SG8 7 E5
Tedder Ave SG16 10 B5
Tedder Rd HP2 125 A4
Tee Side SG13 114 B7
Tees Cl SG1 36 F3
Teesdale
Hemel Hempstead HP2 124 E6
Luton LU4 44 C5
Telford Ave SG2 51 B6
Telford Cl WD25 154 D4
Telford Ct Hatfield AL10 129 F3
St Albans AL1 127 E2
Telford Rd AL2 142 C4
Telford Way LU1 63 D8
Telmere Ind Est 16 LU1 63 E6
Telscombe Way LU2 46 C3
Temperance St AL3 127 C3
Tempest Ave EN6 159 D7
Templar Ave SG7 23 F6
Templars Dr HA3 176 D4
Templars La SG4 48 D6
Temple Bank CM20 118 B5
Temple Cl Cheshunt EN7 162 A8
Luton LU2 45 E5
Preston SG5 34 B4
Watford WD17 166 F7
Temple Ct Hertford SG14 92 D1
Potters Bar EN6 158 D8
Temple Fields SG14 92 D1
Temple Gdns
Letchworth SG6 23 C8
Moor Park WD3 174 B6
Temple Ho EN7 162 A6
Temple La SG12 92 F8
Temple Mead
Hemel Hempstead HP2 124 D5
Roydon CM19 116 B1
Temple View AL3 127 C5
Templefields Ent Ctr CM20 118 A3
Templepan La WD3 152 E2
Templewood AL8 89 D1
Templewood Prim Sch AL8 110 D8
Tempsford AL7 111 D6
Tempsford Ave WD6 170 D5
Temsford Cl HA2 176 C1
Tenby Dr LU4 44 F3
Tenby Mews LU4 44 E3
Tene The SG7 23 F8
Tennand Cl EN7 147 F5
Tennison Ave WD6 170 B4
Tennyson Ave Hitchin SG4 35 C7
Waltham Abbey EN9 163 E5
Tennyson Cl SG8 2 E1
Tennyson Ho LU1 63 E5
Tennyson Rd
Chiswell Green AL2 141 B5
Harpenden AL5 86 A2
Luton LU1 63 E5
Tennyson Road Prim Sch LU1 63 E5
Tenterfield Ho AL6 89 C4
Tenth Ave LU3 44 C7
Tenzing Gr LU1 63 C6
Tenzing Rd HP2 125 A3
Teresa Gdns EN8 162 D5
Terminus St CM20 117 D1
Terrace Gdns WD17 167 B7
Terrace The
Essendon AL9 131 E6
Redbourn AL3 106 A5
Tring HP23 100 A3
Westmill SG9 40 F2
Tethys Rd HP2 124 F6
Tewin Cl St Albans AL4 128 C7
Tewin AL6 90 C5
Tewin Cowper CE Prim Sch AL6 90 E2
Tewin Ct AL7 110 F7
Tewin Hill AL6 90 F5
Tewin Rd
Hemel Hempstead HP2 125 C3
Welwyn Garden City AL7 110 F7
Thackeray Cl SG8 2 D1
Thames Ave HP2 124 F8
Thames Ct LU3 45 B3
Thamesdale AL2 142 F4
Thanet Ho 1 WD18 166 F3
Thatchers Croft HP2 124 E7
Thatchers End SG4 35 D8
Thatchers The CM23 76 C5
Thaxted Cl LU2 46 F2
Thaxted Way EN9 163 D6
Thaynesfield EN6 159 D8
Theabald's Grove Sta EN8 162 D7
Thelby Cl LU3 44 F6
Thele Ave SG12 115 D4
Thele Est SG12 115 E4
Theleway Cl EN11 115 B1
Thellusson Way WD3 165 A2
Thelusson Ct WD7 156 A3
Theobald Bsns Ctr SG4 22 A3
Theobald Cres HA3 176 C2
Theobald Ct WD6 170 A6
Theobald St
Borehamwood WD6 169 F7
Radlett WD6,WD7 156 D2
Theobald's La
Cheshunt EN8 162 B7
Cheshunt EN8 162 D7
Theobald's Rd EN6 146 F1
Theobalds Cl EN6 146 F1
Theobalds Park Camp Site EN7 162 A5
Theobalds Park Coll EN7 162 A6
Theobalds Park Rd EN2 161 B3
Therfield Fst Sch SG8 15 F7
Therfield Heath Nature Reserve★ SG8 7 A5
Therfield Rd AL3 127 D6
Thetford Gdns LU2 45 E6
Thieves' La SG14 112 F7
Third Ave Letchworth SG6 23 C7
Luton LU3 44 D7
Watford WD25 154 D4
Thirlestane AL1 127 F4
Thirlestone Rd LU4 44 D1
Thirlmere SG1 37 C2
Thirlmere Dr AL1 128 B1
Thirlmere Gdns HA6 174 C4
Thirsk Rd WD6 157 A1
Thirston Path 1 WD6 170 A7
Thistle Cl HP1 123 E2
Thistle Dr AL10 129 F8
Thistle Gr AL7 111 C3
Thistle Rd LU1 63 F7
Thistlecroft HP1 124 B2
Thistles The HP1 124 B4
Thistley La SG4 34 F1
Thomas Alleyne Sch The SG1 50 C8
Thomas Bourne Ho 9 HP4 122 D4
Thomas Coram CE Mid Sch The HP4 122 D2
Thomas Ct HP4 121 F5
Thomas Heskin Ct 11 CM23 77 A7
Thomas Rochford Way EN8 148 F4

Thomas Watson Cottage Homes The EN5 171 E4
Thomas Way SG8 2 D1
Thompson Way WD3 165 A1
Thompsons Cl
Goff's Oak EN7 147 F2
Harpenden AL5 86 A1
Thompsons Mdw SG8 1 F4
Thorley Ctr The CM23 76 D3
Thorley High CM23 76 F2
Thorley Hill CM23 76 F5
Thorley Hill Prim Sch CM23 76 F4
Thorley La CM23 76 F3
Thorley La E CM23 76 D3
Thorley La W CM23 76 B4
Thorley Park Rd CM23 76 F4
Thorn Ave WD23 168 C1
Thorn Gr CM23 77 B6
Thorn Grove Prim Sch CM23 77 B6
Thorn Tree Dr HP23 99 F4
Thornage Cl LU2 45 D7
Thornbera Cl CM23 76 F4
Thornbera Gdns CM23 76 F4
Thornbera Rd CM23 76 F4
Thornbury AL5 86 D1
Thornbury Cl
Hoddesdon EN11 115 B2
Stevenage SG2 69 A8
Thornbury Gdns WD6 170 C5
Thorncroft HP3 125 B1
Thorndyke Ct HA5 175 F3
Thorne Cl HP1 124 B1
Thorne Ho AL1 127 E4
Thorne Way HP22 99 B4
Thorneycroft Cl LU3 44 F4
Thorneycroft Dr EN3 163 A2
Thornfield Rd CM23 76 E8
Thornhill Rd Luton LU4 44 F2
Moor Park HA6 174 C6
Thornton Gr HA5 176 A4
Thornton Rd Barnet EN5 171 E6
Potters Bar EN6 145 C1
Thornton St
Hertford SG14 113 D6
St Albans AL3 127 C4
Thorntondale 5 LU4 44 C5
Thorpe Cres WD19 167 C2
Thorpe Rd AL1 127 D2
Thorpefield Cl AL4 128 D6
Thrales Cl LU3 44 E7
Three Cherry Trees La HP2 125 B7
Three Close La HP4 122 C4
Three Closes SG5 20 C4
Three Corners HP3 125 A1
Three Houses La SG4 67 D5
Three Meadows Mews HA3 176 F2
Three Rivers Mus of Local History* WD3 165 E2
Three Star Cvn Pk SG16 10 A3
Three Stiles SG2 52 E4
Three Valleys Way WD23 167 E4
Thremhall Ave CM23 77 F8
Thresher Cl CM23 76 C5
Thricknells Cl LU3 44 E7
Thrift Farm La WD6 170 C7
Thriftfield HP2 124 D5
Thrimley La CM23 58 C6
Thristers Cl SG6 23 B3
Throcking La SG9 27 C1
Throcking Rd SG9 39 D8
Thrums WD24 154 B2
Thrush Ave AL10 130 A3
Thrush Gn WD3 165 C2
Thrush La EN6 146 F3
Thumbswood AL7 111 A3
Thumpers HP2 124 E5
Thunder Hall 1 SG12 93 D2
Thundercourt SG12 93 D2
Thundridge Bsns Pk SG12 93 D7
Thundridge CE Prim Sch SG12 93 D7
Thundridge Cl AL7 111 B5
Thurgood Rd EN11 135 A8
Thurlow Cl SG1 36 D2
Thurnall Ave SG8 7 D5
Thurnall Cl SG7 23 F8
Thyme Cl LU2 45 E7
Tibbles Cl WD25 154 E4
Tibbs Hill Rd WD5 139 F1
Tiberius Rd LU3 44 F6
Tichborne WD3 172 D5
Tile Kiln Cl HP3 125 B2
Tile Kiln Cres HP3 125 B2
Tile Kiln La HP3 125 B2
Tilecroft AL8 89 D1
Tilehouse Cl WD6 169 F6
Tilehouse La UB9 172 E2
Tilehouse St SG5 34 E6
Tilekiln Cl EN7 147 F2
Tilgate LU2 46 D3
Tillers Link SG2 51 A2
Tillotson Rd HA3 176 B3
Tilsworth Wlk AL4 128 C8
Timber Orch SG14 92 A2
Timbercroft AL7 89 F1
Timberidge WD3 165 D5
Timbers Ct AL5 85 F2
Times Cl SG5 21 D2
Timplings Row HP1 124 B5
Timworth Cl LU2 46 D1
Tingeys Cl AL3 106 A5
Tinkers La HP23 121 A6
Tinsley Cl LU1 63 B5
Tintagel Cl
Hemel Hempstead HP2 124 D8
Luton LU3 45 B4
Tintern Cl Harpenden AL5 85 C4
Stevenage SG2 69 A7
Tinwell Mews WD6 170 D4
Tippendell La AL2 141 C5
Tippet Ct SG1 50 D3
Tiree Cl HP3 125 B1
Titan Ct LU4 44 F1
Titan Rd HP2 124 F6
Titchfield Rd EN3 162 E2
Tithe Barn Cl AL1 141 C8
Tithe Barn Ct WD5 139 F2
Tithe Cl SG4 67 F1
Titian Ave WD23 168 E2
Titmore Ct SG4 35 E2
Titmus Cl SG1 50 E6
Tiverton Ct AL5 107 E6
Tiverton Rd EN6 159 E8
Toddington Rd LU4 44 C6
Toland Cl LU4 44 C1
Tolcarne Dr HA5 175 A1
Tollgate Cl WD3 164 F5
Tollgate Rd
Colney Heath AL4,AL9 143 E7
Enfield EN3 162 D4
Welham Green AL9 144 A6
Tollpit End HP1 124 A6
Tollsworth Way SG11 55 D3
Tolmers Ave EN6 146 E3
Tolmers Gdns EN6 146 F2
Tolmers Mews SG13 146 E6
Tolmers Rd EN6 146 E3
Tolpits Cl WD18 166 F4
Tolpits La WD18 166 E2
Tom's Hill WD3 152 E3
Tomkins Cl WD6 169 E8
Tomlins Cl SG8 8 F1
Toms Croft HP2 124 E2
Toms Field AL10 129 E4
Toms Hill Cl HP23 101 D5
Toms Hill Rd HP23 101 D5
Toms La WD4,WD5 139 D3
Tonwell St Mary's CE Prim Sch SG12 92 E7
Tooke Cl HA5 175 E2
Toorack Rd HA3 176 D1
Tooveys Mill Cl WD4 139 A2
Topstreet Way AL5 107 C8
Tormead HA6 174 D4
Toronto Ho EN8 162 D8
Torquay Cres SG1 50 B7
Torquay Dr LU4 44 D4
Torridge Wlk 2 HP2 124 F8
Torrington Dr EN6 159 D7
Torrington Rd HP4 122 B4
Tortoiseshell Way HP4 121 F6
Torwood Cl HP4 121 F4
Torworth Rd WD6 157 A1
Tot La CM23,CM24 59 D4
Totteridge Comm N20 171 D1
Totteridge Pk N20 171 C1
Totteridge Rd EN3 162 D2
Totteridge Village N20 171 F1
Totton Mews AL3 106 B5
Totts La SG2 38 C1
Toulmin Dr AL3 127 C7
Tovey Cl
London Colney AL2 142 D5
Lower Nazeing EN9 149 F8
Tower Cl
Berkhamsted HP4 122 A3
Hertford Heath SG13 114 C2
Kneesworth SG8 2 A5
Little Wymondley SG4 35 F3
Tower Ct LU2 46 A1
Tower Ctr EN11 135 A6
Tower Hill
Chipperfield WD4 137 F1
Much Hadham SG10 74 F2
Tower Hill La AL4 108 F4
Tower Hts EN11 135 A6
Tower Prim Sch SG12 93 E3
Tower Rd Codicote SG4 67 F2
Luton LU2 64 A8
Ware SG12 93 F2
Tower St SG14 113 C8
Tower View SG4 66 D6
Tower Way LU2 64 A8
Towers Rd
Hemel Hempstead HP2 124 E4
Pinner HA5 175 E2
Stevenage SG1 50 D4
Towers The SG1 50 D4
Town Ctr AL10 130 A6
Town Farm
Cheddington LU7 80 A7
Wheathampstead AL4 108 D8
Town Farm Cl SG8 1 F4
Town Farm Cres SG11 55 F2
Town Fields AL10 130 A6
Town La SG2 52 E4
Town Mead Rd EN9 163 C5
Town Mill Mews 3 SG14 113 C6
Town Sq SG1 50 D5
Towne Rd SG8 7 D5
Townfield WD3 165 C2
Townley SG6 23 D4
Townsend HP2 124 D5
Townsend Ave AL1 127 E4
Townsend CE Sch AL3 127 C8
Townsend Cl
Barkway SG8 17 C3
Harpenden AL5 85 F1
St Ippolyts SG4 35 A3
Townsend Dr AL3 127 D5
Townsend La AL5 85 F1
Townsend Rd AL5 86 A2
Townsend Way HA6 175 A3
Townshend St SG13 113 E6
Townsley Cl LU1 63 E6
Tracey Ct 15 LU1 63 E6
Trafalgar Ave EN10 134 F2
Trafford Cl Shenley WD7 156 E7
Stevenage SG1 36 E1
Traherne Cl SG4 34 F5
Trajan Gate SG2 37 D1
Trapstyle Rd SG12 93 A2
Travellers Cl AL9 144 C8
Travellers La
Hatfield AL10 130 B2
Welham Green AL9 130 C1
Treacle La SG9 25 F3
Treacy Cl WD23 176 C8
Trebellan Dr HP2 124 F4
Treeby Ct EN3 163 A2
Treehanger Cl HP23 100 B4
Treetops AL6 89 E7
Treetops Cl HA6 174 D5
Trefoil Cl LU4 44 A4
Trefusis Wlk WD17 166 E8
Tremaine Gr HP2 124 E7
Trent Cl Shenley WD7 156 E7
Stevenage SG1 50 E8
Trent Rd LU3 45 B4
Tresco Rd HP4 121 F5
Trescott Cl LU2 46 E2
Tresilian Sq HP2 125 A8
Treslian Sq 1 HP2 124 F8
Trevalga Way HP2 124 E7
Trevellance Way WD25 154 D6
Trevelyan Pl AL1 127 C1
Trevelyan Way HP4 122 B6
Trevera Ct Cheshunt EN8 162 E6
Hoddesdon EN11 135 A7
Trevor Cl HA3 176 F3
Trevor Rd SG4 35 A8
Trevose Way WD19 175 C7
Trewenna Dr EN6 159 D7
Triangle The SG4 34 F6
Trident Ctr WD24 167 C8
Trident Ind Est EN11 135 C7
Trident Rd WD25 153 F5
Trigg Terr SG1 50 E6
Triggs Way LU2 46 E3
Trimley Cl LU4 44 B5
Trinder Rd EN5 171 C4
Tring Bsns Ctr HP23 99 E4
Tring Ford Rd HP23 100 A7
Tring Hill HP23 99 C3
Tring Ho WD18 166 E2
Tring Rd
Berkhamsted HP4 121 D7
Long Marston HP23 79 C3
Wingrave HP22 60 C1
Tring Sch HP23 100 B4
Tring Sta HP23 101 A5
Trinity Cl
Bishop's Stortford CM23 76 F6
Northwood HA6 174 E4
Trinity Ct SG14 113 C8
Trinity Gr SG14 113 C8
Trinity Hall Cl WD24 167 C6
Trinity Ho
2 Borehamwood WD6 170 A5
Cheshunt EN8 162 E7
Trinity La EN8 162 E7
Trinity Mews HP2 125 D2
Trinity Pl SG1 50 D6
Trinity Rd
Hertford Heath SG13 114 C3
Luton LU3 45 A4
Stevenage SG1 50 C6
Stotfold SG5 11 F7
Ware SG12 93 E2
Trinity St CM23 76 F6
Trinity Way CM23 76 F6
Trinity Wlk
Hemel Hempstead HP2 125 D2
Hertford Heath SG13 114 C3
Tristram Rd SG4 22 B2
Triton Way HP2 124 F5
Trojan Terr CM21 97 E3
Troon Gdns LU2 45 E7
Trooper Rd HP23 101 C5
Trotter's Gap SG12 115 E4
Trotters Bottom EN5 158 B2
Trotts Hill Prim Sch SG1 36 F1
Trout Rise WD3 165 B6
Troutstream Way WD3 165 B5
Trouvere Pk HP1 124 B5
Trowbridge Gdns LU2 45 E3
Trowley Bottom AL3 105 B8
Trowley Hts AL3 84 B2
Trowley Rise WD5 153 F8
Truemans Rd SG5 21 D2
Trumper Rd SG1 36 F1
Trumpington Dr AL1 141 D8
Truncals LU1 63 D5
Trundlers Way WD23 168 E1
Truro Gdns LU3 45 C5
Trust Cotts HP4 81 A1
Trust Rd EN8 162 E5
Tucker St WD18 167 C4
Tucker's Row 4 CM23 76 F6
Tudor Ave Cheshunt EN7 162 B8
Watford WD24 154 D2
Tudor Cl Cheshunt EN7 162 B8
Hatfield AL10 129 F2
Tudor Cl *continued*
Hunsdon SG12 116 D8
Stevenage SG1 36 C1
Tudor Cres EN2 161 C1
Tudor Ct Barnet EN5 171 F5
Borehamwood WD6 169 E7
Hitchin SG5 34 D6
Kneesworth SG8 2 B4
Rickmansworth WD3 165 A1
Sawbridgeworth CM21 97 E3
Tudor Dr WD24 154 D2
Tudor Gdns HA3 176 D1
Tudor Jun Mix & Inf Sch HP3 124 E1
Tudor Lodge 3 HA6 174 E3
Tudor Manor Gdns WD25 154 D7
Tudor Par WD3 165 A2
Tudor Rd Harrow HA3 176 D1
Luton LU3 45 B2
Pinner HA5 175 C1
St Albans AL3 127 E7
Welwyn AL6 89 B3
Wheathampstead AL4 108 E8
Tudor Rise EN10 134 E2
Tudor Sq 18 SG12 93 D1
Tudor Way
Hertford SG14 113 A7
Rickmansworth WD3 165 A2
Waltham Abbey EN9 163 D6
Tudor Wlk 17 Ware SG12 93 D1
Watford WD24 154 D2
Tuffnells Way AL5 85 D4
Tunfield Rd EN11 115 B1
Tunnel Wood Cl WD17 153 F2
Tunnel Wood Rd WD17 153 F2
Tunnmeade CM20 118 A1
Turf La SG4 36 B4
Turkey St EN1,EN3 162 C2
Turkey Street Sta EN3 162 C2
Turmore Dale AL8 110 C5
Turnberry Ct WD19 175 C7
Turnberry Dr AL2 140 E1
Turner Cl SG1 36 C2
Turner Rd WD23 168 C5
Turners Cl Bramfield SG14 91 C4
Harpenden AL5 86 C4
Turners Cres CM23 76 C4
Turners Ct EN8 162 D8
Turners Hill
Cheshunt EN8 148 D1
Hemel Hempstead HP2 124 E2
Turners Rd N LU2 46 A2
Turners Rd S LU2 46 A2
Turneys Orch WD3 164 D4
Turnford Sch EN8 148 E3
Turnford Villas EN8 148 F5
Turnpike Dr LU3 31 C1
Turnpike Gn HP2 124 F7
Turnpike La SG5 21 E3
Turnstones The WD25 154 E3
Turpin Cl EN3 163 A2
Turpin's Ride SG8 7 D5
Turpin's Rise SG2 50 F1
Turpin's Way SG7 23 F7
Turpins Chase AL6 89 F7
Turpins Cl SG14 112 F6
Turpins Ride AL6 89 F7
Tussauds Cl WD3 166 A4
Tuthill Ct SG8 15 E7
Tuxford Cl WD6 156 E1
Tweed Cl HP4 122 B5
Twelve Acres AL7 110 E4
Twelve Leys HP22 60 B3
Twickenham Gdns HA3 176 E3
Twigden Ct LU3 44 E5
Twin Foxes SG3 69 A1
Twinwoods SG1 50 F4
Twist The HP23 100 D2
Twitchell The SG7 23 F8
Two Acres AL7 110 F3
Two Beeches HP2 124 F8
Two Dells La HP5 136 A4
Two Oaks Dr AL6 90 C6
Two Waters Prim Sch HP3 138 D6
Two Waters Rd
Hemel Hempstead HP3 124 C1
Hemel Hempstead HP3 138 D8
Twyford Bsns Ctr The CM23 77 A4
Twyford Bury La CM22, CM23 77 A4
Twyford Cl CM23 77 A5
Twyford Dr LU2 46 D1
Twyford Gdns CM23 76 F4
Twyford Mews CM22 77 A3
Twyford Mill CM22 77 A3
Twyford Rd
Bishop's Stortford CM23 77 A5
St Albans AL4 128 D7
Twysdens Terr AL9 144 C7
Tye End SG2 69 B8
Tyfield Cl EN8 148 C1
Tylers AL5 86 D1
Tylers Cl Buntingford SG9 40 D7
Kings Langley WD4 138 F3
Tylers Cswy SG13 132 C1
Tylers Hill Rd HP5 150 A8
Tylers Mead LU2 45 E5
Tylers Way WD23,WD25 168 E4
Tylers Wood AL6 90 C6
Tylersfield WD5 154 A8
Tynedale AL2 142 F4
Tynemouth Dr EN1 162 A1
Typleden Cl HP2 124 D5
Tysoe Ave EN3 162 F2
Tythe Rd LU4 44 C6
Tyttenhanger Gn AL4 142 E8

U

Uckfield Rd EN3 162 D2
Ufford Cl HA3 176 B3
Ufford Rd HA3 176 B3
Ullswater Cl SG1 37 C2
Ullswater Rd HP3 125 C1
Ulverston Cl AL1 127 F3
Underacres Cl HP2 125 A4
Underhill Jun & Inf Schs EN5 171 E4
Underwood Rd SG1 36 C2
Union Chapel Ho 1 LU1 63 E6
Union Ct 19 HP4 122 D4
Union Gn HP2 124 D4
Union St Barnet EN5 171 E6
Luton LU1 63 E6
Union Terr SG9 40 E7
Unity Rd EN3 162 D2
Univ of Hertfordshire AL10 129 F3
Univ of Hertfordshire (Hertford Campus) SG13 113 E4
University Cl WD23 168 A5
Unwin Cl SG6 22 E4
Unwin Pl SG2 51 C3
Unwin Rd SG2 51 C3
Updale Cl EN6 158 E6
Upland Dr AL9 145 B6
Uplands Braughing SG11 55 F6
Croxley Green WD3 165 F3
Luton LU3 44 D8
Stevenage SG2 51 D7
Ware SG12 93 F2
Welwyn Garden City AL8 89 C2
Uplands Ave SG4 35 B6
Uplands Ct
3 Bushey WD23 168 D1
Luton LU1 63 E4
Uplands The
Bricket Wood AL2 140 E1
Harpenden AL5 107 A4
Upper Ashlyns Rd HP4 122 B3
Upper Barn HP3 138 F8
Upper Bourne End La HP1 137 B8
Upper Clabdens SG12 93 F2
Upper Culver Rd AL1 127 F5
Upper Dagnall St AL3 127 D3
Upper George St LU1 63 D7
Upper Gn AL6 90 D3
Upper Green Rd AL6 90 E3
Upper Hall Pk HP4 122 E2
Upper Heath Rd AL1 127 F5
Upper Highway WD5 153 D6
Upper Hill Rise WD3 165 B3
Upper Hitch WD19 167 E1
Upper Icknield Way
Aldbury LU7 80 E1
Aston Clinton HP22 99 A3
Tring HP23 100 D8
Upper King St SG8 7 D6
Upper Lattimore Rd AL1 127 E3
Upper Marlborough Rd AL1 127 E3
Upper Marsh La EN11 135 A5
Upper Maylins SG6 23 C3
Upper Paddock Rd WD19 167 E3
Upper Pk CM20 117 B1
Upper Sales HP1 123 F2
Upper Sean SG2 51 A3
Upper Shot AL7 111 A7
Upper Shott EN7 147 F5
Upper Station Rd WD7 156 A4
Upper Tail WD19 175 E7
Upper Tilehouse St SG5 34 E7
Upperfield Rd AL7 110 F5
Upperstone Cl SG5 11 F6
Upshire Rd EN9 163 F7
Upton Ave AL3 127 D4
Upton Cl Luton LU2 45 D6
Park Street AL2 141 D6
Upton Lodge Cl WD23 168 C2
Upton Rd WD18 167 B6
Upwell Rd LU2 46 B2
Uranus Rd HP2 124 F5
Urban Hive LU3 44 C8
Urban Rd CM23 77 B7
Uxbridge Rd WD3 173 A8
Uxbridge Rd (Harrow Weald) HA3 176 D3
Uxbridge Rd (Hatch End) HA5 175 F3
Uxbridge Rd (Pinner) HA5 175 D2
Uxbridge Rd (Stanmore) HA7 176 F4

V

Vadis Cl LU3 44 E7
Vale Ave WD6 170 B4
Vale Cl AL5 85 D4
Vale Cotts SG11 54 D5
Vale Ct AL4 108 D7
Vale Dr EN5 171 F5
Vale Ind Pk WD18 166 C1
Vale Rd WD23 167 E4
Valence Dr EN7 148 A3
Valency Cl HA6 174 F6
Valerian Way SG2 51 D8

Valerie Cl AL1 .....128 B3
Valerie Ct WD23 .....168 C2
Valeside SG14 .....113 A5
Vallance Pl AL5 .....107 C7
Vallans Cl SG12 .....93 D3
Vallansgate SG2 .....51 B1
Valley Cl Hertford SG13 ..113 D5
Pinner HA5 .....175 B1
Studham LU6 .....82 B4
Waltham Abbey EN9 .....163 C7
Ware SG12 .....93 B2
Whipsnade HP4 .....81 E7
Valley Ct CM23 .....76 E5
Valley Gn HP2 .....105 B1
Valley Gn The AL8 .....110 C7
Valley Ho EN8 .....162 D8
Valley La AL3 .....83 E1
Valley Rd
Berkhamsted HP4 .....121 F6
Codicote SG4 .....67 F1
Letchworth SG6 .....22 D7
Rickmansworth WD3 .....165 B3
St Albans AL3 .....127 F7
Studham LU6 .....82 B3
Welwyn Garden City AL8 ..110 B6
Valley Rise Lea Valley AL4 .86 F2
Royston SG8 .....7 E6
Watford WD25 .....154 B6
Valley Road S SG4 .....88 F8
Valley Sch The SG2 .....50 F2
Valley The SG4 .....66 E7
Valley View Barnet EN5 ..171 E3
Goff's Oak EN7 .....147 C3
Valley Way SG2 .....51 A3
Valley Wlk WD3 .....166 C4
Valleyside HP1 .....123 F3
Valpy Cl HP23 .....100 D1
Vancouver Rd EN10 .....148 E6
Vanda Cres AL1 .....127 F2
Vantorts Cl CM21 .....97 E2
Vantorts Rd CM21 .....97 E2
Vardon Rd SG1 .....50 F8
Varna Cl LU3 .....45 A3
Varney Cl
Hammond Street EN7 ...148 A4
Hemel Hempstead HP1 ...123 F3
Varney Rd HP1 .....123 F3
Vaughan Mead AL3 .....106 A4
Vaughan Rd
Harpenden AL5 .....86 B1
Stotfold SG5 .....11 E7
Vauxhall Rd
Hemel Hempstead HP2 ...125 B3
Luton LU1,LU2 .....64 B5
Vauxhall Way LU2 .....46 B1
Vega Cres HA6 .....175 A5
Vega Rd WD23 .....168 C2
Velizy Ave CM20 .....117 D1
Venetia Rd LU2 .....46 A4
Ventnor Gdns LU3 .....45 A7
Ventura Pk AL2 .....141 F2
Venus Hill HP3 .....151 A8
Ver Mdw Cvn Site AL3 .106 C5
Ver Rd Redbourn AL3 .....106 C6
St Albans AL3 .....127 C3
Vera Ct WD19 .....167 D2
Vera La AL6 .....90 B4
Verdure Cl WD25 .....154 E7
Verity Way SG1 .....51 B8
Veritys AL10 .....130 A5
Verney Cl
Berkhamsted HP4 .....121 F5
Tring HP23 .....100 C5
Vernon Ave EN3 .....162 E3
Vernon Ct CM23 .....76 E4
Vernon Dr UB9 .....173 C2
Vernon Rd Luton LU1 .....63 C8
Watford WD23 .....167 E4
Vernon's Cl AL1 .....127 E2
Veronica Ho AL7 .....111 B4
Verulam Cl AL7 .....110 F6
Verulam Gdns LU3 .....44 F6
Verulam Ind Est AL1 .....127 F1
Verulam Rd Hitchin SG5 ..34 F8
St Albans AL3 .....127 C4
Verulam Sch AL1 .....128 A4
Verulamium Mus★ AL3 .127 B3
Verulamium Roman City Walls★ AL3 .....127 B2
Verulamium Roman Town★ AL3 .....127 A3
Verwood Rd HA2 .....176 C1
Vespers Cl LU4 .....44 A2
Vesta Ave AL1 .....141 C8
Vesta Rd HP2 .....124 F5
Vestry Cl LU1 .....63 D7
Veysey Cl HP1 .....124 B1
Viaduct Cotts LU1 .....85 F8
Viaduct Rd SG12 .....114 E8
Viaduct Way AL7 .....89 F2
Vian Ave EN3 .....162 E4
Vicarage Cl Arlesey SG15 .11 A8
18 Bishop's Stortford CM23 76 F7
Hemel Hempstead HP1 ...124 C2
Northaw EN6 .....145 F1
Shillington SG5 .....19 F8
St Albans AL1 .....141 C8
Standon SG11 .....55 E2
Vicarage Cswy SG13 ...114 B4
Vicarage Gdns
Flamstead AL3 .....84 B1
Marsworth HP23 .....80 A2
Potten End HP4 .....123 B7
Vicarage La
Bovingdon HP3 .....137 B4
Kings Langley WD4 .....138 F2
Pitstone LU7 .....80 F5
Stapleford SG14 .....92 B2
Vicarage Rd
Buntingford SG9 .....40 E8
Marsworth HP23 .....80 A2
Pitstone LU7 .....80 D3
Potten End HP4 .....123 A7
Ware SG12 .....93 E1
Watford WD18 .....167 A4
Wigginton HP23 .....100 D1
Vicarage Road Prec WD18 .....167 B5
Vicarage St LU1 .....63 F7
Vicarage Wood CM20 ...118 A1
Vicerons Pl CM23 .....76 D4
Victoria CE Fst Sch HP4 .....122 C4
Victoria Cl
Rickmansworth WD3 .....165 D2
Stevenage SG1 .....50 D7
Victoria Cres SG8 .....7 D7
Victoria Ct Harlow CM20 .117 E1
Watford WD17 .....167 C6
Victoria Dr SG5 .....12 A5
Victoria La EN5 .....171 F5
Victoria Mews SG13 .....113 A1
Victoria Pl HP2 .....124 D3
Victoria Rd
Berkhamsted HP4 .....122 C4
Bushey WD23 .....168 B1
7 Harpenden AL5 .....86 B1
Waltham Abbey EN9 .....163 C5
Watford WD24 .....154 B1
Victoria Sq AL1 .....127 F2
Victoria St Luton LU1 .....63 E6
St Albans AL1 .....127 E3
Victoria Way SG5 .....34 D8
Victors Way EN5 .....171 F6
Victory Ct SG8 .....7 E5
Victory Rd HP4 .....122 A5
View Point SG1 .....50 A5
View Rd EN6 .....159 C7
Vigors Croft AL10 .....129 F4
Villa Ct 6 LU2 .....63 D8
Villa Rd LU2 .....63 D8
Village Cl EN11 .....135 D8
Village Ct AL4 .....128 D7
Village Mews HP3 .....137 A4
Village St SG4 .....49 F1
Villiers Cl LU4 .....44 D3
Villiers Cres AL4 .....128 D6
Villiers Rd WD19 .....167 E3
Villiers St SG13 .....113 E6
Villiers-Sur-Marne Ave CM23 .....76 D4
Vincent SG6 .....23 C4
Vincent Cl EN8 .....148 E3
Vincent Ct HA6 .....174 F2
Vincent Rd LU4 .....44 D5
Vincenzo Cl AL9 .....144 C8
Vine Cl AL8 .....110 E8
Vine Gr CM20 .....117 E5
Vine Tree Ct WD3 .....173 B8
Vines The SG5 .....11 E6
Vineyard The
Hertford SG14 .....113 D8
Ware SG12 .....94 A2
Welwyn Garden City AL8 ..110 E8
Vineyards Hill EN6 .....146 B2
Vineyards Rd EN6 .....146 A2
Vinters Ave SG1 .....50 F5
Violet Ave EN2 .....161 D1
Violet Way WD3 .....165 C5
Violets La SG9 .....43 B5
Virgil Dr EN10 .....148 F8
Virginia Cl LU2 .....45 F3
Viscount Cl LU3 .....45 A5
Viscount Ct 11 LU2 .....45 D1
Vivian Cl WD19 .....167 A1
Vivian Gdns WD19 .....167 A1
Vixen Dr SG13 .....114 A6
Vyse Cl EN5 .....171 C5

W

Wacketts EN7 .....148 A4
Waddesdon Cl LU2 .....46 D2
Waddesdon Ct EN2 .....161 E1
Waddington Rd 1 AL3 .127 D3
Waddling La AL4 .....87 D1
Wade The AL7 .....111 A3
Wades The AL10 .....130 A2
Wadesmill Rd
Tonwell SG12,SG14 .....92 D3
Ware SG12 .....93 D2
Wadham Rd WD5 .....153 F8
Wadhurst Ave LU3 .....45 C4
Wadley Cl 1 HP2 .....124 F2
Wadnall Way SG3 .....68 F3
Waggon Rd EN4 .....159 E2
Waggoners Yd 4 SG12 ..93 D2
Wagon Mead CM22 .....98 F3
Wagon Rd EN4 .....159 B2
Wagon Way WD3 .....165 C6
Waight Cl AL10 .....129 E7
Wain Cl EN6 .....145 B2
Wainwright St CM23 .....76 C5
Wakefields Wlk EN8 .....162 E8
Walace Ct EN3 .....163 A2
Walcot Ave LU2 .....46 B1
Waldeck Rd LU3 .....63 C8
Waldegrave Pk AL5 .....86 D1
Walden End SG1 .....50 E4
Walden Pl AL8 .....110 D8
Walden Rd AL8 .....110 D8
Waleran Cl HA7 .....176 F4
Waleys Cl LU3 .....44 E8
Walfords Cl CM17 .....118 C3
Walk The Hertford SG14 .113 A5
Walk The continued
Potters Bar EN6 .....159 B7
Walkern Prim Sch SG2 ..52 B8
Walkern Rd
Benington SG2 .....52 D5
Stevenage SG1 .....50 D8
Watton at S SG14 .....70 C6
Walkers Cl AL5 .....107 C7
Walkers Rd AL5 .....107 B7
Walkers' Ct SG7 .....23 F8
Wall Hall (Univ Campus) WD25 .....155 B3
Wallace Way SG4 .....22 A2
Walled Gdn The AL6 .....90 B2
Waller Ave LU4 .....44 F3
Waller Dr HA6 .....175 A2
Waller Street Mall 3 LU1 .....63 E7
Waller's Cl SG8 .....9 F2
Wallers Way EN11 .....115 B1
Wallingford Wlk AL1 .....141 D8
Wallington Rd SG7 .....13 D1
Wallis Ct EN9 .....163 B4
Walnut Ave SG7 .....24 A7
Walnut Cl
Chiswell Green AL2 .....141 B4
Hitchin SG4 .....35 A6
Luton LU2 .....46 B4
Much Hadham SG10 .....74 F2
Royston SG8 .....7 D6
Stotfold SG5 .....11 F6
Walnut Cotts CM21 .....97 E3
Walnut Ct
Welwyn Garden City AL7 ..110 E3
Wheathampstead AL4 .....108 D8
Walnut Dr CM23 .....76 D3
Walnut Gn WD23 .....167 F7
Walnut Gr
Hemel Hempstead HP2 ...124 D3
Welwyn Garden City AL7 ..110 E3
Walnut Ho AL7 .....110 F3
Walnut Tree Ave CM21 ...97 E4
Walnut Tree Cl Aston SG2 51 D4
Cheshunt EN8 .....162 D8
Hoddesdon EN11 .....135 A6
Walnut Tree Cres CM21 ..97 E3
Walnut Tree Rd SG5 .....20 D3
Walnut Tree Wlk SG12 ..114 E6
Walnut Way SG5 .....21 E4
Walpole Bldg WD3 .....165 E1
Walpole Cl HA5 .....176 A4
Walpole Ct SG2 .....69 C7
Walsh Cl SG5 .....34 D7
Walsham Cl SG2 .....69 C7
Walshford Way WD6 .....157 A1
Walsingham Cl
Hatfield AL10 .....129 F6
Luton LU2 .....45 D7
Walsingham Way AL2 ..142 C4
Walsworth Rd SG4 .....35 A8
Walter Rothschild Zoological Mus The★ HP23 .....100 A3
Walters Cl EN7 .....147 B6
Waltham Abbey★ EN9 .163 C6
Waltham Cross Sta EN8 162 F5
Waltham Ct LU2 .....46 C3
Waltham Gate EN8 .....148 F5
Waltham Gdns EN3 .....162 C2
Waltham Holy Cross Inf Sch EN9 .....163 D6
Waltham Holy Cross Jun Sch EN9 .....163 D6
Waltham Rd
4 Hitchin SG4 .....34 F6
Waltham Abbey EN9 .....149 F5
Walton Ct EN11 .....135 C8
Walton Gdns EN9 .....163 B6
Walton Rd
Hoddesdon EN11 .....135 C8
Ware SG12 .....114 D8
Watford WD23 .....167 E5
Walton St AL1 .....127 F5
Walverns Cl WD19 .....167 C3
Wandon Cl LU2 .....46 C4
Wannions Cl HP5 .....136 A1
Wansbeck Cl SG1 .....37 A3
Wansford Pk WD6 .....170 E5
Warburton Cl HA3 .....176 D4
Ward Cl
Hammond Street EN7 ...148 A4
Ware SG12 .....93 C2
Ward Cres CM23 .....76 E6
Ward Hatch CM20 .....118 A3
Warden Ct 5 LU2 .....63 E8
Warden Hill Cl LU2 .....45 C8
Warden Hill Gdns LU2 ..45 C8
Warden Hill Inf Sch LU3 .45 C7
Warden Hill Jun Sch LU3 45 C7
Warden Hill Rd LU2 .....45 C8
Wardown Cres LU2 .....45 E2
Wardown Ct LU3 .....45 D2
Wards Cotts WD6 .....168 F7
Ware Mus★ SG12 .....93 D1
Ware Park Rd SG12, SG14 .....113 E8
Ware Rd Hertford SG13 ..113 E6
Hoddesdon EN11 .....115 A1
Tonwell SG12 .....92 F6
Watton at S SG14,SG12 ...71 C3
Widford SG12 .....95 D4
Ware Sta SG12 .....114 E8
Wareham's La SG14 .....113 C5
Warenford Way WD6 ...170 A8
Wareside HP2 .....105 A1
Wareside CE Prim Sch SG12 .....94 E3
Wareside Cl AL7 .....111 B5
Warham Rd HA3 .....176 F1
Warlow Cl EN3 .....163 A2
Warmark Rd HP1 .....123 E5
Warminster Cl LU2 .....46 F1
Warneford Pl WD19 .....167 E3
Warner Rd SG12 .....114 D8
Warners Ave EN11 .....134 F4
Warners Cl SG2 .....51 C3
Warners End Rd HP1 ...124 B4
Warren Cl Hatfield AL10 .130 B8
Letchworth SG6 .....22 D7
Warren Cotts SG8 .....9 A1
Warren Ct SG8 .....7 D5
Warren Dale AL8 .....89 D1
Warren Dell Prim Sch WD19 .....175 C7
Warren Dr The LU1 .....64 C1
Warren Gn AL10 .....130 B8
Warren Gr WD6 .....170 D5
Warren La Clothall SG7 ..24 D7
Cottered SG9 .....39 B6
Stanmore HA7 .....176 F8
Warren Park Rd SG14 ..113 D7
Warren Pl 18 SG14 .....113 D6
Warren Rd Bushey WD23 168 D1
Luton LU1 .....62 F8
St Albans AL1 .....141 C7
Warren Terr SG14 .....113 D8
Warren The
Harpenden AL5 .....107 A6
Radlett WD7 .....156 B6
Royston SG8 .....7 D5
Warren Way AL6 .....89 E4
Warren Wood Ind Est SG14 .....91 F6
Warrenfield Cl EN7 .....162 A8
Warrengate La EN6 .....158 C8
Warrengate Rd AL9 .....144 C4
Warrensgreen La SG4 ...37 D5
Warton Gn LU2 .....46 E2
Warwick Ave EN6 .....146 D4
Warwick Cl
Bushey WD23 .....168 E2
Cuffley EN6 .....146 D4
Hertford SG13 .....113 C4
Warwick Ct
Chorleywood WD3 .....164 F6
Luton LU4 .....63 B8
Warwick Dr EN8 .....148 D3
Warwick Rd
Bishop's Stortford CM23 ...77 B6
Borehamwood WD6 .....170 D6
Enfield EN3 .....162 F2
Pitstone LU7 .....80 D3
St Albans AL1 .....127 F5
Stevenage SG2 .....51 C6
Warwick Rd E LU4 .....63 B8
Warwick Rd W LU4 .....63 B8
Warwick Way WD3 .....166 C5
Wash La Dancers Hill EN6 158 C3
South Mimms EN6 .....158 C5
Wash The
Furneux Pelham SG9 .....43 D5
Hertford SG14 .....113 D6
Washington Ave HP2 ...124 E8
Watchlytes AL7 .....111 C6
Watchlytes Jun Mix Inf Sch AL7 .....111 C6
Watchmead AL7 .....111 A6
Water End HP1 .....103 F2
Water End Cl WD6 .....169 F7
Water End Rd HP4 .....123 C7
Water Hall Farm & Craft Ctr★ SG4 .....66 F7
Water La
Abbots Langley WD4 .....139 B2
Berkhamsted HP4 .....122 C4
Bishop's Stortford CM23 ...76 F8
Bovingdon HP3 .....137 B1
Hertford SG14 .....113 C5
Hitchin SG5 .....21 F1
Stansted Mountfitchet CM24 .....59 E6
Watford WD17 .....167 D5
Water Row 11 SG12 .....93 D1
Waterbeach AL7 .....111 D6
Watercress Cl SG2 .....51 D5
Watercress Rd EN7 .....147 D5
Waterdale SG13 .....113 C4
Waterdell La SG4 .....35 A2
Waterdell Pl WD3 .....173 B8
Waterend La
Ayot St Peter AL4,AL6 .....88 E1
Redbourn AL3 .....106 B5
Waterfield
Chorleywood WD3 .....164 C2
Welwyn Garden City AL7 ...111 B7
Waterfields Ret Pk WD17 .....167 D5
Waterfields Way WD17, WD23 .....167 D4
Waterford Comm SG14 ..92 B2
Waterford Gn AL7 .....111 B6
Watergate The WD19 ...175 D8
Waterhall Cotts SG13 ..132 D7
Waterhouse St HP1 .....124 C2
Waterhouse The HP1 ...124 C3
Waterloo La SG5 .....21 A6
Waterlow Mews SG4 .....35 E3
Waterman Cl WD19 .....167 B3
Watermark Way SG13 ..113 F6
Watermead Rd LU3 .....44 F6
Watermeadow AL2 .....141 E3
Watermill Ind Est SG9 ...40 E6
Watermill La
Hertford SG14 .....113 D8
Stansted Mountfitchet CM24 .....59 C6
Waters Dr WD3 .....165 E1
Waters End SG5 .....11 E6
Waterside
Berkhamsted HP4 .....122 D4
Kings Langley WD4 .....139 A2
London Colney AL2 .....142 E4
Radlett WD7 .....156 B5
Stansted Mountfitchet CM24 .....59 E6
Welwyn Garden City AL7 ...90 B1
Waterside Cotts AL9 ...130 E8
Waterside Ct WD4 .....139 B2
Waterside Ind Est EN11 135 D5
Waterside Mews UB9 ..173 A4
Waterside Pl CM22 .....98 A2
Waterslade Gn LU3 .....45 B6
Watersplash Ct AL2 .....142 F4
Waterways Bsns Ctr EN3 .....163 A1
Watery La
Flamstead AL3,AL5 .....84 E3
Hatfield AL10 .....129 E4
Marsworth HP23 .....79 F1
Watford Arches Ret Pk WD17 .....167 D4
Watford By-pass WD6 ..169 C2
Watford Coll (annex) WD23 .....167 D6
Watford County Ct WD18 .....167 C5
Watford Ent Ctr WD18 ..166 E3
Watford Field Rd WD18 167 C4
Watford Football Gd & Saracens RFC WD18 ...167 B4
Watford General Hospl (Shrodells Wing) WD18 .....167 B4
Watford Gram Sch for Boys WD18 .....166 F5
Watford Gram Sch for Girls WD18 .....167 B5
Watford Heath WD19 ...167 D2
Watford Heath Farm WD19 .....167 D2
Watford High Street Sta WD17 .....167 C5
Watford Junction Sta WD17 .....167 C7
Watford Mus★ WD17 ...167 C5
Watford North Sta WD24 .....154 C2
Watford Rd
Abbots Langley WD4 .....153 C6
Chiswell Green AL2 .....141 A6
Croxley Green WD3 .....166 B3
Elstree WD6 .....169 C3
Kings Langley WD4 .....139 A1
Moor Park HA6 .....175 A4
Radlett WD7 .....155 F4
Watford Sch of Music WD17 .....154 A1
Watford Sta WD18 .....166 F6
Watkin Mews EN3 .....163 A2
Watkins Cl HA6 .....174 F2
Watkins Rise EN6 .....159 B7
Watling Cl 1 HP2 .....124 E6
Watling Ct WD6 .....169 D3
Watling Knoll WD7 .....155 F6
Watling Mans WD7 .....156 B3
Watling St
Park Street AL2 .....141 D6
St Albans AL1 .....141 C8
Watling View AL1 .....141 C8
Watling View Sch AL1 ..141 D7
Watlington Rd CM17 ...118 D4
Watson Ave AL3 .....127 F6
Watson's Wlk AL1 .....127 E2
Watton at Stone Prim Sch SG14 .....70 D3
Watton at Stone Sta SG14 .....70 D3
Watton Ho SG14 .....70 F3
Watton Rd Knebworth SG3 69 A5
Ware SG12 .....93 C2
Watton at S SG3,SG14 .....70 B2
Watts Cl SG11 .....57 C2
Waulud Prim Sch LU3 ...44 E7
Wauluds Bank Dr LU3 ...44 E7
Wavell Cl EN8 .....148 E4
Wavell Ho AL1 .....128 A2
Waveney HP2 .....124 F8
Waveney Rd AL5 .....86 C3
Waverley Cl SG2 .....69 A8
Waverley Gdns HA6 ...175 A2
Waverley Lodge AL3 ...127 D5
Waverley Rd AL3 .....127 D5
Waxhouse Gate AL1 ...127 D3
Waxwell Cl HA5 .....175 D1
Waxwell La HA5 .....175 D1
Wayfarers Pk HP4 .....121 F4
Wayletts Dr CM23 .....77 B7
Waynes Ct 9 LU1 .....63 E7
Wayre St CM17 .....118 C4
Wayre The CM17 .....118 C4
Waysbrook SG6 .....23 B5
Wayside
Chipperfield WD4 .....138 B1
Potters Bar EN6 .....159 D6
Shenley WD7 .....156 D6
Wayside Ave WD23 .....168 D3
Wayside Ct AL2 .....140 F1
Wayside The HP3 .....125 C2
Waysmeet SG6 .....23 B4
Waytemore Castle★ CM23 .....77 A7
Waytemore Rd CM23 ...76 E6

Weald Fst Sch HA3 . . . . .176 F3
Weald La HA3 . . . . .176 D2
Weald Mid Sch HA3 . . . .176 F3
Weald Rise HA3 . . . . .176 F2
Wealdwood Gdns HA5 . .176 B4
Weall Gn WD25 . . . . . . .154 B7
Weardale Ct EN5 . . . . . .171 C4
Weatherby Rd LU4 . . . . . .44 D2
Weaver St CM23 . . . . .76 C4
Weavers Orch SG15 . . . . . .11 A4
Weavers Rd HP23 . . . . . . .99 E4
Weavers Way SG7 . . . . . . .24 A8
Webb Cl SG6 . . . . .23 C5
Webb Rise SG1 . . . . .50 F7
Webber Cl WD6 . . . . . . .169 D3
Webley Ct EN3 . . . . .163 A2
Wedgewood Cl HA6 . . . .174 C4
Wedgewood Pk SG1 . . . . .37 C2
Wedgewood Rd SG4 . . . . .35 B7
Wedgewood Way SG1 . . . .37 B2
Wedgwood Ct SG1 . . . . . .37 C2
Wedgwood Gate SG1 . . . .37 B2
Wedmore Rd SG4 . . . . . . .35 A6
Wedon Way SG7 . . . . .13 C4
Weedon Cl SG16 . . . . .10 C5
Weighton Rd HA3 . . . . . .176 D2
Welbeck Cl WD6 . . . . . . .170 A6
Welbeck Rd 3 LU2 . . . . . .63 E8
Welbeck Rise AL5 . . . . . .107 D6
Welbury Ave LU3 . . . . . . .45 C7
Welch Pl HA5 . . . . .175 C2
Welclose St AL3 . . . . . . .127 C3
Welcote Dr HA6 . . . . . . .174 D4
Weldon Cl LU2 . . . . .46 E1
Welham Cl
Borehamwood WD6 . . . . .170 A8
Welham Green AL9 . . . . . .144 C7
Welham Ct AL9 . . . . .144 C7
Welham Green Sta AL9 .144 D8
Welham Manor AL9 . . . .144 C7
Welkin Gn HP2 . . . . .125 C4
Well App EN5 . . . . .171 C4
Well Croft HP1 . . . . .124 B4
Well End Rd WD6 . . . . . .157 D1
Well Garth AL7 . . . . .110 E5
Well Gn SG14 . . . . .91 C4
Well La Harlow CM19 . . . .117 A1
Mentmore LU7 . . . . .61 B8
Well Rd Barnet EN5 . . . . .171 C4
Northaw EN6 . . . . .145 E2
Well Row SG13 . . . . .132 F6
Wellands AL10 . . . . .130 A7
Wellbrook Mews HP23 . .100 B4
Wellbury Terr HP2 . . . . .125 C3
Wellcroft LU7 . . . . .80 F5
Wellcroft Cl AL7 . . . . . . .111 A4
Wellcroft Rd AL7 . . . . . . .111 A4
Wellen Rise HP3 . . . . . . .138 E8
Wellers Gr EN7 . . . . .148 A3
Wellesley Ave HA6 . . . . .174 F5
Wellesley Cres EN6 . . . .158 E6
Wellfield Ave LU3 . . . . . .44 C8
Wellfield Cl AL10 . . . . . .130 A6
Wellfield Ct SG1 . . . . .37 B1
Wellfield Rd AL10 . . . . . .130 A7
Wellgate Rd LU4 . . . . .44 D2
Wellhouse Cl LU1 . . . . . . .63 A7
Wellhouse La EN5 . . . . . .171 D5
Wellingham Ave SG5 . . . .21 D1
Wellington Ave HA5 . . . .175 F2
Wellington Cl WD19 . . . .175 F7
Wellington Cotts SG11 . . .73 B7
Wellington Ct 3 LU1 . . . . .63 D6
Wellington Dr AL7 . . . . . .111 C6
Wellington Ho 1 WD24 167 C7
Wellington Pl
Cheshunt EN10 . . . . .148 C8
Kneesworth SG8 . . . . .2 B5
Wellington Rd
London Colney AL2 . . . . . .142 D5
Pinner HA5 . . . . .175 F2
St Albans AL1 . . . . .128 B2
Stevenage SG2 . . . . .51 C5
Watford WD17 . . . . .167 B7
Wellington St
Hertford SG14 . . . . .113 B7
Luton LU1 . . . . .63 D7
Wells Cl
Hammond Street EN7 . . . .147 C6
Harpenden AL5 . . . . .85 E4
St Albans AL3 . . . . .127 C4
Wells Yd 8 Ware SG12 . . . .93 D1
Watford WD17 . . . . .167 B6
Wellside Cl EN5 . . . . . . .171 C5
Wellstones WD18 . . . . . .167 B5
Wellswood Cl HP2 . . . . .125 B4
Welsummer Way EN8 . . .148 D3
Weltmore Rd LU3 . . . . . . .44 F6
Welwyn By Pass Rd AL6 .89 C5
Welwyn Ct HP2 . . . . .124 F7
Welwyn Garden City Sta
AL8 . . . . .110 D6
Welwyn Hall Gdns AL6 . .89 C5
Welwyn North Sta AL6 . . .89 F3
Welwyn Rd SG14 . . . . . . .112 F7
Wendover Cl
Harpenden AL5 . . . . .86 D1
St Albans AL4 . . . . .128 C8
Wendover Ct AL6 . . . . . . .89 C5
Wendover Dr AL6 . . . . . . .89 C5
Wendover Ho WD18 . . . .166 E2
Wendover Way
Bushey WD23 . . . . .168 C3
Luton LU2 . . . . .45 F3
Wengeo La SG12 . . . . .93 B2
Wenham Ct SG2 . . . . .52 B8
Wenlock CE Jun Sch LU2 64 B8
Wenlock St LU2 . . . . .63 E8
Wensley Cl AL5 . . . . .107 D6
Wensleydale
Hemel Hempstead HP2 . . .124 F6
Luton LU2 . . . . .45 E1
Wensum Rd SG1 . . . . .36 F3
Wensum Way WD3 . . . . .165 D1
Wenta Bsns Ctr WD24 . .154 D2
Wentbridge Path WD6 .157 A1
Wentworth Ave
Borehamwood WD6 . . . . . .169 F4
Luton LU4 . . . . .44 C6
Wentworth Cl
Potters Bar EN6 . . . . .159 A8
Watford WD17 . . . . .153 F1
Wentworth Cotts
Dane End SG11 . . . . .53 F2
Hoddesdon EN10 . . . . . . .134 E1
Wentworth Ct EN5 . . . . .171 E6
Wentworth Dr CM23 . . . . .76 D6
Wentworth Rd
Barnet EN5 . . . . .171 D6
Hertford SG13 . . . . .113 C3
Wenwell Cl HP22 . . . . . . .99 A3
Wesley Cl Arlesey SG15 . . .11 A4
Goff's Oak EN7 . . . . .147 C3
Wesley Ho 7 AL1 . . . . . .127 D3
Wesley Rd AL3 . . . . .83 E5
Wessex Ct 7 EN5 . . . . . .171 D5
Wessex Dr HA5 . . . . .175 E3
West Alley 3 SG5 . . . . . . .34 E7
West Ave Baldock SG7 . . . .23 E8
Chiswell Green AL2 . . . . . .141 B6
West Burrowfield AL7 . .110 D4
West Chantry HA3 . . . . .176 B2
West Cl Barnet EN5 . . . . .171 B4
Hitchin SG4 . . . . .22 B1
Hoddesdon EN11 . . . . . . .135 A8
Stevenage SG1 . . . . .50 F5
West Comm
Harpenden AL5 . . . . .107 B6
Redbourn AL3 . . . . .106 A4
West Common Cl AL5 . .107 B5
West Common Gr AL5 . .107 B5
West Common Way
AL5 . . . . .107 A5
West Ct CM21 . . . . .97 E3
West Dene HP2 . . . . .104 A8
West Dr Arlesey SG15 . . . .11 B4
Stanmore HA3 . . . . .176 D4
Watford WD25 . . . . .154 B3
West Drive Gdns HA3 . .176 D4
West End SG7 . . . . .4 C3
West End La Barnet EN5 171 D5
Essendon AL9 . . . . .131 C5
West End Rd EN7 . . . . . .147 F8
West Gate CM20 . . . . . . .117 C1
West Herts Bsns Ctr
WD6 . . . . .170 B6
West Herts Coll (Dacorum
Campus) HP1 . . . . .124 C4
West Herts Coll Cassio
Campus WD17 . . . . . . .154 A1
West Herts Coll Leggatts
Campus WD24 . . . . . . .154 A3
West Herts Coll Watford
Campus WD17 . . . . . . .167 A6
West Hill SG5 . . . . .34 D7
West Hill Rd
Hoddesdon EN11 . . . . . . .134 F8
Luton LU1 . . . . .63 E5
West Hyde La SL9 . . . . . .172 A4
West La Great Offley SG5 . .33 C2
Pirton SG5 . . . . .20 D5
West Lieth HP23 . . . . .99 F1
West Lodge Cotts LU2 . . .46 D5
West Mead AL7 . . . . .111 B3
West Pas HP23 . . . . .100 A3
West Pl CM20 . . . . .118 A3
West Rd
Berkhamsted HP4 . . . . . . .122 A5
Bishop's Stortford CM23 . . .76 E6
Harlow CM20 . . . . .118 A4
Sawbridgeworth CM21 . . . .97 C3
Stansted Mountfitchet
CM24 . . . . .59 E6
West Reach SG2 . . . . .50 F2
West Riding
Bricket Wood AL2 . . . . . . .140 F1
Tewin AL6 . . . . .90 D5
West Side EN10 . . . . .148 E6
West Sq CM20 . . . . .117 C1
West St Hertford SG13 . . .113 C5
Lilley LU2 . . . . .32 D1
Ware SG12 . . . . .93 D1
Watford WD17 . . . . .167 B7
West Valley Rd HP3 . . . .138 D7
West View Hatfield AL10 .130 A7
Letchworth SG6 . . . . .22 E5
Standon SG11 . . . . .73 A6
West View Ct WD6 . . . . .169 D3
West View Gdns WD6 . . .169 D3
West View Rd AL3 . . . . .127 D4
West Way Harpenden AL5 .86 C2
Luton LU2 . . . . .46 C4
Rickmansworth WD3 . . . . .165 B1
West Ways HA6 . . . . .175 A1
Westall Cl SG13 . . . . . . .113 C5
Westall Mews SG13 . . . .113 C5
Westbourne Mews AL1 .127 D3
Westbourne Rd LU4 . . . . .45 B1
Westbrook Cl SG8 . . . . .5 B8
Westbrook Ct SG4 . . . . . . .34 F5
Westbrook Hay Prep Sch
HP1 . . . . .137 D7
Westbury EN8 . . . . .148 D1
Westbury Cl SG5 . . . . .34 D8
Westbury Farm Cl SG5 . .33 C3
Westbury Gdns LU2 . . . . .45 E3
Westbury Pl SG6 . . . . .22 E5
Westbury Prim Sch SG6 .22 E5
Westbury Rd
Moor Park HA6 . . . . .174 E7
Watford WD18 . . . . .167 B4
Westbush Cl EN11 . . . . .114 F1
Westcott AL7 . . . . .111 D7
Westcroft HP23 . . . . .100 A3
Westcroft Cl EN3 . . . . . .162 C1
Westcroft Ct EN10 . . . . .135 A4
Westell Cl SG7 . . . . .24 A8
Westerdale
Hemel Hempstead HP2 . . .124 E6
Luton LU4 . . . . .44 B5
Western Ave SG16 . . . . . . .10 B3
Western Cl SG6 . . . . .11 E1
Western House Hospl
SG12 . . . . .93 E2
Western Rd
Lower Nazeing EN9 . . . . . .135 E1
Luton LU1 . . . . .63 D6
Tring HP23 . . . . .99 F3
Western Terr 1 EN11 . . .115 B1
Western Way SG6 . . . . . . .11 E1
Westfield
Welham Green AL9 . . . . . .144 F8
Welwyn Garden City AL7 . .111 A7
Westfield Ave
Harpenden AL5 . . . . .86 A3
Watford WD24 . . . . .154 D1
Westfield Cl
Bishop's Stortford CM23 . . .76 E8
Cheshunt EN8 . . . . .162 F8
Hitchin SG5 . . . . .34 D7
Westfield Com Prim Sch
EN11 . . . . .134 F7
Westfield Com Tech Coll
WD18 . . . . .166 F3
Westfield Ct AL4 . . . . . .128 D6
Westfield Dr AL5 . . . . .86 B4
Westfield Fst Sch HP4 . .121 F5
Westfield La SG5 . . . . .34 D7
Westfield Pk HA5 . . . . . .175 F3
Westfield Pl AL5 . . . . .86 B4
Westfield Rd
Berkhamsted HP4 . . . . . . .121 F5
Bishop's Stortford CM23 . . .76 E8
Harpenden AL5 . . . . .86 B4
Hertford SG14 . . . . .113 C8
Hoddesdon EN11 . . . . .134 F7
Pitstone LU7 . . . . .80 C3
Westfield Wlk EN8 . . . . .162 F8
Westfields AL3 . . . . .141 A8
Westgate SG1 . . . . .50 D5
Westgate Ct EN3 . . . . . .162 D4
Westholm SG6 . . . . .22 F8
Westland Cl WD25 . . . . .153 F5
Westland Dr AL9 . . . . . . .144 E4
Westland Rd
Watford WD17 . . . . .167 B7
Knebworth SG3 . . . . .69 A5
Westlea Ave WD25 . . . . .154 E2
Westlea Cl EN10 . . . . . . .148 F8
Westlea Rd EN10 . . . . . .148 F8
Westlecote Gdns LU2 . . . .45 D4
Westly Wood AL7 . . . . . .111 A7
Westmeade Cl EN7 . . . . .148 B2
Westmill La Hitchin SG5 . .21 C2
Ickleford SG5 . . . . .21 C3
Westmill Lawns SG5 . . . . .21 D1
Westmill Rd Hitchin SG5 . .21 D1
Thundridge SG12 . . . . .93 A3
Westminster Ct
Cheshunt EN8 . . . . .162 F6
St Albans AL1 . . . . .127 C1
Westminster Ho 6
WD24 . . . . .167 C7
Westmorland Ave LU3 . . .44 F5
Weston Ave SG8 . . . . .7 C7
Weston Cl EN6 . . . . .158 F7
Weston Prim Sch SG4 . . .24 C1
Weston Rd SG1 . . . . .36 E1
Weston Way SG7 . . . . .23 E7
Westonia Ct EN3 . . . . . . .162 E3
Westray HP3 . . . . .125 C1
Westridge Cl HP1 . . . . . .123 F3
Westron Gdns HP23 . . . .100 B4
Westview Rise HP2 . . . . .124 D4
Westwick Cl HP2 . . . . . . .125 D2
Westwick Pl WD25 . . . . .154 C5
Westwick Row HP2 . . . . .125 E2
Westwood Ave SG4 . . . . . .35 A6
Westwood Cl EN6 . . . . . .145 A1
Wetherby Cl SG1 . . . . . . .51 C8
Wetherby Rd
Borehamwood WD6 . . . . . .169 E8
Enfield EN2 . . . . .161 C1
Wetherfield CM24 . . . . . . .59 D7
Wetherly Cl CM17 . . . . . .118 F4
Wetherne Link LU4 . . . . . .44 C5
Wexham Cl LU3 . . . . .44 E8
Weybourne Cl AL5 . . . . . .86 D2
Weybourne Dr LU2 . . . . . .45 C7
Weybridge Cl AL3 . . . . . .106 A5
Weymouth St HP3 . . . . .138 D7
Weyver Ct 3 AL1 . . . . . .127 E4
Whaley Rd EN6 . . . . .159 C6
Wharf La
Berkhamsted HP4 . . . . . . .121 C8
Rickmansworth WD3 . . . . .165 E1
Wharf Pl CM23 . . . . .77 A6
Wharf Rd
12 Bishop's Stortford CM23 76 F6
Hemel Hempstead HP1 . . .124 B1
Hoddesdon EN10 . . . . .148 F8
Wharf Row HP22 . . . . .99 B4
Wharf Villas HP1 . . . . . . .124 B1
Wharfdale 7 LU4 . . . . . . .44 C5
Wharfedale HP2 . . . . . . .124 E6
Wheat Cl AL4 . . . . .128 A7
Wheat Croft CM23 . . . . . .76 E4
Wheat Hill SG6 . . . . .22 F8
Wheatbarn AL7 . . . . .111 B7
Wheatcotes SG3 . . . . .69 C1
Wheatcroft EN7 . . . . . . .148 B3
Wheatcroft Prim Sch
SG13 . . . . .114 A7
Wheatfield Hatfield AL10 130 B6
Hemel Hempstead HP2 . . .124 D5
Wheatfield Ave AL5 . . . .107 A5
Wheatfield Cres SG8 . . . . .7 E6
Wheatfield Rd AL5 . . . . .107 A4
Wheatfields CM17 . . . . .118 D6
Wheatfields Inf Sch
AL4 . . . . .128 B7
Wheatfields Jun Mix Sch
AL4 . . . . .128 B7
Wheathampstead Rd
Harpenden AL5 . . . . .107 E8
Wheathampstead AL5,AL4 108 A8
Wheatlands SG2 . . . . .51 C7
Wheatley Cl
Sawbridgeworth CM21 . . . .97 C1
Welwyn Garden City AL7 . .111 A4
Wheatley Dr WD25 . . . . .154 C5
Wheatley Rd AL7 . . . . . .111 A4
Wheatleys AL4 . . . . .128 C5
Wheatlock Mead AL3 . . .106 A5
Wheatsheaf Dr SG12 . . . .93 B3
Wheatsheaf Rd SG12 . . . .95 D1
Wheelers Cl EN9 . . . . . .135 F1
Wheelers La HP3 . . . . . .124 E1
Wheelright Cl WD23 . . . .168 B3
Wheelwrights SG4 . . . . . .66 C1
Wheelwrights Cl CM23 . . .76 C4
Whempstead La SG12 . . . .71 B6
Whempstead Rd SG12 . . .71 B7
Whetstone Cl AL6 . . . . . . .89 E8
Whetstone Ct AL6 . . . . . . .89 E8
Whinbush Gr SG5 . . . . . . .34 F8
Whinbush Rd SG5 . . . . . . .34 F8
Whippendell Hill WD4 .138 C1
Whippendell Rd WD18 .166 F4
Whipperley Ct LU1 . . . . . .63 C5
Whipperley Inf Sch LU1 .63 A6
Whipperley Ring LU1 . . . .63 A6
Whipperley Way LU1 . . . .63 C5
Whipsnade Wild Animal Pk★
LU6 . . . . .81 E7
Whisper Mews LU4 . . . . .44 D4
Whisper Wood WD3 . . . .165 B6
Whisperwood Cl HA3 . . .176 E3
Whit Hern Ct EN8 . . . . . .148 C1
Whitby Rd LU3 . . . . .45 C1
Whitchurch Cl LU2 . . . . . .46 D2
White Beams AL2 . . . . . .141 C3
White Bear CM24 . . . . . . .59 E8
White Craig Cl HA5 . . . .176 A5
White Gate Gdns HA3 . .176 F3
White Hart Cl SG9 . . . . . .40 E8
White Hart Ct HP2 . . . . .125 A2
White Hart Dr HP2 . . . . .124 F2
White Hart Rd HP2 . . . . .125 A2
White Hedge Dr AL3 . . .127 C5
White Hill
Ashley Green HP3,HP5 . . .136 C7
Flamstead AL3 . . . . .105 B8
Hemel Hempstead HP1 . . .123 F2
Rickmansworth WD3 . . . . .174 A4
Walkern SG2 . . . . .38 C2
White Ho The 6 EN8 . . . .148 D3
White Horse La
London Colney AL2 . . . . . .142 E5
Welwyn AL6 . . . . .90 C7
White House Cl SG14 . . . .70 E3
White House The SG6 . . .23 B5
White La SG4 . . . . .49 C7
White Lion St HP3 . . . . .138 D7
White Orchards N20 . . . .171 F1
White Post Field CM21 . . .97 D2
White Shack La WD3 . . .152 F2
White Stubbs La EN10,
SG13 . . . . .133 C2
White Way The SG2 . . . . .51 C7
Whitebarns SG9 . . . . .43 A5
Whitebarns La SG9 . . . . .43 A6
Whitebeam Cl
4 Hammond Street EN7 .147 E5
Shenley WD7 . . . . .156 F6
Whitebeams AL10 . . . . . .130 A2
Whitebroom Rd HP1 . . . .123 E5
Whitechurch Gdns SG6 . .23 C3
Whitecroft AL1 . . . . .142 B8
Whitecroft Rd LU2 . . . . . .64 A8
Whitecrofts SG5 . . . . .11 F6
Whitefield Ave LU3 . . . . .44 C7
Whitefield Ho AL10 . . . .130 C7
Whitefield Inf Sch LU3 . .44 E8
Whitefield Jun Sch LU3 .44 E8
Whitefields Rd EN8 . . . .148 C3
Whitefriars Ave HA3 . . .176 E1
Whitefriars Dr HA3 . . . .176 E1
Whitefriars Fst & Mid Sch
HA3 . . . . .176 E1
Whitefriars Teaching Sch
HA3 . . . . .176 D1
Whitefriars Trad Est
HA3 . . . . .176 D1
Whitegale Cl SG4 . . . . . . .35 A6
Whitegates Cl WD3 . . . .166 A5
Whitehall Cl EN9 . . . . . .135 E1
Whitehall Coll CM23 . . . . .58 E1
Whitehall Cotts SG12 . .116 D8
Whitehall La CM23 . . . . . .58 F1
Whitehall Rd CM23 . . . . . .58 E1
Whitehands Cl EN11 . . .134 F6
Whitehart Cross HP3 . .136 F3
Whitehaven Cl EN7 . . . .147 E3
Whitehicks SG6 . . . . .12 A1
Whitehill
Berkhamsted HP4 . . . . . . .122 D5
Welwyn AL6 . . . . .89 A3
Whitehill Ave LU1 . . . . . .63 D5
Whitehill Cotts AL6 . . . . .89 A3
Whitehill Ct HP4 . . . . . .122 D5
Whitehill Jun Sch SG4 . .35 A5
Whitehill La LU7 . . . . .80 D3
Whitehill Rd SG4 . . . . . . .35 A6
Whitehills Cl SG4 . . . . . . .35 A6
Whitehorse St SG7 . . . . . .23 F8
Whitehorse Vale LU3 . . . .31 A1
Whitehouse Ave WD6 . .170 B5
Whitehouse Ct SG8 . . . . .17 D4
Whitehouse La WD5 . . .140 C4
Whitehurst Ave SG5 . . . . .21 F1
Whitelands Ave WD3 . . .164 C5
Whiteleaf Rd HP3 . . . . . .138 C8
Whiteley Cl SG12 . . . . . . .71 E7
Whiteley La SG9 . . . . .27 C8
Whitesmead Rd SG1 . . . .50 E7
Whitestone Wlk HP1 . . .124 A6
Whitethorn AL7 . . . . . . .111 B5
Whitethorn La SG6 . . . . . .23 A4
Whitethorn Way LU1 . . . .63 A6
Whitewaites CM20 . . . . .117 E1
Whiteway SG6 . . . . .23 C4
Whitewaybottom La LU2,
SG4 . . . . .66 A3
Whitewebbs La EN2 . . . .161 F4
Whitewebbs Mus of
Transport★ EN2 . . . . . .161 B4
Whitewebbs Pk★ EN2 . .161 D4
Whitewebbs Rd EN2 . . .161 C4
Whitewood Rd HP4 . . . .122 A4
Whitfield Way WD3 . . . .164 F1
Whitings Cl AL5 . . . . .86 D4
Whitings Hill Prim Sch
EN5 . . . . .171 C4
Whitings Rd EN5 . . . . . .171 C4
Whitlars Dr WD4 . . . . . .138 F3
Whitley Cl WD5 . . . . . . .154 A7
Whitley Ct EN11 . . . . . . .135 B8
Whitley Rd EN11 . . . . . .135 B8
Whitmores Wood HP2 . .125 B4
Whitney Dr SG1 . . . . .36 C1
Whittingham Cl LU2 . . . . .46 F1
Whittingstall Rd EN11 . .135 C8
Whittington La SG1 . . . . .50 E4
Whittington Way CM23 . .76 F3
Whittle Cl
Lower Stondon SG16 . . . . . .10 B4
Watford WD25 . . . . .153 F5
Whittlesea Cl HA3 . . . . .176 C3
Whittlesea Path HA3 . . .176 C2
Whittlesea Rd HA3 . . . .176 C2
Whitwell Cl LU3 . . . . .45 B8
Whitwell Rd WD25 . . . . .154 D4
Whitworth Cres EN3 . . .163 A2
Whitworth Jones Ave
SG16 . . . . .10 C5
Whitworth Rd SG1 . . . . . .37 B3
Whomerley Rd SG1 . . . . .50 E4
Whybrow Gdns HP4 . . . .122 E6
Whydale Rd SG8 . . . . .7 E5
Whytingham Rd HP23 . .100 C4
Wick Ave AL4 . . . . .108 D8
Wick Hill LU6 . . . . .82 F8
Wick Rd HP23 . . . . .120 D8
Wick The Hertford SG14 . .92 C1
Kimpton SG4 . . . . .66 D1
Wicken Fields SG12 . . . . .93 C3
Wickets End WD7 . . . . . .156 E6
Wickets The LU2 . . . . . . .45 E1
Wickfield SG3 . . . . .69 A2
Wickfield Cl SG3 . . . . . . .69 A2
Wickham Cl UB9 . . . . . . .173 D2
Wickham Rd HA3 . . . . . .176 D1
Wickham Way SG11 . . . . .55 E3
Wickhams Wharf SG12 . . .93 E1
Wicklands Rd SG12 . . . .116 D8
Wickmere Cl LU2 . . . . . . .45 C7
Wickstead Ave LU4 . . . . . .44 E4
Wickwood Ct AL1 . . . . . .128 B5
Widbury Gdns SG12 . . . . .93 F1
Widbury Hill SG12 . . . . . .93 F1
Widbury Ho SG12 . . . . . . .94 A1
Widford Rd Hunsdon SG12 95 D2
Much Hadham SG10 . . . . . .95 F7
Welwyn Garden City AL7 . .111 B6
Widford Sch SG12 . . . . . . .95 D4
Widford Terr HP2 . . . . . .105 A1
Widgeon Way WD25 . . . .154 E2
Widmore Dr HP2 . . . . . . .125 A5
Wieland Rd HA6 . . . . . . .175 A3
Wiggenhall Rd WD18 . . .167 C4
Wigginton Bottom
HP23 . . . . .120 E8
Wiggles La HP23 . . . . . . .99 F7
Wight Ho WD18 . . . . . . .166 F4
Wigmore La LU2 . . . . . . .46 D2
Wigmore Park Sh Ctr
LU2 . . . . .46 E1
Wigmore Pl LU2 . . . . .46 E1
Wigmore Prim Sch LU2 . .46 E2
Wigmores N AL8 . . . . . .110 D7
Wigmores S AL8 . . . . . .110 D6
Wigram Way SG2 . . . . . . .51 B3
Wilbraham's Almshouses
EN5 . . . . .171 F7
Wilbury Cl SG6 . . . . .22 C7
Wilbury Hills Rd SG6 . . . .22 C7

Wilbury Jun Sch SG6 ...22 D6
Wilbury Lodge 2 EN5 ..171 D5
Wilbury Rd SG6 ...22 E8
Wilbury Way SG4 ...22 A3
Wilcon Way WD25 ...154 D5
Wilcot Ave WD19 ...167 E2
Wilcot Cl WD19 ...167 E2
Wilcox Cl WD6 ...170 C8
Wild Cherry Dr LU1 ...63 D5
Wild Marsh Ct EN8 ...162 E2
Wildacres HA6 ...174 F7
Wilderness The 3 HP4 .122 C4
Wildhill rd AL9 ...131 B2
Wildman Ct SG13 ...114 A7
Wildoaks Cl HA6 ...174 F4
Wildwood HA6 ...174 D4
Wildwood Ave AL2 ...140 F1
Wildwood Ct WD3 ...164 F5
Wildwood La SG1 ...50 E3
Wilford Cl HA6 ...174 D3
Wilga Rd AL6 ...89 B5
Wilkin's Green La AL4 ..129 C4
Wilkins Gr AL8 ...110 D5
Wilkinsgreen Terr AL4 ..129 B3
Wilkinson Cl EN7 ...147 C6
Willenhall Cl LU3 ...45 A7
Willetts Mews EN11 ...135 A7
William Austin Inf Sch LU3 ...45 C4
William Austin Jun Sch LU3 ...45 C4
William Covell Cl EN2 ..160 F1
William Crook Ho HP1 .123 F3
William Ct HP3 ...138 D7
William Pl SG2 ...51 A3
William Ransom Prim Sch SG4 ...35 B7
William St
18 Berkhamsted HP4 ...122 D4
Luton LU2 ...45 E1
Markyate AL3 ...83 E5
Watford WD23 ...167 D6
William Sutton Ct LU2 ..46 B5
Williams Way WD7 ...156 C4
Williamson St 1 LU1 ...63 E7
Williamson Way WD3 ..165 A1
Willian Church Rd SG6 ..23 A2
Willian Rd
Great Wymondley SG4 ...35 F7
Hitchin SG4,SG6 ...22 E1
Willian Way Baldock SG7 ..23 E6
Letchworth SG6 ...23 A3
Willinghall Cl EN9 ...163 D7
Williton Rd LU2 ...46 C2
Willoughby Cl EN10 ...134 E2
Willoughby Ct AL2 ...142 D5
Willoughby Rd AL5 ...86 B4
Willoughby Way SG4 ...35 A6
Willow Cl
Bishop's Stortford CM23 ..76 E8
Great Hormead SG9 ...42 A8
Hammond Street EN7 ...147 E5
Reed SG8 ...16 D5
Willow Cnr SG13 ...132 F5
Willow Cres AL1 ...128 C3
Willow Ct Harrow HA2 ..176 C1
Harrow HA3 ...176 F2
Luton LU3 ...44 E5
Willow Dene
Bushey WD23 ...168 E2
Pinner HA5 ...175 D1
Willow Dr EN5 ...171 E5
Willow Edge WD4 ...139 A2
Willow End HA6 ...175 A4
Willow Gn WD6 ...170 D4
Willow Gr AL8 ...89 D3
Willow La Hitchin SG5 ...34 D6
St Ippolyts SG4 ...35 B2
Watford WD18 ...167 A4
Willow Mead CM21 ...97 E2
Willow Path EN9 ...163 E5
Willow Tree Way SG5 ...21 F2
Willow Trees Cvn Site SG16 ...10 A4
Willow View SG12 ...114 E8
Willow Way
Chiswell Green AL2 ...141 A4
Harpenden AL5 ...86 C4
Hatfield AL10 ...129 F2
Hemel Hempstead HP1 ..124 B5
Luton LU3 ...44 E5
Potters Bar EN6 ...159 B6
Radlett WD7 ...155 E3
Willow Wlk AL6 ...89 C8
Willowdene EN8 ...148 E4
Willowfield Lower Sch LU1 ...62 F4
Willowgate Trad Est LU3 .44 B8
Willowmead SG14 ...113 B5
Willows Cl HA5 ...175 C1
Willows La HP1 ...103 F1
Willows Link SG2 ...51 A1
Willows The
Buntingford SG9 ...40 D8
Hemel Hempstead HP2 ..125 B5
Hitchin SG4 ...35 A5
Rickmansworth WD3 ...173 A8
St Albans AL1 ...142 B7
Stevenage SG2 ...51 A1
Watford WD19 ...167 B2
Willowside AL2 ...142 E4
Willowside Way SG8 ...7 C8
Willowtree Lo HA6 ...174 F5
Willowtree Lodge 1 HA6 ...174 F5
Wilsden Ave LU1 ...63 C6
Wilshere Ave AL1 ...127 C1
Wilshere Cres SG4 ...35 C8
Wilshere Rd AL6 ...89 A5
Wilshere-Dacre Jun Sch SG5 ...34 E8
Wilsmere Dr HA3 ...176 E3
Wilson Cl
Bishop's Stortford CM23 ..76 F5
Stevenage SG1 ...36 D1
Wilsons La SG7 ...4 C4
Wilstone Dr AL4 ...128 C8
Wilton Cl CM23 ...77 B7
Wilton Cres SG13 ...113 C4
Wilton Ct WD17 ...167 C6
Wilton Rd SG5 ...21 E1
Wilton Way SG13 ...113 C4
Wiltshire Rd SG2 ...51 A4
Wimborne Cl CM21 ...97 D2
Wimborne Gr WD17 ...153 E2
Wimborne Rd LU1 ...63 C8
Wimple Rd LU4 ...44 A2
Winch Cl SG4 ...88 F8
Winch St LU2 ...45 F1
Winchdells HP3 ...139 A8
Winchester Cl
Bishop's Stortford CM23 ..76 D4
Stevenage SG1 ...37 B2
Winchester Ho AL3 ...127 C2
Winchester Rd HA6 ...174 F1
Winchester Way WD3 ..166 B4
Winchfield LU1 ...62 E4
Winchfield Way WD3 ..165 C2
Windermere Ave AL1 ..128 B1
Windermere Cl
Chorleywood WD3 ...164 D4
Hemel Hempstead HP3 ..125 C2
Stevenage SG1 ...37 D2
Windermere Cres LU3 ..44 F5
Windermere Ct 5 WD17 ...167 A7
Windermere Prim Sch AL1 ...128 B1
Windhill
Bishop's Stortford CM23 ..76 E7
Welwyn Garden City AL7 ..111 A7
Windhill Old Rd CM23 ..76 E7
Winding Hill SG10 ...75 A4
Winding Shot HP1 ...124 A4
Winding Shott SG14 ...91 C4
Windmill Ave AL4 ...128 C7
Windmill Cl Barkway SG8 .17 C5
Pitstone LU7 ...80 F5
Stansted Mountfitchet CM24 ...59 D6
Waltham Abbey EN9 ...163 E5
Windmill Cotts SG12 ...93 D6
Windmill Dr WD3 ...165 F3
Windmill Field SG12 ...114 D8
Windmill Fields CM17 ..118 F4
Windmill Hill
Buntingford SG9 ...40 F6
Chipperfield WD4 ...151 F7
Hitchin SG4 ...34 F7
Windmill La Barnet EN5 .170 F3
Bushey WD23 ...168 E1
Cheshunt EN8 ...148 E1
Windmill Rd
Breachwood Green SG4 ..47 D2
Hemel Hempstead HP2 ..124 F2
Luton LU1 ...63 F6
Markyate AL3,LU1 ...84 B6
Windmill St WD23 ...168 E1
Windmill Way
Much Hadham SG10 ...74 E1
Tring HP23 ...99 F4
Windmills SG12 ...71 E8
Windmore Ave EN6 ...158 C8
Windmore Hall EN6 ...158 C8
Windridge Cl AL3 ...127 A1
Windrush Cl SG1 ...37 A3
Winds End Cl HP2 ...125 A5
Windsor Cl
Borehamwood WD6 ...170 A8
Bovingdon HP3 ...137 A3
Cheshunt EN7 ...148 A1
Hemel Hempstead HP3 ..124 E2
Northwood HA6 ...175 A1
Stevenage SG2 ...69 B7
Welwyn AL6 ...89 B3
Windsor Ct
Borehamwood WD6 ...170 C7
Bushey WD23 ...168 C2
Kings Langley WD4 ...139 B2
11 Luton LU1 ...63 D6
St Albans AL1 ...128 A2
Windsor Gdns CM23 ...76 C7
Windsor Rd Barnet EN5 .171 E3
Enfield EN3 ...162 D3
Harrow HA3 ...176 D2
Pitstone LU7 ...80 D3
Royston SG8 ...7 F6
Watford WD24 ...154 C1
Welwyn AL6 ...89 B3
Windsor St LU1 ...63 D6
Windsor Way WD3 ...165 A1
Windsor Wlk 8 LU1 ...63 D6
Windsor Wood EN9 ...163 E6
Windward Cl EN3 ...162 D4
Windy Rise SG12 ...71 F7
Winford Dr EN10 ...134 F1
Wingate Ct LU4 ...44 F2
Wingate Gdns AL6 ...89 B5
Wingate Rd LU4 ...44 F2
Wingate Way AL1 ...128 A2
Wingrave CE Comb Sch HP22 ...60 A3
Wingrave Rd Tring HP23 .100 B6
Wilstone HP23 ...79 D1
Winifred Cl NW7 ...170 F3
Winifred Rd HP3 ...138 D7
Winkfield Cl LU4 ...44 B1
Winnington Rd EN3 ...162 C2
Winsdon Ct 1 LU1 ...63 D6
Winsdon Rd LU1 ...63 D6
Winslow Cl LU3 ...45 C4
Winslow Rd HP22 ...60 B3
Winston Churchill Way EN8 ...162 D6
Winston Cl Harrow HA3 .176 F4
Hitchin SG5 ...34 D7
Winston Ct HA3 ...176 B3
Winston Gdns HP4 ...121 F4
Winston Way EN6 ...159 A6
Winstre Rd WD6 ...170 A8
Winters La SG2 ...38 C1
Winterscroft Rd EN11 ..134 F7
Winton App WD3 ...166 C4
Winton Cl Letchworth SG6 .23 D8
Luton LU2 ...45 D6
Winton Cres WD3 ...166 B4
Winton Dr Cheshunt EN8 .148 E2
Croxley Green WD3 ...166 C4
Winton Rd SG12 ...93 F1
Winton Terr AL1 ...127 E2
Wintons CM20 ...117 C2
Wisden Rd SG1 ...36 F1
Wisdom Dr SG13 ...113 E6
Wiseman Cl LU2 ...45 E7
Wisemans Gdns CM21 ...97 C1
Wistaria Dr AL2 ...142 B5
Wistlea Cres AL4 ...129 B1
Wistow Rd LU3 ...45 A6
Witchford AL7 ...111 D6
Withy Cl LU4 ...44 B4
Withy Pl AL2 ...141 C3
Witley Gn LU2 ...46 D2
Witney Cl HA5 ...175 F4
Witter Ave SG5 ...21 E4
Wiveton Cl LU2 ...45 D7
Woburn Ave CM23 ...76 C7
Woburn Cl Bushey WD23 168 C3
Stevenage SG2 ...69 C7
Woburn Ct LU4 ...44 D5
Wodecroft Rd LU3 ...45 B6
Wodson Park Sports & L Ctr SG12 ...93 D4
Wolfsburg Ct 4 LU4 ...44 C5
Wolsey Ave EN7 ...147 F2
Wolsey Bsns Pk WD18 .166 D2
Wolsey Mans HA6 ...174 C7
Wolsey Rd
Hemel Hempstead HP2 ..124 D2
Moor Park HA6 ...174 D7
Wolston Cl LU1 ...63 C7
Wolverley Ho SG7 ...4 D4
Wolves Mere SG3 ...69 A2
Wolvescroft SG3 ...69 A2
Wonnacott Pl EN3 ...162 D3
Wood Cl AL10 ...130 B5
Wood Comm AL10 ...130 B8
Wood Cres HP3 ...124 E1
Wood Dr SG2 ...51 B2
Wood End AL2 ...141 C3
Wood End Cl HP2 ...125 C4
Wood End Hill AL5 ...85 D4
Wood End La AL3 ...104 E8
Wood End Rd AL5 ...85 D3
Wood End Sch AL5 ...85 D3
Wood Farm Rd HP2 ...124 E2
Wood Green Cl LU2 ...46 B5
Wood Green Rd LU2 ...46 C5
Wood Green Way EN8 ..162 E8
Wood House La EN10 ..134 A2
Wood La Birchanger CM23 .59 E2
Hemel Hempstead HP2 ..124 D2
Meesden SG9 ...30 A6
Wood Lane End HP2 ..125 B4
Wood St Barnet EN5 ...171 D5
Luton LU1 ...63 F6
Wood Vale AL10 ...130 B5
Wood View Cuffley EN6 .146 E4
Hemel Hempstead HP1 ..124 B5
Woodacre Dr AL6 ...90 A8
Woodbine Gr EN2 ...161 D1
Woodbridge Cl LU4 ...44 E4
Woodbrook Gdns EN9 ..163 E6
Woodbury Hill LU2 ...45 E2
Woodcock Hill
Rickmansworth WD3 ...173 E4
Sandridge AL4 ...108 E1
Woodcock Rd Luton LU1 ..63 A7
Royston SG8 ...7 E8
Stevenage SG2 ...51 D2
Woodcote Cl EN8 ...148 C1
Woodcote Ho 1 SG4 ...34 F7
Woodcroft SG5 ...34 E6
Woodcroft Ave SG12 ...115 E4
Woodfall Ave EN5 ...171 F4
Woodfield Ave HA6 ...174 E6
Woodfield Cl CM24 ...59 E6
Woodfield Dr HP3 ...125 D1
Woodfield Gdns HP3 ...125 D1
Woodfield La AL9 ...145 E8
Woodfield Rd
Radlett WD7 ...156 A3
Stevenage SG1 ...36 C1
Welwyn Garden City AL7 ..110 F6
Woodfield Rise WD23 ..168 D2
Woodfield Sch HP3 ...125 C1
Woodfield Terr
Harefield UB9 ...173 B1
Stansted Mountfitchet CM24 ...59 E6
Woodfield Way AL4 ...128 C6
Woodfields
Stansted Mountfitchet CM24 ...59 E6
2 Watford WD18 ...167 C5
Woodford Cres HA5 ...175 B1
Woodford Rd WD17 ...167 C7
Woodforde Cl SG7 ...4 E4
Woodgate WD25 ...154 B6
Woodgate Ave EN6 ...160 B7
Woodgate Cres HA6 ...175 A4
Woodgrange Ct EN11 ..135 A5
Woodhall Ave HA5 ...175 E2
Woodhall Cl SG14 ...113 C8
Woodhall Ct AL7 ...110 E5
Woodhall Dr HA5 ...175 E2
Woodhall Gate HA5 ...175 D2
Woodhall Gr CM23 ...76 D6
Woodhall Ho AL7 ...110 F4
Woodhall La
Hemel Hempstead HP2 ..124 E4
Shenley WD7 ...156 F4
South Oxhey WD19 ...175 E6
Welwyn Garden City AL7 ..110 E4
Woodhall Sch WD19 ...175 E6
Woodham Way SG12 ..115 C4
Woodhill Ho AL9 ...145 D8
Woodhouse Eaves HA6 .175 A5
Woodhurst SG6 ...22 F8
Woodhurst Ave WD25 ..154 D4
Woodland Ave
Hemel Hempstead HP1 ..124 B2
Luton LU3 ...45 B2
Woodland Cl
Hemel Hempstead HP1 ..124 B2
Tring HP23 ...99 F2
Woodland Ct AL3 ...127 F7
Woodland Dr
St Albans AL4 ...128 C4
Watford WD17 ...166 F8
Woodland La WD3 ...164 D6
Woodland Mount SG13 .113 F6
Woodland Pl
Chorleywood WD3 ...164 F5
Hemel Hempstead HP1 ..124 B2
Woodland Rd
Hertford Heath SG13 ...114 C3
Maple Cross WD3 ...172 D5
Woodland Rise
Studham LU6 ...82 B7
Welwyn Garden City AL8 ..110 C8
Woodland Way
Baldock SG7 ...23 F6
Bedmond WD5 ...139 F4
Goff's Oak EN7 ...147 B3
Stevenage SG2 ...51 A1
Welwyn AL6 ...90 A7
Woodlands
Bishop's Stortford CM23 ..77 C8
Brookmans Park AL9 ...145 B4
Caddington LU1 ...62 E3
Chiswell Green AL2 ...141 C4
Harpenden AL5 ...85 E3
Radlett WD7 ...156 A5
Royston SG8 ...7 E6
Woodlands Ave HP4 ...122 D3
Woodlands Cl
Borehamwood WD6 ...170 B5
Hoddesdon EN11 ...135 A5
Woodlands Dr
Bedmond WD4 ...139 C3
Harrow HA7 ...176 F4
Hoddesdon EN11 ...135 A4
Woodlands Meade SG4 ..37 B8
Woodlands Prim Sch WD6 ...170 A8
Woodlands Rd
Enfield EN2 ...161 D1
Hertford SG13 ...113 F6
Kings Langley HP3 ...139 A4
Thundridge SG12 ...93 D6
Watford WD23 ...167 E4
Woodlands Sec Sch LU3 .44 F7
Woodlea AL2 ...141 A6
Woodlea Gr HA6 ...174 C4
Woodley Rd SG12 ...93 F2
Woodleys CM20 ...118 A1
Woodman Rd 4 HP3 ...124 E1
Woodmere LU3 ...31 A1
Woodmere Ave WD24 ..154 E1
Woodmill Mews EN11 ..135 B8
Woodpecker Cl
Bishop's Stortford CM23 ..76 C6
Bushey WD23 ...168 C1
Harrow HA3 ...176 F2
Hatfield AL10 ...129 F2
Woodridge Way HA6 ...174 E4
Woodridings Ave HA5 ..175 F2
Woodridings Cl HA5 ...175 F3
Woods Ave AL10 ...130 B4
Woods Pl HP23 ...100 A3
Woods The Radlett WD7 .156 B5
South Oxhey HA6 ...175 A5
Woodshots Mdw WD18 .166 D4
Woodside
Bishop's Stortford CM23 ..77 D8
Borehamwood WD6 ...169 F5
Cheshunt EN7 ...162 A8
Hertford Heath SG13 ...114 C2
Watford WD24 ...154 A3
Woodside Farm & Wildfowl Pk★ LU1 ...84 A8
Woodside Gdns SG4 ...34 F7
Woodside Ho AL8 ...110 C7
Woodside Ind Pk SG6 ...23 B7
Woodside La AL9 ...131 A1
Woodside Prim Sch EN7 ...147 B2
Woodside Rd
Abbots Langley WD25 ...154 B8
Bricket Wood AL2 ...140 F2
Welwyn AL6 ...89 F3
Woodside LU1 ...63 B3
Woodstock SG3 ...68 F3
Woodstock Cl SG13 ...114 B4
Woodstock Rd
Bushey WD23 ...168 F2
Hoddesdon EN10 ...134 E4
Woodstock Rd N AL1 ..128 B4
Woodstock Rd S AL1 ..128 B3
Woodvale EN8 ...162 C4
Woodville Court Mews WD17 ...167 A7
Woodville Ct WD17 ...167 A7
Woodville Pl SG14 ...113 B8
Woodward Gdns HA7 ...176 F3
Woodwaye WD19 ...167 C2
Woodwicks WD3 ...172 D5
Woolenwick Inf Sch SG1 50 B6
Woolenwick Jun Sch SG1 ...50 B6
Woolgrove Ct SG4 ...22 B1
Woolgrove Rd SG4 ...22 B1
Woolgrove Sch SG6 ...23 D5
Woollam Cres AL3 ...127 C7
Woollams AL3 ...106 A4
Woollard St EN9 ...163 C5
Woolmans Cl EN10 ...134 F1
Woolmer Cl WD6 ...157 A1
Woolmer Dr HP2 ...125 C3
Woolmer's Park Mews SG14 ...112 B1
Woolmerdine Ct WD23 .167 D6
Woolmers La SG14 ...112 B2
Woolners Way SG1 ...50 C6
Woolston Ave SG6 ...23 A4
Wootton Cl LU3 ...45 B7
Wootton Dr HP2 ...124 F8
Worboys Ct SG8 ...1 F5
Worcester Ct AL1 ...128 A2
Worcester Ho 12 WD6 ..170 A7
Worcester Rd AL10 ...129 F6
Worcesters Ave EN1 ..162 A1
Worcesters Prim Sch EN1 ...161 F1
Wordsworth Cl SG8 ...2 D1
Wordsworth Gdns WD6 170 A4
Wordsworth Rd
Harpenden AL5 ...86 A3
Luton LU4 ...44 A2
Works Rd SG6 ...23 C7
Worley Rd AL3 ...127 D4
Wormley Ct EN10 ...148 F7
Wormley Lodge Cl EN10 148 F8
Wormley Prim Sch EN10 ...148 E8
Wormleybury EN10 ...148 D8
Worsdell Way SG4 ...35 B7
Worsted La SG9 ...41 E7
Wortham Rd SG8 ...7 E4
Wortham Way SG2 ...51 B3
Wraglings The CM23 ...77 B5
Wratten Cl SG5 ...34 E6
Wratten Rd E SG5 ...34 E6
Wratten Rd W SG5 ...34 E6
Wrayfields SG5 ...12 B8
Wraysbury Cl LU4 ...44 D3
Wren Cl Kimpton SG4 ...66 B1
Luton LU2 ...46 C6
Stevenage SG2 ...51 B6
Wren Cres WD23 ...168 C1
Wren Wood AL7 ...111 B7
Wrenbrook Rd CM23 ...76 F6
Wrensfield HP1 ...124 B3
Wrestlers Cl AL10 ...130 C7
Wrexham Terr SG8 ...7 D7
Wright Cl AL4 ...108 E7
Wright's Bldgs WD17 ..167 B7
Wrights Green La CM22 .98 D7
Wrights Mdw SG2 ...52 B8
Wrights Orch SG2 ...51 E2
Wrotham Pk★ EN5 ...158 F3
Wrotham Rd EN5 ...171 E7
Wroxham Ave HP3 ...124 D1
Wroxham Gdns
Crews Hill EN2 ...161 B4
Potters Bar EN6 ...158 D8
Wroxham Sch The EN6 .158 D8
Wroxham Way AL5 ...86 C3
Wulfrath Way SG12 ...93 C3
Wulstan Pk EN6 ...159 D7
Wulwards Cl LU1 ...63 B6
Wulwards Ct LU1 ...63 B6
Wyatt Cl Bushey WD23 .168 E2
Ickleford SG5 ...21 D4
Wyatt's Cl WD3 ...165 A6
Wyatt's Rd WD3 ...165 A6
Wyburn Ave EN5 ...171 F6
Wych Elm CM20 ...117 C1
Wych Elm La AL6,SG3 ...68 F2
Wych Elms AL2 ...141 B3
Wychdell SG2 ...69 C8
Wychford Dr CM21 ...97 C1
Wychwood Ave LU2 ...45 E3
Wychwood Way HA6 ...174 F3
Wycklond Cl SG5 ...11 E6
Wycliffe Cl LU3 ...45 C6
Wycliffe Ct WD5 ...153 E7
Wycombe Pl AL4 ...128 B6
Wycombe Way Luton LU3 .45 C8
St Albans AL4 ...128 B6
Wyddial Gn AL7 ...111 B6
Wyddial Rd SG9 ...40 E8
Wye The HP2 ...125 A8
Wyedale AL2 ...142 F4
Wykeham Rise N20 ...171 E1
Wyken Cl LU3 ...45 A7
Wyldwood Cl CM17 ...118 C6

Wyllyotts Cl EN6 ....158 F7
Wyllyotts La EN6 ....158 F7
Wyllyotts Pl EN6 ....158 F7
Wylo Dr EN5 ....171 A3
Wymondley Cl SG4 .....35 A7
Wymondley Jun Mix Inf Sch
  SG4 ....35 E4
Wymondley Rd
  Hitchin SG4 ....35 B6
  Letchworth SG6 ....23 A1
Wynches Farm Dr AL4 .128 D3
Wynchgate HA3 ....176 E3
Wynchlands Cres AL4 .128 D3
Wynd The SG6 ....22 F6
Wyndham Rd LU4 ....44 C2
Wyndhams End AL7 ....110 F2
Wynlie Gdns HA5 .....175 B1
Wynn Cl SG7 ....13 A1

Wyrley Dell SG6 ....23 A3
Wysells Ct SG6 ....22 D7
Wyton AL7 ....111 D6
Wyvern Cl LU4 ....44 E3

Y

Yardley SG6 ....23 C4
Yardley Ave LU7 ....80 D4
Yardley Ct 14 AL5 ......86 B1
Yarmouth Rd
  Stevenage SG1 ....50 A7
  Watford WD24 ....154 C1
Yarra Ho 3 AL1 ....127 E3
Yately Cl LU2 ....45 D7
Ye Cnr WD19 ....167 E3
Yearling Cl SG12 ......114 F7
Yeatman Ho WD24 ....154 B3
Yeats Cl SG8 ....2 D1
Yeomanry Dr SG7 ......13 A1

Yeomans Ave AL5 ......85 D3
Yeomans Cl CM23 ......76 D6
Yeomans Dr SG2 ....51 E2
Yeomans Ride HP2 ....105 A1
Yeovil Ct LU2 ....46 B2
Yeovil Rd LU2 ....46 B2
Yew Cl EN7 ....147 E4
Yew Gr AL7 ....111 C5
Yew Tree Cl HP5 ......136 A1
Yew Tree Ct
  Elstree WD6 ....169 D3
  Hemel Hempstead HP1 ..124 A1
Yew Tree Dr HP3 ......137 B3
Yew Tree Pl CM23 ......76 F8
Yew Wlk EN11 ....135 A5
Yewlands
  Hoddesdon EN11 ......135 A5
  Sawbridgeworth CM21 ...97 E1
Yewlands Dr EN11 .....135 A5
Yews Ave EN1 ....162 B3
Yewstone Ct WD18 .....167 A6

Yewtree Cl LU7 ....80 E5
Yewtree End AL2 ......141 B4
York Cl WD4 ....139 A2
York Cres WD6 ....170 D7
York Ho
  18 Borehamwood WD6 ..170 A7
  St Albans AL3 ....127 C2
York House Sch WD3 ...165 F7
York Rd Cheshunt EN8 ..162 E6
  Hitchin SG5 ....34 E8
  Northwood HA6 ....175 A1
  St Albans AL1 ....127 F4
  Stevenage SG1 ....36 F1
  Watford WD18 ....167 C4
York St LU2 ....63 F8
York Terr EN2 ....161 C1
York Way
  Hemel Hempstead HP2 ..124 E2
  Royston SG8 ....7 B8
  Watford WD25 ....154 E3
  Welwyn AL6 ....89 C3

Yorke Gate WD17 .....167 A7
Yorke Mead Prim Sch
  WD3 ....166 A4
Yorke Rd WD3 ....166 A3
Yorkes Mews 16 SG12 ..93 D1
Youngfield Rd HP1 ....123 F4
Youngs Mews SG14 ...113 C6
Youngs Rise AL8 ......110 C6
Youngsbury La SG12 ...93 E8
Yule Cl AL2 ....140 F1

Z

Zambesi Rd CM23 ......76 F5